Systems of Linear Equations (Two Variables):

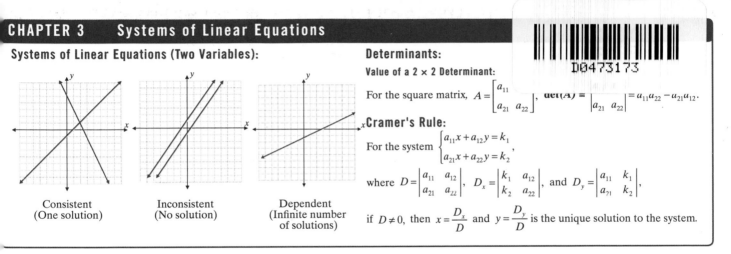

Consistent
(One solution)

Inconsistent
(No solution)

Dependent
(Infinite number
of solutions)

Determinants:

Value of a 2 × 2 Determinant:

For the square matrix, $A = \begin{bmatrix} a_{11} & \\ a_{21} & a_{22} \end{bmatrix}$, $\det(A) = \begin{vmatrix} a_{11} & \\ a_{21} & a_{22} \end{vmatrix} = a_{11}a_{22} - a_{21}a_{12}$.

Cramer's Rule:

For the system $\begin{cases} a_{11}x + a_{12}y = k_1 \\ a_{21}x + a_{22}y = k_2 \end{cases}$,

where $D = \begin{vmatrix} a_{11} & a_{12} \\ a_{21} & a_{22} \end{vmatrix}$, $D_x = \begin{vmatrix} k_1 & a_{12} \\ k_2 & a_{22} \end{vmatrix}$, and $D_y = \begin{vmatrix} a_{11} & k_1 \\ a_{21} & k_2 \end{vmatrix}$,

if $D \neq 0$, then $x = \dfrac{D_x}{D}$ and $y = \dfrac{D_y}{D}$ is the unique solution to the system.

Classification of Polynomials:

Monomial: polynomial with one term
Binomial: polynomial with two terms
Trinomial: polynomial with three terms

FOIL Method:

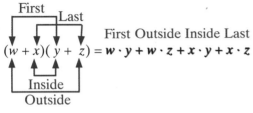

First Outside Inside Last
$(w + x)(y + z) = w \cdot y + w \cdot z + x \cdot y + x \cdot z$

Division Algorithm:

$\dfrac{P(x)}{D(x)} = Q(x) + \dfrac{R(x)}{D(x)}$, $(D(x) \neq 0)$

Zero-Factor Property:

If a and b are real numbers, and $a \cdot b = 0$, then $a = 0$ or $b = 0$ or both.

Special Products of Polynomials:

1. $(X + A)(X - A) = X^2 - A^2$: Difference of two squares

2. $(X + A)^2 = X^2 + 2AX + A^2$: Perfect square trinomial

3. $(X - A)^2 = X^2 - 2AX + A^2$: Perfect square trinomial

4. $(X - A)(X^2 + AX + A^2) = X^3 - A^3$: Difference of two cubes

5. $(X + A)(X^2 - AX + A^2) = X^3 + A^3$: Sum of two cubes

Quadratic Equation:

An equation that can be written in the form $ax^2 + bx + c = 0$ where a, b, and c are real numbers and $a \neq 0$ is called a **quadratic equation**.

The Pythagorean Theorem:

In a right triangle, the square of the hypotenuse is equal to the sum of the squares of the legs.

$$c^2 = a^2 + b^2$$

Rational Expression:

A **rational expression** is an expression of the form $\dfrac{P}{Q}$ (or in function notation, $\dfrac{P(x)}{Q(x)}$) where P and Q are polynomials and $Q \neq 0$.

Fundamental Principle of Fractions:

If $\dfrac{P}{Q}$ is a rational expression and K is a polynomial and $K \neq 0$, then

$\dfrac{P}{Q} = \dfrac{P}{Q} \cdot \dfrac{K}{K} = \dfrac{P \cdot K}{Q \cdot K}$.

Negative Signs in Rational Expressions:

$-\dfrac{P}{Q} = \dfrac{P}{-Q} = \dfrac{-P}{Q}$ and $\dfrac{P}{Q} = \dfrac{-P}{-Q} = -\dfrac{-P}{Q} = -\dfrac{P}{-Q}$.

Opposites in Rational Expressions:

In general, $\dfrac{-P}{P} = -1$ if $P \neq 0$. In particular, $\dfrac{a-x}{x-a} = -1$ if $x \neq a$.

Multiplication with Rational Expressions:

$\dfrac{P}{Q} \cdot \dfrac{R}{S} = \dfrac{P \cdot R}{Q \cdot S}$ where $Q, S \neq 0$.

Division with Rational Expressions:

$\dfrac{P}{Q} \div \dfrac{R}{S} = \dfrac{P}{Q} \cdot \dfrac{S}{R}$ where $Q, R, S \neq 0$.

Addition and Subtraction with Rational Expressions:

$\dfrac{P}{Q} + \dfrac{R}{Q} = \dfrac{P+R}{Q}$ and $\dfrac{P}{Q} - \dfrac{R}{Q} = \dfrac{P-R}{Q}$ where $Q \neq 0$.

Complex Fractions:

A **complex fraction** is a fraction in which the numerator or denominator is a fraction or the sum or difference of fractions.

Variation:

Direct Variation: $\dfrac{y}{x} = k$ or $y = kx$.

Indirect Variation: $x \cdot y = k$ or $y = \dfrac{k}{x}$.

Combined Variation: If a variable varies either directly or inversely with more than one other variable.

Joint Variation: If a combined variation is all direct variation (the variables are multiplied).

INTERMEDIATE ALGEBRA

FIFTH EDITION

INTERMEDIATE
ALGEBRA

FIFTH EDITION

D. FRANKLIN WRIGHT
CERRITOS COLLEGE

HAWKES
PUBLISHING

Editor: Mary Janelle Cady
Developmental Editor: Marcel Prevuznak
Production Editors: Ann Lucius, Mandy Glover, Kim Scott, Priyanka Bihani
Answer Key Editors: Amanda Matlock, Lindsay Stevens, Emily Stegman, Heather Lloyd
Editorial Assistants: Ashley Rankin, John Thomas, Dottie Chappell,
                  Sue Wang, Phillip Kramp
Layout: QSI (Pvt.) Ltd.
Art: Ayvin Samonte
Cover Art and Design: Johnson Design

HAWKES
PUBLISHING
A division of Quant Systems, Inc.

Library of Congress Control Number: 2003107598

Printed in the United States of America

ISBN:
Student (paperback): 0-918091-80-2
Student (hardcover): 0-918091-81-0
Student Solution Manual: 0-918091-83-7

CONTENTS

Preface   ix

Hawkes Learning Systems: Intermediate Algebra   xxii

CHAPTER 1 Real Numbers, Solving Equations, and Exponents   1

1.1	Properties of Real Numbers 2	
1.2	Operations with Real Numbers 17	
1.3	First-Degree (or Linear) Equations and Absolute Value Equations 32	
1.4	Evaluating and Solving Formulas 44	
1.5	Applications 51	
1.6	Linear Inequalities and Absolute Value Inequalities 64	
1.7	Properties of Exponents 76	
1.8	More on Exponents and Scientific Notation 84	

Chapter 1 Index of Key Ideas and Terms   94
Chapter 1 Test   100

CHAPTER 2 Straight Lines and Functions   103

2.1	Cartesian Coordinate System and Straight Lines: $Ax + By = C$ 104	
2.2	Slope-intercept Form: $y = mx + b$ 113	
2.3	Point-slope Form: $y - y_1 = m(x - x_1)$ 126	
2.4	Introduction to Functions 140	
2.5	Graphing Linear Inequalities 158	

Chapter 2 Index of Key Ideas and Terms   166
Chapter 2 Test   168
Cumulative Review: Chapters 1 – 2   171

CHAPTER 3 Systems of Linear Equations 175

3.1 Systems of Linear Equations (Two Variables)   176
3.2 Applications   187
3.3 Systems of Linear Equations (Three Variables)   194
3.4 Matrices and Gaussian Elimination   205
3.5 Determinants   220
3.6 Determinants and Systems of Linear Equations:
Cramer's Rule   229
3.7 Graphing Systems of Linear Inequalities   236

Chapter 3 Index of Key Ideas and Terms   242
Chapter 3 Test   247
Cumulative Review: Chapters 1 − 3   249

CHAPTER 4 Polynomials 253

4.1 Addition and Subtraction of Polynomials   254
4.2 Multiplication of Polynomials   262
4.3 Division with Polynomials and Synthetic Division   271
4.4 Introduction to Factoring   283
4.5 Special Factoring Techniques   295
4.6 Polynomial Equations and Applications   303
4.7 Using a Graphing Calculator to Solve
Equations and Absolute Values   314

Chapter 4 Index of Key Ideas and Terms   321
Chapter 4 Test   324
Cumulative Review: Chapters 1 − 4   325

CHAPTER 5 Rational Expressions — 329

5.1 Multiplication and Division of Rational Expressions 330
5.2 Addition and Subtraction of Rational Expressions 341
5.3 Complex Fractions 351
5.4 Equations and Inequalities with Rational Expressions 356
5.5 Applications 368
5.6 Applications (Variation) 378

Chapter 5 Index of Key Ideas and Terms 388
Chapter 5 Test 391
Cumulative Review: Chapters 1 – 5 392

CHAPTER 6 Roots, Radicals and Complex Numbers — 397

6.1 Roots and Radicals 398
6.2 Rational Exponents 412
6.3 Arithmetic with Radicals 423
6.4 Functions with Radicals 433
6.5 Introduction to Complex Numbers 443
6.6 Multiplication and Divison with Complex Numbers 450

Chapter 6 Index of Key Ideas and Terms 457
Chapter 6 Test 461
Cumulative Review: Chapters 1 – 6 462

CHAPTER 7 Quadratic Equations — 467

7.1 Quadratic Equations: Completing the Square 468
7.2 Quadratic Equations: The Quadratic Formula 479
7.3 Applications 487
7.4 Equations with Radicals 497
7.5 Equations in Quadratic Form 503

Chapter 7 Index of Key Ideas and Terms 507
Chapter 7 Test 510
Cumulative Review: Chapters 1 – 7 511

CHAPTER 8 Quadratic Functions and Conic Sections — 515

8.1	Quadratic Functions: Parabolas	516
8.2	Quadratic Inequalities	532
8.3	f(x) Notation and Translations	542
8.4	Parabolas as Conic Sections	557
8.5	Distance Formula, Midpoint Formula, and Circles	566
8.6	Ellipses and Hyperbolas	579
8.7	Nonlinear Systems of Equations	592

Chapter 8 Index of Key Ideas and Terms   598
Chapter 8 Test   602
Cumulative Review: Chapters 1 - 8   604

CHAPTER 9 Exponential and Logarithmic Functions — 607

9.1	Algebra of Functions	608
9.2	Composition of Functions and Inverse Functions	619
9.3	Exponential Functions	635
9.4	Logarithmic Functions	647
9.5	Properties of Logarithms	660
9.6	Logarithmic and Exponential Equations	669
9.7	Applications	679

Chapter 9 Index of Key Ideas and Terms   685
Chapter 9 Test   690
Cumulative Review: Chapters 1 − 9   691

CHAPTER 10 Sequences, Series, and the Binomial Theorem — 697

10.1	Sequences	698
10.2	Sigma Notation	705
10.3	Arithmetic Sequences	711
10.4	Geometric Sequences and Series	721
10.5	The Binomial Theorem	734
10.6	Permutations	743
10.7	Combinations	749

Chapter 10 Index of Key Ideas and Terms   753
Chapter 10 Test   757
Cumultive Review: Chapters 1 − 10   758

Appendix 763

A.1   Pi   763
A.2   Powers, Roots, and Prime Factorizations   765

Answers 769

Index 839

PREFACE

Purpose and Style

Intermediate Algebra (fifth edition) provides a solid base for further studies in mathematics. In particular, business and social science majors who will continue their studies in statistics and calculus will be well prepared for success in those courses. With feedback from users, insightful comments from reviewers, and skillful editing and design by the editorial staff at Hawkes Publishing, we have confidence that students and instructors alike will find that this text is indeed a superior teaching and learning tool. The text may be used independently or in conjunction with the software package ***Hawkes Learning Systems: Intermediate Algebra*** developed by Quant Systems.

We have provided very little overlap with material covered in a beginning algebra course. While chapter 1 provides a review of topics from beginning algebra, students will find that the review is comprehensive and that the pace of coverage is somewhat faster and in more depth than they have seen in previous courses. As with any text in mathematics, students should read the text carefully and thoroughly.

The style of the text is informal and nontechnical while maintaining mathematical accuracy. Each topic is developed in a straightforward step-by-step manner. Each section contains many carefully developed and worked out examples to lead the students successfully through the exercises and prepare them for examinations. Whenever appropriate, information is presented in list form for organized learning and easy reference. Common errors are highlighted and explained so that students can avoid such pitfalls and better understand the correct corresponding techniques. Practice problems with answers are provided in nearly every section to allow the students to "warm up" and to provide the instructor with immediate classroom feedback.

The NCTM and AMATYC curriculum standards have been taken into consideration in the development of the topics throughout the text. In particular:

- there is emphasis on reading and writing skills as they relate to mathematics
- techniques for using a graphing calculator are discussed early
- a special effort has been made to make the exercises motivating and interesting
- geometric concepts are integrated throughout
- statistical concepts, such as interpreting bar graphs and calculating elementary statistics, are included where appropriate

Real Numbers, Solving Equations, and Exponents

C H A P T E R

1

Did You Know?

In Chapter 1, you will find a great many symbols defined, as well as rules of manipulation for these symbolic expressions. Most people think that algebra has always existed, complete with all the common symbols in use today. That is not the case, since modern symbols did not appear consistently until the beginning of the sixteenth century. Prior to that, algebra was rhetorical. That is, all problems were written out in words using either Latin, Arabic, or Greek, and some nonstandard abbreviations. Numbers were written out. The common use of Hindu-Arabic numerals did not begin until the sixteenth century, although these numerals had been introduced into Europe in the twelfth century.

The sign for addition, +, was a contraction of the Latin *et*, which means "and." Gradually, the *e* was contracted and the crossed *t* became the plus sign. The minus sign or bar, –, is thought to be derived from the habit of early scribes of using a bar to represent the letter *m*. Thus the word *summa* was often written *sum̄a*. Thus, the bar came to represent the missing *m*, the first letter of the word *minus*. The radical symbol, $\sqrt{}$, is derived from a small printed *r*, which stood for the Latin word *radix*, or root. The symbol for times, a cross, ×, was developed from cross multiplication or for the purpose of indicating products in proportions. Thus

$$\frac{2}{3} \times \frac{6}{9} \quad \text{stood for } \frac{2}{3} = \frac{6}{9}.$$

The cross is not well suited for algebra, since it resembles the symbol *x*, which is used for variables. Therefore, a dot is usually used to indicate multiplication in algebra. The dot seemed to have developed from an Italian practice of separating columns in multiplication tables with a dot. Exponents were used as early as the fourteenth century by the mathematician Oresme (1330? – 1382), who gave the first known use of the rules for fractional exponents in a text book he wrote. The equal sign is attributed to Robert Recorde (1510? – 1558), who wrote, "I will sette as I doe often in woorke use, a paire of paralleles, or Gemowe [twin] lines of one lengthe, thus: = , because noe .2. thynges, can be moare equalle." As you can tell, the development of algebraic symbols occurred over a long period of time, and symbols became standardized through usage and con-

1.1   Properties of Real Numbers

1.2   Operations with Real Numbers

1.3   First-Degree (or Linear) Equations and Absolute Value Equations

1.4   Evaluating and Solving Formulas

1.5   Applications

1.6   Linear Inequalities and Absolute Value Inequalities

1.7   ...

1.8   ...

*"The Mat...
flood of ...
purely for...
of endless...
the physi...*

Karl Pear...

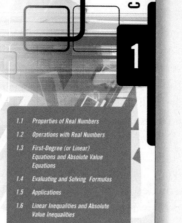

Introduction:

Presented before the first section of every chapter, this feature provides an introduction to the subject of the chapter and its purpose.

Did You Know?:

A feature at the beginning of every chapter that presents some interesting math history related to the chapter at hand.

Objectives:

The objectives provide the students with a clear and concise list of skills presented in each section.

CHAPTER 1   **Real Numbers, Solving Equations and Exponents**

Welcome to your second course in algebra. You will find that many of the topics presented, such as solving equations, factoring, working with fractional expressions, and solving word problems, are familiar because they were discussed in beginning algebra. However, you will also find that the coverage of each topic, including many new topics, is in greater depth and that the pace is somewhat faster. The intent is to prepare you for success with the algebraic content in your future studies in mathematics, science, business, and economics. You should be prepared to expend considerable time and effort throughout the semester.

We begin in Chapter 1 with a review of the properties and operations with real numbers. These ideas form the foundation for the study of algebra and need to be understood thoroughly. As an example of a deeper analysis of familiar topics, we will discuss solving first-degree equations, then expand the techniques to include solving absolute value equations and solving formulas for specified variables. Also, you will be introduced to the new topic of intervals of real numbers. Intervals and interval notation are related to graphs and are used frequently in higher level mathematics courses.

There is much to look forward to in this course. With hard work and perseverance, you should have a very rewarding experience.

1.1   Properties of Real Numbers

Objectives

After completing this section, you will be able to:

1. *Identify given numbers as members of one or more of the following sets: natural numbers, whole numbers, integers, rational numbers, irrational numbers, and real numbers.*

2. *Write rational numbers as infinite repeating decimals.*

3. *Graph sets of numbers on real number lines.*

4. *Describe sets of numbers using set-builder notation given their graphs.*

5. *Name the properties of real numbers that justify given statements.*

6. *Complete statements using the real number properties.*

We begin with a development of the terminology and properties of numbers that form the foundation for the study of algebra. The following kinds of numbers are studied in some detail in beginning algebra courses.

2

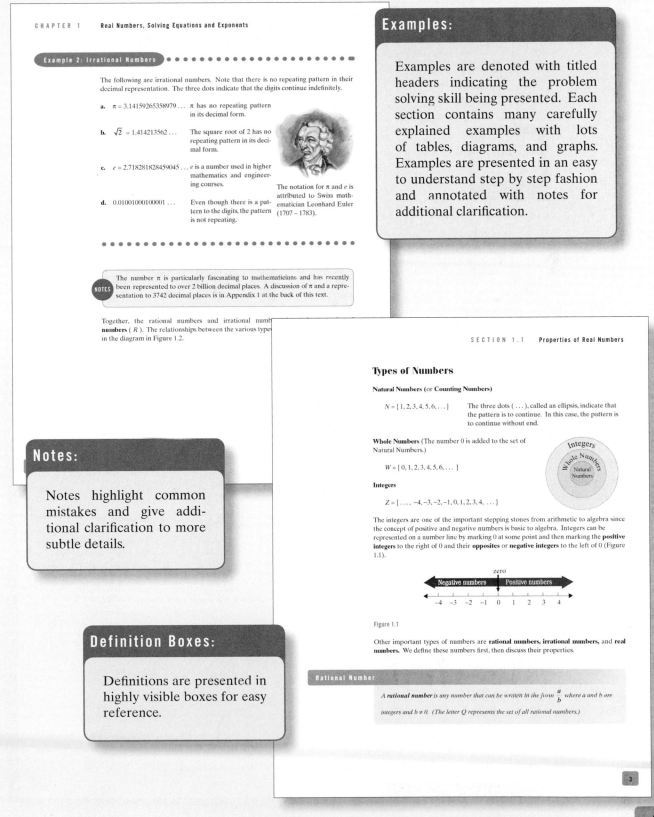

CHAPTER 1   Real Numbers, Solving Equations and Exponents

Example 2: Irrational Numbers

The following are irrational numbers. Note that there is no repeating pattern in their decimal representation. The three dots indicate that the digits continue indefinitely.

a. $\pi = 3.14159265358979\ldots$ π has no repeating pattern in its decimal form.

b. $\sqrt{2} = 1.414213562\ldots$ The square root of 2 has no repeating pattern in its decimal form.

c. $e = 2.718281828459045\ldots$ e is a number used in higher mathematics and engineering courses.

d. $0.01001000100001\ldots$ Even though there is a pattern to the digits, the pattern is not repeating.

The notation for π and e is attributed to Swiss mathematician Leonhard Euler (1707 – 1783).

NOTES The number π is particularly fascinating to mathematicians and has recently been represented to over 2 billion decimal places. A discussion of π and a representation to 3742 decimal places is in Appendix 1 at the back of this text.

Together, the rational numbers and irrational numb[ers] **numbers** (R). The relationships between the various type[s] in the diagram in Figure 1.2.

Examples:

Examples are denoted with titled headers indicating the problem solving skill being presented. Each section contains many carefully explained examples with lots of tables, diagrams, and graphs. Examples are presented in an easy to understand step by step fashion and annotated with notes for additional clarification.

Notes:

Notes highlight common mistakes and give additional clarification to more subtle details.

Definition Boxes:

Definitions are presented in highly visible boxes for easy reference.

SECTION 1.1   Properties of Real Numbers

Types of Numbers

Natural Numbers (or **Counting Numbers**)

$N = \{1, 2, 3, 4, 5, 6, \ldots\}$ The three dots (. . .), called an ellipsis, indicate that the pattern is to continue. In this case, the pattern is to continue without end.

Whole Numbers (The number 0 is added to the set of Natural Numbers.)

$W = \{0, 1, 2, 3, 4, 5, 6, \ldots\}$

Integers

$Z = \{\ldots, -4, -3, -2, -1, 0, 1, 2, 3, 4, \ldots\}$

The integers are one of the important stepping stones from arithmetic to algebra since the concept of positive and negative numbers is basic to algebra. Integers can be represented on a number line by marking 0 at some point and then marking the **positive integers** to the right of 0 and their **opposites** or **negative integers** to the left of 0 (Figure 1.1).

Figure 1.1

Other important types of numbers are **rational numbers, irrational numbers,** and **real numbers.** We define these numbers first, then discuss their properties.

Rational Number

A **rational number** is any number that can be written in the form $\dfrac{a}{b}$ where a and b are integers and $b \neq 0$. (The letter Q represents the set of all rational numbers.)

3

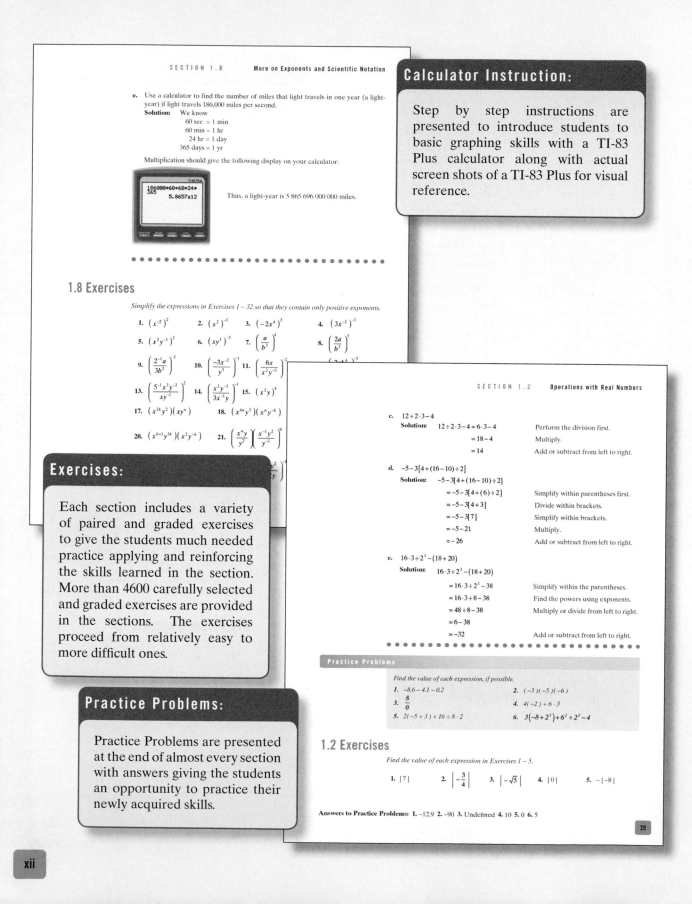

SECTION 1.8   **More on Exponents and Scientific Notation**

e. Use a calculator to find the number of miles that light travels in one year (a light-year) if light travels 186,000 miles per second.

Solution: We know

$$60 \text{ sec} = 1 \text{ min}$$
$$60 \text{ min} = 1 \text{ hr}$$
$$24 \text{ hr} = 1 \text{ day}$$
$$365 \text{ days} = 1 \text{ yr}$$

Multiplication should give the following display on your calculator:

186000*60*60*24*
365
     5.8657ᴇ12

Thus, a light-year is 5 865 696 000 000 miles.

Calculator Instruction:

Step by step instructions are presented to introduce students to basic graphing skills with a TI-83 Plus calculator along with actual screen shots of a TI-83 Plus for visual reference.

1.8 Exercises

Simplify the expressions in Exercises 1 – 32 so that they contain only positive exponents.

1. $\left(x^{-2}\right)^2$ 2. $\left(x^2\right)^{-3}$ 3. $\left(-2x^4\right)^2$ 4. $\left(3x^{-2}\right)^{-1}$

5. $\left(x^2y^{-3}\right)^2$ 6. $\left(xy^3\right)^{-2}$ 7. $\left(\dfrac{a}{b^2}\right)^4$ 8. $\left(\dfrac{2a}{b^2}\right)^3$

9. $\left(\dfrac{2^{-1}a}{3b^2}\right)^2$ 10. $\left(\dfrac{-3x^{-2}}{y^3}\right)^{-1}$ 11. $\left(\dfrac{6x}{x^2y^{-3}}\right)^{-2}$

13. $\left(\dfrac{5^{-1}x^3y^{-2}}{xy^{-1}}\right)^2$ 14. $\left(\dfrac{x^2y^{-3}}{3x^{-1}y}\right)^{-1}$ 15. $\left(x^2y\right)^4$

17. $\left(x^{2k}y^2\right)\left(xy^n\right)$ 18. $\left(x^{4n}y^3\right)\left(x^ny^{-k}\right)$

20. $\left(x^{k+1}y^{3k}\right)\left(x^2y^{-k}\right)$ 21. $\left(\dfrac{x^4y}{y^2}\right)\left(\dfrac{x^{-1}y^2}{y^{-1}}\right)^0$

Exercises:

Each section includes a variety of paired and graded exercises to give the students much needed practice applying and reinforcing the skills learned in the section. More than 4600 carefully selected and graded exercises are provided in the sections. The exercises proceed from relatively easy to more difficult ones.

SECTION 1.2   **Operations with Real Numbers**

c. $12 \div 2 \cdot 3 - 4$

Solution: $\quad 12 \div 2 \cdot 3 - 4 = 6 \cdot 3 - 4 \qquad$ Perform the division first.
$\qquad\qquad\qquad\qquad = 18 - 4 \qquad$ Multiply.
$\qquad\qquad\qquad\qquad = 14 \qquad$ Add or subtract from left to right.

d. $-5 - 3[4 + (16 - 10) \div 2]$

Solution: $\quad -5 - 3[4 + (16 - 10) \div 2]$
$\qquad\qquad = -5 - 3[4 + (6) \div 2] \qquad$ Simplify within parentheses first.
$\qquad\qquad = -5 - 3[4 + 3] \qquad$ Divide within brackets.
$\qquad\qquad = -5 - 3[7] \qquad$ Simplify within brackets.
$\qquad\qquad = -5 - 21 \qquad$ Multiply.
$\qquad\qquad = -26 \qquad$ Add or subtract from left to right.

e. $16 \cdot 3 \div 2^3 - (18 + 20)$

Solution: $\quad 16 \cdot 3 \div 2^3 - (18 + 20)$
$\qquad\qquad = 16 \cdot 3 \div 2^3 - 38 \qquad$ Simplify within the parentheses.
$\qquad\qquad = 16 \cdot 3 \div 8 - 38 \qquad$ Find the powers using exponents.
$\qquad\qquad = 48 \div 8 - 38 \qquad$ Multiply or divide from left to right.
$\qquad\qquad = 6 - 38$
$\qquad\qquad = -32 \qquad$ Add or subtract from left to right.

Practice Problems

Find the value of each expression, if possible.

1. $-8.6 - 4.1 - 0.2$ 2. $(-3)(-5)(-6)$

3. $\dfrac{8}{0}$ 4. $4(-2) + 6 \cdot 3$

5. $2(-5 + 3) + 16 \div 8 \cdot 2$ 6. $3\left(-8 + 2^3\right) + 6^2 \div 2^2 - 4$

Practice Problems:

Practice Problems are presented at the end of almost every section with answers giving the students an opportunity to practice their newly acquired skills.

1.2 Exercises

Find the value of each expression in Exercises 1 – 5.

1. $|7|$ 2. $\left|-\dfrac{3}{4}\right|$ 3. $\left|-\sqrt{5}\right|$ 4. $|0|$ 5. $-|-8|$

Answers to Practice Problems: 1. -12.9 2. -90 3. Undefined 4. 10 5. 0 6. 5

29

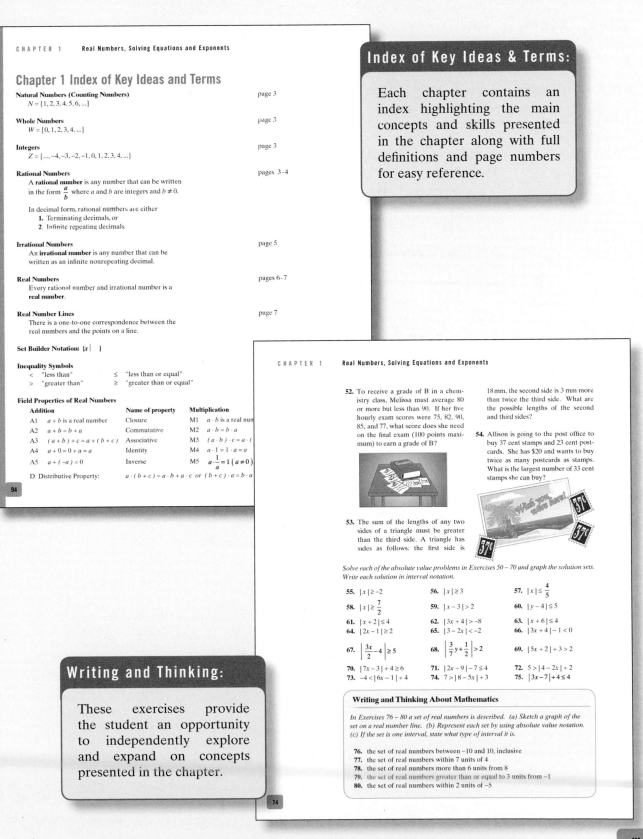

Chapter 1 Index of Key Ideas and Terms

Natural Numbers (Counting Numbers)   page 3
$$N = \{1, 2, 3, 4, 5, 6, \dots\}$$

Whole Numbers   page 3
$$W = \{0, 1, 2, 3, 4, \dots\}$$

Integers   page 3
$$Z = \{\dots, -4, -3, -2, -1, 0, 1, 2, 3, 4, \dots\}$$

Rational Numbers   pages 3-4
A **rational number** is any number that can be written in the form $\frac{a}{b}$ where a and b are integers and $b \neq 0$.

In decimal form, rational numbers are either
1. Terminating decimals, or
2. Infinite repeating decimals.

Irrational Numbers   page 5
An **irrational number** is any number that can be written as an infinite nonrepeating decimal.

Real Numbers   pages 6-7
Every rational number and irrational number is a **real number**.

Real Number Lines   page 7
There is a one-to-one correspondence between the real numbers and the points on a line.

Set Builder Notation: $\{x \mid \quad \}$

Inequality Symbols

<	"less than"	≤	"less than or equal"
>	"greater than"	≥	"greater than or equal"

Field Properties of Real Numbers

Addition		Name of property	Multiplication	
A1	$a + b$ is a real number	Closure	M1	$a \cdot b$ is a real num
A2	$a + b = b + a$	Commutative	M2	$a \cdot b = b \cdot a$
A3	$(a + b) + c = a + (b + c)$	Associative	M3	$(a \cdot b) \cdot c = a \cdot ($
A4	$a + 0 = 0 + a = a$	Identity	M4	$a \cdot 1 = 1 \cdot a = a$
A5	$a + (-a) = 0$	Inverse	M5	$a \cdot \frac{1}{a} = 1 \ (a \neq 0)$

D Distributive Property: $a \cdot (b + c) = a \cdot b + a \cdot c$ or $(b + c) \cdot a = b \cdot a$

94

---

52. To receive a grade of B in a chemistry class, Melissa must average 80 or more but less than 90. If her five hourly exam scores were 75, 82, 90, 85, and 77, what score does she need on the final exam (100 points maximum) to earn a grade of B?

53. The sum of the lengths of any two sides of a triangle must be greater than the third side. A triangle has sides as follows: the first side is 18 mm, the second side is 3 mm more than twice the third side. What are the possible lengths of the second and third sides?

54. Allison is going to the post office to buy 37 cent stamps and 23 cent postcards. She has $20 and wants to buy twice as many postcards as stamps. What is the largest number of 33 cent stamps she can buy?

Solve each of the absolute value problems in Exercises 50 – 70 and graph the solution sets. Write each solution in interval notation.

55. $|x| \geq -2$ **56.** $|x| \geq 3$ **57.** $|x| \leq \frac{4}{5}$

58. $|x| \geq \frac{7}{2}$ **59.** $|x - 3| > 2$ **60.** $|y - 4| \leq 5$

61. $|x + 2| \leq 4$ **62.** $|3x + 4| > -8$ **63.** $|x + 6| \leq 4$

64. $|2x - 1| \geq 2$ **65.** $|3 - 2x| < -2$ **66.** $|3x + 4| - 1 < 0$

67. $\left|\frac{3x}{2} - 4\right| \geq 5$ **68.** $\left|\frac{3}{7}y + \frac{1}{2}\right| > 2$ **69.** $|5x + 2| + 3 > 2$

70. $|7x - 3| + 4 \geq 6$ **71.** $|2x - 9| - 7 \leq 4$ **72.** $5 > |4 - 2x| + 2$

73. $-4 < |6x - 1| + 4$ **74.** $7 > |8 - 5x| + 3$ **75.** $|3x - 7| + 4 \leq 4$

Writing and Thinking About Mathematics

In Exercises 76 – 80 a set of real numbers is described. (a) Sketch a graph of the set on a real number line. (b) Represent each set by using absolute value notation. (c) If the set is one interval, state what type of interval it is.

76. the set of real numbers between −10 and 10, inclusive
77. the set of real numbers within 7 units of 4
78. the set of real numbers more than 6 units from 8
79. the set of real numbers greater than or equal to 3 units from −1
80. the set of real numbers within 2 units of −5

74

Index of Key Ideas & Terms:

Each chapter contains an index highlighting the main concepts and skills presented in the chapter along with full definitions and page numbers for easy reference.

Writing and Thinking:

These exercises provide the student an opportunity to independently explore and expand on concepts presented in the chapter.

Additional Features

Calculator Problems: Each problem is designed to highlight the usefulness of a calculator in solving certain complex problems, but maintain the necessity of understanding the concepts behind the problem.

Chapter Test: Provides an opportunity for the students to practice the skills presented in the chapter in a test format.

Cumulative Review: As new concepts build on previous concepts, the cumulative review provides the student with an opportunity to continually reinforce existing skills while practicing newer skills.

Answers: Answers are provided for odd numbered section exercises and answers to all even and odd numbered exercises in the cumulative reviews and chapter tests.

Teachers' Edition:

Answers: Answers to all the exercises are conveniently located in the margins next to the problems.

Teaching Notes: Suggestions for more in depth classroom discussions and alternate methods and techniques are located in the margins.

Changes included in the new edition:

- New, reader friendly, layout
- Rearrangement of chapters for better flow, continuity and progression
- Writing and Thinking About Mathematics
- Calculator Instructions (New emphasis on the graphing calculator)
- Calculator Problems

Content

The TI-83 Plus graphing calculator has been made an integral part of many of the presentations in this textbook. To get maximum benefits from the use of this text, the student must have one of these calculators (or a calculator with similar features). Directions are given for using the related calculator commands as they are needed throughout.

Chapter 1, Real Numbers, Solving Equations, and Exponents, is a review of topics from beginning algebra. Real numbers and their properties, sets and set-builder notation, properties of exponents, scientific notation, absolute values, solving equations, and solving for terms in formulas are all reviewed. Other topics include a variety of word problems, interval notation (possibly new for some students), solving linear and absolute value inequalities, and graphing the solution sets of inequalities by testing points in intervals.

Chapter 2, Straight Lines and Functions, includes complete discussions on the three basic forms for equations of straight lines in a plane: the standard form, the slope-intercept form, and the point-slope form. Slope is discussed for parallel and perpendicular lines and treated as a rate of change. Functions are introduced and the vertical line test is used to tell whether or not a graph represents a function. Use of a TI-83 Plus graphing calculator is an integral part of this introduction to functions as well as part of graphing linear inequalities in the last section.

Chapter 3, Systems of Linear Equations, covers solving systems of two equations in two variables and systems of three equations in three variables. The basic methods of graphing, substitution, and addition are included along with matrices and Gaussian elimination, determinants and Cramer's Rule. Double subscript notation is now used with matrices for an easy transition to use of matrices in solving systems of equations with the TI-83 Plus calculator. Applications involve mixture, interest, work, algebra, and geometry. The last section discusses half-planes and graphing systems of linear inequalities, again including the use of a graphing calculator.

Chapter 4, Polynomials, discusses polynomials, and the operations of addition, subtraction, multiplication, and division, including synthetic division. Factoring of polynomials includes factoring the greatest common factor, the FOIL method and recognizing special forms such as the sum and difference of cubes. A special section on factoring with negative exponents is included. Equations are solved by factoring and applications involve topics such as the use of function notation to represent area and volume, the Pythagorean Theorem, and consecutive integers. A new section on using a graphing calculator to solve equations and inequalities provides the student with the opportunity to become more familiar with the calculator and to solve more difficult equations.

Chapter 5, Rational Expressions, applies the factoring skills from Chapter 4 in operations with rational expressions. Included are the topics of multiplication, division, addition and subtraction with rational expressions, simplifying complex fractions and solving equations and inequalities containing rational expressions. Applications are related to work, distance-rate-time, and variation.

Chapter 6, Roots, Radicals, and Complex Numbers, introduces roots and fractional exponents and the use of a calculator to find estimated values. Arithmetic with radicals includes simplifying radical expressions, addition, subtraction, and rationalizing numerators and denominators. A new section on functions with radicals shows how to analyze the domain and range of radical functions and how to graph these functions by using a graphing calculator. Complex numbers are introduced along with the basic operations of addition, subtraction, multiplication, and division. These are skills needed for the work with quadratic equations and quadratic functions in Chapters 7 and 8.

Chapter 7, Quadratic Equations and Inequalities, reviews solving quadratic equations by factoring and introduces the methods of using the square root property and completing the square. The quadratic formula is developed by completing the square and students are encouraged to use the most efficient method for solving any particular quadratic equation. Applications are related to the Pythagorean Theorem, projectiles, geometry, and cost per person. The last two sections cover solving equations with radicals and solving equations in quadratic form.

Chapter 8, Quadratic Functions and Conic Sections, provides a basic understanding of conic sections (parabolas, circles, ellipses, and hyperbolas) and their graphs. The first section gives detailed analyses of parabolas as functions involving horizontal and vertical shifting and finding maximum and minimum values with applications. Quadratic inequalities are solved algebraically with factoring and the aid of number lines and with techniques using the graphing calculator. Function notation is used in discussing reflections and translations of a variety of types of functions. Then vertical and horizontal parabolas are developed as conic sections. The distance formula and midpoint formula are included along with the discussion of circles. The thorough development of ellipses and hyperbolas includes graphs with centers not at the origin. Solving systems with nonlinear equations is the final topic of the chapter.

Chapter 9, Exponential and Logarithmic Functions, begins with a new section on the algebra of functions and leads to the development of the composition of functions and methods for finding the inverses of one-to-one functions. This introduction lays the groundwork for understanding the relationship between exponential functions and logarithmic functions. While the properties of real exponents and logarithms are presented completely, most numerical calculations are performed with the aid of a calculator. Special emphasis is placed on the number e and applications with natural logarithms. Students will find the applications with exponential and logarithmic functions among the most interesting and useful in their mathematical studies. Those students who plan to take a course in calculus should be aware that many of the applications found in calculus involve exponential and logarithmic expressions in some form.

Chapter 10, Sequences, Series, and the Binomial Theorem, provides flexibility for the instructor and reference material for the students. The topics presented here, including permutations and combinations, are likely to appear in courses in probability and statistics, finite mathematics, and higher level courses in mathematics. Any of these topics covered at this time will give students additional mathematical experience and insight for future studies.

I recommend that the topics be covered in the order presented because most sections assume knowledge of the material in previous sections. This is particularly true of the cumulative review sections at the end of each chapter. Of course, time and other circumstances may dictate another sequence of topics. For example, in some programs, Chapters 1 and 2 might be considered review. In case of any changes, the instructor should be sure that the students are somewhat familiar with a graphing calculator.

Acknowledgements

I would like to thank Editor Mary Janelle Cady and Developmental Editor Marcel Prevuznak for their hard work and invaluable assistance in the development and production of this text.

Many thanks go to the following manuscript reviewers who offered their constructive and critical comments: Peggie Smith at Bowie State University; Leah Pierce at Crafton Hills College; Lois Miller and Jack Wadhams at Golden West College; Linda Buchanan at Howard College-Big Spring; Rob Van Kirk at Idaho State University; Elaine Elkind and Terry Fung at Kean University; Virginia Puckett at Miami-Dade Community College; Theresa Hert at Mount San Jacinto College; Michael Sanchez at Sacramento City College; Thom Clark at Trident Technical College.

Finally, special thanks go to James Hawkes for his faith in this fifth edition and his willingness to commit so many resources to guarantee a top-quality product for students and teachers.

D. Franklin Wright

TO THE STUDENT

The goal of this text and of your instructor is for you to succeed in intermediate algebra. Certainly, you should make this your goal as well. What follows is a brief discussion about developing good work habits and using the features of this text to your best advantage. For you to achieve the greatest return on your investment of time and energy you should practice the following three rules of learning.

1. Reserve a block of time for study every day.
2. Study what you don't know.
3. Don't be afraid to make mistakes.

How to use this book

The following seven-step guide will not only make using this book a more worthwhile and efficient task, but it will also help you benefit more from classroom lectures or the assistance that you receive in a math lab.

1. Try to look over the assigned section(s) before attending class or lab. In this way, new ideas may not sound so foreign when you hear them mentioned again. This will also help you see where you need to ask questions about material that seems difficult to you.

2. Read examples carefully. They have been chosen and written to show you all of the problem-solving steps that you need to be familiar with. You might even try to solve example problems on your own before studying the solutions that are given.

3. Work the section exercises faithfully as they are assigned. Problem-solving practice is the single most important element in achieving success in any math class, and there is no good substitute for actually doing this work yourself. Demonstrating that you can think independently through each step of each type of problem will also give you confidence in your ability to answer questions on quizzes and exams. Check the Answer Key periodically while working section exercises to be sure that you have the right ideas and are proceeding in the right manner.

4. Use the Writing and Thinking About Mathematics questions as an opportunity to explore the way that you think about math. A big part of learning and understanding mathematics is being able to talk about mathematical ideas and communicate the thinking that you do when you approach new concepts and problems. These questions can help you analyze your own approach to mathematics and, in class or group discussions, learn from ideas expressed by your fellow students.

5. Use the Chapter Index of Key Ideas and Terms as a recap when you begin to prepare for a Chapter Test. It will reference all the major ideas that you should be familiar with from that chapter and indicate where you can turn if review is needed. You can also use the Chapter Index as a final checklist once you feel you have completed your review and are prepared for the Chapter Test.

6. Chapter Tests are provided so that you can practice for the tests that are actually given in class or lab. To simulate a test situation, block out a one-hour, uninterrupted period in a quiet place where your only focus is on accurately completing the Chapter Test. Use the Answer Key at the back of the book as a self-check only after you have completed all of the questions on the test.

7. Cumulative Reviews will help you retain the skills that you acquired in studying earlier chapters. They appear after every chapter beginning with Chapter 2. Approach them in much the same manner as you would the Chapter Tests in order to keep all of your skills sharp throughout the entire course.

How to Prepare for an Exam

Gaining Skill and Confidence

The stress that many students feel while trying to succeed in mathematics is what you have probably heard called "math anxiety." It is a real-life phenomenon, and many students experience such a high level of anxiety during mathematics exams in particular that they simply cannot perform to the best of their abilities. It is possible to overcome this stress simply by building your confidence in your ability to do mathematics and by minimizing your fears of making mistakes.

No matter how much it may seem that in mathematics you must either be right or wrong, with no middle ground, you should realize that you can be learning just as much from the times that you make mistakes as you can from the times that your work is correct. Success will come. Don't think that making mistakes at first means that you'll never be any good at mathematics. Learning mathematics requires lots of practice. Most importantly, it requires a true confidence in yourself and in the fact that with practice and persistence the mistakes will become fewer, the successes will become greater, and you will be able to say, "I can do this."

Showing What You Know

If you have attended class or lab regularly, taken good notes, read your textbook, kept up with homework exercises, and asked for help when it was needed, then you have already made significant progress in preparing for an exam and conquering any anxiety. Here are a few other suggestions to maximize your preparedness and minimize your stress.

1. Give yourself enough time to review. You will generally have several days advance notice before an exam. Set aside a block of time each day with the goal of reviewing a manageable portion of the material that the test will cover. Don't cram!

2. Work lots of problems to refresh your memory and sharpen you skills. Go back to redo selected exercises from all of your homework assignments.

3. Reread your text and your notes, and use the Chapter Index of Key Ideas and Terms and the Chapter Test to recap major ideas and do a self-evaluated test simulation.

4. Be sure that you are well-rested so that you can be alert and focused during the exam.

5. Don't study up to the last minute. Give yourself some time to wind down before the exam. This will help you to organize your thoughts and feel more calm as the test begins.

6. As you take the test, realize that its purpose is not to trick you, but to give you and your instructor an accurate idea of what you have learned. Good study habits, a positive attitude, and confidence in your own ability will be reflected in your performance on any exam.

7. Finally, you should realize that your responsibility does not end with taking the exam. When your instructor returns your corrected exam, you should review your instructor's comments and any mistakes that you might have made. Take the opportunity to learn from this important feedback about what you have accomplished, where you could work harder, and how you can best prepare for future exams.

HAWKES LEARNING SYSTEMS: INTERMEDIATE ALGEBRA

Overview

This multimedia courseware allows students to become better problem-solvers by creating a mastery level of learning in the classroom. The software includes a "demonstrate," "instruct," "practice," "tutor," and "certify" mode in each lesson, allowing students to learn through step-by-step interactions with the software. These automated homework system's tutorial and assessment modes extend instructional influence beyond the classroom. Intelligence is what makes the tutorials so unique. By offering intelligent tutoring and mastery level testing to measure what has been learned, the software extends the instructor's ability to influence students to solve problems. This courseware can be ordered either seperately or bundled together with this text.

Minimum Requirements

In order to run *HLS: Intermediate Algebra*, you will need:

400 MHz or faster processor or equivalent
Windows® 98SE or later
64 MB RAM (128 MB recommended)
150 MB hard drive space
256 color display (800x600, 16-bit color recommended)
Internet Explorer 5.5 or later
CD-ROM drive

Getting Started

Before you can run *HLS: Intermediate Algebra*, you will need an access code. This 30 character code is <u>your</u> personal access code. To obtain an access code, go to **http://www.quantsystems.com** and follow the links to the access code request page (unless directed otherwise by your instructor.)

Installation

Insert the *HLS: Intermediate Algebra* Installation CD-ROM into the CD-ROM drive. Select the Start/Run command, type in the CD-ROM drive letter followed by \setup.exe. (For example, d:\setup.exe where d is the CD-ROM drive letter.)

The complete installation will use over 140 MB of hard drive space and will install the entire product, except the multimedia files, on your hard drive.

After selecting the desired installation option, follow the on-screen instructions to complete your installation of *HLS: Intermediate Algebra*.

Starting the Courseware

After you installed *HLS: Intermediate Algebra* on your computer, to run the courseware select Start/Programs/Quant Systems/Intermediate Algebra.

You will be prompted to enter your access code with a message box similar to the following:

Login

Enter your access code

| F1 - Load from Disk | Ok | Cancel |

Type your access code into the box(es) provided. When you are finished, press OK.

If you typed in your access code correctly, you will be prompted to save the code to disk. If you choose to save your code to disk, typing in the access code each time you run *HLS: Intermediate Algebra* will not be necessary. Instead, select the [F1 - Load from Disk] button when prompted to enter your access code and choose the path to your saved access code.

Now that you have entered your access code and saved it to diskette, you are ready to run a lesson. From the table of contents screen, choose the appropriate chapter and then choose the lesson you wish to run.

Features

Each lesson in *HLS: Intermediate Algebra* has five modes: Demonstrate, Instruct, Practice, Tutor, and Certify.

Demonstrate: Demonstrate provides you with a brief overview of the lesson. It presents an example of the type of question you will see in Practice and Certify, shows you how to input an answer, lists some of the specific features of the lesson, and tells you how many correct answers are needed to pass Certify.

Instruct: Instruct provides an expository on the material covered in the lesson in a multimedia environment. This same instruct mode can be accessed via the tutor mode.

Practice: Practice allows you to hone your problem-solving skills. It provides an unlimited number of randomly generated problems. Practice also provides access to the Tutor mode by selecting the Tutor button located by the Submit button.

Tutor: Tutor mode is broken up into several parts: Instruct, Explain Error, Step by Step, and Solution.

1. Instruct, which can also be selected directly from Practice mode, contains a multimedia lecture of the material covered in a lesson.

2. Explain Error is active whenever a problem is incorrectly answered. It will attempt to explain the error that caused you to incorrectly answer the problem.

3. Step by Step is an interactive "step through" of the problem. It breaks each problem into several steps, explains to you each step in solving the problem, and asks you a question about the step. After you answer the last step correctly, you have solved the problem.

4. Solution will provide you with a detailed "worked-out" solution to the problem.

Throughout the Tutor, you will see words or phrases colored green with a dashed underline. These are called Hot Words. Clicking on a Hot Word will provide you with more information on these word(s) or phrases.

Certify: Certify is the testing mode. You are given a finite number of problems and a certain number of strikes (problems you can get wrong). If you answer the required number of questions, you will receive a certification code and a certificate. Write down your certification code and/or print out your certificate. The certification code will be used by your instructor to update your records. Note that the Tutor is not available in Certify.

Integration of Courseware and Textbook

Throughout this text, you will see an icon that helps to integrate the Intermediate Algebra textbook and *HLS: Intermediate Algebra* courseware.

This icon indicates which *HLS: Intermediate Algebra* lessons you should run in order to test yourself on the subject material and to review the contents of a chapter.

Support

If you have questions about *HLS: Intermediate Algebra* or are having technical difficulties, we can be contacted as follows:

Phone: (843) 571-2825
Email: tcchsupport@quantsystems.com
Web: www.quantsystems.com

Our support hours are 8:30 am to 5:30 pm, Eastern Time, Monday through Friday.

Real Numbers, Solving Equations, and Exponents

Did You Know?

In Chapter 1, you will find a great many symbols defined, as well as rules of manipulation for these symbolic expressions. Most people think that algebra has always existed, complete with all the common symbols in use today. That is not the case, since modern symbols did not appear consistently until the beginning of the sixteenth century. Prior to that, algebra was rhetorical. That is, all problems were written out in words using either Latin, Arabic, or Greek, and some nonstandard abbreviations. Numbers were written out. The common use of Hindu-Arabic numerals did not begin until the sixteenth century, although these numerals had been introduced into Europe in the twelfth century.

The sign for addition, +, was a contraction of the Latin *et*, which means "and." Gradually, the *e* was contracted and the crossed *t* became the plus sign. The minus sign or bar, −, is thought to be derived from the habit of early scribes of using a bar to represent the letter *m*. Thus the word *summa* was often written *sum̄a*. Thus, the bar came to represent the missing *m*, the first letter of the word *minus*. The radical symbol, $\sqrt{}$, is derived from a small printed *r*, which stood for the Latin word *radix*, or root. The symbol for times, a cross, ×, was developed from cross multiplication or for the purpose of indicating products in proportions. Thus

$$\frac{2}{3} \times \frac{6}{9} \quad \text{stood for} \quad \frac{2}{3} = \frac{6}{9}.$$

The cross is not well suited for algebra, since it resembles the symbol *x*, which is used for variables. Therefore, a dot is usually used to indicate multiplication in algebra. The dot seemed to have developed from an Italian practice of separating columns in multiplication tables with a dot. Exponents were used as early as the fourteenth century by the mathematician Oresme (1330? – 1382), who gave the first known use of the rules for fractional exponents in a text book he wrote. The equal sign is attributed to Robert Recorde (1510? – 1558), who wrote, "I will sette as I doe often in woorke use, a paire of paralleles, or Gemowe [twin] lines of one lengthe, thus: = , because noe .2. thynges, can be moare equalle." As you can tell, the development of algebraic symbols occurred over a long period of time, and symbols became standardized through usage and convenience. If you are interested in the history of numerical symbolism, you will find more information in D.E Smith's *History of Mathematics*, Volume II.

Recorde

1.1   **Properties of Real Numbers**

1.2   **Operations with Real Numbers**

1.3   **First-Degree (or Linear) Equations and Absolute Value Equations**

1.4   **Evaluating and Solving Formulas**

1.5   **Applications**

1.6   **Linear Inequalities and Absolute Value Inequalities**

1.7   **Properties of Exponents**

1.8   **More on Exponents and Scientific Notation**

"The Mathematician, carried along on his flood of symbols, dealing apparently with purely formal truths, may still reach results of endless importance for our description of the physical universe."

Karl Pearson (1857 – 1936)

Welcome to your second course in algebra. You will find that many of the topics presented, such as solving equations, factoring, working with fractional expressions, and solving word problems, are familiar because they were discussed in beginning algebra. However, you will also find that the coverage of each topic, including many new topics, is in greater depth and that the pace is somewhat faster. The intent is to prepare you for success with the algebraic content in your future studies in mathematics, science, business, and economics. You should be prepared to expend considerable time and effort throughout the semester.

We begin in Chapter 1 with a review of the properties and operations with real numbers. These ideas form the foundation for the study of algebra and need to be understood thoroughly. As an example of a deeper analysis of familiar topics, we will discuss solving first-degree equations, then expand the techniques to include solving absolute value equations and solving formulas for specified variables. Also, you will be introduced to the new topic of intervals of real numbers. Intervals and interval notation are related to graphs and are used frequently in higher level mathematics courses.

There is much to look forward to in this course. With hard work and perseverance, you should have a very rewarding experience.

Properties of Real Numbers

Objectives

After completing this section, you will be able to:

1. *Identify given numbers as members of one or more of the following sets:*
   natural numbers, whole numbers, integers, rational numbers, irrational numbers,
   and real numbers.
2. *Write rational numbers as infinite repeating decimals.*
3. *Graph sets of numbers on real number lines.*
4. *Describe sets of numbers using set-builder notation given their graphs.*
5. *Name the properties of real numbers that justify given statements.*
6. *Complete statements using the real number properties.*

We begin with a development of the terminology and properties of numbers that form the foundation for the study of algebra. The following kinds of numbers are studied in some detail in beginning algebra courses.

Types of Numbers

Natural Numbers (or Counting Numbers)

$N = \{ 1, 2, 3, 4, 5, 6, \ldots \}$ The three dots (. . .), called an ellipsis, indicate that the pattern is to continue. In this case, the pattern is to continue without end.

Whole Numbers (The number 0 is added to the set of Natural Numbers.)

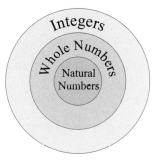

$W = \{ 0, 1, 2, 3, 4, 5, 6, \ldots \}$

Integers

$Z = \{ \ldots, \ -4, -3, -2, -1, 0, 1, 2, 3, 4, \ldots \}$

The integers are one of the important stepping stones from arithmetic to algebra since the concept of positive and negative numbers is basic to algebra. Integers can be represented on a number line by marking 0 at some point and then marking the **positive integers** to the right of 0 and their **opposites** or **negative integers** to the left of 0 (Figure 1.1).

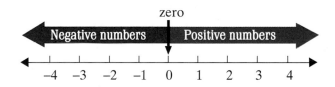

Figure 1.1

Other important types of numbers are **rational numbers, irrational numbers,** and **real numbers**. We define these numbers first, then discuss their properties.

Rational Number

*A **rational number** is any number that can be written in the form $\dfrac{a}{b}$ where a and b are integers and $b \neq 0$. (The letter Q represents the set of all rational numbers.)*

Example 1: Rational Numbers •

a. $\dfrac{2}{3}, \dfrac{7}{1}, \dfrac{-5}{3}, \dfrac{27}{10}$, and $\dfrac{3}{-10}$ are all rational numbers. Each is in the form $\dfrac{a}{b}$ where a and b are integers and $b \neq 0$.

b. $1\dfrac{3}{4}$ and 2.33 are also rational numbers. They are not in the form $\dfrac{a}{b}$, but they **can be written** in that form:

$$1\frac{3}{4} = \frac{7}{4} \quad \text{and} \quad 2.33 = 2\frac{33}{100} = \frac{233}{100}.$$

c. $\dfrac{\pi}{6}$ and $\dfrac{\sqrt{2}}{3}$ are in the form $\dfrac{a}{b}$ but the numerator in each case is not an integer and cannot be written as an integer. In fact, both fractions are **not** rational numbers and, as we will see, they are called **irrational numbers**.

• •

Rational numbers have been defined as numbers that can be written in the form $\dfrac{a}{b}$ where a and b are integers and $b \neq 0$. With this definition, we can show that in decimal form a rational number is either

    1. a terminating decimal, or
    2. an infinite repeating decimal.

Examples of terminating decimals are:

$$\frac{1}{4} = 0.25, \quad \frac{3}{8} = 0.375, \text{ and } 1\frac{4}{5} = \frac{9}{5} = 1.8$$

Examples of infinite repeating decimals are: $\dfrac{2}{3}, \dfrac{1}{7}$ and $\dfrac{4}{11}$. Long division shows the repeating decimal pattern for each:

$$
\begin{array}{r}
0.6666.. \\
3\overline{)2.0000...} \\
\underline{18} \\
20 \\
\underline{18} \\
20 \\
\underline{18} \\
20 \\
\underline{18} \\
2
\end{array}
\qquad
\begin{array}{r}
0.14285714... \\
7\overline{)1.00000000...} \\
\underline{7} \\
30 \\
\underline{28} \\
20 \\
\underline{14} \\
60 \\
\underline{56} \\
40 \\
\underline{35} \\
50 \\
\underline{49} \\
10 \\
\underline{7} \\
30 \\
\underline{28} \\
2
\end{array}
\qquad
\begin{array}{r}
0.3636... \\
11\overline{)4.0000...} \\
\underline{33} \\
70 \\
\underline{66} \\
40 \\
\underline{33} \\
70 \\
\underline{66} \\
4
\end{array}
$$

Thus,

$$\frac{2}{3} = 0.6666..., \quad \frac{1}{7} = 0.14285714..., \quad \text{and} \quad \frac{4}{11} = 0.3636...$$

Or we can write a bar over the repeating pattern of digits as:

$$\frac{2}{3} = 0.\overline{6}, \quad \frac{1}{7} = 0.\overline{142857}, \quad \text{and} \quad \frac{4}{11} = 0.\overline{36}.$$

As the following definition indicates, decimal numbers that cannot be written as terminating or infinite repeating decimals have a nonrepeating pattern to their digits and are called **irrational numbers**.

Irrational Number

*An **irrational number** is any number that can be written as an infinite, nonrepeating decimal.*

Example 2: Irrational Numbers ●

The following are irrational numbers. Note that there is no repeating pattern in their decimal representation. The three dots indicate that the digits continue indefinitely.

a. $\pi = 3.14159265358979\ldots$ π has no repeating pattern in its decimal form.

b. $\sqrt{2} = 1.414213562\ldots$ The square root of 2 has no repeating pattern in its decimal form.

c. $e = 2.718281828459045\ldots$ e is a number used in higher mathematics and engineering courses.

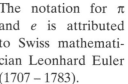

d. $0.01001000100001\ldots$ Even though there is a pattern to the digits, the pattern is not repeating.

The notation for π and e is attributed to Swiss mathematician Leonhard Euler (1707 – 1783).

● ●

NOTES The number π is particularly fascinating to mathematicians and has recently been represented to 1.24 trillion decimal places. A discussion of π and a representation to 3742 decimal places is in Appendix 1 at the back of this text.

Together, the rational numbers and irrational numbers form the set of **real numbers** (R). The relationships between the various types of real numbers can be seen in the diagram in Figure 1.2.

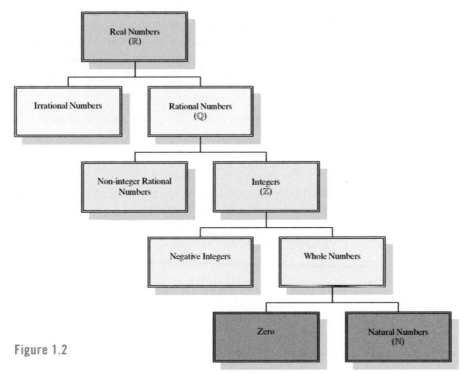

Figure 1.2

Understanding these relationships is critical for success in algebra. For example, if a problem calls for integer solutions and your solution is $\frac{3}{5}$, then you need to understand that you have not found an **integer** solution.

Summary of Relationships Among Various Types of Numbers

1. *Every natural number is also a whole number, an integer, a rational number, and a real number.*

2. *Every whole number is also an integer, a rational number, and a real number.*

3. *Every integer is also a rational number and a real number.*

4. *Every rational number is also a real number.*

5. *Every irrational number is also a real number.*

Real Number Lines

There is a one-to-one correspondence between the real numbers and the points on a line. Thus, number lines are also called **real number lines** (Figure 1.3), and every rational and irrational number has a corresponding point on a real number line.

Figure 1.3

Irrational numbers in the form of various roots, such as $\sqrt{3}$, will be discussed thoroughly in Chapter 6. For now, to estimate the placement of numbers such as $\sqrt{3}$, $\sqrt{6}$, or $\sqrt{27}$ on a real number line, you can note their relationships to the square roots of perfect square integers such as 1, 4, 9, 16, 25, and so on, or use a calculator to find a decimal estimation. Thus,

$\sqrt{3}$ is slightly less than $\sqrt{4} = 2$ (With a calculator: $\sqrt{3} = 1.732050808...$)

$\sqrt{6}$ is slightly more than $\sqrt{4} = 2$ (With a calculator: $\sqrt{6} = 2.449489743...$)

$\sqrt{27}$ is slightly more than $\sqrt{25} = 5$ (With a calculator: $\sqrt{27} = 5.196152423...$)

To understand how an infinite, nonrepeating decimal corresponds to a single point on a line, we will illustrate how $\pi = 3.14159265...$ can be marked. If a circle has a diameter of 1 unit, then its circumference is π units because the formula for circumference $(C = \pi d)$ gives $C = \pi \cdot 1 = \pi$. By rolling such a circle along a line, the number π can be located (Figure 1.4).

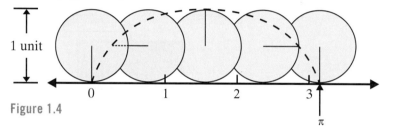

Figure 1.4

Sets and Set-Builder Notation

A **set** is a collection of objects or numbers. The items in the set are called **elements**, and sets are indicated with braces, { }, and named with capital letters. If the elements are listed within the braces, as we have done earlier with the set of natural numbers, N, the set of whole numbers, W, and the set of integers, Z, the set is said to be in **roster form**. The symbol $\in$ is read "is an element of" and is used to indicate that a particular number belongs to a set. For example, $0 \in W$ and $-3 \in Z$.

If the elements in a set can be counted, the set is said to be **finite**. If the elements cannot be counted, as for N, W, and Z, the set is said to be **infinite**. If a set has absolutely no elements, it is called the **empty set** or **null set** and is written in the form { } or with the special symbol $\varnothing$. For example, the set of all people over 12 feet tall is the empty set, $\varnothing$.

The notation $\{x \mid \quad \}$ is read "the set of all x such that..." and is called **set-builder notation**. The bar (|) is read "such that." This notation, along with the inequality symbols below, is used to indicate sets of real numbers.

$<$	*"less than"*	$\leq$	*"less than or equal to"*
$>$	*"greater than"*	$\geq$	*"greater than or equal to"*

Notation	Meaning	Graph
$\{\,x \mid x \le a\,\}$	"the set of all x such that x is less than or equal to a"	
$\{\,x \mid x \ge b\,\}$	"the set of all x such that x is greater than or equal to b"	
$\{\,x \mid x < a \text{ or } x > b\,\}$ (This is also known as the **union** of two sets of numbers.)	"the set of all x such that x is less than a or x is greater than b"	
$\{\,x \mid x > a \text{ and } x < b\,\}$ or $\{\,x \mid a < x < b\,\}$ (This is also known as the **intersection** of two sets of numbers.)	"the set of all x such that x is greater than a **and** x is less than b"	

NOTES

Comment about Union and Intersection

The concepts of union and intersection are part of set theory which is very useful in a variety of courses including abstract algebra, probability and statistics. These concepts are also used in analyzing inequalities and analyzing relationships among sets in general. The **union** (symbolized $\cup$, as in $A \cup B$) of two (or more) sets is the set of all elements that belong to either one set or the other set or to both sets. The **intersection** (symbolized $\cap$, as in $A \cap B$) of two (or more) sets is the set of all elements that belong to both sets. The word **or** is used to indicate union and the word **and** is used to indicate intersection. For example, if $A = \{1, 2, 3\}$ and $B = \{2, 3, 4\}$, then the numbers that belong to A **or** B is the set $A \cup B = \{1, 2, 3, 4\}$. The set of numbers that belong to A **and** B is the set $A \cap B = \{2, 3\}$. Also, we can write $2 \in (A \cap B)$ and $3 \in (A \cap B)$. Similarly, the union and intersection notation can be used for sets with the inequalities.

For example, $\{\,x \mid x < a \text{ or } x > b\,\}$ can be written in the form
$$\{\,x \mid x < a\,\} \cup \{\,x \mid x > b\,\}.$$

Also, $\{\,x \mid x > a \text{ and } x < b\,\}$ can be written in the form
$$\{\,x \mid x > a\,\} \cap \{\,x \mid x < b\,\}$$

The following examples show how various sets of real numbers can be graphed. **Note that an open circle means that the point is not included in the set, and a closed circle means that the point is included in the set.**

Example 3: Graph

a. Graph the set of real numbers $\{\,x\mid -1 \leq x < 2\,\}$.
Solution:

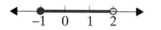

This graph shows all points between -1 and 2, including -1 but not 2.

b. Graph the set $\{\,x\mid x > 3\,\}$.
Solution:

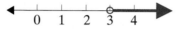

This graph shows all points greater than 3, but not including 3.

In Examples 3c and 3d, note carefully the use of the two key words **or** and **and**.

c. Graph the set $\{\,x\mid x \leq 2\ \textbf{and}\ x \geq 0\,\}$. The word **and** implies those values of x that satisfy **both** inequalities.
Solution:

$x \leq 2$

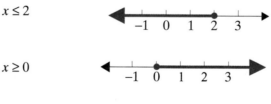

$x \geq 0$

Note that the third graph shows the points in common between the first two graphs in this example.

$x \leq 2$ **and** $x \geq 0$

This set can also be indicated as $\{\,x\mid 0 \leq x \leq 2\,\}$.

d. Graph the set $\{\,x\mid x > 5\ \textbf{or}\ x \leq 4\,\}$. The word or implies those values of x that satisfy **either** inequality.
Solution:

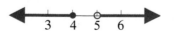

e. Given the set $\{\,-2,\ -\sqrt{3},\ -1.1,\ -\dfrac{1}{2},\ 0,\ \dfrac{5}{8},\ \sqrt{1.7},\ 1.7\,\}$,

    i.   graph the set of numbers on a number line;
    ii. tell which numbers are integers;
    iii. tell which numbers are rational numbers;
    iv. tell which numbers are irrational numbers.

Solutions: **i.**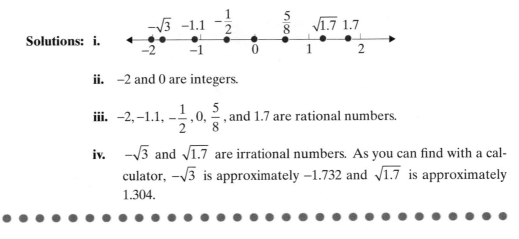

ii. −2 and 0 are integers.

iii. $-2, -1.1, -\dfrac{1}{2}, 0, \dfrac{5}{8}$, and 1.7 are rational numbers.

iv. $-\sqrt{3}$ and $\sqrt{1.7}$ are irrational numbers. As you can find with a calculator, $-\sqrt{3}$ is approximately −1.732 and $\sqrt{1.7}$ is approximately 1.304.

• •

The **operations** of addition and multiplication with real numbers have five properties each, and there is one property that combines both operations. These eleven properties are called the **field properties of real numbers** and, as we will discuss in the next section, are used whenever real numbers are added or multiplied.

For real numbers $a, b,$ and c:

Field Properties of the Real Numbers

Addition	*Name of property*	*Multiplication*
A1 $\ a + b$ is a real number	Closure	**M1** $\ a \cdot b$ is a real number
A2 $\ a + b = b + a$	Commutative	**M2** $\ a \cdot b = b \cdot a$
A3 $\ (a + b) + c = a + (b + c)$	Associative	**M3** $\ (a \cdot b) \cdot c = a \cdot (b \cdot c)$
A4 $\ a + 0 = 0 + a = a$	Identity	**M4** $\ a \cdot 1 = 1 \cdot a = a$
A5 $\ a + (-a) = 0$	Inverse	**M5** $\ a \cdot \dfrac{1}{a} = 1 \ (a \neq 0)$
D Distributive Property:		$a \cdot (b + c) = a \cdot b + a \cdot c$ or $(b + c) \cdot a = b \cdot a + c \cdot a$

When 0 is added to a number, the result is that same number. Similarly, when a number is multiplied by 1, the result is that same number. These properties lead to the following terminology.

Identities
1. The number 0 is called the **additive identity**.
2. The number 1 is called the **multiplicative identity**.

Example 4: Identify the Property •

Tell which field property justifies each statement.

a. $-3 \cdot 1 = -3$ Identity of multiplication

b. $\dfrac{1}{2} + 0 = \dfrac{1}{2}$ Identity of addition

c. $7 + 1.6 = 1.6 + 7$ Commutative property of addition

d. $(2 \cdot 3) \cdot 8 = 2 \cdot (3 \cdot 8)$ Associative property of multiplication

e. $6 + (-6) = 0$ Inverse property of addition

f. $9 \cdot \dfrac{1}{9} = 1$ Inverse property of multiplication

g. $4 \cdot (2 + 3) = 4 \cdot 2 + 4 \cdot 3$ Distributive property

h. $4 \cdot (x + 3) = 4 \cdot x + 12$ Distributive property

• •

As the following examples illustrate, subtraction and division are neither commutative nor associative.

Subtraction is not commutative: $a - b \neq b - a$

   Example: $6 - 2 \neq 2 - 6$

               because $6 - 2 = 4$

               and $2 - 6 = -4$

               and $4 \neq -4$.

Subtraction is not associative: $a - (b - c) \neq (a - b) - c$

   Example: $10 - (5 - 3) \neq (10 - 5) - 3$

               because $10 - (5 - 3) = 10 - (2) = 8$

               and $(10 - 5) - 3 = 5 - 3 = 2$

               and $8 \neq 2$.

Division is not commutative: $a \div b \neq b \div a$

   Example: $6 \div 2 \neq 2 \div 6$

               because $6 \div 2 = 3$

               and $2 \div 6 = \dfrac{1}{3}$

               and $3 \neq \dfrac{1}{3}$.

Division is not associative: $a \div (b \div c) \neq (a \div b) \div c$

   Example: $24 \div (4 \div 2) \neq (24 \div 4) \div 2$

               because $24 \div (4 \div 2) = 24 \div (2) = 12$

               and $(24 \div 4) \div 2 = (6) \div 2 = 3$

               and $12 \neq 3$.

The **multiplicative inverse** of a, $\dfrac{1}{a}$, is also called the **reciprocal** of a and is defined only for $a \neq 0$. For $a = 0$,

$$\dfrac{1}{0} \text{ is \textbf{undefined}.} \text{ (0 is the only real number that does not have a reciprocal.)}$$

(That is, if $\dfrac{1}{0} = x$, then we must have $1 = 0 \cdot x$. But this is not possible because $0 \cdot x = 0$ for all x. Therefore, we say that $\dfrac{1}{0}$ is **undefined**.)

There are two basic properties related to inequalities (or order) with real numbers. You have probably used these before, but you may not have known their names.

Properties of Inequality (Order)

For real numbers a, b, and c:

O1   Trichotomy Property: *Exactly one of the following is true: $a < b$, $a = b$, or $a > b$.*

O2   Transitive Property: *If $a < b$ and $b < c$, then $a < c$.*

Example 5: Identify the Property

State which property of inequality or order is illustrated.

a. If $x < 3$ and $3 < y$, then $x < y$.   Transitive property of order

b. If a is a real number, then either   Trichotomy property of order
$a = 5$ or $a > 5$ or $a < 5$.

c. If x and y are real numbers, then either   Trichotomy property of order
$x = y$ or $x > y$ or $x < y$.

d. If $t > x$ and $x > -7$, then $t > -7$.   Transitive property of order
(Note that this property applies to $>$, $\geq$, $<$, and $\leq$.)

Practice Problems

1. List the integers.

2. What type of number is π?

3. Graph the set $\{ x \mid 0 < x \leq 1 \}$.

4. $a + 3 = 3 + a$ illustrates which property of addition?

5. $2(x + y) = 2x + 2y$ illustrates which field property?

1.1 Exercises

For Exercises 1 – 6, list the numbers in the set

$$A = \left\{ -8, -\sqrt{5}, -\sqrt{4}, -\frac{4}{3}, -1.2, -\frac{\sqrt{3}}{2}, 0, \frac{4}{5}, \sqrt{3}, \sqrt{11}, \sqrt{16}, 4.2, 6 \right\} \text{ that are described in}$$

each exercise.

1. $\{ x \mid x$ is a whole number $\}$
2. $\{ x \mid x$ is a natural number $\}$
3. $\{ x \mid x$ is an integer $\}$
4. $\{ x \mid x$ is an irrational number $\}$
5. $\{ x \mid x$ is a rational number $\}$
6. $\{ x \mid x$ is a real number $\}$

In Exercises 7 – 12, choose the word that correctly completes each statement.

7. If x is a rational number, then x is (always, sometimes, never) a real number.
8. If x is a rational number, then x is (always, sometimes, never) an irrational number.
9. If x is an integer, then x is (always, sometimes, never) a whole number.
10. If x is a real number, then x is (always, sometimes, never) a rational number.
11. If x is a rational number, then x is (always, sometimes, never) an integer.
12. If x is a natural number, then x is (always, sometimes, never) a whole number.

Write each of the rational numbers in Exercises 13 – 18 as a terminating decimal or an infinite repeating decimal.

13. $\dfrac{5}{8}$
14. $\dfrac{9}{16}$
15. $-\dfrac{7}{3}$
16. $-\dfrac{8}{9}$
17. $\dfrac{71}{20}$
18. $\dfrac{5}{7}$

Graph each of the sets of numbers in Exercises 19 – 26 on a number line. Note that in each exercise a restriction is placed on the variable.

19. $\{ x \mid x < 7, x$ is a whole number $\}$
20. $\{ x \mid x < -12, x$ is an integer $\}$
21. $\{ x \mid x \geq -4, x$ is an integer $\}$
22. $\{ x \mid -9 < x \leq 2, x$ is an integer $\}$
23. $\{ x \mid -5 < x < 6, x$ is a natural number $\}$
24. $\{ x \mid -8 < x < 0, x$ is a whole number $\}$
25. $\{ x \mid x < 12$ and $x > 0, x$ is an integer $\}$
26. $\{ x \mid x > 0$ and $x \leq 8, x$ is an integer $\}$

For Exercises 27 – 30, use set-builder notation to indicate each set of numbers as described.

27. the set of all real numbers between 3 and 5, including 3.
28. the set of all real numbers between −4 and 4.
29. the set of all real numbers greater than or equal to −2.5.
30. the set of all real numbers between −1.8 and 5, including both of these numbers.

Answers to Practice Problems: 1. $\{ \ldots, -4, -3, -2, -1, 0, 1, 2, \ldots \}$ **2.** Irrational (or real)
3. **4.** Commutative property of addition **5.** Distributive property

Graph each of the sets of real numbers in Exercises 31 – 38 on a number line. Note that since no restriction is placed on the variable, it is understood to represent real numbers.

31. $\{\, x \mid x < 2 \text{ or } x > 8 \,\}$

32. $\{\, x \mid x \le -5 \text{ or } x \ge \dfrac{9}{5} \,\}$

33. $\{\, x \mid -\sqrt{2} < x < 0 \,\}$

34. $\{\, x \mid -4 \le x < -\sqrt{5} \,\}$

35. $\{\, x \mid x \ge -1 \text{ and } -3 \le x \le 0 \,\}$

36. $\{\, x \mid -\dfrac{7}{4} < x \le 2 \text{ and } x < 1 \,\}$

37. $\{\, x \mid -1.6 < x < 0 \text{ or } 2 \le x \le 3.7 \,\}$

38. $\{\, x \mid -\dfrac{3}{5} < x < 0 \text{ or } 0 \le x < \pi \,\}$

Name the property of real numbers that justifies each statement in Exercises 39 – 62. All variables represent real numbers and no denominator is 0.

39. $6 + (-3)$ is a real number.

40. $9 + (-9) = 0$

41. Either $x < y, x = y,$ or $x > y$

42. $4 + 0 = 4$

43. $5 + (a + b) = (5 + a) + b$

44. $9 \cdot (x + 5) = 9 \cdot x + 45$

45. $3 \cdot y = y \cdot 3$

46. $7 \cdot \dfrac{1}{7} = 1$

47. Exactly one of the following is true: $x < 5, x = 5,$ or $x > 5$

48. If $x < 11$ and $11 < y$, then $x < y$.

49. $\sqrt{5} \cdot y$ is a real number.

50. $\left(\sqrt{2} \cdot x \right) \cdot y = \sqrt{2} \cdot (x \cdot y)$

51. $6 + y = y + 6$

52. Either $s = t, s > t,$ or $s < t$.

53. $x \cdot (y + 5) = x \cdot y + x \cdot 5$

54. $\sqrt{7} + (-\sqrt{7}) = 0$

55. $(y + z) \times 1 = y + z$

56. $x + (y + 7) = (x + y) + 7$

57. If $a < -2$ and $-2 < b,$ then $a < b$.

58. $8 \cdot x + 3 \cdot x = (8 + 3) \cdot x$

59. $11 + (y + 4) = (11 + y) + 4$

60. $(x + y) \cdot \dfrac{1}{x + y} = 1$

61. $s + (-s) = 0$

62. If $a < b$ and $b < (x - 2),$ then $a < (x - 2)$.

Complete the expressions in Exercises 63 – 74 by using the given property.

63. $x + 7 = $ _____ Commutative property of addition

64. $x \cdot 3 = $ _____ Commutative property of multiplication

65. $x \cdot (6 + y) = $ _____ Distributive property

66. $x + (3 + y) = $ _____ Associative property of addition

67. $3 \cdot (x \cdot z) = $ _____ Associative property of multiplication

68. Either $x < y, x > y,$ or _____. Trichotomy property of order

69. $2 \cdot (y + 3) = $ _____ Distributive property

70. If $x < a$ and $a < 10,$ then _____. Transitive property of order

71. The multiplicative inverse of 6 is _____ because _____. Inverse of multiplication

72. The reciprocal of –4 is _____ because _____ .
Inverse of multiplication

73. The additive inverse of –7 is _____ because _____ .
Inverse of addition

74. The additive inverse of 15 is _____ because _____ .
Inverse of addition

Writing and Thinking About Mathematics

75. The inequality $x > 5$ is used to indicate all real numbers greater than 5. Is there a "first" real number greater than 5? Or, in other words, is there a real number greater than 5 that is "closest to" 5? Write, in your own words, a paragraph or two with examples to indicate your understanding of this question. Show your analysis to a friend to see if he or she understands and agrees or disagrees with your thinking. A related question would be "What is the real number closest to 0?".

Hawkes Learning Systems: Intermediate Algebra

Name That Real Number
Properties of Real Numbers

1.2 Operations with Real Numbers

After completing this section, you will be able to:

1. *Evaluate absolute value expressions.*
2. *Determine the values, if any, that satisfy absolute value equations.*
3. *Add, subtract, multiply, and divide real numbers.*
4. *Evaluate expressions by using the rules for order of operations.*

Absolute Value

To understand how to actually perform the operations of addition, subtraction, multiplication, and division, we need the concept of **absolute value** of a number, symbolized $|x|$. Geometrically, the absolute value of a number is its distance from 0 on a real number line. Thus, $|3| = 3$ and $|-3| = 3$, since both 3 and -3 are 3 units from 0 (Figure 1.5).

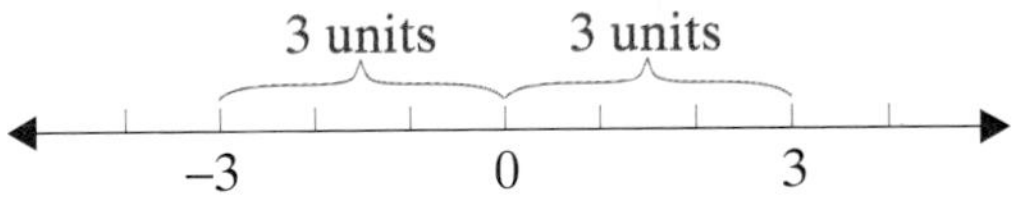

$$|-3| = 3 \text{ and } |3| = 3$$

Figure 1.5

For a variable x, $-x$ represents the **opposite** of x.

Thus,   if x represents a **positive** number, then $-x$ represents a **negative** number.
However,   if x represents a **negative** number, then $-x$ represents a **positive** number.

For example,

If $x = 3$, then $-x = -3$.
But, if $x = -5$, then $-x = -(-5) = 5$.

By thinking of $-x$ as the **opposite of x** rather than being negative, you will better understand the following definition of absolute value.

Absolute Value

For any real number x,

$$if\ x\ is\ positive\ or\ 0, \qquad |x| = x;$$

$$if\ x\ is\ negative, \qquad |x| = -x.$$

Another form of this same definition is the following:

$$|x| = \begin{cases} x\ if\ x \geq 0 \\ -x\ if\ x < 0 \end{cases}$$

In any case, remember that the absolute value of any real number is **nonnegative**. To reinforce this relatively abstract definition, consider the following examples:

For $a = 4$,   Here, a is positive.

$$|a| = |4| = 4 = a.$$

For $a = -7$,   Here, $-a$ is positive because a is negative.

$$|a| = |-7| = +7 = -(-7) = -a. \quad \text{In this case } -a = -(-7) = 7.$$

Remember that the symbol $-x$ represents a positive number whenever the variable represents a negative number.

Example 1: Absolute Value

a. $|5| = 5$ **b.** $|-6| = -(-6) = 6$

c. $\left|-\sqrt{2}\right| = -\left(-\sqrt{2}\right) = \sqrt{2}$ **d.** $|\pi| = \pi$

e. $\left|-\dfrac{3}{4}\right| = -\left(-\dfrac{3}{4}\right) = \dfrac{3}{4}$ **f.** $|0| = 0$

g. If $|x| = 6$, what are the possible values for x?
     Solution: $x = 6$ or $x = -6$ since both $|6| = 6$ and $|-6| = 6$. (We say that $\{6, -6\}$ is the
          solution set of the equation.)

h. If $|x| = -5$, what are the possible values for x?
     Solution: There is no value for x for which $|x| = -5$ because the absolute value of
          a number is always nonnegative. The solution set is the empty set, $\varnothing$.

Addition and Subtraction

The rules for addition with positive and negative real numbers are stated here for easy reference. They illustrate the need for understanding absolute value. They also illustrate how mathematical symbols can simplify an idea that is rather difficult to state in words.

Rules for Adding Real Numbers

1. To add two real numbers with like signs, add their absolute values and use the common sign.

$$(+7) + (+3) = +(|+7| + |+3|) = +(7 + 3) = 10$$
$$(-7) + (-3) = -(|-7| + |-3|) = -(7 + 3) = -10$$

2. To add two real numbers with unlike signs, subtract their absolute values (the smaller from the larger), and use the sign of the number with the larger absolute value.

$$(-15) + (+9) = -(|-15| - |+9|) = -(15 - 9) = -6$$
$$(+15) + (-9) = +(|+15| - |-9|) = +(15 - 9) = 6$$

Example 2: Addition

a. Sums with like signs:

i. $(+10) + (+2) = +(|+10| + |+2|) = +(10 + 2) = 12$

ii. $\left(\dfrac{1}{5}\right) + \left(\dfrac{3}{5}\right) = \left(\left|\dfrac{1}{5}\right| + \left|\dfrac{3}{5}\right|\right) = \dfrac{1}{5} + \dfrac{3}{5} = \dfrac{4}{5}$

iii. $(-10) + (-2) = -(|-10| + |-2|) = -(10 + 2) = -12$

b. Sums with unlike signs:

i. $(-10) + (+2) = -(|-10| - |+2|) = -(10 - 2) = -8$

ii. $\left(-\dfrac{7}{11}\right) + \left(\dfrac{5}{11}\right) = -\left(\left|-\dfrac{7}{11}\right| - \left|\dfrac{5}{11}\right|\right) = -\left(\dfrac{7}{11} - \dfrac{5}{11}\right) = -\dfrac{2}{11}$

iii. $(+10) + (-2) = +(|+10| - |-2|) = +(10 - 2) = 8$

c. Application:

Jeremy is planning a cookout. He wants to buy $3\dfrac{1}{2}$ lbs ground beef, 3 lbs pork chops, 2 lbs chicken, and $3\dfrac{1}{4}$ lbs steak. How much meat does Jeremy intend to buy?

continued on next page ...

Solution:

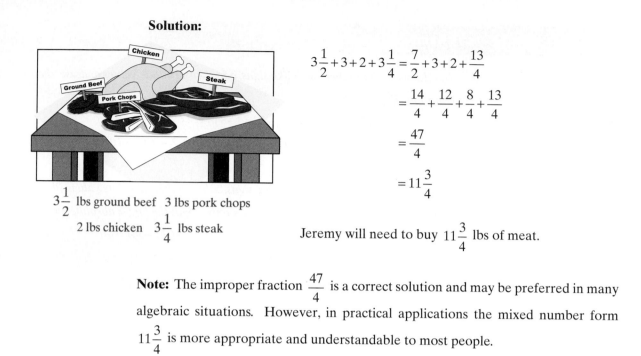

$$3\frac{1}{2}+3+2+3\frac{1}{4}=\frac{7}{2}+3+2+\frac{13}{4}$$

$$=\frac{14}{4}+\frac{12}{4}+\frac{8}{4}+\frac{13}{4}$$

$$=\frac{47}{4}$$

$$=11\frac{3}{4}$$

$3\frac{1}{2}$ lbs ground beef   3 lbs pork chops

2 lbs chicken $3\frac{1}{4}$ lbs steak

Jeremy will need to buy $11\frac{3}{4}$ lbs of meat.

Note: The improper fraction $\frac{47}{4}$ is a correct solution and may be preferred in many algebraic situations. However, in practical applications the mixed number form $11\frac{3}{4}$ is more appropriate and understandable to most people.

● ●

The difference between two real numbers is defined as the sum of the first number and the opposite of the second number, as follows:

Subtraction

For real numbers a and b,

$$a - b = a + (-b).$$

Subtraction is defined in terms of addition. This means that any subtraction problem can be thought of as an addition problem. Thus, to find the difference between −20 and +13, we can write

$$(-20)-(+13)=(-20)+(-13)=-33.$$

To subtract −7 from −18, we have

$$(-18)-(-7)=(-18)+(+7)=-11.$$

The operation of subtraction can be done mentally in terms of addition. For example,

$$-8-10 \ = -8+(-10) \qquad \text{This step can be done mentally.}$$
$$= -18.$$

Example 3: Subtraction

a. $18 - 13 = 18 + (-13) = 5$

b. $-20 - 9 = -20 + (-9) = -29$

c. $14 - (-6) = 14 + (+6) = 20$

d. $-3 - 4 = -3 + (-4) = -7$

e. $\dfrac{17}{3} - \dfrac{25}{3} = \dfrac{17}{3} + \left(-\dfrac{25}{3}\right) = -\dfrac{8}{3}$

If more than two numbers are involved, add or subtract from left to right.

f. $8 - 12 - 21 = 8 + (-12) + (-21) = -4 + (-21) = -25$

g. $\dfrac{3}{5} + \dfrac{4}{5} - \dfrac{7}{5} = \dfrac{7}{5} - \dfrac{7}{5} = 0$

h. $8.2 - 3.1 - 0.6 = 5.1 - 0.6 = 4.5$

Applications

i. Susan is a salesperson for a shoe store. Last week, her sales were as follows:

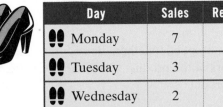

Day	Sales	Returns	Daily Net Sales
Monday	7	1	6
Tuesday	3	0	3
Wednesday	2	4	-2
Thursday	6	1	5
Friday	8	3	5

What were Susan's net sales for last week?

Solution: $6 + 3 + (-2) + 5 + 5 = 17$

Susan's net sales for the week were 17 pairs of shoes.

continued on next page ...

ii. During the first hour of trading, a stock trader has a profit of $1973.27. During the second hour, the trader has a loss of $797.53. During the third hour, he has a profit of $925.87. What was the trader's net profit during the first three hours of trading?

Solution: $1973.27 - 797.53 + 925.87 = 2101.61$
The trader's net profit during the first three hours of trading was $2101.61.

iii. At noon on Tuesday, the temperature was 34° F. By noon on Thursday, the temperature had dropped to −5° F. How much did the temperature drop between Tuesday and Thursday?

Solution: $(-5) - (+34) = -5 + (-34) = -39$

Between Tuesday and Thursday, the temperature changed −39° F (or dropped 39° F).

Multiplication and Division

If two real numbers are multiplied together, the result is called the **product**, and the two numbers are called **factors** of the product. For example, since $5 \cdot 3 = 15$, the numbers 5 and 3 are factors of the product 15.

$$5 \cdot 3 \ = \ 15$$

factors   product

Multiplication can be indicated by any of the following conventions:

Symbols for Multiplication

Symbol		Example
·	raised dot	$4 \cdot 7$
( )	numbers inside or next to parentheses	$5(10)$ or $(5)10$ or $(5)(10)$
×	cross sign	6×12 or $\begin{array}{r} 12 \\ \underline{\times 6} \end{array}$
	number written next to variable	$8x$
	variable written next to variable	xy

From previous experience, we know that **the product of two positive real numbers is positive**. For the product of a positive integer and a negative integer, consider the product $5(-3)$. We can think of this as repeated addition,

$$(-3) + (-3) + (-3) + (-3) + (-3) = 5(-3)$$
$$= -15$$

More generally, by using the commutative and associative properties and the relationship $-a = -1 \cdot a$, it can be proven that **the product of a positive real number and a negative real number is negative**. The theorem is stated here without proof.

Theorem

For positive real numbers a and b,

$$a(-b) = (-a)b = -ab$$

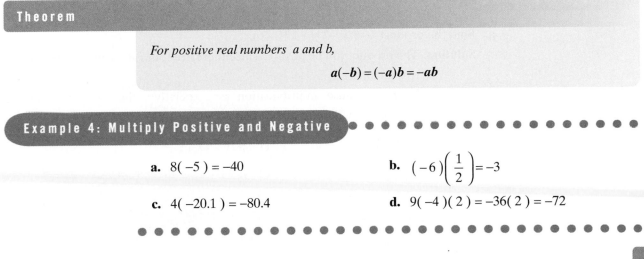

Example 4: Multiply Positive and Negative

a. $8(-5) = -40$

b. $(-6)\left(\dfrac{1}{2}\right) = -3$

c. $4(-20.1) = -80.4$

d. $9(-4)(2) = -36(2) = -72$

The fact that the product of two negative numbers is positive is stated in the following theorem without proof.

Theorem

For positive real numbers a and b,

$$(-a)(-b) = ab.$$

Example 5: Multiply Negative and Negative ● ● ● ● ● ● ● ● ● ● ● ● ● ● ● ● ● ● ●

a. $(-3)(-4) = 12$

b. $\left(-\dfrac{3}{4}\right)\left(-\dfrac{1}{2}\right) = \dfrac{3}{8}$

c. $(-2.1)(-0.03) = 0.063$

d. $(-2)(-5)(-7) = (10)(-7) = -70$

● ●

Since the product of two negative numbers is positive, we can make the following useful observations:

1. If a product of nonzero factors contains an **even** number of negative factors, the product will be positive.
2. If a product of nonzero factors contains an **odd** number of negative factors, the product will be negative.

Example 6 illustrates these two ideas.

Example 6: Multiply ●

a. Find the product $(-6)(-2)(-1)(-8)$.

Solution: The product will be positive since there are four (an even number) negative factors.

[**Note:** Because multiplication is associative, the numbers can be "grouped" without violating the rules for order of operations.]

$$(-6)(-2)(-1)(-8) = \big[(-6)(-2)\big]\big[(-1)(-8)\big]$$
$$= \big[12\big]\big[8\big]$$
$$= 96$$

b. Find the product $(-7)(5)(-2)(-9)$.

Solution: The product will be negative since there are three (an odd number) negative factors.

$$(-7)(5)(-2)(-9) = \left[(-7)(5)\right]\left[(-2)(-9)\right]$$
$$= \left[-35\right]\left[18\right]$$
$$= -630$$

The rule for division follows from the rule for multiplication and is given below.

NOTES

Note that division can be indicated in any of the following forms:

$$\frac{a}{b}, \quad a \div b, \quad a/b, \quad \text{and} \quad b\overline{)a}$$

The fraction form is used in this discussion.

Division

For real numbers a and b (b ≠ 0),

$$\frac{a}{b} = x \; \text{if and only if } a = b \cdot x.$$

Since division is defined in terms of multiplication, the rules for dividing with positive and negative real numbers are related to the rules for multiplication. With this definition and the rules for multiplication, we have results as follows:

$\frac{15}{3} = 5$	because	$15 = 3 \cdot 5$
$\frac{-24}{6} = -4$	because	$-24 = 6(-4)$
$\frac{14}{-2} = -7$	because	$14 = (-2)(-7)$
$\frac{-36}{-12} = 3$	because	$-36 = (-12)(3)$

Example 7: Divide

a. $\frac{30.6}{-2} = -15.3$ **b.** $\frac{-18}{-6} = 3$ **c.** $-\frac{51}{3} = -17$

Rules for Multiplication and Division with Real Numbers

1. *If two nonzero numbers have like signs, then both their product and their quotients will be positive.*

2. *If two nonzero numbers have unlike signs, then both their product and their quotients will be negative.*

For the number 0, we have the following two properties.

Multiplication Property of Zero

For any real number a, $a \cdot 0 = 0$.

Division by 0

Division by 0 is undefined*. To understand why division by 0 is undefined, consider the following discussion.*

Suppose that $\dfrac{a}{0} = x$. Then, by the definition of division, $a = 0 \cdot x$.

If $a \neq 0$, then this is impossible because $0 \cdot x = 0$ and $a \neq 0$.

If $a = 0$, then $0 \cdot x = 0 = a$ is true for any value of x and there is no unique value for x. (This means that $\dfrac{0}{0}$ is undefined.)

Therefore, $\dfrac{a}{0}$ is undefined for all real values of a.

However, if $b \neq 0$, then $\dfrac{0}{b} = 0$ since $0 = b \cdot 0$ for any nonzero real value of b.

Example 8: Division and 0

a. $\dfrac{7}{0}$ is undefined.

b. $\dfrac{0}{-6} = 0$

A positive integer **exponent** is a number used to indicate repeated multiplication by the same factor. An exponent is written to the right and slightly above the factor, and this factor is called the **base** of the exponent. (**Note:** Properties of exponents will be discussed in detail in Sections 1.7 and 1.8. Fractional exponents and their meanings will be discussed in Chapter 6.)

Exponent

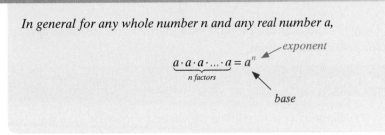

In general for any whole number n and any real number a,

$$\underbrace{a \cdot a \cdot a \cdot \ldots \cdot a}_{n \text{ factors}} = a^n$$

with labels: *exponent* pointing to n, *base* pointing to a.

$$3 \cdot 3 \cdot 3 \cdot 3 = 3^4 \qquad\qquad \text{read “ 3 to the fourth power”}$$

with labels: exponent 4, base 3.

The **power** is the value of the expression:

$$3^4 = 81$$

with labels: exponent 4, base 3, power pointing to 81.

The equation $3^4 = 81$ can be read as "Three to the fourth power is 81." or "81 is the fourth power of 3." This is the sense in which 81 is the "power." Similarly, 1, 10, 100, and 1000 are powers of 10.

The base is said to be "squared" if the exponent is 2 and "cubed" if the exponent is 3. Thus,

$$5^2 = 25 \qquad \text{is read "5 squared equals 25."}$$

and

$$2^3 = 8 \qquad \text{is read "2 cubed equals 8."}$$

Example 9: Exponents ●

    a. $2^5 = 2 \cdot 2 \cdot 2 \cdot 2 \cdot 2 = 32$

    b. $(-6)^3 = (-6)(-6)(-6) = -216$

    c. $-2^4 = -1 \cdot (2 \cdot 2 \cdot 2 \cdot 2) = -1 \cdot 16 = -16$

● ●

Order of Operations

Consider the problem of evaluating an expression with more than one operation, such as $5 + 2 \cdot 3$.

Addition first gives: $5 + 2 \cdot 3 = 7 \cdot 3 = 21.$
Multiplication first gives: $5 + 2 \cdot 3 = 5 + 6 = 11.$
But $21 \neq 11.$

Only one answer can be right, and mathematicians have agreed on the following **rules for order of operations**.

Rules for Order of Operations

1. *Simplify within symbols of inclusion (parentheses, brackets, braces, fraction bar, absolute value bars) beginning with the innermost symbols.*
2. *Find any powers indicated by exponents or roots.*
3. *Multiply or divide from **left to right**.*
4. *Add or subtract from **left to right**.*

Using these rules, we find that the correct value for $5 + 2 \cdot 3$ is found by multiplying first. Thus,

$5 + 2 \cdot 3 = 5 + 6 = 11$ is correct.

A well-known mnemonic device for remembering these rules is the following:

Please	**E**xcuse	**M**y	**D**ear	**A**unt	**S**ally
↑	↑	↑	↑	↑	↑
Parentheses	**Exponents**	**Multiplication**	**Division**	Addition	Subtraction

Example 10: Order of Operations

Using the rules for order of operations, find the value of each of the following expressions.

a. $10 - 21 \div 3 + 2$

Solution:

$10 - 21 \div 3 + 2 = 10 - 7 + 2$ Perform the division first.

$= 3 + 2 = 5$ Add or subtract from left to right.

b. $5(-2) + 6 \cdot 4 - 2$

Solution:

$5(-2) + 6 \cdot 4 - 2 = -10 + 24 - 2$ Multiply from left to right first.

$= 14 - 2$ Add or subtract from left to right.

$= 12$

c. $12 \div 2 \cdot 3 - 4$

    Solution: $12 \div 2 \cdot 3 - 4 = 6 \cdot 3 - 4$ Perform the division first.

                               $= 18 - 4$ Multiply.

                               $= 14$ Add or subtract from left to right.

d. $-5 - 3[4 + (16 - 10) \div 2]$

    Solution: $-5 - 3[4 + (16 - 10) \div 2]$

                     $= -5 - 3[4 + (6) \div 2]$ Simplify within parentheses first.

                     $= -5 - 3[4 + 3]$ Divide within brackets.

                     $= -5 - 3[7]$ Simplify within brackets.

                     $= -5 - 21$ Multiply.

                     $= -26$ Add or subtract from left to right.

e. $16 \cdot 3 \div 2^3 - (18 + 20)$

    Solution: $16 \cdot 3 \div 2^3 - (18 + 20)$

                     $= 16 \cdot 3 \div 2^3 - 38$ Simplify within the parentheses.

                     $= 16 \cdot 3 \div 8 - 38$ Find the powers using exponents.

                     $= 48 \div 8 - 38$ Multiply or divide from left to right.

                     $= 6 - 38$

                     $= -32$ Add or subtract from left to right.

Practice Problems

Find the value of each expression, if possible.

1. $-8.6 - 4.1 - 0.2$

2. $(-3)(-5)(-6)$

3. $\dfrac{8}{0}$

4. $4(-2) + 6 \cdot 3$

5. $2(-5 + 3) + 16 \div 8 \cdot 2$

6. $3(-8 + 2^3) + 6^2 \div 2^2 - 4$

1.2 Exercises

Find the value of each expression in Exercises 1 – 5.

1. $|7|$ **2.** $\left| -\dfrac{3}{4} \right|$ **3.** $\left| -\sqrt{5} \right|$ **4.** $|0|$ **5.** $-|-8|$

Answers to Practice Problems: **1.** -12.9 **2.** -90 **3.** Undefined **4.** 10 **5.** 0 **6.** 5

Find the set of values for x in Exercises 6 – 15 that make true statements. If a statement is never true, indicate this by writing the empty set, ∅.

6. $|x| = 4$　　**7.** $|x| = 7$　　**8.** $|x| = 0$　　**9.** $|x| = 2$　　**10.** $|x| = -3$

11. $|x| = \dfrac{4}{5}$　　**12.** $|x| = 2.6$　　**13.** $|x| = -2.8$　　**14.** $|x| = -x$　　**15.** $|x| = x$

Perform the indicated operation in Exercises 16 – 65.

16. $(-16) + 20$　　**17.** $(-2) + (-9)$　　**18.** $-5 + |-3|$　　**19.** $(-8) + (-6) + 5$

20. $-3 + |7| + (-2)$　　**21.** $\left(-\dfrac{3}{8}\right) + \dfrac{7}{8}$　　**22.** $\dfrac{9}{16} + \left|-\dfrac{5}{16}\right|$　　**23.** $12 - 15$

24. $-4 - (-8)$　　**25.** $(-9) - (-9)$　　**26.** $0 - (-12)$　　**27.** $17 - |-4|$

28. $-\dfrac{4}{13} - \dfrac{3}{13}$　　**29.** $\dfrac{3}{5} - \dfrac{9}{5}$　　**30.** $\left|-\dfrac{8}{3}\right| - \left(-\dfrac{2}{3}\right)$

31. $(-1.7) + (-5.2)$　　**32.** $(8.5) + (-7.9)$　　**33.** $-7 - (-2) + 6$

34. $-18 - 22 - 41$　　**35.** $-8 + (-7) - (-15)$　　**36.** $9 - (-3) + (-2)$

37. $21 + |-3| - |-4|$　　**38.** $|13| - |-9| + |-3|$　　**39.** $-\dfrac{7}{6} + \left(-\dfrac{5}{6}\right) - \dfrac{1}{6}$

40. $\dfrac{4}{15} + \left|-\dfrac{7}{15}\right| - \left|\dfrac{16}{15}\right|$　　**41.** $\left(-\dfrac{9}{16}\right) + \left(-\dfrac{7}{8}\right)$　　**42.** $\dfrac{1}{8} - \left(-\dfrac{1}{2}\right) + \dfrac{1}{4}$

43. $\dfrac{4}{5} + \left(-\dfrac{2}{3}\right) - \dfrac{1}{6}$　　**44.** $-\dfrac{3}{8} - \dfrac{5}{6} + \left(-\dfrac{1}{2}\right)$　　**45.** $(-8)(-7)$

46. $(-3)(17)$　　**47.** $(-8)(-1)(-5)(6)(-2)$

48. $(12)\left(-\dfrac{5}{6}\right)$　　**49.** $\dfrac{3}{8} \cdot \dfrac{5}{2}$　　**50.** $-\dfrac{5}{16} \cdot \dfrac{3}{4}$

51. $\left(-\dfrac{3}{10}\right)\left(\dfrac{5}{6}\right)\left(-\dfrac{8}{7}\right)\left(\dfrac{1}{2}\right)\left(-\dfrac{1}{4}\right)$　　**52.** $6(5.3)$

53. $(-0.8)(4.9)$　　**54.** $(11.7)(-2.06)(-1.3)$　　**55.** $(-20) \div (-10)$

56. $\dfrac{-39}{-13}$　　**57.** $\dfrac{-91}{-7}$　　**58.** $\dfrac{52}{13}$　　**59.** $\dfrac{6}{16} \div 0$

60. $60 \div (-15)$　　**61.** $0 \div \dfrac{11}{12}$　　**62.** $\dfrac{28.4}{-7}$　　**63.** $-68.05 \div 5$

64. $-88.64 \div (-8)$　　**65.** $-6.084 \div (-9)$

Find the value of each expression in Exercises 66 – 80 by using the rules for order of operations.

66. $18 \div 3 \cdot 6 + 3$　　**67.** $7(4 - 2) \div 7 + 3$　　**68.** $2^2 - 15 \div 3$

69. $2^2 \cdot 3 \div 3 + 6 \div 3$

70. $-6 \cdot 3 \div (-1) + 4 - 2$

71. $5(-2) \div (-5) + 5 - 3$

72. $\left(4^2 + 6\right) - 2 \cdot 19$

73. $\left(12 \cdot 4 \div 2^3\right) - \left[\left(3 \cdot 2^3\right) \div (4 \cdot 6)\right]$

74. $\left[(3 \cdot 0) \div (2 \cdot 1)\right] - \left(24 - 6^2\right) \div \left(4^2 - 3 \cdot 4\right)$

75. $\left(3 \cdot 2^3\right) \div (3 \cdot 4) + (2 \cdot 3 + 4) \div (6 - 1)$

76. $-6 + (-2)(12 \cdot 2 \div 3)4$

77. $14 - \left[11 \cdot 4 - \left(2 \cdot 3^2 + 1\right)\right]$

78. $6 + 3\left[-4 - 2(3 - 1)\right]$

79. $7 - \left[4 \cdot 3 - (4 - 3 \cdot 2)\right]$

80. $-2\left[6 + 4(1 + 7)\right] \div 4$

81. $\dfrac{(-3)(-6)}{5 - (-4)} - 2$

82. $\dfrac{4 - (-10)}{-2 - 5} \div (-2)$

83. $\dfrac{16 - (-4)}{-3 + 9} \div \dfrac{10^2 + 10}{-5 \cdot 11}$

84. $\dfrac{3^3 - (-27)}{2 \cdot 3^2} + \dfrac{-6 \cdot 5}{-2 \cdot 5}$

*Use a calculator to evaluate each expression in Exercises 85 – 90. Note that for a leading negative sign you must use the (–) key next to **ENTER** or the (+/–) key on some calculators. Also, brackets must be replaced with parentheses on the calculator.*

85. $12^2 \div 3 \cdot 2 + (17 - 5)^3$

86. $5^3 - 7^3 + (5 - 7)^3$

87. $0.8 + 2.1(17 - 14.1 \div 2) \div 7$

88. $(140 - 20 \cdot 6 \div 2^3) \div 5^3$

89. $16 - [18 \cdot 4 - (11.1 \cdot 5^2 + 1)]$

90. $-10\left[45 + 40(10 - 76.5)\right] \div 4$

Hawkes Learning Systems: Intermediate Algebra

Introduction to Absolute Values
Addition with Real Numbers
Subtraction with Real Numbers
Multiplication and Division with Real Numbers
Order of Operations

First-Degree (or Linear) Equations and Absolute Value Equations

Objectives

After completing this section, you will be able to:

1. *Simplify expressions by removing grouping symbols and combining like terms.*

2. *Solve first-degree (or linear) equations.*

3. *Solve first-degree (or linear) absolute value equations.*

Combining Like Terms

An **algebraic expression** is an expression involving variables and numbers using any of the operations of addition, subtraction, multiplication, or division as well as exponents and roots. For example,

$$2x + 5, \quad 3y^2, \quad x^2 - 7x + 10, \quad \sqrt{x} + 9, \quad \text{and} \quad \frac{-b + \sqrt{b^2 - 4ac}}{2a}$$

are all algebraic expressions. You will be learning throughout this course how to work with a variety of types of algebraic expressions.

At this time, we are particularly interested in algebraic expressions called **terms**. A **term** is an expression that involves only multiplication and/or division with constants and variables. A term consisting of only a real number (and no variables) is called a **constant** or a **constant term**. Exponents can be used to indicate repeated factors. The following are four examples of terms:

$$2x^5, \quad \frac{1}{3}x^2y, \quad -14, \quad \text{and} \quad 6x$$

Like terms (or **similar terms**) are those terms that have the same variable factors with the same exponents. That is, whatever power a variable is raised to in one term, it is raised to that same power in other like terms. Constants are also like terms. For example,

Like Terms	
$-5, 1.3,$ and 144	are **like terms** because each term is a constant.
$x^2y, 9x^2y,$ and $-3x^2y$	are **like terms** because each term contains the same two variables with x having an exponent of 2 and y having an exponent of 1.

Unlike Terms	
$9x$ and $5x^3$	are **unlike terms** (**not** like terms) because the variable x is not to the same power in both terms.
$8xy, 13x^2$, and $17y$	are **unlike terms** because not all terms have the same variables and the variables are not to the same power in all terms.

The numerical factor of a term is called the **coefficient** of the variables. Thus, in the term $4x^2y$, 4 is the coefficient of x^2y. If no coefficient is written, then it is understood to be 1. If a negative sign is in front of a variable expression, then the coefficient is understood to be -1. For example,

$$x = 1 \cdot x, \quad n^2 = 1 \cdot n^2, \quad -y = -1 \cdot y, \quad \text{and} -p^3 q^2 = -1 \cdot p^3 q^2$$

The distributive property (see page 11) was stated in both

a left-hand sense with a on the left: $a(b+c) = ab + ac$

and a right-hand sense with a on the right: $(b+c)a = ba + ca$

Each of these forms is equivalent to the other because of the commutative property of multiplication. Now, to **combine like terms** we use the distributive property in the right-hand sense. For example,

$$9x + 2x = (9+2)x \quad \text{and} \quad 5n + n - 2n = (5+1-2)n$$
$$= 11x \qquad\qquad\qquad\qquad\quad = 4n$$

Example 1: Combine Like Terms •

Combine like terms in the following expressions.

a. $4x^2 + 11x^2$

  Solution: $4x^2 + 11x^2$
  $$= (4+11)x^2$$
  $$= 15x^2$$

b. $-6y + 4y$

  Solution: $-6y + 4y$
  $$= (-6+4)y$$
  $$= -2y$$

continued on next page ...

c. $3x^2 - x + 3 - (x^2 - 5x + 6)$

Solution:

$$3x^2 - x + 3 - (x^2 - 5x + 6)$$
$$= 3x^2 - x + 3 + (-1)(x^2 - 5x + 6)$$
$$= 3x^2 - x + 3 + (-x^2 + 5x - 6)$$
$$= 3x^2 - x + 3 - x^2 + 5x - 6$$
$$= (3 - 1)x^2 + (-1 + 5)x + (3 - 6)$$
$$= 2x^2 + 4x - 3$$

The − sign in front of $x^2 - 5x + 6$, can be interpreted as multiplication by −1. Thus, each term in parentheses is multiplied by −1, and each term in parentheses is changed.

d. $\dfrac{3x + 5x}{4} + 9x$

Solution:

$$\frac{3x + 5x}{4} + 9x$$
$$= \frac{8x}{4} + 9x$$
$$= 2x + 9x$$
$$= 11x$$

Note that the fraction bar is treated as a symbol of inclusion, and $3x$ and $5x$ are added first.

e. $4x^2 - [3x - (x^2 + x)]$

Solution:

$$4x^2 - [3x - (x^2 + x)]$$
$$= 4x^2 - [3x - x^2 - x]$$
$$= 4x^2 - [2x - x^2]$$
$$= 4x^2 - 2x + x^2$$
$$= 5x^2 - 2x$$

Remove the innermost symbol of inclusion first. The coefficient of x (and of x^2) is 1. With practice, this step can be done mentally.

First-Degree (or Linear) Equations

Replacing x with 5 in the equation $3x + 4 = 10$ gives the false statement $3 \cdot 5 + 4 = 10$. Replacing x with 2 gives the true statement $3 \cdot 2 + 4 = 10$. Therefore, the number 2 is a **solution** of the equation. The objective of solving equations is to find the **solution set** of the equation. The solution set consists of all values of the variable that make a true statement when substituted for the variable.

First-Degree Equation

An equation of the form **$ax + b = c$**, where a, b, and c are real numbers and $a \neq 0$, is called a **first-degree (or linear) equation** in x.

In this course we will study various types of equations that have more than one solution. However, one important fact, stated here without proof, refers to the number of solutions of a linear equation.

Theorem

Every first-degree (or linear) equation has exactly one solution.

To **solve** (or **find the solution set** of) a first-degree equation, we need the following two properties of equality.

Addition Property of Equality

If the same algebraic expression is added to both sides of an equation, the new equation has the same solutions as the original equation. Symbolically, if A, B, and C are algebraic expressions,

$$\text{and if} \qquad A = B$$

$$\text{then} \qquad A + C = B + C$$

$$\text{and} \qquad A - C = B - C$$

Note: *Subtracting C is the same as adding its opposite, $-C$.*

Multiplication Property of Equality

If both sides of an equation are multiplied by the same nonzero algebraic expression, the new equation has the same solutions as the original equation. Symbolically, if A, B, and C are algebraic expressions,

$$\text{and if} \qquad A = B$$

$$\text{then} \qquad AC = BC \qquad (where\ C \neq 0)$$

$$\text{and} \qquad \frac{A}{C} = \frac{B}{C} \qquad (where\ C \neq 0)$$

Note: *Dividing by C is the same as multiplying by its reciprocal, $\frac{1}{C}$.*

Two equations that have the same solution set are **equivalent**. The numbers in the solution set are said to **satisfy** the equation, and solving the equation is the process used to find the solution set. For example, the equations

$$5x + 3 = 13$$

and $$5x = 10$$

and $$x = 2$$

are all equivalent since the solution to all three equations is the same number, namely 2.

The basic strategy in solving first-degree equations is to find equivalent equations until one is found with only variable terms on one side and constants on the other. Then an equation such as $x = 5$ or $x = 7$, in which the variable has a coefficient of 1, gives the solution to the original equation.

To Solve a First-Degree (or Linear) Equation in One Variable

1. *Simplify each side of the equation by removing any grouping symbols and combining like terms. (In some cases, you may want to multiply both sides of the equation by a constant to clear fractional or decimal coefficients.)*

2. *Use the addition property of equality to add the opposites of constants or variable expressions so that variable expressions are on one side of the equation and constants on the other.*

3. *Use the multiplication property of equality to multiply both sides by the reciprocal of the coefficient of the variable (that is, divide both sides by the coefficient) so that the new coefficient is 1.*

4. *Check your answer by substituting it into the **original** equation.*

Example 2: Solving First-Degree Equations ●●●●●●●●●●●●●●●●●●●

Solve the following first-degree equations.

a. $3x - 5 = 4x + 7 + x$

Solution:

$3x - 5 = 4x + 7 + x$	Write the equation.
$3x - 5 = 5x + 7$	Combine like terms.
$3x - 5 + 5 = 5x + 7 + 5$	Add 5 to both sides of the equation.
$3x = 5x + 12$	Simplify.

$$3x - 5x = 5x + 12 - 5x \qquad \text{Add } -5x \text{ to both sides of the equation.}$$

$$-2x = 12 \qquad \text{Simplify.}$$

$$\frac{-2x}{-2} = \frac{12}{-2} \qquad \text{Divide both sides of the equation by } -2.$$

$$x = -6 \qquad \text{Simplify.}$$

Check: $3(-6) - 5 \overset{?}{=} 4(-6) + 7 + (-6)$

$$-18 - 5 \overset{?}{=} -24 + 7 - 6$$

$$-23 = -23$$

The solution is –6. We usually write just $x = -6$ (or $-6 = x$) to indicate the solution to the original equation. But, writing {–6} as the **solution set** is also acceptable.

As the following examples illustrate, many of the steps shown in Example 2a can be done mentally. Also, there is generally more than one correct way to proceed. In Example 2a, you may choose to add –7 to both sides of the equation where 5 was added to both sides. In this case, the steps that follow will be different, too. However, the solution will be the same.

NOTES

To avoid errors and to help make your work easy to read and understand, try to align the = signs in a vertical format so that each new equation is directly below the previous equation.

---

b. $7(x - 3) = x + 3(x + 5)$

Solution:

$$7(x - 3) = x + 3(x + 5) \qquad \text{Write the equation.}$$

$$7x - 21 = x + 3x + 15 \qquad \text{Use the distributive property (twice).}$$

$$7x - 21 = 4x + 15 \qquad \text{Combine like terms.}$$

$$3x - 21 = 15 \qquad \text{Add } -4x \text{ to both sides.}$$

$$3x = 36 \qquad \text{Add 21 to both sides.}$$

$$x = 12 \qquad \text{Divide both sides by 3.}$$

Check: $7(12 - 3) \overset{?}{=} 12 + 3(12 + 5)$

$$7(9) \overset{?}{=} 12 + 3(17)$$

$$63 \overset{?}{=} 12 + 51$$

$$63 = 63$$

continued on next page ...

c. $\dfrac{x-5}{4} + \dfrac{3}{2} = \dfrac{x+2}{3}$

Solution:

$$\dfrac{x-5}{4} + \dfrac{3}{2} = \dfrac{x+2}{3}$$ Write the equation.

$$12\left(\dfrac{x-5}{4}\right) + 12\left(\dfrac{3}{2}\right) = 12\left(\dfrac{x+2}{3}\right)$$ Multiply both sides by 12, the LCM of the denominators. The LCM of the denominators is also called the LCD or least common denominator.

$$3(x-5) + 6(3) = 4(x+2)$$

$$3x - 15 + 18 = 4x + 8$$ Use the distributive property.

$$3x + 3 = 4x + 8$$ Combine like terms.

$$3 = x + 8$$ Add $-3x$ to both sides.

$$-5 = x$$ Add -8 to both sides.

Check:

$$\dfrac{-5-5}{4} + \dfrac{3}{2} \overset{?}{=} \dfrac{-5+2}{3}$$

$$\dfrac{-10}{4} + \dfrac{6}{4} \overset{?}{=} \dfrac{-3}{3}$$

$$\dfrac{-4}{4} \overset{?}{=} \dfrac{-3}{3}$$

$$-1 = -1$$

Conditional Equations, Identities, and Contradictions

There are times when solving equations that we are concerned with the number of solutions that an equation has. If an equation has a finite number of solutions (the number of solutions is a countable number), the equation is said to be a **conditional equation**. As stated earlier, every linear equation has exactly one solution. Thus, **every linear equation is a conditional equation**. However, in some cases, simplifying an equation will lead to a statement that is always true, such as $0 = 0$. In these cases the original equation has an infinite number of solutions and is called an **identity**. If the equation simplifies to a statement that is never true, such as $0 = 2$, then the original equation is called a **contradiction** and its solution set is the empty set, $\emptyset$. Table 1.1 summarizes these ideas.

Types of Equations	Number of Solutions
Conditional	Finite number of solutions
Identity	Infinite number of solutions
Contradiction	No solutions

Table 1.1

Example 3: Solutions of Equations •

Determine whether each of the following equations is a conditional equation, an identity, or a contradiction.

a. $0.3x + 15 = -1.2$

Solution:	$0.3x + 15 = -1.2$	Write the equation.
	$0.3x = -16.2$	Add -15 to both sides.
	$x = -54$	Solve for x.

The equation has one solution and it is a conditional equation.

b. $3(x - 25) + 3x = 6(x + 10)$

Solution:	$3(x - 25) + 3x = 6(x + 10)$	Write the equation.
	$3x - 75 + 3x = 6x + 60$	Use the distributive property.
	$6x - 75 = 6x + 60$	Simplify.
	$-75 = 60$	Add $-6x$ to both sides.

The last equation is never true. Therefore, the original equation is a contradiction.

c. $-2(x - 7) + x = 14 - x$

Solution:	$-2(x - 7) + x = 14 - x$	Write the equation.
	$-2x + 14 + x = 14 - x$	Use the distributive property.
	$14 - x = 14 - x$	Simplify.
	$14 = 14$	Add x to both sides.

The last equation is always true. Therefore, the original equation is an identity and has an infinite number of solutions. Every real number is a solution.

• •

Absolute Value Equations

The definition of **absolute value** was given in Section 1.2 and is stated again here for easy reference.

Absolute Value

For any real number x,

$$|x| = \begin{cases} x & \text{if } x \geq 0 \\ -x & \text{if } x < 0 \end{cases}$$

Equations involving absolute value may have more than one solution (all of which must be included when giving an answer). For example, suppose that $|x| = 3$. Since $|3| = 3$ and $|-3| = -(-3) = 3$, we have either $x = 3$ or $x = -3$. We can say that the solution set is $\{3, -3\}$. In general, **any number and its opposite have the same absolute value**.

Solving Absolute Value Equations

For c > 0:

a. If $|x| = c$, then $x = c$ or $x = -c$.

b. If $|ax + b| = c$, then $ax + b = c$ or $ax + b = -c$.

Example 4: Solving Absolute Value Equations

Solve the following equations involving absolute value.

a. $|x| = 5$
   Solution: $x = 5$ or $x = -5$

b. $|3x - 4| = 5$
   Solution:

$$3x - 4 = 5 \qquad \text{or} \qquad 3x - 4 = -5$$
$$3x = 9 \qquad\qquad\qquad 3x = -1$$
$$x = 3 \qquad\qquad\qquad x = \frac{-1}{3}$$

c. $|4x - 1| = -8$
   Solution: There is no number that has a negative absolute value. Therefore, this equation has no solution. (The solution is $\varnothing$ and the equation is a contradiction.)

d. $|3x + 7| - 4 = 2$
   Solution: $\quad |3x + 7| - 4 = 2 \qquad\qquad$ Add 4 to both sides so that the absolute value
   $\qquad\qquad\quad |3x + 7| = 6 \qquad\qquad$ expression is by itself.

$$3x + 7 = 6 \qquad \text{or} \qquad 3x + 7 = -6$$
$$3x = -1 \qquad\qquad\qquad 3x = -13$$
$$x = -\frac{1}{3} \qquad\qquad\qquad x = -\frac{13}{3}$$

If two numbers have the same absolute value, then either they are equal or they are opposites of each other. This fact can be used to solve equations that involve two absolute values.

Two Absolute Values

If $|a| = |b|$, then either $a = b$ or $a = -b$.

More generally,

if $|ax + b| = |cx + d|$, then either $ax + b = cx + d$ or $ax + b = -(cx + d)$.

Example 5: Solving Equations with Two Absolute Values • • • • • • • • • • • •

Solve $|x + 5| = |2x + 1|$.

In this case, the two expressions ($x + 5$) and ($2x + 1$) either are equal to each other or are opposites of each other.

Solution:

$$|x + 5| = |2x + 1|$$

$$x + 5 = 2x + 1 \quad \text{or} \quad x + 5 = -(2x + 1)$$

$$5 = x + 1 \qquad\qquad x + 5 = -2x - 1$$

$$4 = x \qquad\qquad\quad 3x + 5 = -1$$

$$3x = -6$$

$$x = -2$$

Note the use of parentheses. We want the opposite of the entire expression ($2x + 1$).

Note: You should check that both 4 and −2 satisfy the original equation.

• •

Practice Problems

1. *Combine like terms:* $3x^2 - \left[x^2 + \left(3x - 2x^2 \right) \right]$

Solve the following equations.

2. $3x - 4 = 2x + 6 - x$

3. $6(x - 4) + x = 4(1 - x) + 4x$

4. $|2x - 1| = 8.2$ $2x - 1 = 8.2 \ OR \ 2x - 1 = -8.2$

1.3 Exercises

In each of the expressions in Exercises 1 – 16, simplify by combining like terms.

1. $-2x + 5y + 6x - 2y$

2. $4x + 2x - 3y - x$

3. $4x - 3y + 2(x + 2y)$

4. $5(x - y) + 2x - 3y$

5. $(3x^2 + x) - (7x^2 - 2x)$

6. $-(4x^2 - 2x) - (5x^2 + 2x)$

7. $4x - [5x + 3 - (7x - 4)]$

8. $3x - [2y - (3x + 4y)]$

9. $\dfrac{-4x - 2x}{3} + 7x$

10. $\dfrac{2(4x - x)}{3} - \dfrac{3(6x - x)}{3}$

11. $\dfrac{8(5x + 2x)}{7} - \dfrac{2(3x + x)}{4}$

12. $\dfrac{6(5x - x)}{8} + \dfrac{5(x + 5x)}{3}$

Answers to Practice Problems: **1.** $4x^2 - 3x$ **2.** $x = 5$ **3.** $x = 4$ **4.** $x = 4.6$ or $x = -3.6$

13. $2x + [\, 9x - 4(\, 3x + 2\,) - 7\,]$

14. $7x - 3[\, 4 - (\, 6x - 1\,) + x\,]$

15. $6x^2 - [\, 9 - 2(\, 3x^2 - 1\,) + 7x^2\,]$

16. $2x^2 + [\, 4x^2 - (\, 8x^2 - 3x\,) + (\, 2x^2 + 7x\,)]$

Solve each of the equations in Exercises 17 – 60.

17. $7x - 4 = 17$

18. $9x + 6 = -21$

19. $4 - 3x = 19$

20. $18 + 11x = 23$

21. $6x - 2.5 = 1.1$

22. $5x + 4.06 = 2.31$

23. $7x + 3.4 = -1.5$

24. $8.2 = 2.6 + 8x$

25. $7x - 6 = 2x + 9$

26. $x - 7 = 4x + 11$

27. $\dfrac{x}{5} - 1 = -6$

28. $\dfrac{3x}{4} + 11 = 20$

29. $\dfrac{2x}{3} - 4 = 8$

30. $\dfrac{5x}{4} + 1 = 11$

31. $2(\, x - 2\,) = 2x - 4$

32. $3x - 7 = 4(\, x + 3\,)$

33. $3(\, 2x - 3\,) = 4x + 5$

34. $3(\, x - 1\,) = 4x + 6$

35. $4(\, 3 - 2x\,) = 2(\, x - 4\,)$

36. $-3(\, x + 5\,) = 6(\, x + 2\,)$

37. $4x + 3 - x = 3x - 9$

38. $5x + 13 = x - 8 - 3x$

39. $x + 7 = 6x + 4 - x$

40. $x - 9 + 5x = 2x - 3$

41. $x - 2 = \dfrac{x + 2}{4} + 5$

42. $x + 8 = \dfrac{x}{3}$

43. $\dfrac{4x}{5} + 2 = 2x - 4$

44. $\dfrac{3x}{2} + 1 = x - 1$

45. $0.8x + 6.2 = 0.2x - 1.0$

46. $2.4x - 8.5 = 1.1x + 0.6$

47. $2.5x + 2.0 = 0.7x + 5.6$

48. $3.2x + 9.5 = 1.8x - 1.7$

49. $12x - (\, 4x - 6\,) = 3x - (\, 9x - 27\,)$

50. $5(\, x - 3\,) - 3 = 2x - 6(\, 2 - x\,)$

51. $\dfrac{x}{4} + 2 = \dfrac{3x}{2} - 3$

52. $\dfrac{2x + 1}{8} - \dfrac{1}{4} = \dfrac{x - 3}{2} + 1$

53. $\dfrac{x}{2} - \dfrac{2x}{3} = \dfrac{3}{4} + \dfrac{x}{3}$

54. $\dfrac{1}{3}x + \dfrac{1}{4} = \dfrac{1}{5}x + \dfrac{1}{6}$

55. $5(\, x - 4\,) = 3(\, 4x - 7\,) - 2(\, 3x + 4\,)$

56. $5(\, x + 1\,) - 4(\, 3 - x\,) = 2x - 7(\, 1 - x\,)$

57. $2(\, 4 - x\,) - (\, 3x + 2\,) = 7 + 4(\, x - 7\,)$

58. $3(\, x - 1\,) - (\, 4x + 2\,) = 3[(\, 2x - 1\,) - 2(\, x + 3\,)]$

59. $3 - x = \dfrac{1}{4}(\, 7 - x\,) - \dfrac{1}{3}(\, 2x - 3\,)$

60. $\dfrac{3}{2}(\, x - 1\,) = \dfrac{1}{2}(\, x - 3\,) - \dfrac{7}{10}$

Solve each of the absolute value equations in Exercises 61 – 80.

61. $|\, x\,| = 8$

62. $|\, x\,| = 6$

63. $|\, z\,| = -\dfrac{1}{5}$

64. $|\, z\,| = \dfrac{1}{5}$

65. $|\, x + 3\,| = 2$

66. $|\, y + 5\,| = -7$

67. $|x - 4| = \dfrac{1}{2}$ **68.** $|3x + 1| = 8$ **69.** $|5x - 2| + 4 = 7$

70. $|2x - 7| - 1 = 0$ **71.** $\left|\dfrac{x}{4} + 1\right| - 2 = 1$ **72.** $\left|\dfrac{x}{3} - 2\right| + 3 = 4$

73. $|2x - 1| = |x + 2|$ **74.** $|2x - 5| = |x - 3|$ **75.** $|3x + 1| = |4 - x|$

76. $|5x + 4| = |1 - 3x|$ **77.** $\left|\dfrac{3x}{2} + 2\right| = \left|\dfrac{x}{4} + 3\right|$ **78.** $\left|\dfrac{x}{3} - 4\right| = \left|\dfrac{5x}{6} + 1\right|$

79. $\left|\dfrac{2x}{5} - 3\right| = \left|\dfrac{x}{2} - 1\right|$ **80.** $\left|\dfrac{4x}{3} + 7\right| = \left|\dfrac{x}{4} + 2\right|$

In Exercises 81 – 90, determine whether each of the equations is a conditional equation, an identity, or a contradiction.

81. $2x + 3x = 17.4 - x$ **82.** $2(3x - 1) + 5 = 3$

83. $7(x - 1) = -3(3 - x) + 4x$ **84.** $5x + 13 = -2(x - 7) + 3$

85. $5x + 12 - 9x = -4(x - 3) - x$ **86.** $5.2x + 3.4x = 0.2(x - 0.42)$

87. $\dfrac{1}{2}(x - 24) = \dfrac{1}{3}(x - 24)$ **88.** $4(3x - 5) = x + 3(x - 1) + 10$

89. $3(x - 2) + 4x = 6(x - 1) + x$ **90.** $\dfrac{1}{4}(2x + 1) - 7 = \dfrac{1}{2}(2x - 1)$

Hawkes Learning Systems: Intermediate Algebra

Simplifying Expressions
Solving Linear Equations
Solving Absolute Value Expressions

1.4 Evaluating and Solving Formulas

Objectives

After completing this section, you will be able to:

1. *Solve applied problems by using known formulas.*

2. *Solve formulas for specified variables in terms of the other variables.*

A **formula** is an equation that represents a general relationship between two or more quantities or measurements. Several variables may appear in a formula, and the formula is not always in the most convenient form for application in some word problems. In such situations, we may want to solve a formula for a particular variable and use the formula in a different form. For example, the formula $d = rt$ (distance equals rate times time) is solved for d. Solving for r or t gives

$$r = \frac{d}{t} \quad \text{or} \quad t = \frac{d}{r}$$

Formulas are useful in many fields of study, such as business, economics, medicine, physics, technology, and chemistry, as well as mathematics. Some formulas and their meanings are shown here and will be used with others in the exercises.

Formula	Meaning
1. $I = Prt$	The simple interest (I), earned by investing money, is equal to the product of the principal (P) times the rate of interest (r) times the time (t) in years.
2. $C = \frac{5}{9}(F - 32)$	Temperature in degrees Celsius (C) equals $\frac{5}{9}$ times the difference between the Fahrenheit temperature (F) and 32.
3. $IQ = \frac{100M}{C}$	Intelligence Quotient (IQ) is calculated by multiplying 100 times mental age (M), as measured by some test, and dividing by chronological age (C).
4. $\alpha + \beta + \gamma = 180°$	The sum of the measures of the angles (α, β, γ) of a triangle is 180°. (**Note**: α, β, and γ are the Greek letters alpha, beta, and gamma, respectively.)

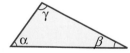

Formulas for the perimeter (P) and the area (A) of geometric figures are as follows:

Formula	Figure Name	Figure
5. $P = 4s$ $A = s^2$	SQUARE	
6. $P = 2l + 2w$ $A = lw$	RECTANGLE	
7. $P = 2b + 2a$ $A = bh$	PARALLELOGRAM	
8. $P = a + b + c$ $A = \dfrac{1}{2}bh$	TRIANGLE	
9. $C = 2\pi r$ $C = \pi d$ $A = \pi r^2$	CIRCLE r = radius d = diameter C = circumference or perimeter of a circle	
10. $P = a + b + c + d$ $A = \dfrac{1}{2}h(b+c)$	TRAPEZOID	

If the values for all but one variable in a formula are known, they can be substituted into the formula, and the unknown value can be found by solving the equation as we did in Section 1.3. This is essentially how formulas are used in solving applications.

Example 1: Triangle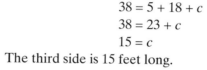

a.   The perimeter of a triangle is 38 feet. One side is 5 feet long and a second side is 18 feet long. How long is the third side?

Solution 1:   Using the formula $P = a + b + c$, substitute $P = 38$, $a = 5$, and $b = 18$.
Then solve for the third side.

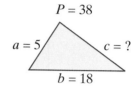

$$38 = 5 + 18 + c$$
$$38 = 23 + c$$
$$15 = c$$

The third side is 15 feet long.

Solution 2:   First solve for c in terms of P, a, and b. Then substitute for P, a, and b.

$$P = a + b + c$$
$$P - a - b = c$$ Treat a and b as constants.
    Add $-a - b$ to both sides.
or $$c = P - a - b$$

Substituting gives $c = 38 - 5 - 18$
$$= 33 - 18 = 15$$

Many times, we simply want the formula solved for one of the variables without substituting in particular values. In this situation, we treat all the other variables as if they were constants and follow the same procedure for solving an equation as we did in Section 1.3. Thus, in Solution 2, we solved the formula $P = a + b + c$ for c to obtain $c = P - a - b$.

Example 2: Solving Formulas

a.   Given $P = a + b + c$, solve for a in terms of P, b, and c.

Solution: $P = a + b + c$ Treat P, b, and c as if they are constants.

$$P - b - c = a + b + c - b - c$$ Add $-b - c$ to both sides.
$$P - b - c = a$$ Simplify.
or $$a = P - b - c$$

b. Given $C = \dfrac{5}{9}(F-32)$, solve for F in terms of C.

Solution:

$$C = \frac{5}{9}(F-32) \qquad \text{Treat } C \text{ as a constant.}$$

$$\frac{9}{5}C = \frac{9}{5} \cdot \frac{5}{9}(F-32) \quad \text{Multiply both sides by } \frac{9}{5}.$$

$$\frac{9}{5}C = F - 32 \qquad\qquad \text{Simplify.}$$

$$\frac{9}{5}C + 32 = F - 32 + 32 \qquad \text{Add 32 to both sides.}$$

$$\frac{9}{5}C + 32 = F \qquad\qquad \text{Simplify.}$$

Thus, the formula for Celsius and Fahrenheit solved for C is

$$C = \frac{5}{9}(F-32)$$

and the same formula solved for F is

$$F = \frac{9}{5}C + 32.$$

These are two forms of the same formula.

c. Solve for l given $P = 2l + 2w$.

Solution:

$$P = 2l + 2w$$

$$P - 2w = 2l + 2w - 2w \qquad \text{Add } -2w \text{ to both sides.}$$

$$P - 2w = 2l \qquad\qquad\qquad \text{Simplify.}$$

$$\frac{P-2w}{2} = \frac{2l}{2} \qquad\qquad \text{Divide both sides by 2.}$$

$$\frac{P-2w}{2} = l$$

d. Solve the formula $y = mx + b$ for x.

Solution:

$$y = mx + b$$

$$y - b = mx \qquad\qquad \text{Add } -b \text{ to both sides.}$$

$$\frac{y-b}{m} = x \qquad\qquad \text{Divide both sides by } m.$$

continued on next page ...

e. Solve for R given the formula $F = \dfrac{1}{R+r}$.

Solution:

$$F = \frac{1}{R+r}$$

$$(R+r)F = (R+r)\frac{1}{R+r} \qquad \text{Multiply both sides by the denominator, } R+r.$$

$$RF + rF = 1 \qquad \text{Use the distributive property.}$$

$$RF = 1 - rF \qquad \text{Add } -rF \text{ to both sides.}$$

$$\frac{R\!\!\!/F}{\!\!\!/F} = \frac{1-rF}{F} \qquad \text{Divide both sides by } F.$$

$$R = \frac{1-rF}{F}$$

This problem illustrates the importance of writing the correct form of a variable in a formula. Note that the uppercase R and the lowercase r represent completely different quantities.

● ●

Practice Problems

In each formula, solve for the indicated variable.

1. $P = a + 2b$; *solve for b.*

2. $y = mx + b$; *solve for m.*

3. $\alpha + \beta + \gamma = 180$; *solve for α.*

4. $F = \dfrac{1}{R+r}$; *solve for r.*

1.4 Exercises

For Exercises 1 – 10, (a) state the formula that relates to the given information, (b) solve the formula for the unknown quantity, and (c) substitute the given values in the formula to determine the value of the unknown quantity.

1. The interest earned in 2 years on an investment is $297. If the rate of interest is 9%, find the amount invested.

2. The Celsius temperature is 45°. Find the Fahrenheit temperature.

Answers to Practice Problems: 1. $b = \dfrac{P-a}{2}$ **2.** $m = \dfrac{y-b}{x}$ **3.** $\alpha = 180 - \beta - \gamma$ **4.** $r = \dfrac{1-FR}{F}$

3. Two angles of a triangle measure 72° and 65°. Find the measure of the third angle.

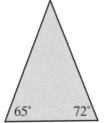

4. The perimeter of a square is $10\frac{2}{3}$ meters. Find the length of the sides.

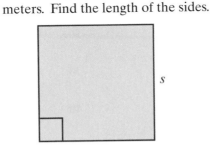

5. The perimeter of a rectangle is 88 feet. If the length is 31 feet, find the width.

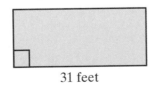

31 feet

6. The area of a parallelogram is 1081 square inches. If the height is 23 inches, find the length of the base.

23 inches

7. The perimeter of a triangle is 147 inches. Two of the sides measure 38 inches and 48 inches. Find the length of the third side.

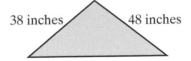

38 inches   48 inches

8. The circumference of a circle is 26π centimeters. Find the radius.

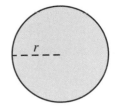

r

9. The radius of a circle is 14 feet. Find the area.

14 feet

10. The area of a trapezoid is 51 square meters. One base is 7 meters long, and the other is 10 meters long. Find the height of the trapezoid.

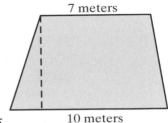

7 meters

10 meters

Solve for the indicated variables in Exercises 11 – 55.

11. $P = a + b + c$; solve for b.   **12.** $P = 3s$; solve for s.   **13.** $f = ma$; solve for m.

14. $C = \pi d$; solve for d.   **15.** $A = lw$; solve for w.   **16.** $P = R - C$; solve for C.

17. $R = np$; solve for n.   **18.** $v = k + gt$; solve for k.   **19.** $I = A - p$; solve for p.

20. $L = 2\pi rh$; solve for h.   21. $A = \dfrac{m+n}{2}$; solve for m.   22. $W = Rl^2t$; solve for R.

23. $P = 4s$; solve for s.   24. $C = 2\pi r$; solve for r.   25. $d = rt$; solve for t.

26. $P = a + 2b$; solve for a.   27. $I = Prt$; solve for t.   28. $R = \dfrac{E}{I}$; solve for E.

29. $P = a + 2b$; solve for b.   30. $c^2 = a^2 + b^2$; solve for b^2.

31. $S = \dfrac{a}{1-r}$; solve for a.   32. $A = \dfrac{h}{2}(a+b)$; solve for h.

33. $y = mx + b$; solve for x.   34. $V = lwh$; solve for h.

35. $A = 4\pi r^2$; solve for r^2.   36. $V = \pi r^2 h$; solve for h.

37. $IQ = \dfrac{100M}{C}$; solve for M.   38. $A = \dfrac{R}{2L}$; solve for R.

39. $V = \dfrac{1}{3}\pi r^2 h$; solve for h.   40. $A = \dfrac{1}{2}bh$; solve for b.

41. $R = \dfrac{E}{I}$; solve for I.   42. $IQ = \dfrac{100M}{C}$; solve for C.

43. $A = \dfrac{R}{2L}$; solve for L.   44. $K = \dfrac{mv^2}{2g}$; solve for g.

45. $A = \dfrac{h}{2}(a+b)$; solve for b.   46. $L = a + (n-1)d$; solve for d.

47. $L = 2\pi rh$; solve for h.   48. $S = 2\pi rh + 2\pi r^2$; solve for h.

49. $S = \dfrac{a}{1-r}$; solve for r.   50. $P = \dfrac{A}{1+ni}$; solve for n.

51. $W = \dfrac{2PR}{R-r}$; solve for P.   52. $V^2 = v^2 + 2gh$; solve for g.

53. $I = \dfrac{nE}{R+nr}$; solve for R.   54. $A = P + Prt$; solve for t.

55. $S = \dfrac{rL-a}{b-a}$; solve for r.

Hawkes Learning Systems: Intermediate Algebra

Evaluating Formulas

1.5   Applications

Objectives

After completing this section, you will be able to:

Solve the following by using first degree equations:

1. *Number problems,*

2. *Distance-rate-time problems,*

3. *Cost-profit problems, and*

4. *Simple interest problems*

Word problems (or applications) are designed to teach you to read carefully, to organize, and to think clearly. Whether or not a particular problem is easy for you depends a great deal on your personal experiences and general reasoning abilities. The problems generally do not give specific directions to add, subtract, multiply, or divide. You must decide what relationships are indicated through careful analysis of the problem.

George Pòlya (1887-1985), a famous professor at Stanford University, studied the process of discovery learning. Among his many accomplishments, he developed the following four-step process as an approach to problem solving:

1. Understand the problem.
2. Devise a plan.
3. Carry out the plan.
4. Look back over the results.

For a complete discussion of these ideas, see *How to Solve It* by Pòlya (Princeton University Press, 1945, 2nd edition, 1957). The following strategy is recommended for all word problems involving one variable and one equation.

Strategy for Solving Word Problems

1. *Understand the problem.*

    a. *Read the problem carefully. (Read it several times if necessary.)*

    b. *If it helps, restate the problem in your own words.*

continued on next page ...

Strategy for Solving Word Problems (continued)

2. *Devise a plan.*

   a. *Decide what is asked for; assign a variable to the unknown quantity. Label this variable so you know exactly what it represents.*

   b. *Draw a diagram or set up a chart whenever possible.*

   c. *Write an equation that relates the information provided.*

3. *Carry out the plan.*

   a. *Study your picture or diagram for insight into the solution.*

   b. *Solve the equation.*

4. *Look back over the results.*

   a. *Does your solution make sense in terms of the wording of the problem?*

   b. *Check your solution in the equation.*

Problems involving numerical expressions will usually contain key words indicating the operations to be performed. Learn to look for words such as those in the following list.

Addition	Subtraction	Multiplication	Division	Equality
add	subtract	multiply	divide	gives
sum	difference	product	quotient	represents
plus	minus	times	ratio	amounts to
more than	less than	twice		is / was
increased by	decreased by	of (with fractions and percents)		is the same as

Example 1: Number Problem •

The sum of two numbers is 36. If $\dfrac{1}{2}$ of the smaller number is equal to $\dfrac{1}{4}$ of the larger number, find the two numbers.

Solution: Analyze the problem and identify the key words.

The key words are **sum** (indicating addition) and **of** (indicating multiplication when used with fractions).

Assign variables to the unknown quantities.

Let x = smaller number
Since x + (larger number) = 36,
$36 - x$ = larger number.

Write an equation relating the given information.

$\dfrac{1}{2}$ of the smaller number   is equal to $\dfrac{1}{4}$ of the larger number

$$\dfrac{1}{2}x \qquad = \qquad \dfrac{1}{4}(36-x)$$

Solve the equation.

$$\dfrac{1}{2}x = \dfrac{1}{4}(36-x)$$

$$4 \cdot \dfrac{1}{2}x = 4 \cdot \dfrac{1}{4}(36-x) \qquad \text{Multiplying both sides of the equation by 4 yields integer coefficients.}$$

$$2x = 1(36-x)$$

$$2x = 36 - x$$

$$3x = 36$$

$$x = 12 \qquad \text{Smaller number}$$

$$36 - x = 24 \qquad \text{Larger number}$$

Check:

$$12 + 24 \overset{?}{=} 36$$

$$\dfrac{1}{2}(12) \overset{?}{=} \dfrac{1}{4}(24)$$

$$6 = 6$$

The two numbers are 12 and 24.

● ●

Problems involving distance usually make use of the relationship indicated by the formula $d = rt$, where r = rate, t = time, and d = distance. A chart or table showing the known and unknown values is quite helpful and is illustrated in the next example.

Example 2: Distance-Rate-Time

A motorist averaged 45 mph for the first part of a trip and 54 mph for the last part of the trip. If the total trip of 303 miles took 6 hours, what was the time for each part of the trip?

Solution:

Let t = time for 1st part of trip

$6 - t$ = time for 2nd part of trip

Analysis of Strategy

What is being asked for?

Total time minus time for 1st part of trip gives time for 2nd part of trip.

	rate	·	time	=	distance
1st Part	45		t		$45 \cdot t$
2nd Part	54		$6 - t$		$54(6 - t)$

45 mph   54 mph

t hrs   6 – t hrs

303 mi

$$\underbrace{\text{1st part distance}} + \underbrace{\text{2nd part distance}} = \underbrace{\text{total distance}}$$

Form the equation relating the given information.

$$45t + 54(6 - t) = 303$$ Solve the equation.

$$45t + 324 - 54t = 303$$

$$324 - 9t = 303$$

$$-9t = -21$$

$$t = \frac{21}{9} = \frac{7}{3}$$ 1st part of the trip

$$6 - t = 6 - \frac{7}{3} = \frac{11}{3}$$ 2nd part of the trip

Check: $$45 \cdot \frac{7}{3} = 15 \cdot 7 = 105 \, \text{miles} \, (1\text{st part})$$

$$54 \cdot \frac{11}{3} = 18 \cdot 11 = 198 \, \text{miles} \, (2\text{nd part})$$

$$105 + 198 = 303 \, \text{miles total}$$

The first part took $\frac{7}{3}$ hr or $2\frac{1}{3}$ hr. The second part took $\frac{11}{3}$ hr or $3\frac{2}{3}$ hr.

Problems involving cost come in a variety of forms. The next two examples illustrate the types of problems you will find in the exercises.

Example 3: Cost

a. The Berrys sold their house. After paying the real estate agent a commission of 6% of the selling price and then paying $1,486 in other costs and $90,000 on the mortgage, they received $49,514. What was the selling price of the house?

Solution: Use the relationship $SP - C = P$,
that is,   selling price − cost = profit.
Let s = selling price.
    cost = $0.06s + 1{,}486 + 90{,}000$

selling price	−	cost	=	profit

$$s \quad - (0.06s + 1{,}486 + 90{,}000) = 49{,}514$$
$$s - 0.06s - 1{,}486 - 90{,}000 = 49{,}514$$
$$0.94s = 141{,}000$$
$$s = 150{,}000$$

Check:

$150,000	selling price		$9,000	commission		$150,000	selling price
0.06	commission %		1,486	costs		−100,486	expenses
$9,000	commission		+ 90,000	mortgage		$49,514	profit received
			$100,486	total expenses			

The selling price was $150,000.

b. A jeweler paid $350 for a ring. He wants to price the ring for sale so that he can give a 30% discount on the selling price (or marked price) and still make a profit of 20% on his cost. What selling price should he mark for the ring?

Solution: Again, we make use of the relationship $SP - C = P$.
Let x = the selling price,
then $0.30x + 350$ = the cost

selling price	−	cost	=	profit

$$x \quad - (0.30x + 350) = 0.20(350)$$
$$x \quad - 0.30x - 350 = 70$$
$$0.70x = 420$$
$$x = 600$$

His total cost is the discount plus what he paid for the ring.

The profit is 20% of what he paid originally.

continued on next page ...

30% OFF

Check:

$600 selling price	$180 discount	$600 selling price
× 0.30 discount %	+350 cost	−530 total cost
$180 discount	$530 total cost	$70 profit

As a double check, $350 original cost

$\times 0.20$ profit %

$70 profit

The jeweler should set the selling price at $600.

● ●

To work problems related to interest on money invested for one year, you need to know the basic relationship between the principal P (amount invested), the annual rate of interest r, and the amount of interest I (money earned). This relationship is described in the formula $P \cdot r = I$. (This is the formula for simple interest, $I = Prt$, with $t = 1$.) We use this relationship in Example 4.

Example 4: Interest ●

A woman has had $40,000 invested for one year, some with a savings and loan which paid 7%, the rest in a high-risk stock which yielded 12% for the year. If her interest income last year was $3,550, how much did she have in the savings and loan and how much did she invest in the stock?

Solution: Let x = amount invested at 7%

$40,000 - x$ = amount invested at 12%

Total amount invested minus amount invested at 7% represents amount invested at 12%.

	principal	·	rate	=	interest
Savings and loan	x		0.07		$0.07(x)$
Stock	$40,000 - x$		0.12		$0.12(40,000 - x)$

interest @ 7% + interest @ 12% = total interest

$$0.07(x) + 0.12(40,000 - x) = 3,550$$

$$7x + 12(40,000 - x) = 355,000$$

$$7x + 480,000 - 12x = 355,000$$

$$-5x = -125,000$$

$$x = 25,000$$

$$40,000 - x = 15,000$$

Multiply both sides of the equation by 100.

Check: 25,000(0.07) = 1,750 and 15,000(0.12) = 1,800
and $1,750 + $1,800 = $3550.
The woman had $25,000 in the savings and loan at 7% interest and
invested $15,000 in the stock at 12% interest.

• •

Average (or Mean)

You are probably already familiar with the concept of **average** of a set of numbers. The average is also called the **arithmetic average** or **mean**. Your grade in most courses is related to an "average" of your exam scores. Magazines and newspapers report average income, average price of homes, average sales, batting averages, and so on. The mean is particularly important in the study of statistics. For example, traffic studies are interested in average speeds, census studies are concerned with the mean number of people living in a house, and universities study the mean test scores of incoming freshmen students.

Average

*The **average** (or **mean**) of a set of numbers is the value found by adding the numbers and then dividing the sum by the number of numbers in the set.*

Example 5: Average (or Mean)   •

Suppose that you have scores of 85, 92, 82 and 88 on four exams in your English class. What score will you need on the fifth exam to have an average of 90?

Solution: Let x = your score on the fifth exam
The sum of all the scores, including the unknown fifth exam, divided by 5 must equal 90.

$$\frac{85+92+82+88+x}{5} = 90$$

$$\frac{347+x}{5} = 90$$

$$5 \cdot \frac{347+x}{5} = 5 \cdot 90$$

$$347 + x = 450$$

$$x = 103$$

Assuming that each exam is worth 100 points, you cannot attain an average of 90 on the five exams.

• •

1.5 Exercises

Refer to the formulas listed in Section 1.4 as necessary.

1. If 15 is added to a number, the result is 56 less than twice the number. Find the number.

2. A number subtracted from 20 is equal to three times the number. Find the number.

3. Nine less than twice a number is equal to the number. What is the number?

4. Find a number such that −64 is 12 more than four times the number.

5. What number gives a result of −2 when 5 is subtracted from the quotient of the number and 4?

6. If 6 is added to the quotient of a number and 3, the result is 1. What is the number?

7. Seven times a certain number is equal to the sum of three times the number and 28. What is the number?

8. Twelve more than five times a number is equal to the difference between 5 and twice the number. Find the number.

9. Four added to the quotient of a number and 6 is equal to 11 less than the number. What is the number?

10. The quotient of twice a number and 8 is equal to 3 more than the number. What is the number?

11. One number is 6 more than three times another. If their sum is 38, what are the two numbers?

12. The sum of two numbers is 98 and their difference is 20. Find the two numbers.

13. The length of a rectangular-shaped backyard is 8 feet less than twice the width. If 260 feet of fencing is needed to enclose the yard, find the dimensions of the yard.

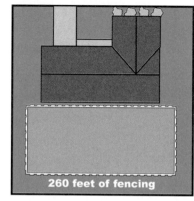

260 feet of fencing

14. The price of a pair of trousers is reduced 15%. The sale price is $39.95. Find the original price.

15% OFF
TROUSERS
NOW
$39⁹⁵

15. After a raise of 8%, Juan's salary is $1620 per month. What was his salary before the increase?

16. The U-Drive Company charges $20 per day plus 22¢ per mile driven. For a one-day trip, Louis paid a rent charge of $66.20. How many miles did he drive?

17. For a long-distance call, the telephone company charges 35¢ for each of the first three minutes and 15¢ for each additional minute. If the cost of a call was $12.30, how many minutes did the call last?

18. Willis bought a shirt and necktie for $85. The shirt cost $15 more than the tie. Find the cost of each.

19. Two planes, which are 2475 miles apart, fly toward each other. Their speeds differ by 75 mph. If they pass each other in 3 hours, what is the speed of each?

	rate ·	time	= distance
1st plane	r	3	
2nd plane	$r + 75$	3	

2475 miles

20. Jane rides her bike to Blue Lake. Going to the lake, she averages 12 mph. On the return trip, she averages 10 mph. If the round trip takes a total of 5.5 hours, how long does the return trip take?

	rate ·	time	= distance
Going	12	$5.5 - t$	
Returning	10	t	

BLUE LAKE

21. A car travels from one town to another in 6 hours. On the return trip, the speed is increased by 10 mph and the trip takes 5 hours. Find the rate on the return trip. How far apart are the towns?

	rate ·	time	= distance
Going	r	6	
Returning	$r + 10$	5	

22. The Reeds are moving across the state. Mr. Reed leaves $3\frac{1}{2}$ hours before Mrs. Reed. If he averages 40 mph and she averages 60 mph, how long will it take Mrs. Reed to overtake Mr. Reed?

23. Carol has 8 hours to spend on a mountain hike. She can walk up the trail at an average of 2 mph and can walk down at an average of 3 mph. How long should she plan to spend on the uphill part of the hike?

24. After traveling for 40 minutes, Mr. Koole had to slow to $\frac{2}{3}$ his original speed for the rest of the trip due to heavy traffic. The total trip of 84 miles took 2 hours. Find his original speed.

25. A train leaves Los Angeles at 2:00 PM. A second train leaves the same station in the same direction at 4:00 PM. The second train travels 24 mph faster than the first. If the second train overtakes the first at 7:00 PM, what is the speed of each of the two trains?

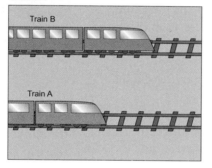

26. Maria jogs to the country at a rate of 10 mph. She returns along the same route at 6 mph. If the total trip took 1 hour 36 minutes, how far did she jog?

27. A particular style of shoe costs the dealer $81 per pair. At what price should the dealer mark them so he can sell them at a 10% discount off the selling price and still make a 25% profit?

28. A grocery store bought ice cream for $2.60 a half gallon and stored it in two freezers. During the night, one freezer malfunctioned and ruined 15 half gallons. If the remaining ice cream is sold for $3.98 per half gallon, how many half gallons did the store buy if it made a profit of $64.50?

29. A farmer raises strawberries. They cost him $0.80 a basket to produce. He is able to sell only 85% of those he produces. If he sells his strawberries at $2.40 a basket, how many must he produce to make a profit of $2480?

30. Mary builds cabinets in her spare time. Good quality cabinet plywood costs $4.00 per square foot. There is approximately a 10% waste of material due to cutting and fitting. She also figures $240 per month for finishing material, glue, tools, etc. If she charges $9.20 per square foot of finished cabinet, how many square feet of plywood would she use if her profit is $1129.60 in one month?

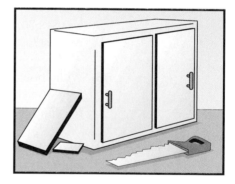

31. A citrus farmer figures that his fruit costs 96¢ a pound to grow. If he lost 20% of the crop he produced due to a frost and he sold the remaining 80% at $1.80 a pound, how many pounds did he produce to make a profit of $30,000?

32. Mr. Wise bought $1950 worth of stock, some at $3.00 per share and some at $4.50 per share. If he bought a total of 450 shares of stock, how many of each did he buy?

33. Last summer, Ernie sold surfboards. One style sold for $300 and the other sold for $250. He sold a total of 44 surfboards. How many of each style did he sell if the receipts from each style were equal?

34. The pro shop at the Divots Country Club ordered two brands of golf balls. Titleless balls cost $1.80 each and the Done Lob balls cost $1.50 each. The total cost of Titleless balls exceeded the total cost of the Done Lob balls by $108. If an equal number of each brand was ordered, how many dozen of each brand were ordered?

35. Amanda invests $25,000, part at 5% and the rest at 6%. The annual return on the 5% investment exceeds the annual return on the 6% investment by $40. How much did she invest at each rate?

36. The annual interest earned on a $6000 investment was $120 less than the interest earned on $10,000 invested at 1% less interest per year. What was the rate of interest on each amount?

37. The annual interest on a $4000 investment exceeds the interest earned on a $3000 investment by $80. The $4000 is invested at a 0.5% higher rate of interest than the $3000. What is the interest rate of each investment?

38. Mr. Hill invests ten thousand dollars, part at 5.5% and part at 6%. The interest from the 5.5% investment exceeds the interest from the 6% investment by $251. How much did he invest at each rate?

39. Two investments totaling $16,000 produce an annual income of $1140. One investment yields 6% a year, while the other yields 8% per year. How much is invested at each rate?

40. Sellit Realty Company gets a 6% fee for selling improved properties and 10% for selling unimproved land. Last week, the total sales were $220,000 and their total fees were $16,400. What were the sales from each of the two types of properties?

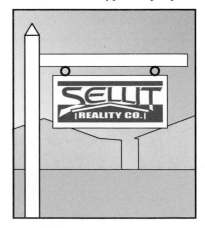

41. Given the monthly temperatures over a year for Christchurch, New Zealand:

  a. Find the average temperature for the year.

  b. Find the minimum temperature for the year.

  c. Find the difference in temperature between the months of June and December.

Source: http://www.weather.com

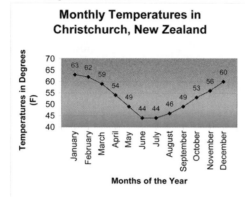

42. Given the enrollment at the Main Campuses of the following Big Ten Universities:

  a. Find the average enrollment over the six schools. (Round to the nearest whole number.)

  b. Find the University with the lowest enrollment.

  c. Find the difference in enrollment between Ohio State and Penn State.

Source: Peterson's, 2002

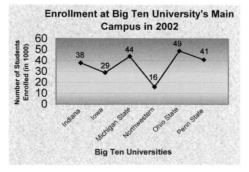

43. Given the monthly rainfall averages over a year for Vishakhapatnam, India:

  a. Find the average rainfall for the year. (Round to the nearest tenth.)

  b. Find the maximum rainfall for the year. (Round to the nearest tenth.)

  c. Find the difference in rainfall between the months of October and December. (Round to the nearest tenth.)

Source: http://www.weather.com

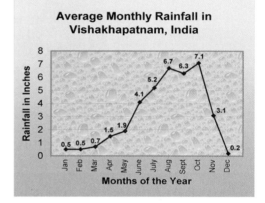

44. Given the length of each Space Shuttle flight:

  a. Find the average duration of the flights in the year 1995. (Round to the nearest tenth.)

  b. Find the length of the flight on March 2nd.

  c. Which two flights had the same duration?

Source: NASA

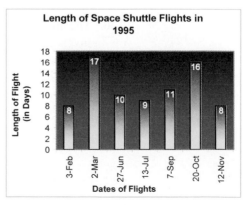

45. Given the number of passengers at the following airports:
  a. Find the average number of passengers.
  b. Find the difference in passengers between JFK and LAX.
  c. What was the total number of passengers to go through ATL?
Source: Airports Council International – North America

Number of Passengers at US Airports in 2001

Writing and Thinking About Mathematics

46. List the four steps in Polya's approach to problem solving. Then, in your own words, discuss how you used these steps in solving a "problem" you have had recently. Did you have trouble finding your car keys this morning? How did you decide what movie to see last weekend?

Hawkes Learning Systems: Intermediate Algebra

Applications of Linear Equations

Linear Inequalities and Absolute Value Inequalities

After completing this section, you will be able to:

1. Solve linear inequalities.

2. Solve absolute value inequalities.

3. Write the solutions for inequalities using interval notation.

4. Graph the solutions for inequalities on real number lines.

Linear Inequalities

In Section 1.1, we graphed the sets of real numbers on real number lines. Some of those graphs represented **intervals** of real numbers. Various types of intervals and the corresponding **interval notation** are listed in Table 1.2.

As an aid in reading inequalities and graphing inequalities correctly, note that an inequality may be read either from right to left or left to right. Also, read the variable first. For example,

$$x > 7 \quad \text{is read from left to right as } \text{``}x \text{ is greater than 7.''}$$
and $\quad 7 < x \quad$ is read from right to left as **"x is greater than 7."**

A compound interval such as $-3 < x < 6$ is read
"x is greater than -3 and x is less than 6."

Types of Intervals			
Name of Interval	**Algebraic Notation**	**Interval Notation**	**Graph**
Open Interval	$a < x < b$	(a, b)	
Closed Interval	$a \leq x \leq b$	$[a, b]$	
Half-open Interval	$a \leq x < b$	$[a, b)$	
	$a < x \leq b$	$(a, b]$	

continued on next page ...

Open Interval	$\begin{cases} x > a \\ x < b \end{cases}$	(a, ∞) $(-\infty, b)$	
Half-open Interval	$\begin{cases} x \geq a \\ x \leq b \end{cases}$	$[a, \infty)$ $(-\infty, b]$	

Table 1.2

In this section, we will solve **linear inequalities** such as $6x + 5 \leq -7$ and write the solution in interval notation as $(-\infty, -2]$. We say that "x is in $(-\infty, -2]$." [**Note:** The symbol for infinity, ∞ (or $-\infty$), is not a number. It is used to indicate that the interval is to continue without end.]

Linear Inequality

For real numbers a, b, and c ($a \neq 0$), $ax + b < c$ is called a **linear inequality** in x.

(The definition also holds if $\leq$, $>$, or $\geq$ is used instead of $<$.)

Solving linear inequalities is similar to solving linear equations, with one important difference: **Multiplying or dividing both sides of an inequality by a negative number reverses the sense of the inequality**. "Is less than" becomes "is greater than," and vice versa. For example,

Multiplying by −1	Multiplying by −4	Dividing by −6
a. $\quad 3 < 6$ $-1(3)\,?\,-1(6)$ $-3 > -6$ $\uparrow$ reversed	**b.** $\quad -2 \leq 5$ $-4(-2)\,?\,-4(5)$ $8 \geq -20$ $\uparrow$ reversed	**c.** $\quad -6x > 12$ $\dfrac{-6x}{-6}\,?\,\dfrac{12}{-6}$ $x < -2$ $\uparrow$ reversed

To solve first-degree inequalities, perform the following procedures and use the properties on the following page.

To Solve a Linear Inequality

1. *Simplify each side of the inequality by removing any grouping symbols and combining like terms.*

2. *Add the opposites of constants and/or variable expressions to both sides so that variables are on one side and constants are on the other.*

3. *Divide both sides by the coefficient of the variable and*

    a. *leave the direction of the inequality unchanged if the coefficient is positive; or*

    b. *reverse the direction of the inequality if the coefficient is negative.*

 NOTES Unless otherwise stated, we will assume that the set of values allowed for the variable (called the **replacement set**) in an inequality is the set of all real numbers. The **solution set** must be a part of the replacement set.

The procedure for solving linear inequalities uses the following procedures for finding equivalent inequalities just as we used the properties of equations to solve linear equations.

Addition Property of Inequality

If the same algebraic expression is added to both sides of an inequality, the new inequality is equivalent to the original inequality.

$$\text{If } A < B, \text{ then } A + C < B + C.$$

$$\text{If } A < B, \text{ then } A - C < B - C.$$

Multiplication Property of Inequality

If both sides of an inequality are multiplied (or divided) by the same positive expression, then the new inequality is equivalent to the original inequality.

$$\begin{cases} \text{If } A < B \text{ and } C > 0, \text{ then } AC < BC. \\ \text{If } A < B \text{ and } C > 0, \text{ then } \dfrac{A}{C} < \dfrac{B}{C}. \end{cases}$$

If both sides of an inequality are multiplied (or divided) by the same negative expression and the inequality is reversed, then the new inequality is equivalent to the original inequality.

$$\begin{cases} \text{If } A < B \text{ and } C < 0, \text{ then } AC > BC. \\ \text{If } A < B \text{ and } C < 0, \text{ then } \dfrac{A}{C} > \dfrac{B}{C}. \end{cases}$$

Example 1: Solving Linear Inequalities •

Solve the following inequalities and graph their solution sets. Write the solutions in interval notation. As a check, you can substitute a number into the original inequality. (Any number will do. 0 is always easy to use.) If the result is a true statement, then this number should be in the solution interval. If the result is false, then this number should not be in the solution interval. **This check does not guarantee that the solution interval is correct**, but it can help determine whether the interval is headed in the right direction.

a. $6x + 5 \le -1$

   Solution: $6x + 5 \le -1$

$$6x \le -6$$ Add -5 to both sides.

$$x \le -1$$ Divide both sides by 6.

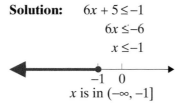

x is in $(-\infty, -1]$ Use interval notation. Note that the interval $(-\infty, -1]$ is a half-open interval.

As a check, substituting 0 for x in the original inequality gives

$$6 \cdot 0 + 5 \le -1$$

$$0 + 5 \le -1$$

$$5 \le -1$$

This last statement is false and we see that 0 is not in the solution interval. This result indicates that the solution interval is going in the right direction.

b. $x - 3 > 3x + 4$

   Solution: $x - 3 > 3x + 4$

$$-3 > 2x + 4$$ Add $-x$ to both sides.

$$-7 > 2x$$ Add -4 to both sides.

$$\frac{-7}{2} > x$$ Divide both sides by 2.

or $$x < -\frac{7}{2}$$

x is in $\left(-\infty, -\frac{7}{2}\right)$ Use interval notation. Note that the interval $\left(-\infty, -\frac{7}{2}\right)$ is an open interval.

continued on next page ...

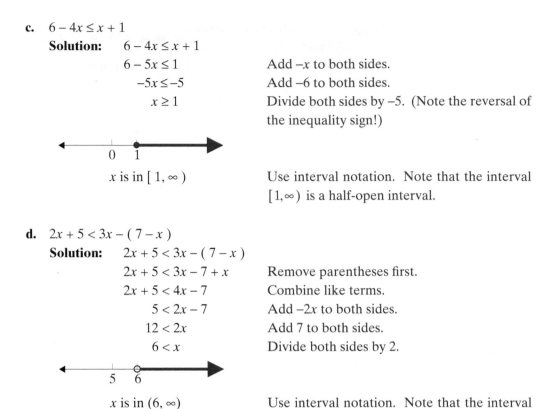

c. $6 - 4x \leq x + 1$

Solution:

$6 - 4x \leq x + 1$	
$6 - 5x \leq 1$	Add $-x$ to both sides.
$-5x \leq -5$	Add -6 to both sides.
$x \geq 1$	Divide both sides by -5. (Note the reversal of the inequality sign!)

x is in $[\,1, \infty\,)$ — Use interval notation. Note that the interval $[1, \infty)$ is a half-open interval.

d. $2x + 5 < 3x - (\,7 - x\,)$

Solution:

$2x + 5 < 3x - (\,7 - x\,)$	
$2x + 5 < 3x - 7 + x$	Remove parentheses first.
$2x + 5 < 4x - 7$	Combine like terms.
$5 < 2x - 7$	Add $-2x$ to both sides.
$12 < 2x$	Add 7 to both sides.
$6 < x$	Divide both sides by 2.

x is in $(6, \infty)$ — Use interval notation. Note that the interval $(6, \infty)$ is an open interval.

Inequalities with Three Parts

Inequalities with three parts can arise when a variable or variable expression is to be between two numbers. (We will see this with some absolute value inequalities, too.) For example, the inequality

$$5 < x + 3 < 10$$

indicates that $x + 3$ is between 5 and 10. To solve this inequality (to isolate the variable x), subtract 3 from each part of the inequality as follows:

$$5 < x + 3 < 10$$
$$5 - 3 < x + 3 - 3 < 10 - 3$$
$$2 < x < 7$$

Thus, the values of x must be between 2 and 7. The solution set is the open interval $(2, 7)$ and its graph is the following.

> **NOTES**
>
> Be careful when you write a three part inequality that the transitive property holds. For example writing $10 \leq x + 3 \leq 5$ would be wrong because the transitive property indicates $10 \leq 5$ which is false, With three part inequalities, both of the inequality symbols should point in the same direction and point toward the smaller number.

Example 2: Solving Inequalities with Three Parts

Solve the three part inequality $-3 \leq 4x - 1 \leq 11$ and graph the solution set.

Solution:

$-3 \leq 4x - 1 \leq 11$	Write the inequality.
$-3 + 1 \leq 4x - 1 + 1 \leq 11 + 1$	Add 1 to each part.
$-2 \leq 4x \leq 12$	Simplify.
$\dfrac{-2}{4} \leq \dfrac{4x}{4} \leq \dfrac{12}{4}$	Divide each part by 4.
$-\dfrac{1}{2} \leq x \leq 3$	Simplify.

The solution set is the closed interval $\left[-\dfrac{1}{2}, 3\right]$.

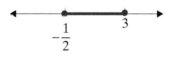

Absolute Value Inequalities

Now consider an inequality with absolute value such as $|x| < 3$. For a number to have an absolute value less than 3, it must be within 3 units of 0. That is, the numbers between -3 and 3 have their absolute values less than 3 because they are within 3 units of 0. Thus, for $|x| < 3$,

Algebraic Notation	Graph		Interval Notation
$-3 < x < 3$	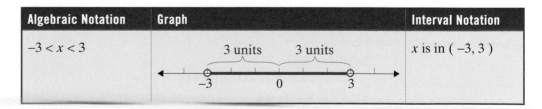		x is in $(-3, 3)$

The inequality $|x - 5| < 3$ means that the distance between x and 5 is less than 3. That is, we want all the values of x that are within 3 units of 5. The inequality is solved algebraically as follows:

69

$$|x - 5| < 3$$
$$-3 < x - 5 < 3$$ $x - 5$ is between -3 and 3.
$$-3 + 5 < x - 5 + 5 < 3 + 5$$ Add $+5$ to each part of the expression, just as in solving linear inequalities.
$$2 < x < 8$$ Simplify each expression.
x is in $(2, 8)$ Using interval notation

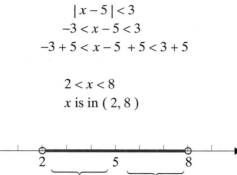

The values for x are between 2 and 8 and are within 3 units of 5.

Solving Absolute Value Inequalities

For $c > 0$;

a.   If $|x| < c$, then $-c < x < c$.

b.   If $|ax + b| < c$, then $-c < ax + b < c$.

Note: *These inequalities are true if $<$ is replaced by $\leq$.*

Example 3: Solving Absolute Value Inequalities

Solve the following absolute value inequalities and graph the solution sets.

a. $|x| \leq 6$

Solution: $|x| \leq 6$
$$-6 \leq x \leq 6$$
or x is in $[-6, 6]$

b. $|x + 3| < 2$

Solution: $|x + 3| < 2$
$$-2 < x + 3 < 2$$
$$-2 - 3 < x + 3 - 3 < 2 - 3$$
$$-5 < x < -1$$
or x is in $(-5, -1)$

c. $|2x - 7| < 1$

Solution: $|2x - 7| < 1$
$$-1 < 2x - 7 < 1$$
$$6 < 2x < 8$$
$$3 < x < 4$$
or x is in $(3, 4)$

We have been discussing inequalities in which the absolute value is less than some positive number. Now consider an inequality where the absolute value is greater than some positive number, such as $|x| > 3$. For a number to have an absolute value greater than 3, its distance from 0 must be greater than 3. That is, numbers that are greater than 3 **or** less than −3 will have absolute values greater than 3. Thus, for $|x| > 3$,

Algebraic Notation	Graph	Interval Notation
$x > 3$ or $x < -3$	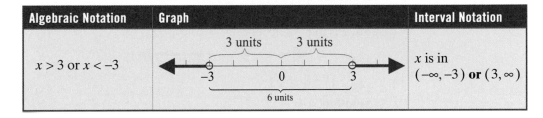	x is in $(-\infty, -3)$ **or** $(3, \infty)$

NOTES

The expression $x > 3$ **or** $x < -3$ **cannot** be combined into one inequality expression. The word **or** must separate the inequalities since any number that satisfies one **or** the other is a solution to the absolute value inequality. There are **no** numbers that satisfy **both** inequalities.

The inequality $|x - 5| > 6$ means that the distance between x and 5 is more than 6. That is, we want all values of x that are more than 6 units from 5. The inequality is solved algebraically as follows:

$$|x - 5| > 6 \text{ indicates that}$$
$$x - 5 < -6 \quad \textbf{or} \quad x - 5 > 6 \qquad x - 5 \text{ is less than } -6 \text{ or greater than } 6$$

Solving both inequalities gives,

$$x - 5 + 5 < -6 + 5 \text{ or } x - 5 + 5 > 6 + 5, \quad \text{Add 5 to each side, just as in solving linear inequalities.}$$
$$x < -1 \quad \textbf{or} \quad x > 11. \qquad \text{Simplify.}$$

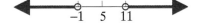

Note: The values for x less than −1 or greater than 11 are more than 6 units from 5. Thus, we can interpret the equality $|x - 5| > 6$ to mean that the distance from x to 5 is greater than 6.

Solving Absolute Value Inequalities

For $c > 0$;

a. If $|x| > c$, then $x > c$ *or* $x < -c$.

b. If $|ax + b| > c$, then $ax + b < -c$ *or* $ax + b > c$.

Note: *The inequalities in a. and b. are true if $>$ and $<$ are replaced by $\geq$ and $\leq$, respectively.*

Example 4: Solving Absolute Value Inequalities

Solve the following absolute value inequalities and graph the solution set.

a. $|x| \geq 5$

Solution: $|x| \geq 5$

$$x \leq -5 \quad \text{or} \quad x \geq 5$$

So, x is in $(-\infty, -5]$ or $[5, \infty)$.

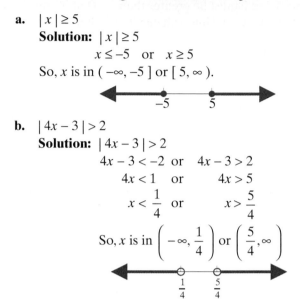

b. $|4x - 3| > 2$

Solution: $|4x - 3| > 2$

$$4x - 3 < -2 \quad \text{or} \quad 4x - 3 > 2$$
$$4x < 1 \quad \text{or} \quad 4x > 5$$
$$x < \frac{1}{4} \quad \text{or} \quad x > \frac{5}{4}$$

So, x is in $\left(-\infty, \frac{1}{4}\right)$ or $\left(\frac{5}{4}, \infty\right)$

c. $|3x - 8| > -6$

Solution: There is nothing to do here except observe that no matter what is substituted for x, the absolute value will be greater than -6. Absolute value is always nonnegative (greater than or equal to 0). The solution to the inequality is all real numbers, so shade the entire number line. In interval notation, x is in $(-\infty, \infty)$.

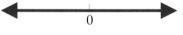

d. $|x + 9| < -\dfrac{1}{2}$

Solution: Since absolute value is always nonnegative (greater than or equal to 0), there is no solution to this inequality. No number has an absolute value less than $-\dfrac{1}{2}$.

e. $|2x + 6| + 4 < 9$

Solution: $|2x + 6| + 4 < 9$

$|2x + 6| < 5$ Add -4 to both sides in order to isolate the

$-5 < 2x + 6 < 5$ absolute value expression on one side. Then

$-11 < 2x < -1$ rewrite as a double inequality.

$$-\frac{11}{2} < x < -\frac{1}{2}$$

So, x is in $\left(-\dfrac{11}{2}, -\dfrac{1}{2}\right)$.

1.6 Exercises

Solve the inequalities in Exercises 1 – 45 and graph the solution sets. Write each solution in interval notation. Assume that x is a real number.

1. $2x + 3 < 5$ **2.** $4x - 7 \geq 9$ **3.** $14 - 5x < 4$

4. $23 < 7x - 5$ **5.** $6x - 15 > 1$ **6.** $9 - 2x < 8$

7. $5.6 + 3x \geq 4.4$ **8.** $12x - 8.3 < 6.1$ **9.** $1.5x + 9.6 < 12.6$

10. $0.8x - 2.1 \geq 1.1$ **11.** $2x - 1 > 3x + 2$ **12.** $6x + 6 < 4x - 2$

13. $3x - 5 > 3 - x$ **14.** $2 + 3x \geq x + 8$ **15.** $x - 6 \leq 4 - x$

16. $3x - 1 \leq 11 - 3x$ **17.** $5x + 6 \geq 2x - 2$ **18.** $4 - 2x < 5 + x$

19. $4 + x > 1 - x$ **20.** $x - 6 > 3x + 5$ **21.** $\dfrac{x}{2} - 1 \leq \dfrac{5x}{2} - 3$

22. $\dfrac{x}{4} + 1 \leq 5 - \dfrac{x}{4}$ **23.** $\dfrac{4x}{5} - 2 > x + 1$ **24.** $\dfrac{x}{3} - 2 > 1 - \dfrac{x}{3}$

25. $\dfrac{5x}{3} + 2 > \dfrac{x}{3} - 1$ **26.** $3.5 + 2x < 4x - 2.5$ **27.** $6x + 5.91 < 1.11 - 2x$

28. $4.3x + 21.5 \geq 1.7x + 0.7$ **29.** $6.2x - 5.7 > 4.8x + 3.1$

30. $0.9x - 11.3 < 3.1 - 0.7x$ **31.** $4(6 - x) < -2(3x + 1)$

32. $-3(2x - 5) \leq 3(x - 1)$ **33.** $3x + 8 \leq -3(2x - 3)$

34. $6(3x + 1) < 5(1 - 2x)$ **35.** $4 + 7x \leq 3x - 8 + x$

36. $11x + 8 - 5x \geq 2x - (4 - x)$ **37.** $1 - (2x + 8) < (9 + x) - 4x$

38. $5 - 3(4 - x) + x \leq -2(3 - 2x) - x$ **39.** $x - (2x + 5) \geq 7 - (4 - x) + 10$

40. $\dfrac{2(x-1)}{3} < \dfrac{3(x+1)}{4}$ **41.** $\dfrac{x+2}{2} \geq \dfrac{2x}{3}$ **42.** $\dfrac{x-2}{4} > \dfrac{x+2}{2} + 6$

43. $\dfrac{x+4}{9} \leq \dfrac{x}{3} - 2$ **44.** $\dfrac{2x+7}{4} \leq \dfrac{x+1}{3} - 1$ **45.** $\dfrac{4x}{7} - 3 > \dfrac{x-6}{2} - 4$

46. $-4 < x + 5 < 6$ **47.** $1 \leq \dfrac{2}{3}x - 1 \leq 9$ **48.** $14 > -2x - 6 > 4$

49. $-11 \geq -3x + 2 > -20$ **50.** $-1.5 < 2x + 4.1 < 3.5$

51. A statistics student has grades of 82, 95, 93, and 78 on four hourly exams. He must average 90 or higher to receive an A for the course. What scores can he receive on the final exam and earn an A if:

a. the final is equivalent to a single hourly exam (100 points maximum)?

b. the final is equivalent to two hourly exams (200 points maximum)?

52. To receive a grade of B in a chemistry class, Melissa must average 80 or more but less than 90. If her five hourly exam scores were 75, 82, 90, 85, and 77, what score does she need on the final exam (100 points maximum) to earn a grade of B?

53. The sum of the lengths of any two sides of a triangle must be greater than the third side. A triangle has sides as follows: the first side is 18 mm, the second side is 3 mm more than twice the third side. What are the possible lengths of the second and third sides?

54. Allison is going to the post office to buy 37 cent stamps and 23 cent postcards. She has $20 and wants to buy twice as many postcards as stamps. What is the largest number of 37 cent stamps she can buy?

Solve each of the absolute value problems in Exercises 55 – 75 and graph the solution sets. Write each solution in interval notation.

55. $|x| \geq -2$

56. $|x| \geq 3$

57. $|x| \leq \dfrac{4}{5}$

58. $|x| \geq \dfrac{7}{2}$

59. $|x - 3| > 2$

60. $|y - 4| \leq 5$

61. $|x + 2| \leq 4$

62. $|3x + 4| > -8$

63. $|x + 6| \leq 4$

64. $|2x - 1| \geq 2$

65. $|3 - 2x| < -2$

66. $|3x + 4| - 1 < 0$

67. $\left|\dfrac{3x}{2} - 4\right| \geq 5$

68. $\left|\dfrac{3}{7}y + \dfrac{1}{2}\right| > 2$

69. $|5x + 2| + 3 > 2$

70. $|7x - 3| + 4 \geq 6$

71. $|2x - 9| - 7 \leq 4$

72. $5 > |4 - 2x| + 2$

73. $-4 < |6x - 1| + 4$

74. $7 > |8 - 5x| + 3$

75. $|3x - 7| + 4 \leq 4$

Writing and Thinking About Mathematics

In Exercises 76 – 80 a set of real numbers is described. (a) Sketch a graph of the set on a real number line. (b) Represent each set by using absolute value notation. (c) If the set is one interval, state what type of interval it is.

76. the set of real numbers between −10 and 10, inclusive
77. the set of real numbers within 7 units of 4
78. the set of real numbers more than 6 units from 8
79. the set of real numbers greater than or equal to 3 units from −1
80. the set of real numbers within 2 units of −5

Hawkes Learning Systems: Intermediate Algebra

Solving Linear Inequalities
Solving Absolute Value Inequalities

Properties of Exponents

After completing this section, you will be able to:

Simplify expressions with constant or single-variable bases using the properties of integer exponents.

In this section, we will discuss the properties of **integer exponents**, including the exponent zero and negative integer exponents. These properties are particularly useful in simplifying algebraic expressions. Of course, all the definitions and facts about natural number exponents discussed in Section 1.2 are still valid. (Fractional exponents will be discussed in Chapter 6.)

The Exponent 1

In the expression x^5, x is called the base and 5 is called the exponent. If the expression can be evaluated, then the value is called the power. For example, $2^5 = 32$ and 32 is the power. If a variable or constant is written without an exponent, then the exponent is understood to be 1. Thus,

$$x = x^1,\ 17 = 17^1,\text{ and } -5a = -5a^1.$$

The Exponent 1

For any real number a, $\boldsymbol{a = a^1}$*.*

Product Rule for Exponents

To multiply $4^2 \cdot 4^3$ or $x^3 \cdot x^5$ or $(-2)^3(-2)$, we could write

$$4^2 \cdot 4^3 = (4 \cdot 4) \cdot (4 \cdot 4 \cdot 4) = 4^5$$

$$x^3 \cdot x^5 = (x \cdot x \cdot x) \cdot (x \cdot x \cdot x \cdot x \cdot x) = x^8$$

$$(-2)^3(-2) = (-2)(-2)(-2) \cdot (-2) = (-2)^4$$

As these examples illustrate, when **multiplying** terms with the **same base**, we **add** the exponents. This rule is stated as the Product Rule for exponents.

Product Rule for Exponents

If a is a nonzero real number and m and n are integers, then

$$a^m \cdot a^n = a^{m+n}.$$

Two different expressions with negative signs and exponents, such as $(-2)^4$ and -2^4, need special clarification. In the expression $(-2)^4$, -2 is the base and 4 is the exponent. Thus, we can write

$$(-2)^4 = (-2)(-2)(-2)(-2) = 16$$

In contrast, in the expression -2^4, only the 2 is the base of the exponent 4. Thus, we have a different result:

$$-2^4 = (-1) \cdot 2^4 = (-1)(2)(2)(2)(2) = -16$$

This type of expression may be easier to understand with a variable. For example, $-x^2$ is understood to have the coefficient -1. Therefore,

$$-x^2 = -1 \cdot x^2.$$

Here x is the base and -1 is the coefficient.

and $\quad (-x)^2 = (-x)(-x) = x^2$

Here $(-x)$ is the base.

The Exponent 0

The Product Rule is stated for integer exponents and, applying this property with the exponent 0, we get the following results:

$2^0 \cdot 2^3 = 2^{0+3} = 2^3$ We also know that $1 \cdot 2^3 = 2^3$. This implies, $2^0 = 1$.

$3^0 \cdot 3^4 = 3^{0+4} = 3^4$ We also know that $1 \cdot 3^4 = 3^4$. This implies, $3^0 = 1$.

$5^0 \cdot 5^2 = 5^{0+2} = 5^2$ We also know that $1 \cdot 5^2 = 5^2$. This implies, $5^0 = 1$.

In the analysis of these examples, we see that $2^0 = 1, 3^0 = 1$, and $5^0 = 1$. Therefore, if the exponent is 0, then the value of the expression is 1 with one exception. The exception is that the expression 0^0 is undefined.

The Exponent 0

If a is a nonzero real number, then

$$a^0 = 1.$$

The expression 0^0 is undefined.

NOTES Throughout this text, unless specifically stated otherwise, we will assume that the bases of exponents are nonzero.

Negative Exponents

The following examples, applying the Product Rule with negative exponents and the exponent 0, lead to the meaning of negative exponents.

With Exponents	With Fractions
$2 \cdot 2^{-1} = 2^{1+(-1)} = 2^0 = 1$	$2 \cdot \dfrac{1}{2} = 1$
$2^2 \cdot 2^{-2} = 2^{2+(-2)} = 2^0 = 1$	$2^2 \cdot \dfrac{1}{2^2} = 4 \cdot \dfrac{1}{4} = 1$
$2^3 \cdot 2^{-3} = 2^{3+(-3)} = 2^0 = 1$	$2^3 \cdot \dfrac{1}{2^3} = 8 \cdot \dfrac{1}{8} = 1$
$3^2 \cdot 3^{-2} = 3^{2+(-2)} = 3^0 = 1$	$3^2 \cdot \dfrac{1}{3^2} = 9 \cdot \dfrac{1}{9} = 1$

These examples indicate that

$$2^{-1} = \frac{1}{2^1} = \frac{1}{2}, \quad 2^{-2} = \frac{1}{2^2} = \frac{1}{4}, \quad 2^{-3} = \frac{1}{2^3} = \frac{1}{8}, \quad \text{and } 3^{-2} = \frac{1}{3^2} = \frac{1}{9}$$

We now have the following Rule for Negative Exponents:

Rule for Negative Exponents

If a is a nonzero real number and n is an integer, then

$$a^{-n} = \frac{1}{a^n}.$$

Remember that a negative exponent indicates a fraction, not a negative number.

Example 1: Negative Exponents •

Using the Product Rule, the Exponent 0, and Rule for Negative Exponents, simplify the following expressions so that they contain only positive exponents.

a. $x^2 \cdot x^5$

Solution: $x^2 \cdot x^5 = x^{2+5} = x^7$

b. $3^2 \cdot 3^5 \cdot 3$

Solution: $3^2 \cdot 3^5 \cdot 3 = 3^{2+5+1} = 3^8 = 6561$

c. $2y^3 \cdot 3y^4$

Solution: $2y^3 \cdot 3y^4 = 2 \cdot 3 \cdot y^{3+4} = 6y^7$

d. 11^0

Solution: $11^0 = 1$

e. $x^0 \cdot x^4$

Solution: $x^0 \cdot x^4 = x^{0+4} = x^4$

f. 7^{-1}

Solution: $7^{-1} = \dfrac{1}{7}$

g. $x^{-10} \cdot x^7 \cdot x$

Solution: $x^{-10} \cdot x^7 \cdot x = x^{-10+7+1} = x^{-2} = \dfrac{1}{x^2}$

h. $2x^{-3} \cdot 5x^{-4}$

Solution: $2x^{-3} \cdot 5x^{-4} = 2 \cdot 5 \cdot x^{-3+(-4)} = 10x^{-7} = 10 \cdot \dfrac{1}{x^7} = \dfrac{10}{x^7}$

• •

The Quotient Rule for Exponents

In the Product Rule, when two (or more) expressions are multiplied, the exponents are added. As shown here, when two expressions with like bases are divided, the exponent in the denominator is subtracted from the exponent in the numerator. For example,

$$\frac{2^5}{2^2} = 2^5 \cdot \frac{1}{2^2} = 2^5 \cdot 2^{-2} = 2^{5-2} = 2^3 = 8$$

and

$$\frac{6}{6^3} = 6 \cdot \frac{1}{6^3} = 6^1 \cdot 6^{-3} = 6^{1-3} = 6^{-2} = \frac{1}{6^2} = \frac{1}{36}.$$

Or we can reduce as fractions:

$$\frac{2^5}{2^2} = \frac{\cancel{2} \cdot \cancel{2} \cdot 2 \cdot 2 \cdot 2}{\cancel{2} \cdot \cancel{2}} = 2^3 = 8$$

and

$$\frac{6}{6^3} = \frac{\overset{1}{\cancel{6}}}{\cancel{6} \cdot 6 \cdot 6} = \frac{1}{6^2} = \frac{1}{36}.$$

Quotient Rule for Exponents

If a is a nonzero real number and m and n are integers, then

$$\frac{a^m}{a^n} = a^{m-n}.$$

Example 2: Quotient Rule

Use the Quotient Rule to simplify the following expressions so that they contain only positive exponents.

a. $\dfrac{x^7}{x}$

Solution: $\dfrac{x^7}{x} = x^{7-1} = x^6$

b. $\dfrac{y^{-3}}{y^{-8}}$

Solution: $\dfrac{y^{-3}}{y^{-8}} = y^{-3-(-8)} = y^{-3+8} = y^5$

Having negative exponents in the denominator can be confusing. Remember to subtract the exponent in the denominator even if it is negative.

c. $\dfrac{a^{-10}}{a^{-6}}$

Solution: $\dfrac{a^{-10}}{a^{-6}} = a^{-10-(-6)} = a^{-10+6} = a^{-4} = \dfrac{1}{a^4}$

The Power Rule for Exponents

The last property in this section involves raising a power to a power. Consider an expression such as $\left(2^2\right)^3$ or $\left(x^4\right)^5$. We can write

$$\left(2^2\right)^3 = 2^2 \cdot 2^2 \cdot 2^2 = 2^{2+2+2} = 2^6$$

and

$$\left(x^4\right)^5 = x^4 \cdot x^4 \cdot x^4 \cdot x^4 \cdot x^4 = x^{4+4+4+4+4} = x^{20}.$$

Repeated addition with the same number is the same as multiplication with that number. Thus, we can use the following shorter method with the exponents:

$$\left(2^2\right)^3 = 2^{2 \cdot 3} = 2^6 \text{ and } \left(x^4\right)^5 = x^{4 \cdot 5} = x^{20}.$$

These examples illustrate the Power Rule for Exponents.

Power Rule for Exponents

If a is a nonzero real number and m and n are integers, then

$$\left(a^m \right)^n = a^{mn}.$$

Example 3: Power Rule ●

Use the Power Rule for Exponents to simplify the following expressions so that they contain only positive exponents.

a. $\left(x^3 \right)^2$

Solution: $\left(x^3 \right)^2 = x^{3 \cdot 2} = x^6$

b. $\left(a^{-3} \right)^7$

Solution: $\left(a^{-3} \right)^7 = a^{-3 \cdot 7} = a^{-21} = \dfrac{1}{a^{21}}$

In the following examples, simplify each of the expressions using any of the five properties of exponents that apply. You might try each example on scratch paper first and then look at the solution shown in the example. There may be more than one correct procedure, and **you should apply whichever property you "see" first.**

c. $\dfrac{x^{10} x^2}{x^3}$

Solution: $\dfrac{x^{10} x^2}{x^3} = \dfrac{x^{10+2}}{x^3} = \dfrac{x^{12}}{x^3} = x^{12-3} = x^9$ or

$\dfrac{x^{10} x^2}{x^3} = x^{10+2-3} = x^9$

d. $\dfrac{x^6 x^{-2}}{x^7}$

Solution: $\dfrac{x^6 x^{-2}}{x^7} = \dfrac{x^{6+(-2)}}{x^7} = \dfrac{x^{6-2}}{x^7} = \dfrac{x^4}{x^7} = x^{4-7} = x^{-3} = \dfrac{1}{x^3}$ or

$\dfrac{x^6 x^{-2}}{x^7} = x^{6-2-7} = x^{-3} = \dfrac{1}{x^3}$

e. $\dfrac{3^{-5} \cdot 3^9}{3^3 \cdot 3}$

Solution: $\dfrac{3^{-5} \cdot 3^9}{3^3 \cdot 3} = \dfrac{3^{-5+9}}{3^{3+1}} = \dfrac{3^4}{3^4} = 3^{4-4} = 3^0 = 1$

f. $\left(\dfrac{y^{-2}}{y^{-5}} \right)^{-2}$

Solution: $\left(\dfrac{y^{-2}}{y^{-5}} \right)^{-2} = \left(y^{-2-(-5)} \right)^{-2} = \left(y^{-2+5} \right)^{-2} = \left(y^3 \right)^{-2} = y^{-6} = \dfrac{1}{y^6}$

g. $\dfrac{2y^3 \cdot 6y}{4y^{-1}}$

Solution: $\dfrac{2y^3 \cdot 6y}{4y^{-1}} = \dfrac{12y^{3+1}}{4y^{-1}} = \dfrac{\overset{3}{\cancel{12}}\, y^4}{\underset{1}{\cancel{4}}\, y^{-1}} = 3y^{4-(-1)} = 3y^{4+1} = 3y^5$

In Examples 3h and 3i, assume that k represents a nonzero integer. Follow the appropriate rules for exponents.

h. $x^{2k} \cdot x^{2k}$

Solution: $x^{2k} \cdot x^{2k} = x^{2k+2k} = x^{4k}$

i. $\dfrac{x^3 \cdot x^k}{\left(x^2 \right)^k}$

Solution: $\dfrac{x^3 \cdot x^k}{\left(x^2 \right)^k} = \dfrac{x^{k+3}}{x^{2k}} = x^{k+3-2k} = x^{3-k} \text{ or } \dfrac{1}{x^{k-3}}$

• •

1.7 Exercises

Use any of the appropriate properties of exponents to simplify the expressions in Exercises 1 – 70 so that they contain only positive exponents.

1. $(-2)^4(-2)$ **2.** $\left(7^2 \right)\left(7^0 \right)$ **3.** 8^0 **4.** 7^{-2}

5. -6^2 **6.** $3 \cdot 2^2$ **7.** 5^{-1} **8.** -5^{-2}

9. $(-4)^{-3}$ **10.** $(-8)^{-2}$ **11.** $x^5 \cdot x^7$ **12.** $x^3 \cdot x^5$

13. $x^4 \cdot x^0 \cdot x$ **14.** $x^2 \cdot x^{-1}$ **15.** $y^{-2} \cdot y^{-1}$ **16.** $x^{-2} \cdot x^3 \cdot x^5$

17. $x^3 \cdot x^{-7} \cdot x^2$ **18.** $y^{-3} \cdot y^{-2} \cdot y^0$ **19.** $\dfrac{x^3}{x^4}$ **20.** $\dfrac{x^{12}}{x^4}$

21. $\dfrac{y^5}{y^0}$ **22.** $\dfrac{x^2}{x^{-1}}$ **23.** $\dfrac{y^{-2}}{y^2}$ **24.** $\dfrac{y^2}{y^{-5}}$

25. $\dfrac{x^2 x^4}{x^{-4}}$ **26.** $\dfrac{x^3 x^5}{x^4}$ **27.** $\dfrac{x^0 x^3}{x^6}$ **28.** $\dfrac{x \cdot x^3}{x^5}$

29. $\dfrac{x^2 x^4}{x^{-2}}$ **30.** $\dfrac{x^{-1} x^3}{x^{-4}}$ **31.** $\dfrac{x \cdot x^{-2}}{x^2 x^{-3}}$ **32.** $\dfrac{x^{16}}{x^{-2} x^{-8}}$

33. $\left(x^2 \right)^3$ **34.** $\left(x^4 \right)^2$ **35.** $\left(-x^4 \right)^3$ **36.** $\left(-x^3 \right)^4$

37. $\left(x^5 \right)^{-2}$ **38.** $\left(x^{-2} \right)^{-1}$ **39.** $\left(x^3 \right)^{-3}$ **40.** $\left(x^2 \right)^{-2}$

41. $\left(x^2 x^{-3} \right)^4$ **42.** $\left(y^4 y^{-1} \right)^5$ **43.** $\left(x^3 x^{-2} \right)^{-1}$ **44.** $\left(x^3 x^{-3} \right)^3$

45. $\dfrac{y^3 y^3}{y^2}$ **46.** $\dfrac{y^2 y^4}{y}$ **47.** $\dfrac{y^{10} y^4}{y^6}$ **48.** $\dfrac{y \cdot y^4}{y}$

49. $\dfrac{x^5 x^2}{\left(x^2 \right)^2}$ **50.** $\dfrac{x^{10} x^{-3}}{x^3 x^{-1}}$ **51.** $\dfrac{x^8 x^{-2}}{\left(x^2 \right)^3}$ **52.** $\dfrac{\left(x^{-2} \right)^3}{x \cdot x^{-3}}$

53. $\dfrac{\left(y^2 \right)^4}{y^{-2} y^{-1}}$ **54.** $\left(\dfrac{y^2 y^{-1}}{y^5 y^2} \right)^{-2}$ **55.** $\left(\dfrac{x^2 x^0}{x^4 x^{-1}} \right)^{-3}$ **56.** $\left(\dfrac{x^{-3} x^0}{x^2 x} \right)^3$

57. $\left(\dfrac{x^5 x^{-2}}{x \cdot x^{-3}} \right)^2$ **58.** $x^k \cdot x$ **59.** $x^k \cdot x^3$ **60.** $x^k \cdot x^{2k}$

61. $x^{3k} \cdot x^4$ **62.** $\dfrac{x^k}{x^2}$ **63.** $\dfrac{x^{2k}}{x^k}$ **64.** $\dfrac{x^{k+1}}{x^3}$

65. $\left(x^k \right)^2$ **66.** $\left(x^5 \right)^k$ **67.** $x \left(x^2 \right)^k$ **68.** $\dfrac{x^2 x^k}{\left(x^2 \right)^k}$

69. $\dfrac{x^{k+1} x^{-2}}{x^4}$ **70.** $\dfrac{x^{k+3} x}{x^{-2}}$

Writing and Thinking About Mathematics

71. Discuss, briefly, why each of the following statements is WRONG.

    a. $3^2 \cdot 3^2 = 6^2$ **b.** $3^2 \cdot 2^2 = 6^4$ **c.** $3^2 \cdot 3^2 = 9^4$

Hawkes Learning Systems: Intermediate Algebra

Simplifying Integer Exponents I
Simplifying Integer Exponents II

More on Exponents and Scientific Notation

After completing this section, you will be able to:

1. *Simplify expressions by using the properties of integer exponents.*

2. *Write numbers given in scientific notation as decimal numbers.*

3. *Write decimal numbers in scientific notation.*

In Section 1.7, the base of each exponent was one constant or one variable. Two more properties of exponents will help in simplifying expressions such as $(4x)^3$, $(-3x^2y)^5$, and $\left(\dfrac{a^2b}{b^7}\right)^3$, in which the base is a product, a quotient, or a combination of products and quotients. Using the associative and commutative properties of multiplication, we can write

$$(4x)^3 = (4x)\cdot(4x)\cdot(4x)$$
$$= 4\cdot4\cdot4\cdot x\cdot x\cdot x$$
$$= 4^3\cdot x^3$$
$$= 64x^3$$

$$(-3x^2y)^5 = (-3x^2y)\cdot(-3x^2y)\cdot(-3x^2y)\cdot(-3x^2y)\cdot(-3x^2y)$$
$$= (-3)\cdot(-3)\cdot(-3)\cdot(-3)\cdot(-3)\cdot x^2\cdot x^2\cdot x^2\cdot x^2\cdot x^2\cdot y\cdot y\cdot y\cdot y\cdot y$$
$$= (-3)^5\cdot(x^2)^5\cdot y^5$$
$$= -243x^{10}y^5$$

Note carefully that in the expression $(-3x^2y)^5$, the negative sign goes with the 3, and −3 is treated as a factor.

In the previous example, we could write −3 as −1 · 3 and then use both −1 and 3 as bases. In fact, for an expression such as −x, we will do just that, as illustrated in Example 1e.

These examples illustrate the following Power Rule for Products.

Power Rule for Products

If a and b are nonzero real numbers and n is an integer, then

$$(ab)^n = a^n b^n.$$

Example 1: Power Rule for Products • • • • • • • • • • • • • • • • • • •

Simplify the following expressions by using the Power Rule for Products.

a. $(2x)^5$
Solution: $(2x)^5 = 2^5 \cdot x^5 = 32x^5$

b. $(-5y)^2$
Solution: $(-5y)^2 = (-5)^2 \cdot y^2 = 25y^2$

c. $(-6x^5)^3$
Solution: $(-6x^5)^3 = (-6)^3(x^5)^3 = -216x^{15}$

d. $(3x^{-2}y^3)^2$
Solution: $(3x^{-2}y^3)^2 = (3)^2(x^{-2})^2(y^3)^2$

$$= 9x^{-4}y^6 \text{ or } \frac{9y^6}{x^4}$$

e. $(-a^2b^4c)^3$
Solution: $(-a^2b^4c)^3 = (-1 \cdot a^2b^4c)^3$
$$= (-1)^3(a^2)^3(b^4)^3c^3$$
$$= -a^6b^{12}c^3$$

• •

Example 1e illustrates the important relationship concerning exponents and the coefficient -1. In the expression $-a^2$, -1 is the coefficient and a is the base of the exponent 2.
That is,

$$-a^2 = -1 \cdot a^2, \quad -y^3 = -1 \cdot y^3, \quad \text{and} \quad -x^4 = -1 \cdot x^4.$$

The same is true with constant bases. Thus,

$$-5^2 = -1 \cdot 5^2 = -25.$$
$$[-5^2 \neq (-5)^2 \quad \text{and} \quad -a^2 \neq (-a)^2]$$

This distinction is critical only with even exponents. With odd exponents, the results are the same whether or not you apply the exponent to the coefficient -1. For example,

$$-2^3 = -1 \cdot 2^3 = -1 \cdot 8 = -8$$
and $$(-2)^3 = -8.$$

Power Rule for Fractions

Expressions with fractions (or quotients) are treated much the same as expressions with products. For example,

$$\left(\frac{y}{3}\right)^4 = \frac{y}{3} \cdot \frac{y}{3} \cdot \frac{y}{3} \cdot \frac{y}{3} = \frac{y \cdot y \cdot y \cdot y}{3 \cdot 3 \cdot 3 \cdot 3} = \frac{y^4}{3^4} = \frac{y^4}{81}$$

and

$$\left(\frac{a}{x}\right)^3 = \frac{a}{x} \cdot \frac{a}{x} \cdot \frac{a}{x} = \frac{a \cdot a \cdot a}{x \cdot x \cdot x} = \frac{a^3}{x^3}.$$

These examples illustrate the Power Rule for Fractions.

Power Rule for Fractions

If a and b are nonzero real numbers and n is an integer, then

$$\left(\frac{a}{b}\right)^n = \frac{a^n}{b^n}.$$

Example 2: Properties of Exponents

Simplify the following expressions by using any of the properties of exponents that apply.

a. $\left(\dfrac{5x}{3b}\right)^3$

     Solution: $\left(\dfrac{5x}{3b}\right)^3 = \dfrac{(5x)^3}{(3b)^3} = \dfrac{5^3 x^3}{3^3 b^3} = \dfrac{125x^3}{27b^3}$

b. $\left(\dfrac{a^3 b^{-3}}{4}\right)^2$

     Solution: $\left(\dfrac{a^3 b^{-3}}{4}\right)^2 = \dfrac{(a^3 b^{-3})^2}{4^2} = \dfrac{(a^3)^2 (b^{-3})^2}{4^2} = \dfrac{a^6 b^{-6}}{16}$ **or** $\dfrac{a^6}{16b^6}$

c. $\dfrac{(3^{-2} x^{-3})^{-1}}{(x^{-2} y^3)^3 (2x^{-1} y^2)^{-1}}$

     Solution: $\dfrac{(3^{-2} x^{-3})^{-1}}{(x^{-2} y^3)^3 (2x^{-1} y^2)^{-1}} = \dfrac{3^2 x^3}{x^{-6} y^9 \cdot 2^{-1} x^1 y^{-2}} = \dfrac{2^1 \cdot 9 x^3}{x^{-5} y^7}$

$$= \frac{18 x^{3-(-5)}}{y^7} = \frac{18 x^8}{y^7} \text{ or } 18 x^8 y^{-7}$$

d. $\left(\dfrac{2x^2 y^{-3}}{x^{-3} y} \right)^{-2}$

Solution: $\left(\dfrac{2x^2 y^{-3}}{x^{-3} y} \right)^{-2} = \left(2x^{2-(-3)} y^{-3-1} \right)^{-2} = \left(2x^{2+3} y^{-3-1} \right)^{-2} = \left(2x^5 y^{-4} \right)^{-2}$

$$= 2^{-2} x^{-10} y^8 \quad \textbf{or} \quad \dfrac{1}{4} x^{-10} y^8 \quad \textbf{or} \quad \dfrac{y^8}{4x^{10}}$$

e. $\left(\dfrac{x^{2k} y^k}{x^k y} \right)^2$

Solution: $\left(\dfrac{x^{2k} y^k}{x^k y} \right)^2 = \left(x^{2k-k} y^{k-1} \right)^2$

$$= \left(x^k y^{k-1} \right)^2 = x^{2k} y^{2(k-1)} = x^{2k} y^{2k-2}$$

f. $\dfrac{1}{5x^{-2}}$

Solution: $\dfrac{1}{5x^{-2}} = \dfrac{1}{5 \cdot \dfrac{1}{x^2}} = \dfrac{1}{\dfrac{5}{x^2}} = 1 \cdot \dfrac{x^2}{5} = \dfrac{x^2}{5}$

Notice that the exponent −2 applies only to the x and has no effect on the coefficient 5.

● ●

NOTES

Another general approach with fractions involving negative exponents is to note that

$$\left(\dfrac{a}{b} \right)^{-n} = \dfrac{a^{-n}}{b^{-n}} = \dfrac{b^n}{a^n} = \left(\dfrac{b}{a} \right)^n$$

In effect, there are two basic shortcuts with negative exponents and fractions:

1. Taking the reciprocal of a fraction changes the sign of any exponent on the fraction.
2. Moving any factor from numerator to denominator or vice versa, changes the sign of the corresponding exponent.

Example 3: Two Approaches ●

a. Either of the following approaches can be used to simplify $\left(\dfrac{a^2}{b^3} \right)^{3}$.

i. $\left(\dfrac{a^2}{b^3} \right)^{-3} = \left(\dfrac{b^3}{a^2} \right)^3 = \dfrac{\left(b^3 \right)^3}{\left(a^2 \right)^3} = \dfrac{b^9}{a^6}$ **ii.** $\left(\dfrac{a^2}{b^3} \right)^{-3} = \dfrac{\left(a^2 \right)^{-3}}{\left(b^3 \right)^{-3}} = \dfrac{a^{-6}}{b^{-9}} = \dfrac{b^9}{a^6}$

continued on next page ...

b. Either of the following approaches can be used to simplify $\left(\dfrac{x}{3y^4}\right)^{-2}$.

i. $\left(\dfrac{x}{3y^4}\right)^{-2} = \left(\dfrac{3y^4}{x}\right)^{2} = \dfrac{\left(3y^4\right)^2}{x^2} = \dfrac{9y^8}{x^2}$

ii. $\left(\dfrac{x}{3y^4}\right)^{-2} = \dfrac{x^{-2}}{\left(3y^4\right)^{-2}} = \dfrac{\left(3y^4\right)^2}{x^2} = \dfrac{9y^8}{x^2}$

• •

In general,

$$\frac{1}{a^{-n}} = a^n \quad \text{and} \quad \frac{a^{-n}}{b^{-m}} = \frac{b^m}{a^n} \quad \text{and} \quad \left(\frac{a}{b}\right)^{-n} = \left(\frac{b}{a}\right)^{n}.$$

Remember that the choice of steps is yours and that, as long as you correctly apply the properties of exponents, the answer will be the same regardless of the order of the steps. The following table provides a summary of the properties of exponents for easy reference.

Summary of Properties of Exponents

For nonzero real numbers a and b and integers m and n,

The Exponent 1:	$a = a^1$ (*a is any real number.*)
The Exponent 0:	$a^0 = 1$ ($a \neq 0$)
Product Rule:	$a^m \cdot a^n = a^{m+n}$
Quotient Rule:	$\dfrac{a^m}{a^n} = a^{m-n}$
Power Rule:	$\left(a^m\right)^n = a^{mn}$
Negative Exponents:	$a^{-n} = \dfrac{1}{a^n}, \quad \dfrac{1}{a^{-n}} = a^n$
Power Rule for Products:	$(ab)^n = a^n b^n$
Power Rule for Fractions:	$\left(\dfrac{a}{b}\right)^n = \dfrac{a^n}{b^n}$

Scientific Notation

A basic application of integer exponents occurs in scientific disciplines, such as astronomy and biology, when very large and very small numbers are involved. For example, the distance from the earth to the sun is approximately 93,000,000 miles, and the approximate radius of a carbon atom is 0.000 000 007 7 centimeters.

In **scientific notation** (an option in all scientific and graphing calculators), **decimal numbers are written as the product of a number greater than or equal to 1 and less than 10, and an integer power of 10**. In scientific notation there is just one digit to the left of the decimal point. For example,

$$93,000,000 = 9.3 \times 10^7 \quad \text{and} \quad 0.000\,000\,007\,7 = 7.7 \times 10^{-9}$$

The exponent tells how many places the decimal point is to be moved and in what direction. If the exponent is positive, the decimal point is moved to the right:

$$2.7 \times 10^3 = 2700. \qquad \text{3 places right}$$

A negative exponent indicates that the decimal point should move to the left:

$$3.92 \times 10^{-6} = 0.00000392 \qquad \text{6 places left}$$

Scientific Notation

> If N is a decimal number, then in **scientific notation**
>
> $N = a \times 10^n$ where $1 \le a < 10$ and n is an integer.

Example 4: Decimals in Scientific Notation

Write the following decimal numbers in scientific notation.

a. 867,000,000,000   **b.** 420,000
c. 0.0036   **d.** 0.000 000 025

Solution:

a. $867,000,000,000 = 8.67 \times 10^{11}$

b. $420,000 = 4.2 \times 10^5$

c. $0.0036 = 3.6 \times 10^{-3}$

d. $0.000\,000\,025 = 2.5 \times 10^{-8}$

Example 5: Properties of Exponents

Simplify the following expressions by first writing the decimal numbers in scientific notation and then using the properties of exponents.

a. $\dfrac{0.0023 \times 560{,}000}{0.00014}$

Solution: $\dfrac{0.0023 \times 560{,}000}{0.00014} = \dfrac{2.3 \times 10^{-3} \times 5.6 \times 10^{5}}{1.4 \times 10^{-4}}$

$$= \dfrac{2.3 \times \overset{4}{\cancel{5.6}}}{\cancel{1.4}} \times \dfrac{10^{-3} \times 10^{5}}{10^{-4}}$$

$$= 9.2 \times \dfrac{10^{2}}{10^{-4}} = 9.2 \times 10^{2-(-4)}$$

$$= 9.2 \times 10^{6}$$

b. $\dfrac{8.1 \times 8200}{9{,}000{,}000 \times 4.1}$

Solution: $\dfrac{8.1 \times 8200}{9{,}000{,}000 \times 4.1} = \dfrac{8.1 \times 8.2 \times 10^{3}}{9.0 \times 10^{6} \times 4.1}$

$$= \dfrac{\overset{0.9}{\cancel{8.1}} \times \overset{2}{\cancel{8.2}}}{\cancel{9.0} \times \cancel{4.1}} \times \dfrac{10^{3}}{10^{6}}$$

$$= 1.8 \times 10^{3-6} = 1.8 \times 10^{-3}$$

c. Light travels approximately 3×10^{8} meters per second. How many meters per minute does light travel?

Solution: Since there are 60 seconds in one minute, multiply by 60.

$$3 \times 10^{8} \times 60 = 180 \times 10^{8} = 1.8 \times 10^{2} \times 10^{8} = 1.8 \times 10^{10}$$

Thus light travels 1.8×10^{10} meters per minute.

d. Use a calculator to evaluate the expression $\dfrac{8600(3.0 \times 10^{5})}{1.5 \times 10^{-6}}$. Leave the answer in scientific notation.

(**Note:** The caret key 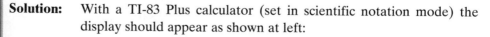 is used to indicate an exponent.)

Solution: With a TI-83 Plus calculator (set in scientific notation mode) the display should appear as shown at left:

Note that the numerator and denominator must be set in parentheses.

e. Use a calculator to find the number of miles that light travels in one year (a light-year) if light travels 186,000 miles per second.

Solution: We know

$$60 \text{ sec} = 1 \text{ min}$$
$$60 \text{ min} = 1 \text{ hr}$$
$$24 \text{ hr} = 1 \text{ day}$$
$$365 \text{ days} = 1 \text{ yr}$$

Multiplication should give the following display on your calculator:

Thus, a light-year is 5,865,696,000,000 miles.

1.8 Exercises

Simplify the expressions in Exercises 1 – 32 so that they contain only positive exponents.

1. $\left(x^{-2} \right)^2$

2. $\left(x^2 \right)^{-3}$

3. $\left(-2x^4 \right)^2$

4. $\left(3x^{-2} \right)^{-1}$

5. $\left(x^2 y^{-3} \right)^2$

6. $\left(xy^3 \right)^{-2}$

7. $\left(\dfrac{a}{b^2} \right)^4$

8. $\left(\dfrac{2a}{b^2} \right)^3$

9. $\left(\dfrac{2^{-1} a}{3b^2} \right)^{-2}$

10. $\left(\dfrac{-3x^{-2}}{y^3} \right)^{-1}$

11. $\left(\dfrac{6x}{x^2 y^{-3}} \right)^{-2}$

12. $\left(\dfrac{2ab^4}{3b^2} \right)^{-3}$

13. $\left(\dfrac{5^{-1} x^3 y^{-2}}{xy^{-1}} \right)^2$

14. $\left(\dfrac{x^2 y^{-3}}{3x^{-1} y} \right)^{-1}$

15. $\left(x^2 y \right)^k$

16. $\left(x^k y^m \right)^2$

17. $\left(x^{2k} y^2 \right)\left(xy^n \right)$

18. $\left(x^{4n} y^3 \right)\left(x^n y^{-k} \right)$

19. $\left(x^{n+2} y^k \right)\left(x^{-2} y \right)$

20. $\left(x^{k+1} y^{3k} \right)\left(x^2 y^{-k} \right)$

21. $\left(\dfrac{x^4 y}{y^2} \right)\left(\dfrac{x^{-1} y^2}{y^{-1}} \right)^0$

22. $\left(\dfrac{a^2 b}{ab^{-2}} \right)\left(\dfrac{a^{-3} b}{b^{-3}} \right)$

23. $\left(\dfrac{x^2 y}{y^2} \right)^{-1}\left(\dfrac{3x^{-2} y}{y^{-2}} \right)^2$

24. $\left(\dfrac{x^2 y^{-3}}{y^{-1}} \right)^2\left(\dfrac{xy^2}{2y} \right)^{-1}$

25. $\left(\dfrac{a^3 b^{-1}}{ab^{-2}} \right)\left(\dfrac{a^0 b^3}{a^4 b^{-1}} \right)^{-1}$

26. $\left(\dfrac{5x^3 y}{x^{-2}y^3}\right)^{-1}\left(\dfrac{4x^{-2}y^{-1}}{15xy^4}\right)^{-1}$ **27.** $\left(\dfrac{7x^{-2}y}{xy^4}\right)^{2}\left(\dfrac{14xy^{-3}}{x^4y^2}\right)^{-1}$ **28.** $\dfrac{\left(4^{-2}x^{-3}y\right)^{-1}}{\left(x^{-2}y^2\right)^3\left(5xy^{-2}\right)^{-1}}$

29. $\dfrac{\left(xy^{-2}\right)^4\left(x^{-2}y^3\right)^{-2}}{\left(xy^2\right)^{-1}\left(xy^{-2}\right)^{-4}}$ **30.** $\dfrac{\left(6x^2y\right)\left(x^{-1}y^3\right)^2}{\left(x^{-1}y\right)^2\left(3x^2y\right)^3}$ **31.** $\dfrac{\left(x^3y^4\right)^{-1}\left(x^{-2}y\right)^2}{\left(xy^2\right)^{-3}\left(xy^{-1}\right)^2}$

32. $\dfrac{\left(x^{-3}y^{-5}\right)^{-2}\left(x^2y^{-3}\right)^3}{\left(x^3y^{-4}\right)^2\left(x^{-1}y^{-2}\right)^{-2}}$

Write each expression in Exercises 33 – 38 in decimal notation.

33. 4.72×10^5 **34.** 6.91×10^{-4} **35.** 1.28×10^{-7}

36. 1.63×10^8 **37.** 9.23×10^{-3} **38.** 5.88×10^6

For Exercises 39 – 54, write each expression in scientific notation. Show the steps you use as in Examples 5a and 5b in the text. Do not use your calculator.

39. 479,000   **40.** 0.000367   **41.** 0.000000871

42. $52,800\times1,000$ **43.** $143,000\times0.0003$ **44.** 0.007×0.00012

45. $0.036\times4,000,000$ **46.** $\dfrac{27,000}{0.0009}$ **47.** $\dfrac{1800\times0.00045}{1350}$

48. $\dfrac{0.0032\times120}{0.0096}$ **49.** $\dfrac{0.084\times0.0093}{0.21\times0.031}$ **50.** $\dfrac{0.0070\times50\times0.55}{1.4\times0.0011\times0.25}$

51. $\dfrac{0.36\times5200}{0.00052\times720}$ **52.** $\dfrac{0.0016\times0.09\times460}{0.00012\times0.023}$ **53.** $\dfrac{760\times84\times0.063}{900\times0.38\times210}$

54. $\dfrac{420\times0.016\times80}{0.028\times120\times0.2}$

For Exercises 55 – 60, use your calculator and leave all answers in scientific notation.

55. Light travels approximately 3×10^{10} centimeters per second. How many centimeters would this be per minute? per hour?

56. An atom of gold weighs approximately 3.25×10^{-22} grams. What would be the weight of 3,000 atoms of gold?

57. One light-year is approximately 9.46×10^{15} meters. The distance to a certain star is about 4.3 light years. How many meters is this?

58. One light-year is about 5.87×10^{12} miles. The mean distance from the sun to Pluto is 3.675×10^{9} miles. How many light years is this?

59. The weight of an atom is measured in atomic weight units (amu), where 1 amu $= 1.6605 \times 10^{-27}$ kilograms. The atomic weight of carbon 12 is 12 amu. Express the atomic weight of carbon 12 in kilograms.

60. The atomic weight of argon is about 40 amu. Express this weight in kilograms. (See Exercise 59.)

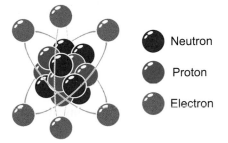

Neutron

Proton

Electron

In Exercises 61 – 66, use your calculator (set in scientific notation mode) to evaluate each expression. Leave the answer in scientific notation.

61. $\dfrac{5.4 \cdot 0.003 \cdot 5000}{15 \cdot 0.0027 \cdot 20}$

62. $\dfrac{0.0005 \cdot 650 \cdot 3.3}{0.00011 \cdot 2500}$

63. $\dfrac{\left(1.4 \times 10^{-3}\right)\left(922\right)}{\left(3.5 \times 10^{3}\right)\left(2.0 \times 10^{-6}\right)}$

64. $\dfrac{0.0084 \cdot 0.003}{0.21 \cdot 600}$

65. $\dfrac{0.02\left(3.9 \times 10^{3}\right)}{0.013\left(5.0 \times 10^{-3}\right)}$

66. $\dfrac{(43,000)\left(3.0 \times 10^{5}\right)}{\left(8.6 \times 10^{-2}\right)\left(1.5 \times 10^{-3}\right)}$

Hawkes Learning Systems: Intermediate Algebra

Simplifying Integer Exponents II

Chapter 1 Index of Key Ideas and Terms

Natural Numbers (Counting Numbers)   page 3

$N = \{1, 2, 3, 4, 5, 6, ...\}$

Whole Numbers   page 3

$W = \{0, 1, 2, 3, 4, ...\}$

Integers   page 3

$Z = \{..., -4, -3, -2, -1, 0, 1, 2, 3, 4, ...\}$

Rational Numbers   pages 3-4

A **rational number** is any number that can be written in the form $\dfrac{a}{b}$ where a and b are integers and $b \neq 0$.

In decimal form, rational numbers are either

    1. Terminating decimals, or
    2. Infinite repeating decimals.

Irrational Numbers   page 5

An **irrational number** is any number that can be written as an infinite nonrepeating decimal.

Real Numbers   pages 6-7

Every rational number and irrational number is a **real number**.

Real Number Lines   page 7

There is a one-to-one correspondence between the real numbers and the points on a line.

Set Builder Notation: $\{\, x \mid \quad \}$ pages 8-9

Inequality Symbols   page 8

$<$	"less than"	$\leq$	"less than or equal"
$>$	"greater than"	$\geq$	"greater than or equal"

Field Properties of Real Numbers   page 11

Addition		Name of property	Multiplication	
A1	$a + b$ is a real number	Closure	M1	$a \cdot b$ is a real number
A2	$a + b = b + a$	Commutative	M2	$a \cdot b = b \cdot a$
A3	$(a + b) + c = a + (b + c)$	Associative	M3	$(a \cdot b) \cdot c = a \cdot (b \cdot c)$
A4	$a + 0 = 0 + a = a$	Identity	M4	$a \cdot 1 = 1 \cdot a = a$
A5	$a + (-a) = 0$	Inverse	M5	$a \cdot \dfrac{1}{a} = 1 \, (a \neq 0)$

D Distributive Property: $a \cdot (b + c) = a \cdot b + a \cdot c \ or \ (b + c) \cdot a = b \cdot a + c \cdot a$

Properties of Inequality (Order)   page 13

For real numbers a, b, and c:

O1 **Trichotomy Property**:   Exactly one of the following is true:

$a < b$, $a = b$,   or $a > b$.

O2 **Transitive Property**:   If $a < b$ and $b < c$, then $a < c$.

Absolute Value   pages 17-18

For any real number x, $|x| = \begin{cases} x \text{ if } x \geq 0 \\ -x \text{ if } x < 0 \end{cases}$

Operations with Real Numbers

Addition   page 19

1.   To add two real numbers with like signs, add
     their absolute values and use thc common sign.
2.   To add two numbers with unlike signs, subtract
     their absolute values and use the sign of the
     number with the larger absolute value.

Subtraction   page 20

For real numbers a and b, $a - b = a + (-b)$

Multiplication   pages 23-24

1.   For positive numbers a and b, $a(-b) = (-a)b = -ab$.
2.   For positive numbers a and b, $(-a)(-b) = ab$.

Division   page 25

For real numbers a and b $(b \neq 0)$, $\dfrac{a}{b} = x$ **if and only if** $a = b \cdot x$.

Rules for Multiplication and Division   page 26

1.   If two nonzero numbers have like signs, then both
     the product and quotients will be positive
2.   If two nonzero numbers have unlike signs, then both
     the product and quotients will be negative.

Multiplication Property of Zero   page 26

For any real number a, $a \cdot 0 = 0$

Division by 0   page 26

Division by 0 is undefined.

Exponents   page 27

An **exponent** is a number written to the right and slightly
above another number (called the **base**) that indicates repeated
multiplication of the base by itself.

95

Rules for Order of Operations   page 28
1. Simplify within symbols of inclusion (parentheses, brackets, braces, fraction bar, or absolute value bars) beginning with the innermost symbols.
2. Find any powers indicated by exponents.
3. Multiply or divide from left to right.
4. Add or subtract from left to right.

Terms   page 32
A **term** is an expression that involves only multiplication and/or division with constants and variables.

Like Terms   page 32
Like terms (or similar terms) are those terms that have the same variable factors with the same exponents.

Combining Like Terms   page 33

First-degree (or Linear) Equations   page 34
An equation of the form $ax + b = c$, where a, b, and c are real numbers and $a \neq 0$, is called a first-degree (or linear) equation in x.

Addition Property of Equality   page 35
If the same algebraic expression is added to both sides of an equation, the new equation has the same solutions as the original equation.
Symbolically, if A, B, and C are algebraic expressions,

and if	$A = B$
then	$A + C = B + C$
and	$A - C = B - C$

Note: Subtracting C is the same as adding its opposite, $-C$

Multiplication Property of Equality   page 35
If both sides of an equation are multiplied by the same nonzero algebraic expression, the new equation has the same solutions as the original equation.
Symbolically, if A, B, and C are algebraic expressions,

and if	$A = B$	
then	$AC = BC$	(where $C \neq 0$)
and	$\dfrac{A}{C} = \dfrac{B}{C}$	(where $C \neq 0$)

Note: Dividing by C is the same as multiplying by its reciprocal, $\dfrac{1}{C}$.

Solving a Linear Equation   page 36

1. Simplify each side of the equation by removing any grouping symbols and combining like terms. (In some cases, you may want to multiply each term by a constant to clear fractional or decimal coefficients.)
2. Use the addition property of equality to add the opposites of constants or variable expressions so that variable expressions are on one side of the equation and constants on the other.
3. Use the multiplication property of equality to multiply both sides by the reciprocal of the coefficient of the variable (that is, divide both sides by the coefficient) so that the new coefficient is 1.
4. Check your answer by substituting it into the original equation.

Types of Equations   page 38

Types of Equations	Number of Solutions
Conditional	Finite number of solutions
Identity	Infinite number of solutions
Contradiction	No solutions

Absolute Value Equations   page 40

For $c > 0$,
1. If $|x| = c$, then $x = c$ or $x = -c$.
2. If $|ax + b| = c$, then $ax + b = c$ or $ax + b = -c$.

Evaluating and Solving Formulas   page 44

Applications   pages 51-57

Number problems
Distance-rate-time
Cost
Interest
Average

Interval Notation   pages 64-65

Types of intervals:

Open	(a, b), (a, ∞), $(-\infty, b)$
Closed	$[a, b]$
Half-open	$[a, \infty)$, $(-\infty, b]$, $[a, b)$, $(a, b]$

Linear Inequalities   page 65

For real numbers $a, b,$ and c $(a \neq 0)$, $\boldsymbol{ax + b} < \boldsymbol{c}$ is called a **linear inequality** in x. (The definition also holds if $\leq, >,$ or $\geq$ is used instead of $<$.)

To Solve a Linear Inequality   page 66
   1. Simplify each side of the inequality by removing any grouping symbols
       and combining like terms.
   2. Add the opposites of constants and/or variable expressions to both sides so
       that variables are on one side and constants are on the other.
   3. Divide both sides by the coefficient of the variable and
       a. leave the direction of the inequality unchanged if the coefficient is positive; or
       b. reverse the direction of the inequality if the coefficient is negative.

Addition Property of Inequality   page 66
   If the same algebraic expression is added to both sides of an inequality, the new
   inequality is equivalent to the original inequality.
       If $A < B$, then $A + C < B + C$.
       If $A < B$, then $A - C < B - C$.

Multiplication Property of Inequality   page 66
   If both sides of an inequality are multiplied (or divided) by the same
   positive expression, then the new inequality is equivalent to the original inequality.

$$\left\{ \begin{array}{l} \text{If } A < B \text{ and } C > 0, \text{ then } AC < BC. \\ \text{If } A < B \text{ and } C > 0, \text{ then } \dfrac{A}{C} < \dfrac{B}{C}. \end{array} \right.$$

   If both sides of an inequality are multiplied (or divided) by the same
   negative expression and the inequality is reversed, then the new inequality is
   equivalent to the original inequality.

$$\left\{ \begin{array}{l} \text{If } A < B \text{ and } C < 0, \text{ then } AC > BC. \\ \text{If } A < B \text{ and } C < 0, \text{ then } \dfrac{A}{C} > \dfrac{B}{C}. \end{array} \right.$$

Absolute Value Inequalities   pages 69 - 71
   For $c > 0$;
   1. If $|x| < c$, then $-c < x < c$.
   2. If $|ax + b| < c$, then $-c < ax + b < c$.

   For $c > 0$;
   1. If $|x| > c$, then $x > c$ **or** $x < -c$.
   2. If $|ax + b| > c$, then $ax + b < -c$ **or** $ax + b > c$.

Properties of Exponents   page 88

For nonzero real numbers a and b and integers m and n,

The Exponent 1: $a = a^1$ (*a* is any real number.)

The Exponent 0: $a^0 = 1$ ($a \neq 0$)

Product Rule: $a^m \cdot a^n = a^{m+n}$

Quotient Rule: $\dfrac{a^m}{a^n} = a^{m-n}$

Power Rule: $\left(a^m\right)^n = a^{mn}$

Negative Exponents: $a^{-n} = \dfrac{1}{a^n}, \qquad \dfrac{1}{a^{-n}} = a^n$

Power Rule for Products: $(ab)^n = a^n b^n$

Power Rule for Fractions: $\left(\dfrac{a}{b}\right)^n = \dfrac{a^n}{b^n}$

Scientific Notation   page 89

If N is a decimal number, then in scientific notation
$N = a \times 10^n$ where $1 \leq a < 10$ and n is an integer.

Chapter 1 Review

For a review of the topics and problems from Chapter 1, look at the following lessons from *Hawkes Learning Systems: Intermediate Algebra*

Name that Real Number
Properties of Real Numbers
Introduction to Absolute Values
Addition with Real Numbers
Subtraction with Real Numbers
Multiplication and Division with
Real Numbers
Order of Operations
Simplifying Expressions

Solving Linear Equations
Solving Absolute Value Expressions
Evaluating Formulas
Applications of Linear Equations
Solving Linear Inequalities
Solving Absolute Value Inequalities
Simplifying Integer Exponents I
Simplifying Interger Exponents II

Chapter 1 Test

1. List the numbers in the set $A = \left\{ -\sqrt{11},\ -2,\ -\dfrac{5}{3},\ 0,\ \dfrac{1}{2},\ \sqrt{3},\ 2,\ \pi \right\}$ that are described below.

    a. $\{\, x \mid x \text{ is an integer} \,\}$ **b.** $\{\, x \mid x \text{ is a rational number} \,\}$

2. Write the rational number $\dfrac{5}{12}$ as an infinite repeating decimal.

Graph each of the sets in Exercises 3 – 6 on a real number line.

3. $\{\, x \mid x \le 7,\ x \text{ is a whole number} \,\}$ **4.** $\{\, x \mid -8 < x \le 0,\ x \text{ is an integer} \,\}$

5. $\left\{ x \,\middle|\, -2 \le x < \dfrac{5}{8} \right\}$ **6.** $\left\{ x \,\middle|\, -1.5 < x < 3 \text{ or } x \ge \sqrt{17} \right\}$

Name the property that justifies each statement in Exercises 7 and 8. All variables represent real numbers.

7. $3x + 15y = 3(\, x + 5y \,)$ **8.** $3 + (\, x + y \,) = (\, 3 + x \,) + y$

Complete the expressions in Exercises 9 and 10 using the given property.

9. $7y \cdot 0 =$ _____   Zero factor law

10. If $x < 17$ and $17 < a$, then _____   Transitive property

Perform the indicated operations in Exercises 11 – 15.

11. $|-19| + 43 - (\, -8 \,)$ **12.** $(\, -96 \,) \div (\, -12 \,)$ **13.** $\left(\dfrac{5}{8} \right)(\, -3 \,)$

14. $\dfrac{3}{5} + \left(\dfrac{-7}{10} \right) - \dfrac{1}{6}$ **15.** $4(\, -6 \,)(\, -2 \,)(\, -3 \,)$

Find the value of each expression in Exercises 16 and 17 by using the rules for order of operations.

16. $6 + (\, 7^2 - 3^2 \,) \div 5 \cdot 4$ **17.** $\left(\dfrac{-1}{3} \right) + \dfrac{3}{4} \div \dfrac{1}{6}$

Simplify each expression in Exercises 18 and 19 by combining like terms.

18. $4(\, x + 6 \,) - (\, 8 - 2x \,)$ **19.** $-2x + 3 [\, 5x - (\, 2x + 4 \,)]$

Solve each of the equations in Exercises 20 – 24.

20. $5x - 3(x - 2) = 4$

21. $4x + (5 - x) = 3(x + 2)$

22. $\dfrac{3x - 2}{8} = \dfrac{x}{4} - 1$

23. $|2x + 1| = 2.8$

24. $|5 - 3x| + 1 = 4$

25. Determine whether each equation is a conditional equation, an identity, or a contradiction.

   a. $\dfrac{3}{4}x + 5 = \dfrac{2}{3}x - 1$

   b. $5x + 7 = 3(x - 2) + 2x$

   c. $-4(x + 2) = -2(2x + 4)$

26. Solve the formula $P = 2l + 2w$ for w.

27. Solve the formula $A = P + Prt$ for t.

Solve the inequalities in Exercises 26 – 29, then graph each solution on a real number line and write the solution in interval notation.

28. $3x + 7 < 4(x + 3)$

29. $\dfrac{2x + 5}{4} > x + 3$

30. $|7 - 2x| < 3$

31. $|2(x - 3) + 5| > 2.7$

32. A bus leaves Kansas City headed for Phoenix traveling at a rate of 48 mph. Thirty minutes later, a second bus follows, traveling at 54 mph. How long will it take the second bus to overtake the first?

33. The Candy Shack sells a particular candy in two different size packages. One size sells for $1.25 and the other sells for $1.75. If the store received $65.50 for 42 packages of candy, how many of each size were sold?

34. Given the amount of U.S. cellular telephone subscribers:
  a. Find the average number of subscribers from 1995-1999.
  b. Find the difference in the number of subscribers from 1985-2001.
  c. How many subscribers were there in 1991?

Source: The CTIA Semi-Annual Wireless Survey (All numbers have been rounded to the nearest hundred)

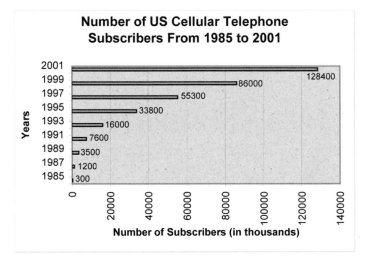

Use the properties of exponents to simplify each of the expressions in Exercises 35 – 38. Leave the answers with positive exponents.

35. $(4x^2y)(-5.2xy^{-3})$

36. $\dfrac{\left(xy^{-2}\right)^3}{\left(x^3y^{-1}\right)^2}$

37. $\left(\dfrac{x^2y^{-2}}{3y^5}\right)^{-2}$

38. $\dfrac{x^{k+3}\cdot x^{2k-1}}{x^{3k+1}}$

39. Write each number in the following expressions in scientific notation and simplify. Show all the steps you use and do not use a calculator. Leave the answers in scientific notation.

  a. $\dfrac{0.27\times0.0016}{120}$

  b. $\dfrac{650\times35,000}{0.0025}$

40. Use a calculator to simplify the following expression. Leave the answer in scientific notation.

$$\dfrac{\left(3.4\times10^6\right)\left(4.5\times10^3\right)}{5400}$$

Straight Lines and Functions

Did You Know?

One of the most difficult problems for students in algebra is to become comfortable with the idea that letters or symbols can be manipulated just like numbers in arithmetic. These symbols may be the cause of "math anxiety."

A great deal of publicity has recently been given to the concept that a large number of people suffer from math anxiety, a painful uneasiness caused by mathematical symbols or a problem-solving situation. Persons affected by math anxiety find it difficult to learn mathematics, or they may be able to learn but be unable to apply their knowledge or do well on tests. Persons suffering from math anxiety often develop math avoidance, and they avoid careers, majors, or classes that will require mathematics courses or skills. Sociologist Lucy Sells has determined that mathematics is a critical filter in the job market. Persons who lack quantitative skills are often channeled into high unemployment, low-paying, non-technical careers.

What causes math anxiety? Researchers are investigating the following hypotheses:

1. a lack of skills which leads to lack of confidence and, therefore, to anxiety;
2. an attitude that mathematics is not useful or significant to society;
3. career goals that seem to preclude mathematics;
4. a self-concept that differs radically from the stereotype of a mathematician;
5. perceptions that parents, peers, or teachers have low expectations for the person in mathematics;
6. social conditioning to avoid mathematics (a particular problem for women).

We hope that you are finding your present experience with algebra successful and that the skills you are acquiring now will enable you to approach mathematical problems with confidence.

2.1 **Cartesian Coordinate System and Straight Lines: $Ax + By = C$**

2.2 **Slope - Intercept Form: $y = mx + b$**

2.3 **Point - Slope Form: $y - y_1 = m(x - x_1)$**

2.4 **Introduction to Functions**

2.5 **Graphing Linear Inequalities**

"The Science of Pure Mathematics, in its modern developments, may claim to be the most original creation of the human spirit."

Alfred North Whitehead (1861-1947)

This chapter is designed to develop graphing skills with linear equations and inequalities in two variables. The graphs of linear equations are straight lines. The graphs of linear inequalities are half-planes separated by straight lines. The related skills learned in this chapter will be particularly helpful when dealing with applications involving linear equations and linear inequalities that will be discussed later.

Three useful forms of linear equations are the standard form, the slope-intercept form, and the point-slope form. Each form is equally important and useful depending on the information given and the application of the equation. Your algebraic skills should allow you to change from one form to another and to recognize when the same equation is in a different form.

The concept of slope underlies all our work with straight lines. Even in the cases of horizontal lines (with slope 0) and vertical lines (with undefined slope), we can relate to the slopes. Relationships between two or more lines can be discussed in terms of their slopes; parallel lines have the same slope, and perpendicular lines have slopes that are negative reciprocals of each other.

Slope also is a part of our daily lives, such as in the slope of the roof of a building, the approaching slope of a landing airplane, or the slope of a mountain road.

Cartesian Coordinate System and Straight Lines: $Ax + By = C$

Objectives

After completing this section, you will be able to:

1. Find ordered pairs that satisfy given linear equations.

2. Graph lines in a Cartesian coordinate system by locating points that satisfy given linear equations.

The linear (or first-degree) equations and inequalities we have discussed so far in this text have involved only one variable. In this chapter, we will discuss linear equations and inequalities that contain two variables. The context of the material should indicate clearly which type of linear equation is being discussed. As we will see in Section 2.4, except for special cases, linear equations in two variables are also called **linear functions**.

Descartes

Cartesian Coordinate System

We begin with the concept of **ordered pairs** of real numbers of the form (x, y) and show how these are related to the solutions and graphs of equations. For example, the pair of numbers (5, 2) enclosed in parentheses is called an **ordered pair**. The first number, 5, is called the **first coordinate** (or *x*-coordinate), and the second number, 2, is called the **second coordinate** (or *y*-coordinate). The ordered pair (5, 2) is not the same as the ordered pair (2, 5) because the order of the numbers is not the same.

Just as there is a one-to-one correspondence between points on a real number line and the real numbers (See Section 1.1), **there is a one-to-one correspondence between the points in a plane and ordered pairs of real numbers**. Ordered pairs of real numbers are graphed as points in a plane using the **Cartesian coordinate system**, named after seventeenth century French mathematician René Descartes (1596 – 1650). It is also known as a **rectangular coordinate system**.

This system uses two perpendicular number lines to separate a plane into four **quadrants**. By convention, the horizontal number line is the *x*-axis and the vertical number line is the *y*-axis. The point (0, 0) is called the **origin**. The quadrants, axes, and the graphs of several points are shown in Figure 2.1.

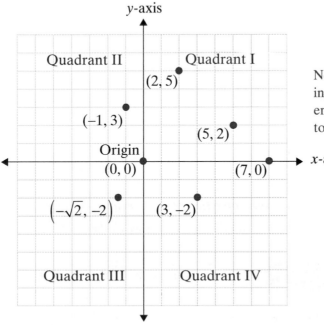

Note that the point corresponding to (5, 2) is completely different from the point corresponding to (2, 5).

Figure 2.1

Solutions to Equations

Now, consider the equation in two variables

$$2x + 3y = 6$$

or, solved for y, $y = \dfrac{6 - 2x}{3}$

The solution to this equation consists of an infinite set of ordered pairs in the form (x, y) where the first coordinate represents the variable x (sometimes called the **independent variable**), and the second coordinate represents the variable y (sometimes called the **dependent variable**). To find some of these solutions, we form a table by choosing arbitrary values for x and finding the corresponding values for y by using the equation. We say that these ordered pairs **satisfy the equation**.

$x = 0$: $y = \dfrac{6 - 2 \cdot 0}{3} = \dfrac{6}{3} = 2$

$x = -3$: $y = \dfrac{6 - 2 \cdot (-3)}{3} = \dfrac{12}{3} = 4$

$x = 3$: $y = \dfrac{6 - 2 \cdot 3}{3} = \dfrac{0}{3} = 0$

$x = \dfrac{1}{2}$: $y = \dfrac{6 - 2 \cdot \dfrac{1}{2}}{3} = \dfrac{5}{3}$

Choose x	Calculate y
0	2
−3	4
3	0
$\dfrac{1}{2}$	$\dfrac{5}{3}$

Thus, $(0, 2)$, $(-3, 4)$, $(3, 0)$, and $\left(\dfrac{1}{2}, \dfrac{5}{3} \right)$ are ordered pairs that satisfy the equation $2x + 3y = 6$.

Solution of an Equation in Two Variables

*The **solution** (or **solution set**) of an equation in two variables, x and y, consists of all those ordered pairs of real numbers (x, y) that satisfy the equation.*

Example 1: Solution Set ●

a. Given the equation $3x + y = 9$, find the missing coordinate of each ordered pair so that the ordered pair belongs to the solution set of the equation.

    i. $(2, \ )$ **ii.** $(0, \ )$ **iii.** $(6, \ )$ **iv.** $(\ , 0)$

Solution: First solve the equation for y to make evaluations easier: $y = 9 - 3x$

i. For $(2,\ )$, $x = 2$:
$y = 9 - 3 \cdot 2 = 9 - 6 = 3$
The ordered pair is $(2, 3)$.

ii. For $(0,\ )$, $x = 0$:
$y = 9 - 3 \cdot 0 = 9 - 0 = 9$
The ordered pair is $(0, 9)$.

iii. For $(6,\ )$, $x = 6$:
$y = 9 - 3 \cdot 6 = 9 - 18 = -9$
The ordered pair is $(6, -9)$.

iv. For $(\ , 0)$, $y = 0$:
$0 = 9 - 3x$
$3x = 9$
$x = 3$
The ordered pair is $(3, 0)$.

b. Suppose that x belongs to the set $\left\{ 0, \dfrac{2}{3}, 1, 1.6 \right\}$. Find the corresponding ordered pairs that satisfy the equation $x + y = 2$.

Solution: Solve for y to make evaluations easier: $y = 2 - x$
In table form:

x	$y = 2 - x$	(x, y)
0	$y = 2 - 0 = 2$	$(0, 2)$
$\dfrac{2}{3}$	$y = 2 - \dfrac{2}{3} = \dfrac{4}{3}$	$\left(\dfrac{2}{3}, \dfrac{4}{3} \right)$
1	$y = 2 - 1 = 1$	$(1, 1)$
1.6	$y = 2 - 1.6 = 0.4$	$(1.6, 0.4)$

• •

Just as we use the terms **ordered pair** and **point** (graph of an ordered pair) interchangeably, we use the terms **equation** and **graph of an equation** interchangeably. The equations

$$2x + 3y = 4, \quad y = 7, \quad x = -1, \quad \text{and} \quad y = 3x + 5$$

are called **linear equations** (or first-degree equations in two variables) and their graphs will be straight lines.

Standard Form of a Linear Equation

Any equation of the form

$$Ax + By = C \qquad \text{where A and B are not both equal to 0}$$

*is called the **standard form** of a **linear equation**.*

Every straight line corresponds to some linear equation, and the graph of every linear equation is a straight line. Thus, because we know from geometry that two points determine a line, the graph of an equation can be found by locating any two points that satisfy the equation.

To Graph a Linear Equation in Two Variables

1. *Locate any two points that satisfy the equation. (Choose values for x and y that lead to simple solutions. Remember that there are an infinite number of choices for either x or y. But, once a value for x or y is chosen, the corresponding value for the other variable is found by substituting into the equation.)*

2. *Plot these two points on a Cartesian coordinate system.*

3. *Draw a straight line through these two points. (**Note:** Every point on that line will satisfy the equation.)*

4. *To check: Locate a third point that satisfies the equation and check to see that it does indeed lie on the line.*

Example 2: Equation in Two Variables

Graph each of the following linear equations.

a. $2x + 3y = 6$

Solution: Make a table with headings **x** and **y** and, whenever possible, choose values for x or y that lead to simple solutions. (In our previous discussion, we found four ordered pairs that satisfy this equation.)

x	y
0	2
−3	4
3	0
$\dfrac{1}{2}$	$\dfrac{5}{3}$

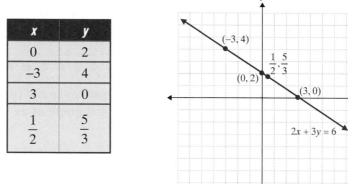

b. $x - 2y = 1$

Solution: Solve for x and substitute 0, 1, and 2 for y: $x = 1 + 2y$

x	y
1	0
3	1
5	2

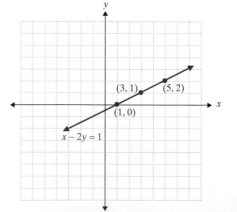

c. $y = 2x$

Solution: Substitute –1, 0, and 1 for x.

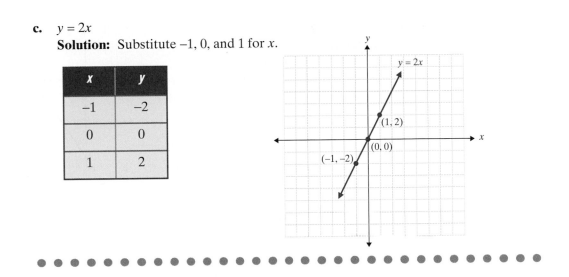

x	y
–1	–2
0	0
1	2

Locating the *y*-intercept and *x*-intercept

While the choice of the values for x or y can be arbitrary, letting $x = 0$ will locate the point on the graph where the line crosses (or intercepts) the y-axis. This point is called the **y-intercept**. The **x-intercept** is the point found by letting $y = 0$. This is the point where the line crosses (or intercepts) the x-axis. These two points are generally easy to locate and are frequently used as the two points for drawing the graph of a linear equation. If the line passes through the point $(0, 0)$, then the y-intercept and the x-intercept are the same point, namely the origin. In this case you will need to locate some other point to draw the graph. Example 3 illustrates this technique.

Example 3: *x*- and *y*-intercepts

Graph the following linear equations by locating the y-intercept and the x-intercept.

a. $x + 3y = 9$

Solution:

$$x = 0 \rightarrow 3y = 9$$
$$y = 3$$
$$y = 0 \rightarrow \ x = 9$$

$(0, 3)$ is the y-intercept.

$(9, 0)$ is the x-intercept.

Graph the two intercepts and draw the line that contains them.

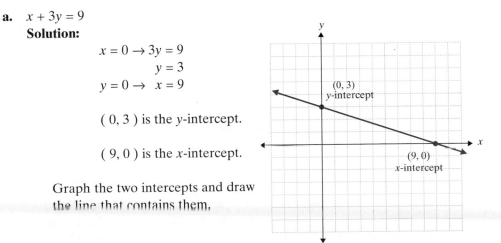

continued on next page ...

b. $3x - 2y = 12$
Solution:

$$x = 0 \rightarrow -2y = 12$$
$$y = -6$$

$$y = 0 \rightarrow 3x = 12$$
$$x = 4$$

(0, −6) is the y-intercept.
(4, 0) is the x-intercept.

Graph the two intercepts and draw
the line that contains them.

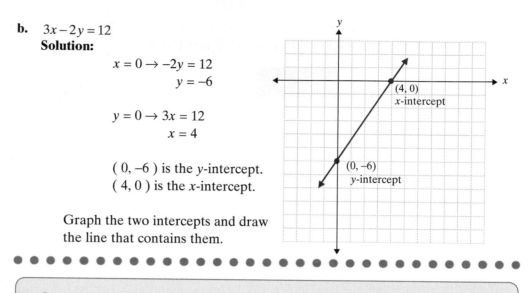

NOTES

In general, the intercepts are easy to find because substituting 0 (for x or y) leads to an easy solution for the other variable. However, when the intercepts result in a point with fraction (or decimal) coordinates and estimation is involved, then a third point that satisfies the equation should be found to verify that the line is positioned correctly.

Practice Problems

1. *For x in the set {−1, 2, 3}, find the corresponding ordered pairs that satisfy the equation x − 2y = 3.*

2. *Find the missing coordinate of each ordered pair so that it belongs to the solution set of the equation 2x + y = 4:*
   (0,   ), (, 0), (, 8), (−1,   ).

3. *Does the ordered pair* $\left(1, \dfrac{3}{2} \right)$ *satisfy the equation 3x + 2y = 6?*

2.1 Exercises

Find the missing coordinate of each ordered pair so that the ordered pair belongs to the solution set of the equation in Exercises 1 − 8.

1. $2x + y = 5$

   a. (0,   )
   b. (, 0)
   c. (−2,   )
   d. (, 3)

2. $x + 2y = 6$

   a. (0,   )
   b. (, 0)
   c. (4,   )
   d. (, −2)

3. $3x - y = 4$

   a. (0,   )
   b. (, 0)
   c. (2,   )
   d. (, 5)

4. $x - 3y = 9$

   a. (0,   )
   b. (, 0)
   c. (−3,   )
   d. (, −1)

5. $y = 5 - 2x$

    a. $(0, \quad)$
    b. $(\quad, 0)$
    c. $(2, \quad)$
    d. $(\quad, 7)$

6. $y = 5x - 3$

    a. $(0, \quad)$
    b. $(\quad, 0)$
    c. $(-1, \quad)$
    d. $(\quad, 7)$

7. $3x - 2y = 6$

    a. $(0, \quad)$
    b. $(\quad, 0)$
    c. $(-2, \quad)$
    d. $(\quad, 3)$

8. $5x + 2y = 10$

    a. $(0, \quad)$
    b. $(\quad, 0)$
    c. $(4, \quad)$
    d. $(\quad, 10)$

Locate at least two ordered pairs of real numbers that satisfy each of the linear equations in Exercises 9 – 34 and graph the corresponding line in a Cartesian coordinate system.

9. $x + y = 3$
10. $x + y = 4$
11. $y = 3x$
12. $2y = x$

13. $2x + y = 0$
14. $3x + 2y = 0$
15. $2x + 3y = 7$
16. $4x + 3y = 11$

17. $3x - 4y = 12$
18. $2x - 5y = 10$
19. $-4x + y = 4$
20. $-3x + 3y = 6$

21. $3y = 2x - 4$
22. $4x = 3y + 8$
23. $3x + 5y = 6$
24. $2x + 7y = -4$

25. $2x + 3y = 1$
26. $5x - 3y = -1$
27. $5x - 2y = 7$
28. $3x + 4y = 7$

29. $\dfrac{2}{3}x - y = 4$
30. $x + \dfrac{3}{4}y = 6$
31. $2x + \dfrac{1}{2}y = 3$
32. $\dfrac{2}{5}x - 3y = 5$

33. $5x = y + 2$
34. $4x = 3y - 5$

Graph the linear equations in Exercises 35 – 42 by locating the y-intercept and the x-intercept.

35. $x - 2y = 8$
36. $x + y = 6$
37. $2x + 3y = 12$

38. $3x - 7y = -21$
39. $4x - y = 10$
40. $\dfrac{1}{2}x + 2y = 3$

41. $3x + 2y = 15$
42. $x - 4y = -6$

Writing and Thinking About Mathematics

43. Explain in your own words why it is sufficient to find the *x*-intercept and *y*-intercept to graph a line.

44. Explain in your own words how you can determine if an ordered pair is a solution to an equation.

Answers to Practice Problems: 1. $(-1, -2)$, $\left(2, -\dfrac{1}{2}\right)$, $(3, 0)$ **2.** $(0, 4), (2, 0), (-2, 8), (-1, 6)$ **3.** Yes

111

Hawkes Learning Systems: Intermediate Algebra

Introduction to the Cartesian Coordinate System
Graphing Linear Equations by Plotting Points

2.2   Slope-intercept Form: $y = mx + b$

After completing this section, you will be able to:

1. *Find the slope of a line containing two given points.*

2. *Graph lines using the slope-intercept method.*

3. *Graph horizontal lines.*

4. *Graph vertical lines.*

Slope of a Line

In Section 2.1, we discussed the **standard form** of a linear equation in two variables:

$$Ax + By = C$$

In this section, we will analyze linear equations in another form using the concept of **slope**.

The term **slope** is common in phrases such as the slope of a roof, the slope of a road, or the slope of a mountain. If you ride a bicycle up a mountain road, you certainly know when the slope increases because you have to pedal harder. In construction, a roof that is to have a 7:12 pitch is constructed so that for every 7 inches of rise (vertical distance) there are 12 inches of run (horizontal distance). That is, the ratio of the rise to the run can be written as $\dfrac{\text{rise}}{\text{run}} = \dfrac{7}{12}$.

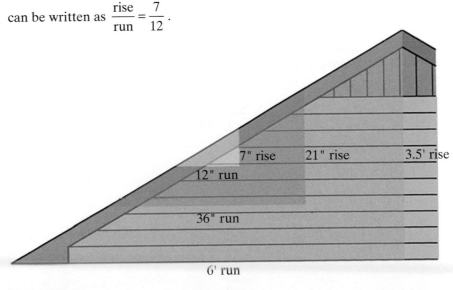

Figure 2.2

$$\frac{\text{rise}}{\text{run}} = \frac{7}{12} = \frac{21}{36} = \frac{3.5}{6}$$

113

If we know any two points on a line, say (x_1, y_1) and (x_2, y_2), we can calculate the **slope** using the following formula. (**Note:** The letter m is standard notation for representing the slope of a line.)

$$\text{slope} = m = \frac{\text{rise}}{\text{run}} = \frac{y_2 - y_1}{x_2 - x_1} = \frac{y_1 - y_2}{x_1 - x_2} \quad \text{where } x_1 \neq x_2$$

NOTES

It does not matter which point is called (x_1, y_1) and which is called (x_2, y_2) as long as we are consistent. That is, be sure to subtract the coordinates in the same order in both the numerator and denominator.

The slope of a line is illustrated in Figure 2.3.

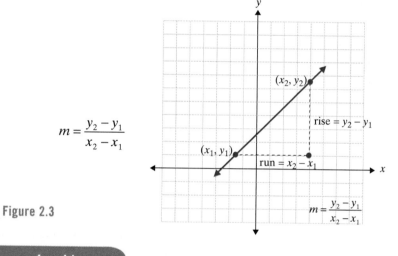

$$m = \frac{y_2 - y_1}{x_2 - x_1}$$

Figure 2.3

Example 1: Slope of a Line ●

a. Find the slope of the line that contains the two points $(-1, 2)$ and $(3, 5)$, and then graph the line.

Solution: Using $(x_1, y_1) = (-1, 2)$ and $(x_2, y_2) = (3, 5)$,

$$m = \frac{5 - 2}{3 - (-1)}$$

$$= \frac{3}{4}$$

or, using $(x_1, y_1) = (3, 5)$ and $(x_2, y_2) = (-1, 2)$,

$$m = \frac{2 - 5}{-1 - 3}$$

$$= \frac{-3}{-4}$$

$$= \frac{3}{4}$$

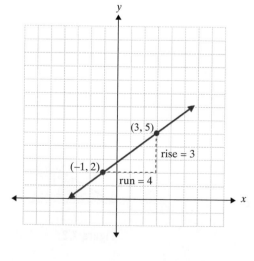

b. Find the slope of the line that contains the two points $(0, 1)$ and $(2, 6)$ and graph the line.

Solution: Using $(x_1, y_1) = (0, 1)$ and $(x_2, y_2) = (2, 6)$,

$$\text{slope} = m = \frac{1-6}{0-2}$$

$$= \frac{-5}{-2}$$

$$= \frac{5}{2}$$

$$\text{or } \ m = \frac{6-1}{2-0}$$

$$= \frac{5}{2}$$

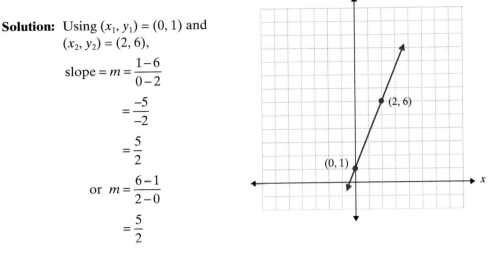

c. Find the slope of the line through the points $(5, 1)$ and $(1, 3)$ and graph the line.

Solution: Using $(x_1, y_1) = (5, 1)$ and $(x_2, y_2) = (1, 3)$,

$$\text{slope} = m = \frac{1-3}{5-1}$$

$$= \frac{-2}{4}$$

$$= -\frac{1}{2}$$

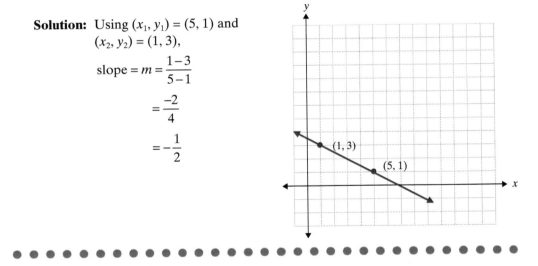

NOTES After studying Examples 1a – 1c and the remaining examples in this section, you should be aware that lines with positive slope slant upward to the right and lines with negative slope slant downward to the right. This observation will be a great help in graphing straight lines and analyzing the graphs of many other types of curves.

Slope-intercept Form: $y = mx + b$

There are certain relationships between the coefficients in the equation of a line and the graph of that line. For example, consider the equation

$$y = 5x - 7.$$

First, find two points on the line and calculate the slope.

$(0, -7)$ and $(2, 3)$ both satisfy the equation.

$$\text{slope} = m = \frac{-7 - 3}{0 - 2} = \frac{-10}{-2} = 5$$

$$\text{or } m = \frac{3 - (-7)}{2 - 0} = \frac{10}{2} = 5$$

Observe that the slope m is the same as the coefficient of x in the equation $y = 5x - 7$. This is not just a coincidence. In fact, if a linear equation is solved for y, then the coefficient of x will always be the slope of the line. The proof of this statement follows:

Consider the equation

$$y = mx + b.$$

Suppose that (x_1, y_1) and (x_2, y_2) are any two points on the line. Then,

$$y_1 = mx_1 + b \qquad \text{and} \qquad y_2 = mx_2 + b$$

$$\text{slope} = \frac{y_2 - y_1}{x_2 - x_1}$$

$$= \frac{(mx_2 + b) - (mx_1 + b)}{x_2 - x_1}$$

$$= \frac{mx_2 + b - mx_1 - b}{x_2 - x_1}$$

$$= \frac{m(x_2 - x_1)}{(x_2 - x_1)}$$

$$= m$$

Therefore, the coefficient m in the equation $y = mx + b$ is the slope of the line.

As we discussed earlier, the **y-intercept** is the point where the graph of a line crosses the x-axis. The x-coordinate of this point will always be 0. If $x = 0$ in the general equation $y = mx + b$, then $y = m(0) + b = b$. Therefore, the y-intercept is the point $(0, b)$. The constant b is also called the y-intercept with the understanding that $x = 0$ when $y = b$.

Slope-intercept Form

Any equation of the form

$$y = mx + b$$

*is called the **slope-intercept** form for the equation of a line. The slope of the line is m and the y-intercept is b.*

An equation in the standard form

$$Ax + By = C \qquad \text{with } B \neq 0$$

can be written in the slope-intercept form by solving for y.

$$Ax + By = C$$

$$By = -Ax + C$$

$$y = -\frac{A}{B}x + \frac{C}{B}$$

Thus, in general,

$$m = -\frac{A}{B} \text{ and } b = \frac{C}{B}$$

Example 2: Slope-intercept Form

a. Find the slope, m, and y-intercept, b, of the line $-2x + 3y = 6$ and graph the line.

Solution: Solving for y, $\quad -2x + 3y = 6$

$$3y = 2x + 6$$

$$y = \frac{2}{3}x + 2$$

Thus,

$$m = \frac{2}{3} \quad \text{and} \quad b = 2.$$

Now that the equation is in the slope-intercept form, the graph can be drawn by locating the y-intercept and using the slope as $\dfrac{\textbf{rise}}{\textbf{run}}$ to locate a second point on the line. **Note that when the rise is negative, move down, and when the run is negative, move left.**

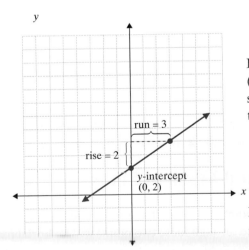

From the y-intercept, count 2 units up (rise) and 3 units right (run) to locate a second point on the line. This illustrates the slope

$$m = \frac{2}{3}.$$

Note: The same point can be located by moving 3 units right and then 2 units up.

continued on next page ...

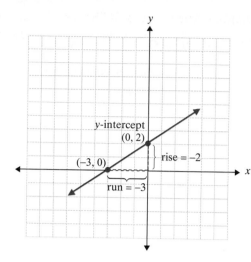

Or locate a second point by counting 2 units down (rise) and 3 units left (run). That is, interpret the slope m as

$$m = \frac{-2}{-3}.$$

b. Find the slope, m, and y-intercept, b, of the line $y = -3x + 2$ and graph the line.
   Solution: The equation is already in the slope-intercept form with

$$m = -3 \quad \text{and} \quad b = 2.$$

To draw the graph, note that the slope $m = -3 = \dfrac{-3}{1} = \dfrac{\textbf{rise}}{\textbf{run}}$.

Treat the rise as -3 and the run as 1.

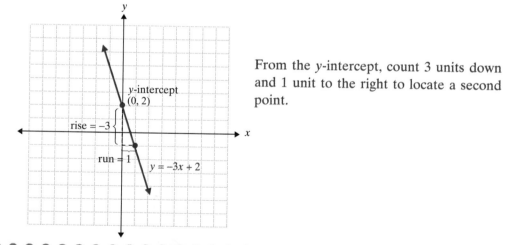

From the y-intercept, count 3 units down and 1 unit to the right to locate a second point.

● ●

Horizontal and Vertical Lines

Suppose that two points on a line have the same y-coordinate, such as $(-2, 3)$ and $(5, 3)$. Then the line through these two points will be **horizontal** as shown in Figure 2.4. The slope is

$$m = \frac{3-3}{5-(-2)} = \frac{0}{7} = 0$$

For any horizontal line, all of the y-values will be the same. Consequently, the formula for slope will always have 0 in the numerator. Therefore, **the slope of every horizontal line is 0**.

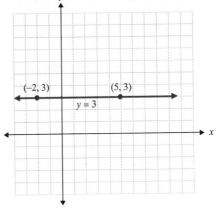

Figure 2.4

The equation of any horizontal line is in the form $y = 0x + b$ or $y = b$. In the case above, the y-coordinates are all 3, and the equation of the line is $y = 0x + 3$ or $y = 3$.

If two points have the same x-coordinates, such as (1, 3) and (1, −2), then the line through these two points will be **vertical** as in Figure 2.5. The slope is

$$m = \frac{-2-3}{1-1} = \frac{-5}{0}, \text{which is } \textbf{undefined}.$$

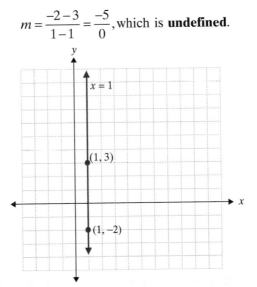

Figure 2.5

The equation of the vertical line in Figure 2.5 is $x = 1$ (in standard form, $x + 0y = 1$).

The x-coordinate is 1 for every point on the line.

In general, the equation $y = b$ restricts y-values to b with no restrictions on x, giving a horizontal line. Similarly, the equation $x = a$ restricts x-values to a with no restrictions on y, giving a vertical line.

Horizontal and Vertical Lines

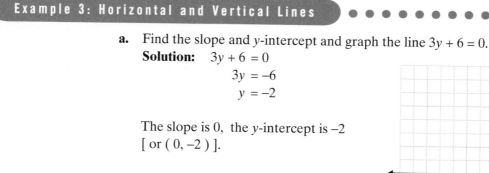

Any equation of the form $y = b$ represents a **horizontal line** with **slope 0**.

Any equation of the form $x = a$ represents a **vertical line** with **undefined slope**.

Example 3: Horizontal and Vertical Lines

a. Find the slope and y-intercept and graph the line $3y + 6 = 0$.
    Solution: $3y + 6 = 0$
    $$3y = -6$$
    $$y = -2$$

    The slope is 0, the y-intercept is -2
    [or $(0, -2)$].

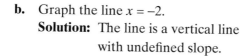

b. Graph the line $x = -2$.
    Solution: The line is a vertical line
    with undefined slope.

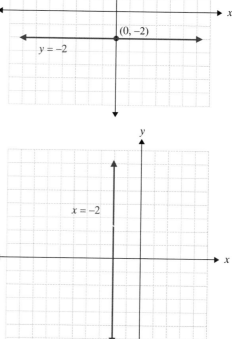

Characteristics of Slopes and Graphs of Lines

1. *Lines that have positive slope slant "upward" to the right.*

2. *Lines that have negative slope slant "downward" to the right.*

3. *Horizontal lines have slope 0.*

4. *Vertical lines have undefined slopes.*

Practice Problems

1. *Find the slope of the line through the two points (1, 3) and (4, 6).*

2. *What is the slope and the y-intercept of the line with the equation $2x + y = 5$?*

3. *Find the slope and y-intercept of the line with equation $5x - 4y = 20$.*

2.2 Exercises

Graph the line determined by each pair of points in Exercises 1 – 12, and then find the slope of the line.

1. $(2, 4), (1, -1)$ **2.** $(5, 1), (3, 0)$ **3.** $(-3, 7), (4, -1)$

4. $(-6, 3), (1, 2)$ **5.** $(-5, 8), (3, 8)$ **6.** $(0, 0), (-2, -3)$

7. $\left(4, \dfrac{1}{2}\right), (-1, 2)$ **8.** $\left(\dfrac{3}{4}, \dfrac{3}{2}\right), (1, 2)$ **9.** $(-2, 3), (-2, -1)$

10. $(1, -2), (1, 4)$ **11.** $\left(\dfrac{3}{2}, \dfrac{4}{5}\right), \left(-2, \dfrac{1}{10}\right)$ **12.** $\left(\dfrac{7}{2}, \dfrac{3}{4}\right), \left(\dfrac{1}{2}, -3\right)$

For Exercises 13 – 40, write the equation in slope-intercept form. Find the slope and the y-intercept, and then draw the graph.

13. $y = 2x - 1$ **14.** $y = 3x - 4$ **15.** $y = 5 - 4x$ **16.** $y = 4 - x$

17. $y = \dfrac{2}{3}x + 2$ **18.** $y = \dfrac{2}{5}x + 2$ **19.** $x + y = 5$ **20.** $x - 2y = 6$

21. $x + 5y = 10$ **22.** $4x + y + 3 = 0$ **23.** $2y - 8 = 0$ **24.** $2x + 7y + 7 = 0$

25. $4x + y = 0$ **26.** $3y - 9 = 0$ **27.** $2x = 3y + 6$ **28.** $4x = y + 2$

29. $3x + 9 = 0$ **30.** $3x + 6 = 6y$ **31.** $5x - 6y = 10$ **32.** $4x + 7 = 0$

33. $5 - 3x = 4y$ **34.** $5x = 11 - 2y$ **35.** $6x + 4y = -7$ **36.** $7x + 2y = 4$

37. $6y = 4 + 3x$ **38.** $6x + 5y = -15$ **39.** $5x - 2y + 5 = 0$ **40.** $4x = 3y - 7$

41. In reference to the equation $y = mx + b$, sketch the graph of three lines for each of the two characteristics listed below.

   a. $m > 0$ and $b > 0$ **b.** $m < 0$ and $b > 0$
   c. $m > 0$ and $b < 0$ **d.** $m < 0$ and $b < 0$

Answers to Practice Problems: 1. $m = 1$ **2.** $m = -2, b = 5$ **3.** $m = \dfrac{5}{4}, b = -5$

*In Exercises 42 – 49 the graph of a line is shown with two points highlighted. Find (**a**) the slope, (**b**) the y-intercept (if there is one), and (**c**) the equation of the line.*

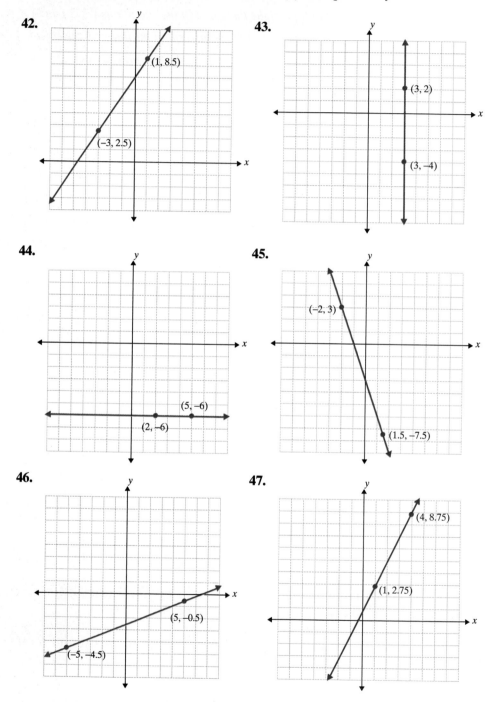

42. (1, 8.5) (−3, 2.5)

43. (3, 2) (3, −4)

44. (5, −6) (2, −6)

45. (−2, 3) (1.5, −7.5)

46. (5, −0.5) (−5, −4.5)

47. (4, 8.75) (1, 2.75)

48.

49.

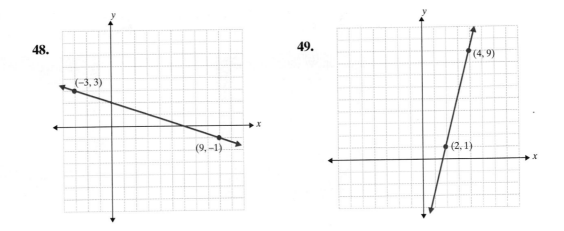

Points are said to be **collinear** if they are on a straight line. If points are collinear, then the slope of the line through any two of them must be the same (because the line is the same line). Use this idea to determine whether or not the three points in each of the sets in Exercises 50 – 54 are collinear.

50. $\{(-1, 3), (0, 1), (5, -9)\}$

51. $\{(-2, -4), (0, 2), (3, 11)\}$

52. $\{(-2, 0), (0, 30), (1.5, 5.25)\}$

53. $\left\{ \left(\dfrac{2}{3}, \dfrac{1}{2} \right), \left(0, \dfrac{5}{6} \right), \left(-\dfrac{3}{4}, \dfrac{29}{24} \right) \right\}$

54. $\{(-1, -7), (1, 1), (4, 12)\}$

In Exercises 55 – 59, the calculator display shows an incorrect graph for the corresponding equation. Explain how you know, by just looking at the graph, that a mistake has been made.

55. $y = 2x + 5$

56. $y = -3x + 4$

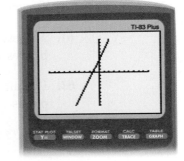

57. $y = \dfrac{2}{3}x - 2$

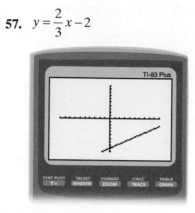

58. $y = -4x$

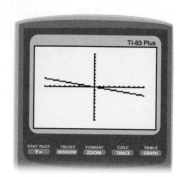

59. $y = -\dfrac{1}{3}x$

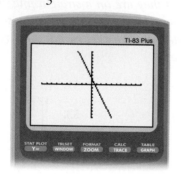

Writing and Thinking About Mathematics

60. a. Explain in your own words why the slope of a horizontal line must be 0.
  b. Explain in your own words why the slope of a vertical line must be undefined.

61. a. Describe the graph of the line $y = 0$.
  b. Describe the graph of the line $x = 0$.

62. Explain, in your own words, how the slope changes if the coordinates of the points (x_1, y_1) and (x_2, y_2) are interchanged in the formula for slope.

63. In the formula $y = mx + b$ explain the meaning of m and the meaning of b.

Hawkes Learning Systems: Intermediate Algebra

Graphing Linear Equations in Slope-Intercept Form

2.3   Point-slope Form: $y - y_1 = m(x - x_1)$

Objectives

After completing this section, you will be able to:

1. Write the equation of a line in standard form given either:
    a. the slope and one point, or
    b. two points.
2. Graph lines by using a point and the slope.
3. Graph lines by finding the x-and y-intercepts.

We have discussed and analyzed the **standard form** ($Ax + By = C$), **the slope-intercept form** ($y = mx + b$), horizontal lines ($y = b$), and vertical lines ($x = a$). In this section, we are going to develop another form for linear equations, and we will discuss parallel lines and perpendicular lines.

The Point-slope Form: $y - y_1 = m(x - x_1)$

The objective here is to develop a formula for a line that passes through a given point, say (x_1, y_1), and has a given slope, say m. Now, if (x, y) is any point on the line, then the slope formula gives the equation

$$\frac{y - y_1}{x - x_1} = m$$

and multiplying both sides by the denominator (assuming the denominator is not 0 because m is defined) we have

$$y - y_1 = m(x - x_1) \qquad \text{The point-slope form}$$

For example, suppose that a point $(x_1, y_1) = (8, 3)$ and the slope $m = -\dfrac{3}{4}$ are given.

If (x, y) represents any point on the line other than $(8, 3)$, then substituting into the formula for slope, gives

$$\frac{y - y_1}{x - x_1} = m \qquad \text{Formula for slope}$$

$$\frac{y - 3}{x - 8} = -\frac{3}{4} \qquad \text{Substituting given information}$$

$$y - 3 = -\frac{3}{4}(x - 8) \qquad \text{Point-slope form}: y - y_1 = m(x - x_1)$$

From this point-slope form, we can manipulate the equation to get the other two forms:

$$y - 3 = -\frac{3}{4}(x - 8)$$

$$y - 3 = -\frac{3}{4}x + 6$$

or $\qquad y = -\frac{3}{4}x + 9$ $\qquad\qquad$ Slope-intercept form : $y = mx + b$

or $\qquad 3x + 4y = 36$ $\qquad\qquad$ Standard form : $Ax + By = C$

Point-slope Form

An equation of the form

$$y - y_1 = m(x - x_1)$$

*is called the **point-slope** form for the equation of a line that contains the point (x_1, y_1) and has slope m.*

In Examples 1a and 1b, the equations of the lines are written in all three forms: point-slope form, slope-intercept form, and standard form. Generally any one of these forms is sufficient. However, there are situations in which one form is preferred over the others. Therefore, manipulation among the forms is an important skill. Also, if the answer in the text is in one form and your answer is in another form, you should be able to recognize that the answers are equivalent.

Example 1: Forms of Equations

a. Find the equation of the line containing the two points $(-1, 2)$ and $(4, -2)$.
    Solution: First, find the slope.

$$m = \frac{y_2 - y_1}{x_2 - x_1}$$

$$m = \frac{-2 - 2}{4 - (-1)}$$

$$= \frac{-4}{5}$$

$$= -\frac{4}{5}$$

continued on next page ...

Now, use one of the given points and the point-slope form for the equation of a line. [(–1, 2) and (4, –2) are used here to illustrate that either point may be used.]

<u>Using (–1, 2)</u>

$$y - y_1 = m(x - x_1)$$ Point-slope form

$$y - 2 = -\frac{4}{5}[x - (-1)]$$ Substitute

$$y - 2 = -\frac{4}{5}x - \frac{4}{5}$$

$$y = -\frac{4}{5}x - \frac{4}{5} + 2$$

$$y = -\frac{4}{5}x + \frac{6}{5}$$ Slope-intercept form

or $4x + 5y = 6$ Standard form

<u>Using (4, –2)</u>

$$y - y_2 = m(x - x_2)$$

$$y - (-2) = -\frac{4}{5}(x - 4)$$

$$y + 2 = -\frac{4}{5}x + \frac{16}{5}$$

$$y = -\frac{4}{5}x + \frac{16}{5} - 2$$

$$y = -\frac{4}{5}x + \frac{6}{5}$$

$$4x + 5y = 6$$

b. Find the equation of the line with a slope of $-\frac{1}{2}$ and passing through the point (2, 3). Graph the line using the point and slope.

Solution: Substitute into the point-slope form:

$$y - y_1 = m(x - x_1)$$ Point-slope form

$$y - 3 = -\frac{1}{2}(x - 2)$$

$$y = -\frac{1}{2}x + 4$$ Slope-intercept form

or $\qquad x + 2y = 8$ Standard form

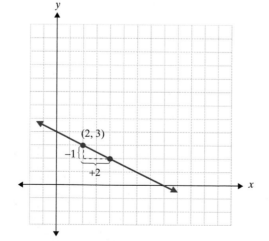

The point one unit down and two units right from (2, 3) will be on the line because the slope is

$$m = \frac{\text{rise}}{\text{run}} = \frac{-1}{2} = -\frac{1}{2}.$$

With a negative slope, either the rise is negative and the run is positive, or the rise is positive and the run is negative. In either case, as the previous figure and the following figure illustrate, the line is the same.

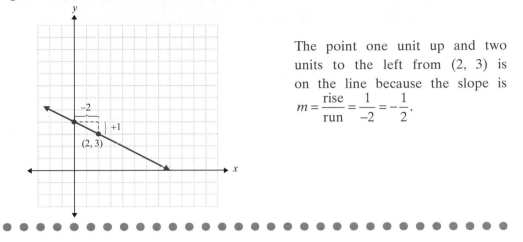

The point one unit up and two units to the left from (2, 3) is on the line because the slope is $m = \dfrac{\text{rise}}{\text{run}} = \dfrac{1}{-2} = -\dfrac{1}{2}$.

Parallel Lines and Perpendicular Lines

Consider two nonvertical parallel lines, L_1 and L_2, with slopes m_1 and m_2, respectively, as shown in Figure 2.6. Since the lines are parallel, the two right triangles AOB and COD are similar triangles (from geometry.) Therefore, the corresponding sides are proportional. Note that in Figure 2.6, AO and CO represent the run for lines L_1 and L_2, respectively. Similarly, BO and DO represent the rise for lines L_1 and L_2, respectively. That is,

$$\frac{BO}{DO} = \frac{AO}{CO} \qquad \text{or, equivalently,} \qquad \frac{BO}{AO} = \frac{DO}{CO}.$$

But,

$$\frac{BO}{AO} = m_1 \qquad \text{and} \qquad \frac{DO}{CO} = m_2.$$

Thus, $m_1 = m_2$, and **parallel lines have the same slope**.

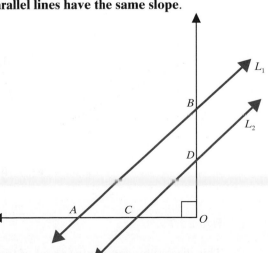

Figure 2.6

129

It can also be shown (using plane geometry) that, conversely, lines with the same slope are parallel. Therefore, we have the following theorem.

Parallel Lines

*Two lines (neither vertical) are **parallel** if and only if they have the same slope.*

All vertical lines are parallel.

In Figure 2.7, the two lines L_1 and L_2 with slopes m_1 and m_2, respectively, are **perpendicular**. That is, the angles formed at the point of intersection are $90°$. Using the Pythagorean Theorem three times, we find the following relationships between the slopes of these lines. (You may need to review some beginning algebra to follow this discussion in detail.)

$$(AO)^2 = (m_1)^2 + 1^2$$

$$(BO)^2 = (m_2)^2 + 1^2$$

$$\text{and} \quad (AB)^2 = (AO)^2 + (BO)^2$$

But, $AB = m_1 - m_2$ (since m_2 is negative). Substituting $m_1 - m_2$ for AB above gives

$$(m_1 - m_2)^2 = (AO)^2 + (BO)^2$$

$$(m_1 - m_2)^2 = (m_1)^2 + 1^2 + (m_2)^2 + 1^2$$

$$m_1^2 - 2m_1m_2 + m_2^2 = (m_1)^2 + (m_2)^2 + 2$$

$$-2m_1m_2 = 2$$

$$\boldsymbol{m_1m_2 = -1} \quad \text{or} \quad \boldsymbol{m_2 = \dfrac{-1}{m_1}}$$

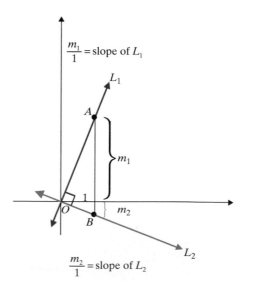

$\dfrac{m_1}{1} = $ slope of L_1

$\dfrac{m_2}{1} = $ slope of L_2

Figure 2.7

This discussion constitutes proof of the following theorem.

Perpendicular Lines

> *Two lines (neither vertical) are* **perpendicular** *if and only if their slopes are negative reciprocals of each other:*
>
> $$m_2 = -\frac{1}{m_1} \qquad \text{or} \qquad m_1 m_2 = -1.$$
>
> *Vertical lines are perpendicular to horizontal lines.*

As illustrated in Figure 2.8, the lines $y = 2x + 1$ and $y = 2x - 3$ are **parallel**. They have the same slope. The lines $y = \frac{2}{3}x + 1$ and $y = -\frac{3}{2}x - 2$ are **perpendicular**. Their slopes are negative reciprocals of each other. In other words, the product of their slopes is -1.

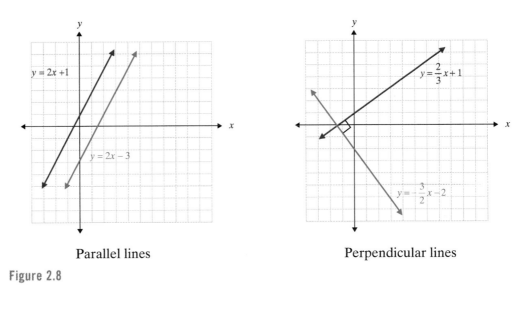

Parallel lines   Perpendicular lines

Figure 2.8

Example 2: Slopes of Lines

Graph the following pairs of lines and state the slope of each line.

a. $y = -1$
$x = \sqrt{2}$

b. $2y = x + 4$
$2y - x = 10$

c. $3x - 4y = 8$
$3y = -4x + 3$

continued on next page ...

a. $y = -1$
    $x = \sqrt{2}$
    Solution:

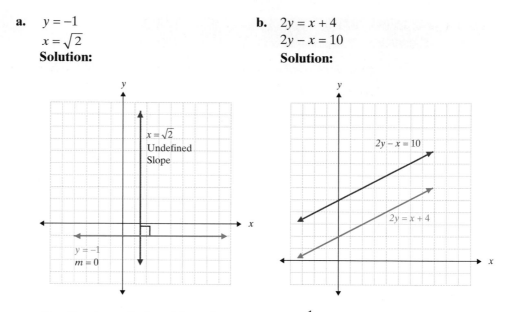

One line is vertical and the other is horizontal. The lines are perpendicular.

b. $2y = x + 4$
    $2y - x = 10$
    Solution:

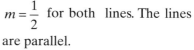

$m = \dfrac{1}{2}$ for both lines. The lines are parallel.

c. $3x - 4y = 8$
    $3y = -4x + 3$
    Solution:

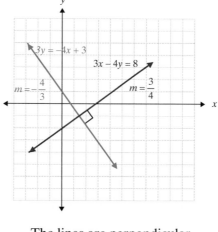

The lines are perpendicular.

$$-\frac{4}{3} \cdot \frac{3}{4} = -1$$

● ●

For easy reference, the following table summarizes what we know about straight lines.

Summary of Formulas and Properties of Straight Lines

1. $Ax + By = C$ *Standard form*

2. $m = \dfrac{y_2 - y_1}{x_2 - x_1}$ *Slope of a line*

3. $y = mx + b$ *Slope-intercept form*

4. $y - y_1 = m(x - x_1)$ *Point-slope form*

5. $y = b$ *Horizontal line, slope 0*

6. $x = a$ *Vertical line, undefined slope*

7. *Parallel lines have the same slope* $(m_1 = m_2)$.

8. *Perpendicular lines have slopes that are negative reciprocals of each other:*

$$\left(m_2 = \frac{-1}{m_1} \text{ or } m_1 m_2 = -1 \right).$$

Example 3 illustrates how to use information about slopes to find the equation of a line.

Example 3: How to use information about slopes

Find the equation in standard form for the line parallel to the line $5x + 3y = 1$ and passing through the point $(2, 3)$.

Solution: First solve for y to find the slope m.

$$5x + 3y = 1$$
$$3y = -5x + 1$$
$$y = -\frac{5}{3}x + \frac{1}{3} \qquad \text{Thus, any line parallel to this line has slope } -\frac{5}{3}.$$

Now use the point-slope form $y - y_1 = m(x - x_1)$ with $m = -\dfrac{5}{3}$ and $(x_1, y_1) = (2, 3)$.

$$y - 3 = -\frac{5}{3}(x - 2) \qquad \text{Point-slope form}$$
$$3(y - 3) = -5(x - 2) \qquad \text{Multiply both sides by 3}$$
$$3y - 9 = -5x + 10 \qquad \text{Simplify}$$
$$5x + 3y = 19 \qquad \text{Standard form}$$

Slope as a Rate of Change

The average speed that you ride your bicycle is the rate of change of distance with respect to time. For example, if you ride your bicycle 24 miles in 2 hours then your average rate is

$$r = \frac{d}{t} = \frac{24 \text{ miles}}{2 \text{ hours}} = \frac{12 \text{ mi}}{1 \text{ hr}} \left(\text{ or } 12 \text{ mph} \right)$$

If time and distance are represented on the horizontal and vertical axes, respectively, then the slope of the line segment joining the two points (0, 0) and (2, 24) is average speed or average rate of change of distance with respect to time.

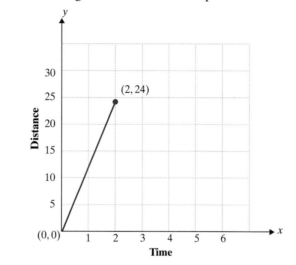

Figure 2.9

In general, the ratio of a change in one variable (say y) to a change in another variable (say x) is called the rate of change of y with respect to x. Graphically, this rate of change is the slope of the line segment joining the appropriate points. Figure 2.10 shows how two different rates of change can be interpreted as slope on a graph.

The rate of change of the average price of a computer rose at $70/yr. from 1985 to 1990, then continued to rise at $90/yr. until 1995, when it began to drop at a rate of $92/yr. The number of households owning computers rose at 4.16 households per yr. from 1994 to 1997, and at 4.8 households per year from 1997 to 2000.

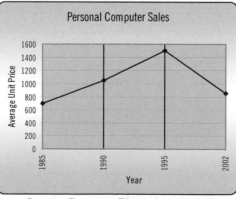

Source: Consumer Electonics Association

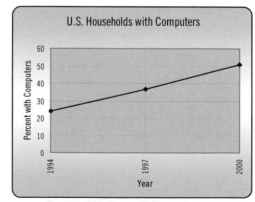

Source: U.S. Dept. of Commerce

Figure 2.10

Practice Problems

Find a linear equation in standard form that satisfies the given conditions.

1. *Passes through the point (4, –1) with m = 2*

2. *Parallel to y = –3x + 4 and contains the point (–1, 5)*

3. *Perpendicular to 2x + y = 1 and passes through the origin (0, 0)*

4. *Contains the two points (6, –2) and (2, 0)*

2.3 Exercises

In Exercises 1 – 15, given either two points on a line or the slope and a point on a line, find an equation in standard form that satisfies the given conditions. Then graph each line.

1. $m = -2; (-2, 1)$ **2.** $m = 3; (3, 4)$ **3.** $(-5, 2); (3, 6)$ **4.** $(-3, 4); (2, 1)$

5. $m = -\dfrac{1}{3}; (5, -1)$ **6.** $m = \dfrac{3}{4}; \left(0, \dfrac{1}{2}\right)$ **7.** $(4, 2); (4, -3)$ **8.** $(5, 2); (1, -3)$

9. $m = 0; (2, 3)$ **10.** $m = -\dfrac{5}{7}; \left(-2, \dfrac{1}{2}\right)$ **11.** $(-2, 7); (3, 1)$

12. $(2, -5); (4, -5)$ **13.** $\left(\dfrac{5}{2}, 0\right); \left(-2, \dfrac{1}{3}\right)$ **14.** $m = 0; (-3, -1)$

15. $m = -\dfrac{4}{3}; \left(\dfrac{2}{3}, 1\right)$

Graph each line in Exercises 16 – 23 by finding the x- and y-intercepts.

16. $2x + y = 4$ **17.** $2x + y = 6$ **18.** $3x - 2y = 6$ **19.** $2x - 3y = 6$
20. $-2x + 5y = 10$ **21.** $-3x + 5y = 15$ **22.** $3x + 4y = 9$ **23.** $3x - 4y = 9$

Find an equation in standard form for each line that satisfies the given conditions in Exercises 24 – 36.

24. Parallel to $3x + y = 5$ and passes through $(2, 1)$

25. Parallel to $2x + 4y = 9$ and passes through $(1, 6)$

26. Parallel to $7x - 3y = 1$ and contains the point $(1, 0)$

27. Parallel to $5x = 7 + y$ and contains the point $(-1, -3)$

28. Parallel to the *x*-axis and passes through $(-1, 3)$

29. Parallel to the *y*-axis and contains the point $(2, -4)$

Answers to Practice Problems: 1. $2x - y = 9$ **2.** $3x + y = 2$ **3.** $x - 2y = 0$ **4.** $x + 2y = 2$

30. Perpendicular to $4x + 3y = 4$ and passes through the point $(2, 2)$

31. Perpendicular to $5x - 3y + 4 = 0$ and passes through the point $(4, -1)$

32. Perpendicular to $5x - 2y - 4 = 0$ and contains $(-3, 5)$

33. Perpendicular to $8 - 3x - 2y = 0$ and contains the point $(-4, -2)$

34. Perpendicular to $3x - y = 4$ and passes through the origin

35. Perpendicular to $2x - y = 7$ and has the same y-intercept as $x - 3y = 6$

36. Perpendicular to $3x - 2y = 4$ and has the same y-intercept as $5x + 4y = 12$

37. Show that the points $A(-2, 4)$, $B(0, 0)$, $C(6, 3)$, and $D(4, 7)$ are the vertices of a rectangle. (Plot the points and show that opposite sides are parallel and that adjacent sides are perpendicular.)

38. Show that the points $(0, -1)$, $(3, -4)$, $(6, 3)$, and $(9, 0)$ are the vertices of a parallelogram. (Plot the points and show that opposite sides are parallel.)

39. John bought his new car for $35,000 in the year 2000. He knows that the value of his car has depreciated linearly. If the value of the car in 2003 was $23,000, what was the annual rate of depreciation of his car? Show this information on a graph.

40. The number of homes in the United States with personal computers was about 33 million in 1995 and about 53 million in 2000. If the growth in personal computers per home was linear, what was the approximate rate of growth per year from 1995 to 2000? Show this information on a graph.

41. The following table shows the estimated number of internet users from 1998 - 2001. The number of users for each year is shown in millions.

Year	Internet Users
1998	73
1999	102
2000	124
2001	143
2002	164

Source: International Telecommunications Union Yearbook of Statistics

  a. plot these points on a graph
  b. connect the points with line segments
  c. find the slope of each line segment
  d. interpret the slope as a rate of change

42. The following table shows the urban growth from 1850 to 2000 in New York, NY.

Year	Population
1850	515,547
1900	3,437,202
1950	7,891,957
2000	8,008,278

Source: U.S. Census Bureau

  a. plot these points on a graph
  b. connect the points with line segments
  c. find the slope of each line segment
  d. interpret the slope as a rate of change

43. The following graph shows the number of female active duty military personnel over a span from 1945 to 2001. The number of women listed include both officers and enlisted personnel from the Army, the Navy, the Marine Corps., and the Air Force.

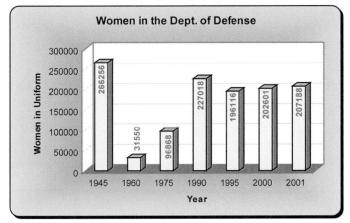

Source: U.S. Dept. of Defense

   a. plot these points on a graph
   b. connect the points with line segments
   c. find the slope of each line segment
   d. interpret the slope as a rate of change

44. The following graph shows the rates of marriage per 1,000 people in the U.S., over a span from 1920 to 2000.

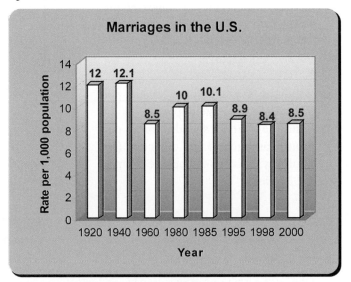

Source: U.S. National Center for Health Statistics

   a. plot these points on a graph
   b. connect the points with line segments
   c. find the slope of each line segment
   d. interpret the slope as a rate of change

The graphs in exercises 45 and 46 show the relationship between time and distance in three different situations. Answer the following questions for each exercise by interpreting the slopes of the appropriate line segments.

   a. *What is the average speed from point a to point b?*
   b. *What is the average speed from point b to point c?*
   c. *What is the average speed from point c to point d?*
   d. *What is the average speed from point a to point d?*

45. Distance walking   **46.** Distance driving a car

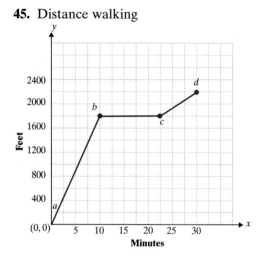

47. Distance of Lance Armstrong riding a bike in his winning stages of the 2002 *Tour de France*
(**Note:** Times have been rounded to the nearest hundredth)

   a. Find the average speed in km per hour for each stage depicted.
   b. Find the average speed in miles per hour for each stage depicted (by multiplying by 0.62, because 1 km = 0.62 miles).

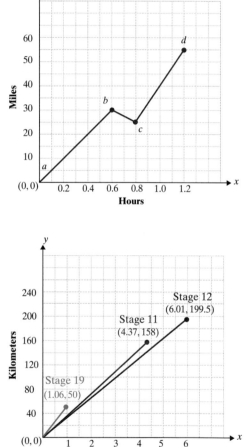

source: www.cyclingnews.com

In Exercises 48 – 53, determine whether each pair of lines is (a) parallel, (b) perpendicular, or (c) neither. Graph both lines.

48. $\begin{cases} y = -2x + 3 \\ y = -2x - 1 \end{cases}$

49. $\begin{cases} y = 3x + 2 \\ y = -\dfrac{1}{3}x + 6 \end{cases}$

50. $\begin{cases} 4x + y = 4 \\ x - 4y = 8 \end{cases}$

51. $\begin{cases} 2x + 3y = 5 \\ 3x + 2y = 10 \end{cases}$

52. $\begin{cases} 2x + 2y = 9 \\ 2x - y = 6 \end{cases}$

53. $\begin{cases} 3x - 4y = 16 \\ 4x + 3y = 15 \end{cases}$

Writing and Thinking About Mathematics

54. Discuss the meaning of slope in five situations that you have observed related to daily life and why this is important. (For example, the slope or "pitch" of the roof of a house in the mountains is particularly important when there is a heavy snow.)

55. Discuss, in your own words, how to find the equation of a line if you are given two points on the line.

56. Discuss the difference between the concepts of a line having "slope 0" and a line having undefined slope.

Hawkes Learning Systems: Intermediate Algebra

Graphing Linear Equations in Point-Slope Form
Finding the Equation of a Line

Introduction to Functions

After completing this section, you will be able to:

1. *State the domain and range of a relation and a function.*
2. *Use the vertical line test to determine whether or not a graph represents a function.*
3. *Write functions as sets of ordered pairs.*
4. *Graph functions by using a graphing calculator.*

Everyday use of the term **function** is not far from the technical use in mathematics. For example, distance traveled is a function of time; profit is a function of sales; heart rate is a function of exertion; and interest earned is a function of principal invested. In this sense, one variable "depends on" (or "is a function of ") another.

Mathematicians distinguish between graphs of real numbers as those that represent **functions** and those that do not. Thus, the concept of a function is one of the most important concepts in mathematics. For example, every equation of the form $y = mx + b$ represents a function and we say that y "is a function of " x. Thus, straight lines that are not vertical are the graphs of functions. As the following discussion indicates, vertical lines do not represent functions.

> **NOTES** The ordered pairs discussed in this text will be ordered pairs of real numbers. However, more generally in some other course, the ordered pairs might be other types of entries such as (parent, child), (city, state), or (name, batting average).

Relations and Functions

*A **relation** is a set of ordered pairs of real numbers.*

*The **domain**, **D**, of a relation is the set of all first coordinates in the relation.*

*The **range**, **R**, of a relation is the set of all second coordinates in the relation.*

In graphing relations, the horizontal is called the **domain axis**, and the vertical is called the **range axis** (See Figure 2.11 on page 142).

Example 1: Relation, Domain, and Range • • • • • • • • • • • • • • • •

Find the domain and range for each of the following relations.

a. $r = \left\{ (5,7), \left(\sqrt{6},2\right), \left(\sqrt{6},3\right), (-1,2) \right\}$

Solution: $D = \left\{ 5, \sqrt{6}, -1 \right\}$ All the first coordinates in r

$R = \{7, 2, 3\}$ All the second coordinates in r

Note that $\sqrt{6}$ is written only once in the domain and 2 is written only once in the range, even though each appears more than once in the relation.

b. $f = \left\{ (-1,1), (1,5), (0,3) \right\}$

Solution: $D = \{-1, 1, 0\}$ All the first coordinates in f

$R = \{1, 5, 3\}$ All the second coordinates in f

• •

The relation $f = \left\{ (-1,1), (1,5), (0,3) \right\}$, used in Example 1b, meets a particular condition in that each first coordinate has a unique corresponding second coordinate. Such a relation is called a **function**. Notice that r in Example 1a is **not** a function because the first coordinate $\sqrt{6}$ has more than one corresponding second coordinate. Also, for ease in discussion and understanding, the relations illustrated in Examples 1 – 4 have only a finite number of ordered pairs. The graphs of these relations would be isolated dots or points. As we will see, the graphs of most relations and functions have an infinite number of points, and their graphs are smooth curves. (**Note:** Straight lines are also deemed to be curves in mathematics.)

The following three definitions of a function are equivalent. That is, each is simply a slightly different way of saying the same thing.

Function

A *function* is a relation in which each domain element has a unique range element.

OR

A *function* is a relation in which each first coordinate appears only once.

OR

A *function* is a relation in which no two ordered pairs have the same first coordinate.

Example 2: Functions •

Determine whether or not each of the following relations is a function.

a. $r = \left\{ (2,3), (1,6), \left(2, \sqrt{5}\right), (0,-1) \right\}$

Solution: r is not a function. The number 2 appears as a first coordinate more than once.

b. $t = \left\{ (1,5), (3,5), \left(\sqrt{2}, 5\right), (-1,5), (-4,5) \right\}$

Solution: t is a function. Each first coordinate appears only once. The fact that the second coordinates are all the same has no effect on the definition of a function.

• •

If one point on the graph of a relation is directly above or below another point on the graph, then these points have the same first coordinate (or x-coordinate). Such a relation is **not** a function. Therefore, the following **vertical line test** can be used to tell whether or not a graph represents a function (See Figure 2.11).

Vertical Line Test

*If **any** vertical line intersects the graph of a relation at more than one point, then the relation graphed is **not** a function.*

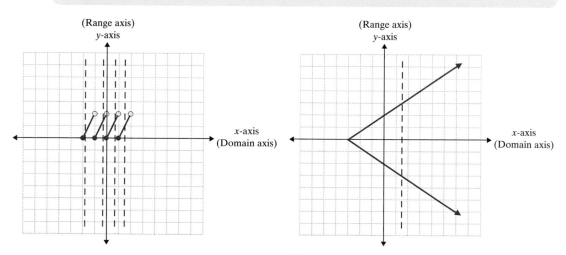

From the graph, we see that the domain of the function is the interval of real numbers $[-2, 2)$ and the range of the function is the interval of real numbers $[0, 2)$.

This graph is **not** a function because the vertical line drawn intersects the graph at more than one point. Thus, for that x-value, there is more than one corresponding y-value.

Figure 2.11

Example 3: Vertical Line Test

Use the vertical line test to determine whether or not each of the following graphs represents a function.

a.

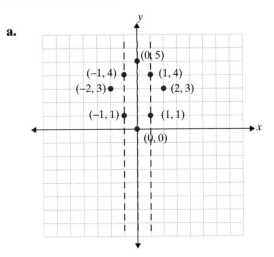

Solution: The relation is **not** a function since a vertical line can be drawn that intersects the graph at more than one point. Listing the ordered pairs shows that several x-coordinates appear more than once:

$$\{(-2,3),(-1,1),(-1,4),(0,0),(0,5),(1,1),(1,4),(2,3)\}$$

For this relation, we see from the graph that $D = \{-2,-1,0,1,2\}$ and $R = \{0,1,3,4,5\}$.

b.

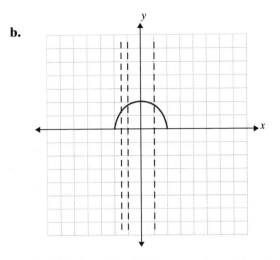

Solution: The relation is a function. No vertical line will intersect the graph at more than one point. Several vertical lines are drawn to illustrate this. For this function, we see from the graph that $D = [-2,2]$ and $R = [0,2]$.

continued on next page ...

c.

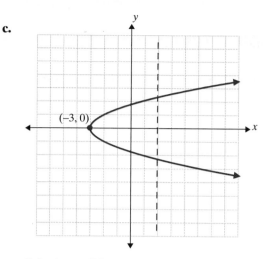

Solution: The relation is **not** a function. At least one vertical line (drawn) intersects the graph at more than one point.

d.

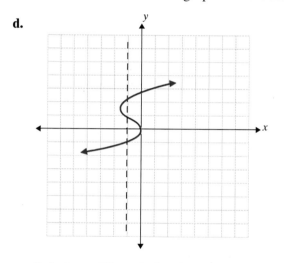

Solution: The relation is **not** a function. At least one vertical line intersects the graph at more than one point.

• •

If only the domain and range of a function are given, the function cannot be determined because there is no way to determine how to pair the coordinates. However, if a rule or equation is given that relates x and y, this rule can be used to determine how values of x and y are paired. **Every equation that can be solved for y represents a function, and we say that y is a function of x.** For example,

given the equation $y = \dfrac{2}{x-1}$ and the domain $\{2, 3, 5\}$,

the ordered pairs can be determined by substituting 2, 3, and 5 for x.

$x = 2:$	$x = 3:$	$x = 5:$
$y = \dfrac{2}{2-1} = 2$	$y = \dfrac{2}{3-1} = 1$	$y = \dfrac{2}{5-1} = \dfrac{1}{2}$

The function is $\left\{ (2,2),(3,1),\left(5,\dfrac{1}{2}\right) \right\}$.

In general, relations or functions involving only a few points are not of interest. In fact, if the domain had not been restricted in the previous discussion, the equation $y = \dfrac{2}{x-1}$ represents a function whose domain consists of all real numbers except 1. That is, $x \neq 1$ because the denominator cannot be 0 (division by 0 is undefined.) We adopt the following rule concerning equations and domains:

> **Unless a finite domain is explicitly stated, the domain will be considered to be the set of all real x-values for which the given equation is defined. That is, the domain consists of all values for x that give real values for y.**

In determining the domain of a function, two facts about real numbers are particularly important:

1. No denominator can equal 0, and
2. Square roots of negative numbers are not real numbers. (**Note:** Such non-real numbers do exist and are part of the complex number system that we will discuss in Chapter 6.)

Example 4: Ordered Pairs

Given the equation (or rule relating x and y)

$$y = x^2 + 1 \qquad \text{and} \qquad D = \{-1,0,1,2,3\},$$

find the function as a set of ordered pairs.

Solution: Find the ordered pairs by setting up a table and substituting for x in the equation.

x	$y = x^2 + 1$
-1	$y = (-1)^2 + 1 = 2$
0	$y = (0)^2 + 1 = 1$
1	$y = (1)^2 + 1 = 2$
2	$y = (2)^2 + 1 = 5$
3	$y = (3)^2 + 1 = 10$

The function is the following set of ordered pairs:

$$\{(-1,2),(0,1),(1,2),(2,5),(3,10)\}.$$

Example 5: Domain •

Find the domain of the function represented by each of the following equations.

   a. $y = \dfrac{2x+1}{x-5}$

       Solution: The domain is all real numbers for which the expression $\dfrac{2x+1}{x-5}$ is defined.   Thus, $D = \{\, x \mid x \neq 5 \,\}$.

       Note: This mathematical notation means that x can be any real number except 5.

   b. $y = \sqrt{x-2}$

       Solution: For $\sqrt{x-2}$ to be a real number, the expression under the square root sign must be non-negative. So we have

$$x - 2 \geq 0 \qquad \text{or} \qquad x \geq 2.$$

       Thus, $D = \{\, x \mid x \geq 2 \,\}$.

• •

Linear Functions

All non-vertical straight lines represent functions. If $B \neq 0$, then an equation in the standard form $Ax + By = C$ can be solved for y, and we have the form

$$y = -\frac{A}{B}x + \frac{C}{B} \qquad \text{or} \qquad y = mx + b$$

Linear Function

*A **linear function** is a function represented by an equation of the form*

$$y = -\frac{A}{B}x + \frac{C}{B} \quad (or \ \ y = mx + b) \ \ where \ B \neq 0.$$

The domain of a linear function is the set of all real numbers.

If the graph of a linear function is not a horizontal line, then the range is also the set of all real numbers. If the line is horizontal, then the domain is still all real numbers; however, the range is just a single number. For example, the graph of the linear equation $y = 5$ is a horizontal line. The domain of the function is all real numbers and the range is the number 5. Figure 2.12 shows two linear functions and the domain and range of each function.

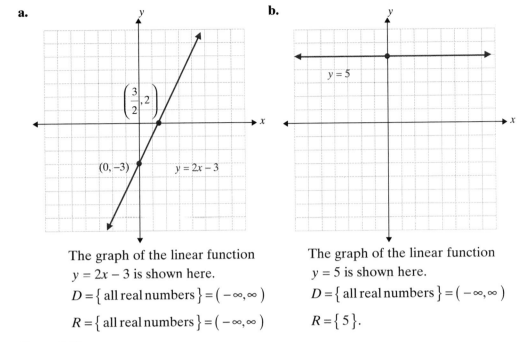

a.

b.

The graph of the linear function $y = 2x - 3$ is shown here.

$D = \{\text{all real numbers}\} = (-\infty, \infty)$

$R = \{\text{all real numbers}\} = (-\infty, \infty)$

The graph of the linear function $y = 5$ is shown here.

$D = \{\text{all real numbers}\} = (-\infty, \infty)$

$R = \{5\}.$

Figure 2.12

Practice Problems

1. State the domain and range of the relation $\{(5,6),(7,8),(9,10),(10,11)\}$. Is the relation a function? Explain briefly.

2. Write the function as a set of ordered pairs, given $y = 2x - 5$ and $D = \left\{-4, 0, \frac{1}{2}, 3\right\}$.

3. State the domain of the function represented by the equation $y = \sqrt{x+3}$.

Using a TI-83 Plus Calculator to Graph Functions

There are many types and brands of graphing calculators available. For convenience and so that directions can be specific, only the TI-83 Plus graphing calculator is used in the related discussions in this text. Other graphing calculators may be used, but the steps required may be different from those indicated in the text. If you do choose to use another calculator, be sure to read the manual for your calculator and follow the related directions.

Answers to Practice Problems: 1. $D = \{5,7,9,10\}; R = \{6,8,10,11\}$ Yes, the relation is a function because each x-coordinate appears only once. **2.** $\left\{(-4,-13),(0,-5),\left(\frac{1}{2},-4\right),(3,1)\right\}$ **3.** $D = \{x \mid x \geq -3\}$

In any case, **remember that a calculator is just a tool to allow for fast calculations and to help in understanding some abstract concepts. A calculator does not replace the need for algebraic knowledge and skills.**

Pressing certain keys will give a list of options called a **menu**. You may choose from the menu by pressing the corresponding numerical key or highlighting your choice by pressing an arrow key and pressing ENTER. Be aware that even for simple calculations, a calculator follows the rules for order of operations. For example,

$$2 + \frac{3}{4} \text{ would be entered as } 2 + \frac{3}{4} \text{ and will give the answer 2.75;}$$

$$\frac{2+3}{4} \text{ would be entered as } \frac{(2+3)}{4} \text{ and will give the answer 1.25.}$$

Note that the parentheses are needed to indicate a numerator (or denominator) with more than one number.

You should practice and experiment with your calculator until you feel comfortable with the results. **Do not be afraid of making mistakes**.

The following six keys and the related menus are important for the exercises in this text. The CLEAR key or 2nd QUIT will get you out of most trouble and allow you to start over.

Some Basics about the TI-83 Plus

1. MODE Turn the calculator ON and press the MODE key. The screen should be highlighted as shown below. If it is not, use the arrow keys in the upper right corner of the keyboard to highlight the correct words and press ENTER. See the manual for the meanings of the terms not highlighted.

   Note: The highlighted 4 in the **Float** setting indicates 4-digit accuracy. This may be changed at any time for more or fewer digits in the accuracy of calculations.

   After these settings have been checked, press 2nd and QUIT.

2. (WINDOW) Press the (WINDOW) key and the standard window will be displayed:

This window can be changed at any time by changing the individual numbers or pressing the (ZOOM) key and whatever number is needed in the menu displayed. Because of the shape of the display screen this standard screen is not a square screen. For example, be aware that the slopes of lines are not truly depicted unless the screen is in a scale of about 3 : 2. For example, a square screen can be attained by setting Xmin = −15 and Xmax = 15 to give the x-axis a length of 30 and the y-axis a length of 20, or a ratio of 3 : 2.

3. (Y=) The (Y=) key is in the upper left corner of the keyboard. This key will allow ten different functions to be entered. These functions are labeled as $Y_1 \dots Y_{10}$. The variable x may be entered by using the (X,T,θ,n) key. The (∧) key can be used to indicate exponents. For example, the equation $y = x^2 + 3x$ would be entered as:

$$Y_1 \ = \ X{\wedge}2 + 3X$$

To change an entry, practice with the keys (DEL), (CLEAR), and (2nd) INS.

4. (GRAPH) If this key is pressed, then the screen will display the graph of whatever functions are indicated in the (Y=) list with the = sign highlighted by using whatever scales are indicated in the current WINDOW. In many cases the WINDOW must be changed to accommodate the domain and range of the function or to show a point where two functions intersect.

5. (TRACE) The (TRACE) key will display the current graph even if it is not already displayed and give the *x*- and *y*- coordinates of a point highlighted on the graph. The curve may be traced by pressing the left and right arrow keys. At each point on the graph, the corresponding *x*- and *y*- coordinates are indicated at the bottom of the screen. **(Remember that because of the limitations of the pixels (lighted dots) on the screen, these *x*- and *y*- coordinates are accurate only part of the time. Generally, they are only approximations.)**

6. CALC   The CALC key (press (2nd) (TRACE)) gives a menu with seven items. Items 2 – 5 are used with graphs.

After displaying a graph, select CALC. Then press (2) and follow the steps outlined below to locate the point where the graph crosses the *x*-axis (the *x*-intercept). The graph must actually cross the axis. This point is called a **zero** of the function because the *y*-value will be 0.

Step 1:   With the left arrow, move the cursor to the left of the *x*-intercept on the graph. Press (ENTER) in response to the question "`LeftBound?`".

Step 2:   With the right arrow, move the cursor to the right of the *x*-intercept on the graph. Press **ENTER** in response to the question "**RightBound?**".

Step 3:   With the left arrow, move the cursor near the *x*-intercept. Press **ENTER** in response to the question "**Guess?**". The calculator's estimate of the zero will appear at the bottom of the display.

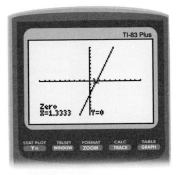

Example 6: Graphing Calculator

Use a graphing calculator to find the graphs of each of the following functions. Use the **TRACE** key to find the point where each graph intersects the *x*-axis. Sketch a copy of each graph on graph paper and label the *x*-intercepts.

a. $y = -3x - 1$ [It is important that the **(−)** key be used to indicate the negative sign in front of $3x$. Use of the subtraction key is a common error.]

Solution:

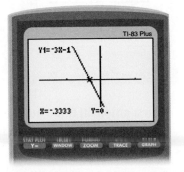

Note: Vertical lines are not functions and cannot be graphed by the calculator.

continued on next page ...

b. $y = \sqrt{x - 4}$

Solution:

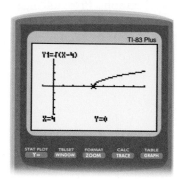

Note: Be sure to include the expression "$(x - 4)$" in parentheses after the $\sqrt{}$ sign.

c. $y = x^2 + 3x$

Solution: Since the graph of this function has two x-intercepts, we have shown the graph twice. Each graph shows the coordinates of a distinct x-intercept.

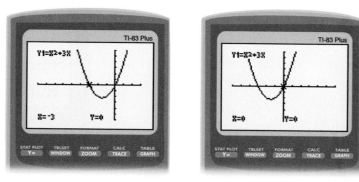

d. $y = 2x - 1;\ \ y = 2x + 1;\ \ y = 2x + 3$

Solution:

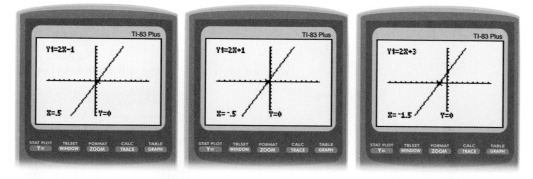

First graph all three functions in the standard window. Then change the window to a square window and notice the difference in the accuracy of the slopes of the lines.

2.4 Exercises

List the sets of ordered pairs corresponding to the points in Exercises 1 – 8. State the domain and range and indicate which of the relations are also functions.

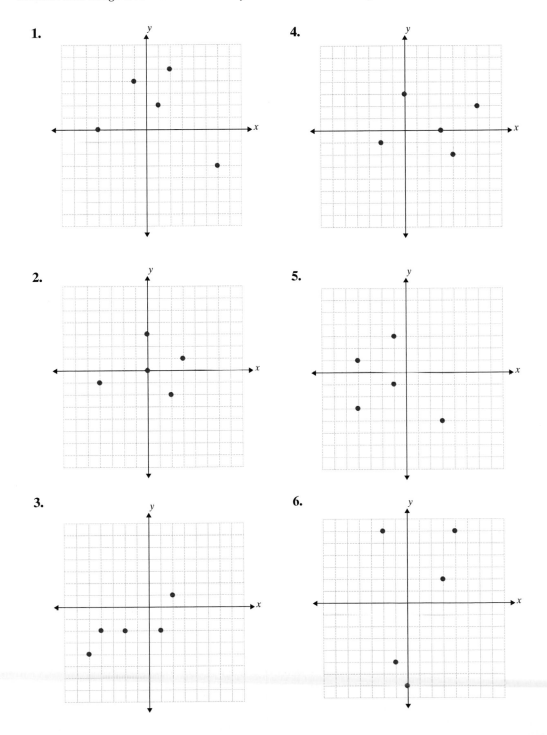

1.

2.

3.

4.

5.

6.

7.

8.

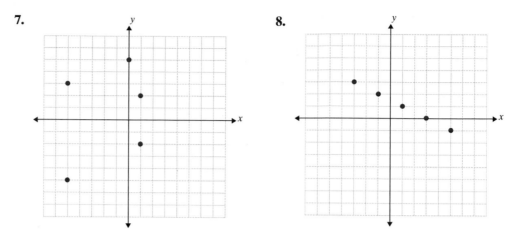

Graph the relations in Exercises 9 – 16. State the domain and range and indicate which of the relations are functions.

9. $\{(0,0),(1,6),(4,-2),(-3,5),(2,-1)\}$

10. $\{(1,-5),(2,-3),(-1,-3),(0,2),(4,3)\}$

11. $\{(-4,4),(-3,4),(1,4),(2,4),(3,4)\}$

12. $\{(-3,-3),(0,1),(-2,1),(3,1),(5,1)\}$

13. $\{(0,2),(-1,1),(2,4),(3,5),(-3,5)\}$

14. $\{(-1,-4),(0,-3),(2,-1),(4,1),(1,1)\}$

15. $\{(-1,4),(-1,2),(-1,0),(-1,6),(-1,-2)\}$

16. $\{(0,0),(-2,-5),(2,0),(4,-6),(5,2)\}$

Use the vertical line test to determine whether or not each graph in Exercises 17 – 26 represents a function. If the graph represents a function, state the domain and range.

17.

18.

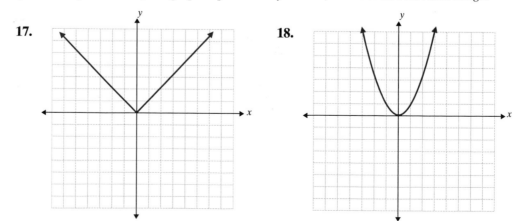

19.

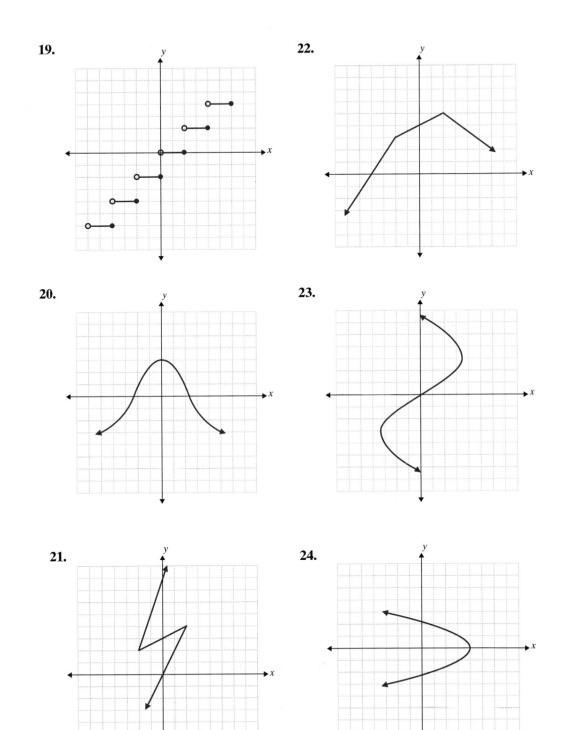

22.

20.

23.

21.

24.

25.

26.

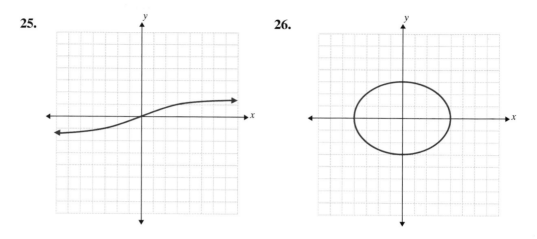

In Exercises 27 – 30, express the function as a set of ordered pairs for the given equation and domain.

27. $y = 3x + 1;\ \ D = \left\{ -9, -\dfrac{1}{3}, 0, \dfrac{4}{3}, 2 \right\}$ **28.** $y = -\dfrac{3}{4}x + 2;\ D = \left\{ -4, -2, 0, 3, 4 \right\}$

29. $y = 1 - 3x^2;\ \ D = \left\{ -2, -1, 0, 1, 2 \right\}$ **30.** $y = x^3 - 4x;\ \ D = \left\{ -1, 0, \dfrac{1}{2}, 1, 2 \right\}$

Find the domain of each function represented by the equations in Exercises 31 – 34.

31. $y = \dfrac{x+5}{x+3}$ **32.** $y = \dfrac{x-1}{2x+1}$ **33.** $y = \sqrt{2x+5}$ **34.** $y = \sqrt{4-3x}$

Use a graphing calculator to graph the functions in Exercises 35 – 46. Use the **TRACE**, **ZOOM**, and **CALC** features of the calculator to estimate x-intercepts, if any. (Remember, at these points the value of y will be 0.) Sketch each function on graph paper. For absolute value functions, select the **MATH** menu, then the **NUM** menu, and then **1: abs(** .

35. $y = 6$ **36.** $y = 4x$ **37.** $y = -2x + 3$ **38.** $y = x^2 - 4x$

39. $y = 1 + 2x - x^2$ **40.** $y = \sqrt{x+5}$ **41.** $y = \sqrt{3-x}$ **42.** $y = |x+2|$

43. $y = |x^2 - 3x|$ **44.** $y = x^3 - 2x^2 + 1$ **45.** $y = -x^3 + 3x - 1$ **46.** $y = x^4 - 13x^2 + 36$

In Exercises 47 and 48, use the **TRACE**, **ZOOM**, and **CALC** features of the calculator to estimate the coordinates of the highest point on the graph. (**HINT:** Item 4 on the **CALC** menu **4: maximum** will help in finding the highest point of a function, if there is one.) Sketch the graph on graph paper and label the coordinates of the highest point.

47. $y = 4x - x^2$ **48.** $y = 3 - 2x - x^2$

*In Exercises 49 and 50, use the **TRACE**, **ZOOM**, and **CALC** features of the calculator to estimate the coordinates of the lowest point on the graph. (**HINT:** Item 3 on the **CALC** menu **3: minimum** will help in finding the lowest point of a function, if there is one.) Sketch the graph on graph paper and label the coordinates of the lowest point.*

49. $y = 2x^2 - x + 1$ **50.** $y = 3(x - 1)^2 + 2$

*In Exercises 51 – 54, use the **TRACE**, **ZOOM**, and **CALC** features of the calculator to estimate the coordinates of the point(s) of intersection on the graphs. (**HINT:** Item 5 on the **CALC** menu **5: intersect** will help in finding the point of intersection of two functions, if there is one.) In the **Y=** menu use both **Y1 =** and **Y2 =** to be able to graph both functions at the same time. Sketch these functions on graph paper and label the point(s) of intersection.*

51. $y = 3x + 2$ **52.** $y = 2 - x$ **53.** $y = 2x - 1$ **54.** $y = x + 3$
   $y = 4 - x$ $y = x$ $y = x^2$ $y = -x^2 + x + 7$

Writing and Thinking About Mathematics

55. Explain in your own words how you find the domain of a function
   a. graphically
   b. algebraically

56. Which, if any, of the following functions has no restriction for the values in the domain? If the function's domain has restrictions, explain why.
   a. $3x - 2y = -1$
   b. $\sqrt{x + 2} = y$
   c. $\dfrac{1}{3x - 1} = y$

Hawkes Learning Systems: Intermediate Algebra

Introduction to Functions

2.5   Graphing Linear Inequalities

Objectives

After completing this section, you will be able to:

Graph linear inequalities.

Graphing Linear Inequalities

A straight line separates a plane into two **half-planes**. The points on one side of the line are in one of the half-planes, and the points on the other side of the line are in the other half-plane. The line itself is called the **boundary line**. If the boundary line is included with a half-plane, then the half-plane is said to be **closed**. If the boundary line is not included, then the half-plane is said to be **open**. (Note the similarity between the terminology for open and closed intervals.)

There are two basic methods for deciding which side of the line is the graph of the solution set of the inequality. In both methods, the boundary line must be graphed first.

Two Methods for Graphing Linear Inequalities

First, graph the boundary line (dashed if the inequality is < or >, solid if the inequality is ≤ or ≥).

Method 1

    a.   *Test any one point obviously on one side of the line.*

    b.   *If the test-point satisfies the inequality, shade the half-plane on that side of the line. Otherwise, shade the other half-plane.*

        *(****Note:*** *The point (0, 0), if it is not on the boundary line, is usually the easiest point to test.)*

Method 2

    a.   *Solve the inequality for y (assuming that the line is not vertical).*

    b.   *If the solution shows y < or y ≤ , then shade the half-plane below the line.*

    c.   *If the solution shows y > or y ≥, then shade the half-plane above the line.*

        *(****Note:*** *If the boundary line is vertical, then it is of the form x = a and Method 1 should be used.)*

Figure 2.13 shows both **a.** an open half-plane and **b.** a closed half-plane with the line $5x - 3y = 15$ as the boundary line.

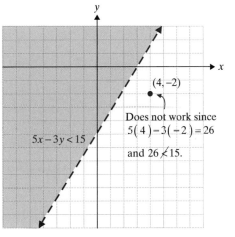

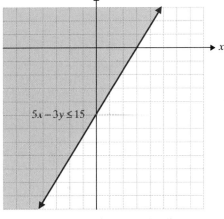

a. The points on the line
$5x - 3y = 15$
are not included so the line is dashed.
The half-plane is open.

b. The points on the line
$5x - 3y = 15$
are included so the line is solid.
The half-plane is closed.

Figure 2.13

Example 1: Graphing Linear Inequalities

Graph the following inequalities.

a. Graph the half-plane that satisfies the inequality $2x + y \leq 6$.

Solution: Method 1 is used in this example.

Step 1:   Graph the line $2x + y = 6$ as a solid line.

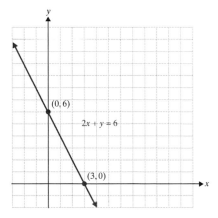

continued on next page ...

Step 2:   Test any point on one side of the line. In this example, we have chosen $(0, 0)$.

$$2 \cdot 0 + 0 \le 6$$
$$0 \le 6$$

This is a true statement.

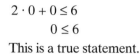

Step 3:   Shade the points on the same side as the point $(0, 0)$.

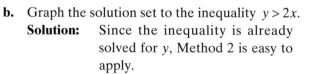

b. Graph the solution set to the inequality $y > 2x$.

Solution: Since the inequality is already solved for y, Method 2 is easy to apply.

Step 1:   Graph the line $y = 2x$ as a dashed line.

Step 2:   By Method 2, the graph consists of those points above the line. Shade the half-plane above the line.

[**Note:** As a check, we see that the points $(3, 0)$ gives $0 > 2 \cdot 3$, a false statement.]

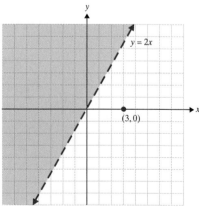

c. Graph the half-plane that satisfies the inequality $y > 1$.

Solution: Again, the inequality is already solved for y and Method 2 is used.

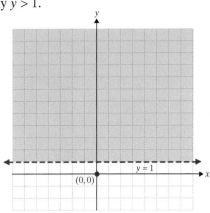

Step 1: Graph the horizontal line $y = 1$ as a dashed line.

Step 2: By Method 2, shade the half-plane above the line.

d. Graph the solution set to the inequality $x \leq 0$.

Solution: The boundary line is a vertical line and Method 1 is used.

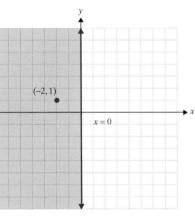

Step 1: Graph the line $x = 0$ as a solid line. Note that this is the y-axis.

Step 2: Test the point $(-2, 1)$.
$$-2 \leq 0$$
This statement is true.

Step 3: Shade the half-plane on the same side of the line as $(-2, 1)$. This half-plane consists of the points with x-coordinate 0 or negative.

● ●

Using a TI-83 Plus Graphing Calculator to Graph Linear Inequalities

The first step in using the TI-83 Plus (or any other graphing calculator) to graph a linear inequality is to solve the inequality for y. This is necessary because this is the way that the boundary line equation can be graphed as a function. Thus, Method 2 for graphing the correct half-plane is appropriate.

Note that when you press the ⬭Y=⬭ key on the calculator, a slash (\ ) appears to the left of the Y expression as in \Y1 =. This slash is actually a command to the calculator to graph the corresponding function as a solid line or curve. If you move the cursor to position over the slash and hit ⬭ENTER⬭, you will find the following options appearing:

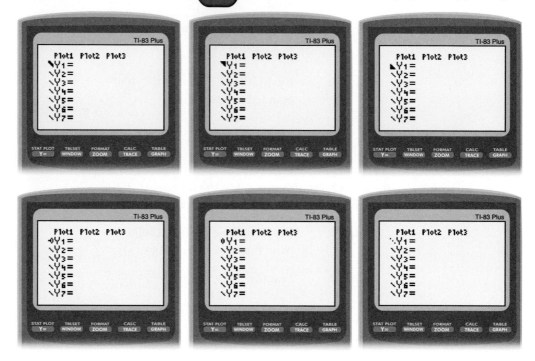

If the slash (which is actually four dots if you look closely) becomes a set of three dots, then the corresponding graph of the function will be dotted. By setting the shading above the dots, the corresponding graph on the display will show shading above the line or curve. By setting the shading below the dots, the corresponding graph on the display will show shading below the line or curve. The actual shading occurs only when the slash is four dots. So, the calculator is not good for determining whether the boundary curve is included or not. The following examples illustrate two situations.

Example 2: Graphing Using a T1 - 83 Plus • • • • • • • • • • • • • • • • • • •

a. Graph the linear inequality $2x + y \le 7$.
Solution:

Step 1: Solving the inequality for y gives: $y \le -2x + 7$.

Step 2: Press the key ⬭Y=⬭ and enter the function: $\Y1 = -2X + 7$.

Step 3:   Go to the \ and hit **ENTER** three times so that the display appears as follows:

Step 4:   Press **GRAPH** and (assuming that the WINDOW settings are the same) the following graph should appear on the display.

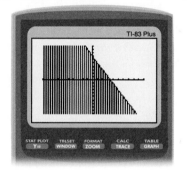

b.   Graph the linear inequality $-5x + 4y > -8$.
Solution:

Step 1:   Solving the inequality for y gives: $y > \dfrac{5}{4}x - 2$.

Step 2:   Press the key **Y=** and enter the function: $\backslash Y1 = (5/4)X - 2$.

Step 3:   Go to the \ and hit **ENTER** two times so that the display appears as follows:

continued on next page ...

Step 4:   Press (GRAPH) and (assuming that the WINDOW settings are the same) the following graph should appear on the display.

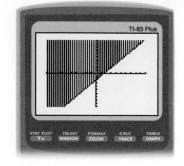

● ●

Practice Problems

1. Which of the following points satisfy the inequality $x + y < 3$?

    a. $(2, 1)$ **b.** $\left(\dfrac{1}{2}, 3\right)$ **c.** $(0, 5)$ **d.** $(-5, 2)$

2. Which of the following points satisfy the inequality $x - 2y \geq 0$?

    a. $(2, 1)$ **b.** $(1, 3)$ **c.** $(4, 2)$ **d.** $(3, 1)$

3. Which of the following points satisfy the inequality $x < 3$?

    a. $(1, 0)$ **b.** $(0, 1)$ **c.** $(4, -1)$ **d.** $(2, 3)$

2.5 Exercises

Graph the solution set of each of the linear inequalities in Exercises 1 – 30.

1. $x + y \leq 7$	**2.** $x - y > -2$	**3.** $x - y > 4$	**4.** $x + y \leq 6$
5. $y < 4x$	**6.** $y < -2x$	**7.** $y \geq -3x$	**8.** $y > x$
9. $x - 2y > 5$	**10.** $x + 3y \leq 7$	**11.** $4x + y \geq 3$	**12.** $5x - y < 4$
13. $y \leq 5 - 3x$	**14.** $y \geq 8 - 2x$	**15.** $2y - x \leq 0$	**16.** $x + y > 0$
17. $x + 4 \geq 0$	**18.** $x - 5 \leq 0$	**19.** $y \geq -2$	**20.** $y + 3 < 0$
21. $4x + 3y < 8$	**22.** $3x < 2y - 4$	**23.** $3y > 4x + 6$	**24.** $5x < 2y - 5$
25. $x + 3y < 7$	**26.** $3x + 4y > 11$	**27.** $\dfrac{1}{2}x - y > 1$	**28.** $\dfrac{1}{3}x + y \geq 3$
29. $\dfrac{2}{3}x + y \geq 4$	**30.** $2x - \dfrac{4}{3}y > 8$		

Answers to Practice Problems: 1. (d)   **2.** (a), (c), (d) **3.** (a), (b), (d)

Use your graphing calculator to graph each of the linear inequalities in Exercises 31 – 40.

31. $y > \dfrac{1}{2}x$

32. $x - y \leq 5$

33. $x + 2y > 8$

34. $3x + 2y \geq 12$

35. $2x + y \leq 6$

36. $y \geq -3$

37. $x - 3y \geq 9$

38. $y \leq -4$

39. $2x + 6y \geq 0$

40. $3x - 4y > 15$

Writing and Thinking About Mathematics

41. Explain in your own words how to test to determine which side of the graph of an inequality should be shaded.

42. Describe the difference between a closed and open half-plane.

Hawkes Learning Systems: Intermediate Algebra

Graphing Linear Inequalities

Chapter 2 Index of Key Ideas and Terms

Ordered Pairs   page 105

An **ordered pair** of real numbers is of the form (x, y)
where the order of x and y is important.

Coordinates   page 105

The first number in an ordered pair is called the **first coordinate**
(or **x-coordinate**). The second number in an ordered pair is called
the **second coordinate** (or **y-coordinate**).

Cartesian Coordinate System   page 105

There is a one-to-one correspondence between the points in   page 105
  a plane and ordered pairs of real numbers.
Quadrants   page 105
x-axis, y-axis   page 105
Origin   page 105

Solution (or Solution Set) of an Equation   page 106

The **solution** (or **solution set**) of an equation in two variables,
x and y, consists of all those ordered pairs of real numbers (x, y)
that satisfy the equation.

Linear Equation   page 107

Any equation of the form $Ax + By = C$, where A and B are
not both 0, is called the **standard form** of a **linear equation.**

To Graph a Linear Equation   page 108

1. Locate any two points that satisfy the equation. (Choose values
    for x and y that lead to simple solutions. Remember that there
    are an infinite number of choices for either x or y. But, once a
    value for x or y is chosen, the corresponding value for the other
    variable is found by substituting into the equation.)
2. Plot these two points on a Cartesian coordinate system.
3. Draw a straight line through these two points. (**Note:** Every
    point on that line will satisfy the equation.)
4. To check: Locate a third point that satisfies the equation and check
    to see that it does indeed lie on the line.

y-intercept   page 109

The **y-intercept** is the point where the graph of a line crosses
the y-axis. The x-coordinate will be 0.

x-intercept   page 109

The **x-intercept** is the point where the graph of a line crosses
the x-axis. The y-coordinate will be 0.

Slope (of a line)   page 114

$$\text{slope} = m = \frac{rise}{run} = \frac{y_2 - y_1}{x_2 - x_1} = \frac{y_1 - y_2}{x_1 - x_2}$$

Slope-Intercept Form   page 116

Any equation of the form $y = mx + b$ is called the **slope-intercept form** of the equation of a line. The slope is m and the y-intercept is b.

Horizontal Lines   page 120

Any equation of the form $y = b$ represents a **horizontal line** with **slope 0**.

Vertical Lines   page 120

Any equation of the form $x = a$ represents a **vertical line** with **undefined slope**.

Point-slope Form   page 127

An equation of the form $y - y_1 = m(x - x_1)$ is called the **point-slope form** for the equation of a line. The line contains the point (x_1, y_1) and has slope m.

Parallel Lines   page 130

Two lines (neither vertical) are **parallel** if and only if they have the same slope. All vertical lines are parallel.

Perpendicular Lines   page 131

Two lines (neither vertical) are **perpendicular** if and only if

their slopes are negative reciprocals of each other:

$$m_2 = -\frac{1}{m_1} \ or \ m_1 \cdot m_2 = -1.$$

Slope as a Rate of Change   page 134

Relations   page 140

A **relation** is a set of ordered pairs of real numbers. The **domain**, **D**, of a relation is the set of all first coordinates in the relation. The **range**, **R**, of a relation is the set of all second coordinates in the relation.

Functions   page 141

A **function** is a relation in which each domain element has a unique range element. OR A **function** is a relation in which each first coordinate appears only once. OR A **function** is a relation in which no two ordered pairs have the same first coordinate.

Vertical Line Test   page 142

If **any** vertical line intersects the graph of a relation at more
than one point, then the relation graphed is **not** a function.

Using a Calculator to Graph Linear Functions   pages 147-152

Linear Inequalities   page 158

Half-planes
Boundary line
Closed Half-plane
Open Half-plane

Using a Calculator to Graph Linear Inequalities   pages 161-164

Chapter 2 Review

For a review of the topics and problems from Chapter 2, look at the following lessons from *Hawkes Learning Systems: Intermediate Algebra*

Introduction to the Cartesian Coordinate System
Graphing Linear Equations by Plotting Points
Graphing Linear Equations in Slope-Intercept Form
Graphing Linear Equations in Point-Slope Form
Finding the Equation of a Line
Introduction to Functions
Graphing Linear Inequalities

Chapter 2 Test

*Find the missing coordinate of each ordered pair so that the ordered pair belongs to the
solution set of the equation in Exercises 1 and 2.*

1. $3x + y = 2$
  a. $(0, \quad)$
  b. $(\quad, 0)$
  c. $(-2, \quad)$
  d. $(\quad, -7)$

2. $x - 5y = 6$
  a. $(0, \quad)$
  b. $(\quad, 0)$
  c. $(11, \quad)$
  d. $(\quad, -2)$

Graph each of the linear equations in Exercises 3 and 4.

3. $x + 4y = 5$

4. $2x - 5y = 1$

Find the slope of the line determined by each pair of points in Exercises 5 and 6. Graph the line.

5. $(1, -2), (9, 7)$

6. $(-2, 5), (8, 3)$

Write each equation in Exercises 7 and 8 in slope-intercept form. Find the slope and y-intercept, and then draw the graph.

7. $x - 3y = 4$

8. $4x - 3y = 3$

Find the equation in standard form for the line determined by the given point and slope or the given two points.

9. $(3, 7)$, $m = -\dfrac{5}{3}$

10. $(-4, 6), (3, -2)$

In Exercises 11 – 13, find an equation in standard form for the line satisfying the given conditions.

11. Passing through $(-1, 6)$ and $(4, -2)$
12. Parallel to $3x + 2y = -1$ and passing through $(2, 4)$
13. Perpendicular to the *y*-axis and passing through the point $(3, -2)$

14. The following table shows the number of miles Sam rode his bicycle from one hour to another.
   a. Plot the points indicated in the table.
   b. Calculate the slope of the line segments from point to point.
   c. Interpret each slope.

Hour	Miles
First	20
Second	31
Third	17

15. Write the definition of a function.

16. List the set of ordered pairs of real numbers corresponding to the points shown in the graph. State the domain and range of the relation and indicate whether or not the relation is a function.

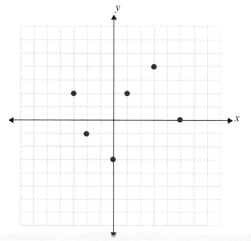

In Exercises 17 and 18, use the vertical line test to determine whether or not each graph represents a function.

17.   **18.**

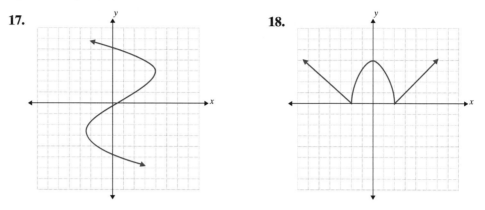

19. Write the function indicated by the equation and given domain as a set of ordered pairs of real numbers. $y = x^2 - 2x + 5$ and $D = \{-2, -1, 0, 1, 2\}$.

20. State the domain of the function $y = \dfrac{x+3}{2x-1}$.

21. a. Use a graphing calculator to graph the functions $y = \sqrt{2x-3}$ and $y = 5 - x$, and then sketch the graphs on graph paper.
b. Use the **TRACE**, **ZOOM**, and **CALC** features of the calculator to estimate the point of intersection of these two functions.

22. a. Use a graphing calculator to graph the function $y = 5 - 2x - 2x^2$ then sketch the graph on graph paper.
b. Use the **TRACE**, **ZOOM**, and **CALC** features of the calculator to estimate the highest on the graph.

Graph the linear inequalities in Exercises 23 and 24.

23. $3x - 5y \leq 10$ **24.** $3x + 4y > 7$

Cumulative Review: Chapters 1 - 2

1. Given the set of numbers $\left\{-10, -\sqrt{25}, -1.6, -\sqrt{7}, 0, \dfrac{1}{5}, \sqrt{9}, \pi, \sqrt{12}\right\}$, list those numbers that belong to each of the following sets:

    a. $\{x \mid x \text{ is a natural number}\}$ **b.** $\{x \mid x \text{ is a whole number}\}$

    c. $\{x \mid x \text{ is a rational number}\}$ **d.** $\{x \mid x \text{ is an integer}\}$

    e. $\{x \mid x \text{ is an irrational number}\}$ **f.** $\{x \mid x \text{ is a real number}\}$

Graph each of the sets of real numbers described in Exercises 2 and 3 on a real number line.

2. $\{x \mid -1.8 < x < 5 \text{ and } x \le 3\}$ **3.** $\{x \mid -5 < x \le -4 \text{ or } 2 < x \le 5\}$

Name the property of real numbers that justifies each statement in Exercises 4 – 9. All variables represent real numbers.

4. $7 + (x + 3) = (7 + x) + 3$ **5.** $3(y + 6) = 3y + 18$

6. $\dfrac{4}{5} + \left(-\dfrac{4}{5}\right) = 0$ **7.** $x \cdot 1 = x$

8. If $x < 10$ and $10 < y$, then $x < y$.   **9.** Either $x < -9$, $x = -9$, or $x > -9$.

Perform the indicated operations in Exercises 10 – 21.

10. $(-13) + (-7)$ **11.** $|-9| + 2$ **12.** $17 - (-5)$ **13.** $|9| - |-10|$

14. $6.5 + (-4.2) - 3.1$ **15.** $\dfrac{3}{4} - \dfrac{2}{3} + \left(-\dfrac{1}{6}\right)$ **16.** $(-7) \cdot (-12)$

17. $8(-5)$ **18.** $22 \div (-11)$ **19.** $(-4) \div (-6)$ **20.** $8 \div 0$

21. $0 \div \dfrac{3}{5}$

Find the value of each expression in Exercises 22 – 25 by using the rules for order of operations.

22. $12 - 6 \div 2 \cdot 3 - 5$ **23.** $5 - (13 \cdot 5 - 5) \div 3 \cdot 2$
24. $3^2 + 5 \cdot 4 - 10 + |7|$ **25.** $6 \cdot 4 - 2^3 - (5 \cdot 10) - 5^2$

Simplify each expression in Exercises 26 – 29 by combining like terms.

26. $-4(x + 3) + 2x$ **27.** $x + \dfrac{x - 5x}{4}$

28. $(x^3 + 4x - 1) - (-2x^3 + x^2)$ **29.** $-2[7x - (2x + 5) + 3]$

Solve each of the equations in Exercises 30 – 35.

30. $9x - 11 = x + 5$

31. $5(1 - 2x) = 3x + 57$

32. $5(2x + 3) = 3(x - 4) - 1$

33. $\dfrac{7x}{8} + 5 = \dfrac{x}{4}$

34. $|2x + 1| = 5.6$

35. $|2(x - 4) + x| = 2$

36. Solve each equation for the indicated variable.

a. Solve for n: $A = \dfrac{m + n}{2}$

b. Solve for d: $C = \pi d$

37. The difference between twice a number and 3 is equal to the difference between five times the number and 2. Find the number.

38. The local supermarket charges a flat rate of $5, plus $3 per hour for rental of a carpet cleaner. If it cost Ron $26 to rent the machine, how many hours did he keep it?

39. Stephanie rode her new moped to Rod's house. Traveling the side streets, she averaged 20 mph. To save time on the return trip, they loaded the bike into Rod's truck and took the freeway, averaging 50 mph. The freeway distance is 2 miles less than the distance on the side streets and saves 24 minutes. Find the distance traveled on the return trip.

40. On a placement exam for English, a group of ten students had the following scores: 3 students scored 76, 2 students scored 79, 1 student scored 81, 3 students scored 85 and 1 student scored 88. What was the mean score for this group of students?

41. The mathematics component of the entrance exam at a certain Midwestern college consists of three parts: one part on geometry, one part on algebra, and one part on trigonometry. Prospective students must score at least 50 on each part and average at least 70 on the three parts. Beth learned that she had scored 60 and 66 on the first two parts of the exam. What minimum score did she need on the third part for her to pass this portion of the exam to gain entrance to the college?

Solve the inequalities in Exercises 42 – 47 and graph the solutions. Write the solution set in interval notation. Assume that x is a real number.

42. $5x - 7 > x + 9$

43. $5x + 10 \leq 6(x + 3.8)$

44. $x + 8 - 5x \geq 2(x - 2)$

45. $\dfrac{2x + 1}{3} \leq \dfrac{3x}{5}$

46. $|5x + 2| > 7$

47. $|3x + 2| + 4 < 10$

Use the properties of exponents to simplify each expression in Exercises 48 – 57.

48. $(-3)^5(-3)^2$ **49.** $y^5 \cdot y^{-2}$ **50.** $\left(4x^2y\right)^3$ **51.** $\left(7x^5y^2\right)^2$

52. $\left(\dfrac{-3xy^4}{x^2}\right)^2$ **53.** $\left(\dfrac{2x^2y^0}{xy}\right)^{-3}$ **54.** $\left(x^3y^2\right)^2\left(x^2y\right)^{-3}$

55. $\dfrac{x^2y^{-3}}{x^{-3}y^{-2}}$ **56.** $\left(\dfrac{x^2y^3}{x^{-1}y}\right)^{-1}\left(\dfrac{x^4y}{xy^2}\right)^2$ **57.** $\left(\dfrac{2}{x^{-1}y^{-1}}\right)^{-2}\left(\dfrac{x^5y}{x^{-1}y^2}\right)$

In Exercises 58 and 59, write each number in scientific notation and simplify.

58. $(2100)(0.000005)$ **59.** $\dfrac{(270,000)(0.00014)}{42,000}$

In Exercises 60 and 61, find the missing coordinate of each ordered pair so that the ordered pair belongs to the solution set of the given equation.

60. $2x - y = 4$
   a. $(0, \quad)$
   b. $(\quad, 0)$
   c. $(1, \quad)$
   d. $(\quad, 2)$

61. $x + 3y = 6$
   a. $(0, \quad)$
   b. $(\quad, 0)$
   c. $(2, \quad)$
   d. $(\quad, -1)$

Write each equation in Exercises 62 – 64 in slope-intercept form. Find the slope and the y-intercept and draw the graph.

62. $x + 5y = 10$ **63.** $3x + y = 1$ **64.** $3x - 7y = 7$

Find the equation in standard form for the line determined by the given point and slope or two points in Exercises 65 – 70.

65. $(6, -1)$, $m = \dfrac{2}{5}$ **66.** $(-1, 2)$, $m = \dfrac{4}{3}$ **67.** $(0, 0)$, $m = 2$

68. $(5, 2)$, undefined slope   **69.** $(0, 3)$, $(5, -1)$ **70.** $(5, -2)$, $(1, 6)$

Find the equation in standard form for the line satisfying the conditions in Exercises 71 – 74.

71. Parallel to $3x + 2y - 6 = 0$, passing through $(2, 3)$
72. Parallel to the y-axis, passing through $(1, -7)$
73. Perpendicular to $4x + 3y = 5$, passing through $(4, 0)$
74. Perpendicular to $3x - 5y = 1$, passing through $(6, -2)$

Graph the linear inequalities in Exercises 75 and 76.

75. $y \geq 4x$

76. $3x + y < 2$

77. List the set of ordered pairs corresponding to the points in the given graph. State the domain and range and whether or not the relation is a function.

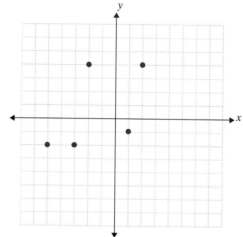

78. Use the vertical line test to determine whether or not the given graph represents a function.

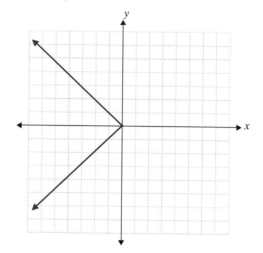

79. State the domain of the function $y = \sqrt{3x+6}$.

80. **a.** Use a graphing calculator to graph the linear functions $y = -2x + 7$ and $y = 3x$, and then sketch the graphs on graph paper.

   b. Use the **TRACE**, **ZOOM**, and **CALC** features of the calculator to estimate the point of intersection of these two linear functions.

81. **a.** Use a graphing calculator to graph the function $y = \frac{1}{2}x^2 + x$, and then sketch the graph on graph paper.

   b. Use the **TRACE**, **ZOOM**, and **CALC** features of the calculator to estimate the lowest point on the graph.

82. **a.** Use a graphing calculator to graph the function $y = x^4 - 3x^3 + 1$.

   b. Use the trace and zoom features of the calculator to estimate the values of the x-intercepts.

Systems of Linear Equations

Did You Know?

The subject of solutions to systems of linear equations, especially using determinants, received a great deal of attention in nineteenth-century mathematics. However, problems of this type are very old in the history of mathematics. As a matter of fact, determinants (or rules that were the equivalent of determinants) are found in pre-Christian, Chinese mathematical manuscripts. The solution to simultaneous systems of equations was well known in China and carried to Japan also. The great Japanese mathematician Seki Shinsuku Kowa (1642–1708) wrote a book on the subject in 1683 that was well in advance of European work on the subject. Seki Kowa is probably the most distinguished of all Japanese mathematicians. Born into a samurai family, he showed great mathematical talent at an early age. He is credited with the independent development of calculus and is sometimes referred to as "the Newton of Japan." There is a traditional story that Seki Kowa made a journey to the Buddhist shrines at Nara. There, ancient Chinese mathematical manuscripts were preserved, and Seki is supposed to have spent three years learning the contents of the manuscripts that previously no one had been able to understand. As was the custom, much of Seki Kowa's work was done through finding solutions of very intricate problems. In 1907, the Emperor of Japan presented a posthumous award to the memory of Seki Kowa, who did so much to awaken interest in scientific and mathematical research in Japan.

Native Japanese mathematics (the **wasan**) flourished until the nineteenth century when western mathematics and notation were completely adopted. In the 1940s, solutions to large systems of equations became a part of the new branch of mathematics called **operations research**. Operations research is concerned with deciding how best to design and operate man-machine systems, usually under conditions requiring the allocation of scarce resources. Although this new science initially had only military applications, recent applications have been made in the areas of business, industry, transportation, meteorology, and ecology. Computers now make it possible to solve extremely large systems of linear equations that are used to model the operating system being studied. Although computers do much of the work involved in solving systems of equations, it is necessary for you to understand the principles involved by studying small systems involving two or three unknowns, as presented in Chapter 3.

3.1   Systems of Linear Equations (Two Variables)

3.2   Applications

3.3   Systems of Linear Equations (Three Variables)

3.4   Matrices and Gaussian Elimination

3.5   Determinants

3.6   Determinants and Systems of Linear Equations: Cramer's Rule

3.7   Graphing Systems of Linear Inequalities

"The advancement and perfection of mathematics are intimately connected with the prosperity of the state."

Napoleon Bonaparte (1769 – 1821)

Many applications involve two (or more) quantities and, by using two (or more) variables, a set of two or more equations can be formed by using the given information. If the equations are linear, then the set of equations is called a **system of linear equations**. The purpose of this chapter is to develop techniques for solving systems of linear equations.

Graphing systems of two equations in two variables is helpful in visualizing the relationships between the equations. However, this approach is somewhat limited in finding solutions since numbers might be quite large, or solutions might involve fractions that must be estimated on the graph. Therefore, algebraic techniques are necessary to accurately solve systems of linear equations. Graphing in three dimensions will be left to later courses.

Two ideas probably new to students at this level are matrices and determinants. Matrices and determinants provide powerful general approaches to solving large systems of equations with many variables. Discussions in this chapter will be restricted to two linear equations in two variables and three linear equations in three variables.

3.1   Systems of Linear Equations (Two Variables)

Objectives

After completing this section, you will be able to:

Solve systems of linear equations in two variables using three methods:

a. *graphing,*

b. *substitution, and*

c. *addition.*

Two (or more) linear equations considered at one time are said to form a **system of equations** or a **set of simultaneous equations**. For example, consider the following system of two equations

$$\begin{cases} 2x + y = 5 \\ x - y = 1 \end{cases}$$

Each equation has an infinite number of solutions. That is, there is an infinite number of ordered pairs that satisfy each equation. But, the question of interest is, "Are there any ordered pairs that satisfy both equations at the same time?" In this example, the answer is yes. The ordered pair (2, 1) satisfies both equations:

$$2(2) + 1 = 5 \qquad \text{substituting into the first equation}$$
$$2 - 1 = 1 \qquad \text{substituting into the second equation}$$

There are several questions that need to be answered.

How do we find the solution, if there is one?
Will there always be a solution to a system of linear equations?
Can there be more than one solution?

Graphing linear equations provides initial insight to the answers to these questions. However, as the chapter progresses we will see that other algebraic techniques are even more informative.

Table 3.1 illustrates the three possibilities for a system of two linear equations in two variables. The system can be

1. **consistent**   (has exactly one solution)
2. **inconsistent**   (has no solution)
3. **dependent**   (has an infinite number of solutions)

System	Graph	Intersection	Terms
$\begin{cases} 2x + y = 5 \\ x - y = 1 \end{cases}$		$(2, 1)$ or $\begin{cases} x = 2 \\ y = 1 \end{cases}$ (The lines intersect at one point.)	**Consistent**
$\begin{cases} 3x - 2y = 2 \\ 6x - 4y = -4 \end{cases}$		No Solution (The lines are parallel.)	**Inconsistent**
$\begin{cases} 2x - 4y = 6 \\ x - 2y = 3 \end{cases}$		Any ordered pair that satisfies $x - 2y = 3$. (The lines are the same line. There are an infinite number of solutions: $\{(x, y) \mid x - 2y = 3\}$.)	**Dependent**

Table 3.1

The three basic methods for solving a system of two linear equations in two variables that will be discussed in this section are:

1. **graphing**   (as illustrated in Table 3.1)
2. **substitution** (algebraically substituting from one equation into the other)
3. **addition**   (combining like terms from both equations)

The Graphing Method

To solve a system of two linear equations in two variables by graphing,

> **1.** graph both lines on the same set of axes, and
> **2.** observe the point of intersection (if there is one).

  a. If the slopes of the two lines are different, then the lines will intersect in one and only one point. The system is consistent and has a single point solution.
  b. If the lines are distinct and have the same slope, then the lines will be parallel and the system is inconsistent. The system will have no solution.
  c. If the lines are the same line, the system is dependent and all the points on both lines constitute the solution.

Solving by graphing can involve estimating the solutions whenever the intersection of the two lines is at a point not represented by a pair of integers. (There is nothing wrong with this technique. Just be aware that at times it can lack accuracy. See Example 1b.)

Example 1: Graphing ●

Solve each of the following systems by graphing.

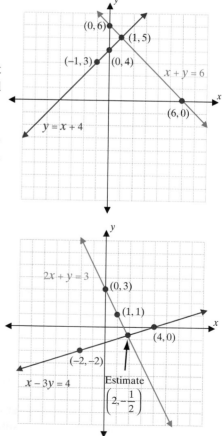

  a. $\begin{cases} x+y=6 \\ \quad y=x+4 \end{cases}$

   Solution: The two lines intersect at the point $(1, 5)$. The system is consistent and the solution is $x = 1$ and $y = 5$.

   Check: Substitution shows that $(1, 5)$ satisfies both of the equations in the system.

  b. $\begin{cases} x-3y=4 \\ 2x+y=3 \end{cases}$

   Solution: The two lines intersect, but we can only estimate the point of intersection at $\left(2, -\dfrac{1}{2}\right)$. In this situation be aware that, while graphing gives a good "estimate," finding exact solutions to the system is not likely.

Check: Substituting $x = 2$ and $y = -\dfrac{1}{2}$ gives:

$$2 - 3\left(-\frac{1}{2}\right) \overset{?}{=} 4 \quad \text{and} \quad 2(2) + \left(-\frac{1}{2}\right) \overset{?}{=} 3$$

$$\frac{7}{2} \neq 4 \qquad\qquad\qquad \frac{7}{2} \neq 3$$

Thus, checking shows that the estimated solution $\left(2, -\dfrac{1}{2}\right)$ does not satisfy either equation. The estimated point of intersection is just that – an estimate. The following discussion develops an algebraic technique that gives the exact solution as $\left(\dfrac{13}{7}, -\dfrac{5}{7}\right)$.

The Substitution Method

The objective in the substitution method is to eliminate one of the variables so that a new equation is formed with just one variable. If this new equation has one solution, then the system is **consistent**. If this new equation is never true, then the system is **inconsistent**. If this new equation is always true, then the system is **dependent**.

To Solve a System of Linear Equations by Substitution

1. *Solve one of the equations for one of the variables.*
2. *Substitute the resulting expression into the other equation.*
3. *Solve this new equation, if possible, and then substitute back into one of the original equations to find the value of the other variable. (This is known as **back substitution**.)*

Example 2: Substitution

Solve the following systems of equations by substitution.

a. $\begin{cases} x - 3y = 4 \\ 2x + y = 3 \end{cases}$ b. $\begin{cases} 6x + 3y = 14 \\ 2x + y = -3 \end{cases}$

continued on next page ...

a. $\begin{cases} x - 3y = 4 \\ 2x + y = 3 \end{cases}$

Solution:

$$x - 3y = 4$$

$$x = 4 + 3y \qquad \text{Solve the first equation for } x.$$

$$2(4 + 3y) + y = 3 \qquad \text{Substitute } 4 + 3y \text{ for } x \text{ in the second equation.}$$

$$8 + 6y + y = 3 \qquad \text{Solve the new equation for } y.$$

$$7y = -5$$

$$y = -\frac{5}{7}$$

To find x, we "**back substitute**" $-\dfrac{5}{7}$ for y in one of the original equations.

$$x - 3\left(-\frac{5}{7}\right) = 4$$

$$x = 4 - \frac{15}{7} = \frac{13}{7}$$

The system is consistent, and the solution is $x = \dfrac{13}{7}$ and $y = -\dfrac{5}{7}$, or $\left(\dfrac{13}{7}, -\dfrac{5}{7}\right)$.

In this example, the second equation could have been solved for y and the substitution made into the first equation. The solution would have been the same.

NOTES Either equation can be solved for either variable, and the result substituted into the other equation. For simplicity, we generally solve for the variable that has a coefficient of 1 if there is such a variable.

b. $\begin{cases} 6x + 3y = 14 \\ 2x + y = -3 \end{cases}$

Solution:

$$2x + y = -3$$

$$y = -3 - 2x \qquad \text{Solve the second equation for } y.$$

$$6x + 3(-3 - 2x) = 14 \qquad \text{Substitute } -3 - 2x \text{ for } y \text{ in the first equation.}$$

$$6x - 9 - 6x = 14 \qquad \text{Solve for } x.$$

$$-9 = 14$$

The variable x is eliminated, and this last equation is never true.
Therefore, the system is **inconsistent**.
There is no solution to this system of equations.

The Addition Method

In arithmetic, we can show that if $a = b$ and $c = d$, then $a + c = b + d$. Similarly, in algebra, we can show that any solution to **both** linear equations

$$a_1 x + b_1 y = c_1$$

and

$$a_2 x + b_2 y = c_2$$

will also be a solution to the equation

$$k_1 \left(a_1 x + b_1 y \right) + k_2 \left(a_2 x + b_2 y \right) = k_1 c_1 + k_2 c_2$$

where k_1 and k_2 are not both 0.

Thus, to find a common solution to the original two equations, form a new equation by combining like terms of the two equations. As with the substitution method, the objective is to eliminate one of the variables so that the new equation has just one variable. If this new equation has one solution, then the system is **consistent**. If this new equation is never true, then the system is **inconsistent**. If this new equation is always true, then the system is **dependent**. The procedure is outlined as follows:

To Solve a System of Linear Equations by Addition

1. *Write the equations one under the other so that like terms are aligned.*

2. *Multiply all terms of one equation by a constant (and possibly all terms of the other equation by another constant) so that two like terms have opposite coefficients.*

3. *Add like terms and solve the resulting equation, if possible. Then, back substitute into one of the original equations to find the value of the other variable.*

NOTES When solving a system of equations, two equations may be interchanged. That is, the order in which the equations are written has no bearing on the solutions. If for some reason you think that writing one equation before another will make the system easier to solve, you may do so without affecting the solutions.

Example 3: Addition ●

Solve the following systems of equations by addition.

a.
$$\begin{cases} 4x+3y=1 \\ 5x+y=-7 \end{cases}$$

Solution: Multiply each term in the second equation by −3 so that the y-coefficients will be opposites. Add like terms to eliminate y. Solve for x.

[**Note:** We could have eliminated x by multiplying the first equation by −5 and the second equation by 4 then adding like terms. The result will be the same. Because the coefficient for y in the second equation is +1, it was less work to multiply this one equation by −3.]

$$\begin{cases} 4x + 3y = 1 \\ [-3]\ 5x + y = -7 \end{cases} \qquad \begin{array}{rcl} 4x + 3y & = & 1 \\ -15x - 3y & = & 21 \\ \hline -11x & = & 22 \\ x & = & -2 \end{array}$$

Now, back substitute x = −2 in one of the original equations and solve for y.

$$5(-2)+y=-7$$

$$-10+y=-7$$

$$y=3$$

The system is consistent, and the solution is x = −2 and y = 3, or (−2, 3).

[**Check:** As a thorough check, substitute the solution, in this case (−3, 2), into **both** of the original equations.]

b.
$$\begin{cases} 2x=-17-3y \\ 3x-\dfrac{51}{2}=4y \end{cases}$$

Solution: Rewriting the equations in standard form yields $\begin{cases} 2x+3y=-17 \\ 3x-4y=\dfrac{51}{2} \end{cases}$.

Multiply each term in the first equation by −3 and each term in the second equation by 2 so that the x-coefficients will be opposites.

[**Note:** We could just as easily have eliminated y by multiplying the first equation by 4 and the second equation by 3 then adding like terms. The result will be the same.]

$$\begin{cases} [-3]\ 2x + 3y = -17 \\ [2]\ 3x - 4y = \dfrac{51}{2} \end{cases} \qquad \begin{array}{rcl} -6x - 9y & = & 51 \\ 6x - 8y & = & 51 \\ \hline -17y & = & 102 \\ y & = & -6 \end{array}$$

Now, back substitute $y = -6$ in one of the original equations and solve for x.

$$2x + 3(-6) = -17$$
$$2x = -17 + 18$$
$$2x = 1$$
$$x = \frac{1}{2}$$

The system is consistent. The solution is $x = \frac{1}{2}$ and $y = -6$, or $\left(\frac{1}{2}, -6\right)$.

c. $\begin{cases} 3x - \dfrac{1}{2}y = 6 \\ 6x - y = 12 \end{cases}$

Solution: Multiply the first equation by -2.

$$\begin{cases} [-2] \quad 3x \;-\; \dfrac{1}{2}y \;=\; 6 \\ \quad 6x \;-\; \phantom{\dfrac{1}{2}}y \;=\; 12 \end{cases}$$

$$\begin{array}{rcrcr} -6x & + & y & = & -12 \\ 6x & - & y & = & 12 \\ \hline & & 0 & = & 0 \end{array}$$

The last equation, $0 = 0$, is always true so the system is **dependent**. There are an infinite number of solutions. Any ordered pair that satisfies the equation $6x - y = 12$ is a solution to the system, written in set-builder notation as $\{(x, y)\mid 6x - y = 12\}$.

● ●

Solving a System of Linear Equations by Using a TI-83 Plus Calculator

Consider the system of two linear equations $\begin{cases} x + y = 4 \\ 3x - 2y = 7 \end{cases}$.

To solve this system by using a TI-83 Plus graphing calculator, we can proceed as follows:

Step 1: To be able to use the calculator's function mode, solve each equation for y:

$$\begin{cases} y = 4 - x \\ y = \dfrac{3}{2}x - \dfrac{7}{2} \end{cases}$$

Step 2: Press the `Y=` key and enter the two functions for Y1 and Y2 as shown here:

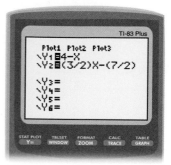

Step 3: Press GRAPH.
(You may need to check the WINDOW to be sure that both lines appear.)

Step 4: Press `2nd` CALC
Choose **5: intersect**.
Move the cursor to one of the lines and press ENTER in response to the question **First curve?**.
Move the cursor to the second line and press ENTER in response to the question **Second curve?**.
Move the cursor near the point of intersection and press ENTER in response to the question **Guess?**.

We see that the solution is $x = 3$ and $y = 1$.

[**Note:** In this case the solution shown is exact. In many cases the solution shown will be only an estimate. Thus, even with a calculator, the graphing method is limited.]

Practice Problems

Solve each of the following systems of linear equations algebraically.

1. $\begin{cases} y = 3x + 4 \\ 2x + y = -1 \end{cases}$ **2.** $\begin{cases} 2x - 3y = 0 \\ 6x + 3y = 4 \end{cases}$ **3.** $\begin{cases} 4x + y = 3 \\ 4x + y = 2 \end{cases}$

3.1 Exercises

Solve each of the systems in Exercises 1 – 10 by graphing.

1. $\begin{cases} x+y=5 \\ x-4y=5 \end{cases}$ **2.** $\begin{cases} 3x-y=6 \\ 2x+y=-1 \end{cases}$ **3.** $\begin{cases} 2x-y=8 \\ y=2x \end{cases}$ **4.** $\begin{cases} 5x+2y=21 \\ x=y \end{cases}$

5. $\begin{cases} y=\dfrac{5}{6}x+1 \\ x-2y=2 \end{cases}$ **6.** $\begin{cases} 4x-2y=10 \\ -6x+3y=-15 \end{cases}$ **7.** $\begin{cases} 2x+y+1=0 \\ 3x+4y-1=0 \end{cases}$ **8.** $\begin{cases} 2x+3y=4 \\ 4x-y=1 \end{cases}$

9. $\begin{cases} x-2y=11 \\ 2x-3y=18 \end{cases}$ **10.** $\begin{cases} 4x+3y+7=0 \\ 5x=2y-3 \end{cases}$

Use the Substitution Method or the Addition Method to solve the systems of linear equations in Exercises 11 – 36. State whether each system is consistent, inconsistent, or dependent.

11. $\begin{cases} x+4y=6 \\ 2x+y=5 \end{cases}$ **12.** $\begin{cases} 2x+y=0 \\ x-2y=-10 \end{cases}$ **13.** $\begin{cases} 5x-y=-2 \\ x+2y=-7 \end{cases}$ **14.** $\begin{cases} 7x-y=18 \\ x+2y=9 \end{cases}$

15. $\begin{cases} x+2y=3 \\ 4x+8y=8 \end{cases}$ **16.** $\begin{cases} 2x+3y=3 \\ x+4y=4 \end{cases}$ **17.** $\begin{cases} 6x+2y=16 \\ 3x+y=8 \end{cases}$ **18.** $\begin{cases} 4x-y=18 \\ 3x+5y=2 \end{cases}$

19. $\begin{cases} y=3x+3 \\ y=-2x+8 \end{cases}$ **20.** $\begin{cases} x=5-4y \\ x=2y-7 \end{cases}$ **21.** $\begin{cases} 2x+y=4 \\ 4x+5y=11 \end{cases}$

22. $\begin{cases} x+6y=4 \\ 2x+3y=5 \end{cases}$ **23.** $\begin{cases} 3x+4y=6 \\ x-8y=9 \end{cases}$ **24.** $\begin{cases} 3x+5y=3 \\ 9x-y=-7 \end{cases}$

25. $\begin{cases} 2x=5y-1 \\ 4x-10y=0 \end{cases}$ **26.** $\begin{cases} 6x+2y=5 \\ 2x+y=1 \end{cases}$ **27.** $\begin{cases} 4x+12y=5 \\ 5x-6y=1 \end{cases}$

28. $\begin{cases} 2x-3y=18 \\ 5x+4y=-1 \end{cases}$ **29.** $\begin{cases} x+y=7 \\ 2x+3y=16 \end{cases}$ **30.** $\begin{cases} 5x-7y=8 \\ 3x+11y=-12 \end{cases}$

31. $\begin{cases} 6x-y=15 \\ 0.2x+0.5y=2.1 \end{cases}$ **32.** $\begin{cases} 3x+y=14 \\ 0.1x-0.2y=1.4 \end{cases}$ **33.** $\begin{cases} x+y=12 \\ 0.05x+0.25y=1.6 \end{cases}$

Answers to Practice Problems: 1. $x=-1, y=1$ **2.** $x=\dfrac{1}{2}, y=\dfrac{1}{3}$ **3.** Inconsistent

34. $\begin{cases} x + y = 20 \\ 0.1x + 2.5y = 3.8 \end{cases}$ **35.** $\begin{cases} 0.6x + 0.5y = 5.9 \\ 0.8x + 0.4y = 6 \end{cases}$ **36.** $\begin{cases} 0.5x - 0.3y = 7 \\ 0.3x + 0.4y = 2 \end{cases}$

*In Exercises 37 – 44, use a graphing calculator and the ZOOM, TRACE, and CALC features to estimate the solutions to the systems of linear equations. (**HINT:** The **CALC** and **5: intersect** commands may give the most accurate answers. Remember to solve each equation for y. Use both Y1 and Y2 in the* Y= *menu.)*

37. $\begin{cases} 2x + y = 3 \\ x - y = 5 \end{cases}$ **38.** $\begin{cases} 3x + y = 6 \\ 2x + y = -1 \end{cases}$ **39.** $\begin{cases} 8x - 2y = 8 \\ y = -2x \end{cases}$ **40.** $\begin{cases} x + y = -5 \\ 4x - y = 5 \end{cases}$

41. $\begin{cases} x - 3y = 6 \\ -2x + y = -1 \end{cases}$ **42.** $\begin{cases} x + \dfrac{1}{2}y = 0 \\ 6x - y = 3 \end{cases}$ **43.** $\begin{cases} 2x + 3y = 2 \\ x + 2y = -3 \end{cases}$ **44.** $\begin{cases} x - 3y = 5 \\ 2x + 3y = 4 \end{cases}$

Hawkes Learning Systems: Intermediate Algebra

Solving Systems of Linear Equations by Graphing
Solving Systems of Linear Equations by Substitution
Solving Systems of Linear Equations by Addition

3.2   Applications

Objectives

After completing this section, you will be able to:

Solve applied problems by using systems of two linear equations in two variables.

In Chapters 1 and 2, a variety of word problems were solved by using one variable and one equation. However, many applications can be solved, and in fact are easier to solve, by using two variables and two equations. That is, the information given in a problem can be represented with a system of two linear equations. Then the system can be solved using the methods discussed in the previous section.

Example 1: Mixture

A manufacturer receives an order for 30 tons of a 40% copper alloy. He has only 20% alloy and 50% alloy in stock. How much of each will he need to fill the order?

Solution: Let x = amount of 20% alloy in tons
y = amount of 50% alloy in tons

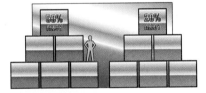

Form two equations based on the information given.

Phrase from problem	Equation formed
The total order is 30 tons.	$x + y = 30$
The total amount of copper is 40% of 30.	$0.20x + 0.50y = 0.40(30)$

Now solve the system. We will use the addition method.

$$\begin{cases} [-2] & x + y = 30 \\ [10] & 0.20x + 0.50y = 0.40(30) \end{cases}$$

$$\begin{aligned} -2x - 2y &= -60 \\ 2x + 5y &= 120 \\ \hline 3y &= 60 \\ y &= 20 \end{aligned}$$

Substituting $y = 20$ into the first equation yields
$$x + 20 = 30$$
$$x = 10$$

The manufacturer will need 10 tons of the 20% alloy and 20 tons of the 50% alloy.

Example 2: Interest ●

A savings and loan company pays 7% interest on long-term savings, and a high-risk stock indicates that it should yield 12% interest. If a woman has $40,000 to invest and wants an annual income of $3550 from her investments, how much should she put in the savings and loan and how much in the stock?

Solution: Let x = amount invested at 7%
y = amount invested at 12%

Phrase from problem	Equation formed
The total invested is $40,000.	$\begin{cases} x + y = 40,000 \\ 0.07x + 0.12y = 3,550 \end{cases}$
The total interest is $3,550.	

$$\begin{cases} [-7] & x + y = 40,000 \\ [100] & 0.07x + 0.12y = 3,550 \end{cases}$$

$$\begin{array}{rcl} -7x - 7y &=& -280,000 \\ 7x + 12y &=& 355,000 \\ \hline 5y &=& 75,000 \\ y &=& 15,000 \end{array}$$

Back substituting gives:

$$x + 15,000 = 40,000$$

$$x = 25,000$$

She should put $25,000 in the long-term savings at 7% and $15,000 in stock at 12%.

● ●

Example 3: Work ●

Working his way through school, Richard works two part-time jobs for a total of 25 hours a week. Job A pays $4.50 per hour and job B pays $6.30 per hour. How many hours did he work at each job the week he made $137.70?

Solution: Let x = number of hours at job A at $4.50 per hour
y = number of hours at job B at $6.30 per hour

Job A   Job B

Phrase from problem	Equation formed
The total hours worked is 25.	$\begin{cases} x + y = 25 \\ 4.50x + 6.30y = 137.70 \end{cases}$
The total earnings were $137.70.	

$$\begin{cases} [-45] & x + y = 25 \\ [10] & 4.50x + 6.30y = 137.70 \end{cases}$$

$$\begin{array}{rcl} -45x - 45y &=& -1125 \\ 45x + 63y &=& 1377 \\ \hline 18y &=& 252 \\ y &=& 14 \end{array}$$

Back substitute to obtain:

$$x + 14 = 25$$

$$x = 11$$

Richard worked 11 hours at job A and 14 hours at job B.

Example 4: Algebra •

Determine the value of a and b such that the straight line $ax + by = 11$ passes through the point $(3, -1)$ and has slope $-\dfrac{5}{4}$.

Solution: Here, the unknown quantities are a and b, not x and y.

Since the point $(3, -1)$ is on the line, substitute $x = 3$ and $y = -1$ into the equation $ax + by = 11$.

$$3a - b = 11 \qquad \text{A linear equation in } a \text{ and } b$$

To find the slope in terms of a and b, write the equation $ax + by = 11$ in slope-intercept form.

$$ax + by = 11$$
$$by = -ax + 11$$
$$y = -\frac{a}{b}x + \frac{11}{b}$$

Thus, the slope is $-\dfrac{a}{b}$. Therefore,

$$-\frac{a}{b} = -\frac{5}{4} \qquad \text{Since the slope is given as} -\frac{5}{4}$$

or $\qquad 4a - 5b$

or $\quad 4a - 5b = 0 \qquad$ Another linear equation in a and b

Now we have two linear equations in a and b so we can use the addition method to solve the system of equations.

$$\begin{cases}[-5] & 3a & - & b & = & 11 \\ & 4a & - & 5b & = & 0\end{cases}$$

$$\begin{array}{rcrcr} -15a & + & 5b & = & -55 \\ 4a & - & 5b & = & 0 \\ \hline -11a & & & = & -55 \\ a & & & = & 5 \end{array}$$

Back substituting $a = 5$ yields:

$$3(5) - b = 11$$
$$-b = -4$$
$$b = 4$$

Thus, $a = 5$ and $b = 4$, so the line $5x + 4y = 11$ passes through the point $(3, -1)$ and has slope $-\dfrac{5}{4}$.

• •

NOTES

The equation $\dfrac{a}{b} = \dfrac{5}{4}$ does not necessarily mean that $a = 5$ and $b = 4$. It means that the **ratio** of a to b is 5 to 4. For example, if $a = 10$ and $b = 8$, then the ratio of a to b is still 5 to 4.

3.2 Exercises

1. The sum of two integers is 102, and the larger number is 10 more than three times the smaller. Find the two integers.

2. The difference between two integers is 13, and their sum is 87. What are the two integers?

3. Two angles are supplementary if the sum of their measures is 180°. Find two supplementary angles such that the smaller is 30° more than one-half of the larger.

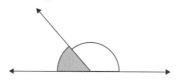

4. Two angles are complementary if the sum of their measures is 90°. Find two complementary angles such that one is 15° less than six times the other.

5. At present, the length of a rectangular soccer field is 55 yards longer than the width. The city council is thinking of rearranging the area containing the soccer field into two square playing fields. A math teacher on the council decided to test the council members' mathematical skills. (You know how math teachers are.) He told them that if the width of the current field were to be increased by 5 yards and the length cut in half, the field would be a square.

What are the dimensions of the field currently?

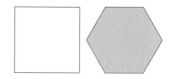

w + 55 yards

6. Consider a square and a regular hexagon (a six-sided figure with sides of equal length). One side of the square is 5 feet longer than a side of the hexagon, and the two figures have the same perimeter. What are the lengths of the sides of each figure?

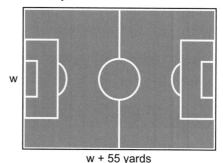

7. How many liters each of a 12% iodine solution and a 30% iodine solution must be used to produce a total mixture of 90 liters of a 22% iodine solution?

8. A meat market has ground beef that is 40% fat and extra lean ground beef that is only 15% fat. How many pounds of each (ground beef and extra lean) must be ground together to get a total of 50 pounds of "lean" ground beef that is 25% fat?

9. A dairy needs 360 gallons of milk containing 4% butterfat. How many gallons each of milk containing 5% butterfat and milk containing 2% butterfat must be used to obtain the desired 360 gallons?

10. A druggist has two solutions of alcohol. One is 25% alcohol. The other is 45% alcohol. He wants to mix these two solutions to get 36 ounces that will be 30% alcohol. How many ounces of each of these two solutions should he mix together?

11. Roxanne inherited $124,000 from her Uncle Jake. She invested a portion in bonds and the remainder in a long-term certificate account. The amount invested in bonds was $24,000 less than 3 times the amount invested in certificates. How much was invested in bonds and how much in certificates?

12. Sang has invested $48,000, part at 6% and the rest in a higher risk investment at 10%. How much did she invest at each rate to receive $4000 in interest after one year?

13. An investor bought 500 shares of stock, some at $3.50 per share and some at $6.00 per share. If the total cost was $2187.50, how many shares of each stock did the investor buy?

14. Inez has 20 coins consisting of dimes and quarters. How many of each type does she have if all together she has $4.10?

15. A confectioner is going to mix candy worth $3.90 per pound with candy worth $2.50 per pound to obtain 70 pounds of candy worth $3.30 per pound. How many pounds of each kind should she use?

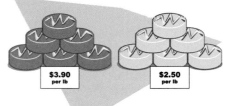

16. The postal service charges 33 cents for letters that weigh 1 ounce or less and 22 cents more for letters that weigh between 1 and 2 ounces. Jeffery, testing his father's math skills, gave his father $37.40 and asked him to purchase 80 stamps for his stamp collection, some 33-cent stamps and some 55-cent stamps. How many of each type stamp did he buy?

17. A grocer wants to mix two kinds of nuts. One kind sells for 70 cents per pound, and the other sells for $1.30 per pound. He wants to mix a total of 20 pounds and sell it for 82 cents per pound. How many pounds of each kind should he use in the new mix?

18. A manufacturing plant is going to use two different stamping machines to complete an order of 975 units. One produces 100 units per hour, while the other produces 75 units per hour. How long must each machine operate to complete the order if the faster machine needs to be shut down for two and one-half hours for repairs?

19. The bookstore can buy a popular book with either paper back or hard back cover. A hard back book costs $3.50 more than the paper back book. What is the cost of each if 90 paper back books cost the same as 55 hard back books?

20. In an election, the winner received 430 votes more than twice as many votes as the loser. If there was a total of 2290 votes cast, how many did each candidate receive?

21. A bill was defeated in the legislature by 50 votes. If one-fifth of those voting against the bill had voted for it, the bill would have passed by 30 votes. How many legislators voted for the bill?

22. Andrea made a trip of 440 kilometers. She averaged 54 kilometers per hour for the first part of the trip and 80 kilometers per hour for the second part. If the total trip took 6 hours, how long was she traveling at 80 kilometers per hour?

23. A boat left Dana Point Marina at 11:00 A.M. traveling at 10 knots (nautical miles per hour). Two hours later, a Coast Guard boat left the same marina traveling at 14 knots trying to catch the first boat. If both boats traveled the same course, at what time did the Coast Guard captain anticipate overtaking the other boat?

24. Two cars are to start at the same place in Knoxville and travel in opposite directions (assume in straight lines). The drivers know that one driver drives an average of 5 mph faster than the other. (They have been married for 20 years.) They have agreed to stop and call each other after driving for 3 hours. In the telephone conversation they realize that they are 355 miles apart. What was the average speed of each driver?

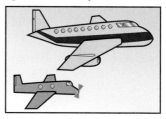

25. A private jet flies the same distance in 6 hours that a commercial jet flies in 2.5 hours. If the speed of the commercial jet was 75 mph less than three times the speed of the private jet, find the speed of each jet.

26. Determine a and b such that the line with equation $ax + by = 7$ passes through the two points $(2, 1)$ and $(-1, 10)$.

27. Determine a and b such that the line with equation $ax + by = 6$ passes through the points $(-6, -2)$ and $(3, 4)$.

28. Determine a and b such that the line with equation $ax + by = 4$ passes through the point $(5, 2)$ and has a slope of $\frac{2}{3}$.

29. Determine a and b such that the line with equation $ax + by = -4$ contains the point $(-1, -3)$ and has a slope of 5.

30. A manufacturer produces two models of the same toy, Model A and Model B. Model A takes 4 hours to produce and costs $8 each. Model B takes 3 hours to produce and costs $7 each. If the manufacturer allots a total of 5800 hours and $12,600 for production each week, how many of each model will be produced?

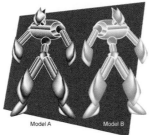

Model A   Model B

31. A company manufactures two products. One requires 2.5 hours of labor, 3 pounds of raw materials, and costs $42.40 each to produce. The second product requires 4 hours of labor, 4 pounds of raw materials, and costs $64 each to produce. Find the cost of labor per hour and the cost of raw materials per pound.

32. A furniture shop refinishes chairs. Employees use two methods to refinish a chair. Method I takes 1 hour, and the material costs $6. Method II takes an hour and a half, and the material costs $3. Next week, they plan to spend 144 hours in labor and $600 in material for refinishing chairs. How many chairs should they plan to refinish with each method?

33. A large feed lot uses two feed supplements, Ration I and Ration II. Each pound of Ration I contains 4 units of protein and 2 units of carbohydrates. Each pound of Ration II contains 3 units of protein and 6 units of carbohydrates. If the dietary requirement calls for 42 units of protein and 30 units of carbohydrates, how many pounds of each ration should be used to satisfy the requirements?

34. The sum of the measures of the three angles of a triangle is $180°$. In an isosceles triangle, two of the angles have the same measure. What are the measures of the angles of an isosceles triangle in which one angle measures $15°$ more than each of the other two equal angles?

35. The sum of the measures of the three angles of a triangle is $180°$. In an isosceles triangle, two of the angles have the same measure. What are the measures of the angles of an isosceles triangle in which each of the two equal angles measures $15°$ more than the third angle?

Hawkes Learning Systems: Intermediate Algebra

Applications (Systems of Equations)

3.3 Systems of Linear Equations (Three Variables)

Objectives

After completing this section, you will be able to :

1. *Solve systems of linear equations in three variables.*

2. *Solve applied problems by using systems of linear equations in three variables.*

The equation $2x + 3y - z = 16$ is called a **linear equation in three variables**. The general form is

$$Ax + By + Cz = D \text{ where } A, B, \text{ and } C \text{ are not all 0.}$$

The solutions to such equations are called **ordered triples** and are of the form (x_0, y_0, z_0) or $x = x_0$, $y = y_0$, and $z = z_0$. One ordered triple that satisfies the equation $2x + 3y - z = 16$ is $(1, 4, -2)$. To check this, substitute $x = 1$, $y = 4$, and $z = -2$ into the equation to see if the result is 16:

$$2(1) + 3(4) - (-2) = 2 + 12 + 2$$
$$= 16$$

There are an infinite number of ordered triples that satisfy any linear equation in three variables in which at least two of the coefficients are nonzero. Any two values may be substituted for two of the variables, and then the value for the third variable can be calculated. For example, by letting $x = -1$ and $y = 5$, we find:

$$2(-1) + 3(5) - z = 16$$
$$-2 + 15 - z = 16$$
$$-z = 3$$
$$z = -3$$

Hence, the ordered triple $(-1, 5, -3)$ satisfies the equation $2x + 3y - z = 16$.

Graphs can be drawn in three dimensions by using a coordinate system involving three mutually perpendicular number lines labeled as the x-axis, y-axis, and z-axis. Three planes are formed: the xy-plane, the xz-plane, and the yz-plane. The three axes separate space into eight regions called **octants**. You can "picture" the first octant as the region bounded by the floor of a room and two walls with the axes meeting in a corner. The floor is the xy-plane. The axes can be ordered in a "right-hand" or "left-hand" format. Figure 3.1 shows the point represented by the ordered triple $(2, 3, 1)$ in a right-hand system.

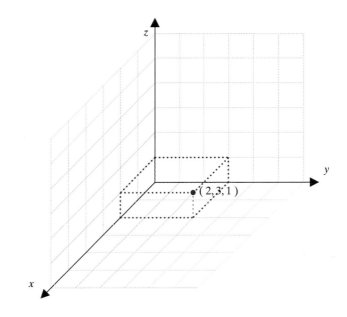

Figure 3.1

The graphs of linear equations in three variables are planes in three dimensions. A portion of the graph of $2x + 3y - z = 16$ appears in Figure 3.2.

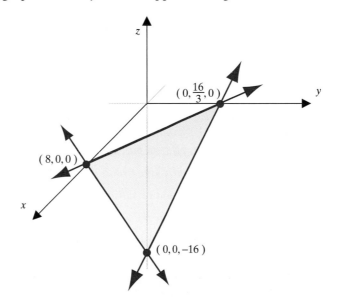

Figure 3.2

Two distinct planes will either be parallel or they will intersect. If they intersect, their intersection will be a straight line. If three distinct planes intersect, they will intersect in a straight line, or they will intersect in a single point represented by an ordered triple.

The graphs of systems of three linear equations in three variables can be both interesting and informative, but they can be difficult to sketch and points of intersection difficult to estimate. Also, most graphing calculators are limited to graphs in two dimensions, so they are not useful in graphically analyzing systems of linear equations in three variables.

Therefore, in this text, only algebraic techniques for solving these systems will be discussed. Figure 3.3 illustrates four different possibilities for the relative positions of three planes.

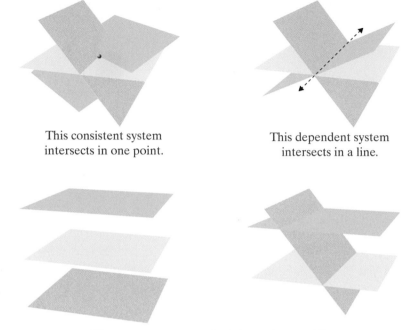

This consistent system
intersects in one point.

This dependent system
intersects in a line.

These two systems are both inconsistent. All
three planes do not have a common intersection.

Figure 3.3

To Solve Three Linear Equations in Three Variables

Step 1: *Select two equations and eliminate one variable by using the addition method.*

Step 2: *Select a different pair of equations and eliminate the **same** variable.*

Step 3: *Steps 1 and 2 give **two** linear equations in **two** variables. Solve these equations by either addition or substitution as discussed in Section 3.1.*

Step 4: *Back substitute the values found in Step 3 into any one of the original equations to find the value of the third variable.*

The solution possibilities for a system of three equations in three variables are as follows:

1. There will be exactly one ordered triple solution.
   (Graphically, the three planes intersect in one point.)
2. There will be an infinite number of solutions.
   (Graphically, the three planes intersect in a line or are the same plane.)
3. There will be no solutions.
   (Graphically, the three planes have no points in common.)

The technique is illustrated with the following system:

$$\begin{cases} 2x + 3y - z = 16 & \text{(I)} \\ x - y + 3z = -9 & \text{(II)} \\ 5x + 2y - z = 15 & \text{(III)} \end{cases}$$

Step 1: Using equations (I) and (II), eliminate y.

[**Note**: We could just as easily have chosen to eliminate x or z. To be sure that you understand the process you might want to solve the system by first eliminating x and then again by first eliminating z. In any case, the answer will be the same.]

$$\begin{cases} & 2x + 3y - z = 16 \\ [3] & x - y + 3z = -9 \end{cases} \qquad \begin{array}{r} 2x + 3y - z = 16 \\ 3x - 3y + 9z = -27 \\ \hline 5x + 8z = -11 \end{array}$$

Step 2: Using a different pair of equations, (II) and (III), eliminate the same variable y.

$$\begin{cases} [2] & x - y + 3z = -9 \\ & 5x + 2y - z = 15 \end{cases} \qquad \begin{array}{r} 2x - 2y + 6z = -18 \\ 5x + 2y - z = 15 \\ \hline 7x + 5z = -3 \end{array}$$

Step 3: Using the results of Steps 1 and 2, solve the two equations for x and z.

$$\begin{cases} [-7] & 5x + 8z = -11 \\ [5] & 7x + 5z = -3 \end{cases} \qquad \begin{array}{r} -35x - 56z = 77 \\ 35x + 25z = -15 \\ \hline -31z = 62 \\ z = -2 \end{array}$$

Back substitute $z = -2$ into the equation $5x + 8z = -11$ to find x.

$$5x + 8(-2) = -11$$
$$5x = 5$$
$$x = 1$$

Step 4: Using $x = 1$ and $z = -2$, back substitute to find y.

$$\begin{array}{ll} 1 - y + 3(-2) = -9 & \text{Using equation (II)} \\ -y = -4 \\ y = 4 \end{array}$$

The solution is $(1, 4, -2)$ or $x = 1$, $y = 4$, and $z = -2$. The solution can be checked by substituting the results into **all three** of the original equations.

$$\begin{cases} 2(1)+3(4)-(-2)=16 & \text{(I)} \\ 1-(4)+3(-2)=-9 & \text{(II)} \\ 5(1)+2(4)-(-2)=15 & \text{(III)} \end{cases}$$

Example 1: Three Variables (Consistent System) ● ● ● ● ● ● ● ● ● ● ● ● ● ●

Solve the following systems of linear equations:

$$\begin{cases} x-y+2z=-4 & \text{(I)} \\ 2x+3y+z=\dfrac{1}{2} & \text{(II)} \\ x+4y-2z=4 & \text{(III)} \end{cases}$$

Solution   Using equations (I) and (III), eliminate z.

$$\begin{array}{rcrcrcr} x & - & y & + & 2z & = & -4 \\ x & + & 4y & - & 2z & = & 4 \\ \hline 2x & + & 3y & & & = & 0 \end{array}$$

Using equations (I) and (II), eliminate z.

$$\begin{cases} \;\; x & - & y & + & 2z & = & -4 \\ [-2]\;\; 2x & + & 3y & + & z & = & \dfrac{1}{2} \end{cases} \qquad \begin{array}{rcrcrcr} x & - & y & + & 2z & = & -4 \\ -4x & - & 6y & - & 2z & = & -1 \\ \hline -3x & - & 7y & & & = & -5 \end{array}$$

Eliminate the variable x using the two equations in x and y.

$$\begin{cases} [3]\;\; 2x & + & 3y & = & 0 \\ [2]\; -3x & - & 7y & = & -5 \end{cases} \qquad \begin{array}{rcrcr} 6x & + & 9y & = & 0 \\ -6x & - & 14y & = & -10 \\ \hline & & -5y & = & -10 \\ & & y & = & 2 \end{array}$$

Back substituting to find x yields:

$$\begin{aligned} 2x + 3(2) &= 0 \\ 2x &= -6 \\ x &= -3 \end{aligned}$$

Finally, using $x = -3$ and $y = 2$, back substitute into (I).

$$\begin{aligned} -3-2+2z &= -4 \\ 2z &= 1 \\ z &= \frac{1}{2} \end{aligned}$$

The solution is $\left(-3, 2, \dfrac{1}{2}\right)$.

The solution can be checked by substituting $\left(-3, 2, \dfrac{1}{2}\right)$ into **all three** of the original equations.

$$\begin{cases} -3 - 2 + 2\left(\dfrac{1}{2}\right) = -4 & \text{(I)} \\[2mm] 2(-3) + 3(2) + \dfrac{1}{2} = \dfrac{1}{2} & \text{(II)} \\[2mm] -3 + 4(2) - 2\left(\dfrac{1}{2}\right) = 4 & \text{(III)} \end{cases}$$

● ●

Example 2: Three Variables (Inconsistent System) ● ● ● ● ● ● ● ● ● ● ● ●

Solve the following systems of linear equations:

$$\begin{cases} 3x - 5y + z = 6 & \text{(I)} \\ x - y + 3z = -1 & \text{(II)} \\ 2x - 2y + 6z = 5 & \text{(III)} \end{cases}$$

Solution: Using equations (I) and (II), eliminate z.

$$\begin{cases} [-3] \quad 3x - 5y + z = 6 \\ \qquad\quad x - y + 3z = -1 \end{cases} \qquad \begin{array}{rcl} -9x + 15y - 3z &=& -18 \\ x - y + 3z &=& -1 \\ \hline -8x + 14y &=& -19 \end{array}$$

Using equations (II) and (III), eliminate z.

$$\begin{cases} [-2] \quad x - y + 3z = -1 \\ \qquad\quad 2x - 2y + 6z = 5 \end{cases} \qquad \begin{array}{rcl} -2x + 2y - 6z &=& 2 \\ 2x - 2y + 6z &=& 5 \\ \hline 0 &=& 7 \end{array}$$

This last equation is false, and the system **does not have a solution**.

● ●

Example 3: Three Variables (Application) ●

A cash register contains $341 in $20, $5, and $2 bills. There are twenty-eight bills in all and three more twos than fives. How many bills of each kind are there?

Solution: Let x = number of $20 bills

y = number of $5 bills

z = number of $2 bills

$$\begin{cases} x + y + z = 28 \\ 20x + 5y + 2z = 341 \\ z = y + 3 \end{cases}$$

(I)   There are twenty-eight bills.

(II) The total value is $341.

(III) There are three more twos than fives.

Using equations (I) and (II), eliminate x.

$$\begin{cases} [-20] & x & + & y & + & z & = & 28 \\ & 20x & + & 5y & + & 2z & = & 341 \end{cases}$$

$$\begin{array}{rrrrrrr} -20x & - & 20y & - & 20z & = & -560 \\ 20x & + & 5y & + & 2z & = & 341 \\ \hline & - & 15y & - & 18z & = & -219 \end{array}$$

We rewrite equation (III) in the form $y - z = -3$ and use this equation along with the results just found:

$$\begin{cases} [15] & y & - & z & = & -3 \\ & -15y & - & 18z & = & -219 \end{cases}$$

$$\begin{array}{rrrrr} 15y & - & 15z & = & -45 \\ -15y & - & 18z & = & -219 \\ \hline & - & 33z & = & -264 \\ & & z & = & 8 \end{array}$$

Back substituting to solve for y gives:

$$y - 8 = -3$$
$$y = 5.$$

Now we can use the values $z = 8$ and $y = 5$ to substitute into equation (I).

$$x + 5 + 8 = 28$$
$$x = 15$$

There are fifteen $20 bills, five $5 bills, and eight $2 bills.

● ●

Practice Problems

Solve the following system of linear equations:

$$\begin{cases} 2x + y + z = 4 \\ x + 2y + z = 1 \\ 3x + y - z = -3 \end{cases}$$

3.3 Exercises

Solve each of the systems of equations in Exercises 1 – 20. State which systems have no solution or an infinite number of solutions.

1. $\begin{cases} x + y - z = 0 \\ 3x + 2y + z = 4 \\ x - 3y + 4z = 5 \end{cases}$

2. $\begin{cases} x - y + 2z = 3 \\ -6x + y + 3z = 7 \\ x + 2y - 5z = -4 \end{cases}$

3. $\begin{cases} 2x - y - z = 1 \\ 2x - 3y - 4z = 0 \\ x + y - z = 4 \end{cases}$

4. $\begin{cases} y + z = 6 \\ x + 5y - 4z = 4 \\ x - 3y + 5z = 7 \end{cases}$

5. $\begin{cases} x + y - 2z = 4 \\ 2x + y = 1 \\ 5x + 3y - 2z = 6 \end{cases}$

6. $\begin{cases} 2y + z = -4 \\ 3x + 4z = 11 \\ x + y = -2 \end{cases}$

7. $\begin{cases} x - y + 5z = -6 \\ x + 2z = 0 \\ 6x + y + 3z = 0 \end{cases}$

8. $\begin{cases} x - y + 2z = -3 \\ 2x + y - z = 5 \\ 3x - 2y + 2z = -3 \end{cases}$

9. $\begin{cases} y + z = 2 \\ x + z = 5 \\ x + y = 5 \end{cases}$

10. $\begin{cases} x - y - 2z = 3 \\ x + 2y + z = 1 \\ 3y + 3z = -2 \end{cases}$

11. $\begin{cases} 2x - y + 5z = -2 \\ x + 3y - z = 6 \\ 4x + y + 3z = -2 \end{cases}$

12. $\begin{cases} 2x - y + 5z = 5 \\ x - 2y + 3z = 0 \\ x + y + 4z = 7 \end{cases}$

13. $\begin{cases} 3x + y + 4z = -6 \\ 2x + 3y - z = 2 \\ 5x + 4y + 3z = 2 \end{cases}$

14. $\begin{cases} 2x + y - z = -3 \\ -x + 2y + z = 5 \\ 2x + 3y - 2z = -3 \end{cases}$

15. $\begin{cases} x - 2y + z = 4 \\ x - y - 4z = 1 \\ 2x - 4y + 2z = 8 \end{cases}$

16. $\begin{cases} 2x - 2y + 3z = 4 \\ x - 3y + 2z = 2 \\ x + y + z = 1 \end{cases}$

17. $\begin{cases} 2x - 3y + z = -1 \\ 6x - 9y - 4z = 4 \\ 4x + 6y - z = 5 \end{cases}$

18. $\begin{cases} x + y + z = 3 \\ 2x - y - 2z = -3 \\ 3x + 2y + z = 4 \end{cases}$

19. $\begin{cases} 2x + 3y + z = 4 \\ 3x - 5y + 2z = -5 \\ 4x - 6y + 3z = -7 \end{cases}$

20. $\begin{cases} x + 6y + z = 6 \\ 2x + 3y - 2z = 8 \\ 2x + 4z = 3 \end{cases}$

Answers to Practice Problems: $x = 1, y = -2, z = 4$

21. The sum of three integers is 67. The sum of the first and second integers exceeds the third by 13. The third integer is 7 less than the first. Find the three integers.

22. The sum of three integers is 189. The first integer is 28 less than the second. The second integer is 21 less than the sum of the first and third integers. Find the three integers.

23. Sally is trying to get her brother Robert to learn to think algebraically. She tells him that she has 23 coins in her purse, including nickels, dimes, and quarters. She has two more dimes than quarters, and the total value of the coins is $2.50. How many of each kind of coin does she have?

24. A wallet contains $218 in $10, $5, and $1 bills. There are forty-six bills in all and four more fives than tens. How many bills of each kind are there?

25. Find values for *a*, *b*, and *c* so that the points (−1, −4), (2, 8), and (−2, −4) lie on the graph of the function $y = ax^2 + bx + c$.

26. Find values for *a*, *b*, and *c* so that the points (1, 1), (−3, 13), and (0, −2) lie on the graph of the function $y = ax^2 + bx + c$.

27. The perimeter of a triangle is 73 cm. The longest side is 13 cm less than the sum of the other two sides. The short-est side is 11 cm less than the longest side. Find the lengths of the three sides.

28. At Tony's Fruit Stand, 4 pounds of bananas, 2 pounds of apples, and 3 pounds of grapes cost $16.40. Five pounds of bananas, 4 pounds of apples, and 2 pounds of grapes cost $16.60. Two pounds of bananas, 3 pounds of apples, and 1 pound of grapes cost $9.60. Find the price per pound of each kind of fruit.

29. The Marshalls are having a house built. The cost of building the house is $24,000 more than three times the cost of the lot. The cost of the landscaping, sidewalks, and upgrades is one-half the cost of the lot. If the total cost is $123,000, what is the cost of each part of the construction (the home, the lot, and the improvements)?

30. At the Happy Burger Drive-In, you can buy 2 hamburgers, 1 chocolate shake, and 2 orders of fries, or 3 hamburgers and 1 order of fries, for $9.50. One hamburger, 2 chocolate shakes, and 1 order of fries cost $7.30. How much does a hamburger cost?

31. Kirk inherited $100,000 dollars from his aunt and decided to invest in three different accounts: savings, bonds, and stocks. His bond account was $10,000 more than three times the stock account. At the end of the first year, the savings returned 5%, the bonds 8%, and the stocks 10% for total interest of $7400. How much did he invest in each account?

32. Melissa has saved a total of $30,000 and wants to invest in three different stocks: Pepsico, IBM, and Microsoft. She wants the Pepsico amount to be $1000 less than twice the IBM amount and the Microsoft amount to be $2000 more than the total in the other two stocks. How much should she invest in each stock?

33. The sum of the measures of the three angles of a triangle is 180°. In one particular triangle, the largest angle is 10° more than three times the smallest angle, and the third angle is one-half the largest angle. What are the measures of the three angles?

34. The local theater has three types of seats for Broadway plays: main floor, balcony, and mezzanine. Main floor tickets are $60, balcony tickets are $45, mezzanine tickets are $30. On one particular night the sales totaled $29,400. Main floor sales were 20 more than the total of balcony and mezzanine sales. Balcony sales were 40 more than two times mezzanine sales. How many of each type of ticket were sold?

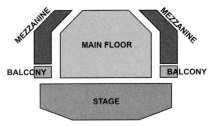

35. A chemist wants to mix 9 liters of a 25% acid solution. Because of limited amounts on hand, the mixture is to come from three different solutions, one with 10% acid, another with 30% acid, and a third with 40% acid. The amount of the 10% solution must be twice the amount of the 40% solution, and the amount of the 30% solution must equal the total amount of the other two solutions. How much of each solution must be used?

Writing and Thinking About Mathematics

36. Is it possible for three linear equations in three unknowns to have exactly two solutions? Explain your reasoning in some detail.

37. In geometry, we know that three non-collinear points determine a plane. (That is, if three points are not on a line, then there is a unique plane that contains all three points.) Find the values of A, B, and C (and therefore the equation of the plane) given $Ax + By + Cz = 3$ and the three points on the plane (0, 3, 2), (0, 0, 1) and (−3, 0, 3). Sketch the plane in three dimensions as best you can by locating the three given points.

continued on next page ...

38. As stated in Exercise 37, three non-collinear points determine a plane. Find the values of A, B, and C (and therefore the equation of the plane) given $Ax + By + Cz = 10$ and the three points on the plane (2, 0, –2), (3, –1, 0) and (–1, 5, –4). Sketch the plane in three dimensions as best you can by locating the three given points.

Hawkes Learning Systems: Intermediate Algebra

Solving Systems of Linear Equations with Three Variables

3.4   Matrices and Gaussian Elimination

Objectives

After completing this section, you will be able to:

1. *Transform a matrix into triangular form by using elementary row operations.*

2. *Solve systems of linear equations by using the Gaussian elimination method.*

Matrices

A rectangular array of numbers is called a **matrix** (plural **matrices**). Matrices are usually named with capital letters, and each number in the matrix is called an **entry**. Entries written horizontally are said to form a **row**, and entries written vertically are said to form a **column**. The matrix A shown below has two rows and three columns and is a **2 × 3 matrix** (read "two by three matrix"). We say that the **dimension** of the matrix is two by three (or 2×3). Similarly, if a matrix has three rows and three columns then its dimension is 3×3.

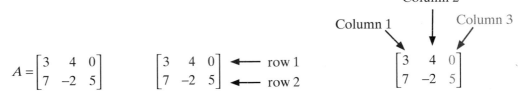

Three more examples are:

$$B = \begin{bmatrix} 5 & -1 \\ 2 & 3 \end{bmatrix} \qquad C = \begin{bmatrix} 5 & -1 & 0 & 7 \\ 2 & 3 & 2 & 8 \\ 1 & -3 & 0 & 6 \end{bmatrix} \qquad D = \begin{bmatrix} 0 & 4 \\ 1 & 6 \\ -1 & 3 \end{bmatrix}$$

2×2 matrix 3×4 matrix 3×2 matrix

A matrix with the same number of rows as columns is called a **square matrix**. Matrix B (shown above) is a square 2×2 matrix.

Elementary Row Operations

Matrices have many uses and are generated from various types of problems because they allow data to be presented in a systematic and orderly manner. (Business majors may want to look up a topic called Markov chains.)

Also, matrices can sometimes be added, subtracted, and multiplied. Some square matrices have inverses, much the same as multiplicative inverses for real numbers. Matrix methods of solving systems of linear equations can be done manually or with graphing calculators and computers. These topics are presented in courses such as finite mathematics and linear algebra.

In this text we will see that matrices can be used to solve systems of linear equations in which the equations are written in standard form. The two matrices derived from such a system are the **coefficient matrix** (made up of the coefficients of the variables) and the **augmented matrix** (including the coefficients and the constant terms). For example,

System	**Coefficient Matrix**	**Augmented Matrix**

$$\begin{cases} x - y + z = -6 \\ 2x + 3y \quad\; = 17 \\ x + 2y + 2z = 7 \end{cases} \qquad \begin{bmatrix} 1 & -1 & 1 \\ 2 & 3 & 0 \\ 1 & 2 & 2 \end{bmatrix} \qquad \left[\begin{array}{ccc|c} 1 & -1 & 1 & -6 \\ 2 & 3 & 0 & 17 \\ 1 & 2 & 2 & 7 \end{array} \right]$$

Note that 0 is the entry in the second row, third column of both matrices. This 0 corresponds to the missing z-variable in the second equation. The second equation could have been written $2x + 3y + 0z = 17$.

In Sections 3.1 and 3.3, systems of linear equations were solved by the addition method and back substitution. In solving these systems, we can make any of the following three manipulations **without changing the solution set of the system**.

The system $\begin{cases} x - y + z = -6 \\ 2x + 3y + 0z = 17 \\ x + 2y + 2z = 7 \end{cases}$ is used here to illustrate some possibilities.

1. Any two equations may be interchanged.

$$\begin{cases} 2x + 3y + 0z = 17 \\ x - y + z = -6 \\ x + 2y + 2z = 7 \end{cases}$$ Here we have interchanged the first two equations.

2. All terms of any equation may be multiplied by a constant.

$$\begin{cases} -2x + 2y - 2z = 12 \\ 2x + 3y + 0z = 17 \\ x + 2y + 2z = 7 \end{cases}$$ Here we have multiplied each term of the first equation by –2.

3. All terms of any equation may be multiplied by a constant and these new terms may be added to like terms of another equation. (The original equation remains unchanged.)

$$\begin{cases} x - y + z = -6 \\ 2x + 3y + 0z = 17 \\ 0x + 3y + z = 13 \end{cases}$$

Here we have multiplied the first equation by -1 (mentally) and added the results to the third equation.

When dealing with matrices, the three corresponding operations are called **elementary row operations**. These operations are listed below and illustrated in Example 1. Follow the steps outlined in Example 1 carefully, and note how the row operations are indicated, such as $\frac{1}{2}R3$ to indicate that all numbers in row 3 are multiplied by $\frac{1}{2}$. (Reasons for using these row operations are discussed under **Gaussian Elimination** on page 211.)

Elementary Row Operations

1. Interchange two rows.

2. Multiply a row by a nonzero constant.

3. Add a multiple of a row to another row.

*If any elementary row operation is applied to a matrix, the new matrix is said to be **row-equivalent** to the original matrix.*

Example 1: Coefficient and Augmented Matrices

a. For the system $\begin{cases} y + z = 6 \\ x + 5y - 4z = 4 \\ 2x - 6y + 10z = 14 \end{cases}$

write the corresponding coefficient matrix and the corresponding augmented matrix.

Solution: Coefficient Matrix

$$\begin{bmatrix} 0 & 1 & 1 \\ 1 & 5 & -4 \\ 2 & -6 & 10 \end{bmatrix}$$

Augmented Matrix

$$\begin{bmatrix} 0 & 1 & 1 & | & 6 \\ 1 & 5 & -4 & | & 4 \\ 2 & -6 & 10 & | & 14 \end{bmatrix}$$

continued on next page ...

b. In the augmented matrix, interchange rows 1 and 2 and multiply row 3 by $\frac{1}{2}$.

Solution:

$$\begin{array}{l} R2 \rightarrow \\ R1 \rightarrow \\ \frac{1}{2}R3 \rightarrow \end{array} \left[\begin{array}{ccc|c} 1 & 5 & -4 & 4 \\ 0 & 1 & 1 & 6 \\ 1 & -3 & 5 & 7 \end{array}\right]$$

c. For the system $\begin{cases} x - y = 5 \\ 3x + 4y = 29 \end{cases}$

write the corresponding coefficient matrix and the corresponding augmented matrix.

Solution: Coefficient Matrix   Augmented Matrix

$$\begin{bmatrix} 1 & -1 \\ 3 & 4 \end{bmatrix} \qquad\qquad \left[\begin{array}{cc|c} 1 & -1 & 5 \\ 3 & 4 & 29 \end{array}\right]$$

d. In the augmented matrix in Example 1c, add −3 times row 1 to row 2.

Solution: $R2 - 3 \cdot R1 \rightarrow \left[\begin{array}{cc|c} 1 & -1 & 5 \\ 0 & 7 & 14 \end{array}\right]$ Mentally $\left[\begin{array}{cc|c} 1 & -1 & 5 \\ 3-3(1) & 4-3(-1) & 29-3(5) \end{array}\right]$

Note that row 1 is left unchanged.

• •

General Notation for a Matrix and a System of Equations

Notation with a small number to the right and below a variable is called **subscript** notation. For example, a_1 is read "a sub one" and b_3 is read "b sub three."

$a_1 \longleftarrow$ subscript $b_1 \longleftarrow$ subscript

variable   variable

With matrices we use capital letters to name a matrix and **double subscript** notation with corresponding lower case letters to indicate both the row and column location of an entry. For example in a matrix A the entries will be designated as shown on the following page.

a_{11} is read "*a* sub one one" and indicates the entry in the first row and first column;
a_{12} is read "*a* sub one two" and indicates the entry in the first row and second column;
a_{13} is read "*a* sub one three" and indicates the entry in the first row and third column;
a_{21} is read "*a* sub two one" and indicates the entry in the second row and first column;
and so on.

NOTES

We will see in dealing with polynomials later that a_{11} can be read simply as "*a* sub eleven". However, with matrices, we need to indicate the row and column corresponding to the entry. If there are more than nine rows or columns, then commas are used to separate the numbers as $a_{10,10}$. You will see the commas in use on your calculator.

With double subscript notation we can write the general form of a 2×3 matrix A and a 3×3 matrix B as follows:

$$A = \begin{bmatrix} a_{11} & a_{12} & a_{13} \\ a_{21} & a_{22} & a_{23} \end{bmatrix} \qquad B = \begin{bmatrix} b_{11} & b_{12} & b_{13} \\ b_{21} & b_{22} & b_{23} \\ b_{31} & b_{32} & b_{33} \end{bmatrix}$$

We will use this notation when discussing the use of calculators to define matrices and to operate with matrices. The general form of a system of three linear equations might use this notation in the following way:

$$\begin{cases} a_{11}x + a_{12}y + a_{13}z = k_1 \\ a_{21}x + a_{22}y + a_{23}z = k_2 \\ a_{31}x + a_{32}y + a_{33}z = k_3 \end{cases}$$

A matrix is in **upper triangular form** (or just **triangular form** for our purposes) if its entries in the lower left triangular region are all 0's. The entries with the same numbers in the double subscript such as b_{11}, b_{22}, and b_{33} are said to form the **main diagonal** of a matrix. Thus, if all the entries below the main diagonal of a matrix are all 0's, the matrix is in triangular form as shown below:

$$B = \begin{bmatrix} b_{11} & b_{12} & b_{13} \\ 0 & b_{22} & b_{23} \\ 0 & 0 & b_{33} \end{bmatrix}$$

The upper triangular form of a matrix is also called the **row echelon form** (or **ref form**), and we will see that a graphing calculator can be used to change a matrix into the ref form.

Gaussian Elimination

Another method of solving a system of linear equations is the **Gaussian elimination** method (named after the famous German mathematician Carl Friedrich Gauss, 1777 – 1855). This method makes use of augmented matrices and elementary row operations. The objective is to transform an augmented matrix into triangular form (or ref form) and then use back substitution to find the values of the variables. The method is outlined as follows:

Strategy for Gaussian Elimination

1. *Write the augmented matrix for the system.*

2. *Use elementary row operations to transform the matrix into triangular form.*

3. *Solve the corresponding system of equations by using back substitution.*

The following examples illustrate the method. Study the steps and the corresponding comments carefully.

Example 2: Gaussian Elimination ●

a. Solve the following system of linear equations by using the Gaussian elimination method with back substitution.

$$\begin{cases} 2x + 4y = -6 \\ 5x - y = 7 \end{cases}$$

Solution:

Step 1: Write the augmented matrix.
[The following steps show how to use elementary row operations to get the matrix in triangular form (or ref form) with 0 in the lower left corner.]

$$\begin{bmatrix} 2 & 4 & | & -6 \\ 5 & -1 & | & 7 \end{bmatrix}$$

Step 2: Multiply row 1 by $\dfrac{1}{2}$ so that the entry in the upper left corner will be 1. This will help to get 0 below the 1 in the next step.

$$\begin{bmatrix} 2 & 4 & | & -6 \\ 5 & -1 & | & 7 \end{bmatrix} \qquad \tfrac{1}{2}R1 \rightarrow \begin{bmatrix} 1 & 2 & | & -3 \\ 5 & -1 & | & 7 \end{bmatrix}$$

Step 3: To get 0 in the lower left corner, add −5 times row 1 to row 2.

$$\begin{bmatrix} 1 & 2 & | & -3 \\ 5 & -1 & | & 7 \end{bmatrix} \qquad R2 - 5 \cdot R1 \rightarrow \begin{bmatrix} 1 & 2 & | & -3 \\ 0 & -11 & | & 22 \end{bmatrix}$$

Step 4: The triangular matrix in Step 3 represents the following system of linear equations.

$$\begin{cases} x + 2y = -3 \\ 0x - 11y = 22 \end{cases}$$

Solving the last equation for y gives:

$$-11y = 22$$
$$y = -2$$

Back substitute to find the value for x.

$$x + 2(-2) = -3$$
$$x - 4 = -3$$
$$x = 1$$

Thus, the solution is $x = 1$ and $y = -2$. Or we can write $(1, -2)$

b. Solve the following system of linear equations by using the Gaussian elimination method with back substitution.

$$\begin{cases} 2x - 3y - z = -4 \\ -x + 2y + z = 6 \\ x - y + 2z = 14 \end{cases}$$

Solution:

Step 1: Write the augmented matrix.

$$\begin{bmatrix} 2 & -3 & -1 & | & -4 \\ -1 & 2 & 1 & | & 6 \\ 1 & -1 & 2 & | & 14 \end{bmatrix}$$

continued on next page ...

Step 2:   Exchange row 1 and row 3 so that the entry in the upper left corner will be 1.

$$\begin{bmatrix} 1 & -1 & 2 & \vdots & 14 \\ -1 & 2 & 1 & \vdots & 6 \\ 2 & -3 & -1 & \vdots & -4 \end{bmatrix}$$

Step 3:   To get the 0's under the 1 in Column 1, add row 1 to row 2 and add -2 times row 1 to row 3.

$$\begin{matrix} \\ R2 + R1 \rightarrow \\ R3 - 2 \cdot R1 \rightarrow \end{matrix} \begin{bmatrix} 1 & -1 & 2 & \vdots & 14 \\ 0 & 1 & 3 & \vdots & 20 \\ 0 & -1 & -5 & \vdots & -32 \end{bmatrix}$$

Step 4:   Add row 2 to row 3 to arrive at the triangular form.

$$\begin{matrix} \\ \\ R3 + R2 \rightarrow \end{matrix} \begin{bmatrix} 1 & -1 & 2 & \vdots & 14 \\ 0 & 1 & 3 & \vdots & 20 \\ 0 & 0 & -2 & \vdots & -12 \end{bmatrix}$$

Step 5:   The triangle matrix in Step 4 represents the following system of linear equations:

$$\begin{cases} x - y + 2z = 14 \\ \quad\ y + 3z = 20 \\ \qquad\quad -2z = -12 \end{cases}$$

Solving the last equation for z gives:

$$-2z = -12$$
$$z = 6$$

Back substitution into the equation $y + 3z = 20$ gives:

$$y + 3(6) = 20$$
$$y = 2$$

Back substitution into the equation $x - y + 2z = 14$ gives:

$$x - 2 + 2(6) = 14$$
$$x = 4$$

Thus, the solution is $x = 4$, $y = 2$, and $z = 6$. Or, we can write the solution in the form of an ordered triple as $(4, 2, 6)$.

If the final matrix, in triangular form, has a row with all entries 0, then the system has an infinite number of solutions.

For example, solving the system $\begin{cases} x + 3y = 8 \\ 2x + 6y = 16 \end{cases}$ will result in the matrix $\begin{bmatrix} 1 & 3 & | & 8 \\ 0 & 0 & | & 0 \end{bmatrix}$.

The last line indicates that $0x + 0y = 0$ which is always true. Therefore, the solution to the system is the set of all solutions of the equation $x + 3y = 8$. The system is **dependent.**

If the triangular form of the augmented matrix shows the coefficient entries in one or more rows to be all 0's and the constant not 0, then the system has no solution.

For example, the last row of the augmented matrix $\begin{bmatrix} 1 & 2 & 2 & | & 7 \\ 0 & 1 & 3 & | & 6 \\ 0 & 0 & 0 & | & 15 \end{bmatrix}$ indicates that $0 = 15$.

Since this is not true, the system has no solution. That is, the system is **inconsistent.**

Using the TI-83 Plus Calculator to Solve a System of Linear Equations

The TI-83 Plus calculator can be used to define and operate with matrices. The Gaussian elimination technique can be employed by the calculator by entering the coefficients and constants of a system of linear equations as an augmented matrix and then having the calculator reduce the matrix to ref form.

Pressing the matrix key (spelled MATRX on the keyboard) (found by pressing 2nd x^{-1}) will give the menu shown here:

Pressing the right arrow and moving to **MATH** will give the following choices:

Pressing the right arrow again and moving to **EDIT** will give the following choices:

Example 3 shows how to use the calculator to solve a system of three linear equations in three variables. Study each step carefully.

Example 3: System of Equations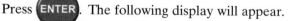

Use a TI-83 Plus calculator to solve the following system of linear equations.

$$\begin{cases} x + 2y + z = 1 \\ -x + y + z = -6 \\ 4x - y + 3z = -1 \end{cases}$$

Solution:

Step 1: Press the MATRX key and move to the **EDIT** menu.

Press ENTER. The following display will appear.

Step 2: The augmented matrix is a 3 × 4 matrix. So, in the top line enter 3, press ENTER, enter 4, press ENTER and the display will appear as follows:

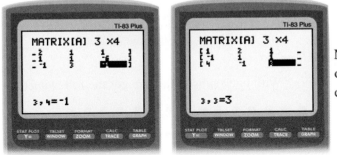

(**Note**: If other numbers are already present on the display, just type over them. The calculator will adjust automatically.)

Step 3: Move the cursor to the upper left entry position and enter the coefficients and constants in the matrix. As you enter each number press ENTER and the cursor will automatically move to the next position in the matrix. Note that the double subscripts appear at the bottom of the display as each number is entered. The final display for matrix [A] should appear as follows:

Note: The display only shows three columns at a time.

Step 4: Press 2nd QUIT; press MATRX again; go to **MATH**; move the cursor down to **A: ref (**; press ENTER. The display will appear as follows:

continued on next page ...

Step 5: Press MATRX again; press ENTER ; enter a right parenthesis) ; press the MATH key on the keyboard; choose `1:>Frac` by pressing ENTER . The display will appear as follows:

Step 6: Press ENTER and the ref form of matrix will appear as follows:

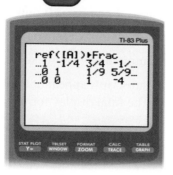

With back substitution we get the following solution: $x = 3, y = 1, z = -4$.

Practice Problems

Solve the following system of linear equations by using the Gaussian elimination method with back substitution.

$$\begin{cases} x - 2y + 3z = 4 \\ 2x + y = 0 \\ 3x + y - z = -4 \end{cases}$$

3.4 Exercises

In Exercises 1 – 6, form the coefficient matrix and the augmented matrix for the given systems of linear equations.

1. $\begin{cases} 2x+2y=13 \\ 5x-y=10 \end{cases}$

2. $\begin{cases} x+4y=-1 \\ 2x-3y=7 \end{cases}$

3. $\begin{cases} 7x-2y+7z=2 \\ -5x+3y=2 \\ 4y+11z=8 \end{cases}$

4. $\begin{cases} -8x+2y-z=6 \\ 2x+3z=-3 \\ -4x-2y+5z=13 \end{cases}$

5. $\begin{cases} 3x+y-z+2w=6 \\ x-y+2z-w=-8 \\ 2y+5z+w=2 \\ x+3y+3w=14 \end{cases}$

6. $\begin{cases} 4x+y+3z-2w=13 \\ x-2y+z-4w=-3 \\ x+y+4z+2w=12 \\ -2x+3y-z-3w=5 \end{cases}$

In Exercises 7 – 10, write the system of linear equations represented by each of the augmented matrices. Use x, y, and z as the variables.

7. $\begin{bmatrix} -3 & 5 & | & 1 \\ -1 & 3 & | & 2 \end{bmatrix}$

8. $\begin{bmatrix} 3 & -1 & | & 5 \\ -2 & 10 & | & 9 \end{bmatrix}$

9. $\begin{bmatrix} 1 & 3 & 4 & | & 1 \\ 2 & -3 & -2 & | & 0 \\ 1 & 1 & 0 & | & -4 \end{bmatrix}$

10. $\begin{bmatrix} 2 & -9 & 14 & | & 0 \\ -3 & 0 & -8 & | & 5 \\ 2 & -6 & 1 & | & 3 \end{bmatrix}$

In Exercises 11 – 26, use the Gaussian elimination method with back substitution to solve the given system of linear equations.

11. $\begin{cases} x+2y=3 \\ 2x-y=-4 \end{cases}$

12. $\begin{cases} 4x+3y=5 \\ -x-2y=0 \end{cases}$

13. $\begin{cases} -8x+2y=6 \\ x-2y=1 \end{cases}$

14. $\begin{cases} 2x+y=-2 \\ 4x+3y=-2 \end{cases}$

15. $\begin{cases} x-3y+2z=11 \\ -2x+4y+z=-3 \\ x-2y+3z=12 \end{cases}$

16. $\begin{cases} x+2y-z=6 \\ 3x-y+2z=9 \\ x+y+z=6 \end{cases}$

17. $\begin{cases} x+2y+3z=4 \\ x-y-z=0 \\ 4x-3y+z=5 \end{cases}$

18. $\begin{cases} x+y-2z=-1 \\ 3x+4y-2z=0 \\ x-y+z=4 \end{cases}$

19. $\begin{cases} x-y-2z=3 \\ x+2y-z=5 \\ 2x-3y-2z=3 \end{cases}$

20. $\begin{cases} x-y+5z=-6 \\ x+2z=0 \\ 6x+y+3z=0 \end{cases}$

21. $\begin{cases} x-3y-z=-4 \\ 3x-2y+z=1 \\ -2x+y+2z=13 \end{cases}$

22. $\begin{cases} 2x-y-5z=-9 \\ x-3y+2z=0 \\ 3x+2y+10z=4 \end{cases}$

Answers to Practice Problems: $x=-1, y=2, z=3$

23. $\begin{cases} x - 2y + 3z = 0 \\ x + y + 4z = 7 \\ 2x - y + 5z = 5 \end{cases}$ **24.** $\begin{cases} 2x - y + 5z = -2 \\ 4x + y + 3z = -2 \\ x + 3y - z = 6 \end{cases}$ **25.** $\begin{cases} 3x + 4z = 11 \\ x + y = -2 \\ 2y + z = -4 \end{cases}$

26. $\begin{cases} y + z = 2 \\ x + y = 5 \\ x + z = 5 \end{cases}$

For Exercises 27 – 30, set up a system of linear equations that represents the information and solve the system using Gaussian elimination.

27. The sum of three integers is 169. The first integer is twelve more than the second integer. The third integer is fifteen less than the sum of the first and second integers. What are the integers?

28. Julie bought a pound of bacon, a dozen eggs, and a loaf of bread. The total cost was $8.52. The eggs cost $0.94 more than the bacon. The combined cost of the bread and eggs was $2.34 more than the cost of the bacon. Find the cost of each item.

29. A pizzeria sells three sizes of pizzas: small, medium, and large. The pizzas sell for $6.00, $8.00, and $9.50, respectively. One evening they sold 68 pizzas for a total of $528.00. If they sold twice as many medium sized pizzas as large-sized pizzas, how many of each size did they sell?

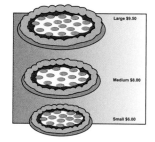

30. An investment firm is responsible for investing $250,000 from an estate according to three conditions in the will of the deceased. The money is to be invested in three accounts paying 6%, 8%, and 11% interest. The amount invested in the 6% account is to be $5000 more than the total invested in the other two accounts, and the total annual interest for the first year is to be $19,250. How much is the firm supposed to invest in each account?

Use your graphing calculator to solve the systems of linear equations in Exercises 31 – 38.

31. $\begin{cases} x + y = -4 \\ 2x + 3y = -12 \end{cases}$ **32.** $\begin{cases} 2x + 3y = 1 \\ x - 5y = -19 \end{cases}$

33. $\begin{cases} x + y + z = 10 \\ 2x - y + z = 10 \\ -x + 2y + 2z = 14 \end{cases}$

34. $\begin{cases} 2x + y + 2z = -1 \\ x - y + 4z = -3 \\ 3x - y + \dfrac{1}{2}z = -\dfrac{25}{4} \end{cases}$

35. $\begin{cases} x - 3y + z = 0 \\ 2x + 2y - z = 2 \\ x + y + z = 5 \end{cases}$

36. $\begin{cases} x + 5y = 13 \\ 2x + z = 6 \\ 4y - z = 8 \end{cases}$

37. $\begin{cases} x - 2y - 2z = -13 \\ 2x + y - z = -5 \\ x + y + z = 6 \end{cases}$

38. $\begin{cases} x + y + z + w = 0 \\ x - y - z + w = -2 \\ 3x + 3y - z - w = 11 \\ y - 2z = 6 \end{cases}$

Writing and Thinking About Mathematics

39. Suppose that Gaussian elimination with a system of three linear equations in three unknowns results in the following triangular matrix. Discuss how you can use back substitution to find that the system has an infinite number of solutions. That is, the system is dependent. (**HINT:** Solve the second equation for z.)

$$\begin{bmatrix} 1 & 2 & -1 & 4 \\ 0 & 3 & 1 & 2 \\ 0 & 0 & 0 & 0 \end{bmatrix}$$

Hawkes Learning Systems: Intermediate Algebra

Matrices and Gaussian Elimination

Determinants

After completing this section, you will be able to:

1. *Evaluate 2 × 2 and 3 × 3 determinants.*

2. *Solve equations involving determinants.*

As was discussed in Section 3.4, a rectangular array of numbers is called a matrix, and matrices arise in connection with solving systems of linear equations such as:

$$\begin{cases} a_{11}x + a_{12}y = k_1 \\ a_{21}x + a_{22}y = k_2 \end{cases}$$

The **matrix of the coefficients** (or the **coefficient matrix**) is

$$A = \begin{bmatrix} a_{11} & a_{12} \\ a_{21} & a_{22} \end{bmatrix}$$

If a matrix is **square** (the number of rows is equal to the number of columns), then there is a number associated with the matrix called its **determinant**. In this section, we will show how to evaluate determinants and, in the next section, we will show how determinants can be used to solve systems of linear equations by using a method called **Cramer's Rule**.

Determinant

*A **determinant** is a real number associated with a square array of real numbers and is indicated by enclosing the array between two vertical bars. For a matrix A, the corresponding determinant is designated as det(A) and is read "determinant of A."*

Examples of determinants are:

(a) For the matrix, $A = \begin{bmatrix} 3 & 4 \\ 7 & -2 \end{bmatrix}$, $\det(A) = \begin{vmatrix} 3 & 4 \\ 7 & -2 \end{vmatrix}$

(b) For the matrix, $B = \begin{bmatrix} 1 & 6 & -3 \\ 4 & 5 & 5 \\ -1 & -1 & -1 \end{bmatrix}$, $\det(B) = \begin{vmatrix} 1 & 6 & -3 \\ 4 & 5 & 5 \\ -1 & -1 & -1 \end{vmatrix}$

Example (a) is a 2 × 2 determinant and has two rows and two columns.
Example (b) is a 3 × 3 determinant and has three rows and three columns.

column 1   column 2
↓   ↓

$$\begin{array}{l} \text{row } 1 \to \\ \text{row } 2 \to \end{array} \begin{vmatrix} 3 & 4 \\ 7 & -2 \end{vmatrix} \qquad \begin{vmatrix} 3 & 4 \\ 7 & -2 \end{vmatrix}$$

A 4 × 4 determinant has four rows and four columns. A determinant may be of any size $n \times n$ where n is a positive integer and $n \geq 2$. In this text, the discussion will be restricted to 2 × 2 and 3 × 3 determinants, and the entries will be real numbers. [Huge matrices and determinants (1000 × 1000 or larger) are common in industry, and their values are calculated by computers. Even then, someone must understand the algebraic techniques to be able to write the necessary programs.]

Every determinant with real entries has a real value. The method for finding the value of 3 × 3 determinants involves finding the value of 2 × 2 determinants. Determinants of larger matrices can be evaluated by using techniques similar to those shown here. Their applications occur in higher mathematics such as linear algebra and differential equations.

Value of a 2×2 Determinant

$$\textit{For the square matrix, } A = \begin{bmatrix} a_{11} & a_{12} \\ a_{21} & a_{22} \end{bmatrix}, \quad \textit{det}(A) = \begin{vmatrix} a_{11} & a_{12} \\ a_{21} & a_{22} \end{vmatrix} = a_{11}a_{22} - a_{21}a_{12}.$$

As the definition indicates and the following examples illustrate, the value of a 2 × 2 determinant is the **product of the numbers in the diagonal containing the term in the first row, first column, minus the product of the numbers in the other diagonal.**

Example 1: 2×2 Determinant

Evaluate the following 2 × 2 determinants.

a. $\begin{vmatrix} 3 & 4 \\ 7 & -2 \end{vmatrix} = 3(-2) - 7(4) = -6 - 28 = -34$

b. $\begin{vmatrix} -5 & -\dfrac{1}{2} \\ 6 & 3 \end{vmatrix} = -5(3) - 6\left(-\dfrac{1}{2}\right) = -15 + 3 = -12$

c. $\begin{vmatrix} 1 & 7 \\ 2 & 14 \end{vmatrix} = 1(14) - 2(7) = 14 - 14 = 0$

One method of evaluating 3×3 determinants is called **expanding by minors**. In this method, **one row is chosen** and each entry in that row has a minor. Each minor is found by mentally crossing out both the row and column (shown here in the shaded regions) that contain that entry. The minors of the entries in the first row are illustrated here:

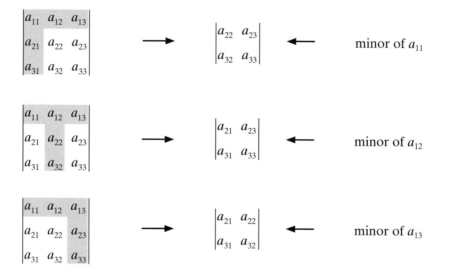

$$\begin{vmatrix} a_{22} & a_{23} \\ a_{32} & a_{33} \end{vmatrix} \qquad \longleftarrow \qquad \text{minor of } a_{11}$$

$$\begin{vmatrix} a_{21} & a_{23} \\ a_{31} & a_{33} \end{vmatrix} \qquad \longleftarrow \qquad \text{minor of } a_{12}$$

$$\begin{vmatrix} a_{21} & a_{22} \\ a_{31} & a_{32} \end{vmatrix} \qquad \longleftarrow \qquad \text{minor of } a_{13}$$

To find the value of a determinant (of any dimension other than 2×2), first choose a row (or column) and find the product of each entry in that row (or column) with its corresponding minor. Then the value is determined by adding these products with appropriate adjustments of alternating signs of the minors. We say that the determinant has been expanded by that row (or column). The following illustrates how to find the value of a 3×3 determinant by expanding by the first row.

Value of a 3×3 Determinant

For the square matrix, $A = \begin{bmatrix} a_{11} & a_{12} & a_{13} \\ a_{21} & a_{22} & a_{23} \\ a_{31} & a_{32} & a_{33} \end{bmatrix}$, $\textit{\textbf{det}}(A) = \begin{vmatrix} a_{11} & a_{12} & a_{13} \\ a_{21} & a_{22} & a_{23} \\ a_{31} & a_{32} & a_{33} \end{vmatrix}$

$$= \textit{\textbf{a}}_{\textit{11}}(\textit{minor of } a_{11}) - \textit{\textbf{a}}_{\textit{12}}(\textit{minor of } a_{12}) + \textit{\textbf{a}}_{\textit{13}}(\textit{minor of } a_{13})$$

$$= \textit{\textbf{a}}_{\textit{11}} \begin{vmatrix} a_{22} & a_{23} \\ a_{32} & a_{33} \end{vmatrix} - \textit{\textbf{a}}_{\textit{12}} \begin{vmatrix} a_{21} & a_{23} \\ a_{31} & a_{33} \end{vmatrix} + \textit{\textbf{a}}_{\textit{13}} \begin{vmatrix} a_{21} & a_{22} \\ a_{31} & a_{32} \end{vmatrix}$$

NOTES

CAUTION: The negative sign in the middle term of the expansion (representing -1 times a_{12}) is a critical part of the method and is a source of error for many students. **Be careful**.

Each minor is multiplied by its corresponding entry and +1 or −1 according to the pattern illustrated in Figure 3.4. [**Note:** The signs alternate and this pattern can be extended to apply to any $n \times n$ determinant.]

$$\begin{vmatrix} + & - & + \\ - & + & - \\ + & - & + \end{vmatrix}$$

Figure 3.4

For example, the value of a 3×3 determinant can be found by expanding by the minors of the second row as follows:

$$\det(A) = -a_{21} \,(\text{minor of } a_{21}) + a_{22} \,(\text{minor of } a_{22}) - a_{23} \,(\text{minor of } a_{23})$$

Note the use of the alternating + and − signs from the pattern in Figure 3.4. You may want to try this for practice with some of the exercises.

> **NOTES**
>
> There are methods other than expanding by minors for evaluating 3×3 determinants. Your instructor may wish to show you some of these, but they will not be discussed in the text. The advantage of learning to expand by minors is that this method can be used for evaluating higher order determinants.

Example 2: 3×3 Determinant

Evaluate the following 3×3 determinants.

a. $\begin{vmatrix} 5 & 1 & -4 \\ 2 & 6 & 3 \\ 2 & 2 & 1 \end{vmatrix}$ Using Row 1, mentally delete the shaded region.

Solution: $= 5 \begin{vmatrix} 5 & 1 & -4 \\ 2 & 6 & 3 \\ 2 & 2 & 1 \end{vmatrix} - 1 \begin{vmatrix} 5 & 1 & -4 \\ 2 & 6 & 3 \\ 2 & 2 & 1 \end{vmatrix} - 4 \begin{vmatrix} 5 & 1 & -4 \\ 2 & 6 & 3 \\ 2 & 2 & 1 \end{vmatrix}$

$= 5 \begin{vmatrix} 6 & 3 \\ 2 & 1 \end{vmatrix} - 1 \begin{vmatrix} 2 & 3 \\ 2 & 1 \end{vmatrix} - 4 \begin{vmatrix} 2 & 6 \\ 2 & 2 \end{vmatrix}$

$= 5(6 \cdot 1 - 2 \cdot 3) - 1(2 \cdot 1 - 2 \cdot 3) - 4(2 \cdot 2 - 2 \cdot 6)$

$= 5(6 - 6) - 1(2 - 6) - 4(4 - 12)$

$= 5(0) - 1(-4) - 4(-8)$

$= 0 + 4 + 32$

$= 36$

continued on next page ...

b. $\begin{vmatrix} 6 & -2 & 4 \\ 1 & 7 & 0 \\ -3 & 2 & -1 \end{vmatrix}$

Solution: $= 6\begin{vmatrix} 7 & 0 \\ 2 & -1 \end{vmatrix} + 2\begin{vmatrix} 1 & 0 \\ -3 & -1 \end{vmatrix} + 4\begin{vmatrix} 1 & 7 \\ -3 & 2 \end{vmatrix}$

$= 6(-7 - 0) + 2(-1 - 0) + 4(2 + 21)$

After some practice, many of these steps can be done mentally.

$= -42 - 2 + 92$

$= 48$

Example 3: Equations with Determinants

Solve the following equation for x: $\begin{vmatrix} 2 & 3 & 0 \\ 6 & x & 5 \\ 1 & -2 & 9 \end{vmatrix} = 53.$

Solution: First, evaluate the determinant.

$$\begin{vmatrix} 2 & 3 & 0 \\ 6 & x & 5 \\ 1 & -2 & 9 \end{vmatrix} = 2\begin{vmatrix} x & 5 \\ -2 & 9 \end{vmatrix} - 3\begin{vmatrix} 6 & 5 \\ 1 & 9 \end{vmatrix} + 0\begin{vmatrix} 6 & x \\ 1 & -2 \end{vmatrix}$$

$$= 2(9x + 10) - 3(54 - 5) + 0$$

$$= 18x + 20 - 162 + 15$$

$$= 18x - 127$$

Now solve the equation.

$$18x - 127 = 53$$

$$18x = 180$$

$$x = 10$$

The technique of expanding by minors may be used (with appropriate adjustments) to evaluate any $n \times n$ determinant. For example, in a 4×4 determinant, the minors of the entries in a particular row will be 3×3 determinants. Also, there are techniques for simplifying determinants and there are rules for arithmetic with determinants. The general rules governing these operations are discussed in courses in precalculus mathematics, finite mathematics, and linear algebra.

Using the TI-83 Plus Calculator to Evaluate a Determinant

A TI-83 Plus calculator (and other graphing calculators) can be used to find the value of the determinant of a square matrix. The determinant command, **1: det(** is found as the first entry in the MATRIX MATH menu. Example 4 shows, in a step by step format, how to find the determinant of a given 3×3 matrix.

Example 4: Evaluating Determinants with a Calculator

Use a TI-83 Plus calculator to find the value of det(A) for the matrix

$$A = \begin{bmatrix} 2 & 5 & 7 \\ 3 & 1 & 0 \\ 4 & 0 & 3 \end{bmatrix}$$

Step 1: Press MATRX, go to the **EDIT** menu and enter the numbers in the matrix A. The display should appear as follows:

Step 2: Press QUIT then MATRX again and go to the **MATH** menu. On the **MATH** menu choose **1: det(** and press ENTER. The display should appear as follows:

continued on next page ...

Step 3: Press MATRX again and on the **NAMES** menu choose **1:[A] 3×3.** Press
ENTER and the display should appear as follows:

Step 4: Press ENTER and the display should appear as follows with the answer:

• •

Practice Problems

Evaluate each of the following determinants.

1. $\begin{vmatrix} -3 & 2 \\ 4 & 7 \end{vmatrix}$ **2.** $\begin{vmatrix} 6 & 3 \\ 4 & 2 \end{vmatrix}$ **3.** $\begin{vmatrix} 1 & 4 & 0 \\ 2 & -1 & 5 \\ 0 & 7 & -1 \end{vmatrix}$

Use a TI-83 Plus calculator to find the value of the determinant.

4. $\begin{vmatrix} 5 & -1 & 3 \\ 0 & 4 & 2 \\ -3 & 1 & 3 \end{vmatrix}$

3.5 Exercises

In Exercises 1 – 4, the matrix A is given. Find det(A).

1. $A = \begin{bmatrix} 2 & 7 \\ 4 & 3 \end{bmatrix}$ **2.** $A = \begin{bmatrix} 7 & 3 \\ 8 & 5 \end{bmatrix}$ **3.** $A = \begin{bmatrix} -5 & 2 & 1 \\ 4 & 8 & 0 \\ -2 & 3 & 5 \end{bmatrix}$ **4.** $A = \begin{bmatrix} -6 & 5 & -3 \\ 4 & 0 & -1 \\ -2 & 7 & -2 \end{bmatrix}$

Answers to Practice Problems: 1. −29   **2.** 0   **3.** −26   **4.** 92

Evaluate the determinants in Exercises 5 – 20.

5. $\begin{vmatrix} 1 & 3 \\ -2 & 5 \end{vmatrix}$ **6.** $\begin{vmatrix} 7 & 2 \\ 3 & -6 \end{vmatrix}$ **7.** $\begin{vmatrix} 6 & 3 \\ -11 & -5 \end{vmatrix}$ **8.** $\begin{vmatrix} 2 & 3 \\ 3 & -4 \end{vmatrix}$

9. $\begin{vmatrix} 9 & 4 \\ 4 & 7 \end{vmatrix}$ **10.** $\begin{vmatrix} 3 & -4 \\ 8 & -6 \end{vmatrix}$ **11.** $\begin{vmatrix} 0 & -1 & 2 \\ 3 & 5 & -7 \\ -3 & 4 & 1 \end{vmatrix}$ **12.** $\begin{vmatrix} 1 & 0 & -1 \\ -2 & 3 & 5 \\ 6 & -3 & 4 \end{vmatrix}$

13. $\begin{vmatrix} 1 & -1 & 2 \\ -2 & 5 & -7 \\ 6 & 4 & 1 \end{vmatrix}$ **14.** $\begin{vmatrix} 2 & -1 & -3 \\ 5 & 9 & 4 \\ 7 & 6 & -2 \end{vmatrix}$ **15.** $\begin{vmatrix} 2 & 1 & 3 \\ 3 & 4 & 5 \\ 1 & 7 & 2 \end{vmatrix}$

16. $\begin{vmatrix} -3 & 2 & 1 \\ 1 & -4 & -1 \\ 2 & 5 & 3 \end{vmatrix}$ **17.** $\begin{vmatrix} 2 & 1 & -1 \\ 4 & 3 & 2 \\ 1 & 5 & 5 \end{vmatrix}$ **18.** $\begin{vmatrix} 6 & 7 & 1 \\ 0 & 3 & 3 \\ 4 & 1 & -5 \end{vmatrix}$

19. $\begin{vmatrix} 3 & -1 & -1 \\ 2 & 4 & 1 \\ -1 & 1 & 2 \end{vmatrix}$ **20.** $\begin{vmatrix} 2 & 3 & 2 \\ 1 & -1 & 5 \\ 0 & 5 & 1 \end{vmatrix}$

Use the method for evaluating determinants to solve the equations for x in Exercises 21 – 25.

21. $\begin{vmatrix} 1 & 3 & 4 \\ 2 & x & 3 \\ 1 & 3 & 5 \end{vmatrix} = 1$ **22.** $\begin{vmatrix} -2 & -1 & 1 \\ x & 1 & -1 \\ 4 & 3 & -2 \end{vmatrix} = 7$ **23.** $\begin{vmatrix} 1 & x & x \\ 2 & -2 & 1 \\ -1 & 3 & 2 \end{vmatrix} = 0$

24. $\begin{vmatrix} x & x & 1 \\ 1 & 5 & 0 \\ 0 & 1 & -2 \end{vmatrix} = -15$ **25.** $\begin{vmatrix} 3 & 1 & -2 \\ 1 & x & 4 \\ 2 & x & 0 \end{vmatrix} = 38$

The equation $\begin{vmatrix} x & y & 1 \\ x_1 & y_1 & 1 \\ x_2 & y_2 & 1 \end{vmatrix} = 0$ *is an equation of the line passing through the two points* $P_1(x_1, y_1)$ *and* $P_2(x_2, y_2)$. *Find an equation for the line determined by the pairs of points given in Exercises 26 – 28.*

26. $(3, 2), (-1, 4)$ **27.** $(-2, 1), (5, 3)$ **28.** $(4, -4), (0, 6)$

The area of the triangle having the vertices $P_1(x_1, y_1), P_2(x_2, y_2)$ *and* $P_3(x_3, y_3)$ *is given by the absolute value of the expression* $\dfrac{1}{2} \begin{vmatrix} x_1 & y_1 & 1 \\ x_2 & y_2 & 1 \\ x_3 & y_3 & 1 \end{vmatrix}$. *In Exercises 29 – 31, draw the triangle with the given points as vertices and then find the area of the triangle.*

29. $(3, 1), (5, 2), (1, -1)$ **30.** $(4, 0), (7, 1), (5, -2)$ **31.** $(-1, 3), (-4, -1), (3, -2)$

32. Explain, in your own words, the position of the three points $P_1(x_1, y_1)$, $P_2(x_2, y_2)$, and $P_3(x_3, y_3)$ if the expression $\dfrac{1}{2}\begin{vmatrix} x_1 & y_1 & 1 \\ x_2 & y_2 & 1 \\ x_3 & y_3 & 1 \end{vmatrix}$ has a value of 0. **Hint:** Refer to the discussion before Exercises 29 – 31.

In Exercises 33 – 35, use a graphing calculator to find the value of the determinant.

33. $\begin{vmatrix} 3 & -4 & 6 \\ 2 & 4 & -1 \\ 7 & 9 & -1 \end{vmatrix}$ **34.** $\begin{vmatrix} 2.1 & 3.5 & -3.4 \\ 2.6 & 5.0 & 1.2 \\ -1.0 & 3.4 & 9.3 \end{vmatrix}$ **35.** $\begin{vmatrix} 1.6 & \frac{1}{2} & -5.9 \\ 0.7 & \frac{3}{4} & 1.7 \\ 5.0 & 8.2 & -4.1 \end{vmatrix}$

Writing and Thinking About Mathematics

36. Suppose that in a 2×2 determinant two rows are identical. What will be the value of this determinant? Give two specific examples and a general example to back up your conclusion.

37. Suppose that in a 3×3 determinant one row is all 0's. What will be the value of this determinant? Give two specific examples and a general example to back up your conclusion.

38. (a) Suppose that in a 2×2 determinant two rows (or columns) are switched. How will the value of this new determinant relate to the value of the original determinant?

(b) Suppose that in a 3×3 determinant two rows (or columns) are switched. How will the value of this new determinant relate to the value of the original determinant?

Give two specific examples and a general example to back up your conclusion in each case.

Hawkes Learning Systems: Intermediate Algebra

Determinants

3.6 Determinants and Systems of Linear Equations: Cramer's Rule

Objectives

After completing this section, you will be able to:

Solve systems of linear equations by using Cramer's Rule.

Cramer's Rule is a method that uses determinants for solving systems of linear equations. To explain the method and how these determinants are generated, we first illustrate the solution to a system of linear equations by the addition method and do not simplify the indicated products and sums of the coefficients. We will see that these products and sums can be represented as determinants.

Consider the following system of linear equations **with the equations in standard form:**

$$\begin{cases} 2x + 3y = -5 \\ 4x + y = 5 \end{cases}$$

Eliminating y gives:

$$\begin{cases} [1] & 2x + 3y = -5 \\ [-3] & 4x + y = 5 \end{cases}$$

$$1(2x) + 1(3y) = 1(-5)$$
$$-3(4x) - 3(1y) = -3(5)$$
$$\overline{[1(2) - 3(4)]x = 1(-5) - 3(5)}$$
$$x = \frac{1(-5) - 3(5)}{1(2) - 3(4)}$$

Eliminating x gives:

$$\begin{cases} [-4] & 2x + 3y = -5 \\ [2] & 4x + y = 5 \end{cases}$$

$$-4(2x) - 4(3y) = -4(-5)$$
$$2(4x) + 2(1y) = 2(5)$$
$$\overline{[2(1) - 4(3)]y = 2(5) - 4(-5)}$$
$$y = \frac{2(5) - 4(-5)}{2(1) - 4(3)}$$

Notice that the denominators for both x and y are the same number. This number is the value of the determinant of the coefficients. (Remember that the equations are in standard form.)

$$\text{Determinant of coefficients} = D = \begin{vmatrix} 2 & 3 \\ 4 & 1 \end{vmatrix} = 2 \cdot 1 - 4 \cdot 3 = -10 \,.$$

In determinant form, the numerators are

$$D_x = \begin{vmatrix} -5 & 3 \\ 5 & 1 \end{vmatrix} = 1(-5) - 3(5) = -20$$

and

$$D_y = \begin{vmatrix} 2 & -5 \\ 4 & 5 \end{vmatrix} = 2(5) - 4(-5) = 30.$$

Therefore, the values for x and y can be written in fraction form using determinants as follows:

$$x = \frac{D_x}{D} = \frac{-20}{-10} = 2 \qquad \text{and} \qquad y = \frac{D_y}{D} = \frac{30}{-10} = -3$$

The determinant D_x is formed as follows:

1. Form D, the determinant of the coefficients.
2. Replace the coefficients of x with the corresponding constants on the right hand side of the equations.

The determinant D_y is formed as follows:

1. Form D, the determinant of the coefficients.
2. Replace the coefficients of y with the corresponding constants on the right hand side of the equations.

Cramer's Rule is stated here only for 2×2 systems (systems of two linear equations in two variables) and 3×3 systems (systems of three linear equations in three variables). However, Cramer's Rule applies to all $n \times n$ systems of linear equations.

Cramer's Rule for 2 × 2 Matrices

For the system $\begin{cases} a_{11}x + a_{12}y = k_1 \\ a_{21}x + a_{22}y = k_2 \end{cases}$,

where

$$D = \begin{vmatrix} a_{11} & a_{12} \\ a_{21} & a_{22} \end{vmatrix} \qquad D_x = \begin{vmatrix} k_1 & a_{12} \\ k_2 & a_{22} \end{vmatrix} \qquad \text{and} \qquad D_y = \begin{vmatrix} a_{11} & k_1 \\ a_{21} & k_2 \end{vmatrix},$$

if $D \neq 0$, then

$$x = \frac{D_x}{D} \qquad \text{and} \qquad y = \frac{D_y}{D}$$

is the unique solution to the system.

Cramer's Rule for 3 × 3 Matrices

For the system $\begin{cases} a_{11}x + a_{12}y + a_{13}z = k_1 \\ a_{21}x + a_{22}y + a_{23}z = k_2 \\ a_{31}x + a_{32}y + a_{33}z = k_3 \end{cases}$,

where

$$D = \begin{vmatrix} a_{11} & a_{12} & a_{13} \\ a_{21} & a_{22} & a_{23} \\ a_{31} & a_{32} & a_{33} \end{vmatrix}$$

$$D_x = \begin{vmatrix} k_1 & a_{12} & a_{13} \\ k_2 & a_{22} & a_{23} \\ k_3 & a_{32} & a_{33} \end{vmatrix} \qquad D_y = \begin{vmatrix} a_{11} & k_1 & a_{13} \\ a_{21} & k_2 & a_{23} \\ a_{31} & k_3 & a_{33} \end{vmatrix} \qquad \text{and} \qquad D_z = \begin{vmatrix} a_{11} & a_{12} & k_1 \\ a_{21} & a_{22} & k_2 \\ a_{31} & a_{32} & k_3 \end{vmatrix}$$

if $D \neq 0$, then

$$x = \frac{D_x}{D}, \quad y = \frac{D_y}{D}, \quad \text{and} \quad z = \frac{D_z}{D},$$

is the unique solution to the system.

Possibilities if $D = 0$

If $D = 0$:

For the 2 × 2 Case	For the 3 × 3 Case
1. If either $D_x \neq 0$ or $D_y \neq 0$, the system is **inconsistent and there is no solution.**	**1.** If $D_x \neq 0$ or $D_y \neq 0$ or $D_z \neq 0$, the system is **inconsistent and has no solution.**
2. If both $D_x = 0$ and $D_y = 0$, the system is **dependent and has an infinite number of solutions.**	**2.** If $D_x = 0$ and $D_y = 0$ and $D_z = 0$, the system is **dependent and has an infinite number of solutions.**

Example 1: Cramer's Rule

Using Cramer's Rule, solve the following systems of linear equations. The solutions are not checked here, but they can be checked by substituting the solutions into all of the equations in the system.

a. $\begin{cases} 2x + y = 3 \\ 3x - 2y = 5 \end{cases}$

Solution: $D = \begin{vmatrix} 2 & 1 \\ 3 & -2 \end{vmatrix} = -7,$ $\qquad D_x = \begin{vmatrix} 3 & 1 \\ 5 & -2 \end{vmatrix} = -11,$ $\qquad D_y = \begin{vmatrix} 2 & 3 \\ 3 & 5 \end{vmatrix} = 1$

$$x = \frac{D_x}{D} = \frac{-11}{-7} = \frac{11}{7} \qquad\qquad y = \frac{D_y}{D} = \frac{1}{-7} = -\frac{1}{7}$$

b. $\begin{cases} 2x + 2y = 8 \\ -x + 3y = -8 \end{cases}$

Solution: $D = \begin{vmatrix} 2 & 2 \\ -1 & 3 \end{vmatrix} = 8,$ $\qquad D_x = \begin{vmatrix} 8 & 2 \\ -8 & 3 \end{vmatrix} = 40,$ $\qquad D_y = \begin{vmatrix} 2 & 8 \\ -1 & -8 \end{vmatrix} = -8$

$$x = \frac{D_x}{D} = \frac{40}{8} = 5 \qquad\qquad y = \frac{D_y}{D} = \frac{-8}{8} = -1$$

c. $\begin{cases} x + 2y + 3z = 3 \\ 4x + 5y + 6z = 1 \\ 7x + 8y + 9z = 0 \end{cases}$

Solution: $D = \begin{vmatrix} 1 & 2 & 3 \\ 4 & 5 & 6 \\ 7 & 8 & 9 \end{vmatrix} = 1\begin{vmatrix} 5 & 6 \\ 8 & 9 \end{vmatrix} - 2\begin{vmatrix} 4 & 6 \\ 7 & 9 \end{vmatrix} + 3\begin{vmatrix} 4 & 5 \\ 7 & 8 \end{vmatrix}$

$$= 1(-3) - 2(-6) + 3(-3) = 0$$

$$D_x = \begin{vmatrix} 3 & 2 & 3 \\ 1 & 5 & 6 \\ 0 & 8 & 9 \end{vmatrix} = 3\begin{vmatrix} 5 & 6 \\ 8 & 9 \end{vmatrix} - 2\begin{vmatrix} 1 & 6 \\ 0 & 9 \end{vmatrix} + 3\begin{vmatrix} 1 & 5 \\ 0 & 8 \end{vmatrix}$$

$$= 3(-3) - 2(9) + 3(8) = -3$$

The system has no solution because **$D = 0$ and $D_x \neq 0$.**

d. $\begin{cases} x + y + 3z = 7 \\ 2x - y - 3z = -4 \\ 5x - 2y = -5 \end{cases}$

Solution: $D = \begin{vmatrix} 1 & 1 & 3 \\ 2 & -1 & -3 \\ 5 & -2 & 0 \end{vmatrix} = 1\begin{vmatrix} -1 & -3 \\ -2 & 0 \end{vmatrix} - 1\begin{vmatrix} 2 & -3 \\ 5 & 0 \end{vmatrix} + 3\begin{vmatrix} 2 & -1 \\ 5 & -2 \end{vmatrix} = -18$

$D_x = \begin{vmatrix} 7 & 1 & 3 \\ -4 & -1 & -3 \\ -5 & -2 & 0 \end{vmatrix} = 7\begin{vmatrix} -1 & -3 \\ -2 & 0 \end{vmatrix} - 1\begin{vmatrix} -4 & -3 \\ -5 & 0 \end{vmatrix} + 3\begin{vmatrix} -4 & -1 \\ -5 & -2 \end{vmatrix} = -18$

$D_y = \begin{vmatrix} 1 & 7 & 3 \\ 2 & -4 & -3 \\ 5 & -5 & 0 \end{vmatrix} = 1\begin{vmatrix} -4 & -3 \\ -5 & 0 \end{vmatrix} - 7\begin{vmatrix} 2 & -3 \\ 5 & 0 \end{vmatrix} + 3\begin{vmatrix} 2 & -4 \\ 5 & -5 \end{vmatrix} = -90$

$D_z = \begin{vmatrix} 1 & 1 & 7 \\ 2 & -1 & -4 \\ 5 & -2 & -5 \end{vmatrix} = 1\begin{vmatrix} -1 & -4 \\ -2 & -5 \end{vmatrix} - 1\begin{vmatrix} 2 & -4 \\ 5 & -5 \end{vmatrix} + 7\begin{vmatrix} 2 & -1 \\ 5 & -2 \end{vmatrix} = -6$

$$x = \frac{-18}{-18} = 1 \qquad y = \frac{-90}{-18} = 5 \qquad z = \frac{-6}{-18} = \frac{1}{3}$$

● ●

NOTES

The determinants shown in Examples 1c and 1d are expanded by the first row. However, you should remember that any row or column can be used in the expansion as long as the corresponding adjustments in the + and − signs are used with the minors. This may be particularly useful when a row or column has one or more 0's because multiplication by 0 will always give 0 and this will reduce the time needed for the expansion.

Practice Problems

1. Solve the following system using Cramer's Rule.

$\begin{cases} 2x - y = 11 \\ x + y = -2 \end{cases}$

2. Find D_x for the following system.

$\begin{cases} x + 2y + z = 0 \\ 2x + y - 2z = 5 \\ 3x - y + z = -3 \end{cases}$

Answers to Practice Problems: 1. $x = 3$, $y = -5$ **2.** $D_x = 0$

3.6 Exercises

Use Cramer's Rule to solve the following systems of linear equations.

1. $\begin{cases} 2x - 5y = -7 \\ 3x - 2y = 6 \end{cases}$
2. $\begin{cases} 3x + 5y = 17 \\ x + 3y = 15 \end{cases}$
3. $\begin{cases} 6x - 4y = 5 \\ 3x + 8y = 0 \end{cases}$
4. $\begin{cases} 3x + 4y = 24 \\ 2x + y = 11 \end{cases}$

5. $\begin{cases} 3x + y = 1 \\ -9x - 3y = 2 \end{cases}$
6. $\begin{cases} 4x + 8y = 12 \\ 3x + 6y = 9 \end{cases}$
7. $\begin{cases} 12x + 4y = 3 \\ -10x + 3y = 7 \end{cases}$
8. $\begin{cases} 4x - 9y = 2 \\ 8x - 15y = 3 \end{cases}$

9. $\begin{cases} 2x + 3y = 4 \\ 3x - 4y = 5 \end{cases}$
10. $\begin{cases} 5x + 2y = 7 \\ 2x - 3y = 4 \end{cases}$
11. $\begin{cases} 7x + 3y = 9 \\ 4x + 8y = 11 \end{cases}$
12. $\begin{cases} 5x - 9y = 3 \\ 11x + 6y = 12 \end{cases}$

13. $\begin{cases} 6x - 13y = 21 \\ 5x - 12y = 18 \end{cases}$
14. $\begin{cases} 10x + 7y = 15 \\ 13x - 4y = 11 \end{cases}$
15. $\begin{cases} 8x - 9y = -14 \\ 15x + 6y = 7 \end{cases}$
16. $\begin{cases} 17x - 5y = 21 \\ 4x + 3y = 6 \end{cases}$

17. $\begin{cases} 0.8x + 0.3y = 4 \\ 0.9x - 1.2y = 5 \end{cases}$
18. $\begin{cases} 0.4x + 0.7y = 3 \\ 0.5x + y = 6 \end{cases}$
19. $\begin{cases} 1.6x - 4.5y = 1.5 \\ 0.4x + 1.2y = 3.1 \end{cases}$

20. $\begin{cases} 2.3x + 1.8y = 4.6 \\ 0.8x - 1.4y = 3.2 \end{cases}$
21. $\begin{cases} x - 2y - z = -7 \\ 2x + y + z = 0 \\ 3x - 5y + 8z = 13 \end{cases}$
22. $\begin{cases} 2x + 3y + z = 0 \\ 5x + y - 2z = 9 \\ 10x - 5y + 3z = 4 \end{cases}$

23. $\begin{cases} 5x - 4y + z = 17 \\ x + y + z = 4 \\ -10x + 8y - 2z = 11 \end{cases}$
24. $\begin{cases} 9x + 10y = 2 \\ 2x + 6z = 4 \\ -3y + 3z = 1 \end{cases}$
25. $\begin{cases} 2x - 3y - z = -4 \\ -x + 2y + z = 6 \\ x - y + 2z = 14 \end{cases}$

26. $\begin{cases} 2x - 3y - z = 4 \\ x - 2y - z = 1 \\ x - y + 2z = 9 \end{cases}$
27. $\begin{cases} 3x + 2y + z = 5 \\ 2x + y - 2z = 4 \\ 5x + 3y - z = 9 \end{cases}$
28. $\begin{cases} 8x + 3y + 2z = 15 \\ 3x + 5y + z = -4 \\ 2x + 3y = -7 \end{cases}$

29. $\begin{cases} 2x - y + 3z = 1 \\ 5x + 2y - z = 2 \\ x - 2y + 5z = 2 \end{cases}$
30. $\begin{cases} 2x + 3y + 2z = -5 \\ 2x - 2y + z = -1 \\ 5x + y + z = 1 \end{cases}$

For exercises 31 – 35, set up a system of linear equations that represents the information, then solve the system by using Cramer's Rule.

31. The three sides of a triangle are related as follows: the perimeter is 43 feet, the second side is 5 feet more than twice the first side, and the third side is 3 feet less than the sum of the other two sides. Find the lengths of the three sides of the triangle.

32. Joel loves candy bars and ice cream, and they have fat and calories as follows: each candy bar contains 5 gm of fat and 280 calories; each serving of ice cream contains 10 gm of fat and 150 calories. How many candy bars and how many servings of ice cream did he eat the week that he consumed 85 gm of fat and 2300 calories from these two foods?

33. A financial advisor has $6 million to invest for her clients. She chooses, for one month, to invest in mutual funds and technology stocks. If the mutual funds earned 2% and the stocks earned 4% for a total of $170,000 in earnings for the month, how much money did she invest in each type of investment?

34. A farmer plants corn, wheat, and soybeans and rotates the planting each year on his 500-acre farm. In one particular year, the profits were: $120 per acre for corn, $100 per acre for wheat, and $80 per acre for soybeans. He planted twice as many acres with corn as with soybeans. How many acres did he plant with each crop the year he made a total profit of $51,800?

Hawkes Learning Systems: Intermediate Algebra

Determinants and Systems of Linear Equations: Cramer's Rule

Graphing Systems of Linear Inequalities

After completing this section, you will be able to:

Solve systems of linear inequalities graphically.

In some branches of mathematics, in particular a topic called (interestingly enough) game theory, the solution to a very sophisticated problem can involve the set of points that satisfy a system of several **linear inequalities.** In business these ideas relate to problems such as minimizing the cost of shipping goods from several warehouses to distribution outlets. In this section we will consider graphing the solution sets to only two inequalities. We will leave the problem solving techniques to another course.

First, we review the ideas related to systems of equations discussed in Section 3.1. Systems of two linear equations were solved by using three methods: graphing, substitution, and addition. We found that such systems can be:

    a. consistent   (one point satisfies both equations, and the lines intersect in one point),

    b. inconsistent (no point satisfies both equations, and the lines are parallel), or

    c. dependent (an infinite number of points satisfy both equations, and the lines are the same).

Figure 3.5 shows an example of each case.

System	Graph	Intersection	
$\begin{cases} y = 3x - 1 \\ y = -x + 3 \end{cases}$	$y = 3x - 1$ $y = -x + 3$ $(1,2)$	*One point: (1, 2)*	*Consistent*
$\begin{cases} 2x + y = 4 \\ y = -2x + 1 \end{cases}$	$2x + y = 4$ $y = -2x + 1$	*No points;* *lines are parallel*	*Inconsistent*

continued on next page ...

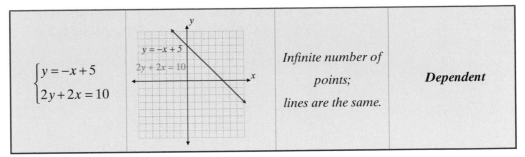

| $\begin{cases} y = -x + 5 \\ 2y + 2x = 10 \end{cases}$ | | Infinite number of points; lines are the same. | **Dependent** |

Figure 3.5

In this section, we will develop techniques for graphing (and therefore solving) **systems of two linear inequalities**. The solution set (if there are any solutions) to a system of two linear inequalities consists of the points in the intersection of two half-planes and portions of boundary lines indicated by the inequalities. We know that a straight line separates a plane into two **half-planes**. The line itself is called the **boundary line**, and the boundary line may be included (the half-plane is **closed**) or the boundary line may not be included (the half-plane is **open**). The following procedure may be used to solve a system of linear inequalities.

To Solve a System of Two Linear Inequalities

1. *Graph the boundary lines for both half-planes.*
2. *Shade the region that is common to both of these half-planes.*
    *(This region is called the **intersection** of the two half-planes.)*
3. *To check, pick one test-point in the intersection and verify that it satisfies both*
    inequalities.

*(**Note:** If there is no intersection, then the system is inconsistent and has no solution.)*

Example 1: Graphing Systems of Linear Inequalities

a. Graph the points that satisfy the system of inequalities $\begin{cases} x \le 2 \\ y \ge -x + 1 \end{cases}$.

Solution: **Step 1:** For $x \le 2$, the points are to the left of and on the line $x = 2$.

Step 2: For $y \ge -x + 1$, the points are above and on the line $y = -x + 1$.

continued on next page ...

Step 3: Shade only the region with points that satisfy both inequalities. In this case, we test the point $(0, 3)$:

$0 \leq 2$ A true statement

$3 \geq -0 + 1$ A true statement

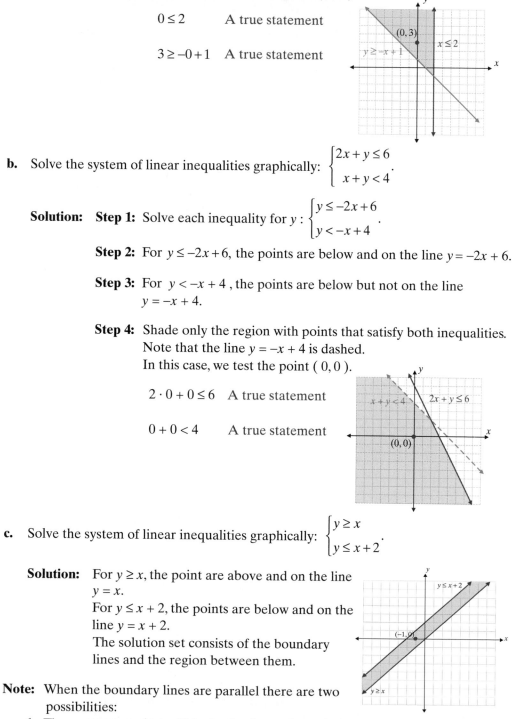

b. Solve the system of linear inequalities graphically: $\begin{cases} 2x + y \leq 6 \\ x + y < 4 \end{cases}$.

Solution: **Step 1:** Solve each inequality for y: $\begin{cases} y \leq -2x + 6 \\ y < -x + 4 \end{cases}$.

Step 2: For $y \leq -2x + 6$, the points are below and on the line $y = -2x + 6$.

Step 3: For $y < -x + 4$, the points are below but not on the line $y = -x + 4$.

Step 4: Shade only the region with points that satisfy both inequalities. Note that the line $y = -x + 4$ is dashed. In this case, we test the point $(0, 0)$.

$2 \cdot 0 + 0 \leq 6$ A true statement

$0 + 0 < 4$ A true statement

c. Solve the system of linear inequalities graphically: $\begin{cases} y \geq x \\ y \leq x + 2 \end{cases}$.

Solution: For $y \geq x$, the point are above and on the line $y = x$.
For $y \leq x + 2$, the points are below and on the line $y = x + 2$.
The solution set consists of the boundary lines and the region between them.

Note: When the boundary lines are parallel there are two possibilities:
1. The common region will be in the form of a strip between two lines (as in this example), or
2. There will be no common region and the solution set will be the empty set, $\emptyset$.

Using a TI-83 Plus Graphing Calculator to Graph Systems of Linear Inequalities

To graph a system of linear inequalities with a TI-83 Plus graphing calculator, first solve each inequality for y and then enter both of the corresponding functions after pressing the ⬤ Y= key. By setting the graphing symbol to the left of Y1 and Y2 to the desired form and then pressing GRAPH, the desired region will be graphed as a cross-hatched area on the display (assuming that the window is set correctly). The following example shows how this can be done.

Example 2: Graphing Systems of Linear Inequalities ● ● ● ● ● ● ● ● ● ● ● ● ● ●

Use a TI-83 Plus graphing calculator to graph the following system of linear

inequalities: $\begin{cases} 2x + y < 4 \\ 2x - y \leq 0 \end{cases}$.

Solution: **Step 1:** Solve each inequality for y: $\begin{cases} y < -2x + 4 \\ y \geq 2x \end{cases}$.

(**Note:** Solving $2x - y \leq 0$ for y can be written as $2x \leq y$ and then as $y \geq 2x$.)

Step 2: Press the ⬤ Y= key and enter both functions and the corresponding symbols as they appear here:

Step 3: Press GRAPH. The display should appear as follows. The solution is the cross-hatched region.

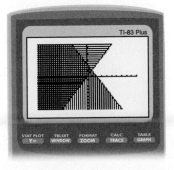

3.7 Exercises

In Exercises 1 – 20, solve the systems of two linear inequalities graphically.

1. $\begin{cases} y > 2 \\ x \geq -3 \end{cases}$ **2.** $\begin{cases} 2x + 5 < 0 \\ \quad y \geq 2 \end{cases}$ **3.** $\begin{cases} x < 3 \\ y > -x + 2 \end{cases}$ **4.** $\begin{cases} y \leq -5 \\ y \geq x - 5 \end{cases}$

5. $\begin{cases} \quad x \leq 3 \\ 2x + y > 7 \end{cases}$ **6.** $\begin{cases} 2x - y > 4 \\ \quad y < -1 \end{cases}$ **7.** $\begin{cases} x - 3y \leq 3 \\ \quad x < 5 \end{cases}$ **8.** $\begin{cases} 3x - 2y \geq 8 \\ \quad y \geq 0 \end{cases}$

9. $\begin{cases} \quad x - y \geq 0 \\ 3x - 2y \geq 4 \end{cases}$ **10.** $\begin{cases} y \geq x - 2 \\ x + y \geq -2 \end{cases}$ **11.** $\begin{cases} 3x + y \leq 10 \\ 5x - y \geq 6 \end{cases}$ **12.** $\begin{cases} \quad y \geq 2x - 5 \\ 3x + 2y > -3 \end{cases}$

13. $\begin{cases} 3x + 4y \geq -7 \\ \quad y < 2x + 1 \end{cases}$ **14.** $\begin{cases} 2x - 3y \geq 0 \\ 8x - 3y < 36 \end{cases}$ **15.** $\begin{cases} \quad x + y < 4 \\ 2x - 3y < 3 \end{cases}$ **16.** $\begin{cases} 2x + 3y < 12 \\ 3x + 2y > 13 \end{cases}$

17. $\begin{cases} x + y \geq 0 \\ x - 2y \geq 6 \end{cases}$ **18.** $\begin{cases} y \geq 2x + 3 \\ y \leq x - 2 \end{cases}$ **19.** $\begin{cases} x + 3y \leq 9 \\ x - y \geq 5 \end{cases}$ **20.** $\begin{cases} x - y \geq -2 \\ x + 2y < -1 \end{cases}$

21. $\begin{cases} y \leq -2x \\ y > -2x - 6 \end{cases}$ **22.** $\begin{cases} \quad y > 3x + 1 \\ -3x + y < -1 \end{cases}$ **23.** $\begin{cases} \quad y \leq x + 3 \\ x - y \leq -5 \end{cases}$

24. $\begin{cases} y > x - 4 \\ y < x + 2 \end{cases}$

Use a graphing calculator to solve the systems of linear inequalities in Exercises 25 – 35.

25. $\begin{cases} \quad y \geq 0 \\ 3x - 5y \leq 10 \end{cases}$ **26.** $\begin{cases} 3x + 2y \leq 15 \\ 2x + 5y \geq 10 \end{cases}$ **27.** $\begin{cases} 4x - 3y \geq 6 \\ \quad 3x - y \leq 3 \end{cases}$ **28.** $\begin{cases} \quad y \leq 0 \\ 3x + y \leq 11 \end{cases}$

29. $\begin{cases} 3x - 4y \geq -6 \\ 3x + 2y \leq 12 \end{cases}$ **30.** $\begin{cases} \quad 3y \leq 2x \\ x + 2y \leq 11 \end{cases}$ **31.** $\begin{cases} \quad x + y \leq 8 \\ 3x - 2y \geq -6 \end{cases}$ **32.** $\begin{cases} x + y \leq 7 \\ 2x - y \leq 8 \end{cases}$

33. $\begin{cases} y \leq x \\ y < 2x + 1 \end{cases}$ **34.** $\begin{cases} \quad x - y \geq -2 \\ 4x - y < 16 \end{cases}$ **35.** $\begin{cases} y \geq x \\ y \leq x + 7 \end{cases}$

Writing and Thinking About Mathematics

36. Example 1c discusses a system of two linear inequalities in which the boundary lines are parallel. Describe, in your own words, how you might test whether or not you have graphed the correct solution set. Solve the following systems graphically and indicate how your method of testing works in each case.

a. $\begin{cases} y \le 2x - 5 \\ y \ge 2x + 3 \end{cases}$

b. $\begin{cases} y \le -x + 2 \\ y \ge -x - 1 \end{cases}$

c. $\begin{cases} y \le \dfrac{1}{2}x + 3 \\ y \ge \dfrac{1}{2}x - 3 \end{cases}$

Hawkes Learning Systems: Intermediate Algebra

Systems of Linear Inequalities

Chapter 3 Index of Key Ideas and Terms

Systems of Linear Equations (Two Variables)   page 176

Two (or more) linear equations considered at one time
are said to form a **system of linear equations** or a set
of **simultaneous equations**.

Simultaneous Equations   page 176

Consistent   page 177

If a system of linear equations has a unique solution,
it is said to be **consistent**.

Inconsistent   page 177

If a system has no solutions, it is said to be **inconsistent**.

Dependent   page 177

If a system has an infinite number of solutions, it is said
to be **dependent**.

Solving a System by Graphing   page 178

To solve a system of two linear equations by graphing,
graph both equations on the same set of axes and observe
the point of intersection of the two lines (if there is one).

Solving a System by Substitution   page 179

1. Solve one of the equations for one of the variables.
2. Substitute the resulting expression into the other equation.
3. Solve this new equation, if possible, and then substitute
   back into one of the original equations to find the value
   of the other variable. (This is known as **back substitution**.)

Solving a System by Addition   page 181

1. Write the equations one under the other so that
   like terms are aligned.
2. Multiply all terms of one equation by a constant (and possibly
   the terms of the other equation by another constant)
   so that two like terms have opposite coefficients.
3. Add like terms and solve the resulting equation, if possible.
   Then, back substitute into one of the original equations
   to find the value of the other variable.

Applications

　　Mixture　　　　　　　　　　　　　　　　　　　　　page 187
　　Interest　　　　　　　　　　　　　　　　　　　　　page 188
　　Work　　　　　　　　　　　　　　　　　　　　　　page 188
　　Algebra　　　　　　　　　　　　　　　　　　　　　page 189

Ordered Triples　　　　　　　　　　　　　　　　　　　page 194

　　An **ordered triple** is an ordering of three real numbers
　　in the form (x, y, z).

Graphs in Three Dimensions　　　　　　　　　　　　　page 194

　　Three mutually perpendicular axes labeled as the x-axis, y-axis,
　　and z-axis are used to separate space into eight regions called **octants**.

Solving a System of Three Linear Equations　　　　　　page 196

　　Step 1:　Select two equations and eliminate one variable by using the
　　　　　　　addition method.
　　Step 2:　Select a different pair of equations and eliminate the **same** variable.
　　Step 3:　Steps 1 and 2 give **two** linear equations in **two** variables.
　　　　　　　Solve these equations by either addition or substitution
　　　　　　　as discussed in Section 3.1.
　　Step 4:　Back substitute the values found in Step 3 into any one
　　　　　　　of the original equations to find the value of the third variable.

Matrices　　　　　　　　　　　　　　　　　　　　　　page 205

　　　Entries, Rows, Columns, Dimensions, Square

Coefficient Matrix　　　　　　　　　　　　　　　　　　page 206

　　A matrix formed from the coefficients of the variables in a system
　　of linear equations is called a **coefficient matrix**.

Augmented Matrix　　　　　　　　　　　　　　　　　　page 206

　　A matrix that includes the coefficients and the constant terms
　　is called an **augmented matrix**.

Elementary Row Operations　　　　　　　　　　　　　　page 207

　　There are three elementary row operations with matrices:
　　1.　Interchange two rows.
　　2.　Multiply a row by a nonzero constant.
　　3.　Add a multiple of a row to another row.

　　If any elementary row operation is applied to a matrix,
　　the new matrix is said to be **row-equivalent** to the original matrix.

Upper Triangular Form (or ref Form)　　　　　　　　　　page 209

　　If all the entries below the main diagonal of a matrix are 0's,
　　the matrix is said to be in **upper triangular form**.

Gaussian Elimination

To solve a system of linear equations by using Gaussian elimination:

1. Write the augmented matrix for the system.
2. Use elementary row operations to transform the matrix into triangular form.
3. Solve the corresponding system of equations by using back substitution.

page 210

Using a TI-83 Plus Calculator to Solve a System of Linear Equations

page 213 - 216

Determinants

page 220

A **determinant** is a real number associated with a square array of real numbers and is indicated by enclosing the array between two vertical bars. For a matrix A, the corresponding determinant is designated as $\det(A)$.

Value of a 2 × 2 Determinant

page 221

For the square matrix $A = \begin{bmatrix} a_{11} & a_{12} \\ a_{21} & a_{22} \end{bmatrix}$,

$$\det(A) = \begin{vmatrix} a_{11} & a_{12} \\ a_{21} & a_{22} \end{vmatrix} = a_{11}a_{22} - a_{21}a_{12}.$$

Value of a 3 × 3 Determinant

page 222

For the square matrix $A = \begin{bmatrix} a_{11} & a_{12} & a_{13} \\ a_{21} & a_{22} & a_{23} \\ a_{31} & a_{32} & a_{33} \end{bmatrix}$,

$$\det(A) = \begin{vmatrix} a_{11} & a_{12} & a_{13} \\ a_{21} & a_{22} & a_{23} \\ a_{31} & a_{32} & a_{33} \end{vmatrix}$$

$$= a_{11}\left(\text{minor of } a_{11}\right) - a_{12}\left(\text{minor of } a_{12}\right) + a_{13}\left(\text{minor of } a_{13}\right)$$

$$= a_{11}\begin{vmatrix} a_{22} & a_{23} \\ a_{32} & a_{33} \end{vmatrix} - a_{12}\begin{vmatrix} a_{21} & a_{23} \\ a_{31} & a_{33} \end{vmatrix} + a_{13}\begin{vmatrix} a_{21} & a_{22} \\ a_{31} & a_{32} \end{vmatrix}$$

Sign Table for Minors of a 3 × 3 Determinant

page 223

$$\begin{vmatrix} + & - & + \\ - & + & - \\ + & - & + \end{vmatrix}$$

Using a TI-83 Plus Calculator to Evaluate a Determinant

page 225 - 226

Cramer's Rule   page 230

For 2 × 2 Matrices

For the system $\begin{cases} a_{11}x + a_{12}y = k_1 \\ a_{21}x + a_{22}y = k_2 \end{cases}$, where

$$D = \begin{vmatrix} a_{11} & a_{12} \\ a_{21} & a_{22} \end{vmatrix} \quad D_x = \begin{vmatrix} k_1 & a_{12} \\ k_2 & a_{22} \end{vmatrix} \quad \text{and} \quad D_y = \begin{vmatrix} a_{11} & k_1 \\ a_{21} & k_2 \end{vmatrix},$$

if $D \neq 0$, then $x = \dfrac{D_x}{D}$ and $y = \dfrac{D_y}{D}$

is the unique solution to the system.

For 3 × 3 Matrices   page 231

For the system $\begin{cases} a_{11}x + a_{12}y + a_{13}z = k_1 \\ a_{21}x + a_{22}y + a_{23}z = k_2 \\ a_{31}x + a_{32}y + a_{33}z = k_3 \end{cases}$, where $D = \begin{vmatrix} a_{11} & a_{12} & a_{13} \\ a_{21} & a_{22} & a_{23} \\ a_{31} & a_{32} & a_{33} \end{vmatrix}$

$$D_x = \begin{vmatrix} k_1 & a_{12} & a_{13} \\ k_2 & a_{22} & a_{23} \\ k_3 & a_{32} & a_{33} \end{vmatrix} \quad D_y = \begin{vmatrix} a_{11} & k_1 & a_{13} \\ a_{21} & k_2 & a_{23} \\ a_{31} & k_3 & a_{33} \end{vmatrix} \quad \text{and} \quad D_z = \begin{vmatrix} a_{11} & a_{12} & k_1 \\ a_{21} & a_{22} & k_2 \\ a_{31} & a_{32} & k_3 \end{vmatrix}$$

if $D \neq 0$, then $x = \dfrac{D_x}{D}$, $y = \dfrac{D_y}{D}$, and $z = \dfrac{D_z}{D}$,

is the unique solution to the system.

Possibilities if $D = 0$ page 231

For the 2 × 2 Case

1. If either $D_x \neq 0$ or $D_y \neq 0$, the system is **inconsistent and there is no solution**.
2. If both $D_x = 0$ and $D_y = 0$, the system is **dependent and has an infinite number of solutions**.

For the 3 × 3 Case

1. If $D_x \neq 0$ or $D_y \neq 0$ or $D_z \neq 0$, the system is **inconsistent and has no solution**.
2. If $D_x = 0$ and $D_y = 0$ and $D_z = 0$, the system is **dependent and has an infinite number of solutions**.

Solving a System of Linear Inequalities   page 237

To solve a system of two linear inequalities:
1. Graph both half-planes.
2. Shade the region that is common to both of these half-planes.
    (This region is called the **intersection** of the two half-planes.)
3. To check, pick one test-point in the intersection and verify that it
    satisfies both inequalities.
    (**Note:** If there is no intersection, then the system is inconsistent
    and has no solution.)

Using a TI-83 Plus Calculator to Graph Systems of Linear Inequalities   page 239

Chapter 3 Review

For a review of the topics and problems from Chapter 3, look at the following lessons from *Hawkes Learning Systems: Intermediate Algebra*

Solving Systems of Linear Equations by Graphing
Solving Systems of Linear Equations by Substitution
Solving Systems of Linear Equations by Addition
Applications (Systems of Equations)
Solving Systems of Linear Equations with Three Variables
Matrices and Gaussian Elimination
Determinants
Determinants and Systems of Linear Equations: Cramer's Rule
Systems of Linear Inequalities

Chapter 3 Test

1. Solve the system by graphing: $\begin{cases} 4x - y = 13 \\ 2x - 3y = 9 \end{cases}$.

Solve each system of linear equations in Exercises 2 – 5 by the substitution method or the addition method. State which systems are dependent or inconsistent.

2. $\begin{cases} x + y = 9 \\ x - y = 5 \end{cases}$ 3. $\begin{cases} 6x + 3y = 5 \\ 4x + 2y = -3 \end{cases}$ 4. $\begin{cases} 7x - 6y = 2 \\ 5x + 2y = 3 \end{cases}$ 5. $\begin{cases} 2x + 3y = 1 \\ 5x + 7y = 6 \end{cases}$

6. Determine a and b such that the line $ax + by = 17$ passes through the two points $(-3, 2)$ and $(1, 5)$.

7. The length of a rectangle is 7 ft more than twice its width. The perimeter is 62 ft. Find the dimensions of the rectangle.

8. Solve the following system of equations algebraically: $\begin{cases} x - 2y - 3z = 3 \\ x + y - z = 2 \\ 2x - 3y - 5z = 5 \end{cases}$.

9. Solve the following system of equations algebraically: $\begin{cases} x + 2y - 2z = 0 \\ x - y + z = 2 \\ -x + 4y - 4z = -8 \end{cases}$.

10. For the following system of equations:
    a. write the coefficient matrix and the augmented matrix and state the dimension of each, and
    b. solve the system by using the Gaussian elimination method.
    $$\begin{cases} x + 2y - 3z = -11 \\ x - y - z = 2 \\ x + 3y + 2z = -4 \end{cases}$$

11. Kimberly bought 90 stamps in denominations of 33¢, 55¢, and 78¢. To test her daughter, who is taking an algebra class, she said that she bought three times as many 33¢ stamps as 55¢ stamps and that the total cost of the stamps was $38.60. How many stamps of each denomination did she buy?

Evaluate the determinants in Exercises 12 and 13.

12. $\begin{vmatrix} 6 & -3 \\ 4 & 5 \end{vmatrix}$

13. $\begin{vmatrix} 1 & 3 & 2 \\ 2 & 5 & 1 \\ 0 & 2 & 1 \end{vmatrix}$

Solve for x in Exercises 14 and 15.

14. $\begin{vmatrix} 3 & x \\ 5 & 7 \end{vmatrix} = -9$

15. $\begin{vmatrix} -2 & 3 & 1 \\ 1 & 3 & x \\ 2 & 3 & x \end{vmatrix} = 14$

Solve Exercises 16 and 17 by using Cramer's Rule.

16. $\begin{cases} 3x + 8y = 14 \\ 2x + 7y = 22 \end{cases}$

17. $\begin{cases} x + 2y - z = 2 \\ x - 4y - 5z = -7 \\ x + 3y + 4z = 5 \end{cases}$

18. The sum of the measures of the three angles of a triangle is $180°$. If the largest angle is $40°$ less than the sum of the other two, and the middle angle is $40°$ less than twice the smallest angle, find the measures of the angles.

19. Solve the following system of linear inequalities graphically:

$$\begin{cases} y < 3x + 4 \\ 2x + y \geq 1 \end{cases}$$

Use a TI-83 Plus calculator to answer Exercises 20 and 21.

20. Solve the system of equations using the row echelon form command, ref:

$$\begin{cases} x - 3y - 4z = -12 \\ 3x + 4y + \dfrac{1}{2}z = -4 \\ -x - y + z = 2 \end{cases}$$

21. Find the value of the determinant D_x for the system of equations in Exercise 20.

Cumulative Review: Chapters 1 – 3

1. Given the set of numbers $\left\{-\sqrt{13}, -3, -\frac{1}{2}, 0, \frac{5}{8}, 1, \sqrt{2}, \pi\right\}$, list those in the set that are
   a. integers
   b. rational numbers
   c. irrational numbers
   d. real numbers

In Exercises 2 and 3, simplify each expression using the rules for order of operations.

2. $16 + (3^2 - 7^2) \div 5 \cdot 2$

3. $15 - 3(4^2 - 10^3 \div 2^3 + 6 \cdot 3) + 2^5$

Solve each equation in Exercises 4 – 6.

4. $4(x + 2) - (8 - 2x) = 12$

5. $\dfrac{3x - 2}{8} = \dfrac{x}{4} - 1$

6. $| 2x + 1 | = 28$

7. Solve the formula $K = \dfrac{mv^2}{2g}$ for m.

Solve the inequalities in Exercises 8 – 10. Write the solutions in interval notation then graph each solution on a real number line.

8. $5x - 13 > 7(x - 3)$

9. $\dfrac{x}{3} - 21 \le \dfrac{x}{2} + 3$

10. $| 3x + 2 | + 4 < 10$

In Exercises 11 – 13, simplify the expressions by using the rules for exponents.

11. $\left(x^2 y^3\right)^{-1} \left(x^{-2} y\right)^3$

12. $\dfrac{x^2 y^{-3}}{x^{-3} y^{-2}}$

13. $\left(\dfrac{5x^2 y^2}{3xy^3}\right)^{-1} \left(\dfrac{10x^{-1}}{y}\right)$

14. Write each number in scientific notation and simplify:

    $$\dfrac{810,000 \times 0.00014}{42,000}$$

15. Given the two points $(-5, 2)$ and $(5, -3)$:
    a. Find the slope of the line that passes through the two points.
    b. Find the equation of the line.
    c. Graph the line.

16. Find the equation of the line that is parallel to the line $2x - 5y = 1$ and passes through the origin.

17. Graph the function $y = 5 - 2x - x^2$ on a graphing calculator. With the trace and zoom features, estimate the x-intercepts and the maximum value for y on the curve.

18. Using a graphing calculator, graph the two functions $y = x^2 - 3$ and $y = 2x + 3$ and estimate their points of intersection.

19. Solve the system of linear equations by graphing.
$$\begin{cases} 2x + y = 6 \\ 3x - 2y = -5 \end{cases}$$

20. Solve the system of linear equations by the addition method.
$$\begin{cases} x + 3y = 10 \\ 5x - y = 2 \end{cases}$$

21. Solve the system of linear equations by using the Gaussian elimination method.
$$\begin{cases} x - 3y + 2z = -1 \\ -2x + y + 3z = 1 \\ x - y + 4z = 9 \end{cases}$$

22. Solve the system of linear equations by using Cramer's Rule.
$$\begin{cases} 3x - 5y + 2z = 3 \\ 2x + 2z = 3 \\ -x + 5y - 4z = 2 \end{cases}$$

23. Karl makes two kinds of cookies. Choc-O-Nut requires 4 oz of peanuts for each 10 oz of chocolate chips. Chocolate Krunch requires 12 oz of peanuts per 8 oz of chocolate chips. How many batches of each can he make if he has 46 oz of chocolate chips and 36 oz of peanuts?

24. Alicia has $7000 invested, some at 7% and the remainder at 8%. After one year, the interest from the 7% investment exceeds the interest from the 8% investment by $70. How much is invested at each rate?

25. The points (0, 4), (–2, 6), and (1, 9) lie on the curve described by the function $y = ax^2 + bx + c$. Find the values of $a, b,$ and c.

Use a TI-83 Plus calculator to answer Exercises 26 – 32.

26. Solve the system $\begin{cases} 6x + y = 0 \\ -3x + 2y = -15 \end{cases}$ by graphing.

27. Solve the system of equations by using the row echelon form command, ref:
$$\begin{cases} x + 2y = 7 \\ -x + 3y = \dfrac{13}{2} \end{cases}$$

28. Solve the system of equations by using the row echelon form command, ref:

$$\begin{cases} x+y-z=-8 \\ 2x-3y=-6 \\ x+y+z=2 \end{cases}$$

29. Solve the system of equations $\begin{cases} x-y=0 \\ 2x+y=3 \end{cases}$ by using Cramer's rule.

30. Solve the system of equations $\begin{cases} x+y-z=0 \\ 2x+3z=11 \\ 3y-z=3 \end{cases}$ by using Cramer's rule.

31. Solve the following system of linear inequalities graphically:

$$\begin{cases} x+2y>4 \\ x-y>7 \end{cases}$$

32. Solve the following system of linear inequalities graphically:

$$\begin{cases} y\le x-5 \\ 3x+y\ge 2 \end{cases}$$

Polynomials

Did You Know?

Throughout history, teachers of mathematics have tried to develop calculation methods that were easy to use or to memorize. One of the more interesting of these techniques is the Rule of Double False Position. As a student of algebra, it may seem strange to you that such a complicated method would be developed to solve a simple first-degree equation of the form $ax + b = 0$. But remember that you have modern symbolism at your disposal. To use the rule, we will make two guesses as to the solution of the equation. We shall designate the guesses as g_1 and g_2. Now we will let $e_1 = ag_1 + b$ and $e_2 = ag_2 + b$, where e_1 and e_2 represent the amount of error in our guesses. Then the solution is

$$x = \frac{e_1 g_2 - e_2 g_1}{e_1 - e_2}.$$

We now illustrate the Rule of Double False Position with an example: $3x + 6 = 0$. Suppose we guess that the solution is either 1 or 2. That is, let $g_1 = 1$ and $g_2 = 2$. Then $e_1 = 3(1) + 6 = 9$ and $e_2 = 3(2) + 6 = 12$, and the solution to the equation would be

$$\frac{9(2) - 12(1)}{9 - 12} = \frac{18 - 12}{-3} = \frac{6}{-3} = -2.$$

This unnecessarily complicated method of solving first-degree equations was taught until the nineteenth century. One of the most popular English texts of the sixteenth century, *The Grounde of Arte* by Robert Recorde (1510?–58), gives the Rule of Double False Position in verse:

Recorde

Gesse at this woorke as happe doth leade.
By chance to truthe you may procede.
And firste woorke by the question,
Although no truthe therein be don.
Suche falsehode is so good a grounde,
That truth by it will soone be founde.
From many bate to many mo,
From to fewe take to fewe also.
With to much ioyne to fewe againe,
To to fewe adde to manye plaine.
To crossewaies multiplye contrary kinde,
All truthe by falsehode for to fynde.

Students memorized the poem as a method of remembering the rule, which they generally did not understand. Can you figure out why making two false guesses can lead to the correct answer? After studying Chapters 3 and 4, you may be able to verify the Rule of Double False Position.

4.1   Addition and Subtraction of Polynomials

4.2   Multiplication of Polynomials

4.3   Division with Polynomials and Synthetic Division

4.4   Introduction to Factoring

4.5   Special Factoring Techniques

4.6   Polynomial Equations and Applications

4.7   Using a Graphing Calculator to Solve Equations and Absolute Values

"But it should always be required that a mathematical subject not be considered exhausted until it has become intuitively evident"

Felix Klein (1849-1925)

The basic operations of addition, subtraction, and multiplication with polynomials are used throughout all levels of mathematics. (You may want to review the properties of exponents discussed in Sections 1.7 and 1.8.) Division with polynomials is developed in Chapter 5. The importance of developing the related skills in operating with polynomials cannot be overstated.

Equally important are the factoring techniques discussed in Sections 4.4 - 4.6. As we will see in Chapter 5, these techniques are an integral part of operating with and simplifying rational expressions (fractions with polynomials in the numerator and denominator) and in solving equations. **Skill in factoring polynomials may be one of the determining factors in successfully completing this course**, so work particularly hard at this early stage.

Factoring with negative exponents, discussed in Section 4.4, deserves special mention. This skill gives an added dimension to equation-solving skills and is particularly useful in simplifying expressions in calculus.

4.1   Addition and Subtraction of Polynomials

Objectives

After completing this section, you will be able to:

1. *Identify polynomial expressions.*

2. *Classify certain polynomials as monomials, binomials, or trinomials.*

3. *Add and subtract polynomials.*

4. *Evaluate polynomials for given values of the variables.*

Monomial

A **monomial** is a term that has no variable in its denominator, and its variables have only whole number exponents. Thus, a monomial does **not** have variables with negative exponents in the numerator, positive exponents in the denominator, or fractional exponents. For example:

Monomial terms: $5x, \quad -7y^2, \quad 4, \quad \dfrac{1}{8}x^2y^2$

Not monomial terms: $\dfrac{2x^2}{y^2}, \quad -6x^{-1}, \quad 3y^{\frac{1}{2}}$

Monomial

> *A **monomial in x** is an expression of the form*
>
> $$kx^n$$
>
> *where n is a whole number and k is any real number.*
>
> ***n** is called the **degree** of the monomial, and **k** is the **coefficient**.*

A monomial may be in more than one variable. For example, $7x^2y$ is a monomial in x and y. The **degree of a monomial in more than one variable** is the sum of the exponents of its variables. Thus, $7x^2y$ is third degree ($2 + 1 = 3$) in x and y, and $8a^2b^3$ is fifth degree in a and b.

In the case of a constant monomial, such as 5, we can write $5 = 5 \cdot 1 = 5 \cdot x^0$. Therefore, a nonzero constant is considered to be a monomial of **degree 0**. Because there is more than one way of writing 0 with a variable, as $0 = 0x = 0x^3 = 0x^{16}$, 0 is considered to be a monomial of **no degree**.

Polynomials

Any monomial or algebraic sum of monomials is a **polynomial**. For example:

Polynomials:	$18, \ 3x^2 + 2, \ 5x^2y + 4xy^2,$ and $3x - 5.4w^2 - \dfrac{3}{2}xy$
Not polynomials:	$2x^{\frac{1}{3}} + 1, \dfrac{x}{y}, \dfrac{1}{x-2},$ and $x^{-1} + 5x$

In general, expressions with variables in the denominator, or variables with fractional or negative exponents are not polynomials.

The **degree of a polynomial** is the largest of the degrees of its terms after like terms have been combined. For example,

$$x^3 - 2x + 4x^2 - x^3 + 5x + 1 = 4x^2 + 3x + 1 \text{ is \textbf{second degree} in } x.$$

For consistency and easy identification, we will write polynomials in the generally accepted form with terms in **descending order** of degree from left to right. Thus, the polynomial

$$3x + 5x^2 - 14 + 2x^3 \text{ will be written as } 2x^3 + 5x^2 + 3x - 14.$$

Polynomials with one, two, or three terms are classified as follows.

Classification of Polynomials

Term	Description	Example
Monomial:	*polynomial with one term*	$15x^3$ *(third-degree monomial)*
Binomial:	*polynomial with two terms*	$4x - 10$ *(first-degree binomial)*
Trinomial:	*polynomial with three terms*	$-x^4 + 2x - 1$ *(fourth-degree trinomial)*

No special name is given to polynomials with more than three terms. They are referred to simply as polynomials. Of course, monomials, binomials, and trinomials can be referred to as polynomials as well.

A polynomial can be classified in reference to its degree as follows:

If a polynomial is of
  a. degree 0 or 1, it is called a **linear** polynomial.
  b. degree 2, it is called a **quadratic** polynomial.
  c. degree 3, it is called a **cubic** polynomial.

For example,
  $3x + 8$ is a linear polynomial (and a first-degree binomial).
  $5x^2 - 3x + 7$ is a quadratic polynomial (and a second-degree trinomial).
  $-10y^3$ is a cubic polynomial (and a third-degree monomial).

Addition of Polynomials

The **sum** of two or more polynomials can be found by combining like terms. (See Section 1.3.)

Example 1: Addition of Polynomials

Simplify each of the following expressions.

a. $(x^3 - 2x + 1) + (3x^2 + 4x + 5)$
  Solution:
$$(x^3 - 2x + 1) + (3x^2 + 4x + 5) = x^3 - 2x + 1 + 3x^2 + 4x + 5$$
$$= x^3 + 3x^2 - 2x + 4x + 1 + 5$$
$$= x^3 + 3x^2 + 2x + 6$$

b. $(2x^2 + 4x - 7) + (x^2 + 6x + 8)$
  Solution:
$$(2x^2 + 4x - 7) + (x^2 + 6x + 8) = 2x^2 + 4x - 7 + x^2 + 6x + 8$$
$$= 2x^2 + x^2 + 4x + 6x - 7 + 8$$
$$= 3x^2 + 10x + 1$$

As illustrated in Example 2 below, polynomials can be added vertically with like terms aligned. The polynomials are written in descending order and a 0 is written as a placeholder for any missing powers of the variable.

Example 2: Addition in Vertical Format

Write the sum $(5x^3 - 9x^2 - 10x + 12) + (3x^3 + 6x^2 - 7)$ in a vertical format and evaluate.

Solution:

$$5x^3 - 9x^2 - 10x + 12$$

$$\underline{3x^3 + 6x^2 + 0x - 7}$$ Note that $0x$ is written as a placeholder.

$$8x^3 - 3x^2 - 10x + 5$$

Subtraction of Polynomials

To find the **difference** of two polynomials, either

a. add the opposite of each term being subtracted, or equivalently,

b. use the distributive property and multiply each term being subtracted by –1, then add.

Example 3: Subtraction of Polynomials

Find the difference in simplest form: $(x^2y + 3y - 4x) - (2x^2y - 7x)$.

Solution:

a.   Add the opposites of the terms being subtracted.
$$(x^2y + 3y - 4x) - (2x^2y - 7x) = x^2y + 3y - 4x - 2x^2y + 7x$$
$$= x^2y - 2x^2y + 3y - 4x + 7x$$
$$= -x^2y + 3y + 3x$$

b.   Multiply each term being subtracted by –1.
$$(x^2y + 3y - 4x) - (2x^2y - 7x) = (x^2y + 3y - 4x) + (-1) (2x^2y - 7x)$$
$$= x^2y + 3y - 4x + (-2x^2y + 7x)$$
$$= x^2y + 3y - 4x - 2x^2y + 7x$$
$$= -x^2y + 3y + 3x$$

Adding the opposites of the terms or multiplying by –1 and then adding both have the effect of changing the sign of each term in the polynomial being subtracted. Subtraction can be performed using either the horizontal or vertical format.

• •

a. Find the difference $(x^2 + 12x - 23) - (2x^2 + 7x - 20)$

> **Solution:** Change the sign of each term in the polynomial being subtracted and combine like terms.
>
> $$(x^2 + 12x - 23) - (2x^2 + 7x - 20) = x^2 + 12x - 23 - 2x^2 - 7x + 20$$
> $$= -x^2 + 5x - 3$$
>
> If the polynomials are written in a vertical format, one beneath the other, we change the signs of the terms of the polynomial being subtracted and then combine like terms.
>
> $$\begin{array}{r} x^2 + 12x - 23 \\ -(2x^2 + 7x - 20) \\ \hline \end{array} \quad \rightarrow \quad \begin{array}{r} x^2 + 12x - 23 \\ -2x^2 - 7x + 20 \\ \hline -x^2 + 5x - 3 \end{array}$$

b. Find the difference $(6x^4 + 2x^3 - 4x^2 - 8) - (3x^4 + 5x^3 - x^2 + 6x - 10)$ by writing the terms in a vertical format and changing the signs of the polynomial being subtracted.

> **Solution:**
>
> $$\begin{array}{r} 6x^4 + 2x^3 - 4x^2 + 0x - 8 \\ -\left(3x^4 + 5x^3 - x^2 + 6x + 10\right) \\ \hline \end{array} \quad \rightarrow \quad \begin{array}{r} 6x^4 + 2x^3 - 4x^2 + 0x - 8 \\ -3x^4 - 5x^3 + x^2 - 6x - 10 \\ \hline 3x^4 - 3x^3 - 3x^2 - 6x - 18 \end{array}$$
>
> Note that $0x$ is written as a placeholder.

• •

$P(x)$ Notation and Evaluation of Polynomials

The evaluation of a polynomial for given values of the variable(s) provides an opportunity for the introduction of function notation in the form of $P(x)$. $P(x)$ is read "P of x," and **does not** mean multiplication. P is the name of the polynomial, and x is the variable. With this notation, $P(3)$ [read "P of 3"] indicates that the value of the polynomial P is to be calculated for $x = 3$, and $P(-2)$ indicates that the value of P is to be calculated for $x = -2$. If a polynomial is in more than one variable, such as x and y, then the notation can be written as $P(x, y)$ [read "P of x and y"]. Function notation is common to much of mathematics and it will be discussed again throughout Chapters 8 and 9.

Evaluating polynomials for given values of the variables gives excellent practice in following the rules for order of operations. **Be sure to put negative numbers in parentheses as illustrated in Example 5b.**

Example 5: Notation and Evaluation of Polynomials

a. For the polynomial $P(x) = x^3 - 2x^2 + 3x + 5$, find $P(4)$.

   Solution: Substitute 4 for x throughout the polynomial.

$$P(4) = 4^3 - 2 \cdot 4^2 + 3 \cdot 4 + 5 = 64 - 32 + 12 + 5$$
$$= 32 + 12 + 5$$
$$= 49$$

b. Evaluate the polynomial $P(x, y) = 2x^2y - xy + 3x - 4y + 15$ for $x = -1$ and $y = -6$.

   Solution: Substitute -1 for x and -6 for y throughout the polynomial.

$$P(-1, -6) = 2(-1)^2(-6) - (-1)(-6) + 3(-1) - 4(-6) + 15$$
$$= -12 - 6 - 3 + 24 + 15$$
$$= -21 + 39$$
$$= 18$$

Practice Problems

Add or subtract as indicated and simplify the result.

1. $(3x^2 - 2x + 5) + (2x^2 - x + 3)$ **2.** $(x^3 - 2x^2) - (x^2 - 1)$

3. $(5x^2 - 9x - 11) - (x^2 - 3x + 1)$

4. For $P(x) = x^3 - 8x^2 - 5x + 10$, find $P(-2)$.

4.1 Exercises

In Exercises 1 – 12, state whether the expression is or is not a polynomial. If the expression is a polynomial, state its degree and its classification as a monomial, binomial, or trinomial.

1. $x^3 - x^2$ **2.** 9 **3.** $x^2 - 3x^{\frac{1}{2}}$

4. $x^4 + 8x^2y - y^2$ **5.** $\dfrac{5}{4}x^2y - \dfrac{7}{4}y + \dfrac{1}{2}y^2$ **6.** $x^2 + xy - \dfrac{1}{y}$

7. 0 **8.** $-\sqrt{2}$ **9.** $\left(x^2y^3 - xy^2\right)^{\frac{1}{2}}$

10. $\dfrac{3}{2}x^2 - \sqrt{3}x - 7$ **11.** $7x^2 - 6x + 9x^{\frac{2}{3}}$ **12.** $\dfrac{x^2y - 3y^2}{x}$

In Exercises 13 – 35, add or subtract as indicated and simplify the result.

13. $\left(3x^2 - 5x + 1\right) + \left(x^2 + 2x - 7\right)$ **14.** $\left(5x^2 + 8x - 3\right) + \left(-2x^2 + 6x - 4\right)$

Answers to Practice Problems: 1. $5x^2 - 3x + 8$ **2.** $x^3 - 3x^2 + 1$ **3.** $4x^2 - 6x - 12$ **4.** -20

15. $\left(x^2 - 9x + 2 \right) + \left(-x^2 + 2x - 8 \right)$ **16.** $\left(7x^2 - 4x + 6 \right) + \left(4x^2 - 2x + 5 \right)$

17. $\left(x^2 + y^2 \right) + \left(2x^2 - 5y^2 \right)$ **18.** $\left(x^2 - 3xy + y^2 \right) + \left(2x^2 - 5xy - y^2 \right)$

19. $\left(2x^2 + 3x + 8 \right) - \left(x^2 + 4x - 2 \right)$ **20.** $\left(6x^3 - 5x + 1 \right) - \left(2x^3 + 3x - 4 \right)$

21. $\left(2x^4 + 3x \right) - \left(5x^3 + 4x + 3 \right)$ **22.** $\left(2x^3 - 3x^2 + 6 \right) - \left(x^4 + x + 1 \right)$

23. $\left(5x^2 + 6x - 1 \right) + \left(x^4 - 3x^2 + 2x \right)$ **24.** $\left(7x^2 - 2xy + 3y^2 \right) + \left(-3x^2 - 2xy + 5y^2 \right)$

25. $\left(4x^3 - 7x^2 + 3x + 2 \right) - \left(-2x^3 - 5x - 1 \right)$

26. $\left(4x^2 - 8xy - 2y^2 \right) + \left(-9x^2 + 5xy - 6y^2 \right)$

27. $\left(3x^2 - 2y^2 \right) + \left(7xy + 4y^2 \right) - \left(-6x^2 - 6xy + 8y^2 \right)$

28. $\left(9xy + 8y^2 \right) - \left(6x^2 - 8xy \right) + \left(5x^2 - 3xy + 7y^2 \right)$

29. $\left(5x^3 - 14x^2 \right) - \left(5x^2 + 2x + 1 \right) - \left(-7x^3 + 2x^2 - 13 \right)$

30. $\left(7x^3 + 4x^2 - x \right) + \left(3x^3 - 4x + 5 \right) - \left(8x^3 + x^2 - x + 3 \right)$

31. $x^3 - \left[3x^2 - 1 - \left(x^3 + 4x^2 + 1 \right) \right] + \left(3x^3 - 3x^2 - 2 \right)$

32. $3x - 4xy + \left[6y + \left(4x + 3xy + 2y \right) \right] - \left[-6x - \left(xy - 4y \right) \right]$

33. $x^2 - 2xy + \left[y^2 - \left(3xy + 2y^2 \right) - \left(3x^2 - xy - 2y^2 \right) \right]$

34. $\left[\left(4x^2 - 3x \right) - \left(2x^2 + 5x \right) \right] + \left[\left(x^2 - 6x \right) + \left(-3x^2 + x \right) \right]$

35. $\left[\left(2x + xy - y \right) + \left(x - 2xy + 4y \right) \right] - \left[\left(-3x + 5xy + y \right) - \left(2x + 3xy - 2y \right) \right]$

Find each sum in Exercises 36 – 40.

36. $\begin{aligned} 2x^2 &- 5x - 6 \\ \underline{-3x^2} &+ 2x - 1 \end{aligned}$ **37.** $\begin{aligned} x^3 + 2x^2 &+ x - 2 \\ \underline{x^3 - 2x^2} &- 3x - 1 \end{aligned}$

38. $\begin{aligned} 5x^3 - 4x^2 & - 9 \\ \underline{2x^3 - 3x^2} &- 6x + 5 \end{aligned}$ **39.** $\begin{aligned} 3x^4 + 3x^3 &+ x^2 + x + 2 \\ \underline{7x^4 - x^3} &- 5x^2 + x - 1 \end{aligned}$

40. $\begin{aligned} 14x^3 + 13x^2 &+ 10x - 13 \\ \underline{20x^3 } &- 18x + 25 \end{aligned}$

Find each difference in Exercises 41 – 45.

41. $9x^2 - 2x + 3$
$-\left(4x^2 + 5x - 2\right)$

42. $-3x^2 + 7x - 6$
$-\left(2x^2 - x + 6\right)$

43. $5x^3 \qquad -10x + 15$
$-\left(x^3 - 4x^2 - 3x - 9\right)$

44. $x^3 - 8x^2 + 12x + 5$
$-\left(-3x^3 + 8x^2 + 2x + 5\right)$

45. $2x^4 - 5x^3 - 6x^2 + 7x + 7$
$-\left(x^4 \qquad + 2x^2 + 4x + 10\right)$

Evaluate each polynomial in Exercises 46 – 55 for the specified value of the variable(s).

46. $P(x) = 2x^2 - x + 3;\ x = 1$

47. $P(x) = 3x^2 - 2x + 5;\ x = 2$

48. $P(x) = 3 - x^2;\ x = -2$

49. $P(x) = x^3 - 2x^2 + x - 1;\ x = 2$

50. $P(x) = x^3 + x^2 - 4;\ x = -3$

51. $P(x) = 4x^3 - 2x^2 - 1;\ x = -4$

52. $P(x, y) = 2x^2 - 3xy + y^2;\ x = 2,\ y = -2$

53. $P(x, y) = 4x - 2xy + 5y;\ x = 1,\ y = 1$

54. $P(x, y, z) = 3x + 4xy - 2yz + z;\ x = 1,\ y = 0,\ z = 2$

55. $P(x, y, z) = 2xyz - 3x + yz - xz;\ x = 2,\ y = -1,\ z = 2$

Writing and Thinking About Mathematics

56. Write the definition of a polynomial.

57. Explain, in your own words, how to subtract one polynomial from another.

58. Describe what is meant by the degree of a polynomial.

59. Give two examples that show how the sum of two binomials might not be a binomial.

60. Give two examples that show
   a. how the sum of two cubic polynomials might not be a cubic polynomial.
   b. how the difference of two quadratic polynomials might not be a quadratic polynomial.

Hawkes Learning Systems: Intermediate Algebra

Identifying Polynomials
Adding and Subtracting Polynomials

Multiplication of Polynomials

After completing this section, you will be able to:

1. *Multiply polynomials.*

2. *Recognize special products of polynomials.*

Multiplication by Monomials

Using the distributive property $a(b+c) = ab + ac$ with multiplication indicated on the left, we can find the product of a monomial and a polynomial of two or more terms as follows:

$$5x(2x^3 + 3) = 5x \cdot 2x^3 + 5x \cdot 3$$
$$= 10x^4 + 15x$$

and
$$3x^2(x^2 - 5x + 1) = 3x^2 \cdot x^2 + 3x^2(-5x) + 3x^2 \cdot 1$$
$$= 3x^4 - 15x^3 + 3x^2.$$

Multiplication of Polynomials

For a product of a binomial times a binomial, such as $(x+3)(x+8)$, we consider the distributive property in the form

$$(b+c)a = ba + ca$$

and replace a in the formula with the binomial $(x+8)$.

$$(b+c)a = ba + ca$$

$$(x+3)(x+8) = x(x+8) + 3(x+8)$$

Continue to apply the distributive property.

$$= x \cdot x + x \cdot 8 + 3 \cdot x + 3 \cdot 8$$
$$= x^2 + 8x + 3x + 24$$
$$= x^2 + 11x + 24$$

Similarly,

$$(2x - 1)(x^2 + x - 4) = 2x(x^2 + x - 4) - 1(x^2 + x - 4)$$
$$= 2x \cdot x^2 + 2x \cdot x + 2x(-4) - 1 \cdot x^2 - 1 \cdot x - 1(-4)$$
$$= 2x^3 + 2x^2 - 8x - x^2 - x + 4$$
$$= 2x^3 + x^2 - 9x + 4$$

Example 1: Multiplication of Polynomials ●

a.　$x^2 y(x^2 + 3y^2) = x^2 y \cdot x^2 + x^2 y \cdot 3y^2$　　　Use the distributive property.

$$= x^4 y + 3x^2 y^3$$

b.　$(2x + 1)(x - 5) = 2x(x - 5) + 1(x - 5)$　　　Use the distributive property.

$$= 2x^2 - 10x + x - 5$$

$$= 2x^2 - 9x - 5$$　　　Simplify.

c.　$x^{3k}(x^k + x) = x^{3k} \cdot x^k + x^{3k} \cdot x$　　　Use the distributive property.

$$= x^{3k+k} + x^{3k+1}$$　　　Add the exponents.

$$= x^{4k} + x^{3k+1}$$　　　Simplify.

● ●

The FOIL Method

In the case of the **product of two binomials** such as $(2x + 5)(3x - 7)$, the **FOIL** method is useful. **F-O-I-L** is a mnemonic device (memory aid) to help in remembering which terms of the binomials to multiply together. First, by using the distributive property we can see how the terms are multiplied:

$$(2x + 5)(3x - 7) = 2x(3x - 7) + 5(3x - 7)$$

$$= 2x \cdot 3x + 2x(-7) + 5 \cdot 3x + 5(-7)$$

　　　　↑　　　↑　　　↑　　　↑

First　Outside　Inside　Last
Terms　Terms　Terms　Terms
　F　　　O　　　I　　　L

Now, by using the FOIL method (mentally), except for combining like terms we can go directly to the answer:

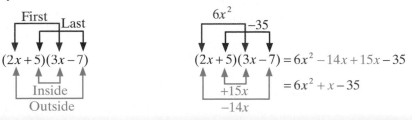

Example 2: FOIL Method

a. Find the product $(x+3)(2x+8)$ by using the **FOIL** method.
Solution:

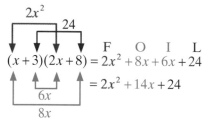

$$(x+3)(2x+8) = 2x^2 + 8x + 6x + 24$$
$$= 2x^2 + 14x + 24$$

b. Find the product $(2x-3)(3x-5)$ by using the **FOIL** method.
Solution:

$$(2x-3)(3x-5) = 6x^2 - 10x - 9x + 15$$
$$= 6x^2 - 19x + 15$$

Special Products

We have discussed the following two techniques for multiplying polynomials:
1. Use the distributive property to multiply by monomials.
2. Use the FOIL method to multiply two binomials.

However, there are five types of products that occur so frequently that they are given in the forms of formulas with names. All five formulas listed here can be developed by using the distributive property and collecting like terms.

Special Products of Polynomials

Formula	Classification
I. $(X+A)(X-A) = X^2 - A^2$	*Difference of two squares*
II. $(X+A)^2 = X^2 + 2AX + A^2$	*Perfect square trinomial*
III. $(X-A)^2 = X^2 - 2AX + A^2$	*Perfect square trinomial*
IV. $(X-A)(X^2 + AX + A^2) = X^3 - A^3$	*Difference of two cubes*
V. $(X+A)(X^2 - AX + A^2) = X^3 + A^3$	*Sum of two cubes*

> **NOTES**
>
> **CAUTION!**
> Be careful to note that the two trinomials $X^2 + AX + A^2$ and $X^2 - AX + A^2$ in Formulas **IV** and **V** are not perfect square trinomials.

You should memorize these formulas. Along with the FOIL method of multiplication of two binomials, they are part of the foundation for our work with factoring in the next section and with algebraic fractions in the next chapter.

Example 3: Special Products

Find each of the indicated products by applying the appropriate formula and name the product.

a. $(3y+2)(3y-2)$

Solution: Using Formula **I**, the result is the difference of two squares.

Formula **I**:
$$(X + A)(X - A) = X^2 - A^2$$
$$(3y+2)(3y-2) = (3y)^2 - (2)^2$$
$$= 9y^2 - 4 \qquad \text{Difference of two squares}$$

b. $(5x+7)^2$

Solution: Using Formula **II**, the result is a perfect square trinomial.

Formula **II**:
$$(X + A)^2 = X^2 + 2AX + A^2$$
$$(5x+7)^2 = (5x+7)(5x+7)$$
$$= (5x)^2 + 7(5x) + 7(5x) + 7^2$$
$$= (5x)^2 + 2(7)(5x) + 7^2$$
$$= 25x^2 + 70x + 49 \qquad \text{Perfect square trinomial}$$

c. $(x-3)(x^2+3x+9)$

Solution: Using Formula **IV**, the result is the difference of two cubes.

Formula **IV**:
$$(X - A)(X^2 + AX + A^2) = X^3 - A^3$$
$$(x-3)(x^2+3x+9) = (x)^3 - (3)^3$$
$$= x^3 - 27 \qquad \text{Difference of two cubes}$$

To verify this product, multiply and combine like terms.

$$(x-3)(x^2+3x+9) = x(x^2+3x+9) - 3(x^2+3x+9)$$
$$= x^3 + 3x^2 + 9x - 3x^2 - 9x - 27$$
$$= x^3 - 27$$

The squares of binomials represented in Formulas **II** and **III** sometimes lead to the following common error.

Common Error

*For **products** raised to a power, we have $(ab)^n = a^n b^n$ and $(ab)^2 = a^2 b^2$. However, this rule does not apply to sums. In particular, it does **not** apply to binomials.*

$$(a+b)^2 \neq a^2 + b^2$$

$$(a-b)^2 \neq a^2 - b^2$$

Remember, the squares of binomials are trinomials:

$$(a+b)^2 = (a+b)(a+b) = a^2 + 2ab + b^2$$

and

$$(a-b)^2 = (a-b)(a-b) = a^2 - 2ab + b^2$$

The following examples illustrate a few more abstract applications of the general forms.

Example 4: Abstract Products •

a. $[(x+3)-y]^2$

Solution: Treat $(x+3)$ as a single term and use Formula **III** for the square of a binomial.

Formula **III**:
$$(X-A)^2 = X^2 - 2AX + A^2$$
$$[(x+3)-y]^2 = (x+3)^2 - 2(x+3)y + y^2$$
$$= x^2 + 6x + 9 - 2xy - 6y + y^2$$

b. $(x^k + 3)(x^k - 3)$ (Assume that k represents a whole number.)

Solution: Using Formula **I** and the fact that $(x^k)^2 = x^{2k}$,

Formula **I**:
$$(X+A)(X-A) = X^2 - A^2$$
$$(x^k + 3)(x^k - 3) = (x^k)^2 - 3^2$$
$$= x^{2k} - 9 \qquad \text{Difference of two squares}$$

c. $(3y^{2k} - 5)(3y^{2k} - 5)$

> **Solution:**   Using the FOIL method (or Formula **III** could be used),
> $$(3y^{2k} - 5)(3y^{2k} - 5) = 3y^{2k} \cdot 3y^{2k} - 5 \cdot 3y^{2k} - 5 \cdot 3y^{2k} - 5(-5)$$
> $$= 9y^{4k} - 30y^{2k} + 25$$

● ●

Just as with addition and subtraction, multiplication with polynomials can be performed in a vertical format. Align the terms vertically and, in turn, multiply every term in the bottom polynomial by every term in the top polynomial. That is, apply the distributive property in a vertical format and align like terms in the partial products so they can be added. Example 5 illustrates this technique.

Example 5: Vertical Format   ●

Find the product $(2x + 3)(5x^2 + 4x - 5)$.

> **Solution:**   Arrange the polynomials in a vertical format and multiply each term in the top polynomial by 3.
> $$\begin{array}{rrrrrr} & 5x^2 & + & 4x & - & 5 \\ & & & 2x & + & 3 \\ \hline 15x^2 & + & 12x & - & 15 \end{array}$$
>
> Next, multiply each term in the top polynomial by $2x$ and align like terms,
> $$\begin{array}{rrrrrr} & & 5x^2 & + & 4x & - & 5 \\ & & & & 2x & + & 3 \\ \hline & & 15x^2 & + & 12x & - & 15 \\ 10x^3 & + & 8x^2 & - & 10x \end{array}$$
>
> Now, combine like terms to find the product.
> $$\begin{array}{rrrrrr} & & 5x^2 & + & 4x & - & 5 \\ & & & & 2x & + & 3 \\ \hline & & 15x^2 & + & 12x & - & 15 \\ 10x^3 & + & 8x^2 & - & 10x \\ \hline 10x^3 & + & 23x^2 & + & 2x & - & 15 \end{array}$$ ⟵ product

● ●

Practice Problems

Find each of the following products.

1. $(x+5)(x^2-5x+25)$

2. $x^k(x^k-1)$

3. $(7x-1)(2x+3)$

4. $(x-8)^2$

5. $\begin{array}{r} x^2 + 3x - 2 \\ \underline{5x - 1} \end{array}$

4.2 Exercises

Find the indicated products and simplify in Exercises 1 – 62. If a product involves three polynomials, find the product of any two and multiply this product by the third polynomial.

1. $5x(x^2-2x+3)$

2. $2x^2(3x^2+5x-1)$

3. $xy^2(x^2+4y)$

4. $x^2z(x-4y+z)$

5. $(x+3)(x-6)$

6. $(x-2)(x-5)$

7. $(x-8)(x-1)$

8. $(x+2)(x+4)$

9. $(2y+1)(y-6)$

10. $(y+5)(3y+2)$

11. $(3x-4)(x-5)$

12. $(2x-1)(x-2)$

13. $(2y+3)(3y+2)$

14. $(5y-2)(3y+1)$

15. $(8x+3)(x-5)$

16. $(7x+6)(2x-3)$

17. $(9x+1)(3x-2)$

18. $(5x-11)(3x+4)$

19. $(3x+1)^2$

20. $(4x-3)^2$

21. $(5x-2y)^2$

22. $(7x+4y)^2$

23. $(4x+7)(4x-7)$

24. $(3x+5)(3x-5)$

25. $(2x-3y)(2x+3y)$

26. $(6x-y)(6x+y)$

27. $x(3x^2-4)(3x^2+4)$

28. $3x(7x^2+8)(7x^2-8)$

29. $(x-1)(x^2+x+1)$

30. $(y+4)(y^2-4y+16)$

31. $(x+3)(x^2+6x+9)$

32. $(y-5)(y^2+3y+2)$

33. $(x^3+2)^2$

34. $(2x^3-3)^2$

35. $(2x^3-7)(2x^3+7)$

36. $(x+2y)(x^2-2xy+4y^2)$

37. $(x-3y)(x^2+3xy+9y^2)$

Answers to Practice Problems: **1.** x^3+125 **2.** $x^{2k}-x^k$ **3.** $14x^2+19x-3$ **4.** $x^2-16x+64$
  5. $5x^3+14x^2-13x+2$

38. $(8y^2 - 7)(3y^2 + 2)$

39. $4x^2y(x^2 + 6y^2)(x^2 - 6y^2)$

40. $3xy(x^2 - 6y^2)(x^2 + 3y^2)$

41. $x^2y(5x^2 + y^2)(2x^2 - 3y^2)$

42. $x^3(x - 2y)(x^2 + 2xy + 4y^2)$

43. $[(x+y)+2][(x+y)-2]$

44. $[(x+1)+y][(x+1)-y]$

45. $[(5x-y)+3]^2$

46. $[(2x+1)-y]^2$

47. $[(x+4)-2y]^2$

48. $[(x-3y)+5]^2$

49. $x^2(x^k + 3)$

50. $x^3(x^{2k} + x)$

51. $(x^k + 3)(x^k - 5)$

52. $(x^k + 6)(x^k - 6)$

53. $(x^k + 1)(x^k + 4)$

54. $(2x^k - 3)(x^k + 2)$

55. $(3x^k + 2)(x^k + 5)$

56. $\left(x + \dfrac{1}{4}\right)\left(x - \dfrac{1}{4}\right)$

57. $\left(x + \dfrac{5}{8}\right)\left(x - \dfrac{5}{8}\right)$

58. $\left(x + \dfrac{2}{3}\right)^2$

59. $\left(y - \dfrac{1}{5}\right)^2$

60. $\left(y + \dfrac{1}{4}\right)\left(y - \dfrac{3}{4}\right)$

61. $(x + 2.5)(x - 2.5)$

62. $(x + 2.1)^2$

Find the indicated products in Exercises 63 – 68.

63.
$$
\begin{array}{r}
2x^2 - 5x - 6 \\
3x + 1 \\
\hline
\end{array}
$$

64.
$$
\begin{array}{r}
x^2 + 2x + 1 \\
x^2 + 2x + 1 \\
\hline
\end{array}
$$

65.
$$
\begin{array}{r}
x^3 - 3x + 4 \\
2x - 3 \\
\hline
\end{array}
$$

66.
$$
\begin{array}{r}
2x^3 + 6x^2 + 5 \\
x^2 + 5 \\
\hline
\end{array}
$$

67.
$$
\begin{array}{r}
x^3 - 7x - 4 \\
4x - 6 \\
\hline
\end{array}
$$

68.
$$
\begin{array}{r}
x^3 - 5x + 14 \\
2x - 3 \\
\hline
\end{array}
$$

69. In the case of binomial probabilities, if x is the probability of success in one trial of an event, then the expression $P(x) = 10x^3(1-x)^2$ is the probability of three successes in 5 trials where $0 \le x \le 1$.

a. Represent the expression $P(x)$ as a single polynomial function.

b. If a fair coin is tossed, the probability of heads occurring is $\dfrac{1}{2}$. That is, $x = \dfrac{1}{2}$. Find the probability of 3 heads occurring in 5 tosses.

c. A basketball player is known to make 80% of his free throws. What is the probability that he will make exactly 3 of his next 5 attempts?

70. A square is 30 inches on each side. A square x inches on each side is cut from each corner of the square.

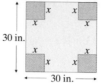

30 in.
30 in.

a. Represent the area of the remaining portion of the square in the form of a polynomial function $A(x)$.

b. Represent the perimeter of the remaining portion of the square in the form of a polynomial function $P(x)$.

71. A swimming pool, 25 meters by 50 meters, is surrounded by a concrete deck that is x meters wide.

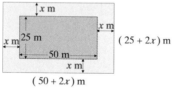

x m
x m
25 m
$(25 + 2x)$ m
50 m
x m
$(50 + 2x)$ m

a. Represent the area covered by the deck and the pool in the form of a polynomial function.

b. Represent the area covered by the deck only in the form of a polynomial function.

72. A rectangle has sides $(x + 5)$ ft and $(x + 10)$ ft. A square x feet on a side is cut from one corner of the rectangle.

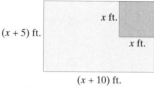

x ft.
$(x + 5)$ ft.
x ft.
$(x + 10)$ ft.

a. Represent the remaining area (light area in the figure shown) in the form of a polynomial function $A(x)$.

b. Represent the perimeter of the remaining figure (after the square in the corner has been removed) in the form of a polynomial function $P(x)$.

Writing and Thinking About Mathematics

73. Explain how the sum of the areas of the rectangles within the square with sides of length $(x + 5)$ can represent the perfect square trinomial in the formula for $(X + A)^2$.

[Hopefully, this exercise will help remind you that the square of a binomial always has three terms.]

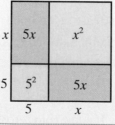

x | $5x$ | x^2
5 | 5^2 | $5x$
5 | x

Multiplying Polynomials
The FOIL Method

4.3   Division with Polynomials and Synthetic Division

Objectives

After completing this section, you will be able to:

1.   Divide a polynomial by a monomial.

2.   Divide polynomials by using the long division algorithm.

3.   Divide polynomials by using synthetic division.

In this section we will investigate three forms of division with polynomials. In each case the dividend is the same or higher degree than the divisor. The three cases are:

    1. A polynomial divided by a monomial

    2. The division algorithm (known as long division)

    3. Synthetic division (a special case of long division)

Division by a Monomial

As with real numbers, division with polynomials can be indicated by writing the polynomials in fraction form. That is, the fractions

$$\frac{x^3 - 6x^2 + 2x}{3x}, \quad \frac{6x^2 - 7x - 2}{2x - 1}, \quad \text{and} \quad \frac{5x^3 + 11x^2 - 3x + 1}{x + 3}$$

all indicate that the numerator is to be divided by the denominator.

When the denominator (or divisor) is a monomial (as in the first fraction above), simply divide each term in the numerator by the denominator and simplify each fraction. (You may want to review the rules for exponents in Sections 1.7 and 1.8.) Examples 1a and 1b illustrate this technique.

Example 1: Division by a Monomial •

a. Divide $x^3 - 6x^2 + 2x$ by $3x$.

    Solution: Write the quotient as a sum of fractions by dividing each term in the numerator by the denominator.

$$\frac{x^3 - 6x^2 + 2x}{3x} = \frac{x^3}{3x} - \frac{6x^2}{3x} + \frac{2x}{3x} \qquad \text{Divide each term in the numerator by } 3x.$$

$$= \frac{x^2}{3} - 2x + \frac{2}{3} \qquad \text{Simplify each fraction.}$$

continued on next page ...

b. Divide $\dfrac{15y^3 + 20y^2 - 5y}{5y}$ by dividing each term in the numerator by the denominator.

Solution: $\dfrac{15y^3 + 20y^2 - 5y}{5y} = \dfrac{15y^3}{5y} + \dfrac{20y^2}{5y} - \dfrac{5y}{5y}$

$$= 3y^2 + 4y - 1$$

• •

The Division Algorithm

When we first learn to divide with whole numbers the dividend (the numerator) is larger than the divisor (the denominator). The process is called long division and the remainder must be a number less than the divisor. For example,

the fraction $\dfrac{64}{5}$ can indicate long division as

$$\begin{array}{r} 12 \\ 5\overline{)64} \\ \underline{5} \\ 14 \\ \underline{10} \\ 4 \end{array}$$

and the result can be written as a mixed number $12\dfrac{4}{5}$

which can be written in the form of a sum $12 + \dfrac{4}{5}$.

Long division with polynomials is a similar process. If the denominator is not a monomial, and the degree of the numerator is equal to or greater than the degree of the denominator, the division can be indicated in fraction form as $\dfrac{P}{D}$ where P and D are polynomials. This method of division is called the **division algorithm** or **long division**. (An algorithm is a process or series of steps for solving a problem.)

The Division Algorithm

*For polynomials P and D, the **division algorithm** gives*

$$\frac{P}{D} = Q + \frac{R}{D}, D \neq 0 \ \ [\textit{or, in function notation, } \frac{P(x)}{D(x)} = Q(x) + \frac{R(x)}{D(x)}, D(x) \neq 0]$$

*where Q and R are polynomials and **the degree of R < degree of D**.*

The actual process of long division is not clear from this abstract definition. Although you are familiar with the process of long division with integers, this same procedure seems more complicated with polynomials. Long division with polynomials is illustrated in detail in the following three examples. Study them carefully.

Example 2: The Division Algorithm •

a. Simplify $\dfrac{6x^2 - 7x - 2}{2x - 1}$ by using long division.

Solution: **Step 1:** $2x - 1 \overline{)6x^2 - 7x - 2}$

Write the expression in the long division format with both polynomials written in descending powers of the variables.

Step 2: $2x - 1 \overline{)\begin{array}{c} 3x \\ 6x^2 - 7x - 2 \end{array}}$

Mentally divide $6x^2$ by $2x$. Since $6x^2 \div 2x = 3x$, write $3x$ in the quotient.

Step 3: $2x - 1 \overline{)\begin{array}{c} 3x \\ 6x^2 - 7x - 2 \\ \underline{6x^2 - 3x} \end{array}}$ ⟵ $3x(2x - 1)$

Multiply $3x$ times $2x - 1$ and write the product $6x^2 - 3x$ below the polynomial $6x^2 - 7x - 2$.

Step 4: $2x - 1 \overline{)\begin{array}{c} 3x \\ 6x^2 - 7x - 2 \\ \underline{-6x^2 + 3x} \\ -4x - 2 \end{array}}$

Subtract $6x^2 - 3x$ by changing signs and adding. Bring down the next term, -2.

Step 5: $2x - 1 \overline{)\begin{array}{c} 3x - 2 \\ 6x^2 - 7x - 2 \\ \underline{-6x^2 + 3x} \\ -4x - 2 \end{array}}$

Divide $-4x$ by $2x$. Since $-4x \div 2x = -2$, write -2 in the quotient.

Step 6: $2x - 1 \overline{)\begin{array}{c} 3x - 2 \\ 6x^2 - 7x - 2 \\ \underline{-6x^2 + 3x} \\ -4x - 2 \\ \underline{-4x + 2} \end{array}}$ ⟵ $-2(2x - 1)$

Multiply -2 times $2x - 1$. Write the product $-4x + 2$ below $-4x - 2$.

continued on next page ...

273

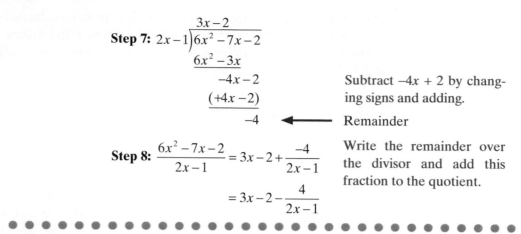

Step 7:

$$3x - 2$$
$$2x - 1 \overline{)6x^2 - 7x - 2}$$
$$\underline{6x^2 - 3x}$$
$$-4x - 2$$
$$\underline{(+4x - 2)}$$
$$-4 \quad \longleftarrow$$

Subtract $-4x + 2$ by changing signs and adding.

Remainder

Step 8: $\dfrac{6x^2 - 7x - 2}{2x - 1} = 3x - 2 + \dfrac{-4}{2x - 1}$

Write the remainder over the divisor and add this fraction to the quotient.

$$= 3x - 2 - \dfrac{4}{2x - 1}$$

• •

In Example 3, we show the same sequence of steps as in Example 2, but they are written in the normal compact form that should be used. Note that 0 is written as a placeholder for any missing powers of the variable, and like terms are aligned vertically.

Example 3: Long Division •

a. Simplify $\dfrac{25x^3 + 9x + 2}{5x + 1}$ by using long division.

Solution:

$$5x^2 - x + 2$$
$$5x + 1 \overline{)25x^3 + 0x^2 + 9x + 2}$$
$$\underline{25x^3 + 5x^2}$$
$$-5x^2 + 9x$$
$$\underline{-5x^2 - x}$$
$$10x + 2$$
$$\underline{10x + 2}$$
$$0$$

Divide $25x^3 \div 5x = 5x^2$. Write $5x^2$ in the quotient. Multiply $5x^2$ times $5x + 1$ and **subtract**. Continue the process **until the degree of the remainder is smaller than the degree of the divisor**.

$$\dfrac{25x^3 + 9x + 2}{5x + 1} = 5x^2 - x + 2$$

NOTES

Because the remainder is 0, both $5x + 1$ and $(5x^2 - x + 2)$ are **factors** of the polynomial $25x^3 + 9x + 2$. That is, the product of the divisor and the quotient is the dividend:

$$(5x + 1)(5x^2 - x + 2) = 25x^3 + 9x + 2$$

In general, if $\dfrac{P}{D} = Q$ or $D \cdot Q = P$, then D and Q are **factors** of P.

(We will discuss factors and factoring in detail in Sections 4.4 and 4.5.)

b. Divide $\dfrac{x^4 - 5x^3 + 2x^2 - 6x + 1}{x^2 + 1}$ by using the division algorithm.

Solution:

$$
\begin{array}{r}
x^2 - 5x + 1 \\
x^2 + 1 \overline{\smash{\big)}\, x^4 - 5x^3 + 2x^2 - 6x + 1} \\
\underline{x^4 \qquad + \; x^2} \\
-5x^3 + \; x^2 - 6x \\
\underline{-5x^3 \qquad -5x} \\
x^2 - x + 1 \\
\underline{x^2 \qquad +1} \\
-x
\end{array}
$$

Note that the divisor is second degree, and the remainder, $-x$, is less than second degree.

So,

$$\frac{x^4 - 5x^3 + 2x^2 - 6x + 1}{x^2 + 1} = x^2 - 5x + 1 + \frac{-x}{x^2 + 1}$$

$$= x^2 - 5x + 1 - \frac{x}{x^2 + 1}$$

• •

Synthetic Division

In the special case **when the divisor is first-degree with leading coefficient 1**, the division can be simplified by omitting the variables entirely and writing only certain coefficients. The procedure is called **synthetic division**. The following analysis describes how the procedure works for $\dfrac{5x^3 + 11x^2 - 3x + 1}{x + 3}$. (Note that $x + 3$ is first-degree with leading coefficient 1.)

a. With Variables

$$
\begin{array}{r}
5x^2 - 4x + 9 \\
x + 3 \overline{\smash{\big)}\, 5x^3 + 11x^2 - \; 3x + 1} \\
\underline{5x^3 + 15x^2} \\
-4x^2 - \; 3x \\
\underline{-4x^2 - 12x} \\
9x + \; 1 \\
\underline{9x + 27} \\
-26
\end{array}
$$

b. Without Variables

$$
\begin{array}{r}
5 - 4 + 9 \\
1 + 3 \overline{\smash{\big)}\, 5 + 11 - 3 + 1} \\
\underline{\boxed{5} + 15} \\
-4 \boxed{-3} \\
\underline{\boxed{-4} - 12} \\
9 \boxed{+1} \\
\underline{\boxed{9} + 27} \\
-26
\end{array}
$$

continued on next page ...

275

The boxed numbers in step **b** can be omitted since they are repetitions of the numbers directly above them.

c. Boxed numbers omitted

$$
\begin{array}{r}
5-\ 4+\ 9 \\
1+3\overline{)5+11-\ 3+\ 1} \\
+15 \\
\overline{-4} \\
-12 \\
\overline{9} \\
+27 \\
\overline{-26}
\end{array}
$$

d. Numbers moved up to fill in spaces

$$
\begin{array}{r}
5-\ 4+\ 9 \\
1+3\overline{)5+11-\ 3+\ 1} \\
+15\ -12+27 \\
\overline{-4\ +\ 9-26}
\end{array}
$$

Next, we omit the 1 in the divisor, change +3 to −3, and write the opposites of the boxed numbers (because the quotient coefficient will now be multiplied by −3 instead of +3), as shown in steps **e** and **f**. This allows the numbers to be added instead of subtracted. The number 5 is written on the bottom line, and the top line is omitted. The quotient and remainder can now be read from the bottom line.

e.
$$
\begin{array}{r}
5-\ 4\ +9 \\
1+3\overline{)5+11\ -\ 3\ +\ 1} \\
\boxed{+15}\,\boxed{-12}\,\boxed{+27} \\
\overline{-4\ +\ 9\ -26}
\end{array}
$$

f.
$$
\begin{array}{r}
-3\overline{)5+11-\ 3+\ 1} \\
\downarrow -15+12-27 \\
\overline{5\ -\ 4+\ 9-26}
\end{array}
$$

Represents

$$5x^2 - 4x + 9 + \frac{-26}{x+3}$$

The numbers on the bottom now represent the coefficients of a polynomial of **one degree less than the dividend**, along with the remainder. The last number to the right is the remainder.

In summary, synthetic division can be accomplished as follows:

1. Write only the coefficients of the dividend and the opposite of the constant in the divisor.

$$
\begin{array}{r|rrrr}
-3 & 5 & 11 & -3 & 1 \\
\hline
& & & &
\end{array}
$$

2. Rewrite the first coefficient as the first coefficient in the quotient.

$$
\begin{array}{r|rrrr}
-3 & 5 & 11 & -3 & 1 \\
& \downarrow & & & \\
\hline
& 5 & & &
\end{array}
$$

3. Multiply the coefficient by the constant divisor and **add** this product to the second coefficient.

$$
\begin{array}{r|rrrr}
-3 & 5 & 11 & -3 & 1 \\
& \downarrow & -15 & & \\
\hline
& 5 \nearrow & -4 & &
\end{array}
$$

4. Continue to multiply each new coefficient by the constant divisor and add this product to the next coefficient in the dividend.

$$\begin{array}{r|rrrr} -3 & 5 & 11 & -3 & 1 \\ & \downarrow & -15 & 12 & -27 \\ \hline & 5 \nearrow & -4 \nearrow & 9 \nearrow & -26 \end{array}$$

5. The constants on the bottom line are the coefficients of the quotient and the remainder.

$$\frac{5x^3 + 11x^2 - 3x + 1}{x + 3} = 5x^2 - 4x + 9 + \frac{-26}{x + 3}$$

$$= 5x^2 - 4x + 9 - \frac{26}{x + 3}$$

Example 4: Synthetic Division ●

Use synthetic division to write each expression in the form $Q + \dfrac{R}{D}$.

a. $\dfrac{4x^3 + 10x^2 + 11}{x + 5}$

Solution: $\begin{array}{r|rrrr} -5 & 4 & 10 & 0 & 11 \\ & \downarrow & -20 & 50 & -250 \\ \hline & 4 & -10 & 50 & -239 \end{array}$ Since there is no x-term, 0 is the coefficient. The coefficient is 0 for any missing term.

$$\frac{4x^3 + 10x^2 + 11}{x + 5} = 4x^2 - 10x + 50 + \frac{-239}{x + 5}$$

$$= 4x^2 - 10x + 50 - \frac{239}{x + 5}$$

b. $\dfrac{2x^4 - x^3 - 5x^2 - 2x + 7}{x - 2}$

Solution: $\begin{array}{r|rrrrr} 2 & 2 & -1 & -5 & -2 & 7 \\ & \downarrow & 4 & 6 & 2 & 0 \\ \hline & 2 & 3 & 1 & 0 & 7 \end{array}$

$$\frac{2x^4 - x^3 - 5x^2 - 2x + 7}{x - 2} = 2x^3 + 3x^2 + x + \frac{7}{x - 2}$$

● ●

NOTES

Remember that synthetic division is used only when the divisor is first-degree of the form $(x + c)$ or $(x - c)$.

The Remainder Theorem

Synthetic division can be used for several purposes, one of which is to find the value of a polynomial for a particular value of x. For example, we know (from Section 4.1) that if

$$P(x) = x^3 - 5x^2 + 7x - 10$$

then

$$P(2) = 2^3 - 5 \cdot 2^2 + 7 \cdot 2 - 10 = -8.$$

With synthetic division of $x^3 - 5x^2 + 7x - 10$ by $x - 2$ we have

$$
\begin{array}{r|rrrr}
2 & 1 & -5 & +7 & -10 \\
  &   & 2 & -6 & +2 \\
\hline
  & 1 & -3 & +1 & -8
\end{array}
\quad \longleftarrow \text{Remainder}
$$

The fact that the remainder is the same as $P(2)$ is not an accident. In fact, as the following theorem states, the remainder when a polynomial is divided by a first-degree factor of the form $(x - c)$ will always be $P(c)$.

The Remainder Theorem

If a polynomial, $P(x)$, is divided by $(x - c)$, then the remainder will be $P(c)$.

Proof:

By the division algorithm we know that $\dfrac{P(x)}{x - c} = Q(x) + \dfrac{R}{x - c}$ where R is a constant. (Remember that the degree of the remainder must be less than the degree of the divisor.)

Now, multiplying through by $(x - c)$, we have

$$P(x) = (x - c) \cdot Q(x) + R$$

and substituting $x = c$ gives

$$
\begin{aligned}
P(c) &= (c - c) \cdot Q(c) + R \\
&= 0 \cdot Q(c) + R \\
&= 0 + R \\
&= R
\end{aligned}
$$

The proof is complete.

Example 5: The Remainder Theorem and Synthetic Division

a. Use synthetic division to find $P(5)$ given $P(x) = -2x^2 + 15x - 50$.

Solution:

$$
\begin{array}{r|rrr}
5 & -2 & 15 & -50 \\
  &   & -10 & 25 \\
\hline
  & -2 & 5 & -25
\end{array}
\quad \longleftarrow \text{Remainder} = P(5)
$$

Thus, $P(5) = -25$.

[Checking shows $P(5) = -2 \cdot 5^2 + 15 \cdot 5 - 50 = -50 + 75 - 50 = -25$.]

b. Use synthetic division to find $P(-3)$ given $P(x) = 3x^4 + 10x^3 - 5x^2 + 125$.

Note: To evaluate $P(-3)$ we must think of the divisor of the form $(x+3) = (x-(-3))$. That is, in the form $(x-c)$, $c = -3$.

Solution:

$$
\begin{array}{r|rrrrr}
-3 & 3 & 10 & -5 & 0 & 125 \\
   &   & -9 & -3 & 24 & -72 \\
\hline
   & 3 & 1 & -8 & 24 & 53
\end{array}
$$
← Remainder $= P(-3)$

Thus, $P(-3) = 53$.

c. Use synthetic division to show that $(x-6)$ is a factor of $P(x) = x^3 - 14x^2 + 53x - 30$.

Solution:

$$
\begin{array}{r|rrrr}
6 & 1 & -14 & 53 & -30 \\
  &   & 6 & -48 & 30 \\
\hline
  & 1 & -8 & 5 & 0
\end{array}
$$
← Remainder $= P(6)$

Thus, the remainder is $P(6) = 0$ and **$x-6$ is a factor of $P(x)$**.

[**Note:** The coefficients in the quotient tell us that $x^2 - 8x + 5$ is also a factor of $P(x)$.]

• •

4.3 Exercises

In Exercises 1 – 10, find each quotient by dividing each term in the numerator by the monomial denominator. Simplify each resulting fraction. Assume that no divisor is 0.

1. $\dfrac{8y^3 - 16y^2 + 24y}{8y}$

2. $\dfrac{18x^4 + 24x^3 + 36x^2}{6x^2}$

3. $\dfrac{34x^5 - 51x^4 + 17x^3}{17x^3}$

4. $\dfrac{14y^4 + 28y^3 + 12y^2}{2y^2}$

5. $\dfrac{110x^4 - 121x^3 + 11x^2}{11x}$

6. $\dfrac{15x^7 + 36x^6 - 25x^3}{15x^3}$

7. $\dfrac{-56x^4 + 98x^3 - 35x^2}{14x^2}$

8. $\dfrac{108x^6 - 72x^5 + 63x^4}{18x^4}$

9. $\dfrac{16y^6 - 56y^5 - 120y^4 + 64y^3}{16y^3}$

10. $\dfrac{20y^5 - 14y^4 + 21y^3 + 42y^2}{4y^2}$

Use the division algorithm to divide in Exercises 11 – 40 and write the answer in the form $Q + \dfrac{R}{D}$ where the degree of R is less than the degree of D. Assume that no divisor is 0.

11. $\dfrac{21x^2 + 25x - 3}{7x - 1}$

12. $\dfrac{15x^2 - 14x - 11}{3x - 4}$

13. $\dfrac{2x^3 + 7x^2 + 10x - 6}{2x + 3}$

14. $\dfrac{6x^3 - 7x^2 + 14x - 8}{3x - 2}$

15. $\dfrac{21x^3 + 41x^2 + 13x + 5}{3x + 5}$

16. $\dfrac{6x^3 - 4x^2 + 5x - 7}{x - 2}$

17. $\dfrac{x^3 - x^2 - 10x - 10}{x - 4}$

18. $\dfrac{2x^3 - 3x^2 + 7x + 4}{2x - 1}$

19. $\dfrac{10x^3 + 11x^2 - 12x + 9}{5x + 3}$

20. $\dfrac{6x^3 + 19x^2 - 3x - 7}{6x + 1}$

21. $\dfrac{2x^3 - 7x + 2}{x + 4}$

22. $\dfrac{2x^3 + 4x^2 - 9}{x + 3}$

23. $\dfrac{9x^3 - 19x + 9}{3x - 2}$

24. $\dfrac{16x^3 + 7x + 12}{4x + 3}$

25. $\dfrac{6x^3 + 11x^2 + 25}{2x + 5}$

26. $\dfrac{4x^3 - 8x^2 - 9x}{2x - 3}$

27. $\dfrac{3x^3 + 5x^2 + 7x + 9}{x^2 + 2}$

28. $\dfrac{2x^4 + 2x^3 + 3x^2 + 6x - 1}{2x^2 + 3}$

29. $\dfrac{x^4 + x^3 - 4x + 1}{x^2 + 4}$

30. $\dfrac{2x^4 + x^3 - 8x^2 + 3x - 2}{x^2 - 5}$

31. $\dfrac{6x^3 + 5x^2 - 8x + 3}{3x^2 - 2x - 1}$

32. $\dfrac{x^3 - 9x^2 + 20x - 38}{x^2 - 3x + 5}$

33. $\dfrac{3x^4 - 7x^3 + 5x^2 + x - 2}{x^2 + x + 1}$

34. $\dfrac{2x^4 + 9x^3 - x^2 + 6x + 9}{x^2 - 3x + 1}$

35. $\dfrac{x^4 + 3x - 7}{x^2 + 2x - 3}$

36. $\dfrac{3x^4 - 2x^3 + 4x^2 - x + 3}{3x^2 + x - 1}$

37. $\dfrac{x^3 - 27}{x - 3}$

38. $\dfrac{x^3 + 125}{x + 5}$

39. $\dfrac{x^5 - 1}{x^2 + 1}$

40. $\dfrac{x^6 - 1}{x^3 - 1}$

In Exercises 41 – 60, divide by using synthetic division. ***a.*** *Write the answer in the form $Q + \dfrac{R}{D}$ where R is a constant.* ***b.*** *In each exercise, $D = (x - c)$. State the value of c and the value of P(c).*

41. $\dfrac{x^2 - 12x + 27}{x - 3}$

42. $\dfrac{x^2 - 12x + 35}{x - 5}$

43. $\dfrac{x^3 + 4x^2 + x - 1}{x + 8}$

44. $\dfrac{x^3 - 6x^2 + 8x - 5}{x - 2}$

45. $\dfrac{4x^3 + 2x^2 - 3x + 1}{x + 2}$

46. $\dfrac{3x^3 + 6x^2 + 8x - 5}{x + 1}$

47. $\dfrac{x^3+6x+3}{x-7}$

48. $\dfrac{2x^3-7x+2}{x+4}$

49. $\dfrac{2x^3+4x^2-9}{x+3}$

50. $\dfrac{4x^3-x^2+13}{x-1}$

51. $\dfrac{x^4-3x^3+2x^2-x+2}{x-3}$

52. $\dfrac{x^4+x^3-4x^2+x-3}{x+6}$

53. $\dfrac{x^4+2x^2-3x+5}{x-2}$

54. $\dfrac{3x^4+2x^3+2x^2+x-1}{x+1}$

55. $\dfrac{x^4-x^2+3}{x-\dfrac{1}{2}}$

56. $\dfrac{x^3+2x^2+1}{x-\dfrac{2}{3}}$

57. $\dfrac{x^5-1}{x-1}$

58. $\dfrac{x^5-x^3+x}{x+\dfrac{1}{2}}$

59. $\dfrac{x^4-2x^3+4}{x+\dfrac{4}{5}}$

60. $\dfrac{x^6+1}{x+1}$

Writing and Thinking About Mathematics

61. State and prove the Remainder Theorem.

62. Suppose that a polynomial is divided by $(3x-2)$ and the answer is given as $x^2+2x+4+\dfrac{20}{3x-2}$. What is the polynomial? Explain how you arrived at this conclusion.

Collaborative Learning Exercise

63. The class should be divided into teams of 3 or 4 students. Each team should then develop answers to the following questions and be prepared to discuss these answers in class.

   a. First use long division to divide the polynomial $P(x)=2x^3-8x^2+10x+15$ by $2x-1$.

   Then use synthetic division to divide the same polynomial by $x-\dfrac{1}{2}$.

   Do the same process with two or three other polynomials and divisors. Next compare the corresponding long and synthetic division answers and explain how the answers are related.

   b. Use the results from part a and explain algebraically the relationship of the answers when a polynomial is divided (using long division) by $ax-b$ and (using synthetic division) by $x-\dfrac{b}{a}$.

   c. Show how the Remainder Theorem should be restated if $x-c$ is replaced by $ax-b$.

Hawkes Learning Systems: Intermediate Algebra

Division by a Monomial
The Division Algorithm
Synthetic Division

4.4   Introduction to Factoring

After completing this section, you will be able to:

1. *Factor out the greatest common factors of polynomials.*

2. *Factor trinomials (including perfect squares).*

3. *Factor the differences of squares.*

In Section 4.2, products of polynomials were found by using the distributive property, the FOIL method, and applying various formulas. For example, using the distributive property,

$$2x(x^2 - 8x + 3) = 2x(x^2) + 2x(-8x) + 2x(3)$$
$$= 2x^3 - 16x^2 + 6x$$

The expressions $2x$ and $x^2 - 8x + 3$ are called **factors** of the product.

$$\underbrace{2x(x^2 - 8x + 3)}_{\text{factors}} = \underbrace{2x^3 - 16x^2 + 6x}_{\text{product}}$$

Factoring is the reverse of multiplication. That is, to factor a polynomial means to find polynomials that will multiply together to produce the given polynomial as a product. Factoring relies heavily on the multiplication techniques developed in Section 4.2. That is, you must remember how to multiply in order to be able to factor. This is similar to basic arithmetic.

For example, in order to be able to divide 45 by 5, you must remember that $9 \cdot 5 = 45$.

Furthermore, we will find that the skill of factoring polynomials is necessary when simplifying rational expressions (Chapter 5) and when solving equations. In other words, Sections 4.4 and 4.5 are particularly important, so study them with extra care.

Greatest Common Factor

To find the **greatest common factor (GCF)** of a polynomial:

1. Find the expression of highest degree and largest integer coefficient that is a factor of each term of the polynomial.

2. Divide this factor into each term of the polynomial resulting in another polynomial factor.
   (**Note:** This process is called "factoring out" the common factor.)

For example, factoring out $3x$ in the polynomial $6x^4 + 3x^3 - 21x^2$ gives

$$6x^4 + 3x^3 - 21x^2 = 3x \cdot 2x^3 + 3x \cdot x^2 + 3x(-7x)$$
$$= 3x(2x^3 + x^2 - 7x)$$

Note that the polynomial $2x^3 + x^2 - 7x$ has x as a common factor. Therefore, we have not factored **completely**. **An expression is factored completely if none of its factors can be factored**. Thus, $3x$ is not the **greatest** common factor. The greatest common factor is $3x^2$. Factoring out $3x^2$ gives the factored form

$$6x^4 + 3x^3 - 21x^2 = 3x^2 \cdot 2x^2 + 3x^2 \cdot x + 3x^2 \cdot (-7)$$
$$= 3x^2(2x^2 + x - 7)$$

A common factor may be an expression other than a monomial. It might be a binomial or a polynomial with three or more terms. In the following example, the binomial $x^2 + 1$ is the common factor and is factored out.

$$x^2(x^2 + 1) + 5x(x^2 + 1) + 2(x^2 + 1) = (x^2 + 1)(x^2 + 5x + 2)$$

In this text, we attempt to factor polynomials into products of polynomials of lesser degree, all with integer coefficients. If this cannot be done, we say that the polynomial is **irreducible** (or **not factorable** or **prime**). For example, the polynomials $x^2 + 36$ and $x^2 + 5x + 2$ cannot be factored over the integers and are both irreducible (or not factorable or prime).

Example 1: Greatest Common Factor ●

Factor out the greatest common factor in each polynomial.

a. $4x^2 + 24x + 8$

Solution: In this case, the greatest common factor is the constant 4.

$$4x^2 + 24x + 8 = 4(x^2 + 6x + 2)$$

b. $-14x^4 + 21x^3 - 84x^2$

Solution: In this case, the leading term is negative, and $-7x^2$ can be considered the greatest common factor. With this approach, the polynomial factor in parentheses will have a positive leading term and will be easier to factor, if possible. However, factoring out $7x^2$ would still be considered correct.

$$-14x^4 + 21x^3 - 84x^2 = -7x^2(2x^2 - 3x + 12) \qquad \text{Preferred}$$

or $\qquad -14x^4 + 21x^3 - 84x^2 = 7x^2(-2x^2 + 3x - 12) \qquad \text{Still correct}$

● ●

Basic Forms

Finding the greatest common factor, whether a monomial or other polynomial, is just the first step in factoring. Certain products should be recognized quickly, while others may involve the **FOIL** method and some experimentation. Consider the first three formulas from Section 4.2:

Formulas of Squares

I.	*Difference of two squares*	$X^2 - A^2 = (X + A)(X - A)$
II.	*Perfect square trinomial*	$X^2 + 2AX + A^2 = (X + A)^2$
III.	*Perfect square trinomial*	$X^2 - 2AX + A^2 = (X - A)^2$

With these formulas firmly committed to memory, many binomials and trinomials can be factored directly simply by replacing *x* and *a* with the terms in the same positions.

Example 2: Basic Forms

Factor completely.

a. $x^2 - 25$

Solution: Formula: $X^2 - A^2 = (X + A)(X - A)$

(In this example we used $X = x$ and $A = 5$.)

$$x^2 - 25 = x^2 - 5^2$$
$$= (x + 5)(x - 5)$$

b. $4x^2 - 121$

Solution: Formula: $X^2 - A^2 = (X + A)(X - A)$

(In this example we used $X = 2x$ and $A = 11$.)

$$4x^2 - 121 = (2x)^2 - 11^2$$
$$= (2x + 11)(2x - 11)$$

c. $4y^2 + 12y + 9$

Solution: Formula: $X^2 + 2AX + A^2 = (X + A)^2$

(In this example we used $X = 2y$ and $A = 3$.)

$$4y^2 + 12y + 9 = (2y)^2 + 2(2y)(3) + 3^2$$
$$= (2y + 3)^2$$

continued on next page ...

Factor completely.

d. $(z+2)^2 - 12(z+2) + 36$

Solution: Formula: $X^2 - 2AX + A^2 = (X-A)^2$

$$(z+2)^2 - 2\cdot 6(z+2) + 6^2 = \left[(z+2)-6\right]^2$$

(In this example we used $X = z+2$ and $A = 6$.)

$$= (z-4)^2$$

e. $2x^2 - 128$

Solution: Factor out the GCF first. Then factor $(x^2 - 64)$.

$$2x^2 - 128 = 2(x^2 - 64)$$
$$= 2(x+8)(x-8)$$

f. $x(x-3) - (3x+1)(x-3)$

Solution: Factor out $(x-3)$ first.

$$x(x-3) - (3x+1)(x-3) = (x-3)\left[x-(3x+1)\right]$$
$$= (x-3)\left[x-3x-1\right]$$
$$= (x-3)(-2x-1) \text{ or } -1(x-3)(2x+1)$$

g. $2a^3 - 8a^2b + 8ab^2$

Solution: Factor out GCF first. Then factor the perfect square trinomial.

$$2a^3 - 8a^2b + 8ab^2 = 2a(a^2 - 4ab + 4b^2)$$
$$= 2a(a-2b)^2$$

● ●

ac-Method (Grouping)

Not all polynomials can be factored by using the known formulas. Two general methods for factoring trinomials in the form

$$ax^2 + bx + c \qquad\qquad \text{where } a, b, \text{ and } c \text{ are integers}$$

are the *ac*-**method** (or **grouping**) and the **FOIL method** (or **trial and error**).

The **ac-method** is very systematic. It also involves a technique called factoring by grouping that we will develop here on a limited basis. Factoring by grouping will be discussed in more detail in Section 4.5.

Consider the problem of factoring $2x^2 + 9x + 10$ in which $a = 2$, $b = 9$, and $c = 10$.

Analysis of Factoring by the *ac*-method

	General Method	**Example**
	$ax^2 + bx + c$	$2x^2 + 9x + 10$
Step 1:	*Multiply* $a \cdot c$	*Multiply* $2 \cdot 10 = 20$
Step 2:	*Find two integers whose product is ac and whose sum is b. If this is not possible, then the trinomial is* **not factorable.**	*Find two integers whose product is 20 and whose sum is 9. (In this case, $4 \cdot 5 = 20$ and $4 + 5 = 9$).*
Step 3:	*Rewrite the middle term* (bx) *using the two numbers found in step 2 as coefficients.*	*Rewrite the middle term* $(9x)$ *using 4 and 5 as coefficients.* $2x^2 + 9x + 10$ $= 2x^2 + 4x + 5x + 10$
Step 4:	*Factor by grouping the first two terms and the last two terms.*	*Factor by grouping the first two terms and the last two terms.* $2x^2 + 4x + 5x + 10$ $= (2x^2 + 4x) + (5x + 10)$ $= 2x(x + 2) + 5(x + 2)$
Step 5:	*Factor out the common binomial factor. This will give two binomial factors of the trinomial $ax^2 + bx + c$.*	*Factor out the common binomial factor $(x + 2)$. Thus,* $2x^2 + 9x + 10$ $= 2x^2 + 4x + 5x + 10$ $= 2x(x + 2) + 5(x + 2)$ $= (x + 2)(2x + 5)$

Example 3: ac-method

a. Factor $x^2 - 2x - 15$ using the *ac*-method.
Solution: $a = 1, b = -2,$ and $c = -15$

Step 1: Find the product $a \cdot c$: $1(-15) = -15$.

Step 2: Find two integers whose product is -15 and whose sum is -2.
$(-5)(+3) = -15$ and $-5 + 3 = -2$

Step 3: Rewrite $-2x$ as $-5x + 3x$ to obtain
$x^2 - 2x - 15 = x^2 - 5x + 3x - 15$.

Step 4: Factor by grouping.
$x^2 - 2x - 15 = x^2 - 5x + 3x - 15 = x(x - 5) + 3(x - 5)$

Step 5: Factor out the common binomial factor $(x - 5)$.
$x^2 - 2x - 15 = x(x - 5) + 3(x - 5) = (x - 5)(x + 3)$

b. Factor $18x^3 - 39x^2 + 18x$ using the *ac*–method.
Solution: First factor out the greatest common factor $3x$.

$$18x^3 - 39x^2 + 18x = 3x(6x^2 - 13x + 6)$$

Now factor the trinomial $6x^2 - 13x + 6$ with $a = 6, b = -13,$ and $c = 6$.

Step 1: Find the product $a \cdot c$: $6(6) = 36$.

Step 2: Find two integers whose product is 36 and whose sum is -13.
Note: This may take some time and experimentation. We do know that both numbers must be negative since the product is positive and the sum is negative.

$(-9)(-4) = +36$ and $-9 + (-4) = -13$

Step 3: Rewrite $-13x$ as $-9x - 4x$ to obtain
$6x^2 - 13x + 6 = 6x^2 - 9x - 4x + 6$.

Step 4: Factor by grouping.
$6x^2 - 13x + 6 = 6x^2 - 9x - 4x + 6$
$$= (6x^2 - 9x) + (-4x + 6)$$
$$= 3x(2x - 3) - 2(2x - 3)$$

Note: -2 is factored from the last two terms so that there will be a common binomial factor $(2x - 3)$.

Step 5:   Factor out the common binomial factor $(2x-3)$.

$$6x^2 - 13x + 6 = 6x^2 - 9x - 4x + 6$$
$$= 3x(2x-3) - 2(2x-3)$$
$$= (2x-3)(3x-2)$$

Thus, for the original expression,

$$18x^3 - 39x^2 + 18x = 3x(6x^2 - 13x + 6)$$
$$= 3x(2x-3)(3x-2)$$

Remember to include the original GCF in the final product.

● ●

FOIL Method (Trial and Error)

The **FOIL method** (or **Trial and Error method**) of factoring trinomials is actually applying the FOIL method of multiplication of two binomials in reverse. We consider two basic forms:

1. The leading coefficient is 1: ⟶ $x^2 + bx + c$

2. The leading coefficient is not 1: ⟶ $ax^2 + bx + c$

For example, consider factoring a trinomial with leading coefficient 1 such as

$$x^2 + 17x + 30.$$

Because the leading coefficient is 1, we know that the first terms in the two binomial factors are x and x:

$$\mathbf{F} = x^2 \qquad \mathbf{L} = 30$$
$$x^2 + 17x + 30 = (x \quad)(x \quad)$$
$$\mathbf{I}$$
$$\mathbf{O}$$

For **O** and **I**, we need two factors of 30 whose sum is 17.
Possible pairs are $30 \cdot 1$, $15 \cdot 2$, $10 \cdot 3$, and $6 \cdot 5$.

Because $15 \cdot 2 = 30$ and $15 + 2 = 17$, we have

$$\mathbf{F} = x^2 \qquad \mathbf{L} = 30$$
$$x^2 + 17x + 30 = (x + 2)(x + 15)$$
$$\mathbf{I} = 2x$$
$$\mathbf{O} = 15x$$

Similarly, to factor $x^2 + 11x + 30$, we need the factors of 30 whose sum is 11.

$6 \cdot 5 = 30$ and $6 + 5 = 11$.

$$x^2 + 11x + 30 = (x + 6)(x + 5)$$

To factor a trinomial with leading coefficient other than 1, we use the FOIL method also, but with more of a trial and error approach. For example, to factor

$$4x^2 - x - 5,$$

the product of the first two terms of the binomial factors is to be $4x^2$, so we might have

$\mathbf{F} = 4x^2$ $\mathbf{F} = 4x^2$

$(2x\quad)(2x\quad)$ **OR** $(4x\quad)(x\quad)$

The product of the last terms, **L**, is to be –5. The factors could be –5(1) or 5(–1). Try each of the possible combinations until the correct product is found. If all possible pairs are tried and none gives the correct product, then the trinomial is **not factorable using integer coefficients**.

1. $(2x + 1)(2x - 5) = 4x^2 - 10x + 2x - 5 = 4x^2 - 8x - 5 \neq 4x^2 - x - 5$

2. $(2x - 1)(2x + 5) = 4x^2 + 10x - 2x - 5 = 4x^2 + 8x - 5 \neq 4x^2 - x - 5$

3. $(4x + 1)(x - 5) = 4x^2 - 20x + x - 5 = 4x^2 - 19x - 5 \neq 4x^2 - x - 5$

4. $(4x - 1)(x + 5) = 4x^2 + 20x - x - 5 = 4x^2 + 19x - 5 \neq 4x^2 - x - 5$

5. $(4x + 5)(x - 1) = 4x^2 - 4x + 5x - 5 = 4x^2 + x - 5 \neq 4x^2 - x - 5$

6. $(4x - 5)(x + 1) = 4x^2 + 4x - 5x - 5 = 4x^2 - x - 5$

We have found the factors on the last try. With practice, most of the steps can be done mentally, and the final form can be found more quickly.

a. For example, in the above discussion, since the first pair did not work, there is no point in trying the second pair because the only difference is the sign of the middle term. The same is true with the third and fourth pairs. Thus, two attempts could have been eliminated immediately.

b. Also, by looking at the fifth attempt, we can see that the middle term is only incorrect by the sign.

c. Therefore, we know the sixth pair must work before we even try it.

Example 4: FOIL Method (Trial and Error) ● ● ● ● ● ● ● ● ● ● ● ● ● ● ● ●

a. Factor $x^2 - 10x + 16$.

   Solution: The coefficient of x^2 is 1. We know $(-8)(-2) = 16$ and $(-8) + (-2) = -10$.
   Thus, we have

$$\mathbf{F} = x^2 \qquad \mathbf{L} = 16$$

$$x^2 - 10x + 16 = (x - 8)(x - 2)$$

$$\mathbf{I} = -8x$$
$$\mathbf{O} = -2x$$

b. Factor $3x^2 + 3x - 36$.

   Solution: $3x^2 + 3x - 36 = 3(x^2 + x - 12)$ The greatest common factor is 3.

   $\qquad\qquad\qquad = 3(x - 3)(x + 4)$ $(-3)(4) = -12$ and $-3x + 4x = x$

c. Factor $5x^2 + 23x - 10$.

   Solution: $(5x - 10)(x + 1)$ $5x - 10x = -5x \neq 23x$

   $-10x$
   $5x$

   $(5x - 1)(x + 10)$ $50x - x = 49x \neq 23x$

   $-x$
   $50x$

   $(5x + 2)(x - 5)$ $-25x + 2x = -23x \neq 23x$

   $2x$
   $-25x$

   $(5x - 2)(x + 5)$ $25x - 2x = 23x$

   $-2x$
   $25x$

$$5x^2 + 23x - 10 = (5x - 2)(x + 5)$$

● ●

> **NOTES**
>
> **Summary Note:** When factoring polynomials, always look for a common monomial factor first. Then, if there is one, remember to include this common monomial factor as part of the answer. Not all polynomials are factorable. For example, no matter what combinations are tried, $x^2 + 3x + 5$ does not have two binomial factors with integer coefficients. (There are no factors of +5 that will add to +3.) We say that the polynomial is **irreducible** (or **not factorable** or **prime**). **An irreducible (or prime) polynomial is one that cannot be factored as the product of polynomials with integer coefficients**.

Practice Problems

Factor completely.

1. $x^2 - 12x + 36$

2. $x^2 + 2x - 35$

3. $15 - 2x - x^2$

4. $50y^6 - 2y^4$

5. $8x^2 + 13x - 6$

6. $2x^2(x+1) + 9x(x+1) - 18(x+1)$

4.4 Exercises

Completely factor each expression in Exercises 1 – 60. In Exercises 53 – 60, treat the expression in parentheses as a single term.

1. $5x^2 + 15$

2. $7x^3 - 14x^2$

3. $x^2y - 2xy + xy^2$

4. $8x^2y - 4xy^2$

5. $5x^2y^2 + 20x^2y$

6. $6x^2y + 3xy - 9xy^2$

7. $3x^2y + 21x^3y^2 + 3x^2y^3$

8. $10x^3y^2 - 5x^2y - 15x^2$

9. $x^2 + 64$

10. $y^2 + 81$

11. $9x^2 - 25$

12. $4x^2 - 49$

13. $x^2 - 10x + 25$

14. $y^2 + 12y + 36$

15. $9y^2 + 12y + 4$

16. $49x^2 - 14x + 1$

17. $x^2 + 9x + 18$

18. $y^2 - 7y - 30$

19. $x^2 - 6x - 27$

20. $x^2 - 144$

21. $y^2 - 5y - 14$

22. $x^2 - 27x + 50$

23. $x^2 + 14x + 49$

24. $2x^2 + 15x - 8$

25. $6x^2 + 13x + 6$

26. $8x^2 + 10x - 25$

27. $2x^2 + 9x - 35$

Answers to Practice Problems: 1. $(x-6)^2$ **2.** $(x+7)(x-5)$ **3.** $(5+x)(3-x)$ **4.** $2y^4(5y+1)(5y-1)$

5. $(8x-3)(x+2)$ **6.** $(x+1)(2x-3)(x+6)$

28. $3x^2 + 2x - 8$

29. $16x^2 - 40x + 25$

30. $6x^2 - 35x - 5$

31. $35x^2 + 9x - 18$

32. $18x^2 - 7xy - y^2$

33. $4x^3 - 64x$

34. $2x^3y + 32x^2y + 128xy$

35. $21x^4 - 4x^3 - 32x^2$

36. $2x^4y^3 - 5x^3y^3 - 18x^2y^3$

37. $6x^5y^2 - 28x^4y^3 - 6x^3y^4$

38. $16x^4 + 8x^2y + y^2$

39. $12x^5 + 38x^3 + 20x$

40. $14x^5y^2 - 11x^3y^2$

41. $9x^5 - 16x$

42. $x^4 + 10x^2y + 25y^2$

43. $2x^4 + x^2y - 15y^2$

44. $4x^6 - 49$

45. $2x^4 - 7x^2y + 4y^2$

46. $2x^4 + 11x^2y - 21y^2$

47. $2x^6 + 9x^3y^2 + 4y^4$

48. $5x^4 + 17x^2y^2 + 6y^4$

49. $x^2(x-5) + 4x(x-5) - 21(x-5)$

50. $x^2(x+4) - 6x(x+4) - 15(x+4)$

51. $2x^2(2x+1) - 9x(2x+1) - 18(2x+1)$

52. $3x^2(4x-1) + 19x(4x-1) + 28(4x-1)$

53. $(x+y)^2 + 6(x+y) + 9$

54. $(x-y)^2 - 81$

55. $(x+2y)^2 - 25$

56. $(4x+y)^2 + 4(4x+y) + 4$

57. $(x+5y)^2 + 8(x+5y) + 12$

58. $(6x-y)^2 + 8(6x-y) + 7$

59. $(3x-y)^2 + 3(3x-y) - 4$

60. $(2x+y)^2 + (2x+y) - 6$

61. The area (in square inches) of the rectangle shown is given by the polynomial function $A(x) = 8x^2 + 120x$. If the width of the rectangle is $4x$ inches, what is the representation of the length?

62. The area (in square meters) of the rectangle shown is given by the polynomial function $A(x) = x^2 + 13x + 30$. If the length of the rectangle is $(x+10)$ meters, what is the representation of the width?

$A(x) = 8x^2 + 120x$

$4x$

l

w

$A(x) = x^2 + 13x + 30$

$x + 10$

63. The volume of an open box is found by cutting equal squares (x units on a side) from a sheet of cardboard that is 12 inches by 36 inches. The function representing the volume is $V(x) = 4x^3 - 96x^2 + 432x$, where $0 < x < 6$.

    a. Factor this function in such a way that the factors represent the lengths of the sides of the box.

    b. What is the value of and the meaning of $V(2)$? $V(4)$?

64. The area of a triangle is $\dfrac{1}{2}$ the product of its base and its height. The area (in square feet) of the triangle shown is given by the function $A(x) = \dfrac{1}{2}x^2 + 16x$

    a. Find representations for the lengths of its base and its height.

    b. What is the value of and the meaning of $A(2)$? $A(3)$?

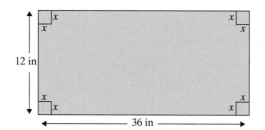

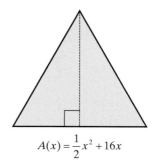

$A(x) = \dfrac{1}{2}x^2 + 16x$

Writing and Thinking About Mathematics

65. It is true that

$$4x^2 + 24x + 20 = (4x + 20)(x + 1) = (x + 5)(4x + 4) = (2x + 10)(2x + 2).$$

Explain how the trinomial can be factored in three ways. Is there some kind of error?

66. It is true that $5x^2 + 5x - 60 = (5x + 20)(x - 3)$.
Explain why this is not the completely factored form of the trinomial.

67. Explain, in your own words, what is meant by factoring a polynomial.

Hawkes Learning Systems: Intermediate Algebra

GCF of a Polynomial
Special Factorizations - Squares
Factoring Trinomials by Grouping
Factoring Trinomials by Trial and Error

Special Factoring Techniques

Objectives

After completing this section, you will be able to:

1. Factor the sums and differences of cubes.

2. Factor by grouping.

3. Factor special expressions in which there are common factors with negative exponents.

This section covers three different special techniques for factoring:

   1. factoring sums and differences of cubes,

   2. factoring by grouping with four terms,

   3. factoring with negative exponents.

Sums and Differences of Cubes

Recall formulas **IV** and **V** from Section 4.2:

IV. $(X - A)(X^2 + AX + A^2) = X^3 - A^3$ Difference of two cubes

V. $(X + A)(X^2 - AX + A^2) = X^3 + A^3$ Sum of two cubes

 NOTES

Caution: Note that the trinomials $(X^2 + AX + A^2)$ and $(X^2 - AX + A^2)$ in Formulas **IV** and **V** are **not** perfect square trinomials. Perfect square trinomials are in the form $(X^2 + 2AX + A^2)$ and $(X^2 - 2AX + A^2)$.

For convenience and understanding, we rewrite these formulas so that the factors are on the right:

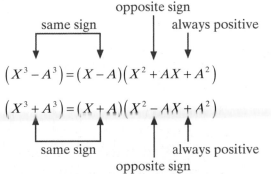

The differences and sums of two cubes can be factored by mentally substituting for X and A in these two formulas. As shown in the following examples, a variety of expressions must be substituted for X and A.

Example 1: Sums and Differences of Cubes ● ● ● ● ● ● ● ● ● ● ● ● ● ● ● ● ●

Factor completely.

a. $x^3 - 27$

Solution:

$$x^3 - 27 = x^3 - (3)^3$$
$$= (x - 3)(x^2 + 3x + 9)$$
$$(X - A)(X^2 + AX + A^2)$$

b. $x^6 + 64$

Solution:

$$x^6 + 64 = (x^2)^3 + (4)^3$$
$$= (x^2 + 4)(x^4 - 4x^2 + 16)$$
$$(X + A)(X^2 - AX + A^2)$$

c. $8y^{12} - 125$

Solution:

$$8y^{12} - 125 = (2y^4)^3 - (5)^3$$
$$= (2y^4 - 5)(4y^8 + 10y^4 + 25)$$
$$(X - A)(X^2 + AX + A^2)$$

d. $x^{3k} + y^{6k}$

Solution: $x^{3k} + y^{6k} = (x^k)^3 + (y^{2k})^3$
$$= (x^k + y^{2k})(x^{2k} - x^k y^{2k} + y^{4k})$$
$$(X + A) \ (X^2 - AX + A^2)$$

● ●

Factoring by Grouping

Not all products are binomials or trinomials. For example,

$$(a+b)(c+d) = (a+b)c + (a+b)d$$
$$= ac + bc + ad + bd$$

and
$$(x+3)(y-7) = (x+3)y + (x+3)(-7)$$
$$= xy + 3y - 7x - 21$$

In both examples, there are no like terms to be combined, and the product has four terms. Now, given a product such as $xy + 3y - 7x - 21$, try to **group** terms in such a way that a common binomial factor can be recognized.

Example 2: Factoring by Grouping

Factor each of the following by grouping terms.

a. $ax - ay + bx - by$

Solution: $ax - ay + bx - by = (ax - ay) + (bx - by)$

$$= a(x - y) + b(x - y)$$ $(x - y)$ is treated as a common factor.

$$= (x - y)(a + b)$$

b. $xy - 8x - 2y + 16$

Solution: $xy - 8x - 2y + 16 = (xy - 8x) + (-2y + 16)$

$$= x(y - 8) + 2(-y + 8)$$ Since $y - 8$ and $-y + 8$ are not the same factor, we factor -2 instead of 2 from the last two terms.

$$= x(y - 8) - 2(y - 8)$$

$$= (y - 8)(x - 2)$$

c. $4xy - 28x + 3y - 15$

Solution: $4xy - 28x + 3y - 15 = 4x(y - 7) + 3(y - 5)$

But $y - 7$ and $y - 5$ are not the same factor. In fact, $4xy - 28x + 3y - 15$ is not factorable. That is, **the fact that some of the terms are factorable does not necessarily imply that the entire expression is factorable**. To be factored, the entire expression must be a product of factors.

continued on next page ...

d. $x^2 + 6x + 9 - y^2$

Solution: $x^2 + 6x + 9 - y^2 = \left(x^2 + 6x + 9\right) - y^2$ Special grouping

$$= (x+3)^2 - y^2$$ Difference of the two squares

$$= \left[(x+3) + y\right]\left[(x+3) - y\right]$$

The special grouping provided here shows that the expression can be treated as the difference of two squares.

● ●

Factoring with Negative Exponents

Students continuing their mathematics studies into trigonometry, algebra, or calculus will find expressions with negative exponents that can be factored. These expressions cannot be classified as polynomials. However, many times one of the factors is a polynomial. We will consider expressions in which a common term with negative exponents can be factored out. For example,

$$x^2 + 4x^{-1} = x^{-1}\left(x^3 + 4\right)$$

The powers of x are x^2 and x^{-1}. The smallest power is x^{-1}. The following format may help in understanding the technique of factoring with negative exponents. Multiply the expression by $1 = x^0$ in the form $x^{-n} \cdot x^n$ where x^{-n} is the **smallest power of the variable**, x^{-1} in this case.

$$x^2 + 4x^{-1} = x^{-1} \cdot x^1 \left(x^2 + 4x^{-1}\right) \qquad x^0 = x^{-1} \cdot x^1$$

$$= x^{-1}\left(x^2 \cdot x^1 + 4x^{-1} \cdot x^1\right) \qquad \text{Distribute } x^1.$$

$$= x^{-1}\left(x^3 + 4\right)$$

Similarly, in the expression $x^2 + 5 - x^{-2}$, the smallest power of x is x^{-2}.

$$x^2 + 5 - x^{-2} = x^{-2} \cdot x^2 \left(x^2 + 5 - x^{-2}\right) \qquad x^0 = x^{-2} \cdot x^2$$

$$= x^{-2}\left(x^2 \cdot x^2 + 5x^2 - x^{-2} \cdot x^2\right) \quad \text{Distribute } x^2.$$

$$= x^{-2}\left(x^4 + 5x^2 - 1\right)$$

In effect, factoring out x^{-n} can be accomplished by adding n to the exponent of x in each term.

When factoring, **factor out the smallest power of any variable or factor that is to be factored out**. Remember that negative numbers are smaller than positive numbers.

Recall that factoring can be checked by multiplying. If the product is not the original expression, then an error has been made. This is particularly helpful and reassuring when factoring out terms with negative exponents.

Example 3: Factoring with Negative Exponents

a. $2x^2 + x + 3x^{-1}$

Solution: $2x^2 + x + 3x^{-1} = x^{-1}\left(2x^3 + x^2 + 3\right)$

In this example, adding 1 to each exponent of the variable x has the effect of multiplying by x^1, which gives the correct polynomial factor:

$$2x^{2+1} + x^{1+1} + 3x^{-1+1} = 2x^3 + x^2 + 3$$

b. $x^2 y^{-1} + 4xy^{-1} + y^{-2}$

Solution: $x^2 y^{-1} + 4xy^{-1} + y^{-2} = y^{-2}\left(x^2 y + 4xy + 1\right)$

To factor out y^{-2}, add 2 to each exponent of the variable y.

c. $9x^2 y^{-2} - 36y^{-2}$

Solution: $9x^2 y^{-2} - 36y^{-2} = 9y^{-2}\left(x^2 - 4\right)$

$$= 9y^{-2}(x+2)(x-2)$$

In this case, the polynomial $x^2 - 4$ can be factored.

Practice Problems

Factor completely.

1. $x^6 - 125$

2. $4x^{3k} + 32$

3. $2xy - 6x + 4y - 12$

4. $49x^{-1} - x^{-3}$

4.5 Exercises

Factor each expression in Exercises 1 – 68. If an expression has negative exponents, factor out the smallest power of the variable.

1. $x^3 - 125$

2. $x^3 - 64$

3. $x^3 - 8y^3$

4. $x^3 - y^3$

5. $x^3 + 216$

6. $x^3 + 125$

7. $x^3 + y^3$

8. $x^3 + 27y^3$

9. $x^3 - 1$

Answers to Practice Problems: **1.** $\left(x^2 - 5\right)\left(x^4 + 5x^2 + 25\right)$ **2.** $4\left(x^k + 2\right)\left(x^{2k} - 2x^k + 4\right)$
3. $2(x+2)(y-3)$ **4.** $x^{-3}\left(7x+1\right)\left(7x-1\right)$

10. $8x^3 + 1$

11. $27x^3 + 8$

12. $x^3 + 125$

13. $3x^3 + 81$

14. $4x^3 - 32$

15. $125x^3 - 64y^3$

16. $64x^3 + 27y^3$

17. $54x^3 - 2y^3$

18. $3x^4 + 375xy^3$

19. $x^3y + y^4$

20. $x^4y^3 - x$

21. $x^2y^2 - x^2y^5$

22. $2x^2 - 16x^2y^3$

23. $24x^4y + 81xy^4$

24. $x^6 - 64y^3$

25. $x^6 - y^9$

26. $x^3 + (x - y)^3$

27. $27x^3 + (y^2 - 1)^3$

28. $(x - 3y)^3 - 64z^3$

29. $(x + 2)^3 + (y - 3)^3$

30. $(x + y)^3 + (y - 4)^3$

31. $(x + 2y)^3 - (y + 4)^3$

32. $(3x + 2y)^3 + (y - 3)^3$

33. $xy + 4x - 3y - 12$

34. $xy + 5y + 2x + 10$

35. $6x + 4y + xy + 24$

36. $7x - 3y + xy - 21$

37. $3xy + 6y - x - 1$

38. $2xy + 10x + 3y + 15$

39. $4xy - 28x + 3y - 21$

40. $6xy - 9x + 4y - 6$

41. $5x^2 + 10x + 3y + 15$

42. $(x^2 + 2x + 1) - y^2$

43. $(x^2 - 2xy + y^2) - 36$

44. $(x^2 + 4xy + 4y^2) - 25$

45. $(16x^2 + 8x + 1) - y^2$

46. $x^2 - y^2 - 6y - 9$

47. $x^3 - 5x^2 + 6x - 30$

48. $4x^3 - 6x^2 - 14x + 21$

49. $x^3 + 12x^2 - 4x - 48$

50. $x^3 + 3x^2 - 9x - 27$

51. $x^3 + 2x^2 - 4x - 8$

52. $x^3 + 7x^2 - 4x - 28$

53. $x^2y + 5x^2 - 9y - 45$

54. $x^{2k} - 4y^2$

55. $x^{3k} + 8$

56. $x^{3k} + 27y^{3k}$

57. $3x^{3k} - 24x^{3k}y^{3k}$

58. $108x^{3k} - 32y^{3k}$

59. $4x^{-1} + 8x^{-2}$

60. $3x^{-2} + 15x^{-4}$

61. $2x^{-2} + 3x^{-3}y - 6x^{-3}$

62. $x^{-1} + 3x^{-2} + x^{-3}$

63. $5x^{-2} - 20x^{-4}$

64. $8x^{-1} - 50x^{-3}$

65. $x^{-1} + 4x^{-2} + 3x^{-3}$

66. $2x^{-2} + 3x^{-3} + x^{-4}$

67. $2 - 8x^{-1} - 10x^{-2}$

68. $3 - 3x^{-1} - 18x^{-2}$

69. a. Represent the shaded region of the square shown below as the difference of two squares.

b. Use the factors of the expression in part a to draw (and label the sides) of a rectangle that has the same area as the shaded region.

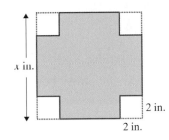

70. a. Use a polynomial function to represent the shaded region of the square.

b. Use a polynomial function to represent the perimeter of the shaded figure.

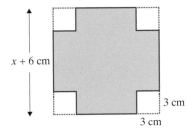

Writing and Thinking About Mathematics

71. **a.** Show that the sum of the areas of the rectangles and squares in the figure is a perfect square trinomial.
b. Rearrange the rectangles and squares in the form of a square and represent its area as the square of a binomial.

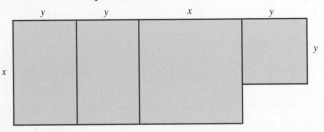

72. Compound interest is interest earned on interest. If a principal, P, is invested and compounded annually (once a year) at a rate of r, then the amount, A_1, accumulated in one year is $A_1 = P + Pr$.
In factored form, we have: $A_1 = P + Pr = P(1 + r)$.
At the end of the second year the amount accumulated is
$$A_2 = P + Pr + (P + Pr)r.$$

a. Write the expression for A_2 in factored form similar to that for A_1.
b. Write an expression for the amount accumulated in three years, A_3, in factored form.
c. Write an expression for A_n the amount accumulated in n years.
d. Use the formula you developed in part (c) and your calculator to find the amount accumulated if $10,000 is invested at 6% and compounded annually for 20 years.

73. You may have heard of (or studied) the following rules for division of an integer by 3 and 9:

    I. An integer is divisible by 3 if the sum of its digits is divisible by 3.

    II. An integer is divisible by 9 if the sum of its digits is divisible by 9. The proofs of both I and II can be started as follows:

Let abc represent a three digit integer.

Then $abc = 100a + 10b + c$

$$= (99 + 1)a + (9 + 1)b + c$$

$$= (\text{now you finish the proofs})$$

Use the pattern just shown and prove both **I** and **II** for a four-digit integer.

Hawkes Learning Systems: Intermediate Algebra

Special Factorizations - Cubes
Factoring Expressions by Grouping

Polynomial Equations and Applications

After completing this section, you will be able to:

1.   Solve equations by factoring.

2.   Write equations given the roots.

The equations that we have solved to this point have been linear equations, identities, or contradictions. Each linear equation is first-degree and has exactly one solution. In order to solve equations of higher degree, with more than one solution, new methods must be developed. These methods include factoring, completing the square, and using the quadratic formula. In this section, we will discuss only solving equations by factoring. The other methods will be discussed in Chapter 7. The solutions to an equation are also called the **roots** of the equation, and finding the solutions can be termed **finding the roots**.

Solving Equations by Factoring

Just as not every polynomial can be factored, not every equation can be solved by factoring. However, those equations that can be solved by factoring depend on the following property of the number 0, called the **zero-factor property**.

Zero-Factor Property

If the product of two factors is 0, then one or both of the factors must be 0.

That is, if a and b are real numbers,

$$\text{if } a \cdot b = 0, \text{ then } a = 0 \text{ or } b = 0.$$

Example 1: Solving Equations by Factoring • • • • • • • • • • • • • • • • • • •

Use the zero-factor property to solve the equation $(x - 5)(2x + 7) = 0$.

Solution: In this case, the expression is already factored, and the product is 0. By the zero-factor property, either $x - 5 = 0$ or $2x + 7 = 0$. Solving these two linear equations gives the two solutions of the original equation.

$$x - 5 = 0 \qquad 2x + 7 = 0$$

$$x = 5 \qquad 2x = -7$$

$$x = -\frac{7}{2} \qquad \textit{continued on next page...}$$

These solutions can be checked by substituting them, one at a time, into the original equation. Thus,

Check: $(5-5)(2\cdot5+7)\overset{?}{=}0$ $\left(-\frac{7}{2}-5\right)\left(2\cdot\left(-\frac{7}{2}\right)+7\right)\overset{?}{=}0$

$(0)(17)\overset{?}{=}0$ $\left(-\frac{17}{2}\right)(-7+7)\overset{?}{=}0$

$0=0$ $\left(-\frac{17}{2}\right)(0)\overset{?}{=}0$

$0=0$

We say that the solutions are $x=5$ and $x=-\frac{7}{2}$ or that the solution set is $\left\{5,-\frac{7}{2}\right\}$.

● ●

In Example 1, the polynomial was given in factored form. However, multiplying the factors gives the product $(x-5)(2x+7)=2x^2-3x-35$, and the equation could have been given in the following form:

$$2x^2-3x-35=0$$

The expression $2x^2-3x-35$ is a quadratic expression and the equation $2x^2-3x-35=0$ is called a **quadratic equation**.

Quadratic Equation

An equation that can be written in the form

   $ax^2 + bx + c = 0$ *where a, b, and c are real numbers and $a \neq 0$*

*is called a **quadratic equation**.*

Many polynomial equations, including quadratic equations, can be solved by factoring and using the zero-factor property. The following list of steps outlines the procedure.

To Solve an Equation by Factoring

1. Add or subtract terms so that one side of the equation is 0.

2. Factor the polynomial expression.

3. Set each factor equal to 0 and solve for the variable.

Example 2: Quadratic Equation •

Solve the following quadratic equations by factoring.

a. $y^2 - 6y = 27$

   Solution: $y^2 - 6y = 27$

              $y^2 - 6y - 27 = 0$ Add -27 to both sides. **One side must be 0.**

              $(y-9)(y+3) = 0$ Factor the left-hand side.

              $y-9 = 0$ or $y+3 = 0$ Set each factor equal to 0.

              $y = 9$ $y = -3$ Solve each linear equation.

b. $4x^2 + 4x = 0$

   Solution: $4x^2 + 4x = 0$

              $4x(x+1) = 0$ Factor out $4x$.
                              [Caution: Do not divide both sides
                              by $4x$. You will lose a solution.]

              $4x = 0$ or $x+1 = 0$ Set each factor equal to 0.

              $x = 0$ $x = -1$ Solve each linear equation.

c. $(3z+6)(4z+12) = -3$

   Solution: $(3z+6)(4z+12) = -3$

              $12z^2 + 60z + 72 = -3$ Multiply factors on left-hand side.

              $12z^2 + 60z + 75 = 0$ **One side must be 0.**

              $3(4z^2 + 20z + 25) = 0$ Factor out the GCF.

              $4z^2 + 20z + 25 = 0$ Divide both sides by the constant 3.

              $(2z+5)^2 = 0$ Factor the perfect square trinomial.

              $2z+5 = 0$ Since both factors are the same, there
                              is only one equation to solve.

              $z = -\dfrac{5}{2}$

There is only one root because the factor $2z + 5$ is repeated. In this case, the root is called a **double root** or a **root of multiplicity two**.

continued on next page...

Check: $\left[3\left(-\dfrac{5}{2}\right)+6\right]\left[4\left(-\dfrac{5}{2}\right)+12\right]\overset{?}{=}-3$

$$\left(-\dfrac{15}{2}+6\right)\left(-10+12\right)\overset{?}{=}-3$$

$$\left(-\dfrac{3}{2}\right)\left(2\right)\overset{?}{=}-3$$

$$-3=-3$$

Sometimes higher-degree polynomial equations can be solved by factoring. In particular, factoring is relatively easy if one of the factors is a monomial. This may give a second factor that is quadratic or some other familiar form.

Example 3: Cubic Equations

Solve the following **third-degree** (or **cubic**) equation by factoring. $100x = 4x^3$

Solution: $\quad 100x = 4x^3$ Add $-100x$ to both sides. **Either the left side or the right side must be 0.**

$$0 = 4x^3 - 100x$$

$0 = 4x\left(x^2 - 25\right)$ Factor out the monomial $4x$.

$0 = 4x\left(x+5\right)\left(x-5\right)$ Factor the difference of two squares.

$4x = 0 \;$ or $\; x+5 = 0 \;$ or $\; x-5 = 0$ Set each factor equal to 0 and solve.

$\quad x = 0 \qquad\qquad x = -5 \qquad x = 5$

Checking will show that each of the numbers 0, −5, and 5 is a solution.

Finding an Equation Given the Roots

To help develop a complete understanding of the concepts of factors, factoring, and solutions to equations, we consider the problem of finding an equation that has certain given solutions (or roots). For example, to find an equation that has the roots

$$x = 4 \;\text{ and }\; x = -7$$

we proceed as follows:

1. Write the corresponding linear equations with 0 on one side.

$$x - 4 = 0 \text{ and } x + 7 = 0$$

2. Form the product of the factors $(x-4)$ and $(x+7)$ and set this product equal to 0.
$$(x-4)(x+7)=0$$

3. Multiply the factors. The resulting quadratic equation
$$x^2+3x-28=0$$

has the two roots 4 and –7.

The reasoning is based on the following theorem called the **Factor Theorem**.

Factor Theorem

If $x = c$ is a root of a polynomial equation in the form $P(x) = 0$, then $x - c$ is a factor of the polynomial $P(x)$.

Proof:

The division algorithm says that
$$P(x)=(x-c)\cdot Q(x)+r$$
Now, by the Remainder Theorem (See page 278), $r = P(c)$.
But, because c is a root of the equation, we know that $P(c) = 0$.
Thus, $P(x)=(x-c)\cdot Q(x)+0=(x-c)\cdot Q(x)$
and $(x - c)$ is a factor of $P(x)$.

Example 4: Factor Theorem

Find a polynomial equation that has the given roots: $x = 3$ and $x = -\dfrac{2}{3}$

Solution: $x = 3$ $x = -\dfrac{2}{3}$

$x - 3 = 0$ $x + \dfrac{2}{3} = 0$ Set each equation equal to zero.

$3x + 2 = 0$ Multiplying both sides by 3 yields integer coefficients.

Form an equation by setting the product of the two factors equal to 0.

$$(x-3)(3x+2)=0$$

$$3x^2 - 7x - 6 = 0$$ This equation has the given roots.

Consecutive Integers

Applications related to integers often involve one of the following three categories: **consecutive integers**, **consecutive odd integers**, or **consecutive even integers**.

Consecutive Integers

Integers are consecutive if each is 1 more than the previous integer.

Three consecutive integers can be represented as **n, n + 1**, and **n + 2**.

For example: 5, 6, 7

Consecutive Even Integers

Even integers are consecutive if each is 2 more than the previous even integer.

Three consecutive even integers can be represented as **n, n + 2**, and **n + 4**.

For example: 24, 26, 28

Consecutive Odd Integers

Odd integers are consecutive if each is 2 more than the previous odd integer.

Three consecutive odd integers can be represented as **n, n + 2**, and **n + 4**.

For example: 41, 43, 45

Note that consecutive even and consecutive odd integers are represented in the same way. The value of the first integer *n* determines whether the remaining integers are even or odd.

Example 5: Consecutive Integers

a. Find two consecutive positive integers such that the sum of their squares is 265.

Solution: Let n = first integer
$n + 1$ = next consecutive integer
Set up and solve the related equation.

$$n^2 + (n+1)^2 = 265$$

$$n^2 + n^2 + 2n + 1 = 265$$

$$2n^2 + 2n - 264 = 0$$

$$n^2 + n - 132 = 0$$

$$(n+12)(n-11) = 0$$

$$
\begin{array}{ccc}
n + 12 = 0 & \text{or} & n - 11 = 0 \\
n = -12 & & n = 11 \\
n + 1 = -11 & & n + 1 = 12
\end{array}
$$

Consider the solution $n = -12$. The next consecutive integer, $n + 1$, is -11. While it is true that the sum of their squares is 265, we must remember that the problem calls for **positive** consecutive integers. Therefore, we can only consider positive solutions. Hence, the two integers are 11 and 12.

b. Find three consecutive odd integers such that the product of the first and second is 68 more than the third.

Solution: Let n = first integer
and $n + 2$ = second consecutive odd integer
and $n + 4$ = third consecutive odd integer
Set up and solve the related equation.

$$n(n+2) = n + 4 + 68$$

$$n^2 + 2n = n + 72$$

$$n^2 + n - 72 = 0$$

$$(n+9)(n-8) = 0$$

$$
\begin{array}{ll}
n + 9 = 0 \quad \text{or} & n - 8 = 0 \\
n = -9 & n = 8 \\
n + 2 = -7 & n + 2 = 10 \\
n + 4 = -5 & n + 4 = 12
\end{array}
$$

The three consecutive odd integers are -9, -7, and -5. Note that 8, 10 and 12 are even and therefore cannot be considered a solution to the problem.

● ●

The Pythagorean Theorem

A geometric topic that often generates quadratic equations is right triangles. In a **right triangle**, one of the angles is a right angle (measures 90°), and the side opposite this angle (the longest side) is called the **hypotenuse**. The other two sides are called **legs**. Pythagoras (c. 585 – 501 B.C.), a famous Greek mathematician, is given credit for proving the following very important and useful theorem (even though history indicates that the Chinese knew of this theorem centuries before Pythagoras). Now, there are entire books written that contain only proofs of the Pythagorean Theorem developed by mathematicians since the time of Pythagoras. (You might want to visit the library!)

Pythagoras

You will see the Pythagorean Theorem stated again in Chapter 7 and used throughout your studies in mathematics.

The Pythagorean Theorem

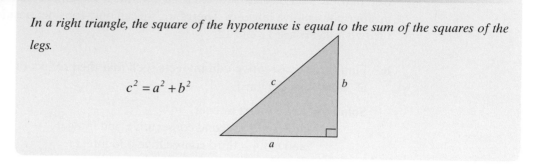

In a right triangle, the square of the hypotenuse is equal to the sum of the squares of the legs.

$$c^2 = a^2 + b^2$$

Example 6: The Pythagorean Theorem

A support wire is to be 25 feet long and stretched from a tree to a point on the ground. The point of attachment on the tree is to be 5 feet higher than the distance from the base of the tree to the point on the ground. How far up the tree is the point of attachment?

Solution:
Let $\quad x$ = distance from base of tree to point on ground (See diagram.)
then $\quad x + 5$ = height of point of attachment
By the Pythagorean Theorem, we have

$$(x+5)^2 + x^2 = 25^2$$

$$x^2 + 10x + 25 + x^2 = 625$$

$$2x^2 + 10x - 600 = 0$$

$$2(x^2 + 5x - 300) = 0$$

$$2(x - 15)(x + 20) = 0$$

$$x = 15 \ \text{ or } \ x = -20$$

Because distance is positive, –20 is not a possible solution.
The solution is
$$x = 15$$
and $x + 5 = 20$.

Thus, the point of attachment is to be 20 feet up the tree.

Practice Problems

Solve the following equations by factoring.

1. $y^2 - 4y = 21$

2. $3x^2 - 16x + 5 = 0$

3. $z^2 + 6z = -9$

4. $x^3 = 25x$

5. *Find a quadratic equation with integer coefficients that has the roots* $\dfrac{2}{3}$ *and* $\dfrac{1}{2}$.

4.6 Exercises

For Exercises 1 – 10, write a polynomial equation with integer coefficients that has the given roots.

1. $y = 3, y = -2$

2. $x = 5, x = 7$

3. $x = \dfrac{1}{2}, x = \dfrac{3}{4}$

4. $y = \dfrac{2}{3}, y = \dfrac{1}{6}$

5. $p = 0, p = 3, p = -2$

6. $m = 0, m = -4, m = 1$

7. $x = -5, x = -3$

8. $z = \dfrac{1}{4}, z = -1$

9. $y = -2, y = 3, y = 3$ (3 is a double root.)

10. $x = -1, x = -1, x = -1$ (–1 is a triple root.)

Solve the equations in Exercises 11 – 52 by factoring.

11. $x^2 + 13x + 36 = 0$

12. $x^2 + 17x + 72 = 0$

13. $5x^2 - 70x + 240 = 0$

14. $2y^2 - 24y + 70 = 0$

15. $4x^2 = 20x + 200$

16. $7x^2 + 14x = 168$

17. $3x^2 = 147$

18. $64 - 49x^2 = 0$

19. $3x^2 + 10 = 17x$

20. $2x^2 = 3x - 1$

21. $6x^2 - 11x + 4 = 0$

22. $4y^2 = 14y - 6$

23. $2x^2 - 72 = 0$

24. $3x^2 - 27 = 0$

25. $4z^2 - 49 = 0$

26. $9x^2 - 16 = 0$

27. $2z^2 + 3 = 7z$

28. $34x + 6 = 12x^2$

29. $12x^2 = 6 - x$

30. $12x^2 + 5x = 3$

31. $6x^2 + x = 35$

32. $50y^2 - 98 = 0$

33. $150y^2 - 96 = 0$

34. $8y^2 + 6y = 35$

35. $(x + 5)(x - 7) = 13$

36. $(2x + 3)(x - 1) = -2$

37. $x(x - 5) + 9 = 3(x - 1)$

38. $x(2x + 3) - 2 = 2(x + 4)$

39. $2x(x + 3) - 14 = x(x - 2) + 19$

40. $x(3x + 5) = x(x + 2) + 14$

41. $18y^2 - 15y + 2 = 0$

42. $14 + 11y = 15y^2$

43. $63x^2 = 40x + 12$

44. $12z^2 - 47z + 11 = 0$

45. $3x^3 + 15x^2 + 18x = 0$

46. $x^3 = 4x^2 + 12x$

47. $16x^3 - 100x = 0$

48. $112x - 2x^2 = 2x^3$

49. $12x^3 + 2x^2 = 70x$

50. $21x^3 = 13x^2 - 2x$

51. $63x = 3x^2 + 30x^3$

52. $14x^3 + 60x^2 = 50x$

Find the solution sets for the polynomial equations in Exercises 53 – 58.

53. $x(2x - 1)(3x + 1) = 0$

54. $2x(x - 5)(2x + 3) = 0$

55. $(x + 1)(x - 2)(x - 6) = 0$

56. $(x - 3)(2x - 5)(x - 4)(4x + 9) = 0$

57. $(4x + 1)(3x - 2)(x - 8.5)(6x - 1) = 0$

58. $x^3(5x - 1)(2x + 3) = 0$

Answers to Practice Problems: 1. $y = 7, y = -3$ **2.** $x = \dfrac{1}{3}, x = 5$ **3.** $z = -3$ **4.** $x = 0, x = 5, x = -5$
5. $6x^2 - 7x + 2 = 0$

59. Find two consecutive positive integers such that the sum of their squares is 113.

60. The product of two consecutive even integers is 168. Find the integers.

61. The product of two consecutive odd integers is 420 more than three times the smaller integer. Find the integers.

62. Find three consecutive positive integers such that twice the product of the two smaller integers is 88 more than the product of the two larger integers.

63. Find three consecutive even integers such that the sum of their squares is 440.

64. Find three consecutive odd integers such that the product of the first and third is 71 more than 10 times the second.

65. Four consecutive integers are such that if the product of the first and third is multiplied by 6, the result is equal to the sum of the second and the square of the fourth. What are the integers?

66. Find four consecutive even integers such that the square of the sum of the first and second is equal to 516 more than twice the product of the third and fourth.

67. An architect wants to draw a rectangle with a diagonal of 13 inches. The length of the rectangle is to be 2 inches more than twice the width. What dimensions should she make the rectangle?

68. A Christmas tree is supported by a wire that is 1 foot longer than the height of the tree. The wire is anchored at a point whose distance from the base of the tree is 49 feet shorter than the height of the tree. What is the height of the tree?

69. Two mountain peaks are known to be 29 miles apart. A person located at a vista point such that a right angle is spanned when he looks from one peak to the other is told that the distances from the vista point to each peak differ by 1 mile. How far is the vista point from each mountain peak?

70. A telephone pole is to have a guy wire attached to its top and anchored to the ground at a point that is 34 feet less than the height of the pole. If the wire is to be 2 feet longer than the height of the pole, what is the height of the pole?

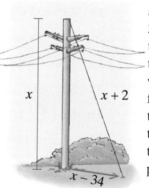

71. A ball is dropped from the top of a building that is known to be 256 feet high. The formula for finding the height of the ball at any time is $h = 256 - 16t^2$ where t is measured in seconds.

   a. How many seconds will it take for the ball to hit the ground?

   b. How many seconds did it take for the ball to reach a height of 192 feet above the ground?

   c. How many seconds did it take for the ball to fall 64 feet?

Writing and Thinking About Mathematics

72. If three positive integers satisfy the Pythagorean Theorem, they are called a **Pythagorean Triple**. For example, 3, 4, and 5 are a Pythagorean Triple because $3^2 + 4^2 = 5^2$. There are an infinite number of such triples. To see how some triples can be found, fill out the following table and verify that the last three numbers are indeed Pythagorean Triples.

u	v	$2uv$	$u^2 - v^2$	$u^2 + v^2$
2	1	4	3	5
3	2	___	___	___
5	2	___	___	___
4	3	___	___	___
7	1	___	___	___
6	5	___	___	___

73. The pattern in linoleum flooring is in the shape of a square 8 inches on a side with right triangles of sides x inches placed on each side of the original square so that a new larger square is formed. What is the area of the new square? Explain why you do not need to find the value of x.

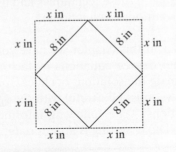

74. Write and prove the Factor Theorem.

Solving Equations by Factoring

Using a Graphing Calculator to Solve Equations and Absolute Values

After completing this section, you will be able to:

1. Use a TI-83 Plus graphing calculator to solve (or estimate the solutions of) polynomial equations by using one of the following strategies:

    a. graph one function and find the zeros of the function, or

    b. graph two functions and find the points of intersection of the functions.

2. Use a TI-83 Plus graphing calculator to solve absolute value equations and inequalities.

In Section 2.4 we introduced functions, showed how to use a graphing calculator to graph functions, and listed steps for finding the zeros of a function. Remember that the zeros of a function are the values for *x* at the points, if any, where the function crosses the *x*-axis. These are the points where *y* is equal to 0. In this section we will simply expand on these techniques and use the related ideas to solve equations (or to estimate the solutions of equations).

So far in this chapter we have solved second degree (quadratic) equations and a few higher degree equations by factoring. With the calculator as a tool we can solve (or estimate the solutions of) linear, quadratic, or higher degree real polynomial equations, but we must be careful with the ⬚WINDOW settings or the display may not show all of the solutions. The following information will help in determining whether or not your WINDOW setting is appropriate:

Information About Zeros of Polynomial Functions

1. *Nonconstant linear functions have 1 zero.*

2. *Second degree (or quadratic) functions have 2 zeros or none.*

3. *Third degree polynomial functions have 1 zero or 3.*

4. *Fourth degree polynomial functions have 4 zeros, 2 zeros, or none.*

NOTES   When a polynomial is second degree or higher, the same zero may appear more than once. That is, a binomial factor may be to a power, say *n*, and the zero factor is said to be a zero of multiplicity *n* of the polynomial. Thus, the polynomial $p(x) = x^3 - 3x^2 - 24x + 80 = (x+5)(x-4)^2$ has the three zeros, -5, 4, and 4. Because 4 appears twice, 4 is a zero of multiplicity 2.

[**Note:** We will discuss nonreal zeros in detail in Chapter 6.]

For example, if you are graphing a third degree polynomial function and the display shows only 1 zero, you may need a larger WINDOW setting to determine whether or not there are more zeros. If you see 3 zeros, then you know that there are no more and the WINDOW setting is sufficient.

Important Comment About the Graphs of Polynomial Functions

The graph of every polynomial function is a smooth continuous graph. (That is, there are no holes, jumps from one point to another, or sharp points in the graph of a polynomial function.)

Now, there are two basic strategies to solving equations using the graphing calculator. We need to either:

a. graph one function and find the zeros of the function, or

b. graph two functions and find the points of intersection of the functions.

The following examples illustrate both of these strategies and the steps to use with the graphing calculator.

Example 1: Solving a Polynomial Equation ● ● ● ● ● ● ● ● ● ● ● ● ● ● ● ● ● ● ●

Use a graphing calculator to solve the polynomial equation $x^3 - 3x^2 = 13x - 15$.

Solution:

Strategy: Manipulate the equation so that one side is 0. Graph the indicated function on the nonzero side. The zeros of this function are the roots of the original equation.

$$x^3 - 3x^2 = 13x - 15$$

$$x^3 - 3x^2 - 13x + 15 = 0$$

Enter the function as follows:

continued on next page ...

With the standard window the graph will appear as follows:

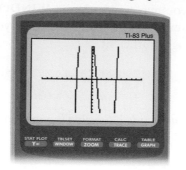

Note: You may want to increase the y-values on the window to see a more complete graph. This will not change the zeros.

With the (2nd) > CALC > **2:zero** sequence of commands you will find the following zeros (and therefore solutions to the equation):

$x = -3$, $x = 1$, and $x = 5$

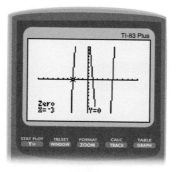

[**Note:** With the TRACE command you will find only approximations to the zeros.]

• •

Example 2: Solving a Polynomial Equation •

Solve the polynomial equation $2x^2 = 3x + 1$.

Solution:

Strategy: Graph the function indicated on each side of the equation. Find the points of intersection of these two graphs. The x-values of these points are the roots of the original equation.

Enter the functions as follows:

With the standard window the graphs will appear as follows:

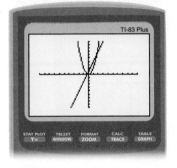

With the (2nd) > **CALC** > **5:intersect** sequence of commands you will find the following approximate x-values of the points of intersection (and therefore approximate solutions to the equation):

$x = -.28$ and $x = 1.78$ (accurate to two decimal places)

Example 3: Solving an Absolute Value Equation

Solve the equation $|2x - 5| = 8$.

Solution:

Strategy: Graph the function indicated on each side of the equation. This includes the constant function. Find the points of intersection of these two graphs. The x-values of these points are the roots of the original equation. Remember that the absolute value command can be found in the (**MATH**) > **NUM** menu.

continued on next page ...

Enter the functions as follows:

With the standard window the graphs will appear as follows:

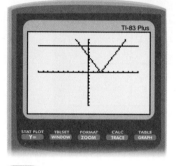

With the (2nd) > CALC > 5:intersect sequence of commands you will find the following *x*-values of the points of intersection (and therefore solutions to the equation):

$x = -1.5$ and $x = 6.5$

[**Note:** These values of *x* are exact. The TRACE command will not give these exact values.]

● ●

Example 4: Solving an Absolute Value Inequality ● ● ● ● ● ● ● ● ● ● ● ● ●

Use a graphing calculator to solve the inequalities:

    a. $\left|2x - 5\right| < 8$ **b.** $\left|2x - 5\right| > 8$

One graph can be used to solve the two inequalities.

Solution: We change the window for a clearer view: Use the interval $[-10, 10]$ for x and the interval $[-1, 15]$ for y. Now use the graph for Example 3 just shown:

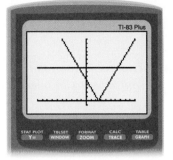

a. From Example 3, we know that the intersections occur at $x = -1.5$ and $x = 6.5$. Looking at the graph we see that the absolute value is below the line $y = 8$ on the interval $(-1.5, 6.5)$. Thus, the interval $(-1.5, 6.5)$ is the solution set for $|2x - 5| < 8$.

b. Looking at the graph we see that the absolute value curve is above the line $y = 8$ on the intervals $(-\infty, -1.5)$ and $(6.5, \infty)$. Thus, the solution set is $(-\infty, -1.5)$ or $(6.5, \infty)$ for $|2x - 5| > 8$.

● ●

4.7 Exercises

Use a graphing calculator to solve (or estimate the solutions of) the equations in Exercises 1 – 35. Sketch the graphs that you use and find any approximations accurate to two decimal places.

1. $x^2 - 4 = 0$

2. $x^2 - 9 = 0$

3. $x^2 - 2 = 0$

4. $x^2 - 15 = 0$

5. $x^2 - 4x = 12$

6. $x^2 + 6x = 7$

7. $x^2 + 2x - 11 = 0$

8. $3x^2 - x - 6 = 0$

9. $-x^2 + 3x + 8 = 0$

10. $-2x^2 + 4x - 5 = 0$

11. $2x^2 + x + 2 = 0$

12. $3x + 15 = x^2$

13. $3x^2 - 9 = x$

14. $x^3 = 2x^2 - 5$

15. $5x - 3 = x^3$

16. $x^3 + 2x^2 = 4x + 6$

17. $x(x - 1)(x - 3) = 0$

18. $(x - 2)(x + 1)(x + 4) = 0$

19. $(x + 3)(x + 1)(x - 5) = 0$

20. $(x + 2)(x - 1)(x - 6) = 0$

21. $2x^3 - 8x^2 + 7x - 1 = 9$

22. $3x^3 - x^2 + 4 = 10$

23. $-x^3 + 4x^2 - x = 5$

24. $x^4 - 10x^2 = 0$

25. $x^4 = 3x^2$

26. $x^4 - x^3 + 2x = 0$

27. $|2x - 3| = 11$

28. $|2x + 1| = 7$

29. $|3x - 2| = 7$

30. $|4x + 1| = 19$

31. $|2x+1| = |x-1|$ **32.** $|x-3| = |x+2|$ **33.** $\left|\dfrac{x}{2}+1\right| = \dfrac{3}{2}$

34. $\left|\dfrac{x}{5}-1\right| = |x|$ **35.** $|x-2| = |5-x|$

Use a graphing calculator to solve (or estimate the solutions of) the inequalities in Exercises 36 – 45. Write your answers in interval notation. Sketch the graphs that you use.

36. $|x| > 6$ **37.** $|x| \le 3$ **38.** $|x-3| \le 1$

39. $|x-5| > 2$ **40.** $|x-4| \ge 2$ **41.** $|3x-8| > 4$

42. $|x+2| - 10 \le 17$ **43.** $|x-4| - 2 > 10$ **44.** $\left|\dfrac{x}{3}-1\right| < 2$

45. $\left|\dfrac{x}{4}+3\right| \ge 1$

Writing and Thinking About Mathematics

In Exercise 46, use a graphing calculator and three graphs to solve the inequalities. Write the answer in interval notation. Explain how you might solve these inequalities algebraically.

46. $1 \le |x-4| \le 5$

Hawkes Learning Systems: Intermediate Algebra

Using a Graphing Calculator to Solve Equations

Chapter 4 Index of Key Ideas and Terms

Monomial   page 255

> A **monomial in x** is an expression of the form kx^n where n is a whole number and k is any real number. n is called the **degree** of the monomial and k is the **coefficient**.

Polynomial   page 255

> Any monomial or algebraic sum of monomials is a **polynomial**. The **degree of a polynomial** is the largest of the degrees of its terms after like terms have been combined.

Classification of Polynomials   page 256

> **Monomial:** polynomial with one term
> **Binomial:** polynomial with two terms
> **Trinomial:** polynomial with three terms

Addition of Polynomials   page 256

Subtraction of Polynomials   page 257

***P(x)* Notation**   page 258

> $P(x)$ is function notation and is read "P of x."

Multiplication by Monomials   page 262

Multiplication of Polynomials   page 262

FOIL Method   page 263

Special Products (Formulas)   page 264

> **I.** $(X+A)(X-A)=X^2-A^2$: Difference of two squares
>
> **II.** $(X+A)^2=X^2+2AX+A^2$: Perfect square trinomial
>
> **III.** $(X-A)^2=X^2-2AX+A^2$: Perfect square trinomial
>
> **IV.** $(X-A)(X^2+AX+A^2)=X^3-A^3$: Difference of two cubes
>
> **V.** $(X+A)(X^2-AX+A^2)=X^3+A^3$: Sum of two cubes

Division with Polynomials   page 272

> Division Algorithm: $\dfrac{P(x)}{D(x)}=Q(x)+\dfrac{R(x)}{D(x)}$

Synthetic Division   page 275

Remainder Theorem page 278

> If a polynomial, $P(x)$, is divided by $(x - c)$,
> then the remainder will be $P(c)$.

Greatest Common Factor page 283

Irreducible (or Not Factorable or Prime) page 284

> An irreducible (or prime) polynomial is one that cannot be
> factored as the product of polynomials with integer coefficients.

ac-Method of Factoring page 286

FOIL Method of Factoring (Trial and Error) page 289

Factoring by Grouping page 297

Factoring with Negative Exponents page 298

Solving Equations by Factoring page 303

Zero-Factor Property page 303

> If the product of two factors is 0, then one or both of the factors
> must be 0. That is, if a and b are real numbers, if $a \cdot b = 0$, then
> $a = 0$ or $b = 0$.

Quadratic Equation page 304

> An equation that can be written in the form $ax^2 + bx + c = 0$ where
> a, b, and c are real numbers and $a \neq 0$ is called a **quadratic equation**.

Factor Theorem page 307

> If $x = c$ is a root of a polynomial equation in the form $P(x) = 0$,
> then $x - c$ is a factor of the polynomial $P(x)$.

Consecutive Integers page 308

> Integers are consecutive if each is 1 more than the previous integer.

Consecutive Even Integers page 308

> Even integers are consecutive if each is 2 more
> than the previous even integer.

Consecutive Odd Integers page 308

> Odd integers are consecutive if each is 2 more
> than the previous odd integer.

Pythagorean Theorem

page 309

In a right triangle, the square of the hypotenuse is equal to
the sum of the squares of the legs.

Solving Equations and Inequalities with a Graphing Calculator

pages 314 - 315

Chapter 4 Review

For a review of the topics and problems from Chapter 4, look at the following lessons from *Hawkes Learning Systems: Intermediate Algebra.*

Identifying Polynomials
Adding and Subtracting Polynomials
Multiplying Polynomials
The FOIL Method
Division by a Monomial
The Division Algorithm
Synthetic Division
GCF of a Polynomial
Special Factorizations - Squares
Factoring Trinomials by Grouping
Factoring Trinomials by Trial and Error
Special Factorization - Cubes
Factoring Expressions by Grouping
Solving Equations by Factoring
Using a Graphing Calculator to Solve Equations

Chapter 4 Test

In Exercises 1 – 6, add or subtract as indicated and simplify the results.

1. $\left(6x^2 + x - 10 \right) - \left(x^3 + x^2 + x - 4 \right)$ **2.** $\left(x^3 + 4x^2 - x \right) + \left(-2x^3 + 6x - 3 \right)$

3. $\left[\left(2x^2 - x \right) + \left(3x + 2 \right) \right] + \left[\left(x - 3 \right) - \left(x^2 + 1 \right) \right]$

4. $\left(5x^2 - 3x + 7 \right) - \left(2x^2 - 5x - 6 \right)$

5. $\left(2x^2 - 6xy + y^2 \right) - \left(4x^2 + 3xy - y^2 + 2y \right)$

6. $\left[\left(3x - y \right) - \left(y - 2 \right) \right] + \left[y + 3 - \left(x + 2 \right) \right]$

Find each product in Exercises 7 – 12.

7. $\left(7x - 3 \right)\left(4x + 5 \right)$ **8.** $\left(2x - 7 \right)^2$ **9.** $\left(8x + 3 \right)\left(8x - 3 \right)$

10. $\left(x^3 + 5 \right)^2$ **11.** $\left[\left(x + 1 \right) - y \right]\left[\left(x + 1 \right) + y \right]$ **12.** $3x^2 + x - 1$
$$\underline{\hphantom{3x^2 + x - 1} 2x + 1}$$

13. Divide by using long division. Write the answer in the form $Q(x) + \dfrac{R(x)}{D(x)}$.

$$\frac{4x^3 - 6x^2 + x - 3}{2x^2 + 1}$$

14. Divide by using synthetic division: $\dfrac{2x^3 + 11x - 6}{x - 4}$.

15. **a.** Use synthetic division to find $P(3)$ given that $P(x) = 2x^3 - 8x^2 + 15x + 20$.
    b. Is $x - 3$ a factor of $P(x)$? Explain.

16. Find an equation that has $x = 3$ and $x = -7$ as roots.

Completely factor each expression in Exercises 17 – 24.

17. $30x^2 y - 18xy^2 + 24xy$ **18.** $x^2 - 9x - 36$ **19.** $3x^2 y - 18xy^2 + 27y^3$

20. $9x^2 - 81y^2$ **21.** $7x^2 - 26x - 8$ **22.** $x^{2k} - y^{2k}$

23. $3x^3 + 81y^3$ **24.** $2x^2 + 4xy + x + 2y$

Solve the equations in Exercises 25 and 26 by factoring.

25. $3x^2 + 14x - 5 = 0$ **26.** $2x(x + 2) = 3(x + 5)$

27. Find three consecutive odd integers such that the sum of the first and second is 201 less than the square of the third.

28. In a right triangle, the hypotenuse is 1 meter more than the length of one of the legs and this leg is 17 meters more than the length of the shortest leg. What are the lengths of the three sides of the triangle?

Use a graphing calculator to solve the equations in Exercises 29 and 30. Sketch the graphs that you use and find any approximations accurate to two decimal places.

29. $x^2 + 4x = 8$

30. $x^3 - 5x^2 + 4x = 0$

In Exercise 31, use a graphing calculator to find the solution set for the inequality.

31. $\left| \dfrac{x}{3} - 1 \right| < 3$

Cumulative Review: Chapters 1 - 4

Evaluate each expression.

1. $\dfrac{1}{3} + \dfrac{11}{15} + \left(-\dfrac{7}{30} \right)$

2. $\dfrac{2}{3} \cdot \dfrac{7}{5} \div \dfrac{7}{12}$

Simplify the expressions in Exercises 3 and 4 by using the rules for order of operations..

3. $2 \cdot 3^2 \div 6 \cdot 3 - 3$

4. $6 + 3 \left[4 - 2 \left(3^3 - 1 \right) \right]$

Simplify each of the expressions in Exercises 5 – 8.

5. $\left(4x^2 y \right)^3$

6. $\left(7x^5 y^2 \right)^2$

7. $\left(-2x^3 y^2 \right)^{-3}$

8. $\left(\dfrac{6x^2}{y^5} \right)^2$

Combine like terms in Exercises 9 and 10.

9. $8x - \left[2x + 4(x - 3) - 5 \right]$

10. $9x + \left[8 - 5(3 - 2x) - 7x \right]$

Solve each of the equations in Exercises 11 – 14.

11. $4(2x - 3) + 2 = 5 - (2x + 6)$

12. $\dfrac{4x}{7} - 3 = 9$

13. $\dfrac{2x + 3}{6} - \dfrac{x + 1}{4} = 2$

14. $\left| \dfrac{2x}{5} - 1 \right| = 3$

Solve the inequalities in Exercises 15 and 16 and graph the solution sets on real number lines.

15. $2x - 3 \geq 5x + 12$

16. $|3x + 2| < 5$

17. Write the equation $4x + 3y = 7$ in slope-intercept form and then graph the line.

18. Find an equation in standard form for the line determined by the two points $(-2, 1)$ and $(5, 3)$.

19. Find the equation in standard form for the line parallel to the line $3x + 2y = -4$ and passing through the point $(2, -2)$. Graph both lines.

Solve the systems of equations in Exercises 20 and 21.

20. $\begin{cases} 3x + y = 10 \\ 5x - y = 6 \end{cases}$

21. $\begin{cases} y = 2x - 5 \\ 3x + 2y = -3 \end{cases}$

22. Solve the following system of equations by using the Gaussian elimination method.

$$\begin{cases} 2x + y - z = 5 \\ x + 2y - 2z = 4 \\ 4x + 5y - 5z = 13 \end{cases}$$

23. Solve the following system of equations by using Cramer's Rule.

$$\begin{cases} 3x - y = 15 \\ 2x + y = 5 \end{cases}$$

24. For the matrix $A = \begin{bmatrix} 1 & 4 & 7 \\ 2 & 1 & 0 \\ -3 & 1 & 5 \end{bmatrix}$, find the value of det (A).

25. Graph the solution set to the following inequality: $3x + y \leq 10$.

26. Graph the solution set to the following system of inequalities:

$$\begin{cases} y > -5x + 1 \\ y < 2x - 3 \end{cases}$$

27. Use a graphing calculator to find the solution set to the following system of inequalities: $\begin{cases} 2x - y > 5 \\ 3x + y > 6 \end{cases}$

28. Divide by using long division. Write the answer in the form $Q(x) + \dfrac{R(x)}{D(x)}$.

$$\frac{4x^3 - 5x^2 + 7x - 13}{x^2 - 3}$$

29. Divide by using synthetic division: $\dfrac{5x^3 + 10x^2 - 4x - 16}{x + 5}$.

30. a. Use synthetic division to find $P(6)$ given that $P(x) = 5x^3 + 8x^2 - 12x - 3$.
b. Is $(x-6)$ a factor of $P(x)$? Explain.

31. Find an equation that has $x = -10$ and $x = -5$ as roots.

32. Find an equation that has $x = 0$, $x = 4$ and $x = 13$ as roots.

Perform the indicated operations in Exercises 33 – 36.

33. $(2x^2 + 9x - 3) - (5x^2 - 2x + 1)$ **34.** $(3x^2 + x - 9) - (-2x^2 + 5x - 3)$

35. $(5x + 3)(x - 8)$ **36.** $(4x + 1)(2x + 3)$

Completely factor the expressions in Exercises 37 – 40.

37. $4x^2 - 4x - 15$ **38.** $6x^2 - 7x + 2$ **39.** $6x^3 - 22x^2 - 8x$

40. $8x^3 + 125$

Solve the equations in Exercises 41 – 44 by factoring.

41. $x^2 - 10x + 21 = 0$ **42.** $4x^2 + 20x + 25 = 0$

43. $3x(x - 2) = x^2 - 2x + 16$ **44.** $x^3 - x^2 = 20x$

45. Olivia invested $7000, some at 7%, and the remainder at 8%. During the first year, the interest from the 7% investment exceeded the interest from the 8% investment by $70. How much did she have invested at each rate?

46. One number is 4 more than another and the sum of their squares is 976. What are the numbers?

47. Find the values for a, b, and c so that the points $(-1, 0), (0, 1)$, and $(1, 0)$ lie on the graph of the function $y = ax^2 + bx + c$.

48. How many liters each of a 6% iodine solution and a 15% iodine solution must be used to produce 30 liters of a 12% iodine solution?

49. The following table shows the number of miles Kim drove from one hour to another:

Hours	Miles
1	70
2	85
3	60
4	72
5	68

    a. Plot the points indicated in the table.
    b. Calculate the slope of the line segments from point to point.
    c. Interpret each slope.

50. The graphs of three curves are shown. Use the vertical line test to determine whether or not each graph represents a function. If the graph represents a function, state its domain and its range.

    a.   **b.**   **c.**

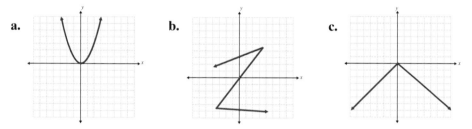

In Exercises 51 – 55, use a graphing calculator to estimate the real number solutions, if any, to the equations. Sketch the graphs that you use.

51. $2x^2 - 8 = x$ **52.** $x^2 - 4x = 1$ **53.** $-x^2 + 3x + 5 = 0$

54. $x^3 - x^2 - 2x + 1 = 0$ **55.** $2x^2 = 5x - 4$

In Exercises 56 – 58, use a graphing calculator to solve the inequalities. Write the answers in interval notation and sketch the graphs that you use.

56. $|x - 5| < 6$ **57.** $|2x - 4| \geq 4$ **58.** $\left| \dfrac{x}{2} + 1 \right| \leq 5$

Rational Expressions

Did You Know?

Chapter 5 deals with rational expressions, and one of the first properties listed for such expressions is the **cross-multiplication property**, which states that two rational expressions are equal if the cross products are equal. Symbolically, this property is stated as $\frac{a}{b} = \frac{c}{d}$ if and only if $a \cdot d = b \cdot c$. This property is the key to understanding how a missing term of a proportion can be found if the remaining three terms are known. For example, using the cross-multiplication property to solve the proportion $\frac{x}{6} = \frac{3}{4}$ yields $4x = 18$, and the solution of this simple linear equation is $x = \frac{9}{2}$, the missing term of the proportion. This type of solution illustrates the so-called Rule of Three, which has been known for over 3000 years. The Hindu mathematician Brahmagupta (c. 628) called the rule by that name in his writings, although problems of this type exist in ancient Egyptian and Chinese writings. Brahmagupta taught and wrote in the town of Ujjain in Central India, a center of Hindu science in the seventh century. Brahmagupta is one of the most famous Hindu mathematicians and he stated the Rule of Three as follows: "In the Rule of Three, argument, fruit and requisition are the names of the terms. Requisition multiplied by fruit and divided by argument is the produce;" or, as in our example, $x = 3 \cdot \left(\frac{6}{4}\right)$. In this case, the terms of the proportion have been given very fanciful names, and the cross-multiplication property has been concealed in an arbitrary rule.

The Rule of Three appears in Arabic and Latin works without explanation until the Renaissance. It was used in commercial arithmetic and occasionally was called the Merchant's Key or the Golden Rule. A popular seventeenth-century English arithmetic states: "The Rule of Three is commonly called The Golden Rule; and indeed it might be so termed; for as gold transcends all other mettals, so doth this rule all others in Arithmetick." The Rule of Three often appeared in verse as a memory aid.

Arithmetic texts of the sixteenth and seventeenth centuries had pages or chapters called Practice. At that time, the term "practice" was used to mean commercial arithmetic usually involving the Rule of Three and other short processes for solving applied problems. Sometimes such problems were called Italian Practice because the problems often related to the methods developed in Italian commercial arithmetic.

5.1 Multiplication and Division of Rational Expressions

5.2 Addition and Subtraction of Rational Expressions

5.3 Complex Fractions

5.4 Equations and Inequalities with Rational Expressions

5.5 Applications

5.6 Applications (Variation)

*"Multiplication is vexation,
Division is as bad;
The Rule of three doth puzzle me,
And practice drives me mad."*

Mother Goose Rhyme

$\mathbf{R}$ational expressions are fractions in which the numerator and denominator are polynomials. All of the rules you learned in arithmetic about operating with fractions are going to be applied. For example, to add or subtract rational expressions, you need a common denominator, just as with fractions in arithmetic. To find common denominators and to multiply, divide, and simplify rational expressions, you are going to apply all the factoring skills you learned in Chapter 4. Thus, all those skills will be reinforced and, even if you had some difficulty with factoring, you probably will be very comfortable with factoring after Chapter 5.

The use of rational expressions opens the way to a variety of algebraic expressions, equations, and applications not available otherwise. In Section 5.4, you will learn to solve inequalities involving fractions, graph the solutions, and represent the solutions in interval notation in a manner similar to that discussed in Section 1.6. In Section 5.5, the applied problems involve fractions using some familiar formulas from a different point of view. You should find them particularly interesting.

Multiplication and Division of Rational Expressions

Objectives

After completing this section, you will be able to:

1. *Define rational expressions.*

2. *Raise rational expressions to higher terms.*

3. *Reduce rational expressions to lowest terms.*

4. *Multiply rational expressions.*

5. *Divide rational expressions.*

Basic Properties

Expressions such as

$$x-5, \quad x^2+1, \quad x^5-3x^4+2, \quad \text{and} \quad 2y^3+4y^2-8y+6$$

are polynomials. Any fraction formed with a polynomial as numerator and a polynomial as denominator is called a **rational expression**. Thus,

$$\frac{2x}{x^2+1}, \quad \frac{x+3}{x-5} \quad \text{and} \quad \frac{y^3-3y^2}{y^2-7y+12}$$

are all rational expressions.

Rational Expression

A ***rational expression*** *is an expression of the form* $\dfrac{P}{Q}$ *(or in function notation,* $\dfrac{P(x)}{Q(x)}$ *)*

where P and Q are polynomials and $Q \neq 0$.

In the definition, the denominator $Q \neq 0$ means that for any rational expression we assume that **the variable will not equal any value that will cause a denominator to be 0**. For example, in the rational expression

$$\frac{P}{Q} = \frac{x^2 + 2x + 1}{3x - 6} \qquad Q = 3x - 6 \text{ , and we assume that } 3x - 6 \neq 0 \text{ (or } x \neq 2\text{).}$$

All of the basic properties of real numbers hold for rational expressions because rational expressions represent real numbers. The rules for operating with rational expressions are essentially the same as those for operating with fractions in arithmetic. That is, addition, subtraction, multiplication, and division with rational expressions are operations involving factoring and common denominators just as with fractions in arithmetic. The following rules for operating with rational numbers apply to operating with real numbers and rational expressions.

Arithmetic Rules for Rational Numbers (or Fractions)

A ***rational number*** *is a number that can be written in the fraction form* $\dfrac{a}{b}$ *where a and b are integers and* $b \neq 0$. *No denominator can be 0.*

The Fundamental Principle: $\dfrac{a}{b} = \dfrac{a \cdot k}{b \cdot k}$ *where* $k \neq 0$

*The **reciprocal** of* $\dfrac{a}{b}$ *is* $\dfrac{b}{a}$ *and* $\dfrac{a}{b} \cdot \dfrac{b}{a} = 1$.

Multiplication: $\dfrac{a}{b} \cdot \dfrac{c}{d} = \dfrac{a \cdot c}{b \cdot d}$

Division: $\dfrac{a}{b} \div \dfrac{c}{d} = \dfrac{a}{b} \cdot \dfrac{d}{c}$

Addition: $\dfrac{a}{b} + \dfrac{c}{b} = \dfrac{a + c}{b}$

Subtraction: $\dfrac{a}{b} - \dfrac{c}{b} = \dfrac{a - c}{b}$

Each rule can be restated by replacing a and b with P and Q where P and Q represent polynomials. In particular, the Fundamental Principle can be restated as follows:

Fundamental Principle of Fractions

If $\dfrac{P}{Q}$ is rational expression and K is a polynomial and $K \neq 0$, then

$$\frac{P}{Q} = \frac{P}{Q} \cdot \frac{K}{K} = \frac{P \cdot K}{Q \cdot K}.$$

The Fundamental Principle can be used to build a rational expression to **higher terms** (for addition or subtraction) and to **reduce** a rational expression to **lower terms** (for multiplication or division). Just as with rational numbers, a rational expression is said to be **reduced to lowest terms** if the numerator and denominator have no common factors other than 1 and −1.

Example 1: Fundamental Principle •

Use the Fundamental Principle to build up each expression as indicated. State any restrictions on the variable using the fact that no denominator can be 0.

a. $\dfrac{7}{8} = \dfrac{?}{24}$

Solution: Because $24 = 8 \cdot 3$

$$\frac{7}{8} = \frac{7 \cdot 3}{8 \cdot 3} = \frac{21}{24}$$

Building up a fraction to higher terms by using the Fundamental Principle

b. $\dfrac{5x}{x+3} = \dfrac{?}{x^2 - x - 12}$

Solution: Because $x^2 - x - 12 = (x+3)(x-4)$,

$$\frac{5x}{x+3} = \frac{5x(x-4)}{(x+3)(x-4)}$$

$$= \frac{5x^2 - 20x}{x^2 - x - 12}$$

Building up a rational expression by using the Fundamental Principle ($x \neq -3$ and $x \neq 4$ because either of these values for x would make the denominator 0.)

Use the Fundamental Principle to reduce each expression to lowest terms. State any restrictions on the variable using the fact that no denominator can be 0.

c. $\dfrac{2x-10}{3x-15}$

Solution: $\dfrac{2x-10}{3x-15} = \dfrac{2(x-5)}{3(x-5)} = \dfrac{2}{3} \quad (x \neq 5)$

Note that $x-5$ is a common **factor**. The key word here is **factor**. We reduce using **factors** only.

d. $\dfrac{x^2 - 16}{x^3 - 64}$

Solution: $\dfrac{x^2 - 16}{x^3 - 64} = \dfrac{(x+4)(x-4)}{(x-4)(x^2 + 4x + 16)}$

Reduce; the common **factor** is $x - 4$. Note that $x^3 - 64$ is the difference of two cubes.

$$= \dfrac{(x+4)}{(x^2 + 4x + 16)} \quad (x \neq 4)$$

• •

The following properties are concerned with the placement of negative signs. These properties are particularly useful in addition and subtraction with rational expressions. In other words, these properties state that a negative sign can be in front of an expression, or with the denominator, or with the numerator, and the expression will have the same value. Additionally, negative signs can be introduced into a rational expression as long as they are placed in two positions, as shown. This means that we can use the form that best suits our purposes when simplifying particular expressions.

Negative Signs

$$-\frac{P}{Q} = \frac{P}{-Q} = \frac{-P}{Q} \qquad and \qquad \frac{P}{Q} = \frac{-P}{-Q} = -\frac{-P}{Q} = -\frac{P}{-Q}$$

Example 2: Negative Signs •

a. $-\dfrac{35}{5} = \dfrac{35}{-5} = \dfrac{-35}{5} = -7$

b. $-\dfrac{y-3}{y^2} = \dfrac{y-3}{-y^2} = \dfrac{-(y-3)}{y^2} \qquad (y \neq 0)$

c. $\dfrac{24}{6} = \dfrac{-24}{-6} = -\dfrac{-24}{6} = -\dfrac{24}{-6} = 4$

d. $-\dfrac{5-x}{x-5} = \dfrac{-(5-x)}{x-5} = \dfrac{(x-5)}{x-5} = 1 \quad (x \neq 5)$

• •

Closely related to the placement of negative signs is the following statement about opposites. If any number or algebraic expression is divided by its opposite, the quotient is −1.

Opposites

In general,

$$\frac{-P}{P} = -1 \qquad \text{if } P \neq 0$$

In particular,

$$\frac{a-x}{x-a} = -1 \qquad \text{if } x \neq a$$

Note carefully that $a - x$ and $x - a$ are opposites. Thus,

$$a - x = -x + a = -(x - a) \quad \text{which leads to} \quad \frac{a-x}{x-a} = \frac{-(x-a)}{x-a} = -1$$

Example 3: Opposites

a. $\dfrac{x^2 - 2x - 3}{-x^2 + 2x + 3} = -1$ 　　　　　$x^2 - 2x - 3 = -\left(-x^2 + 2x + 3\right)$

　　　　　　　　　　　　　　　　　　$x \neq 3, -1$

b. $\dfrac{17 - x}{x - 17} = \dfrac{-(-17 + x)}{x - 17} = \dfrac{-1 \cdot (x - 17)}{+1 \cdot (x - 17)} = -1 \quad x \neq 17$

Common Errors

*Reduce only **common factors**. Do not reduce terms unless they are **factors** common to both the numerator and denominator. Remember that **factors** imply multiplication.*

$\dfrac{x + 2}{2}$ 　　　　　　← **WRONG** 　　　*2 is not a common factor.*

$\dfrac{x^2 - 9}{x - 3}$ 　　　　　　← **WRONG** 　　　*3 and x are not common factors.*

$\dfrac{x^2 - 9}{x - 3} = \dfrac{(x+3)(x-3)}{(x-3)}$ 　　← **RIGHT** 　　　*x − 3 is a common factor.*

$\dfrac{2x + 8}{2} = \dfrac{2(x+4)}{2}$ 　　← **RIGHT** 　　　*2 is a common factor.*

Multiplication of Rational Expressions

As stated earlier, multiplication of rational expressions is accomplished in the same manner as multiplication of rational numbers. For example, the products $\frac{2}{3} \cdot \frac{5}{9}$ and $\frac{15}{7} \cdot \frac{49}{65}$ can be found by multiplying the numerators and denominators, factoring, and reducing.

$$\frac{2}{3} \cdot \frac{5}{9} = \frac{2 \cdot 5}{3 \cdot 9} = \frac{10}{27} \quad \text{and} \quad \frac{15}{7} \cdot \frac{49}{65} = \frac{3 \cdot \cancel{5} \cdot \cancel{7} \cdot 7}{\cancel{7} \cdot \cancel{5} \cdot 13} = \frac{21}{13}$$

The same techniques are used to multiply rational expressions.

$$\frac{2x}{x-6} \cdot \frac{x+5}{x-4} = \frac{2x(x+5)}{(x-6)(x-4)} = \frac{2x^2+10x}{x^2-10x+24}$$

$$\frac{y^2-4}{y^3} \cdot \frac{y^2-3y}{y^2-y-6} = \frac{(y+2)(y-2)\cdot \cancel{y}\,(y-3)}{\cancel{y^3}\,(y-3)(y+2)} = \frac{y-2}{y^2}$$

Multiplication of Rational Expressions

$$\frac{P}{Q} \cdot \frac{R}{S} = \frac{P \cdot R}{Q \cdot S} \qquad \text{where } Q,\, S \neq 0$$

Example 4: Multiplication of Rational Expressions

Find the following products and reduce to lowest terms by factoring whenever possible. Assume that no denominator has a value of 0.

a. $\dfrac{5x^2y}{9xy^3} \cdot \dfrac{6x^3y^2}{15xy^4} = \dfrac{\cancel{5}\cdot 2\cdot \cancel{3}x^5y^3}{3\cdot 3\cdot \cancel{5}\cdot \cancel{3}x^2y^7} = \dfrac{2x^{5-2}y^{3-7}}{9} = \dfrac{2x^3y^{-4}}{9} = \dfrac{2x^3}{9y^4}$

b. $\dfrac{x}{x-2} \cdot \dfrac{x^2-4}{x^2} = \dfrac{\cancel{x}(x+2)(\cancel{x-2})}{(\cancel{x-2})\,\cancel{x^2}} = \dfrac{x+2}{x}$

c. $\dfrac{3x-3}{x^2+x} \cdot \dfrac{x^2+2x+1}{3x^2-6x+3} = \dfrac{\cancel{3}\,(\cancel{x-1})\,(x+1)^{\cancel{2}\,(x+1)}}{x(x+1)\cdot \cancel{3}\,(x-1)^{\cancel{2}}_{(x-1)}} = \dfrac{x+1}{x(x-1)}$

Division of Rational Expressions

The rational expression $\dfrac{S}{R}$ is the **reciprocal** of $\dfrac{R}{S}$. Just as in division with rational numbers, division with rational expressions is accomplished by performing multiplication by the reciprocal of the divisor.

Division of Rational Expressions

$$\frac{P}{Q} \div \frac{R}{S} = \frac{P}{Q} \cdot \frac{S}{R} \qquad \textit{where } Q,\ R,\ S \neq 0$$

Example 5: Division of Rational Expressions ● ● ● ● ● ● ● ● ● ● ● ● ● ● ●

Find the following quotients and reduce to lowest terms by factoring whenever possible. Assume that no denominator has a value of 0. Write the final answer using only positive exponents.

a. $\dfrac{12x^2y}{10xy^2} \div \dfrac{3x^4y}{xy^3}$

Solution: $\dfrac{12x^2y}{10xy^2} \div \dfrac{3x^4y}{xy^3} = \dfrac{12x^2y}{10xy^2} \cdot \dfrac{xy^3}{3x^4y}$

$$= \frac{\cancel{2} \cdot 2 \cdot \cancel{3} x^3 y^4}{\cancel{2} \cdot 5 \cdot \cancel{3} x^5 y^3} = \frac{2x^{3-5}y^{4-3}}{5} = \frac{2x^{-2}y}{5} = \frac{2y}{5x^2}$$

b. $\dfrac{x^3 - y^3}{x^3} \div \dfrac{y - x}{xy}$

Solution: $\dfrac{x^3 - y^3}{x^3} \div \dfrac{y - x}{xy} = \dfrac{x^3 - y^3}{x^3} \cdot \dfrac{xy}{y - x}$

$$= \frac{\overset{-1}{\cancel{(x - y)}}(x^2 + xy + y^2)\cancel{x}y}{\cancel{x^3}_{x^2}\,\cancel{(y - x)}} \qquad \text{Note that } \frac{x - y}{y - x} = -1$$

$$= \frac{-y(x^2 + xy + y^2)}{x^2}$$

c. $\dfrac{x^2 - 8x + 15}{2x^2 + 11x + 5} \div \dfrac{2x^2 - 5x - 3}{4x^2 - 1}$

Solution: $\dfrac{x^2 - 8x + 15}{2x^2 + 11x + 5} \div \dfrac{2x^2 - 5x - 3}{4x^2 - 1} = \dfrac{x^2 - 8x + 15}{2x^2 + 11x + 5} \cdot \dfrac{4x^2 - 1}{2x^2 - 5x - 3}$

$$= \dfrac{(x-3)(x-5)(2x-1)(2x+1)}{(2x+1)(x+5)(x-3)(2x+1)}$$

$$= \dfrac{(x-5)(2x-1)}{(2x+1)(x+5)} = \dfrac{2x^2 - 11x + 5}{(2x+1)(x+5)}$$

● ●

NOTES

As illustrated in the answer in Example 5c, generally the denominator will be left in factored form, and the numerator will be multiplied out. This form makes the results easier to add or subtract, as we will see in the next section. However, be aware that leaving the denominator in factored form is just an option, and multiplying out the denominator is not an error. Thus in Example 5c we can write the answer either as

$$\dfrac{2x^2 - 11x + 5}{(2x+1)(x+5)} \quad \text{or as} \quad \dfrac{2x^2 - 11x + 5}{2x^2 + 11x + 5}.$$

Practice Problems

Reduce to lowest terms. State any restrictions on the variables.

1. $\dfrac{5x + 20}{7x + 28}$

2. $\dfrac{4 - 2x}{2x - 4}$

3. $\dfrac{x^2 + x - 2}{x^2 + 3x + 2}$

Perform the following operations and simplify the results. Assume that no denominator is 0.

4. $\dfrac{x - 7}{x^3} \cdot \dfrac{x^2}{49 - x^2}$

5. $\dfrac{y^2 - y - 6}{y^2 - 5y + 6} \cdot \dfrac{y^2 - 4}{y^2 + 4y + 4}$

6. $\dfrac{x^3 + 3x}{2x + 1} \div \dfrac{x^2 + 3}{x + 1}$

7. $\dfrac{x^2 + 2x - 3}{x^2 - 3x - 10} \cdot \dfrac{2x^2 - 9x - 5}{x^2 - 2x + 1} \div \dfrac{4x + 2}{x^2 - x}$

Answers to Practice Problems: 1. $\dfrac{5}{7}$, $x \neq -4$ **2.** -1, $x \neq 2$ **3.** $\dfrac{x - 1}{x + 1}$, $x \neq -1$, -2 **4.** $\dfrac{-1}{x(x + 7)}$ **5.** 1 **6.** $\dfrac{x^2 + x}{2x + 1}$

7. $\dfrac{x^2 + 3x}{2(x + 2)}$

5.1 Exercises

In Exercises 1 – 10, build each rational expression to higher terms as indicated. Assume that no denominator equals 0.

1. $\dfrac{3x^2}{-8y^2} = \dfrac{?}{32x^2y^3}$

2. $\dfrac{3y}{16x^2} = \dfrac{?}{96x^3y^2}$

3. $\dfrac{4x}{x+4} = \dfrac{?}{(x+2)(x+4)}$

4. $\dfrac{5x}{x-3} = \dfrac{?}{(x-3)(x+5)}$

5. $\dfrac{x-1}{x+1} = \dfrac{?}{x^2+3x+2}$

6. $\dfrac{5}{9x^2-3x} = \dfrac{?}{9x^3+15x^2-6x}$

7. $\dfrac{8}{x-4} = \dfrac{?}{8+2x-x^2}$

8. $\dfrac{6}{3-y} = \dfrac{?}{y^2-11y+24}$

9. $\dfrac{7}{x+4} = \dfrac{?}{x^3+64}$

10. $\dfrac{12}{x+3} = \dfrac{?}{x^3+27}$

Reduce each rational expression in Exercises 11 – 30. State any restrictions on the variable using the fact that no denominator can equal 0.

11. $\dfrac{9x^2y^3}{12xy^4}$

12. $\dfrac{18xy^4}{27x^2y}$

13. $\dfrac{20x^5}{30x^2y^3}$

14. $\dfrac{15y^4}{20x^3y^2}$

15. $\dfrac{x}{x^2-3x}$

16. $\dfrac{3x}{x^2+5x}$

17. $\dfrac{7x-14}{x-2}$

18. $\dfrac{4-2x}{2x-4}$

19. $\dfrac{9-3x}{4x-12}$

20. $\dfrac{6x^2+4x}{3xy+2y}$

21. $\dfrac{3x-9}{12-4x}$

22. $\dfrac{x+3y}{4x^2+12xy}$

23. $\dfrac{x^2+6x}{x^2+5x-6}$

24. $\dfrac{x^2-5x+6}{x^2-x-2}$

25. $\dfrac{x^2-y^2}{3x^2+3xy}$

26. $\dfrac{x^2-4}{x^3-8}$

27. $\dfrac{x^3+64}{2x^2+x-28}$

28. $\dfrac{3x^2+14x-24}{18-9x-2x^2}$

29. $\dfrac{x^3-2x^2+5x-10}{x^3-8}$

30. $\dfrac{xy-3y+2x-6}{y^2-4}$

Perform the indicated operations in Exercises 31 – 80. Assume that no denominator equals 0.

31. $\dfrac{ax^2}{b} \cdot \dfrac{b^2}{x^2y}$

32. $\dfrac{18x^3}{5y^2} \cdot \dfrac{30y^3}{9x^4}$

33. $\dfrac{24x^3}{25y^2} \cdot \dfrac{10y^5}{18x}$

34. $\dfrac{16x^8}{3y^{11}} \cdot \dfrac{-21y^9}{10x^7}$

35. $\dfrac{x^2-9}{x^2+2x} \cdot \dfrac{x+2}{x-3}$

36. $\dfrac{16x^2-9}{3x^2-15x} \cdot \dfrac{6}{4x+3}$

37. $\dfrac{x^2+2x-3}{x^2+3x} \cdot \dfrac{x}{x+1}$

38. $\dfrac{4x+16}{x^2-16} \cdot \dfrac{x-4}{x}$

39. $\dfrac{x^2+6x-16}{x^2-64} \cdot \dfrac{1}{2-x}$

40. $\dfrac{4-x^2}{x^2-4x+4} \cdot \dfrac{3}{x+2}$

41. $\dfrac{x^2-5x+6}{x^2-4x} \cdot \dfrac{x-4}{x-3}$

42. $\dfrac{2x^2+x-3}{x^2+4x} \cdot \dfrac{2x+8}{x-1}$

43. $\dfrac{2x^2+10x}{3x^2+5x+2} \cdot \dfrac{6x+4}{x^2}$

44. $\dfrac{x+3}{x^2-16} \cdot \dfrac{x^2-3x-4}{x^2-1}$

45. $\dfrac{x}{x^2+7x+12} \cdot \dfrac{x^2-2x-24}{x^2-7x+6}$

46. $\dfrac{x^2-2x-3}{x+5} \cdot \dfrac{x^2-5x-14}{x^2-x-6}$

47. $\dfrac{8-2x-x^2}{x^2-2x}\cdot\dfrac{x-4}{x^2-3x-4}$

48. $\dfrac{3x^2+21x}{x^2-49}\cdot\dfrac{x^2-5x+4}{x^2+3x-4}$

49. $\dfrac{(x-2y)^2}{x^2-5xy+6y^2}\cdot\dfrac{x+2y}{x^2-4xy+4y^2}$

50. $\dfrac{4x^2+6x}{x^2+3x-10}\cdot\dfrac{x^2+4x-12}{x^2+5x-6}$

51. $\dfrac{2x^2+5x+2}{3x^2+8x+4}\cdot\dfrac{3x^2-x-2}{4x^3-x}$

52. $\dfrac{x^2+5x}{4x^2+12x+9}\cdot\dfrac{6x^2+7x-3}{x^2+10x+25}$

53. $\dfrac{x^2+x+1}{x^2-1}\cdot\dfrac{x^2-2x+1}{x^3-1}$

54. $\dfrac{x-2}{x^2-2x+4}\cdot\dfrac{x^3+8}{x^2-4x+4}$

55. $\dfrac{2x^2-7x+3}{x^2-9}\cdot\dfrac{3x^2+8x-3}{6x^2+x-1}$

56. $\dfrac{12x^2y}{9xy^9}\div\dfrac{4x^4y}{x^2y^3}$

57. $\dfrac{35xy^3}{24x^3y}\div\dfrac{15x^4y^3}{84xy^4}$

58. $\dfrac{45xy^4}{21x^2y^2}\div\dfrac{40x^4}{112xy^5}$

59. $\dfrac{x-3}{15x}\div\dfrac{4x-12}{5}$

60. $\dfrac{x-1}{6x+6}\div\dfrac{2x-2}{x^2+x}$

61. $\dfrac{7x-14}{x^2}\div\dfrac{x^2-4}{x^3}$

62. $\dfrac{6x^2-54}{x^4}\div\dfrac{x-3}{x^2}$

63. $\dfrac{x^2-25}{6x+30}\div\dfrac{x-5}{x}$

64. $\dfrac{2x-1}{x^2+2x}\div\dfrac{10x^2-5x}{6x^2+12x}$

65. $\dfrac{x+3}{x^2+3x-4}\div\dfrac{x+2}{x^2+x-2}$

66. $\dfrac{6x^2-7x-3}{x^2-1}\div\dfrac{2x-3}{x-1}$

67. $\dfrac{x^2-9}{2x^2+7x+3}\div\dfrac{x^2-3x}{2x^2+11x+5}$

68. $\dfrac{x^2-8x+15}{x^2-9x+14}\div\dfrac{x^2+4x-21}{x-1}$

69. $\dfrac{2x+1}{4x-x^2}\div\dfrac{4x^2-1}{x^2-16}$

70. $\dfrac{x^2-6x+9}{x^2-4x+3}\div\dfrac{2x^2-7x+3}{x^2-3x+2}$

71. $\dfrac{x^2-4x+4}{x^2+5x+6}\div\dfrac{x^2+2x-8}{x^2+7x+12}$

72. $\dfrac{x^2-x-6}{x^2+6x+8}\div\dfrac{x^2-4x+3}{x^2+5x+4}$

73. $\dfrac{x^2-x-12}{6x^2+x-9}\div\dfrac{x^2-6x+8}{3x^2-x-6}$

74. $\dfrac{6x^2+5x+1}{4x^3-3x^2}\div\dfrac{3x^2-2x-1}{3x^2-2x+1}$

75. $\dfrac{8x^2+2x-15}{3x^2+13x+4}\div\dfrac{2x^2+5x+3}{6x^2-x-1}$

76. $\dfrac{3x^2+13x+14}{4x^3-3x^2}\div\dfrac{6x^2-x-35}{4x^2+5x-6}$

77. $\dfrac{3x^2+2x}{9x^2-4}\div\dfrac{27x^3-8}{9x^2-6x+4}$

78. $\dfrac{x^3+2x^2}{x^3+64}\cdot\dfrac{4x^2}{x^2-4x+16}$

79. $\dfrac{6-11x-10x^2}{2x^2+x-3}\div\dfrac{5x^3-2x^2}{3x^2-5x+2}$

80. $\dfrac{x-6}{x^2-7x+6}\cdot\dfrac{x^2-3x}{x+3}\cdot\dfrac{x^2-9}{x^2-4x+3}$

81. $\dfrac{3x^2 + 11x + 10}{2x^2 + x - 6} \cdot \dfrac{x^2 + 2x - 3}{2x - 1} \cdot \dfrac{2x - 3}{3x^2 + 2x - 5}$ **82.** $\dfrac{x^3 + 3x^2}{x^2 + 7x + 12} \cdot \dfrac{2x^2 + 7x - 4}{2x^2 - x} \div \dfrac{2x^2 - x - 1}{x^2 + 4x - 5}$

83. $\dfrac{x^2 + 2x - 3}{x^2 + 10x + 21} \div \dfrac{x^2 - 7x - 8}{x^2 + 6x + 5} \cdot \dfrac{x^2 - x - 56}{x^2 - 3x - 40}$ **84.** $\dfrac{2x^2 - 5x + 2}{4xy - 2y + 6x - 3} \div \dfrac{xy - 2y + 3x - 6}{2y^2 + 9y + 9}$

Writing and Thinking About Mathematics

85. a. Define rational expression.
   b. Give an example of a rational expression that is undefined for $x = -2$ and $x = 3$ and has a value of 0 for $x = 1$. Explain how you determined this expression.
   c. Give an example of a rational expression that is undefined for $x = -5$ and never has a value of 0. Explain how you determined this expression.

86. Write the opposite of each of the following expressions.
   a. $3 - x$ **b.** $2x - 7$ **c.** $x + 5$ **d.** $-3x - 2$

87. Given the rational function $f(x) = \dfrac{x - 4}{x^2 - 100}$.

   a. For what values, if any, will $f(x) = 0$?
   b. For what values, if any, is $f(x)$ undefined?

Hawkes Learning Systems: Intermediate Algebra

Defining Rational Expressions
Multiplication and Division of Rational Expressions

5.2	# Addition and Subtraction of Rational Expressions

After completing this section, you will be able to:

1. *Find the least common multiple of a set of algebraic expressions.*
2. *Add rational expressions.*
3. *Subtract rational expressions.*

Adding and Subtracting Rational Expressions with Common Denominators

To add or subtract rational expressions with a common denominator, proceed just as you would with numerical fractions. That is, add (or subtract) the numerators and keep the common denominator. For example,

$$\frac{x}{x+2}+\frac{3}{x+2}=\frac{x+3}{x+2} \quad \text{and} \quad \frac{x}{x+2}-\frac{3}{x+2}=\frac{x-3}{x+2} \qquad (x \neq -2)$$

Just as with numerical fractions, the sum (or difference) should be reduced if possible. For example in the following sum, the result can be reduced.

$$\frac{x}{x^2-1}+\frac{1}{x^2-1}=\frac{x+1}{x^2-1}$$ Factor and reduce the sum.

$$=\frac{\overset{1}{\cancel{(x+1)}}}{\cancel{(x+1)}(x-1)}=\frac{1}{x-1} \quad x^2-1 \neq 0 \,(\text{or } x \neq \pm 1)$$

A difference such as $\dfrac{x^2}{x^2+4x+4}-\dfrac{2x+8}{x^2+4x+4}$ is found by subtracting the numerators and using the common denominator.

$$\frac{x^2}{x^2+4x+4}-\frac{2x+8}{x^2+4x+4}=\frac{x^2-(2x+8)}{x^2+4x+4}$$

$$=\frac{x^2-2x-8}{x^2+4x+4}$$

Again, the result can be reduced.

$$\frac{x^2-2x-8}{x^2+4x+4}=\frac{(x-4)\cancel{(x+2)}}{(x+2)\cancel{(x+2)}}$$

$$=\frac{x-4}{x+2} \quad (x \neq -2)$$

Addition and Subtraction of Rational Expressions

$$\frac{P}{Q} + \frac{R}{Q} = \frac{P+R}{Q} \quad and \quad \frac{P}{Q} - \frac{R}{Q} = \frac{P-R}{Q} \quad where \ Q \neq 0$$

Note that the expression $P - R$ indicates the difference of two polynomials and this will affect all of the signs in R. **A good idea is to put P in parentheses and R in parentheses so that all changes in sign will be done correctly.**

Example 1: Addition and Subtraction of Rational Expressions

Find the indicated sum or difference. Reduce if possible. Assume that no denominator is 0.

a.
$$\frac{2x+1}{3x-3} + \frac{x+2}{3x-3} = \frac{(2x+1)+(x+2)}{3x-3}$$

$$= \frac{3x+3}{3x-3} = \frac{\cancel{3}(x+1)}{\cancel{3}(x-1)} = \frac{x+1}{x-1}$$

b.
$$\frac{2x-5y}{x+y} - \frac{3x-7y}{x+y} = \frac{(2x-5y)-(3x-7y)}{x+y}$$

$$= \frac{2x-5y-3x+7y}{x+y} = \frac{-x+2y}{x+y}$$

NOTES

Common Error

Many students make a **mistake** in subtracting fractions by not subtracting the entire numerator. They make a mistake similar to the following.

Error

WRONG →
$$\frac{7}{x+6} - \frac{x+3}{x+6} = \frac{7-x+3}{x+6} = \frac{10-x}{x+6}$$

By using parentheses, you can avoid such mistakes.

RIGHT →
$$\frac{7}{x+6} - \frac{x+3}{x+6} = \frac{7-(x+3)}{x+6} = \frac{7-x-3}{x+6} = \frac{4-x}{x+6}$$

Finding the Least Common Multiple (LCM)

The rational expressions added and subtracted in Examples 1a and 1b had common denominators. To add or subtract expressions with different denominators, each expression must be built to higher terms with a common denominator. This common denominator is the **least common denominator** (**LCD**) and represents the **least common multiple** (**LCM**) of the denominators. The technique for finding the LCD is developed in the following discussion.

To Find the LCM for a Set of Polynomials

1. Completely factor each polynomial (including the prime factors for numerical factors).

2. Form the product of all distinct factors that appear, using each factor the most number of times it appears in any one factorization.

NOTES   Recall that the prime numbers are $\{2, 3, 5, 7, 11, 13, 17, 19, 23, 31, 37, 41, 43, 47, 53,...\}$. Also, 0 and 1 are **not** prime numbers.

Consider the three terms in the set $\left\{18x^3,\ 24xy,\ 63\right\}$. To find the **LCM**:

1. Find the complete factorization of each term, including prime factors.

$$18x^3 = 2 \cdot 3 \cdot 3 \cdot x^3 \quad \longleftarrow \text{one 2, two 3's, } x^3$$
$$24xy = 2 \cdot 2 \cdot 2 \cdot 3 \cdot x \cdot y \longleftarrow \text{three 2's, one 3, } x, y$$
$$63 = 3 \cdot 3 \cdot 7 \quad \longleftarrow \text{two 3's, one 7}$$

2. Form a product using each prime factor and each variable the most number of times it appears in **any one** of the factorizations.

$$\text{LCM} = 2 \cdot 2 \cdot 2 \cdot 3 \cdot 3 \cdot 7 \cdot x^3 \cdot y \quad \longleftarrow \text{three 2's, two 3's, one 7, } x^3, y$$
$$= 504x^3 y$$

This product, $504x^3 y$, is the least common multiple. This is the smallest number with the smallest positive exponents on the variables that is divisible by all three terms.

Now, use the same technique to find the LCM for the polynomial expressions

$$x^2 + 6x + 9,\quad x^2 - 9,\quad \text{and}\quad 2x + 6.$$

1. Factor each expression completely.

$$x^2 + 6x + 9 = (x+3)^2$$
$$x^2 - 9 = (x+3)(x-3)$$
$$2x + 6 = 2(x+3)$$

2. To determine the LCM, form the product of 2, $(x+3)^2$, and $(x-3)$. That is, use each factor the most number of times it appears in **any one** factorization.

$$LCM = 2(x+3)^2(x-3)$$

Adding and Subtracting Rational Expressions with Different Denominators

Use the following procedure when adding or subtracting rational expressions with different denominators.

Procedure for Adding or Subtracting Rational Expressions with Different Denominators

1. *Find the LCD (the LCM of the denominators).*

2. *Rewrite each fraction in an equivalent form with the LCD.*

3. *Add (or subtract) the numerators and keep the common denominator.*

4. *Reduce if possible.*

The procedure is outlined in detail in finding the following sum:

$$\frac{1}{x^2+6x+9} + \frac{1}{x^2-9} + \frac{1}{2x+6}$$

First, find the LCD which is the LCM as just discussed above:

$$LCD = LCM = 2(x+3)^2(x-3)$$

Next, by using the Fundamental Theorem of Fractions, each rational expression is multiplied by 1 in a form that will give an equivalent expression with the desired denominator. Thus,

$$\frac{1}{x^2+6x+9} = \frac{1}{(x+3)^2} \cdot \frac{2(x-3)}{2(x-3)} = \frac{1\cdot 2(x-3)}{(x+3)^2 \cdot 2(x-3)}$$

$$\frac{1}{x^2-9} = \frac{1}{(x+3)(x-3)} \cdot \frac{2(x+3)}{2(x+3)} = \frac{1\cdot 2(x+3)}{(x+3)(x-3)\cdot 2(x+3)}$$

$$\frac{1}{2x+6} = \frac{1}{2(x+3)} \cdot \frac{(x+3)(x-3)}{(x+3)(x-3)} = \frac{1\cdot(x+3)(x-3)}{2(x+3)\cdot(x+3)(x-3)}$$

Each rational expression now has the same denominator $2(x+3)^2(x-3)$, and the resulting fractions can be added.

$$\frac{1}{x^2+6x+9} \qquad +\frac{1}{x^2-9} \qquad +\frac{1}{2x+6}$$

$$=\frac{1}{(x+3)^2} \qquad +\frac{1}{(x+3)(x-3)} \qquad +\frac{1}{2(x+3)}$$

$$=\frac{1\cdot 2(x-3)}{(x+3)^2\cdot 2(x-3)}+\frac{1\cdot 2(x+3)}{(x+3)(x-3)\cdot 2(x+3)}+\frac{1\cdot(x+3)(x-3)}{2(x+3)\cdot(x+3)(x-3)}$$

$$=\frac{(2x-6)+(2x+6)+(x^2-9)}{2(x+3)^2(x-3)}$$

$$=\frac{x^2+4x-9}{2(x+3)^2(x-3)}$$

NOTES The denominator is left in factored form as a convenience for possibly reducing or adding to some other expression later. Denominators are left in factored form in the answers in the back of the text.

Example 2: Adding and Subtracting Rational Expressions

Perform the indicated operation. Reduce if possible. Assume that no denominator is 0.

a. $\dfrac{x}{x-3}+\dfrac{6}{x+4}$

Solution: Here, neither denominator can be factored so the LCD is the product of these factors. That is, LCD $=(x-3)(x+4)$.

$$\frac{x}{x-3}+\frac{6}{x+4}=\frac{x(x+4)}{(x-3)(x+4)}+\frac{6(x-3)}{(x+4)(x-3)}$$

$$=\frac{(x^2+4x)+(6x-18)}{(x-3)(x+4)}$$

$$=\frac{x^2+4x+6x-18}{(x-3)(x+4)}$$

$$=\frac{x^2+10x-18}{(x-3)(x+4)}$$

NOTES Again, the denominator is left in factored form as a convenience for possibly reducing or adding to some other expression later. You may choose to multiply these factors. Either form is correct.

continued on next page …

b. $\dfrac{x}{x-5} - \dfrac{3}{5-x}$

Solution: Because each denominator is the opposite of the other, the numerator and denominator of one fraction can both be multiplied by -1. Then both denominators will be the same.

Note: $(5-x)(-1) = -5 + x = x - 5$.

$$\dfrac{x}{x-5} - \dfrac{3}{5-x} \cdot \dfrac{(-1)}{(-1)} = \dfrac{x}{x-5} - \dfrac{-3}{x-5} = \dfrac{x-(-3)}{x-5} = \dfrac{x+3}{x-5}$$

c. $\dfrac{x+5}{x-5} - \dfrac{100}{x^2-25}$

Solution: $\left. \begin{aligned} x - 5 &= x - 5 \\ x^2 - 25 &= (x+5)(x-5) \end{aligned} \right\} \quad \text{LCD} = (x+5)(x-5)$

$$\dfrac{x+5}{x-5} - \dfrac{100}{x^2-25} = \dfrac{(x+5)(x+5)}{(x-5)(x+5)} - \dfrac{100}{(x+5)(x-5)}$$

$$= \dfrac{(x^2+10x+25)-100}{(x+5)(x-5)}$$

$$= \dfrac{x^2+10x+25-100}{(x+5)(x-5)}$$

$$= \dfrac{x^2+10x-75}{(x+5)(x-5)} = \dfrac{(x+15)\,\cancel{(x-5)}}{\cancel{(x-5)}\,(x+5)} = \dfrac{x+15}{x+5}$$

d. $\dfrac{x+y}{(x-y)^2} + \dfrac{x}{2x^2-2y^2}$

Solution: $\left. \begin{aligned} (x-y)^2 &= (x-y)^2 \\ 2x^2 - 2y^2 &= 2(x+y)(x-y) \end{aligned} \right\} \quad \text{LCD} = 2(x-y)^2(x+y)$

$$\dfrac{x+y}{(x-y)^2} + \dfrac{x}{2x^2-2y^2}$$

$$= \dfrac{(x+y)\cdot 2(x+y)}{(x-y)^2 \cdot 2(x+y)} + \dfrac{x(x-y)}{2(x-y)(x+y)(x-y)}$$

$$= \dfrac{2x^2+4xy+2y^2+x^2-xy}{2(x-y)^2(x+y)}$$

$$= \dfrac{3x^2+3xy+2y^2}{2(x-y)^2(x+y)}$$

e. $\dfrac{3x-12}{x^2+x-20}-\dfrac{x^2+5x}{x^2+9x+20}$

Hint: In this problem, both expressions can be reduced before looking for the LCD.

Solution: $\dfrac{3x-12}{x^2+x-20}-\dfrac{x^2+5x}{x^2+9x+20}$

$=\dfrac{3(x-4)}{(x+5)(x-4)}-\dfrac{x(x+5)}{(x+5)(x+4)}$

$=\dfrac{3}{x+5}-\dfrac{x}{x+4}$

Now subtract these two expressions with LCD $=(x+5)(x+4)$.

$\dfrac{3}{x+5}-\dfrac{x}{x+4}=\dfrac{3(x+4)}{(x+5)(x+4)}-\dfrac{x(x+5)}{(x+4)(x+5)}$

$=\dfrac{(3x+12)-(x^2+5x)}{(x+5)(x+4)}$

$=\dfrac{3x+12-x^2-5x}{(x+5)(x+4)}$

$=\dfrac{-x^2-2x+12}{(x+5)(x+4)}$

f. $\dfrac{4}{x^2-1}+\dfrac{4}{x+1}+\dfrac{2}{1-x}$

Solution: $x^2-1=(x+1)(x-1)$

$x+1=x+1$

$1-x=-1(x-1)$

Note that $1-x=-1(x-1)$.

Rewrite the problem by changing $1-x$ to $-1(x-1)$. In this situation, the addition problem becomes a subtraction problem, and -1 is not considered to be part of the LCD.

$\dfrac{4}{x^2-1}+\dfrac{4}{x+1}+\dfrac{2}{-1(x-1)}$

$=\dfrac{4}{(x+1)(x-1)}+\dfrac{4(x-1)}{(x+1)(x-1)}-\dfrac{2(x+1)}{(x-1)(x+1)}$ LCD $=(x+1)(x-1)$

$=\dfrac{4+4(x-1)-2(x+1)}{(x+1)(x-1)}$

$=\dfrac{4+4x-4-2x-2}{(x+1)(x-1)}$

$=\dfrac{2x-2}{(x+1)(x-1)}=\dfrac{2(x-1)}{(x+1)(x-1)}=\dfrac{2}{x+1}$

continued on next page ...

g. $\dfrac{x+1}{xy-3y+4x-12} + \dfrac{x-3}{xy+6y+4x+24}$

Solution: $\left. \begin{aligned} xy-3y+4x-12 &= y(x-3)+4(x-3) \\ &= (x-3)(y+4) \\ xy+6y+4x+24 &= y(x+6)+4(x+6) \\ &= (x+6)(y+4) \end{aligned} \right\}$ LCD $= (y+4)(x-3)(x+6)$

$$\dfrac{x+1}{xy-3y+4x-12} + \dfrac{x-3}{xy+6y+4x+24} = \dfrac{(x+1)(x+6)}{(y+4)(x-3)(x+6)} + \dfrac{(x-3)(x-3)}{(y+4)(x-3)(x+6)}$$

$$= \dfrac{x^2+7x+6+x^2-6x+9}{(y+4)(x-3)(x+6)}$$

$$= \dfrac{2x^2+x+15}{(y+4)(x-3)(x+6)}$$

Practice Problems

Perform the indicated operations and reduce if possible. Assume that no denominator is 0.

1. $\dfrac{x}{x^2-1} + \dfrac{1}{x-1}$

2. $\dfrac{x+3}{x^2+x-6} + \dfrac{x-2}{x^2+4x-12}$

3. $\dfrac{1}{y+2} - \dfrac{1}{y^3+8}$

4. $\dfrac{1}{1-y} + \dfrac{2}{y^2-1}$

5.2 Exercises

Perform the indicated operations and reduce if possible. Assume that no denominator is 0.

1. $\dfrac{3x}{x+4} + \dfrac{12}{x+4}$

2. $\dfrac{7x}{x+5} + \dfrac{35}{x+5}$

3. $\dfrac{x-1}{x+6} + \dfrac{x+13}{x+6}$

4. $\dfrac{3x-1}{2x-6} + \dfrac{x-11}{2x-6}$

5. $\dfrac{3x+1}{5x+2} + \dfrac{2x+1}{5x+2}$

6. $\dfrac{x^2+3}{x+1} + \dfrac{4x}{x+1}$

7. $\dfrac{x-5}{x^2-2x+1} + \dfrac{x+3}{x^2-2x+1}$

8. $\dfrac{2x^2+5}{x^2-4} + \dfrac{3x-1}{x^2-4}$

9. $\dfrac{13}{7-x} - \dfrac{1}{x-7}$

Answers to Practice Problems: 1. $\dfrac{2x+1}{(x+1)(x-1)}$ **2.** $\dfrac{2x+4}{(x-2)(x+6)}$ **3.** $\dfrac{y^2-2y+3}{y^3+8}$ **4.** $\dfrac{-1}{y+1}$

10. $\dfrac{6x}{x-6} + \dfrac{36}{6-x}$

11. $\dfrac{3x}{x-4} + \dfrac{16-x}{4-x}$

12. $\dfrac{20}{x-10} - \dfrac{3}{10-x}$

13. $\dfrac{x^2+2}{x^2+x-12} + \dfrac{x+1}{12-x-x^2}$

14. $\dfrac{10}{x^2-x-6} - \dfrac{5x}{6+x-x^2}$

15. $\dfrac{x^2+2}{x^2-4} - \dfrac{4x-2}{x^2-4}$

16. $\dfrac{2x+5}{2x^2-x-1} - \dfrac{4x+2}{2x^2-x-1}$

17. $\dfrac{x+3}{7x-2} + \dfrac{2x-1}{14x-4}$

18. $\dfrac{3x+1}{4x+10} + \dfrac{4-x}{2x+5}$

19. $\dfrac{5}{x-3} + \dfrac{x}{x^2-9}$

20. $\dfrac{x+1}{x^2-3x-10} + \dfrac{x}{x-5}$

21. $\dfrac{x}{x-1} - \dfrac{4}{x+2}$

22. $\dfrac{x-1}{3x-1} - \dfrac{8+4x}{x+2}$

23. $\dfrac{x+2}{x+3} - \dfrac{4}{3-x}$

24. $\dfrac{x}{4-x} + \dfrac{3x}{x+5}$

25. $\dfrac{x+2}{3x+9} + \dfrac{2x-1}{2x-6}$

26. $\dfrac{x}{4x-8} - \dfrac{3x+2}{3x+6}$

27. $\dfrac{3x}{6+x} - \dfrac{2x}{x^2-36}$

28. $\dfrac{3x-4}{x^2-x-20} - \dfrac{2}{5-x}$

29. $\dfrac{4x+1}{7-x} + \dfrac{x-1}{x^2-8x+7}$

30. $\dfrac{4}{x+5} - \dfrac{2x+3}{x^2+4x-5}$

31. $\dfrac{4x}{x^2+3x-28} + \dfrac{3}{x^2+6x-7}$

32. $\dfrac{3x}{x^2+2x+1} - \dfrac{x}{x^2+4x+4}$

33. $\dfrac{x+1}{x^2+4x+4} - \dfrac{x-3}{x^2-4}$

34. $\dfrac{x-4}{x^2-5x+6} + \dfrac{2x}{x^2-2x-3}$

35. $\dfrac{3x}{9-x^2} + \dfrac{5}{x^2-7x+12}$

36. $\dfrac{4x}{3x^2+4x+1} - \dfrac{x+4}{x^2+7x+6}$

37. $\dfrac{x-6}{7x^2-3x-4} + \dfrac{7-x}{7x^2+18x+8}$

38. $\dfrac{x+5}{9x^2-26x-3} - \dfrac{8x}{9x^2+11x+3}$

39. $\dfrac{x-3}{4x^2-5x-6} - \dfrac{4x+10}{2x^2+x-10}$

40. $\dfrac{2x+1}{8x^2-37x-15} + \dfrac{2-x}{8x^2+11x+3}$

41. $\dfrac{3x}{4-x} + \dfrac{7x}{x+4} - \dfrac{x-3}{x^2-16}$

42. $\dfrac{x}{x+3} + \dfrac{x+1}{3-x} + \dfrac{x^2+4}{x^2-9}$

43. $2 - \dfrac{4x+1}{x-4} + \dfrac{x-3}{x^2-6x+8}$

44. $-4 + \dfrac{1-2x}{x+6} + \dfrac{x^2+1}{x^2+4x-12}$

45. $\dfrac{2}{x^2-4} - \dfrac{3}{x^2-3x+2} + \dfrac{x-1}{x^2+x-2}$

46. $\dfrac{x}{x^2+4x-21} + \dfrac{1-x}{x^2+8x+7} + \dfrac{3x}{x^2-2x-3}$

47. $\dfrac{3(x+3)}{x^2-5x+4} + \dfrac{49}{12+x-x^2} + \dfrac{3x+21}{x^2+2x-3}$

48. $\dfrac{4}{x^2+3x-10} + \dfrac{3}{x^2-25} - \dfrac{5}{x^2-7x+10}$

49. $\dfrac{5x+22}{x^2+8x+15}+\dfrac{4}{x^2+4x+3}+\dfrac{6}{x^2+6x+5}$

50. $\dfrac{x+1}{2x^2-x-1}+\dfrac{2x}{2x^2+5x+2}-\dfrac{2x}{3x^2+4x-4}$

51. $\dfrac{x-6}{3x^2+10x+3}-\dfrac{2x}{5x^2-3x-2}+\dfrac{2x}{3x^2-2x-1}$

52. $\dfrac{x}{xy+x-2y-2}+\dfrac{x+2}{xy+x+y+1}$

53. $\dfrac{4x}{xy-3x+y-3}+\dfrac{x+2}{xy+2y-3x-6}$

54. $\dfrac{3y}{xy+2x+3y+6}+\dfrac{x}{x^2-2x-15}$

55. $\dfrac{2}{xy-4x-2y+8}+\dfrac{5y}{y^2-3y-4}$

56. $\dfrac{x+6}{x^2+x+1}-\dfrac{3x^2+x-4}{x^3-1}$

57. $\dfrac{2x-5}{8x^2-4x+2}+\dfrac{x^2-2x+5}{8x^3+1}$

58. $\dfrac{x+1}{x^3-3x^2+x-3}+\dfrac{x^2-5x-8}{x^4-8x^2-9}$

59. $\dfrac{x+4}{x^3-5x^2+6x-30}-\dfrac{x-7}{x^3-2x^2+6x-12}$

60. $\dfrac{x+2}{9x^2-6x+4}+\dfrac{10x-5x^2}{27x^3+8}-\dfrac{2}{3x+2}$

Writing and Thinking About Mathematics

61. Discuss the steps in the process you go through when adding two rational expressions. That is, discuss how you find the least common denominator when adding two fractions (rational expressions) and how you use this LCD in finding equivalent fractions that you can add.

Hawkes Learning Systems: Intermediate Algebra

Addition and Subtraction of Rational Expressions

5.3   Complex Fractions

Objectives

After completing this section, you will be able to:

Simplify complex fractions.

A **complex fraction** is a fraction in which the numerator or denominator is itself a fraction or the sum or difference of fractions. Examples of complex fractions are

$$\frac{\dfrac{6x}{5y^2}}{\dfrac{8x^2}{10y^3}}, \quad \frac{x+y}{x^{-1}+y^{-1}}, \quad \text{and} \quad \frac{\dfrac{1}{x+3}-\dfrac{1}{x}}{1+\dfrac{3}{x}}.$$

In the first example, the numerator and denominator are both single fractions; no sum or difference is indicated. To simplify this expression, we simply divide and reduce as with rational expressions.

Example 1: Complex Fraction

Simplify $\dfrac{\dfrac{6x}{5y^2}}{\dfrac{8x^2}{10y^3}}$

Solution: $\dfrac{\dfrac{6x}{5y^2}}{\dfrac{8x^2}{10y^3}} = \dfrac{6x}{5y^2} \div \dfrac{8x^2}{10y^3} = \dfrac{6x}{5y^2} \cdot \dfrac{10y^3}{8x^2} = \dfrac{2 \cdot 3 \cdot 2 \cdot \cancel{5} \cancel{x} \cancel{y^3}^{y}}{\cancel{5} \cdot \cancel{2} \cdot \cancel{2} \cdot 2 y^2 x^2}_{x} = \dfrac{3y}{2x}$

There are two methods for simplifying a complex fraction when a sum or difference of fractions is indicated. The method you choose depends on which method is easier to apply or better fits the particular problem.

To Simplify a Complex Fraction (First Method)

1.   *Simplify the numerator and denominator separately so that the numerator and denominator are simple fractions.*

2.   *Divide by multiplying by the reciprocal of the denominator.*

Example 2: First Method ●

a. $\dfrac{x+y}{x^{-1}+y^{-1}}$

Solution: $\dfrac{x+y}{x^{-1}+y^{-1}} = \dfrac{x+y}{\dfrac{1}{x}+\dfrac{1}{y}}$

Recall that $x^{-1}=\dfrac{1}{x}$ and $y^{-1}=\dfrac{1}{y}$.

$= \dfrac{\dfrac{x+y}{1}}{\dfrac{1}{x}\cdot\dfrac{y}{y}+\dfrac{1}{y}\cdot\dfrac{x}{x}}$

Add the two fractions in the denominator.

$= \dfrac{\dfrac{x+y}{1}}{\dfrac{y}{xy}+\dfrac{x}{xy}} = \dfrac{\dfrac{x+y}{1}}{\dfrac{y+x}{xy}}$

$= \dfrac{x\!\!\!/+y}{1}\cdot\dfrac{xy}{y\!\!\!/+x} = \dfrac{xy}{1} = xy$

Multiply by the reciprocal of the denominator.

b. $\dfrac{\dfrac{1}{x+3}-\dfrac{1}{x}}{1+\dfrac{3}{x}}$

Solution: $\dfrac{\dfrac{1}{x+3}-\dfrac{1}{x}}{1+\dfrac{3}{x}} = \dfrac{\dfrac{1\cdot x}{(x+3)\cdot x}-\dfrac{1(x+3)}{x(x+3)}}{\dfrac{x}{x}+\dfrac{3}{x}}$

Combine the fractions in the numerator and in the denominator separately.

Note that $1=\dfrac{x}{x}$.

$= \dfrac{\dfrac{x-(x+3)}{x(x+3)}}{\dfrac{x+3}{x}} = \dfrac{\dfrac{x-x-3}{x(x+3)}}{\dfrac{x+3}{x}}$

$= \dfrac{-3}{x\!\!\!/(x+3)}\cdot\dfrac{x\!\!\!/}{x+3} = \dfrac{-3}{(x+3)^2}$

Multiply by the reciprocal of the denominator.

● ●

To Simplify a Complex Fraction (Second Method)

1. Find the LCM of all the denominators in the original numerator and denominator.

2. Multiply both the numerator and denominator by this LCM.

Example 3: Second Method

a. $\dfrac{x+y}{x^{-1}+y^{-1}}$

Solution: $\dfrac{x+y}{x^{-1}+y^{-1}} = \dfrac{\dfrac{x+y}{1}}{\dfrac{1}{x}+\dfrac{1}{y}}$

$= \dfrac{\left(\dfrac{x+y}{1}\right)xy}{\left(\dfrac{1}{x}+\dfrac{1}{y}\right)xy} = \dfrac{(x+y)xy}{\dfrac{1}{x}\cdot xy+\dfrac{1}{y}\cdot xy}$ The LCM for $\{x, y, 1\}$ is xy.

$= \dfrac{(x+y)xy}{y+x} = xy$

Note that this multiplication can be done because the net effect is that the fraction is multiplied by 1.

b. $\dfrac{\dfrac{1}{x+3}-\dfrac{1}{x}}{1+\dfrac{3}{x}}$

Solution: $\dfrac{\dfrac{1}{x+3}-\dfrac{1}{x}}{1+\dfrac{3}{x}} = \dfrac{\left(\dfrac{1}{x+3}-\dfrac{1}{x}\right)\cdot x(x+3)}{\left(1+\dfrac{3}{x}\right)\cdot x(x+3)}$ The LCM for $\{x, x+3\}$ is $x(x+3)$.

$= \dfrac{\dfrac{1}{x+3}\cdot x(x+3)-\dfrac{1}{x}\cdot x(x+3)}{1\cdot x(x+3)+\dfrac{3}{x}\cdot x(x+3)}$

$= \dfrac{x-(x+3)}{x(x+3)+3(x+3)} = \dfrac{x-x-3}{(x+3)(x+3)}$

$= \dfrac{-3}{(x+3)^{2}}$

5.3 Exercises

Simplify each complex fraction in Exercises 1 – 36.

1. $\dfrac{\dfrac{2x}{3y^2}}{\dfrac{5x^2}{6y}}$

2. $\dfrac{\dfrac{6x^2}{5y}}{\dfrac{x}{10y^2}}$

3. $\dfrac{\dfrac{12x^3}{7y^2}}{\dfrac{3x^5}{2y}}$

4. $\dfrac{\dfrac{9x^2}{7y^3}}{\dfrac{3xy}{14}}$

5. $\dfrac{\dfrac{x+3}{2x}}{\dfrac{2x-1}{4x^2}}$

6. $\dfrac{\dfrac{x-2}{6x}}{\dfrac{x+3}{3x^2}}$

7. $\dfrac{\dfrac{3}{x}+\dfrac{1}{2x}}{1+\dfrac{2}{x}}$

8. $\dfrac{\dfrac{2x-1}{x}}{\dfrac{2}{x}+3}$

9. $\dfrac{1+\dfrac{1}{x}}{1-\dfrac{1}{x^2}}$

10. $\dfrac{\dfrac{2}{y}+1}{\dfrac{4}{y^2}-1}$

11. $\dfrac{\dfrac{1}{x}+\dfrac{1}{3x}}{\dfrac{x+6}{x^2}}$

12. $\dfrac{\dfrac{3}{x}-\dfrac{6}{x^2}}{\dfrac{x-2}{x^2}}$

13. $\dfrac{\dfrac{7}{x}-\dfrac{14}{x^2}}{\dfrac{1}{x}-\dfrac{4}{x^3}}$

14. $\dfrac{\dfrac{3}{x}-\dfrac{6}{x^2}}{\dfrac{1}{x}-\dfrac{2}{x^2}}$

15. $\dfrac{\dfrac{x}{y}-\dfrac{1}{3}}{\dfrac{6}{y}-\dfrac{2}{x}}$

16. $\dfrac{\dfrac{3}{x}+\dfrac{5}{2x}}{\dfrac{1}{x}+4}$

17. $\dfrac{\dfrac{2}{x}+\dfrac{3}{4y}}{\dfrac{3}{2x}-\dfrac{5}{3y}}$

18. $\dfrac{1+x^{-1}}{1-x^{-2}}$

19. $\dfrac{1}{x^{-1}+y^{-1}}$

20. $\dfrac{x^{-1}+y^{-1}}{x+y}$

21. $\dfrac{x^{-1}+y^{-1}}{x^{-1}-y^{-1}}$

22. $\dfrac{x^{-1}+y^{-1}}{x^{-2}-y^{-2}}$

23. $\dfrac{2-\dfrac{4}{x}}{\dfrac{x^2-4}{x^2+x}}$

24. $\dfrac{\dfrac{1}{x}}{1-\dfrac{1}{x-2}}$

25. $\dfrac{x+\dfrac{3}{x-4}}{1-\dfrac{1}{x}}$

26. $\dfrac{1-\dfrac{4}{x+3}}{1-\dfrac{2}{x+1}}$

27. $\dfrac{1+\dfrac{4}{2x-3}}{1+\dfrac{x}{x+1}}$

28. $\dfrac{\dfrac{1}{x+h}-\dfrac{1}{x}}{h}$

29. $\dfrac{\dfrac{1}{(x+h)^2}-\dfrac{1}{x^2}}{h}$

30. $\dfrac{\left(2+\dfrac{1}{x+h}\right)-\left(2+\dfrac{1}{x}\right)}{h}$

31. $\dfrac{x^2-4y^2}{1-\dfrac{2x+y}{x-y}}$

32. $\dfrac{\dfrac{x+1}{x-1}-\dfrac{x-1}{x+1}}{\dfrac{x+1}{x-1}+\dfrac{x-1}{x+1}}$

33. $\dfrac{\dfrac{1}{x^2-1}-\dfrac{1}{x+1}}{\dfrac{1}{x-1}+\dfrac{1}{x^2-1}}$

34. $\dfrac{\dfrac{x}{x-4}-\dfrac{1}{x-1}}{\dfrac{x}{x-1}+\dfrac{2}{x-3}}$

35. $\dfrac{x-y}{x^{-2}-y^{-2}}$

36. $\dfrac{y^{-2}-x^{-2}}{x+y}$

Writing and Thinking About Mathematics

37. In electronics, when resistors R_1 and R_2 are in series, one after the other, then the total resistance is the sum

$$R_{\text{total}} = R_1 + R_2.$$

When resistors are studied in parallel, the total resistance, R_{total}, of two resistors with resistance R_1 and R_2 can be found by using the formula $\dfrac{1}{R_{\text{total}}} = \dfrac{1}{R_1} + \dfrac{1}{R_2}$ which means that

$$R_{\text{total}} = \dfrac{1}{\dfrac{1}{R_1} + \dfrac{1}{R_2}}.$$

Simplify the complex fraction in the right hand side of the last formula in the form of a single fraction.

38. By using the concepts discussed in Exercise 37, write a single fraction for R_{total} if three resistors, $R_1, R_2,$ and R_3 are in parallel.

Hawkes Learning Systems: Intermediate Algebra

Complex Fractions

Equations and Inequalities with Rational Expressions

Objectives

After completing this section, you will be able to:

1. *Solve equations containing rational expressions.*

2. *Solve inequalities containing rational expressions.*

3. *Graph the solutions for inequalities containing rational expressions.*

Solving Equations with Rational Expressions

To solve an equation that has fractions, such as $\dfrac{x}{5} - \dfrac{x}{2} = -6$, we can multiply both sides of the equation by the LCM of the denominators so that the new coefficients will be integers. The new equation will have integer coefficients and constants and be easier to work with. Thus,

$$\frac{x}{5} - \frac{x}{2} = -6$$

$$10 \cdot \left(\frac{x}{5} - \frac{x}{2} \right) = 10 \cdot (-6) \qquad \text{10 is the LCM of the denominators.}$$

$$2x - 5x = -60 \qquad \text{Use the distributive property.}$$

$$-3x = -60 \qquad \text{Simplify.}$$

$$x = 20 \qquad \text{Divide both sides by } -3.$$

A **rational equation** is an equation that contains at least one rational expression. To solve rational equations we use the following procedure.

To Solve a Rational Equation

1. *Find the LCM of all the denominators of all the rational expressions in the equation.*

2. *Multiply both sides of the equation by this LCM. Use the distributive property if necessary.*

3. *Simplify both sides of the resulting equation.*

4. *Solve this equation.*

5. *Check each solution in the **original equation**. (Remember that no denominator can be 0.)*

Step 5 is critical when solving rational equations. **If both sides of an equation are multiplied by the same nonzero number or expression, the solution set of the new equation will contain the solutions to the original equation.** However, if the multiplication is by a variable expression, then the new equation may actually have more solutions than the original equation. These extra solutions are called **extraneous solutions** or **extraneous roots**. Therefore, it is absolutely necessary to check all solutions in the original equation to identify the actual solutions and any extraneous solutions.

Example 1: Solving Equations with Rational Expressions

Find the solution set for each of the following equations. Multiply both sides of each equation by the LCM of the denominators.

a. $\dfrac{x-5}{2x} = \dfrac{6}{3x}$ $\hspace{2cm}$ LCM $= 6x$.

$\hspace{2cm}$ **Solution:** $\hspace{0.5cm} 6x \cdot \left(\dfrac{x-5}{2x} \right) = 6x \cdot \left(\dfrac{6}{3x} \right) \hspace{1cm} (x \neq 0)$

$$3(x-5) = 2(6)$$
$$3x - 15 = 12$$
$$3x = 27$$
$$x = 9$$

$\hspace{1.5cm}$ **Check:** $\hspace{0.3cm} \dfrac{9-5}{2 \cdot 9} \overset{?}{=} \dfrac{6}{3 \cdot 9}$

$$\dfrac{4}{18} \overset{?}{=} \dfrac{6}{27}$$

$$\dfrac{2}{9} = \dfrac{2}{9}$$

$\hspace{1.5cm}$ The solution is $x = 9$.

b. $\dfrac{3}{x-6} = \dfrac{5}{x}$ $\hspace{2cm}$ LCM $= x(x-6)$

$\hspace{2cm}$ **Solution:** $\hspace{0.5cm} x(x-6) \cdot \dfrac{3}{x-6} = x(x-6) \cdot \dfrac{5}{x} \hspace{0.5cm} (x \neq 0, 6)$

$$3x = 5x - 30$$
$$30 = 2x$$
$$15 = x$$

continued on next page ...

Check: $\dfrac{3}{15-6} \overset{?}{=} \dfrac{5}{15}$

$$\dfrac{1}{3} = \dfrac{1}{3}$$

The solution is $x = 15$.

c. $\dfrac{2}{x^2-9} = \dfrac{1}{x^2} + \dfrac{1}{x^2-3x}$

Solution: First find the LCM of the denominators and then multiply both sides of the equation by the LCM.

$$x^2-9 = (x+3)(x-3)$$
$$x^2 = x^2$$
$$x^2-3x = x(x-3)$$

$\left. \right\}$ $\text{LCM}=x^2(x+3)(x-3)$

$x^2\,\cancel{(x+3)}\,\cancel{(x-3)}\cdot\dfrac{2}{\cancel{(x+3)}\,\cancel{(x-3)}} = \cancel{x^2}(x+3)(x-3)\cdot\dfrac{1}{\cancel{x^2}} + \overset{x}{\cancel{x^2}}(x+3)\,\cancel{(x-3)}\cdot\dfrac{1}{\cancel{x}\,\cancel{(x-3)}}$

$$2x^2 = (x\ +\ 3)(x-3)\ +\ x(x+3) \qquad (x \neq 0, -3, 3)$$
$$2x^2 = x^2-9\ +\ x^2+\ 3x$$
$$2x^2 = 2x^2+3x-9$$
$$9 = 3x$$
$$\cancel{3 = x}$$

3 is not allowed since no denominator can be 0.

There is no solution. The solution set is the empty set, $\varnothing$. The original equation is a contradiction. (Multiplying by the factor $x-3$ was, in effect, multiplying by 0.)

d. $\dfrac{1}{x-7} = \dfrac{2}{x^2-12x+35} + \dfrac{x}{x^2-5x}$

Solution: First find the LCM of the denominators and then multiply both sides of the equation by the LCM.

$$x-7 = x-7$$
$$x^2-12x+35 = (x-5)(x-7)$$
$$x^2-5x = x(x-5)$$

$\left. \right\}$ $\text{LCM} = x(x-5)(x-7)$

$$x(x-5)\cancel{(x-7)} \cdot \frac{1}{\cancel{x-7}} = x\cancel{(x-5)}\cancel{(x-7)} \cdot \frac{2}{\cancel{(x-5)}\cancel{(x-7)}} + \cancel{x}\cancel{(x-5)}(x-7) \cdot \frac{x}{\cancel{x}\cancel{(x-5)}}$$

$$x(x-5) = 2x + x(x-7) \qquad\qquad (x \neq 0, 5, 7)$$

$$x^2 - 5x = 2x + x^2 - 7x$$

$$x^2 - 5x = x^2 - 5x$$

$$0 = 0$$

The equation 0 = 0 is true for all real numbers. Therefore, x can be any real number with the exception of 0, 5, or 7. We indicated $x \neq 0, 5, 7$. These values are not included since each of them would give a 0 denominator. The implication is that all other values are allowed. The original equation is an **identity**.

e. The formula $C = \dfrac{5}{9}(F - 32)$ is solved for C and represents the relationship between

temperature measured in degrees Celsius and degrees Fahrenheit. Solve this formula for F.

Solution:

$$C = \frac{5}{9}(F - 32) \qquad \text{Write the formula.}$$

$$\frac{9}{5} \cdot C = \frac{9}{5} \cdot \frac{5}{9}(F - 32) \qquad \text{Multiply both sides of the equation by } \frac{9}{5}.$$

$$\frac{9}{5}C = F - 32 \qquad \text{Simplify.}$$

$$\frac{9}{5}C + 32 = F \qquad \text{Add 32 to both sides.}$$

Thus, the formula solved for F is: $F = \dfrac{9}{5}C + 32$.

● ●

Proportions and Similar Triangles

Proportions are equations of the form $\dfrac{a}{b} = \dfrac{c}{d}$ that state that two ratios (or rational expressions) are equal. Proportions can be solved by multiplying both sides of the equation by the LCM of the denominators:

$$\frac{a}{b} = \frac{c}{d}$$

$$bd \cdot \frac{a}{b} = \frac{c}{d} \cdot bd$$

$$ad = bc$$

Proportions are used when working with similar geometric figures. Similar figures are figures that meet the following two conditions:

1. The corresponding angles are equal.
2. The corresponding sides are proportional.

In similar triangles, corresponding sides are those sides opposite the equal angles. (See Figure 5.1.)

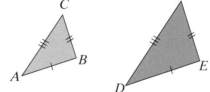

Figure 5.1

We write $\triangle ABC \sim \triangle DEF$. ($\sim$ is read "**is similar to**".) The corresponding sides are proportional and

$$\frac{AB}{DE} = \frac{BC}{EF} \quad \text{and} \quad \frac{AB}{DE} = \frac{AC}{DF} \quad \text{and} \quad \frac{BC}{EF} = \frac{AC}{DF}$$

In a pair of similar triangles, we can often find the length of an unknown side by setting up a proportion and solving. Example 2 illustrates such a situation.

Example 2: Similar Triangles ●

In the figure shown, $\triangle ABC \sim \triangle PQR$. Find the lengths of the sides AB and QR.

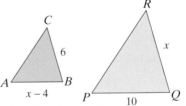

Solution: Set up a proportion involving the corresponding sides and solve for x.

$$\frac{x-4}{10} = \frac{6}{x}$$

$$10x \cdot \frac{x-4}{10} = \frac{6}{x} \cdot 10x$$

$$x(x-4) = 6 \cdot 10$$

$$x^2 - 4x = 60$$

$$x^2 - 4x - 60 = 0$$

$$(x-10)(x+6) = 0$$

$$x - 10 = 0 \qquad \text{or} \qquad x + 6 = 0$$

$$x = 10 \qquad\qquad\qquad x = -6$$

Because the length of a triangle cannot be negative, the only acceptable solution is $x = 10$. Substituting 10 for x gives $AB = 10 - 4 = 6$ and $QR = 10$.

Solving Inequalities with Rational Expressions

In Chapter 1, we solved linear (or first-degree) inequalities and introduced intervals and interval notation. For example,

if $\qquad\qquad\qquad\qquad x - 4 \le 0$

then $\qquad\qquad\qquad\qquad x \le 4 \qquad$ or $\qquad x$ is in $(-\infty, 4]$

Graphically,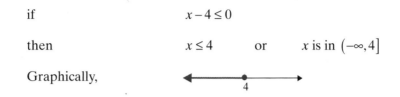

Notice that the solution consists of the point where $x - 4 = 0$ ($x = 4$) and all the points to the left of this point. For linear inequalities, the solution always contains the points to one side or the other of the point where the inequality has value 0. We use this idea in the following discussion.

A rational inequality may involve the product or quotient of several first-degree expressions. For example, the inequality

$$\frac{x+3}{x-2} > 0$$

involves the two first-degree expressions $x + 3$ and $x - 2$.

The following procedure for solving such an inequality is based on the fact that an expression of the form $x - a$ changes sign when x has values on either side of a. That is, if $x < a$, then $x - a$ is negative; if $x > a$, then $x - a$ is positive.

The steps are as follows:

a. Find the points where each linear factor has value 0.

$$x + 3 = 0 \qquad\qquad x - 2 = 0$$
$$x = -3 \qquad\qquad\quad x = 2$$

b. Mark each of these points on a number line. (Consider these points as endpoints of intervals.)

Three intervals, $(-\infty, -3), (-3, 2), \text{and} (2, \infty)$ are formed.

c. Choose any number from each interval as a **test value** to determine the sign of the expression for all values in that interval. Remember, we are not interested in the value of the expression, only whether it is positive (>0) or negative (<0).

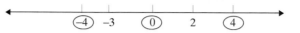

We have chosen the convenient test values $-4, 0$, and 4. Substituting these values into the original inequality gives the following results:

Results	Explanation
$\dfrac{x+3}{x-2} = \dfrac{-4+3}{-4-2} = \dfrac{1}{6} > 0$	This means that $\dfrac{x+3}{x-2}$ is positive $(+)$ for all x in $(-\infty, -3)$.
$\dfrac{x+3}{x-2} = \dfrac{0+3}{0-2} = -\dfrac{3}{2} < 0$	This means that $\dfrac{x+3}{x-2}$ is negative $(-)$ for all x in $(-3, 2)$.
$\dfrac{x+3}{x-2} = \dfrac{4+3}{4-2} = \dfrac{7}{2} > 0$	This means that $\dfrac{x+3}{x-2}$ is positive $(+)$ for all x in $(2, \infty)$.
$\begin{array}{ccccc} & & 0 & & 0 \\ +\,+\,+\,+\,+ & | & & -\,-\,-\,-\,- & | & +\,+\,+\,+ \\ & -3 & & & 2 \end{array}$	

d. The solution to the inequality consists of all the intervals that indicate the desired sign: $+$ (for >0) or $-$ (for <0). The solution for $\dfrac{x+3}{x-2} > 0$ is

all x in $(-\infty, -3)$ or $(2, \infty)$.

In algebraic notation: $x < -3$ or $x > 2$; In set notation $x \in (-\infty, -3) \cup (2, \infty)$. Graphically,

Example 3: Solving and Graphing Inequalities

Solve and graph the solution for each of the following inequalities.

a. $\dfrac{x+3}{x-2} < 0$

Solution: From the previous discussion, we know that $\dfrac{x+3}{x-2}$ is negative whenever x is in $(-3, 2)$. Similarly, $\dfrac{x+3}{x-2} < 0$ if $-3 < x < 2$.

Graphically,

b. $\dfrac{x+5}{x-4} \geq -1$

Solution:

$$\frac{x+5}{x-4} + 1 \geq 0 \qquad \text{One side must be 0.}$$

$$\frac{x+5}{x-4} + \frac{x-4}{x-4} \geq 0$$

$$\frac{2x+1}{x-4} \geq 0 \qquad \text{Simplify to get one fraction.}$$

Set each linear expression equal to 0 to find the interval endpoints.

$$2x + 1 = 0 \qquad x - 4 = 0$$

$$x = -\frac{1}{2} \qquad x = 4$$

Test a value from each of the intervals:

$$\left(-\infty, \ \frac{1}{2}\right), \left(-\frac{1}{2}, \ 4\right), \text{ and } (4, \ \infty)$$

continued on next page ...

Using the values circled on the previous page, we obtain the following results:

Results	Explanation
$\dfrac{2(-2)+1}{-2-4}=\dfrac{-3}{-6}>0$	This means that $\dfrac{2x+1}{x-4}>0$ for all x in $\left(-\infty,-\dfrac{1}{2}\right)$.
$\dfrac{2(1)+1}{1-4}=\dfrac{3}{-3}<0$	This means that $\dfrac{2x+1}{x-4}<0$ for all x in $\left(-\dfrac{1}{2},4\right)$.
$\dfrac{2(5)+1}{5-4}=\dfrac{11}{1}>0$	This means that $\dfrac{2x+1}{x-4}>0$ for all x in $(4,\infty)$.

$\dfrac{2x+1}{x-4}=0$ if the numerator $2x+1=0$ or $x=-\dfrac{1}{2}$. Since $x-4\neq 0$, 4 is not included in the solution. Thus, the solution is all x in the interval $\left(-\infty,-\dfrac{1}{2}\right]$ or $(4,\infty)$. In algebraic notation, $x\leq-\dfrac{1}{2}$ or $x>4$. Graphically,

• •

We can summarize the technique for solving rational inequalities as follows:

Procedure for Solving Inequalities with Rational Expressions

1. *Simplify the inequality so that one side is 0 and on the other side both the numerator and denominator are in factored form.*
2. *Find the points where each linear factor is 0.*
3. *Mark each of these points on a number line.*
4. *Choose a number from each indicated interval as a test value.*
5. *The intervals where the test values satisfy the conditions of the inequality are the solution intervals.*
6. *Mark a solid circle for endpoints that are included and an open circle for endpoints that are not included.*

NOTES

Notice that in the first step, we do **not** multiply by the denominator $x-4$. The reason is that the variable expression is positive for some values of x and negative for other values of x. Therefore, if we did multiply by $x-4$, we would not be able to determine whether the inequality should stay as $\geq$ or be reversed to $\leq$.

5.4 Exercises

Solve each equation in Exercises 1 – 34.

1. $\dfrac{4x}{7} = \dfrac{x+5}{3}$

2. $\dfrac{3x+1}{-4} = \dfrac{2x+1}{-3}$

3. $\dfrac{5x+2}{11x} = \dfrac{x-6}{4x}$

4. $\dfrac{x+3}{5x} = \dfrac{x-1}{6x}$

5. $\dfrac{5x}{4} - \dfrac{1}{2} = -\dfrac{3}{16}$

6. $\dfrac{x}{6} - \dfrac{1}{42} = \dfrac{1}{7}$

7. $\dfrac{4x}{3} - \dfrac{3}{4} = \dfrac{5x}{6}$

8. $\dfrac{x-2}{3} - \dfrac{x-3}{5} = \dfrac{13}{15}$

9. $\dfrac{2+x}{4} - \dfrac{5x-2}{12} = \dfrac{8-2x}{5}$

10. $\dfrac{8x+10}{5} = 2x+3 - \dfrac{6x+1}{4}$

11. $\dfrac{2}{3x} = \dfrac{1}{4} - \dfrac{1}{6x}$

12. $\dfrac{x-4}{x} + \dfrac{3}{x} = 0$

13. $\dfrac{3}{8x} - \dfrac{7}{10} = \dfrac{1}{5x}$

14. $\dfrac{1}{x} - \dfrac{8}{21} = \dfrac{3}{7x}$

15. $\dfrac{3}{4x} - \dfrac{1}{2} = \dfrac{7}{8x} + \dfrac{1}{6}$

16. $\dfrac{7}{x-3} = \dfrac{6}{x-4}$

17. $\dfrac{2}{3x+2} = \dfrac{4}{5x+1}$

18. $\dfrac{-3}{2x+1} = \dfrac{4}{3x+1}$

19. $\dfrac{9}{5x-3} = \dfrac{5}{3x+7}$

20. $\dfrac{5x+2}{x-6} = \dfrac{11}{4}$

21. $\dfrac{x+9}{3x+2} = \dfrac{5}{8}$

22. $\dfrac{8}{2x+3} = \dfrac{9}{4x-5}$

23. $\dfrac{x}{x-4} - \dfrac{4}{2x-1} = 1$

24. $\dfrac{x}{x+3} + \dfrac{1}{x+2} = 1$

25. $\dfrac{x+2}{x+1} + \dfrac{x+2}{x+4} = 2$

26. $\dfrac{x-2}{x-3} + \dfrac{x-3}{x-2} = \dfrac{2x^2}{x^2-5x+6}$

27. $\dfrac{2}{4x-1} + \dfrac{1}{x+1} = \dfrac{3}{x+1}$

28. $\dfrac{3x-2}{15} - \dfrac{16-3x}{x+6} = \dfrac{x+3}{5}$

29. $\dfrac{x}{x-4} - \dfrac{12x}{x^2+x-20} = \dfrac{x-1}{x+5}$

30. $\dfrac{x-2}{x+4} - \dfrac{3}{2x+1} = \dfrac{x-7}{x+4}$

31. $\dfrac{3x+5}{3x+2} - \dfrac{4-2x}{3x^2+8x+4} = \dfrac{x+4}{x+2}$

32. $\dfrac{3}{3x-1} + \dfrac{1}{x+1} = \dfrac{4}{2x-1}$

33. $\dfrac{5}{2x+1} - \dfrac{1}{2x-1} = \dfrac{2}{x-2}$

34. $\dfrac{2}{x+1} + \dfrac{4}{2x-3} = \dfrac{4}{x-5}$

Solve and graph the solution set of each of the inequalities in Exercises 35 – 50.

35. $\dfrac{x+4}{2x} \geq 0$

36. $\dfrac{x}{x-4} \geq 0$

37. $\dfrac{x+6}{x^2} < 0$

38. $\dfrac{3-x}{x+1} < 0$

39. $\dfrac{x+3}{x+9} > 0$

40. $\dfrac{2x+3}{x-4} < 0$

41. $\dfrac{3x-6}{2x-5} < 0$

42. $\dfrac{4-3x}{2x+4} \le 0$

43. $\dfrac{x+5}{x-7} \ge 1$

44. $\dfrac{x+4}{2x-1} > 2$

45. $\dfrac{2x+5}{x-4} \le -3$

46. $\dfrac{3x+2}{4x-1} < 3$

47. $\dfrac{5-2x}{3x+4} < -1$

48. $\dfrac{8-x}{x+5} < -4$

49. $\dfrac{x(x+4)}{x-3} \le 0$

50. $\dfrac{(x+3)(x-2)}{x+1} > 0$

Solve each of the formulas in Exercises 51 – 60 for the indicated variables.

51. $S = \dfrac{a}{1-r}$; solve for r (formula used in mathematics)

52. $z = \dfrac{x - \bar{x}}{s}$; solve for x (formula used in statistics)

53. $z = \dfrac{x - \bar{x}}{s}$; solve for s (formula used in statistics)

54. $a_n = a_1 + (n-1)d$; solve for d (formula used in mathematics)

55. $\dfrac{1}{R_{\text{total}}} = \dfrac{1}{R_1} + \dfrac{1}{R_2}$; solve for R_{total} (formula used in electronics)

56. $m = \dfrac{y - y_1}{x - x_1}$; solve for y (formula used for slope of a line)

57. $A = P + Pr$; solve for P (formula used for compound interest)

58. $v_{\text{ave}} = \dfrac{d_2 - d_1}{t_2 - t_1}$; solve for d_2 (formula for average velocity)

59. $y = \dfrac{ax + b}{cx + d}$; solve for x (formula used in mathematics)

60. $\dfrac{1}{x} = \dfrac{1}{t_1} + \dfrac{1}{t_2}$; solve for x (formula used in mathematics)

Writing and Thinking About Mathematics

In simplifying rational expressions, the result is a rational expression. However, in solving equations with rational expressions, the goal is to find a value (or values) for the variable that will make the equation a true statement. Many students confuse these two ideas. To avoid confusing the techniques for adding and subtracting rational expressions with the techniques for solving equations, simplify the expression in part (a) and solve the equation in part (b). Explain, in your own words, the differences in your procedures.

61. a. $\dfrac{10}{x} + \dfrac{31}{x-1} + \dfrac{4x}{x-1}$ **b.** $\dfrac{10}{x} + \dfrac{31}{x-1} = \dfrac{4x}{x-1}$

62. a. $\dfrac{-4}{x^2-16} + \dfrac{x}{2x+8} - \dfrac{1}{4}$ **b.** $\dfrac{-4}{x^2-16} + \dfrac{x}{2x+8} = \dfrac{1}{4}$

Hawkes Learning Systems: Intermediate Algebra

Solving Equations Involving Rational Expressions.

Applications

Objectives

After completing this section, you will be able to:

Solve the following types of applied problems by using equations containing rational expressions:

    a. fractions,

    b. jobs, and

    c. distance-rate-time.

The following Strategy for Solving Word Problems is valid for all word problems that involve algebraic equations (or inequalities).

Strategy for Solving Word Problems

1. *Read the problem carefully. Read it several times if necessary.*
2. *Decide what is asked for and assign a variable to the unknown quantity.*
3. *Draw a diagram or set up a chart whenever possible.*
4. *Form an equation (or inequality) that relates the information provided.*
5. *Solve the equation (or inequality).*
6. *Check your solution with the wording of the problem to be sure it makes sense.*

We now introduce word problems involving rational expressions with problems relating the numerator and denominator of a fraction. Let one variable represent either the numerator or denominator, then write the equation to be solved using the information given.

Example 1: Fractions

a.   The denominator of a fraction is 8 more than the numerator. If both the numerator and denominator are increased by 3, the resulting fraction is equal to $\frac{1}{2}$. Find the original fraction.

    Solution: Reread the problem to be sure that you understand it. Assign variables to the unknown quantities.

Let $n = $ original numerator

$n + 8 = $ original denominator

$\dfrac{n}{n+8} = $ original fraction

$\dfrac{n+3}{(n+8)+3} = \dfrac{1}{2}$ The numerator and the denominator are each increased by 3, making a new

$\dfrac{n+3}{n+11} = \dfrac{1}{2}$ fraction that is equal to $\dfrac{1}{2}$.

$2\left(n+11\right)\cdot\left(\dfrac{n+3}{n+11}\right) = 2\left(n+11\right)\cdot\dfrac{1}{2}$

$2n + 6 = n + 11$

$n = 5$ ← Original numerator

$n + 8 = 13$ ← Original denominator

Check: $\dfrac{5+3}{13+3} \overset{?}{=} \dfrac{8}{16} \overset{?}{=} \dfrac{1}{2}$

The original fraction is $\dfrac{5}{13}$.

● ●

Problems involving jobs (sometimes called **work problems**) usually translate into equations involving rational expressions. The basic idea is to **represent what part of a job is done in one unit of time**. For example, if a manuscript was typed in 35 hours, what part was typed in 1 hour? Assuming an even typing speed, $\dfrac{1}{35}$ of the manuscript was typed in 1 hour. Similarly, if a boy can paint a fence in 2 days, then he can do $\dfrac{1}{2}$ the job in 1 day.

Example 2: Work Problems ●

a.   A carpenter can build a certain type of patio cover in 6 hours. His partner takes 8 hours to build the same cover. How long would it take them working together to build this type of patio cover?

Solution: Let $x = $ number of hours to build the cover working together

continued on next page ...

369

Person(s)	Time of Work (in Hours)	Part of Job Done in 1 Hour
Carpenter	6	$\dfrac{1}{6}$
Partner	8	$\dfrac{1}{8}$
Together	x	$\dfrac{1}{x}$

$$\underbrace{\text{Part done in 1 hr by carpenter}} \quad + \quad \underbrace{\text{Part done in 1 hr by partner}} \quad = \quad \underbrace{\text{Part done in 1 hr together}}$$

$$\frac{1}{6} \quad + \quad \frac{1}{8} \quad = \quad \frac{1}{x}$$

$$\frac{1}{6}(24x) + \frac{1}{8}(24x) = \frac{1}{x}(24x)$$

Multiply each term on both sides by $24x$, the LCM of the denominators.

$$4x + 3x = 24$$
$$7x = 24$$
$$x = \frac{24}{7}$$

Together, they can build the patio cover in $\dfrac{24}{7}$ hours, or $3\dfrac{3}{7}$ hours.

(Note that this answer is reasonable because the time is less than either person would take working alone.)

b. A man can wax his car three times as fast as his daughter can. Together they can do the job in 4 hours. How long does it take each of them working alone?

Solution: Let t = number of hours for man alone
$3t$ = number of hours for daughter alone

Person(s)	Time of Work (in Hours)	Part of Job Done in 1 Hour
Man	t	$\dfrac{1}{t}$
Daughter	$3t$	$\dfrac{1}{3t}$
Together	4	$\dfrac{1}{4}$

$$\underbrace{\begin{array}{c}\text{part done by man}\\\text{alone in 1 hour}\end{array}} + \underbrace{\begin{array}{c}\text{part done by daughter}\\\text{alone in 1 hour}\end{array}} = \underbrace{\begin{array}{c}\text{part done working}\\\text{together in 1 hour}\end{array}}$$

$$\frac{1}{t} \quad + \quad \frac{1}{3t} \quad = \quad \frac{1}{4}$$

$$\frac{1}{t}(12t) + \frac{1}{3t}(12t) = \frac{1}{4}(12t)$$

Multiply each term on both sides by $12t$, the LCM of the denominators.

$$12 + 4 = 3t$$

$$16 = 3t$$

$$\frac{16}{3} = t$$

Check: Man's part in 1 hr $\overset{?}{=} \dfrac{1}{t} = \dfrac{1}{\frac{16}{3}} = \dfrac{3}{16}$

Daughter's part in 1 hr $\overset{?}{=} \dfrac{1}{3t} = \dfrac{1}{3 \cdot \frac{16}{3}} = \dfrac{1}{16}$

Man's part in 4 hr $\overset{?}{=} \dfrac{3}{16} \cdot 4 = \dfrac{3}{4}$

Daughter's part in 4 hr $\overset{?}{=} \dfrac{1}{16} \cdot 4 = \dfrac{1}{4}$

$\dfrac{3}{4} + \dfrac{1}{4} = 1$ car waxed in 4 hours.

Working alone, the man takes $\dfrac{16}{3}$ or $5\dfrac{1}{3}$ hours, and his daughter takes 16 hours.

c. An inlet pipe on a swimming pool can be used to fill the pool in 36 hours. The drain pipe can be used to empty the pool in 40 hours. If the pool is $\dfrac{2}{3}$ filled and then the drain pipe is accidentally opened, how long from that time will it take to fill the pool?

Solution: Let t = hours to fill pool with both pipes open

Pipe(s)	Time of work (in Hours)	Part of Job Done in 1 Hour
Inlet	36	$\dfrac{1}{36}$
Outlet	40	$\dfrac{1}{40}$
Together	t	$\dfrac{1}{t}$

continued on next page ...

part filled   part emptied   part filled in 1
by inlet pipe –   by drain pipe   =   hour when both
in 1 hour   in 1 hour   pipes are open

$$\frac{1}{36} \quad - \quad \frac{1}{40} \quad = \quad \frac{1}{t}$$

$$\frac{1}{36}(360t) - \frac{1}{40}(360t) = \frac{1}{t}(360t)$$

$$10t - 9t = 360$$

$$t = 360$$

However, 360 hours is the time it would take if the pool was empty at the beginning. Only $\frac{1}{3}$ this time will be used since the pool is $\frac{2}{3}$ filled.

$$\frac{1}{3} \cdot 360\,\text{hr} = 120\,\text{hr}$$

Check: Part filled in 120 hr $\overset{?}{=} \dfrac{1}{36}(120) = \dfrac{10}{3} = 3\dfrac{1}{3}$

Part drained in 120 hr $\overset{?}{=} \dfrac{1}{40}(120) = 3$

$3\dfrac{1}{3}$ Part filled

-3 Part drained

$\dfrac{1}{3}$ Part filled in 120 hr

It will take 120 hours to fill the remaining third of the pool.

● ●

Problems involving distance, rate, and time were discussed in Section 1.5. You may recall that the basic formula is $r \cdot t = d$. However, this relationship can also be stated in the forms $t = \dfrac{d}{r}$ and $r = \dfrac{d}{t}$.

If distance and rate are known or can be represented, then $t = \dfrac{d}{r}$ is the way to represent time. Similarly, if the distance and time are known or can be represented, then $r = \dfrac{d}{t}$ is the way to represent rate.

Example 3: Rate Problems

a. A man can row his boat 5 miles per hour on a lake. On a river, it takes him the same time to row 5 miles downstream as it does to row 3 miles upstream. What is the speed of the river current in miles per hour?

Solution:

Rate and distance are represented in the following table.

	Rate	Distance
Downstream	$5 + c$	5
Upstream	$5 - c$	3

c represents speed of the current.

Now, represent the time going downstream and coming back upstream in terms of the rate and distance. If the rate is in miles per hour, then the distance is in miles and the time is in hours.

	Rate	$t = \dfrac{d}{r}$	Distance
Downstream	$5 + c$	$\dfrac{5}{5+c}$	5
Upstream	$5 - c$	$\dfrac{3}{5-c}$	3

$$\frac{5}{5+c} = \frac{3}{5-c} \qquad \text{The times are equal.}$$

$$(5+c)(5-c)\cdot\frac{5}{5+c} = (5+c)(5-c)\cdot\frac{3}{5-c}$$

$$25 - 5c = 15 + 3c$$

$$10 = 8c$$

$$c = \frac{5}{4} \text{ miles per hour}$$

Check:

$$\text{Time downstream} = \frac{5}{5+\dfrac{5}{4}} = \frac{5}{\dfrac{20}{4}+\dfrac{5}{4}} = \frac{5}{\dfrac{25}{4}} = 5\cdot\frac{4}{25} = \frac{4}{5} \text{ hr.}$$

$$\text{Time upstream} = \frac{3}{5-\dfrac{5}{4}} = \frac{3}{\dfrac{20}{4}-\dfrac{5}{4}} = \frac{3}{\dfrac{15}{4}} = 3\cdot\frac{4}{15} = \frac{4}{5} \text{ hr.}$$

The times are equal. The rate of the river current is $\dfrac{5}{4}$ mph $\left(\text{or } 1\dfrac{1}{4} \text{ mph}\right)$.

continued on next page ...

b. If a passenger train travels three times as fast as a freight train, and the freight train takes 4 hours longer to travel 210 miles, what is the speed of each train?

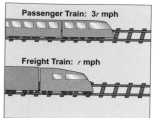

Passenger Train: 3*r* mph

Freight Train: *r* mph

Solution: Let r = rate of freight train in miles per hour
$3r$ = rate of passenger train in miles per hour

	Rate	$t = \dfrac{d}{r}$	Distance
Freight	r	$\dfrac{210}{r}$	210
Passenger	$3r$	$\dfrac{210}{3r}$	210

(**Note:** If the rate is faster, then the time is shorter. Thus, the fraction $\dfrac{210}{3r}$ is smaller than the fraction $\dfrac{210}{r}$.)

$$\frac{210}{r} - \frac{210}{3r} = 4 \qquad \text{The difference between their times is 4 hours.}$$

$$\frac{210}{r} - \frac{70}{r} = 4$$

$$\frac{210}{r} \cdot r - \frac{70}{r} \cdot r = 4 \cdot r$$

$$210 - 70 = 4r$$

$$140 = 4r$$

$$35 = r$$

$$105 = 3r$$

Check: Time for freight train = $\dfrac{210}{35} = 6\,\text{hr}$

Time for passenger train = $\dfrac{210}{105} = 2\,\text{hr}$

$6 - 2 = 4$ hours difference in time.

The freight travels 35 mph, and passengers travels 105 mph.

5.5 Exercises

1. If 4 is subtracted from a certain number and the difference is divided by 2, the result is 1 more than $\frac{1}{5}$ of the original number. Find the original number.

2. What number must be added to both numerator and denominator of $\frac{16}{21}$ to make the resulting fraction equal to $\frac{5}{6}$?

3. Find the number that can be subtracted from both numerator and denominator of the fraction $\frac{69}{102}$ so that the result is $\frac{5}{8}$.

4. The denominator of a fraction exceeds the numerator by 7. If the numerator is increased by 3 and the denominator is increased by 5, the resulting fraction is equal to $\frac{1}{2}$. Find the original fraction.

5. The numerator of a fraction exceeds the denominator by 5. If the numerator is decreased by 4 and the denominator is increased by 3, the resulting fraction is equal to $\frac{4}{5}$. Find the original fraction.

6. One number is $\frac{3}{4}$ of another number. Their sum is 63. Find the numbers.

7. The sum of two numbers is 24. If $\frac{2}{5}$ the larger number is equal to $\frac{2}{3}$ the smaller number, find the numbers.

8. One number exceeds another by 5. The sum of their reciprocals is equal to 19 divided by the product of the two numbers. Find the numbers.

9. One number is 3 less than another. The sum of their reciprocals is equal to 7 divided by the product of the two numbers. Find the numbers.

10. A manufacturer sold a group of shirts for $1026. One-fifth of the shirts were priced at $18 each, and the remainder at $24 each. How many shirts were sold?

11. Luis spent $\frac{1}{5}$ of his monthly salary for rent and $\frac{1}{6}$ of his monthly salary for his car payment. If $950 was left, what was his monthly salary?

12. It takes Rosa, traveling at 50 mph, 45 minutes longer to go a certain distance than it takes Maria traveling at 60 mph. Find the distance traveled.

13. It takes a plane flying at 450 mph 25 minutes longer to travel a certain distance than it takes a second plane to fly the same distance at 500 mph. Find the distance.

14. Toni needs 4 hours to complete the yard work. Her husband, Sonny, needs 6 hours to do the work. How long will the job take if they work together?

15. Ben's secretary can address the weekly newsletters in $4\frac{1}{2}$ hours. Charlie's secretary needs only 3 hours. How long will it take if they both work on the job?

16. Working together, Greg and Cindy can clean the snow from the driveway in 20 minutes. It would have taken Cindy, working alone, 36 minutes. How long would it have taken Greg alone?

17. A carpenter and his partner can put up a patio cover in $3\frac{3}{7}$ hours. If the partner needs 8 hours to complete the patio alone, how long would it take the carpenter working alone?

18. Beth can travel 208 miles in the same length of time it takes Anna to travel 192 miles. If Beth's speed is 4 mph greater than Anna's, find both rates.

19. A commercial airliner can travel 750 miles in the same length of time that it takes a private plane to travel 300 miles. The speed of the airliner is 60 mph more than twice the speed of the private plane. Find the speed of each aircraft.

20. Gabriela travels 350 miles at a certain speed. If the average speed had been 9 mph less, she could have traveled only 300 miles in the same length of time. What was the average rate of speed?

21. A jet flies twice as fast as a propeller plane. On a trip 1500 miles, the propeller plane took 3 hours longer than the jet. Find the speed of each plane.

22. A family travels 18 miles downriver and returns. It takes 8 hours to make the round trip. Their rate in still water is twice the rate of the current. How long will the return trip take?

23. An airplane can fly 650 mph in calm air. If it can travel 2800 miles with the wind in the same time it can travel 2400 miles against the wind, find the wind speed.

24. Using a small inlet pipe, it takes 3 hours longer to fill a pool than if a larger pipe is used. If both are used, it takes $3\frac{3}{5}$ hours to fill the pool. Using each pipe alone, how long would it take to fill the pool?

25. A contractor hires two bulldozers to clear the trees from a 20-acre tract of land. One works twice as fast as the other. It takes them 3 days to clear the tract working together. How long would it take each of them alone?

26. John, Ralph, and Denny, working together, can clean the store in 6 hours. Working alone, Ralph takes twice as long to clean the store as does John. Denny needs three times as long as does John. How long would it take each man working alone?

27. Francois went 36 miles downstream and returned. The round trip took $5\frac{1}{4}$ hours. Find the speed of the boat in still water and the speed of the current if the speed of the current is $\frac{1}{7}$ the speed of the boat.

28. Town A is 12 miles upstream from Town B (on the same side of the river). A motorboat that can travel 8 mph in still water leaves A and travels downstream toward B. At the same time, another boat that can travel 10 mph leaves B and travels upstream toward A. Each boat completes the trip at the same time. Find the rate of the current.

Writing and Thinking About Mathematics

29. If n is any integer, then $2n$ is an even integer and $2n + 1$ is an odd integer. Use these ideas to solve the following problems.

    a. Find two consecutive odd integers such that the sum of their reciprocals is $\dfrac{12}{35}$.

    b. Find two consecutive even integers such that the sum of the first and the reciprocal of the second is $\dfrac{9}{4}$.

Hawkes Learning Systems: Intermediate Algebra

Applications Involving Rational Expressions

5.6

Applications (Variation)

After completing this section, you will be able to:

Solve applied problems using the principles of variation:

 a. direct variation,

 b. inverse variation, and

 c. combined variation.

Direct Variation

Suppose that you ride your bicycle at a steady rate of 15 miles per hour (not quite as fast as Lance Armstrong, but you are enjoying yourself). If you ride for 1 hour, the distance you travel would be 15 miles. If you ride for two hours, the distance you travel would be 30 miles. This relationship can be written in the form of the formula $d = 15t$ (or $\dfrac{d}{t} = 15$) where d is the distance traveled and t is the time in hours. We say that distance  and time **vary directly** (or are in **direct variation** or are **directly proportional**). The term proportional implies that the ratio is constant. In this example, 15 is the constant and is called the **constant of variation**. When two variables vary directly, an increase in the value of one variable indicates an increase in the other, and the ratio of the two quantities is constant.

Direct Variation:

*A variable quantity y **varies directly** as (or is **directly proportional to**) a variable x if*

there is a constant k such that

$$\frac{y}{x} = k \text{ or } y = kx$$

*The constant k is called the **constant of variation**.*

Example 1: Direct Variation ●

A spring will stretch a greater distance as more weight is placed on the end of the spring. The distance, s, the spring stretches varies directly as the weight, w, placed at the end of the spring. This is a property of springs studied in physics and is known as Hooke's Law. If a weight of 10 grams stretches a certain spring 6 centimeters, how far will the spring stretch with a weight of 15 g? (**Note:** We assume that the weight is not so great as to break the spring.)

Solution: Because the two variables are directly proportional, the relationship can be indicated with the formula

$$s = k \cdot w$$

where s = distance spring stretches,
w = weight in g,
and k = constant of proportionality.

First substitute the given information to find the value for k. (The value of k will depend on the particular spring. Springs made of different material or which are wound more tightly, will have different values for k.)

$$s = k \cdot w$$

$$6 = k \cdot 10 \qquad \text{Substitute the known values into the formula.}$$

$$\frac{3}{5} = k \qquad \text{Find the value of } k \text{ to substitute into the formula.}$$

So, $\qquad s = \frac{3}{5}w \qquad$ The constant of proportionality is $\frac{3}{5}$ (or 0.6).

If $w = 15$, we have

$$s = \frac{3}{5} \cdot 15 = 9 \text{ cm}$$

The spring will stretch 9 cm if a weight of 15 g is placed at its end.

● ●

Listed here are several formulas involving direct variation.

$d = \frac{3}{5}w \qquad$ Hooke's Law for a spring where $k = \frac{3}{5}$.

$C = 2\pi r \qquad$ The circumference of a circle varies directly as the radius.

$A = \pi r^2 \qquad$ The area of a circle is directly proportional to the **square** of its radius.

$P = 625d \qquad$ Water pressure is proportional to the depth of the water.

Inverse Variation

When two variables vary in such a way that their product is constant, we say that the two variables **vary inversely** (or are **inversely proportional**). For example, if a gas is placed in a container (as in an automobile engine) and pressure is increased on the gas, then the product of the pressure and the volume of gas will remain constant. That is, pressure and volume are related by the formula $V \cdot P = k \left(\text{ or } V = \dfrac{k}{P} \right)$.

Note that if a product of two variables is to remain constant, then an increase in the value of one variable must be accompanied by a decrease in the other. Or, in the case of a fraction with a constant numerator, if the denominator increases in value, then the fraction decreases in value. For the gas in an engine, an increase in pressure indicates a decrease in the volume of gas.

Inverse Variation:

*A variable quantity y **varies inversely** as (or is **inversely proportional to**) a variable x if*

there is a constant k such that

$$x \cdot y = k \text{ or } y = \frac{k}{x}.$$

*The constant k is called the **constant of variation.***

Example 2: Inverse Variation

The gravitational force, F, between an object and the earth is inversely proportional to the square of the distance, d, from the object to the center of the earth. Hence, we have the formula

$$F \cdot d^2 = k \text{ or } F = \frac{k}{d^2}, \qquad \text{where } F = \text{force, } d = \text{distance}$$

$$\text{and } k = \text{constant of proportionality}$$

(As the distance of an object from the earth becomes larger, the gravitational force exerted by the earth on the object becomes smaller.)

If an astronaut weighs 200 pounds on the surface of the earth, what will he weigh 100 miles above the earth? Assume that the radius of the earth is 4000 miles.

Solution: We know $F = 200 = 2 \times 10^2$ pounds
when $d = 4000 = 4 \times 10^3$ miles

$$2 \times 10^2 = \frac{k}{\left(4 \times 10^3\right)^2} \qquad \text{Substitute and solve for } k.$$

$$k = 2 \times 10^2 \times 16 \times 10^6 = 32 \times 10^8 = 3.2 \times 10^9$$

So, $F = \dfrac{3.2 \times 10^9}{d^2}$

Let $d = 4100 = 4.1 \times 10^3$ miles. Then,

$$F = \frac{3.2 \times 10^9}{16.81 \times 10^6} \approx 0.190 \times 10^3 = 190 \text{ pounds.}$$

That is, 100 miles above the earth the astronaut will weigh 190 pounds.

● ●

Combined Variation

If a variable varies either directly or inversely with more than one other variable, the variation is said to be a **combined variation**. If the combined variation is all direct variation (the variables are multiplied), then it is called **joint variation**. For example, the volume of a cylinder varies jointly as its height and the square of its radius.

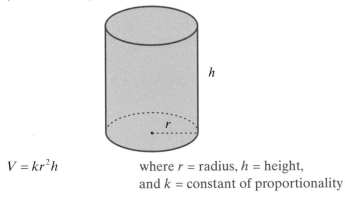

$V = kr^2h$ where r = radius, h = height, and k = constant of proportionality

For example, what is the value of k, the constant of proportionality, if a cylinder has the approximate measurements $V = 198$ cubic feet, $r = 3$ feet, and $h = 7$ feet?

Solution: $V = k \cdot r^2 \cdot h$ V **varies jointly** as r^2 and h.

$198 = k \cdot 3^2 \cdot 7$ Substitute the known values.

$\dfrac{198}{9 \cdot 7} = k$

$k = \dfrac{22}{7} \approx 3.14$ We know from experience that $k = \pi$. Since the measurements are only approximate, the estimate for k is only approximate.

The formula is $V = \pi r^2 h$.

Example 3: Variations •

a. If y is **directly proportional** to x^2, and $y = 9$ and $x = 2$, what is y when $x = 4$?

    Solution: $y = k \cdot x^2$ First substitute known values and solve for k.

                        $9 = k \cdot 2^2$ Use this value for k in the formula.

$$\frac{9}{4} = k$$

    So, $y = \frac{9}{4}x^2.$

If $x = 4$, then

$$y = \frac{9}{4} \cdot 4^2$$
$$= 36.$$

b. The distance an object falls **varies directly** as the square of the time it falls (until it hits the ground and assuming little or no air resistance). If an object fell 64 feet in two seconds, how far would it have fallen by the end of 3 seconds?

    Solution: $d = k \cdot t^2$ where d = distance, t = time (in seconds), and k = constant of proportionality

                        $64 = k \cdot 2^2$ Substitute the known values and solve for k.

                        $16 = k$ Use this value for k in the formula.

    So, $d = 16t^2$

$$d - 16 \cdot 3^2 = 144 \text{ feet}$$

The object would have fallen 144 feet in 3 seconds.

c. The volume of a gas in a container **varies inversely** as the pressure on the gas. If a gas has a volume of 200 cubic inches under pressure of 5 pounds per square inch, what will be its volume if the pressure is increased to 8 pounds per square inch?

Pressure
5 lbs. psi

200 in³

Solution:

$$V = \frac{k}{P}$$
        where V = volume, P = pressure, and k = constant of proportionality

$$200 = \frac{k}{5}$$
        Substitute the known values and solve for k.

$$k = 1000$$

So, $V = \dfrac{1000}{P}$ Substitute 1000 for k

$$V = \dfrac{1000}{8} = 125\,\text{cu in.}$$

The volume will be 125 cubic inches.

d. The illumination (in foot-candles, fc) of a light source **varies directly** as the intensity (in candlepower, cp) of the source and **inversely** as the square of the distance from the source. If a certain light source with intensity of 300 cp provides an illumination of 10 fc at a distance of 20 feet, what is the illumination at a distance of 40 feet? (**Note:** This is an illustration of combined variation.)

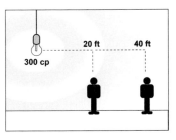

Solution: $I = \dfrac{k \cdot i}{d^2}$ Where I = illumination, i = intensity, and d = distance

$$10 = \dfrac{k \cdot 300}{\left(20 \right)^2}$$

$$k = \dfrac{400 \cdot 10}{300}$$

$$k = \dfrac{40}{3}$$ Value to be used in the formula

So, $I = \dfrac{\dfrac{40}{3} \cdot i}{d^2}$

$$I = \dfrac{\dfrac{40}{3} \cdot 300}{\left(40 \right)^2} = \dfrac{40 \cdot 100}{40 \cdot 40} = \dfrac{5}{2} = 2.5\ \text{fc}$$

The illumination at 40 feet is 2.5 fc.

● ●

5.6 Exercises

For Exercises 1 – 38, write an equation or formula that represents the general relationship indicated. Then use the given information to find the unknown value.

1. If y varies directly as x, and $y = 3$ when $x = 9$, find y if $x = 7$.

2. If y is directly proportional to x^2, and $y = 9$ when $x = 2$, what is y when $x = 4$?

3. If y varies inversely as x, and $y = 5$ when $x = 8$, find y if $x = 20$.

4. If y varies inversely as x^2, and $y = -8$ when $x = 2$, find y if $x = 3$.

5. If y is inversely proportional to x, and $y = 5$ when $x = 4$, what is y when $x = 2$?

6. If y is inversely proportional to x^3, and $y = 40$ when $x = \dfrac{1}{2}$, what is y when $x = \dfrac{1}{3}$?

7. If y is proportional to the square root of x, and $y = 6$ when $x = \dfrac{1}{4}$, what is y when $x = 9$?

8. If y is proportional to the square of x, and $y = 80$ when $x = 4$, what is y when $x = 6$?

9. If y varies directly as x^3, and $y = 81$ when $x = 3$, find y if $x = 2$.

10. z varies jointly as x and y, and $z = 60$ when $x = 2$ and $y = 3$. Find z if $x = 3$ and $y = 4$.

11. z varies jointly as x and y, and $z = -6$ when $x = 5$ and $y = 8$. Find z if $x = 12$ and $y = 3$.

12. z varies jointly as x^2 and y, and $z = 20$ when $x = 2$ and $y = 3$. Find z if $x = 4$ and $y = \dfrac{7}{10}$.

13. z varies directly as x and inversely as y^2. If $z = 5$ when $x = 1$ and $y = 2$, find z if $x = 2$ and $y = 1$.

14. z varies directly as x^3 and inversely as y^2. If $z = 24$ when $x = 2$ and $y = 2$, find z if $x = 3$ and $y = 2$.

15. z varies directly as $\sqrt{x}$ and inversely as y. If $z = 24$ when $x = 4$ and $y = 3$, find z if $x = 9$ and $y = 2$.

16. z is jointly proportional to x^2 and y^3. If $z = 192$ when $x = 4$ and $y = 2$, find z when $x = 2$ and $y = 4$.

17. z varies directly as x^2 and inversely as $\sqrt{y}$. If $z = 108$ when $x = 6$ and $y = 4$, find z if $x = 4$ and $y = 9$.

18. s varies directly as the sum of r and t and inversely as w. If $s = 24$ when $r = 7$ and $t = 8$ and $w = 9$, find s if $r = 9$ and $t = 3$ and $w = 18$

19. L varies jointly as m and n and inversely as p. If $L = 6$ when $m = 7$ and $n = 8$ and $p = 12$, find L if $m = 15$ and $n = 14$ and $p = 10$.

20. If an astronaut weighs 250 pounds on the surface of the earth, what will the astronaut weigh 150 miles above the earth? (Assume that the radius of the earth is 4000 miles, and round off to the nearest tenth.)

21. The distance a free falling object falls is directly proportional to the square of the time it falls (before it hits the ground). If an object fell 144 feet in 3 seconds, how far will it have fallen by the end of 4 seconds?

22. The volume of gas in a container is 300 cm^3 when the pressure on the gas is 20 gm per cm^2. What will be the volume of the gas if the pressure is increased to 30 gm per cm^2?

23. A hanging spring will stretch 5 in. if a weight of 10 lbs is placed at its end. How far will the spring stretch if the weight is increased to 12 lbs?

24. The circumference of a circle varies directly as the diameter. A circular pizza pie with a diameter of 1 foot has a circumference of 3.14 feet. What will be the circumference of a pizza pie with a diameter of 1.5 feet?

25. The area of a circle varies directly as the square of its radius. A circular pizza pie with a diameter of 12 inches has an area of 113.04 in.^{2}. What will be the area of a pizza pie with a diameter of 18 inches?

26. The total price, P, of gasoline purchased varies directly with the number of gallons purchased. If 10 gallons are purchased for $12.50, what will be the price of 15 gallons?

27. Several triangles are to have the same area. In this set of triangles the height and base are inversely proportional. In one such triangle the height is 5 m and the base is 12 m. Find the height of the triangle in this set with a base of 10 m.

28. W varies jointly as x and y and inversely as z. If $W = 10$ when $x = 6$ and $y = 5$ and $z = 2$, find W if $x = 12$ and $y = 6$ and $z = 3$.

29. The resistance, R, of a wire varies directly as its length and inversely as the square of its diameter. The resistance of a wire 500 feet long with diameter 0.01 inch is 20 ohms. What is the resistance of a wire 1500 feet long with diameter 0.02 inch?

30. The resistance of a wire 100 feet long and 0.01 inch in diameter is 8 ohms. What is the resistance of 150 feet of the same type of wire but with diameter 0.015 inch? (See Exercise 29.)

31. The lifting force, F, exerted on an airplane wing varies jointly as the area, A, of the wing's surface and the square of the plane's velocity, v. The lift for a wing with an area of 120 square feet is 1600 pounds when the plane is going 80 mph. Find the lift if the speed is increased to 90 mph.

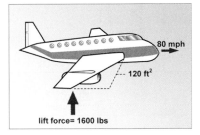

32. The lift for a wing of area 280 sq ft is 34,300 lb when the plane is going 210 mph. What is the lift if the speed is decreased to 180 mph? (See Exercise 31.)

33. The elongation, E, in a wire when a mass, m, is hung at its free end varies jointly as the mass and the length, l, of the wire and inversely as the cross-sectional area, A, of the wire. The elongation is 0.0055 cm when a mass of 120 gm is attached to a wire 330 cm long with a cross-sectional area of 0.4 sq cm. Find the elongation if a mass of 160 gm is attached to the same wire.

34. When a mass of 240 oz is suspended by a wire 49 inches long whose cross-sectional area is 0.035 sq in., the elongation of the wire is 0.016 in. Find the elongation if the same mass is suspended by a 28-in. wire of the same material with a cross-sectional area of 0.04 sq in. (See Exercise 33.)

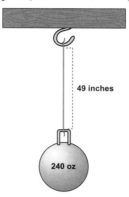

49 inches

240 oz

35. The safe load, L, of a wooden beam supported at both ends varies jointly as the width, w, and the square of the depth, d, and inversely as the length, l. A wooden beam 2 in. wide, 8 in. deep, and 14 ft long holds up 2400 lbs. What load would a beam 3 in. × 6 in. × 15 ft, of the same material, support?

36. A 4 in. × 6 in. beam 12 ft. long supports a load of 4800 lb. What is the safe load of a beam of the same material that is 6 in. × 10 in. × 15 ft long? (See Exercise 35.)

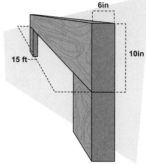

6in

15 ft

10in

37. The gravitational force of attraction, F, between two bodies varies directly as the product of their masses, m_1 and m_2, and inversely as the square of the distance, d, between them. The gravitational force between a 5-kg mass and a 2-kg mass 1 m apart is 1.5×10^{-10} N. Find the force between a 24-kg mass and a 9-kg mass that are 6 m apart. (N represents a unit of force called a **newton**.)

38. In exercise 37, what happens to the force if the distance between the bodies is cut in half?

Writing and Thinking About Mathematics

39. Explain in your own words, the meaning of the terms
    a. direct variation,
    b. inverse variation,
    c. joint variation, and
    d. combined variation.

Discuss an example of each type of variation that you have observed in your daily life.

Hawkes Learning Systems: Intermediate Algebra

Applications (Variation)

Chapter 5 Index of Key Ideas and Terms

Rational Expression   page 331

A **rational expression** is an expression of the form

$\dfrac{P}{Q}$ where P and Q are polynomials and $Q \neq 0$.

Arithmetic Rules for Rational Numbers (or Fractions)   page 331

Fundamental Principle of Fractions   page 332

If $\dfrac{P}{Q}$ is a rational expression and K is a polynomial

and $K \neq 0$, then $\dfrac{P}{Q} = \dfrac{P}{Q} \cdot \dfrac{K}{K} = \dfrac{P \cdot K}{Q \cdot K}$.

Negative Signs in Rational Expressions   page 333

$-\dfrac{P}{Q} = \dfrac{P}{-Q} = \dfrac{-P}{Q}$ and $\dfrac{P}{Q} = \dfrac{-P}{-Q} = -\dfrac{-P}{Q} = -\dfrac{P}{-Q}$

Opposites in Rational Expressions   page 334

In general, $\dfrac{-P}{P} = -1$ if $P \neq 0$.

In particular, $\dfrac{a-x}{x-a} = -1$ if $x \neq a$.

Multiplication of Rational Expressions   page 335

$\dfrac{P}{Q} \cdot \dfrac{R}{S} = \dfrac{P \cdot R}{Q \cdot S}$ where $Q, S \neq 0$.

Division of Rational Expressions   page 336

$\dfrac{P}{Q} \div \dfrac{R}{S} = \dfrac{P}{Q} \cdot \dfrac{S}{R}$ where $Q, R, S \neq 0$.

Addition and Subtraction of Rational Expressions   page 342

$\dfrac{P}{Q} + \dfrac{R}{Q} = \dfrac{P+R}{Q}$ and $\dfrac{P}{Q} - \dfrac{R}{Q} = \dfrac{P-R}{Q}$ where $Q \neq 0$.

Finding the LCD for a Set of Polynomials   page 343

1. Completely factor each polynomial (including prime factors for numerical factors).
2. Form the product of all distinct factors that appear, using each factor the most number of times it appears in any one factorization.

**Procedure for Adding or Subtracting Rational
Expressions with Different Denominators**   page 344
  1. Find the LCD (the LCM of the denominators).
  2. Rewrite each fraction in an equivalent form with the LCD.
  3. Add (or subtract) the numerators and keep the common
     denominator.
  4. Reduce if possible.

Complex Fraction   page 351
  A **complex fraction** is a fraction in which the numerator or
  denominator is a fraction or the sum or difference of fractions.

Simplifying Complex Fractions   pages 351 - 353
  Method 1   page 351
  1. Simplify the numerator and denominator separately so
     that the numerator and denominator are simple fractions.
  2. Divide by multiplying by the reciprocal of the denominator.
  Method 2   page 353
  1. Find the LCM of all the denominators in the original
     numerator and denominator.
  2. Multiply both the numerator and denominator by this
     LCM.

Rational Equation   page 356
  A **rational equation** is an equation that contains at least one
  rational expression.

To Solve a Rational Equation   page 356
  1. Find the LCM of all the denominators of all the rational
     expressions in the equation.
  2. Multiply both sides of the equation by this LCM.
     Use the distributive property if necessary.
  3. Simplify both sides of the resulting equation.
  4. Solve this equation.
  5. Check each solution in the **original equation**.
     (Remember that no denominator can be 0.)

Proportions and Similar Triangles   pages 359 - 360

Solving Inequalities with Rational Expressions   page 364
  1. Simplify the inequality so that one side is 0 and on the other
     side both the numerator and denominator are in factored form.
  2. Find the points where each linear factor is 0.
  3. Mark each of these points on a number line.
  4. Choose a number from each indicated interval as a test value.
  5. The intervals where the test values satisfy the conditions of the
     inequality are the solution intervals.
  6. Mark a solid circle for endpoints that are included and an open
     circle for points that are not included.

Strategy for Solving Word Problems page 368
1. Read the problem carefully. Read it several times if necessary.
2. Decide what is asked for and assign a variable to the unknown quantity.
3. Draw a diagram or set up a chart whenever possible.
4. Form an equation (or inequality) that relates the information provided.
5. Solve the equation (or inequality).
6. Check your solution with the wording of the problem to be sure it makes sense.

Direct Variation page 378

A variable quantity y **varies directly** as (or is **directly proportional to**) a variable x if there is a constant k such that

$$\frac{y}{x} = k \text{ or } y = kx$$

The constant k is called the **constant of variation**.

Inverse Variation page 380

A variable quantity y **varies inversely** as (or is **inversely proportional** to) a variable x if there is a constant k such that

$$x \cdot y = k \text{ or } y = \frac{k}{x}$$

The constant k is called the **constant of variation**.

Combined Variation page 381

If a variable varies either directly or inversely with more than one other variable, the variation is said to be **combined variation**.

Joint Variation page 381

If a combined variation is all direct variation (the variables are multiplied), then it is called **joint variation**.

Chapter 5 Review

For a review of the topics and problems from Chapter 5, look at the following lessons from *Hawkes Learning Systems: Intermediate Algebra*

Defining Rational Expressions
Multiplication and Division of
    Rational Expressions
Addition and Subtraction of
    Rational Expressions
Complex Fractions

Solving Equations Involving
    Rational Expressions
Applications Involving Rational
    Expressions
Applications (Variation)

Chapter 5 Test

Assume that none of the denominators in the rational expressions on this test has a value of 0.

Write each expression in Exercises 1 and 2 in lowest terms.

1. $\dfrac{x^2 + 3x}{x^2 + 7x + 12}$

2. $\dfrac{x^3 - 64}{16 - x^2}$

3. Determine the missing numerator that will make the following rational expressions equivalent.

   a. $\dfrac{x-5}{3-x} = \dfrac{?}{x-3}$

   b. $\dfrac{x-1}{3x+1} = \dfrac{?}{(3x+1)(x+2)}$

Perform the indicated operations in Exercises 4 – 9. Reduce all answers to lowest terms.

4. $\dfrac{x+3}{x^2+3x-4} \cdot \dfrac{x^2+x-2}{x+2}$

5. $\dfrac{6x^2-x-2}{12x^2+5x-2} \div \dfrac{4x^2-1}{8x^2-6x+1}$

6. $\dfrac{x}{x^2+3x-10} + \dfrac{3x}{4-x^2}$

7. $\dfrac{x-4}{3x^2+5x+2} - \dfrac{x-1}{x^2-3x-4}$

8. $\dfrac{x^2-16}{x^2-4x} \cdot \dfrac{x^2}{x+4} \div \dfrac{x-1}{2x^2-2x}$

9. $\dfrac{x}{x+3} - \dfrac{x+1}{x-3} + \dfrac{x^2+4}{x^2-9}$

10. Simplify each of the following complex fractions.

   a. $\dfrac{\dfrac{4}{3x}+\dfrac{1}{6x}}{\dfrac{1}{x^2}-\dfrac{1}{2x}}$

   b. $\dfrac{1-4x^{-2}}{1+2x^{-1}}$

Solve each of the equations in Exercises 11 and 12.

11. $\dfrac{4}{7} - \dfrac{1}{2x} = 1 + \dfrac{1}{x}$

12. $\dfrac{4}{x+4} + \dfrac{3}{x-1} = \dfrac{1}{x^2+3x-4}$

Solve each of the inequalities in Exercises 13 and 14. Graph each solution set on a number line and write the answer in interval notation.

13. $\dfrac{2x+5}{x-3} \ge 0$

14. $\dfrac{x-3}{2x+1} < 2$

15. The denominator of fraction is three more than twice the numerator. If eight is added to both the numerator and the denominator, the resulting fraction is equal to $\dfrac{2}{3}$. Find the original fraction.

16. Sonya can clean the apartment in 6 hours. It takes Lucy 12 hours to clean it. If they work together, how long will it take them?

17. Mario can travel 228 miles in the same time that Carlos travels 168 miles. If Mario's speed is 15 mph faster than Carlos', find their rates.

18. Bob travels 4 miles upstream. In the same time, he could have traveled 7 miles downstream. If the speed of the current is 3 mph, find the speed of the boat in still water.

19. z varies directly as x^2 and inversely as $\sqrt{y}$. If $z = 24$ when $x = 3$ and $y = 4$, find z if $x = 5$ and $y = 9$.

20. Hooke's Law states that the distance a spring will stretch vertically is directly proportional to the weight placed at its end. If a particular spring will stretch 5 cm when a weight of 4 g is placed at its end, how far will the spring stretch if a weight of 6 g is placed at its end?

Cumulative Review: Chapters 1 - 5

Solve each of the equations in Exercises 1 – 3.

1. $4(3x-1)=2(2x-5)-3$ **2.** $\dfrac{4x-1}{3}+\dfrac{x-5}{2}=2$ **3.** $\left|\dfrac{3x}{4}-1\right|=2$

Solve the inequalities in Exercises 4 – 6 and graph the solutions. Write the solutions in interval notation.

4. $x+4-3x \ge 2x+5$ **5.** $\dfrac{x}{5}-3.4 > \dfrac{x}{2}+1.6$ **6.** $\left|\dfrac{3x}{2}-1\right|-2 \le 3$

Simplify each expression in Exercises 7 – 9.

7. $\left(3x^2y^{-3}\right)^{-2}$ **8.** $\left(\dfrac{x^4y}{x^2y^3}\right)^3$ **9.** $\left(\dfrac{5x^2y^{-1}}{2xy}\right)\left(\dfrac{3x^{-3}y}{5x^2y^0}\right)$

Write Exercises 10 and 11 in scientific notation.

10. $(17000)(0.0004)$ **11.** $\dfrac{6300}{0.006}$

12. Find an equation in standard form for the line that has slope $m = -\dfrac{4}{5}$ and contains the point $(-2, 2)$. Then graph the line.

13. Find an equation in standard form for the line that passes through the point $(3, -4)$ and is parallel to the line $2x - y = 5$. Graph both lines.

14. Solve the following system of linear equations by using Cramer's Rule:
$$\begin{cases} 3x + 8y = -2 \\ -x + 2y = -4 \end{cases}$$

15. Solve the following system of linear equations by using the Gaussian elimination technique:
$$\begin{cases} x + y + z = 6 \\ 2x - 3y - z = -3 \\ -x + y - 3z = 6 \end{cases}$$

16. Determine the values of a and b such that the straight line $ax + by = 14$ passes through the two points $(-1, 19)$ and $(2, 4)$.

17. Solve the following system of equations by using the Gaussian elimination method. You may use your calculator.
$$\begin{cases} x + y + z = -2 \\ 2x - 3y - z = 15 \\ -x + y - 3z = -12 \end{cases}$$

18. Find the value of $\det(A)$ for the matrix $A = \begin{bmatrix} 4 & 3 & -1 \\ 2 & -1 & 5 \\ 0 & 6 & -3 \end{bmatrix}$

Factor each expression in Exercises 19 – 22 completely.

19. $15x^2 + 22x + 8$

20. $2x^3 + 8x^2 + 3x + 12$

21. $16x^3 - 54$

22. $2x^{-1} - 5x^{-2} - 3x^{-3}$

23. a. Use synthetic division to find $P(2)$ given that $P(x) = 4x^3 - 5x^2 + 2x - 1$.
   b. Is $x - 2$ a factor of $P(x)$? Explain.

24. a. Find an equation that has $x = -5$ and $x = -4$ as roots.
   b. Find an equation that has $x = 1$, $x = 2$, and $x = 3$ as roots.

25. Use a graphing calculator to find the solution set to the following system of inequalities:
$$\begin{cases} y \leq 2x - 3 \\ y \geq -\dfrac{1}{2}x \end{cases}$$

In Exercises 26 and 27, divide by using long division. Write the answer in the form $Q(x)+\dfrac{R(x)}{D(x)}$.

26. $\dfrac{2x^3+5x^2-x+3}{x+2}$

27. $\dfrac{x^3-4x^2+9}{x^2-6}$

Perform the indicated operations in Exercises 28 and 29.

28. $\dfrac{x+1}{x^2+3x-4}\cdot\dfrac{2x^2+7x-4}{x^2-1}\div\dfrac{x+1}{x-1}$

29. $\dfrac{x}{x^2-2x-8}+\dfrac{x-3}{2x^2-5x-12}-\dfrac{2x-5}{2x^2+7x+6}$

30. Solve each of the following inequalities. Graph each solution set on a number line and write the answer in interval notation.

 a. $\dfrac{3x-10}{x+2}\le 1$

 b. $\dfrac{x+1}{2x-1}>1$

31. The following table shows the number of feet that Juan drove his car from one minute to another. (Sometimes he backed up.)

Minutes	Feet
1	1496
2	2024
3	1056
4	440
5	−704

 a. Plot the points indicated in the table.
 b. Calculate the slope of the line segments from point to point.
 c. Interpret each slope.

32. Three graphs are shown below. Use the vertical line test to determine whether or not each graph represents a function. If the graph represents a function, state its domain and range.

 a.   **b.**   **c.**

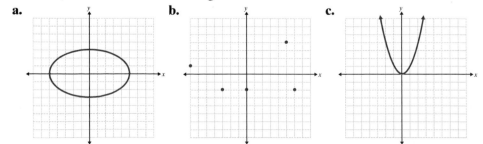

33. The distance an object falls (in feet) varies directly as the square of the time (in seconds) that it falls. If an object falls 16 feet in 1 sec., how far will it fall in 4 sec.?

34. A right triangle is formed when a ladder is leaned against a building. If the ladder is 26 ft. long and its bottom is placed 10 feet from the base of the building, how far up the building does the ladder reach?

35. The sum of the squares of two consecutive positive even integers is 580. What are the integers?

36. The sum of two numbers is 14. Twice the larger number added to three times the smaller is equal to thirty-one. Find both numbers.

37. Emily started walking to a town 10 miles away at a rate of 3 mph. After walking part of the way, she got a ride on a bus. The bus traveled at an average rate of 48 mph, and Emily reached the town 50 minutes after she started. How long did she walk?

38. LeAnn is a carpet layer. She has agreed to carpet a house for $18 per square yard. The carpet will cost her $11 per square yard, and she knows that there is approximately 12% waste in cutting and matching. If she plans to make a profit of $580.80, how many yards of carpet will she buy?

Roots, Radicals and Complex Numbers

Did You Know?

An important method of reasoning related to mathematical proofs is proof by contradiction. See if you can follow the reasoning in the following proof that $\sqrt{2}$ is an irrational number.

We need the following statement (which can be proven algebraically):

The square of an integer is even if and only if the integer is even.

Proof: $\sqrt{2}$ is either an irrational number or a rational number.

Suppose that $\sqrt{2}$ is a rational number and

$\dfrac{a}{b} = \sqrt{2}$ Where a and b are integers and $\dfrac{a}{b}$ is reduced.

6.1   **Roots and Radicals**

6.2   **Rational Exponents**

6.3   **Arithmetic with Radicals**

6.4   **Functions with Radicals**

6.5   **Introduction to Complex Numbers**

6.6   **Multiplication and Division with Complex Numbers**

$\dfrac{a^2}{b^2} = 2$ Square both sides.

$a^2 = 2b^2$ This means a^2 is an even integer.

So $a = 2n$ Since a^2 is even, a must be even.

$a^2 = 4n^2$ Square both sides.

$a^2 = 4n^2 = 2b^2$ Substitution.

$2n^2 = b^2$ This means b^2 is an even integer.

Therefore, b is an even integer.

But if a and b are both even, 2 is a common factor.

This contradicts the statement that $\dfrac{a}{b}$ is reduced.

Thus, our original supposition that $\sqrt{2}$ is rational is false, and $\sqrt{2}$ is an irrational number.

"The number of grains of sand on the beach at Coney Island is much less than a googol $-10,000,000,000,000,000,000,000,000,$ $000,000,000,000,000,000,000,000,000,$ $000,000,000,000,000,000,000,000,000,$ $000,000,000,000,000,000,000.$"

Edward Kasner

$\mathbf{I}$n this chapter, we will discuss expressions with exponents and their close relationship with radical expressions such as square roots ($\sqrt{x}$) and cube roots ($\sqrt[3]{x}$). This relationship allows translation from one type of expression to the other with relative ease and a choice for the form of an answer that best suits the purposes of the problem. For example, in higher level mathematics courses, particularly in calculus, an expression with a square root such as $\sqrt{x^2+1}$ may be changed into an equivalent expression with a fractional exponent such as $\left(x^2+1\right)^{\frac{1}{2}}$. Operations learned in calculus can be performed on expressions in the fractional exponent form. Then, if desired, answers can be changed back into a form with radical notation.

An important concern is under what conditions an expression with fractional exponents (or radicals) will be defined to be a real number. This concern leads to the definition of a new category of numbers called complex numbers. These numbers include the real numbers and a type of number called imaginary numbers. The term "imaginary" is somewhat unfortunate and misleading because these numbers have many practical applications and are no more imaginary than any other type of number. In fact, at one time negative numbers were thought of as "imaginary" since they represent an impossible quantity. However, complex numbers are particularly useful in electrical engineering and hydrodynamics. As we will see in Chapter 7, complex numbers evolve quite naturally as solutions to second-degree equations.

6.1   Roots and Radicals

Objectives

After completing this section, you will be able to:

1. *Evaluate square roots.*
2. *Simplify expressions with square roots.*
3. *Evaluate cube roots.*
4. *Simplify expressions with cube roots.*
5. *Rationalize denominators of fractional expressions.*

You are probably familiar with the concept of **square roots** and the **square root symbol** (or **radical sign**) ($\sqrt{\ }$) from your work in beginning algebra and our discussions of real numbers in Chapter 1. For example, the **radical notation** for the square root of 2 is $\sqrt{2}$, and $\sqrt{3}$ represents the square root of 3. In this section, we discuss the meanings of square roots and cube roots and methods for simplifying expressions with square roots and cube roots. In Section 6.2, we will expand these ideas to nth roots in general and the meanings of fractional exponents (rational exponents).

Square Roots: $\sqrt{a}$

A number is squared when it is multiplied by itself. The exponent 2 is used to indicate squares. For example,

$$6^2 = 6 \cdot 6 = 36 \quad \text{and} \quad (-15)^2 = (-15) \cdot (-15) = 225$$

If an integer is squared, the result is called a **perfect square**. For understanding and easy reference, Table 6.1 shows the squares of the integers from 1 to 20 and thus the perfect squares from 1 to 400.

Table 6.1 Squares of Integers from 1 to 20 (Perfect Squares)										
Integers (n)	1	2	3	4	5	6	7	8	9	10
Perfect Squares (n^2)	1	4	9	16	25	36	49	64	81	100
Integers (n)	11	12	13	14	15	16	17	18	19	20
Perfect Squares (n^2)	121	144	169	196	225	256	289	324	361	400

Now, we want to reverse the process of squaring. That is, given a number, we want to find a number that when squared will result in the given number. This is called **finding a square root** of the given number. In general,

if $b^2 = a$, then b is a square root of a.

For example,

- because $5^2 = 25$, then 5 is a **square root** of 25 and we write $\sqrt{25} = 5$.

- because $9^2 = 81$, then 9 is a **square root** of 81 and we write $\sqrt{81} = 9$.

Terminology

*The symbol $\sqrt{}$ is called a **radical sign**.*

*The number under the radical sign is called the **radicand**.*

*The complete expression, such as $\sqrt{64}$, is called a **radical** or **radical expression**.*

Every positive real number has two square roots, one positive and one negative. The positive square root is called the **principal square root**. For example,

- because $(8)^2 = 64$, then $\sqrt{64} = 8$ ←——— the **principal square root**

- because $(-8)^2 = 64$, then $-\sqrt{64} = -8$ ←———the **negative square root**

The number 0 has only one square root, namely 0.

Square Root

If a is a nonnegative real number and b is a real number such that
$$b^2 = a \text{, then } b \text{ is called a } \textbf{square root } of a.$$
If b is nonnegative, then we write
$$\sqrt{a} = b \text{ ←——— } b \text{ is called the } \textbf{principal square root}$$
$$and \ -\sqrt{a} = -b \text{ ←———} -b \text{ is called the } \textbf{negative square root.}$$

Example 1: Evaluating Square Roots

(**Note:** As these examples illustrate, the radicand may be an integer, a fraction, or a decimal number.)

Evaluate each of the following radical expressions.

a. $\sqrt{121}$ **b.** $\sqrt{\dfrac{16}{25}}$ **c.** $-\sqrt{0.0036}$ **d.** $\sqrt{16+9}$ **e.** $\sqrt{16} + \sqrt{9}$

Solutions:

a. $\sqrt{121} = 11$ The principal square root of 121 is 11 because $11^2 = 121$.

b. $\sqrt{\dfrac{16}{25}} = \dfrac{4}{5}$ The principal square root of $\dfrac{16}{25}$ is $\dfrac{4}{5}$ because $\left(\dfrac{4}{5}\right)^2 = \dfrac{16}{25}$.

c. $-\sqrt{0.0036} = -0.06$ The negative square root of 0.0036 is –0.06 because $(-0.06)^2 = (-0.06)(-0.06) = 0.0036$.

d. $\sqrt{16+9} = \sqrt{25} = 5$ Note that the sum under the radical sign is found first. Then the square root is found. In this situation, the radical sign is similar to parentheses.

e. $\sqrt{16} + \sqrt{9} = 4 + 3 = 7$ Note that as illustrated in examples 1d and 1e, in general, $\sqrt{a+b} \neq \sqrt{a} + \sqrt{b}$.

Example 2: Using a Calculator to Find Square Roots

Many real numbers have square roots that are not terminating decimals or fractions. The square roots of these numbers are infinite nonrepeating decimals (irrational numbers). Your calculator will find these values accurate to as many as nine decimal places.

Follow the steps outlined here with your calculator and the $\sqrt{}$ key to find the following square roots accurate to four decimal places.

a. $\sqrt{200}$ **b.** $-\sqrt{35}$

Solutions:

a.   **Step 1:** Press (2nd) and then the $\sqrt{}$ key.

Step 2: Enter 200) and then press (ENTER).

The display on the screen should appear as follows:

Thus, $\sqrt{200} = 14.1421$ accurate to four decimal places.

b.   **Step 1:** Press the ((−)) key (located next to (ENTER)).

Step 2: Press (2nd) and then the $\sqrt{}$ key.

Step 3: Enter 35) and then press (ENTER).

The display on the screen should appear as follows:

Thus, $-\sqrt{35} = -5.9161$ accurate to four decimal places.

Next, consider the square root of a negative number. For example, what is the value of $\sqrt{-49}$? There is no real number whose square is –49. The square of every real number is nonnegative. Thus, $\sqrt{-49}$ is a not a real number. In general,

$\sqrt{x}$ **is not a real number if** x **is negative** ($x < 0$).

We will discuss these nonreal numbers (part of the complex number system) later in this chapter.

Simplifying Expressions with Square Roots

Various roots can be related to solutions of equations, and we want such numbers to be in a **simplified form** for easier calculations and algebraic manipulations. We need the two properties of radicals stated here for square roots. (Similar properties are true for other roots.)

Properties of Square Roots

*If a and b are **positive** real numbers, then*

1. $\sqrt{ab} = \sqrt{a}\sqrt{b}$ **2.** $\sqrt{\dfrac{a}{b}} = \dfrac{\sqrt{a}}{\sqrt{b}}$

As an example, we know that 144 is a perfect square and $\sqrt{144}$ = 12. However, in a situation where you may have forgotten this, you can proceed as follows using Property 1 of Square Roots:

$$\sqrt{144} = \sqrt{36} \cdot \sqrt{4} = 6 \cdot 2 = 12$$

Similarly, using Property 2, we can write

$$\sqrt{\frac{49}{36}} = \frac{\sqrt{49}}{\sqrt{36}} = \frac{7}{6}$$

Simplest Form

*A square root is considered to be in **simplest form** when the radicand has no perfect square as a factor.*

The number 648 is not a perfect square, and to simplify $\sqrt{648}$ we can use Property 1 of Square Roots and any of the following three approaches.

Approach 1: Factor 648 as $36 \cdot 18$ because 36 is a perfect square. Then,

$$\sqrt{648} = \sqrt{36 \cdot 18} = \sqrt{36} \cdot \sqrt{18} = 6\sqrt{18}.$$

However, $6\sqrt{18}$ is **not in simplest form** because 18 has a perfect square factor, 9. Thus to complete the process, we have

$$\sqrt{648} = 6\sqrt{18} = 6\sqrt{9 \cdot 2} = 6\sqrt{9} \cdot \sqrt{2} = 6 \cdot 3\sqrt{2} = 18\sqrt{2}.$$

Approach 2: Note that 324 is a perfect square factor of 648 and $648 = 324 \cdot 2$.

$$\sqrt{648} = \sqrt{324 \cdot 2} = \sqrt{324} \cdot \sqrt{2} = 18\sqrt{2}$$

Approach 3: Use prime factors.

$$\sqrt{648} = \sqrt{12 \cdot 54}$$
$$= \sqrt{2 \cdot 2 \cdot 3 \cdot 2 \cdot 3 \cdot 3 \cdot 3}$$
$$= \sqrt{2 \cdot 2 \cdot 3 \cdot 3 \cdot 3 \cdot 3} \cdot \sqrt{2}$$
$$= 2 \cdot 3 \cdot 3 \cdot \sqrt{2}$$
$$= 18\sqrt{2}$$

Of these three approaches, the second appears to be the easiest because it has the fewest steps. However, "seeing" the largest perfect square factor may be difficult. If you do not immediately see a perfect square factor, then proceed to find other factors or prime factors as illustrated.

Example 3: Simplifying Expressions with Square Roots

Simplify the following square roots.

a. $\sqrt{48}$ b. $\sqrt{\dfrac{75}{16}}$ c. $\dfrac{2 - \sqrt{20}}{2}$

Solutions:

a. $\sqrt{48} = \sqrt{16 \cdot 3} = \sqrt{16} \cdot \sqrt{3} = 4\sqrt{3}$ Find the largest perfect square factor.

b. $\sqrt{\dfrac{75}{16}} = \dfrac{\sqrt{75}}{\sqrt{16}} = \dfrac{\sqrt{25 \cdot 3}}{\sqrt{16}} = \dfrac{5\sqrt{3}}{4}$

c. $\dfrac{2 - \sqrt{20}}{2} = \dfrac{2 - \sqrt{4 \cdot 5}}{2} = \dfrac{2 - 2\sqrt{5}}{2} = \dfrac{2}{2} - \dfrac{2\sqrt{5}}{2} = 1 - \sqrt{5}$

$$\left[\text{or factoring and reducing.} \quad \dfrac{2 - 2\sqrt{5}}{2} = \dfrac{2\left(1 - \sqrt{5}\right)}{2} = 1 - \sqrt{5} \right]$$

Simplifying Square Roots with Variables

Now, we consider simplifying square root expressions that contain variables. To simplify the expression $\sqrt{x^2}$ we must consider the fact that we do not know whether x represents a positive number ($x > 0$) or a negative number ($x < 0$) along with the two squares

$$x \cdot x = x^2 \text{ and } (-x)(-x) = x^2$$

For example,

$$\text{If } x = 5, \text{ then } \sqrt{x^2} = \sqrt{5^2} = \sqrt{25} = 5 = x.$$

$$\text{But, if } x = -5, \text{ then } \sqrt{x^2} = \sqrt{(-5)^2} = \sqrt{25} = 5 \neq x.$$

$$\text{In fact, if } x = -5, \text{ then } \sqrt{x^2} = \sqrt{(-5)^2} = \sqrt{25} = 5 = |-5| = |x|.$$

Thus, simplifying radical expressions with variables involves more detailed analysis than simplifying radical expressions with only constants. The following definition indicates the correct way to simplify $\sqrt{x^2}$.

Square Root of x^2

If x is a real number, then $\sqrt{x^2} = |x|$.

Note: *If $x \geq 0$ is given, then we can write $\sqrt{x^2} = x$.*

Example 4: Simplifying Square Root Expressions with Variables

Simplify each of the following radical expressions.

    a. $\sqrt{16x^2}$ **b.** $\sqrt{72a^2}$ **c.** $\sqrt{12x^2y^2}$

Solutions:

    a. $\sqrt{16x^2} = \sqrt{16}\sqrt{x^2} = 4|x|$

    b. $\sqrt{72a^2} = \sqrt{72}\sqrt{a^2} = \sqrt{36}\sqrt{2}\sqrt{a^2} = 6\sqrt{2}|a|$

    c. $\sqrt{12x^2y^2} = \sqrt{12}\sqrt{x^2}\sqrt{y^2} = \sqrt{4}\sqrt{3}\sqrt{x^2}\sqrt{y^2} = 2\sqrt{3}|x||y|$ (or $2\sqrt{3}|xy|$)

When expressions with the same base are multiplied, the exponents are added. Thus, if an expression is multiplied by itself, the exponents (if there are any) will be doubled and, therefore, even. This means that, to find the square root of an expression with even exponents, the exponents can be divided by 2.

For example,

$$x^2 \cdot x^2 = x^4 \qquad a^3 \cdot a^3 = a^6 \qquad y^5 \cdot y^5 = y^{10}$$

and $\quad \sqrt{x^4} = x^2 \qquad \sqrt{a^6} = |a^3| \qquad \sqrt{y^{10}} = |y^5|$

To find the square root of an expression with odd exponents, factor the expression into two terms, one with exponent 1 and the other with an even exponent. For example,

$$x^3 = x^2 \cdot x \qquad \text{and} \qquad y^9 = y^8 \cdot y$$

which means that

$$\sqrt{x^3} = \sqrt{x^2 \cdot x} = \sqrt{x^2} \cdot \sqrt{x} - |x| \cdot \sqrt{x} \qquad \text{and} \qquad \sqrt{y^9} = \sqrt{y^8 \cdot y} = y^4 \sqrt{y}$$

Square Roots of Expressions with Even and Odd Exponents

For any real number x and positive integer m,

$$\sqrt{x^{2m}} = |x^m| \qquad \text{and} \qquad \sqrt{x^{2m+1}} = x^m \sqrt{x}$$

Note that the absolute value sign is necessary only if m is odd.

Also, note that for $\sqrt{x^{2m+1}}$ to be defined as real, x cannot be negative.

Note: *If m is any integer, then 2m is even and 2m + 1 is odd.*

Example 5: Simplifying Radical Expressions with Variables

Simplify each of the following radical expressions.

a. $\sqrt{81x^4}$ **b.** $\sqrt{64x^5y}$, assume that $x, y \geq 0$ **c.** $\sqrt{18a^4b^6}$ **d.** $\sqrt{\dfrac{9a^{13}}{b^4}}$

Solutions:

a. $\sqrt{81x^4} = 9x^2$ The exponent 4 is divided by 2 and x can be positive or negative.

b. $\sqrt{64x^5y} = \sqrt{64 \cdot x^4 \cdot x \cdot y} = 8x^2\sqrt{xy}$ Assuming that $x, y \geq 0$

Result of odd numbered exponent answer?

c. $\sqrt{18a^4b^6} = \sqrt{9 \cdot 2 \cdot a^4 \cdot b^6} = 3\sqrt{2}a^2|b^3|$ Each exponent is divided by 2.

d. $\sqrt{\dfrac{9a^{13}}{b^4}} = \dfrac{\sqrt{9 \cdot a^{12} \cdot a}}{\sqrt{b^4}} = \dfrac{3a^6\sqrt{a}}{b^2}$ We have assumed that $b \neq 0$ and $a \geq 0$. Thus, both $\sqrt{a^{13}}$ and $\sqrt{a}$ are real.

Cube Roots: $\sqrt[3]{a}$

For understanding and easy reference, the cubes of the integers from 1 to 10 are shown in Table 6.2. These perfect cubes occur frequently in the exercises and should be memorized.

Table 6.2 Cubes of Integers from 1 to 10 (Perfect Cubes)									
Integers (n)	1	2	3	4	5	6	7	8	9	10
Perfect Cubes (n^3)	1	8	27	64	125	216	343	512	729	1000

Cube Root

If a and b are real numbers such that

$b^3 = a$, then b is called the **cube root** of a.

We write $\sqrt[3]{a} = b$ ◀—— the **cube root**.

NOTES   In the cube root expression $\sqrt[3]{a}$ the number 3 is called the **index**. In a square root expression such as $\sqrt{a}$ the index is understood to be 2 and is not written. That is, $\sqrt{a}$ and $\sqrt[2]{a}$ have the same meaning. We will discuss indices in more detail in Section 6.2.

Example 6: Evaluating Cube Roots

Find the value of each of the following cube roots.

    a. $\sqrt[3]{216}$ **b.** $\sqrt[3]{-8}$ **c.** $\sqrt[3]{500}$

Solutions:

    a. $\sqrt[3]{216} = 6$ As we can see in Table 6.2, $6^3 = 216$ and 216 is a perfect cube.

    b. $\sqrt[3]{-8} = -2$ Note that the cube root of a negative number is negative. In this example $\sqrt[3]{-8} = -2$ because $(-2)^3 = -8$.

c. $\sqrt[3]{500}$ 500 is not a perfect cube.

A TI-83 Plus calculator can be used to estimate the value by using the following steps.

Step 1: Press **MATH** and press **4** (This will select $\sqrt[3]{(}$.)

Step 2: Enter 500) and press **ENTER**.

The display should appear as follows:

```
                                    TI-83 Plus
 ³√(500)
            7.93700526
```

Thus, the cube root of 500 is approximately 7.93700526 (or 7.9370 to four decimal places).

Simplifying Cube Roots

When simplifying expressions with cube roots, we need to be aware of perfect cube numbers and variables with exponents that are multiples of 3. (Multiples of 3 are 3, 6, 9, 12, 15, and so on.) Thus, exponents are divided by 3 in simplifying cube root expressions.

Simplest Form

A cube root is considered to be in **simplest form** when the radicand has no perfect cube as a factor.

Example 7: Simplifying Expressions with Cube Roots

Simplify each of the following cube root expressions by finding the largest perfect cube factor.

a. $\sqrt[3]{54x^6}$ **b.** $\sqrt[3]{-40x^4y^{13}}$ **c.** $\sqrt[3]{250a^8b^{11}}$

Solutions:

a. $\sqrt[3]{54x^6} = \sqrt[3]{27 \cdot 2 \cdot x^6}$ Note that 27 is a perfect cube and the exponent 6 is divided by 3 because we are finding a cube root.

$= 3x^2 \sqrt[3]{2}$

continued on next page ...

b. $\sqrt[3]{-40x^4y^{13}} = \sqrt[3]{(-8)\cdot 5\cdot x^3\cdot x\cdot y^{12}\cdot y}$
$= -2xy^4\sqrt[3]{5xy}$

Note that –8 is a perfect cube because $(-2)^3 = -8$, and each variable expression is separated so that one exponent is a multiple of 3. In simplifying, these exponents are divided by 3.

c. $\sqrt[3]{250a^8b^{11}} = \sqrt[3]{125\cdot 2\cdot a^6\cdot a^2\cdot b^9\cdot b^2}$
$= 5a^2b^3\sqrt[3]{2a^2b^2}$

Note that 125 is a perfect cube and each variable expression is separated so that one exponent is a multiple of 3.

Rationalizing Denominators in Radical Expressions

An expression with a radical in the denominator may not be in the simplest form for further algebraic manipulation or operations. If this is the case, then we may want to rationalize the denominator. That is, we want to find an equivalent fraction in which the denominator does not have a radical. The numerator may still have a radical in it, but a rational denominator definitely makes arithmetic with radicals much easier. (**Note:** In this section we will deal with radicals that are square roots or cube roots. Other roots will be discussed in Section 6.2.)

To Rationalize the Denominator of a Radical Expression

1. *If the denominator contains a square root, multiply both the numerator and denominator by a square root. Choose this square root so that the denominator will be a perfect square.*

2. *If the denominator contains a cube root, multiply both the numerator and denominator by a cube root. Choose this cube root so that the denominator will be a perfect cube.*

Example 8: Rationalizing Denominators

Simplify each of the following radical expressions so that the denominator is a rational expression. Assume that each variable is positive.

a. $\sqrt{\dfrac{5}{4x}}$ **b.** $\dfrac{7}{\sqrt[3]{32y}}$ **c.** $\sqrt{\dfrac{18a^2b}{30ac}}$

Solutions:

a. Multiply the numerator and denominator by $\sqrt{x}$ because $4x \cdot x = 4x^2$ and $4x^2$ is a perfect square expression.

$$\sqrt{\frac{5}{4x}} = \frac{\sqrt{5}}{\sqrt{4x}} = \frac{\sqrt{5} \cdot \sqrt{x}}{\sqrt{4x} \cdot \sqrt{x}} = \frac{\sqrt{5x}}{\sqrt{4x^2}} = \frac{\sqrt{5x}}{2x}$$

Or, multiply by $\dfrac{x}{x}$ under the radical first as follows:

$$\sqrt{\frac{5}{4x}} = \sqrt{\frac{5}{4x} \cdot \frac{x}{x}} = \frac{\sqrt{5x}}{\sqrt{4x^2}} = \frac{\sqrt{5x}}{2x}$$

b. Multiply the numerator and denominator by $\sqrt[3]{2y^2}$ because $32y \cdot 2y^2 = 64y^3$ and $64y^3$ is a perfect cube expression since $(4y)^3 = 64y^3$.

$$\frac{7}{\sqrt[3]{32y}} = \frac{7 \cdot \sqrt[3]{2y^2}}{\sqrt[3]{32y} \cdot \sqrt[3]{2y^2}} = \frac{7\sqrt[3]{2y^2}}{\sqrt[3]{64y^3}} = \frac{7\sqrt[3]{2y^2}}{4y}$$

c. In this case we can simplify under the radical first and then rationalize the denominator.

$$\sqrt{\frac{18a^2b}{30ac}} = \sqrt{\frac{3ab}{5c}} = \frac{\sqrt{3ab} \cdot \sqrt{5c}}{\sqrt{5c} \cdot \sqrt{5c}} = \frac{\sqrt{15abc}}{\sqrt{25c^2}} = \frac{\sqrt{15abc}}{5c}$$

● ●

Practice Problems

Use a calculator to find the value of each number accurate to four decimal places.

1. $\sqrt{40}$ ⠀⠀⠀⠀ **2.** $\sqrt[3]{40}$

Simplify the following radical expressions. Assume that x may be positive or negative, but that a and b must be positive.

3. $\sqrt{80x^3}$ ⠀⠀ **4.** $\sqrt[3]{-27x^9}$ ⠀⠀ **5.** $\sqrt{18x^2}$ ⠀⠀ **6.** $\sqrt{128a^2b^5}$

Simplify each expression so that the denominator is a rational expression.

7. $\sqrt{\dfrac{3}{8a^2}}$ ⠀⠀ **8.** $\dfrac{\sqrt[3]{4ab}}{\sqrt[3]{2a^2b^4}}$

Answers to Practice Problems: 1. 6.3246 **2.** 3.4200 **3.** $4|x|\sqrt{5x}$ **4.** $-3x^3$ **5.** $3|x|\sqrt{2}$ **6.** $8ab^2\sqrt{2b}$ **7.** $\dfrac{\sqrt{6}}{4a}$ **8.** $\dfrac{\sqrt[3]{2a^2}}{ab}$

6.1 Exercises

In Exercises 1 – 10, use a calculator to find the value of each radical accurate to four decimal places.

1. $\sqrt{0.0004}$ **2.** $\sqrt{0.0025}$ **3.** $\sqrt{1024}$ **4.** $\sqrt{720}$ **5.** $\sqrt{4500}$

6. $\sqrt[3]{343}$ **7.** $\sqrt[3]{0.000008}$ **8.** $\sqrt[3]{50,000}$ **9.** $\sqrt[3]{12.5}$ **10.** $\sqrt[3]{100}$

In Exercises 11 – 40, simplify each radical expression. Assume that the variables are positive. Say "nonreal" if the expression does not represent a real number.

11. $\sqrt{12}$ **12.** $\sqrt{18}$ **13.** $\sqrt{98}$ **14.** $\sqrt{216}$ **15.** $-\sqrt{162}$

16. $-\sqrt{27}$ **17.** $\sqrt[3]{16}$ **18.** $\sqrt[3]{40}$ **19.** $\sqrt[3]{108}$ **20.** $\sqrt[3]{-54}$

21. $\sqrt{-25}$ **22.** $\sqrt{-100}$ **23.** $\sqrt{24x^{11}y^2}$ **24.** $\sqrt{20x^{15}y^3}$

25. $\sqrt[3]{a^5b^2c^3}$ **26.** $\sqrt[3]{-xy^6}$ **27.** $\sqrt{-4x^5}$ **28.** $\sqrt{-9a^2}$

29. $\sqrt[3]{8x^9y^{12}}$ **30.** $\sqrt[3]{512a^3b^{27}}$ **31.** $\sqrt[3]{729a^4b^8}$ **32.** $\sqrt[3]{125x^2y^2}$

33. $\sqrt{125x^3y^6}$ **34.** $\sqrt{8x^5y^4}$ **35.** $\sqrt{12ab^2c^3}$ **36.** $\sqrt{45a^2b^3c^4}$

37. $-\sqrt{75x^4y^6z^8}$ **38.** $-\sqrt{200x^2y^2z^2}$ **39.** $\sqrt[3]{24x^5y^7z^9}$ **40.** $\sqrt[3]{250x^6y^9z^{15}}$

In Exercises 41 – 50, simplify each radical expression. Assume that the variables may be positive or negative.

41. $\sqrt{25y^2}$ **42.** $-\sqrt{81x^2}$ **43.** $-\sqrt{64a^6}$ **44.** $\sqrt{18x^2y^2}$ **45.** $\sqrt{32x^4y^8}$

46. $\sqrt[3]{-24x^3y^6}$ **47.** $\sqrt[3]{108ab^9}$ **48.** $\sqrt[3]{-64a^{12}}$ **49.** $\sqrt[3]{81x^5y^7}$ **50.** $\sqrt[3]{54a^4b^2}$

In Exercises 51 – 62, simplify each expression so that the denominator is a rational expression. Assume that the variables are positive.

51. $\sqrt{\dfrac{1}{64x}}$ **52.** $\sqrt{\dfrac{81}{x}}$ **53.** $-\sqrt{\dfrac{2}{3y}}$ **54.** $-\sqrt{\dfrac{25}{x^3}}$ **55.** $\dfrac{\sqrt{5y^2}}{\sqrt{8x}}$

56. $\dfrac{\sqrt{4x}}{\sqrt{3y^2}}$ **57.** $\dfrac{\sqrt{16y^2}}{\sqrt{2y^3}}$ **58.** $\dfrac{\sqrt{24a^3b}}{\sqrt{6ab^2}}$ **59.** $\sqrt[3]{\dfrac{2y^3}{27x^2}}$ **60.** $\sqrt[3]{\dfrac{7x}{2y^4}}$

61. $\sqrt[3]{\dfrac{6a^2}{25b}}$ **62.** $\dfrac{\sqrt[3]{x^5}}{\sqrt[3]{9xy}}$

Writing and Thinking About Mathematics

63. Explain, in your own words, why we cannot just say that $\sqrt{x^2} = x$. That is, why do we write $\sqrt{x^2} = |x|$?

64. Under what conditions is the expression $\sqrt{a}$ not a real number?

65. Explain why the expression $\sqrt[3]{y}$ is a real number regardless of whether $y > 0$ or $y < 0$ or $y = 0$.

66. Explain the technique for rationalizing the denominator when the denominator is a radical with index greater than 2.

Hawkes Learning Systems: Intermediate Algebra

Evaluating Radicals
Simplifying Radicals
Division of Radicals

6.2

Rational Exponents

After completing this section, you will be able to:

1. *Understand the meaning of nth root.*

2. *Simplify expressions using the properties of rational exponents.*

3. *Evaluate expressions of the form $a^{\frac{m}{n}}$ with a calculator.*

n^{th} Roots: $\sqrt[n]{a} = a^{\frac{1}{n}}$

In Section 6.1 we restricted our discussions to radicals involving square roots and cube roots. In this section we will expand on those ideas by discussing radicals indicating n^{th} roots in general and how to relate radical expressions to expressions with rational (fractional) exponents. For example, the fifth root of x can be written in radical form as $\sqrt[5]{x}$ and with a fractional exponent as $x^{\frac{1}{5}}$.

To understand roots in general, consider the following analysis (assuming that $b > 0$):

For square roots,	if $b^2 = a$, then $b = \sqrt{a}$ (or $b = a^{\frac{1}{2}}$).
For cube roots,	if $b^3 = a$, then $b = \sqrt[3]{a}$ (or $b = a^{\frac{1}{3}}$).
For fourth roots,	if $b^4 = a$, then $b = \sqrt[4]{a}$ (or $b = a^{\frac{1}{4}}$).
For n^{th} roots,	if $b^n = a$, then $b = \sqrt[n]{a}$ (or $b = a^{\frac{1}{n}}$).

(**Note:** In this discussion, we assume that $n \neq 0$.)

For example:

Because $2^4 = 16$ we can say that $\sqrt[4]{16} = 2$ (or $2 = 16^{\frac{1}{4}}$).

Because $3^5 = 243$ we can say that $\sqrt[5]{243} = 3$ (or $3 = 243^{\frac{1}{5}}$).

The following notation is used for all radical expressions.

Radical Notation

If n is a positive integer and $b^n = a$, then $b = \sqrt[n]{a} = a^{\frac{1}{n}}$ (assuming $\sqrt[n]{a}$ is a real number).

The expression $\sqrt[n]{a}$ is called a **radical**.

The symbol $\sqrt[n]{}$ is called a **radical sign**.

n is called the **index**.

a is called the **radicand**.

(**Note:** If no index is given, it is understood to be 2. For example, $\sqrt{3} = \sqrt[2]{3} = 3^{\frac{1}{2}}$.)

Special Note About the Index n:

For the expression $\sqrt[n]{a}$ (or $a^{\frac{1}{n}}$) to be a real number:

    1. n can be any index when a is nonnegative.

    2. n must be odd when a is negative.

    (If a is negative and n is even, then $\sqrt[n]{a}$ is nonreal.)

Example 1: Principal n^{th} Root

a. $49^{\frac{1}{2}} = \sqrt{49} = 7$ because $7^2 = 49$.

b. $81^{\frac{1}{4}} = \sqrt[4]{81} = 3$ because $3^4 = 81$.

c. $(-8)^{\frac{1}{3}} = \sqrt[3]{-8} = -2$ because $(-2)^3 = -8$.

d. $(0.00001)^{\frac{1}{5}} = \sqrt[5]{0.00001} = 0.1$ because $(0.1)^5 = 0.00001$.

e. $(-16)^{\frac{1}{2}} = \sqrt{-16}$ is not a real number. (Any even root of a negative number is non-real.)

Example 2: Odd Powers

Use a TI-83 Plus calculator to find the value of each of the following roots accurate to four decimal places.

a. $\sqrt[5]{200}$ **b.** $\sqrt[6]{1.25}$

continued on next page ...

Solutions:

a. To find $\sqrt[5]{200}$ proceed as follows:

> **Step 1:** Enter 5. (Note: This 5 is the index.)
>
> **Step 2:** Press **MATH**.
>
> **Step 3:** Choose **5 :** $\sqrt[x]{\ }$.
>
> **Step 4:** Enter 200 and press **ENTER**.

The display will appear as follows:

```
                              TI-83 Plus
 5×√200
              2.885399812
```

Thus, $\sqrt[5]{200} = 2.8854$ accurate to four decimal places.

(**Note:** Another approach is to use the fractional exponent as follows: 200 **∧** (1/5). Be sure to put parentheses around the exponent. The exponent form will give the same result as the radical form.)

b. To find $\sqrt[6]{1.25}$ proceed as follows:

> **Step 1:** Enter 6. (**Note:** This 6 is the index.)
>
> **Step 2:** Press **MATH**
>
> **Step 3:** Choose **5:** $\sqrt[x]{\ }$.
>
> **Step 4:** Enter 1.25 and press **ENTER**.

The display will appear as follows:

```
                              TI-83 Plus
 6×√1.25
              1.037890816
```

Thus, $\sqrt[6]{1.25} = 1.0379$ accurate to four decimal places.

(**Note:** Again, the exponent form 1.25 **∧** (1/6) will give the same result. Be sure to put the exponent in parentheses.)

Rational Exponents of the Form $\dfrac{m}{n}$: $\sqrt[n]{a^m} = a^{\frac{m}{n}}$

In Chapter 1 we discussed the properties of exponents using only integer exponents. These same properties of exponents apply to rational exponents (fractional exponents) as well and are repeated here for emphasis and easy reference.

Summary of Properties of Exponents

For nonzero real numbers a and b and rational numbers m and n,

The Exponent 1: $a = a^1$ *(a is any real number.)*

The Exponent 0: $a^0 = 1$ $(a \neq 0)$

Product Rule: $a^m \cdot a^n = a^{m+n}$

Quotient Rule: $\dfrac{a^m}{a^n} = a^{m-n}$

Power Rule: $\left(a^m\right)^n = a^{mn}$

Negative Exponents: $a^{-n} = \dfrac{1}{a^n}, \quad \dfrac{1}{a^{-n}} = a^n$

Power Rule for Products: $(ab)^n = a^n b^n$

Power Rule for Fractions: $\left(\dfrac{a}{b}\right)^n = \dfrac{a^n}{b^n}$

Now consider the problem of evaluating the expression $8^{\frac{2}{3}}$ where the exponent, $\dfrac{2}{3}$, is of the form $\dfrac{m}{n}$. By using the Power Rule for exponents, we can write

$$8^{\frac{2}{3}} = \left(8^{\frac{1}{3}}\right)^2 = (2)^2 = 4$$

or, $8^{\frac{2}{3}} = \left(8^2\right)^{\frac{1}{3}} = (64)^{\frac{1}{3}} = 4$

The result is the same with either approach. That is we can take the cube root first and then square the answer. Or, we can square first and then take the cube root. In general, for an exponent of the form $\dfrac{m}{n}$, taking the nth root first and then raising this root to the power m is easier because the numbers are smaller.

For example,

$$81^{\frac{3}{4}} = \left(81^{\frac{1}{4}}\right)^3 = (3)^3 = 27$$

is easier to calculate and work with than

$$81^{\frac{3}{4}} = \left(81^3\right)^{\frac{1}{4}} = (531,441)^{\frac{1}{4}} = 27.$$

The fourth root of 81 is more commonly known than the fourth root of 531,441.

The General Form $a^{\frac{m}{n}}$

If n is a positive integer and m is any integer and $a^{\frac{1}{n}}$ is a real number, then

$$a^{\frac{m}{n}} = \left(a^{\frac{1}{n}}\right)^m = \left(a^m\right)^{\frac{1}{n}}$$

In radical notation:

$$a^{\frac{m}{n}} = \left(\sqrt[n]{a}\right)^m = \sqrt[n]{a^m}$$

Example 3: Conversion

Assume that each variable represents a positive real number.
Each expression is changed to an equivalent expression in radical notation.

a. $x^{\frac{2}{3}} = \sqrt[3]{x^2}$ Note that the index, 3, is the denominator in the rational exponent.

b. $3x^{\frac{4}{5}} = 3\sqrt[5]{x^4}$ Note that the coefficient, 3, is not affected by the exponent.

c. $-a^{\frac{3}{2}} = -\sqrt{a^3}$ Note that -1 is the understood coefficient.

d. $\sqrt[6]{a^5} = a^{\frac{5}{6}}$ Note that the index is the denominator of the rational exponent.

e. $5\sqrt{x} = 5x^{\frac{1}{2}}$ Note that, in a square root, the index is understood to be 2.

f. $-\sqrt[3]{4} = -4^{\frac{1}{3}}$ Note that the coefficient, -1, is not affected by the exponent. Also, we could write $-4^{\frac{1}{3}} = -1 \cdot 4^{\frac{1}{3}}$.

Simplifying Expressions with Rational Exponents

Expressions with rational exponents such as

$$x^{\frac{2}{3}} \cdot x^{\frac{1}{6}}, \quad \frac{x^{\frac{3}{4}}}{x^{\frac{1}{3}}}, \text{ and } \left(2a^{\frac{1}{4}}\right)^{3}$$

can be simplified by using the properties of exponents.

NOTES   Unless otherwise stated, we will assume, for the remainder of this chapter, that all variables represent non-negative real numbers.

Example 4: Simplifying Expressions with Rational Exponents

Each expression is simplified by using one or more of the rules of exponents.

a. $x^{\frac{2}{3}} \cdot x^{\frac{1}{6}} = x^{\frac{2}{3} + \frac{1}{6}}$ Find a common denominator and add the exponents.

$$= x^{\frac{4}{6} + \frac{1}{6}} = x^{\frac{5}{6}}$$

b. $\dfrac{x^{\frac{3}{4}}}{x^{\frac{1}{3}}} = x^{\frac{3}{4} - \frac{1}{3}}$ Subtract the exponents.

$$= x^{\frac{9}{12} - \frac{4}{12}} = x^{\frac{5}{12}}$$

c. $\left(2a^{\frac{1}{4}}\right)^{3} = 2^{3} \cdot a^{\frac{1}{4} \cdot 3} = 8a^{\frac{3}{4}}$

d. $\left(27y^{-\frac{9}{10}}\right)^{-\frac{1}{3}} = 27^{-\frac{1}{3}} \cdot y^{-\frac{9}{10}\left(-\frac{1}{3}\right)}$

$$= \frac{y^{\frac{3}{10}}}{27^{\frac{1}{3}}} = \frac{y^{\frac{3}{10}}}{3}$$ Multiply the exponents of y and reduce the fraction to $\dfrac{3}{10}$.

e. $(-36)^{-\frac{1}{2}} = \dfrac{1}{(-36)^{\frac{1}{2}}}$ This is not a real number because $(-36)^{\frac{1}{2}} = \sqrt{-36}$ is not real.

f. $9^{\frac{2}{4}} = 9^{\frac{1}{2}} = 3$ The exponent can be reduced as long as the expression is real.

g. $\left(\dfrac{49x^{6}y^{-2}}{z^{-4}}\right)^{\frac{1}{2}} = \dfrac{49^{\frac{1}{2}}x^{3}y^{-1}}{z^{-2}}$ **Study this example carefully.**

$$= \frac{7x^{3}z^{2}}{y}$$

Example 5 shows how to use fractional exponents to simplify rather complicated looking radical expressions. The results may seem surprising at first.

Example 5: Simplifying Radical Notation by Changing to Exponential Notation

Each radical expression is changed to an equivalent expression with exponential notation and simplified in this form. Then, the result is returned to radical notation.

a. $\sqrt[4]{\sqrt[3]{x}} = \left(\sqrt[3]{x}\right)^{\frac{1}{4}} = \left(x^{\frac{1}{3}}\right)^{\frac{1}{4}} = x^{\frac{1}{12}} = \sqrt[12]{x}$ Note that $\dfrac{1}{3} \cdot \dfrac{1}{4} = \dfrac{1}{12}$.

b. $\sqrt[3]{a}\sqrt{a} = a^{\frac{1}{3}} \cdot a^{\frac{1}{2}} = a^{\frac{1}{3}+\frac{1}{2}} = a^{\frac{2}{6}+\frac{3}{6}} = a^{\frac{5}{6}} = \sqrt[6]{a^5}$

c. $\dfrac{\sqrt{x^3}\sqrt[3]{x^2}}{\sqrt[5]{x^2}} = \dfrac{x^{\frac{3}{2}} \cdot x^{\frac{2}{3}}}{x^{\frac{2}{5}}} = \dfrac{x^{\frac{3}{2}+\frac{2}{3}}}{x^{\frac{2}{5}}} = \dfrac{x^{\frac{13}{6}}}{x^{\frac{2}{5}}}$

$= x^{\frac{13}{6}-\frac{2}{5}} = x^{\frac{65}{30}-\frac{12}{30}} = x^{\frac{53}{30}}$

$= x^{\frac{30}{30}} \cdot x^{\frac{23}{30}} = x\sqrt[30]{x^{23}}$

Evaluating Roots with a TI-83 Plus Calculator (The $\boxed{\wedge}$ key)

The up arrow key (or caret key) $\boxed{\wedge}$ on the TI-83 Plus calculator (and most graphing calculators) is used to indicate exponents. By using this key, roots of real numbers can be calculated with up to nine digit accuracy. To set the number of decimal places you wish in any calculations, press the $\boxed{\text{MODE}}$ key and highlight the digit opposite the word **FLOAT** that indicates the desired accuracy. If no digit is highlighted, then the accuracy will be to nine decimal places (in some cases ten decimal places).

To Find the Value of $a^{\frac{m}{n}}$ with a Calculator

Step 1: *Enter the value of the base, a.*

Step 2: *Press the up arrow key* .

Step 3: *Enter the fractional exponent enclosed in parentheses.*
(This exponent may be positive or negative.)

Step 4: *Press* $\boxed{\text{ENTER}}$.

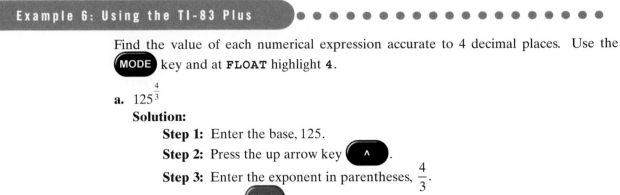

Find the value of each numerical expression accurate to 4 decimal places. Use the MODE key and at **FLOAT** highlight **4**.

a. $125^{\frac{4}{3}}$

Solution:

Step 1: Enter the base, 125.

Step 2: Press the up arrow key ⌃.

Step 3: Enter the exponent in parentheses, $\frac{4}{3}$.

Step 4: Press ENTER.

The display should read as follows:

```
                          TI-83 Plus
      125^(4/3)
                  625.0000
```

(**Note:** This particular result can be found by using our knowledge of roots as

follows: $125^{\frac{4}{3}} = \left(125^{\frac{1}{3}}\right)^4 = 5^4 = 625$.)

b. $36^{\frac{3}{5}}$

Solution:

Step 1: Enter the base, 36.

Step 2: Press the up arrow key ⌃.

Step 3: Enter the exponent in parentheses, $\frac{3}{5}$.

Step 4: Press ENTER.

The display should read as follows:

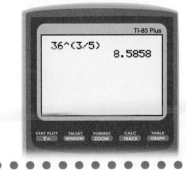

```
                          TI-83 Plus
      36^(3/5)
                  8.5858
```

Practice Problems

Simplify each of the following expressions. Leave the answers with rational exponents.

1. $64^{\frac{2}{3}}$ **2.** $x^{\frac{3}{4}} \cdot x^{\frac{1}{5}} \cdot x^{\frac{1}{2}}$ **3.** $\dfrac{x^{\frac{1}{6}} \cdot y^{\frac{1}{2}}}{x^{\frac{1}{3}} \cdot y^{\frac{1}{4}}}$ **4.** $\left(\dfrac{16x^{-\frac{1}{6}}}{x^{-\frac{2}{3}}}\right)^{\frac{1}{4}}$ **5.** $-81^{\frac{1}{4}}$

Simplify each radical expression and leave the answers in simplest radical form.

6. $\sqrt[4]{x} \cdot \sqrt{x}$ **7.** $\sqrt[5]{\sqrt[3]{a^2}}$ **8.** $\dfrac{\sqrt{36x}}{\sqrt[3]{8x^2}}$

Use a TI-83 Plus calculator to find the following values accurate to 4 decimal places.

9. $128^{\frac{1}{5}}$ **10.** $100^{-\frac{1}{4}}$

6.2 Exercises

Simplify each numerical expression in Exercises 1 – 25.

1. $9^{\frac{1}{2}}$ **2.** $121^{\frac{1}{2}}$ **3.** $100^{-\frac{1}{2}}$ **4.** $25^{-\frac{1}{2}}$ **5.** $-64^{\frac{3}{2}}$

6. $(-64)^{\frac{3}{2}}$ **7.** $\left(-\dfrac{4}{25}\right)^{\frac{1}{2}}$ **8.** $-\left(\dfrac{4}{25}\right)^{\frac{1}{2}}$ **9.** $\left(\dfrac{9}{49}\right)^{\frac{1}{2}}$ **10.** $\left(\dfrac{225}{144}\right)^{\frac{1}{2}}$

11. $(-64)^{\frac{1}{3}}$ **12.** $64^{\frac{2}{3}}$ **13.** $(-125)^{\frac{1}{3}}$ **14.** $(-216)^{-\frac{1}{3}}$ **15.** $8^{-\frac{2}{3}}$

16. $\left(\dfrac{8}{125}\right)^{-\frac{1}{3}}$ **17.** $-\left(\dfrac{16}{81}\right)^{-\frac{3}{4}}$ **18.** $\left(-\dfrac{1}{32}\right)^{\frac{2}{5}}$ **19.** $\left(\dfrac{27}{64}\right)^{\frac{2}{3}}$ **20.** $3 \cdot 16^{-\frac{3}{4}}$

21. $2 \cdot 25^{-\frac{1}{2}}$ **22.** $-100^{-\frac{3}{2}}$ **23.** $\left[(-27)^{\frac{2}{3}}\right]^{-2}$ **24.** $\left[\left(\dfrac{1}{32}\right)^{\frac{2}{5}}\right]^{-3}$ **25.** $-49^{-\frac{5}{2}}$

In Exercises 26 – 40, use a calculator to find the value of each numerical expression accurate to 4 decimal places.

26. $25^{\frac{2}{3}}$ **27.** $81^{\frac{7}{4}}$ **28.** $100^{\frac{7}{2}}$ **29.** $100^{\frac{1}{3}}$ **30.** $250^{\frac{5}{6}}$

31. $18^{-\frac{3}{2}}$ **32.** $24^{-\frac{3}{4}}$ **33.** $2000^{\frac{2}{3}}$ **34.** $\sqrt[4]{0.0025}$ **35.** $\sqrt[4]{3600}$

36. $\sqrt[5]{35.4}$ **37.** $\sqrt[10]{1.8}$ **38.** $\sqrt[6]{4500}$ **39.** $\sqrt[9]{72}$ **40.** $\sqrt[5]{0.00032}$

Answers to Practice Problems: 1. 16 **2.** $x^{\frac{29}{20}}$ **3.** $\dfrac{y^{\frac{1}{4}}}{x^{\frac{1}{6}}}$ **4.** $2x^{\frac{1}{8}}$ **5.** -3 **6.** $\sqrt[4]{x^3}$ **7.** $\sqrt[15]{a^2}$ **8.** $\dfrac{3\sqrt[6]{x^5}}{x}$ **9.** 2.6390 **10.** 0.3162

Simplify each algebraic expression in Exercises 41 – 77. Leave the answers in rational exponent form.

41. $\left(2x^{\frac{1}{3}}\right)^3$ **42.** $\left(3x^{\frac{1}{2}}\right)^4$ **43.** $\left(9a^4\right)^{\frac{1}{2}}$ **44.** $\left(16a^3\right)^{-\frac{1}{4}}$ **45.** $8x^2 \cdot x^{\frac{1}{2}}$

46. $3x^3 \cdot x^{\frac{2}{3}}$ **47.** $5a^2 \cdot a^{-\frac{1}{3}} \cdot a^{\frac{1}{2}}$ **48.** $a^{\frac{2}{3}} \cdot a^{-\frac{3}{5}} \cdot a^0$ **49.** $\dfrac{a^2}{a^{\frac{2}{5}}}$ **50.** $\dfrac{x^{\frac{3}{4}}}{x^{\frac{1}{6}}}$

51. $\dfrac{x^{\frac{2}{5}}}{x^{-\frac{1}{10}}}$ **52.** $\dfrac{a^{\frac{2}{3}}}{a^{\frac{1}{9}}}$ **53.** $\dfrac{a^{\frac{1}{2}}}{a^{-\frac{2}{3}}}$ **54.** $\dfrac{a^{\frac{3}{4}} \cdot a^{\frac{1}{8}}}{a^2}$ **55.** $\dfrac{a^{\frac{1}{2}} \cdot a^{-\frac{3}{4}}}{a^{-\frac{1}{2}}}$

56. $\dfrac{x^{\frac{2}{3}} \cdot x^{\frac{4}{3}}}{x^2}$ **57.** $\dfrac{x^{\frac{2}{3}}y}{x^2 y^{\frac{1}{2}}}$ **58.** $\dfrac{a^{\frac{3}{2}}b^{\frac{4}{5}}}{a^{-\frac{1}{2}}b^2}$ **59.** $\dfrac{a^{\frac{3}{4}}b^{-\frac{1}{3}}}{a^{\frac{3}{2}}b^{\frac{1}{6}}}$ **60.** $\left(2x^{\frac{1}{2}}y^{\frac{1}{3}}\right)^3$

61. $\left(4x^{-\frac{3}{4}}y^{\frac{1}{5}}\right)^{-2}$ **62.** $\left(a^{\frac{1}{2}}a^{\frac{1}{3}}\right)^6$ **63.** $\left(-x^3 y^6 z^{-6}\right)^{\frac{2}{3}}$ **64.** $\left(\dfrac{x^2 y^{-3}}{z^4}\right)^{-\frac{1}{2}}$

65. $\left(\dfrac{27a^3 b^6}{c^9}\right)^{-\frac{1}{3}}$ **66.** $\left(81a^{-8}b^2\right)^{-\frac{1}{4}}$ **67.** $\left(\dfrac{16a^{-4}b^3}{c^4}\right)^{\frac{3}{4}}$ **68.** $\left(\dfrac{-27a^2 b^3}{c^{-3}}\right)^{\frac{1}{3}}$

69. $\dfrac{\left(x^{\frac{1}{4}}y^{\frac{1}{2}}\right)^3}{x^{\frac{1}{2}}y^{\frac{1}{4}}}$ **70.** $\dfrac{\left(x^{\frac{1}{2}}y\right)^{-\frac{1}{3}}}{x^{\frac{2}{3}}y^{-1}}$ **71.** $\dfrac{\left(8x^2 y\right)^{-\frac{1}{3}}}{\left(5x^{\frac{1}{3}}y^{-\frac{1}{2}}\right)^2}$ **72.** $\dfrac{\left(25a^4 b^{-1}\right)^{\frac{1}{2}}}{\left(2a^{\frac{1}{5}}b^{\frac{3}{5}}\right)^3}$

73. $\left(\dfrac{5a^{-3}}{21b^2}\right)^{-1} \cdot \left(\dfrac{49a^4}{100b^{-8}}\right)^{-\frac{1}{2}}$ **74.** $\left(\dfrac{x^2 y^{\frac{1}{3}}}{x^{\frac{1}{2}}y^{\frac{3}{2}}}\right)^{\frac{1}{2}} \cdot \left(\dfrac{x^{-\frac{1}{2}}y^{\frac{2}{3}}}{x^{-1}y^{\frac{3}{4}}}\right)^2$

75. $\left(\dfrac{a^{-3}b^{\frac{1}{3}}}{a^{\frac{1}{2}}b}\right)^{\frac{1}{2}} \cdot \left(\dfrac{ab^{\frac{1}{2}}}{a^{-\frac{2}{3}}b^{-1}}\right)^{\frac{1}{2}}$ **76.** $\left(\dfrac{a^3 b^{-2}}{ab^4}\right)^{\frac{1}{6}} \cdot \left(\dfrac{a^{\frac{1}{5}}b^{\frac{1}{3}}}{a^{-\frac{1}{2}}}\right)^3$ **77.** $\dfrac{\left(27xy^2\right)^{\frac{1}{3}}}{\left(25x^{-\frac{1}{2}}y\right)^{\frac{1}{2}}} \cdot \dfrac{\left(x^{\frac{1}{2}}y\right)^{\frac{1}{6}}}{\left(16x^{\frac{1}{3}}y\right)^{\frac{1}{2}}}$

In Exercises 78 – 91, simplify each expression by first changing to an equivalent expression with rational exponents. Rewrite the answer in simplified radical form.

78. $\sqrt[3]{a} \cdot \sqrt{a}$ **79.** $\sqrt[3]{x^2} \cdot \sqrt[5]{x^3}$ **80.** $\dfrac{\sqrt[4]{y^3}}{\sqrt[6]{y}}$ **81.** $\dfrac{\sqrt[4]{x}}{\sqrt[3]{x^4}}$ **82.** $\dfrac{\sqrt[3]{x^2}\sqrt[5]{x^4}}{\sqrt{x^3}}$

83. $\dfrac{a\sqrt[4]{a}}{\sqrt[3]{a}\sqrt{a}}$ **84.** $\sqrt{\sqrt[3]{y}}$ **85.** $\sqrt[5]{\sqrt{x}}$ **86.** $\sqrt[3]{\sqrt[3]{x}}$ **87.** $\sqrt{\sqrt{a}}$

88. $\sqrt[15]{(7a)^5}$ **89.** $\left(\sqrt[4]{a^3b^6c}\right)^{12}$ **90.** $\sqrt[5]{\sqrt[4]{\sqrt[3]{x}}}$ **91.** $\left(\sqrt[3]{a^4bc^2}\right)^{15}$

Writing and Thinking About Mathematics

92. Is $\sqrt[5]{a}\cdot\sqrt{a}$ the same as $\sqrt[5]{a^2}$? Explain why or why not.

Hawkes Learning Systems: Intermediate Algebra

Rational Exponents

6.3

Arithmetic with Radicals

After completing this section, you will be able to:

1. *Perform arithmetic operations with radical expressions.*

2. *Rationalize the denominators of radicals.*

Addition and Subtraction with Radical Expressions

To find the sum $2x^2 + 3x^2 - 8x^2$, you can use the distributive property and write

$$2x^2 + 3x^2 - 8x^2 = (2 + 3 - 8)x^2$$
$$= -3x^2$$

Recall that the terms $2x^2$, $3x^2$, and $-8x^2$ are called **like terms** because each term contains the same variable expression, x^2. Similarly,

$$2\sqrt{5} + 3\sqrt{5} - 8\sqrt{5} = (2 + 3 - 8)\sqrt{5}$$
$$= -3\sqrt{5}$$

and $2\sqrt{5}$, $3\sqrt{5}$, and $-8\sqrt{5}$ are called **like radicals** because each term contains the same radical expression, $\sqrt{5}$. The terms $2\sqrt{3}$ and $2\sqrt{7}$ are not like radicals because the radical expressions are not the same, and neither expression can be simplified. Therefore, a sum such as

$$2\sqrt{3} + 2\sqrt{7}$$

cannot be simplified. That is, the terms cannot be combined.

In some cases, radicals that are not like radicals can be simplified, and the results may lead to like radicals. For example, $4\sqrt{12}$, $\sqrt{75}$, and $-\sqrt{108}$ are not like radicals. However, simplification of each radical allows the sum of these radicals to be found as follows:

$$4\sqrt{12} + \sqrt{75} - \sqrt{108} = 4\sqrt{4 \cdot 3} + \sqrt{25 \cdot 3} - \sqrt{36 \cdot 3}$$
$$= 4 \cdot 2\sqrt{3} + 5\sqrt{3} - 6\sqrt{3}$$
$$= (8 + 5 - 6)\sqrt{3}$$
$$= 7\sqrt{3}$$

423

Example 1: Radicals with Positive Variables

Perform the indicated operation and simplify, if possible. Assume that all variables are positive.

a. $\sqrt{32x} + \sqrt{18x}$

Solution: $\sqrt{32x} + \sqrt{18x} = \sqrt{16 \cdot 2x} + \sqrt{9 \cdot 2x}$

$$= 4\sqrt{2x} + 3\sqrt{2x}$$

$$= 7\sqrt{2x}$$

b. $\sqrt{12} + \sqrt{18} + \sqrt{27}$

Solution: $\sqrt{12} + \sqrt{18} + \sqrt{27} = \sqrt{4 \cdot 3} + \sqrt{9 \cdot 2} + \sqrt{9 \cdot 3}$

$$= 2\sqrt{3} + 3\sqrt{2} + 3\sqrt{3}$$

$$= 5\sqrt{3} + 3\sqrt{2}$$

Note that $\sqrt{3}$ and $\sqrt{2}$ are **not** like radicals. Therefore, the last expression cannot be simplified.

c. $\sqrt[3]{5x} - \sqrt[3]{40x}$

Solution: $\sqrt[3]{5x} - \sqrt[3]{40x} = \sqrt[3]{5x} - \sqrt[3]{8 \cdot 5x}$

$$= \sqrt[3]{5x} - 2\sqrt[3]{5x}$$

$$= (1-2)\sqrt[3]{5x}$$

$$= -\sqrt[3]{5x}$$

d. $x\sqrt{4y^3} - 5\sqrt{x^2 y^3}$

Solution: $x\sqrt{4y^3} - 5\sqrt{x^2 y^3} = x\sqrt{4y^2}\sqrt{y} - 5\sqrt{x^2 y^2}\sqrt{y}$

$$= 2xy\sqrt{y} - 5xy\sqrt{y}$$

$$= -3xy\sqrt{y}$$

Multiplication with Radical Expressions

To find a product such as $\left(\sqrt{3}+5\right)\left(\sqrt{3}-7\right)$ treat the two expressions as two binomials and multiply just as with polynomials. For example, using the FOIL method, we get

$$\left(\sqrt{3}+5\right)\left(\sqrt{3}-7\right) = \left(\sqrt{3}\right)^2 + 5\sqrt{3} - 7\sqrt{3} + 5(-7)$$

$$= \left(\sqrt{3}\right)^2 + 5\sqrt{3} - 7\sqrt{3} - 35$$

$$= 3 - 2\sqrt{3} - 35$$

$$= -32 - 2\sqrt{3}$$

Example 2: Multiplication ●

Multiply and simplify the following expressions.

a. $\left(3\sqrt{7}-2\right)\left(\sqrt{7}+3\right)$

Solution: $\left(3\sqrt{7}-2\right)\left(\sqrt{7}+3\right)=3\left(\sqrt{7}\right)^2-2\sqrt{7}+9\sqrt{7}-2(3)$

$$=21-2\sqrt{7}+9\sqrt{7}-6$$

$$=21-6-2\sqrt{7}+9\sqrt{7}$$

$$=15+7\sqrt{7}$$

b. $\left(\sqrt{6}+\sqrt{2}\right)^2$

Solution: $\left(\sqrt{6}+\sqrt{2}\right)^2=\left(\sqrt{6}\right)^2+2\sqrt{6}\sqrt{2}+\left(\sqrt{2}\right)^2$ $(a+b)^2=a^2+2ab+b^2$

$$=6+2\sqrt{12}+2$$

$$=8+2\sqrt{4}\sqrt{3}$$

$$=8+4\sqrt{3}$$

c. $\left(\sqrt{2x}+5\right)\left(\sqrt{2x}-5\right)$

Solution: $\left(\sqrt{2x}+5\right)\left(\sqrt{2x}-5\right)=\left(\sqrt{2x}\right)^2-(5)^2$ $(a+b)(a-b)=a^2-b^2$

$$=2x-25$$

● ●

Rationalizing Denominators of Rational Expressions

We discussed **rationalizing the denominator** in Section 6.1. In that discussion, all denominators were single terms. If the denominator has a radical expression with **a sum or difference involving square roots** such as

$$\frac{2}{4-\sqrt{2}} \quad \text{or} \quad \frac{12}{3+\sqrt{5}}$$

then the method of rationalizing the denominator must be changed. In this situation, think of the denominator in the form of $a-b$ or $a+b$. Thus,

if $4-\sqrt{2}=a-b$ then $4+\sqrt{2}=a+b$,

and if $3+\sqrt{5}=a+b$, then $3-\sqrt{5}=a-b$.

The two expressions $(a-b)$ and $(a+b)$ are called **conjugates** of each other, and the product $(a-b)(a+b)$ results in the difference of two squares.

$$(a-b)(a+b)=a^2-b^2$$

Thus, even if either a or b (or both) is a square root, the difference of the squares will not contain a square root. With this in mind, we can proceed as follows to rationalize a denominator with square roots.

Rationalizing Denominators with Sums or Differences of Square Roots

1. *If the denominator is of the form a − b, multiply both the numerator and denominator by its conjugate a + b.*

2. *If the denominator is of the form a + b, multiply both the numerator and denominator by its conjugate a − b.*

In either case, the new denominator becomes

$$a^2 - b^2, \text{ the difference of two squares}$$

and this denominator is a rational number or a rational expression.

Example 3: Rationalization

Simplify the following expressions by rationalizing the denominators.

a. $\dfrac{2}{4-\sqrt{2}}$

Solution: Multiply the numerator and denominator by $4+\sqrt{2}$.

$$\frac{2}{4-\sqrt{2}} = \frac{2\left(4+\sqrt{2}\right)}{\left(4-\sqrt{2}\right)\left(4+\sqrt{2}\right)} \qquad \text{If } a-b=4-\sqrt{2} \text{ , then } a+b=4+\sqrt{2} \text{ .}$$

$$= \frac{2\left(4+\sqrt{2}\right)}{4^2-\left(\sqrt{2}\right)^2} \qquad \text{The denominator is the difference of two squares.}$$

$$= \frac{2\left(4+\sqrt{2}\right)}{16-2} \qquad \text{The denominator is a rational number.}$$

$$= \frac{2\left(4+\sqrt{2}\right)}{14} = \frac{4+\sqrt{2}}{7} \qquad \text{Note that the numerator is now irrational. However, this is generally preferred to having an irrational denominator.}$$

b. $\dfrac{31}{6+\sqrt{5}}$

Solution: Multiply the numerator and denominator by $6-\sqrt{5}$.

$$\frac{31}{6+\sqrt{5}} = \frac{31\left(6-\sqrt{5}\right)}{\left(6+\sqrt{5}\right)\left(6-\sqrt{5}\right)}$$

$$= \frac{31\left(6-\sqrt{5}\right)}{36-5}$$

$$= \frac{31\left(6-\sqrt{5}\right)}{31} = 6-\sqrt{5}$$

c. $\dfrac{1}{\sqrt{7}-\sqrt{2}}$

Solution: Multiply the numerator and denominator by $\sqrt{7}+\sqrt{2}$.

$$\frac{1}{\sqrt{7}-\sqrt{2}} = \frac{1\left(\sqrt{7}+\sqrt{2}\right)}{\left(\sqrt{7}-\sqrt{2}\right)\left(\sqrt{7}+\sqrt{2}\right)}$$

$$= \frac{\left(\sqrt{7}+\sqrt{2}\right)}{7-2}$$

$$= \frac{\sqrt{7}+\sqrt{2}}{5}$$

d. $\dfrac{6}{1-\sqrt{x}}$

Solution: $\dfrac{6}{1-\sqrt{x}} = \dfrac{6\left(1+\sqrt{x}\right)}{\left(1-\sqrt{x}\right)\left(1+\sqrt{x}\right)}$

$$= \frac{6\left(1+\sqrt{x}\right)}{1-x}$$

e. $\dfrac{x-y}{\sqrt{x}-\sqrt{y}}$

Solution: $\dfrac{x-y}{\sqrt{x}-\sqrt{y}} = \dfrac{\left(x-y\right)\left(\sqrt{x}+\sqrt{y}\right)}{\left(\sqrt{x}-\sqrt{y}\right)\left(\sqrt{x}+\sqrt{y}\right)}$

$$= \frac{\cancel{\left(x-y\right)}\left(\sqrt{x}+\sqrt{y}\right)}{\cancel{\left(x-y\right)}}$$

$$= \sqrt{x}+\sqrt{y}$$

Evaluating Radical Expressions with a Calculator

In Sections 6.1 and 6.2, we showed how to use a TI-83 Plus calculator to evaluate expressions in radical form and in exponential form. These same basic techniques are used to evaluate numerical expressions that contain sums, differences, products, and quotients of radicals. Be careful to use parentheses to ensure that the rules for order of operations are maintained. In particular, sums and differences in numerators and denominators of fractions must be enclosed in parentheses.

Example 4: Using a Calculator

Use a TI-83 Plus calculator to evaluate each expression accurate to 4 decimal places.

a. $3 + 2\sqrt{5}$

b. $\left(\sqrt{2} + 5\right)\left(\sqrt{2} - 5\right)$

c. $\dfrac{3}{\sqrt{6} - \sqrt{2}}$

Solutions:

The displays should appear as follows:

a. $3 + 2\sqrt{5}$

```
TI-83 Plus
3+2√(5)
            7.4721
```

b. $\left(\sqrt{2} + 5\right)\left(\sqrt{2} - 5\right)$

```
TI-83 Plus
(√(2)+5)(√(2)-5)
           -23.0000
```

Note that the right parenthesis on 2 must be included. Otherwise, the calculator will interpret the expression as $\sqrt{(2 + 5)}$ $\left(\text{or } \sqrt{7}\right)$ which is not intended.

c. $\dfrac{3}{\sqrt{6} - \sqrt{2}}$

```
TI-83 Plus
3/(√(6)-√(2))
           2.8978
```

Count the parentheses in pairs.

Practice Problems

Simplify the following expressions. Assume that all variables are positive.

1. $2\sqrt{10} - 6\sqrt{10}$

2. $\sqrt{5} + \sqrt{45} - \sqrt{15}$

3. $\sqrt{8x} - 3\sqrt{2x} + \sqrt{18x}$

4. $\sqrt[3]{x^5} + x\sqrt[3]{27x^2}$

5. $\sqrt[3]{x^3 y^6 z} + 4xy^2 \sqrt[3]{z}$

6. $\left(\sqrt{6} - 2\sqrt{5}\right)\left(\sqrt{6} + \sqrt{5}\right)$

7. $\dfrac{4}{\sqrt{2} + \sqrt{6}}$

8. $\dfrac{x - 5}{\sqrt{x} - \sqrt{5}}$

9. $\left(\sqrt{3} + \sqrt{2}\right)^2$

10. $\left(3 + \sqrt{2}\right)^2$

11. $\left(\sqrt{3} + \sqrt{8}\right)^2$

12. $\dfrac{\sqrt{5} - 3\sqrt{2}}{\sqrt{6} + \sqrt{10}}$

6.3 Exercises

Perform the indicated operations and simplify for Exercises 1 – 45. Assume that all variables are positive.

1. $\sqrt{2} - 7\sqrt{2}$

2. $6\sqrt{11} + 4\sqrt{11} - 3\sqrt{11}$

3. $2\sqrt{x} + 4\sqrt{x} - \sqrt{x}$

4. $8\sqrt[3]{xy} - 3\sqrt[3]{xy} + 4\sqrt[3]{xy}$

5. $9\sqrt[3]{7x^2} - 4\sqrt[3]{7x^2} - 8\sqrt[3]{7x^2}$

6. $12\sqrt[3]{4x} - 10\sqrt[3]{4x} - 6\sqrt[3]{4x}$

7. $2\sqrt{3} + 4\sqrt{12}$

8. $2\sqrt{48} - 3\sqrt{75}$

9. $2\sqrt{18} + \sqrt{8} - 3\sqrt{50}$

10. $2\sqrt{12} + \sqrt{72} - \sqrt{75}$

11. $5\sqrt{48} + 2\sqrt{45} - 3\sqrt{20}$

12. $3\sqrt{28} - \sqrt{63} + 8\sqrt{10}$

13. $2\sqrt{96} + \sqrt{147} - \sqrt{150}$

14. $7\sqrt{12x} - 4\sqrt{27x} + \sqrt{108x}$

15. $6\sqrt{45x^3} + \sqrt{80x^3} - \sqrt{20x^3}$

16. $2\sqrt{18xy^2} + \sqrt{8xy^2} - 3y\sqrt{50x}$

17. $\sqrt{125} - \sqrt{63} + 3\sqrt{45}$

18. $5\sqrt{48} + 2\sqrt{24} - \sqrt{75}$

19. $\sqrt{32x} + 7\sqrt{12x} + \sqrt{98x}$

20. $\sqrt[3]{81x^2} - 5\sqrt[3]{48x^2} - 5\sqrt[3]{24x^2}$

21. $\sqrt[3]{16} - 5\sqrt[3]{54} + 2\sqrt[3]{40}$

22. $x\sqrt{y} + \sqrt{x^2 y} - \sqrt{xy^3}$

23. $x\sqrt{2x^3} - 3\sqrt{8x^5} + x\sqrt{72x^3}$

24. $x\sqrt{y^3} - 2\sqrt{x^2 y^3} - y\sqrt{x^2 y}$

Answers to Practice Problems: 1. $-4\sqrt{10}$ **2.** $4\sqrt{5} - \sqrt{15}$ **3.** $2\sqrt{2x}$ **4.** $4x\sqrt[3]{x^2}$ **5.** $5xy^2\sqrt[3]{z}$ **6.** $-4 - \sqrt{30}$

7. $\sqrt{6} - \sqrt{2}$ **8.** $\sqrt{x} + \sqrt{5}$ **9.** $5 + 2\sqrt{6}$ **10.** $11 + 6\sqrt{2}$ **11.** $11 + 4\sqrt{6}$ **12.** $\dfrac{5\sqrt{2} + 6\sqrt{3} - 6\sqrt{5} - \sqrt{30}}{4}$

25. $x\sqrt{9x^3y^2} - 5x^2\sqrt{xy^2} + 6y\sqrt{x^5}$

26. $(3+\sqrt{2})(5-\sqrt{2})$

27. $(\sqrt{3x}-8)(\sqrt{3x}-1)$

28. $(2\sqrt{7}+4)(\sqrt{7}-3)$

29. $(6+\sqrt{2x})(4+\sqrt{2x})$

30. $(5\sqrt{3}-2)(2\sqrt{3}-7)$

31. $(\sqrt{6}+2)(\sqrt{6}-2)$

32. $(3\sqrt{2}+\sqrt{5})(\sqrt{2}+\sqrt{5})$

33. $(\sqrt{5}+2\sqrt{2})^2$

34. $(2\sqrt{5}+3\sqrt{2})^2$

35. $(3\sqrt{5}+4\sqrt{3})(3\sqrt{5}-4\sqrt{3})$

36. $(\sqrt{2}+\sqrt{3})(\sqrt{5}-\sqrt{3})$

37. $(\sqrt{6}+\sqrt{5})(\sqrt{6}-\sqrt{2})$

38. $(3\sqrt{7}+\sqrt{5})(3\sqrt{7}-\sqrt{5})$

39. $(\sqrt{11}+\sqrt{3})(\sqrt{11}-2\sqrt{3})$

40. $(\sqrt{x}+\sqrt{6})(\sqrt{x}-3\sqrt{6})$

41. $(7\sqrt{x}+\sqrt{2})(7\sqrt{x}-\sqrt{2})$

42. $(\sqrt{x}+5\sqrt{y})^2$

43. $(3\sqrt{x}+\sqrt{y})^2$

44. $(4\sqrt{x}+3\sqrt{y})(\sqrt{x}-3\sqrt{y})$

45. $(2\sqrt{2x}+\sqrt{y})(3\sqrt{2x}+2\sqrt{y})$

In Exercises 46 – 60, rationalize the denominator and simplify if possible.

46. $\dfrac{1}{\sqrt{2}+1}$

47. $\dfrac{3}{\sqrt{3}-5}$

48. $\dfrac{\sqrt{3}}{\sqrt{5}-4}$

49. $\dfrac{\sqrt{6}}{\sqrt{7}+3}$

50. $\dfrac{2}{\sqrt{2}+\sqrt{3}}$

51. $\dfrac{8}{\sqrt{5}-\sqrt{3}}$

52. $\dfrac{\sqrt{5}}{\sqrt{7}-\sqrt{3}}$

53. $\dfrac{\sqrt{10}}{\sqrt{5}-2\sqrt{2}}$

54. $\dfrac{2-\sqrt{6}}{\sqrt{6}-3}$

55. $\dfrac{7+2\sqrt{5}}{7-\sqrt{5}}$

56. $\dfrac{\sqrt{3}+\sqrt{7}}{\sqrt{3}-\sqrt{7}}$

57. $\dfrac{2\sqrt{3}+\sqrt{2}}{\sqrt{3}-\sqrt{2}}$

58. $\dfrac{2\sqrt{x}-y}{\sqrt{x}-y}$

59. $\dfrac{x+2\sqrt{y}}{x-2\sqrt{y}}$

60. $\dfrac{y}{\sqrt{x}+\sqrt{2y}}$

In Exercises 61 – 70, rationalize the numerator (by using the same technique used to rationalize the denominator in Exercises 46 – 60) and simplify if possible.

61. $\dfrac{\sqrt{7}-2}{3}$

62. $\dfrac{\sqrt{5}+1}{2}$

63. $\dfrac{\sqrt{15}+\sqrt{3}}{6}$

64. $\dfrac{\sqrt{10}-\sqrt{2}}{-8}$

65. $\dfrac{\sqrt{x}+\sqrt{5}}{x-5}$

66. $\dfrac{\sqrt{y}+\sqrt{2}}{y-2}$

67. $\dfrac{\sqrt{2y}-\sqrt{x}}{x}$

68. $\dfrac{3\sqrt{x}-y}{3x}$

69. $\dfrac{\sqrt{2+h}-\sqrt{2}}{h}$

70. $\dfrac{\sqrt{5+h}-\sqrt{5}}{h}$

In Exercises 71 – 80, use a calculator to find the value of each expression accurate to 5 decimal places.

71. $13 - \sqrt{75}$

72. $5 - \sqrt{67}$

73. $\sqrt{900} + \sqrt{2.56}$

74. $\sqrt{1600} - \sqrt{1.69}$

75. $(\sqrt{7} + 8)(\sqrt{7} - 8)$

76. $(\sqrt{3} + \sqrt{2})(\sqrt{5} - \sqrt{10})$

77. $(6\sqrt{8} + 5\sqrt{7})(3\sqrt{39} - 2\sqrt{27})$

78. $\dfrac{19}{35 - \sqrt{60}}$

79. $\dfrac{\sqrt{5}}{1 + 2\sqrt{5}}$

80. $\dfrac{\sqrt{10} - \sqrt{2}}{\sqrt{10} + \sqrt{2}}$

Writing and Thinking About Mathematics

81. One of the most studied and interesting visual and numerical concepts in algebra is the **Golden Ratio**. Ancient Greeks thought (and many people still do) that a rectangle was most aesthetically pleasing to the eye if the ratio of its length to its width is the Golden Ratio (about 1.618). In fact, the Parthenon, built by Greeks in the fifth century B.C. utilizes the Golden Ratio. A rectangle is "golden" if its length, l, and width, w, satisfy the equation $\dfrac{l}{w} = \dfrac{w}{l - w}$.

a. By letting $w = 1$ unit in the equation above, we get the equation $\dfrac{l}{1} = \dfrac{1}{l - 1}$.

Solve this equation for l and find the algebraic expression for the golden ratio (a positive number).

b. Suppose that an architect is constructing a building with a rectangular front that is to be 60 feet high. About how long should the front be if he wants the appearance of a golden rectangle?

c. Look at the two rectangles shown here. Which seems most pleasing to your eye? Measure the length and width of each rectangle and see if you chose the golden rectangle.

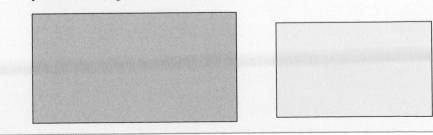

Hawkes Learning Systems: Intermediate Algebra

Addition and Subtraction of Radicals
Multiplication of Radicals

6.4 Functions with Radicals

Objectives

After completing this section, you will be able to:

1. Recognize radical functions.

2. Evaluate radical functions.

3. Find the domain and range of radical functions.

4. Graph radical functions.

The concept of functions is among the most important and useful ideas in all of mathematics. We introduced functions in Chapter 2 and used the function notation, $P(x)$ (read "P of x"), with polynomials in Chapter 4. In this section we will expand the function concept to include **radical functions** (functions with radicals). More functions will be discussed in Chapters 8 and 9. For review and easy reference, we restate the definitions of relations and functions and the vertical line test as stated in Chapter 2.

Relation

*A **relation** is a set of ordered pairs of real numbers.*

*The **domain**, **D**, of a relation is the set of all first coordinates in the relation.*

*The **range**, **R**, of a relation is the set of all second coordinates in the relation.*

Function

*A **function** is a relation in which each domain element has a unique range element.*

OR

*A **function** is a relation in which each first coordinate appears only once.*

OR

*A **function** is a relation in which no two ordered pairs have the same first coordinate.*

Vertical Line Test

*If **any** vertical line intersects the graph of a relation at more than one point, then the relation graphed is **not** a function.*

433

Evaluating Radical Functions

We have used the ordered pair notation (x, y) to represent points on the graphs of relations and functions. For example,

$y = 2x - 5$ represents a linear function and its graph is a straight line.

We define radical functions (functions with radical expressions) as follows.

Radical Function

*A **radical function** is a function of the form $y = \sqrt[n]{g(x)}$ in which the radicand contains a variable expression.*

*The **domain** of such a function depends on the index, n:*

1. *If n is an even number, the domain is the set of all x such that $g(x) \geq 0$.*

2. *If n is an odd number, the domain is the set of all real numbers, $(-\infty, \infty)$.*

Examples of radical functions are

$$y = 3\sqrt{x}, \quad f(x) = \sqrt{2x+3}, \quad y = \sqrt[3]{x-7}$$

The functions

$$y = \sqrt{2}x \quad \text{and} \quad f(x) = x^2 + \sqrt{3}$$

are **not** radical functions because the radicand does not contain the variable.

The function notation, $f(x)$ (read "f of x"), is very useful when evaluating a function for a particular value of x. For example,

$f(9)$ means to substitute 9 for x in the function.

Thus,

if $f(x) = \sqrt{x-5}$,

then $f(9) = \sqrt{9-5} = \sqrt{4} = 2$

We can use a calculator to find decimal approximations. Such approximations are particularly helpful when estimating the locations of points on a graph. For example,

if $f(x) = \sqrt{x-5}$, then $f(8) = \sqrt{3} \approx 1.7321$ and $f(25) = \sqrt{20} = 2\sqrt{5} \approx 4.4721$.

Example 1: Evaluating a Radical Function

Complete each table by finding each value of the function for the related value of x.

a. $f(x) = 3\sqrt{x}$

x	f(x)
0	?
4	?
6	?

b. $y = \sqrt[3]{x-7}$

x	y
7	?
6	?
−1	?

Solutions:

a.

x	f(x)
0	$3\sqrt{0} = 0$
4	$3\sqrt{4} = 3 \cdot 2 = 6$
6	$3\sqrt{6} \approx 7.3485$

with a calculator

b.

x	y
7	$\sqrt[3]{7-7} = \sqrt[3]{0} = 0$
6	$\sqrt[3]{6-7} = \sqrt[3]{-1} = -1$
−1	$\sqrt[3]{-1-7} = \sqrt[3]{-8} = -2$

Example 2: Domain of a Radical Function

Determine the domain of each radical function:

a. $y = \sqrt{2x+3}$ **b.** $f(x) = \sqrt[3]{x-5}$

Solutions:

a. $y = \sqrt{2x+3}$

Because the index is 2 (understood), an even number, the radicand must be nonnegative. Thus, we have

$$2x + 3 \geq 0$$

$$2x \geq -3$$

$$x \geq -\frac{3}{2}$$

The domain is the interval $\left[-\frac{3}{2}, \infty\right)$.

b. $f(x) = \sqrt[3]{x-5}$

Because the index is 3, an odd number, the radicand may be any real number. The domain is $(-\infty, \infty)$.

Graphing Radical Functions

To graph a radical function, we need to be aware of its domain and to plot at least a few points to see the nature of the resulting curve. Example 3 shows how to proceed, at least in the beginning, to graph the radical function $y = \sqrt{x+5}$.

Example 3: Graphing a Radical Function

Graph the function $y = \sqrt{x+5}$.
Solution:

For the domain we have
$$x + 5 \geq 0$$
$$x \geq -5$$

To see the nature of the graph we select a few values for x in the domain and find the corresponding values of y:

x	y
–5	0
–4	1
–3	$\sqrt{2} \approx 1.41$
0	$\sqrt{5} \approx 2.24$
4	3

Now we plot these points on a graph.

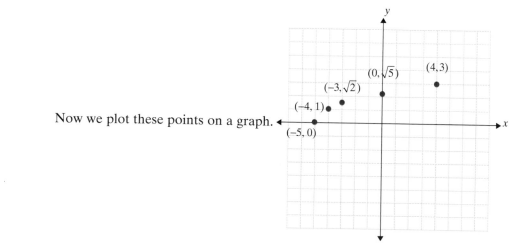

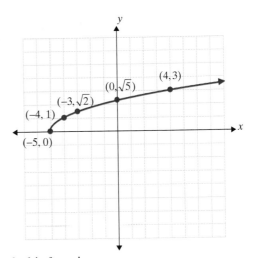

Next we complete the graph by drawing a smooth curve that passes through the selected points. This is the graph of the function.

To use a TI-83 Plus graphing calculator to graph this function,

Step 1. Press   Y=   and enter the function as follows:

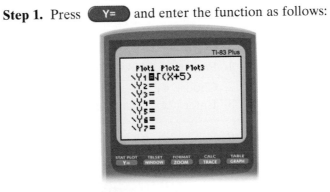

Step 2. Press **GRAPH** (You may need to adjust the **WINDOW**.)

The result will be the graph as shown here:

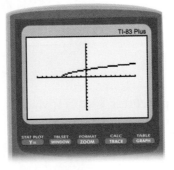

Example 4 shows how to use a TI-83 Plus graphing calculator to find a lot of points on the graph of a radical function and then how to graph the function.

Example 4: Using a TI-83 Plus to Graph a Radical Function

a. Use the **TABLE** feature of a TI-83 Plus graphing calculator to locate many points on the graph of the function $y = \sqrt[3]{2x-3}$.

b. Plot several points (approximately) on a graph and then connect them with a smooth curve.

c. Use a TI-83 Plus graphing calculator to graph the function.

Solutions:

a. Using the **TABLE** feature of a TI-83 Plus:

Step 1. Press **Y=** and enter the function as follows:

1. Press **MATH**
2. Choose **4 :** $\sqrt[3]{\ }$
3. Enter $(2x - 3)$ and press **ENTER**

Step 2. Press **TBLSET** (which is **2nd** **WINDOW**) and set the display as shown here:

Step 3. Press **TABLE** (which is **2nd** **GRAPH**) and the display will appear as follows:

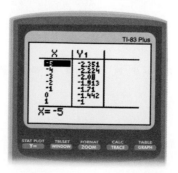

b. You may scroll up and down the display to find as many points as you like. A few are shown here to see the nature of the graph.

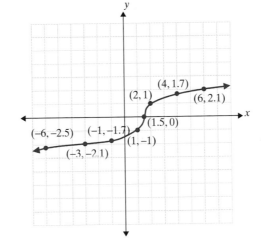

c. Press **GRAPH** and the display will appear with the curve as follows:

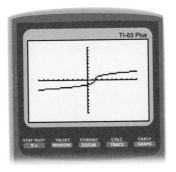

6.4 Exercises

In Exercises 1 – 4, write answers in both radical notation and decimal notation (accurate to 4 decimal places.)

1. Given $f(x) = \sqrt{2x+1}$, find
    a. $f(2)$ **b.** $f(4)$ **c.** $f(24.5)$ **d.** $f(1.5)$

2. Given $f(x) = \sqrt{5-3x}$, find
    a. $f(0)$ **b.** $f(-2)$ **c.** $f\left(-\dfrac{20}{3}\right)$ **d.** $f(-2.4)$

3. Given $g(x) = \sqrt[3]{x+6}$, find
    a. $g(21)$ **b.** $g(-7)$ **c.** $g(-14)$ **d.** $g(18)$

4. Given $h(x) = \sqrt[3]{4-x}$, find
    a. $h(4)$ **b.** $h(-4)$ **c.** $h(3.999)$ **d.** $h(-2.5)$

In Exercises 5 – 14, use interval notation to indicate the domain of each radical function.

5. $y = \sqrt{x+8}$ **6.** $y = \sqrt{2x-1}$ **7.** $y = \sqrt{2.5-5x}$ **8.** $y = \sqrt{1-3x}$

9. $f(x) = \sqrt[3]{x+4}$ **10.** $f(x) = \sqrt[3]{6x}$ **11.** $g(x) = \sqrt[4]{x}$ **12.** $g(x) = \sqrt[4]{7-x}$

13. $y = \sqrt[5]{4x-1}$ **14.** $y = \sqrt[5]{8+x}$

Match the function given in Exercises 15 – 20, with the graph of that function (A) – (F).

15. $y = \sqrt{x-2}$ **16.** $y = \sqrt{2-x}$ **17.** $y = -\sqrt{x-3}$

18. $y = -\sqrt{3-x}$ **19.** $y = \sqrt{x+4}$ **20.** $y = \sqrt{x-4}$

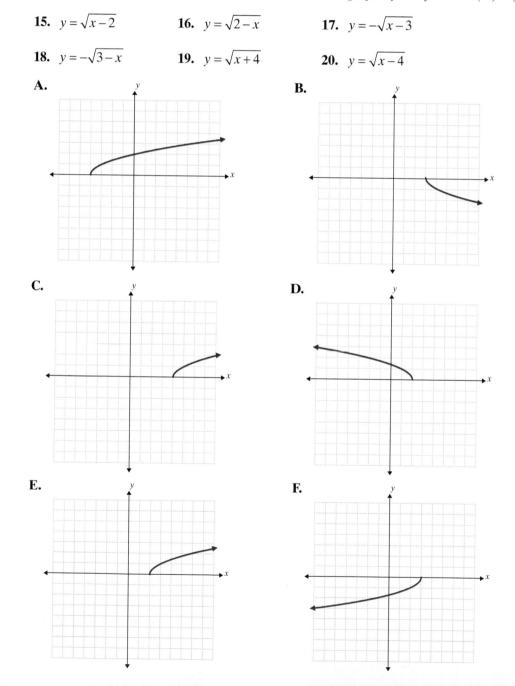

A.   **B.**

C.   **D.**

E.   **F.**

In Exercises 21 – 25, find and label at least 5 points on the graph of the function and then sketch the graph of the function.

21. $f(x) = \sqrt[3]{x+2}$ **22.** $g(x) = \sqrt[3]{x-6}$ **23.** $y = \sqrt[4]{x}$

24. $y = \sqrt[4]{2x+8}$ **25.** $y = \sqrt[5]{x-1}$

Use a TI-83 Plus graphing calculator to graph each of the functions in Exercises 26 – 35.

26. $y = 3\sqrt{x+2}$ **27.** $y = 2\sqrt{3-x}$ **28.** $f(x) = -\sqrt{x+2.5}$

29. $f(x) = -\sqrt{3-x}$ **30.** $y = -\sqrt[3]{x+2}$ **31.** $y = \sqrt[3]{3x+4}$

32. $g(x) = -\sqrt{2x}$ **33.** $g(x) = -\sqrt[4]{x+5}$ **34.** $y = \sqrt[4]{2x+6}$

35. $y = \sqrt[5]{x+7}$

Writing and Thinking About Mathematics

36. The graph of the radical function $f(x) = \sqrt{x}$ is shown with two values of x on the x-axis, 3 and $3 + h$.

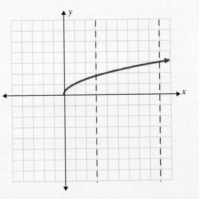

  a. Rationalize the numerator and simplify the resulting expression

$$\frac{f(3+h) - f(3)}{h} = \frac{\sqrt{3+h} - \sqrt{3}}{h}$$

  by multiplying both the numerator and denominator by the conjugate of the numerator.

  b. What do you think that this expression represents graphically?
    (**Hint:** Two points determine a line.)

  c. Using your result from part **b.**, what do you see happening on the graph if the value of h shrinks slowly to 0?

  d. Using your analysis from part **c.**, what happens to the value of your simplified expression in part **a.** and what do you think this value represents?

Hawkes Learning Systems: Intermediate Algebra

Functions with Radicals

Introduction to Complex Numbers

After completing this section, you will be able to:

1. *Identify the real parts and the imaginary parts of complex numbers.*

2. *Simplify square roots of negative numbers.*

3. *Add and subtract complex numbers.*

4. *Solve linear equations with complex numbers by setting the real and imaginary parts equal.*

One of the properties of real numbers is that the square of any real number is nonnegative. That is, for any real number x, $x^2 \geq 0$. The square roots of negative numbers, such as $\sqrt{-4}$ and $\sqrt{-5}$, are not real numbers. However, they can be defined by expanding the real number system into the system of **complex numbers**.

Complex numbers include all the real numbers and the even roots of negative numbers. In Chapter 7, we will see how these numbers occur as solutions to quadratic equations. At first such numbers seem to be somewhat impractical because they are difficult to picture in any type of geometric setting and they are not solutions to the types of word problems that are familiar. However, complex numbers do occur quite naturally in trigonometry and higher level mathematics and have practical applications in such fields as electrical engineering.

The first step in the development of complex numbers is to define $\sqrt{-1}$.

$\sqrt{-1}$

$$i = \sqrt{-1} \text{ and } i^2 = \left(\sqrt{-1}\right)^2 = -1$$

With this definition, the following definition of the square root of any negative number can be made.

$\sqrt{-a}$

$$\sqrt{-a} = \sqrt{a} \cdot \sqrt{-1} = \sqrt{a}\, i$$

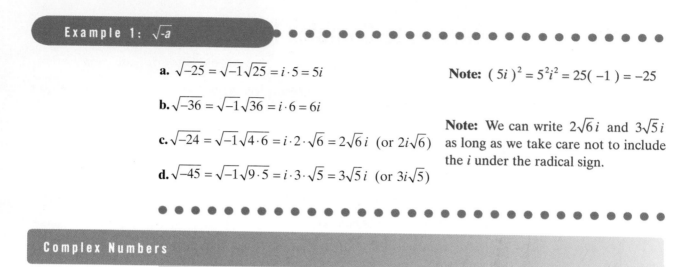

Example 1: $\sqrt{-a}$

a. $\sqrt{-25} = \sqrt{-1}\sqrt{25} = i \cdot 5 = 5i$

Note: $(5i)^2 = 5^2 i^2 = 25(-1) = -25$

b. $\sqrt{-36} = \sqrt{-1}\sqrt{36} = i \cdot 6 = 6i$

Note: We can write $2\sqrt{6}\,i$ and $3\sqrt{5}\,i$ as long as we take care not to include the i under the radical sign.

c. $\sqrt{-24} = \sqrt{-1}\sqrt{4 \cdot 6} = i \cdot 2 \cdot \sqrt{6} = 2\sqrt{6}\,i$ (or $2i\sqrt{6}$)

d. $\sqrt{-45} = \sqrt{-1}\sqrt{9 \cdot 5} = i \cdot 3 \cdot \sqrt{5} = 3\sqrt{5}\,i$ (or $3i\sqrt{5}$)

Complex Numbers

A **complex number** is a number of the form **a + bi**, where a and b are real numbers. a is called the **real part** and b is called the **imaginary part**.

If $b = 0$, then $a + bi = a + 0i = a$ is a **real number**.

If $a = 0$, then $a + bi = 0 + bi = bi$ is called a **pure imaginary number** (or an **imaginary number**).

Complex Number: **a + bi**

real part ⟶ ⟵ *imaginary part*

NOTES

The term "imaginary" is somewhat unfortunate. Complex numbers and imaginary numbers are no more "imaginary" than any other type of number. In fact, all the types of numbers that we have studied (whole numbers, integers, rational numbers, irrational numbers, and real numbers) are products of human imagination.

Example 2: Real and Imaginary Parts

Identify the real and imaginary parts of each complex number.

a. $4 - 2i$ — 4 is the real part; –2 is the imaginary part.

b. $\sqrt{5} + 3\sqrt{2}\,i$ — $\sqrt{5}$ is the real part; $3\sqrt{2}$ is the imaginary part.

c. $7 = 7 + 0i$ — 7 is the real part; 0 is the imaginary part. (Remember, if $b = 0$, the complex number is a real number.)

d. $-\sqrt{3}\,i = 0 - \sqrt{3}\,i$ — 0 is the real part; $-\sqrt{3}$ is the imaginary part. (If $a = 0$ and $b \neq 0$, then the complex number is a pure imaginary number.)

In general, if a is a real number, then we can write $a = a + 0i$. This means that a is a complex number. Thus, **every real number is a complex number**. Figure 6.1 illustrates the relationships among the various types of numbers we study.

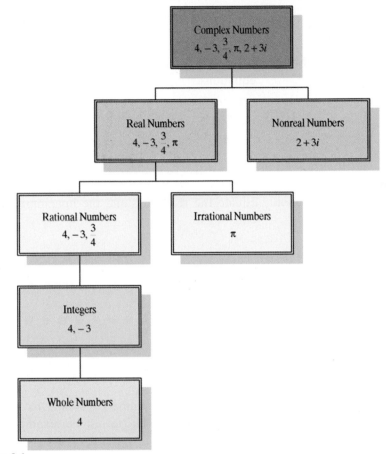

Figure 6.1

If two complex numbers are equal, then the real parts are equal and the imaginary parts are equal. For example, if

$$x + yi = 7 + 2i$$

then

$$x = 7 \quad \text{and} \quad y = 2$$

This relationship can be used to solve equations involving complex numbers.

Equality of Complex Numbers

For complex numbers $a + bi$ and $c + di$,

$$a + bi = c + di \quad \textit{if and only if} \quad a = c \textbf{ and } b = d.$$

Example 3: Solving Equations ● ● ● ● ● ● ● ● ● ● ● ● ● ● ● ● ●

Solve each equation for the unknown numbers.

a. $(x + 3) + 2yi = 7 - 6i$

Solution: Equate the real parts and the imaginary parts and solve the resulting equations.

$$x + 3 = 7 \quad \text{and} \quad 2y = -6$$
$$x = 4 \qquad\qquad y = -3$$

b. $2y + 3 - 8i = 9 + 4xi$

Solution: Equate the real parts and the imaginary parts and solve the resulting equations.

$$2y + 3 = 9 \quad \text{and} \quad -8 = 4x$$
$$2y = 6 \qquad\qquad -2 = x$$
$$y = 3$$

Addition and Subtraction with Complex Numbers

Adding and subtracting complex numbers is similar to adding and subtracting polynomials. That is, simply combine the like terms. For example,

$$(2 + 3i) + (9 - 8i) = 2 + 9 + 3i - 8i$$
$$= (2 + 9) + (3 - 8)i$$
$$= 11 - 5i$$

Similarly,

$$(5 - 2i) - (6 + 7i) = 5 - 2i - 6 - 7i$$
$$= (5 - 6) + (-2 - 7)i$$
$$= -1 - 9i$$

Addition and Subtraction with Complex Numbers

For complex numbers $a + bi$ and $c + di$

$$(a + bi) + (c + di) = (a + c) + (b + d)i$$

and

$$(a + bi) - (c + di) = (a - c) + (b - d)i$$

Example 4: Addition and Subtraction with Complex Numbers • • • • • • • •

Find each sum or difference as indicated.

a. $(6 - 2i) + (1 - 2i)$

Solution: $(6 - 2i) + (1 - 2i) = (6 + 1) + (-2 - 2)i$
$$= 7 - 4i$$

b. $\left(-8 - \sqrt{2}\,i\right) - \left(-8 + \sqrt{2}\,i\right)$

Solution: $\left(-8 - \sqrt{2}\,i\right) - \left(-8 + \sqrt{2}\,i\right) = -8 - \sqrt{2}\,i + 8 - \sqrt{2}\,i$
$$= -8 + 8 - \sqrt{2}\,i - \sqrt{2}\,i$$
$$= 0 + \left(-\sqrt{2} - \sqrt{2}\right)i$$
$$= -2\sqrt{2}\,i$$

NOTES When an expression with a radical is the coefficient of i, be sure that the radical sign does not cover the i. For example, in a case such as $-2\sqrt{2}i$ the square root symbol might extend too far. To avoid this error and confusion, you may choose to write the expression in the form $-2i\sqrt{2}$.

c. $\left(\sqrt{3} - 2i\right) + \left(1 + \sqrt{5}\,i\right)$

Solution: $\left(\sqrt{3} - 2i\right) + \left(1 + \sqrt{5}\,i\right) = \sqrt{3} + 1 - 2i + \sqrt{5}\,i$
$$= \left(\sqrt{3} + 1\right) + \left(\sqrt{5} - 2\right)i$$

Note: Here, the coefficients do not simplify, and the real part is $\sqrt{3} + 1$ and the imaginary part is $\sqrt{5} - 2$.

• •

Practice Problems

1. *Find the imaginary part and the real part of* $2 - \sqrt{39}i$.

Add or subtract as indicated. Simplify your answers.

2. $\left(-7 + \sqrt{3}i\right) + (5 - 2i)$

3. $(4 + i) - (5 + 2i)$

Solve for x and y.

4. $x + yi = \sqrt{2} - 7i$

5. $3y + (x - 7)i = -9 + 2i$

Answers to Practice Problems: 1. Imaginary part is $-\sqrt{39}$ and real part is 2 **2.** $-2 + \left(-2 + \sqrt{3}\right)i$ **3.** $-1 - i$
4. $x = \sqrt{2}$ and $y = -7$ **5.** $x = 9$ and $y = -3$

6.5 Exercises

Find the imaginary part and the real part of each of the complex numbers in Exercises 1 – 10.

1. $4 - 3i$ **2.** $6 + \sqrt{3}\,i$ **3.** $-11 + \sqrt{2}\,i$ **4.** $\dfrac{3}{4} + i$ **5.** $\dfrac{2}{3} + \sqrt{17}\,i$

6. $\dfrac{4}{7}i$ **7.** $\dfrac{4 + 7i}{5}$ **8.** $\dfrac{2 - i}{4}$ **9.** $\dfrac{3}{8}$ **10.** $-\sqrt{5} + \dfrac{\sqrt{2}}{2}\,i$

Simplify the radicals Exercises 11 – 24.

11. $\sqrt{-49}$ **12.** $\sqrt{-121}$ **13.** $-\sqrt{-64}$ **14.** $\sqrt{-169}$ **15.** $3\sqrt{147}$

16. $\sqrt{128}$ **17.** $2\sqrt{-150}$ **18.** $4\sqrt{-99}$ **19.** $-2\sqrt{-108}$ **20.** $2\sqrt{175}$

21. $\sqrt{242}$ **22.** $\sqrt{-192}$ **23.** $\sqrt{-1000}$ **24.** $\sqrt{-243}$

Find each sum or difference as indicated in Exercises 25 – 46.

25. $(2 + 3i) + (4 - i)$ **26.** $(7 - i) + (3 + 6i)$ **27.** $(4 + 5i) - (3 - 2i)$
28. $(-3 + 2i) - (6 + 2i)$ **29.** $-3i + (2 - 3i)$ **30.** $(7 + 5i) + (6 - 2i)$
31. $(8 + 9i) - (8 - 5i)$ **32.** $(-6 + i) - (2 + 3i)$ **33.** $\left(\sqrt{5} - 2i\right) + (3 - 4i)$
34. $(4 + 3i) - \left(\sqrt{2} + 3i\right)$ **35.** $\left(7 + \sqrt{6}\,i\right) + (-2 + i)$ **36.** $\left(\sqrt{11} + 2i\right) + (5 - 7i)$
37. $\left(\sqrt{3} + \sqrt{2}\,i\right) - \left(5 + \sqrt{2}\,i\right)$ **38.** $\left(\sqrt{5} + \sqrt{3}\,i\right) + (1 - i)$
39. $\left(5 + \sqrt{-25}\right) - \left(7 + \sqrt{-100}\right)$ **40.** $\left(1 + \sqrt{-36}\right) - \left(-4 - \sqrt{-49}\right)$
41. $\left(13 - 3\sqrt{-16}\right) + \left(-2 - 4\sqrt{-1}\right)$ **42.** $\left(7 + \sqrt{-9}\right) - \left(3 - 2\sqrt{-25}\right)$
43. $(4 + i) + (-3 - 2i) - (-1 - i)$ **44.** $(-2 - 3i) + (6 + i) - (2 + 5i)$
45. $(7 + 3i) + (2 - 4i) - (6 - 5i)$ **46.** $(-5 + 7i) + (4 - 2i) - (3 - 5i)$

Solve the equations in Exercises 47 – 60 for x and y.

47. $x + 3i = 6 - yi$ **48.** $2x - 8yi = -2 + 4yi$ **49.** $\sqrt{5} - 2i = y + xi$

50. $\dfrac{2}{3} - 2yi = 2x + \dfrac{4}{5}$ **51.** $\sqrt{2} + i - 3 = x + yi$ **52.** $\sqrt{5}\,i - 3 + 4i = x + yi$

53. $2x + 3 + 6i = 7 - (y + 2)i$ **54.** $x + yi + 8 = 2i + 4 - 3yi$
55. $x + 2i = 5 - yi - 3 - 4i$ **56.** $3x + 2 - 7i = i - 2yi + 5$
57. $2 + 3i + x = 5 - 7i + yi$ **58.** $11i - 2x + 4 = 10 - 3i + 2yi$
59. $2x - 2yi + 6 = 6i - x + 2$ **60.** $x + 4 - 3x + i = 8 + yi$

Writing and Thinking About Mathematics

61. Answer the following questions and give a brief explanation of your answer.
    a. Is every real number a complex number?
    b. Is every complex number a real number?

62. If you can, list 5 numbers that do and 5 numbers that do not fit each of the following categories.
    a. rational number
    b. integer
    c. real number
    d. pure imaginary number
    e. complex number
    f. irrational number

Hawkes Learning Systems: Intermediate Algebra

Complex Numbers

Multiplication and Division with Complex Numbers

After completing this section, you will be able to:

1. Multiply complex numbers.

2. Divide complex numbers.

3. Simplify powers of i.

Multiplication with Complex Numbers

The product of two complex numbers can be found using the same procedure as in multiplying two binomials. This is similar to multiplying binomial expressions with the sums and differences of radicals as we did in Section 6.3. **Remember that $i^2 = -1$.** For example,

$$(3 + 5i)(2 + i) = (3 + 5i)2 + (3 + 5i)i$$
$$= 6 + 10i + 3i + 5i^2$$
$$= 6 + 13i - 5 \qquad\qquad 5i^2 = 5(-1) = -5$$
$$= 1 + 13i$$

Multiplication with Complex Numbers

For complex numbers a + bi and c + di,

$$(a + bi)(c + di) = (ac - bd) + (bc + ad)i$$

This definition is an application of the FOIL method of multiplying two binomials. **Memorizing the definition is not recommended.** An easier approach is simply to use the FOIL method for each product and do as many steps as you can mentally. **Remember that $i^2 = -1$.**

Example 1: Multiplication with Complex Numbers

Find the following products.
a. $(6 + 3i)(2 - 7i)$
Solution: $(6 + 3i)(2 - 7i) = 12 + 6i - 42i - 21i^2$
$$= 12 - 36i + 21$$
$$= 33 - 36i$$

b. $\left(\sqrt{2}-i\right)\left(\sqrt{2}-i\right)$

    Solution: $\left(\sqrt{2}-i\right)\left(\sqrt{2}-i\right) = \left(\sqrt{2}\right)^2 - \sqrt{2}\cdot i - \sqrt{2}\cdot i + i^2$

$$= 2 - 2\sqrt{2}\,i - 1$$

$$= 1 - 2\sqrt{2}\,i$$

c. $(-1+i)(2-i)$

    Solution: $(-1+i)(2-i) = -2 + 2i + i - i^2$

$$= -2 + 3i + 1$$

$$= -1 + 3i$$

● ●

Common Error

Remember that $\sqrt{a}\cdot\sqrt{b} = \sqrt{ab}$ only if a and b are nonnegative real numbers.

Applying this rule to negative real numbers can lead to an error. The error can be avoided by first changing the radicals to imaginary form.

<table>
<tr><td align="center">WRONG</td><td align="center">RIGHT</td></tr>
<tr><td align="center">$\sqrt{-6}\cdot\sqrt{-2} = \sqrt{12}$</td><td align="center">$\sqrt{-6}\cdot\sqrt{-2} = \sqrt{6}\,i\cdot\sqrt{2}\,i$</td></tr>
<tr><td align="center">$= \sqrt{4}\cdot\sqrt{3}$</td><td align="center">$= \sqrt{12}\,i^2$</td></tr>
<tr><td align="center">$= 2\sqrt{3}$</td><td align="center">$= 2\sqrt{3}\,(-1)$</td></tr>
<tr><td align="center"></td><td align="center">$= -2\sqrt{3}$</td></tr>
</table>

Division with Complex Numbers

The two complex numbers $a + bi$ and $a - bi$ are called **complex conjugates** or simply **conjugates** of each other. As the following steps show, **the product of two complex conjugates will always be a non-negative real number**.

$$(a + bi)(a - bi) = (a + bi)a + (a + bi)(-bi)$$
$$= a^2 + abi - abi - b^2i^2$$
$$= a^2 - b^2i^2$$
$$= a^2 + b^2$$

The resulting product, $a^2 + b^2$, is a real number, and it is non-negative since it is the sum of the squares of real numbers.

The form $a + bi$ is called the **standard form** of a complex number. The standard form allows easy identification of the real and imaginary parts. Thus,

$$\frac{1+3i}{5} = \frac{1}{5} + \frac{3}{5}i \text{ in standard form.}$$

The real part is $\dfrac{1}{5}$ and the imaginary part is $\dfrac{3}{5}$.

A fraction formed with complex numbers, such as $\dfrac{1+i}{2-3i}$, indicates division of the numerator by the denominator. However, we do not divide these numbers in the usual sense. The objective is to find an equivalent expression that is in standard form, $a + bi$.

To write the fraction $\dfrac{1+i}{2-3i}$ in standard form, multiply both the numerator and denominator by $2 + 3i$ and simplify. This will give a positive real number in the denominator.

$$\frac{1+i}{2-3i} = \frac{(1+i)(2+3i)}{(2-3i)(2+3i)} \qquad 2 + 3i \text{ is the conjugate of the denominator}$$

$$= \frac{2+2i+3i+3i^2}{2^2 - 6i + 6i - 3^2 i^2}$$

$$= \frac{2+5i-3}{2^2 + 3^2} = \frac{-1+5i}{13}$$

$$= -\frac{1}{13} + \frac{5}{13}i$$

To Write a Fraction with Complex Numbers in Standard Form

1. *Multiply both the numerator and denominator by the complex conjugate of the denominator.*
2. *Simplify the resulting products in both the numerator and denominator.*
3. *Write the simplified result in standard form.*

Remember the following special product. We restate it here to emphasize its importance.

$$(a + bi)(a - bi) = a^2 + b^2$$

Example 2: Division with Complex Numbers

Write the following fractions in standard form.

a. $\dfrac{4}{-1-5i}$

Solution: $\dfrac{4}{-1-5i} = \dfrac{4(-1+5i)}{(-1-5i)(-1+5i)}$

$$= \frac{-4+20i}{(-1)^2 + (5)^2}$$

$$= \frac{-4+20i}{26}$$

$$= -\frac{4}{26} + \frac{20}{26}i$$

$$= -\frac{2}{13} + \frac{10}{13}i$$

b. $\dfrac{\sqrt{3}+i}{\sqrt{3}-i}$

Solution: $\dfrac{\sqrt{3}+i}{\sqrt{3}-i}=\dfrac{\left(\sqrt{3}+i\right)\left(\sqrt{3}+i\right)}{\left(\sqrt{3}-i\right)\left(\sqrt{3}+i\right)}$

$$=\dfrac{3+2\sqrt{3}\,i+i^{2}}{\left(\sqrt{3}\right)^{2}-i^{2}}=\dfrac{2+2\sqrt{3}\,i}{3+1}$$

$$=\dfrac{2+2\sqrt{3}\,i}{4}=\dfrac{2}{4}+\dfrac{2\sqrt{3}\,i}{4}$$

$$=\dfrac{1}{2}+\dfrac{\sqrt{3}\,i}{2}$$

c. $\dfrac{6+i}{i}$

Solution: $\dfrac{6+i}{i}=\dfrac{(6+i)(-i)}{i(-i)}$ Since $i = 0 + i$ and $-i = 0 - i$, the number $-i$ is the conjugate of i.

$$=\dfrac{-6i-i^{2}}{-i^{2}}=\dfrac{-6i+1}{1}$$

$$=1-6i$$

d. $\dfrac{\sqrt{2}+i}{-\sqrt{2}+i}$

Solution: $\dfrac{\sqrt{2}+i}{-\sqrt{2}+i}=\dfrac{\left(\sqrt{2}+i\right)\left(-\sqrt{2}-i\right)}{\left(-\sqrt{2}+i\right)\left(-\sqrt{2}-i\right)}$

$$=\dfrac{-\left(\sqrt{2}\right)^{2}-\sqrt{2}\,i-\sqrt{2}\,i-i^{2}}{\left(-\sqrt{2}\right)^{2}-(i)^{2}}$$

$$=\dfrac{-2-2\sqrt{2}\,i+1}{2+1}=\dfrac{-1-2\sqrt{2}\,i}{3}$$

$$=-\dfrac{1}{3}-\dfrac{2\sqrt{2}}{3}\,i$$

● ●

Powers of *i*

The powers of *i* form an interesting pattern. Regardless of the particular integer exponent, there are only four possible values for any power of *i*:

$$i, \quad -1, \quad -i, \quad \text{and} \quad 1$$

The fact that these are the only four possibilities for powers of i becomes apparent from studying the following powers.

$$i^1 = i$$
$$i^2 = -1$$
$$i^3 = i^2 \cdot i = -1 \cdot i = -i$$
$$i^4 = i^2 \cdot i^2 = (-1)(-1) = 1$$
$$i^5 = i^4 \cdot i = +1 \cdot i = i$$
$$i^6 = i^4 \cdot i^2 = (1)(-1) = -1$$
$$i^7 = i^4 \cdot i^3 = (1)(-i) = -i$$
$$i^8 = i^4 \cdot i^4 = (1)(1) = 1$$

Higher powers of i can be simplified by using the fact that when i is raised to a power that is a multiple of 4, the result is 1. Thus, if n is a positive integer, then

$$i^{4n} = (i^4)^n = 1^n = 1$$
$$i^{4n+1} = i^{4n} \cdot i = 1 \cdot i = i$$
$$i^{4n+2} = i^{4n} \cdot i^2 = 1 \cdot (-1) = -1$$
$$i^{4n+3} = i^{4n} \cdot i^3 = 1 \cdot (-i) = -i$$

Example 3: Powers of i

a. $i^{45} = i^{44} \cdot i = (i^4)^{11} \cdot i = 1^{11} \cdot i = i$

b. $i^{59} = i^{56} \cdot i^3 = (i^4)^{14} \cdot i^2 \cdot i = 1^{14} \cdot (-1)i = -i$

c. $i^{-6} = \dfrac{1}{i^6} = \dfrac{1}{i^4 \cdot i^2} = \dfrac{1}{1(-1)} = \dfrac{1}{-1} = -1$

Practice Problems

Write each of the following numbers in standard form.

1. $-2i(3-i)$ **2.** $(2+4i)(1+i)$ **3.** i^{13}

4. i^{-2} **5.** $\dfrac{2}{1+5i}$ **6.** $\dfrac{7+i}{2-i}$

6.6 Exercises

Write each of the following numbers in standard form. Assume k is a positive integer.

1. $8(2+3i)$ **2.** $-3(7-4i)$ **3.** $-7\left(\sqrt{2}-i\right)$ **4.** $\sqrt{3}\left(\sqrt{3}+2i\right)$

5. $3i(4-i)$ **6.** $-4i(6-7i)$ **7.** $-i\left(\sqrt{3}+i\right)$ **8.** $2i\left(\sqrt{5}+2i\right)$

9. $5i(2-\sqrt{2}\,i)$ **10.** $\sqrt{3}\,i(2-\sqrt{3}\,i)$ **11.** $(5+3i)(1+i)$ **12.** $(2+7i)(6+i)$

13. $(-3+5i)(-1+2i)$ **14.** $(6+2i)(3-i)$ **15.** $(2-3i)(2+3i)$

16. $(4+3i)(7-2i)$ **17.** $(-2+5i)(i-1)$ **18.** $(5+7i)^2$

19. $(3+2i)^2$ **20.** $(4+5i)(4-5i)$ **21.** $(\sqrt{3}+i)(\sqrt{3}-2i)$

22. $(2\sqrt{5}+3i)(\sqrt{5}-i)$ **23.** $(4+\sqrt{5}\,i)(4-\sqrt{5}\,i)$ **24.** $(\sqrt{7}+3i)(\sqrt{7}+i)$

25. $(5-\sqrt{2}\,i)(5-\sqrt{2}\,i)$ **26.** $(7+2\sqrt{3}\,i)(7-2\sqrt{3}\,i)$ **27.** $(\sqrt{5}+2i)(\sqrt{2}-i)$

28. $(2\sqrt{3}+i)(4+3i)$ **29.** $(3+\sqrt{5}\,i)(3+\sqrt{6}\,i)$ **30.** $(2-\sqrt{3}\,i)(3-\sqrt{2}\,i)$

31. $\dfrac{-3}{i}$ **32.** $\dfrac{7}{i}$ **33.** $\dfrac{5}{4i}$ **34.** $\dfrac{-3}{2i}$ **35.** $\dfrac{2+i}{-4i}$

36. $\dfrac{3-4i}{3i}$ **37.** $\dfrac{-4}{1+2i}$ **38.** $\dfrac{7}{5-2i}$ **39.** $\dfrac{6}{4-3i}$ **40.** $\dfrac{-8}{6+i}$

41. $\dfrac{2i}{5-i}$ **42.** $\dfrac{-4i}{1+3i}$ **43.** $\dfrac{2-i}{2+5i}$ **44.** $\dfrac{6+i}{3-4i}$ **45.** $\dfrac{2-3i}{-1+5i}$

46. $\dfrac{-3+i}{7-2i}$ **47.** $\dfrac{1+4i}{\sqrt{3}+i}$ **48.** $\dfrac{9-2i}{\sqrt{5}+i}$ **49.** $\dfrac{\sqrt{3}+2i}{\sqrt{3}-2i}$ **50.** $\dfrac{\sqrt{6}-3i}{\sqrt{6}+3i}$

51. i^{13} **52.** i^{20} **53.** i^{30} **54.** i^{15} **55.** i^{-3}

56. $(i)^{-5}$ **57.** $(i)^{4k}$ **58.** i^{4k+2} **59.** i^{4k+3} **60.** i^{4k+1}

61. $(x+3i)(x-3i)$ **62.** $(y+5i)(y-5i)$ **63.** $(x+\sqrt{2}\,i)(x-\sqrt{2}\,i)$

64. $(2x+\sqrt{7}\,i)(2x-\sqrt{7}\,i)$ **65.** $(\sqrt{5}y+2i)(\sqrt{5}y-2i)$ **66.** $(y-\sqrt{3}\,i)(y+\sqrt{3}\,i)$

67. $[(x+2)+6i][(x+2)-6i]$ **68.** $\left[(x+1)-\sqrt{8}\,i\right]\left[(x+1)+\sqrt{8}\,i\right]$

69. $[(y-3)+2i][(y-3)-2i]$ **70.** $[(x-1)+5i][(x-1)-5i]$

Writing and Thinking About Mathematics

71. Explain why the product of every complex number and its conjugate is a positive real number.

72. Explain why $\sqrt{-4}\cdot\sqrt{-4}\neq 4$. What is the correct value of $\sqrt{-4}\cdot\sqrt{-4}$?

73. What condition is necessary for the conjugate of a complex number, $a+bi$, to be equal to the reciprocal of this number?

Answers to Practice Problems: 1. $-2-6i$ **2.** $-2+6i$ **3.** i **4.** -1 **5.** $\dfrac{1}{13}-\dfrac{5}{13}i$ **6.** $\dfrac{13}{5}+\dfrac{9}{5}i$

Hawkes Learning Systems: Intermediate Algebra

Multiplication and Division of Complex Numbers

Chapter 6 Index of Key Ideas and Terms

Perfect Squares (Table of)   page 399

Square Roots   page 399

   If $b^2 = a$, then b is a **square root** of a.

Terminology   page 399

   The symbol $\sqrt{\ }$ is called a **radical sign**.
   The number under the radical sign is called the **radicand**.
   The complete expression, such as $\sqrt{64}$, is called
   a **radical** or **radical expression**.

Square Root   page 400

   If a is a nonnegative real number and b is a real number such that

   $b^2 = a$, then b is called a **square root** of a.
   If b is nonnegative, then we write
      $\sqrt{a} = b \leftarrow$ b is called the **principal square root**

   and $-\sqrt{a} = -b \leftarrow$ $-b$ is called the **negative square root**

Simplest Form of Square Roots   page 402

   A square root is considered to be in simplest form
   when the radicand has no perfect square as a factor.

Square Roots of Expressions with Even and Odd Exponents   page 405

   For any real number x and positive integer m,

      $\sqrt{x^{2m}} = \left| x^m \right|$ and $\sqrt{x^{2m+1}} = \left| x^m \right| \sqrt{x}$

   Note that the absolute value sign is necessary only if m is odd.
   Also, note that for $\sqrt{x^{2m+1}}$ to be defined as real, x cannot be negative.

   Comment: If m is any integer, then $2m$ is even and $2m + 1$ is odd.

Perfect Cubes (Table of)   page 406

Cube Root   page 406

   If a and b are real numbers such that $b^3 = a$, then b is called the
   cube root of a. We write $\sqrt[3]{a} = b \leftarrow$ the **cube root**.

Simplest Form of Cube Roots   page 407

   A cube root is considered to be in simplest form
   when the radicand has no perfect cube as a factor.

To Rationalize the Denominator of a Radical Expression   page 408
(with Square Roots or Cube Roots)
   1. If the denominator contains a square root, multiply both the
   numerator and denominator by a square root. Choose this square root
   so that the denominator will be a perfect square.   *continued on next page ...*

2. If the denominator contains a cube root, multiply both the numerator and denominator by a cube root. Choose this cube root so that the denominator will be a perfect cube.

Radical Notation   page 413

If n is a positive integer and $b^n = a$, then
$b = \sqrt[n]{a} = a^{\frac{1}{n}}$ (assuming $\sqrt[n]{a}$ is a real number).

The expression $\sqrt[n]{a}$ is called a **radical**.

The symbol $\sqrt[n]{}$ is called a **radical sign**.
n is called the **index**.
a is called the **radicand**.
(**Note**: If no index is given, it is understood to be 2.

For example, $\sqrt{3} = \sqrt[2]{3} = 3^{\frac{1}{2}}$.)

Special Note About the Index n   page 413

For the expression $\sqrt[n]{a}$ (or $a^{\frac{1}{n}}$) to be a real number:
1. n can be any index when a is nonnegative.
2. n must be odd when a is negative.
(If a is negative and n is even, then $\sqrt[n]{a}$ is nonreal.)

Properties of Exponents   page 415

For nonzero real numbers a and b and rational numbers m and n,

The Exponent 1:	$a = a^1$ (a is any real number.)
The Exponent 0:	$a^0 = 1$ ($a \neq 0$)
Product Rule:	$a^m \cdot a^n = a^{m+n}$
Quotient Rule:	$\dfrac{a^m}{a^n} = a^{m-n}$
Power Rule:	$\left(a^m\right)^n = a^{mn}$
Negative Exponents:	$a^{-n} = \dfrac{1}{a^n}, \quad \dfrac{1}{a^{-n}} = a^n$
Power Rule for Products:	$(ab)^n = a^n b^n$
Power Rule for Fractions:	$\left(\dfrac{a}{b}\right)^n = \dfrac{a^n}{b^n}$

The General Form $a^{\frac{m}{n}}$ page 416

If n is a positive integer and m is any integer and $a^{\frac{1}{n}}$ is a real number, then

$$a^{\frac{m}{n}} = \left(a^{\frac{1}{n}}\right)^m = (a^m)^{\frac{1}{n}}$$

In radical notation:

$$a^{\frac{m}{n}} = \left(\sqrt[n]{a}\right)^m = \sqrt[n]{a^m}$$

To Find the Value of $a^{\frac{m}{n}}$ with a Calculator　　　　　　　page 419

　　Step 1: Enter the value of the base, a.

　　Step 2: Press the up arrow key 〔 ^ 〕.

　　Step 3: Enter the fractional exponent enclosed in parentheses.
　　　　　　(This exponent may be positive or negative.)

Step 4: Press 〔ENTER〕.

Addition and Subtraction with Radical Expressions　　　　　page 423

　　Like radicals

Multiplication with Radical Expressions　　　　　　　　　　page 424

Rationalizing Denominators of Rational Expressions　　　　page 426

　　If the denominator is a sum or difference with square roots:

　　1. If the denominator is of the form $a - b$, multiply both
　　　the numerator and denominator by $a + b$.

　　2. If the denominator is of the form $a + b$, multiply both
　　　the numerator and denominator by $a - b$.

Evaluating Radical Expressions with a Calculator　　　　　page 427

Radical Function　　　　　　　　　　　　　　　　　　　　page 434

　　A **radical function** is a function of the form $y = \sqrt[n]{g(x)}$ in which
　　the radicand contains the variable.

　　The **domain** of such a function depends on the index, n:

　　　　1. If n is an even number, the domain is the set of all x
　　　　　such that $g(x) \geq 0$.

　　　　2. If n is an odd number, the domain is the set of all real
　　　　　numbers $(-\infty, \infty)$.

Complex Numbers　　　　　　　　　　　　　　　　　　　　page 443

　　$i = \sqrt{-1}$　and　$i^2 = -1$

　　If a is a positive real number, then $\sqrt{-a} = \sqrt{a} \cdot \sqrt{-1} = \sqrt{a}\,i$.

Standard Form: $a + bi$　　　　　　　　　　　　　　　　　page 444

　　A **complex number** is a number of the form $a + bi$, where
　　a and b are real numbers.

　　a is called the **real part** and b is called the **imaginary part**.

　　If $b = 0$, then $a + bi = a + 0i = a$ is a real number.

　　If $a = 0$, then $a + bi = 0 + bi = bi$ is called a **pure imaginary
　　　　number** (or an **imaginary number**).

Equality of Complex Numbers　　　　　　　　　　　　　　page 445

　　For complex numbers $a + bi$ and $c + di$,

　　　　$a + bi = c + di$ if and only if $a = c$ and $b = d$.

Addition and Subtraction with Complex Numbers   page 446
For complex numbers $a+bi$ and $c+di$

$$(a+bi)+(c+di)=(a+c)+(b+d)i$$

and $(a+bi)-(c+di)=(a-c)+(b-d)i$

Multiplication with Complex Numbers   page 450
For complex numbers $a+bi$ and $c+di$

$$(a+bi)(c+di)=(ac-bd)+(bc+ad)i$$

Complex Conjugates   page 451
$a+bi$ and $a-bi$ are complex conjugates
The product of complex conjugates will always be
a nonnegative real number: $(a+bi)(a-bi)=a^2+b^2$.

To Simplify a Fraction with Complex Numbers   page 452
1. Multiply both the numerator and denominator by the
   complex conjugate of the denominator.
2. Simplify the resulting products in both the numerator
   and denominator.
3. Write the simplified result in standard form.

Powers of i: i^n   page 454
$$i^{4n}=\left(i^4\right)^n=1^n\ \ \ \ =1$$
$$i^{4n+1}=i^{4n}\cdot i\ =1\cdot i\ \ \ \ =i$$
$$i^{4n+2}=i^{4n}\cdot i^2=1\cdot(-1)=-1$$
$$i^{4n+3}=i^{4n}\cdot i^3=1\cdot(-i)=-i$$

Chapter 6 Review

For a review of the topics and problems from Chapter 6, look at the following lessons from *Hawkes Learning Systems: Intermediate Algebra*

Evaluating Radicals
Simplifying Radicals
Division of Radicals
Rational Exponents
Addition and Subtraction of Radicals
Multiplication of Radicals
Functions with Radicals
Complex Numbers
Multiplication and Division of Complex Numbers

Chapter 6 Test

Simplify each expression in Exercises 1 – 5. Assume that all variables are positive.

1. $(-8)^{\frac{2}{3}}$

2. $(9)^{\frac{-3}{2}}$

3. $4x^{\frac{1}{2}} \cdot x^{\frac{2}{3}}$

4. $\left(49x^{\frac{1}{2}}y^{\frac{-2}{3}}\right)^{\frac{1}{2}}$

5. $\left(\dfrac{16x^{-4}y}{y^{-1}}\right)^{\frac{3}{4}}$

6. Write $(2x)^{\frac{2}{3}}$ in radical notation.

7. Write $\sqrt[6]{8x^2y^4}$ in exponential notation.

8. Simplify the expression $\sqrt[3]{x^2} \cdot \sqrt[4]{x}$.

9. $\sqrt{112}$

10. $\sqrt[3]{48x^2y^5}$

11. $\sqrt{\dfrac{5y^2}{8x^3}}$

In Exercises 12 – 17, perform the indicated operations and simplify. Assume that all variables are positive.

12. $2\sqrt{75} + 3\sqrt{27} - \sqrt{12}$

13. $\sqrt{16x^3} + \sqrt{9x^3} - \sqrt{36x}$

14. $\sqrt[3]{24} + 2\sqrt[3]{81}$

15. $\left(\sqrt{3} - \sqrt{2}\right)^2$

16. $5x\sqrt{y^3} - 2\sqrt{x^2y^3} - 4y\sqrt{x^2y}$

17. $\left(6 + \sqrt{3x}\right)\left(5 - 2\sqrt{3x}\right)$

18. Rationalize the denominator and simplify the quotient.

a. $\dfrac{2}{\sqrt{3} - \sqrt{5}}$

b. $\dfrac{1-x}{1-\sqrt{x^3}}$

19. Find the domain of each of the following radical functions. Write the answer in interval notation.

a. $y = \sqrt{3x + 4}$

b. $f(x) = \sqrt[3]{2x + 5}$

20. Use a TI-83 Plus graphing calculator to graph each of the following radical functions. Sketch the graph on your test paper and label 3 points.

a. $f(x) = -\sqrt{x + 3}$

b. $y = \sqrt[3]{x - 4}$

In Exercises 21 – 24, perform the indicated operations and write the results in standard form.

21. $(5 + 8i) + (11 - 4i)$

22. $(2 + 3\sqrt{-4}) - (7 - 2\sqrt{-25})$

23. $(4 + 3i)(2 - 5i)$

24. $\dfrac{2+i}{3+2i}$

25. Solve for x and y: $(2x + 3i) - (6 + 2yi) = 5 - 3i$

26. Write i^{23} in the standard form, $a + bi$.

27. Find the product and simplify: $(x + 2i)(x - 2i)$

28. Find the product and simplify: $\left(x+3-\sqrt{3}i\right)\left(x+3+\sqrt{3}i\right)$

29. Explain, in your own words, why the product of a nonzero complex number and its conjugate will always result in a positive real number.

In Exercises 30 – 32, use a calculator to find the value of each expression accurate to 4 decimal places.

30. $32^{\frac{-3}{5}}$

31. $\left(\sqrt{2}+6\right)\left(\sqrt{2}-1\right)$

32. $\dfrac{\sqrt{3}-\sqrt{5}}{\sqrt{7}-\sqrt{10}}$

Cumulative Review: Chapters 1 - 6

Perform the indicated operations in Exercises 1 – 3.

1. $\left(x^2+7x-5\right)-\left(-2x^3+5x^2-x-1\right)$ **2.** $\left(2x+7\right)\left(3x-1\right)$

3. $\left(5x+2\right)\left(4-x\right)$

Solve for the indicated variable in Exercises 4 and 5.

4. Solve $s=a+\left(n-1\right)d$ for n **5.** Solve $A=p+prt$ for p

In Exercises 6 – 9, factor completely.

6. $12x^2-7x-12$ **7.** $28+x-2x^2$ **8.** $5x^3-320$

9. x^3+4x^2-x-4

Perform the indicated operations in Exercises 10 and 11 and reduce if possible.

10. $\dfrac{x+1}{x^2+x-6}+\dfrac{3x-2}{x^2-2x-15}$ **11.** $\dfrac{2x+5}{4x^2-1}-\dfrac{2-x}{2x^2+7x+3}$

Simplify the complex fractions in Exercises 12 and 13.

12. $\dfrac{1-\dfrac{1}{x^2}}{\dfrac{2}{x}-\dfrac{4}{x^2}}$ **13.** $\dfrac{x+2-\dfrac{12}{x+3}}{x-5+\dfrac{16}{x+3}}$

Solve each equation in Exercises 14 and 15.

14. $\dfrac{3}{x}+\dfrac{2}{x+5}=\dfrac{8}{3x}$ **15.** $\dfrac{9}{x+7}+\dfrac{3x}{x^2+4x-21}=\dfrac{8}{x-3}$

Solve the inequalities in Exercises 16 and 17 and graph the solutions on a real number line. Write the solutions in interval notation.

16. $\dfrac{5x-3}{2x+4}\le 0$ **17.** $\dfrac{x-5}{3x-1}\ge 1$

18. V (volume) varies inversely as P (pressure) when a gas is enclosed in a container. In a particular situation, the volume of gas is 25 in^3 when a force of 10 pounds is exerted. What would be the volume of gas if a force of 15 pounds were to be used?

19. The resistance, R (in ohms), in a wire is directly proportional to the length, L, and inversely proportional to the square of the diameter of the wire. The resistance of a wire 500 ft long with a diameter of 0.01 in. is 20 ohms. What is the resistance of a wire of the same type that is 200 ft long?

In Exercises 20 – 22, solve each quadratic equation by factoring.

20. $x^2 - 13x - 48 = 0$ **21.** $x = 2x^2 - 6$ **22.** $0 = 15x^2 - 11x + 2$

23. Find the value of $\det(A)$ for the matrix

$$A = \begin{bmatrix} 5 & -2 & 0 \\ -1 & 1 & 6 \\ 7 & 8 & -3 \end{bmatrix}$$

24. Solve the following system of linear equations by graphing both equations and locating the point of intersection.

$$\begin{cases} 3x - 2y = 7 \\ x + 3y = -5 \end{cases}$$

25. Solve the following system of linear equations by using the Gaussian elimination technique. You may use your calculator.

$$\begin{cases} x + y - z = 1 \\ 3x - y + z = 3 \\ -x + 2y + 2z = 3 \end{cases}$$

26. Solve the following system of linear equations by using Cramer's Rule.

$$\begin{cases} -2x + 5y = 10 \\ 6x - 2y = 30 \end{cases}$$

27. a. Use synthetic division to find $P(3)$ given that $P(x) = x^3 - 8x^2 + 19x - 12$
    b. Use synthetic division to find $P(4)$.
    c. Use synthetic division to find $P(1)$.
    d. What are the factors of $P(x)$?

28. a. Find an equation that has $x = 4$ and $x = 7$ as roots.

    b. Find an equation that has $x = -2$, $x = 12$, and $x = 1$ as roots.

29. Use a graphing calculator to find the solution set to the following system of inequalities: $\begin{cases} x+y \le 4 \\ 3x-y \le 2 \end{cases}$

30. Divide by using long division. Write the answer in the form $Q(x) + \dfrac{R(x)}{D(x)}$.

$$\frac{x^3 - 7x^2 + 2x - 15}{x^2 + 2x - 1}$$

31. The following table shows the number of feet that Linda skied downhill from one second to another. (She never skied uphill, but she did stop occasionally.)

Distance Traveled (in feet)	Time Elapsed (in seconds)
24	3
48	6
96	8
96	15
200	20

a. Plot the points indicated in the table.
b. Calculate the slope of the line segments from point to point.
c. Interpret each slope.

32. The graphs of three curves are shown. Use the vertical line test to determine whether or not each graph represents a function. If the graph represents a function, state its domain and range.

a.   b.   c.

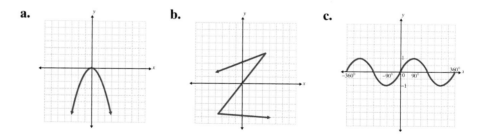

33. The sum of the squares of two consecutive positive odd integers is 514. What are the integers?

Use a graphing calculator to solve (or estimate the solutions of) the equations in Exercises 34 and 35. Sketch the graphs that you use and find any approximations accurate to two decimal places.

34. $x^3 = 3x^2 - 3x + 1$ **35.** $\left| x^2 - 9 \right| = 3$

Simplify the expressions in Exercises 36 – 39. Assume that all variables are positive.

36. $8^{\frac{-4}{3}}$

37. $\left(x^{\frac{1}{2}} \cdot x^{\frac{2}{3}}\right)^2$

38. $\sqrt{288}$

39. $\sqrt[3]{16x^6 y^{10}}$

Perform the indicated operations in Exercises 40 and 41 and simplify. Write your answers in standard form.

40. $(2+2i)(3-4i)$

41. $\dfrac{4-3i}{1+4i}$

42. Susan traveled 25 miles downstream. In the same length of time, she could have traveled 15 miles upstream. If the speed of the current is 2.5 mph, find the speed of Susan's boat in still water.

43. Robin can prepare a monthly sales report in 5 hours. If Mac helps her, together they can prepare the report in 3 hours. How long would it take Mac if he worked alone?

44. Harold has $50,000 that he wants to invest in two accounts. One pays 6% interest, and the other (at a higher risk) pays 10% interest. If he wants a $3600 annual return on these two investments, how much should he put into each account?

45. A grocer plans to make up a special mix of two popular kinds of candy for Halloween. He wants to mix a total of 100 pounds to sell for $1.75 per pound. Individually, the two types sell for $1.25 and $2.50 per pound. How many pounds of each of the two kinds should he put in the mix?

In Exercises 46 – 48, use a graphing calculator to graph each function and use the trace and zoom features to estimate the x-intercepts.

46. $y = x^2 - 3x - 6$

47. $y = x^3 - 4x + 3$

48. $y = -x^3 + 2x^2 + 19x - 20$

In Exercises 49 – 52, use a calculator to find the value of each expression accurate to 5 decimal places.

49. $36^{\frac{7}{2}}$

50. $125^{\frac{-2}{3}}$

51. $\sqrt{5}\left(\sqrt{21} - 4\right)$

52. $\dfrac{13+\sqrt{12}}{5-\sqrt{6}}$

Quadratic Equations

Did You Know?

Much of classical algebra has focused on the problem of solving equations such as the second-degree equation $ax^2 + bx + c = 0$, which is studied in this chapter. In Section 7.2, you will be introduced to the quadratic formula, a formula that has been known since approximately 2000 B.C. This formula expresses the roots of the quadratic equation in terms of the coefficients a, b, and c. Italian mathematicians during the 16th century also discovered that general cubic equations, in the form $ax^3 + bx^2 + cx + d = 0$, and general fourth-degree equations, in the form $ax^4 + bx^3 + cx^2 + dx + e = 0$ could be solved by similar types of formulas. Not many people are aware that these general formulas exist. They can be found in a book of mathematical formulas or in a theory of equations text.

After the discovery of general formulas for the first four cases of polynomial equations (linear, quadratic, cubic, and quartic), it was assumed that the fifth-degree equation also could be solved. However, in the early 1800s, two brilliant young mathematicians proved that the fifth-degree equation was not solvable by algebraic formulas involving the coefficients, as the previous four cases had been. The mathematicians were Neils Henrick Abel (1802–1829) and Evariste Galois (1811–1832).

Galois

Galois was a fascinating person whose life ended in a romantic duel that may have been arranged by right-wing politicians to eliminate the brilliant young radical. He was involved in the French Revolution and was expelled from school because of his political activity. His brilliance in mathematics was unrecognized because of his youth, his bitterness toward organized science, his radical politics, and the sophistication of his work. The night before his duel, anticipating his death, Galois sat down and wrote out all of the creative mathematics that he could—much of it abstract algebra that he had worked out mentally but not recorded. Included in this work was the unsolvability of fifth-degree equations. Galois' turbulent life has been fictionalized in a novel, *Whom the Gods Love*, by Leopold Infield. Galois' proof that fifth-degree equations could not be solved kept mathematicians from trying to do the impossible and also opened a whole new field in higher mathematics known as **group theory**.

Abel's life ended less dramatically, but also tragically. He died of tuberculosis brought about by poverty because no one recognized his talent. Ironically, he died two days before he was offered a professorship at the University of Berlin. Abel and Galois both left mathematical legacies that kept future mathematicians engaged in developing their ideas up to the present time.

7.1 **Quadratic Equations: Completing the Square**

7.2 **Quadratic Equations: The Quadratic Formula**

7.3 **Applications**

7.4 **Equations with Radicals**

7.5 **Equations in Quadratic Form**

"Through and through the world is infested with quantity: To talk sense is to talk quantities. It is no use saying the nation is large—How large? It is no use saying that radium is scarce—How scarce? You cannot evade quantity. You may fly to poetry and music, and quantity and number will face you in your rhythms and your octaves."

Alfred North Whitehead (1861-1947)

Abel

Quadratic equations appear in one form or another in almost every course in mathematics and in many courses in related fields such as business, biology, engineering, and computer science. In this chapter, we will discuss three techniques for solving quadratic equations: factoring, completing the square, and the quadratic formula. Factoring has already been discussed in Section 4.6 and, when possible, is generally considered the method of first choice because it is easier to apply, and factoring quadratic expressions is useful in other mathematical situations. However, the quadratic formula is very important and should be memorized as it works in all cases. A part of the formula, called the discriminant, gives ready information about the nature of the solutions. Additionally, the formula is easy to use in computer programs.

The wide variety of applications presented in Section 7.3 illustrates the practicality of knowing how to recognize and solve quadratic equations.

7.1   Quadratic Equations: Completing the Square

Objectives

After completing this section, you will be able to:

1. *Solve quadratic equations by factoring.*

2. *Solve quadratic equations by using the definition of square root.*

3. *Solve quadratic equations by completing the square.*

Review of Solving Equations by Factoring

Not every polynomial can be factored so that the factors have integer coefficients, and not every polynomial equation can be solved by factoring. However, when the solutions of a polynomial equation can be found by factoring, the method depends on the **zero-factor property**, which is restated here for easy reference.

Zero-Factor Property

If the product of two factors is 0, then one or both of the factors must be zero. Symbolically, for factors a and b,

$$\textit{if } a \cdot b = 0, \textit{ then } a = 0 \textit{ or } b = 0$$

Also as discussed in Section 4.6, polynomial equations of second-degree are called **quadratic equations** and, since these are the equations of interest in this chapter, the definition is restated here.

Quadratic Equation

An equation that can be written in the form

$$ax^2 + bx + c = 0 \qquad \text{where a, b, and c are real numbers and } a \neq 0$$

is called a **quadratic equation**.

The procedure for solving quadratic equations by factoring involves making sure that one side of the equation is 0 and then applying the zero-factor property. The following list of steps outlines the procedure.

To Solve an Equation By Factoring

1. *Add or subtract terms so that* <u>*one side of the equation is 0*</u>.

2. *Factor the polynomial expression.*

3. *Set each factor equal to 0 and solve each of the resulting equations.*

(**Note:** *If two of the factors are the same, then the solution is said to be a* **double root** *or a* **root of multiplicity two**.)

NOTES

We will see throughout this chapter that quadratic equations may have nonreal solutions.

Also, you will need to remember that the sum of two squares can be factored as complex conjugates. For example,

$$x^2 + 9 = (x + 3i)(x - 3i).$$

Example 1: Factorization

Solve the following equations by factoring.

a. $x^2 - 15x = -50$

Solution:

$$x^2 - 15x = -50$$

$$x^2 - 15x + 50 = 0 \qquad \text{Add 50 to both sides. \textbf{One side must be 0.}}$$

$$(x - 5)(x - 10) = 0 \qquad \text{Factor the left-hand side.}$$

$$x - 5 = 0 \quad \text{or} \quad x - 10 = 0 \qquad \text{Set each factor equal to 0.}$$

$$x = 5 \qquad\qquad x = 10 \qquad \text{Solve each linear equation.}$$

Check: $\qquad 5^2 - 15 \cdot 5 \overset{?}{=} -50 \qquad 10^2 - 15 \cdot 10 \overset{?}{=} -50$

$$25 - 75 \overset{?}{=} -50 \qquad\qquad 100 - 150 \overset{?}{=} -50$$

$$-50 = -50 \qquad\qquad -50 = -50 \qquad \textit{continued on next page ...}$$

469

b. $x^2 - 8x = -16$

  Solution: $x^2 - 8x = -16$

   $x^2 - 8x + 16 = 0$ Add 16 to both sides.

   $(x-4)^2 = 0$ The trinomial is a perfect square.

   $x - 4 = 0$ The two factors are the same.

   $x = 4$ The solution is a **double root**.

  Check: $4^2 - 8 \cdot 4 \stackrel{?}{=} -16$

   $16 - 32 \stackrel{?}{=} -16$

   $-16 = -16$

c. $x^2 + 4 = 0$

  Solution: $x^2 + 4 = 0$

   $(x + 2i)(x - 2i) = 0$

   $x + 2i = 0$ or $x - 2i = 0$

   $x = -2i$ $x = 2i$

Note that $x^2 + 4$ is the sum of two squares and can be factored into the product of conjugates of complex numbers.

  Check: $(-2i)^2 + 4 \stackrel{?}{=} 0$ $(2i)^2 + 4 \stackrel{?}{=} 0$

   $4i^2 + 4 \stackrel{?}{=} 0$ $4i^2 + 4 \stackrel{?}{=} 0$

   $-4 + 4 \stackrel{?}{=} 0$ $-4 + 4 \stackrel{?}{=} 0$

   $0 = 0$ $0 = 0$

• •

Using the Definition of Square Root and the Square Root Property

Consider the equation

$$x^2 = 13.$$

The definition of square root, $\left[\sqrt{x^2} = |x|\right]$, leads to two solutions, as follows:

Taking the square root of both sides of the equation gives:

$$|x| = \sqrt{13}.$$

So,

$$x = \sqrt{13} \quad \text{or} \quad x = -\sqrt{13}$$

For both solutions, we write

$$x = \pm\sqrt{13}.$$

Similarly, for the equation

$$(x - 3)^2 = 5$$

the definition of square root gives

$$x - 3 = \pm\sqrt{5}$$

which leads to the two equations and the two solutions, as follows:

$$x - 3 = \sqrt{5} \quad \text{or} \quad x - 3 = -\sqrt{5}$$
$$x = 3 + \sqrt{5} \qquad x = 3 - \sqrt{5}$$

We can write the two solutions in the form

$$x = 3 \pm \sqrt{5}.$$

These examples illustrate how the definition of square root can be used to solve some quadratic equations. In particular, if one side of the equation is a squared expression and the other side is a constant, we can simply take the square roots of each side. However, we must keep in mind that the square roots of negative numbers are nonreal complex numbers and will involve the number i. We have the following **Square Root Property**.

Square Root Property

If $x^2 = c$, then $x = \pm\sqrt{c}$.

If $(x - a)^2 = c$, then $x - a = \pm\sqrt{c}$ (or $x = a \pm \sqrt{c}$).

Example 2: Solving Quadratic Equations by Using the Square Root Property

Solve the following quadratic equations.

a. $x^2 = -25$

Solution: $x^2 = -25$

$$x = \pm\sqrt{-25}$$
$$x = \pm 5i$$

continued on next page ...

b. $(y + 4)^2 = 8$

Solution: $(y + 4)^2 = 8$

$$y + 4 = \pm\sqrt{8}$$

$$y = -4 \pm 2\sqrt{2}$$

Completing the Square

Recall that a perfect square trinomial (Section 4.3) is the result of squaring a binomial. Our objective here is to find the third term of a perfect square trinomial when the first two terms are given. This is called **completing the square**. We will find this procedure useful in solving quadratic equations and in developing the quadratic formula.

Study the following examples to help in your understanding.

Perfect Square Trinomials		Equal Factors		Square of a Binomial
$x^2 - 8x + 16$	$=$	$(x - 4)(x - 4)$	$=$	$(x - 4)^2$
$x^2 + 20x + 100$	$=$	$(x + 10)(x + 10)$	$=$	$(x + 10)^2$
$x^2 - 9x + \dfrac{81}{4}$	$=$	$\left(x - \dfrac{9}{2}\right)\left(x - \dfrac{9}{2}\right)$	$=$	$\left(x - \dfrac{9}{2}\right)^2$
$x^2 - 2hx + h^2$	$=$	$(x - h)(x - h)$	$=$	$(x - h)^2$
$x^2 + 2hx + h^2$	$=$	$(x + h)(x + h)$	$=$	$(x + h)^2$

The last two examples are in the form of formulas. We see two things in each case:

1. The leading coefficient (the coefficient of x^2) is 1.

2. The constant term is the square of $\dfrac{1}{2}$ of the coefficient of x.

    For example, $\dfrac{1}{2}(2h) = h$ and the square of this result is the constant h^2.

What constant should be added to $x^2 - 16x$ to get a perfect square trinomial? By following the ideas just discussed, we find that $\dfrac{1}{2}(-16) = -8$ and $(-8)^2 = 64$. Therefore, to complete the square, we add 64. Thus,

$$x^2 - 16x + 64 = (x - 8)^2.$$

By adding 64, we have completed the square for $x^2 - 16x$.

Example 3: Completing the Square •

Add the constant that will complete the square for each expression, and write the new expression as the square of a binomial.

a. $x^2 + 10x$

    Solution: $x^2 + 10x + \underline{\quad} = (\quad\quad)^2$

$$\frac{1}{2}(10) = 5 \text{ and } (5)^2 = 25$$

So, add 25: $x^2 + 10x + 25 = (x+5)^2$

b. $x^2 - 7x$

    Solution: $x^2 - 7x + \underline{\quad} = (\quad\quad)^2$

$$\frac{1}{2}(-7) = -\frac{7}{2} \text{ and } \left(-\frac{7}{2}\right)^2 = \frac{49}{4}$$

So, add $\dfrac{49}{4}$: $x^2 - 7x + \dfrac{49}{4} = \left(x - \dfrac{7}{2}\right)^2$

• •

Solving Quadratic Equations by Completing the Square

Now we want to use the process of completing the square to help in solving quadratic equations. This technique involves the following steps.

To Solve a Quadratic Equation by Completing the Square

1. *If necessary, divide or multiply both sides of the equation so that the leading coefficient (the coefficient of x^2) is 1.*

2. *If necessary, isolate the constant term on one side of the equation.*

3. *Find the constant that completes the square of the polynomial and add this constant to both sides.*

4. *Use the Square Root Property to find the solutions of the equation.*

Example 4: Solving Quadratic Equations by Completing the Square • • • • • •

Solve the following quadratic equations by completing the square.

a. $x^2 - 8x = 25$

Solution:

$$x^2 - 8x = 25 \qquad \text{The coefficient of } x^2 \text{ is already 1.}$$

$$x^2 - 8x + 16 = 25 + 16 \qquad \frac{1}{2}(-8) = -4 \text{ and } (-4)^2 = 16.$$

Therefore, add 16 to both sides.

$$(x - 4)^2 = 41$$

$$x - 4 = \sqrt{41} \quad \text{or} \quad x - 4 = -\sqrt{41} \qquad \text{Use the Square Root Property.}$$

$$x = 4 + \sqrt{41} \qquad\qquad x = 4 - \sqrt{41}$$

There are two real solutions: $4 + \sqrt{41}$ and $4 - \sqrt{41}$. We write $x = 4 \pm \sqrt{41}$.

b. $3x^2 + 6x - 15 = 0$

Solution: $3x^2 + 6x - 15 = 0$

$$\frac{3x^2}{3} + \frac{6x}{3} - \frac{15}{3} = \frac{0}{3} \qquad \text{Divide each term by 3. } \textbf{The leading coefficient}$$

must be 1.

$$x^2 + 2x - 5 = 0 \qquad \text{Isolate the constant term and complete the}$$

$$x^2 + 2x = 5 \qquad \text{square: } \frac{1}{2}(2) = 1 \text{ and } 1^2 = 1.$$

$$x^2 + 2x + 1 = 5 + 1 \qquad \text{Therefore, add 1 to both sides.}$$

$$(x + 1)^2 = 6$$

$$x + 1 = \pm\sqrt{6}$$

$$x = -1 \pm \sqrt{6}$$

c. $2x^2 + 2x - 7 = 0$

Solution: $2x^2 + 2x - 7 = 0$

$$x^2 + x - \frac{7}{2} = 0 \qquad \text{Divide each term by 2 so that the leading coef-}$$

ficient will be 1.

$$x^2 + x = \frac{7}{2} \qquad \text{Isolate the constant term and complete the}$$

$$x^2 + x + \frac{1}{4} = \frac{7}{2} + \frac{1}{4} \qquad \text{square: } \frac{1}{2}(1) = \frac{1}{2} \text{ and } \left(\frac{1}{2}\right)^2 = \frac{1}{4}.$$

$$\left(x + \frac{1}{2}\right)^2 = \frac{15}{4}$$

$$x + \frac{1}{2} = \pm\sqrt{\frac{15}{4}}$$

$$x = -\frac{1}{2} \pm \frac{\sqrt{15}}{2}$$

$$x = \frac{-1 \pm \sqrt{15}}{2}$$

d. $x^2 - 2x + 13 = 0$

Solution: $x^2 - 2x + 13 = 0$

$$x^2 - 2x = -13$$

$$x^2 - 2x + 1 = -13 + 1$$

$$(x - 1)^2 = -12$$

$$x - 1 = \pm\sqrt{-12} = \pm i\sqrt{12} = \pm 2i\sqrt{3}$$

$$x = 1 \pm 2i\sqrt{3} \qquad \text{The solutions are nonreal complex numbers.}$$

Writing Equations with Known Roots

In Section 4.6, we found equations with known roots by setting the product of factors equal to 0 and simplifying. The same method is applied here with roots that are nonreal and roots that involve radicals.

Example 5: Equations with Known Roots

Find polynomial equations that have the given roots.

a. $y = 3 + 2i$ and $y = 3 - 2i$

Solution: $\qquad y = 3 + 2i \qquad\qquad y = 3 - 2i$

$\qquad y - 3 - 2i = 0 \qquad y - 3 + 2i = 0 \qquad$ Get 0 on one side of each equation.

Set the product of the two factors equal to 0 and simplify.

$$[y - 3 - 2i][y - 3 + 2i] = 0$$

$$[(y - 3) - 2i][(y - 3) + 2i] = 0$$

$$(y - 3)^2 - 4i^2 = 0$$

$$y^2 - 6y + 9 + 4 = 0$$

$$y^2 - 6y + 13 = 0$$

Regroup the terms to represent the product of complex conjugates. This makes the multiplication easier.

$i^2 = -1$

This equation has two solutions: $y = 3 + 2i$ and $y = 3 - 2i$

b. $x = 5 - \sqrt{2}$ and $x = 5 + \sqrt{2}$

Solution: $\qquad x = 5 - \sqrt{2} \qquad\qquad x = 5 + \sqrt{2}$

$\qquad x - 5 + \sqrt{2} = 0 \qquad x - 5 - \sqrt{2} = 0 \qquad$ Get 0 on one side of each equation.

continued on next page ...

Set the product of the two factors equal to 0 and simplify

$$\left[x-5+\sqrt{2}\right]\left[x-5-\sqrt{2}\right]=0$$

$$\left[(x-5)+\sqrt{2}\right]\left[(x-5)-\sqrt{2}\right]=0 \qquad \text{Regroup the terms to make the multiplication easier.}$$

$$(x-5)^2-\left(\sqrt{2}\right)^2=0$$

$$x^2-10x+25-2=0$$

$$x^2-10x+23=0 \qquad \text{This equation has two solutions:} \; x=5-\sqrt{2} \; \text{and} \; x=5+\sqrt{2}.$$

c. $x=3+i\sqrt{5}$ and $x=3-i\sqrt{5}$

Solution: $x=3+i\sqrt{5}$ $\qquad\qquad$ $x=3-i\sqrt{5}$

$x-3-i\sqrt{5}=0$ $\qquad\qquad$ $x-3+i\sqrt{5}=0$ $\qquad$ Get 0 on one side of each equation.

Set the product of the two factors equal to 0 and simplify.

$$\left[x-3-i\sqrt{5}\right]\left[x-3+i\sqrt{5}\right]=0$$

$$\left[(x-3)-i\sqrt{5}\right]\left[(x-3)+i\sqrt{5}\right]=0 \qquad \text{Regroup the terms to make the multiplication easier.}$$

$$(x-3)^2-\left(i\sqrt{5}\right)^2=0$$

$$x^2-6x+9-\left(i\sqrt{5}\right)^2=0$$

$$x^2-6x+9-i^2\left(\sqrt{5}\right)^2=0$$

$$x^2-6x+9-(-1)(5)=0 \qquad \text{Remember,} \; i^2=-1.$$

$$x^2-6x+14=0 \qquad \text{This equation has two solutions:} \; x=3+i\sqrt{5} \; \text{and} \; x=3-i\sqrt{5}.$$

Practice Problems

Solve each of the following quadratic equations by completing the square.

1. $2x^2+5x-3=0$ $\qquad$ **2.** $x^2+2x+2=0$ $\qquad$ **3.** $x^2-24x+72=0$

4. $x^2-3x+1=0$ $\qquad$ **5.** $3x^2-6x+15=0$

6. *Find a quadratic equation that has the roots $x=2\pm 3i$.*

Answers to Practice Problems: $\quad$ **1.** $x=-3, \; x=\dfrac{1}{2}$ $\quad$ **2.** $x=-1\pm i$ $\quad$ **3.** $x=12\pm 6\sqrt{2}$ $\quad$ **4.** $x=\dfrac{3\pm\sqrt{5}}{2}$

5. $x=1\pm 2i$ $\qquad$ **6.** $x^2-4x+13=0$

7.1 Exercises

Add the correct constant to complete the square in Exercises 1 – 10; then factor the trinomial as indicated.

1. $x^2 - 12x + \underline{\quad} = (\quad)^2$ **2.** $y^2 + 14y + \underline{\quad} = (\quad)^2$ **3.** $x^2 + 6x + \underline{\quad} = (\quad)^2$

4. $x^2 + 8x + \underline{\quad} = (\quad)^2$ **5.** $x^2 - 5x + \underline{\quad} = (\quad)^2$ **6.** $x^2 + 7x + \underline{\quad} = (\quad)^2$

7. $y^2 + y + \underline{\quad} = (\quad)^2$ **8.** $x^2 + \dfrac{1}{2}x + \underline{\quad} = (\quad)^2$ **9.** $x^2 + \dfrac{1}{3}x + \underline{\quad} = (\quad)^2$

10. $y^2 + \dfrac{3}{4}y + \underline{\quad} = (\quad)^2$

Solve the equations in Exercises 11 – 25.

11. $x^2 - 144 = 0$ **12.** $x^2 - 169 = 0$ **13.** $x^2 + 25 = 0$

14. $x^2 + 24 = 0$ **15.** $x^2 + 18 = 0$ **16.** $(x - 2)^2 = 9$

17. $(x - 4)^2 = 25$ **18.** $x^2 = 5$ **19.** $x^2 = 12$

20. $2(x + 3)^2 = 6$ **21.** $3(x - 1)^2 = 15$ **22.** $(x - 3)^2 = -4$

23. $(x + 8)^2 = -9$ **24.** $(x + 2)^2 = -7$ **25.** $(x - 5)^2 = -10$

Solve the quadratic equations in Exercises 26 – 55 by completing the square.

26. $x^2 + 4x - 5 = 0$ **27.** $x^2 + 6x - 7 = 0$ **28.** $y^2 + 2y = 5$

29. $x^2 + 3 = 8x$ **30.** $x^2 - 10x + 3 = 0$ **31.** $z^2 + 4z = 2$

32. $x^2 - 6x + 10 = 0$ **33.** $x^2 + 2x + 6 = 0$ **34.** $x^2 + 11 = 12x$

35. $y^2 - 10y + 4 = 0$ **36.** $z^2 + 3z - 5 = 0$ **37.** $x^2 - 5x + 5 = 0$

38. $x^2 + 5x + 2 = 0$ **39.** $x^2 + x + 2 = 0$ **40.** $x^2 - 2x + 5 = 0$

41. $x^2 = 3 - 4x$ **42.** $3y^2 + 9y + 9 = 0$ **43.** $4x^2 + 8x + 16 = 0$

44. $x^2 = 6 - x$ **45.** $3y^2 = 4 - y$ **46.** $3x^2 - 10x + 5 = 0$

47. $7x + 2 = -4x^2$ **48.** $3y^2 + 5y - 3 = 0$ **49.** $4x^2 - 2x + 3 = 0$

50. $2x + 2 = -6x^2$ **51.** $5y^2 + 15y + 25 = 0$ **52.** $2x^2 + 9x + 4 = 0$

53. $2x^2 - 8x + 4 = 0$ **54.** $3 = 3x - 6x^2$ **55.** $4x^2 + 20x + 32 = 0$

For Exercises 56 – 70, write a quadratic equation with integer coefficients that has the given roots.

56. $x = \sqrt{7}, x = -\sqrt{7}$ **57.** $x = \sqrt{5}, x = -\sqrt{5}$

58. $x = 1 + \sqrt{3}, x = 1 - \sqrt{3}$ **59.** $z = 2 + \sqrt{2}, z = 2 - \sqrt{2}$

60. $y = -2 + \sqrt{5}, y = -2 - \sqrt{5}$ **61.** $x = 1 + 2\sqrt{3}, x = 1 - 2\sqrt{3}$

62. $x = 4i, x = -4i$ **63.** $x = 7i, x = -7i$

64. $y = i\sqrt{6}, y = -i\sqrt{6}$ **65.** $y = i\sqrt{5}, y = -i\sqrt{5}$

66. $x = 2 + i, x = 2 - i$ **67.** $x = -3 + 2i, x = -3 - 2i$

68. $x = 1 + i\sqrt{2}, x = 1 - i\sqrt{2}$ **69.** $x = 2 + i\sqrt{3}, x = 2 - i\sqrt{3}$

70. $x = -5 + 2i\sqrt{6}, x = -5 - 2i\sqrt{6}$

Writing and Thinking About Mathematics

71. Explain, in your own words, the steps involved in the process of solving a quadratic equation by completing the square.

Hawkes Learning Systems: Intermediate Algebra

SQE: The Square Root Method
SQE: Completing the Square

7.2   Quadratic Equations: The Quadratic Formula

After completing this section, you will be able to:

1. *Determine the nature of the solutions (one real, two real, or two nonreal) for quadratic equations by using the discriminant.*
2. *Solve quadratic equations by using the quadratic formula.*

The **quadratic formula** gives the roots of any quadratic equation in terms of the coefficients a, b, and c of the **general quadratic equation**

$$ax^2 + bx + c = 0.$$

Therefore, if you have memorized the quadratic formula, you can solve any quadratic equation by simply substituting the coefficients into the formula. To develop the quadratic formula, we solve the general quadratic equation by completing the square as follows:

$ax^2 + bx + c = 0$ The general quadratic equation.

$x^2 + \dfrac{b}{a}x + \dfrac{c}{a} = \dfrac{0}{a}$ Divide each term of the equation by a. Since $a \neq 0$ this is permissible.

$x^2 + \dfrac{b}{a}x = -\dfrac{c}{a}$ Add $-\dfrac{c}{a}$ to both sides of the equation.

$x^2 + \dfrac{b}{a}x + \dfrac{b^2}{4a^2} = \dfrac{b^2}{4a^2} - \dfrac{c}{a}$ $\dfrac{1}{2}\left(\dfrac{b}{a}\right) = \dfrac{b}{2a}$ and $\left(\dfrac{b}{2a}\right)^2 = \dfrac{b^2}{4a^2}$. Add $\dfrac{b^2}{4a^2}$ to both sides of the equation.

$\left(x + \dfrac{b}{2a}\right)^2 = \dfrac{b^2}{4a^2} - \dfrac{4ac}{4a^2}$ Factor the left side. $4a^2$ is the common denominator on the right side.

$\left(x + \dfrac{b}{2a}\right)^2 = \dfrac{b^2 - 4ac}{4a^2}$ Simplify.

$x + \dfrac{b}{2a} = \pm\sqrt{\dfrac{b^2 - 4ac}{4a^2}}$ Use the Square Root Property.

$x + \dfrac{b}{2a} = \pm\dfrac{\sqrt{b^2 - 4ac}}{2a}$ Simplify.

$x = -\dfrac{b}{2a} + \dfrac{\sqrt{b^2 - 4ac}}{2a}$ Solve for x.

$x = \dfrac{-b \pm \sqrt{b^2 - 4ac}}{2a}$ **This equation is called the Quadratic Formula.**

Note about the coefficient _a_

For convenience and without loss of generality, in the development of the quadratic formula (and in the examples and exercises) the leading coefficient, _a_, is positive. If _a_ is a negative number, we can multiply both sides of the equation by −1. This will make the leading coefficient positive without changing any solutions of the original equation.

The Quadratic Formula

For the general quadratic equation

$$ax^2 + bx + c = 0 \qquad where\ a \neq 0$$

the solutions are

$$x = \frac{-b \pm \sqrt{b^2 - 4ac}}{2a}.$$

The quadratic formula should be memorized.

Applications of quadratic equations are found in such fields as economics, business, computer science, and chemistry, and in almost all branches of mathematics. Most instructors assume that their students know the quadratic formula and how to apply it. You should recognize that the importance of the quadratic formula lies in the fact that it allows you to solve **any** quadratic equation.

Example 1: Quadratic Formula

Solve the following quadratic equations by using the quadratic formula.

a. $x^2 - 5x + 3 = 0$

    Solution: Substitute $a = 1$, $b = -5$, and $c = 3$ into the formula:

$$x = \frac{-b \pm \sqrt{b^2 - 4ac}}{2a} = \frac{-(-5) \pm \sqrt{(-5)^2 - 4 \cdot 1 \cdot 3}}{2 \cdot 1}$$

$$= \frac{5 \pm \sqrt{25 - 12}}{2}$$

$$= \frac{5 \pm \sqrt{13}}{2}$$

b. $7x^2 - 2x + 1 = 0$

    Solution: Substitute $a = 7$, $b = -2$, and $c = 1$ into the formula:

$$x = \frac{-b \pm \sqrt{b^2 - 4ac}}{2a} = \frac{-(-2) \pm \sqrt{(-2)^2 - 4 \cdot 7 \cdot 1}}{2 \cdot 7}$$

$$= \frac{2 \pm \sqrt{4 - 28}}{14}$$

$$= \frac{2 \pm \sqrt{-24}}{14}$$

$$= \frac{2 \pm 2i\sqrt{6}}{14}$$

$$= \frac{\cancel{2}\left(1 \pm i\sqrt{6}\right)}{\cancel{2} \cdot 7} \qquad \text{Factor and reduce.}$$

$$= \frac{1 \pm i\sqrt{6}}{7} \qquad \text{The solutions are nonreal complex}$$
numbers.

c. $\dfrac{3}{4}x^2 - \dfrac{1}{2}x = \dfrac{1}{3}$

    Solution: Multiply each term by the LCM, 12, so that the coefficients will be integers. The quadratic formula is easier to use with integer coefficients.

$$12 \cdot \frac{3}{4}x^2 - 12 \cdot \frac{1}{2}x = 12 \cdot \frac{1}{3}$$

$$9x^2 - 6x = 4$$

$$9x^2 - 6x - 4 = 0 \qquad \textbf{To apply the formula, one side must be 0.}$$

$$x = \frac{-(-6) \pm \sqrt{(-6)^2 - 4(9)(-4)}}{2 \cdot 9}$$

$$= \frac{6 \pm \sqrt{36 + 144}}{18}$$

$$= \frac{6 \pm \sqrt{180}}{18} = \frac{6 \pm 6\sqrt{5}}{18}$$

$$= \frac{\cancel{6}\left(1 \pm \sqrt{5}\right)}{\cancel{6} \cdot 3} = \frac{1 \pm \sqrt{5}}{3} \qquad \text{Factor out 6 and reduce.}$$

COMMON ERROR

NOTES

Many students make a mistake when simplifying fractions by dividing the denominator into only one of the terms in the numerator.

$$\text{WRONG} \qquad \frac{4 + \cancel{2}\sqrt{3}}{\cancel{2}} = 4 + \sqrt{3}$$

The correct method is to divide both terms by the denominator or to factor out a common factor in the numerator and then reduce.

$$\text{RIGHT} \qquad \frac{4 + 2\sqrt{3}}{2} = \frac{4}{2} + \frac{2\sqrt{3}}{2} = 2 + \sqrt{3}$$

$$\text{RIGHT} \qquad \frac{4 + 2\sqrt{3}}{2} = \frac{\cancel{2}\left(2 + \sqrt{3}\right)}{\cancel{2}} = 2 + \sqrt{3}$$

In Example 2, the equation is third-degree (a cubic equation) and one of the factors is quadratic. The quadratic formula can be applied to this factor.

Example 2: Cubic Equation •

Solve the following cubic equation using the quadratic formula.
$$2x^3 - 10x^2 + 6x = 0$$

Solution: $2x^3 - 10x^2 + 6x = 0$

$\qquad 2x\left(x^2 - 5x + 3\right) = 0$ Factor out $2x$.

$\qquad 2x = 0 \quad \text{or} \quad x^2 - 5x + 3 = 0$ Set each factor equal to 0.

$\qquad\quad x = 0 \qquad\qquad\qquad x = \dfrac{5 \pm \sqrt{13}}{2}$ Solve each equation. (The quadratic equation was solved in Example 1a by using the quadratic formula.)

• •

The Discriminant

The expression $b^2 - 4ac$, the part of the quadratic formula that lies under the radical sign, is called the **discriminant**. The discriminant identifies the kind of numbers that are solutions to a quadratic equation. Assuming a, b, and c are all real numbers, there are three possibilities: the discriminant is either positive, negative, or zero.

In Example 1a $\left(x^2 - 5x + 3 = 0\right)$, the discriminant was positive, $b^2 - 4ac = (-5)^2 - 4(1)(3)$ $= 13$, and there were two real solutions: $x = \dfrac{5 \pm \sqrt{13}}{2}$. In Example 1b, the discriminant was negative, $b^2 - 4ac = (-2)^2 - 4(7)(1) = -24$, and there were two nonreal solutions: $x = \dfrac{1 \pm i\sqrt{6}}{7}$.

The discriminant gives the following information:

Discriminant	Nature of Solutions
$b^2 - 4ac > 0$	Two real solutions
$b^2 - 4ac = 0$	One real solution, $x = \dfrac{-b \pm 0}{2a} = -\dfrac{b}{2a}$
$b^2 - 4ac < 0$	Two nonreal solutions

In the case where $b^2 - 4ac = 0$, we say $x = -\dfrac{b}{2a}$ is a **double root**. Additionally, if the discriminant is a perfect square, the equation is factorable.

Example 3: Finding the Discriminant ● ● ● ● ● ● ● ● ● ● ● ● ● ● ● ● ●

Find the discriminant and determine the nature of the solutions to each of the following quadratic equations.

a. $3x^2 + 11x - 7 = 0$

   Solution: $b^2 - 4ac = 11^2 - 4(3)(-7)$

$$= 121 + 84$$

$$= 205 > 0$$

   There are two real solutions.

b. $x^2 + 6x + 9 = 0$

   Solution: $b^2 - 4ac = 6^2 - 4(1)(9)$

$$= 36 - 36$$

$$= 0$$

   There is one real solution.

c. $x^2 + 1 = 0$

   Solution: Here $b = 0$. We could write $x^2 + 0x + 1 = 0$.

$$b^2 - 4ac = 0^2 - 4(1)(1)$$

$$= 0 - 4$$

$$= -4$$

   There are two nonreal solutions.

Example 4: Using the Discriminant ● ● ● ● ● ● ● ● ● ● ● ● ● ● ● ● ●

a. Determine the values for k so that $x^2 + 8x - k = 0$ will have one real solution.
   Hint: Set the discriminant equal to 0 and solve the equation for k.
   Solution: $b^2 - 4ac = 8^2 - 4(1)(-k) = 0$

$$64 + 4k = 0$$

$$4k = -64$$

$$k = -16$$

continued on next page ...

Check: $x^2 + 8x - (-16) \overset{?}{=} 0$

$$x^2 + 8x + 16 \overset{?}{=} 0$$

$$(x+4)^2 \overset{?}{=} 0$$

$$x = -4$$

There is only one real solution. Thus, -4 is a double root.

b. Determine the values for k so that $kx^2 - 8x + 4 = 0$ will have two nonreal solutions.

Solution: $b^2 - 4ac = 64 - 4(k)(4)$

$$64 - 4(k)(4) < 0$$

$$64 - 16k < 0$$

$$-16k < -64$$

$$k > 4$$

Thus, if k is any real number greater than 4, the discriminant will be negative and the equation will have two nonreal soutions.

● ●

Practice Problems

Solve each of the following quadratic equations by using the quadratic formula.

1. $x^2 + 2x - 4 = 0$ **2.** $2x^2 - 3x + 4 = 0$ **3.** $5x^2 - x - 4 = 0$

4. $\frac{1}{4}x^2 - \frac{1}{2}x = -\frac{1}{4}$ **5.** $3x^2 + 5 = 0$

7.2 Exercises

Find the discriminant and determine the nature of the solutions to each quadratic equation in Exercises 1 – 12.

1. $x^2 + 6x - 8 = 0$ **2.** $x^2 + 3x + 1 = 0$ **3.** $x^2 - 8x + 16 = 0$

4. $x^2 + 3x + 5 = 0$ **5.** $4x^2 + 2x + 3 = 0$ **6.** $3x^2 - x + 2 = 0$

7. $5x^2 + 8x + 3 = 0$ **8.** $4x^2 + 12x + 9 = 0$ **9.** $100x^2 - 49 = 0$

10. $9x^2 + 121 = 0$ **11.** $3x^2 + x + 1 = 0$ **12.** $5x^2 - 3x - 2 = 0$

Answers to Practice Problems: **1.** $x = -1 \pm \sqrt{5}$ **2.** $x = \dfrac{3 \pm i\sqrt{23}}{4}$ **3.** $x = 1, x = \dfrac{-4}{5}$ **4.** $x = 1$

      5. $x = \dfrac{\pm i\sqrt{15}}{3}$

In Exercises 13 – 24, find the indicated values for k.

13. Determine the values for k so that $x^2 - 8x + k = 0$ will have two real solutions.

14. Determine the values for k so that $x^2 + 5x + k = 0$ will have two real solutions.

15. Determine the values for k so that $x^2 + 9x + k = 0$ will have one real solution.

16. Determine the values for k so that $x^2 - 7x + k = 0$ will have one real solution.

17. Determine the values for k so that $kx^2 - 6x + 3 = 0$ will have two nonreal solutions.

18. Determine the values for k so that $kx^2 + 4x - 2 = 0$ will have two nonreal solutions.

19. Determine the values for k so that $kx^2 + x - 9 = 0$ will have two real solutions.

20. Determine the values for k so that $kx^2 + 6x + 3 = 0$ will have two real solutions.

21. Determine the values for k so that $kx^2 + 7x + 12 = 0$ will have one real solution.

22. Determine the values for k so that $kx^2 - 2x + 8 = 0$ will have one real solution.

23. Determine the values for k so that $3x^2 + 4x + k = 0$ will have two nonreal solutions.

24. Determine the values for k so that $2x^2 + 3x + k = 0$ will have two nonreal solutions.

Solve the equations in Exercises 25 – 52. You may use any of the techniques discussed for solving quadratic equations: factoring, completing the square, or the quadratic formula.

25. $x^2 + 3x - 5 = 0$

26. $x^2 = 7x + 3$

27. $x^2 - 5x + 2 = 0$

28. $x^2 + 4x + 3 = 0$

29. $2x^2 + 7x + 2 = 0$

30. $3x^2 + 2x - 2 = 0$

31. $6x^2 = 5x + 1$

32. $4x^2 + x - 4 = 0$

33. $3x^2 - 4 = 0$

34. $7x^2 + 6x + 1 = 0$

35. $x^3 - 9x^2 + 4x = 0$

36. $x^3 - 8x^2 = 3x^2 + 3x$

37. $x^3 + 3x^2 + x = 0$

38. $4x^3 + 10x^2 - 3x = 0$

39. $x^2 - 3x - 4 = 0$

40. $9x^2 - 6x + 1 = 0$

41. $2x^2 + 8x + 9 = 0$

42. $3x^2 + 7x - 4 = 0$

43. $x^2 - 7 = 0$

44. $3x^2 - 6x + 4 = 0$

45. $x^2 + 4x = x - 2x^2$

46. $3x^2 + 4x = 0$

47. $5x^2 - 7x + 5 = 0$

48. $4x^2 - 5x + 3 = 0$

49. $6x^2 + 2x - 20 = 0$

50. $10x^2 + 35x + 30 = 0$

51. $4x^2 + 9 = 0$

52. $3x^2 - 8x + 6 = 0$

In Exercises 53 – 60, first multiply each side of the equation by the LCM of the denominator to get integer coefficients and then solve the resulting equation.

53. $3x^2 - 4x + \dfrac{1}{3} = 0$

54. $\dfrac{3}{4}x^2 - 2x + \dfrac{1}{8} = 0$

55. $\dfrac{3}{7}x^2 - \dfrac{1}{2}x + 1 = 0$

56. $2x^2 + 3x + \dfrac{5}{4} = 0$

57. $\dfrac{1}{2}x^2 - x + \dfrac{1}{4} = 0$

58. $\dfrac{2}{3}x^2 - \dfrac{1}{3}x + \dfrac{1}{2} = 0$

59. $\dfrac{1}{4}x^2 + \dfrac{7}{8}x + \dfrac{1}{2} = 0$

60. $\dfrac{5}{12}x^2 - \dfrac{1}{2}x - \dfrac{1}{4} = 0$

In Exercises 61 – 68, solve the quadratic equations by using the quadratic formula and your calculator. Write the solutions accurate to 4 decimal places.

61. $0.02x^2 - 1.26x + 3.14 = 0$

62. $0.5x^2 + 0.07x - 5.6 = 0$

63. $\sqrt{2}x^2 - \sqrt{3}x - \sqrt{5} = 0$

64. $x^2 - 2\sqrt{10}x + 10 = 0$

65. $0.3x^2 + \sqrt{2}x + 0.72 = 0$

66. $\sqrt[3]{4}x^2 - \sqrt[4]{2}x - \sqrt{11} = 0$

67. $x^2 + 2\sqrt{15} + 15 = 0$

68. $0.05x^2 - \sqrt{30} = 0$

Writing and Thinking About Mathematics

69. Find an equation of the form $Ax^4 + Bx^2 + C = 0$ that has the four roots ± 2 and ± 3. Explain how you arrived at this equation.

70. The surface area of a circular cylinder can be found with the following formula:

$$S = 2\pi r^2 + 2\pi rh \quad \text{where } r \text{ is the radius of the cylinder and } h \text{ is the height.}$$

Estimate the radius of a circular cylinder of height 30 cm and surface area 300 cm^2. Explain how you used your knowledge of quadratic equations.

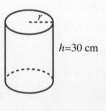

h=30 cm

Hawkes Learning Systems: Intermediate Algebra

SQE: The Quadratic Formula

7.3 Applications

After completing this section, you will be able to:

Solve applied problems by using quadratic equations.

The following Strategy for Solving Word Problems, given in Section 1.5 and again in Section 5.6, is a valid approach to solving word problems at all levels.

Strategy for Solving Word Problems

1. Understand the problem.

   a. Read the problem carefully. (Read it several times if necessary.)

   b. If it helps, restate the problem in your own words.

2. Devise a plan.

   a. Decide what is asked for; assign a variable to the unknown quantity. Label this variable so you know exactly what it represents.

   b. Draw a diagram or set up a chart whenever possible.

   c. Write an equation that relates the information provided.

3. Carry out the plan.

   a. Study your picture or diagram for insight into the solution.

   b. Solve the equation.

4. Look back over the results.

   a. Does your solution make sense in terms of the wording of the problem?

   b. Check your solution in the equation.

The problems in this section can be solved by setting up quadratic equations and then solving these equations by factoring, completing the square, or using the quadratic formula.

The Pythagorean Theorem

The **Pythagorean Theorem** is one of the most interesting and useful ideas in mathematics. We discussed the Pythagorean Theorem in Section 4.6 and do so again here because problems with right triangles often generate quadratic equations.

In a **right triangle**, one of the angles is a right angle (measures 90º), and the side opposite this angle (the longest side) is called the **hypotenuse**. The other two sides are called **legs**.

The Pythagorean Theorem

In a right triangle, the square of the hypotenuse is equal to the sum of the squares of the legs.

$$c^2 = a^2 + b^2$$

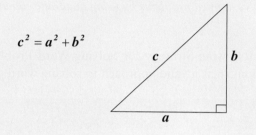

Example 1: The Pythagorean Theorem

The length of a rectangular field is 6 meters more than its width. If the diagonal foot path is 30 meters, what are the dimensions of the field?

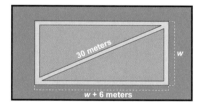

Solution: Let w = width
$w + 6$ = length

$$(w+6)^2 + w^2 = 30^2 \quad \text{Use the Pythagorean Theorem.}$$
$$w^2 + 12w + 36 + w^2 = 900$$
$$2w^2 + 12w - 864 = 0$$
$$w^2 + 6w - 432 = 0$$
$$(w+24)(w-18) = 0$$

$\cancel{w = -24}$ or $w = 18$ A negative number does not fit the conditions of the problem.

$w = 18$ meters
$w + 6 = 24$ meters

The length is 24 meters and the width is 18 meters.

Projectiles

The formula $h = -16t^2 + v_0 t + h_0$ is used in physics and relates to the height of a projectile such as a thrown ball, a bullet, or a rocket.

$$h = \text{height of object, in feet}$$
$$t = \text{time object is in the air, in seconds}$$
$$v_0 = \text{beginning velocity, in feet per second}$$
$$h_0 = \text{beginning height} \quad (h_0 = 0 \text{ if the object is initially at ground level.})$$

Example 2: Projectiles •

A bullet is fired straight up from ground level with a muzzle velocity of 320 ft per sec.
  a. When will the bullet hit the ground?
  b. When will the bullet be 1200 ft above the ground?

Solution: In this problem, $v_0 = 320$ ft per sec
                            and $h_0 = 0$

a. The bullet hits the ground when $h = 0$.

$$h = -16t^2 + v_0 t + h_0$$

$$0 = -16t^2 + 320t + 0$$

$$0 = t^2 - 20t \qquad\qquad \text{Divide both sides by } -16.$$

$$0 = t(t - 20) \qquad\qquad \text{Factor.}$$

$$t = 0 \quad \text{or} \quad t = 20$$

The bullet hits the ground in 20 seconds. The solution $t = 0$ confirms the fact that the bullet was fired from the ground.

b. Let $h = 1200$

$$1200 = -16t^2 + 320t$$

$$0 = -16t^2 + 320t - 1200$$

$$0 = t^2 - 20t + 75$$

$$0 = (t - 5)(t - 15)$$

$$t = 5 \quad \text{or} \quad t = 15$$

Both solutions are meaningful. The bullet is at 1200 ft twice; once in 5 sec going up and once in 15 sec coming down.

• •

Example 3: Geometry

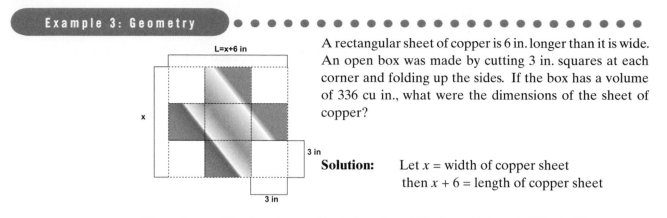

A rectangular sheet of copper is 6 in. longer than it is wide. An open box was made by cutting 3 in. squares at each corner and folding up the sides. If the box has a volume of 336 cu in., what were the dimensions of the sheet of copper?

Solution: Let x = width of copper sheet
then $x + 6$ = length of copper sheet

The volume of the box is equal to 3 times its width times its length. $[V = lwh]$

$$3x(x-6) = 336$$
$$3x^2 - 18x = 336$$
$$3x^2 - 18x - 336 = 0$$
$$x^2 - 6x - 112 = 0$$
$$(x+8)(x-14) = 0$$
$$\cancel{x = -8} \text{ or } x = 14$$
$$x + 6 = 20$$

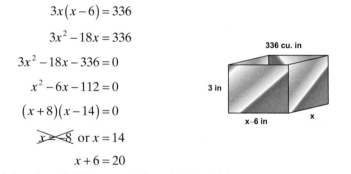

The length of the sheet is 20 in., and the width is 14 in.

Cost Per Person

In the following example, note that the **cost per person** is found by dividing the total cost by the number of people going to the tournament. The cost per person changes because the total cost remains fixed but the number of people changes.

Example 4: Cost Per Person

The members of a bowling club were going to fly commercially to a tournament at a total cost of $2420, which was to be divided equally among the members. At the last minute, two of the members decided to fly their own private planes. The cost to the remaining members increased $11 each. How many members flew commercially?

Solution: Let x = number of club members
then $x - 2$ = number of club members that flew commercially

$$\underbrace{\frac{\text{final cost}}{\text{per member}}} - \underbrace{\frac{\text{initial cost}}{\text{per member}}} = \underbrace{\frac{\text{difference in cost}}{\text{per member}}}$$

$$\frac{2420}{x-2} - \frac{2420}{x} = 11$$

$$x(x-2)\frac{2420}{x-2} - x(x-2)\frac{2420}{x} = x(x-2)\cdot 11$$

$$2420x - 2420(x-2) = 11x(x-2)$$

$$2420x - 2420x + 4840 = 11x^2 - 22x$$

$$0 = 11x^2 - 22x - 4840$$

$$0 = 11(x^2 - 2x - 440)$$

$$0 = 11(x-22)(x+20)$$

$$x = 22 \text{ or } x = -20$$

$$x - 2 = 20$$

(−20 does not fit the conditions. That is, the number of people in a club is a positive number.)

Check: Final cost per member $= \dfrac{2420}{20} = \$121$

Initial cost per member $= \dfrac{2420}{22} = \$110$

$\$121 - \$110 = \$11$ Difference in cost per member.

Twenty members flew commercially.

7.3 Exercises

1. A positive integer is one more than twice another. Their product is 78. Find the two integers.

2. One number is equal to the square of another. Find the numbers if their sum is 72.

3. Find two positive numbers whose difference is 10 and whose product is 56.

4. One number is three more than twice a second number. Their product is 119. Find the numbers.

5. The sum of two numbers is −17. Their product is 66. Find the numbers.

6. Find a positive real number such that its square is equal to twice the number increased by 2.

7. Find a negative real number such that the square of the sum of the number and 5 is equal to 48.

8. The square of a negative real number is decreased by 2.25 and the result is equal to 3 times the number. What is the number?

9. Twice the square of a positive real number is equal to 4 more than the number. What is the number?

10. The sum of three positive integers is 68. The second is one more than twice the first. The third is three less than the square of the first. Find the integers.

11. A right triangle has two equal sides. The hypotenuse is 14 centimeters. Find the length of the sides.

12. The length of one leg of a right triangle is twice the length of the second leg. The hypotenuse is 15 meters. Find the lengths of the two legs.

13. Mel and John leave Desert Point at the same time. Mel drives north and John drives east. Mel's average speed is 10 mph slower than John's. At the end of one hour they are 50 miles apart. Find the average speed of each driver.

14. A flag pole was bent over at a point $\frac{4}{9}$ of the distance from its base to the top. The top of the pole reached a point on the ground 9 meters from the base of the pole. What was the original height of the pole?

15. The length of a rectangle is 2 feet less than three times the width. If the area of the rectangle is 40 square feet, find the dimensions.

16. A rectangle is 3 meters longer than it is wide. If the width is doubled and the length decreased by 4 meters, the area is unchanged. Find the original dimensions.

17. A rectangular piece of cardboard twice as long as it is wide has a small square 4 cm by 4 cm cut from each corner. The edges are then folded up to form an open box with a volume of 1536 cu cm. What are the dimensions of the box? (See example 3.)

18. An orchard has 2030 trees. The number of trees in each row exceeds twice the number of rows by 12. How many trees are in each row?

19. A rectangular auditorium seats 960 people. The number of seats in each row exceeds the number of rows by 16. Find the number of seats in each row.

20. The perimeter of a rectangle is 24 meters and its area is 27 square meters. Find the dimensions of the rectangle.

21. The area of a rectangle is 102 square inches and the perimeter of the rectangle is 46 inches. Find the length and width.

22. The length of a rectangle is 2 cm greater than its width. If the length and the width are each increased by 3 cm, the area is increased by 57 sq cm. Find the dimensions of the original rectangle.

23. A picture 9 in. wide and 12 in. long is surrounded by a frame of uniform width. The area of the frame only is 162 sq in. Find the width of the frame.

24. A 40-volt generator with a resistance of 4 ohms delivers power externally of $40I - 4I^2$ watts, where I is the current measured in amperes. Find the current needed for the generator to deliver 100 watts of power.

25. Find the current needed for the 40-volt generator in Exercise 24 to deliver 64 watts of power.

26. Vince operates a small sign-making business. He finds that if he charges x dollars for each sign, he sells $40 - x$ signs per week. What is the least number of signs he can sell to have an income of $336 in one week?

27. Sam operates a small peanut stand. He estimates that he can sell 600 bags of peanuts per day if he charges 50¢ for each bag. He determines that he can sell 20 more bags for each 1¢ reduction in price.
   a. What would his revenue be if he charged 48¢ per bag?
   b. What should he charge in order to have receipts of $315?

28. It costs Ms. Snow $3 to build a picture frame. She estimates that if she charges x dollars each, she can sell $60 - x$ frames per week. What is the lowest price necessary to make a profit of $432 each week?

29. J.B. bought some shirts and pants. He bought two more pairs of pants than shirts. He spent $154 on pants and $65 for shirts. Find the price of each type of clothing if the price of a pair of pants exceeds the price of a shirt by $9.

30. The Piton Rock Climbing Club planned a climbing expedition. The total cost was $900, which was to be divided equally among the members going. While practicing, three members fell and were hurt so they were unable to go. If the cost per person increased by $15, how many people went on the expedition?

31. Mark traveled 240 miles to a convention. Later, his wife Ann drove up to meet him. Ann's average speed exceeded Mark's by 4 mph, and the trip took her 15 minutes less time. Find Ann's speed.

32. In two hours, a motorboat can travel 8 miles down a river and return 4 miles back. If the river flows at a rate of 2 miles per hour, how fast can the boat travel in still water?

33. It takes Bob 5 hours longer to assemble a machine than it does Sam. After Bob works for as many hours as it would take Sam to do the entire job, Sam can finish the job in 3 hours. How long would it take each man working alone to assemble the machine? (**Hint:** Represent the total job by the number 1.)

34. Two employees together can prepare a large order in 2 hrs. Working alone, one employee takes three hours longer than the other. How long does it take each person working alone?

35. Fern can fly her plane 240 miles against the wind in the same time it takes her to fly 360 miles with the wind. The speed of the plane in still air is 30 mph more than four times the speed of the wind. Find the speed of the plane in still air.

36. A grocer mixes $9.00 worth of Grade A coffee with $12.00 worth of Grade B coffee to obtain 30 pounds of a blend. If Grade A costs 30¢ a pound more than Grade B, how many pounds of each were used?

37. The Andersonville Little Theater Group sold 340 tickets to their spring production. Receipts from the sale of reserved tickets were $855. Receipts from general admission tickets were $375. How many of each type ticket were sold if the cost of a reserved ticket is $2 more than a general admission ticket?

38. It takes a young man 2 hours longer to build a wall than it does his father. After the son has worked for 1 hour, his father joins him and they finish the job together in 6 more hours. How long would it take the father working alone?

In Exercises 39 – 42, use the formula $h = -16t^2 + v_0t + h_0$.

39. A ball is thrown vertically from ground level with an initial speed of 108 ft per sec.
   a. When will the ball hit the ground?
   b. When will the ball be 180 ft above the ground?

40. A ball is thrown vertically from the ground with an initial speed of 160 ft per sec.
   a. When will the ball strike the ground?
   b. When will the ball be 400 ft above the ground?

41. An arrow is shot vertically upward from a platform 40 ft high at a rate of 224 ft per sec.
   a. When will the arrow be 824 ft above the ground?
   b. When will it be 424 ft above the ground?

224 ft/sec

40 ft

42. A stone is dropped from a platform 196 ft high.
   a. When will it hit the ground?
   b. How far will it fall during the third second of time? **Hint:** Since the stone is dropped, $v_0 = 0$.

43. If a triangle is inscribed in a circle so that one side of the triangle is a diameter of the circle, the triangle will be a right triangle (every time). If an isosceles triangle (two sides equal) is inscribed in this manner in a circle with diameter 20 cm, find the length of the two equal sides to the nearest tenth of a centimeter.

44. If a triangle is inscribed in a semicircle such that one side of the triangle is the diameter of a circle with radius 6 in., and one side of the triangle is 5 in., what is the length of the third side? (See Exercise 43.)

In Exercises 45 – 50, use your calculator to find the answers accurate to two decimal places.

45. A square is said to be inscribed in a circle if each corner of the square lies on the circle. (Use $\pi = 3.14$.)
   a. Find the circumference and area of a circle with diameter 30 feet.
   b. Find the perimeter and area of a square inscribed in the circle.

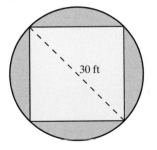

46. The shape of a baseball infield is a square with sides 90 feet long.
   a. Find the distance (to the nearest hundredth of a foot) from home plate to second base.

b. Find the distance (to the nearest hundredth of a foot) from first base to third base.

47. The distance from home plate to the pitcher's mound for the field in question 46 is 60.5 feet.
   a. Is the pitcher's mound exactly half way between home plate and second base?
   b. If not, which base is it closer to, home plate or second base?
   c. Do the two diagonals of the square intersect at the pitcher's mound?

48. The GE Building in New York is 850 feet tall (70 stories). At a certain time of day, the building casts a shadow 100 feet long. Find the distance from the top of the building to the tip of the shadow (to the nearest hundredth of a foot)

49. To create a square inside a square, a quilting pattern requires four triangular pieces like the one shaded in the figure shown here. If the square in the center measures 12 centimeters on a side, and the two legs of each triangle are of equal length, how long are the legs of each triangle, to the nearest hundredth of a centimeter?

50. If an airplane passes directly over your head at an altitude of 1 mile, how far (to the nearest hundredth of a mile) is the airplane from your position after it has flown 2 miles farther at the same altitude?

Writing and Thinking About Mathematics

51. Develop the Quadratic Formula by using the technique of completing the square with the general quadratic equation $ax^2 + bx + c = 0$.

Hawkes Learning Systems: Intermediate Algebra

Applications: Quadratic

7.4   Equations with Radicals

Objectives

After completing this section, you will be able to:

Solve equations that contain one or more radical expressions.

Each of the following equations involves at least one radical expression:

$$x + 3 = \sqrt{x+5} \qquad \sqrt{x} - \sqrt{2x-14} = 1 \qquad \sqrt[3]{x+1} = 5$$

If the radicals are square roots, we solve by squaring both sides of the equations. If the radical is some other root and this root can be isolated on one side of the equation, we solve by raising both sides of the equation to the integer power corresponding to the root. For example, with a cube root both sides are raised to the third power.

Squaring both sides of an equation may introduce new solutions. For example, the first-degree equation $x = -3$ has only one solution, namely, -3. However, squaring both sides gives the quadratic equation

$$x^2 = (-3)^2 \qquad \text{or} \qquad x^2 = 9.$$

The quadratic equation $x^2 = 9$ has two solutions, 3 and -3. Thus, a new solution that is not a solution to the original equation has been introduced. Such a solution is called an **extraneous solution**.

When both sides of an equation are raised to a power, an extraneous solution may be introduced. Be sure to check all solutions in the original equation.

The following examples illustrate a variety of situations involving radicals. The steps used are related to the following general method.

Method for Solving Equations with Radicals

Step 1: Isolate one of the radicals on one side of the equation. (An equation may have more than one radical.)

Step 2: Raise both sides of the equation to the power corresponding to the index of the radical.

Step 3: If the equation still contains a radical, repeat Steps 1 and 2.

Step 4: Solve the equation after all the radicals have been eliminated.

Step 5: Be sure to check all possible solutions in the original equation and eliminate any extraneous solutions.

Example 1: Radical Equations •

Solve the following equations.

a. $x + 3 = \sqrt{x+5}$

Solution: The radical is by itself on one side of the equation, so square both sides.

$$x + 3 = \sqrt{x+5}$$

$$(x+3)^2 = \left(\sqrt{x+5}\right)^2 \quad \text{Square both sides.}$$

$$x^2 + 6x + 9 = x + 5 \qquad \text{This new equation contains no radical.}$$

$$x^2 + 5x + 4 = 0$$

$$(x+4)(x+1) = 0 \qquad \text{Solve by factoring.}$$

$$x = -4 \quad \text{or} \quad x = -1$$

Check both answers in the original equation: $\overset{?}{-4+3=\sqrt{-4+5}} \qquad \overset{?}{-1+3=\sqrt{-1+5}}$

$$\overset{?}{-1 = \sqrt{1}} \qquad\qquad \overset{?}{2 = \sqrt{4}}$$

$$-1 \neq 1 \qquad\qquad\quad 2 = 2$$

–4 is **not** a solution. The only solution is –1.

b. $\sqrt{y^2 - 10y - 11} = 1 + y$

Solution: Since there is only one radical and it is by itself on one side of the equation, square both sides.

$$\sqrt{y^2 - 10y - 11} = 1 + y$$

$$\left(\sqrt{y^2 - 10y - 11}\right)^2 = (1+y)^2$$

$$y^2 - 10y - 11 = 1 + 2y + y^2$$

$$-12y - 12 = 0 \qquad \text{Simplifying gives a first-degree equation.}$$

$$-12y = 12$$

$$y = -1$$

Check in the original equation: $\overset{?}{\sqrt{(-1)^2 - 10(-1) - 11} = 1 + (-1)}$

$$\overset{?}{\sqrt{1 + 10 - 11} = 0}$$

$$\overset{?}{\sqrt{0} = 0}$$

$$0 = 0$$

There is one solution, –1.

c. $\sqrt{x+4} = \sqrt{3x-2}$

    Solution: There are two radicals on opposite sides of the equation. Squaring both sides will give a new equation with no radicals.

$$\sqrt{x+4} = \sqrt{3x-2}$$

$$\left(\sqrt{x+4}\right)^2 = \left(\sqrt{3x-2}\right)^2$$

$$x+4 = 3x-2$$

$$6 = 2x \qquad\qquad \text{Simplifying gives a first-degree equation.}$$

$$3 = x$$

Check in the original equation: $\sqrt{3+4} \overset{?}{=} \sqrt{3\cdot 3 - 2}$

$$\sqrt{7} = \sqrt{7}$$

There is one solution, 3.

d. $\sqrt{3x+13} + 3 = 2x$

    Solution: $\sqrt{3x+13} + 3 = 2x$

$$\sqrt{3x+13} = 2x-3 \qquad\qquad \text{Isolate the radical.}$$

$$\left(\sqrt{3x+13}\right)^2 = (2x-3)^2 \qquad\qquad \text{Square both sides.}$$

$$3x+13 = 4x^2 - 12x + 9$$

$$0 = 4x^2 - 15x - 4$$

$$0 = (4x+1)(x-4)$$

$$x = \frac{-1}{4} \quad \text{or} \quad x = 4$$

Check both answers in the original equation:

$$\sqrt{3\left(\frac{-1}{4}\right)+13} + 3 \overset{?}{=} 2\left(\frac{-1}{4}\right) \qquad\qquad \sqrt{3(4)+13} + 3 \overset{?}{=} 2(4)$$

$$\sqrt{\frac{49}{4}} + 3 \overset{?}{=} \frac{-1}{2} \qquad\qquad\qquad\qquad \sqrt{25} + 3 \overset{?}{=} 8$$

$$\frac{7}{2} + 3 \overset{?}{=} \frac{-1}{2} \qquad\qquad\qquad\qquad 5+3 \overset{?}{=} 8$$

$$\frac{13}{2} \neq \frac{-1}{2} \qquad\qquad\qquad\qquad 8 = 8$$

$-\dfrac{1}{4}$ is **not** a solution. The only solution is 4.

continued on next page ...

499

e. $\sqrt[3]{2x+1}+1=3$

Solution: First, get the radical by itself on one side of the equation. Then, since this radical is a cube root, cube both sides of the equation.

$$\sqrt[3]{2x+1}+1=3$$

$$\sqrt[3]{2x+1}=2 \qquad \text{Add } -1 \text{ to both sides.}$$

$$\left(\sqrt[3]{2x+1}\right)^3=2^3 \qquad \text{Cube both sides.}$$

$$2x+1=8 \qquad \text{Solve the equation.}$$

$$x=\frac{7}{2}$$

Check in the original equation: $\sqrt[3]{2\left(\frac{7}{2}\right)+1}+1\overset{?}{=}3$

$$\sqrt[3]{7+1}+1\overset{?}{=}3$$

$$\sqrt[3]{8}+1\overset{?}{=}3$$

$$2+1\overset{?}{=}3$$

$$3=3$$

There is one solution, $\frac{7}{2}$.

f. $\sqrt{x}-\sqrt{2x-14}=1$

Solution: Where there is a sum or difference of radicals, squaring is easier if the radicals are on different sides of the equation. Also, squaring both sides of the equation is easier if one of the radicals is by itself on one side of the equation.

$$\sqrt{x}-\sqrt{2x-14}=1$$

$$\sqrt{x}=1+\sqrt{2x-14} \qquad \text{Arrange a radical on each side.}$$

$$\left(\sqrt{x}\right)^2=\left(1+\sqrt{2x-14}\right)^2 \qquad \text{Square both sides.}$$

$$x=1+2\sqrt{2x-14}+(2x-14) \qquad \text{Remember, the right-hand side is the square of a binomial.}$$

$$-x+13=2\sqrt{2x-14} \qquad \text{Simplify so that the radical is on one side by itself.}$$

$$\left(-x+13\right)^2=\left(2\sqrt{2x-14}\right)^2 \qquad \text{Square both sides \textbf{again}.}$$

$$x^2-26x+169=4(2x-14)$$

$$x^2-26x+169=8x-56$$

$$x^2 - 34x + 225 = 0$$

$$(x-9)(x-25) = 0$$ Solve by factoring. Use the quadratic formula if you do not see the factors.

$$x = 9 \quad \text{or} \quad x = 25$$

Check both answers in the original equation:

$$\sqrt{9} - \sqrt{2 \cdot 9 - 14} \overset{?}{=} 1 \qquad \sqrt{25} - \sqrt{2 \cdot 25 - 14} \overset{?}{=} 1$$

$$3 - 2 \overset{?}{=} 1 \qquad\qquad 5 - 6 \overset{?}{=} 1$$

$$1 = 1 \qquad\qquad\qquad -1 \neq 1$$

25 is **not** a solution. The only solution is 9.

● ●

Practice Problems

Solve the following equations.

1. $2\sqrt{x+4} = x+1$ **2.** $\sqrt{3x+1} + 1 = \sqrt{x}$ **3.** $\sqrt[3]{2x-9} + 4 = 3$

7.4 Exercises

Solve the following equations.

1. $\sqrt{8x+1} = 5$ **2.** $\sqrt{7x+1} = 6$ **3.** $\sqrt{4x-3} = 7$

4. $\sqrt{5x-6} = 8$ **5.** $\sqrt{2x+5} = \sqrt{4x-1}$ **6.** $\sqrt{5x-1} = \sqrt{x+7}$

7. $\sqrt{3x+2} = \sqrt{9x-10}$ **8.** $\sqrt{2-x} = \sqrt{2x-7}$ **9.** $\sqrt{x(x+3)} = 2$

10. $\sqrt{x(x-5)} = 6$ **11.** $\sqrt{x(2x+5)} = 5$ **12.** $\sqrt{x(3x-14)} = 7$

13. $\sqrt{x+6} = x+4$ **14.** $\sqrt{x+7} = 2x-1$ **15.** $\sqrt{x^2-16} = 3$

16. $\sqrt{x^2-25} = 12$ **17.** $5x + \sqrt{x+7} - 13 = 0$ **18.** $x - 6 - \sqrt{x+1} = 2$

19. $2x = \sqrt{7x-3} + 3$ **20.** $x - \sqrt{3x-8} = 4$ **21.** $\sqrt{3x+1} = 1 - \sqrt{x}$

22. $\sqrt{x} = \sqrt{x+16} - 2$ **23.** $\sqrt{x+4} = \sqrt{x+11} - 1$ **24.** $\sqrt{1-x} + 2 = \sqrt{13-x}$

25. $\sqrt{x+1} = \sqrt{x+6} + 1$ **26.** $\sqrt{x+4} = \sqrt{x+20} - 2$ **27.** $\sqrt{x+5} + \sqrt{x} = 5$

28. $\sqrt{5x-18} - 4 = \sqrt{5x+6}$ **29.** $\sqrt{2x+3} = 1 + \sqrt{x+1}$ **30.** $\sqrt{x} + \sqrt{x-3} = 3$

31. $\sqrt{3x+1} - \sqrt{x+4} - 1$ **32.** $\sqrt{3x+4} - \sqrt{x+5} = 1$ **33.** $\sqrt{5x-1} - 4 - \sqrt{x-1}$

Answers to Practice Problems: **1.** $x = 5$ **2.** No Solution   **3.** $x = 4$

34. $\sqrt{2x-5} - 2 = \sqrt{x-2}$ 35. $\sqrt{2x-3} + \sqrt{x+3} = 6$ 36. $\sqrt{2x+3} - \sqrt{x+5} = 1$

37. $\sqrt[3]{4+3x} = -2$ 38. $\sqrt[3]{2+9x} = 9$ 39. $\sqrt[3]{5x+4} = 4$

40. $\sqrt[3]{7x+1} = -5$ 41. $\sqrt{2x+1} = -4$ 42. $\sqrt{3x-5} = -2$

43. $\sqrt[4]{2x+1} = 3$ 44. $\sqrt[4]{x-6} = 2$

Writing and Thinking About Mathematics

45. Explain, in your own words, why, in general, $(a+b)^2 \neq a^2 + b^2$.

Hawkes Learning Systems: Intermediate Algebra

Solving Radical Equations

7.5   Equations in Quadratic Form

After completing this section, you will be able to:

1. *Solve the equations that can be written in quadratic form by appropriate substitutions.*
2. *Solve equations that contain rational expressions.*

The general quadratic equation is $ax^2 + bx + c = 0$, where $a \neq 0$.

The equations

$$x^4 - 7x^2 + 12 = 0 \quad \text{and} \quad x^{\frac{2}{3}} - 4x^{\frac{1}{3}} - 21 = 0$$

are **not** quadratic equations, but they are in **quadratic form** because the degree of the middle term is one-half the degree of the first term. Specifically,

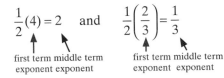

$$\frac{1}{2}(4) = 2 \quad \text{and} \quad \frac{1}{2}\left(\frac{2}{3}\right) = \frac{1}{3}$$

first term middle term   first term middle term
exponent exponent   exponent exponent

Equations in quadratic form can be solved by using the quadratic formula or by factoring just as if they were quadratic equations. In each case, a substitution can be made to clarify the problem. Try to follow these suggestions:

Solving Equations in Quadratic Form by Substitution

1. *Look at the middle term.*
2. *Substitute a first-degree variable, say, u, for the variable expression in the middle term.*
3. *Substitute the square of this variable, u^2, for the variable expression in the first term.*
4. *Solve the resulting quadratic equation for u.*
5. *Substitute the results "back" for u in the beginning substitution and solve for the original variable.*

The following examples illustrate how such a substitution may help. Study these examples carefully and note the variety of algebraic manipulations used.

Example 1: Substitution •

Solve the following equations. Equations a-d are in quadratic form, and a substitution will help.

a. $x^4 - 7x^2 + 12 = 0$

Solution: $x^4 - 7x^2 + 12 = 0$

$$u^2 - 7u + 12 = 0$$ Substitute $u = x^2$ and $u^2 = x^4$.

$$(u-3)(u-4) = 0$$ Solve for u by factoring.

$$u = 3 \qquad \text{or} \quad u = 4$$

$$x^2 = 3 \qquad \text{or} \quad x^2 = 4$$ Now substitute back: x^2 for u.

$$x = \pm\sqrt{3} \qquad\qquad x = \pm 2$$ Solve quadratic equations for x.

There are four solutions: $\sqrt{3}, -\sqrt{3}, 2,$ and -2.

b. $x^{\frac{2}{3}} - 4x^{\frac{1}{3}} - 21 = 0$

Solution: $x^{\frac{2}{3}} - 4x^{\frac{1}{3}} - 21 = 0$

$$u^2 - 4u - 21 = 0$$ Let $u = x^{\frac{1}{3}}$ and $u^2 = x^{\frac{2}{3}}$.

$$(u-7)(u+3) = 0$$ Solve for u by factoring.

$$u = 7 \qquad\qquad \text{or} \qquad\qquad u = -3$$

$$x^{\frac{1}{3}} = 7 \qquad\qquad \text{or} \qquad\qquad x^{\frac{1}{3}} = -3$$ Substitute back: $x^{\frac{1}{3}}$ for u.

$$\left(x^{\frac{1}{3}}\right)^3 = 7^3 \qquad \text{or} \quad \left(x^{\frac{1}{3}}\right)^3 = (-3)^3$$ Cube both sides.

$$x = 343 \qquad\qquad\qquad x = -27$$

There are two solutions: 343 and −27.

c. $x^{-4} - 7x^{-2} + 10 = 0$

Solution: $x^{-4} - 7x^{-2} + 10 = 0$

$$u^2 - 7u + 10 = 0$$ Let $u = x^{-2}$ and $u^2 = x^{-4}$.

$$(u-2)(u-5) = 0$$ Solve for u by factoring.

$$u = 2 \quad \text{or} \quad u = 5$$

$$x^{-2} = 2 \qquad x^{-2} = 5$$ Substitute back: x^{-2} for u.

$$\frac{1}{x^2} = 2 \qquad \frac{1}{x^2} = 5$$ Remember $x^{-2} = \frac{1}{x^2}$.

$$x^2 = \frac{1}{2} \qquad x^2 = \frac{1}{5}$$ Reciprocals.

$$x = \pm\sqrt{\frac{1}{2}} \qquad x = \pm\sqrt{\frac{1}{5}}$$

$$x = \pm\frac{1}{\sqrt{2}} \qquad x = \pm\frac{1}{\sqrt{5}}$$

Rationalizing denominators, we have $x = \pm \dfrac{\sqrt{2}}{2}$ $x = \pm \dfrac{\sqrt{5}}{5}$

There are four solutions: $\dfrac{\sqrt{2}}{2}, \dfrac{-\sqrt{2}}{2}, \dfrac{\sqrt{5}}{5}, \dfrac{-\sqrt{5}}{5}$.

d. $(x + 2)^2 - (x + 2) - 12 = 0$

Solution: $(x + 2)^2 - (x + 2) - 12 = 0$

$$u^2 - u - 12 = 0 \qquad \text{Let } u = x + 2.$$

$$(u - 4)(u + 3) = 0 \qquad \text{Solve for } u \text{ by factoring.}$$

$$u = 4 \qquad \text{or} \qquad u = -3$$
$$x + 2 = 4 \qquad \qquad x + 2 = -3 \qquad \text{Substitute back: } x + 2 \text{ for } u.$$
$$x = 2 \qquad \qquad x = -5$$

There are two solutions: 2 and –5.

e. $x^5 - 16x = 0$

Solution: $x^5 - 16x = 0$

$$x(x^4 - 16) = 0 \qquad \qquad \text{Factor out the common term } x.$$

$$x(x^2 + 4)(x^2 - 4) = 0 \qquad \qquad \text{Factor the difference of two squares.}$$

$$x = 0 \quad \text{or} \quad x^2 = -4 \quad \text{or} \quad x^2 = 4$$
$$x = \pm 2i \qquad \quad x = \pm 2$$

There are five solutions: $0, 2i, -2i, 2, -2$.

f. $\dfrac{2}{3x - 1} + \dfrac{1}{x + 1} = \dfrac{x}{x + 1}$

Solution: This equation is not in quadratic form. However, multiplying both sides of the equation by the LCM of the denominators gives a quadratic equation.

$$(x + 1)\,(3x - 1) \cdot \frac{2}{3x - 1} + (x + 1)(3x - 1) \cdot \frac{1}{x + 1} = (x + 1)(3x - 1) \cdot \frac{x}{x + 1}$$

$$2(x + 1) + 3x - 1 = (3x - 1)x$$

$$2x + 2 + 3x - 1 = 3x^2 - x$$

$$0 = 3x^2 - 6x - 1$$

$$x = \frac{6 \pm \sqrt{36 - 4 \cdot 3(-1)}}{6}$$

$$= \frac{6 \pm \sqrt{48}}{6}$$

$$= \frac{6 \pm 4\sqrt{3}}{6}$$

$$= \frac{3 \pm 2\sqrt{3}}{3}$$

Practice Problems

Solve the following equations.

1. $x - x^{\frac{1}{2}} - 2 = 0$

$(Let\ u = x^{\frac{1}{2}}\ and\ u^2 = x.)$

2. $x^4 + 16x^2 = -48$

$(Let\ u = x^2\ and\ u^2 = x^4.)$

3. $\dfrac{3(x-2)}{x-1} = \dfrac{2(x+1)}{x-2} + 2$

7.5 Exercises

Solve the following equations.

1. $x^4 - 13x^2 + 36 = 0$

2. $x^4 - 29x^2 + 100 = 0$

3. $x^4 - 9x^2 + 20 = 0$

4. $y^4 - 11y^2 + 18 = 0$

5. $y^4 - 3y^2 - 28 = 0$

6. $y^4 + y^2 - 12 = 0$

7. $y^4 - 25 = 0$

8. $x^{-2} - 12x^{-1} + 35 = 0$

9. $z^{-2} - 2z^{-1} - 24 = 0$

10. $16x^3 + 100x = 0$

11. $2x - 9x^{\frac{1}{2}} + 10 = 0$

12. $2x - 3x^{\frac{1}{2}} + 1 = 0$

13. $x^3 - 9x^{\frac{3}{2}} + 8 = 0$

14. $y^3 - 28y^{\frac{3}{2}} + 27 = 0$

15. $2x^{\frac{2}{3}} + 3x^{\frac{1}{3}} - 2 = 0$

16. $2x^{\frac{-2}{3}} + x^{\frac{-1}{3}} - 6 = 0$

17. $x^{-1} + 5x^{\frac{-1}{2}} - 50 = 0$

18. $2x^{-2} - 7x^{-1} + 6 = 0$

19. $3x^{-2} + x^{-1} - 24 = 0$

20. $3y^{-1} - 7y^{\frac{-1}{2}} + 2 = 0$

21. $3x^{\frac{5}{3}} + 15x^{\frac{4}{3}} + 18x = 0$

22. $2x^2 - 30x^{\frac{3}{2}} + 112x = 0$

23. $(3x - 5)^2 + (3x - 5) - 2 = 0$

24. $(x - 1)^2 + (x - 1) - 6 = 0$

25. $(2x + 3)^2 + 7(2x + 3) + 12 = 0$

26. $(5x - 4)^2 + 2(5x - 4) - 8 = 0$

27. $(x - 3)^2 - 2(x - 3) - 15 = 0$

28. $(x + 4)^2 - 2(x + 4) = 3$

29. $(2x + 1)^2 + (2x + 1) = 0$

30. $(x + 7)^2 + 5(x + 7) = 50$

31. $x^4 - 2x^2 + 2 = 0$

32. $x^4 - 4x^2 + 5 = 0$

33. $x^4 - 2x^2 + 10 = 0$

34. $x^4 + 16 = 0$

35. $x^4 - 4x^2 + 7 = 0$

36. $x^4 - 6x^2 + 11 = 0$

37. $x^{-4} - 6x^{-2} + 5 = 0$

38. $3x^{-4} - 5x^{-2} + 2 = 0$

39. $3x^{-4} + 25x^{-2} - 18 = 0$

40. $2x^{-4} + 3x^{-2} - 20 = 0$

41. $\dfrac{2}{4x-1} + \dfrac{1}{x+1} = \dfrac{-x}{x+1}$

42. $\dfrac{3x-2}{15} - \dfrac{16-3x}{x+6} = \dfrac{x+3}{5}$

43. $\dfrac{2x}{x-4} - \dfrac{12x}{x^2+x-20} = \dfrac{x-1}{x+5}$

44. $\dfrac{x+1}{x+3} + \dfrac{2x-1}{x-2} = \dfrac{12x-2}{x^2+x-6}$

45. $\dfrac{x+5}{3x+2} - \dfrac{4-2x}{3x^2+8x+4} = \dfrac{x+4}{x+2}$

46. $\dfrac{x+5}{3x+4} + \dfrac{16x^2+5x+6}{3x^2-2x-8} = \dfrac{4x}{x-2}$

47. $\dfrac{4x+1}{x-6} - \dfrac{3x^2-8x+20}{2x^2-13x+6} = \dfrac{3x+7}{2x-1}$

Answers to Practice Problems: **1.** $x = 4$ **2.** $x = \pm 2i, x = \pm 2i\sqrt{3}$ **3.** $x = -3 \pm \sqrt{19}$

48. $\dfrac{3x+2}{x+3} + \dfrac{22x-31}{x^2-x-12} = \dfrac{3(x+4)}{x+3}$

49. $\dfrac{5(x-10)}{x-7} = \dfrac{2(x+1)}{x-4} + 3$

50. $2 + \dfrac{2-x}{x+2} = \dfrac{x-3}{x+5}$

Writing and Thinking About Mathematics

51. Consider the following equation: $x - x^{\frac{1}{2}} - 6 = 0$

In your own words, explain why, even though it is in quadratic form, this equation has only one solution.

Hawkes Learning Systems: Intermediate Algebra

Equations in Quadratic Form

Chapter 7 Index of Key Ideas and Terms

Zero-Factor Property   page 468

If the product of two factors is 0, then one or both of the factors must be 0. Symbolically, for factors a and b,

if $a \cdot b = 0$, then $a = 0$ or $b = 0$.

Quadratic Equation   page 469

An equation that can be written in the form

$ax^2 + bx + c = 0$ where a, b, and c are real numbers and $a \neq 0$

is called a **quadratic equation**.

To Solve an Equation by Factoring   page 469

1. Add or subtract terms so that <u>one side of the equation is 0</u>.
2. Factor the polynomial expression.
3. Set each factor equal to 0 and solve each of the resulting equations.

(**Note:** If two of the factors are the same, then the solution is said to be a **double root** or a **root of multiplicity two**.)

Square Root Property

page 471

If $x^2 = c$, then $x = \pm\sqrt{c}$.

If $(x - a)^2 = c$, then $x - a = \pm\sqrt{c}$ (or $x = a \pm \sqrt{c}$).

To Solve a Quadratic Equation by Completing the Square

page 473

1. If necessary, divide or multiply both sides of the equation so that the leading coefficient (the coefficient of x^2) is 1.
2. If necessary, isolate the constant term on one side of the equation.
3. Find the constant that completes the square of the polynomial and add this constant to both sides.
4. Use the Square Root Property to find the solutions of the equation.

Writing Equations with Known Roots

pages 475 - 476

Quadratic Formula

page 480

For the general quadratic equation $ax^2 + bx + c = 0$ where $a \neq 0$

the solutions are $x = \dfrac{-b \pm \sqrt{b^2 - 4ac}}{2a}$.

Discriminant

pages 482 - 486

The expression $b^2 - 4ac$, that part of the quadratic formula that lies under the radical sign, is called the **discriminant**.

If $b^2 - 4ac > 0$, there are two real solutions.

If $b^2 - 4ac = 0$, there is one real solution.

If $b^2 - 4ac < 0$, there are two nonreal solutions.

Applications

Pythagorean Theorem

Projectiles

Geometry

Cost Per Person

pages 487 - 488
page 489
page 490
pages 490 - 491

The Pythagorean Theorem

page 488

In a right triangle, the square of the hypotenuse is equal to the sum of the squares of the legs.

Equations with Radicals

page 497

Method for Solving Equations with Radicals

Step 1: Isolate one of the radicals on one side of the equation.

Step 2: Raise both sides of the equation to the power corresponding to the index of the radical.

Step 3: If the equation still contains a radical, repeat Steps 1 and 2.

Step 4: Solve the equation after all the radicals have been eliminated.

Step 5: Be sure to check all possible solutions in the original equation and eliminate any extraneous solutions.

Equations in Quadratic Form   page 503
> **Solving Equations in Quadratic Form by Substitution**
> **1.** Look at the middle term.
> **2.** Substitute a first-degree variable, say, u, for the variable expression in the middle term.
> **3.** Substitute the square of this variable, u^2, for the variable expression in the first term.
> **4.** Solve the resulting quadratic equation for u.
> **5.** Substitute the results "back" for u in the beginning substitution and solve for the original variable.

Chapter 7 Review

For a review of the topics and problems from Chapter 7, look at the following lessons from *Hawkes Learning Systems: Intermediate Algebra*

SQE: The Square Root Method   Applications (Quadratic)
SQE: Completing the Square   Solving Radical Equations
SQE: The Quadratic Formula   Equations in Quadratic Form

Chapter 7 Test

Solve the equations in Exercises 1 and 2 by factoring.

1. a. $x^2 - 16 = 0$

   b. $x^2 + 16 = 0$

2. $4x^3 = -4x^2 - x$

3. Add the constant that will complete the square in each expression and write the new expression as the square of a binomial.

   a. $x^2 - 30x + \underline{\hphantom{xx}} = (\quad)^2$

   b. $x^2 + 5x + \underline{\hphantom{xx}} = (\quad)^2$

4. Write a quadratic equation in the form $ax^2 + bx + c = 0$ that

   a. has the two numbers $\pm 2\sqrt{2}i$ as roots.

   b. has the two numbers $1 \pm \sqrt{5}$ as roots.

5. Solve the following equation by completing the square. Show all the steps.

$$x^2 + 4x + 1 = 0$$

6. What is the discriminant of the quadratic equation $4x^2 + 5x - 3 = 0$? Without finding the roots, tell how many roots the equation has and what type of number they are.

7. By using the discriminant, determine the values for k so that the equation $2x^2 - kx + 3 = 0$ will have exactly one real root.

Solve the equations in Exercises 8 – 15 by using any method.

8. $2x^2 + x + 1 = 0$

9. $2x^2 - 3x - 4 = 0$

10. $2x^2 + 3 = 4x$

11. $\sqrt{x+8} - 2 = x$

12. $\sqrt{2x+9} = \sqrt{x} + 3$

13. $x^4 = 10x^2 - 9$

14. $3x^{-2} + x^{-1} - 2 = 0$

15. $\dfrac{2x}{x-3} - \dfrac{2}{x-2} = 1$

16. Determine whether a triangle with sides of 6 ft, 8 ft, and 11 ft is a right triangle. Explain your answer in detail. Sketch a graph of the triangle and label the sides.

17. A person standing at the edge of a cliff 112 ft above the beach throws a ball into the air with a velocity of 96 ft per sec. (Use the formula $h = -16t^2 + v_0t + h_0$.)

   a. When will the ball hit the beach?

   b. When will the ball be 64 ft above the beach?

18. The length of a rectangle is 4 inches longer than the width. If the diagonal is 20 inches long, what are the dimensions of the rectangle?

19. Sandy made a business trip to a city 200 miles away and then returned home. Her average speed on the return trip was 10 mph less than her average speed going. If her total travel time was 9 hours, what was her average rate in each direction?

20. Use your calculator and your knowledge of the quadratic formula to estimate the solutions to the following quadratic equation: $0.02x^2 + 3.5x - 0.25 = 0$

Cumulative Review: Chapters 1 - 7

Solve the equations in Exercises 1 and 2.

1. $7(2x - 5) = 5(x + 3) + 4$

2. $(2x + 1)(x - 4) = (2x - 3)(x + 6)$

Solve the inequalities in Exercises 3 and 4 and graph the solutions. Write the solutions in interval notation.

3. $4(x + 3) - 1 \geq 2(x - 4)$

4. $\dfrac{7}{2}x + 3 \leq x + \dfrac{13}{2}$

Solve for the indicated variable in Exercises 5 and 6.

5. $3x + 2y = 6$ for y

6. $\dfrac{3}{4}x + \dfrac{1}{2}y = 5$ for y

Simplify Exercises 7 – 14. Assume that all variables are positive.

7. $\left(4x^{-3}\right)\left(2x\right)^{-2}$

8. $\dfrac{x^{-2}y^4}{x^{-5}y^{-2}}$

9. $\left(27x^{-3}y^{\frac{3}{4}}\right)^{\frac{2}{3}}$

10. $\left(\dfrac{9x^{\frac{4}{3}}}{4y^{\frac{2}{3}}}\right)^{\frac{3}{2}}$

11. $\sqrt[3]{-27x^6y^8}$

12. $\sqrt[4]{32x^9y^{15}}$

13. $\dfrac{\sqrt{72}}{3} + 5\sqrt{\dfrac{1}{2}}$

14. $\dfrac{1}{2}\sqrt{\dfrac{4}{3}} + 3\sqrt{\dfrac{1}{3}}$

In Exercises 15 and 16, find an equation with integer coefficients that has the indicated roots.

15. $x = \dfrac{3}{4}, x = -5$

16. $x = 1 - 2\sqrt{5}, x = 1 + 2\sqrt{5}$

17. Solve the following system graphically. $\begin{cases} -2x + 3y = -4 \\ x - 2y = 3 \end{cases}$

18. Solve the following system using Cramer's Rule. $\begin{cases} 3x - 2y = 7 \\ -2x + y = -6 \end{cases}$

19. If $A = \begin{bmatrix} 1 & 5 & 2 \\ -3 & 4 & 6 \\ -2 & -5 & 3 \end{bmatrix}$ find the value of det (A).

20. Use Gaussian elimination to solve the following system. $\begin{cases} x - 3y - z = 1 \\ 2x + y - 2z = -5 \\ 3x - y + 2z = 10 \end{cases}$

Solve the equations in Exercises 21 – 24.

21. $10x^2 + 11x - 6 = 0$

22. $4x^2 + 7x + 1 = 0$

23. $\sqrt{x+5} - 2 = x + 1$

24. $8x^{-2} - 2x^{-1} - 3 = 0$

25. Use synthetic division and the Remainder Theorem to find the following:

    a. $P(3)$ if $P(x) = 2x^3 - 5x^2 + 8x - 33$

    b. $f(-2)$ if $f(x) = x^3 - 10x^2 + 2x + 20$

    c. $g(4)$ if $g(x) = x^4 - 7x^2 + 3x$

26. a. Use synthetic division to find $p(2)$ for the polynomial function
$$p(x) = x^4 - 10x^3 + 20x^2 - 8x - 2$$
    b. What does this result tell you about the expression $(x - 2)$?

    c. What theorem are you using to come to this conclusion?

27. Use a calculator to estimate the value of each number accurate to 4 decimal places.

    a. $\sqrt{6} + 2\sqrt{3}$
    b. $\sqrt{2}\left(1 + 3\sqrt{10}\right)$
    c. $\dfrac{\sqrt{2} + 2}{\sqrt{2} - 2}$

Rationalize the denominator and simplify each expression in Exercises 28 – 30.

28. $\dfrac{5}{\sqrt{2} + \sqrt{3}}$

29. $\dfrac{x^2 - 81}{3 + \sqrt{x}}$

30. $\dfrac{\sqrt{125}}{1 + \sqrt{6}}$

In Exercises 31 – 33, perform the indicated operations and write the results in the standard form a + bi.

31. $(2 + 5i) + (2 - 3i)$
    32. $(2 + 5i)(2 - 3i)$
    33. $\dfrac{2 + 5i}{2 - 3i}$

Use a graphing calculator and trace and zoom features to graph the functions in Exercises 34 – 37 and estimate the x-intercepts.

34. $f(x) = 2x^2 - 5$

35. $y = -x^3 + 2x^2 - 1$

36. $g(x) = x^4 - x^2 + 8$

37. $h(x) = x^3 + 3x + 2$

Use a graphing calculator to graph each of the functions in Exercises 38 – 40. State the domain and range of each function.

38. $f(x) = \sqrt{x - 3}$
    39. $g(x) = \sqrt{1 - x}$
    40. $y = -\sqrt{x + 1}$

41. A car rental agency rents 200 cars per day at a rate of $30 per day for each car. For each $1 increase in the daily rate, the owners have found that they will rent 5 fewer cars per day. What daily rate would give total receipts of $6125?

(**Hint:** Let x = the number of $1 increases.)

42. Find the dimensions of a rectangle that has an area of 520 m^2 and a perimeter of 92 m.

43. Find three consecutive even integers such that the square of the first added to the product of the second and third gives a result of 368.

44. The base of a triangle is 3 cm more than twice its altitude. If the area of the triangle is 76 cm^2, find the lengths of the base and altitude of the triangle.

45. What is the vertical line test for functions? Why does it work?

Quadratic Functions and Conic Sections

Did You Know?

Euler

The mathematician who invented the notation for functions, $f(x)$, which you will study in this chapter, was Leonhard Euler (1707–1783) of Switzerland. Euler was one of the most prolific mathematical researchers of all time, and he lived during a period in which mathematics was making great progress. He studied mathematics, theology, medicine, astronomy, physics, and oriental languages before he began a career as a court philosopher-mathematician. His professional life was spent at St. Petersburg Academy by invitation of Catherine I of Russia, at the Berlin Academy under Frederick the Great of Prussia, and again at the St. Petersburg Academy under Catherine the Great. The collected works of Euler fill 80 volumes, and for almost 50 years after Euler's death, the publications of the St. Petersburg Academy continued to include articles by him.

Euler was blind the last 17 years of his life, but he continued his mathematical research by writing on a large slate and dictating to a secretary. He was responsible for the conventionalization of many mathematical symbols such as $f(x)$ for function notation, i for $\sqrt{-1}$, e for the base of the natural logarithms, π for the ratio of circumference to diameter of a circle, and Σ for the summation symbol.

From the age of 20 to his death, Euler was busy adding to knowledge in every branch of mathematics. He wrote with modern symbolism, and his work in calculus was particularly outstanding. Euler had a rich family life, having had 13 children, and he not only contributed to mathematics but reformed the Russian system of weights and measures, supervised the government pension system in Prussia and the government geographic office in Russia, designed canals, and worked in many areas of physics, including acoustics and optics. It was said of Euler, by the French academician François Arago, that he could calculate without apparent effort "just as men breathe and eagles sustain themselves in the air."

An interesting story is told about Euler's meeting with the French philosopher Diderot at the Russian court. Diderot had angered the czarina by his antireligious views, and Euler was called to the court to debate Diderot. Diderot was told that the great mathematician Euler had an algebraic proof that God existed. Euler walked in towards Diderot and said, "Monsieur, $\dfrac{a+b^n}{n} = x$, therefore God exists, respond." Diderot, who had no understanding of algebra, was unable to respond.

8.1   Quadratic Functions: Parabolas

8.2   Quadratic Inequalities

8.3 $f(x)$ Notation and Translations

8.4   Parabolas as Conic Sections

8.5   Distance Formula, Midpoint Formula, and Circles

8.6   Ellipses and Hyperbolas

8.7   Nonlinear Systems of Equations

"I have not hesitated in 1900, at the Congress of Mathematicians in Paris to call the nineteenth century the century of the theory of functions."

Vito Volterra (1860 – 1940)

The speed at which you drive your car is a **function** of how far you depress the accelerator; your energy level is a **function** of the amount and type of food you eat; your grade in this class is a **function** of the quality time you spend studying. Obviously, the concept of a **function** is present in many aspects of our daily lives. In this text we quantify these ideas by dealing only with functions involving pairs of real numbers. As we have seen in Chapters 2, 4, and 6, this restriction allows us to analyze functions in terms of their graphs in the Cartesian coordinate system. In this chapter, we will be particularly interested in a special category of function called quadratic functions whose graphs are parabolas (curves that, among other things, can be used to describe the paths of projectiles).

Throughout the remainder of the text, we continue to build a list of general properties of functions that form the basis for all our work with functions and lead to the topics of exponential and logarithmic functions in Chapter 9. The function notation, $f(x)$, is particularly useful in understanding, evaluating, and manipulating functions. Mathematical models for applications depend on the concept of functions and use this function notation. For example, we might represent the depreciated value in dollars of a piece of equipment as $f(t) = 10,000 + 4000 \cdot 2^{-0.3t}$ where t is time in years. Or, the profit in dollars from selling x items might be a more familiar polynomial function such as $P(x) = 500 + 3x - 2x^2$. In any case we will find that the concept of functions and related topics, such as graphs and domain and range, provides the basic tools for understanding many applied problems.

8.1 Quadratic Functions: Parabolas

Objectives

After completing this section, you will be able to:

1. *Graph a parabola by finding the zeros (if any) and completing the square, if*

necessary, to determine the vertex, range, and line of symmetry.

2. *Solve applied problems by using quadratic functions.*

Quadratic Functions: $y = ax^2 + bx + c,\ a \neq 0$

We have studied various types of functions, linear functions, polynomial functions, and functions with radicals. In each case we have been interested in the corresponding graphs and the concepts of domain and range and the points where the graph crosses the x–axis (**zeros of the function**). Also, recall that the vertical line test can be used to tell whether or not a graph represents a function.

Vertical Line Test

> If **any** vertical line intersects a graph in more than one point, then the relation graphed is **not** a function.

In this section, we expand our interest in functions to include a detailed analysis of **quadratic functions**, functions that are represented by quadratic expressions. For example, consider the function

$$y = x^2 - 4x + 3$$

What is the graph of this function? Since the equation is not linear, the graph will not be a straight line. The nature of the graph can be investigated by plotting several points (See Figure 8.1.).

x	$x^2 - 4x + 3 = y$
-1	$(-1)^2 - 4(-1) + 3 = 8$
0	$0^2 - 4(0) + 3 = 3$
$\dfrac{1}{2}$	$\left(\dfrac{1}{2}\right)^2 - 4\left(\dfrac{1}{2}\right) + 3 = \dfrac{5}{4}$
1	$1^2 - 4(1) + 3 = 0$
2	$2^2 - 4(2) + 3 = -1$
3	$3^2 - 4(3) + 3 = 0$
$\dfrac{7}{2}$	$\left(\dfrac{7}{2}\right)^2 - 4\left(\dfrac{7}{2}\right) + 3 = \dfrac{5}{4}$
4	$4^2 - 4(4) + 3 = 3$
5	$5^2 - 4(5) + 3 = 8$

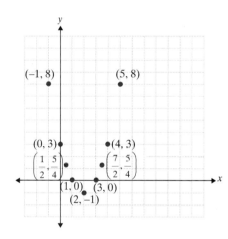

Figure 8.1

The complete graph of $y = x^2 - 4x + 3$ is shown in Figure 8.2. The curve is called a **parabola**. The point $(2, -1)$ is the "turning point" of the parabola and is called the **vertex** of the parabola. The line $x = 2$ is the **line of symmetry** or **axis of symmetry** for the parabola. That is, the curve is a "mirror image" of itself with respect to the line $x = 2$.

Vertex is $(2, -1)$.
$y = x^2 - 4x + 3$ is a parabola.
$x = 2$ is the line of symmetry.

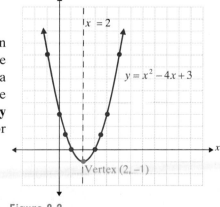

Figure 8.2

517

Quadratic Function

Any function that can be written in the form

$$y = ax^2 + bx + c$$

*where a, b, c are real constants and $a \neq 0$ is a **quadratic function**.*

The graph of every quadratic function is a parabola. The position of the parabola, its shape, and whether it "opens up" or "opens down" can be determined by investigating the function itself. For convenience, we will refer to parabolas that open up or down as **vertical parabolas**. Parabolas that open left or right will be called **horizontal parabolas**. As we will see in Section 8.3, **horizontal parabolas do not represent functions**.

We will discuss quadratic functions in each of the following five forms where $a, b, c, h,$ and k are constants:

$$y = ax^2 \qquad y = ax^2 + k \qquad y = a(x-h)^2 \qquad y = a(x-h)^2 + k \qquad y = ax^2 + bx + c$$

Functions of the form $y = ax^2$

For any real number x, $x^2 \geq 0$. So, $ax^2 \geq 0$ if $a > 0$ and $ax^2 \leq 0$ if $a < 0$. This means that the graph of $y = ax^2$ is "above" the x-axis if $a > 0$ and "below" the x-axis if $a < 0$. The **vertex** is at the origin $(0, 0)$ in either of these cases and is the one point where each graph touches (or is tangent to) the x-axis.

For all quadratic functions, the **domain** is the set of all real numbers. That is, x can be replaced by any real number and there will be one corresponding y-value. The **range** of the function depends on the value of a. If $a > 0$, then $y \geq 0$. If $a < 0$, then $y \leq 0$.

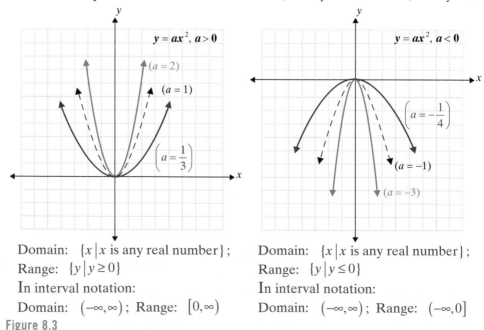

Domain: $\{x \mid x \text{ is any real number}\}$;
Range: $\{y \mid y \geq 0\}$
In interval notation:
Domain: $(-\infty, \infty)$;   Range: $[0, \infty)$

Domain: $\{x \mid x \text{ is any real number}\}$;
Range: $\{y \mid y \leq 0\}$
In interval notation:
Domain: $(-\infty, \infty)$;   Range: $(-\infty, 0]$

Figure 8.3

Figure 8.3 illustrates several properties of quadratic functions of the form $y = ax^2$. If $a > 0$, the parabola "opens upward." If $a < 0$, the parabola "opens downward." The bigger $|a|$ is, the narrower the opening; the smaller $|a|$ is, the wider the opening. The line $x = 0$ (the y-axis) is the line of symmetry.

Functions of the form $y = ax^2 + k$

Adding k to ax^2 simply changes each y-value of $y = ax^2$ by k units (increase if k is positive, decrease if k is negative). That is, the graph of $y = ax^2 + k$ can be found by "sliding or shifting" the graph of $y = ax^2$ up k units if $k > 0$ or down $|k|$ units if $k < 0$ (Figure 8.4).

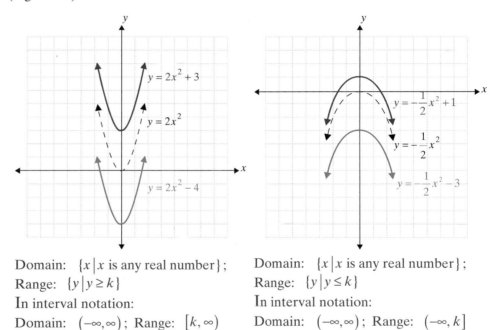

Domain: $\{x \mid x \text{ is any real number}\}$;   Domain: $\{x \mid x \text{ is any real number}\}$;
Range: $\{y \mid y \geq k\}$ Range: $\{y \mid y \leq k\}$
In interval notation: In interval notation:
Domain: $(-\infty, \infty)$; Range: $[k, \infty)$ Domain: $(-\infty, \infty)$; Range: $(-\infty, k]$

Figure 8.4

The vertex of $y = ax^2 + k$ is at the point $(0, k)$. The graph of $y = ax^2 + k$ is a **vertical shift** (or **vertical translation**) of the graph of $y = ax^2$. The line $x = 0$ (the y-axis) is the line of symmetry just as with equations of the form $y = ax^2$.

Functions of the form $y = a(x - h)^2$

We know that $(x - h)^2 \geq 0$. So, if $a > 0$, then $y = a(x - h)^2 \geq 0$. If $a < 0$, then $y = a(x - h)^2 \leq 0$. Also notice that $ax^2 = 0$ when $x = 0$, and $a(x - h)^2 = 0$ when $x = h$. Thus the vertex is at $(h, 0)$, and the parabola "opens upward" if $a > 0$ and "opens downward" if $a < 0$. (Figure 8.5).

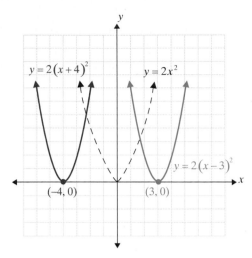

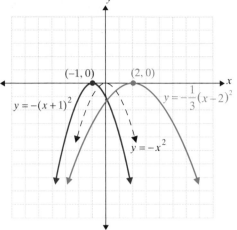

Domain: $\{x \mid x \text{ is any real number}\}$;
Range: $\{y \mid y \geq 0\}$
In interval notation:
Domain: $(-\infty, \infty)$; Range: $[0, \infty)$

Figure 8.5

Domain: $\{x \mid x \text{ is any real number}\}$;
Range: $\{y \mid y \leq 0\}$
In interval notation:
Domain: $(-\infty, \infty)$; Range: $(-\infty, 0]$

The graph of $y = a(x-h)^2$ is a **horizontal shift** (or **horizontal translation**) of the graph of $y = ax^2$. The shift is to the right if $h > 0$ and to the left if $h < 0$. As a special comment, note that if $h = -3$, then

$$y = a(x-h)^2$$

$$\text{gives } y = a(x-(-3))^2$$

$$\text{or } y = a(x+3)^2.$$

Thus, if h is negative, the expression $(x-h)^2$ appears with a plus sign. If h is positive, the expression $(x-h)^2$ appears with a minus sign. In either case, the line $x = h$ is the **line of symmetry**.

Example 1: Quadratic Functions

Graph the following quadratic functions. Set up a table of values for x and y as an aid and choose values of x on each side of the line of symmetry. Find the line of symmetry and the vertex and state the domain and range of each function.

a. $y = 2x^2 - 3$

    Solution: Line of symmetry is $x = 0$. [The parabola opens upward since a is positive.]

            Vertex is at $(0, -3)$. Domain: $\{x \mid x \text{ is any real number}\}$ or $(-\infty, \infty)$

            Range: $\{y \mid y \geq -3\}$ or $[-3, \infty)$

x	y
0	−3
$\frac{1}{2}$	$-\frac{5}{2}$
$-\frac{1}{2}$	$-\frac{5}{2}$
1	−1
−1	−1
2	5
−2	5

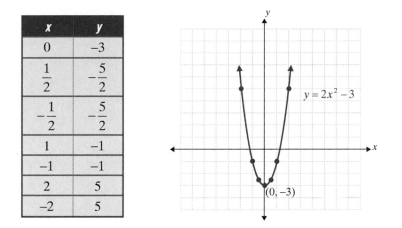

b. $y = -\left(x - \dfrac{5}{2}\right)^2$

Solution: Line of symmetry is $x = \dfrac{5}{2}$. [The parabola opens down since a is negative.]

Vertex is at $\left(\dfrac{5}{2}, 0\right)$. Domain: $\{x \mid x \text{ is any real number}\}$ or $(-\infty, \infty)$

Range: $\{y \mid y \le 0\}$ or $(-\infty, 0]$

x	y
$\dfrac{5}{2}$	0
2	$-\dfrac{1}{4}$
3	$-\dfrac{1}{4}$
1	$-\dfrac{9}{4}$
4	$-\dfrac{9}{4}$
0	$-\dfrac{25}{4}$
5	$-\dfrac{25}{4}$

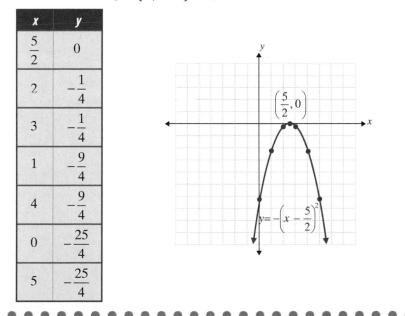

Functions of the form $y = a(x - h)^2 + k$ and $y = ax^2 + bx + c$

The graphs of equations of the form

$$y = a(x - h)^2 + k$$

combine both the vertical shift of k units and the horizontal shift of h units. The vertex is at (h, k). For example, the graph of the function $y = -2(x - 3)^2 + 5$ is a shift of the graph of $y = -2x^2$ up 5 units and to the right 3 units and has its vertex at $(3, 5)$.

The graph of $y = \left(x + \dfrac{1}{2}\right)^2 - 2$ is the same as the graph of $y = x^2$ but is shifted left $\dfrac{1}{2}$ unit and down 2 units. The vertex is at $\left(-\dfrac{1}{2}, -2\right)$ (Figure 8.6).

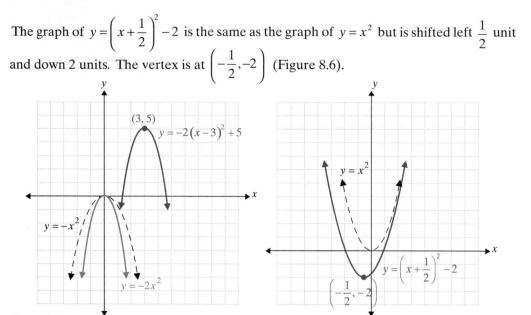

Figure 8.6

The general form of a quadratic function is $y = ax^2 + bx + c$. However, this form does not give as much information about the graph of the corresponding parabola as the form $y = a(x - h)^2 + k$. Therefore, to easily find the vertex, line of symmetry, and range, and to graph the parabola, we want to change the general form $y = ax^2 + bx + c$ into the form $y = a(x - h)^2 + k$. This can be accomplished by completing the square using the following technique. This technique is also useful in other courses in mathematics and should be studied carefully. (Be aware that you are not solving an equation. You do not "do something" to both sides. You are **changing the form** of a function.) **Note:** A graphing calculator will give the same graph regardless of the form of the function.

$y = ax^2 + bx + c$ Write the function.

$= a\left(x^2 + \dfrac{b}{a}x\right) + c$ Factor a from just the first two terms.

$= a\left(x^2 + \dfrac{b}{a}x + \dfrac{b^2}{4a^2} - \dfrac{b^2}{4a^2}\right) + c$ Complete the square of $x^2 + \dfrac{b}{a}x$.

$\dfrac{1}{2} \cdot \dfrac{b}{a} = \dfrac{b}{2a}$ and $\left(\dfrac{b}{2a}\right)^2 = \dfrac{b^2}{4a^2}$.

Add and subtract $\dfrac{b^2}{4a^2}$ inside the parentheses.

$= a\left(x^2 + \dfrac{b}{a}x + \dfrac{b^2}{4a^2}\right) - \dfrac{b^2}{4a} + c$ Multiply $a\left(\dfrac{-b^2}{4a^2}\right)$ and write this term outside the parentheses.

$= a\left(x + \dfrac{b}{2a}\right)^2 + \dfrac{4ac - b^2}{4a}$ Write the square of the binomial and simplify the fraction to get the form $y = a(x - h)^2 + k$.

In terms of the coefficients a, b, and c,

$$x = -\frac{b}{2a} \quad \text{is the line of symmetry}$$

and

$$(h, k) = \left(-\frac{b}{2a}, \frac{4ac - b^2}{4a} \right) \quad \text{is the vertex.}$$

NOTES Rather than memorize the formula for the coordinates of the vertex, you should just remember that the x-coordinate of the vertex is $x = -\frac{b}{2a}$. Substituting this value for x in the function will give the y-value for the vertex.

Zeros of a Quadratic Function

The points where a parabola crosses the x-axis, if any, are the x-intercepts. This is where $y = 0$. These points are called the **zeros of the function**. We find these points by substituting 0 for y and solving the resulting quadratic equation:

$$y = ax^2 + bx + c \quad \textbf{quadratic function}$$

$$0 = ax^2 + bx + c \quad \textbf{quadratic equation}$$

If the solutions are nonreal complex numbers, then the graph does not cross the x-axis. It is either entirely above the x-axis or entirely below the x-axis.

The following examples illustrate how to apply all our knowledge about quadratic functions.

Example 2: Zeros of a Function •

a. $y = x^2 - 6x + 1$

Solution: Find the zeros of the function, the line of symmetry, the vertex, the domain, the range, and graph the parabola.

$$x^2 - 6x + 1 = 0$$

$$x = \frac{6 \pm \sqrt{36 - 4}}{2}$$

$$= \frac{6 \pm \sqrt{32}}{2}$$

$$= \frac{6 \pm 4\sqrt{2}}{2}$$

$$= 3 \pm 2\sqrt{2}$$

continued on next page ...

Change the form of the function for easier graphing.

$$y = x^2 - 6x + 1$$

$$= \left(x^2 - 6x + 9 - 9\right) + 1$$

$$= \left(x^2 - 6x + 9\right) - 9 + 1$$

$$= (x-3)^2 - 8$$

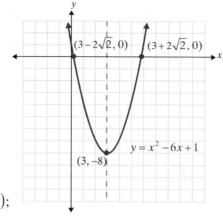

Line of symmetry is $x = 3$. Vertex: $(3, -8)$.
Domain: $\{x \mid x \text{ is any real number}\}$ or $(-\infty, \infty)$;
Range: $\{y \mid y \geq -8\}$ or $[-8, \infty)$.

b. $y = -x^2 - 4x + 2$

Solution: Find the zeros of the function, the line of symmetry, the vertex, the domain, the range, and graph the parabola.

$$-x^2 - 4x + 2 = 0$$

$$x = \frac{4 \pm \sqrt{16 + 8}}{-2}$$

$$= \frac{4 \pm \sqrt{24}}{-2}$$

$$= \frac{4 \pm 2\sqrt{6}}{-2}$$

$$= -2 \pm \sqrt{6}$$

The zeros are $-2 \pm \sqrt{6}$.

Change the form of the function for easier graphing.
$$y = -x^2 - 4x + 2$$

$$= -\left(x^2 + 4x\right) + 2 \qquad \text{Factor } -1 \text{ from the first two terms only.}$$

$$= -\left(x^2 + 4x + 4 - 4\right) + 2 \qquad \text{Add } 0 = 4 - 4 \text{ inside the parentheses.}$$

$$= -\left(x^2 + 4x + 4\right) + 4 + 2 \qquad \text{Multiply } -1(-4) \text{ and put this outside the parentheses.}$$

$$= -(x + 2)^2 + 6$$

Line of symmetry is $x = -2$. Vertex: $(-2, 6)$.
Domain: $\{x \mid x \text{ is any real number}\}$ or $(-\infty, \infty)$;
Range: $\{y \mid y \leq 6\}$ or $(-\infty, 6]$.

c. $y = 2x^2 - 6x + 5$

Solution: Find the zeros of the function, the line of symmetry, the vertex, the domain, the range, and graph the parabola.

$$2x^2 - 6x + 5 = 0$$

$$x = \frac{6 \pm \sqrt{36 - 40}}{4} = \frac{6 \pm \sqrt{-4}}{4} \qquad \text{Quadratic formula}$$

There are no real zeros since the discriminant is negative. The graph will not cross the x–axis.   Now, change the form of the function for easier graphing.

$$y = 2x^2 - 6x + 5$$

$$= 2\left(x^2 - 3x\right) + 5 \qquad \text{Factor 2 from the first two terms only.}$$

$$= 2\left(x^2 - 3x + \frac{9}{4} - \frac{9}{4}\right) + 5 \qquad \text{Add } 0 = \frac{9}{4} - \frac{9}{4} \text{ inside the parentheses.}$$

$$= 2\left(x^2 - 3x + \frac{9}{4}\right) + 2\left(-\frac{9}{4}\right) + 5 \quad \text{Multiply } 2\left(-\frac{9}{4}\right) \text{ and put this outside the parentheses.}$$

$$= 2\left(x - \frac{3}{2}\right)^2 + \frac{1}{2} \qquad \text{Simplify: } 2\left(-\frac{9}{4}\right) + 5 = -\frac{9}{2} + \frac{10}{2} = \frac{1}{2}$$

Line of symmetry is $x = \dfrac{3}{2}$. Vertex: $\left(\dfrac{3}{2}, \dfrac{1}{2}\right)$

Domain: $\{x \mid x \text{ is any real number}\}$ or $(-\infty, \infty)$;

Range: $\left\{ y \mid y \geq \dfrac{1}{2} \right\}$ or $\left[\dfrac{1}{2}, \infty\right)$

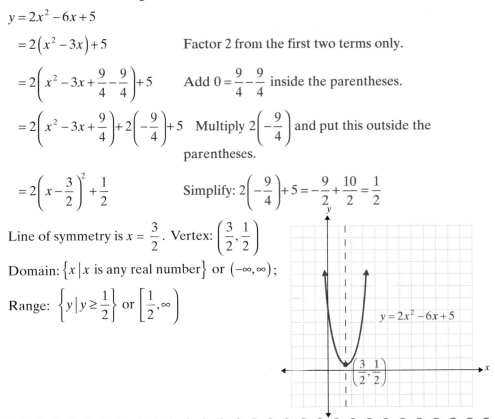

$y = 2x^2 - 6x + 5$

$\left(\dfrac{3}{2}, \dfrac{1}{2}\right)$

Maximum and Minimum Values

The vertex of a vertical parabola is either the lowest point or the highest point on the parabola.

Minimum and Maximum Values

For a parabola with equation in the form $y = a(x - h)^2 + k$,

1.   If $a > 0$, then (h, k) is the lowest point and $y = k$ is called the **minimum value** of the function.

2.   If $a < 0$, then (h, k) is the highest point and $y = k$ is called the **maximum value** of the function.

If the function is in the general quadratic form $y = ax^2 + bx + c$, then the maximum or minimum value can be found by letting $x = -\dfrac{b}{2a}$ and solving for y.

The concepts of maximum and minimum values of a function help not only in graphing but also in solving many types of applications. Applications involving quadratic functions are discussed here. Other types of applications are discussed in Chapter 9 and in more advanced courses in mathematics.

Example 3: Minimum and Maximum Values

a. A sandwich company sells hot dogs at the local baseball stadium for $3.00 each and sells 2000 hot dogs per game. The company estimates that each time the price is raised by 25¢, they will sell 100 fewer hot dogs.

   i. What price should they charge to maximize their revenue (income) per game?
   ii. What will be the maximum revenue?

   Solution: Let x = number of 25¢ increases in price.

   Then $3.00 + 0.25x = $ price per hot dog
   and $2000 - 100x = $ number of hot dogs sold.

   Revenue = (price per unit) · (number of units sold)

   So, $R = (3.00 + 0.25x)(2000 - 100x)$

   $$= 6000 + 500x - 300x - 25x^2$$

   $$= 6000 + 200x - 25x^2$$

   The revenue is represented by a quadratic function and the maximum revenue occurs at the point where

   $$x = -\frac{b}{2a} = -\frac{200}{-50} = 4.$$

   For $x = 4$,

   price per hot dog $= 3.00 + 0.25(4) = \$4.00$

   and   Revenue $= R = (4)(2000 - 400) = \$6400.$

   Thus, the company will make its maximum revenue of $6400 by charging $4 per hot dog.

b. A rancher is going to build three sides of a rectangular corral next to a river. He has 240 feet of fencing and wants to enclose the maximum area possible inside the corral. What are the dimensions of the corral with the maximum area and what is this area?

Solution: Let x = length of one of the two equal sides of the rectangle.
Then $240 - 2x$ = length of third side of the rectangle.
Since the area is the length times the width, the area is represented by the quadratic function $A = x(240 - 2x) = 240x - 2x^2$, the maximum area

occurs at the point where $x = -\dfrac{b}{2a} = -\dfrac{240}{-4} = 60$.

Two sides of the rectangle are 60 feet and the third side is $240 - 2x = 120$ feet.
The maximum area possible is $60(120) = 7200 \text{ ft}^2$.

● ●

Practice Problems

1. Write the function $y = 2x^2 - 4x + 3$ in the form $y = a(x - h)^2 + k$.

2. Find the zeros of the function $y = x^2 - 7x + 10$.

3. Find the vertex and the range of the function $y = -x^2 + 4x - 5$.

8.1 Exercises

For each of the quadratic functions in Exercises 1 – 20, determine the line of symmetry, the vertex, and the domain and range.

1. $y = 3x^2 - 4$ **2.** $y = \dfrac{2}{3}x^2 + 7$ **3.** $y = 7x^2 + 9$

4. $y = 5x^2 - 1$ **5.** $y = -4x^2 + 1$ **6.** $y = -2x^2 - 6$

7. $y = -\dfrac{3}{4}x^2 + \dfrac{1}{5}$ **8.** $y = \dfrac{5}{3}x^2 + \dfrac{7}{8}$ **9.** $y = (x + 1)^2$

10. $y = (x - 1)^2$ **11.** $y = -\dfrac{2}{3}(x - 4)^2$ **12.** $y = -5(x + 2)^2$

13. $y = 2(x + 3)^2 - 2$ **14.** $y = 4(x - 5)^2 + 1$ **15.** $y = \dfrac{3}{4}(x + 2)^2 - 6$

Answers to Practice Problems: **1.** $y = 2(x - 1)^2 + 1$ **2.** $x = 5, x = 2$ **3.** Vertex: $(2, -1)$, Range: $y \le -1$

16. $y = -2(x+1)^2 - 4$ **17.** $y = -\dfrac{1}{2}\left(x - \dfrac{3}{2}\right)^2 + \dfrac{7}{2}$ **18.** $y = -\dfrac{5}{3}\left(x - \dfrac{9}{2}\right)^2 + \dfrac{3}{4}$

19. $y = \dfrac{1}{4}\left(x - \dfrac{4}{5}\right)^2 - \dfrac{11}{5}$ **20.** $y = \dfrac{10}{3}\left(x + \dfrac{7}{8}\right)^2 - \dfrac{9}{16}$

21. Graph the function $y = x^2$. Then, without additional computation, graph the following translations.

    a. $y = x^2 - 2$ **b.** $y = (x-3)^2$ **c.** $y = -(x-1)^2$ **d.** $y = 5 - (x+1)^2$

22. Graph the function $y = 2x^2$. Then, without additional computation, graph the following translations.

    a. $y = 2x^2 - 3$ **b.** $y = 2(x-4)^2$ **c.** $y = -2(x+1)^2$ **d.** $y = -2(x+2)^2 - 4$

23. Graph the function $y = \dfrac{1}{2}x^2$. Then, without additional computation, graph the following translations.

    a. $y = \dfrac{1}{2}x^2 + 3$ **b.** $y = \dfrac{1}{2}(x+2)^2$ **c.** $y = -\dfrac{1}{2}x^2$ **d.** $y = \dfrac{1}{2}(x-1)^2 - 4$

24. Graph the function $y = \dfrac{1}{4}x^2$. Then, without additional computation, graph the following translations.

    a. $y = -\dfrac{1}{4}x^2$ **b.** $y = \dfrac{1}{4}x^2 - 5$ **c.** $y = \dfrac{1}{4}(x+4)^2$ **d.** $y = 2 - \dfrac{1}{4}(x+2)^2$

Rewrite each of the quadratic functions in Exercises 25 – 40 in the form $y = a(x-h)^2 + k$ Find the vertex, range, and zeros of each function. Graph the function.

    25. $y = 2x^2 - 4x + 2$ **26.** $y = -3x^2 + 12x - 12$ **27.** $y = x^2 - 2x - 3$

    28. $y = x^2 - 4x + 5$ **29.** $y = x^2 + 6x + 5$ **30.** $y = x^2 - 8x + 12$

    31. $y = 2x^2 - 8x + 5$ **32.** $y = 2x^2 - 6x + 5$ **33.** $y = -3x^2 - 12x - 9$

    34. $y = 3x^2 - 6x - 1$ **35.** $y = 5x^2 - 10x + 8$ **36.** $y = -4x^2 + 16x - 11$

    37. $y = -x^2 - 5x - 2$ **38.** $y = x^2 + 3x - 1$ **39.** $y = 2x^2 + 7x + 5$

    40. $y = 2x^2 + x - 3$

In Exercises 41–44, graph the two given functions and answer the following questions:

   a. Are the graphs the same?

   b. Do the functions have the same zeros?

   c. Briefly, discuss your interpretation of the results in parts **a** and **b**.

41. $\begin{cases} y = x^2 - 3x - 10 \\ y = -x^2 + 3x + 10 \end{cases}$
      42. $\begin{cases} y = x^2 - 5x + 6 \\ y = -x^2 + 5x - 6 \end{cases}$

43. $\begin{cases} y = 2x^2 - 5x - 3 \\ y = -2x^2 + 5x + 3 \end{cases}$
      44. $\begin{cases} y = -4x^2 - 15x + 4 \\ y = 4x^2 + 15x - 4 \end{cases}$

In Exercises 45 – 48, use the function $h = -16t^2 + v_0 t + h_0$ where h is the height of the object after time t; v_0 is the initial velocity; and h_0 is the initial height.

45. A ball is thrown vertically upward from the ground with an initial velocity of 112 ft per sec.

   a. When will the ball reach its maximum height?

   b. What will be the maximum height?

46. A ball is thrown vertically upward from the ground with an initial velocity of 104 ft per sec.

   a. When will the ball reach its maximum height?

   b. What will be the maximum height?

47. A stone is projected vertically upward from a platform that is 32 ft high, at a rate of 128 ft per sec.

   a. When will the stone reach its maximum height?

   b. What will be the maximum height?

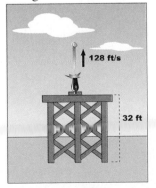

128 ft/s

32 ft

48. A stone is projected vertically upward from a platform that is 20 ft high, at a rate of 160 ft per sec.

   a. When will the stone reach its maximum height?

   b. What will be the maximum height?

49. A store owner estimates that by charging x dollars each for a certain lamp, he can sell $40 - x$ lamps each week. What price will give him maximum receipts?

50. A retailer sells radios. He estimates that by selling them for x dollars each, he will be able to sell $100 - x$ radios each month.

   a. What price will yield maximum revenue?

   b. What will be the maximum revenue?

51. Ms. Richey can sell 72 picture frames each month if she charges $24 each. She estimates that for each $1 increase in price, she will sell 2 fewer frames.

   a. Find the price that will yield maximum revenue.

   b. What will be the maximum revenue?

52. A contractor is to build a brick wall 6 feet high to enclose a rectangular garden. The wall will be on three sides of the rectangle because the fourth side is a building. The owner wants to enclose the maximum area but wants to pay for only 150 feet wall. What dimensions should the contractor make the garden?

*In Exercises 53 – 58, use a graphing calculator to graph each function and use the **ZOOM** and **TRACE** features of the calculator to estimate the zeros of the function (if any) and the coordinates of the vertex.*

53. $y = x^2 - 2x - 2$ **54.** $y = 3x^2 + x - 1$ **55.** $y = -2x^2 + 2x + 5$

56. $y = -x^2 - 2x + 7$ **57.** $y = x^2 + 3x + 3$ **58.** $y = -4x^2 - x - 6$

Writing and Thinking About Mathematics

59. Discuss the following features of the general quadratic function $y = ax^2 + bx + c$.
  a. What type of curve is its graph?
  b. What is the value of x at the vertex of the parabola?
  c. What is the equation of the line of symmetry?
  d. Does the graph always cross the x–axis? Explain.

60. Discuss the discriminant of the general quadratic equation $y = a(x-h)^2 + k$ and how the value of the discriminant is related to the graph of the corresponding quadratic function $y = ax^2 + bx + c$.

61. Discuss the domain and range of a quadratic function in the form $y = a(x-h)^2 + k$.

Hawkes Learning Systems: Intermediate Algebra

Graphing Parabolas

8.2   Quadratic Inequalities

After completing this section, you will be able to:

1. *Solve quadratic inequalities.*
2. *Solve higher degree inequalities.*
3. *Graph the solutions for inequalities on real number lines.*

In Section 1.6, we solved first-degree (or linear) inequalities and, in Section 5.4, we solved inequalities involving rational expressions. In this section we will solve polynomial inequalities of second-degree or higher with emphasis on second-degree or quadratic inequalities. For example,

$$x^2 + 3x + 2 \geq 0, \quad x^2 - 2x > 8, \quad \text{and} \quad x^3 + 4x^2 - 5x < 0$$

We will use two basic methods: solving algebraically by factoring or by using the quadratic formula, and solving by using a graphing calculator.

Quadratic Inequalities: Solved Algebraically

The technique used is based on the same concepts that were used in Section 5.4. That is, the sign of a factor in the form $(x - a)$ changes for x on either side of a. In other words,

if $x > a$, then $(x - a)$ is positive.

if $x < a$, then $(x - a)$ is negative.

The procedure for solving polynomial inequalities algebraically involves getting 0 on one side of the inequality and then factoring (if possible) the polynomial on the other side. The values that make each factor 0 are used to determine intervals over which the polynomial is positive or negative.

To Solve a Polynomial Inequality

1. *Arrange the terms so that one side of the inequality is 0.*
2. *Factor the algebraic expression, if possible, and find the points (numbers) where each factor is 0. (Use the quadratic formula, if necessary.)*
3. *Mark these points on a number line.*
4. *Test one point from each interval to determine the sign of the polynomial expression for all points in that interval.*
5. *The solution consists of those intervals where the test points satisfy the original inequality.*

The following examples illustrate the technique.

Example 1: Solving Polynomial Inequalities Algebraically ● ● ● ● ● ● ● ● ● ●

Solve the following inequalities by factoring and using a number line. Graph the solution set on a number line.

a. $x^2 - 2x > 8$

Solution: $x^2 - 2x > 8$

$x^2 - 2x - 8 > 0$ Add -8 to both sides so that one side is 0.

$(x+2)(x-4) > 0$ Factor.

Set each factor equal to 0 to find endpoints of intervals.

$x+2 = 0$ $x-4 = 0$

$x = -2$ $x = 4$

Mark these points on a number line and test one point from each of the intervals formed.

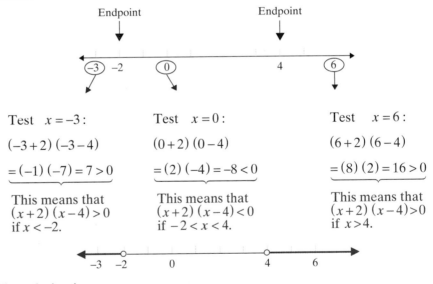

Test $x = -3$:

$(-3+2)(-3-4)$

$= (-1)(-7) = 7 > 0$

This means that
$(x+2)(x-4) > 0$
if $x < -2$.

Test $x = 0$:

$(0+2)(0-4)$

$= (2)(-4) = -8 < 0$

This means that
$(x+2)(x-4) < 0$
if $-2 < x < 4$.

Test $x = 6$:

$(6+2)(6-4)$

$= (8)(2) = 16 > 0$

This means that
$(x+2)(x-4) > 0$
if $x > 4$.

The solution is:

(algebraic notation)   or   (interval notation)

$x < -2$ or $x > 4$ x is in $(-\infty, -2) \cup (4, \infty)$

b. $2x^2 + 15 \le 13x$

Solution: $2x^2 + 15 \le 13x$

$2x^2 - 13x + 15 \le 0$ Add $-13x$ to both sides so that one side is 0.

$(2x-3)(x-5) \le 0$ Factor.

continued on next page ...

Set each factor equal to 0 to locate interval endpoints.

$$2x - 3 = 0 \qquad x - 5 = 0$$

$$x = \frac{3}{2} \qquad x = 5$$

Test one point from each interval formed.

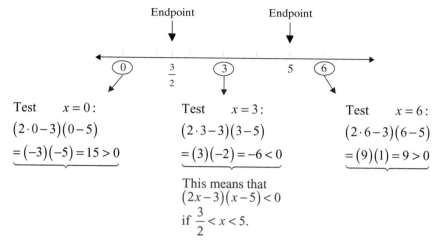

Test $\quad x = 0$:

$(2 \cdot 0 - 3)(0 - 5)$

$= (-3)(-5) = 15 > 0$

Test $\quad x = 3$:

$(2 \cdot 3 - 3)(3 - 5)$

$= (3)(-2) = -6 < 0$

This means that
$(2x - 3)(x - 5) < 0$
if $\dfrac{3}{2} < x < 5$.

Test $\quad x = 6$:

$(2 \cdot 6 - 3)(6 - 5)$

$= (9)(1) = 9 > 0$

The solution includes both endpoints since the inequality ($\leq$) includes 0:

The solution is:

(algebraic notation)   or   (interval notation)

$$\frac{3}{2} \leq x \leq 5 \qquad\qquad x \text{ is in } \left[\frac{3}{2}, 5\right]$$

c. $x^3 + 4x^2 - 5x < 0$

Solution: $x^3 + 4x^2 - 5x < 0$

$$x\left(x^2 + 4x - 5\right) < 0$$

$$x(x + 5)(x - 1) < 0$$

Set each factor equal to 0 to locate interval endpoints.

$$x = 0 \qquad x + 5 = 0 \qquad x - 1 = 0$$

$$x = -5 \qquad\quad x = 1$$

Test one point from each interval formed.

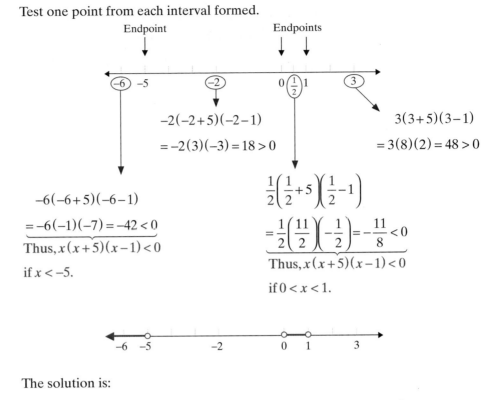

The solution is:

(algebraic notation)	or	(interval notation)
$x < -5$ or $0 < x < 1$		x is in $(-\infty, -5) \cup (0, 1)$

d. $x^2 - 2x - 1 > 0$

Solution: The quadratic expression $x^2 - 2x - 1$ will not factor with integer coefficients. Use the quadratic formula and find the roots of the equation. $x^2 - 2x - 1 = 0$. Then use these roots as endpoints for the intervals. The test points can themselves be integers.

$$x^2 - 2x - 1 = 0$$

$$x = \frac{2 \pm \sqrt{(-2)^2 - 4(1)(-1)}}{2} \quad \text{Use the quadratic formula.}$$

$$x = \frac{2 \pm \sqrt{4 + 4}}{2}$$

$$x = \frac{2 \pm 2\sqrt{2}}{2} = 1 + \sqrt{2}$$

The endpoints are $x = 1 - \sqrt{2}$ and $x = 1 + \sqrt{2}$.

continued on next page ...

535

Test one point from each interval in the expression $x^2 - 2x - 1$.

Note: With a calculator, you can determine that $1 - \sqrt{2} \approx -0.414$ and $1 + \sqrt{2} \approx 2.414$.

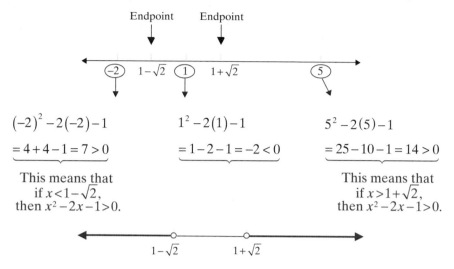

$$(-2)^2 - 2(-2) - 1$$

$$= 4 + 4 - 1 = 7 > 0$$

This means that
if $x < 1 - \sqrt{2}$,
then $x^2 - 2x - 1 > 0$.

$$1^2 - 2(1) - 1$$

$$= 1 - 2 - 1 = -2 < 0$$

$$5^2 - 2(5) - 1$$

$$= 25 - 10 - 1 = 14 > 0$$

This means that
if $x > 1 + \sqrt{2}$,
then $x^2 - 2x - 1 > 0$.

The solution is:

(algebraic notation)   or   (interval notation)

$x < 1 - \sqrt{2}$ or $x > 1 + \sqrt{2}$ x is in $\left(-\infty, 1 - \sqrt{2}\right) \cup \left(1 + \sqrt{2}, \infty\right)$

e. $x^2 - 2x + 13 > 0$

Solution: To find where $x^2 - 2x + 13 > 0$, use the quadratic formula:

$$x = \frac{2 \pm \sqrt{(-2)^2 - 4(1)(13)}}{2} = \frac{2 \pm \sqrt{-48}}{2}$$

$$= \frac{2 \pm 4i\sqrt{3}}{2} = 1 \pm 2i\sqrt{3}$$

Since these values are nonreal, the polynomial is either always positive or always negative for real values of x. Therefore, we only need to test one point. If that point satisfies the inequality, then the solution is all real numbers. Otherwise, there is no solution. In this example, we test $x = 0$ because the polynomial is easy to evaluate for $x = 0$.

$$0^2 - 2(0) + 13 = 13 > 0$$

Since the real number 0 satisfies the inequality, the solution is all real numbers. In interval notation, we write $(-\infty, \infty)$. Graphically,

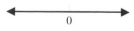

Quadratic Inequalities: Solved with a Graphing Calculator

In Section 1.6, we solved linear inequalities with a graphing calculator by shading on one side of a straight line. To solve quadratic (or other polynomial) inequalities we will simply graph the corresponding function and find intervals over which the function is positive or negative by noting where the graph is above the *x*-axis and where it is below the *x*-axis.

To Solve a Polynomial Inequality with a Graphing Calculator

1. *Arrange the terms so that one side of the inequality is 0.*

2. *Set the quadratic (or other polynomial) equal to y and graph the function.*

   *[Be sure to set the **WINDOW** so that all of the zeros are easily seen.]*

3. *Use the **TRACE** key or **CALC** key to approximate the zeros of the function.*

4. **a.** *If the inequality is of the form y > 0, then the solution consists of those intervals of x where the graph is above the x-axis.*

   b. *If the inequality is of the form y < 0, then the solution consists of those intervals of x where the graph is below the x-axis.*

5. *Endpoints of the intervals are included if the inequality is $y \geq 0$ or $y \leq 0$.*

Example 2: Solving a Polynomial Inequality with a Graphing Calculator ● ● ● ●

Solve the following inequalities by using a graphing calculator. Graph the solution set on a number line.

a. $x^2 - 2x > 8$

Solution: This inequality has been solved algebraically in Example 1a. We repeat the solution here to show how the two methods are related.

$$x^2 - 2x > 8$$

$$x^2 - 2x - 8 > 0 \quad \text{Add} -8 \text{ to both sides so that one side is 0.}$$

$$y = x^2 - 2x - 8 \quad \text{Set the quadratic expression equal to } y.$$

Now graph the function (in this case a parabola).

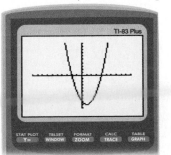

continued on next page ...

537

Pressing 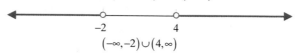 CALC > 2:zero and following the directions for **LeftBound?** and **RightBound?** and **Guess?** will give $x = -2$ and $x = 4$ (the same two values for x that we found in Example 1a). Because we want to know where $y > 0$, we look for the intervals on the x-axis where the parabola is above the x-axis.

The solution set is (as we expected) $(-\infty, -2)$ or $(4, \infty)$.

$$(-\infty, -2) \cup (4, \infty)$$

CAUTION: Choose the Left Bound and Right Bound so that only one zero is between them. Otherwise, you will get an ERROR message.

b. $2x^2 + 3x - 10 \le 0$

Solution: $2x^2 + 3x - 10 \le 0$

$$y = 2x^2 + 3x - 10 \quad \text{Set the expression equal to } y.$$

Now graph the function (in this case a parabola).

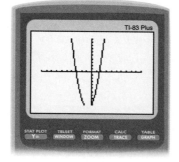

Pressing  CALC > 2:zero and following the directions for **Left Bound?** and **RightBound?** and **Guess?** will give the approximate values $x = -3.1085$ and $x = 1.6085$. Because we want to know where $y \le 0$, we look for the intervals on the x-axis where the parabola is below the x-axis.

The solution is the closed interval $[-3.1085, 1.6085]$ (with the understanding that we have only 4 decimal place accuracy).

$$-3.1085 \qquad 1.6085$$

c. $x^3 + 2x^2 - 11x - 12 > 0$

Solution: $x^3 + 2x^2 - 11x - 12 > 0$

$$y = x^3 + 2x^2 - 11x - 12 \quad \text{Set the quadratic expression equal to } y.$$

Now graph the function (in this case not a parabola).

Pressing ⟨ **2nd** ⟩ CALC > **2:zero** and following the directions for **LeftBound?**
and **RightBound?** and **Guess?** will give the three values $x = -4$, $x = -1$, and
$x = 3$.

Because we want to know where $y > 0$, we look for the intervals on the x-axis
where the curve is above the x-axis.

The solution is the union of two intervals $(-4, -1) \cup (3, \infty)$.

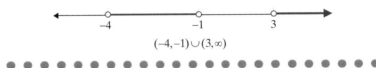

$(-4, -1) \cup (3, \infty)$

8.2 Exercises

*In Exercises 1 – 50, solve the inequalities algebraically and graph each solution set on
a number line. Write the answers in interval notation. (**Note:** You may need to use the
quadratic formula to find endpoints of intervals.)*

1. $(x-6)(x+2) < 0$ **2.** $(x+4)(x-2) > 0$ **3.** $(3x-2)(x-5) > 0$

4. $(4x+1)(x+1) \leq 0$ **5.** $(x+7)(2x-5) \geq 0$ **6.** $(x-3)(5x-3) \leq 0$

7. $(3x+1)(x+2) \leq 0$ **8.** $(x-4)(3x-8) > 0$ **9.** $x(3x+4)(x-5) < 0$

10. $(x-1)(x+4)(2x+5) < 0$ **11.** $x^2 + 4x + 4 \leq 0$ **12.** $5x^2 + 4x - 12 > 0$

13. $2x^2 > x + 15$ **14.** $6x^2 + x > 2$ **15.** $8x^2 < 10x + 3$

16. $2x^2 < x + 10$ **17.** $2x^2 - 5x + 2 \geq 0$ **18.** $15y^2 - 21y - 18 < 0$

19. $6y^2 + 7y < -2$ **20.** $3x^2 + 3 \geq 10x$ **21.** $4z^2 - 20z + 25 > 0$

22. $14 + 11x \geq 15x^2$

23. $8x^2 + 6x \leq 35$

24. $7x < 6x^2 + x^3$

25. $x^3 > 2x^2 + 3x$

26. $x^3 < 6x^2 - 9x$

27. $x^3 > 5x^2 - 4x$

28. $4x^2 \leq x^3 + 3x$

29. $(x+2)(x-2) > 3x$

30. $(x+4)(x-1) < 2x + 2$

31. $x^4 - 5x^2 + 4 > 0$

32. $x^4 - 25x^2 + 144 < 0$

33. $y^4 - 13y^2 + 36 \leq 0$

34. $y^4 - 13y^2 - 48 \geq 0$

35. $(x+1)^2 - 9 \geq 0$

36. $(3x-1)^2 - 16 < 0$

37. $(2x-3)(3x+2) - (3x+2) < 0$

38. $2(x-1)(x-3) > (x-1)(x-6)$

39. $x^2 + 2x - 4 > 0$

40. $x^2 - 8x + 14 < 0$

41. $x^2 + 6x + 7 \geq 0$

42. $2x^2 + 4x - 3 < 0$

43. $3x^2 + 5x + 1 < 0$

44. $3x^2 + 8x + 5 \geq 0$

45. $2x^3 \leq 7x^2 + 4x$

46. $2x^2 > 9x - 8$

47. $x^2 - 2x + 2 > 0$

48. $x^2 + 3x + 3 < 0$

49. $2x - 1 > 3x^2$

50. $6x - 10 < x^2$

Use a graphing calculator to solve the inequalities in Exercises 51 – 60. Graph each solution set on a number line and write the answers in interval notation. (Estimate endpoints, when necessary, to 4 decimal place accuracy.)

51. $x^2 > 10$

52. $20 \geq x^2$

53. $x^2 - 2.5x + 6.25 < 0$

54. $x^2 + 2x \geq -1$

55. $x^3 - 9x < 0$

56. $x^3 - 4x^2 + 4x \leq 0$

57. $2x^3 - 5x + 4 \geq 0$

58. $x^3 - 4x^2 + 3 < 0$

59. $-x^4 + 6x^2 - 3 > 0$

60. $x^4 - 2x^3 - x^2 - 1 < 0$

In Exercises 61 – 64, the graph of a quadratic function is given. Use the information in the graph to solve the related equations and inequalities.

61. $f(x) = x^2 - 7x - 10$

62. $f(x) = x^2 + 5x - 6$

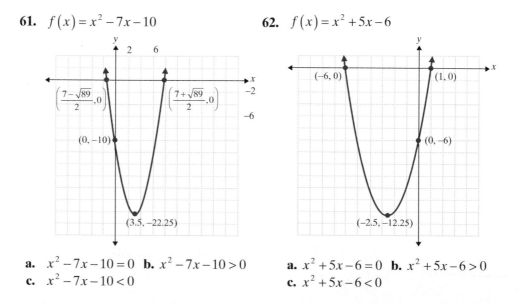

a. $x^2 - 7x - 10 = 0$ **b.** $x^2 - 7x - 10 > 0$
c. $x^2 - 7x - 10 < 0$

a. $x^2 + 5x - 6 = 0$ **b.** $x^2 + 5x - 6 > 0$
c. $x^2 + 5x - 6 < 0$

63. $f(x) = -x^2 - 4x + 5$

64. $f(x) = -3x^2 - 6x + 15$

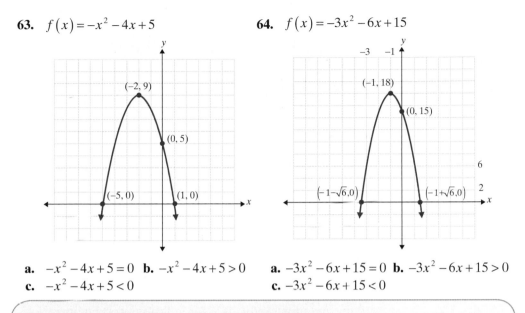

a. $-x^2 - 4x + 5 = 0$ **b.** $-x^2 - 4x + 5 > 0$
c. $-x^2 - 4x + 5 < 0$

a. $-3x^2 - 6x + 15 = 0$ **b.** $-3x^2 - 6x + 15 > 0$
c. $-3x^2 - 6x + 15 < 0$

Writing and Thinking About Mathematics

65. Use a graphing calculator to graph the rational function $y = \dfrac{x^2 + 3x - 4}{x}$.

    a. Use the graph to find the solution set for $y > 0$.
    b. Use the graph to find the solution set for $y < 0$.
    c. Explain the effect of $x = 0$ on the graph and why 0 is not included in either (a) or (b).

66. In your own words, explain why (as in Example 1e), when the quadratic formula gives nonreal values, the quadratic polynomial is either always positive or always negative.

Hawkes Learning Systems: Intermediate Algebra

Solving Quadratic Inequalities

$f(x)$ Notation and Translations

After completing this section, you will be able to:

1.   *Evaluate functions for given values of the independent variables.*
2.   *Graph translations of functions. That is, given the graph of a function $y = f(x)$, you will be able to graph a translation of the form $y = \pm f(x - h) + k$.*

We have used the $f(x)$ (read "f of x") notation in Chapters 2, 4, and 6. As we will see in this section, this notation is particularly convenient for evaluating functions and representing shifts (called **translations**) of graphs of functions. In Chapter 9 we will discuss how this notation can be used for indicating certain operations with functions.

Using $f(x)$ Notation to Evaluate Functions

We have already used the function notation $f(x)$ to evaluate polynomials in Chapter 4 and functions with radicals in Chapter 6. Here, we review and expand the use of the $f(x)$ notation to indicate not only the value of a function for a particular value of x but also for the value when x is replaced by some expression such as $(a + 1)$ or $(x + h)$.

Remember: The function notation $f(x)$ does not mean to multiply f by x.

In discussing functions, the notation $f(x)$ is another notation for y. For example, we can write

$$y = 2x - 4$$

or $$f(x) = 2x - 4.$$

Then $f(3)$ (read "f of 3") means that the function f is to be evaluated for $x = 3$. This is accomplished by replacing x with 3 in the function:

$$f(3) = 2 \cdot 3 - 4 = 6 - 4 = 2.$$

Thus, in the notation for a point on the graph of $y = 2x - 4$, we can label the point

$$(3, 2) \text{ or } (3, f(3)).$$

In general, as shown in Figure 8.7, a point can be labeled as (x, y) or $(x, f(x))$.

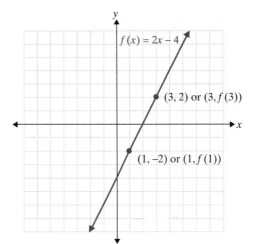

Figure 8.7

Example 1: *f(x)* Notation

a. Let $f(x) = 3x + 5$. Find the following:
  i. $f(2)$ **ii.** $f(-1)$
  iii. $f(a)$ **iv.** $f(a+1)$

Solution: In each case, replace *x* with whatever number or expression is in the parentheses.

$$f(x) = 3x + 5$$

  i. $f(2) = 3 \cdot 2 + 5 = 6 + 5 = 11$
  ii. $f(-1) = 3(-1) + 5 = -3 + 5 = 2$
  iii. $f(a) = 3a + 5$
  iv. $f(a+1) = 3(a+1) + 5 = 3a + 3 + 5 = 3a + 8$

b. Let $g(x) = 2x^2 - 4$. Find the following:
  i. $g(2)$ **ii.** $g(-1)$
  iii. $g(a)$ **iv.** $g(a+1)$

Solution: Substitute whatever number or expression is in parentheses for *x*.

$$g(x) = 2x^2 - 4$$

  i. $g(2) = 2 \cdot 2^2 - 4 = 8 - 4 = 4$

  ii. $g(-1) = 2(-1)^2 - 4 = 2 \cdot 1 - 4 = -2$

  iii. $g(a) = 2a^2 - 4$

  iv. $g(a+1) = 2(a+1)^2 - 4$

$$= 2(a^2 + 2a + 1) - 4$$

$$= 2a^2 + 4a + 2 - 4$$

$$= 2a^2 + 4a - 2$$

continued on next page ...

c.   Let $h(x) = \sqrt{2-x}$. Find the following:

   i. $h(3)$ **ii.** $h(-3)$ **iii.** $h(x+5)$

Solution: $h(x) = \sqrt{2-x}$

   i. $h(3) = \sqrt{2-3} = \sqrt{-1}$, a nonreal number. Because we are concerned only with functions that are sets of ordered pairs of real numbers, we say that 3 is not in the domain of h.

   ii. $h(-3) = \sqrt{2-(-3)} = \sqrt{2+3} = \sqrt{5}$

   iii. $h(x+5) = \sqrt{2-(x+5)} = \sqrt{2-x-5} = \sqrt{-x-3}$

   This substitution is allowed as long as $-x-3 \geq 0$ or $x \leq -3$.

● ●

The formula

$$\frac{f(x+h)-f(x)}{h}$$

is called the **difference quotient** and is particularly useful in calculus. Simplifying the resulting expression is a good algebraic exercise that is a necessary step for finding a new function in calculus called a **derivative**. Be careful to supply parentheses and brackets so that all the algebra is done correctly.

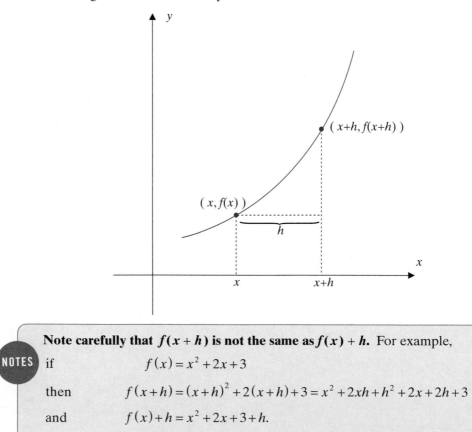

NOTES

   Note carefully that $f(x+h)$ is not the same as $f(x)+h$. For example,

   if $f(x) = x^2 + 2x + 3$

   then $f(x+h) = (x+h)^2 + 2(x+h) + 3 = x^2 + 2xh + h^2 + 2x + 2h + 3$

   and $f(x) + h = x^2 + 2x + 3 + h$.

Example 2: Applying the Formula •

a. Use the function $f(x) = 2x^2 - 5x$ in the formula $\dfrac{f(x+h)-f(x)}{h}$ and simplify.

Solution: $f(x+h) = 2(x+h)^2 - 5(x+h)$ and $f(x) = 2x^2 - 5x$

Substituting gives

$$\frac{f(x+h)-f(x)}{h} = \frac{\left[2(x+h)^2 - 5(x+h)\right] - \left[2x^2 - 5x\right]}{h}$$

$$= \frac{2x^2 + 4xh + 2h^2 - 5x - 5h - 2x^2 + 5x}{h} \qquad \text{Expand } (x+h)^2 \text{ and multiply by 2.}$$

$$= \frac{4xh + 2h^2 - 5h}{h}$$

$$= \frac{h(4x + 2h - 5)}{h} \qquad \text{Factor out } h.$$

$$= 4x + 2h - 5$$

b. Use the function $f(x) = 2 - 6x$ in the formula $\dfrac{f(x+h)-f(x)}{h}$ and simplify.

Solution: $f(x+h) = 2 - 6(x+h)$ and $f(x) = 2 - 6x$

Substituting gives:

$$\frac{f(x+h)-f(x)}{h} = \frac{\left[2 - 6(x+h)\right] - \left[2 - 6x\right]}{h}$$

$$= \frac{2 - 6x - 6h - 2 + 6x}{h}$$

$$= \frac{-6h}{h} = -6$$

• •

Horizontal and Vertical Translations

Function notation is very helpful in understanding a technique for graphing functions called **translations**. There are two kinds of translations: **horizontal translations** (or horizontal shifts) and **vertical translations** (or vertical shifts) (Figure 8.8). We have already discussed the fact that the graph of $y = a(x-h)^2$ is a horizontal shift (or horizontal translation), and the graph of $y = ax^2 + k$ is a vertical shift (or vertical translation) of the graph of $y = ax^2$. (See Section 8.1).

545

In function notation,

if $f(x) = ax^2$,

then $f(x-h) = a(x-h)^2$ is a horizontal translation of $f(x)$

and $f(x) + k = ax^2 + k$ is a vertical translation of $f(x)$.

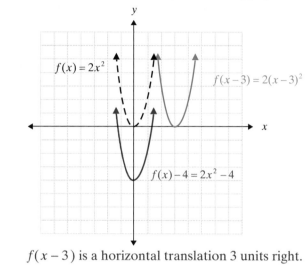

$f(x-3)$ is a horizontal translation 3 units right.
$f(x) - 4$ is a vertical translation 4 units down.

Figure 8.8

The following general approach can be used to help graph a translation of any function.

Horizontal and Vertical Translations

Given the graph of $y = f(x)$, the graph of $y = f(x-h) + k$ is

1. *a horizontal translation of h units, and*

2. *a vertical translation of k units of the graph of $y = f(x)$.*

Think of the origin (0, 0) being moved to the point (h, k).

Then draw the graph of $y = f(x)$ in the same relation to (h, k) as it was to (0, 0).

This new graph will be the graph of $y = f(x-h) + k$.

A good example to use in illustrating translations is the function $f(x) = |x|$. First we need to know what the graph of $f(x) = |x|$ or $y = |x|$ looks like. The definition of $|x|$ gives

$$f(x) = |x| = \begin{cases} x & \text{if } x \ge 0 \\ -x & \text{if } x < 0 \end{cases}$$

The graph can be analyzed in two pieces.

First Piece:

The graph of $f(x) = x$ is a straight line, as shown in Figure 8.9(a), but we want only the part where $x \geq 0$, as shown in Figure 8.9(b).

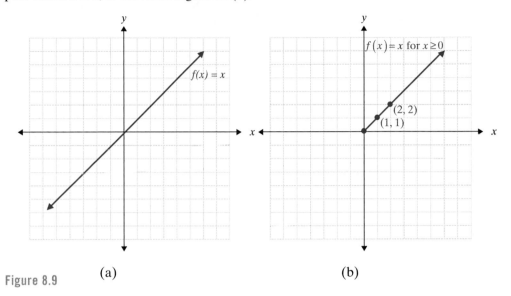

Figure 8.9   (a)   (b)

Second Piece:

The graph of $f(x) = -x$ is also a straight line, as shown in Figure 8.10(a), but we want only the part where $x < 0$, as shown in Figure 8.10(b).

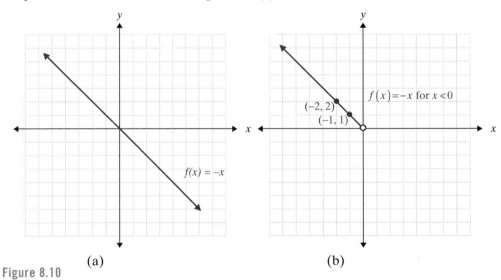

(a)   (b)

Figure 8.10

The two graphs in Figures 8.9(b) and 8.10(b) together give the graph of $f(x) = |x|$, as shown in Figure 8.11 on the following page.

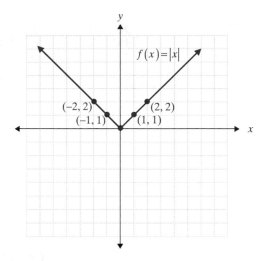

Figure 8.11

The following examples illustrate the graphs of horizontal and vertical translations of the graph of the function $f(x) = |x|$.

Example 3: Horizontal and Vertical Translations

Graph each of the following functions.

a. $y = |x - 3| + 2$

   Solution: Here $(h, k) = (3, 2)$, so there is a horizontal translation of 3 units and a vertical translation of 2 units. In effect, $(3, 2)$ is the vertex of the graph just as $(0, 0)$ is the vertex for $y = |x|$. The points $(2, 3)$ and $(4, 3)$ are shown to make sure that the graph is in the right position. You should check that both points satisfy the function.

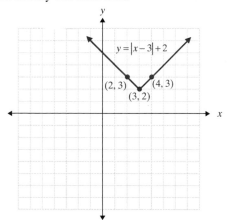

b. $y = |x + 4| - 1$

   Solution: Here $(h, k) = (-4, -1)$, so there is a horizontal translation of -4 and a vertical translation of -1. The effect is that the vertex is now at the point $(-4, -1)$.

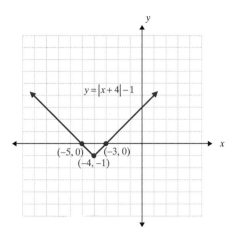

c. $y = |x + 2|$

Solution: Here $(h, k) = (-2, 0)$, so there is a horizontal translation of -2 units. There is no vertical translation.

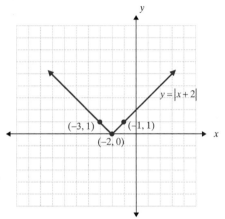

d.   Graph the function $y = |x + 4| - 7$.

Solution: Here $(h, k) = (-4, -7)$, so the graph of $y = |x|$ is translated -4 units horizontally and -7 units vertically.

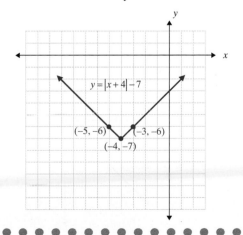

Reflections and Translations

The graph of $y = -f(x)$ is a **reflection across the x-axis** of the graph of $y = f(x)$. In the case of $y = |x|$ and the graph of $y = -|x|$, each graph is the mirror image of the other across the x-axis. The first "opens" upward and the second "opens" downward as illustrated in Figure 8.12.

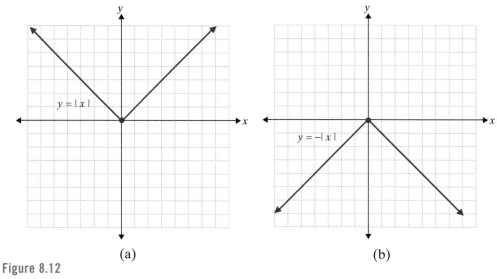

(a)   (b)

Figure 8.12

Example 4: Reflections and Translations

a. Graph the function $y = -|x+2| + 5$.

   Solution: Here $(h,k) = (-2,5)$, and the graph is reflected across the x-axis and "opens" downward. We show step-by-step how to "arrive" at the graph. (You should do these steps mentally and graph only the last step.)

   Step 1:
   Graph the reflection $y = -|x|$.

   Step 2:
   Translate the graph horizontally 2 units left.

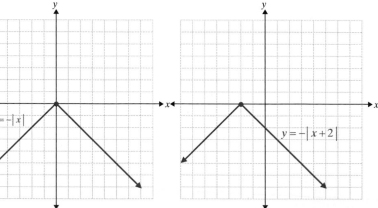

Step 3:

Translate the graph vertically 5 units.

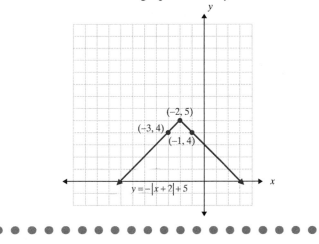

$$y = -|x+2| + 5$$

Example 5 illustrates how the concept of translation can be applied to the graph of any function if the graph of the function is known.

Example 5: Translations of Functions

a.   Graph the function $y = \sqrt{x-2} + 1$. The graph of $y = \sqrt{x}$ is given.

Solution: If $y = \sqrt{x}$ is written $y = f(x)$, then $y = \sqrt{x-2} + 1$ is the same as $y = f(x-2) + 1$. So, $(h, k) = (2, 1)$, and there is a horizontal translation of 2 units and a vertical translation of 1 unit.

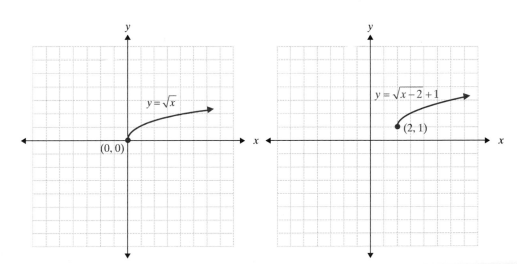

continued on next page ...

b.   The graph of $y = f(x)$ is given. Draw the graph $y = f(x-3)-2$.

Solution: Here $(h, k) = (3, -2)$, so translate horizontally 3 units and vertically -2 units. (Add 3 to each x-value and -2 to each y-value.)

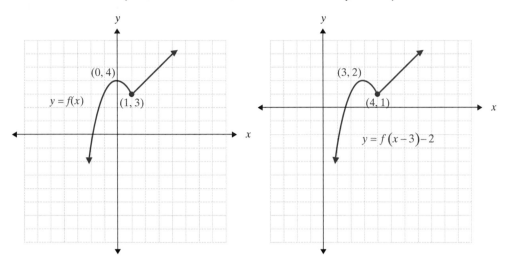

Practice Problems

1. For $f(x) = x^2 - 5$, *find:*

  a. $f(0)$

  b. $f(a)$

  c. $f(a+2)$

2. If $g(x) = 3x + 7$, *find:*

  a. $g(0)$

  b. $g(x+h)$

  c. $\dfrac{g(x+h)-g(x)}{h}$

8.3 Exercises

1. Let $f(x) = x + 7$. Find:
  a. $f(5)$
  b. $f(-3)$
  c. $f(a+1)$

2. Let $f(x) = 2x - 3$. Find:
  a. $f(0)$
  b. $f(7)$
  c. $f(x+4)$

3. Let $f(x) = x^2 - 5$. Find:
  a. $f(3)$
  b. $f(-6)$
  c. $f(x-2)$

4. Let $g(x) = x^2 + 1$. Find:
  a. $g(-4)$
  b. $g(5)$
  c. $g(x-3)$

5. Let $g(x) = 4x - 3$. Find:
  a. $g(1)$
  b. $g(a+2)$
  c. $g(x+h)$
  d. $\dfrac{g(x+h)-g(x)}{h}$

6. Let $f(x) = 5 - 2x$. Find:
  a. $f(-1)$
  b. $f(a+2)$
  c. $f(x+h)$
  d. $\dfrac{f(x+h)-f(x)}{h}$

7. Let $f(x) = x^2 - 4$. Find:

   a. $f(-2)$

   b. $f(a-3)$

   c. $f(x+h)$

   d. $\dfrac{f(x+h)-f(x)}{h}$

8. Let $g(x) = 2 - x^2$. Find:

   a. $g\left(\sqrt{2}\right)$

   b. $g(a-1)$

   c. $g(x+h)$

   d. $\dfrac{g(x+h)-g(x)}{h}$

9. Let $f(x) = 2x^2 - 3$. Find:

   a. $f(0)$

   b. $f(a-2)$

   c. $f(x+h)$

   d. $\dfrac{f(x+h)-f(x)}{h}$

10. Let $f(x) = 3x^2 - x$. Find:

   a. $f(4)$

   b. $f(a+2)$

   c. $f(x+h)$

   d. $\dfrac{f(x+h)-f(x)}{h}$

Using the graph of $y = |x|$, graph the functions in Exercises 11 – 20 without additional computation. (See Example 3)

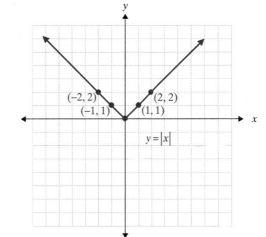

11. $y = |x - 1| - 2$

12. $y = |x - 2| + 6$

13. $y = -|x + 3|$

14. $y = -|x - 4|$

15. $y = -|x + 5| + 4$

16. $y = \left|x + \dfrac{3}{4}\right| - 3$

17. $y = |x - 3| + 5$

18. $y = |x + 2| - 3$

19. $y = \left|x + \dfrac{1}{2}\right| - \dfrac{3}{2}$

20. $y = \dfrac{5}{2}\left|x - \dfrac{2}{3}\right|$

Answers to Practice Problems: **1. a.** $f(0) = -5$ **b.** $f(a) = a^2 - 5$ **c.** $f(a+2) = (a+2)^2 - 5 = a^2 + 4a - 1$

2. a. $g(0) = 7$ **b.** $g(x+h) = 3(x+h) + 7$ **c.** $\dfrac{g(x+h)-g(x)}{h} = 3$

Using the graph of $y = \sqrt{x}$, graph the functions in Exercises 21 – 30 without additional computation. (See Example 5).

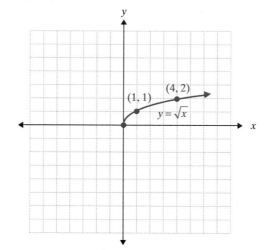

21. $y = \sqrt{x} - 2$ **22.** $y = \sqrt{x} + 1$ **23.** $y = -\sqrt{x+1}$ **24.** $y = -\sqrt{x-6}$

25. $y = \sqrt{x-4} - 3$ **26.** $y = \sqrt{x-2} - 4$ **27.** $y = \sqrt{x-3} + \dfrac{1}{2}$ **28.** $y = \sqrt{x + \dfrac{3}{2}} + 2$

29. $y = 5 + \sqrt{x+2}$ **30.** $y = \sqrt{x+4} - 3$

Using the graph of $y = \dfrac{1}{x}$, graph the functions in Exercises 31 – 40 without additional computation.

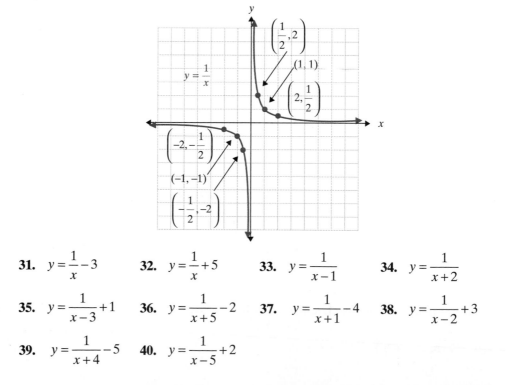

31. $y = \dfrac{1}{x} - 3$ **32.** $y = \dfrac{1}{x} + 5$ **33.** $y = \dfrac{1}{x-1}$ **34.** $y = \dfrac{1}{x+2}$

35. $y = \dfrac{1}{x-3} + 1$ **36.** $y = \dfrac{1}{x+5} - 2$ **37.** $y = \dfrac{1}{x+1} - 4$ **38.** $y = \dfrac{1}{x-2} + 3$

39. $y = \dfrac{1}{x+4} - 5$ **40.** $y = \dfrac{1}{x-5} + 2$

Using the graph y = f(x), graph the functions in Exercises 41– 50 without additional computation.

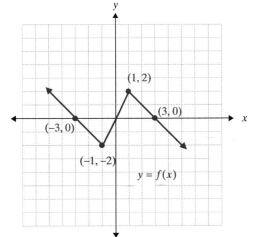

41. $y = f(x) - 1$ **42.** $y = f(x) + 2$ **43.** $y = f(x - 3)$ **44.** $y = f(x + 1)$

45. $y = -f(x)$ **46.** $y = -f(x - 4)$ **47.** $y = f(x + 5) + 3$

48. $y = f(x - 1) + 5$ **49.** $y = f(x + 2) - 4$ **50.** $y = f(x + 3) + 2$

In Exercises 51 – 54, match each equation with its corresponding graph.

51. $y = x^2 - 3$ **52.** $y = -x^2 + 5$ **53.** $y = (x - 1)^2 + 1$ **54.** $y = (x + 3)^2 - 2$

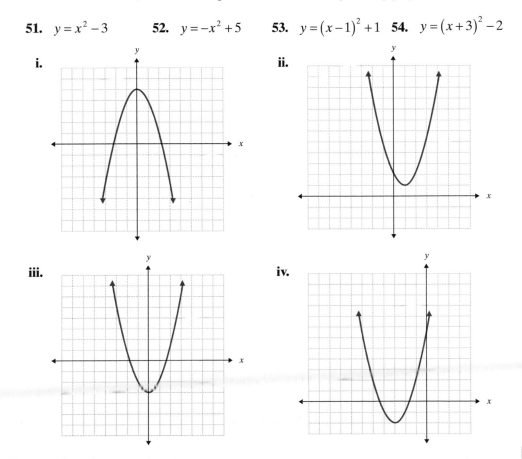

In Exercises 55 – 60, use a graphing calculator to graph each pair of functions on the same set of axes.

55. $y = 2x^2$ and $y = -3x^2$

56. $y = x^2 + 5$ and $y = (x-1)^2$

57. $y = (x+1)^2 - 4$ and $y = x^2 - 4$

58. $y = 2(x+3)^2 - 4$ and $y = 2x^2 + 3$

59. $y = -3(x-2)^2 + 1$ and $y = -x^2 + 1$

60. $y = 4x^2 + 4x - 4$ and $y = x^2 + x - 1$

Hawkes Learning Systems: Intermediate Algebra

Function Notation and Translations

8.4 Parabolas as Conic Sections

Objectives

After completing this section, you will be able to:

1. *Graph parabolas with lines of symmetry parallel to the x-axis.*

2. *Find the vertices, y-intercepts, and lines of symmetry for parabolas that open left or right.*

Conic sections are curves in a plane that are found when the plane intersects a cone. Four such sections are the circle, ellipse, parabola, and hyperbola, as shown in Figure 8.13 respectively.

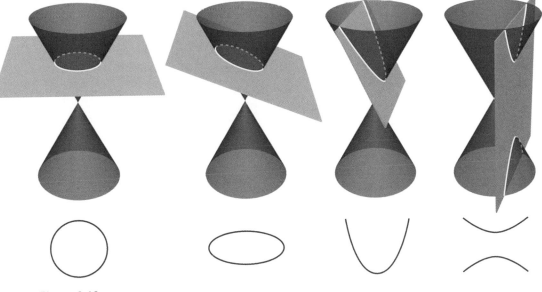

Figure 8.13

The corresponding equations for these conic sections are called quadratic equations because they are second-degree in x and/or y. After some practice you will be able to look at one of these equations and tell immediately what type of curve it represents and where the curve is located with respect to a Cartesian coordinate system. The technique is similar to that used in Chapter 2 in discussing straight lines. By looking at a linear equation, possibly with some algebraic manipulations, you can identify the slope of the line, its y-intercept, and where it is located. By looking at a quadratic equation, you will be able to identify the type of curve it represents and, additionally, you will be able to

 a. identify the center and radius for a circle;
 b. identify the center and intercepts for an ellipse;
 c. identify the vertex and line of symmetry for a parabola; and
 d. identify the vertices and asymptotes for a hyperbola.

Parabolas

As discussed in Section 8.1, the equations of **quadratic functions** are of the basic form $y = ax^2$, and the corresponding graphs are parabolas. From the general view of **conic sections**, not all parabolas are functions. Parabolas that open upward or downward are functions, but those that open to the left or to the right are not functions.

The basic form for equations of parabolas that open left or right is $x = ay^2$, and several graphs of equations of this type are shown in Figure 8.14. As the vertical line test will confirm, these graphs do not represent functions.

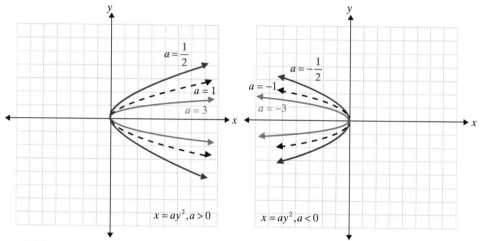

Figure 8.14

In general, the equations of **vertical parabolas** (parabolas that open upward or downward) are in the form

$$y = ax^2 + bx + c \quad \text{or} \quad y = a(x-h)^2 + k \quad (\text{where } a \neq 0)$$

and the parabolas open down (if $a < 0$) or up (if $a > 0$) with vertex at (h, k). The line $x = h$ is the line of symmetry.

By exchanging the roles of x and y, the equations of **horizontal parabolas** (parabolas that open to the left or right) can be written in the following form.

Equations of Horizontal Parabolas

Equations of horizontal parabolas (parabolas that open to the left or right) are of the form

$$x = ay^2 + by + c \quad \text{or} \quad x = a(y-k)^2 + h \quad (\text{where } a \neq 0).$$

The parabola opens left if a is negative and right if a is positive.

The vertex is at ***(h, k)***.

The line $y = k$ *is the line of symmetry.*

In a manner similar to the discussion in Section 8.3, adding h to the right hand side and replacing y with $(y-k)$ in the equation $x=ay^2$ gives an equation whose graph is a horizontal translation of h units and a vertical translation of k units of the graph of $x=ay^2$.

For example, the graph of $x=2(y-3)^2-1$ is shown in Figure 8.15 with a table of y- and x-values. The vertex is at $(h,k)=(-1,3)$, and the line of symmetry is $y=3$. The y-values in the table are chosen on each side of the line of symmetry.

y	$2(y-3)^2-1=x$
3	$2(3-3)^2-1=-1$
4	$2(4-3)^2-1=1$
2	$2(2-3)^2-1=1$
5	$2(5-3)^2-1=7$
1	$2(1-3)^2-1=7$

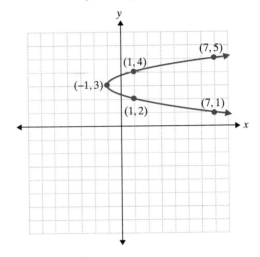

Figure 8.15

The graph of an equation of the form $x=ay^2+by+c$ can be found by completing the square (as in Section 8.3) and writing the equation in the form

$$x=a(y-k)^2+h.$$

Also, by setting $x=0$ and solving the following quadratic equation

$$0=ay^2+by+c$$

we can determine at what points, if any, the graph intersects the **y-axis**. These points are called **y-intercepts**.

Example 1: Horizontal Parabolas ●

a. For $x=y^2-6y+6$, find the vertex, the points where the graph intersects the y-axis, and the line of symmetry. Then sketch the graph.

Solution: To find the vertex, complete the square:

$$x=y^2-6y+6$$

$$x=(y^2-6y+9)-9+6$$

$$x=(y-3)^2-3$$

continued on next page ...

559

To find the y-intercepts, let $x = 0$:

$$y^2 - 6y + 6 = x$$

$$y^2 - 6y + 6 = 0$$

$$y = \frac{6 \pm \sqrt{(-6)^2 - 4 \cdot 1 \cdot 6}}{2}$$

$$y = \frac{6 \pm \sqrt{12}}{2}$$

$$y = 3 \pm \sqrt{3}$$

Since $a = 1$, the parabola has the same shape as $x = y^2$. The vertex is at $(-3, 3)$.

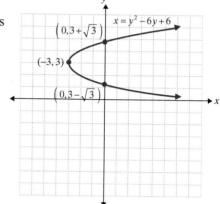

Vertex $= (-3, 3)$.

y-intercepts: $(0, 3 + \sqrt{3})$ and $(0, 3 - \sqrt{3})$.

Line of symmetry is $y = 3$.

b.   For $x = -2y^2 - 4y + 6$, locate the vertex, the y-intercepts, and the line of symmetry. Then sketch the graph.

Solution: To find the vertex, complete the square:

$$x = -2y^2 - 4y + 6$$

$$x = -2(y^2 + 2y) + 6$$

$$x = -2(y^2 + 2y + 1 - 1) + 6$$

$$x = -2(y^2 + 2y + 1) + 2 + 6$$

$$x = -2(y^2 + 2y + 1) + 8$$

$$x = -2(y + 1)^2 + 8$$

To find the y-intercepts, let $x = 0$:

$$-2y^2 - 4y + 6 = 0$$

$$-2(y^2 + 2y - 3) = 0$$

$$-2(y + 3)(y - 1) = 0$$

$$y = -3 \quad \text{or} \quad y = 1$$

Since $a = -2$, the graph opens to the left and is slightly narrower than $x = y^2$.
The vertex is at $(8, -1)$.

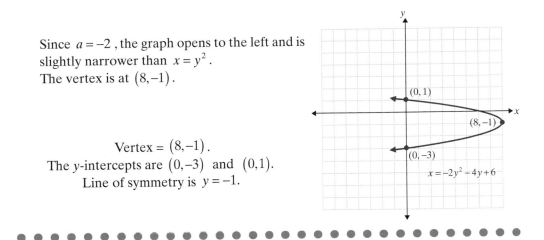

Vertex = $(8, -1)$.
The y-intercepts are $(0, -3)$ and $(0, 1)$.
Line of symmetry is $y = -1$.

Using a Calculator to Graph Horizontal Parabolas

Horizontal parabolas are not functions and the graphing calculator is designed to graph only functions. Therefore to graph a horizontal parabola, solve the given equation for y. For example, from the previous discussion we know that the graph of the equation $x = y^2 - 2$ is a horizontal parabola opening right with vertex at $(-2, 0)$.

To use a graphing calculator, we must first solve for y since equations must be entered with y (to the first power) on the left hand side. By using the definition of square root, we can find two functions that we will designate as y_1 and y_2 as follows:

$$x = y^2 - 2$$

$$y^2 = x + 2 \qquad \text{First solve for } y^2.$$

$$\left.\begin{array}{l} y_1 = \sqrt{x+2} \\ y_2 = -\sqrt{x+2} \end{array}\right\} \quad \begin{array}{l}\text{Solving for } y \text{ gives two equations} \\ \text{that represent two functions.}\end{array}$$

Graphing these equations individually gives the upper and lower halves of the parabola.

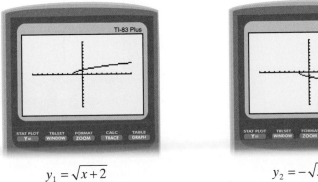

$y_1 = \sqrt{x+2}$
(upper half)

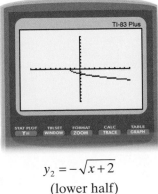

$y_2 = -\sqrt{x+2}$
(lower half)

561

Graphing both halves at the same time gives the entire parabola $x = y^2 - 2$.

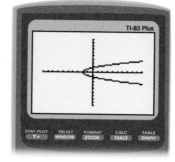

Example 2: Horizontal Parabola

Use a graphing calculator to graph the horizontal parabola $x = y^2 - 4y + 5$. Estimate the y-intercepts by using the trace and zoom features of the calculator.

Solution: To solve for y, complete the square and use the definition of square root as follows.

$$x = y^2 - 4y + 5$$

$$y^2 - 4y = x - 5$$

$$y^2 - 4y + 4 = x - 5 + 4$$

$$(y - 2)^2 = x - 1$$

$$y - 2 = \pm\sqrt{x - 1}$$

$$\left.\begin{array}{l} y_1 = \sqrt{x - 1} + 2 \\ y_2 = -\sqrt{x - 1} + 2 \end{array}\right\} \quad \text{Graph both of these equations.}$$

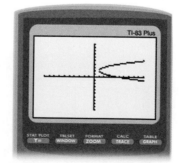

From this graph, we can determine that there are no y-intercepts.

Practice Problems

1. Write the equation $x = -y^2 - 10y - 24$ in the form $x = a(y-k)^2 + h$.

2. Find the vertex, y-intercepts, and line of symmetry for the curve $x = y^2 - 4$.

3. Find the y-intercepts for the curve $x = y^2 + 2y + 2$.

8.4 Exercises

In each of the Exercises 1 – 30, find the vertex, y-intercepts, and the line of symmetry; then draw the graph.

1. $x = y^2 + 4$

2. $x = y^2 - 5$

3. $x + 3 = y^2$

4. $x - 2 = y^2$

5. $x = 2y^2 + 3$

6. $x = 3y^2 + 1$

7. $x = (y-3)^2$

8. $x = (y-2)^2$

9. $x - 4 = (y+2)^2$

10. $x + 3 = (y-5)^2$

11. $x + 1 = (y-1)^2$

12. $x - 5 = (y-3)^2$

13. $x = y^2 + 4y + 4$

14. $x = -y^2 + 10y - 25$

15. $x = y^2 - 8y + 16$

16. $x = y^2 + 6y + 1$

17. $y = -x^2 - 4x + 5$

18. $y = x^2 + 5x + 6$

19. $y = x^2 + 6x + 5$

20. $y = x^2 - 2x - 5$

21. $x = -y^2 + 4y - 3$

22. $x = y^2 + 8y + 10$

23. $y = 2x^2 + x - 1$

24. $y = -2x^2 + x + 3$

25. $x = 3y^2 + 6y - 5$

26. $x = 3y^2 + 5y + 2$

27. $x = -2y^2 + 5y - 2$

28. $x = 4y^2 - 4y - 15$

29. $y = 4x^2 - 12x + 9$

30. $y = -5x^2 + 10x + 2$

Use a graphing calculator to graph each of the parabolas in Exercises 31 – 40. Use the trace and zoom features of the calculator to estimate the y-intercepts of the parabolas.

31. $x = 2y^2 - 3$

32. $x = -3y^2 + 1$

33. $x = -y^2 + 2y$

34. $x = y^2 - 5y$

35. $x = 2y^2 + y + 1$

36. $x = -y^2 - 4y + 1$

37. $x = 4y^2 + 8y - 7$

38. $x = 3y^2 + 3y + 2$

39. $x = -2y^2 + 4y + 3$

40. $x = -5y^2 - 10y - 4$

Answers to Practice Problems: 1. $x = -(y+5)^2 + 1$ **2.** Vertex: $(-4, 0)$, y-intercepts: $(0, 2)$ and $(0, -2)$, Line of symmetry: $y = 0$ **3.** There are no y-intercepts. The solutions to the equation $0 = y^2 + 2y + 2$ are nonreal.

In Exercises 41 – 44, use your knowledge of parabolas and equations to match the equation with the graph.

41. $x = 2(y-3)^2 + 4$

42. $x = -(y+1)^2 + 5$

43. $x = y^2 - 6$

44. $x = -y^2 - 1$

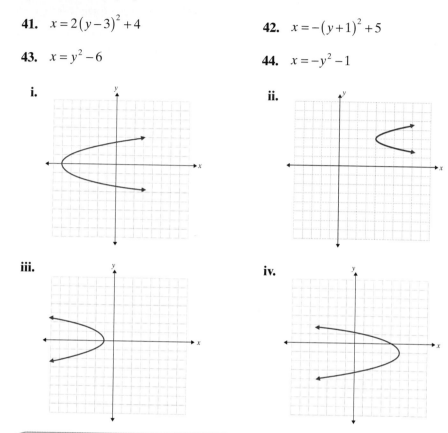

i.

ii.

iii.

iv.

Writing and Thinking About Mathematics

45. For $x = ay^2 + by + c$ we know that the graph of the parabola opens to the right if $a > 0$ and to the left if $a < 0$. Discuss what values of a will cause the parabola to be "wider" and "narrower".

Hawkes Learning Systems: Intermediate Algebra

Parabolas as Conic Sections

8.5   Distance Formula, Midpoint Formula, and Circles

Objectives

After completing this section, you will be able to:

1. *Find the distance between any two points in a plane.*

2. *Write the equations of a circle given its center and radius.*

3. *Graph circles centered at the point (h, k).*

Distance Between Two Points

The formula for the distance between two points in a plane is needed to develop the equations of circles. The **Pythagorean Theorem**, previously discussed in Section 5.4, is the basis for the formula and is repeated here for easy reference.

In a right triangle, the square of the length of the hypotenuse is equal to the sum of the squares of the lengths of the two legs.

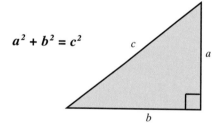

$$a^2 + b^2 = c^2$$

To find the distance between the two points $P(-1, 2)$ and $Q(5, 6)$, as shown in Figure 8.16(a), form a right triangle, as shown in Figure 8.16(b), and find the lengths of the sides a and b. Then, using a and b and the Pythagorean Theorem, we can find the length of the hypotenuse, which is the distance between the two points.

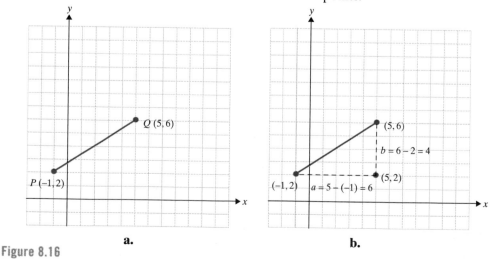

a.   **b.**

Figure 8.16

From Figure 8.16 b,

$$d^2 = a^2 + b^2$$
$$= 6^2 + 4^2$$
$$= 36 + 16$$
$$= 52$$
$$d = \sqrt{52}$$
$$= 2\sqrt{13}$$

By going directly to the Pythagorean Theorem, the distance can be represented by the formula

$$d = \sqrt{a^2 + b^2}.$$

More generally, we can write the formula for d involving the coordinates of two points $P(x_1, y_1)$ and $Q(x_2, y_2)$ as illustrated in Figure 8.17. With $a = |x_2 - x_1|$ and $b = |y_2 - y_1|$, the distance formula is

$$d = \sqrt{(x_2 - x_1)^2 + (y_2 - y_1)^2}.$$

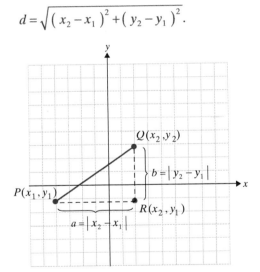

Figure 8.17

Note that in Figure 8.17, the calculations for a and b involve absolute value. These absolute values guarantee nonnegative values for a and b to represent the lengths of legs. In the distance formula, the absolute values are disregarded because $x_2 - x_1$ and $y_2 - y_1$ are squared. **In the actual calculations of d, be sure to add the squares before taking the square root.**

Example 1: The Distance Formula

Each of the following examples illustrates how to use the distance formula:

$$d = \sqrt{(x_2 - x_1)^2 + (y_2 - y_1)^2}.$$

a. Find the distance between the two points $(3, 4)$ and $(-2, 7)$.

Solution: $d = \sqrt{[3 - (-2)]^2 + (4 - 7)^2}$

$$= \sqrt{5^2 + (-3)^2} = \sqrt{25 + 9} = \sqrt{34}$$

b. Determine whether or not the triangle determined by the three points, $A\ (-5, -1)$, $B\ (2, 1)$, and $C\ (0, 7)$ is a right triangle.

Solution: Find the lengths of the three line segments $\overline{AB}$, $\overline{AC}$, and $\overline{BC}$, and decide whether or not the Pythagorean Theorem is satisfied.

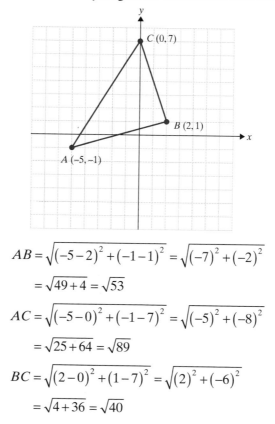

$$AB = \sqrt{(-5 - 2)^2 + (-1 - 1)^2} = \sqrt{(-7)^2 + (-2)^2}$$

$$= \sqrt{49 + 4} = \sqrt{53}$$

$$AC = \sqrt{(-5 - 0)^2 + (-1 - 7)^2} = \sqrt{(-5)^2 + (-8)^2}$$

$$= \sqrt{25 + 64} = \sqrt{89}$$

$$BC = \sqrt{(2 - 0)^2 + (1 - 7)^2} = \sqrt{(2)^2 + (-6)^2}$$

$$= \sqrt{4 + 36} = \sqrt{40}$$

The longest side is $AC = \sqrt{89}$.

The triangle is **not** a right triangle since $\left(\sqrt{89}\right)^2 \neq \left(\sqrt{53}\right)^2 + \left(\sqrt{40}\right)^2$ or $89 \neq 53 + 40$.

The Midpoint Formula

Another useful formula that involves the coordinates of two points is that for finding the **midpoint** of the segment joining two points. The two points are called **endpoints** of the segment. The midpoint is found by averaging the corresponding coordinates of the endpoints.

Midpoint Formula

The formula for the midpoint between two points $P(x_1, y_1)$ and $Q(x_2, y_2)$ is

$$\left(\frac{x_1 + x_2}{2}, \frac{y_1 + y_2}{2} \right)$$

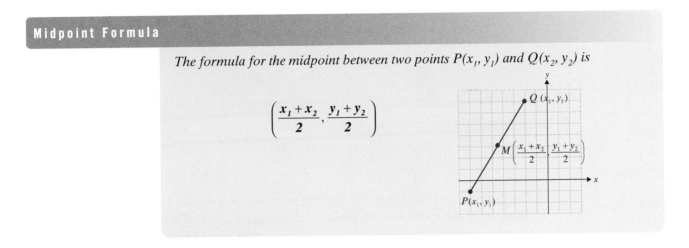

Example 2: Midpoint Formula

Find the coordinates of the midpoint of the line segment joining the two points $P(-4, 6)$ and $Q(1, 2)$.

Solution: The midpoint is $\left(\dfrac{-4+1}{2}, \dfrac{6+2}{2} \right) = \left(-\dfrac{3}{2}, 4 \right)$.

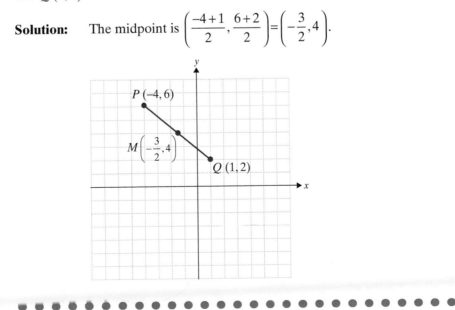

Equations of Circles

Circles and the terms related to circles (**center**, **radius**, and **diameter**) are defined as follows:

Circle, Center, Radius, and Diameter

*A **circle** is the set of all points in a plane that are a fixed distance from a fixed point. The fixed point is called the **center** of the circle.*

*The distance from the center to any point on the circle is called the **radius** of the circle.*

*The distance from one point on the circle to another point on the circle measured through the center is called the **diameter** of the circle.*

Note: *The diameter is twice the length of the radius.*

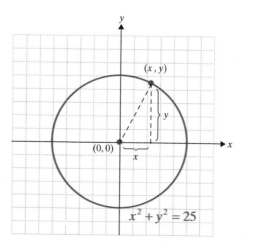

The distance formula is used to find the equation of a circle. For example, to find the equation of the circle with its center at the origin $(0,0)$ and radius 5, for any point on the circle (x,y) the distance from (x,y) to $(0,0)$ must be 5. Therefore, using the distance formula,

$$\sqrt{(x_2-x_1)^2+(y_2-y_1)^2}=d$$
$$\sqrt{(x-0)^2+(y-0)^2}=5$$
$$\sqrt{x^2+y^2}=5$$
$$x^2+y^2=25 \qquad \text{Square both sides.}$$

Thus, as shown in Figure 8.18, all points on the circle satisfy the equation $x^2+y^2=25$.

Figure 8.18

In general, any point (x, y) on a circle with center at (h, k) and radius $r > 0$ must satisfy the equation

$$\sqrt{(x-h)^2 + (y-k)^2} = r.$$

Squaring both sides of this equation gives the **standard form** for the equation of a circle:

$$(x-h)^2 + (y-k)^2 = r^2.$$

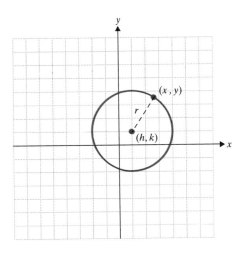

Figure 8.19

The equation for a circle of radius r with **center at the origin** is

$$x^2 + y^2 = r^2.$$

By thinking of this circle translated to have **center at (h, k)**, we can get the standard form by substituting $(x - h)$ for x and $(y - k)$ for y:

$$(x-h)^2 + (y-k)^2 = r^2.$$

Example 3: Equations of Circles ●●●●●●●●●●●●●●●●●●●●●●●●●●●

a. Find the equation of the circle with center at the origin and radius $\sqrt{3}$. Are the points $\left(\sqrt{2}, 1\right)$ and $(1, 2)$ on the circle?

Solution: The equation is $x^2 + y^2 = 3$.

To determine whether or not the points $\left(\sqrt{2}, 1\right)$ and $(1, 2)$ are on the circle, substitute each of these points into the equation.

Substituting $\left(\sqrt{2}, 1\right)$ gives $\left(\sqrt{2}\right)^2 + (1)^2 = 2 + 1 = 3$.

Substituting $(1, 2)$ gives $(1)^2 + (2)^2 = 1 + 4 = 5 \neq 3$.

Therefore, $\left(\sqrt{2}, 1\right)$ is on the circle, but $(1, 2)$ is not on the circle.

continued on next page ...

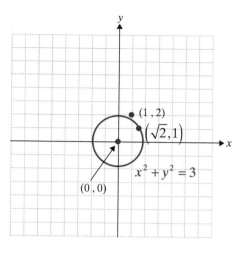

b. Find the equation of the circle with center at $(5, 2)$ and radius 3. Is the point $(5, 5)$ on the circle?

Solution: The equation is $(x-5)^2 + (y-2)^2 = 9$.

Substituting $(5, 5)$ gives $(5-5)^2 + (5-2)^2 = 0^2 + 3^2 = 9$.

Therefore, $(5, 5)$ is on the circle.

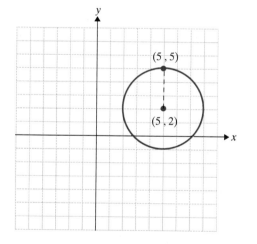

c. Show that $x^2 + y^2 - 8x + 2y = 0$ represents a circle. Find its center and radius. Then graph the circle.

Solution: Rearrange the terms and complete the square for $x^2 - 8x$ and $y^2 + 2y$.

$$x^2 + y^2 - 8x + 2y = 0$$

$$x^2 - 8x + y^2 + 2y = 0$$

$$x^2 - 8x + 16 + y^2 + 2y + 1 = 16 + 1 \qquad \text{Add 16 and 1 to both sides.}$$

Completes the square

$$(x-4)^2 + (y+1)^2 = 17 \qquad \text{Equation of a circle}$$

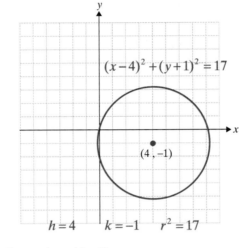

$h = 4 \qquad k = -1 \qquad r^2 = 17$

Center is at $(4, -1)$.

Radius $= \sqrt{17}$.

Using a Graphing Calculator to Graph Circles

The equation of a circle does not represent a function. The upper half (upper semicircle) and the lower half (lower semicircle) do, however, represent separate functions. Therefore, to graph a circle, solve the equation for two values of y just as we did for horizontal parabolas in Section 8.4. For example, consider the circle with equation $x^2 + y^2 = 4$.

$$x^2 + y^2 = 4$$

$$y^2 = 4 - x^2 \qquad \text{First solve for } y^2$$

$$\left. \begin{array}{l} y_1 = \sqrt{4 - x^2} \\ y_2 = -\sqrt{4 - x^2} \end{array} \right\} \quad \begin{array}{l} \text{Solving for } y \text{ gives two equations that} \\ \text{represent two functions.} \end{array}$$

Graphing both of these functions gives the figure pictured in Figure 8.20.

Figure 8.20

The screen on a TI calculator is rectangular and not a square. The ranges for the standard viewing window are from −10 for both Xmin and Ymin to 10 for both Xmax and Ymax. That is, the horizontal scale (x values) and the vertical scale (y values) are the same. Since the rectangular screen is in the approximate ratio of 2 to 3, the graph of a circle using the standard WINDOW will appear flattened as the circle did in Figure 8.20.

To get a more realistic picture of a circle press the (WINDOW) key and set the **Xmin** and **Xmax** values to −6 and 6, respectively. Set the **Ymin** and **Ymax** values to −4 and 4, respectively. Since the numbers 4 and 6 are in the ratio of 2 to 3, the screen is said to show a "square window," and the graphs of y_1 and y_2 will now give a more realistic picture of a circle as shown in Figure 8.21. Alternatively, pressing the (ZOOM) key and choosing option **5:ZSquare** automatically "squares" the window.

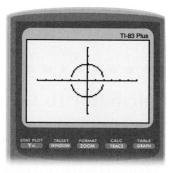

Figure 8.21

Example 4: Using a Graphing Calculator

Use a graphing calculator with a "square window" to graph the circle $x^2 + y^2 = 9$.

Solution: Set the (WINDOW) scales to −6 and 6 for **Xmin** and **Xmax** and −4 and 4 for **Ymin** and **Ymax**, respectively.

Solving for y^2 gives: $y^2 = 9 - x^2$

Solving for y_1 and y_2 gives:
$$\left.\begin{array}{l} y_1 = \sqrt{9 - x^2} \\ y_2 = -\sqrt{9 - x^2} \end{array}\right\}$$

Graphing both y_1 and y_2 gives the following graph of the circle.

Practice Problems

1. *Find the equation of the circle with center at* $(-2,3)$ *and radius 6.*

2. *Write the equation in standard form and find the center and radius for the circle with equation* $x^2 + y^2 + 6y = 7.$

3. *Find the distance between the two points* $(5,3)$ *and* $(-1,-3).$

8.5 Exercises

In Exercises 1 – 12, find the distance between the two given points and the coordinates of the midpoint of the line segment joining the two points.

1. $(2,4),(6,7)$ 2. $(1,0),(6,12)$ 3. $(-3,2),(9,7)$

4. $(-6,3),(-2,0)$ 5. $(1,7),(3,2)$ 6. $(-2,1),(3,-4)$

7. $(4,-3),(7,-3)$ 8. $(-2,6),(5,6)$ 9. $(5,-2),(7,-5)$

10. $(6,4),(8,-5)$ 11. $(-7,3),(1,-12)$ 12. $(3,8),(-2,-4)$

Find equations for each of the circles in Exercises 13 – 32.

13. Center $(0,0)$; $r = 4$ 14. Center $(0,0)$; $r = 6$ 15. Center $(0,0)$; $r = \sqrt{3}$

Answers to Practice Problems: **1.** $(x+2)^2 + (y-3)^2 = 36$ **2.** $x^2 + (y+3)^2 = 16$; center at $(0,-3)$ and radius 4
3. $\sqrt{72} = 6\sqrt{2}$

16. Center $(0,0)$; $r=\sqrt{7}$ **17.** Center $(0,0)$; $r=\sqrt{11}$ **18.** Center $(0,0)$; $r=\sqrt{13}$

19. Center $(0,0)$; $r=\dfrac{2}{3}$ **20.** Center $(0,0)$; $r=\dfrac{7}{4}$ **21.** Center $(0,2)$; $r=2$

22. Center $(0,5)$; $r=5$ **23.** Center $(4,0)$; $r=1$ **24.** Center $(-3,0)$; $r=4$

25. Center $(-2,0)$; $r=\sqrt{8}$ **26.** Center $(5,0)$; $r=\sqrt{2}$ **27.** Center $(3,1)$; $r=6$

28. Center $(-1,2)$; $r=5$ **29.** Center $(3,5)$; $r=\sqrt{12}$

30. Center $(4,-2)$; $r=\sqrt{14}$ **31.** Center $(7,4)$; $r=\sqrt{10}$

32. Center $(-3,2)$; $r=\sqrt{7}$

Write each of the equations in Exercises 33 – 48 in standard form. Find the center and radius of the circle and then sketch the graph.

33. $x^2+y^2=9$ **34.** $x^2+y^2=16$ **35.** $x^2=49-y^2$

36. $y^2=25-x^2$ **37.** $x^2+y^2=18$ **38.** $x^2+y^2=12$

39. $x^2+y^2+2x=8$ **40.** $x^2+y^2-4x=12$ **41.** $x^2+y^2-4y=0$

42. $x^2+y^2+6x=0$ **43.** $x^2+y^2+2x+4y=11$

44. $x^2+y^2-4x+10y+20=0$ **45.** $x^2+y^2+4x+4y-8=0$

46. $x^2+y^2-6x-8y+9=0$ **47.** $x^2+y^2-4x-6y+5=0$

48. $x^2+y^2+10x-2y+14=0$

In Exercises 49 and 50, use the Pythagorean Theorem to decide if the triangle determined by the given points is a right triangle.

49. $A(1,-2)$, $B(7,1)$, $C(5,5)$ **50.** $A(-5,-1)$, $B(2,1)$, $C(-1,6)$

In Exercises 51 and 52, show that the triangle determined by the given points is an isosceles triangle (has two equal sides).

51. $A(1,1)$, $B(5,9)$, $C(9,5)$ **52.** $A(1,-4)$, $B(3,2)$, $C(9,4)$

In Exercises 53 and 54, show that the triangle determined by the given points is an equilateral triangle (all sides equal).

53. $A(1,0)$, $B(3,\sqrt{12})$, $C(5,0)$ **54.** $A(0,5)$, $B(0,-3)$, $C(\sqrt{48},1)$

In Exercises 55 and 56, show that the diagonals (AC and BD) of the rectangle ABCD are equal.

55. $A(2,-2), B(2,3), C(8,3), D(8,-2)$ **56.** $A(-1,1), B(-1,4), C(4,4), D(4,1)$

In Exercises 57 – 60, find the perimeter of the triangle determined by the given points.

57. $A(-5,0), B(3,4), C(0,0)$ **58.** $A(-6,-1), B(-3,3), C(6,4)$

59. $A(-2,5), B(3,1), C(2,-2)$ **60.** $A(1,4), B(-3,3), C(-1,7)$

In Exercises 61 – 64, use a graphing calculator to graph the circles. Be sure to set a square window.

61. $x^2 + y^2 = 16$ **62.** $x^2 + y^2 = 25$

63. $(x+3)^2 + y^2 = 49$ **64.** $(x-2)^2 + (y-5)^2 = 100$

Writing and Thinking About Mathematics

65. For a given line and a point not on the line, a parabola is defined as the set of all points that are the same distance from the point and the line. The point is called the focus and the line is called the directrix. See the figure below.

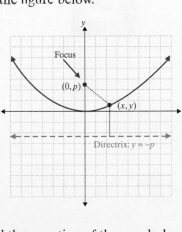

   a. Suppose that (x,y) is any point on a parabola and $(0,p)$ is the focus. Find the distance from (x,y) to the focus.

   b. Suppose that (x,y) is any point on the same parabola in part **a.** and the line $y=-p$ is the directrix. Find the distance from (x,y) to the directrix.

   c. Show that the equation of the parabola is $x^2 = 4py$.

66. Using the equation developed in Exercise 65, find the equation of the parabola with focus at $(0,2)$ and line $y=-2$ as directrix. Draw the graph.

continued on next page ...

67. For a given line and a point not on the line, a parabola is defined as the set of all points that are the same distance from the point and the line. The point is called the focus and the line is called the directrix. See the figure below.

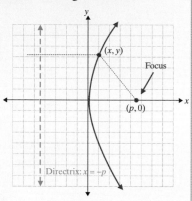

a. Suppose that (x, y) is any point on a parabola and $(p, 0)$ is the focus. Find the distance from (x, y) to the focus.

b. Suppose that (x, y) is any point on the same parabola in part **a.** and the line $x = -p$ is the directrix. Find the distance from (x, y) to the directrix.

c. Show that the equation of the parabola is $y^2 = 4px$.

68. Using the equation developed in Exercise 67, find the equation of the parabola with focus at $(-3, 0)$ and line $x = 3$ as directrix. Draw the graph.

Hawkes Learning Systems: Intermediate Algebra

The Distance Formula and Circles

8.6 Ellipses and Hyperbolas

Objectives

After completing this section, you will be able to:

1. *Graph ellipses centered at the origin or at the point (h, k).*

2. *Graph hyperbolas centered at the origin or at the point (h, k).*

3. *Find the equations for the asymptotes of hyperbolas.*

Equations of Ellipses

An **ellipse** is the set of all points in a plane the sum of whose distances from two fixed points is constant. Each of the fixed points is called a **focus** (plural **foci**). The **center** of an ellipse is the point midway between the foci. Ellipses have many practical applications in the sciences, particularly in astronomy. For example, the planets in our solar system have elliptical orbits and the sun is a focus of each ellipse.

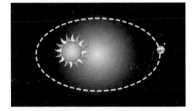

An ellipse with its center at the origin and foci at $(-c, 0)$ and $(c, 0)$ and x-intercepts at $(-a, 0)$ and $(a, 0)$ and y-intercepts at $(0, -b)$ and $(0, b)$ is shown in the Figure below.

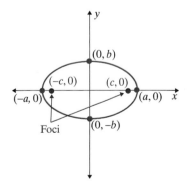

Figure 8.22

As an example, consider the equation

$$\frac{x^2}{25} + \frac{y^2}{9} = 1.$$

Several points that satisfy this equation are given on the following page in tabular form and are graphed in Figure 8.23.

579

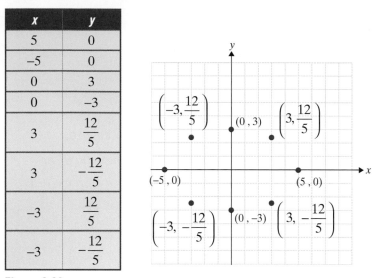

x	y
5	0
−5	0
0	3
0	−3
3	$\dfrac{12}{5}$
3	$-\dfrac{12}{5}$
−3	$\dfrac{12}{5}$
−3	$-\dfrac{12}{5}$

Figure 8.23

Joining the points in Figure 8.23 with a smooth curve, we get the graph of the **ellipse** shown in Figure 8.24. The points $(5,0)$ and $(−5,0)$ are the x-intercepts, and the points $(0,3)$ and $(0,−3)$ are the y-intercepts.

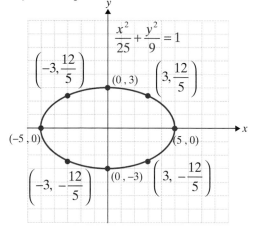

Figure 8.24

Equation of an Ellipse

*The standard form for the equation of an **ellipse** with its center at the origin is*

$$\frac{x^2}{a^2}+\frac{y^2}{b^2}=1 \qquad \text{where} \qquad a^2 \ge b^2.$$

The points $(a,0)$ and $(−a,0)$ are the x-intercepts.

The points $(0,b)$ and $(0,−b)$ are the y-intercepts.

*The segment of length 2a joining the x-intercepts is called the **major axis**.*

*The segment of length 2b joining the y-intercepts is called the **minor axis**.*

Note: Example 2 illustrates a second form, $\dfrac{x^2}{b^2} + \dfrac{y^2}{a^2} = 1,$ and corresponding adjustments in the related terminology. In this form, the major axis is along the *y*-axis.

Example 1: Equation of an Ellipse

Graph the equation $4x^2 + 16y^2 = 64$.

Solution: First divide both sides of the given equation by 64 to find the standard form.

$$4x^2 + 16y^2 = 64$$

$$\frac{4x^2}{64} + \frac{16y^2}{64} = \frac{64}{64}$$

$$\frac{x^2}{16} + \frac{y^2}{4} = 1$$

The curve is an ellipse. The endpoints of the major axis are $(-4, 0)$ and $(4, 0)$. The endpoints of the minor axis are $(0, -2)$ and $(0, 2)$.

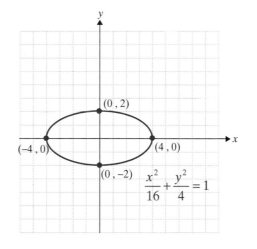

In the general discussion and in Example 1, the major axis is horizontal and the minor axis is vertical. For ellipses in standard form, the larger denominator is treated as a^2 and the smaller denominator as b^2. Thus, if the larger denominator is below y^2, then the major axis is vertical and the minor axis is horizontal. This situation is illustrated in Example 2.

Example 2: The Major and Minor axes •

Graph the equation $\dfrac{x^2}{1} + \dfrac{y^2}{9} = 1$.

Solution: The equation is in standard form. However, since the larger denominator, 9, is below y^2, the major axis is vertical. The ellipse is elongated along the y-axis. The points $(0, -3)$ and $(0, 3)$ are the endpoints of the major axis while $(-1, 0)$ and $(1, 0)$ are the endpoints of the minor axis.

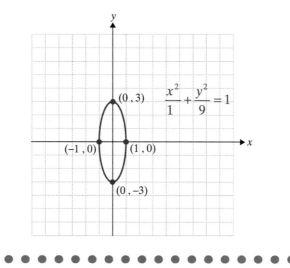

• •

In the equation of an ellipse,

$$\frac{x^2}{a^2} + \frac{y^2}{b^2} = 1 \qquad \left(\text{or } \frac{x^2}{b^2} + \frac{y^2}{a^2} = 1 \right),$$

the coefficients for x^2 and y^2 are both positive. If one of these coefficients is negative, then the equation represents a **hyperbola**.

Equations of Hyperbolas

A **hyperbola** is the set of all points in a plane such that the absolute value of the difference of the distances to two fixed points is constant. Each of the fixed points is called a **focus**. The graph of a hyperbola with its **center** (the point midway between the foci) at the origin and foci at $(-c, 0)$ and $(c, 0)$ and x-intercepts at $(-a, 0)$ and $(a, 0)$ is shown in Figure 8.25.

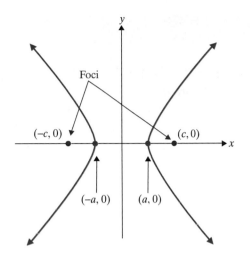

Figure 8.25

Several points that satisfy the equation

$$\frac{x^2}{25} - \frac{y^2}{9} = 1$$

and the curve joining these points (a hyperbola) are shown in Figure 8.26.

x	y
5	0
−5	0
7	$\frac{6\sqrt{6}}{5}$
7	$\frac{-6\sqrt{6}}{5}$
−7	$\frac{6\sqrt{6}}{5}$
−7	$\frac{-6\sqrt{6}}{5}$

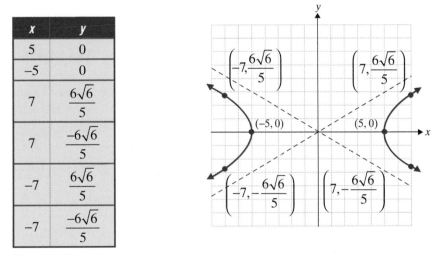

Figure 8.26

The two dotted lines shown in Figure 8.26 are called **asymptotes**. These lines are not part of the hyperbola, but they serve as guidelines for the graph because the curve gets closer and closer to these lines without ever touching them. The equations of these lines are

$$y = \frac{3}{5}x \quad \text{and} \quad y = -\frac{3}{5}x.$$

Standard Form for Equations of Hyperbolas

*In general, there are **two standard forms** for equations of hyperbolas with their **centers** at the origin:*

1. $\dfrac{x^2}{a^2} - \dfrac{y^2}{b^2} = 1$

x-intercepts (vertices) at (a, 0) and (−a, 0); no y-intercepts;

Asymptotes: $y = \dfrac{b}{a}x$ *and* $y = -\dfrac{b}{a}x$ *;*

The curve "opens" left and right.

2. $\dfrac{y^2}{a^2} - \dfrac{x^2}{b^2} = 1$

y-intercepts (vertices) at (0, a) and (0, −a); no x-intercepts;

Asymptotes: $y = \dfrac{a}{b}x$ *and* $y = -\dfrac{a}{b}x$ *;*

The curve "opens" up and down.

Geometrical Aid for Sketching Asymptotes

The asymptotes $y = \dfrac{a}{b}x$ and $y = -\dfrac{a}{b}x$ pass through the diagonals of the **fundamental rectangle** formed by joining the points $(a, 0)$, $(-a, 0)$, $(0, b)$, and $(0, -b)$. Fundamental rectangles are shown in Examples 3a and 3b.

Example 3: Asymptotes

a. Graph the curve $x^2 - 4y^2 = 4$.

Solution: Write the equation in standard form by dividing by 4 which yields

$$\frac{x^2}{4} - \frac{y^2}{1} = 1.$$

Here, $a^2 = 4$ and $b^2 = 1$. So, using $a = 2$ and $b = 1$, the asymptotes are $y = \dfrac{1}{2}x$ and $y = -\dfrac{1}{2}x$. Vertices are $(2, 0)$ and $(-2, 0)$. The curve "opens" left and right. Notice that the asymptotes pass through the diagonals of the fundamental rectangle.

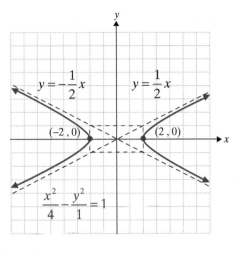

b. Graph the curve $\dfrac{y^2}{1} - \dfrac{x^2}{4} = 1$.

Solution: First locate the asymptotes and the y-intercepts, then sketch the curve. Here, $a = 1$ and $b = 2$. The asymptotes are $y = \dfrac{1}{2}x$ and $y = -\dfrac{1}{2}x$. The y-intercepts are $(0,1)$ and $(0,-1)$. The curve "opens" up and down.

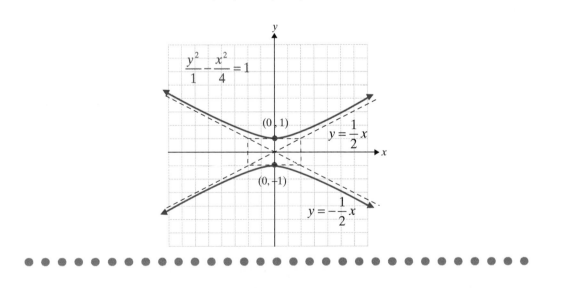

Ellipses and Hyperbolas with Centers at (h, k)

With our knowledge of translations discussed in Section 8.3, we know that replacing x with $x - h$ in an equation gives the graph a horizontal shift of h units, and replacing y with $y - k$ in an equation gives the graph a vertical shift of k units. We used these ideas in Section 8.5 when we discussed the equations and graphs of circles with centers at (h, k), points other than the origin.

For example,

$$x^2 + y^2 = 16: \qquad \text{equation of the circle with center at } (0,0) \text{ and radius } 4$$

$$(x-1)^2 + (y-3)^2 = 16: \quad \text{equation of the circle with center at } (1,3) \text{ and radius } 4$$

The same procedure can be used to obtain the equations of ellipses and hyperbolas with centers at (h, k). That is, the equation of an ellipse and the equation of a hyperbola with center at (h, k) can be found by replacing x with $x - h$ and y with $y - k$ in the standard forms of the equations.

Ellipse with Center at (h, k)

The equation of an ellipse with its center at (h, k) is

$$\frac{(x-h)^2}{a^2} + \frac{(y-k)^2}{b^2} = 1 \ or \ \frac{(x-h)^2}{b^2} + \frac{(y-k)^2}{a^2} = 1 \ where \ a^2 \geq b^2$$

Note: *a and b are distances from (h, k) to the vertices. (See figure 8.27)*

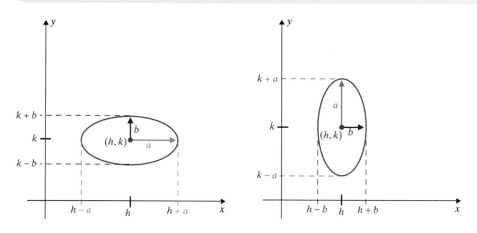

Figure 8.27

Example 4: Ellipse with Center at (h, k)

Graph the ellipse $\dfrac{(x+2)^2}{16} + \dfrac{(y-1)^2}{9} = 1$.

Solution: The graph of $\dfrac{x^2}{16} + \dfrac{y^2}{9} = 1$ is translated 2 units left and 1 unit up so that the center is at $(-2, 1)$ with $a = 4$ and $b = 3$. The graph is shown here with the center and vertices labeled.

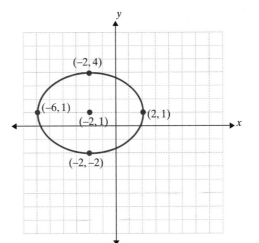

• •

Hyperbola with Center at (h, k)

The equation of a hyperbola with its center at (h, k) is

$$\frac{(x-h)^2}{a^2} - \frac{(y-k)^2}{b^2} = 1 \;\; or \;\; \frac{(y-k)^2}{a^2} - \frac{(x-h)^2}{b^2} = 1$$

Note: *a and b are used as in the standard form but are measured from (h,k). (See figure 8.28)*

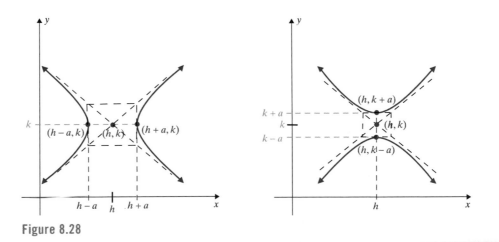

Figure 8.28

Example 5: Hyperbola with Center at (*h*, *k*)

Graph the hyperbola $\dfrac{(x-3)^2}{25} - \dfrac{(y+4)^2}{36} = 1$.

Solution: The graph of $\dfrac{x^2}{25} - \dfrac{y^2}{36} = 1$ is translated 3 units right and 4 units down so that the center is at $(3, -4)$ with $a = 5$ and $b = 6$. The graph is shown here with the asymptotes shown and center and vertices labeled.

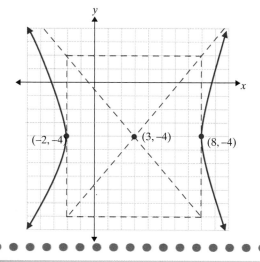

Practice Problems

1. Write the equation $2x^2 + 9y^2 = 18$ in standard form. State the length of the major axis and the length of the minor axis.

2. Write the equation $x^2 - 9y^2 = 9$ in standard form. Write the equations of the asymptotes.

3. Graph the ellipse $\dfrac{(x-2)^2}{4} + \dfrac{(y+1)^2}{1} = 1$

4. Graph the hyperbola $\dfrac{x^2}{16} - \dfrac{(y-3)^2}{4} = 1$

8.6 Exercises

Write each of the equations in Exercises 1 – 30 in standard form, then sketch the graph. For hyperbolas, graph the asymptotes as well.

1. $x^2 + 9y^2 = 36$

2. $x^2 + 4y^2 = 16$

3. $4x^2 + 25y^2 = 100$

4. $4x^2 + 9y^2 = 36$

5. $16x^2 + y^2 = 16$

6. $25x^2 + 9y^2 = 36$

7. $x^2 - y^2 = 1$

8. $x^2 - y^2 = 4$

9. $9x^2 - y^2 = 9$

10. $4x^2 - y^2 = 4$ **11.** $4x^2 - 9y^2 = 36$ **12.** $9x^2 - 16y^2 = 144$

13. $2x^2 + y^2 = 8$ **14.** $3x^2 + y^2 = 12$ **15.** $x^2 + 5y^2 = 20$

16. $x^2 + 7y^2 = 28$ **17.** $y^2 - x^2 = 9$ **18.** $y^2 - x^2 = 16$

19. $y^2 - 2x^2 = 8$ **20.** $y^2 - 3x^2 = 12$ **21.** $y^2 - 2x^2 = 18$

22. $y^2 - 5x^2 = 20$ **23.** $3x^2 + 2y^2 = 18$ **24.** $4x^2 + 3y^2 = 12$

25. $4x^2 + 5y^2 = 20$ **26.** $3x^2 + 8y^2 = 48$ **27.** $3x^2 - 5y^2 = 75$

28. $4x^2 - 7y^2 = 28$ **29.** $3y^2 - 4x^2 = 36$ **30.** $9y^2 - 8x^2 = 72$

In Exercises 31 – 36, match the graph with the given equation.

31. $\dfrac{(x-1)^2}{4} + \dfrac{(y-3)^2}{25} = 1$ **32.** $\dfrac{(x+1)^2}{4} + \dfrac{(y+3)^2}{25} = 1$ **33.** $\dfrac{(x-1)^2}{25} + \dfrac{(y-3)^2}{4} = 1$

34. $\dfrac{(x+1)^2}{25} + \dfrac{(y+3)^2}{4} = 1$ **35.** $\dfrac{(x+1)^2}{25} - \dfrac{(y+3)^2}{4} = 1$ **36.** $\dfrac{(y+3)^2}{4} - \dfrac{(x+1)^2}{25} = 1$

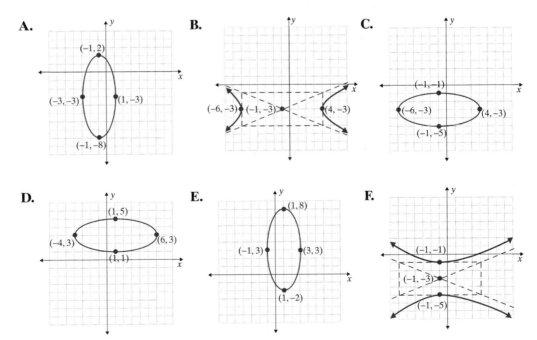

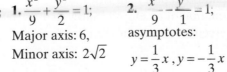

Answers to Practice Problems: **1.** $\dfrac{x^2}{9} + \dfrac{y^2}{2} = 1$;
Major axis: 6,
Minor axis: $2\sqrt{2}$

2. $\dfrac{x^2}{9} - \dfrac{y^2}{1} = 1$,
asymptotes:
$y = \dfrac{1}{3}x$, $y = -\dfrac{1}{3}x$

3.

4.

In Exercises 37 – 42, use your knowledge of translations to graph each of the following equations. These graphs are ellipses and hyperbolas with centers at points other than the origin.

37. $\dfrac{(x-2)^2}{25}+\dfrac{(y-1)^2}{9}=1$ **38.** $\dfrac{(x+1)^2}{16}+\dfrac{(y-4)^2}{1}=1$ **39.** $\dfrac{(x+5)^2}{1}-\dfrac{(y+2)^2}{16}=1$

40. $\dfrac{(x-4)^2}{9}-\dfrac{(y-3)^2}{36}=1$ **41.** $\dfrac{(x+1)^2}{49}+\dfrac{(y-6)^2}{100}=1$ **42.** $\dfrac{(y-2)^2}{9}-\dfrac{(x+2)^2}{4}=1$

Writing and Thinking About Mathematics

43. The definition of an ellipse is given in the text as follows:

An ellipse is the set of all points in a plane the sum of whose distances from two fixed points is constant.

a. Draw an ellipse by proceeding as follows:

Step 1: Place two thumb tacks in a piece of cardboard.

Step 2: Select a piece of string slightly longer than the distance between the two tacks.

Step 3: Tie the string to each thumb tack and stretch the string taut by using a pencil.

Step 4: Use the pencil to trace the path of an ellipse on the cardboard by keeping the string taut. (The length of the string represents the fixed distance from points on the ellipse to the two foci.)

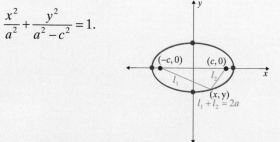

b. Show that the equation of an ellipse with foci at $(-c, 0)$ and $(c, 0)$, center at the origin, and $2a$ as the constant sum of the lengths to the foci can be written in the form

$$\frac{x^2}{a^2}+\frac{y^2}{a^2-c^2}=1.$$

c. In the equation in part b, substitute $b^2 = a^2 - c^2$ to get the standard form for the equation of an ellipse. Show that the points $(0, -b)$ and $(0, b)$ are the y-intercepts and a is the distance from each y-intercept to a focus.

Hawkes Learning Systems: Intermediate Algebra

Ellipses and Hyperbolas

8.7

Nonlinear Systems of Equations

Objectives

After completing this section, you will be able to:

Solve systems of either two quadratic equations or one quadratic and one linear equation in two variables.

The equations for the conic sections that we have discussed all have at least one term that is second-degree. These equations are called **quadratic equations**. (Only the equations for parabolas of the form $y = ax^2 + bx + c$ are **quadratic functions**.) A summary of the equations with their related graphs is shown in Figure 8.29.

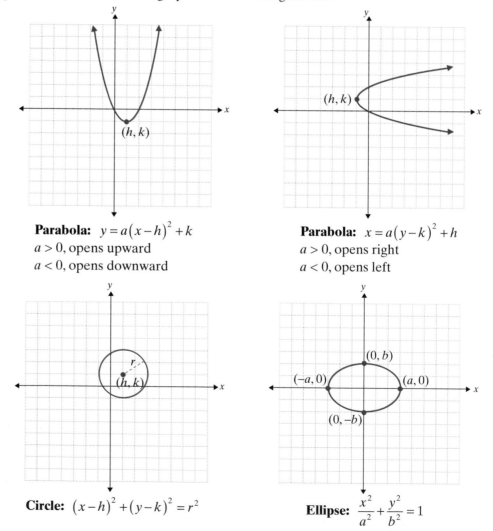

Parabola: $y = a(x - h)^2 + k$
$a > 0$, opens upward
$a < 0$, opens downward

Parabola: $x = a(y - k)^2 + h$
$a > 0$, opens right
$a < 0$, opens left

Circle: $(x - h)^2 + (y - k)^2 = r^2$

Ellipse: $\dfrac{x^2}{a^2} + \dfrac{y^2}{b^2} = 1$

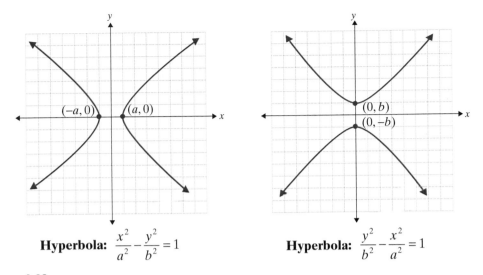

Hyperbola: $\dfrac{x^2}{a^2} - \dfrac{y^2}{b^2} = 1$ **Hyperbola:** $\dfrac{y^2}{b^2} - \dfrac{x^2}{a^2} = 1$

Figure 8.29

If a system of two equations has one quadratic equation and one linear equation, then the method of substitution should be used to solve the system. If the system involves two quadratic equations, then the method used depends on the form of the equations. The following examples show three possible situations. The graphs of the curves are particularly useful for approximating solutions and determining the exact number of solutions.

Example 1: Graphing Curves ●

Solve the following systems and graph both curves in each system.

a. $\begin{cases} x^2 + y^2 = 25 \\ x + y = 5 \end{cases}$

Solution: Solve $x + y = 5$ for y (or x). Then substitute into the other equation.

$$y = 5 - x$$
$$x^2 + (5 - x)^2 = 25$$
$$x^2 + 25 - 10x + x^2 = 25$$
$$2x^2 - 10x = 0$$
$$2x(x - 5) = 0 \qquad \text{Now solve for } x.$$

$$\begin{cases} x = 0 \\ y = 5 - 0 = 5 \end{cases} \qquad \text{or} \qquad \begin{cases} x = 5 \\ y = 5 - 5 = 0 \end{cases}$$

The solutions (points of intersection) are $(0, 5)$ and $(5, 0)$.

continued on next page ...

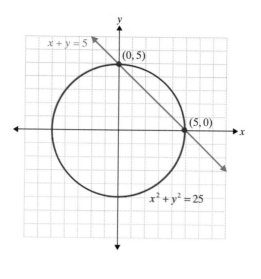

$$\textbf{b.}\quad \begin{cases} x+y=-7 \\ y=x^2-4x-5 \end{cases}$$

Solution: Solve the linear equation for y, then substitute. (In this case, the quadratic equation is already solved for y, and the substitution could be made the other way.)

$$y=-x-7$$
$$-x-7=x^2-4x-5$$
$$0=x^2-3x+2$$
$$0=(x-2)(x-1)$$

$$\begin{cases} x=2 \\ y=-2-7=-9 \end{cases} \quad \text{or} \quad \begin{cases} x=1 \\ y=-1-7=-8 \end{cases}$$

The solutions are $(2,-9)$ and $(1,-8)$.

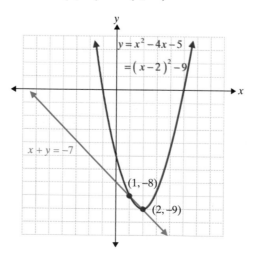

c. $\begin{cases} x^2 - y^2 = 4 \\ x^2 + y^2 = 36 \end{cases}$

Solution: Here addition will eliminate y^2.

$$
\begin{array}{rcl}
x^2 \;-\; y^2 &=& 4 \\
x^2 \;+\; y^2 &=& 36 \\
\hline
2x^2 &=& 40 \\
x^2 &=& 20
\end{array}
$$

$$x = \pm\sqrt{20} = \pm 2\sqrt{5}$$

if $x = 2\sqrt{5}$: $20 + y^2 = 36$ if $x = -2\sqrt{5}$: $20 + y^2 = 36$

$\phantom{if x = 2\sqrt{5} :\;\;} y^2 = 16$ $\phantom{if x = -2\sqrt{5} :\;\;} y^2 = 16$

$\phantom{if x = 2\sqrt{5} :\;\;} y = \pm 4$ $\phantom{if x = -2\sqrt{5} :\;\;} y = \pm 4$

There are four points of intersection:

$$\left(2\sqrt{5}, 4\right), \left(2\sqrt{5}, -4\right), \left(-2\sqrt{5}, 4\right), \left(-2\sqrt{5}, -4\right)$$

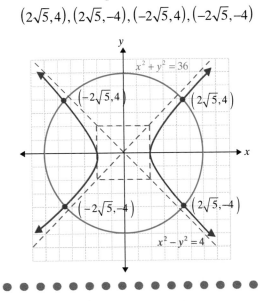

Practice Problems

Solve each of the following systems algebraically.

1. $\begin{cases} y = x^2 - 4 \\ x - y = 2 \end{cases}$ **2.** $\begin{cases} x^2 + y^2 = 72 \\ x = y^2 \end{cases}$

8.7 Exercises

Solve each of the systems of equations in Exercises 1 – 16. Sketch the graphs.

1. $\begin{cases} y = x^2 + 1 \\ 2x + y = 4 \end{cases}$

2. $\begin{cases} y = 3 - x^2 \\ x + y = -3 \end{cases}$

3. $\begin{cases} y = 2 - x \\ y = (x-2)^2 \end{cases}$

4. $\begin{cases} x^2 + y^2 = 25 \\ y + x + 5 = 0 \end{cases}$

5. $\begin{cases} x^2 + y^2 = 20 \\ x - y = 2 \end{cases}$

6. $\begin{cases} x^2 - y^2 = 16 \\ 3x + 5y = 0 \end{cases}$

7. $\begin{cases} y = x - 2 \\ x^2 = y^2 + 16 \end{cases}$

8. $\begin{cases} x^2 + 3y^2 = 12 \\ x = 3y \end{cases}$

9. $\begin{cases} x^2 + y^2 = 9 \\ x^2 - y^2 = 9 \end{cases}$

10. $\begin{cases} x^2 + y^2 = 9 \\ x^2 - y + 3 = 0 \end{cases}$

11. $\begin{cases} 4x^2 + y^2 = 25 \\ 3x - y^2 + 3 = 0 \end{cases}$

12. $\begin{cases} x^2 - 4y^2 = 9 \\ x + 2y^2 = 3 \end{cases}$

13. $\begin{cases} x^2 + y^2 + 4x - 2y = 4 \\ x + y = 2 \end{cases}$

14. $\begin{cases} x^2 - y^2 = 9 \\ x^2 + y^2 - 2x - 3 = 0 \end{cases}$

15. $\begin{cases} x^2 - y^2 = 5 \\ x^2 + 4y^2 = 25 \end{cases}$

16. $\begin{cases} 2x^2 - 3y^2 = 6 \\ 2x^2 + y^2 = 22 \end{cases}$

Solve each of the systems in Exercises 17 – 30.

17. $\begin{cases} x^2 - y^2 = 20 \\ x^2 - 9y = 0 \end{cases}$

18. $\begin{cases} x^2 + 5y^2 = 16 \\ x^2 + y^2 = 4x \end{cases}$

19. $\begin{cases} x^2 + y^2 = 10 \\ x^2 + y^2 - 4y + 2 = 0 \end{cases}$

20. $\begin{cases} x^2 + y^2 = 20 \\ 4x + 8 = y^2 \end{cases}$

21. $\begin{cases} 2x^2 - y^2 = 7 \\ 2x^2 + y^2 = 29 \end{cases}$

22. $\begin{cases} y = x^2 + 2x + 2 \\ 2x + y = 2 \end{cases}$

23. $\begin{cases} 4y + 10x^2 + 7x - 8 = 0 \\ 6x - 8y + 1 = 0 \end{cases}$

24. $\begin{cases} x^2 + y^2 - 4x + 6y + 3 = 0 \\ 2x - y - 2 = 0 \end{cases}$

25. $\begin{cases} x^2 + y^2 - 4y = 16 \\ x - y = 0 \end{cases}$

26. $\begin{cases} 4x^2 + y^2 = 11 \\ y = 4x^2 - 9 \end{cases}$

27. $\begin{cases} x^2 - y^2 - 2y = 22 \\ 2x + 5y + 5 = 0 \end{cases}$

28. $\begin{cases} x^2 + y^2 - 6y = 0 \\ 2x^2 - y^2 + 15 = 0 \end{cases}$

29. $\begin{cases} y = x^2 - 2x + 3 \\ y = -x^2 + 2x + 3 \end{cases}$

30. $\begin{cases} y^2 = x^2 - 5 \\ 4x^2 - y^2 = 32 \end{cases}$

Answers to Practice Problems: 1. $(-1, -3)$ and $(2, 0)$ **2.** $\left(8, 2\sqrt{2}\right)$ and $\left(8, -2\sqrt{2}\right)$

In Exercises 31 – 36, use a graphing calculator to graph and estimate the solutions to the systems of equations.

31. $\begin{cases} y = x^2 + 3 \\ x + y = 3 \end{cases}$

32. $\begin{cases} y = 1 - x^2 \\ x + y = -4 \end{cases}$

33. $\begin{cases} y = 3 - 2x \\ y = (x - 1)^2 \end{cases}$

34. $\begin{cases} x^2 + y^2 = 36 \\ y = x + 5 \end{cases}$

35. $\begin{cases} x^2 + y^2 = 10 \\ x - y = 1 \end{cases}$

36. $\begin{cases} x^2 + y^2 = 4 \\ x^2 - y^2 = 3 \end{cases}$

Hawkes Learning Systems: Intermediate Algebra

Nonlinear Systems of Equations

Chapter 8 Index of Key Ideas and Terms

Function   page 516

Zeros of a Function   page 516
> The zeros of a function are the values of x
> when the graph crosses the x-axis.

Vertical Line Test   page 517
> If **any** vertical line intersects a graph in more than
> one point, then the relation graphed is **not** a function.

Parabola   page 517
> The graph of every quadratic function is a parabola.

Quadratic Function $y = ax^2 + bx + c$ page 518

Equations of Parabolas
> $y = ax^2$ page 518
> $y = ax^2 + k$ page 519
> $y = a(x-h)^2$ page 519
> $y = a(x-h)^2 + k$ page 521
> $y = ax^2 + bx + c$ page 521

Line of Symmetry   page 523
> The line $x = -\dfrac{b}{2a}$ is the line of symmetry of the
>
> graph of the quadratic function $y = ax^2 + bx + c$.

Vertex   page 523
> The vertex of the graph of $y = ax^2 + bx + c$ is at the
>
> point $\left(-\dfrac{b}{2a}, \dfrac{4ac - b^2}{4a} \right)$.

Zeros (of a quadratic function)   page 523

Maximum and Minimum Values   pages 525 - 527
> For a parabola with equation of the form $y = a(x-h)^2 + k$,   page 525
> **1.** If $a > 0$, then (h, k) is the lowest point and $y = k$
> is called the minimum value of the function.
> **2.** If $a < 0$, then (h, k) is the highest point and $y = k$
> is called the maximum value of the function.

To Solve a Polynomial Inequality   page 532
    1. Arrange the terms so that one side of the inequality is 0.
    2. Factor the algebraic expression, if possible, and find the
       points (numbers) where each factor is 0.
       (Use the quadratic formula, if necessary.)
    3. Mark these points on a number line.
    4. Test one point from each interval to determine the sign
       of the polynomial expression for all points in that interval.
    5. The solution consists of those intervals where the test
       points satisfy the original inequality.

To Solve a Polynomial Inequality with a Graphing Calculator   page 537
    1. Arrange the terms so that one side of the inequality is 0.
    2. Set the quadratic (or other polynomial) equal to y and
       graph the function. [Be sure to set the WINDOW so
       that all of the zeros are easily seen.]
    3. Use the TRACE key or CALC key to approximate
       the zeros of the function.
    4. (a) If the inequality is of the form $y > 0$, then the
          solution consists of those intervals of x where the
          graph is above the x-axis
      (b) If the inequality is of the form $y < 0$, then the
          solution consists of those intervals of x where
          the graph is below the x-axis
    5. Endpoints of the intervals are included if the inequality
       is $y \geq 0$ or $y \leq 0$.

$f(x)$ Notation and Evaluating Functions   page 542

Difference Quotient   page 544
    The formula $\dfrac{f(x+h)-f(x)}{h}$ is called the difference
    quotient.

Horizontal and Vertical Translations   pages 546
    Given the graph of $y = f(x)$, the graph of
    $y = f(x-h)+k$ is
    1. a horizontal translation of h units, and
    2. a vertical translation of k units of the graph of $y = f(x)$.

Reflections and Translations   pages 550 - 552

Conic Sections   page 557

    Circles, ellipses, parabolas, and hyperbolas are
    conic sections.

Horizontal Parabolas   page 558

    Equations of horizontal parabolas (parabolas that open
    to the left or right) are of the form
        $x = ay^2 + by + c$ or $x = a(y-k)^2 + h$ where $a \neq 0$.
    The parabola opens left if $a < 0$ and right if $a > 0$.

    The vertex is at (h, k).
    The line $y = k$ is the line of symmetry.

Using a Graphing Calculator to Graph Horizontal Parabolas   pages 561 - 562

Distance Between Two Points   page 566
    The Pythagorean Theorem   page 566

    The Distance Formula: $d = \sqrt{(x_2 - x_1)^2 + (y_2 - y_1)^2}$ page 567

Midpoint Formula: $\left(\dfrac{x_1 + x_2}{2}, \dfrac{y_1 + y_2}{2} \right)$ page 569

Circle   page 570

    A circle is the set of all points in a plane that are a
    fixed distance from a fixed point.
    The fixed point is called the **center** of the circle.

Radius   page 570

    The distance from the center to any point on a circle
    is called the radius of the circle.

Diameter   page 570

    The distance from one point on a circle to another point
    on the circle measured through the center is called
    the diameter of the circle.

Standard form for Equation of a Circle   page 571
    $(x-h)^2 + (y-k)^2 = r^2$
    Center at (h, k) and radius r.

Using a Graphing Calculator to Graph Circles   pages 573 - 575

Ellipse   page 580

The standard form for the equation of an ellipse
with its center at the origin is

$$\frac{x^2}{a^2} + \frac{y^2}{b^2} = 1 \text{ where } a^2 \geq b^2.$$

The points $(a, 0)$ and $(-a, 0)$ are the x-intercepts.
The points $(0, b)$ and $(0, -b)$ are the y-intercepts.
The line segment of length $2a$ joining the x-intercepts is
called the major axis.
The line segment of length $2b$ joining the y-intercepts is
called the minor axis.

Hyperbola   page 584

In general, there are two standard forms for equations of
hyperbolas with their centers at the origin.

1. $\dfrac{x^2}{a^2} - \dfrac{y^2}{b^2} = 1$

   x-intercepts (vertices) at $(a, 0)$ and $(-a, 0)$;
       no y-intercepts

   Asymptotes: $y = \dfrac{b}{a}x$ and $y = -\dfrac{b}{a}x$

   The curve "opens" left and right.

2. $\dfrac{y^2}{a^2} - \dfrac{x^2}{b^2} = 1$

   y-intercepts (vertices) at $(0, a)$ and $(0, -a)$;
       no x-intercepts

   Asymptotes: $y = \dfrac{a}{b}x$ and $y = -\dfrac{a}{b}x$

   The curve "opens" up and down.

Nonlinear Systems of Equations   pages 592 - 595

Chapter 8 Review

For a review of the topics and problems from Chapter 7, look at the
following lessons from *Hawkes Learning Systems: Intermediate Algebra*

Graphing Parabolas   The Distance Formula and Circles
Solving Quadratic Inequalities   Ellipses and Hyperbolas
Function Notation and Translations   Nonlinear Systems of Equations
Parabolas as Conic Sections

Chapter 8 Test

In Exercises 1 – 3, write the quadratic function in the form $y = a(x-h)^2 + k$. Find the vertex, axis of symmetry, domain, range, and zeros. Graph the function.

1. $y = x^2 - 6x + 8$ **2.** $y = -2x^2 + 6x + 3$ **3.** $y = 2x^2 - 12x + 9$

4. For the function $f(x) = 2x^2 + 5$, find:
   a. $f(-2)$

   b. $f(x) + 1$

   c. $f(x+1)$

   d. $\dfrac{f(x+h) - f(x)}{h}$

In Exercises 5 and 6, solve the quadratic inequalities algebraically. Write the solution set in interval notation and graph the solution set on a number line.

5. $x^2 - 2x \geq 15$ **6.** $2x^2 + 9x + 4 < 0$

In Exercises 7 and 8, solve each inequality by using a graphing calculator. Show a sketch of the corresponding graph, write the solution set in interval notation, and graph the solution set on a number line. (Estimate endpoints of intervals accurate to 4 decimal places.)

7. $x^2 \leq 4x - 3$ **8.** $x^3 - 6x^2 + 3x + 5 > 0$

Use the graph of $y = f(x)$ shown below to graph the functions indicated in Exercises 9 – 11.

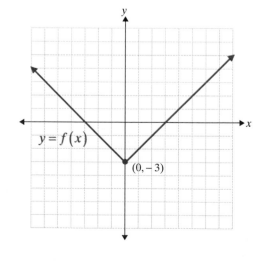

9. $y = -f(x)$ **10.** $y = -f(x) - 3$ **11.** $y = f(x+1) + 2$

12. One number exceeds another by 10. Find the minimum product of the two numbers.

13. The perimeter of a rectangle is 22 inches. Find the dimensions that will maximize the area.

In Exercises 14 and 15, find the vertex, the y-intercepts, and the line of symmetry. Graph the curve.

14. $x = y^2 - 5$

15. $x + 4 = y^2 + 3y$

16. Find the distance between the two points $(5, -2)$ and $(-4, 1)$.

17. Show that the triangle determined by the points $A(-4, -3), B(0, 3), C(6, -1)$ is a right triangle.

18. Find the equation for the circle with center at $(-3, -1)$ and radius 5.

19. Find the center and radius of the circle with equation $x^2 + y^2 - 2y - 8 = 0$, then sketch the graph.

In Exercises 20 – 23, write the equation in standard form, then sketch the graph. If the graph is a hyperbola, write the equations and graph the asymptotes.

20. $9x^2 - 4y^2 = 36$

21. $x^2 + 4y^2 = 9$

22. $16y^2 - 9x^2 = 144$

23. $25x^2 + 4y^2 = 100$

24. Graph the ellipse and label the vertices: $\dfrac{(x-3)^2}{36} + \dfrac{(y-2)^2}{9} = 1$

25. Graph the hyperbola and the asymptotes: $\dfrac{(x+1)^2}{16} - \dfrac{y^2}{9} = 1$

In Exercises 26 – 28, graph each pair of equations, and then solve the system.

26. $\begin{cases} x^2 + y^2 = 29 \\ x - y = 3 \end{cases}$

27. $\begin{cases} x^2 + 2y^2 = 4 \\ x = y^2 - 2 \end{cases}$

28. $\begin{cases} x^2 + y^2 = 25 \\ x^2 - y^2 = 7 \end{cases}$

Cumulative Review: Chapters 1 - 8

Simplify each of the expressions in Exercises 1 – 4. Assume all variables are positive.

1. $\dfrac{x^{-3} \cdot x}{x^2 \cdot x^{-4}}$

2. $\left(\dfrac{2x^{-1}y^2}{3x^3 y^{-2}} \right)^{-2}$

3. $5x^{1/2} \cdot x^{1/4}$

4. $\left(4x^{-2/3} y^{2/5} \right)^{3/2}$

5. Write $\left(7x^3 y \right)^{2/3}$ in radical notation.   **6.** Write $\sqrt[3]{32x^6 y}$ in exponential notation.

Completely factor each expression in Exercises 7 – 9.

7. $2x^3 + 54$

8. $2 + 9x^{-1} - 35x^{-2}$

9. $x^3 - 4x^2 + 3x - 12$

Perform the indicated operations and simplify in Exercises 10 and 11.

10. $2\sqrt{12} + 5\sqrt{108} - 7\sqrt{27}$

11. $3\sqrt{48x} - 2\sqrt{75x} + 5\sqrt{24}$

12. Find an equation for the line parallel to $5x - 2y = 8$ and passing through $(-2, 3)$.

13. Find an equation for the line perpendicular to $4x + 3y = 8$ and passing through $(4, -1)$.

Perform the indicated operations in Exercises 14 and 15.

14. $\dfrac{x}{2x^2 - 5x - 12} - \dfrac{x+1}{6x^2 + 5x - 6}$

15. $\dfrac{x^2 + 2x - 3}{x^2 + x - 2} \div \dfrac{9 - x^2}{x^2 - x - 6}$

Solve each of the equations in Exercises 16 – 18.

16. $3x^2 + 2x - 2 = 0$

17. $\dfrac{5}{x-3} - \dfrac{3}{x+2} = \dfrac{1}{x^2 - x - 6}$

18. $\sqrt{x+14} - 2 = x$

19. Solve the following system by using Cramer's rule.

$$\begin{cases} 2x - 3y = 5 \\ -5x + y = 7 \end{cases}$$

20. Solve the following system by using Gaussian elimination.

$$\begin{cases} 2x - 3y + z = -4 \\ x + 2y - z = 5 \\ 3x + y + 2z = -5 \end{cases}$$

In Exercises 21 and 22, write the quadratic function in the form $y = a(x - h)^2 + k$. Find the vertex, axis of symmetry, domain, range, and zeros. Graph the function.

21. $y = \dfrac{1}{2}x^2 - 3$

22. $y = -x^2 + 4x - 4$

23. Given the graph of $y = f(x)$ shown here,

   a. draw the graph of $y = f(x-2)$

   b. draw the graph of $y = f(x)+2$

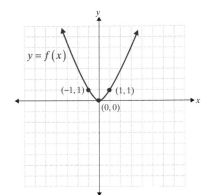

$y = f(x)$

$(-1, 1)$ $(1, 1)$

$(0, 0)$

24. Solve the inequality $\dfrac{x^2 - 4x - 5}{x} \geq 0$.

Graph each of the equations in Exercises 25 – 28.

25. $5x + 2y = 8$ **26.** $y = 2x^2 - 4x - 3$ **27.** $4x^2 - y^2 = 16$

28. $x^2 + 2x + y^2 - 2y = 4$

29. For $f(x) = 4x - 7$, find:

   a. $f(3)$

   b. $f(x-1)$

   c. $f(x)+3$

   d. $\dfrac{f(x+h) - f(x)}{h}$

30. For $g(x) = 2x^2 + 3x - 1$, find:

   a. $g(2)$

   b. $g(x)-2$

   c. $g(x-2)$

   d. $\dfrac{g(x+h) - g(x)}{h}$

31. Lisha has $9000 to invest in two different accounts. One account pays interest at the rate of 7%; the other pays at the rate of 8%. If she wants her annual interest to total $684, how much should she invest at each rate?

32. The average of a number and its square root is 21. Find the number.

33. The height of a ball projected vertically is given by the function $h = -16t^2 + 80t + 48$ where h is the height in feet and t is the time in seconds.
   a. When will the ball reach maximum height?
   b. What will be the maximum height?

34. A store owner estimates that by charging x dollars for a certain shirt, he can sell $60 - 2x$ shirts each week. What price will give him maximum receipts?

Use a graphing calculator to graph the functions in Exercises 35 – 38 and estimate the zeros of each function.

35. $y = 2x - 5$ **36.** $y = x^2 - 3$ **37.** $y = -x^2 + 5$

38. $y = (x+3)^2 - 6$

In Exercises 39 and 40, use a graphing calculator to graph each function. Estimate (accurate to 4 decimal places) the solutions to the equations and write the solutions to the inequalities in interval notation.

39. $f(x) = x^2 - 3x - 10$

    a. $x^2 - 3x - 10 = 0$

    b. $x^2 - 3x - 10 > 0$

    c. $x^2 - 3x - 10 < 0$

40. $f(x) = -2x^2 + 3x + 5$

    a. $-2x^2 + 3x + 5 = 0$

    b. $-2x^2 + 3x + 5 > 0$

    c. $-2x^2 + 3x + 5 < 0$

In Exercises 41 and 42, use a graphing calculator to graph both equations and estimate the solutions to the system.

41. $\begin{cases} x^2 + y^2 = 35 \\ x + y = 4 \end{cases}$

42. $\begin{cases} 3x^2 + 4y^2 = 12 \\ x = y^2 - 3 \end{cases}$

43. a. Use synthetic division and the Remainder Theorem to find $P(5)$ if $P(x) = 2x^3 - 8x^2 + 10x - 100$.

    b. Is $(x-5)$ a factor of $P(x)$? Explain.

44. State the Pythagorean Theorem.

45. Given that $g(x) = \sqrt{x-7}$, state the domain and range of g and sketch the graph of the function.

Exponential and Logarithmic Functions

Did You Know?

In this chapter, you will study exponential functions and their related inverses, logarithmic functions. You will also see how the use of logarithms can simplify calculations involving multiplication and division. Although electronic calculators have made calculation with logarithms obsolete, it is still important to study the logarithmic functions because they have many applications other than computing.

Napier

The inventor of logarithms was John Napier (1550–1617). Napier was a Scottish nobleman, Laird of Merchiston Castle, a stronghold on the outskirts of the town of Edinburgh. An eccentric, Napier was intensely involved in the political and religious struggles of his day. He had interests in many areas, including mathematics. In 1614, Napier published his "Description of the Laws of Logarithms," and thus he is given credit for first publishing and popularizing the idea of logarithms. Napier used a base close to the number *e* for his system, and natural logarithms (base *e*) are often called **Napierian logarithms**. Napier soon saw that a base of 10 would be more appropriate for calculations since our decimal number system uses base 10. Napier began work on a base-10 system but was unable to complete it before his death. John Briggs (1560–1630) completed Napier's work, and base-10 logarithms are often called **Briggsian logarithms** in his honor.

Napier's interest in simplifying calculations was based on the need at that time to do many calculations by hand for astronomical and scientific research. He also invented the forerunner of the slide rule and predicted tanks, submarines, and other advanced war technology. Napier's remarkable ingenuity led the local people to consider him either crazy or a dealer in the black art of magic.

A particularly amusing story is told of Napier's method of identifying which of his servants was stealing from him. He told his servants that his black rooster would identify the thief. Each servant was sent alone into a darkened room to pet the rooster on the back. Napier had coated the back of the rooster with soot, and the guilty servant came out of the room with clean hands.

Napier was a staunch Presbyterian, and he felt that his claim to immortality would be an attack that he had written on the Catholic Church. The scientific community more correctly judged that logarithms would be his one great contribution.

9.1   Algebra of Functions

9.2   Composition of Functions and Inverse Functions

9.3   Exponential Functions

9.4   Logarithmic Functions

9.5   Properties of Logarithms

9.6   Logarithmic and Exponential Equations

9.7   Applications

The invention of logarithms: "by shortening the labors doubled the life of the astronomer."

Pierre de Laplace (1749-1827)

As discussed in Chapters 4, 6, and 8, functions are an important topic in mathematics. The function notation, $f(x)$, is particularly helpful in evaluating functions and in indicating graphical relationships such as horizontal and vertical asymptotes. And, as we will see in this chapter, operating algebraically with functions and understanding and finding the composition and inverses of functions relies heavily on function notation. The composite and inverse function concepts form the basis of the relationship between logarithmic and exponential functions.

Logarithms are exponents. Traditionally, logarithmic and exponential values were calculated with the extensive use of printed tables and techniques for estimating values not found in the tables. Now, hand-held calculators have programs stored in their electronic memories that calculate the values in these tables, with even greater accuracy, and complicated expressions can be evaluated by pressing a few keys.

The irrational number $e = 2.718281828459\ldots$ will be discussed in detail. This number appears quite naturally in many applications and is the base for natural logarithms, indicated on calculators by the key marked **LN** or **ln x**.

Of all the topics discussed in algebra, logarithmic functions and exponential functions probably have the most value in terms of applied problems. For example, the bell-shaped curve (or normal curve) studied in statistics is based on an exponential function. Exponential growth and decay are basic concepts in biology and medicine. (Cancer cells grow exponentially and radium decays exponentially.) In business, depreciation and continuously compounded interest can be calculated by using exponential functions. Learning curves, important in business and education, can be described with logarithmic and exponential functions. Computers use logarithmic and exponential concepts in their design and implementation. Obviously, you are likely to encounter these concepts at some time in almost any field you choose to study.

9.1   Algebra of Functions

Objectives

After completing this section, you will be able to:

1. *Find the sum, difference, product, and quotient of two functions.*
2. *Graph the sum of two functions.*
3. *Graph the sum of two functions with a calculator.*

Algebraic Operations with Functions

In this section we will discuss how to perform the operations of addition, subtraction, multiplication, and division with two functions with the same domain. For example, suppose that

$$f(x) = 2x^2 - 1 \qquad \text{and} \qquad g(x) = x^2 + 2x - 5.$$

Then,

$$f(3) = 2 \cdot 3^2 - 1 = 17 \qquad \text{and} \qquad g(3) = 3^2 + 2 \cdot 3 - 5 = 10$$

Now, we can easily find the sum and difference

$$f(3) + g(3) = 17 + 10 = 27 \qquad \text{and} \qquad f(3) - g(3) = 17 - 10 = 7$$

However, if we want to find, say $f(5) + g(5)$ and $f(5) - g(5)$, we would need to again evaluate both functions, this time at $x = 5$. Another way to find sums and differences of functions is to find the algebraic sum (or difference) between the two algebraic expressions. Then, these new expressions will allow us to find the sum (or difference) directly for any value of x. For example, we find the sum $f + g$

$$(f + g)(x) = f(x) + g(x)$$
$$= (2x^2 - 1) + (x^2 + 2x - 5)$$
$$= 3x^2 + 2x - 6$$

With this new function, we find directly that

$$(f + g)(3) = 3 \cdot 3^2 + 2 \cdot 3 - 6 = 27.$$

Similarly,

$$(f - g)(x) = f(x) - g(x)$$
$$= (2x^2 - 1) - (x^2 + 2x - 5)$$
$$= x^2 - 2x + 4$$

and we have

$$(f - g)(3) = 3^2 - 2 \cdot 3 + 4 = 7.$$

Similar notation is used for the product and quotient of two functions. One important condition is that both functions must have the same domain. If not, then the algebraic sums, differences, products, and quotients are restricted to portions of the domains that are in common. Also, in the case of quotients, no denominator can be 0.

Definitions of Algebraic Operations with Functions

If $f(x)$ and $g(x)$ represent two functions and x is a value in the domain of both functions, then

1. Sum of Two Functions: $\qquad (f + g)(x) = f(x) + g(x)$

2. Difference of Two Functions: $\quad (f - g)(x) = f(x) - g(x)$

3. Product of Two Functions: $\qquad (f \cdot g)(x) = f(x) \cdot g(x)$

4. Quotient of Two Functions: $\qquad \left(\dfrac{f}{g}\right)(x) = \dfrac{f(x)}{g(x)} \qquad$ *where* $g(x) \neq 0$

Example 1: Algebraic Operations with Functions

Let $f(x) = 3x^2 + x - 4$ and $g(x) = x - 6$. Find the following functions:

a. $(f+g)(x)$ **b.** $(f-g)(x)$ **c.** $(f \cdot g)(x)$

d. Evaluate each of the functions found in parts a – c at $x = 2$.

Solutions:

a. $(f+g)(x) = \left(3x^2 + x - 4\right) + (x - 6) = 3x^2 + 2x - 10$

b. $(f-g)(x) = \left(3x^2 + x - 4\right) - (x - 6) = 3x^2 + 2$

c. $(f \cdot g)(x) = \left(3x^2 + x - 4\right)(x - 6) = 3x^3 - 17x^2 - 10x + 24$

d. Evaluating each of these functions at $x = 2$ gives the following results:

$(f+g)(2) = 3 \cdot 2^2 + 2 \cdot 2 - 10 = 6$

$(f-g)(2) = 3 \cdot 2^2 + 2 = 14$

$(f \cdot g)(2) = 3 \cdot 2^3 - 17 \cdot 2^2 - 10 \cdot 2 + 24 = -40$

Example 2: Algebraic Operations with Functions

Let $f(x) = x^2 - x$ and $g(x) = 2x + 1$. Find the following functions:

a. $(f+g)(x)$ **b.** $(g-f)(x)$ **c.** $\left(\dfrac{f}{g}\right)(x)$

d. Evaluate each of the functions found in parts a – c at $x = 3$.

Solutions:

a. $(f+g)(x) = \left(x^2 - x\right) + (2x + 1) = x^2 + x + 1$

b. $(g-f)(x) = (2x + 1) - \left(x^2 - x\right) = -x^2 + 3x + 1$

c. $\left(\dfrac{f}{g}\right)(x) = \dfrac{x^2 - x}{2x + 1}$ where $2x + 1 \neq 0 \left(\text{or } x \neq -\dfrac{1}{2}\right)$

d. Evaluating each of these functions at $x = 3$ gives the following results:

$(f+g)(3) = 3^2 + 3 + 1 = 13$

$(g-f)(3) = -3^2 + 3 \cdot 3 + 1 = 1$

$\left(\dfrac{f}{g}\right)(3) = \dfrac{3^2 - 3}{2 \cdot 3 + 1} = \dfrac{6}{7}$

Note that, except for Example 2c, the domain for all of the functions discussed in Examples 1 and 2 is the set of all real numbers, $(-\infty,\infty)$. In Example 2c, we noted that the denominator cannot equal 0. In Example 3, we show how the domain may need to be limited before performing algebra with functions that contain radical expressions.

Example 3: Algebraic Operations with Functions • • • • • • • • • • • • • • • •

Let $f(x) = x+5$ and $g(x) = \sqrt{x-2}$. Find the following functions and state the domain of each function.

    a. $(f+g)(x)$ **b.** $\left(\dfrac{f}{g}\right)(x)$

Solutions:

    a. $(f+g)(x) = x+5+\sqrt{x-2}$

        The domain of f is the set of all real numbers. However, the domain of the sum is restricted to the domain of the radical function. In this case we must have $x-2 \geq 0$. Thus, in interval notation, the domain is $[2,\infty)$.

    b. $\left(\dfrac{f}{g}\right)(x) = \dfrac{x+5}{\sqrt{x-2}}$

        For this function, the denominator cannot be 0. Therefore, we must have $x-2 > 0$ and the domain, in interval notation, is $(2,\infty)$.

• •

Graphing the Sum of Two Functions

In this section, we discuss how to graph the sum of two functions. (Graphing the difference, product, and quotient can be accomplished in a similar manner.) Remember that, in any case, algebraic operations with functions can be performed only over a common domain.

We begin with two functions f and g that have the same domain and only a finite number of ordered pairs:

$$f = \{(-2,0),(-1,1),(0,4),(2,4),(3,5),(4,1)\}$$

$$g = \{(-2,3),(-1,4),(0,1),(2,-1),(3,2),(4,6)\}$$

The graphs of these two functions are shown in Figure 9.1.

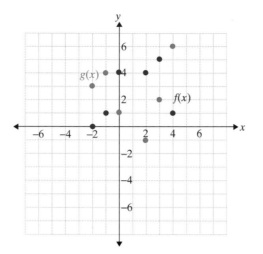

Figure 9.1

Note that the set $\{-2, -1, 0, 2, 3, 4\}$ is the domain of both functions.

The sum of these two functions is found by adding the corresponding y-values for each x in the domain. Thus,

$$f + g = \left\{ (-2, 0+3), (-1, 1+4), (0, 4+1), (2, 4-1), (3, 5+2), (4, 1+6) \right\}$$
$$= \left\{ (-2, 3), (-1, 5), (0, 5), (2, 3), (3, 7), (4, 7) \right\}$$

The graphs of all three functions are shown in Figure 9.2.

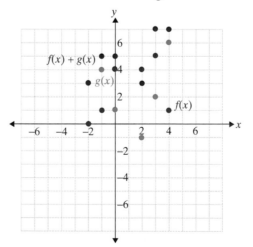

Figure 9.2

In general, graphing the sum of two functions will involve an infinite number of points and we cannot plot all these points one at a time. However, by making a table of a few key points and joining these points with a smooth curve or line segment, we can find the general nature of the sum. In fact, if the two functions consist of line segments, then the sum will also consist of line segments. Figure 9.3 illustrates two such functions and Figure 9.4 illustrates the sum of these functions.

Table 9.1 shows how calculating

$$(f+g)(x) = f(x) + g(x)$$

for some of the points helps in sketching the graph of $f + g$.

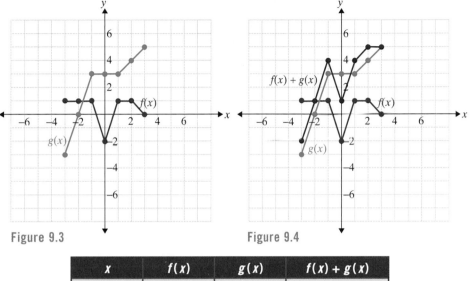

Figure 9.3   Figure 9.4

x	f(x)	g(x)	f(x) + g(x)
−3	1	−3	−2
−2	1	0	1
−1	1	3	4
0	−2	3	1
1	1	3	4
2	1	4	5
3	0	5	5

Table 9.1 (Points Illustrated in Figure 9.3 and Figure 9.4)

Using a Graphing Calculator to Graph the Sum of Two Functions

A graphing calculator can be used to graph the sum (or difference, product, and quotient) of two functions. One interesting way to do this is to enter each function and then assign a third function to be the sum of the first two. Figure 9.5 shows the display for entering two functions.

Figure 9.5

Now, we can add the two functions, $f(x) + g(x)$, as we have been doing. However, the calculator will do this for us if we enter **Y3** as the sum **Y1 + Y2**. This can be accomplished as follows:

1. Press (Y=) and select **Y3**.
2. Press the (VARS) key.
3. Move the cursor to **Y-VARS** at the top of the display.
4. Select **1:Function** and press (ENTER).
5. Select **Y1** and press (ENTER).
6. Press the (+) key.
7. Go to **Y-VARS** again, select **1:Function**, select **Y2**.

The display will appear as follows:

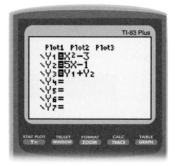

Now press (GRAPH) and the display will show both **Y1** and **Y2** as well as the sum **Y3 = Y1 + Y2**. Your graph may be different if you have different settings for your **WINDOW**.

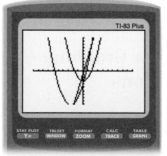

9.1 Exercises

*In Exercises 1 – 10, find **a.** $(f + g)(x)$, **b.** $(f - g)(x)$, **c.** $(f \cdot g)(x)$, and **d.** $\left(\dfrac{f}{g}\right)(x)$.*

1. $f(x) = x + 2$, $g(x) = x - 5$ 2. $f(x) = 2x$, $g(x) = x + 4$

3. $f(x) = x^2$, $g(x) = 3x - 4$ 4. $f(x) = x - 3$, $g(x) = x^2 + 1$

5. $f(x) = x^2 - 9$, $g(x) = x - 3$

6. $f(x) = x^2 - 25$, $g(x) = x + 5$

7. $f(x) = 2x^2 + x$, $g(x) = x^2 + 2$

8. $f(x) = x^3 + 6x$, $g(x) = x^2 + 6$

9. $f(x) = x^2 + 4x + 1$, $g(x) = x^2 - 4x + 1$

10. $f(x) = x^3 - x^2$, $g(x) = 6 - x^2$

For Exercises 11 – 20, let $f(x) = x^2 + 4$ and $g(x) = -x + 3$. Find the value of the indicated expression.

11. $f(2) + g(2)$

12. $f(2) \cdot g(2)$

13. $g(a) - f(a)$

14. $\dfrac{g(a)}{f(a)}$

15. $(f + g)(-4)$

16. $(f - g)(0.5)$

17. $\left(\dfrac{f}{g}\right)(-2)$

18. $(f \cdot g)(-3)$

19. $(g - f)(-6)$

20. $\left(\dfrac{g}{f}\right)(-1)$

In Exercises 21 – 30, find the indicated function and state the domain, in interval notation, of each resulting function.

21. If $f(x) = \sqrt{2x - 6}$ and $g(x) = x + 4$, find $(f + g)(x)$.

22. If $f(x) = x^2 - 2x + 1$ and $g(x) = x - 1$, find $\left(\dfrac{f}{g}\right)(x)$.

23. Find $f(x) \cdot g(x)$ given that $f(x) = 3x + 2$ and $g(x) = x - 7$.

24. Find $f(x) - g(x)$ given that $f(x) = x^2$ and $g(x) = x^2 - 2$.

25. For $f(x) = x - 5$ and $g(x) = \sqrt{x + 3}$ find $\dfrac{f(x)}{g(x)}$.

26. For $f(x) = 2x - 8$ and $g(x) = \sqrt{2 - x}$ find $f(x) \cdot g(x)$.

27. If $f(x) = -\sqrt{x - 3}$ and $g(x) = 3x$, find $(f \cdot g)(x)$.

28. If $f(x) = -\sqrt{4 - x}$ and $g(x) = 5 - x$, find $(g - f)(x)$.

29. If $f(x) = \sqrt[3]{x + 3}$ and $g(x) = \sqrt{5 + x}$, find $f(x) + g(x)$.

30. If $f(x) = \sqrt{x - 1}$ and $g(x) = \sqrt[3]{2x + 1}$, find $f(x) - g(x)$.

In Exercises 31 – 40, graph each pair of functions and the sum of these functions on the same set of axes.

31. $y = x^2$ and $y = -1$

32. $y = x^2$ and $y = 2$

33. $y = x + 1$ and $y = 2x$

34. $y = 2 - x$ and $y = x$

35. $y = x + 4$ and $y = -x$

36. $y = x + 5$ and $y = x - 5$

37. $f(x) = x + 1$ and $g(x) = x^2 - 1$

38. $f(x) = x^2 + 2$ and $g(x) = x^2 - 2$

39. $f(x) = \sqrt{x - 6}$ and $g(x) = 2$

40. $f(x) = \sqrt{3 - x}$ and $g(x) = -1$

Use the graph shown here to find the values indicated in Exercises 41 – 46.

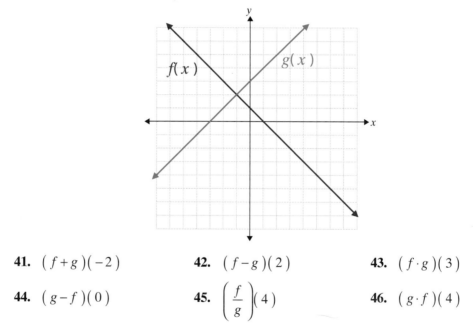

41. $(f + g)(-2)$

42. $(f - g)(2)$

43. $(f \cdot g)(3)$

44. $(g - f)(0)$

45. $\left(\dfrac{f}{g}\right)(4)$

46. $(g \cdot f)(4)$

In Exercises 47 – 52, the graphs of two functions are given. Graph the sum of these two functions.

47.

48.

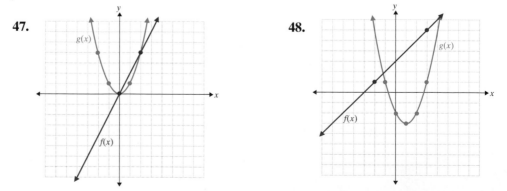

49. **50.**

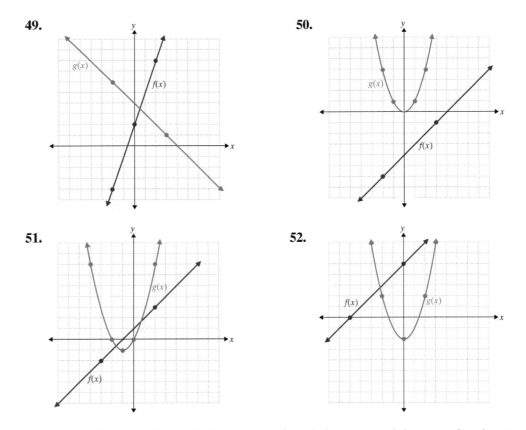

51. **52.**

Use a TI-83 Plus graphing calculator to graph each function and the sum of each pair of functions in Exercises 53 – 60.

53. $y = x^2$ and $y = 2x + 1$

54. $y = x^2 + x$ and $y = 3x + 4$

55. $y = \sqrt{x + 4}$ and $y = -2$

56. $y = -\sqrt{x - 1}$ and $y = 3$

57. $f(x) = \sqrt[3]{x + 5}$ and $h(x) = 2x$

58. $h(x) = \sqrt[3]{x - 1}$ and $g(x) = x - 1$

59. $g(x) = -\sqrt{x - 2}$ and $h(x) = 1$

60. $f(x) = x^2 + 5$ and $g(x) = 4 - x^2$

Writing and Thinking About Mathematics

61. Explain why, in general, $(f - g)(x) \neq (g - f)(x)$.

62. Given the two functions f and g,

$$f = \{(-2, 0), (-1, 1), (0, 4), (2, 4), (3, 5), (4, 1)\}$$

$$g = \{(-2, 3), (-1, 4), (0, 1), (2, -1), (3, 2), (4, 6)\}$$

find and graph

a. $f - g$ **b.** $f \cdot g$ **c.** $\dfrac{f}{g}$

continued on next page ...

63. Use the graphs of the two functions f and g shown in Figure 9.3 on page 613

  a. Sketch the graph of $f - g$.
  b. Sketch the graph of $f \cdot g$.

  c. Is $\dfrac{f}{g}$ defined on the entire interval $[-3, 3]$? Briefly discuss your reasoning.

Hawkes Learning Systems: Intermediate Algebra

Algebra of Functions

Composition of Functions and Inverse Functions

After completing this section, you will be able to:

1. *Form the composition of two functions.*

2. *Determine if functions are one-to-one by using the horizontal line test.*

3. *Show that two functions, f and g, are inverse functions by verifying that $f(g(x)) = x$ and $g(f(x)) = x$.*

4. *Find the inverses of one-to-one functions.*

5. *State the domain and range of one-to-one functions and their inverses.*

6. *Graph the inverses of one-to-one functions by reflecting the graphs of the functions across the line $y = x$.*

Composition of Functions

In Sections 6.4, 8.3, and 9.1, the function notation $f(x)$ was used for evaluating functions for specified values of x, indicating horizontal and vertical translations, and indicating algebraic operations with functions. This same notation can be used to indicate a **function of a function**. For example,

$$\text{If} \quad g(x) = 2x - 4, \qquad \text{then} \quad g(3) = 2 \cdot 3 - 4 = 2$$

$$\text{If} \quad f(x) = x^2 - 4x + 1, \qquad \text{then} \quad f(2) = 2^2 - 4 \cdot 2 + 1 = -3$$

To find the **composite** $f(g(3))$ (read "f of g of 3"), we have

$$f(g(3)) = f(2) = -3 \qquad \text{We see that } g(3) \text{ replaces } x \text{ in the function } f(x).$$

More generally, given two functions $f(x)$ and $g(x)$, a new function $f(g(x))$, called the **composition** (or **composite**) of f and g, is found by substituting the expression for $g(x)$ in place of x in the function f. Thus, for

$$f(x) = x^2 - 4x + 1 \quad \text{and} \quad g(x) = 2x - 4$$

the composition

$$f(g(x)) \qquad \text{read "}f\text{ of }g\text{ of }x\text{"}$$

is found as follows:

continued on next page ...

$$f(g(x)) = (g(x))^2 - 4(g(x)) + 1 \qquad \text{Replace the } x \text{ in } f(x) \text{ with } g(x).$$

$$= (2x-4)^2 - 4(2x-4) + 1 \qquad \text{Replace } g(x) \text{ with } 2x-4.$$

$$= 4x^2 - 16x + 16 - 8x + 16 + 1 \quad \text{Simplify.}$$

$$= 4x^2 - 24x + 33$$

The composition of g and f (reversing the order of f and g) is indicated by

$$g(f(x)) \qquad \text{read} \qquad \text{"g of f of x"}$$

and is found by substituting the expression for $f(x)$ in place of x in the function g. Thus,

$$g(f(x)) = 2(f(x)) - 4 \qquad \text{Replace the } x \text{ in } g(x) \text{ with } f(x).$$

$$= 2(x^2 - 4x + 1) - 4 \qquad \text{Replace } f(x) \text{ with } x^2 - 4x + 1.$$

$$= 2x^2 - 8x + 2 - 4 \qquad \text{Simplify.}$$

$$= 2x^2 - 8x - 2$$

As we can see with these examples, in general, $f(g(x)) \neq g(f(x))$ and substitutions must be done carefully and accurately. The following definition shows another notation (a small raised circle) often used to indicate the composition of functions.

Composite Functions

For two functions f and g, the **composite function** $f \circ g$ is defined as follows:

$$(f \circ g)(x) = f(g(x))$$

Domain of $f \circ g$: *The domain of $f \circ g$ consists of those values of x in the domain of g for which $g(x)$ is in the domain of f.*

Example 1: Compositions

a. Form the compositions $(f \circ g)(x)$ and $(g \circ f)(x)$ if $f(x) = 5x + 2$ and $g(x) = 3x - 7$.
   Solution: $(f \circ g)(x) = f(g(x)) = 5 \cdot g(x) + 2 = 5(3x-7) + 2 = 15x - 33$

   $(g \circ f)(x) = g(f(x)) = 3 \cdot f(x) - 7 = 3(5x+2) - 7 = 15x - 1$

Note: Both $(f \circ g)(x)$ and $(g \circ f)(x)$ are defined for all real numbers.

b. Form the composite functions $(f \circ g)(x)$ and $(g \circ f)(x)$ if $f(x) = \sqrt{x-3}$ and $g(x) = x^2 + 4$

Solution: $(f \circ g)(x) = \sqrt{g(x) - 3}$

$$= \sqrt{(x^2 + 4) - 3} = \sqrt{x^2 + 1}$$

Note: $(f \circ g)(x)$ is defined for all real numbers because $x^2 + 1 \geq 0$ for all real values of x.

$$(g \circ f)(x) = (f(x))^2 + 4$$

$$= (\sqrt{x-3})^2 + 4 = x - 3 + 4 = x + 1$$

Note: $(f \circ g)(x)$ is defined only for $x \geq 3$.

c. Find $f(g(x))$ and $g(f(x))$ if $f(x) = \sqrt{x+3}$ and $g(x) = 2x - 5$.

Solution: $f(g(x)) = \sqrt{g(x) + 3}$

$$= \sqrt{(2x - 5) + 3} = \sqrt{2x - 2}$$

Note: $f(g(x))$ is defined only for $2x - 2 \geq 0$ or $x \geq 1$.

$$g(f(x)) = 2f(x) - 5$$

$$= 2\sqrt{x+3} - 5$$

Note: $g(f(x))$ is defined only for $x \geq -3$.

• •

One-to-One Functions

We know that, in any function, there can be only one value of y for each value of x in the domain. Graphically, the **vertical line test** (See Section 2.5) can be used to help determine whether or not a graph represents a function. Now, in order to develop the concept of **inverse functions**, we need to study functions which have only one value of x for each value of y in the range. That is, for each range element, there is only one corresponding domain element. Such functions are said to be **one-to-one functions** (or **1–1 functions**).

Consider the following two functions:

$$f = \{(1, 2), (2, 4), (3, 6), (4, 8), (5, 10)\}$$

$$g = \{(-2, 6), (0, 6), (1, 5), (2, 4), (4, 1)\}$$

Both sets of ordered pairs are functions because each value of x appears only once. In the function f, each y-value appears only once. But, in function g, the y-value 6 appears twice: in $(-2, 6)$ and $(0, 6)$. Figure 9.5 illustrates both functions.

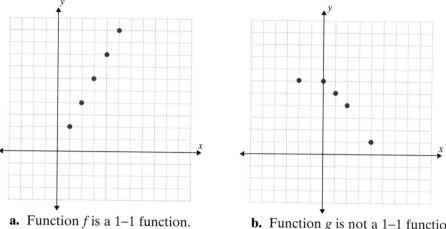

a. Function f is a 1–1 function.   **b.** Function g is not a 1–1 function.

Figure 9.5

One-to-One Functions

*A function is a **one-to-one function** (or **1 – 1 function**) if for each value of y in the range there is only one corresponding value of x in the domain.*

Graphically, as illustrated in Figure 9.5(b), if a horizontal line intersects the graph of a function in more than one point then it is **not** one-to-one. This is, in effect, the **horizontal line test**.

Horizontal Line Test

A function is one-to-one if no horizontal line intersects the graph of the function in more than one point.

The graphs in Figure 9.6 illustrate the concept of one-to-one functions. (Note that each graph is indeed a function and would pass the vertical line test.)

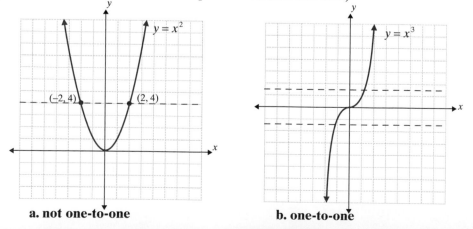

a. not one-to-one   **b. one-to-one**

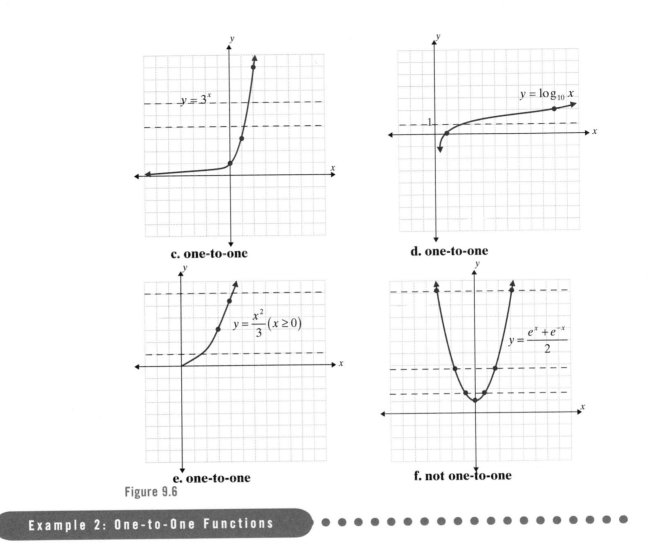

c. one-to-one

d. one-to-one

e. one-to-one

f. not one-to-one

Figure 9.6

Example 2: One-to-One Functions

Determine whether each function is 1–1 or not.

a. $y = \sqrt{x+5}$

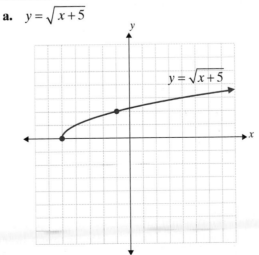

Solution: The horizontal line test shows that this function is 1–1.

continued on next page ...

b. $f = \{(-3,4),(-2,1),(0,4),(3,1)\}$

   Solution: This function is not 1–1. Both y-values, 4 and 1, have more than one corresponding x-value.

c. $y = 2x - 1$

   Solution: The graph of the function $y = 2x - 1$ is a straight line. Straight lines that are not vertical and not horizontal represent 1–1 functions. (Vertical lines are not functions in the first place and horizontal lines fail the horizontal line test.)

d. $y = -x^2 + 1$

   Solution: The graph of the function $y = -x^2 + 1$ is a parabola and the horizontal line test will show that the function is not 1–1.

● ●

Inverse Functions

Now that we have discussed 1–1 functions, we can develop the concept of **inverse functions**. We will find that only 1–1 functions have inverse functions. To find the inverse of a 1–1 function represented by a set of ordered pairs, exchange x and y in each ordered pair. That is, if (x, y) is in the original 1–1 function, then (y, x) is in the inverse function. For example,

$$\text{If } f = \{(-1,1),(0,2),(1,4)\}$$

then interchanging the coordinates in each ordered pair gives

$$g = \{(1,-1),(2,0),(4,1)\}.$$

The functions f and g are called **inverses** of each other. If g is the inverse of f we write

$$f^{-1} \quad (\text{read "}f\text{ inverse"}) \quad \text{rather than use } g.$$

Thus, in this example, we can write $f^{-1} = \{(1,-1),(2,0),(4,1)\}.$

Inverse Function

*If f is a 1–1 function with ordered pairs of the form (x, y), then its **inverse function**, denoted as f^{-1}, is also a 1–1 function with ordered pairs of the form (y, x).*

Note the importance of the original function being 1–1. If it is not 1–1, then interchanging the x- and y-values would yield a relation that is not a function.

> **NOTES** The notation $f^{-1}(x)$ represents the inverse of a 1–1 function. This inverse is a new function in which the *x*- and *y*-values have been interchanged. $f^{-1}(x)$ does NOT mean $\dfrac{1}{f(x)}$ because the –1 is NOT an exponent.

The graph of any point (b, a) is the reflection of the point (a, b) across the line $y = x$. Thus, the points of the inverse function f^{-1} are reflections of the points of the function f across the line $y = x$. We say that the graphs are **symmetric about the line $y = x$**. Figure 9.7 illustrates these reflections and the symmetry.

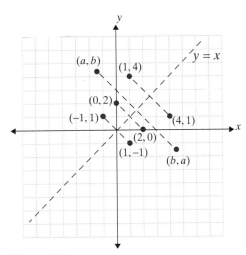

The points of f and f^{-1} are reflections of each other across the line $y = x$.

Figure 9.7

In general, every 1–1 function has an inverse function (or just inverse), and the graph of the inverse function of any 1–1 function f can be found by reflecting the graph of f across the line $y = x$. Figure 9.8 shows two more illustrations of this concept.

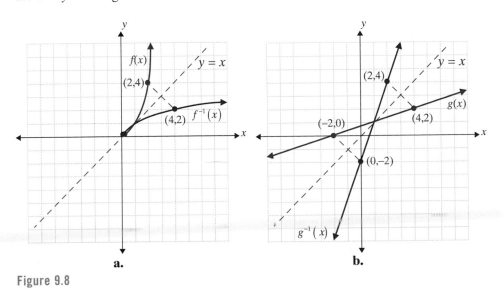

a.   **b.**

Figure 9.8

The following definition of inverse functions helps to determine whether or not two functions are inverses of each other. The notation D_f is used to indicate the domain of the function f.

Inverse Functions

If f and g are one-to-one functions and

$$f(g(x)) = x \qquad \text{for all } x \text{ in } D_g$$
$$g(f(x)) = x \qquad \text{for all } x \text{ in } D_f$$

*then f and g are **inverse functions**.*
That is, $g = f^{-1}$ and $f = g^{-1}$.

Example 3: Inverse Functions

Use the definition of inverse functions to show that f and g are inverse functions.

a. $f(x) = 2x + 6$ and $g(x) = \dfrac{x-6}{2}$.

b. $f(x) = \sqrt{x-3}$ and $g(x) = x^2 + 3$ for $x \geq 0$.

Solutions: a. $f(x) = 2x + 6$ and $g(x) = \dfrac{x-6}{2}$. The domain of both functions is the set of all real numbers.
We have

$$f(g(x)) = 2 \cdot g(x) + 6$$

$$= 2\left(\frac{x-6}{2}\right) + 6 \qquad \text{Replace } x \text{ with } g(x) \text{ and simplify.}$$

$$= (x-6) + 6$$

$$= x$$

Also,

$$g(f(x)) = \frac{f(x) - 6}{2}$$

$$= \frac{(2x+6) - 6}{2} \qquad \text{Replace } x \text{ with } f(x) \text{ and simplify.}$$

$$= \frac{2x}{2}$$

$$= x$$

Therefore, $g = f^{-1}$ and $f = g^{-1}$.

The graph shows that the line $y = x$ is a line of symmetry for the graphs of the inverse functions.

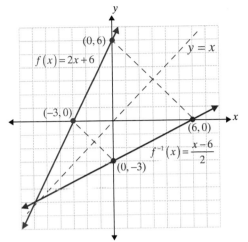

b. $f(x) = \sqrt{x-3}$ and $g(x) = x^2 + 3$ for $x \geq 0$. The domain of f is the interval $[3, \infty)$ and the domain of g is the interval $[0, \infty)$.

We have

$$f(g(x)) = \sqrt{g(x) - 3}$$

$$= \sqrt{(x^2 + 3) - 3} \qquad \text{Replace } x \text{ with } g(x) \text{ and simplify.}$$

$$= \sqrt{x^2}$$

$$= x \qquad \text{for } x \geq 0$$

Also,

$$g(f(x)) = (f(x))^2 + 3$$

$$= (\sqrt{x-3})^2 + 3 \qquad \text{Replace } x \text{ with } f(x) \text{ and simplify.}$$

$$= x - 3 + 3$$

$$= x \qquad \text{for } x \geq 3$$

Therefore, $g = f^{-1}$ and $f = g^{-1}$.

continued on next page ...

The graph shows that the line $y = x$ is a line of symmetry for the graphs of the inverse functions.

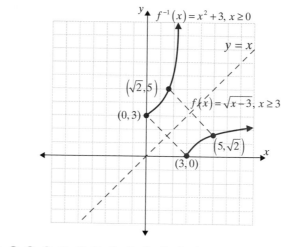

Example 3 shows how to determine whether or not two given functions are inverses of each other. The following procedure shows how to find the inverse of a one-to-one function by using the fact that if (x, y) is in f, then (y, x) is in f^{-1}.

To Find the Inverse of a 1-1 Function

1. Let $y = f(x)$. (In effect, substitute y for $f(x)$.)

2. Interchange x and y.

3. In the new equation, solve for y in terms of x.

4. Substitute $f^{-1}(x)$ for y. (This new function is the inverse of f.)

Example 4: Find the Inverse

a. Find $f^{-1}(x)$ if $f(x) = 5x - 7$.

Solution: $f(x) = 5x - 7$

$\quad\quad y = 5x - 7$ Substitute y for $f(x)$.

$\quad\quad x = 5y - 7$ Interchange x and y.

$\quad\quad x + 7 = 5y$ Solve for y in terms of x.

$\quad\quad \dfrac{x + 7}{5} = y$

$\quad f^{-1}(x) = \dfrac{x + 7}{5}$ Substitute $f^{-1}(x)$ for y.

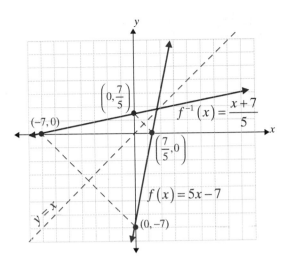

b. Find g^{-1} if $g(x) = x^2 - 2$ for $x \geq 0$.

Solution:

$g(x) = x^2 - 2$	For $x \geq 0$. (Note that g is $1-1$ for $x \geq 0$.)
$y = x^2 - 2$	Substitute y for $g(x)$.
$x = y^2 - 2$	Interchange y and x.
$\pm\sqrt{x+2} = y$	Solve for y in terms of x.
$g^{-1}(x) = \sqrt{x+2}$	Take the positive square root since we must have $y \geq 0$. (The domain of g is $x \geq 0$, so the range of g^{-1} is $y \geq 0$.)

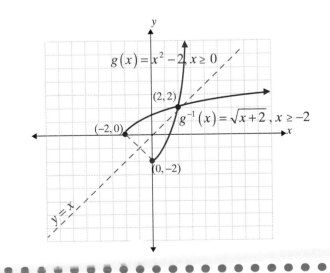

Practice Problems

1. For $f(x) = 2x - 1$ and $g(x) = x^2$, find:

   a. $f(g(x))$ **b.** $g(f(x))$

2. Find the inverse of the function $f(x) = 3x - 1$.

3. Find $f^{-1}(x)$ if $f(x) = x^2 - 4$, $x \geq 0$.   (Note that f is 1–1 for $x \geq 0$.)

9.2 Exercises

Form the compositions $f(g(x))$ and $g(f(x))$ for Exercises 1 – 20.

1. $f(x) = 3x + 5$, $g(x) = \dfrac{x+4}{2}$

2. $f(x) = \dfrac{1}{4}x + 1$, $g(x) = 6x - 7$

3. $f(x) = x^2$, $g(x) = 2x + 3$

4. $f(x) = x^2 + 1$, $g(x) = x - 6$

5. $f(x) = \dfrac{1}{x}$, $g(x) = 5x - 8$

6. $f(x) = \dfrac{1}{x+1}$, $g(x) = x^2 + x - 3$

7. $f(x) = x - 1$, $g(x) = \dfrac{1}{x^2}$

8. $f(x) = \dfrac{1}{x^2}$, $g(x) = x^2 + 1$

9. $f(x) = x^3 + x + 1$, $g(x) = x + 1$

10. $f(x) = x^3$, $g(x) = 2x - 1$

11. $f(x) = \sqrt{x}$, $g(x) = x - 2$

12. $f(x) = \sqrt{x}$, $g(x) = x^2 - 9$

13. $f(x) = \sqrt{x}$, $g(x) = x^2$

14. $f(x) = \dfrac{1}{\sqrt{x}}$, $g(x) = x^2$

15. $f(x) = \dfrac{1}{\sqrt{x}}$, $g(x) = x^2 - 4$

16. $f(x) = x^{3n}$, $g(x) = 2x - 6$

17. $f(x) = \dfrac{1}{x}$, $g(x) = \dfrac{1}{x}$

18. $f(x) = x^{1/3}$, $g(x) = 4x + 7$

19. $f(x) = x^3$, $g(x) = \sqrt{x-8}$

20. $f(x) = x^3 + 1$, $g(x) = \dfrac{1}{x}$

In Exercises 21 – 30, show that the given 1–1 functions are inverses of each other. Graph both functions on the same set of axes and show the line $y = x$ as a dotted line in the graph. (You may use a calculator as an aid in finding the graphs.)

21. $f(x) = 3x + 1$ and $g(x) = \dfrac{x-1}{3}$

22. $f(x) = -2x + 3$ and $g(x) = \dfrac{3-x}{2}$

Answers to Practice Problems: 1. a. $f(g(x)) = 2x^2 - 1$ **b.** $g(f(x)) = (2x-1)^2$ **2.** $f^{-1}(x) = \dfrac{x+1}{3}$

3. $f^{-1}(x) = \sqrt{x+4}$, $x \geq -4$

23. $f(x) = \sqrt[3]{x-1}$ and $g(x) = x^3 + 1$

24. $f(x) = x^3 - 4$ and $g(x) = \sqrt[3]{x+4}$

25. $f(x) = x^2$ for $x \geq 0$ and $g(x) = \sqrt{x}$

26. $f(x) = \sqrt{x+3}$ and $g(x) = x^2 - 3$ for $x \geq 0$

27. $f(x) = x^3 + 2$ and $g(x) = \sqrt[3]{x-2}$

28. $f(x) = \sqrt[5]{x+6}$ and $g(x) = x^5 - 6$

29. $f(x) = x^2 + 4$ for $x \geq 0$ and $g(x) = \sqrt{x-4}$

30. $f(x) = \dfrac{3}{x}$ and $g(x) - \dfrac{3}{x}$

In Exercises 31 – 44, find the inverse of the given function. Graph both functions on the same set of axes and show the line y = x as a dotted line in the graph.

31. $f(x) = 2x - 3$ **32.** $f(x) = 2x - 5$ **33.** $g(x) = x$ **34.** $g(x) = 1 - 4x$

35. $f(x) = 5x + 1$ **36.** $g(x) = \dfrac{2}{3}x + 2$ **37.** $g(x) = -3x + 1$ **38.** $f(x) = -\dfrac{1}{2}x - 3$

39. $f(x) = -\sqrt{x}, x \geq 0$ **40.** $f(x) = -2x + 4$ **41.** $f(x) = x^2 + 1, x \geq 0$

42. $f(x) = x^2 - 1, x \geq 0$ **43.** $f(x) = -x - 2$ **44.** $f(x) = -\sqrt{x-2}, x \geq 2$

Using the horizontal line test, determine which of the graphs in Exercises 45 – 54 are graphs of 1–1 functions. If the graph represents a 1–1 function, graph its inverse by reflecting the graph of the function across the line y = x.

(**Hint:** *If a function is 1–1, label a few points on the graph and use the fact that the x- and y-coordinates are interchanged on the graph of the inverse.*)

45.   **46.**

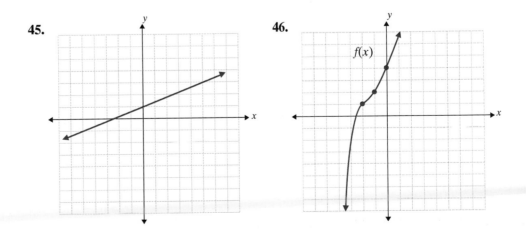

47.

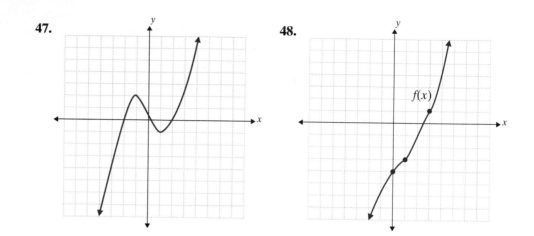

48.

49.

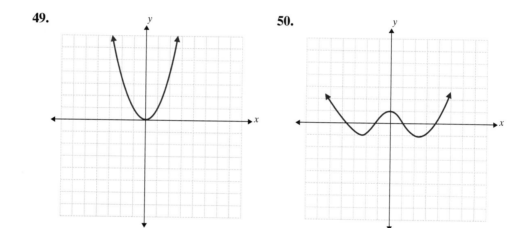

50.

51.

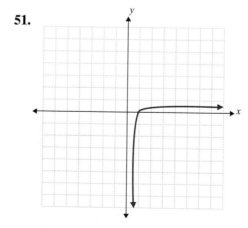

52.

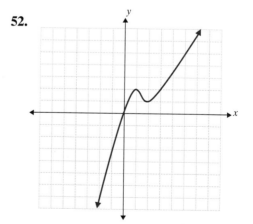

53.

54.

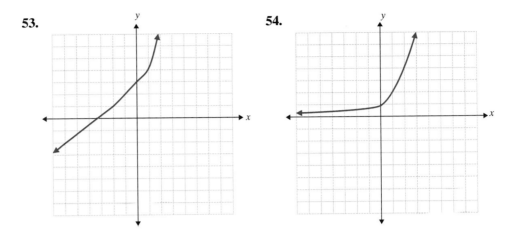

Use a graphing calculator to graph each of the functions in Exercises 55 – 64, and determine which of the functions are 1–1 by inspecting the graph and using the horizontal line test.

55. $f(x) = 2x + 3$ **56.** $f(x) = 7 - 4x$ **57.** $g(x) = x^2 - 2$ **58.** $g(x) = 9 - x^2$

59. $f(x) = x^3 + 2$ **60.** $g(x) = \dfrac{1}{x}$ **61.** $g(x) = \sqrt{x - 3}$ **62.** $f(x) = \sqrt{x + 5}$

63. $f(x) = |x + 1|$ **64.** $f(x) = |x - 5|$

In Exercises 65 – 76, find the inverse of the given function. Then use a graphing calculator to graph both the function and its inverse. Set the **WINDOW** so that it is "square."

65. $f(x) = x^3$ **66.** $f(x) = (x + 1)^3$ **67.** $g(x) = x^3 + 2$

68. $f(x) = \dfrac{1}{x}$ **69.** $f(x) = \dfrac{1}{x - 3}$ **70.** $f(x) = x^2, x \geq 0$

71. $f(x) = x^2 + 2, x \geq 0$ **72.** $g(x) = \sqrt{x + 7}, x \geq -7$ **73.** $f(x) = \sqrt{x + 5}, x \geq -5$

74. $g(x) = \sqrt{x - 3}, x \geq 3$ **75.** $f(x) = -x^2 + 1, x \geq 0$ **76.** $g(x) = -x^2 - 2, x \geq 0$

Hawkes Learning Systems: Intermediate Algebra

Composition of Functions and Inverse Functions

9.3   Exponential Functions

Exponential Functions

You have probably read about exponential growth in the population of the world or studied the exponential growth of bacteria in a biology class. The graphs in Figure 9.9 illustrate that the nature of such exponential growth is a relatively slow beginning and then builds to a relatively rapid growth.

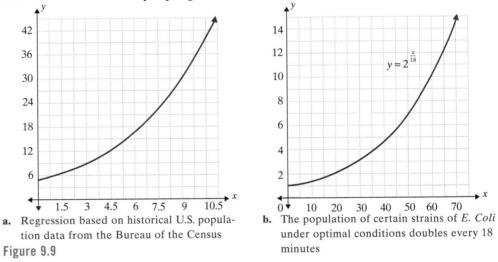

a. Regression based on historical U.S. population data from the Bureau of the Census

b. The population of certain strains of *E. Coli* under optimal conditions doubles every 18 minutes

Figure 9.9

We have studied quadratic functions, such as $f(x) = x^2$, in which the variable is the base and the exponent is a constant. If we reverse this concept and have a function where the base is a constant and the exponent is a variable the resulting function is called an **exponential function**. For example, $f(x) = 2^x$ is an exponential function. We define exponential functions as follows.

Exponential Functions

An exponential function is a function of the form

$$f(x) = b^x$$

where $b > 0$, $b \neq 1$, and x is any real number.

Examples of exponential functions are:

$$f(x) = 2^x, \qquad f(x) = 3^x, \qquad \text{and} \qquad y = \left(\frac{1}{3}\right)^x$$

NOTES

The two conditions $b > 0$ and $b \neq 1$ in the definition are important. We must have $b > 0$ so that b^x is defined for all real x. For example, we do not consider $y = (-2)^x$ to be an exponential function because $(-2)^{\frac{1}{2}}$ is not a real number. Also, $b \neq 1$. Because the function $y = 1^x = 1$ for all real x, this function is not considered to be an exponential function.

Exponential Growth

The following table of values and the graphs of the corresponding points give a very good idea of what the graph of the **exponential growth** function $f(x) = 2^x$ looks like (See Figure 9.10(a).). Because we know that 2^x is defined for all real exponents, points such as $\left(\sqrt{2}, 2^{\sqrt{2}}\right)$, $\left(\pi, 2^{\pi}\right)$, and $\left(\sqrt{5}, 2^{\sqrt{5}}\right)$ are on the graph, and the graph for $f(x) = 2^x$ is a smooth curve as shown in Figure 9.10(b).

x	$y = 2^x$
3	$2^3 = 8$
2	$2^2 = 4$
1	$2^1 = 2$
$\dfrac{1}{2}$	$2^{\frac{1}{2}} = \sqrt{2} \approx 1.41$
0	$2^0 = 1$
$-\dfrac{1}{2}$	$2^{-\frac{1}{2}} = \dfrac{1}{\sqrt{2}} \approx 0.707$
-1	$2^{-1} = \dfrac{1}{2}$
-2	$2^{-2} = \dfrac{1}{2^2} = \dfrac{1}{4}$
-3	$2^{-3} = \dfrac{1}{2^3} = \dfrac{1}{8}$
-4	$2^{-4} = \dfrac{1}{2^4} = \dfrac{1}{16}$

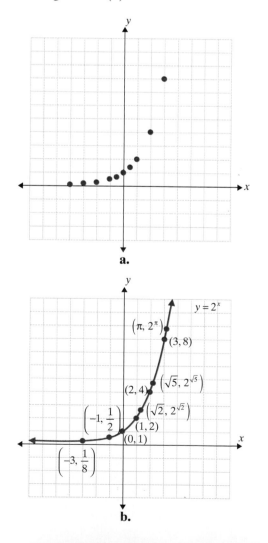

Figure 9.10

Figure 9.11 shows a table of values and the graph of the function $y = 3^x$. Note that the graphs of $y = 2^x$ and $y = 3^x$ are quite similar and that the graph of $y = 3^x$ rises faster. That is, the exponential growth is faster if the base is larger.

x	$y = 3^x$
2	9
1	3
0	1
−1	$\dfrac{1}{3} = 0.3333$
−3	$\dfrac{1}{27} = 0.037$

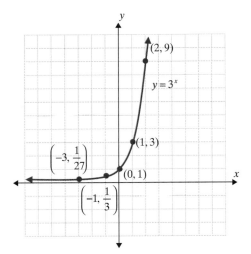

Figure 9.11

Domain $(-\infty, \infty)$
Range $(0, \infty)$

Exponential Decay

Now consider the **exponential decay** function $f(x) = \left(\dfrac{1}{2}\right)^x$. The table and the graph of the corresponding points shown in Figure 9.12 indicate the nature of the graph of this function.

x	$y = \left(\dfrac{1}{2}\right)^x = 2^{-x}$
−3	$2^{-(-3)} = 2^3 = 8$
−2	$2^{-(-2)} = 2^2 = 4$
−1	$2^{-(-1)} = 2^1 = 2$
$-\dfrac{1}{2}$	$2^{-\left(-\frac{1}{2}\right)} = 2^{\frac{1}{2}} = \sqrt{2} \approx 1.41$
0	$2^{-0} = 2^0 = 1$
$\dfrac{1}{2}$	$2^{-\frac{1}{2}} = \dfrac{1}{\sqrt{2}} \approx 0.707$
1	$2^{-1} = \dfrac{1}{2}$
2	$2^{-2} = \dfrac{1}{2^2} = \dfrac{1}{4}$
3	$2^{-3} = \dfrac{1}{2^3} = \dfrac{1}{8}$

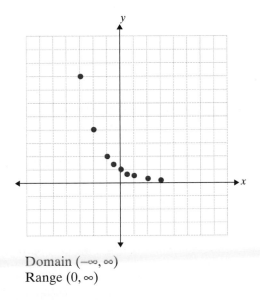

Domain $(-\infty, \infty)$
Range $(0, \infty)$

Figure 9.12

NOTES

Because $\frac{1}{2} = 2^{-1}$, $\frac{1}{3} = 3^{-1}$, $\frac{1}{4} = 4^{-1}$, and so on, for fractions between 0 and 1, we can write an exponential function with a fractional base between 0 and 1 (These are exponential decay functions.) in the form of an exponential function with a base greater than 1 and a negative exponent. Thus, we write

$$y = \left(\frac{1}{2}\right)^x = \left(2^{-1}\right)^x = 2^{-x} \quad \text{and} \quad y = \left(\frac{1}{3}\right)^x = \left(3^{-1}\right)^x = 3^{-x}.$$

Figure 9.13 shows the complete graphs of the two exponential decay functions

$$f(x) = \left(\frac{1}{2}\right)^x = 2^{-x} \quad \text{and} \quad f(x) = \left(\frac{1}{3}\right)^x = 3^{-x}.$$

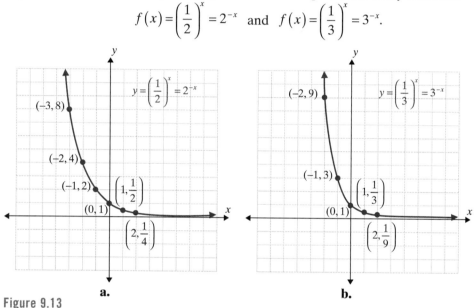

a.   b.

Figure 9.13

The following general concepts are helpful in understanding the graphs and the nature of exponential functions, both exponential growth and exponential decay.

General Concepts of Exponential Functions

For b > 1:

1. $b^x > 0$.

2. b^x *increases to the right and is called an **exponential growth function**.*

3. $b^0 = 1$, *so (0, 1) is on the graph.*

4. b^x *approaches the x-axis for negative values of x. (The x-axis is a horizontal asymptote. See Figure 9.11.)*

For 0 < b < 1:

1. $b^x > 0$.

2. b^x *decreases to the right and is called an **exponential decay function**.*

3. $b^0 = 1$, *so (0, 1) is on the graph.*

4. b^x *approaches the x-axis for positive values of x. (The x-axis is a horizontal asymptote. See Figure 9.13.)*

As with all functions, exponential functions can be multiplied by constants, shifted horizontally, and shifted vertically. Thus,

$$y = a \cdot b^{r \cdot x}, \qquad y = b^{x-h}, \qquad \text{and} \qquad y = b^x + k$$

and various combinations of these expressions are all exponential functions. These types of exponential functions are related to many practical applications, among which are bacterial growth, radioactive decay, compound interest, and light absorption. For example, a bacteria culture kept at a certain temperature may grow according to the function

$$y = y_0 \cdot 2^{0.3t} \qquad \text{where } t = \text{time in hours}$$
$$y_0 = \text{amount of bacteria present when } t = 0.$$

Example 1: Exponential Growth

a. A scientist has 10,000 bacteria present when $t = 0$, and she knows the bacteria grow according to the function $y = y_0 \cdot 2^{0.5t}$ where t is measured in hours. How many bacteria will be present at the end of one day?

Solution: Substitute $t = 24$ hours and $y_0 = 10,000$ into the function.

$$y = 10,000 \cdot 2^{0.5(24)} = 10,000 \cdot 2^{12}$$

$$= 10,000(4096)$$

$$= 40,960,000$$

$$= 4.096 \times 10^7 \text{ bacteria}$$

To use your calculator to evaluate 2^{12}, enter 2, press the ⟨ ^ ⟩ key, enter 12, then press the ⟨ENTER⟩ key.

b. Determine the exponential function that fits the following information: $y_0 = 5000$ bacteria, and there are 135,000 bacteria present after 3 days.

Solution: Use $y = y_0 b^t$ where t is measured in days. Substitute 135,000 for y and 5000 for y_0, then solve for b.

$$135,000 = 5000 b^3$$

$$27 = b^3$$

$$(27)^{\frac{1}{3}} = (b^3)^{\frac{1}{3}}$$

$$3 = b$$

The function is $y = 5000 \cdot 3^t$.

Compound Interest

The topic of compound interest (interest paid on interest) leads to a particularly interesting (and useful) exponential function. The formula $A = P(1+r)^t$ can be used for finding the value (Amount) accumulated when a principal, P, is invested and interest is compounded once a year. If compounding is performed more than once a year, we use the following formula to find A:

$$A = P\left(1+\frac{r}{n}\right)^{nt}$$

where

P = amount invested
r = annual interest rate (in decimal form)
n = number of times per year interest is compounded
t = number of years
A = amount accumulated

Example 2: Compound Interest

a. If P dollars are invested at a rate of interest r (in decimal form) compounded annually for t years, the amount A becomes $A = P(1+r)^t$. Find the value of $1000 invested at 6% for 3 years.

Solution: $A = 1000(1+0.06)^3$ $r = 0.06$ as decimal.

$= 1000(1.06)^3$

$= 1000(1.191016) \approx \$1191.02$

To use your calculator to evaluate $(1.06)^3$, enter 1.06, press the $\boxed{\wedge}$ key, enter 3, then press the $\boxed{\text{ENTER}}$ key.

b. What will be the value of a principal investment of $1000 invested at 6% for 3 years if interest is compounded monthly (12 times per year)?

Solution: We have
$P = 1000, r = 0.06, n = 12,$ and $t = 3$
Using the formula for compound interest,

$$A = 1000\left(1+\frac{0.06}{12}\right)^{12(3)}$$

$= 1000(1+0.005)^{36}$

$= 1000(1.005)^{36}$

$= 1000(1.19668)$ Using a calculator.

$= \$1196.68$

c.   Find the value of A if \$1000 is invested at 6% for 3 years and interest is compounded daily. (Banks and savings institutions sometimes use 360 days per year.)

Solution: Using the formula for compound interest with $n = 360$,

$$A = 1000\left(1 + \frac{0.06}{360}\right)^{360(3)}$$

$$\approx 1000\left(1.000166667\right)^{1080}$$

$$= 1000\left(1.197199838\right) \qquad \text{Using a calculator.}$$

$$\approx \$1197.20$$

• •

Examples 2a, 2b, and 2c illustrate the effects of compounding interest more frequently over 3 years. The formula gives the results

$$A = \$1191.02 \quad \text{for} \quad n = 1,$$
$$A = \$1196.68 \quad \text{for} \quad n = 12,$$
$$A = \$1197.20 \quad \text{for} \quad n = 360.$$

These numbers might not seem very dramatic, only \$6.18 for 3 years; but, if you use your calculator and 20 years you will see a difference of \$112.65 for a \$1000 investment. An investment of \$10,000 for 20 years at 9% will show a difference of \$4438.76. (Try it.) In any case, the results show that more frequent compounding will result in higher income.

Interest Compounded Continuously

The number e ($e \approx 2.718$) can be shown to be the base of an exponential function when interest is **compounded continuously** (even faster than every second). Table 9.2 shows how the number e is generated by using the mathematical concept of a **limit**, or **limiting value**. We find that the value of the expression $\left(1 + \frac{1}{n}\right)^{n}$ approaches the irrational number $e = 2.718281828459\ldots$ as n approaches infinity. The concept of infinity is very abstract, and you should understand that the symbol for infinity, ∞, does not represent a number. The symbol indicates that the numbers under consideration are to continue indefinitely, without end.

n	$\left(1+\dfrac{1}{n}\right)$	$\left(1+\dfrac{1}{n}\right)^n$
1	$\left(1+\dfrac{1}{1}\right)=2$	$2^1=2$
2	$\left(1+\dfrac{1}{2}\right)=1.5$	$(1.5)^2=2.25$
5	$\left(1+\dfrac{1}{5}\right)=1.2$	$(1.2)^5=2.48832$
10	$\left(1+\dfrac{1}{10}\right)=1.1$	$(1.1)^{10}=2.59374246$
100	$\left(1+\dfrac{1}{100}\right)=1.01$	$(1.01)^{100}=2.704813829$
1000	$\left(1+\dfrac{1}{1000}\right)=1.001$	$(1.001)^{1000}=2.716923932$
10,000	$\left(1+\dfrac{1}{10,000}\right)=1.0001$	$(1.0001)^{10,000}=2.718145927$
100,000	$\left(1+\dfrac{1}{100,000}\right)=1.00001$	$(1.00001)^{100,000}=2.718268237$
$\downarrow$		$\downarrow$
∞		$e=2.718281828459...$

Table 9.2

The Number e

The Number e

The number e is defined to be

$$e = \lim_{n\to\infty}\left(1+\frac{1}{n}\right)^n = 2.718281828459\ldots$$

Now, to show how to find the formula for compounding interest continuously, we rewrite the formula for compound interest as follows:

$$A = P\left(1+\frac{r}{n}\right)^{nt} = P\left(1+\frac{r}{n}\right)^{\frac{n}{r}\cdot rt} = P\left[\left(1+\frac{1}{\frac{n}{r}}\right)^{\frac{n}{r}}\right]^{rt}$$

Now, substituting $m = \dfrac{n}{r}$, we can write

$$A = P\left[\left(1 + \frac{1}{m}\right)^m\right]^{rt}$$

Since r is a constant, the value of $m = \dfrac{n}{r}$ approaches ∞ as n approaches ∞. This means that the expression in brackets approaches e as $n \to \infty$, and the formula for **continuously compounded interest** is

$$A = Pe^{rt}.$$

Example 3: Continuously Compounded Interest

Find the value of $1000 invested at 6% for 3 years if interest is compounded continuously. (Use $e = 2.718281828$, or on the TI-83 the number e is in yellow and can be found by pressing (2nd) and then pressing the ($\div$) key.)

Solution: $A = Pe^{rt}$

$= 1000e^{0.06(3)}$

$= 1000\left(2.718281828\right)^{0.18}$

$= 1000\left(1.197217363\right)$

$\approx \$1197.22$

Comparing Examples 2c and 3, we see that there is only 2¢ difference in A when compounding interest daily or continuously over 3 years at 6%.

Practice Problems

1. *Sketch the graph of the exponential function $f(x) = 2 \cdot 3^x$ and label 3 points on the graph.*

2. *Sketch the graph of the exponential decay function $y = 0.5 \cdot 2^{-x}$ and label 3 points on the graph.*

3. *Find the value of $5000 invested at 8% for 10 years if interest is (a) compounded monthly, (b) compounded continuously.*

Answers to Practice Problems: **1.** **2.** **3. a.** $11,098.20 **b.** $11,127.70

9.3 Exercises

Sketch the graph of each of the exponential functions in Exercises 1 – 20, and label three points on each graph. (In some exercises you may need to use your knowledge of horizontal and vertical shifts.)

1. $y = 4^x$

2. $y = \left(\dfrac{1}{3}\right)^x$

3. $y = \left(\dfrac{1}{5}\right)^x$

4. $y = 5^x$

5. $y = 10^x$

6. $y = \left(\dfrac{2}{3}\right)^x$

7. $y = \left(\dfrac{5}{2}\right)^x$

8. $y = \left(\dfrac{1}{2}\right)^{-x}$

9. $y = 2^{x-1}$

10. $y = 3^{x+1}$

11. $f(x) = 2^x + 1$

12. $f(x) = 2^{x+1}$

13. $f(x) = 3^{2x}$

14. $f(x) = 2^{0.5x}$

15. $g(x) = 0.5 \cdot 3^x - 1$

16. $g(x) = 10^{-x} - 3$

17. $g(x) = -2^{-x}$

18. $g(x) = 10^{0.5x}$

19. $y = 3 \cdot \left(\dfrac{1}{2}\right)^{0.2x}$

20. $y = -4 \cdot \left(\dfrac{1}{3}\right)^{x-1}$

21. If $f(t) = 3 \cdot 4^t$ what is the value of $f(2)$?

22. Use your calculator to find the value (to the nearest hundredth) of $f(2)$ if $f(x) = 27.3 \cdot e^{-0.4x}$.

23. For $f(x) = 3 \cdot 10^{2x}$, find the value of $f(0.5)$.

24. Use your calculator to find the value of $f(9)$ if $f(t) = 2000 \cdot e^{0.08t}$. What does this value indicate to you about investing money?

25. Use your calculator to find the value of $f(22)$ if $f(t) = 2000 \cdot e^{0.05t}$. What does this value indicate to you about investing money?

26. A biologist knows that in the laboratory, bacteria in a culture grow according to the function $y = y_0 \cdot 5^{0.2t}$, where y_0 is the initial number of bacteria present and t is time measured in hours. How many bacteria will be present in a culture at the end of 5 hours if there were 5000 present initially?

27. In Exercise 26, how many bacteria were present initially if at the end of 15 hours, there were 2,500,000 bacteria present?

28. Four thousand dollars is deposited into a savings account at the rate of 8% per year. Find the total amount, A, on deposit at the end of 5 years if the interest is compounded
  a. annually
  b. semiannually
  c. quarterly
  d. daily
  e. continuously

29. Find the amount, A, in a savings account if $2000 is invested at 7% for 4 years and the interest is compounded
   a. annually
   b. semiannually
   c. quarterly
   d. daily
   e. continuously

30. Find the value of $1800 invested at 6% for 3 years if the interest is compounded continuously.

31. Find the value of $2500 invested at 5% for 5 years if the interest is compounded continuously.

32. The revenue function is given by $R(x) = x \cdot p(x)$ dollars, where x is the number of units sold and $p(x)$ is the unit price. If $p(x) = 25(2)^{\frac{-x}{5}}$, find the revenue if 15 units are sold.

33. In Exercise 32, if $p(x) = 40(3)^{\frac{-x}{6}}$, find the revenue if 12 units are sold.

34. A radio station knows that during an intense advertising campaign, the number of people, N, who will hear a commercial is given by $N = A(1 - 2^{-0.05t})$, where A is the number of people in the broadcasting area and t is the number of hours the commercial has been run. If there are 500,000 people in the area, how many will hear a commercial during the first 20 hours?

35. Statistics show that the fractional part of flashlight batteries, P, that are still good after t hours of use is given by $P = 4^{-0.02t}$. What fractional part of the batteries are still operating after 150 hours of use?

36. If a principal, P, is invested at a rate, r (expressed as a decimal), compounded continuously, the interest earned is given by $I = A - P$. How much interest will be earned in 20 years on an investment of $10,000 invested at 10% and compounded continuously?

37. In Exercise 36, find the interest earned in 20 years on $10,000 invested at 5% and compounded continuously. Explain why the interest earned at 5% is not just one-half of the interest earned at 10% in Exercise 36.

38. The value of a machine, V, at the end of t years is given by $V = C(1 - r)^t$, where C is the original cost and r is the rate of depreciation. Find the value of a machine at the end of 4 years if the original cost was $1200 and $r = 0.20$.

39. In Exercise 38, find the value of a machine at the end of 3 years if the original cost was $2000 and $r = 0.15$.

40. Use a graphing calculator to graph each of the following functions. In each case the x-axis is a horizontal asymptote. Explain why the graphing calculator does not seem to indicate this fact.
   a. $y = e^x$
   b. $y = e^{-x}$
   c. $y = e^{-x^2}$

645

Writing and Thinking About Mathematics

41. Discuss, in your own words, how the graph of each of the following functions is related to the graph of the exponential function $y = b^x$.

    a. $y = a \cdot b^x$ **b.** $y = b^{x-h}$ **c.** $y = b^x + k$

42. Discuss, in your own words, the symmetrical relationship of the graphs of the two exponential functions $y = 10^x$ and $y = 10^{-x}$.

43. Discuss, in your own words, the symmetrical relationship of the graphs of the two exponential functions $y = 10^x$ and $y = -10^x$.

Hawkes Learning Systems: Intermediate Algebra

Exponential Functions and the Number e

9.4 Logarithmic Functions

After completing this section, you will be able to:

1. *Write exponential expressions in logarithmic form.*
2. *Write logarithmic expressions in exponential form.*
3. *Graph exponential functions and logarithmic functions on the same set of axes.*
4. *Use a calculator to find the values of common logarithms and natural logarithms.*
5. *Use a calculator to find inverse logarithms for common logarithms and for natural logarithms.*

Exponential functions of the form $y = b^x$ are $1-1$ functions and, therefore, have inverses. The inverse functions of exponential functions are called **logarithmic functions**. To find the inverse of a function, we interchange the x and y and solve for y. Thus, for the function

$$y = b^x$$

interchanging x and y gives the inverse function

$$x = b^y$$

Figure 9.14 shows the graphs of these two functions with $b > 1$.

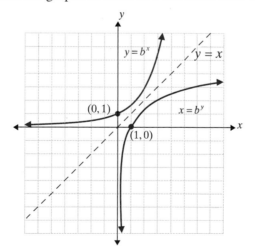

Figure 9.14

Now we need to solve the equation $x = b^y$ for y. But there is no algebraic technique for doing this. Mathematicians have simply created a name for this new function and called it a **logarithm**, abbreviated as **log**. This means that **the inverse of an exponential function is a logarithmic function**.

We have the following relationship:

$$\text{If} \qquad f(x) = b^x$$

$$\text{then} \qquad f^{-1}(x) = \log_b x.$$

The properties of inverse functions give the following two important results:

$$f\left(f^{-1}(x)\right) = b^{f^{-1}(x)} = b^{\log_b x} = x$$

and

$$f^{-1}\left(f(x)\right) = \log_b\left(f(x)\right) = \log_b\left(b^x\right) = x.$$

Logarithm

For $b > 0$ and $b \neq 1$,

$$x = b^y \text{ if and only if } y = \log_b x.$$

Thus, a logarithm is the name of an exponent, and the equations

$$x = b^y \text{ and } y = \log_b x$$

are equivalent.

Example 1: Translations from Exponential Form to Logarithmic Form

	Exponential Form	Logarithmic Form		
a.	$2^3 = 8$	$\log_2 8 = 3$	←	3 is the logarithm.
b.	$2^4 = 16$	$\log_2 16 = 4$	←	4 is the logarithm.
c.	$10^3 = 1000$	$\log_{10} 1000 = 3$	←	3 is the logarithm.
d.	$10^4 = 10,000$	$\log_{10} 10,000 = 4$	←	4 is the logarithm.
e.	$2^0 = 1$	$\log_2 1 = 0$	←	0 is the logarithm.
f.	$3^0 = 1$	$\log_3 1 = 0$	←	0 is the logarithm.
g.	$10^1 = 10$	$\log_{10} 10 = 1$	←	1 is the logarithm.
h.	$5^1 = 5$	$\log_5 5 = 1$	←	1 is the logarithm.
i.	$2^{-2} = \dfrac{1}{4}$	$\log_2 \dfrac{1}{4} = -2$	←	−2 is the logarithm.
j.	$10^{-1} = \dfrac{1}{10}$	$\log_{10} \dfrac{1}{10} = -1$	←	−1 is the logarithm.

REMEMBER, a logarithm is an exponent. For example,

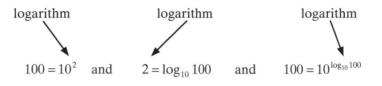

logarithm   logarithm   logarithm

$$100 = 10^2 \quad \text{and} \quad 2 = \log_{10} 100 \quad \text{and} \quad 100 = 10^{\log_{10} 100}$$

are all equivalent. In words,

2 is the **exponent** of the base 10 to get $100 \left(10^2 = 100 \right)$; and

2 is the **logarithm** base 10 of 100 $\left(2 = \log_{10} 100 \right)$.

Evaluating Logarithms

Logarithmic expressions can often be evaluated by changing them to the equivalent exponential form. Several cases are illustrated in Example 2. Note that parentheses are used as in $y = \log_b (x)$ if there is any doubt as to what we are finding the logarithm of or what a base is.

Example 2: Evaluating Logarithms •

a. Evaluate $\log_2 32$.

Solution: Let $\log_2 32 = x$.

Then $2^x = 32$

$2^x = 2^5$

$x = 5$

Thus, $\log_2 32 = 5$.

b. Find the value of $\log_{10} (0.01)$.

Solution: Let $\log_{10} (0.01) = x$.

Then $10^x = 0.01$

$10^x = \dfrac{1}{100}$

$10^x = 10^{-2}$

$x = -2$

Thus, $\log_{10} (0.01) = -2$

continued on next page ...

c. Evaluate $\log_4 8$.

Solution: Let $\log_4 8 = x$.

Then $4^x = 8$

$$\left(2^2\right)^x = 2^3$$

$$2^{2x} = 2^3$$

$$2x = 3$$

$$x = \frac{3}{2}$$

Thus, $\log_4 8 = \dfrac{3}{2}$.

d. Find the value of x if $\log_{16} x = \dfrac{3}{4}$.

Solution: $\log_{16} x = \dfrac{3}{4}$ $\dfrac{3}{4}$ is the **logarithm** of x.

Then $x = 16^{\frac{3}{4}}$ $\dfrac{3}{4}$ is the **exponent** of the base, 16.

$$x = \left(2^4\right)^{\frac{3}{4}}$$

$$x = 2^3 = 8$$

Thus, $\log_{16} 8 = \dfrac{3}{4}$.

● ●

Three Basic Properties of Logarithms

We have previously discussed the following two properties of exponents:

$$b^0 = 1 \quad \text{and} \quad b^1 = b.$$

Since exponents are logarithms, these same two properties can be stated in logarithmic form. Thus,

$$\log_b 1 = 0 \qquad \text{because} \qquad b^0 = 1$$

and $\log_b b = 1$ because $b^1 = b.$

Also, the definition of logarithm states that if $x = b^y$, then

$$y = \log_b x.$$

By substituting for y,

$$y = \log_b x$$
$$\downarrow$$
$$x = b^y$$

we get

$$x = b^{\log_b x}.$$

This equation indicates that $\log_b x$ is the exponent of b that will give x as a result. In summary, we have the following three basic properties of logarithms.

Properties of Logarithms

For $b > 0$, $b \neq 1$, and $x > 0$,

1. $\log_b 1 = 0$ *The logarithm of 1 is always 0.*

2. $\log_b b = 1$ *The logarithm of the base is always 1.*

3. $b^{\log_b x} = x$

REMEMBER: A logarithm is an exponent.

Example 3: Properties of Logarithms

a. $\log_3 1 = 0$ Property 1: $\log_b 1 = 0$. The logarithm of 1 is 0.

b. $\log_8 8 = 1$ Property 2: $\log_b b = 1$. The logarithm of the base is 1.

c. $10^{\log_{10} 20} = 20$ Property 3: $b^{\log_b x} = x$.

d. $10^{\log_{10} 300} = 300$ Property 3: $b^{\log_b x} = x$.

A calculator will show that $\log_{10} 20 = 1.301029996$ and $\log_{10} 300 = 2.477121255$.

Note: The equal sign is used even though the decimals are irrational numbers, infinite nonrepeating decimals. So, Examples 3c and 3d can be written as

$$10^{1.301029996} = 20 \quad \text{and} \quad 10^{2.477121255} = 300.$$

Graphs of Logarithmic Functions

Because logarithmic functions are the inverses of exponential functions, the graphs of logarithmic functions can be found by reflecting the corresponding exponential functions across the line $y = x$. This was illustrated in general for $b > 1$ in Figure 9.14.

Figure 9.15a shows how the graph of $y = \log_2 x$ is related to the graph of $y = 2^x$ and Figure 9.15b shows how the graph of $y = 10^x$ is related to the graph of $y = \log_{10} x$. Note that in the graphs of both logarithmic functions, the logarithms are negative for $0 < x < 1$.

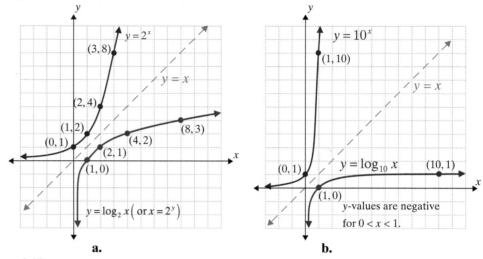

a.   **b.**

Figure 9.15

Notice that points on the graphs of inverse functions can be found by reversing the coordinates of ordered pairs.

Recall that the domain and range of a function and its inverse are interchanged. Thus, for exponential functions and logarithmic functions, we have the following:

For the exponential function $y = b^x$

the domain is all real x, and
the range is all $y > 0$.   (The graph is above the x-axis.)
Horizontal asymptote

For the logarithmic function $y = \log_b x \left(\text{or } x = b^y \right)$,

the domain is all $x > 0$, and
the range is all real y.   (The graph is to the right of the y-axis.)
Vertical asymptote

Common Logarithms(Base-10 Logarithms)

Base-10 logarithms are called **common logarithms.** The notation $\log x$ is used to indicate common logarithms. That is,

$$\log x = \log_{10} x.$$

Using a Calculator

Finding values of common logarithms on a TI-83 is a simple three-step process:

1. *Press the* **LOG** *key.* **log (** *will appear on the display.*

2. *Enter the number and a right hand parenthesis* **)**.

3. *Press* **ENTER**.

Example 4: Finding Logarithms using a Calculator

Use a calculator to find the values of the following common logarithms. To check your understanding, write your estimate of each value on a piece of paper before you use the calculator.

    a. log 200

    b. log 50,000

    c. log 0.0006

Solutions: a. $\log 200 = 2.301029996$ Note that this means $10^{2.301029996} = 200$.

           b. $\log 50{,}000 = 4.698970004$

           c. $\log 0.0006 = -3.22184875$ Note that a logarithm can be negative.

The domain of any logarithmic function is the set of positive real numbers. Negative numbers and 0 are not in the domain. **The logarithm of a negative number or zero is undefined.** For example, $\log_{10}(-2)$ is undefined. That is, $10^x = -2$ is impossible with real exponents. If you try to find the logarithm of a negative number with a calculator, then an error message will appear. For example, enter **LOG** (-2) on the TI-83 and you will get the error message shown here. (If you select **2: Goto**, the cursor will move to the location of the error.)

However, logarithms are exponents and they may be negative or 0. Thus,

$$10^{-2} = \frac{1}{100} \quad \text{and} \quad -2 = \log_{10} \frac{1}{100}$$

$$10^0 = 1 \quad \text{and} \quad 0 = \log_{10} 1.$$

If $\log x = N$, then we know that $x = 10^N$. The number x is called the **inverse log of N**.

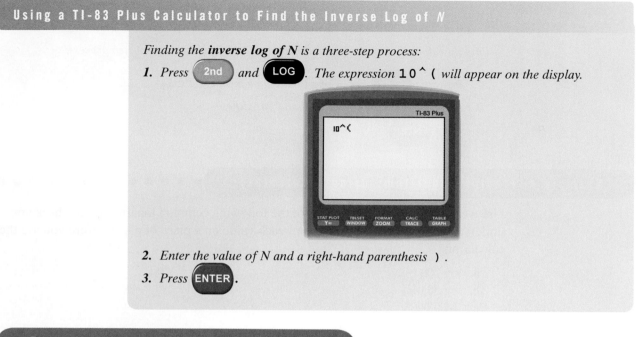

Using a TI-83 Plus Calculator to Find the Inverse Log of N

*Finding the **inverse log of N** is a three-step process:*

1. *Press* 2nd *and* LOG. *The expression* **10^(** *will appear on the display.*

2. *Enter the value of N and a right-hand parenthesis* **)** .

3. *Press* ENTER.

Example 5: Finding the Inverse Log of N ● ● ● ● ● ● ● ● ● ● ● ● ● ● ● ●

Use a TI-83 Plus calculator to find the value of x (which is the ***inverse log of N***). To check your understanding, write your estimate of x on paper before you use the calculator.

a. $\log x = 5$

b. $\log x = -2$

c. $\log x = 2.4142$

d. $\log x = 16.5$

Solutions: **a.** For $\log x = 5$, the calculator shows $x = 10^5 = 100{,}000$.

b. For $\log x = -2$, the calculator shows $x = 10^{-2} = 0.01$.

c. For $\log x = 2.4142$, the calculator shows $x = 10^{2.4142} = 259.5374301$.

d. For $\log x = 16.5$, the calculator shows $x = 10^{16.5} = 3.16227766E16$.

The letter E in the solution is the calculator version of scientific notation. Thus, $3.16227766E16 = 3.16227766 \cdot 10^{16}$.

● ●

Natural Logarithms (Base-*e* Logarithms)

Base-*e* logarithms are called natural logarithms. The notation $\ln x$ (read "natural log of x") is used to indicate that e is the base. That is,

$$\ln x = \log_e x$$

Figure 9.16 shows the graphs of the two functions $y = e^x$ and $y = \ln x$.

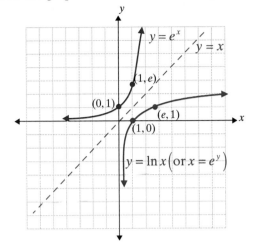

Figure 9.16

Notice again that points on inverse functions can be found by interchanging the coordinates of points.

Using a Calculator

Finding values of natural logarithms on a TI-83 is similar to finding common logarithms:

1. Press the **LN** *key.* `ln (` *will appear on the display.*

2. Enter the number and a right hand parenthesis `)` *.*

3. Press **ENTER** *.*

Example 6: Natural Logarithms

Use a calculator to find the following natural logarithms. To check your understanding, write your estimate of each value on a piece of paper before you use the calculator.

　a. $\ln 1$
　b. $\ln 3$
　c. $\ln (-15)$
　d. $\ln 0.02$

Solutions: a. $\ln 1 = 0$　　　　　　　This means that $e^0 = 1$.

　　　　　b. $\ln 3 = 1.098612289$

　　　　　c. $\ln (-15) = \text{error}$　　　There are no logarithms of negative numbers.

　　　　　d. $\ln 0.02 = -3.912023005$ This means that $e^{-3.912023005} = 0.02$.

If $\ln x = N$, then we know that $x = e^N$. The number x is called **the inverse ln of** N. As the following procedure shows, finding the inverse ln is similar to finding the inverse log.

Using a TI-83 Plus Calculator to Find the Inverse Ln of N

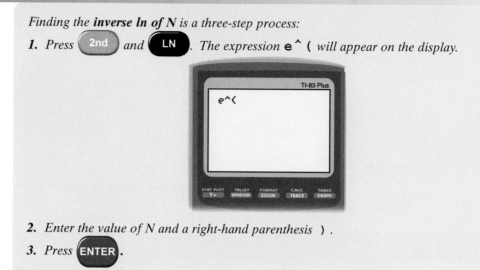

Finding the **inverse ln of** N is a three-step process:

1. Press [2nd] and [LN]. The expression **e** ^ (will appear on the display.

2. Enter the value of N and a right-hand parenthesis) .

3. Press [ENTER].

Example 7: Finding the Inverse ln of N

Use a TI-83 Plus calculator to find the value of x in each of the following expressions. To check your understanding, write an estimate of x on your paper before you use the calculator.

a. $\ln x = 3$ b. $\ln x = -1$ c. $\ln x = -0.1$ d. $\ln x = 50$

Solutions:

a. For $\ln x = 3$, the calculator shows $x = e^3 = 20.08553692$.

b. For $\ln x = -1$, the calculator shows $x = e^{-1} = 0.367879441$.

c. For $\ln x = -0.1$, the calculator shows $x = e^{-0.1} = 0.904837418$.

d. For $\ln x = 50$, the calculator shows $x = e^{50} = 5.184705529E21$.

Practice Problems

1. *Express the given equation in logarithmic form.*
   a. $4^2 = 16$ b. $10^3 = 1000$ c. $5^{-1} = \dfrac{1}{5}$

2. *Express the given equation in exponential form.*
   a. $log_2 x = -1$ b. $log_5 x = 2$ c. $ln\, x = 3$

3. *Find the value of x:*
   a. $x = ln(0.11)$ b. $x = log(1.5)$ c. $x = log_2 32$

4. *Find the value of x:*
   a. $log\, x = 2.46$ b. $ln\, x = -2$ c. $log_4 x = 2.5$

9.4 Exercises

In Exercises 1 – 12, express each equation in logarithmic form.

1. $7^2 = 49$ **2.** $3^3 = 27$ **3.** $5^{-2} = \dfrac{1}{25}$ **4.** $10^2 = 100$

5. $2^{-5} = \dfrac{1}{32}$ **6.** $1 = \pi^0$ **7.** $\left(\dfrac{2}{3}\right)^2 = \dfrac{4}{9}$ **8.** $10^k = 23$

9. $17 = e^x$ **10.** $e^k = 11.6$ **11.** $10^1 = 10$ **12.** $e^0 = 1$

In Exercises 13 – 24, express each equation in exponential form.

13. $log_3 9 = 2$ **14.** $log_5 125 = 3$ **15.** $log_9 3 = \dfrac{1}{2}$ **16.** $log_b 4 = \dfrac{2}{3}$

17. $log_7 \dfrac{1}{7} = -1$ **18.** $log_{\frac{1}{2}} 8 = -3$ **19.** $ln\, N = 1.74$ **20.** $ln\, 42.3 = x$

21. $log_b 18 = 4$ **22.** $log_b 39 = 10$ **23.** $log_n y^2 = x$ **24.** $log_b a = x$

Solve Exercises 25 – 40 by first changing each equation to exponential form.

25. $log_4 x = 2$ **26.** $log_3 x = 4$ **27.** $log_{14} 196 = x$ **28.** $log_5 \dfrac{1}{125} = x$

29. $log_{36} x = -\dfrac{1}{2}$ **30.** $log_x 32 = 5$ **31.** $log_x 121 = 2$ **32.** $log_{81} x = -\dfrac{3}{4}$

Answers to Practice Problems: 1. a. $log_4 16 = 2$ **b.** $log_{10} 1000 = 3$ **c.** $log_5\left(\dfrac{1}{5}\right) = -1$ **2. a.** $x = 2^{-1}$

b. $x = 5^2$ **c.** $x = e^3$ **3. a.** -2.207 **b.** 0.176 **c.** 5 **4. a.** 288.4 **b.** 0.135 **c.** 32

33. $\log_8 x = \dfrac{5}{3}$ **34.** $\log_{25} 125 = x$ **35.** $\log_3 \dfrac{1}{9} = x$ **36.** $\log_8 8^{3.7} = x$

37. $\log_{10} 10^{1.52} = x$ **38.** $\log_5 5^{\log_5 25} = x$ **39.** $\log_4 4^{\log_2 8} = x$ **40.** $\log_p p^{\log_3 81} = x$

In Exercises 41 – 50, graph each function and its inverse on the same set of axes.

41. $f(x) = 6^x$ **42.** $f(x) = 2^x$ **43.** $y = \left(\dfrac{2}{3}\right)^x$ **44.** $y = \left(\dfrac{1}{4}\right)^x$

45. $f(x) = \log_4 x$ **46.** $f(x) = \log_5 x$ **47.** $y = \log_{\frac{1}{2}} x$ **48.** $y = \log_{\frac{1}{3}} x$

49. $y = \log_8 x$ **50.** $y = \log_7 x$

Use a calculator to evaluate the logarithms in Exercises 51 – 62.

51. $\log 173$ **52.** $\log 396$ **53.** $\log 88.4$ **54.** $\log 0.0061$

55. $\log 0.0573$ **56.** $\log(-8.47)$ **57.** $\ln 37.5$ **58.** $\ln 96$

59. $\ln(-14.9)$ **60.** $\ln 157.6$ **61.** $\ln 0.00461$ **62.** $\ln 0.0139$

Use a calculator to find the value of x in each equation in Exercises 63 –74.

63. $\log x = 2.31$ **64.** $\log x = -3$ **65.** $\log x = -1.7$ **66.** $\log x = 4.1$
67. $2 \log x = -0.038$ **68.** $5 \log x = 9.4$ **69.** $\ln x = 5.17$ **70.** $\ln x = 4.9$
71. $\ln x = -8.3$ **72.** $\ln x = 6.74$ **73.** $0.2 \ln x = 0.0079$ **74.** $3 \ln x = -0.066$

In Exercises 75 – 78, use a graphing calculator to graph each function. State the domain and range of each function.

75. $f(x) = \log(x + 1)$ **76.** $f(x) = 1 + \log x$ **77.** $f(x) = \log(-x)$

78. $f(x) = -\log x$

79. Consider the function $y = Ce^x$. Discuss the following:
   a. the domain of the function
   b. the range of the function
   c. any asymptotes of the graph of the function
   Give C two different values and sketch both of the graphs.

80. Consider the function $y = Ce^{-x}$. Discuss the following:
   a. the domain of the function
   b. the range of the function
   c. any asymptotes of the graph of the function
   Give C two different values and sketch both of the graphs.

Writing and Thinking About Mathematics

81. Discuss, in your own words, how the graph of each of the following functions is related to the graph of the logarithmic function $y = \log_b x$.

   a. $y = a \cdot \log_b x$ **b.** $y = \log_b (x - h)$ **c.** $y = \log_b (x) + k$

82. Discuss, in your own words, the symmetrical relationship of the graphs of the two logarithmic functions $y = 10^x$ and $y = \log x$.

83. Discuss, in your own words, the symmetrical relationship of the graphs of the two logarithmic functions $y = \log x$ and $y = -\log x$.

Hawkes Learning Systems: Intermediate Algebra

Logarithmic Functions

Properties of Logarithms

Objectives

After completing this section, you will be able to:

1. Evaluate logarithms using the properties of logarithms.

2. Write logarithmic expressions as the sums and/or differences of logarithms.

3. Write the sums and/or differences of logarithms as single logarithmic expressions.

Although calculators are certainly effective in giving numerical evaluations, they generally do not simplify or solve equations involving exponential or logarithmic expressions. (You might be aware that there are calculators with computer algebra systems, CAS, that do simplify expressions and solve equations.) In this section, we will discuss several properties of logarithms that are helpful in solving equations and simplifying expressions involving logarithms and/or exponential functions.

The following three basic properties have been discussed:

$$\textbf{1.} \quad \log_b 1 = 0$$

$$\textbf{2.} \quad \log_b b = 1$$

$$\textbf{3.} \quad b^{\log_b x} = x$$

With these three properties as a basis, we now develop three more properties (or rules) for logarithms: the Product Rule, the Quotient Rule, and the Power Rule.

The Product Rule

Because logarithms are exponents, their properties are similar to those of exponents. In fact, the properties of exponents are used to prove the rules of logarithms. Consider the following analysis.

We know that $\qquad\qquad 6 = 2 \cdot 3$

Using property 3, we have

$$10^{\log 6} = 6, \quad 10^{\log 2} = 2, \quad \text{and} \quad 10^{\log 3} = 3$$

Thus, we can write

$$
\begin{array}{ccccc}
6 & = & 2 & \cdot & 3 \\
\downarrow & & \downarrow & & \downarrow \\
10^{\log 6} & = & 10^{\log 2} & \cdot & 10^{\log 3} = 10^{\log 2 + \log 3}
\end{array}
$$

Equating the exponents on the left and right, the result is:

$$\log 6 = \log(2 \cdot 3) = \log 2 \quad + \quad \log 3$$
$$\downarrow \qquad\qquad \downarrow \qquad\qquad \downarrow$$

Numerically, $0.7782 = \qquad 0.3010 \quad + \quad 0.4771$

Note: For convenience, we will round off logarithms to 4 decimal place accuracy in the remainder of this chapter.

This technique can be used to prove the following Product Rule of Logarithms.

Product Rule of Logarithms

For b > 0, b ≠ 1, and x, y > 0,

$$log_b xy = log_b x + log_b y$$

In words, the logarithm of a product is equal to the sum of the logarithms of the factors.

Proof of the Product Rule

$$\overbrace{b^{\log_b xy} = xy}^{\text{Property 3}} = \overbrace{x \cdot y = b^{\log_b x} \cdot b^{\log_b y}}^{\text{Property 3 again}} = \overbrace{b^{\log_b x + \log_b y}}^{\text{Add exponents}}$$

Thus,

$$b^{\log_b xy} = b^{\log_b x + \log_b y}$$

Equating the exponents gives the Product Rule of Logarithms:

$$\log_b xy = \log_b x + \log_b y$$

Example 1: Using the Product Rule

A calculator can be used to show the following results:

a. $\log(1000) = \log(10 \cdot 100) = \log 10 + \log 100 = 1 + 2 = 3$

b. $\log(30) = \log(5 \cdot 6) = \log 5 + \log 6 = 0.6990 + 0.7782 = 1.4772$

c. $\ln(16) = \ln(2 \cdot 8) = \ln 2 + \ln 8 = 0.6931 + 2.0794 = 2.7725$

Note: Of course other numbers could be used in these products. The results will be the same.

The Quotient Rule

Now consider the problem of finding the logarithm of a quotient. For example to find $\log \dfrac{3}{2}$, we could proceed as follows:

$$10^{\log\left(\frac{3}{2}\right)} = \frac{3}{2}$$

$$= \frac{10^{\log 3}}{10^{\log 2}}$$

$$= 10^{\log 3 - \log 2}$$

Equating exponents gives

$$\log \frac{3}{2} = \log 3 - \log 2$$

$$\approx 0.4771 - 0.3010$$

$$\approx 0.1761$$

This result can be verified by using a calculator to find log (1.5).

These ideas lead to the following Quotient Rule of Logarithms. The proof is left as an exercise for the student.

Quotient Rule of Logarithms

For b > 0, b ≠ 1, and x,y > 0,

$$\log_b \frac{x}{y} = \log_b x - \log_b y.$$

In words, the logarithm of a quotient is equal to the difference between the logarithm of the numerator and the logarithm of the denominator.

Example 2: Using the Quotient Rule

A calculator can be used to show the following results:

a. $\log\left(\dfrac{1}{2}\right) = \log 1 - \log 2 = 0 - 0.3010 = -0.3010$

b. $\log\left(\dfrac{4}{3}\right) = \log 4 - \log 3 = 0.6021 - 0.4771 = 0.1250$

c. $\ln\left(\dfrac{15}{2}\right) = \ln 15 - \ln 2 = 2.7081 - 0.6931 = 2.0150$

> **NOTES** Because we are rounding off individual logarithms to 4 places there may be a slight difference in answers if a calculator is used to find the logarithm of the original number. For example, a calculator will show that
>
> $$\ln\left(\frac{15}{2}\right) = \ln(7.5) = 2.0149 \text{ to 4 decimal places.}$$

The Power Rule

The next property of logarithms involves a number raised to a power and the multiplication of exponents. For example,

$$10^{\log(2^3)} = 2^3$$
$$= \left[10^{\log 2}\right]^3$$
$$= 10^{3(\log 2)}$$

Equating exponents gives

$$\log(2^3) = 3(\log 2)$$

These ideas lead to the following Power Rule of Logarithms.

Power Rule of Logarithms

For $b > 0$, $b \neq 1$, $x > 0$, and any real number r,

$$log_b x^r = r \cdot log_b x.$$

In words, the logarithm of a number raised to a power is equal to the product of the exponent and the logarithm of the number.

Proof of the Power Rule of Logarithms

$$\overbrace{b^{\log_b(x^r)} = x^r = \left[b^{\log_b x}\right]^r}^{\text{Property 3 twice}} = \overbrace{b^{r \cdot \log_b x}}^{\text{Multiply exponents}}$$

Equating the exponents gives the result called the Power Rule of Logarithms:

$$\log_b x^r = r \cdot \log_b x.$$

Example 3: Using the Power Rule

A calculator can be used to show the following results:

a. $\log\left(\sqrt{2}\right) = \log\left(2\right)^{\frac{1}{2}} = \frac{1}{2}\log\left(2\right) = \frac{1}{2}\left(0.3010\right) = 0.1505$

b. $\log\left(25\right) = \log\left(5^2\right) = 2\log 5 = 2\left(0.6990\right) = 1.3979$

c. $\ln\left(8\right) = \ln\left(2^3\right) = 3 \cdot \ln 2 = 3\left(0.6931\right) = 2.0794$

Table 9.3 summarizes the properties of logarithms for base b. **To emphasize that b could be e, we list the properties separately for natural logarithms.**

Properties of Logarithms		
For $b > 0, b \neq 1, x,y > 0$ and any real number r:	For natural logarithms:	
1. $\log_b 1 = 0$	1. $\ln 1 = 0$	
2. $\log_b b = 1$	2. $\ln e = 1$	
3. $x = b^{\log_b x}$	3. $x = e^{\ln x}$	
4. Product Rule: $\log_b xy = \log_b x + \log_b y$	4. Product Rule: $\ln xy = \ln x + \ln y$	
5. Quotient Rule: $\log_b \dfrac{x}{y} = \log_b x - \log_b y$	5. Quotient Rule: $\ln \dfrac{x}{y} = \ln x - \ln y$	
6. $\log_b x^r = r \cdot \log_b x$	6. $\ln x^r = r \cdot \ln x$	

Table 9.3

Example 4: Properties of Logarithms

Use the properties of logarithms to write each expression as a sum and/or difference of logarithmic expressions.

a. $\log 2x^3$

Solution: $\log 2x^3 = \log 2 + \log x^3$ Product Rule

$\qquad\qquad\quad = \log 2 + 3\log x$ Power Rule

b. $\log\left(\dfrac{ab^2}{c}\right)$

Solution: $\log\left(\dfrac{ab^2}{c}\right) = \log(ab^2) - \log c$ Quotient Rule

$= \log a + \log b^2 - \log c$ Product Rule

$= \log a + 2\log b - \log c$ Power Rule

c. $\ln(xy)^{-3}$

Solution: $\ln(xy)^{-3} = -3\ln(xy)$ Power Rule

$= -3(\ln x + \ln y)$ Product Rule

d. $\ln\left(\sqrt{3x}\right)$

Solution: $\ln\left(\sqrt{3x}\right) = \ln(3x)^{\frac{1}{2}} = \dfrac{1}{2}\ln(3x)$ Power Rule

$= \dfrac{1}{2}(\ln 3 + \ln x)$ Product Rule

● ●

Example 5: Single Logarithm ● ● ● ● ● ● ● ● ● ● ● ● ● ●

Use the properties of logarithms to write each expression as a single logarithm.

a. $2\log_b x - 3\log_b y$

Solution: $2\log_b x - 3\log_b y = \log_b x^2 - \log_b y^3$ Power Rule

$= \log_b\left(\dfrac{x^2}{y^3}\right)$ Quotient Rule

b. $\dfrac{1}{2}\ln 4 + \ln 5 - \ln y$

Solution: $\dfrac{1}{2}\ln 4 + \ln 5 - \ln y = \ln 4^{\frac{1}{2}} + \ln 5 - \ln y$ Power Rule

$= \ln\left(4^{\frac{1}{2}}\cdot 5\right) - \ln y$ Product Rule

$= \ln\dfrac{10}{y}$ Quotient Rule $\left(4^{\frac{1}{2}} = 2\right)$

continued on next page ...

c. $\log(x+1)+\log(x-1)$

Solution: $\log(x+1)+\log(x-1)=\log(x+1)(x-1)$ Product Rule

$$=\log(x^2-1)$$

d. $\ln\sqrt{x}+\ln\sqrt[3]{x}$

Solution: $\ln\sqrt{x}+\ln\sqrt[3]{x}=\ln(x)^{\frac{1}{2}}+\ln(x)^{\frac{1}{3}}=\frac{1}{2}\ln x+\frac{1}{3}\ln x$ Power Rule

$$=\left(\frac{1}{2}+\frac{1}{3}\right)\ln x$$ Algebra

$$=\frac{5}{6}\ln x$$

- -

NOTES

A Note About Common Misunderstandings:
There is no logarithmic property for a sum or a difference. That is, there is no property that will relate to $\log_b(x+y)$ and no property that will relate to $\log_b(x-y)$.

Also,

$$\log_b\frac{x}{y}\neq\frac{\log_b x}{\log_b y}$$

$$\log_b x\cdot\log_b y\neq\log_b x+\log_b y$$

Practice Problems

1. Write $\log(x^3 y)$ as a sum and/or difference of logarithmic expressions.

2. Write the expression $2\ln 5+\ln x-\ln 3$ as a single logarithm.

3. Write $2\log x-\log(x+1)$ as a single logarithm.

9.5 Exercises

In Exercises 1 – 30, use your knowledge of logarithms and exponents to find the value of each expression.

1. $\log_2 32$ **2.** $\log_3 9$ **3.** $\log_4\dfrac{1}{16}$ **4.** $\log_5\dfrac{1}{125}$

5. $\log_3\sqrt{3}$ **6.** $\log_2\sqrt{8}$ **7.** $5^{\log_5 10}$ **8.** $3^{\log_3 17}$

9. $6^{\log_6 \sqrt{3}}$

10. $e^{\ln 5}$

11. $\log 5x^4$

12. $\log 3x^2 y$

13. $\ln 2x^{-3}y$

14. $\ln xy^2 z^{-1}$

15. $\log \dfrac{2x}{y^3}$

16. $\log \dfrac{xy}{4z}$

17. $\ln \dfrac{x^2}{yz}$

18. $\ln \dfrac{xy^2}{z^2}$

19. $\log (xy)^{-2}$

20. $\log (x^2 y)^4$

21. $\log \sqrt[3]{xy^2}$

22. $\log \sqrt{2x^3 y}$

23. $\ln \sqrt{\dfrac{xy}{z}}$

24. $\ln \sqrt[3]{\dfrac{x^2}{y}}$

25. $\log 21x^2 y^{\frac{2}{3}}$

26. $\log 15x^{-\frac{1}{2}} y^{\frac{1}{3}}$

27. $\log \dfrac{x}{\sqrt{x^3 y^5}}$

28. $\log \dfrac{1}{\sqrt{x^4 y}}$

29. $\ln \left(\dfrac{x^3 y^2}{z} \right)^{-3}$

30. $\ln \left(\dfrac{x^{-\frac{1}{2}} y}{z^2} \right)^{-2}$

Use the properties of logarithms to write each expression in Exercises 31 – 52 as a single logarithm.

31. $2\ln 3 + \ln x - \ln 5$

32. $\dfrac{1}{2}\ln 25 + \ln 3 - \ln x$

33. $\log 7 - \log 8 + 2\log x$

34. $\log 4 + \log 6 + \log y$

35. $2\log x + \log y$

36. $\log x + 3\log y$

37. $3\ln x - 2\ln y$

38. $3\ln y - \dfrac{1}{2}\ln x$

39. $\dfrac{1}{2}(\ln x - \ln y)$

40. $\dfrac{1}{3}(\ln x - 2\ln y)$

41. $\log x - \log y + \log z$

42. $\log x + 2\log y - \dfrac{1}{2}\log z$

43. $\log x - 2\log y - 2\log z$

44. $-\dfrac{2}{3}\log x - \dfrac{1}{3}\log y + \dfrac{2}{3}\log z$

45. $\log x + \log(2x+1)$

46. $\log(x+3) + \log(x-3)$

47. $\ln(x-1) + \ln(x+3)$

48. $\ln(3x+1) + 2\ln x$

49. $\log(x^2 - 2x - 3) - \log(x-3)$

50. $\log(x-4) - \log(x^2 - 2x - 8)$

51. $\log(x+6) - \log(2x^2 + 9x - 18)$

52. $\log(3x^2 + 5x - 2) - \log(3x-1)$

Writing and Thinking About Mathematics

53. Prove the Quotient Rule for Logarithms: For $b > 0, b \neq 1$, and $x,y > 0$,

$$\log_b \dfrac{x}{y} = \log_b x - \log_b y.$$

54. Prove the following property of logarithms: For

$b > 0,\ b \neq 1,$ and $x > 0,\ \log_b b^x = x.$

Answers to Practice Problems: 1. $3\log x + \log y$ **2.** $\ln \dfrac{25x}{3}$ **3.** $\log \dfrac{x^2}{x+1}$

Hawkes Learning Systems: Intermediate Algebra

Properties of Logarithmic Functions

9.6   Logarithmic and Exponential Equations

Objectives

After completing this section, you will be able to:

1. *Solve exponential equations in which the bases are not necessarily the same.*

2. *Solve logarithmic equations without necessarily changing to exponential form.*

3. *Use the change-of-base formula and a calculator to evaluate logarithmic expressions.*

Solving Exponential Equations with the Same Base

Both exponential and logarithmic functions involve the meaning of expressions with exponents that are real numbers, including irrational numbers such as $\sqrt{2}$ and π. That is, we are familiar with expressions such as 2^3 and 3^{-2}, but you need to be aware that we have been using (in the definitions of exponential functions and logarithmic functions and in their graphs) the meaning and value of expressions with real exponents such as $2^{\sqrt{2}}$, 2^{π}, and $10^{1.4}$. To be complete in our understanding of exponents, we state, without proof, that all the properties of exponents that have been discussed are valid for real exponents with a positive base.

Properties of Real Exponents

If a and b are positive real numbers and x and y are any real numbers, then:

1. $b^0 = 1$ **2.** $b^{-x} = \dfrac{1}{b^x}$ **3.** $b^x \cdot b^y = b^{x+y}$ **4.** $\dfrac{b^x}{b^y} = b^{x-y}$

5. $\left(b^x\right)^y = b^{xy}$ **6.** $(ab)^x = a^x b^x$ **7.** $\left(\dfrac{a}{b}\right)^x = \dfrac{a^x}{b^x}$

In this section we first show how to solve exponential equations with expressions that have the same base, then exponential equations with different bases, and finally equations that involve logarithms. We need the following properties of equations containing exponents and logarithms to help in solving the related equations.

Properties of Equations with Exponents and Logarithms

For $b > 0$, $b \neq 1$,

1. If $b^x = b^y$, then $x = y$.

2. If $x = y$ then $b^x = b^y$.

3. If $\log_b x = \log_b y$, then $x = y$ $(x > 0$ and $y > 0)$.

4. If $x = y$, then $\log_b x = \log_b y$ $(x > 0$ and $y > 0)$.

Example 1 shows how Property 1 can be used to solve exponential equations with expressions that have the same base.

Example 1: Solving Equations for *x* when the Base is the Same ● ● ● ● ● ● ● ●

Solve each equation for *x*.

a. $3^{x-2} = 3^{\frac{1}{2}}$

Solution:

$$3^{x-2} = 3^{\frac{1}{2}}$$ Both bases are 3.

$$x - 2 = \frac{1}{2}$$ Since the bases are the same, the exponents must be equal.

$$x = \frac{5}{2}$$ Solve for *x*.

b. $2^{x^2-7} = 2^{6x}$

Solution:

$$2^{x^2-7} = 2^{6x}$$ Both bases are 2.

$$x^2 - 7 = 6x$$ The exponents are equal because the bases are the same.

$$x^2 - 6x - 7 = 0$$ Solve for *x*.

$$(x-7)(x+1) = 0$$

$$x = 7 \qquad \text{or} \qquad x = -1$$

c. $8^{4-2x} = 4^{x+2}$

Solution:

$$8^{4-2x} = 4^{x+2}$$ Here, the bases are different.

$$\left(2^3\right)^{4-2x} = \left(2^2\right)^{x+2}$$ Rewrite both sides so that the bases are the same.

$$2^{12-6x} = 2^{2x+4}$$ Use the property $\left(b^x\right)^y = b^{xy}$.

$$12 - 6x = 2x + 4 \qquad \text{The exponents must be equal.}$$

$$8 = 8x \qquad \text{Solve for } x.$$

$$1 = x$$

● ●

Solving Exponential Equations with Different Bases

Example 2 illustrates how to solve exponential equations that have exponential expressions with different bases. The technique is to use Property 4 of equations and take the log (or ln) of the expressions on both sides of the equation or to use the definition of logarithm as an exponent. (As we have seen in Example 1, if the bases are the same there is no need to deal with logarithms.)

Example 2: Solving Exponential Equations with Different Bases ● ● ● ● ● ● ● ●

Solve each of the following exponential equations by taking the log (or ln) of both sides of the equation or by using the definition of logarithm as an exponent.

a. $10^{3x} = 2.1$

Solution: Since the base of $3x$ is 10, we can solve by taking the log of both sides.

$$10^{3x} = 2.1$$

$$\log 10^{3x} = \log 2.1 \qquad \text{Take the log of both sides.}$$

$$3x \log 10 = \log 2.1 \qquad \text{Power Rule}$$

$$3x = \log 2.1 \qquad \log 10 = 1$$

$$x = \frac{\log 2.1}{3}$$

Using a calculator,

$$x = \frac{\log 2.1}{3} \approx \frac{0.3222}{3} \approx 0.1074$$

We could also have simply used the definition of a logarithm as an exponent and stated directly

$$10^{3x} = 2.1$$

$$3x = \log 2.1 \qquad \text{By the definition of logarithm}$$

$$x = \frac{\log 2.1}{3}$$

continued on next page...

b. $e^{0.2x} = 50$

Solution: Using the definition of a logarithm as an exponent, we have

$$e^{0.2x} = 50$$

$$0.2x = \ln 50 \qquad \text{By the definition of logarithm}$$

$$x = \frac{\ln 50}{0.2}$$

Using a calculator,

$$x = \frac{\ln 50}{0.2} \approx \frac{3.912}{0.2} = 19.56$$

c. $6^x = 18$

Solution: The base is 6, not 10 or e, but we can solve by taking the **log** of both sides or by taking the **ln** of both sides. The result is the same.

Taking the log of both sides: Taking the ln of both sides:

$$6^x = 18 \qquad\qquad\qquad\qquad 6^x = 18$$

$$\log 6^x = \log 18 \qquad\qquad\qquad \ln 6^x = \ln 18$$

$$x \cdot \log 6 = \log 18 \qquad\qquad\qquad x \cdot \ln 6 = \ln 18$$

$$x = \frac{\log 18}{\log 6} \qquad\qquad\qquad\qquad x = \frac{\ln 18}{\ln 6}$$

Using a calculator,   Using a calculator

$$x = \frac{\log 18}{\log 6} = \frac{1.2553}{0.7782} \qquad\qquad x = \frac{\ln 18}{\ln 6} = \frac{2.8904}{1.7918}$$

$$= 1.6131 \qquad\qquad\qquad\qquad\qquad = 1.6131$$

d. $5^{2x-1} = 10^x$

Solution:

$$5^{2x-1} = 10^x$$

$$\log 5^{2x-1} = \log 10^x \qquad \text{Take the log of both sides.}$$

$$(2x-1)\log 5 = x \log 10 \qquad \text{Power Rule}$$

$$2x \cdot \log 5 - 1 \cdot \log 5 = x \qquad \text{Log } 10 = 1$$

$$2x \log 5 - x = \log 5 \qquad \text{Arrange } x\text{-terms on one side.}$$

$$x(2\log 5 - 1) = \log 5 \qquad \text{Factor out the } x.$$

$$x = \frac{\log 5}{2\log 5 - 1}$$

As a decimal approximation,

$$x = \frac{\log 5}{2\log 5 - 1} \approx \frac{0.6990}{2(0.6990) - 1} \approx 1.7563$$

Solving Equations with Logarithms

All the various properties of logarithms can be used to solve equations that involve logarithms. Remember that logarithms are defined only for positive real numbers, so each answer should be checked in the original equation.

Example 3: Solving Equations with Logarithms ● ● ● ● ● ● ● ● ● ● ● ● ● ●

Use the properties of logarithms to solve the following equations.

a. $\log(5x) = 3$

Solution: $\log(5x) = 3$

$$5x = 10^3 \qquad \text{Definition of logarithm}$$

$$5x = 1000$$

$$x = 200$$

b. $\log(x-1) + \log(x-4) = 1$

Solution: $\log(x-1) + \log(x-4) = 1$

$$\log(x-1)(x-4) = 1 \qquad \text{Product Rule}$$

$$(x-1)(x-4) = 10^1 \qquad \text{Change to exponential form using base 10.}$$

$$x^2 - 5x + 4 = 10$$

$$x^2 - 5x - 6 = 0$$

$$(x-6)(x+1) = 0 \qquad \text{Solve by factoring.}$$

$$x = 6 \quad \text{or} \quad \cancel{x = -1} \qquad \begin{array}{l}\text{Checking } x = -1 \text{ yields} \\ \log(-1-1) = \log(-2), \\ \text{which is undefined.}\end{array}$$

c. $\log x - \log(x-1) = \log 3$

Solution: $\log x - \log(x-1) = \log 3$

$$\log\left(\frac{x}{x-1}\right) = \log 3 \qquad \text{Quotient Rule}$$

$$\frac{x}{x-1} = 3 \qquad \text{If } \log_b x = \log_b y, \text{ then } x = y$$

continued on next page ...

$$x = 3(x-1) \qquad \text{Solve for } x.$$

$$x = 3x - 3$$

$$3 = 2x$$

$$\frac{3}{2} = x$$

d. $\ln(x^2 - x - 6) - \ln(x+2) = 2$

Solution: $\ln(x^2 - x - 6) - \ln(x+2) = 2$

$$\ln\left(\frac{x^2 - x - 6}{x+2}\right) = 2 \qquad \text{Quotient Rule}$$

$$\ln\left(\frac{(x+2)(x-3)}{(x+2)}\right) = 2 \qquad \text{Factor the numerator.}$$

$$\ln(x-3) = 2 \qquad \text{Simplify.}$$

$$x - 3 = e^2 \qquad \text{Change to exponential}$$

$$x = 3 + e^2 \qquad \text{form with base } e.$$

Or, using a calculator, $x = 3 + e^2 \approx 3 + 7.3891 = 10.3891$

Change-of-Base

Because a calculator can be used to evaluate common logarithms and natural logarithms, we have restricted most of the examples to base 10 or base e expressions. If an equation involves logarithms of other bases, the following discussion shows how to rewrite each logarithm using any base you choose.

Change-of-Base

$$log_b x = \frac{log_a x}{log_a b}$$

The change-of-base formula can be derived by using properties of logarithms as follows:

$$b^{\log_b x} = x \qquad \text{Property 3 in Section 9.5}$$

$$\log_a \left(b^{\log_b x} \right) = \log_a x \qquad \text{Take the } \log(\text{ base } a) \text{ of both sides.}$$

$$\log_b x \left(\log_a b \right) = \log_a x \qquad \begin{array}{l}\text{By the Power Rule using } \log_b x \\ \text{as the exponent } r.\end{array}$$

$$\log_b x = \frac{\log_a x}{\log_a b} \qquad \begin{array}{l}\text{Divide both sides by } \log_a b \text{ to arrive} \\ \\ \text{at the change-of-base formula.}\end{array}$$

Example 4: Change-of-Base

Use the change-of-base formula to evaluate the expressions in (a) and (b) and to solve the equation in (c).

a. $\log_2 3.42$

Solution: This expression can be evaluated by using either base 10 or base e since both are easily available on a calculator.

$$\log_2 3.42 = \frac{\ln 3.42}{\ln 2} = \frac{1.2296}{0.6931} = 1.7741 \qquad \text{Using rounded values}$$

(The student can show that $\dfrac{\log 3.42}{\log 2}$ gives the same result.)

In exponential form: $2^{1.7741} = 3.42$

b. $\log_3 0.3333$

Solution: $\log_3 0.3333 = \dfrac{\log 0.3333}{\log 3} = \dfrac{-0.4772}{0.4771} = -1.0002$

c.   Use the change-of-base formula to find the value of x (accurate to 4 decimal places) in the equation $5^x = 16$

Solution: Because the base is 5, we can take $\log_5$ of both sides. (This method is not necessary, but it does show how the change-of-base formula can be used.)

$$5^x = 16$$

$$\log_5 \left(5^x \right) = \log_5 16$$

$$x = \log_5 16$$

$$x = \frac{\ln 16}{\ln 5} = 1.7227$$

Practice Problems

Solve each of the following equations.

1. $4^x = 64$

2. $10^x = 64$

3. $2^{3x-1} = 0.1$

4. $15 \log x = 45.15$

5. $\ln\left(x^2 - x - 6\right) - \ln\left(x - 3\right) = 1$

9.6 Exercises

Use the properties of exponents and logarithms to solve each of the equations in Exercises 1 – 84.

1. $2^4 \cdot 2^7 = 2^x$

2. $3^7 \cdot 3^{-2} = 3^x$

3. $\left(3^5\right)^2 = 3^{x+1}$

4. $\left(5^x\right)^2 = 5^6$

5. $\left(2^x\right)^3 = \sqrt{2}$

6. $\dfrac{10^4 \cdot 10^{1/2}}{10^x} = 10$

7. $\left(10^2\right)^x = \dfrac{10 \cdot 10^{2/3}}{10^{1/2}}$

8. $2^{5x} = 4^3$

9. $\left(25\right)^x = 5^3 \cdot 5^4$

10. $7^{3x} = 49^4$

11. $10^x \cdot 10^8 = 100^3$

12. $8^{x+3} = 2^{x-1}$

13. $27^x = 3 \cdot 9^{x-2}$

14. $100^{2x+1} = 1000^{x-2}$

15. $2^{3x+5} = 2^{x^2+1}$

16. $10^{x^2+x} = 10^{x+9}$

17. $10^{2x^2+3} = 10^{x+6}$

18. $3^{x^2+5x} = 3^{2x-2}$

19. $\left(3^{x+1}\right)^x = \left(3^{x+3}\right)^2$

20. $\left(10^x\right)^{x+3} = \left(10^{x+2}\right)^{-2}$

21. $3^x = 9$

22. $2^{5x-8} = 4$

23. $4^{x^2} = \left(\dfrac{1}{2}\right)^{3x}$

24. $25^{x^2+2x} = 5^{-x}$

25. $5^{2x-x^2} = \dfrac{1}{125}$

26. $10^{x^2-2x} = 1000$

27. $10^{3x} = 140$

28. $10^{2x} = 97$

29. $10^{0.32x} = 253$

30. $10^{-0.48x} = 88.6$

31. $4.10^{-0.94x} = 126.2$

32. $3 \cdot 10^{-2.1x} = 83.5$

33. $e^{0.03x} = 2.1$

34. $e^{-0.5x} = 47$

35. $e^{-0.006t} = 50.3$

36. $e^{4t} = 184$

37. $3e^{-0.12t} = 3.6$

38. $5e^{2.4t} = 44$

39. $2^x = 10$

40. $3^{x-2} = 100$

41. $5^{2x} = \dfrac{1}{100}$

42. $7^{2x-3} = 10$

43. $5^{1-x} = 1$

44. $4^{2x+5} = 0.01$

45. $4^{2-3x} = 0.1$

Answers to Practice Problems: **1.** $x = 3$ **2.** $x = 1.8062$ **3.** $x = -0.7740$ **4.** $x = 10^{3.01} = 1023.2930$
5. $x = e - 2 = 0.7183$

46. $14^{3x-1} = 10^3$ **47.** $12^{2x+7} = 10^4$ **48.** $12^{5x+2} = 1$

49. $7^x = 9$ **50.** $2^x = 20$ **51.** $3^{x-2} = 23$

52. $5^{2x} = 23$ **53.** $6^{2x-1} = 14.8$ **54.** $4^{7-3x} = 26.3$

55. $5\log x = 7$ **56.** $3\log x = 13.2$ **57.** $4\log x - 6 = 0$

58. $2\log x - 15 = 0$ **59.** $4\log x^{1/2} + 8 = 0$ **60.** $\dfrac{2}{3}\log x^{2/3} + 9 = 0$

61. $5\ln x - 8 = 0$ **62.** $2\ln x + 3 = 0$ **63.** $\ln x^2 + 2.2 = 0$

64. $\ln x^2 - 41.6 = 0$ **65.** $\log x + \log 2x = \log 18$

66. $\log(x+4) + \log(x-4) = \log 9$ **67.** $\log x^2 - \log x = 2$

68. $\log x + \log x^2 = 3$ **69.** $\ln(x-3) + \ln x = \ln 18$

70. $\ln(x^2 - 3x + 2) - \ln(x-1) = \ln 4$ **71.** $\log(x-15) + \log x = 2$

72. $\log(3x-5) + \log(x-1) = 1$ **73.** $\log(2x-17) = 2 - \log x$

74. $\log(x-3) - 1 = \log(x+1)$ **75.** $\log(x^2 + 2x - 3) = 3 + \log(x+3)$

76. $\log(x^2 - 9) - \log(x-3) = -2$ **77.** $\log(x^2 - x - 12) + 2 = \log(x-4)$

78. $\log(x^2 - 4x - 5) - \log(x+1) = 2$ **79.** $\ln(x^2 + 4x - 5) - \ln(x+5) = -2$

80. $\ln(x+1) + \ln(x-1) = 0$ **81.** $\ln(x^2 - 4) - \ln(x+2) = 3$

82. $\ln(x^2 + 2x - 3) = 1 + \ln(x-1)$ **83.** $\log\sqrt[3]{x^2 + 2x + 20} = \dfrac{2}{3}$

84. $\log\sqrt{x^2 - 24} = \dfrac{3}{2}$

Use the Change of Base formula to evaluate each of the expressions or solve the equations in Exercises 85 – 100.

85. $\log_3 12$ **86.** $\log_4 36$ **87.** $\log_5 1.68$ **88.** $\log_{11} 39.6$

89. $\log_8 0.271$ **90.** $\log_7 0.849$ **91.** $\log_{15} 739$ **92.** $\log_2 14.2$

93. $\log_{20} 0.0257$ **94.** $\log_9 2.384$ **95.** $2^x = 5$ **96.** $3^{2x} = 10$

97. $5^{x-1} = 30$ **98.** $9^{2x-1} = 100$ **99.** $4^{3-x} = 20$ **100.** $6^{3x-4} = 25$

Writing and Thinking About Mathematics

101. Solve the following equation for x two different ways: $a^{2x-1} = 1$.

102. Rewrite each of the following expressions as products:
   a. 5^{x+2} **b.** 3^{x-2}

103. Explain, in your own words, why $7 \cdot 7^x \neq 49^x$. Show each of the expressions $7 \cdot 7^x$ and 49^x as a single exponential expression with base 7.

Hawkes Learning Systems: Intermediate Algebra

Exponential and Logarithmic Equations

9.7 Applications

After completing this section, you will be able to:

Solve applied problems by using logarithms and exponential equations.

In Section 9.3, we found that the number *e* appears in a surprisingly natural way in the formula for continuously compounding interest

$$A = Pe^{rt}$$

which was developed from the formula for compounding *n* times per year:

$$A = P\left(1 + \frac{r}{n}\right)^{nt}$$

There are many formulas that involve exponential functions. A few are shown here and in the exercises.

$A = A_0 e^{-0.04t}$ This is a law for decomposition of radium where *t* is in centuries.

$A = A_0 e^{-0.1t}$ This is one law for skin healing where *t* is measured in days.

$A = A_o 2^{-t/5600}$ This law is used for carbon-14 dating to determine the age of fossils where *t* is measured in years.

$T = Ae^{-kt} + C$ This is Newton's law of cooling where *C* is the constant temperature of the surrounding medium. The values of *A* and *k* depend on the particular object that is cooling.

Example 1: Exponential Growth and Exponential Decay

a. Suppose that the formula $y = y_0 e^{0.4t}$ represents the number of bacteria present after *t* days, where y_0 is the initial number of bacteria. In how many days will the bacteria double in number?

Solution: $y = y_0 e^{0.4t}$

$2y_0 = y_0 e^{0.4t}$ $2y_0$ is double the initial number present.

$2 = e^{0.4t}$ Divide both sides by y_0.

$\ln 2 = 0.4t$

continued on next page...

$$t = \frac{\ln 2}{0.4} \approx \frac{0.6931}{0.4}$$

$$t \approx 1.73$$

The number of bacteria will double in approximately 1.73 days. Note that this number is completely independent of the number of bacteria initially present. That is, if $y_0 = 10$ or $y_0 = 1000$ the doubling time is the same, namely 1.73 days.

b.   Suppose that the room temperature is $70°$, and the temperature of a cup of tea is $150°$ when it is placed on the table. In 5 minutes, the tea cools to $120°$. How long will it take for the tea to cool to $100°$?

     Solution: Using the formula $T = Ae^{-kt} + C$ (Newton's law of cooling), first find A and then k. We know that $C = 70°$ and that $T = 150°$ when $t = 0$. Find A by substituting these values:

$$150 = Ae^{-k(0)} + 70$$

$$150 = A \cdot 1 + 70 \qquad\qquad e^{-k(0)} = e^0 = 1$$

$$80 = A$$

Therefore, the formula can be written as $T = 80e^{-kt} + 70$.
Since $T = 120°$ when $t = 5$, substituting these values allows us to find k:

$$120 = 80e^{-k(5)} + 70$$

$$50 = 80e^{-5k}$$

$$\frac{50}{80} = e^{-5k}$$

$$\ln\frac{5}{8} = \ln e^{-5k} \qquad\qquad \text{Take the natural log of both sides.}$$

$$\ln 0.625 = -5k$$

$$k = \frac{\ln 0.625}{-5} = \frac{-0.4700}{-5} = 0.0940$$

The formula can now be written as $T = 80e^{-0.0940t} + 70$.
With all the constants in the formula known, we can find t when $T = 100°$.

$$100 = 80e^{-0.0940t} + 70$$

$$30 = 80e^{-0.0940t}$$

$$\frac{30}{80} = e^{-0.0940t}$$

$$\ln e^{-0.0940t} = \ln\frac{3}{8} \qquad\qquad \text{Take the natural log of both sides.}$$

$$-0.0940t = \ln 0.375$$

$$t = \frac{\ln 0.375}{-0.0940}$$

$$= \frac{-0.9808}{-0.0940} = 10.43 \text{ minutes}$$

The tea will cool to 100° in about 10.43 minutes.

c. If \$1000 is invested at a rate of 6% compounded continuously, in how many years will it grow to \$5000?

Solution: $A = Pe^{rt}$

$$5000 = 1000e^{0.06t}$$

$$5 = e^{0.06t}$$

$$\ln 5 = 0.06t$$

$$t = \frac{\ln 5}{0.06} \approx \frac{1.6094}{0.06}$$

$$t \approx 26.82$$

\$1000 will grow to \$5000 in approximately 26.82 years.

d. The magnitude of an earthquake is measured on the **Richter scale** as a logarithm of the intensity of the shock wave. For magnitude R and intensity I, the formula is $R = \log I$. The 1994 earthquake in Northridge, California measured 6.7 on the Richter scale. What was the intensity of this earthquake?

Solution: Substitute 6.7 for R in the formula and solve for I:
$$6.7 = \log I$$

$$I = 10^{6.7}$$

e. The Long Beach earthquake in 1933 measured 6.2 on the Richter scale. How much stronger was the Northridge earthquake than the 1933 Long Beach earthquake?

Solution: The comparative sizes of the quakes can be found by finding the ratio of the intensities. For the Long Beach quake, $6.2 = \log I$ and $I = 10^{6.2}$. Therefore, the ratio of the two intensities is

$$\frac{I \text{ for Northridge}}{I \text{ for Long Beach}} = \frac{10^{6.7}}{10^{6.2}} = 10^{0.5} \approx 3.2$$

Thus, the Northridge earthquake had an intensity about 3.2 times the Long Beach earthquake.

continued on next page...

f. The **half-life** of a substance is the time needed for the substance to decay to one-half of its original amount. The half-life of radioactive radium is 1620 years. If 10 grams are present today, how many grams will remain in 500 years?

Solution: The model for radioactive decay is $y = y_0 e^{-kt}$. Since the half-life is 1620 years, if we assume $y_0 = 10$ gm, then y would be 5 gm after 1620 years. We solve for k as follows:

$$5 = 10e^{-k(1620)} \qquad \text{Substitute } y = 5, y_0 = 10, \text{and } t = 1620.$$

$$\frac{5}{10} = e^{-1620k} \qquad \text{Solve for } k.$$

$$-1620k = \ln(0.5) \qquad \text{Take the ln of both sides.}$$

$$k = \frac{\ln(0.5)}{-1620} = \frac{-0.6931}{-1620} = 0.0004279$$

The model is $y = 10e^{-0.0004279t}$

Substituting $t = 500$ gives

$$y = 10e^{(-0.0004279)(500)} = 10e^{-0.21395} = 10(0.8074) = 8.074$$

Thus, there will still be about 8.1 gm of the radioactive radium remaining after 500 years.

● ●

9.7 Exercises

1. If $2000 is invested at the rate 7% compounded continuously, what will be the balance after 10 years?

2. Find the amount of money that will be accumulated in a savings account if $3200 is invested at 6.5% for 6 years and the interest is compounded continuously.

3. How long does it take $1000 to double if it is invested at 5% compounded continuously?

4. Four thousand dollars is invested at 6% compounded continuously. How long will it take for the balance to be $8000?

5. The reliability of a certain type of flashlight battery is given by $f = e^{-0.03x}$, where f is the fractional part of the batteries produced that last x hours. What fraction of the batteries produced are good after 40 hours of use?

6. From Exercise 5, how long will at least one-half of the batteries last?

7. The concentration of a drug in the blood stream is given by $C = C_0 e^{-0.8t}$, where C_0 is the initial dosage and t is the time in hours elapsed after administering the dose. If 20 mg of a drug is given, how much time elapses until 5 mg of the drug remains?

8. Using the formula in Exercise 7, determine the amount of insulin present after 3 hours if 0.60 ml are given.

9. A swarm of bees grows according to the formula $P = P_0 e^{0.35t}$, where P_0 is the number present initially and t is the time in days. How many bees will be present in 6 days if there were 1000 present initially?

10. If inversion of raw sugar is given by $A = A_0 e^{-0.03t}$, where A_0 is the initial amount and t is the time in hours, how long will it take for 1000 lb of raw sugar to be reduced to 800 lb?

11. Atmospheric pressure P is related to the altitude h by the formula $P = P_0 e^{-0.00004h}$, where P_0, the pressure at sea level, is approximately 15 lb per sq in. Determine the pressure at 5000 ft.

12. One law for skin healing is $A = A_0 e^{-0.1t}$, where A is the number of sq cm of unhealed area after t days and A_0 is the number of sq cm of the original wound. Find the number of days needed to reduce the wound to one-third the original size.

13. A radioactive substance decays according to $A = A_0 e^{-0.0002t}$, where A_0 is the initial amount and t is the time in years. If $A_0 = 640$ grams, find the time for A to decay to 400 grams.

14. A substance decays according to $A = A_0 e^{-0.045t}$, where t is in hours and A_0 is the initial amount. Determine the half-life of the substance.

15. An employee is learning to assemble remote control units. The number of units per day he can assemble after t days of training is given by $N = 80\left(1 - e^{-0.3t}\right)$. How many days of training will be needed before the employee is able to assemble 40 units per day?

16. The temperature of a carrot cake is 350° when it is removed from the oven. The temperature in the room is 72°. In 10 minutes, the cake cools to 280°. How long will it take for the cake to cool to 160°?

17. How long does it take $10,000 to double if it is invested at 8% compounded quarterly?

18. If $1000 is deposited at 6% compounded monthly, how long before the balance is $1520?

19. The value of a machine, V, at the end of t years is given by $V = C\left(1 - r\right)^t$, where C is the original cost of the machine and r is the rate of depreciation. A machine that originally cost $12,000 in now valued at $3800. How old is the machine if $r = 0.12$?

20. Using the formula in Exercise 19, determine the age of a machine valued at $5800 if its original value was $18,000 and $r = 0.09$.

21. If a principal P is doubled, then $A = 2P$. Use the formula for continuous compounding to find the time that a principal will double in value if the rate of interest is
  a. 5%   **b.** 10%
  (Note that the time for doubling the principal is completely independent of the principal itself.)

22. If a principal P is tripled, then $A = 3P$. Use the formula for continuous compounding to find the time that a principal will triple in value if the interest rate is
  a. 4%   **b.** 8%
  (Note that the time for tripling the principal is completely independent of the principal itself.)

23. Radioactive iodine has a half-life of 60 days. If an accident occurs at a nuclear plant and 30 grams of radioactive iodine are present, in how many days will 1 gram be present?

24. The formula $A = A_0 2^{-t/5600}$ is used for carbon-14 dating to determine the age of fossils where t is measured in years. Determine the half-life of carbon-14.

25. The 1906 earthquake in San Francisco measured 8.6 on the Richter scale. In 1971, an earthquake in the San Fernando Valley measured 6.6 on the Richter scale. How many times greater was the 1906 earthquake than the 1971 earthquake?

26. In 1985, an earthquake in Mexico measured 8.1 on the Richter scale. How many times greater was this earthquake than the one in Landers, California in 1992 that measured 7.3 on the Richter scale?

27. Population does not generally grow in a linear fashion. In fact, population of many species grows exponentially, at least for a limited time. Using the exponential model $y = y_0 e^{kt}$ for population growth, estimate the population of a state in 2020 if the population was 5 million in 1990 and 6 million in 2000. (Assume that t is measured in years and $t = 0$ corresponds to 1990.)

28. Suppose that a lake is stocked with 500 fish, and biologists predict that the population of these fish will be approximated by the function $P(t) = 500\ln(2t + e)$ where t is measured in years. What will be the fish population in 3 years? in 5 years? in 10 years?

29. Sales representatives of a new type of computer predict that sales can be approximated by the function $S(t) = 1000 + 500\ln(3t + e)$ where t is measured in years. What are the predicted sales in 2 years? in 5 years? in 10 years?

30. In chemistry, the pH of a solution is a measure of the acidity or alkalinity of a solution. Water has a pH of 7 and, in general, acids have a pH less than 7 and alkaline solutions have a pH greater than 7. The model for pH is $pH = -\log\left[H^+\right]$ where $\left[H^+\right]$ is the hydrogen ion concentration in moles per liter of a solution.

    a. Find the pH of a solution with a hydrogen ion concentration of 8.6×10^{-7}.

    b. Find the hydrogen ion concentration $\left[H^+\right]$ of a solution if the pH of the solution is 4.5. Write the answer in scientific notation.

Hawkes Learning Systems: Intermediate Algebra

Applications (Exponential and Logarithmic Functions)

Chapter 9 Index of Key Ideas and Terms

Algebraic Operations with Functions   page 609

If $f(x)$ and $g(x)$ represent two functions and x is a value in the domain of both functions, then

1. Sum of Two Functions: $(f+g)(x) = f(x) + g(x)$

2. Difference of Two Functions: $(f-g)(x) = f(x) - g(x)$

3. Product of Two Functions: $(f \cdot g)(x) = f(x) \cdot g(x)$

4. Quotient of Two Functions: $\left(\dfrac{f}{g}\right)(x) = \dfrac{f(x)}{g(x)}$ where $g(x) \neq 0$

Graphing the Sum of Two Functions   page 611

Using a Graphing Calculator to Graph the Sum of Two Functions   page 613

Composition of Two Functions   page 619

Composite Functions   page 620

For two functions f and g, the **composite function** $f \circ g$ is defined as follows: $(f \circ g)(x) = f(g(x))$.

Domain of $f \circ g$: The domain of $f \circ g$ consists of those values x in the domain of g for which $g(x)$ is in the domain of f.

One-to-One Functions   page 622

A function is a **one-to-one function** (or **1-1 function**) if for each value of y in the range there is only one corresponding value of x in the domain.

Horizontal Line Test   page 622

A function is one-to-one if no horizontal line intersects the graph of the function in more than one point.

Inverse Functions   page 624

If f is a 1-1 function with ordered pairs of the form (x, y), then its **inverse function**, denoted as f^{-1}, is also a 1-1 function with ordered pairs of the form (y, x).

Inverse Functions   page 626

If f and g are one-to-one functions and

$$f(g(x)) = x \qquad \text{for all } x \text{ in } D_g$$

$$g(f(x)) = x \qquad \text{for all } x \text{ in } D_f$$

then f and g are **inverse functions.**
That is, $g = f^{-1}$ and $f = g^{-1}$.

To Find the Inverse of a 1-1 Function   page 628

1. Let $y = f(x)$. (In effect, substitute y for $f(x)$.)
2. Interchange x and y.
3. In the new equation, solve for y in terms of x.
4. Substitute $f^{-1}(x)$ for y. (This new function is the inverse of f.)

Exponential Functions   page 635

An exponential function is a function of the form $f(x) = b^x$ where $b > 0, b \neq 1$, and x is any real number.

General Concepts of Exponential Functions

page 638

For $b > 1$:
1. $b^x > 0$.

2. b^x increases to the right and is called an **exponential growth function.**

3. $b^0 = 1$, so $(0, 1)$ is on the graph.

4. b^x approaches the x-axis for negative values of x. (The x-axis is a horizontal asymptote. See Figure 9.11.)

For $0 < b < 1$:
1. $b^x > 0$.

2. b^x decreases to the right and is called an **exponential decay function.**

3. $b^0 = 1$, so $(0, 1)$ is on the graph.

4. b^x approaches the x-axis for positive values of x. (The x-axis is a horizontal asymptote. See Figure 9.13.)

Compound Interest

page 640

Formula for compound interest: $A = P\left(1 + \dfrac{r}{n}\right)^{nt}$

Interest Compounded Continuously

page 641

Formula for compounding continuously: $A = Pe^{rt}$

The Number e

page 642

The number e is defined to be $e = \lim\limits_{n \to \infty}\left(1 + \dfrac{1}{n}\right)^n = 2.718281828459\ldots$

n	$\left(1 + \dfrac{1}{n}\right)$	$\left(1 + \dfrac{1}{n}\right)^n$
1	$\left(1 + \dfrac{1}{1}\right) = 2$	$(2)^1 = 2$
2	$\left(1 + \dfrac{1}{2}\right) = 1.5$	$(1.5)^2 = 2.25$
5	$\left(1 + \dfrac{1}{5}\right) = 1.2$	$(1.2)^5 = 2.48832$
10	$\left(1 + \dfrac{1}{10}\right) = 1.1$	$(1.1)^{10} = 2.59374246$
100	$\left(1 + \dfrac{1}{100}\right) = 1.01$	$(1.01)^{100} = 2.704813829$
1000	$\left(1 + \dfrac{1}{1000}\right) = 1.001$	$(1.001)^{1000} = 2.716923932$
10,000	$\left(1 + \dfrac{1}{10,000}\right) = 1.0001$	$(1.0001)^{10,000} = 2.718145927$
100,000	$\left(1 + \dfrac{1}{100,000}\right) = 1.00001$	$(1.00001)^{100,000} = 2.718268237$
∞		$e = 2.718281828459\ldots$

Logarithm page 647

The inverse of an exponential function is a logarithmic function.

Logarithm page 648

For $b > 0$, and $b \neq 1$, $x = b^y$ if and only if $y = \log_b x$.

Three Basic Properties of Logarithms page 650

For $b > 0$, $b \neq 1$, and $x > 0$

1. $\log_b 1 = 0$

2. $\log_b b = 1$

3. $b^{\log_b x} = x$

Graphs of Logarithmic Functions page 651

Common Logarithms (Base 10 Logarithms) page 652
Using a calculator to find common logarithms page 653

Inverse Logarithms page 653
Using a calculator to find inverse logarithms page 654

Natural Logarithms (Base e Logarithms) page 654
Using a calculator to find natural logarithms page 655
Using a calculator to find inverse natural logarithms page 656

Properties of Logarithms page 664

For $b > 0$, $b \neq 1$, $x,y > 0$ and any real number r:

1. $\log_b 1 = 0$

2. $\log_b b = 1$

3. $x = b^{\log_b x}$

4. Product Rule:

$\log_b xy = \log_b x + \log_b y$

5. Quotient rule:

$\log_b \dfrac{x}{y} = \log_b x - \log_b y$

6. $\log_b x^r = r \cdot \log_b x$

For natural logarithms :

1. $\ln 1 = 0$

2. $\ln e = 1$

3. $x = e^{\ln x}$

4. Product Rule:

$\ln xy = \ln x + \ln y$

5. Quotient rule:

$\ln \dfrac{x}{y} = \ln x - \ln y$

6. $\ln x^r = r \cdot \ln x$

Solving Equations with Exponents and Logarithms   page 669
    Properties of Equations with Exponents and Logarithms   page 670
    For $b > 0, b \neq 1,$

1. If $b^x = b^y$, then $x = y$.

2. If $x = y$, then $b^x = b^y$.

3. If $\log_b x = \log_b y,$ then $x = y$ $(x > 0$ and $y > 0$).

4. If $x = y$, then $\log_b x = \log_b y$ $(x > 0$ and $y > 0$).

Change of Base   page 674
    Change of Base formula: $\log_b x = \dfrac{\log_a x}{\log_a b}$

Applications   page 679
    Exponential growth
    Exponential decay
    Newton's law of cooling
    Earthquakes
    Half-life

Chapter 9 Review

For a review of the topics and problems from Chapter 9, look at the following lessons from *Hawkes Learning Systems: Intermediate Algebra*

Algebra of Functions
Composition of Functions and
    Inverse Functions
Exponential Functions
Logarithmic Functions

Exponential and Logarithmic
    Equations
Applications (Exponential and
    Logarithmic Functions)

Chapter 9 Test

You may use a graphing calculator as an aid for any of the problems on this test. If you are to graph a function, sketch the graph on the test paper and label any points as requested.

1. Given the two functions,

   $$f(x) = \sqrt{x-3} \text{ and } g(x) = x^2 + 1,$$
   find

   a. $(f+g)(x)$ **b.** $(f-g)(x)$,

   c. $(f \cdot g)(x)$,   **d.** $\left(\dfrac{f}{g}\right)(x)$

   e. State the domain of each function in parts (a) – (d).

2. If $f(x) = 2x - 5$ and $g(x) = 3 - 2x^2$, find

   a. $f[g(x)]$ **b.** $g[f(x)]$

3. Determine, algebraically, whether or not each pair of functions are inverses of each other. Graph each pair of functions on the same set of axes and show the line $y = x$ as a dotted line on each graph.

   a. $f(x) = x^2$ and $g(x) = -x^2$

   b. $f(x) = 5x - 3$ and $g(x) = \dfrac{x+3}{5}$

   c. $f(x) = \dfrac{1}{x}$ and $g(x) = \dfrac{1}{x}$

4. Find $f^{-1}(x)$ if $f(x) = \dfrac{1}{x-2}$. Graph both functions.

5. Sketch the graph of $y = 4^x$ and label three points on the graph.

6. Solve each of the following equations for x.
   a. $7^3 \cdot 7^x = 7^{-1}$
   b. $6^{x-1} = 36^{x+1}$

7. A scientist knows that a certain strain of bacteria grows according to the function $y = y_0 \cdot 3^{0.25t}$, where t is a measurement in hours. If she starts a culture with 5000 bacteria, how many will be present after 6 hours?

8. Write the following equations in logarithmic form:
   a. $10^5 = 100,000$ **b.** $\left(\dfrac{1}{2}\right)^{-3} = 8$.

9. Write the following equations in exponential form:
   a. $\ln x = 4$ **b.** $\log_3 \dfrac{1}{9} = -2$.

10. Solve the following equations by first changing them to exponential form.
    a. $\log_7 x = 3$.   **b.** $\log_9 27 = x$.

11. Find the inverse of the function

    $$y = \left(\dfrac{1}{2}\right)^x.$$ Graph both the function and its inverse on the same set of axes. Label three points on each graph and show the line $y = x$ as a dotted line on the graph.

12. Use a calculator to find the value of x.
    a. $x = \log 579$ **b.** $5 \ln x = 9.35$

13. Write each expression as the sum and/or difference of logarithms.

    a. $\ln(x^2 - 25)$ **b.** $\log \sqrt[3]{\dfrac{x^2}{y}}$

14. Write each expression in the form of a single logarithm.
    a. $\ln(x+5) + \ln(x-4)$

    b. $\log \sqrt{x} + \log x^2 - \log 5x$

Solve the equations in Exercises 15 – 19.

15. $10^{x+2} = 283$ **16.** $2e^{0.24x} = 26$ **17.** $4^x = 12$

18. $\log(2x+3) - \log(x+1) = 0$ **19.** $\ln(x^2 + 3x - 4) - \ln(x+4) = 3$

20. If $1000 is invested at 7% compounded continuously, when will the amount be $3800?

21. A substance decomposes according to $A = A_0 e^{-0.0035t}$, where t is measured in years and A_0 is the initial amount.

    a. How long will it take for 800 grams to decompose to 500 grams?
    b. What is the half-life of this substance?

Cumulative Review: Chapters 1 - 9

Perform the indicated operations in Exercises 1 – 4 and simplify the results.

1. $\dfrac{2x^2 + 7x + 3}{x^2 - 3x - 18} \cdot \dfrac{x^2 - x - 30}{2x^2 + 11x + 5}$

2. $\dfrac{9 - x^2}{x^2 + 7x + 6} \div \dfrac{x - 3}{x + 6}$

3. $\dfrac{1}{x - 1} + \dfrac{x - 6}{x^2 + 3x - 4}$

4. $\dfrac{2x}{2x + 3} - \dfrac{7x + 12}{2x^2 + 5x + 3}$

Simplify Exercises 5 and 6. Assume all variables are positive.

5. $\dfrac{x^{\frac{2}{3}} y^{\frac{1}{3}}}{x^{\frac{1}{2}} y^{\frac{2}{3}}}$

6. $\left(x^2 y^{-1} \right)^{\frac{1}{2}} \left(4xy^3 \right)^{-\frac{1}{2}}$

Change each expression in Exercises 7 and 8 to an equivalent exponential expression. Assume variables are positive.

7. $\sqrt{x^4 y^3}$

8. $\sqrt[3]{x^2 y^3}$

9. Use Cramer's Rule to solve the system of linear equations $\begin{cases} 2x - y = -1 \\ x + 2y = 12 \end{cases}$

10. Use the Gaussian elimination method to solve the system of linear equations

$$\begin{cases} x+y+z=2 \\ 2x+y-z=-1 \\ x+3y+2z=2 \end{cases}$$

In Exercises 11 and 12, find the vertex, range, and zeros for the quadratic functions. Graph each function.

11. $y=x^2-6x-2$

12. $y=2x^2+8x+3$

Solve each of the equations in Exercises 13 – 18.

13. $x^2+5x-2=0$

14. $x^4-13x^2+36=0$

15. $x-2=\sqrt{x+10}$

16. $\dfrac{2}{x-2}+\dfrac{3}{x-1}=1$

17. $6^{3x+5}=55$

18. $\ln\left(x^2-7x+10\right)-\ln\left(x-2\right)=2.5$

Find equations for each of the circles indicated in Exercises 19 and 20.

19. Center $\left(0,0\right)$; $r=2\sqrt{3}$

20. Center $\left(1,2\right)$; $r=3$

Solve each of the systems of equations in Exercises 21 – 23. Graph both curves and label the points of intersection.

21. $\begin{cases} x^2+y^2=10 \\ 2x+y=1 \end{cases}$

22. $\begin{cases} 4x^2+y^2=13 \\ x+y=2 \end{cases}$

23. $\begin{cases} 4x^2+y^2=16 \\ y=x^2-4 \end{cases}$

Use the vertical line test to determine whether or not each of the graphs in Exercises 24 – 27 represents a function.

24.   **25.**

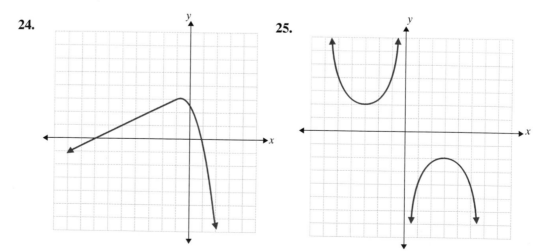

26. **27.**

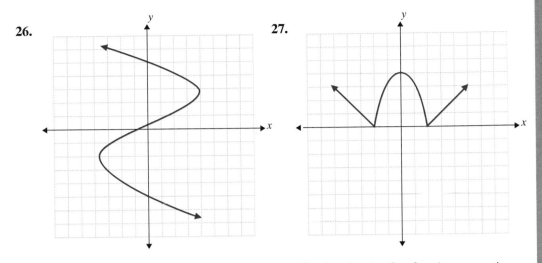

In Exercises 28 and 29, write the function as a set of ordered pairs for the given equation and domain.

28. $y = x^2 - 2x + 5$

$D = \{-2, -1, 0, 1, 2\}$

29. $y = x^3 - 5x^2$

$D = \{-2, -1, 0, 1, 2\}$

Using the following graph of $y = f(x)$, graph the functions in Exercises 30 – 32.

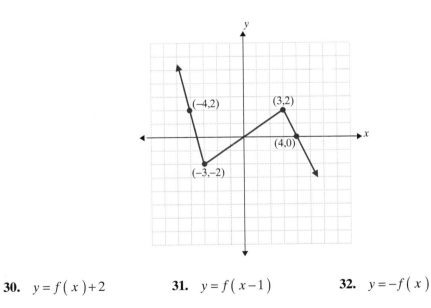

30. $y = f(x) + 2$ **31.** $y = f(x-1)$ **32.** $y = -f(x)$

Which of the functions in Exercises 33 – 36 are 1-1 functions? If a function is 1-1, draw the graph of its inverse.

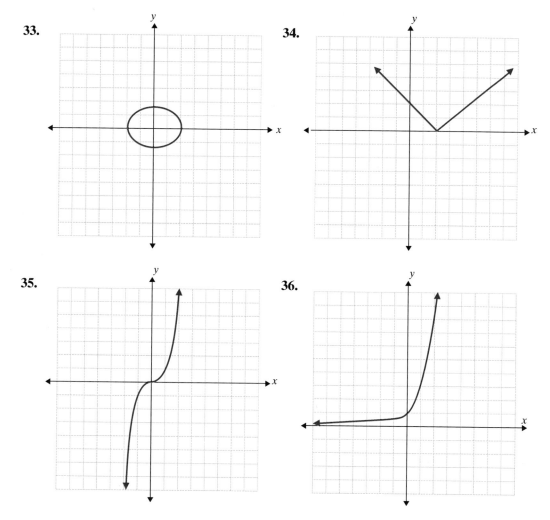

33.

34.

35.

36.

37. Given the two functions, $f(x) = x^2 + x$ and $g(x) = \sqrt{x+2}$, find

    a. $(f+g)(x)$ **b.** $(f-g)(x)$ **c.** $(f \cdot g)(x)$ **d.** $\left(\dfrac{f}{g}\right)(x)$

    e. State the domain of each function in parts (a) – (d).

38. Given the two functions, $f(x) = x^2 + 3$ for $x \geq 0$ and $g(x) = 2x + 1$ for $x \geq 0$, find

    a. $(f+g)(x)$ **b.** $(f-g)(x)$ **c.** $(f \cdot g)(x)$ **d.** $\left(\dfrac{f}{g}\right)(x)$

    e. State the domain of each function in parts (a) – (d).

In Exercises 39 – 42, find the inverse of each function and graph both the function and its inverse on the same set of axes. Include the graph of the line y = x as a dotted line in each graph.

39. $f(x) = 3x + 2$

40. $f(x) = x^2 - 4$ *for* $x \geq 0$

41. $g(x) = (x-2)^3$

42. $g(x) = -\sqrt{x+5}$

43. A book is available in both cloth-bound and paperback. A bookstore sold a total of 43 books during the week. The total receipts were $297.50. If clothbound books sell for $12.50 and paperbacks sell for $4.50, how many of each were sold?

44. Nadine traveled 8 miles upstream and then returned. Her average speed on the return trip was 6 mph faster than her speed upstream. If her total travel time was 2.8 hours, find her rate each way.

45. Find the perimeter of the triangle determined by the points $A(1, 3)$, $B(-2, 2)$, $C(4, 6)$.

46. Show that the triangle determined by the points $A(-3, 1)$, $B(0, -5)$, $C(1, 3)$ is a right triangle.

47. Studies show that the fractional part, P, of light bulbs that have burned out after t hours of use is given by $P = 1 - 2^{-0.03t}$. What fractional part of the light bulbs have burned out after 100 hours of use?

48. If P dollars are invested at a rate, r (expressed as a decimal), and compounded k times a year, the amount, A, due at the end of t years is given by $A = P\left(1 + \dfrac{r}{k}\right)^{kt}$ dollars. Find A if $500 is invested at 10% compounded quarterly for 2 years.

49. Radium decomposes according to $A = A_0 e^{-0.04t}$, where t is measured in centuries and A_0 is the initial amount. Determine the half-life for radium.

50. When friction is used to stop the motion of a wheel, the velocity may be given by $V = V_0 e^{-0.35t}$, where is V_0 the initial velocity and t is the number of seconds the friction has been applied. How long will it take to slow a wheel from 75 ft per sec to 15 ft per sec?

Sequences, Series, and the Binomial Theorem

Did You Know?

One of the outstanding mathematicians of the Middle Ages was Leonardo Fibonacci (Leonardo, son of Bonaccio), also known as Leonardo of Pisa (c. 1175–1250). Fibonacci's name is attached to an interesting sequence of numbers $1, 1, 2, 3, 5, 8, 13, \ldots, x, y, x + y, \ldots$, the so-called Fibonacci sequence, where each term after the first two is obtained by adding the preceding two terms together. The sequence of numbers arises from a problem found in Fibonacci's writings. How many pairs of rabbits can be produced from a single pair in a year if every month each pair begets a new pair that from the second month on becomes productive? The answer to this odd problem is the sum of the first 12 terms of the Fibonacci sequence. Can you verify this?

The Fibonacci sequence itself has been found to have many beautiful and interesting properties. For example, of mathematical interest is the fact that any two successive terms in the sequence are relatively prime; that is, their greatest common divisor is one. In the world of nature, the terms of the Fibonacci sequence also appear. Spirals formed by natural objects such as centers of daisies, pine cone scales, pineapple scales, and leaves generally have two sets of spirals, one clockwise, one counterclockwise. Each set is made up of a specific number of spirals in each direction, the number of spirals being adjacent terms in the Fibonacci sequence. For example, in pine cone

Fibonacci scales, 5 spiral one way and 8 spiral the other; on pineapples, 8 one way and 13 the other.

Leonardo Fibonacci was best known for the texts he wrote in which he introduced the Hindu-Arabic numeral system. He participated in the mathematical tournaments held at the court of the emperor Frederick I, and he used some of the challenge problems in the book he wrote. Fibonacci traveled widely and became acquainted with the different arithmetic systems in use around the Mediterranean. His most famous text, *Liber Abaci* (1202), combined arithmetic and elementary algebra with an emphasis on commercial applied problems. His attempt to reform and improve the study of mathematics in Europe was not too successful; he seemed to be ahead of his time. But his books did much to introduce Hindu-Arabic notation into Europe, and his sequence has provided interesting problems throughout the history of mathematics. In the United States, a Fibonacci Society exists to study the properties of this mysterious and intriguing sequence of numbers.

10.1 Sequences

10.2 Sigma Notation

10.3 Arithmetic Sequences

10.4 Geometric Sequences and Series

10.5 The Binomial Theorem

10.6 Permutations

10.7 Combinations

"There is no branch of mathematics, however abstract, which may not some day be applied to the phenomena of the real world."

Nicolas Ivanovich Lobachevsky
(1793-1856)

$\mathcal{C}$hapter 10 provides an introduction to a powerful notation using the Greek letter Σ, capital sigma. With this Σ-notation and a few basic properties, we will develop some algebraic formulas related to sums of numbers and, in some cases, even infinite sums. The concept of having the sum of an infinite number of numbers equal to some finite number introduces the idea of limits. Consider adding fractions in the following manner:

$$\frac{1}{2} = \frac{1}{2}; \quad \frac{1}{2} + \frac{1}{4} = \frac{3}{4}; \quad \frac{1}{2} + \frac{1}{4} + \frac{1}{8} = \frac{7}{8}; \quad \frac{1}{2} + \frac{1}{4} + \frac{1}{8} + \frac{1}{16} = \frac{15}{16}; \quad \frac{1}{2} + \frac{1}{4} + \frac{1}{8} + \frac{1}{16} + \frac{1}{32} = \frac{31}{32}$$

Continuing to add fractions in this manner, in which the denominators are successive powers of two, will give sums that get closer and closer to 1. We say that the sums "approach" 1, and that 1 is the **limit** of the sum. These fascinating ideas are discussed in Section 10.4 and are fundamental in development of calculus and higher level mathematics.

Other topics in this chapter – permutations, combinations, and the Binomial Theorem – find applications in courses in probability and statistics as well as in more advanced courses in mathematics and computer science.

10.1   Sequences

Objectives

After completing this section, you will be able to:

1. *Write several terms of a sequence given the formula for its general term.*

2. *Find the formula for the general term of a sequence given several terms.*

3. *Determine whether a sequence is increasing, decreasing, or neither.*

In mathematics, a **sequence** is a list of numbers that occur in a certain order. Each number in the sequence is called a **term** of the sequence, and a sequence may have a finite number of terms or an infinite number of terms. For example,

2, 4, 6, 8, 10, 12, 14, 16, 18   is a **finite sequence** consisting of positive even integers less than 20.

3, 6, 9, 12, 15, 18, . . .   is an **infinite sequence** consisting of the multiples of 3.

The infinite sequence of the multiples of 3 can be described in the following way:

For any positive integer n, the corresponding number in the list is $3n$. Thus, we know that

$3 \cdot 6 = 18$ and 18 is the 6th number in the sequence,
$3 \cdot 7 = 21$ and 21 is the 7th number in the sequence,
$3 \cdot 8 = 24$ and 24 is the 8th number in the sequence, and so on.

Infinite Sequence

> An *infinite sequence* (or a *sequence*) is a function that has the positive integers as its domain.

Note: A finite sequence will be so indicated. The term sequence, used alone, indicates an infinite sequence.

Consider the function $f(n) = \dfrac{1}{2^n}$ where n is any positive integer.

For this function,

$$f(1) = \frac{1}{2^1} = \frac{1}{2}$$

$$f(2) = \frac{1}{2^2} = \frac{1}{4}$$

$$f(3) = \frac{1}{2^3} = \frac{1}{8}$$

$$f(4) = \frac{1}{2^4} = \frac{1}{16}$$

$$\vdots$$

$$f(n) = \frac{1}{2^n}$$

$$\vdots$$

Or, using ordered pair notation,

$$f = \left\{ \left(1, \frac{1}{2}\right), \left(2, \frac{1}{4}\right), \left(3, \frac{1}{8}\right), \left(4, \frac{1}{16}\right), \dots, \left(n, \frac{1}{2^n}\right), \dots \right\}.$$

The **terms** of the sequence are the numbers

$$\frac{1}{2}, \frac{1}{4}, \frac{1}{8}, \frac{1}{16}, \dots, \frac{1}{2^n}, \dots$$

Because the order of terms corresponds to the positive integers, it is customary to indicate a sequence by writing only its terms. In general discussions and formulas, a sequence may be indicated with subscript notation as

$$a_1, a_2, a_3, a_4, \dots, a_n, \dots$$

The general term a_n is called the **n^{th} term** of the sequence. The entire sequence can be denoted by writing the nth term in braces as in $\{a_n\}$. Thus,

$$\{a_n\} \quad \text{and} \quad a_1, a_2, a_3, a_4, \ldots, a_n, \ldots$$

are both representations of the sequence with

a_1 as the first term,

a_2 as the second term,

a_3 as the third term,

$$\vdots$$

a_n as the nth term,

$$\vdots$$

Example 1: Sequences ●

a.   Write the first three terms of the sequence $\left\{\dfrac{n}{n+1}\right\}$.

Solution:
$$a_1 = \frac{1}{1+1} = \frac{1}{2}$$

$$a_2 = \frac{2}{2+1} = \frac{2}{3}$$

$$a_3 = \frac{3}{3+1} = \frac{3}{4}$$

b.   If $\{b_n\} = \{2n-1\}$, find $b_1, b_2, b_3,$ and b_{50}.

Solution:
$$b_1 = 2 \cdot 1 - 1 = 1$$

$$b_2 = 2 \cdot 2 - 1 = 3$$

$$b_3 = 2 \cdot 3 - 1 = 5$$

$$b_{50} = 2 \cdot 50 - 1 = 99$$

c.   Determine a_n if the first five terms of $\{a_n\}$ are $0, 3, 8, 15, 24$.

Solution: In this case, study the numbers carefully and make an intelligent guess. That is, keep trying a variety of formulas until you find one that "fits" the given terms. (Questions of this type relating to number patterns are common on intelligence tests.)

The formula is $a_n = n^2 - 1$.

Checking:

$$a_1 = 1^2 - 1 = 0$$

$$a_2 = 2^2 - 1 = 3$$ Although the formula for a_n may not be

$$a_3 = 3^2 - 1 = 8$$ obvious, with practice it becomes easier

$$a_4 = 4^2 - 1 = 15$$ to find.

$$a_5 = 5^2 - 1 = 24$$

An **alternating sequence** is one in which the terms alternate in sign. That is, if one term is positive, then the next term is negative. Alternating sequences generally involve the expression $(-1)^n$. Example 1d illustrates such a sequence.

d. Write the first five terms of the sequence in which $a_n = \dfrac{(-1)^n}{n}$.

Solution: $a_1 = \dfrac{(-1)^1}{1} = -1$

$$a_2 = \dfrac{(-1)^2}{2} = \dfrac{1}{2}$$

$$a_3 = \dfrac{(-1)^3}{3} = -\dfrac{1}{3}$$

$$a_4 = \dfrac{(-1)^4}{4} = \dfrac{1}{4}$$

$$a_5 = \dfrac{(-1)^5}{5} = -\dfrac{1}{5}$$

● ●

As Example 1d illustrates, while the domain of a sequence consists of the positive integers, some (or all) of the terms of a sequence may be negative.

In subscript notation, the term a_{n+1} is the term following a_n, and this term is found by substituting $n + 1$ for n in the formula for the general term. For example,

$$\text{if } a_n = \frac{1}{3n}, \text{ then } a_{n+1} = \frac{1}{3(n+1)} = \frac{1}{3n+3}.$$

Similarly,

$$\text{if } b_n = n^2, \text{ then } b_{n+1} = (n+1)^2.$$

Increasing and Decreasing Sequences

If the terms of a sequence grow increasingly smaller, then the sequence is said to be **decreasing**. If the terms grow successively larger, then the sequence is said to be **increasing**. The following definitions state these ideas algebraically. **Note:** A sequence may be neither decreasing nor increasing.

Decreasing Sequence

A sequence $\{a_n\}$ is

$$\textbf{\textit{decreasing}} \; \textit{if} \; \; a_n > a_{n+1} \; \textit{for all n.}$$

(Successive terms become smaller.)

Increasing Sequence

A sequence $\{a_n\}$ is

$$\textbf{\textit{increasing}} \; \textit{if} \; \; a_n < a_{n+1} \; \textit{for all n.}$$

(Successive terms become larger.)

Example 2: Increasing and Decreasing Sequences

Determine whether each of the following sequences is increasing, decreasing, or neither.

a. $\{a_n\} = \left\{\dfrac{1}{2^n}\right\}$

Solution: Write the formula for terms a_n and a_{n+1} and compare them algebraically.

$$a_n = \frac{1}{2^n} \quad \text{and} \quad a_{n+1} = \frac{1}{2^{n+1}}$$

Note that $2^{n+1} > 2^n$ for all positive integer values of n.

Therefore, $\dfrac{1}{2^n} > \dfrac{1}{2^{n+1}}$. So we have $a_n > a_{n+1}$, and $\{a_n\}$ is **decreasing**.

b. $\{b_n\} = \{n + 3\}$

Solution: $b_n = n + 3$ and $b_{n+1} = (n+1) + 3 = n + 4$

Since $n + 3 < n + 4$, we have $b_n < b_{n+1}$, and $\{b_n\}$ is **increasing**.

c. $\{c_n\} = \{(-1)^n\}$

Solution: The first five terms of the sequence are $-1, 1, -1, 1, -1$. The sequence is alternating and cannot be increasing or decreasing. In general,

$$c_n = (-1)^n \qquad \text{and} \qquad c_{n+1} = (-1)^{n+1}.$$

The value of c_n depends on whether n is even or odd.

If n is even, then $n + 1$ is odd:

$c_n = (-1)^n = 1$ and $c_{n+1} = (-1)^{n+1} = -1$, indicating $c_n > c_{n+1}$.

If n is odd, then $n + 1$ is even:

$c_n = (-1)^n = -1$ and $c_{n+1} = (-1)^{n+1} = 1$, indicating $c_n < c_{n+1}$.

Therefore, the sequence is **neither increasing nor decreasing**.

Practice Problems

Write the first three terms of each sequence.

1. $\{n^2\}$ **2.** $\{2n+1\}$ **3.** $\left\{\dfrac{1}{n+1}\right\}$

4. Find a formula for the general term of sequence $-1, 1, 3, 5, 7, \ldots$

10.1 Exercises

Write the first four terms of each of the sequences in Exercises 1 – 15.

1. $\{2n-1\}$ **2.** $\{4n+1\}$ **3.** $\left\{1+\dfrac{1}{n}\right\}$

4. $\left\{\dfrac{n+3}{n+1}\right\}$ **5.** $\{n^2+n\}$ **6.** $\{n-n^2\}$

7. $\{2^n\}$ **8.** $\left\{\left(\dfrac{1}{2}\right)^n\right\}$ **9.** $\{(-1)^n(n^2+1)\}$

10. $\left\{(-1)^n\left(\dfrac{n}{n+1}\right)\right\}$ **11.** $\left\{(-1)^n\left(\dfrac{1}{2n+3}\right)\right\}$ **12.** $\{(-1)^{n-1}(3^n)\}$

13. $\{2^n-n^2\}$ **14.** $\left\{\dfrac{n(n-1)}{2}\right\}$ **15.** $\left\{\dfrac{1+(-1)^n}{2}\right\}$

Find a formula for the general term of each sequence in Exercises 16 – 23.

16. $2, 5, 8, 11, 14, \ldots$ **17.** $5, 9, 13, 17, 21, \ldots$ **18.** $6, 12, 18, 24, 30, \ldots$

Answers to Practice Problems: **1.** $1, 4, 9$ **2.** $3, 5, 7$ **3.** $\dfrac{1}{2}, \dfrac{1}{3}, \dfrac{1}{4}$ **4.** $a_n = 2n-3$

19. $1, -3, 5, -7, 9, \ldots$ **20.** $-3, 7, -11, 15, -19, \ldots$ **21.** $1, 4, 9, 16, 25, \ldots$

22. $5, 10, 20, 40, 80, \ldots$ **23.** $\dfrac{1}{3}, \dfrac{1}{4}, \dfrac{1}{5}, \dfrac{1}{6}, \dfrac{1}{7}, \ldots$ **24.** $\dfrac{1}{2}, \dfrac{1}{4}, \dfrac{1}{8}, \dfrac{1}{16}, \dfrac{1}{32}, \ldots$

25. $2, 5, 10, 17, 26, \ldots$

For each of the sequences in Exercises 26 – 31, determine whether it is increasing or decreasing. Justify your answer by comparing a_n with a_{n+1}.

26. $\{n+4\}$ **27.** $\{1-2n\}$ **28.** $\left\{\dfrac{1}{n+3}\right\}$

29. $\left\{\dfrac{1}{3^n}\right\}$ **30.** $\left\{\dfrac{2n+1}{n}\right\}$ **31.** $\left\{\dfrac{n}{n+1}\right\}$

Write the finite sequence described by Exercises 32 – 35; then answer the question.

32. A certain automobile costs $29,000 new and depreciates at a rate of $\dfrac{3}{10}$ of its current value each year. What will be its value after 3 years?

33. A ball is dropped from a height of 250 centimeters. Each time it bounces, it rises to $\dfrac{2}{5}$ of its previous height. How high will it rise after the fourth bounce?

34. A culture of bacteria triples everyday. If there were 100 bacteria in the original culture, how many would be present after 4 days?

35. A university is experiencing a declining enrollment of 3% per year. If the present enrollment is 20,000, what is the projected enrollment after 5 years?

Writing and Thinking About Mathematics

36. Use the following formula to generate the first 5 terms of the sequence: $a_{n+2} = a_n + a_{n+1}$ where $a_1 = 1$ and $a_2 = 1$. (This sequence is the famous Fibonacci sequence.) (**Note:** Formulas of this type that use previous answers are said to be **recursive**.)

Hawkes Learning Systems: Intermediate Algebra

Sequences

10.2   Sigma Notation

Objectives

After completing this section, you will be able to:

1. Write sums using Σ-notation.

2. Find the values of sums written in Σ-notation.

Finding the sum of a finite number of terms of a sequence is the same as finding the sum of a finite sequence. Such a sum is called a **partial sum** and can be indicated by using **sigma notation** with the Greek letter capital sigma, Σ. (As we will see in Section 10.4, this notation can be used to indicate the sum of an entire sequence by using the symbol for infinity, ∞.)

Partial Sums Using Sigma Notation

*The **n^{th} partial sum**, S_n, of the first n terms of a sequence $\{a_n\}$ is*

$$S_n = \sum_{k=1}^{n} a_k = a_1 + a_2 + a_3 + \ldots + a_n$$

*k is called the **index of summation**, and k takes the integer values 1, 2, 3, ..., n.*

*n is the **upper limit of summation**, and 1 is the **lower limit of summation**.*

To understand the concept of partial sums, consider the sequence $\left\{\dfrac{1}{n}\right\}$ and the following partial sums:

$$S_1 = a_1 = \frac{1}{1}$$

$$S_2 = a_1 + a_2 = \frac{1}{1} + \frac{1}{2}$$

$$S_3 = a_1 + a_2 + a_3 = \frac{1}{1} + \frac{1}{2} + \frac{1}{3}$$

$$\vdots$$

$$S_n = a_1 + a_2 + a_3 + \ldots + a_n = \frac{1}{1} + \frac{1}{2} + \frac{1}{3} + \ldots + \frac{1}{n}$$

Note: In some cases, the lower limit of summation in sigma notation may be an integer other than 1. Also, letters other than k may be used as the index of summation. The lower case letters i, j, k, l, m, and n are commonly used.

705

For example, the sum of the second through sixth terms of the sequence $\{n^2\}$ can be written in sigma notation as

$$\sum_{i=2}^{6} i^2 = 2^2 + 3^2 + 4^2 + 5^2 + 6^2.$$

If the number of terms is large, then three dots are used to indicate missing terms after a pattern has been established with the first three or four terms. For example,

$$S_{100} = \sum_{k=1}^{100}(k-1) = 0 + 1 + 2 + 3 + \ldots + 99.$$

Example 1: Sigma Notation

Write the indicated sums of the terms and find the value of each sum.

a. $\displaystyle\sum_{k=1}^{4} k^3$

Solution: $\displaystyle\sum_{k=1}^{4} k^3 = 1^3 + 2^3 + 3^3 + 4^3 = 1 + 8 + 27 + 64 = 100$

b. $\displaystyle\sum_{k=5}^{9}(-1)^k k$

Solution: $\displaystyle\sum_{k=5}^{9}(-1)^k k = (-1)^5\,5 + (-1)^6\,6 + (-1)^7\,7 + (-1)^8\,8 + (-1)^9\,9$

$$= -5 + 6 - 7 + 8 - 9 = -7$$

Properties of Σ-Notation

The following properties of Σ-notation are useful in developing systematic methods for finding sums of certain types of finite and infinite sequences.

Properties of Σ-Notation

For sequences $\{a_n\}$ and $\{b_n\}$ and any real number c:

I. $\displaystyle\sum_{k=1}^{n} a_k = \sum_{k=1}^{i} a_k + \sum_{k=i+1}^{n} a_k$ *for any i, $1 \le i \le n-1$*

II. $\displaystyle\sum_{k=1}^{n}(a_k + b_k) = \sum_{k=1}^{n} a_k + \sum_{k=1}^{n} b_k$

III. $\displaystyle\sum_{k=1}^{n} ca_k = c\sum_{k=1}^{n} a_k$

IV. $\displaystyle\sum_{k=1}^{n} c = nc$

These properties follow directly from the associative, commutative, and distributive properties for sums of real numbers.

I. $\displaystyle\sum_{k=1}^{n} a_k = a_1 + a_2 + \ldots + a_i + a_{i+1} + a_{i+2} + \ldots + a_n$

$$= \left(a_1 + a_2 + \ldots + a_i\right) + \left(a_{i+1} + a_{i+2} + \ldots + a_n\right)$$

$$= \sum_{k=1}^{i} a_k + \sum_{k=i+1}^{n} a_k$$

II. $\displaystyle\sum_{k=1}^{n} \left(a_k + b_k\right) = \left(a_1 + b_1\right) + \left(a_2 + b_2\right) + \ldots + \left(a_n + b_n\right)$

$$= \left(a_1 + a_2 + \ldots + a_n\right) + \left(b_1 + b_2 + \ldots + b_n\right)$$

$$= \sum_{k=1}^{n} a_k + \sum_{k=1}^{n} b_k$$

III. $\displaystyle\sum_{k=1}^{n} ca_k = ca_1 + ca_2 + \ldots + ca_n$

$$= c\left(a_1 + a_2 + \ldots + a_n\right)$$

$$= c\sum_{k=1}^{n} a_k$$

IV. $\displaystyle\sum_{k=1}^{n} c = \underbrace{c + c + c + \ldots + c}_{c \text{ appears } n \text{ times}} = nc$

Example 2: Properties of Σ-Notation

a. If $\displaystyle\sum_{k=1}^{7} a_k = 40$ and $\displaystyle\sum_{k=1}^{30} a_k = 75$, find $\displaystyle\sum_{k=8}^{30} a_k$.

Solution: Since $\displaystyle\sum_{k=1}^{7} a_k + \sum_{k=8}^{30} a_k = \sum_{k=1}^{30} a_k$,

then $\displaystyle 40 + \sum_{k=8}^{30} a_k = 75$

$$\sum_{k=8}^{30} a_k = 35$$

continued on next page...

b. If $\displaystyle\sum_{k=1}^{50} 3a_k = 600$, find $\displaystyle\sum_{k=1}^{50} a_k$.

> **Solution:** Since $\displaystyle\sum_{k=1}^{50} 3a_k = 3\sum_{k=1}^{50} a_k$,
>
> then $\displaystyle 3\sum_{k=1}^{50} a_k = 600$
>
> $\displaystyle\sum_{k=1}^{50} a_k = 200$

● ●

Practice Problems

1. Write the indicated sum of the terms and find the value of the sum: $\displaystyle\sum_{k=1}^{4} \left(k^2 - 1\right)$

2. Write the sum $10 + 12 + 14 + 16 + 18$ in Σ-notation.

3. $\displaystyle\sum_{k=1}^{5} a_k = 20$ and $\displaystyle\sum_{k=6}^{10} a_k = 30$. Find $\displaystyle\sum_{k=1}^{10} 2a_k$.

10.2 Exercises

For each of the sequences given in Exercises 1 – 10, write out the partial sums S_1, S_2, S_3, and S_4 and evaluate each partial sum.

1. $\{3k - 1\}$ **2.** $\{2k + 5\}$ **3.** $\left\{\dfrac{k}{k+1}\right\}$ **4.** $\left\{\dfrac{k+1}{k}\right\}$

5. $\left\{(-1)^{k-1} k^2\right\}$ **6.** $\left\{(-1)^k k^3\right\}$ **7.** $\left\{\dfrac{1}{2^k}\right\}$ **8.** $\left\{\left(\dfrac{2}{3}\right)^k\right\}$

9. $\left\{\left(-\dfrac{2}{3}\right)^k\right\}$ **10.** $\left\{k^2 - k\right\}$

Write the sums in Exercises 11 – 26 in expanded form and evaluate.

11. $\displaystyle\sum_{k=1}^{5} 2k$ **12.** $\displaystyle\sum_{k=1}^{11} k(k-1)$ **13.** $\displaystyle\sum_{k=2}^{6} (k+3)$ **14.** $\displaystyle\sum_{k=9}^{11} (2k+1)$

15. $\displaystyle\sum_{k=2}^{4} \dfrac{1}{k}$ **16.** $\displaystyle\sum_{k=1}^{3} \dfrac{1}{2k}$ **17.** $\displaystyle\sum_{k=1}^{3} 2^k$ **18.** $\displaystyle\sum_{k=10}^{15} (-1)^k$

19. $\displaystyle\sum_{k=4}^{8} k^2$ **20.** $\displaystyle\sum_{k=1}^{4} k^3$ **21.** $\displaystyle\sum_{k=3}^{6} (9-2k)$ **22.** $\displaystyle\sum_{k=2}^{7} (4k-1)$

23. $\displaystyle\sum_{k=2}^{5} (-1)^k \left(k^2 + k\right)$ **24.** $\displaystyle\sum_{k=1}^{6} (-1)^k \left(k^2 - 2\right)$

Answers to Practice Problems: 1. $0 + 3 + 8 + 15 = 26$ **2.** $\displaystyle\sum_{k=5}^{9} 2k$ or $\displaystyle\sum_{k=1}^{5} (2k+8)$ **3.** 100

25. $\displaystyle\sum_{k=1}^{5} \frac{k}{k+1}$ **26.** $\displaystyle\sum_{k=3}^{5} (-1)^k \left(\frac{k+1}{k^2} \right)$

Write the sums in Exercises 27 – 35 in sigma notation.

27. $1 + 3 + 5 + 7 + 9$ **28.** $16 + 25 + 36 + 49$

29. $-1 + 1 + (-1) + 1 + (-1)$ **30.** $4 + 7 + 10 + 13 + 16$

31. $\dfrac{1}{8} - \dfrac{1}{27} + \dfrac{1}{64} - \dfrac{1}{125} + \dfrac{1}{216}$ **32.** $\dfrac{1}{8} + \dfrac{1}{16} + \dfrac{1}{32} + \dfrac{1}{64} + \dfrac{1}{128}$

33. $\dfrac{4}{5} + \dfrac{5}{6} + \dfrac{6}{7} + \ldots + \dfrac{15}{16}$ **34.** $8 + 15 + 24 + 35 + 48$

35. $\dfrac{6}{25} + \dfrac{7}{36} + \dfrac{8}{49} + \dfrac{9}{64} + \ldots + \dfrac{13}{144}$

Find the indicated sums in Exercises 36 – 45.

36. $\displaystyle\sum_{k=1}^{14} a_k = 18$ and $\displaystyle\sum_{k=1}^{14} b_k = 21$. Find $\displaystyle\sum_{k=1}^{14} \left(a_k + b_k \right)$.

37. $\displaystyle\sum_{k=1}^{19} a_k = 23$ and $\displaystyle\sum_{k=1}^{19} b_k = 16$. Find $\displaystyle\sum_{k=1}^{19} \left(a_k - b_k \right)$.

38. $\displaystyle\sum_{k=1}^{15} a_k = 19$. Find $\displaystyle\sum_{k=1}^{15} 3a_k$.   **39.** $\displaystyle\sum_{k=1}^{25} a_k = 63$ and $\displaystyle\sum_{k=1}^{11} a_k = 15$. Find $\displaystyle\sum_{k=12}^{25} a_k$.

40. $\displaystyle\sum_{k=1}^{18} a_k = 41$ and $\displaystyle\sum_{k=1}^{18} b_k = 62$. Find $\displaystyle\sum_{k=1}^{18} \left(3a_k - 2b_k \right)$.

41. $\displaystyle\sum_{k=1}^{21} a_k = -68$ and $\displaystyle\sum_{k=1}^{21} b_k = 39$. Find $\displaystyle\sum_{k=1}^{21} \left(a_k + 2b_k \right)$.

42. $\displaystyle\sum_{k=1}^{16} a_k = 56$ and $\displaystyle\sum_{k=17}^{40} a_k = 42$. Find $\displaystyle\sum_{k=1}^{40} a_k$.

43. $\displaystyle\sum_{k=13}^{29} a_k = 84$ and $\displaystyle\sum_{k=1}^{29} a_k = 143$. Find $\displaystyle\sum_{k=1}^{12} 5a_k$.

44. $\displaystyle\sum_{k=1}^{20} b_k = 34$ and $\displaystyle\sum_{k=1}^{20} \left(2a_k + b_k \right) = 144$. Find $\displaystyle\sum_{k=1}^{20} a_k$.

45. $\displaystyle\sum_{k=1}^{27} a_k = 46$ and $\displaystyle\sum_{k=1}^{10} a_k = 122$. Find $\displaystyle\sum_{k=11}^{27} 2a_k$.

Writing and Thinking About Mathematics

46. Use the sum of two Σ notations to represent the following sum:
$-22 + 3 - 24 + 6 - 26 + 9 - 28 + 12 - 30 + 15.$

Hawkes Learning Systems: Intermediate Algebra

 Sigma Notation

10.3 Arithmetic Sequences

Objectives

After completing this section, you will be able to:

1. Determine whether or not a sequence is arithmetic.

2. Find the general term for an arithmetic sequence.

3. Find the sum of the first n terms of an arithmetic sequence.

There are many types of sequences studied in higher levels of mathematics. In the next two sections, we will discuss two types of sequences: **arithmetic sequences** and **geometric sequences**. In this discussion, sigma notation is used, and formulas for finding sums are developed. For arithmetic sequences, we can find sums of only a finite number of terms. For geometric sequences, we can find sums of a finite number of terms and, in some special cases, we define the sum of an infinite number of terms.

Arithmetic Sequences

The sequences

$$3, 5, 7, 9, 11, 13, \ldots$$

$$4, 5, 6, 7, 8, 9, \ldots$$

$$-2, -5, -8, -11, -14, -17, \ldots$$

all have a common characteristic. This characteristic is that **any two consecutive terms in each sequence have the same difference**.

$$3, \ 5, \ 7, \ 9, \ 11, \ 13, \ldots$$
$$2 \ 2 \ \ 2 \ 2 \ \ 2$$
$5 - 3 = 2, 7 - 5 = 2, 9 - 7 = 2,$ and so on

$$4, \ 5, \ 6, \ 7, \ 8, \ 9, \ldots$$
$$1 \ 1 \ \ 1 \ 1 \ \ 1$$
$5 - 4 = 1, 6 - 5 = 1, 7 - 6 = 1,$ and so on

$$-2, \ -5, \ -8, \ -11, \ -14, \ -17, \ldots$$
$$-3 \ \ -3 \ \ -3 \ \ -3 \ \ \ 3$$
$-5 - (-2) = -3, -8 - (-5) = -3,$ and so on

Such sequences are called **arithmetic sequences** or **arithmetic progressions**.

Arithmetic sequences are closely related to linear functions. To see this relationship we can plot the points of an arithmetic sequence and note that the rise from one point to the next is the difference, d, which is the slope of a line passing through all of the points. See Figure 10.1 as an illustration with a positive value for d.

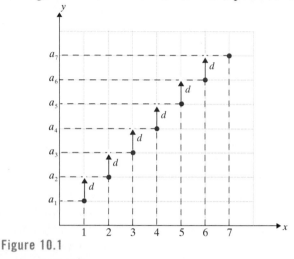

Figure 10.1

Arithmetic Sequence

A sequence $\{a_n\}$ is called an **arithmetic sequence** (or **arithmetic progression**) if for any natural number k,

$$a_{k+1} - a_k = d \qquad \text{where } d \text{ is a constant.}$$

d is called the **common difference**.

Example 1: Arithmetic Sequence

a. Show that the sequence $\{\,2n - 3\,\}$ is arithmetic by finding d.

Solution: $a_k = 2k - 3$ and $a_{k+1} = 2(k+1) - 3 = 2k - 1$

$a_{k+1} - a_k = (2k - 1) - (2k - 3) = 2k - 1 - 2k + 3 = 2$

So, $d = 2$, and the sequence $\{\,2n - 3\,\}$ is arithmetic.

b. Show that the sequence $\{\,n^2\,\}$ is not arithmetic.

Solution: Since $a_3 = 3^2$ and $a_2 = 2^2$ and $a_1 = 1^2$,

$a_3 - a_2 = 9 - 4 = 5$ and $a_2 - a_1 = 4 - 1 = 3$

Therefore, there is no common difference between consecutive terms, and $\{\,n^2\,\}$ is **not arithmetic**.

Note that in Example 1b, we only needed to show that there was **at least one** case in which the difference between two sets of consecutive terms was not the same. However, in Example 1a, showing truth in one case, or even 100 cases, is not enough. We used the general case to show truth in **every** case.

If the first term is a_1 and the common difference is d, then the arithmetic sequence can be indicated as follows:

$$a_1 = a_1 \qquad\qquad \text{first term}$$
$$a_2 = a_1 + d \qquad\qquad \text{second term}$$
$$a_3 = a_2 + d = a_1 + 2d \qquad\qquad \text{third term}$$
$$a_4 = a_3 + d = a_1 + 3d \qquad\qquad \text{fourth term}$$
$$\vdots \qquad\qquad\qquad \vdots$$
$$a_n = a_{n-1} + d = a_1 + (n-1)d \qquad\qquad n^{\text{th}} \text{ term}$$

The nth term of an Arithmetic Sequence

If $\{a_n\}$ is an arithmetic sequence, then the nth term has the form

$$a_n = a_1 + (n-1)d$$

where d is the common difference between the terms.

Example 2: The nth Term

a. If in an arithmetic sequence, $a_1 = 5$ and $d = 3$, find a_{16}.

Solution: To find the 16th term, let $n = 16$ in the formula $a_n = a_1 + (n-1)d$:

$$a_{16} = a_1 + 15d = 5 + 15 \cdot 3 = 50$$

b. Find the 20th term of the arithmetic sequence whose first three terms are –2, 8, and 18.

Solution: In this case, $a_1 = -2$ and $a_2 = 8$.

Since the sequence is arithmetic, $d = a_2 - a_1 = 8 - (-2) = 10$.

To find the 20th term, let $n = 20$ in the formula $a_n = a_1 + (n-1)d$:

$$a_{20} = -2 + (20-1)10 = -2 + 190 = 188$$

continued on next page...

c. Find a_1 and d for the arithmetic sequence in which $a_3 = 6$ and $a_{21} = -48$.

> **Solution:** Using the formula $a_n = a_1 + (n-1)d$ and solving simultaneous equations, we have

$$
\begin{array}{rcl}
-48 = a_1 + 20d \qquad & -48 & = \quad a_1 \quad + \quad 20d \\
6 = a_1 + 2d \qquad & -6 & = \quad -a_1 \quad - \quad 2d \\
\hline
& -54 & = \qquad\qquad\quad 18d \\
& -3 & = \qquad\qquad\quad d
\end{array}
$$

Then

$$
\begin{array}{rcl}
6 & = & a_1 \quad + \quad 2(-3) \\
12 & = & a_1
\end{array}
$$

So, $a_1 = 12$ and $d = -3$.

● ●

Partial Sums of Arithmetic Sequences

Consider the problem of finding the sum $S = \sum_{k=1}^{6}(4k-1)$. We can, of course, write all the terms and then add them:

$$
S = \sum_{k=1}^{6}(4k-1) = 3+7+11+15+19+23 = 78
$$

However, to understand how the general formula is developed, we first write the sum and then write the sum again with the terms in reverse order. Adding vertically gives the same sum six times:

$$
\begin{array}{rcccccccccccc}
S & = & 3 & + & 7 & + & 11 & + & 15 & + & 19 & + & 23 \\
S & = & 23 & + & 19 & + & 15 & + & 11 & + & 7 & + & 3 \\
\hline
2S & = & 26 & + & 26 & + & 26 & + & 26 & + & 26 & + & 26 \\
2S & = & 6 & \cdot & 26 \\
S & = & 78
\end{array}
$$

Using this same procedure with general terms in the subscript notation, we can develop the formula for the sum of any finite arithmetic sequence. Suppose that the n terms are

$$
a_1, \quad a_2 = a_1 + d, \quad a_3 = a_1 + 2d, \quad \ldots, \quad a_{n-1} = a_n - d, a_n.
$$

Thus, writing the terms in both ascending order and descending order and adding vertically, we have

$$S = \quad a_1 + (a_1 + d) + (a_1 + 2d) + \dots + (a_n - 2d) + (a_n - d) + \quad a_n$$
$$S = \quad a_n + (a_n - d) + (a_n - 2d) + \dots + (a_1 + 2d) + (a_1 + d) + \quad a_1$$
$$2S = (a_1 + a_n) + (a_1 + a_n) + (a_1 + a_n) + \dots + (a_1 + a_n) + (a_1 + a_n) + (a_1 + a_n)$$

$$\underbrace{}$$
$(a_1 + a_n)$ appears n times

$$2S = n(a_1 + a_n)$$
$$S = \frac{n}{2}(a_1 + a_n)$$

Partial Sums of Arithmetic Sequences

*The nth **partial sum**, S_n, of the first n terms of an arithmetic sequence $\{a_n\}$ is*

$$S_n = \sum_{k=1}^{n} a_k = \frac{n}{2}(a_1 + a_n)$$

A special case of an arithmetic sequence is $\{n\}$ and the corresponding sum of the first n terms:

$$\sum_{k=1}^{n} k = 1 + 2 + 3 + \dots + n$$

In this case, n = the number of terms, $a_1 = 1$, and $a_n = n$, so

$$\sum_{k=1}^{n} k = \frac{n}{2}(1 + n)$$

Gauss

German mathematician Carl Friedrich Gauss (1777 – 1855) understood and applied this sum at the age of 7 in order to solve an arithmetic problem given to him and his classmates as "busy" work. Gauss probably observed the following pattern when told to find the sum of the whole numbers from 1 to 100:

$$1 + 2 + 3 + \quad . \quad . \quad . \quad + 98 + 99 + 100$$
$$101$$
$$101$$
$$101$$

He saw that 101 was a sum 50 times. Thus, to find the sum he simply multiplied $101 \cdot 50 = 5050$. Not bad for a 7-year old.

Example 3: The Sum of a Finite Arithmetic Sequence ● ● ● ● ● ● ● ● ● ● ● ● ●

First show that the corresponding sequence is an arithmetic sequence by finding $a_{k+1} - a_k = d$. Then find the indicated sum using the formula.

a. $\displaystyle\sum_{k=1}^{75} k = 1 + 2 + 3 + \ldots + 75$

Solution: This is an example of the special case just discussed where the sequence is $\{\,k\,\}$, and the upper limit of summation is $n = 75$.

$$\sum_{k=1}^{75} k = \frac{75}{2}(1 + 75)$$

$$= \frac{75}{2}(76)$$

$$= 2850$$

b. $\displaystyle\sum_{k=1}^{50} 3k = 3 + 6 + 9 + \ldots + 150$

Solution: $a_k = 3k$ and $a_{k+1} = 3(k+1) = 3k + 3$

$$a_{k+1} - a_k = (3k + 3) - 3k = 3 = d$$

So, $\{\,3k\,\}$ is an arithmetic sequence.

$$\sum_{k=1}^{50} 3k = \frac{50}{2}(3 + 150)$$

Here $n = 50$, $a_1 = 3$, and $a_{50} = 150$.

$$= 25(153)$$

$$= 3825$$

Also, Property III of Section 10.2 can be used to find the sum.

$$\sum_{k=1}^{50} 3k = 3\sum_{k=1}^{50} k$$

Property III of Section 10.2

$$= 3 \cdot \frac{50}{2}(1 + 50)$$

Here $n = 50$, $a_1 = 1$, and $a_{50} = 50$.

$$= 3 \cdot 25 \cdot 51$$

$$= 3825$$

c. $\displaystyle\sum_{k=1}^{70}(-2k + 5) = 3 + 1 + (-1) + (-3) + \ldots + (-135)$

Solution: $a_k = -2k + 5$ and $a_{k+1} = -2(k+1) + 5 = -2k + 3$,

$$a_{k+1} - a_k = (-2k + 3) - (-2k + 5) = 3 - 5 = -2 = d$$

So, $\{-2k+5\}$ is an arithmetic sequence.

$$\sum_{k=1}^{70}(-2k+5) = \frac{70}{2}[3+(-135)] \qquad \text{Here } n = 70,\ a_1 = 3,\ a_{70} = -135.$$

$$= 35(-132)$$

$$= -4620$$

Also, Properties II, III, and IV of Section 10.2 and the sum of a finite arithmetic sequence from this section can be used to find the sum.

$$\sum_{k=1}^{70}(-2k+5) = \sum_{k=1}^{70}-2k + \sum_{k=1}^{70}5 \qquad \text{Property II}$$

$$= -2\sum_{k=1}^{70}k + \sum_{k=1}^{70}5 \qquad \text{Property III}$$

$$= -2 \cdot \frac{70}{2}(1+70) + 70 \cdot 5 \qquad \text{Property IV and the sum of a Finite}$$

$$= -2 \cdot 35 \cdot 71 + 350 \qquad \qquad \text{Arithmetic Sequence}$$

$$= -4970 + 350$$

$$= -4620$$

Example 4: Arithmetic Sequence Application

Suppose that you are offered two jobs by the same company. The first job has a starting salary of $25,000, with a "guaranteed" raise of $2000 per year. The second job starts at $30,000 with a "guaranteed" raise of $1200 per year.

a. What would be your salary on the 10th year of each of these jobs?
b. If you were to stay 10 years with the company, which job would pay the most in total salary?

Solution:

Since the salary would increase the same amount each year, the yearly salaries form arithmetic sequences and we can use the corresponding formulas for a_{10} and S_{10}.

a. First job: $a_{10} = a_1 + (10-1)d = 25,000 + 9(2000) = \$43,000$
Second job: $a_{10} = a_1 + (10-1)d = 30,000 + 9(1200) = \$40,800$

You would be making a higher salary on the first job at the end of 10 years.

b. First job: $= 5(25,000 + 43,000) = \$340,000$
Second job: $= 5(30,000 + 40,800) = \$354,000$

At least for 10 years, the second job would pay more in total salary.

Practice Problems

1. *Show that the sequence { 3n + 5 } is arithmetic by finding d.*

2. *Find the 40th term of the arithmetic sequence with 1, 6, and 11 as its first three terms.*

3. *Find $\displaystyle\sum_{k=1}^{50}(3k+5)$.*

10.3 Exercises

Determine which of the sequences in Exercises 1 – 10 are arithmetic. Find the common difference and the nth term for each arithmetic sequence.

1. $2, 5, 8, 11, ...$ **2.** $-3, 1, 5, 9, ...$ **3.** $7, 5, 3, 1, ...$ **4.** $5, 6, 7, 8, ...$

5. $1, 2, 3, 5, 8, ...$ **6.** $2, 4, 8, 16, ...$ **7.** $6, 2, -2, -6, ...$ **8.** $4, -1, -6, -11, ...$

9. $0, \dfrac{1}{2}, 1, \dfrac{3}{2}, ...$ **10.** $2, \dfrac{7}{3}, \dfrac{8}{3}, 3, ...$

In Exercise 11 – 20, write the first five terms of the sequence and determine which of the sequences are arithmetic.

11. $\{2n-1\}$ **12.** $\{4-n\}$ **13.** $\{(-1)^n(3n-2)\}$ **14.** $\left\{n+\dfrac{n}{2}\right\}$

15. $\{5-6n\}$ **16.** $\left\{\dfrac{1}{n+1}\right\}$ **17.** $\left\{7-\dfrac{n}{3}\right\}$ **18.** $\{(-1)^{n+1}(2n+1)\}$

19. $\left\{\dfrac{1}{2n}\right\}$ **20.** $\left\{\dfrac{2}{3}n-\dfrac{7}{3}\right\}$

Find the general term, a_n, for each of the arithmetic sequences in Exercises 21 – 30.

21. $a_1=1,\ d=\dfrac{2}{3}$ **22.** $a_1=9,\ d=-\dfrac{1}{3}$ **23.** $a_1=7,\ d=-2$ **24.** $a_1=-3,\ d=\dfrac{4}{5}$

25. $a_1=10,\ a_3=13$ **26.** $a_1=6,\ a_5=4$ **27.** $a_{10}=13,\ a_{12}=3$ **28.** $a_5=7,\ a_9=19$

29. $a_{13}=60,\ a_{23}=75$ **30.** $a_{11}=54,\ a_{29}=180$

In Exercises 31 – 38, $\{a_n\}$ is an arithmetic sequence.

31. $a_1=8,\ a_{11}=168$. Find a_{15}.   **32.** $a_1=17,\ a_9=-55$. Find a_{20}.

Answers to Practice Problems: 1. $d=3$ **2.** $a_{40}=196$ **3.** 4075

33. $a_6 = 8, a_4 = 2$. Find a_{18}.

34. $a_{16} = 12, a_7 = 30$. Find a_9.

35. $a_{13} = 34, d = 2, a_n = 22$. Find n.

36. $a_4 = 20, d = 3, a_n = 44$. Find n.

37. $a_{10} = 41, d = 4, a_n = 77$. Find n.

38. $a_3 = 15, d = -\dfrac{3}{2}, a_n = 6$. Find n.

Find the indicated sums in Exercises 39 – 54 by using the formula for arithmetic sequences.

39. $-2 + 0 + 2 + 4 + \ldots + 24$

40. $3 + 6 + 9 + \ldots + 33$

41. $1 + 6 + 11 + 16 + \ldots + 46$

42. $5 + 9 + 13 + 17 + \ldots + 49$

43. $\displaystyle\sum_{k=1}^{9} (3k - 1)$

44. $\displaystyle\sum_{k=1}^{12} (4 - 5k)$

45. $\displaystyle\sum_{k=1}^{11} (4k - 3)$

46. $\displaystyle\sum_{k=1}^{10} (2k + 7)$

47. $\displaystyle\sum_{k=1}^{13} \left(\frac{2k}{3} - 1\right)$

48. $\displaystyle\sum_{k=1}^{28} (8k - 5)$

49. $\displaystyle\sum_{k=7}^{15} \left(k + \frac{k}{3}\right)$

50. $\displaystyle\sum_{k=8}^{21} \left(9 - \frac{k}{3}\right)$

51. If $\displaystyle\sum_{k=1}^{33} a_k = -12$, find $\displaystyle\sum_{k=1}^{33} (5a_k + 7)$.

52. If $\displaystyle\sum_{k=1}^{15} a_k = 60$, find $\displaystyle\sum_{k=1}^{15} (-2a_k - 5)$.

53. If $\displaystyle\sum_{k=1}^{100} (-3a_k + 4) = 700$, find $\displaystyle\sum_{k=1}^{100} a_k$.

54. If $\displaystyle\sum_{k=1}^{50} (2b_k - 5) = 32$, find $\displaystyle\sum_{k=1}^{50} b_k$.

55. On a certain project, a construction company was penalized for taking more than the contractual time to finish the project. The company forfeited $75 the first day, $90 the second day, $105 the third day, and so on. How many additional days were needed if the total penalty was $1215?

56. It is estimated that a certain piece of property, now valued at $48,000, will appreciate as follows: $1400 the first year, $1450 the second year, $1500 the third year, and so on. On this basis, what will be the value of the property after 10 years?

57. The rungs of a ladder decrease uniformly in length from 84 cm to 46 cm. What is the total length of the wood in the rungs if there are 25 of them?

58. How many blocks are there in a pile if there are 19 in the first layer, 17 in the second layer, 15 in the third layer, and so on, with only 1 block on the top layer?

Writing and Thinking About Mathematics

59. Explain why an alternating sequence (one in which the terms alternate being positive and negative) cannot be an arithmetic sequence.

Hawkes Learning Systems: Intermediate Algebra

Arithmetic Sequences

10.4 Geometric Sequences and Series

Objectives

After completing this section, you will be able to:

1. Determine whether or not a sequence is geometric.

2. Find the general term for a geometric sequence.

3. Find the specified terms of geometric sequences.

4. Find the sum of the first n terms of a geometric sequence.

5. Find the sum of an infinite geometric series.

Geometric Sequences

Arithmetic sequences are characterized by having the property that any two consecutive terms have the same difference. **Geometric sequences** are characterized by having the property that **any two consecutive terms are in the same ratio**. That is, if consecutive terms are divided, the ratio will be the same regardless of which two consecutive terms are divided. Consider the three sequences

$$\frac{1}{2}, \frac{1}{4}, \frac{1}{8}, \frac{1}{16}, \frac{1}{32}, \ldots$$

$$3, 9, 27, 81, 243, \ldots$$

$$-9, 3, -1, \frac{1}{3}, -\frac{1}{9}, \ldots$$

As the following patterns show, each of these sequences has a **common ratio** when consecutive terms are divided.

$$\frac{1}{2}, \ \frac{1}{4}, \ \frac{1}{8}, \ \frac{1}{16}, \ \frac{1}{32}, \ \ldots \qquad\qquad \frac{\frac{1}{4}}{\frac{1}{2}} = \frac{1}{2}, \frac{\frac{1}{8}}{\frac{1}{4}} = \frac{1}{2}, \frac{\frac{1}{16}}{\frac{1}{8}} = \frac{1}{2}, \text{ and so on}$$

$$\underbrace{\quad}_{\frac{1}{2}} \underbrace{\quad}_{\frac{1}{2}} \underbrace{\quad}_{\frac{1}{2}} \underbrace{\quad}_{\frac{1}{2}}$$

$$3, \ 9, \ 27, \ 81, \ 243, \ldots \qquad\qquad \frac{9}{3} = 3, \frac{27}{9} = 3, \frac{81}{27} = 3, \text{ and so on}$$

$$\underbrace{\quad}_{3} \underbrace{\quad}_{3} \underbrace{\quad}_{3} \underbrace{\quad}_{3}$$

$$-9, 3, -1, \frac{1}{3}, -\frac{1}{9}, \ldots$$

$$\underbrace{}_{-\frac{1}{3}} \underbrace{}_{-\frac{1}{3}} \underbrace{\phantom{-1 \quad \frac{1}{3}}}_{-\frac{1}{3}} \underbrace{\phantom{\frac{1}{3} \quad -\frac{1}{9}}}_{-\frac{1}{3}}$$

$$\frac{3}{-9} = -\frac{1}{3}, \frac{-1}{3} = -\frac{1}{3}, \frac{\frac{1}{3}}{-1} = -\frac{1}{3}, \text{ and so on.}$$

Therefore, these sequences are geometric sequences or geometric progressions.

Geometric Sequence

*A sequence $\{a_n\}$ is called a **geometric sequence** (or **geometric progression**) if for any positive integer k,*

$$\frac{a_{k+1}}{a_k} = r \qquad \text{where } r \text{ is constant, and } r \neq 0.$$

*r is called a **common ratio**.*

Example 1: Geometric Sequence

a. Show that the sequence $\left\{ \dfrac{1}{2^n} \right\}$ is geometric by finding r.

Solution: $a_k = \dfrac{1}{2^k}$ and $a_{k+1} = \dfrac{1}{2^{k+1}}$

$$\frac{a_{k+1}}{a_k} = \frac{\frac{1}{2^{k+1}}}{\frac{1}{2^k}} = \frac{1}{2^k \cdot 2} \cdot \frac{2^k}{1} = \frac{1}{2} = r \qquad \text{Note that } 2^{k+1} = 2^k \cdot 2^1.$$

b. Show that the sequence $\{n^2\}$ is not geometric.

Solution: We want to show that different pairs of consecutive terms have different ratios. For this sequence, $a_3 = 3^2, a_2 = 2^2$, and $a_1 = 1^2$.

So,

$$\frac{a_3}{a_2} = \frac{3^2}{2^2} = \frac{9}{4} \quad \text{and} \quad \frac{a_2}{a_1} = \frac{2^2}{1^2} = 4.$$

Since $\dfrac{9}{4} \neq 4$, there is no common ratio between consecutive terms, and $\{n^2\}$ is **not geometric**.

If the first term is a_1 and the common ratio is r, then the geometric sequence can be indicated as follows:

$$a_1 = a_1 \quad \rightarrow \quad a_1 \qquad\qquad \text{first term}$$

$$\frac{a_2}{a_1} = r \quad \rightarrow \quad a_2 = a_1 r \qquad\qquad \text{second term}$$

$$\frac{a_3}{a_2} = r \quad \rightarrow \quad a_3 = a_2 r = (a_1 r)r = a_1 r^2 \qquad \text{third term}$$

$$\frac{a_4}{a_3} = r \quad \rightarrow \quad a_4 = a_3 r = (a_1 r^2)r = a_1 r^3 \qquad \text{fourth term}$$

$$\vdots \qquad \vdots \qquad\qquad\qquad\qquad \vdots$$

$$\frac{a_n}{a_{n-1}} = r \quad \rightarrow \quad a_n = a_{n-1} \cdot r = (a_1 r^{n-2})r = a_1 r^{n-1} \quad n^{\text{th}} \text{ term}$$

$$\vdots \qquad \vdots \qquad\qquad\qquad\qquad \vdots$$

The nth Term of a Geometric Sequence

If $\{a_n\}$ is a geometric sequence, then the nth term has the form

$$a_n = a_1 r^{n-1}$$

where r is the common ratio.

Example 2: The nth Term of a Geometric Sequence

a. If in a geometric sequence, $a_1 = 4$ and $r = -\dfrac{1}{2}$, find a_8.

Solution: $a_8 = a_1 r^7 = 4\left(-\dfrac{1}{2}\right)^7 = 2^2\left(-\dfrac{1}{2^7}\right) = -\dfrac{1}{2^5} = -\dfrac{1}{32}$

b. Find the seventh term of the following geometric sequence: $3, \dfrac{3}{2}, \dfrac{3}{4}, \ldots$

Solution: Find r using the formula $r = \dfrac{a_{k+1}}{a_k}$ with $a_1 = 3$ and $a_2 = \dfrac{3}{2}$.

$$r = \frac{a_2}{a_1} = \frac{\frac{3}{2}}{3} = \frac{3}{2} \cdot \frac{1}{3} = \frac{1}{2}$$

Now, the seventh term is $a_7 = a_1 r^{7-1} = 3\left(\dfrac{1}{2}\right)^6 = \dfrac{3}{64}$

continued on next page...

c. Find a_1 and r for the geometric sequence in which $a_5 = 2$ and $a_7 = 4$.

Solution: Using the formula $a_n = a_1 r^{n-1}$, we get

$$2 = a_1 r^4 \text{ and } 4 = a_1 r^6.$$

Now, dividing gives

$$\frac{a_1 r^6}{a_1 r^4} = \frac{4}{2}$$

$$r^2 = 2$$

$$r = \pm\sqrt{2}$$

Using these values for r and the fact that $a_5 = 2$, we can find a_1.

For $r = \sqrt{2}$:

$$2 = a_1\left(\sqrt{2}\right)^4$$
$$2 = a_1 \cdot 4$$
$$\frac{1}{2} = a_1$$

For $r = -\sqrt{2}$:

$$2 = a_1\left(-\sqrt{2}\right)^4$$
$$2 = a_1 \cdot 4$$
$$\frac{1}{2} = a_1$$

There are two geometric sequences with $a_5 = 2$ and $a_7 = 4$. In both cases, $a_1 = \frac{1}{2}$. The two possibilities are

$$a_1 = \frac{1}{2} \text{ and } r = \sqrt{2}$$

or $\qquad a_1 = \frac{1}{2} \text{ and } r = -\sqrt{2}.$

The Sum of the Terms of a Geometric Sequence

The following discussion illustrates the method for finding the formula for the sum of the first n terms of a geometric sequence.

To find $S = \sum_{k=1}^{6} \frac{1}{3^k}$, we can write all the terms and then add them.

$$S = \sum_{k=1}^{6} \frac{1}{3^k} = \frac{1}{3} + \frac{1}{3^2} + \frac{1}{3^3} + \frac{1}{3^4} + \frac{1}{3^5} + \frac{1}{3^6}$$

$$= \frac{3^5 + 3^4 + 3^3 + 3^2 + 3 + 1}{3^6} = \frac{364}{729}$$

Or, we can first indicate the sum by writing the terms in order. Then indicate $\frac{1}{3}$ of the sum and multiply each term by $\frac{1}{3}$ (the common ratio). Writing these two sums in a vertical format and subtracting gives the following results.

$$S = \frac{1}{3} + \frac{1}{3^2} + \frac{1}{3^3} + \frac{1}{3^4} + \frac{1}{3^5} + \frac{1}{3^6}$$

$$\frac{1}{3}S = \qquad \frac{1}{3^2} + \frac{1}{3^3} + \frac{1}{3^4} + \frac{1}{3^5} + \frac{1}{3^6} + \frac{1}{3^7}$$

$$S - \frac{1}{3}S = \frac{1}{3} - 0 - 0 - 0 - 0 - 0 - \frac{1}{3^7}$$

$$\left(1 - \frac{1}{3}\right)S = \frac{1}{3} - \frac{1}{3^7} \qquad\qquad \text{Factor out the } S.$$

$$S = \frac{\frac{1}{3} - \frac{1}{3^7}}{1 - \frac{1}{3}} = \frac{\frac{1}{3} - \left(\frac{1}{3}\right)^7}{1 - \frac{1}{3}}$$

This procedure is certainly not necessary when only a few terms are to be added. However, it does illustrate the general method for finding a formula for the sum of the first n terms of any geometric sequence.

Suppose that the n terms are

$$a_1, a_2 = a_1 r, a_3 = a_1 r^2, \dots, a_{n-1} = a_1 r^{n-2}, a_n = a_1 r^{n-1}$$

Thus, the sum can be written

$$S = a_1 + a_1 r + a_1 r^2 + \dots + a_1 r^{n-2} + a_1 r^{n-1}$$

$$rS = a_1 r + a_1 r^2 + a_1 r^3 + \dots + a_1 r^{n-1} + a_1 r^n \qquad \text{Multiply each term by } r.$$

$$S - rS = a_1 - a_1 r^n \qquad\qquad \text{Subtract.}$$

$$(1 - r)S = a_1\left(1 - r^n\right) \qquad\qquad \text{Factor.}$$

$$S = \frac{a_1\left(1 - r^n\right)}{1 - r} \qquad\qquad \text{Simplify.}$$

Partial Sums of Geometric Sequences

The **nth partial sum** S_n of the first n terms of a geometric sequence $\{a_n\}$ is

$$S_n = \sum_{k=1}^{n} a_k = \frac{a_1\left(1 - r^n\right)}{1 - r} \quad \text{where } r \neq 1.$$

Example 3: Partial Sums of Geometric Sequences ● ● ● ● ● ● ● ● ● ● ● ● ● ● ●

First show that the corresponding sequence is a geometric sequence by finding $\dfrac{a_{k+1}}{a_k} = r$.

Then find the indicated sum by using the formula $\displaystyle\sum_{k=1}^{n} a_k = \dfrac{a_1(1-r^n)}{1-r}$.

a. $\displaystyle\sum_{k=1}^{10} \dfrac{1}{2^k}$

Solution: Represent both a_k and a_{k+1} and find the ratio of these two terms.

$$a_k = \dfrac{1}{2^k} \text{ and } a_{k+1} = \dfrac{1}{2^{k+1}}$$

$$\dfrac{a_{k+1}}{a_k} = \dfrac{\dfrac{1}{2^{k+1}}}{\dfrac{1}{2^k}} = \dfrac{1}{2^{k+1}} \cdot \dfrac{2^k}{1} = \dfrac{1}{2 \cdot 2^{k}} \cdot \dfrac{2^{k}}{1} = \dfrac{1}{2} = r$$

So, $\left\{\dfrac{1}{2^n}\right\}$ is a geometric sequence and

$$\sum_{k=1}^{10} \dfrac{1}{2^k} = \dfrac{\dfrac{1}{2}\left(1-\left(\dfrac{1}{2}\right)^{10}\right)}{1-\dfrac{1}{2}} = \dfrac{\dfrac{1}{2}\left(1-\dfrac{1}{1024}\right)}{\dfrac{1}{2}} = \dfrac{1023}{1024}.$$

b. $\displaystyle\sum_{k=1}^{5} (-1)^k \cdot 3^{\frac{k}{2}}$

Solution: Represent both a_k and a_{k+1} and find the ratio of these two terms.

$$\dfrac{a_{k+1}}{a_k} = \dfrac{(-1)^{k+1} \cdot 3^{(k+1)/2}}{(-1)^k \cdot 3^{k/2}} = \dfrac{(-1)^{k} (-1) \cdot 3^{k/2} \cdot 3^{1/2}}{(-1)^{k} \cdot 3^{k/2}}$$

$$= (-1) \cdot 3^{1/2} = -\sqrt{3} = r$$

So, $\left\{(-1^k) \cdot 3^{k/2}\right\}$ is a geometric sequence.

$$\sum_{k=1}^{5} (-1)^k \cdot 3^{k/2} = \dfrac{(-1) \cdot 3^{1/2} \cdot \left(1-\left(-\sqrt{3}\right)^5\right)}{1-\left(-\sqrt{3}\right)} = \dfrac{-\sqrt{3}\left(1+9\sqrt{3}\right)}{1+\sqrt{3}}$$

c. The parents of a small child decide to deposit $1000 annually at the first of each year for 20 years for their child's education. If interest is compounded annually at 8%, what will be the value of the deposits after 20 years? (This type of investment is called an **annuity**.)

Solution: The formula for interest compounded annually is $A = P(1+r)^t$ where A is the amount in the account, r is the annual interest rate (in decimal form), and t is the time (in years).

The first deposit of $1000 will earn interest for 20 years:

$$A_{20} = 1000(1+0.08)^{20} = 1000(1.08)^{20}$$

The second deposit will earn interest for 19 years:

$$A_{19} = 1000(1.08)^{19}$$

$$\vdots$$

The last deposit will earn interest for only one year:

$$A_1 = 1000(1.08)^1$$

The accumulated value of all deposits (plus interest) is the sum of the 20 terms of a geometric sequence:

Value at the end of twenty years:

$$= A_1 + A_2 + \cdots + A_{20} = \sum_{k=1}^{20} 1000(1.08)^k$$

$$= 1000(1.08)^1 + 1000(1.08)^2 + \cdots + 1000(1.08)^{20}$$

$$= \frac{1000(1.08)\left[1-(1.08)^{20}\right]}{1-1.08} \qquad \text{where } a_1 = 1000(1.08) \text{ and } r = 1.08$$

$$= \frac{1080[1-4.660957]}{-0.08}$$

$$= 49,423 \qquad\qquad \text{Rounded to the nearest dollar}$$

Thus, the accumulated value of the annuity is $49,423.

Geometric Series

The indicated sum of all the terms (an infinite number of terms) of a sequence is called a **series**. A thorough study of series is a part of calculus. In this text, we will be concerned only with special cases of geometric series. In the following definition, the symbol ∞ (read "infinity") is used to indicate that the number of terms is unbounded. The symbol ∞ does not represent a number.

Infinite Series

*The indicated sum of all terms of a sequence is called an **infinite series** (or a **series**). For a sequence $\{a_n\}$, the corresponding series can be written as follows:*

$$\sum_{k=1}^{\infty}(a_k) = a_1 + a_2 + a_3 + \ldots + a_n + \ldots$$

For geometric sequences in the case where $|r| < 1$, it can be shown, in higher level mathematics, that r^n approaches 0 as n approaches infinity. This does not mean that r^n is ever equal to 0, only that it gets closer and closer to 0 as n becomes larger and larger. In symbols, we write

$$r^n \to 0 \quad \text{as} \quad n \to \infty.$$

Thus, we have the following result if $|r| < 1$:

$$S_n = \frac{a_1(1-r^n)}{1-r} \quad \to \quad \frac{a_1(1-0)}{1-r} = \frac{a_1}{1-r} \qquad \text{as } n \to \infty.$$

Theorem

If $\{a_n\}$ is a geometric sequence and $|r| < 1$, then sum of the infinite series is

$$S = \sum_{k=1}^{\infty}(a_k) = a_1 + a_1r + a_1r^2 + \ldots = \frac{a_1}{1-r}.$$

Example 4: Infinite Geometric Series ●

Find the sum of each of the following geometric series.

a. $\displaystyle\sum_{k=1}^{\infty}\left(\frac{2}{3}\right)^{k-1} = \left(\frac{2}{3}\right)^0 + \left(\frac{2}{3}\right)^1 + \left(\frac{2}{3}\right)^2 + \left(\frac{2}{3}\right)^3 + \ldots$

$$= 1 + \frac{2}{3} + \frac{4}{9} + \frac{8}{27} + \ldots$$

Solution: Here, $a_1 = 1$ and $r = \dfrac{2}{3}$. Substitution in the formula yields

$$S = \frac{1}{1 - \dfrac{2}{3}} = \frac{1}{\dfrac{1}{3}} = 3.$$

b. $0.3333\ldots = 0.\overline{3}$ Recall that the bar over the 3 indicates a repeating pattern of digits in the decimal.

Solution: $0.33333\ldots = 0.3 + 0.03 + 0.003 + 0.0003 + 0.00003 + \ldots$

This format shows that the decimal number can be interpreted as a geometric series with $a_1 = 0.3 = \dfrac{3}{10}$ and $r = 0.1 = \dfrac{1}{10}$.

Applying the formula gives

$$S = \frac{\dfrac{3}{10}}{1 - \dfrac{1}{10}} = \frac{\dfrac{3}{10}}{\dfrac{9}{10}} = \frac{3}{10} \cdot \frac{10}{9} = \frac{1}{3}.$$

In this way, an infinite repeating decimal can be converted to fraction form:

$$0.33333\ldots = \frac{1}{3}$$

c. $0.99999\ldots = 0.\overline{9}$

Solution: As shown in Example 4b, we can interpret the decimal number

$$0.99999\ldots = 0.9 + 0.09 + 0.009 + 0.0009 + \ldots$$

as a geometric series with $a_1 = 0.9 = \dfrac{9}{10}$ and $r = 0.1 = \dfrac{1}{10}$.

Applying the formula gives

$$S = \frac{\dfrac{9}{10}}{1 - \dfrac{1}{10}} = \frac{\dfrac{9}{10}}{\dfrac{9}{10}} = \frac{9}{10} \cdot \frac{10}{9} = 1.$$

This very interesting result shows that the infinite decimal notation 0.99999... is just another way of writing 1.

In fact, we can prove the results of the following pattern:

$$0.11111\ldots = \frac{1}{9}$$

$$0.22222\ldots - \frac{2}{9}$$

$$\vdots$$

$$0.99999\ldots = \frac{9}{9} = 1$$

continued on next page ...

d. $5 - 1 + \dfrac{1}{5} - \dfrac{1}{25} + \dfrac{1}{125} - \dfrac{1}{625} + \dots$

Solution: Here, $a_1 = 5$ and $r = -\dfrac{1}{5}$. A geometric series that alternates in sign will

always have a negative value for r. Substitution in the formula gives

$$S = \frac{5}{1 - \left(-\dfrac{1}{5}\right)} = \frac{5}{1 + \dfrac{1}{5}} = \frac{5}{\dfrac{6}{5}} = \frac{5}{1} \cdot \frac{5}{6} = \frac{25}{6}.$$

Practice Problems

1. Show that the sequence $\left\{\dfrac{(-1)^n}{3^n}\right\}$ is geometric by finding r.

2. If in a geometric series, $a_1 = 0.1$ and $r = 2$, find a_6.

3. Find the sum $\displaystyle\sum_{k=1}^{5} \dfrac{1}{2^k}$.

4. Represent the decimal $0.\overline{4}$ as a series using Σ-notation.

5. Find the sum of the series in Problem 4.

10.4 Exercises

Which of the sequences in Exercises 1 – 10 are geometric? Find the common ratio for each of the geometric sequences and write a formula for the nth term.

1. $2, 4, 6, 8, \dots$

2. $\dfrac{1}{12}, \dfrac{1}{6}, \dfrac{1}{3}, \dfrac{2}{3}, \dots$

3. $3, -\dfrac{3}{2}, \dfrac{3}{4}, -\dfrac{3}{8}, \dots$

4. $5, 9, 13, 17, \dots$

5. $\dfrac{32}{27}, \dfrac{4}{9}, \dfrac{1}{6}, \dfrac{1}{16}, \dots$

6. $18, 12, 8, \dfrac{16}{3}, \dots$

7. $\dfrac{14}{3}, \dfrac{2}{3}, \dfrac{2}{15}, \dfrac{2}{45}, \dots$

8. $1, -\dfrac{2}{3}, \dfrac{4}{9}, -\dfrac{8}{27}, \dots$

9. $48, -12, 3, -\dfrac{3}{4}, \dots$

10. $4, -8, 12, -16, \dots$

In Exercises 11 – 20 write the first four terms of the sequence and determine which of the sequences are geometric?

11. $\left\{(-3)^{n+1}\right\}$

12. $\left\{3\left(\dfrac{2}{5}\right)^n\right\}$

13. $\left\{\dfrac{2}{3}n\right\}$

14. $\left\{(-1)^{n+1}\left(\dfrac{2}{7}\right)^n\right\}$

Answers to Practice Problems: **1.** $r = -\dfrac{1}{3}$ **2.** $a_6 = 3.2$ **3.** $\dfrac{31}{32}$ **4.** $\displaystyle\sum_{k=1}^{\infty} \dfrac{4}{10^k}$ **5.** $\dfrac{4}{9}$

15. $\left\{2\left(-\dfrac{4}{5}\right)^n\right\}$ **16.** $\left\{1+\dfrac{1}{2^n}\right\}$ **17.** $\left\{3(2)^{n/2}\right\}$ **18.** $\left\{\dfrac{n^2+1}{n}\right\}$

19. $\left\{(-1)^{n-1}(0.3)^n\right\}$ **20.** $\left\{6(10)^{1-n}\right\}$

Find the general term a_n for each of the geometric sequences in Exercises 21 – 30.

21. $a_1 = 3, r = 2$ **22.** $a_1 = -2, r = \dfrac{1}{5}$ **23.** $a_1 = \dfrac{1}{3}, r = -\dfrac{1}{2}$

24. $a_1 = 5, r = \sqrt{2}$ **25.** $a_3 = 2, a_5 = 4, r > 0$ **26.** $a_4 = 19, a_5 = 57$

27. $a_2 = 1, a_4 = 9$ **28.** $a_2 - 5, a_5 = \dfrac{5}{8}$ **29.** $a_3 = -\dfrac{45}{16}, r = -\dfrac{3}{4}$

30. $a_4 = 54, r = 3$

In Exercises 31 – 38, $\{a_n\}$ is a geometric sequence.

31. $a_1 = -32, \ a_6 = 1$. Find a_8.   **32.** $a_1 = 20, \ a_6 = \dfrac{5}{8}$. Find a_7.

33. $a_1 = 18, \ a_7 = \dfrac{128}{81}$. Find a_5.   **34.** $a_1 = -3, \ a_5 = -48$. Find a_7.

35. $a_3 = \dfrac{1}{2}, \ a_7 = \dfrac{1}{32}$. Find a_4.   **36.** $a_5 = 48, \ a_8 = -384$. Find a_9.

37. $a_1 = -2, \ r = \dfrac{2}{3}, \ a_n = -\dfrac{16}{27}$. Find n.   **38.** $a_1 = \dfrac{1}{9}, \ r = \dfrac{3}{2}, \ a_n = \dfrac{27}{32}$. Find n.

In Exercises 39 – 56, find the indicated sums.

39. $3 + 9 + 27 + \ldots + 243$ **40.** $-2 + 4 - 8 + 16$ **41.** $8 + 4 + 2 + \ldots + \dfrac{1}{64}$

42. $3 + 12 + 48 + \ldots + 3072$ **43.** $\displaystyle\sum_{k=1}^{3} -3\left(\dfrac{3}{4}\right)^k$ **44.** $\displaystyle\sum_{k=1}^{6} \left(\dfrac{-5}{3}\right)\left(\dfrac{1}{2}\right)^k$

45. $\displaystyle\sum_{k=1}^{5} \left(\dfrac{2}{3}\right)^k$ **46.** $\displaystyle\sum_{k=1}^{6} \left(\dfrac{1}{3}\right)^k$ **47.** $\displaystyle\sum_{k=4}^{7} 5\left(\dfrac{1}{2}\right)^k$

48. $\displaystyle\sum_{k=3}^{6} -7\left(\dfrac{3}{2}\right)^k$ **49.** $\displaystyle\sum_{k=1}^{\infty} \left(\dfrac{3}{4}\right)^{k-1}$ **50.** $\displaystyle\sum_{k=1}^{\infty} \left(\dfrac{5}{8}\right)^{k-1}$

51. $\displaystyle\sum_{k=1}^{\infty} \left(-\dfrac{1}{2}\right)^k$ **52.** $\displaystyle\sum_{k=1}^{\infty} \left(-\dfrac{2}{5}\right)^k$ **53.** $0.\overline{2}$

54. $0.\overline{6}$ **55.** $0.\overline{36}$ **56.** $0.\overline{81}$

57. Sue deposits $800 annually at the first of each year for 10 years. If the interest is compounded annually at 9%, what will be the value of the deposit at the end of 10 years?

58. If $1200 is deposited annually at the first of each year for 8 years, what will be the value of the deposit if the interest is compounded annually at 10%?

59. An automobile that costs $8500 new depreciates at a rate of 20% of its value each year. What is its value after 3 years?

60. The radiator of a car contains 20 liters of water. Five liters are drained off and replaced by antifreeze. Then 5 liters of the mixture are drained off and replaced by antifreeze, and so on. This process is continued until six drain-offs and replacements have been made. How much antifreeze is in the final mixture?

61. A substance decays at a rate of $\dfrac{2}{5}$ of its weight per day. How much of the substance will be present after 4 days if initially there are 500 grams?

62. A ball rebounds to a height that is $\dfrac{3}{4}$ of its original height. How high will it rise after the fourth bounce if it is dropped from a height of 24 meters?

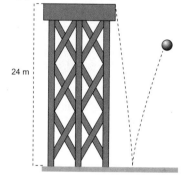

24 m

Writing and Thinking About Mathematics

63. Graph the first 8 partial sums of each geometric series as points to show how the sum of the series approaches a certain value. Show this value as a horizontal line in the graph.

  a. $\displaystyle\sum_{k=1}^{\infty}\left(\frac{1}{2}\right)^{k-1}$

  b. $\displaystyle\sum_{k=1}^{\infty}\frac{(-1)^{k+1}}{3^{k}}$

64. Consider the infinite series $4\cdot\displaystyle\sum_{k=1}^{\infty}\frac{(-1)^{k-1}}{2k-1}$. Write out several (at least 10 to 15) of the partial sums and their values until you can tell what number the partial sums "seem" to be approaching. What is this number?

65. Explain why there is no formula for finding the sum of an infinite geometric series when $|r| > 1$.

Hawkes Learning Systems: Intermediate Algebra

Geometric Sequences and Series

10.5   The Binomial Theorem

After completing this section, you will be able to:

1. Calculate factorials.

2. Expand binomials using the Binomial Theorem.

3. Find specified terms in binomial expressions.

Factorials

The objective in this section is to develop a formula stated as the **Binomial Theorem** (and sometimes called **binomial expansion**) that will allow you to write products such as

$$(a+b)^3, \quad (x+y)^7, \quad \text{and} \quad (x+5)^8$$

without having to multiply the binomial factors. For example, instead of multiplying three factors as follows,

$$
\begin{aligned}
(a+b)^3 &= (a+b)(a+b)(a+b) \\
&= (a^2 + 2ab + b^2)(a+b) \\
&= a^3 + 2a^2 b + ab^2 + a^2 b + 2ab^2 + b^3 \\
&= a^3 + 3a^2 b + 3ab^2 + b^3
\end{aligned}
$$

knowledge of the Binomial Theorem will allow you to go directly to the final polynomial.

Before discussing the theorem itself, we need to understand the concept of **factorial**. For example, 6! (read "six factorial") represents the product of the positive integers from 6 to 1. Thus,

$$6! = 6 \cdot 5 \cdot 4 \cdot 3 \cdot 2 \cdot 1 = 720.$$

Also,

$$10! = 10 \cdot 9 \cdot 8 \cdot 7 \cdot 6 \cdot 5 \cdot 4 \cdot 3 \cdot 2 \cdot 1 = 3,628,800.$$

n Factorial (*n*!)

For any positive integer n,

$$n! = n(n-1)(n-2)...3 \cdot 2 \cdot 1$$

n! is read as "n factorial."

To evaluate an expression such as

$$\frac{7!}{6!}$$

do **not** evaluate each factorial. Instead, write the factorials as products and reduce the fraction.

$$\frac{7!}{6!} = \frac{7 \cdot \cancel{6} \cdot \cancel{5} \cdot \cancel{4} \cdot \cancel{3} \cdot \cancel{2} \cdot \cancel{1}}{\cancel{6} \cdot \cancel{5} \cdot \cancel{4} \cdot \cancel{3} \cdot \cancel{2} \cdot \cancel{1}} = 7$$

Note that $n! = (n)(n-1)(n-2)...(3)(2)(1)$

and $(n-1)! = (n-1)(n-2)(n-3)...(3)(2)(1).$

So $n! = n(n-1)!$

In particular, $\dfrac{7!}{6!} = \dfrac{7 \cdot (6!)}{6!} = 7.$

Also, for work with formulas involving factorials, zero factorial is **defined** to be 1.

0 Factorial

$$0! = 1$$

Using a Calculator

Factorials can be calculated with the TI-83 calculator by pressing the **MATH** *key and going to the menu under* **PRB**. *The fourth item in the list is the factorial symbol,* !. *For example, 6! can be calculated as follows:*

1. *Enter 6.*
2. *Press the* **MATH** *key.*
3. *Go to the* **PRB** *heading and press 4.* (6! *will appear on the display.*)
4. *Press* **ENTER** *and* 720 *will appear on the display.*

Example 1: Factorials •

Simplify the following expressions.

a. $\dfrac{11!}{8!}$

Solution: $\dfrac{11!}{8!} = \dfrac{11 \cdot 10 \cdot 9 \cdot (8 \cdot 7 \cdot 6 \cdot 5 \cdot 4 \cdot 3 \cdot 2 \cdot 1)}{(8 \cdot 7 \cdot 6 \cdot 5 \cdot 4 \cdot 3 \cdot 2 \cdot 1)} = 990$

or $\dfrac{11!}{8!} = \dfrac{11 \cdot 10 \cdot 9 \cdot 8!}{8!} = 990$

b. $\dfrac{n!}{(n-2)!}$

Solution: $\dfrac{n!}{(n-2)!} = \dfrac{n(n-1)(n-2)!}{(n-2)!} = n(n-1)$

c. $\dfrac{30!}{28!2!}$

Solution: $\dfrac{30!}{28!2!} = \dfrac{\overset{15}{\cancel{30}} \cdot 29 \cdot \cancel{28!}}{\cancel{28!} \cdot \cancel{2} \cdot 1} = 15 \cdot 29 = 435$

• •

The expression in Example 1c can be written in the following notation.

$$\binom{30}{2} = \dfrac{30!}{28!2!} \quad \text{and} \quad \binom{30}{28} = \dfrac{30!}{28!2!}$$

Binomial Coefficient $\binom{n}{r}$

For non-negative integers n and r, with $0 \leq r \leq n$, we define

$$\binom{n}{r} = \dfrac{n!}{(n-r)!\,r!}$$

Because this quantity appears repeatedly in the Binomial Theorem, $\binom{n}{r}$ *is often called a*

Binomial Coefficient. *It is read "the combination of n things taken r at a time."*

To get a formula for $\begin{pmatrix} n \\ n-r \end{pmatrix}$, we apply the formula for $\begin{pmatrix} n \\ r \end{pmatrix}$ and replace r with $n - r$. Thus,

$$\begin{pmatrix} n \\ n-r \end{pmatrix} = \frac{n!}{(n-(n-r))!(n-r)!} = \frac{n!}{(n-n+r)!(n-r)!}$$

$$= \frac{n!}{r!(n-r)!} = \begin{pmatrix} n \\ r \end{pmatrix}$$

Thus,

$$\begin{pmatrix} n \\ n-r \end{pmatrix} = \begin{pmatrix} n \\ r \end{pmatrix}$$

Example 2: $\begin{pmatrix} n \\ r \end{pmatrix}$ ●

Evaluate the following.

a. $\begin{pmatrix} 8 \\ 2 \end{pmatrix}$ and $\begin{pmatrix} 8 \\ 6 \end{pmatrix}$

Solution: $\begin{pmatrix} 8 \\ 2 \end{pmatrix} = \frac{8!}{2!6!} = \frac{\overset{4}{\cancel{8}} \cdot 7 \cdot \cancel{6!}}{\cancel{2} \cdot \cancel{6!}} = 28$ $\begin{pmatrix} 8 \\ 6 \end{pmatrix} = \frac{8!}{6!2!} = \frac{\overset{4}{\cancel{8}} \cdot 7 \cdot \cancel{6!}}{\cancel{6!} \cdot \cancel{2}} = 28$

b. $\begin{pmatrix} 17 \\ 0 \end{pmatrix}$

Solution: $\begin{pmatrix} 17 \\ 0 \end{pmatrix} = \frac{17!}{0!17!} = \frac{1}{1} = 1$

● ●

Using a Calculator

Other notations for $\begin{pmatrix} n \\ r \end{pmatrix}$ *are,* $_nC_r$, C_r^n *and* $C(n, r)$. *In particular, the notation* $_nC_r$ *is found in the TI-83 calculator. The "C" in these notations stands for "combination" for reasons which will be discussed in Section 10.7. Expressions of the form* $\begin{pmatrix} n \\ r \end{pmatrix}$ *can be calculated with the TI-83 by pressing the* **MATH** *key and going to the menu under* **PRB***. The third item in the list is the symbol* $_nC_r$ *read "the combination of n things taken r at a time." For example,* $\begin{pmatrix} 8 \\ 2 \end{pmatrix}$ *can be calculated as follows:*

1. Enter 8.

2. Press the **MATH** *key.*

3. Go to the **PRB** *heading and press 3. (* $8 _nC_r$ *will appear on the display.)*

4. Enter 2.

5. Press **ENTER** *and* **28** *will appear on the display.*

The Binomial Theorem

The expansions of the binomial $a + b$ from $(a+b)^0$ to $(a+b)^5$ are shown here.

$$(a+b)^0 = 1$$
$$(a+b)^1 = a+b$$
$$(a+b)^2 = a^2 + 2ab + b^2$$
$$(a+b)^3 = a^3 + 3a^2b + 3ab^2 + b^3$$
$$(a+b)^4 = a^4 + 4a^3b + 6a^2b^2 + 4ab^3 + b^4$$
$$(a+b)^5 = a^5 + 5a^4b + 10a^3b^2 + 10a^2b^3 + 5ab^4 + b^5$$

Three patterns are evident.

1. In each case, the **powers of a decrease by 1** in each term, and the **powers of b increase by 1** in each term.
2. In each term, the sum of the exponents is equal to the exponent on $(a + b)$.
3. A pattern, called Pascal's Triangle, is formed from the coefficients.

Pascal's Triangle

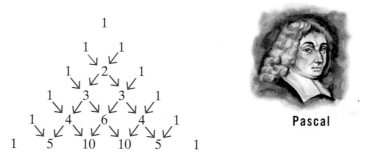

Pascal

In each case, the first and last coefficients are 1, and the other coefficients are the sum of the two numbers above to the left and above to the right of that coefficient. Thus, for $(a+b)^6$, we can construct another row of the triangle as follows:

$$
\begin{array}{ccccccccccccc}
 & 1 & & 5 & & 10 & & 10 & & 5 & & 1 & \\
1 & & 6 & & 15 & & 20 & & 15 & & 6 & & 1
\end{array}
$$

and

$$(a+b)^6 = a^6 + 6a^5b + 15a^4b^2 + 20a^3b^3 + 15a^2b^4 + 6ab^5 + b^6.$$

Note that the coefficients can be written in factorial notation as follows:

$$\binom{6}{0} = \frac{6!}{0!6!} = 1 \qquad \binom{6}{1} = \frac{6!}{1!5!} = 6 \qquad \binom{6}{2} = \frac{6!}{2!4!} = 15 \qquad \binom{6}{3} = \frac{6!}{3!3!} = 20$$

$$\binom{6}{4} = \frac{6!}{4!2!} = 15 \qquad \binom{6}{5} = \frac{6!}{5!1!} = 6 \qquad \binom{6}{6} = \frac{6!}{6!0!} = 1$$

So, the expansion can be written in the following form:

$$(a+b)^6 = \binom{6}{0}a^6 + \binom{6}{1}a^5 b + \binom{6}{2}a^4 b^2 + \binom{6}{3}a^3 b^3 + \binom{6}{4}a^2 b^4 + \binom{6}{5}ab^5 + \binom{6}{6}b^6.$$

This last form is the form used in the statement of the Binomial Theorem, stated here without proof.

The Binomial Theorem

$$(a+b)^n = \binom{n}{0}a^n + \binom{n}{1}a^{n-1}b + \binom{n}{2}a^{n-2}b^2 + \ldots + \binom{n}{k}a^{n-k}b^k + \ldots + \binom{n}{n}b^n$$

In Σ–notation,

$$(a+b)^n = \sum_{k=0}^{n} \binom{n}{k}a^{n-k}b^k$$

NOTES

1. There are $n + 1$ terms in $(a+b)^n$.

2. In each term of $(a+b)^n$, the sum of the exponents of a and b is n.

Example 3: The Binomial Theorem

a. Expand $(x+3)^5$ by using the Binomial Theorem.

Solution: $(x+3)^5 = \sum_{k=0}^{5} \binom{5}{k}x^{5-k}3^k$

$$= \binom{5}{0}x^5 + \binom{5}{1}x^4 \cdot 3 + \binom{5}{2}x^3 \cdot 3^2 + \binom{5}{3}x^2 \cdot 3^3 + \binom{5}{4}x \cdot 3^4 + \binom{5}{5}3^5$$

$$= 1 \cdot x^5 + 5 \cdot x^4 \cdot 3 + 10 \cdot x^3 \cdot 9 + 10 \cdot x^2 \cdot 27 + 5 \cdot x \cdot 81 + 1 \cdot 243$$

$$= x^5 + 15x^4 + 90x^3 + 270x^2 + 405x + 243$$

continued on next page...

b. Expand $\left(y^2 - 1 \right)^6$ by using the Binomial Theorem.

Solution: $\left(y^2 - 1 \right)^6 = \displaystyle\sum_{k=0}^{6} \binom{6}{k} \left(y^2 \right)^{6-k} \left(-1 \right)^k$

$$= \binom{6}{0}\left(y^2 \right)^6 + \binom{6}{1}\left(y^2 \right)^5 \left(-1 \right)^1 + \binom{6}{2}\left(y^2 \right)^4 \left(-1 \right)^2$$

$$+ \binom{6}{3}\left(y^2 \right)^3 \left(-1 \right)^3 + \binom{6}{4}\left(y^2 \right)^2 \left(-1 \right)^4$$

$$+ \binom{6}{5}\left(y^2 \right)^1 \left(-1 \right)^5 + \binom{6}{6}\left(-1 \right)^6$$

$$= 1 \cdot y^{12} + 6 \cdot y^{10} \left(-1 \right) + 15 \cdot y^8 \left(+1 \right) + 20 \cdot y^6 \left(-1 \right)$$

$$+ 15 \cdot y^4 \left(+1 \right) + 6 \cdot y^2 \left(-1 \right) + 1 \left(+1 \right)$$

$$= y^{12} - 6y^{10} + 15y^8 - 20y^6 + 15y^4 - 6y^2 + 1$$

c. Find the sixth term of the expansion of $\left(2x - \dfrac{1}{3} \right)^{10}$.

Solution: Since $\left(2x - \dfrac{1}{3} \right)^{10} = \displaystyle\sum_{k=0}^{10} \binom{10}{k} \left(2x \right)^{10-k} \left(-\dfrac{1}{3} \right)^k$, and the sum begins with

$k = 0$, the sixth term will occur when $k = 5$.

$$\binom{10}{5}\left(2x \right)^{10-5} \left(-\frac{1}{3} \right)^5 = \frac{10!}{5!5!}\left(2x \right)^5 \left(-\frac{1}{3} \right)^5$$

$$= \overset{28}{\cancel{252}} \cdot 32x^5 \left(-\frac{1}{\underset{27}{\cancel{243}}} \right) = \frac{-896x^5}{27}$$

The sixth term is $\dfrac{-896x^5}{27}$.

d. Find the fourth term of the expansion of $\left(x + \dfrac{1}{2}y \right)^8$.

Solution: $\left(x + \dfrac{1}{2}y \right)^8 = \displaystyle\sum_{k=0}^{8} \binom{8}{k} x^{8-k} \left(\dfrac{1}{2}y \right)^k$

The fourth term occurs when $k = 3$.

$$\binom{8}{3} x^{8-3} \left(\frac{1}{2}y \right)^3 = \frac{8!}{3!5!} \cdot x^5 \cdot \frac{1}{8}y^3 = 7x^5 y^3$$

The fourth term is $7x^5 y^3$.

e.   Using the binomial expansion, approximate $(0.99)^4$ to the nearest thousandth.

Solution: $(0.99)^4 = (1-0.01)^4 = \sum_{k=0}^{4}\binom{4}{k}(1)^{4-k}(-0.01)^k$

$$= \binom{4}{0}\cdot 1^4 + \binom{4}{1}\cdot 1^3 \cdot(-0.01) + \binom{4}{2}\cdot 1^2 \cdot(-0.01)^2 + \binom{4}{3}\cdot 1 \cdot(-0.01)^3$$

$$+\binom{4}{4}\cdot(-0.01)^4$$

$$= 1 + 4(-0.01) + 6(-0.01)^2 + 4(-0.01)^3 + 1(-0.01)^4$$

$$= 1 - 0.04 + 0.0006 - 0.000004 + (\text{ small term })$$

$$\approx 0.9606$$

$$\approx 0.961 \qquad\qquad (\text{ to the nearest thousandth })$$

● ●

Practice Problems

1. Simplify $\dfrac{10!}{7!}$.

2. Evaluate $\dbinom{20}{2}$.

3. Expand $(x+2)^4$ by using the Binomial Theorem.

4. Find the third term of the expansion of $(2x-1)^7$.

10.5 Exercises

Simplify the expressions in Exercises 1 – 16.

1. $\dfrac{8!}{6!}$

2. $\dfrac{11!}{7!}$

3. $\dfrac{3!8!}{10!}$

4. $\dfrac{5!7!}{8!}$

5. $\dfrac{5!4!}{6!}$

6. $\dfrac{7!4!}{10!}$

7. $\dfrac{n!}{n}$

8. $\dfrac{n!}{(n-3)!}$

9. $\dfrac{(k+3)!}{k!}$

10. $\dfrac{n(n+1)!}{(n+2)!}$

11. $\dbinom{6}{3}$

12. $\dbinom{5}{4}$

13. $\dbinom{7}{3}$

14. $\dbinom{8}{5}$

15. $\dbinom{10}{0}$

16. $\dbinom{6}{2}$

Answers to Practice Problems: **1.** 720 **2.** 190   **3.** $x^4 + 8x^3 + 24x^2 + 32x + 16$ **4.** $672x^5$

Write the first four terms of the expansions in Exercises 17 – 28.

17. $(x+y)^7$ **18.** $(x+y)^{11}$ **19.** $(x+1)^9$ **20.** $(x+1)^{12}$

21. $(x+3)^5$ **22.** $(x-2)^6$ **23.** $(x+2y)^6$ **24.** $(x+3y)^5$

25. $(3x-y)^7$ **26.** $(2x-y)^{10}$ **27.** $(x^2-4y)^9$ **28.** $(x^2-2y)^7$

Using the Binomial Theorem, expand the expressions in Exercises 29 – 40.

29. $(x+y)^6$ **30.** $(x+y)^8$ **31.** $(x-1)^7$ **32.** $(x-1)^9$

33. $(3x+y)^5$ **34.** $(2x+y)^6$ **35.** $(x+2y)^4$ **36.** $(x+3y)^5$

37. $(3x-2y)^4$ **38.** $(5x+2y)^3$ **39.** $(3x^2-y)^5$ **40.** $(x^2+2y)^4$

Find the specified term in each of the expressions in Exercises 41 – 46.

41. $(x-2y)^{10}$, fifth term **42.** $(x+3y)^{12}$, third term

43. $(2x+3)^{11}$, fourth term **44.** $\left(x-\dfrac{y}{2}\right)^9$, seventh term

45. $(5x^2-y^2)^{12}$, tenth term **46.** $(2x^2+y^2)^{15}$, eleventh term

Approximate the value of each expression in Exercises 47 – 53 correct to the nearest thousandth.

47. $(1.01)^6$ **48.** $(0.96)^8$ **49.** $(0.97)^7$ **50.** $(1.02)^{10}$

51. $(2.3)^5$ **52.** $(2.8)^6$ **53.** $(0.98)^8$

Writing and Thinking About Mathematics

54. Factor the polynomial: $x^4 + 8x^3 + 24x^2 + 32x + 16$.

Hawkes Learning Systems: Intermediate Algebra

The Binomial Theorem

| 10.6 | # Permutations |

Objectives

After completing this section, you will be able to:

1. *Evaluate expressions representing permutations.*
2. *Solve applied problems involving permutations.*
3. *Solve applied problems involving the Fundamental Principle of Counting.*

The Fundamental Principle of Counting

Many problems in statistics require a systematic approach to counting the number of ways several decisions can be made in succession (or several events can occur in succession). For example, if a seven-person board of education must elect a president and a vice-president from its own membership, how many ways can this be done? The reasoning is as follows:

The presidency can be filled by any one of 7.
After the president is elected, the vice-presidency can be filled by any one of 6.
The number of ways these two decisions can be made in succession is $7 \cdot 6 = 42$.

The procedure for counting the number of independent successive decisions (or events) is based on the **Fundamental Principle of Counting.**

The Fundamental Principle of Counting

If an event E_1 can occur in m_1 ways, an event E_2 can occur in m_2 ways, ..., and an event E_k can occur in m_k ways, then the total number of ways that all events may occur is the product $m_1 \cdot m_2 \cdot \ldots \cdot m_k$.

Example 1: Fundamental Principle of Counting

A home contractor offers two basic house plans, each with two possible arrangements for the garage, four color combinations, and three types of landscaping. How many "different" homes can the contractor build?

continued on next page...

743

Solution: The Fundamental Principle of Counting is used with each of the options considered as a decision or event.

$$2 \cdot 2 \cdot 4 \cdot 3 = 48$$

↑   ↑   ↑   ↑

plans garages colors landscaping

He can build 48 "different" homes.

● ●

Permutations

A concept closely related to the Fundamental Principle of Counting is that of counting the number of ways that elements can be arranged (ordered). Each ordering of a set of elements is called a **permutation.**

Permutation

*A **permutation** is an arrangement (or ordering) of the elements of a set.*

In how many ways can the four letters a, b, c, and d be arranged? That is, how many permutations are there for the four letters a, b, c, and d? All the permutations are listed here.

abcd	bacd	cabd	dabc
abdc	badc	cadb	dacb
acbd	bcad	cbad	dbac
acdb	bcda	cbda	dbca
adbc	bdac	cdab	dcab
adcb	bdca	cdba	dcba

The number of permutations is the product

$$4 \cdot 3 \cdot 2 \cdot 1 = 4! = 24.$$

Five letters, such as a, b, c, d, and e, can be arranged in $5 \cdot 4 \cdot 3 \cdot 2 \cdot 1 = 5! = 120$ ways. Finding the number of ways that n elements can be ordered is an application of the Fundamental Principle of Counting and can be indicated with the factorial notation.

Number of Permutations of n Elements

There are $n \cdot (n-1) \cdot \ldots \cdot 2 \cdot 1 = n!$ permutations of n elements.

(That is, n elements can be arranged in n! ways.)

Not all permutation problems use all the elements of a set. For example, suppose that a 5-digit number (no digits are repeated) is to be formed by choosing five digits from the set $\{1,2,3,4,5,6,7,8\}$. How many such 5-digit numbers can be formed? The Fundamental Principle of Counting can be used in the following way.

Leave 5 spaces for the 5 digits.   _ _ _ _ _
8 digits are "eligible" for the first spot.   8_ _ _ _

Once a digit is chosen for the first spot, there are   8·7_ _ _
7 digits "eligible" for the second spot.

Continuing with the same reasoning gives   8·7·6·5·4

Thus, $8 \cdot 7 \cdot 6 \cdot 5 \cdot 4 = 6720$ different 5-digit numbers can be formed using 8 digits. We say that there are 6720 permutations of 8 digits taken 5 at a time.

$$_8P_5 = 8 \cdot 7 \cdot 6 \cdot 5 \cdot 4 = 6720$$ The notation $_8P_5$ is read "the number of permutations of 8 elements taken 5 at a time."

Using the factorial notation,

$$_8P_5 = 8 \cdot 7 \cdot 6 \cdot 5 \cdot 4 = 8 \cdot 7 \cdot 6 \cdot 5 \cdot 4 \left(\frac{3 \cdot 2 \cdot 1}{3 \cdot 2 \cdot 1} \right)$$

$$= \frac{8 \cdot 7 \cdot 6 \cdot 5 \cdot 4 \cdot 3 \cdot 2 \cdot 1}{3 \cdot 2 \cdot 1} = \frac{8!}{3!} = 6720$$

Number of Permutations of *n* Elements Taken *r* at a Time

The symbol $_nP_r$ denotes the number of permutations of n elements taken r at a time.

$$_nP_r = n(n-1)(n-2)...(n-r+1) = \frac{n!}{(n-r)!}$$

NOTES

Other notations for permutations are

$$P_r^n \text{ and } P(n,r).$$

Example 2: Number of Permutations of *n* Elements Taken *r* at a Time   • • • •

a. A sailor has 7 different flags with which he can signal. How many signals can he send using only 3 flags?

Solution: $_7P_3 = \dfrac{7!}{(7-3)!} = \dfrac{7!}{4!} = 7 \cdot 6 \cdot 5 = 210$

He can send 210 different signals using 3 flags.   *continued on next page...*

b. If the digits 1, 2, 3, 4, 5, and 6 are used to form three-digit numbers, how many numbers can be formed:
i. if digits may not be repeated, and
ii. if digits may be repeated?

Solution: i. $_6P_3 = \dfrac{6!}{(6-3)!} = \dfrac{6!}{3!} = 6 \cdot 5 \cdot 4 = 120$

ii. Since any of the digits can be used in more than one position, this part of the problem does not involve permutations. Using the Fundamental Principle of Counting, $6 \cdot 6 \cdot 6 = 216$.

There are 120 three-digit numbers if the digits may not be repeated and 216 three-digit numbers if digits may be repeated.

● ●

How many permutations are there of the letters in the word BEEHIVE? The three E's are not different from each other (that is, they are not distinct), and changing only these letters around would account for 3! permutations. Thus, if N represents the number of distinct permutations, $N \cdot 3! = 7!$ because there are seven letters involved.

This gives

$$N = \frac{7!}{3!} = 7 \cdot 6 \cdot 5 \cdot 4 = 840.$$

The following theorem is stated without proof.

Theorem for Distinct Permutations

If in a collection of n elements, m_1 are of one kind, m_2 are of another kind, ..., m_r are of still another kind, and

$$n = m_1 + m_2 + \ldots + m_r$$

then the total number of distinct permutations of the n elements is

$$N = \frac{n!}{m_1! \cdot m_2! \cdot \ldots \cdot m_r!}$$

Example 3: Permutations ●

a. Find the number of distinct permutations in the word MISSISSIPPI.
Solution: There are four **S**'s, four **I**'s, two **P**'s, and one **M**.

$$\frac{11!}{4!4!2!1!} = \frac{11 \cdot 10 \cdot 9 \cdot 8 \cdot 7 \cdot 6 \cdot 5 \cdot 4 \cdot 3 \cdot 2 \cdot 1}{4 \cdot 3 \cdot 2 \cdot 1 \cdot 4 \cdot 3 \cdot 2 \cdot 1 \cdot 2 \cdot 1 \cdot 1} = 34,650$$

● ●

Using a Calculator

Permutations can be calculated with the TI-83 calculator by pressing the (MATH) key and going to the menu under **PRB**. The second item in the list is the symbol $_n\mathbf{P}_r$. For example, $_7P_3$ can be calculated as follows:

1. Enter 7.
2. Press the (MATH) key.
3. Go to the **PRB** heading and press 2. ($7_n\mathbf{P}_r$ will appear on the display.)
4. Enter 3
5. Press (ENTER) and **210** will appear on the display.

Practice Problems

1. Evaluate $_6P_6$.

2. Evaluate $_6P_2$.

3. How many even numbers with four digits can be formed using the digits 1, 2, 3, 5, 7 if no repetitions are allowed?

4. Find the number of distinct permutations of the letters in the word SCIENTIFIC.

10.6 Exercises

Evaluate the permutations in Exercises 1 – 10.

1. $_7P_4$
2. $_8P_3$
3. $_4P_4$
4. $_6P_2$
5. $_5P_4$

6. $_7P_1$
7. $_9P_6$
8. $_{11}P_9$
9. $_{10}P_8$
10. $_9P_4$

11. A football team of eleven players is electing a captain and a most valuable player. In how many ways can this be done if the awards must be given to two different players?

12. In how many ways can eleven girls be chosen for nine positions in a chorus?

13. There are eight men available for three outfield positions on the baseball team. If each man can play any position, in how many ways can the outfield positions be filled?

14. A president, a vice-president, a secretary, and a treasurer are to be selected for an organization of 20 members. In how many ways can these four people be selected?

Answers to Practice Problems: **1.** 720 **2.** 30 **3.** 24 **4.** 302,400

15. A luxury automobile is available in 6 body colors, 3 different vinyl tops, and 4 choices of interior. How many different cars must the dealer stock if he wishes to have one of each model?

16. In a subdivision, there are five basic floor plans. Each floor plan has three different exterior designs and three plans for landscaping the yard. How many different houses could be built?

17. How many four-digit numbers can be formed from the digits 1, 2, 5, 6, 7, and 9 if no repetitions are allowed?

18. How many **odd** numbers with four digits can be formed from the digits 1, 2, 3, 4, 6, and 7 with no repetitions allowed?

19. How many numbers of not more than four digits can be formed from the digits 2, 5, 7, and 9 if no repetitions are allowed?

20. How many numbers of not more than four digits can be formed from the digits 2, 5, 7, and 9 if repetitions are allowed?

21. A builder recently hired four superintendents and four foremen. He assigned a superintendent and a foreman to each of his four projects. In how many ways can this be done?

22. In how many ways can three math books and four English books be arranged on a shelf if:
a. they may be placed in any position?
b. the math books are together and the English books are together?

23. In how many ways can four algebra texts and three geometry texts be arranged on a shelf, keeping the subjects together?

24. In Exercise 23, if two of the algebra books are identical and two of the geometry books are identical, in how many ways can the books be arranged, keeping those on each subject together?

25. There are eleven flags that are displayed together, one above another. How many signals are possible if four of the flags are blue, two are red, three are yellow, and two are white?

Writing and Thinking About Mathematics

26. How many different ways can 6 people be seated at a round table?

Hawkes Learning Systems: Intermediate Algebra

Permutations

Combinations

After completing this section, you will be able to:

1. *Evaluate expressions representing combinations.*
2. *Solve applied problems involving combinations.*

Permutations indicate the order or arrangement of elements. Arrangements or groupings of elements in which order is not a concern are called **combinations.** For example, if you have ten books and are trying to arrange seven of these books on a shelf, alphabetized from left to right, then the number of arrangements is a permutation problem. However, if you are trying to decide which seven of the ten books to take on vacation, then the number of choices is a combination problem. Other examples of problems involving combinations are how many ways a committee can be formed or how many ways a hand of cards can be formed. In these cases, order is not involved.

Combination

*A **combination** is a collection of some (or all) of the elements of a set without regard to the order of the elements.*

If n distinct elements are given and a combination of r elements is to be selected, then the total number of combinations of n elements taken r at a time is symbolized $_nC_r$. Since each combination of r elements has $r!$ permutations, the product $r! \cdot {}_nC_r$ represents the number of permutations of n elements taken r at a time. Thus,

$$r! \cdot {}_nC_r = {}_nP_r$$

or $\qquad {}_nC_r = \dfrac{{}_nP_r}{r!} = \dfrac{n!}{r!(n-r)!}$

Note that the formula $_nC_r$ for combinations is exactly the same as $\dbinom{n}{r}$ for the coefficients in the Binomial Theorem.

The relationship between combinations and permutations can be illustrated by considering the four letters a, b, c, d and listing both $_4C_3$ and $_4P_3$.

$$\text{Combinations } (_4C_3) \quad \{ abc \quad abd \quad acd \quad bcd \}$$

$$\text{Permutations } (_4P_3) \quad \begin{bmatrix} abc & abd & acd & bcd \\ acb & adb & adc & bdc \\ bac & bad & cad & cbd \\ bca & bda & cda & cdb \\ cab & dab & dac & dbc \\ cba & dba & dca & dcb \end{bmatrix}$$

Notice that each combination of 3 elements has 3! = 6 corresponding permutations. Thus,

$$3! \cdot {_4C_3} = 6 \cdot 4 = 24 = {_4P_3}$$

Example 1: Combinations ●

a.   In how many ways can a hand of 5 cards be dealt from a deck of 52 cards?

Solution: $_{52}C_5 = \dfrac{52!}{5!47!} = \dfrac{52 \cdot 51 \cdot \overset{5}{\cancel{50}} \cdot 49 \cdot \overset{4}{\cancel{48}}}{\cancel{5} \cdot \cancel{4} \cdot \cancel{3} \cdot \cancel{2} \cdot \cancel{1}} = 2,598,960$

There are 2,598,960 possible hands of 5 cards.

b.   A committee of 6 people is to be chosen from a group of 40 members. How many "different" committees are there?

Solution: $_{40}C_6 = \dfrac{40!}{6!34!} = \dfrac{\overset{2}{\cancel{40}} \cdot 39 \cdot 38 \cdot 37 \cdot \overset{1}{\cancel{36}} \cdot 35}{\cancel{6} \cdot \cancel{5} \cdot \cancel{4} \cdot \cancel{3} \cdot \cancel{2} \cdot \cancel{1}} = 3,838,380$

There are 3,838,380 "different" committees.

● ●

These ideas can also be used in conjunction with the Fundamental Principle of Counting, as the following example illustrates.

Example 2: Combinations ●

A Senate committee of 6 members must be chosen with 3 Democrats and 3 Republicans. The eligible members are 10 Democrats and 8 Republicans. How many possible ways can such a committee be formed?

Solution: $_{10}C_3 = \dfrac{10!}{3!7!} = \dfrac{10 \cdot 9 \cdot 8}{3 \cdot 2 \cdot 1} = 120$ groups of Democrats

$_8C_3 = \dfrac{8!}{3!5!} = \dfrac{8 \cdot 7 \cdot 6}{3 \cdot 2 \cdot 1} = 56$ groups of Republicans

Using the Fundamental Principle of Counting,

$$_{10}C_3 \cdot {}_8C_3 = 120 \cdot 56 = 6720.$$

There are 6720 possible ways that this committee can be formed.

● ●

Practice Problems

1. In how many ways can a jury of 6 men and 6 women be selected from a group of 10 men and 14 women?

2. A student senate committee of 5 people is to be chosen from a list of 20 students. In how many ways can this be done?

10.7 Exercises

Evaluate the combinations in Exercises 1 – 10.

1. $_7C_3$ **2.** $_8C_4$ **3.** $_4C_4$ **4.** $_8C_5$ **5.** $_9C_6$

6. $_5C_3$ **7.** $_6C_1$ **8.** $_5C_5$ **9.** $_{10}C_7$ **10.** $_9C_4$

11. A committee of three is selected from the eighteen members of an organization. In how many ways may the committee be chosen?

12. You are permitted to answer any ten questions out of thirteen. In how many different ways can you make your ten selections?

13. If each girl can play any of the positions on a basketball team, how many different starting lineups of five can be formed from a team of twelve girls?

14. A ski club has fifteen members who desire to be on the four-man ski team. How many different ski teams can be formed from the members of the club?

15. Twenty people all shake hands with one another. How many different handshakes occur?

16. How many straight lines are determined by seven distinct points if no three points are collinear? How many triangles are formed? Sketch a picture of this geometric situation.

17. Five women and four men are candidates for the debate team. If the team consists of one woman and two men, in how many ways may the team be chosen?

Answers to Practice Problems: **1.** 630,630 **2.** 15,504

18. In how many ways can a committee of two Republicans and three Democrats be selected from a group of seven Republicans and ten Democrats?

19. Sandy is packing for a trip. She plans to take five blouses and three skirts. In how many different ways can she make her selections if she has twelve blouses and nine skirts to choose from?

20. A department store wishes to fill ten positions with four men and six women. In how many ways can these positions be filled if nine men and ten women have applied for the jobs?

21. A reading list consists of ten books of fiction and eight of nonfiction. In how many ways can a student select four fiction and four nonfiction books?

22. On a geometry test, there are eight theorems and six constructions to choose from. If you are required to do four theorems and three constructions, in how many ways could you work the test?

23. The high school Student Government Committee is composed of three boys and two girls. If there are eight boys and six girls eligible, how many different committees could be formed?

24. In a dozen eggs, three are spoiled. In how many ways can you select four eggs and get two spoiled ones?

25. On a shelf, there are five English books, six algebra books, and three geometry books. Two English books, three algebra books, and two geometry books are selected. How many different selections are there?

26. In California, license plates are formed by a single digit followed by three letters followed by three digits. If the first digit cannot be 0, and all the other letters and digits can be repeated, how many license plates can be formed? (This, of course, does not allow for "vanity" plates.)

27. Find the number of diagonals of each of the following polygons. (A diagonal is a line segment connecting any two nonadjacent corners.) Sketch each figure and its diagonals.
a. square   **b.** pentagon
c. hexagon

28. A lotto drawing consists of a random selection of 6 numbered balls from a set numbered from 1 to 51. In how many ways can six balls be selected?

29. A box contains balls numbered from 0 to 9. If two balls are selected and the balls are placed side by side to form a two digit number, how many of the numbers so formed will be odd?

30. A combination lock has numbers from 1 to 50. If no number may be selected twice, how many combinations to open the lock are possible that use three numbers? (**Hint:** Is this a permutation problem or a combination problem?)

Hawkes Learning Systems: Intermediate Algebra

    Combinations

Chapter 10 Index of Key Ideas and Terms

Sequences: $\{a_n\}$ page 698
    An infinite sequence (or a sequence) is a function that has the positive integers as its domain.

Terms of a sequence   page 698

Alternating Sequence   page 701
    An alternating sequence is one in which the terms alternate in sign. Alternating sequences generally involve the expression $(-1)^n$.

Decreasing Sequence   page 702
    A sequence $\{a_n\}$ is decreasing if $a_n > a_{n+1}$ for all n.

Increasing Sequence   page 702
    A sequence $\{a_n\}$ is increasing if $a_n < a_{n+1}$ for all n.

Partial Sum   page 705

Sigma Notation: $\sum$ page 705

Partial Sums Using Sigma Notation   page 705
    The nth **partial sum**, S_n, of the first n terms of a sequence $\{a_n\}$ is

$$S_n = \sum_{k=1}^{n} a_k = a_1 + a_2 + a_3 + \ldots + a_n.$$

    k is called the **index of summation**, and k takes the integer values $1, 2, 3, \ldots, n$
    n is the **upper limit of summation**, and 1 is the **lower limit of summation**

Properties of Sigma Notation   page 706

For sequences $\{a_n\}$ and $\{b_n\}$ and any real number c:

I. $\displaystyle\sum_{k=1}^{n} a_k = \sum_{k=1}^{i} a_k + \sum_{k=i+1}^{n} a_k$ for any i, $1 \le i \le n-1$

II. $\displaystyle\sum_{k=1}^{n} (a_k + b_k) = \sum_{k=1}^{n} a_k + \sum_{k=1}^{n} b_k$

III. $\displaystyle\sum_{k=1}^{n} ca_k = c\sum_{k=1}^{n} a_k$

IV. $\displaystyle\sum_{k=1}^{n} c = nc$

Arithmetic Sequences   page 712

A sequence $\{a_n\}$ is called an arithmetic sequence (or arithmetic progression) if for any positive integer k, $a_{k+1} - a_k = d$ where d is a constant. d is called the common difference.

n^{th} Term of an Arithmetic Sequence   page 713

If $\{a_n\}$ is an arithmetic sequence, then the nth term has the form

$a_n = a_1 + (n-1)d$ where d is the common difference between the terms.

Partial Sums of Arithmetic Sequences   page 715

If $\{a_n\}$ is an arithmetic sequence, then the sum of the first n terms

is $S_n = \displaystyle\sum_{k=1}^{n} a_k = \frac{n}{2}(a_1 + a_n)$.

Geometric Sequences   page 722

A sequence $\{a_n\}$ is called a geometric sequence, (or geometric progression) if for any positive integer k, $\dfrac{a_{k+1}}{a_k} = r$ where r is constant and $r \ne 0$. r is called the common ratio.

n^{th} Term of a Geometric Sequence   page 723

If $\{a_n\}$ is a geometric sequence, then the nth term has the

form $a_n = a_1 r^{n-1}$ where r is the common ratio.

Partial Sums of Geometric Sequences   page 725

If $\{a_n\}$ is a geometric sequence, then the sum of the first

n terms can be written as $S_n = \displaystyle\sum_{k=1}^{n} a_k = \frac{a_1(1-r^n)}{1-r}$ where $r \ne 1$.

Infinite Series (or Series) page 728

The indicated sum of all the terms of a sequence is called an **infinite series** (or a **series**). For a sequence $\{a_n\}$, the corresponding series can be written as follows:

$$\sum_{k=1}^{\infty}(a_k) = a_1 + a_2 + a_3 + \ldots + a_n + \ldots$$

Sum of a Geometric Series page 728

If $\{a_n\}$ is a geometric sequence and $|r| < 1$, then the sum of the infinite geometric series is

$$S = \sum_{k=1}^{\infty}(a_k) = a_1 + a_1 r + a_1 r^2 + \ldots = \frac{a_1}{1-r}.$$

Factorial ($n!$) page 735

For any positive integer n, $n! = n(n-1)(n-2)\ldots 3 \cdot 2 \cdot 1$.
$n!$ is read as "n factorial."
$0! = 1$ page 735

Using a Calculator to Calculate Factorials page 735

Binomial Coefficient $\begin{pmatrix} n \\ r \end{pmatrix}$ page 736

For non-negative integers n and r, with $0 \leq r \leq n$, we define

$$\begin{pmatrix} n \\ r \end{pmatrix} = \frac{n!}{(n-r)!\,r!}$$

Because this quantity appears repeatedly in the Binomial Theorem, $\begin{pmatrix} n \\ r \end{pmatrix}$ is often called a Binomial Coefficient. It is read "the combination of n things taken r at a time."

Using a Calculator to Calculate Binomial Coefficients: $_nC_r$ page 737

Pascal's Triangle page 738

Binomial Theorem page 739

$$(a+b)^n = \begin{pmatrix} n \\ 0 \end{pmatrix}a^n + \begin{pmatrix} n \\ 1 \end{pmatrix}a^{n-1}b + \begin{pmatrix} n \\ 2 \end{pmatrix}a^{n-2}b^2 + \ldots + \begin{pmatrix} n \\ k \end{pmatrix}a^{n-k}b^k + \ldots + \begin{pmatrix} n \\ n \end{pmatrix}b^n$$

In Σ-notation, $(a+b)^n = \sum_{k=0}^{n} \begin{pmatrix} n \\ k \end{pmatrix}a^{n-k}b^k$.

Fundamental Principle of Counting page 743

If an event E_1 can occur in m_1 ways, an event E_2 can occur in m_2 ways, $\ldots$, and an event E_k can occur in m_k ways, then the total number of ways that all events may occur is the product $m_1 \cdot m_2 \cdot \ldots \cdot m_k$.

Permutations

page 744

A permutation is an arrangement (or ordering) of the elements of a set.

Number of Permutations of n Elements

page 744

There are $n \cdot (n-1) \cdot \ldots \cdot 2 \cdot 1 = n!$ **permutations of n elements.**
(That is, n elements can be arranged in $n!$ ways.)

Number of Permutations of n Elements Taken r at a Time

page 745

The symbol $_nP_r$ denotes the number of permutations of n elements taken r at a time.

$$_nP_r = n(n-1)(n-2)\ldots(n-r+1) = \frac{n!}{(n-r)!}$$

Distinct Permutations (Theorem)

page 746

If in a collection of n elements, m_1 are of one kind, m_2 are of another kind, ... m_r are of still another kind, and

$$n = m_1 + m_2 + \ldots + m_r$$

then the total number of distinct permutations of the n elements is

$$N = \frac{n!}{m_1! \cdot m_2! \cdot \ldots \cdot m_r!}.$$

Using a Calculator to Calculate Permutations

page 747

Combinations

page 749

A combination is a collection of some (or all) of the elements of a set without regard to the order of the elements.

$$r! \cdot {}_nC_r = {}_nP_r$$

or $\qquad {}_nC_r = \frac{_nP_r}{r!} = \frac{n!}{r!(n-r)!}$

Chapter 10 Review

For a review of the topics and problems from Chapter 10, look at the following lessons from *Hawkes Learning Systems: Intermediate Algebra*

Sequences
Sigma Notation
Arithmetic Sequences
Geometric Sequences and Series

The Binomial Theorem
Permutations
Combinations

Chapter 10 Test

1. Write the first four terms of the sequence $\left\{\dfrac{1}{3n+1}\right\}$ and determine whether the sequence is arithmetic, geometric, or neither.

2. Find a general term for the sequence $\dfrac{1}{3}, \dfrac{2}{5}, \dfrac{3}{7}, \dfrac{4}{9}, \ldots$

In Exercises 3 – 5, $\left\{a_k\right\}$ is an arithmetic sequence. Find the indicated quantity.

3. $a_1 = 5$, $d = 3$. Find a_8.

4. $a_2 = 4$, $a_7 = -6$. Find a_n.

5. $a_4 = 22$, $a_7 = 37$. Find $\displaystyle\sum_{k=1}^{9} a_k$.

In Exercises 6 – 8, $\left\{a_k\right\}$ is a geometric sequence. Find the indicated quantity.

6. $a_1 = 8$, $r = \dfrac{1}{2}$. Find a_7.

7. $a_4 = 3$, $a_6 = 9$. Find a_n.

8. $a_2 = \dfrac{1}{3}$, $a_5 = \dfrac{1}{24}$. Find $\displaystyle\sum_{k=1}^{6} a_k$.

Find each of the sums in Exercises 9 and 10.

9. $\displaystyle\sum_{k=1}^{8} (3k - 5)$

10. $\displaystyle\sum_{k=3}^{6} 2\left(-\dfrac{1}{3}\right)^k$

11. Write the decimal number $0.\overline{15}$ in the form of an infinite series and find its sum in the form of a proper fraction.

12. If $\displaystyle\sum_{k=1}^{50} a_k = 88$ and $\displaystyle\sum_{k=1}^{19} a_k = 14$, find $\displaystyle\sum_{k=20}^{50} a_k$.

13. A customer intends to buy a new car for \$25,000 and anticipates that it will depreciate at a rate of 15% of its value each year. What will be the value of the car in 4 years when he wants to trade it in for another new car?

14. Evaluate $\dbinom{11}{5}$.

15. Use the Binomial Theorem to expand $(2x - y)^5$.

16. Write the fifth term of the expansion of $(x + 3y)^8$.

17. Find the value of $_{10}P_6$.

18. Find the value of $_{12}C_7$.

19. There are ten players available for the three different outfield positions on a baseball team. Assuming each player can play any of the positions, in how many ways can the outfield be filled?

20. In a box there are eleven apples, three of which are spoiled. In how many ways could you select three good apples and one bad apple?

21. Explain, in your own words, why defining 0! to be 1 makes sense in mathematics.

Cumulative Review: Chapters 1 - 10

Simplify each expression in Exercises 1 and 2.

1. $10x - \left[2x + (13 - 4x) - (11 - 3x) \right] + (2x + 5)$

2. $(x^2 + 5x - 2) - (3x^2 - 5x - 3) + (x^2 - 7x + 4)$

Factor completely in Exercises 3 – 5.

3. $64x^3 + 27$

4. $6x^2 + 17x - 45$

5. $5x^2 (2x + 1) - 3x (2x + 1) - 14 (2x + 1)$

Perform the indicated operations and simplify in Exercises 6 – 8.

6. $\dfrac{x+3}{3} + \dfrac{2x-1}{5}$

7. $\dfrac{x}{x^2 - 16} - \dfrac{x+1}{x^2 - 5x + 4}$

8. $\dfrac{x^2 - 9}{x^4 + 6x^3} \div \dfrac{x^3 - 2x^2 - 3x}{x^2 + 7x + 6} \cdot \dfrac{x^2}{x+3}$

Simplify each expression in Exercises 9 – 12. Assume that all variables are positive.

9. $\left(\dfrac{8x^{-1} y^{\frac{1}{3}}}{x^3 y^{-\frac{1}{3}}} \right)^{\frac{1}{2}}$

10. $\sqrt[3]{\dfrac{8x^4}{27y^3}}$

11. $\sqrt{12x} - \sqrt{75x} + 2\sqrt{27x}$

12. $\dfrac{1 + 3i}{2 - 5i}$

Solve the inequalities in Exercises 13 – 15. Graph the solution sets on real number lines.

13. $6 (2x - 3) + (x - 5) > 4 (x + 1)$

14. $\left| 7 - 3x \right| - 2 \le 4$

15. $8x^2 + 2x - 45 < 0$

Solve the equations in Exercises 16 – 21.

16. $4 (x - 7) + 2 (3x + 2) = 3x + 2$

17. $2x^2 + 4x + 3 = 0$

18. $x - \sqrt{x} - 2 = 0$

19. $\dfrac{1}{2x} + \dfrac{5}{x+3} = \dfrac{8}{3x}$

20. $2\sqrt{6 - x} = x - 3$

21. $5 \ln x = 12$

22. Solve the formula for *n*: $P = \dfrac{A}{1 + ni}$

Solve the systems of equations in Exercises 23 and 24.

23. Solve the following system by using Cramer's rule. $\begin{cases} 9x + 2y = 8 \\ 4x + 3y = -7 \end{cases}$

24. Solve the following system of equations by using the Gaussian elimination method.

$$\begin{cases} 3x + y - 2z = 4 \\ x - 4y - 3z = -5 \\ 2x + 2y + z = 3 \end{cases}$$

25. If $f(x) = 2x - 7$ and $g(x) = x^2 + 1$, find:

   a. $f^{-1}(x)$

   b. $f[g(x)]$

   c. $g(x+1) - g(x)$

26. The following is a graph of $y = f(x)$. Sketch the graph of $y = f(x - 2) - 1$.

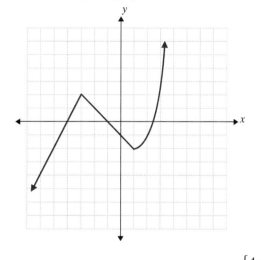

27. Solve the following system by graphing. $\begin{cases} 4x - 3y = 17 \\ 5x + 2y = 4 \end{cases}$

Graph each of the equations in Exercises 28 – 30.

28. $y = 4x^2 - 8x + 9$

29. $\dfrac{x^2}{4} + \dfrac{y^2}{16} = 1$

30. $x^2 - 4x + y^2 + 2y = 4$

31. If $\{a_n\}$ is an arithmetic sequence where $a_3 = 4$ and $a_8 = -6$,

   a. find u_n.

   b. find $\displaystyle\sum_{k=1}^{10} a_k$.

32. If $\{a_k\}$ is a geometric sequence where $a_1 = 16$ and $r = \dfrac{1}{2}$,

   a. find a_n.

   b. find $\displaystyle\sum_{k=1}^{6} a_k$.

33. Use the Binomial Theorem to expand $(x+2y)^6$.

Evaluate each expression in Exercises 34 – 36.

34. $\begin{pmatrix} 10 \\ 4 \end{pmatrix}$

35. $_8P_4$

36. $_{14}C_5$

37. Two cars start together and travel in the same direction, one traveling 3 times as fast as the other. At the end of 3.5 hours, they are 140 miles apart. How fast is each traveling?

38. A grocer mixes two kinds of nuts. One costs $1.40 per pound and the other costs $2.60 per pound. If the mixture weighs 20 pounds and costs $1.64 per pound, how many pounds of each kind did he use?

39. A rectangular yard is 20 ft by 30 ft. A rectangular swimming pool is to be built leaving a strip of grass of uniform width around the pool. If the area of the grass strip is 184 sq ft, find the dimensions of the pool.

40. A radioactive isotope decomposes according to $A = A_0 e^{-0.0552t}$, where t is measured in hours. Determine the half-life of the isotope. Round the solution to two decimal places.

41. Joan started her job exactly 5 years ago. Her original salary was $12,000 per year. Each year she received a raise of 6% of her current salary. What is her salary after this year's raise?

42. A tank holds 1000 liters of a liquid that readily mixes with water. After 150 liters are drained out, the tank is filled by adding water. Then 150 liters of the mixture are drained out and the tank is filled by adding water. If this process is continued 5 times, how much of the original liquid is left? Round the solution to one decimal place.

43. An architect is drawing house plans for a contractor. The contractor requested 4 different floor plans. Each floor plan has 3 different exterior designs. How many different plans must the architect draw?

44. A sailor has 9 different flags to use for signaling. A signal consists of displaying 4 flags in a specific order. How many signals can he send?

45. On a geometry test, there are six theorems and five constructions to choose from. If you are required to do 4 theorems and 2 constructions, in how many ways could you work the test?

Use a graphing calculator to solve (or estimate the solutions of) the equations in Exercises 46 – 50. Proceed by using the following steps:

1. *Get 0 on one side of the equation.*
2. *Press the* **Y=** *key and enter the nonzero side of the equation as the function* **Y1**.
3. *Press* **GRAPH**.
4. *Use the* **TRACE** *and* **ZOOM** *features of the calculator to estimate the zeros of the function. (Remember that the zeros are x-values where the graph intersects the x-axis.)*

46. $x^4 = 2x + 1$

47. $e^x = -x^2 + 4$

48. $\ln x = x^2 - 2x - 1$

49. $x^3 = 3x^2 - 3x + 1$

50. $x^3 = 7x - 6$

A.1   Pi

As discussed in the text on page 6, π is an irrational number, and so the decimal form of π is an infinite nonrepeating decimal. Mathematicians even in ancient times realized that π is a constant value obtained from the ratio of a circle's circumference to its diameter, but they had no sense that it might be an irrational number. As early as about 1800 B.C., the Babylonians gave π a value of 3, and around 1600 B.C., the ancient Egyptians were using the approximation of 256/81, what would be a decimal value of about 3.1605. In the third century B.C., the Greek mathematician Archimedes used polygons approximating a circle to determine that the value of π must lie between 223/71(≈3.1408) and 22/7(≈3.1429). He was thus accurate to two decimal places. About seven hundred years later, in the fourth century A.D., Chinese mathematician Tsu Chung-Chi refined Archimedes' method and expressed the constant as 355/113, which was correct to six decimal places. By 1610, Ludolph van Ceulen of Germany had also used a polygon method to find π accurate to 35 decimal places.

Knowing that the decimal expression of π would not terminate, mathematicians still sought a repeating pattern in its digits. Such a pattern would mean that π was a rational number and that there would be some ratio of two whole numbers that would produce the correct decimal representation. Finally, in 1767, Johann Heinrich Lambert provided a proof to show that π is indeed irrational and thus is nonrepeating as well as nonterminating.

Since Lambert's proof, mathematicians have still made an exercise of calculating π to more and more decimal places. The advent of the computer age in this century has made that work immeasurably easier, and on occasion you will still see newspaper articles pronouncing that mathematics researchers have reached a new high in the number of decimal places in their approximations. In 1988 that number was 201,326,000 decimal places. Within 1 year that record was more than doubled, and most recent approximations of π now reach beyond 1.24 trillion decimal places! For your understanding, appreciation and interest, the value of π is given in the table on the next page to a mere 3742 decimal places as calculated by a computer program. To show π calculated to one billion decimal places would take every page of nearly 400 copies of this text!

The Value of π

π =
3.14159265358979323846264338327950288419716939937510582097494459230781640628620899862803482534211706798214808651328230664709384460955058223172535940812848111745028410270193852110555964462294895493038196442881097566593344612847564823378678316527120190914564856692346034861045432664821339360726024914127372458700660631558817488152092096282925409171536436789259036001133053054882046652138414695194151160943305727036575959195309218611738193261179310511854807446237996274956735188575272489122793818301194912983367336244065664308602139494639522473719070217986094370277053921717629317675238467481846766940513200056812714526356082778577134275778960917363717872146844090122495343014654958537105079227968925892354201995611212902196086403441815981362977477130996051870721134999999837297804995105973173281609631859502445945534690830264252230825334468503526193118817101000313783875288658753320838142061717766914730359825349042875546873115956286388235378759375195778185778053217122680661300192787661119590921642019893809525720106548586327886593615338182796823030195203530185296899577362259941389124972177528347913151557485724245415069595082953311686172785588907509838175463746493931925506040092770167113900984882401285836160356370766010471018194295559619894676783744944825537977472684710404753464620804668425906949129331367702898915210475216205696602405803815019351125338243003558764024749647326391419927260426992279678235478163600934172164121992458631503028618297455570674983850549458858692699569092721079750930295532116534498720275596023648066549911988183479775356636980742654252786255181841757467289097777279380008164706001614524919217321721477235014144197356854816136115735255213347574184946843852332390739414333454477624168625189835694855620992192221842725502542568876717904946016534668049886272327917860857843838279679766814541009538837863609506800642251252051173929848960841284886269456042419652850222106611863067442786220391949450471237137869609563643719172874677646575739624138908658326459958133904780275900994657640789512694683983525957098258226205224894077267194782684826014769909026401363944374455305068203496252451749399651431429809190659250937221696461515709858387410597885959772975498930161753928468138268683868942774155991855925245953959431049972524680845987273644697548685383673622626099124608051243884390451244136549762780797715691435997700129616089441694868555848406353422072225828488648158456028506016842739452267467678895252138522549954666727823986456596116354886230577456498035593634568174324112515076069479451096596094025228797108931456691368672287489405601015033086179286809208747609178249385890097149096759852613655497818931297848216829989487226588048575640142704775551323796414515237462343645428584447952658678210511413547357395231134271661021359695362314429524849371871101457654035902799344037420073105785390621983874478084784896833214457138687519435064302184531910484810053706146806749192781911979399520614196634287544406437451237181921799983910159195618146751426912397489409071864942319615679452080951465502252316038819301420937621378559566389377870830390697920773467221825625996615014215030680384477345492026054146659252014974428507325186660021324340881907104863317346496514539057962685610055081066587969981635747363840525714591028970641401109712062804390397595156771577004203378699360072305587631763594218873125147120532928191826186125867321579198414848829164470609570752706957220917567116722910981690915280173506712748583222871835209353965725121083579151369882091444210067510334671103141267111369908658516398315019701651511685171437657618351556508849099898599823873455283316355076479185358932261854896321329330898570642046752590709154814165498594616371802709819943099244889575712828905923233260972997120844335732654893823911932597...

A.2   Powers, Roots, and Prime Factorizations

No.	Square	Square Root	Cube	Cube Root	Prime Factorization
1	1	1.0000	1	1.0000	
2	4	1.4142	8	1.2599	prime
3	9	1.7321	27	1.4423	prime
4	16	2.0000	64	1.5874	2 · 2
5	25	2.2361	125	1.7100	prime
6	36	2.4495	216	1.8171	2 · 3
7	49	2.6458	343	1.9129	prime
8	64	2.8284	512	2.0000	2 · 2 · 2
9	81	3.0000	729	2.0801	3 · 3
10	100	3.1623	1000	2.1544	2 · 5
11	121	3.3166	1331	2.2240	prime
12	144	3.4641	1728	2.2894	2 · 2 · 3
13	169	3.6056	2197	2.3513	prime
14	196	3.7417	2744	2.4101	2 · 7
15	225	3.8730	3375	2.4662	3 · 5
16	256	4.0000	4096	2.5198	2 · 2 · 2 · 2
17	289	4.1231	4913	2.5713	prime
18	324	4.2426	5832	2.6207	2 · 3 · 3
19	361	4.3589	6859	2.6684	prime
20	400	4.4721	8000	2.7144	2 · 2 · 5
21	441	4.5826	9261	2.7589	3 · 7
22	484	4.6904	10,648	2.8020	2 · 11
23	529	4.7958	12,167	2.8439	prime
24	576	4.8990	13,824	2.8845	2 · 2 · 2 · 3
25	625	5.0000	15,625	2.9240	5 · 5
26	676	5.0990	17,576	2.9625	2 · 13
27	729	5.1962	19,683	3.0000	3 · 3 · 3
28	784	5.2915	21,952	3.0366	2 · 2 · 7
29	841	5.3852	24,389	3.0723	prime
30	900	5.4772	27,000	3.1072	2 · 3 · 5
31	961	5.5678	29,791	3.1414	prime
32	1024	5.6569	32,768	3.1748	2 · 2 · 2 · 2 · 2
33	1089	5.7446	35,937	3.2075	3 · 11
34	1156	5.8310	39,304	3.2396	2 · 17

No.	Square	Square Root	Cube	Cube Root	Prime Factorization
35	1225	5.9161	42,875	3.2711	$5 \cdot 7$
36	1296	6.0000	46,656	3.3019	$2 \cdot 2 \cdot 3 \cdot 3$
37	1369	6.0828	50,653	3.3322	prime
38	1444	6.1644	54,872	3.3620	$2 \cdot 19$
39	1521	6.2450	59,319	3.3912	$3 \cdot 13$
40	1600	6.3246	64,000	3.4200	$2 \cdot 2 \cdot 2 \cdot 5$
41	1681	6.4031	68,921	3.4482	prime
42	1764	6.4807	74,088	3.4760	$2 \cdot 3 \cdot 7$
43	1849	6.5574	79,507	3.5034	prime
44	1936	6.6333	85,184	3.5303	$2 \cdot 2 \cdot 11$
45	2025	6.7082	91,125	3.5569	$3 \cdot 3 \cdot 5$
46	2116	6.7823	97,336	3.5830	$2 \cdot 23$
47	2209	6.8557	103,823	3.6088	prime
48	2304	6.9282	110,592	3.6342	$2 \cdot 2 \cdot 2 \cdot 2 \cdot 3$
49	2401	7.0000	117,649	3.6593	$7 \cdot 7$
50	2500	7.0711	125,000	3.6840	$2 \cdot 5 \cdot 5$
51	2601	7.1414	132,651	3.7084	$3 \cdot 17$
52	2704	7.2111	140,608	3.7325	$2 \cdot 2 \cdot 13$
53	2809	7.2801	148,877	3.7563	prime
54	2916	7.3485	157,464	3.7798	$2 \cdot 3 \cdot 3 \cdot 3$
55	3025	7.4162	166,375	3.8030	$5 \cdot 11$
56	3136	7.4833	175,616	3.8259	$2 \cdot 2 \cdot 2 \cdot 7$
57	3249	7.5498	185,193	3.8485	$3 \cdot 19$
58	3364	7.6158	195,112	3.8709	$2 \cdot 29$
59	3481	7.6811	205,379	3.8930	prime
60	3600	7.7460	216,000	3.9149	$2 \cdot 2 \cdot 3 \cdot 5$
61	3721	7.8103	226,981	3.9365	prime
62	3844	7.8740	238,328	3.9579	$2 \cdot 31$
63	3969	7.9373	250,047	3.9791	$3 \cdot 3 \cdot 7$
64	4096	8.0000	262,144	4.0000	$2 \cdot 2 \cdot 2 \cdot 2 \cdot 2 \cdot 2$
65	4225	8.0623	274,625	4.0207	$5 \cdot 13$
66	4356	8.1240	287,496	4.0412	$2 \cdot 3 \cdot 11$
67	4489	8.1854	300,763	4.0615	prime
68	4624	8.2462	314,432	4.0817	$2 \cdot 2 \cdot 17$
69	4761	8.3066	328,509	4.1016	$3 \cdot 23$
70	4900	8.3666	343,000	4.1213	$2 \cdot 5 \cdot 7$
71	5041	8.4262	357,911	4.1408	prime

No.	Square	Square Root	Cube	Cube Root	Prime Factorization
72	5184	8.4853	373,248	4.1602	$2 \cdot 2 \cdot 2 \cdot 3 \cdot 3$
73	5329	8.5440	389,017	4.1793	prime
74	5476	8.6023	405,224	4.1983	$2 \cdot 37$
75	5625	8.6603	421,875	4.2172	$3 \cdot 5 \cdot 5$
76	5776	8.7178	438,976	4.2358	$2 \cdot 2 \cdot 19$
77	5929	8.7750	456,533	4.2543	$7 \cdot 11$
78	6084	8.8318	474,552	4.2727	$2 \cdot 3 \cdot 13$
79	6241	8.8882	493,039	4.2908	prime
80	6400	8.9443	512,000	4.3089	$2 \cdot 2 \cdot 2 \cdot 2 \cdot 5$
81	6561	9.0000	531,441	4.3267	$3 \cdot 3 \cdot 3 \cdot 3$
82	6724	9.0554	551,368	4.3445	$2 \cdot 41$
83	6889	9.1104	571,787	4.3621	prime
84	7056	9.1652	592,704	4.3795	$2 \cdot 2 \cdot 3 \cdot 7$
85	7225	9.2195	614,125	4.3968	$5 \cdot 17$
86	7396	9.2736	636,056	4.4140	$2 \cdot 43$
87	7569	9.3274	658,503	4.4310	$3 \cdot 29$
88	7744	9.3808	681,472	4.4480	$2 \cdot 2 \cdot 2 \cdot 11$
89	7921	9.4340	704,969	4.4647	prime
90	8100	9.4868	729,000	4.4814	$2 \cdot 3 \cdot 3 \cdot 5$
91	8281	9.5394	753,571	4.4979	$7 \cdot 13$
92	8464	9.5917	778,688	4.5144	$2 \cdot 2 \cdot 23$
93	8649	9.6437	804,357	4.5307	$3 \cdot 31$
94	8836	9.6954	830,584	4.5468	$2 \cdot 47$
95	9025	9.7468	857,375	4.5629	$5 \cdot 19$
96	9216	9.7980	884,736	4.5789	$2 \cdot 2 \cdot 2 \cdot 2 \cdot 2 \cdot 3$
97	9409	9.8489	912,673	4.5947	prime
98	9604	9.8995	941,192	4.6104	$2 \cdot 7 \cdot 7$
99	9801	9.9499	970,299	4.6261	$3 \cdot 3 \cdot 11$
100	10,000	10.0000	1,000,000	4.6416	$2 \cdot 2 \cdot 5 \cdot 5$

Answers

Chapter 1
Exercises 1.1, Pages 14 – 16

1. $0, \sqrt{16}, 6$ **3.** $-8, -\sqrt{4}, 0, \sqrt{16}, 6$ **5.** $-8, -\sqrt{4}, -\dfrac{4}{3}, -1.2, 0, \dfrac{4}{5}, \sqrt{16}, 4.2, 6$ **7.** Always

9. Sometimes   **11.** Sometimes   **13.** 0.625 **15.** $-2.\overline{3}$ **17.** 3.55

19.   **21.**   **23.**

25.   **27.** $\{x \mid 3 \le x < 5\}$ **29.** $\{x \mid x \ge -2.5\}$

31.   **33.**   **35.**

37.   **39.** Closure property for addition   **41.** Trichotomy Property

43. Associative property of addition   **45.** Commutative property of multiplication   **47.** Trichotomy property   **49.** Closure property of multiplication   **51.** Commutative property of addition
53. Distributive property   **55.** Identity for multiplication   **57.** Transitive property   **59.** Associative property of addition   **61.** Inverse property of addition   **63.** $7 + x$ **65.** $x \cdot 6 + xy$ **67.** $(3x) \cdot z$
69. $2 \cdot y + 2 \cdot 3$ **71.** $\dfrac{1}{6}, 6 \cdot \dfrac{1}{6} = 1$ **73.** $7, -7 + 7 = 0$ **75.** Answers will vary

Exercises 1.2, Pages 29 – 31

1. 7 **3.** $\sqrt{5}$ **5.** -8 **7.** $\{7, -7\}$ **9.** $\{2, -2\}$ **11.** $\left\{\dfrac{4}{5}, -\dfrac{4}{5}\right\}$ **13.** $\varnothing$ **15.** $x \ge 0$ **17.** -11

19. -9 **21.** $\dfrac{1}{2}$ **23.** -3 **25.** 0 **27.** 13 **29.** $-\dfrac{6}{5}$ **31.** -6.9 **33.** 1 **35.** 0 **37.** 20 **39.** $-\dfrac{13}{6}$

41. $-\dfrac{23}{16}$ **43.** $-\dfrac{1}{30}$ **45.** 56 **47.** 480 **49.** $\dfrac{15}{16}$ **51.** $-\dfrac{1}{28}$ **53.** -3.92 **55.** 2 **57.** 13

59. Undefined   **61.** 0 **63.** -13.61 **65.** 0.676 **67.** 5 **69.** 6 **71.** 4 **73.** 5 **75.** 4 **77.** -11

79. -7 **81.** 0 **83.** $-\dfrac{5}{3}$ **85.** 1824 **87.** 3.785 **89.** 222.5

Exercises 1.3, Pages 41 – 43

1. $4x + 3y$ **3.** $6x + y$ **5.** $3x - 4x^2$ **7.** $6x - 7$ **9.** $5x$ **11.** $6x$ **13.** $-x - 15$

15. $5x^2 - 11$ **17.** $x = 3$ **19.** $x = -5$ **21.** $x = 0.6$ **23.** $x = -0.7$ **25.** $x = 3$ **27.** $x = -25$

29. $x = 18$ **31.** All real numbers   **33.** $x = 7$ **35.** $x = 2$ **37.** No Solution, $\varnothing$ **39.** $x = \dfrac{3}{4}$

41. $x = 10$ **43.** $x = 5$ **45.** $x = -12$ **47.** $x = 2$ **49.** $x = \dfrac{3}{2}$ **51.** $x = 4$

53. $x = -\dfrac{3}{2}$ **55.** $x = 9$ **57.** $x = 3$ **59.** $x = 3$ **61.** $x = 8$ or $x = -8$ **63.** No solution, $\varnothing$

65. $x = -1$ or $x = -5$ **67.** $x = \dfrac{9}{2}$ or $x = \dfrac{7}{2}$ **69.** $x = -\dfrac{1}{5}$ or $x = 1$ **71.** $x = -16$ or $x = 8$

73. $x = -\dfrac{1}{3}$ or $x = 3$ **75.** $x = -\dfrac{5}{2}$ or $x = \dfrac{3}{4}$ **77.** $x = -\dfrac{20}{7}$ or $x = \dfrac{4}{5}$ **79.** $x = -20$ or $x = \dfrac{40}{9}$

81. conditional   **83.** contradiction   **85.** conditional   **87.** conditional   **89.** identity

Exercises 1.4, Pages 48 – 50

1. $P = \dfrac{I}{rt}$, 16503. $\alpha = 180 - \beta - \gamma$, $43°$ **5.** $w = \dfrac{P - 2l}{2}$, 13 ft   **7.** $a = P - b - c$, 61 in

9. $A = \pi r^2$, 196π sq ft or 615.8 sq ft   **11.** $b = P - a - c$ **13.** $m = \dfrac{f}{a}$ **15.** $w = \dfrac{A}{l}$ **17.** $n = \dfrac{R}{p}$

19. $p = A - I$ **21.** $m = 2A - n$ **23.** $s = \dfrac{P}{4}$ **25.** $t = \dfrac{d}{r}$ **27.** $t = \dfrac{I}{Pr}$ **29.** $b = \dfrac{P - a}{2}$

31. $a = S - Sr$ **33.** $x = \dfrac{y - b}{m}$ **35.** $r^2 = \dfrac{A}{4\pi}$ **37.** $M = \dfrac{(IQ)C}{100}$ **39.** $h = \dfrac{3V}{\pi r^2}$ **41.** $I = \dfrac{E}{R}$

43. $L = \dfrac{R}{2A}$ **45.** $b = \dfrac{2A}{h} - a$ or $b = \dfrac{2A - ah}{h}$ **47.** $h = \dfrac{L}{2\pi r}$ **49.** $r = \dfrac{S - a}{S}$ **51.** $P = \dfrac{WR - Wr}{2R}$

53. $R = \dfrac{nE - Inr}{I}$ **55.** $r = \dfrac{Sb - Sa + a}{L}$

Exercises 1.5, Pages 58 – 63

1. 71   **3.** 9   **5.** 12   **7.** 7   **9.** 18   **11.** 8, 30   **13.** 46 ft by 84 ft   **15.** $1500   **17.** 78 min.

19. 375 mph, 450 mph   **21.** 60 mph, 300 mi   **23.** $4\dfrac{4}{5}$ hr   **25.** 36 mph, 60 mph   **27.** $112.5

29. 2,000 baskets   **31.** 62,500 pounds   **33.** 20 at $300; 24 at $250   **35.** $14,000 at 5%; $11,000 at 6%

37. 6.5% on $4,000; 6% on $3,000   **39.** $7,000 at 6%; $9,000 at 8%   **41. a.** 53.25 **b.** 44 **c.** 16

43. a. 3.2 **b.** 7.1 **c.** 6.9   **45.** a) 51,600,000 b) 33,000,000 c) 76,000,000

Exercises 1.6, Pages 73 – 75

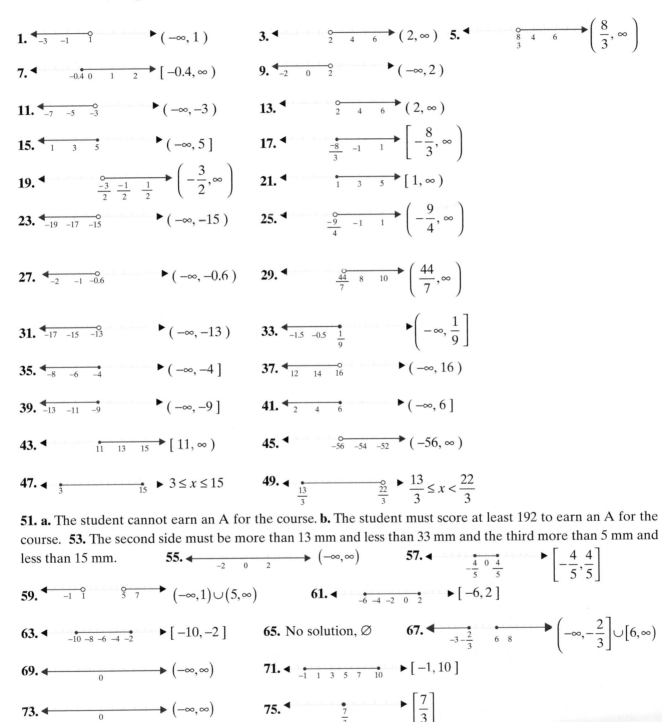

1. $(-\infty, 1)$ **3.** $(2, \infty)$ **5.** $\left(\dfrac{8}{3}, \infty\right)$

7. $[-0.4, \infty)$ **9.** $(-\infty, 2)$

11. $(-\infty, -3)$ **13.** $(2, \infty)$

15. $(-\infty, 5]$ **17.** $\left[-\dfrac{8}{3}, \infty\right)$

19. $\left(-\dfrac{3}{2}, \infty\right)$ **21.** $[1, \infty)$

23. $(-\infty, -15)$ **25.** $\left(-\dfrac{9}{4}, \infty\right)$

27. $(-\infty, -0.6)$ **29.** $\left(\dfrac{44}{7}, \infty\right)$

31. $(-\infty, -13)$ **33.** $\left(-\infty, \dfrac{1}{9}\right]$

35. $(-\infty, -4]$ **37.** $(-\infty, 16)$

39. $(-\infty, -9]$ **41.** $(-\infty, 6]$

43. $[11, \infty)$ **45.** $(-56, \infty)$

47. $3 \le x \le 15$ **49.** $\dfrac{13}{3} \le x < \dfrac{22}{3}$

51. a. The student cannot earn an A for the course. **b.** The student must score at least 192 to earn an A for the course. **53.** The second side must be more than 13 mm and less than 33 mm and the third more than 5 mm and less than 15 mm.   **55.** $(-\infty, \infty)$ **57.** $\left[-\dfrac{4}{5}, \dfrac{4}{5}\right]$

59. $(-\infty, 1) \cup (5, \infty)$ **61.** $[-6, 2]$

63. $[-10, -2]$ **65.** No solution, $\varnothing$ **67.** $\left(-\infty, -\dfrac{2}{3}\right] \cup [6, \infty)$

69. $(-\infty, \infty)$ **71.** $[-1, 10]$

73. $(-\infty, \infty)$ **75.** $\left[\dfrac{7}{3}\right]$

77. a. **b.** $|x - 7| \le 4$ **c.** $[-3, 11]$, closed interval   **79. a.** **b.** $|x + 1| \ge 3$

c. $(-\infty, -4] \cup [2, \infty)$, half-open interval

Exercises 1.7, Pages 82 – 83

1. $(-2)^5 = -32$ **3.** 1 **5.** -36 **7.** $\dfrac{1}{5}$ **9.** $-\dfrac{1}{64}$ **11.** x^{12} **13.** x^5 **15.** $\dfrac{1}{y^3}$ **17.** $\dfrac{1}{x^2}$ **19.** $\dfrac{1}{x}$ **21.** y^5 **23.** $\dfrac{1}{y^4}$

25. x^{10} **27.** $\dfrac{1}{x^3}$ **29.** x^8 **31.** 1 **33.** x^6 **35.** $-x^{12}$ **37.** $\dfrac{1}{x^{10}}$ **39.** $\dfrac{1}{x^9}$ **41.** $\dfrac{1}{x^4}$ **43.** $\dfrac{1}{x}$ **45.** y^4 **47.** y^8

49. x^3 **51.** 1 **53.** y^{11} **55.** x^3 **57.** x^{10} **59.** x^{k+3} **61.** x^{3k+4} **63.** x^k **65.** x^{2k} **67.** x^{2k+1} **69.** x^{k-5}

71. a. $a^m \cdot a^n = a^{m+n}$ **b.** $3^2 \cdot 2^2 = 3 \cdot 3 \cdot 2 \cdot 2 = 6^2$ **c.** $a^m \cdot a^n = a^{m+n}$

Exercises 1.8., Pages 91 – 93

1. $\dfrac{1}{x^4}$ **3.** $4x^8$ **5.** $\dfrac{x^4}{y^6}$ **7.** $\dfrac{a^4}{b^8}$ **9.** $\dfrac{36b^4}{a^2}$ **11.** $\dfrac{x^2}{36y^6}$ **13.** $\dfrac{x^4}{25y^2}$ **15.** $x^{2k}y^k$ **17.** $x^{2k+1}y^{2+n}$ **19.** $x^n y^{k+1}$

21. $\dfrac{x^4}{y}$ **23.** $\dfrac{9y^7}{x^6}$ **25.** $\dfrac{a^6}{b^3}$ **27.** $\dfrac{7}{2x^3y}$ **29.** $\dfrac{x^{13}}{y^{20}}$ **31.** $\dfrac{y^6}{x^6}$ **33.** 472,000 **35.** 0.000000128 **37.** 0.00923

39. $4.79 \cdot 10^5$ **41.** 8.71×10^{-7} **43.** 4.29×10 **45.** 1.44×10^5 **47.** 6×10^{-4} **49.** 1.2×10^{-1} **51.** 5×10^3

53. 5.6×10^{-2} **55.** 1.8×10^{12} cm/min; 1.08×10^{14} cm/hr **57.** 4.0678×10^{16} m **59.** 1.9926×10^{-26} kg

61. 1.0×10^2 **63.** 1.844×10^2 **65.** 1.2×10^6

Chapter 1 Test, Pages 100 – 102

1. a. $-2, 0, 2$ **b.** $-2, -\dfrac{5}{3}, 0, \dfrac{1}{2}, 2$ **2.** $0.41\overline{6}$ **3.** ◄ 0 1 2 3 4 5 6 7 ► **4.** ◄ $-7\,-6\,-5\,-4\,-3\,-2\,-1\,0$ ►

5. ◄ $-2\,-1\;0\;\frac{5}{8}$ ► **6.** ◄ -1.5 $3\;\sqrt{17}$ ► **7.** Distributive property **8.** Associative property of addition

9. 0 **10.** $x < a$ **11.** 70 **12.** 8 **13.** $-\dfrac{15}{8}$ **14.** $-\dfrac{4}{15}$ **15.** -144 **16.** 38 **17.** $\dfrac{25}{6}$ **18.** $6x + 16$

19. $7x - 12$ **20.** $x = -1$ **21.** No solution **22.** $x = -6$ **23.** $x = -1.9$ or $x = 0.9$

24. $x = \dfrac{2}{3}$ or $x = \dfrac{8}{3}$ **25. a.** conditional **b.** contradiction **c.** identity **26.** $w = \dfrac{P - 2l}{2}$ **27.** $t = \dfrac{A - p}{Pr}$

28. ◄ -5 ► $(-5, \infty)$ **29.** ◄ $-\frac{7}{2}$ ► $\left(-\infty, -\dfrac{7}{2}\right)$ **30.** ◄ $2\;3\;4\;5$ ►

$(2, 5)$ **31.** ◄ -0.85 1.85 ► $(-\infty, -0.85)$ or $(1.85, \infty)$ **32.** 4 hr **33.** 16 packages at $1.25;

26 packages at $1.75 **34. a.** 58,367,000 **b.** 128,100,000 **c.** 7,600,000

35. $\dfrac{-20.8x^3}{y^2}$ **36.** $\dfrac{1}{x^3 y^4}$ **37.** $\dfrac{9y^{14}}{x^4}$ **38.** x **39. a.** 3.6×10^{-6} **b.** 9.1×10^9 **40.** 2.83×10^6

Chapter 2

Exercises 2.1, Pages 110 – 112

1. a. $(0, 5)$ **b.** $\left(\dfrac{5}{2}, 0 \right)$ **c.** $(-2, 9)$ **d.** $(1, 3)$ **3. a.** $(0, -4)$ **b.** $\left(\dfrac{4}{3}, 0 \right)$ **c.** $(2, 2)$ **d.** $(3, 5)$ **5. a.** $(0, 5)$

b. $\left(\dfrac{5}{2}, 0 \right)$ **c.** $(2, 1)$ **d.** $(-1, 7)$ **7. a.** $(0, -3)$ **b.** $(2, 0)$ **c.** $(-2, -6)$ **d.** $(4, 3)$

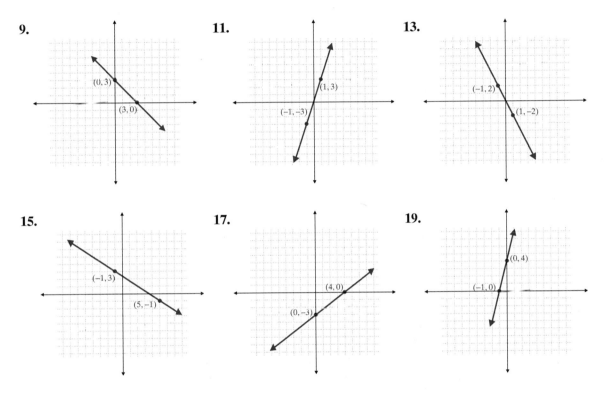

9. (0, 3) (3, 0)

11. (1, 3) (−1, −3)

13. (−1, 2) (1, −2)

15. (−1, 3) (5, −1)

17. (4, 0) (0, −3)

19. (0, 4) (−1, 0)

21. (−1, −2) (2, 0)

23. (−3, 3) (2, 0)

25. (−1, 1) (2, −1)

27. **29.** **31.**

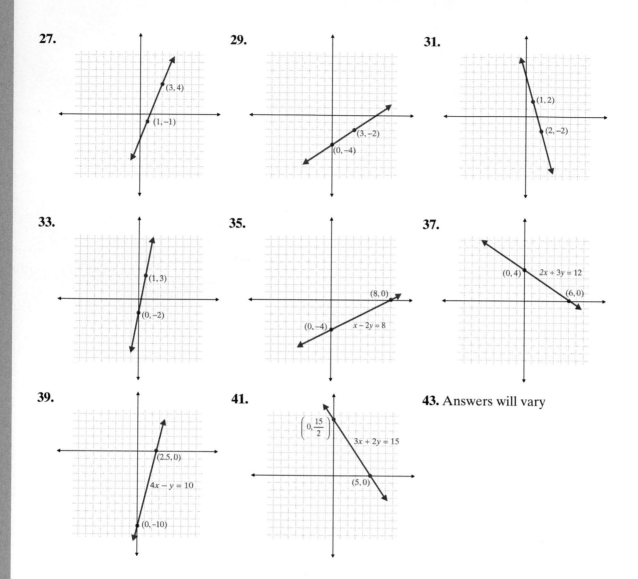

33. **35.** **37.**

39. **41.** **43.** Answers will vary

Exercises 2.2, Pages 121 – 125

1. $m = 5$ **3.** $m = -\dfrac{8}{7}$ **5.** $m = 0$

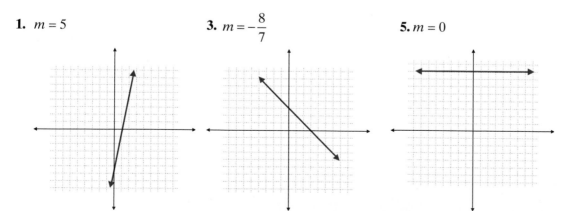

7. $m = -\dfrac{3}{10}$

9. Slope is undefined.

11. $m = \dfrac{1}{5}$

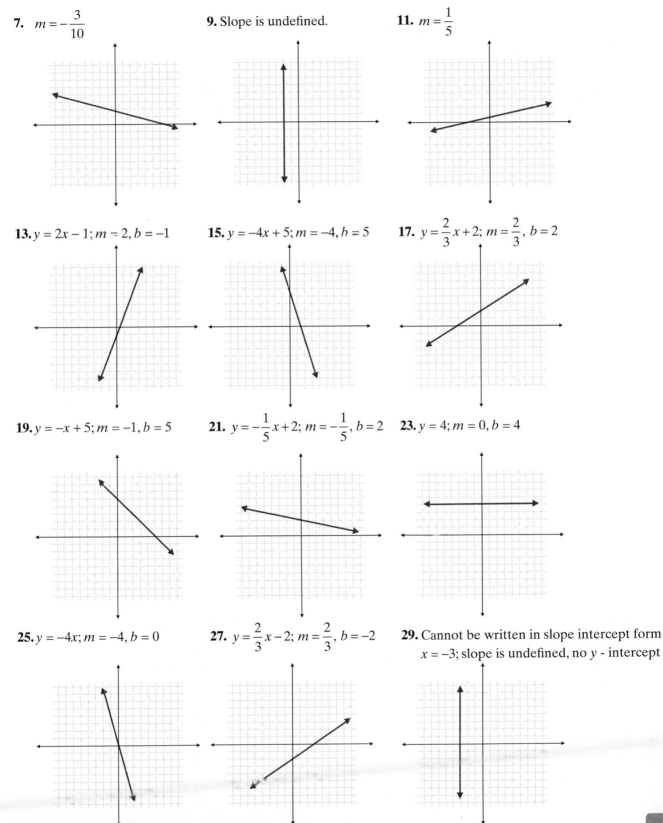

13. $y = 2x - 1; m = 2, b = -1$

15. $y = -4x + 5; m = -4, b = 5$

17. $y = \dfrac{2}{3}x + 2; m = \dfrac{2}{3}, b = 2$

19. $y = -x + 5; m = -1, b = 5$

21. $y = -\dfrac{1}{5}x + 2; m = -\dfrac{1}{5}, b = 2$

23. $y = 4; m = 0, b = 4$

25. $y = -4x; m = -4, b = 0$

27. $y = \dfrac{2}{3}x - 2; m = \dfrac{2}{3}, b = -2$

29. Cannot be written in slope intercept form
$x = -3$; slope is undefined, no y - intercept

31. $y = \dfrac{5}{6}x - \dfrac{5}{3}$; $m = \dfrac{5}{6}$, $b = -\dfrac{5}{3}$ **33.** $y = -\dfrac{3}{4}x + \dfrac{5}{4}$; $m = -\dfrac{3}{4}$, $b = \dfrac{5}{4}$ **35.** $y = -\dfrac{3}{2}x - \dfrac{7}{4}$; $m = -\dfrac{3}{2}$, $b = -\dfrac{7}{4}$

37. $y = \dfrac{1}{2}x + \dfrac{2}{3}$; $m = \dfrac{1}{2}$, $b = \dfrac{2}{3}$ **39.** $y = \dfrac{5}{2}x + \dfrac{5}{2}$; $m = \dfrac{5}{2}$, $b = \dfrac{5}{2}$ **41. a.** Answers will vary

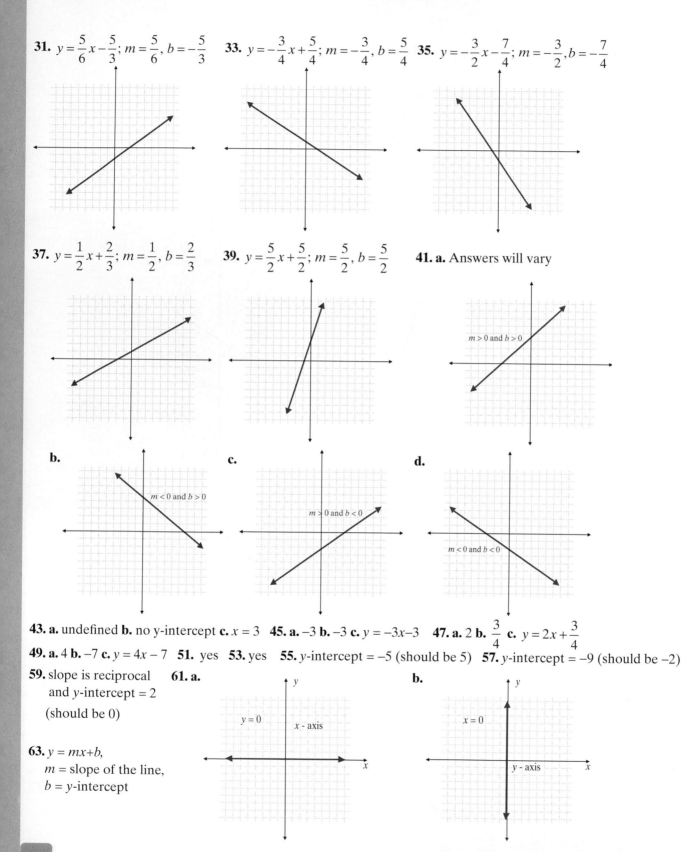

43. a. undefined **b.** no y-intercept **c.** $x = 3$ **45. a.** –3 **b.** –3 **c.** $y = -3x - 3$ **47. a.** 2 **b.** $\dfrac{3}{4}$ **c.** $y = 2x + \dfrac{3}{4}$

49. a. 4 **b.** –7 **c.** $y = 4x - 7$ **51.** yes   **53.** yes   **55.** y-intercept = –5 (should be 5)   **57.** y-intercept = –9 (should be –2)

59. slope is reciprocal and y-intercept = 2 (should be 0)

61. a.

b.

63. $y = mx + b$,
    m = slope of the line,
    b = y-intercept

Exercises 2.3, Pages 135 – 139

1. $2x + y = -3$

3. $x - 2y = -9$

5. $x + 3y = 2$

7. $x = 4$

9. $y = 3$

11. $6x + 5y = 23$

13. $2x + 27y = 5$

15. $12x + 9y = 17$

17.

19.

21.

23.

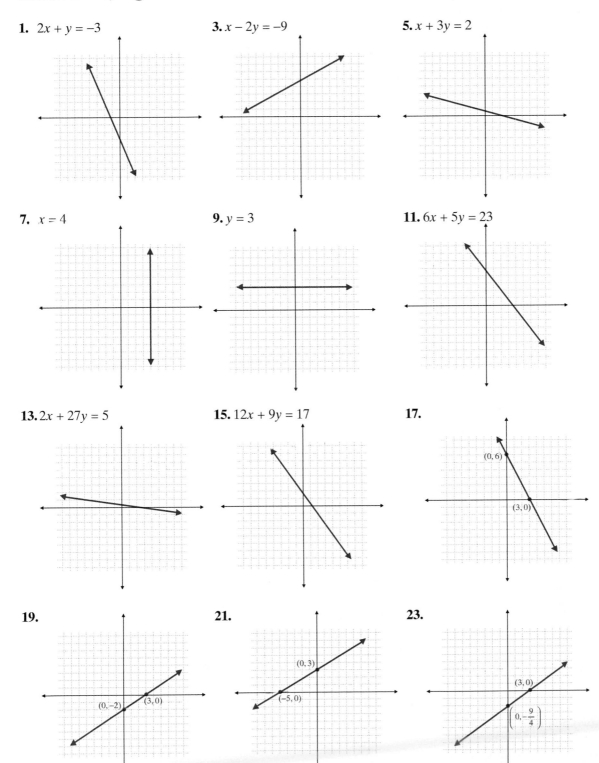

25. $x + 2y = 13$

27. $5x - y = -2$

29. $x = 2$

31. $3x + 5y = 7$

33. $2x - 3y = -2$

35. $x + 2y = -4$

37.

39. \$4000/year

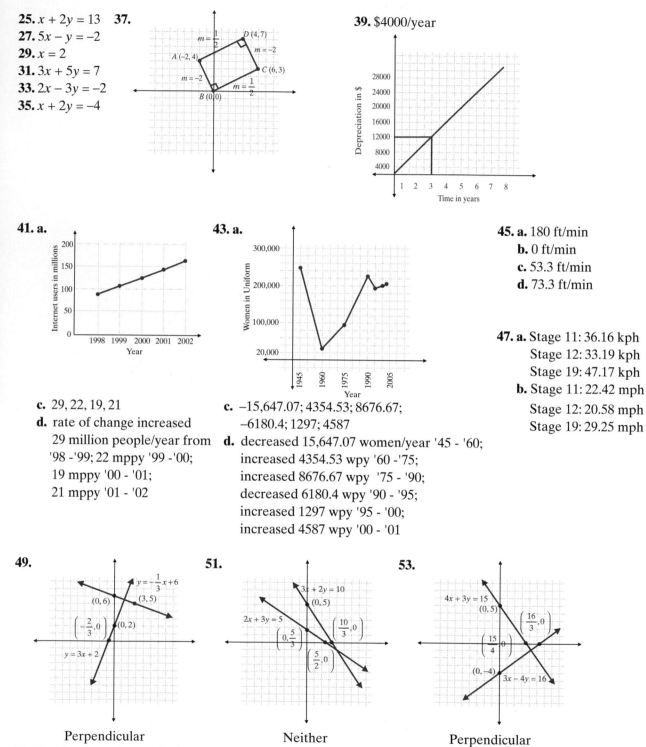

41. a.

c. $29, 22, 19, 21$

d. rate of change increased
29 million people/year from
'98 -'99; 22 mppy '99 -'00;
19 mppy '00 - '01;
21 mppy '01 - '02

43. a.

c. $-15{,}647.07; 4354.53; 8676.67;$
$-6180.4; 1297; 4587$

d. decreased 15,647.07 women/year '45 - '60;
increased 4354.53 wpy '60 -'75;
increased 8676.67 wpy '75 - '90;
decreased 6180.4 wpy '90 - '95;
increased 1297 wpy '95 - '00;
increased 4587 wpy '00 - '01

45. a. 180 ft/min
  b. 0 ft/min
  c. 53.3 ft/min
  d. 73.3 ft/min

47. a. Stage 11: 36.16 kph
     Stage 12: 33.19 kph
     Stage 19: 47.17 kph
  b. Stage 11: 22.42 mph
     Stage 12: 20.58 mph
     Stage 19: 29.25 mph

49.

Perpendicular

51.

Neither

53.

Perpendicular

55. Use the two points to find the slope; then use the slope and one of the points in the point-slope form.

Exercises 2.4, Pages 153 – 157

1. $\{(-4,0),(-1,4),(1,2),(2,5),(6,-3)\}$;

$D=\{-4,-1,1,2,6\}; R=\{0,4,2,5,-3\}$; function

3. $\{(-5,-4),(-4,-2),(-2,-2),(1,-2),(2,1)\}$;

$D=\{-5,-4,-2,1,2\}; R=\{-4,-2,1\}$; function

5. $\{(-4,-3),(-4,1),(-1,-1),(-1,3),(3,-4)\}$;

$D=\{-4,-1,3\}; R=\{-3,1,-1,3,-4\}$; not a function

7. $\{(-5,-5),(-5,3),(0,5),(1,-2),(1,2)\}$;

$D=\{-5,0,1\}; R=\{-5,3,5,-2,2\}$; not a function

9. $D=\{0,1,4,-3,2\}, R=\{0,6,-2,5,-1\}$, function

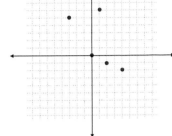

11. $D=\{-4,-3,1,2,3\}, R=\{4\}$, function

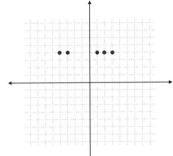

13. $D=\{0,-1,2,3,-3\}, R=\{2,1,4,5\}$, function

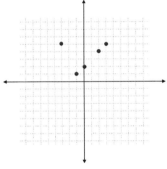

15. $D=\{-1\}, R=\{4,2,0,6,-2\}$, not a function

17. function, $D=(-\infty,\infty), R=[0,\infty)$

19. function, $D=(-6,6], R=\{-6,-4,-2,0,2,4\}$

21. not a function

23. not a function

25. function, $D=(-\infty,\infty), R=\left(-\dfrac{3}{2},\dfrac{3}{2}\right)$

27. $\left\{(-9,-26),\left(-\dfrac{1}{3},0\right),(0,1),\left(\dfrac{4}{3},5\right),(2,7)\right\}$

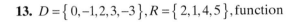

29. $\{(-2,-11),(-1,-2),(0,1),(1,-2),(2,-11)\}$ **31.** $D=\{x \mid x \neq -3\}$ **33.** $D=\left\{x \mid x \geq -\dfrac{5}{2}\right\}$

35.

37.

39.

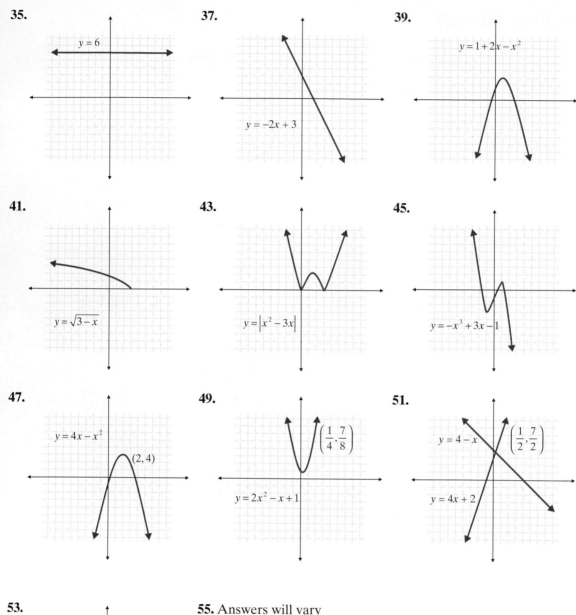

41.

43.

45.

47.

49.

51.

53.

55. Answers will vary

Exercises 2.5, Pages 164 – 165

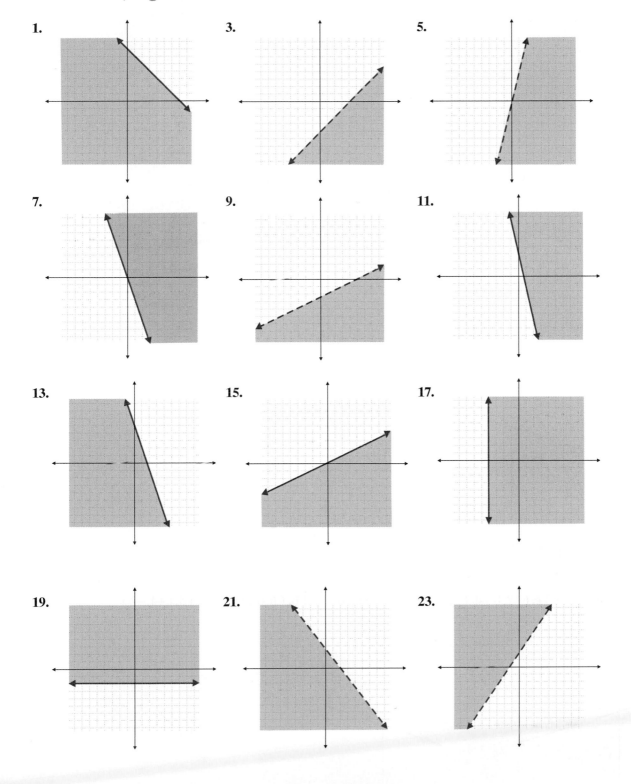

1. **3.** **5.**

7. **9.** **11.**

13. **15.** **17.**

19. **21.** **23.**

25.

27.

29.

31.

33.

35.

37.

39.

41. Answers will vary

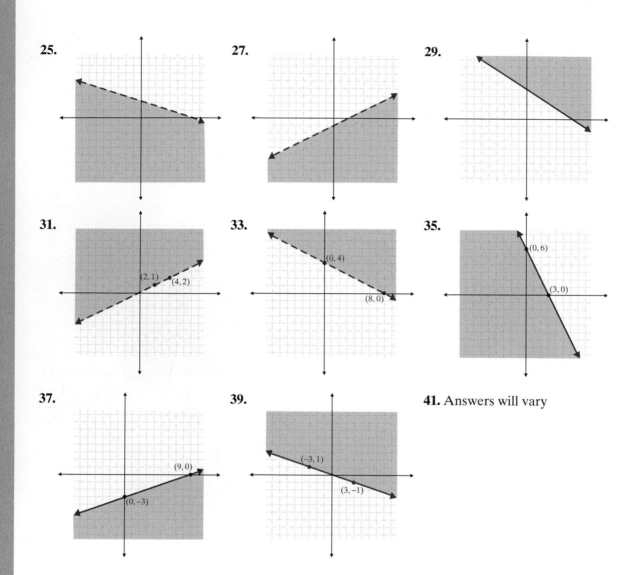

Chapter 2 Test, Pages 168 – 170

1. a. $(0, 2)$ **b.** $\left(\frac{2}{3}, 0\right)$ **c.** $(-2, 8)$ **d.** $(3, -7)$ **2. a.** $\left(0, -\frac{6}{5}\right)$ **b.** $(6, 0)$ **c.** $(11, 1)$ **d.** $(-4, -2)$

3.

4.

5. $m = \dfrac{9}{8}$

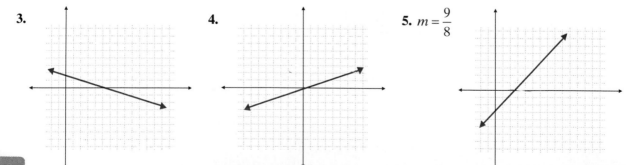

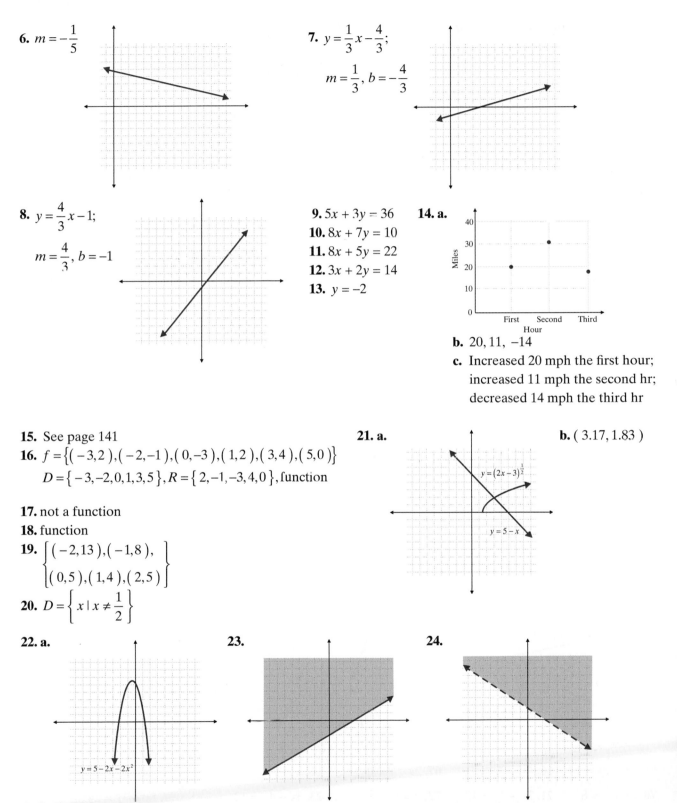

6. $m = -\dfrac{1}{5}$

7. $y = \dfrac{1}{3}x - \dfrac{4}{3};$

$m = \dfrac{1}{3},\ b = -\dfrac{4}{3}$

8. $y = \dfrac{4}{3}x - 1;$

$m = \dfrac{4}{3},\ b = -1$

9. $5x + 3y = 36$
10. $8x + 7y = 10$
11. $8x + 5y = 22$
12. $3x + 2y = 14$
13. $y = -2$

14. a.

b. $20, 11, -14$

c. Increased 20 mph the first hour; increased 11 mph the second hr; decreased 14 mph the third hr

15. See page 141

16. $f = \left\{ (-3,2), (-2,-1), (0,-3), (1,2), (3,4), (5,0) \right\}$

$D = \{-3,-2,0,1,3,5\},\ R = \{2,-1,-3,4,0\},$ function

17. not a function
18. function

19. $\left\{ \begin{matrix} (-2,13), (-1,8), \\ (0,5), (1,4), (2,5) \end{matrix} \right\}$

20. $D = \left\{ x \mid x \neq \dfrac{1}{2} \right\}$

21. a.

b. $(3.17, 1.83)$

22. a.

b. $(-.5, 5.5)$

23.

24.

Chapter 2 Cumulative Review, Pages 171 – 174

1. a. $\{\sqrt{9}\}$ **b.** $\{0,\sqrt{9}\}$ **c.** $\left\{-10,-\sqrt{25},-1.6,0,\dfrac{1}{5},\sqrt{9}\right\}$ **d.** $\left\{-10,-\sqrt{25},0,\sqrt{9}\right\}$ **e.** $\left\{-\sqrt{7},\pi,\sqrt{12}\right\}$

f. $\left\{-10,-\sqrt{25},-1.6,-\sqrt{7},0,\dfrac{1}{5},\sqrt{9},\pi,\sqrt{12}\right\}$ **2.** 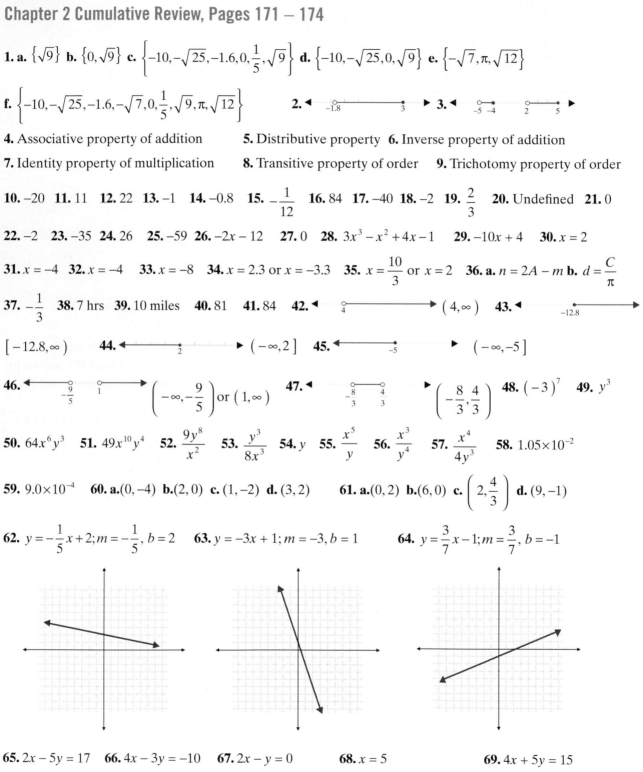 **3.**

4. Associative property of addition   **5.** Distributive property **6.** Inverse property of addition

7. Identity property of multiplication   **8.** Transitive property of order   **9.** Trichotomy property of order

10. -20 **11.** 11 **12.** 22 **13.** -1 **14.** -0.8 **15.** $-\dfrac{1}{12}$ **16.** 84 **17.** -40 **18.** -2 **19.** $\dfrac{2}{3}$ **20.** Undefined **21.** 0

22. -2 **23.** -35 **24.** 26 **25.** -59 **26.** $-2x-12$ **27.** 0 **28.** $3x^{3}-x^{2}+4x-1$ **29.** $-10x+4$ **30.** $x=2$

31. $x=-4$ **32.** $x=-4$ **33.** $x=-8$ **34.** $x=2.3$ or $x=-3.3$ **35.** $x=\dfrac{10}{3}$ or $x=2$ **36. a.** $n=2A-m$ **b.** $d=\dfrac{C}{\pi}$

37. $-\dfrac{1}{3}$ **38.** 7 hrs **39.** 10 miles **40.** 81 **41.** 84 **42.** $(4,\infty)$ **43.**

$[-12.8,\infty)$ **44.** $(-\infty,2]$ **45.** $(-\infty,-5]$

46. $\left(-\infty,-\dfrac{9}{5}\right)$ or $(1,\infty)$ **47.** $\left(-\dfrac{8}{3},\dfrac{4}{3}\right)$ **48.** $(-3)^{7}$ **49.** y^{3}

50. $64x^{6}y^{3}$ **51.** $49x^{10}y^{4}$ **52.** $\dfrac{9y^{8}}{x^{2}}$ **53.** $\dfrac{y^{3}}{8x^{3}}$ **54.** y **55.** $\dfrac{x^{5}}{y}$ **56.** $\dfrac{x^{3}}{y^{4}}$ **57.** $\dfrac{x^{4}}{4y^{3}}$ **58.** 1.05×10^{-2}

59. 9.0×10^{-4} **60. a.** $(0,-4)$ **b.** $(2,0)$ **c.** $(1,-2)$ **d.** $(3,2)$ **61. a.** $(0,2)$ **b.** $(6,0)$ **c.** $\left(2,\dfrac{4}{3}\right)$ **d.** $(9,-1)$

62. $y=-\dfrac{1}{5}x+2;m=-\dfrac{1}{5},b=2$ **63.** $y=-3x+1;m=-3,b=1$ **64.** $y=\dfrac{3}{7}x-1;m=\dfrac{3}{7},b=-1$

65. $2x-5y=17$ **66.** $4x-3y=-10$ **67.** $2x-y=0$ **68.** $x=5$ **69.** $4x+5y=15$

70. $2x+y=8$ **71.** $3x+2y=12$ **72.** $x=1$ **73.** $3x-4y=12$ **74.** $5x+3y=24$

75.

76.

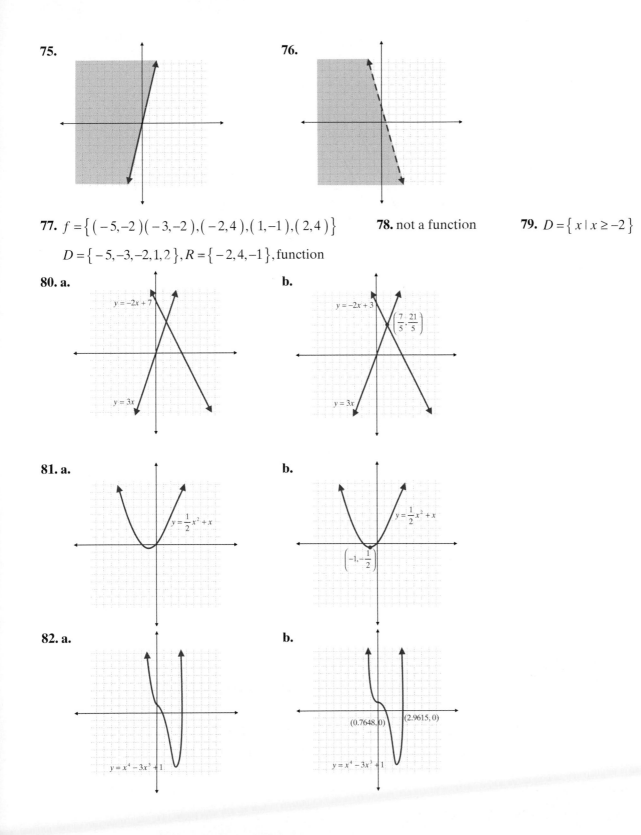

77. $f = \{(-5,-2)(-3,-2),(-2,4),(1,-1),(2,4)\}$ **78.** not a function   **79.** $D = \{x \mid x \geq -2\}$

$D = \{-5,-3,-2,1,2\}, R = \{-2,4,-1\}, \text{function}$

80. a.

$y = -2x + 7$

$y = 3x$

b.

$y = -2x + 3$

$\left(\frac{7}{5}, \frac{21}{5}\right)$

$y = 3x$

81. a.

$y = \frac{1}{2}x^2 + x$

b.

$y = \frac{1}{2}x^2 + x$

$\left(-1, -\frac{1}{2}\right)$

82. a.

$y = x^4 - 3x^3 + 1$

b.

$(0.7648, 0)$

$(2.9615, 0)$

$y = x^4 - 3x^3 + 1$

Chapter 3

Exercises 3.1, Pages 185 – 186

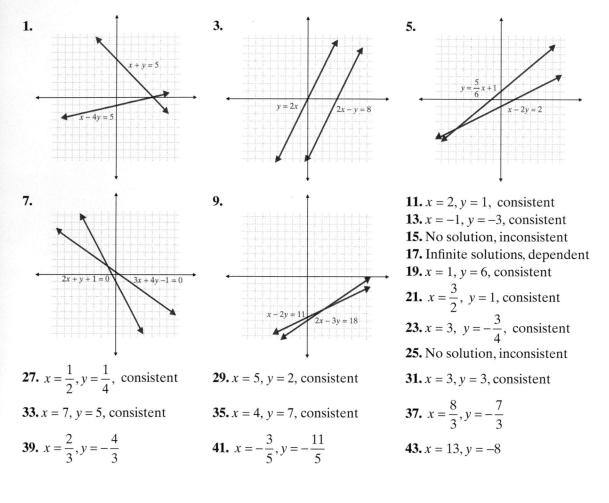

1.

3.

5.

7.

9.

11. $x = 2$, $y = 1$, consistent

13. $x = -1$, $y = -3$, consistent

15. No solution, inconsistent

17. Infinite solutions, dependent

19. $x = 1$, $y = 6$, consistent

21. $x = \dfrac{3}{2}$, $y = 1$, consistent

23. $x = 3$, $y = -\dfrac{3}{4}$, consistent

25. No solution, inconsistent

27. $x = \dfrac{1}{2}$, $y = \dfrac{1}{4}$, consistent

29. $x = 5$, $y = 2$, consistent

31. $x = 3$, $y = 3$, consistent

33. $x = 7$, $y = 5$, consistent

35. $x = 4$, $y = 7$, consistent

37. $x = \dfrac{8}{3}$, $y = -\dfrac{7}{3}$

39. $x = \dfrac{2}{3}$, $y = -\dfrac{4}{3}$

41. $x = -\dfrac{3}{5}$, $y = -\dfrac{11}{5}$

43. $x = 13$, $y = -8$

Exercises 3.2, Pages 190 – 193

1. 23, 79   **3.** $80°, 100°$ **5.** 100 yards $\times$ 45 yards   **7.** 40 liters of 12%, 50 liters of 30%

9. 240 gal of 5%, 120 gal of 2%   **11.** $87,000 in bonds, $37,000 in certificates   **13.** 325 at $3.50/share, 175 at $6.00/share   **15.** 40 lbs at $3.90/lb, 30 lbs at $2.50/lb   **17.** 16 lbs at $.70/lb, 4 lbs at $1.30/lb

19. $5.50 for paperback, $9.00 for hardback   **21.** 150 legislators voted "for" the bill   **23.** 6:00 P.M.

25. Commercial jet: 300 mph, Private: 125 mph   **27.** $a = -2$, $b = 3$ **29.** $a = 10$, $b = -2$

31. $11.20/hr labor, $4.80/lb materials   **33.** 9 lbs of Ration I, 2 lbs of Ration II   **35.** $65°, 65°, 50°$

Exercises 3.3, Pages 201 – 204

1. $x = 1, y = 0, z = 1$ **3.** $x = 1, y = 2, z = -1$ **5.** Infinite solution   **7.** $x = -2, y = 9, z = 1$ **9.** $x = 4,$ $y = 1, z = 1$ **11.** $x = -2, y = 3, z = 1$ **13.** No solution **15.** Infinite solution   **17.** $x = \dfrac{1}{2}, y = \dfrac{1}{3}, z = -1$

19. $x = 2, y = 1, z = -3$ **21.** $34, 6, 27$ **23.** 11 nickels, 7 dimes, 5 quarters   **25.** $a = 1, b = 3, c = -2$
27. 19 cm, 24cm, 30 cm   **29.** home: \$90,000, lot: \$22,000, improve: \$11,000   **31.** savings: \$30,000, bonds: \$55,000, stocks: \$15,000   **33.** $100°, 30°, 50°$ **35.** 3 liters of 10%, 4.5 liters of 30%, 1.5 liters of 40%
37. $A = 2, B = -1, C = 3$

Exercises 3.4, Pages 217 – 219

1. $\begin{bmatrix} 2 & 2 \\ 5 & -1 \end{bmatrix}, \begin{bmatrix} 2 & 2 & | & 13 \\ 5 & -1 & | & 10 \end{bmatrix}$ **3.** $\begin{vmatrix} 7 & -2 & 7 \\ -5 & 3 & 0 \\ 0 & 4 & 11 \end{vmatrix}, \begin{bmatrix} 7 & -2 & 7 & | & 2 \\ -5 & 3 & 0 & | & 2 \\ 0 & 4 & 11 & | & 8 \end{bmatrix}$

5. $\begin{bmatrix} 3 & 1 & -1 & 2 \\ 1 & -1 & 2 & -1 \\ 0 & 2 & 5 & 1 \\ 1 & 3 & 0 & 3 \end{bmatrix} \begin{bmatrix} 3 & 1 & -1 & 2 & | & 6 \\ 1 & -1 & 2 & -1 & | & -8 \\ 0 & 2 & 5 & 1 & | & 2 \\ 1 & 3 & 0 & 3 & | & 14 \end{bmatrix}$ **7.** $\begin{cases} -3x + 5 = 1 \\ -x + 3y = 2 \end{cases}$ **9.** $\begin{cases} x + 3y + 4z = 1 \\ 2x - 3y - 2z = 0 \\ x + y = -4 \end{cases}$ **11.** $x = -1, y = 2$

13. $x = -1, y = -1$ **15.** $x = -1, y = -2, z = 3$ **17.** $x = 1, y = 0, z = 1$ **19.** $x = 2, y = 1, z = -1$
21. $x = -2, y = -1, z = 5$ **23.** $x = 1, y = 2, z = 1$ **25.** $x = 1, y = -3, z = 2$ **27.** $52, 40, 77$
29. 20 small, 32 medium, 16 large   **31.** $x = 0, y = -4$ **33.** $x = 2, y = 1, z = 7$ **35.** $x = \dfrac{13}{12}, y = \dfrac{5}{4}, z = \dfrac{8}{3}$
37. $x = -\dfrac{1}{3}, y = 1, z = \dfrac{16}{3}$ **39.** Answers will vary

Exercises 3.5, Pages 226 – 228

1. -22 **3.** -212 **5.** 11 **7.** 3 **9.** 47 **11.** 36 **13.** -3 **15.** -4 **17.** -25 **19.** 20 **21.** $x = 7$ **23.** $x = -7$

25. $x = -3$ **27.** $2x - 7y = -11$ **29.** $A = 1$ **31.** $A = \dfrac{31}{2}$

33. -25 **35.** -33.28 **37.** 0, Answers will vary

Exercises 3.6, Pages 234 – 235

1. $x = 4, y = 3$ **3.** $x = \dfrac{2}{3}, y = -\dfrac{1}{4}$ **5.** No Solution   **7.** $x = -\dfrac{1}{4}, y = \dfrac{3}{2}$ **9.** $x = \dfrac{31}{17}, y = \dfrac{2}{17}$ **11.** $x = \dfrac{39}{44}, y = \dfrac{41}{44}$

13. $x = \dfrac{18}{7}, y = -\dfrac{3}{7}$ **15.** $x = -\dfrac{7}{61}, y = \dfrac{266}{183}$ **17.** $x = \dfrac{210}{41}, y = -\dfrac{40}{123}$ **19.** $x = \dfrac{525}{124}, y = \dfrac{109}{93}$

21. $x = -2, y = 1, z = 3$ **23.** No Solution   **25.** $x = 4, y = 2, z = 6$ **27.** Infinite Solutions

29. $x = -\dfrac{2}{3}, y = \dfrac{11}{3}, z = 2$ **31.** 6 feet, 17 feet, 20 feet **33.** $3,500,000 in mutual funds $2,500,000 in stock

Exercises 3.7, Pages 240 – 241

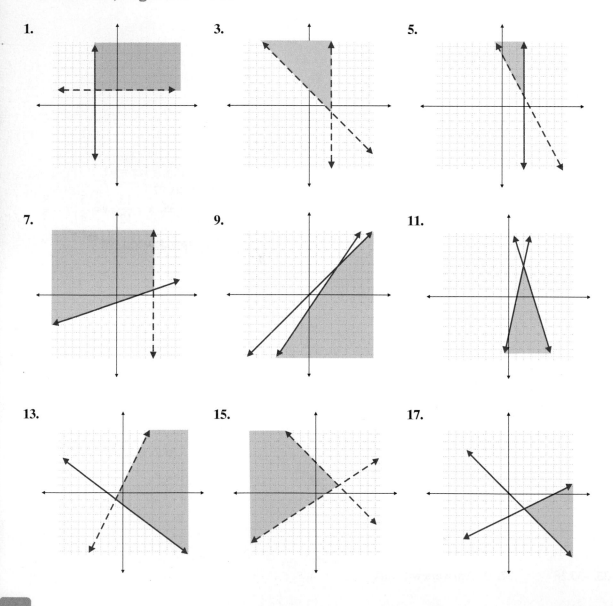

1.

3.

5.

7.

9.

11.

13.

15.

17.

19.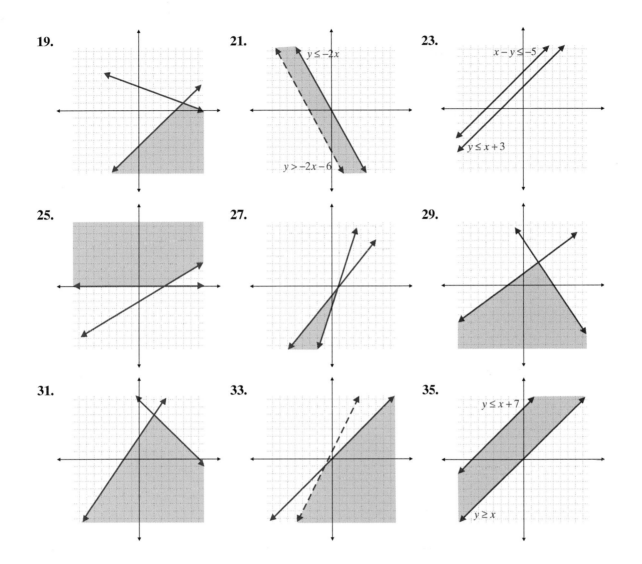

21. $y \leq -2x$ $y > -2x - 6$

23. $x - y \leq -5$ $y \leq x + 3$

25.

27.

29.

31.

33.

35. $y \leq x + 7$ $y \geq x$

Chapter 3 Test, Pages 247 – 248

1. $x = 3, y = -1$

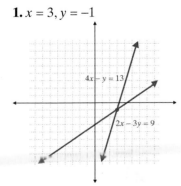

2. $x = 7, y = 2$ **3.** Inconsistent, No Solution **4.** $x = \dfrac{1}{2}, y = \dfrac{1}{4}$

5. $x = 11, y = -7$ **6.** $a = -3, b = 4$ **7.** 8 ft $\times$ 23 ft **8.** $x = -1, y = 1, z = -2$

9. Inconsistent, No Solution **10. a.** $\begin{bmatrix} 1 & 2 & -3 \\ 1 & -1 & -1 \\ 1 & 3 & 2 \end{bmatrix}$ 3×3 **b.** $x = 1, y = -3, z = 2$

$$\begin{bmatrix} 1 & 2 & -3 & | & -11 \\ 1 & -1 & -1 & | & 2 \\ 1 & 3 & 2 & | & -4 \end{bmatrix} \quad 3 \times 4$$

11. 60 33-cent stamps, 20 55-cent stamps, 10 78-cent stamps. **12.** 42 **13.** 5

14. $x = 6$ **15.** $x = \dfrac{17}{3}$ **16.** $x = -\dfrac{78}{5}, y = \dfrac{38}{5}$ **17.** $x = -\dfrac{5}{26}, y = \dfrac{33}{26}, z = \dfrac{9}{26}$ **18.** $50°, 60°, 70°$

19.

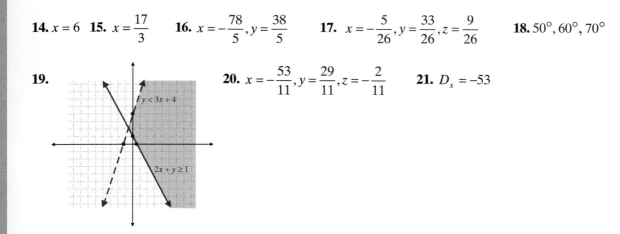

20. $x = -\dfrac{53}{11}, y = \dfrac{29}{11}, z = -\dfrac{2}{11}$ **21.** $D_x = -53$

Chapter 3 Cumulative Review, Pages 249 – 251

1. a. $-3, 0, 1$ **b.** $-3, -\dfrac{1}{2}, 0, \dfrac{5}{8}, 1$ **c.** $-\sqrt{13}, \sqrt{2}, \pi$ **d.** $-\sqrt{13}, -3, -\dfrac{1}{2}, 0, \dfrac{5}{8}, 1, \sqrt{2}, \pi$ **2.** 0 **3.** 320 **4.** $x = 2$

5. $x = -6$ **6.** $x = -\dfrac{29}{2}$ or $x = \dfrac{27}{2}$ **7.** $m = \dfrac{2gK}{V^2}$ **8.** ⟵————○————⟶ $(-\infty, 4)$
                                                                                          4

9. ⟵•————————⟶ $[-144, \infty)$ **10.** ⟵————○————○————⟶ $\left(-\dfrac{8}{3}, \dfrac{4}{3}\right)$ **11.** $\dfrac{1}{x^8}$ **12.** $\dfrac{x^5}{y}$ **13.** $\dfrac{6}{x^2}$
       -144 $-\dfrac{8}{3}$ $\dfrac{4}{3}$

14. 2.7×10^{-3} **15. a.** $m = -\dfrac{1}{2}$ **b.** $x + 2y = -1$ **c.**   **16.** $y = \dfrac{2}{5}x$

17. x-intercepts: $(-3.45, 0)$ and $(1.45, 0)$ maximum: $(-1, 6)$ **18.** $(-1.65, -0.29)$ and $(3.69, 10.29)$

19. $x = 1, y = 4$ **20.** $x = 1, y = 3$ **21.** $x = 4, y = 3, z = 2$ **26.**

22. $x = 2, y = \dfrac{2}{5}, z = -\dfrac{1}{2}$

23. 3 batches of Choc-O-Nut and
   2 batches of Chocolate Krunch
24. \$4,200 at 7%, \$2,800 at 8%
25. $a = 2, b = 3, c = 4$

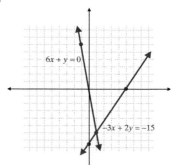

27. $x = \dfrac{8}{5}$, $y = \dfrac{27}{10}$ **31.**

28. $x = -3$, $y = 0$, $z = 5$
29. $x = 1$, $y = 1$
30. $x = 1$, $y = 2$, $z = 3$

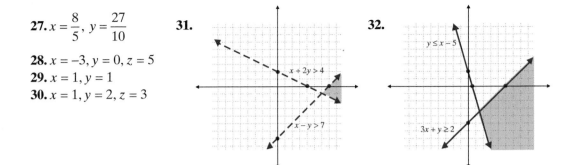

Chapter 4
Exercises 4.1, Pages 259 – 261

1. Bionomial, degree 3   **3.** Not a polynomial   **5.** Trinomial, degree 3   **7.** Monomial, no degree

9. Not a polynomial   **11.** Not a polynomial   **13.** $4x^2 - 3x - 6$ **15.** $-7x - 6$ **17.** $3x^2 - 4y^2$

19. $x^2 - x + 10$ **21.** $2x^4 - 5x^3 - x - 3$ **23.** $x^4 + 2x^2 + 8x - 1$ **25.** $6x^3 - 7x^2 + 8x + 3$

27. $9x^2 + 13xy - 6y^2$ **29.** $12x^3 - 21x^2 - 2x + 12$ **31.** $5x^3 - 2x^2$ **33.** $-2x^2 - 4xy + y^2$

35. $8x - 3xy$ **37.** $2x^3 - 2x - 3$ **39.** $10x^4 + 2x^3 - 4x^2 + 2x + 1$ **41.** $5x^2 - 7x + 5$ **43.** $4x^3 + 4x^2 - 7x + 24$

45. $x^4 - 5x^3 - 8x^2 + 3x - 3$ **47.** 13   **49.** 1   **51.** -289 **53.** 7   **55.** -20

57. Answers will vary   **59.** Answers will vary

Exercises 4.2, Pages 268 – 270

1. $5x^3 - 10x^2 + 15x$ **3.** $x^3y^2 + 4xy^3$ **5.** $x^2 - 3x - 18$ **7.** $x^2 - 9x + 8$ **9.** $2y^2 - 11y - 6$ **11.** $3x^2 - 19x + 20$

13. $6y^2 + 13y + 6$ **15.** $8x^2 - 37x - 15$ **17.** $27x^2 - 15x - 2$ **19.** $9x^2 + 6x + 1$

21. $25x^2 - 20xy + 4y^2$ **23.** $16x^2 - 49$ **25.** $4x^2 - 9y^2$ **27.** $9x^5 - 16x$ **29.** $x^3 - 1$

31. $x^3 + 9x^2 + 27x + 27$ **33.** $x^6 + 4x^3 + 4$ **35.** $4x^6 - 49$ **37.** $x^3 - 27y^3$ **39.** $4x^6y - 144x^2y^5$

41. $10x^6y - 13x^4y^3 - 3x^2y^5$ **43.** $x^2 + 2xy + y^2 - 4$ **45.** $25x^2 + y^2 + 30x - 6y - 10xy + 9$

47. $x^2 + 8x - 4xy - 16y + 4y^2 + 16$ **49.** $x^{k+2} + 3x^2$ **51.** $x^{2k} - 2x^k - 15$ **53.** $x^{2k} + 5x^k + 4$

55. $3x^{2k} + 17x^k + 10$ **57.** $x^2 - \dfrac{25}{64}$ **59.** $y^2 - \dfrac{2}{5}y + \dfrac{1}{25}$ **61.** $x^2 - 6.25$ **63.** $6x^3 - 13x^2 - 23x - 6$

65. $2x^4 - 3x^3 - 6x^2 + 17x - 12$ **67.** $4x^4 - 6x^3 - 28x^2 + 26x + 24$ **69. a.** $10x^5 - 20x^4 + 10x^3$ **b.** $\dfrac{5}{16}$ **c.** $\dfrac{128}{625}$

71. a. $A(x) = 4x^2 + 150x + 1250$ **b.** $A(x) = 4x^2 + 150x$ **73.** Answers will vary

Exercises 4.3, Pages 279 – 282

1. $y^2 - 2y + 3$ **3.** $2x^2 - 3x + 1$ **5.** $10x^3 - 11x^2 + x$ **7.** $-4x^2 + 7x - \dfrac{5}{2}$ **9.** $y^3 - \dfrac{7}{2}y^2 - \dfrac{15}{2}y + 4$

11. $3x + 4 + \dfrac{1}{7x - 1}$ **13.** $x^2 + 2x + 2 + \dfrac{-12}{2x + 3}$ **15.** $7x^2 + 2x + 1$ **17.** $x^2 + 3x + 2 + \dfrac{-2}{x - 4}$

19. $2x^2 + x - 3 + \dfrac{18}{5x + 3}$ **21.** $2x^2 - 8x + 25 + \dfrac{-98}{x + 4}$ **23.** $3x^2 + 2x - 5 + \dfrac{-1}{3x - 2}$ **25.** $3x^2 - 2x + 5$

27. $3x + 5 + \dfrac{x - 1}{x^2 + 2}$ **29.** $x^2 + x - 4 + \dfrac{-8x + 17}{x^2 + 4}$ **31.** $2x + 3 + \dfrac{6}{3x^2 - 2x - 1}$

33. $3x^2 - 10x + 12 + \dfrac{-x - 14}{x^2 + x + 1}$ **35.** $x^2 - 2x + 7 + \dfrac{-17x + 14}{x^2 + 2x - 3}$ **37.** $x^2 + 3x + 9$ **39.** $x^3 - x + \dfrac{x - 1}{x^2 + 1}$

41. a. $x - 9$ **b.** $a = 3, P(3) = 0$ **43. a.** $x^2 - 4x + 33 + \dfrac{-265}{x + 8}$ **b.** $a = -8, P(-8) = -265$

45. a. $4x^2 - 6x + 9 + \dfrac{-17}{x + 2}$ **b.** $a = -2, P(-2) = -17$ **47. a.** $x^2 + 7x + 55 + \dfrac{388}{x - 7}$ **b.** $a = 7, P(7) = 388$

49. a. $2x^2 - 2x + 6 + \dfrac{-27}{x + 3}$ **b.** $a = -3, P(-3) = -27$ **51. a.** $x^3 + 2x + 5 + \dfrac{17}{x - 3}$ **b.** $a = 3, P(3) = 17$

53. a. $x^3 + 2x^2 + 6x + 9 + \dfrac{23}{x - 2}$ **b.** $a = 2, P(2) = 23$ **55. a.** $x^3 + \dfrac{x^2}{2} - \dfrac{3}{4}x - \dfrac{3}{8} + \dfrac{45}{16\left(x - \dfrac{1}{2}\right)}$ **b.** $a = \dfrac{1}{2}, P\left(\dfrac{1}{2}\right) = \dfrac{45}{16}$

57. a. $x^4 + x^3 + x^2 + x + 1$ **b.** $a = 1, P(1) = 0$ **59. a.** $x^3 - \dfrac{14}{5}x^2 + \dfrac{56}{25}x - \dfrac{224}{125} + \dfrac{3396}{625\left(x + \dfrac{4}{5}\right)}$

b. $a = -\dfrac{4}{5}, P\left(-\dfrac{4}{5}\right) = \dfrac{3396}{625}$ **61.** See page 278

63. a. $x^2 - \dfrac{7}{2}x + \dfrac{13}{4} + \dfrac{73}{4(2x - 1)};\ 2x^2 - 7x + \dfrac{13}{2} + \dfrac{73}{4\left(x - \dfrac{1}{2}\right)}$ **b.** Answers will vary   **c.** Answers will vary

Exercises 4.4, Pages 292 – 294

1. $5(x^2 + 3)$ **3.** $xy(x - 2 + y)$ **5.** $5x^2y(y + 4)$ **7.** $3x^2y(1 + 7xy + y^2)$ **9.** Not factorable (or Prime)

11. $(3x + 5)(3x - 5)$ **13.** $(x - 5)^2$ **15.** $(3y + 2)^2$ **17.** $(x + 6)(x + 3)$ **19.** $(x - 9)(x + 3)$

21. $(y - 7)(y + 2)$ **23.** $(x + 7)^2$ **25.** $(2x + 3)(3x + 2)$ **27.** $(2x - 5)(x + 7)$ **29.** $(4x - 5)^2$

31. $(5x - 3)(7x + 6)$ **33.** $4x(x - 4)(x + 4)$ **35.** $x^2(7x + 8)(3x - 4)$ **37.** $2x^3y^2(3x^2 - 14xy - 3y^2)$

39. $2x(3x^2 + 2)(2x^2 + 5)$ **41.** $x(3x^2 - 4)(3x^2 + 4)$ **43.** $(2x^2 - 5y)(x^2 + 3y)$ **45.** Not factorable

47. $(2x^3 + y^2)(x^3 + 4y^2)$ **49.** $(x - 5)(x + 7)(x - 3)$ **51.** $(2x + 1)(2x + 3)(x - 6)$ **53.** $(x + y + 3)^2$

55. $(x + 2y - 5)(x + 2y + 5)$ **57.** $(x + 5y + 6)(x + 5y + 2)$ **59.** $(3x - y - 1)(3x - y + 4)$ **61.** $l = 2x + 30$

63. a. $x(36 - 2x)(12 - 2x)$ **b.** $V(2) = 512 \text{ in}^3, V(4) = 448 \text{ in}^3$ **65.** Answers will vary   **67.** Answers will vary

Exercises 4.5, Pages 299 – 302

1. $(x-5)(x^2+5x+25)$ **3.** $(x-2y)(x^2+2xy+4y^2)$ **5.** $(x+6)(x^2-6x+36)$ **7.** $(x+y)(x^2-xy+y^2)$

9. $(x-1)(x^2+x+1)$ **11.** $(3x+2)(9x^2-6x+4)$ **13.** $3(x+3)(x^2-3x+9)$

15. $(5x-4y)(25x^2+20xy+16y^2)$ **17.** $2(3x-y)(9x^2+3xy+y^2)$ **19.** $y(x+y)(x^2-xy+y^2)$

21. $x^2y^2(1-y)(1+y+y^2)$ **23.** $3xy(2x+3y)(4x^2-6xy+9y^2)$ **25.** $(x^2-y^3)(x^4+x^2y^3+y^6)$

27. $\left[3x+(y^2-1)\right]\left[9x^2-3xy^2+3x+y^4-2y^2+1\right]$ **29.** $[x+y-1]\left[x^2+7x-xy+y^2-8y+19\right]$

31. $[x+y-4]\left[x^2+5xy+7y^2+4x+16y+16\right]$ **33.** $(x-3)(y+4)$ **35.** $(x+4)(y+6)$ **37.** Not factorable

39. $(4x+3)(y-7)$ **41.** Not factorable   **43.** $(x-y-6)(x-y+6)$ **45.** $(4x+1-y)(4x+1+y)$ **47.** $(x^2+6)(x-5)$

49. $(x+12)(x+2)(x-2)$ **51.** $(x+2)(x+2)(x-2)$ **53.** $(y+5)(x+3)(x-3)$ **55.** $(x^k+2)(x^{2k}-2x^k+4)$

57. $3x^{3k}(1-2y^k)(1+2y^k+4y^{2k})$ **59.** $4x^{-2}(x+2)$ **61.** $x^{3}(2x+3y-6)$ **63.** $5x^{-4}(x+2)(x-2)$

65. $x^{-3}(x+3)(x+1)$ **67.** $2x^{-2}(x-5)(x+1)$ **69. a.** x^2-16 **b.** [box] $x-4$ **71. a.** $xy+xy+x^2+y^2$

$=x^2+2xy+y^2$

$=(x+y)^2$

$x+4$

b.

$(x+y)(x+y)=(x+y)^2$

73. I. $abc = 100a + 10b + c$

$ = (99+1)a + (9+1)b + c$

$ = 99a + a + 9b + b + c$

$ = 9(11a+b) + a + b + c$

So, if the sum $(a+b+c)$ is divisible by 3 (or 9), then the number abc will be divisible by 3 (or 9).

II. $abcd = 1000a + 100b + 10c + d$

$ = (999+1)a + (99+1)b + (9+1)c + d$

$ = 999a + a + 99b + b + 9c + c + d$

$ = 9(111a+11b+c) + a + b + c + d$

So, if the sum $(a+b+c+d)$ is divisible by 3 (or 9), then the numbaer $abcd$ will be divisible by 3 (or 9)

Exercises 4.6, Pages 311 – 313

1. $y^2-y-6=0$ **3.** $8x^2-10x+3=0$ **5.** $p^3-p^2-6p=0$ **7.** $x^2+8x+15=0$

9. $y^3-4y^2-3y+18=0$ **11.** $x=-9$ or $x=-4$ **13.** $x=6$ or $x=8$ **15.** $x=-5$ or $x=10$

17. $x=-7$ or $x=7$ **19.** $x=\dfrac{2}{3}$ or $x=5$ **21.** $x=-\dfrac{4}{3}$ or $x=\dfrac{1}{2}$ **23.** $x=-6$ or $x=6$

25. $z=-\dfrac{7}{2}$ or $z=\dfrac{7}{2}$ **27.** $z=\dfrac{1}{2}$ or $z=3$ **29.** $x=-\dfrac{3}{4}$ or $x=\dfrac{2}{3}$ **31.** $x=-\dfrac{5}{2}$ or $x=\dfrac{7}{3}$

33. $y = -\dfrac{4}{5}$ or $y = \dfrac{4}{5}$ **35.** $x = -6$ or $x = 8$ **37.** $x = 2$ or $x = 6$ **39.** $x = -11$ or $x = 3$

41. $y = \dfrac{1}{6}$ or $y = \dfrac{2}{3}$ **43.** $x = -\dfrac{2}{9}$ or $x = \dfrac{6}{7}$ **45.** $x = -3$ or $x = -2$ or $x = 0$

47. $x = -\dfrac{5}{2}$ or $x = 0$ or $x = \dfrac{5}{2}$ **49.** $x = -\dfrac{5}{2}$ or $x = 0$ or $x = \dfrac{7}{3}$ **51.** $x = -\dfrac{3}{2}$ or $x = 0$ or $x = \dfrac{7}{5}$

53. $x = 0, \dfrac{1}{2}, -\dfrac{1}{3}$ **55.** $x = -1, 2, 6$ **57.** $x = -\dfrac{1}{4}, \dfrac{2}{3}, 8.5, \dfrac{1}{6}$ **59.** $7, 8$ **61.** $21, 23$

63. $10, 12, 14$ or $-10, -12, -14$ **65.** $1, 2, 3, 4$ or $-2, -1, 0, 1$ **67.** Length = 12 in, Width = 5 in

69. 20 miles, 21 miles   **71. a.** 4 sec **b.** 2 sec **c.** 2 sec   **73.** 128 in^2; use the Pythagorean Theorem

Exercises 4.7, Pages 319 – 320

1. $x = \pm 2$ **3.** $x = \pm\sqrt{2} = \pm 1.414$ **5.** $x = -2, 6$ **7.** $x = 2.46, -4.46$ **9.** $x = 4.7, -1.70$

11. $\varnothing$ **13.** $x = 1.91, -1.57$ **15.** $x = -2.49, 0.66, 1.83$ **17.** $x = 0, 1, 3$ **19.** $x = -3, -1, 5$
21. $x = 3.40$ **23.** $x = -0.91, 1.71, 3.20$ **25.** $x = -1.73, 0, 1.73$ **27.** $x = -4, 7$ **29.** $x = -1.67, 3$

31. $x = -2, 0$ **33.** $x = -5, 1$ **35.** $x = 3.5$ **37.** $x = [-3, 3]$ **39.** $x = (-\infty, 3)$ or $(7, \infty)$

41. $x = (-\infty, 1.33)$ or $(4, \infty)$ **43.** $x = (-\infty, -8)$ or $(16, \infty)$ **45.** $x = (-\infty, -16]$ or $[-8, \infty)$

Chapter 4 Test, Pages 324 – 325

1. $-x^3 + 5x^2 - 6$ **2.** $-x^3 + 4x^2 + 5x - 3$ **3.** $x^2 + 3x - 2$ **4.** $3x^2 + 2x + 13$ **5.** $-2x^2 - 9xy + 2y^2 - 2y$

6. $2x - y + 3$ **7.** $28x^2 + 23x - 15$ **8.** $4x^2 - 28x + 49$ **9.** $64x^2 - 9$ **10.** $x^6 + 10x^3 + 25$

11. $x^2 + 2x + 1 - y^2$ **12.** $6x^3 + 5x^2 - x - 1$ **13.** $(2x - 3) + \dfrac{-x}{2x^2 + 1}$ **14.** $2x^2 + 8x + 43 + \dfrac{166}{x - 4}$

15. a. $P(3) = 47$ **b.** No, the remainder is not zero   **16.** $x^2 + 4x - 21 = 0$ **17.** $6xy(5x - 3y + 4)$

18. $(x - 12)(x + 3)$ **19.** $3y(x - 3y)^2$ **20.** $9(x + 3y)(x - 3y)$ **21.** $(7x + 2)(x - 4)$

22. $(x^k + y^k)(x^k - y^k)$ **23.** $3(x + 3y)(x^2 - 3xy + 9y^2)$ **24.** $(x + 2y)(2x + 1)$ **25.** $x = \dfrac{1}{3}$ or $x = -5$

26. $x = \dfrac{5}{2}$ or $x = -3$ **27.** $11, 13, 15$ or $-17, -15, -13$ **28.** 7m, 24m, 25m   **29.** $x \approx -5.46$ or $x \approx 1.46$

30. $x = 0, 1, 4$ **31.** $(-6, 12)$

Chapter 4 Cumulative Review, Pages 325 – 328

1. $\dfrac{5}{6}$ **2.** $\dfrac{8}{5}$ **3.** 6 **4.** -138 **5.** $64x^6 y^3$ **6.** $49x^{10} y^4$ **7.** $-\dfrac{1}{8x^9 y^6}$ **8.** $\dfrac{36x^4}{y^{10}}$ **9.** $2x + 17$

10. $12x - 7$ **11.** $x = \dfrac{9}{10}$ **12.** $x = 21$ **13.** $x = 21$ **14.** $x = -5$ or $x = 10$ **15.** 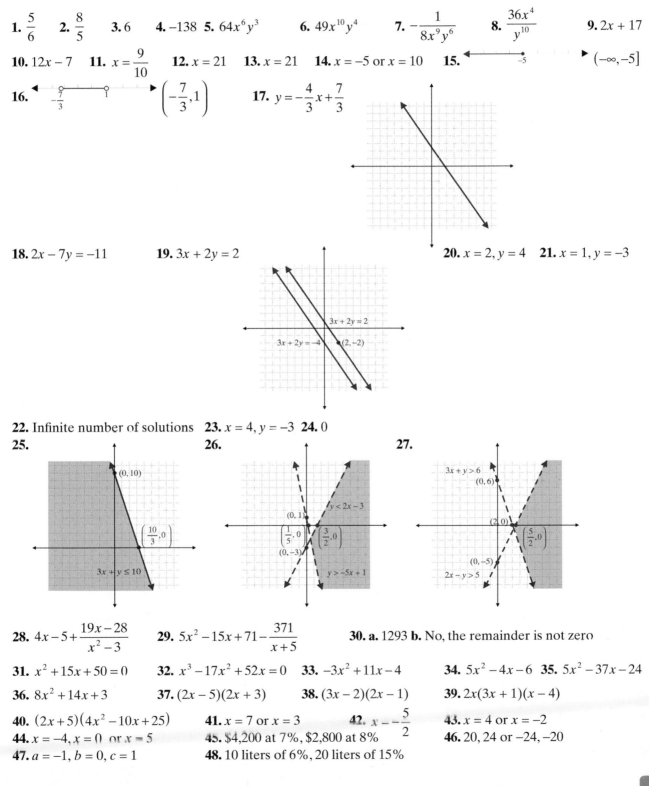 $(-\infty, -5]$

16. $\left(-\dfrac{7}{3}, 1\right)$ **17.** $y = -\dfrac{4}{3}x + \dfrac{7}{3}$

18. $2x - 7y = -11$ **19.** $3x + 2y = 2$ **20.** $x = 2, y = 4$ **21.** $x = 1, y = -3$

22. Infinite number of solutions   **23.** $x = 4, y = -3$ **24.** 0

25.   **26.**   **27.**

28. $4x - 5 + \dfrac{19x - 28}{x^2 - 3}$ **29.** $5x^2 - 15x + 71 - \dfrac{371}{x + 5}$ **30. a.** 1293 **b.** No, the remainder is not zero

31. $x^2 + 15x + 50 = 0$ **32.** $x^3 - 17x^2 + 52x = 0$ **33.** $-3x^2 + 11x - 4$ **34.** $5x^2 - 4x - 6$ **35.** $5x^2 - 37x - 24$

36. $8x^2 + 14x + 3$ **37.** $(2x - 5)(2x + 3)$ **38.** $(3x - 2)(2x - 1)$ **39.** $2x(3x + 1)(x - 4)$

40. $(2x + 5)(4x^2 - 10x + 25)$ **41.** $x = 7$ or $x = 3$ **42.** $x = -\dfrac{5}{2}$ **43.** $x = 4$ or $x = -2$

44. $x = -4, x = 0$ or $x = 5$ **45.** \$4,200 at 7%, \$2,800 at 8%   **46.** $20, 24$ or $-24, -20$

47. $a = -1, b = 0, c = 1$ **48.** 10 liters of 6%, 20 liters of 15%

49. a.

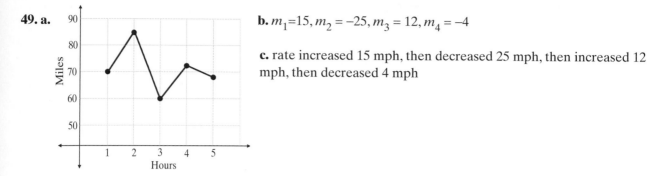

b. $m_1 = 15, m_2 = -25, m_3 = 12, m_4 = -4$

c. rate increased 15 mph, then decreased 25 mph, then increased 12 mph, then decreased 4 mph

50. a. Function $D = (-\infty, \infty), R = [0, \infty)$ **b.** Not a function **c.** function $D = (-\infty, \infty), R = (-\infty, 0]$

51. $x \approx 2.266$ or $x \approx -1.766$ **52.** $x \approx 4.236$ or $x \approx -0.236$ **53.** $x \approx -1.193$ or $x \approx 4.193$

54. $x \approx -1.247$ or $x \approx 0.445$ or $x \approx 1.802$ **55.** none   **56.** $(-1, 11)$ **57.** $(-\infty, 0]$ or $[4, \infty)$

58. $[-12, 8]$

Chapter 5

Exercises 5.1, Pages 338 − 340

1. $-12x^4 y$ **3.** $4x^2 + 8x$ **5.** $x^2 + x - 2$ **7.** $-8(x+2)$ **9.** $7(x^2 - 4x + 16)$

11. $\dfrac{3x}{4y}; x \neq 0; y \neq 0$ **13.** $\dfrac{2x^3}{3y^3}; x \neq 0; y \neq 0$ **15.** $\dfrac{1}{x-3}; x \neq 0, 3$ **17.** $7; x \neq 2$ **19.** $-\dfrac{3}{4}; x \neq 3$

21. $-\dfrac{3}{4}; x \neq 3$ **23.** $\dfrac{x}{x-1}; x \neq -6, 1$ **25.** $\dfrac{x-y}{3x}; x \neq 0, -y$ **27.** $\dfrac{x^2 - 4x + 16}{2x - 7}; x \neq -4, \dfrac{7}{2}$

29. $\dfrac{x^2 + 5}{x^2 + 2x + 4}; x \neq 2$ **31.** $\dfrac{ab}{y}$ **33.** $\dfrac{8x^2 y^3}{15}$ **35.** $\dfrac{x+3}{x}$ **37.** $\dfrac{x-1}{x+1}$ **39.** $-\dfrac{1}{x-8}$ **41.** $\dfrac{x-2}{x}$

43. $\dfrac{4(x+5)}{x(x+1)}$ **45.** $\dfrac{x}{(x+3)(x-1)}$ **47.** $-\dfrac{x+4}{x(x+1)}$ **49.** $\dfrac{x+2y}{(x-3y)(x-2y)}$ **51.** $\dfrac{x-1}{x(2x-1)}$ **53.** $\dfrac{1}{x+1}$

55. $\dfrac{2x-1}{2x+1}$ **57.** $\dfrac{49y^3}{6x^5}$ **59.** $\dfrac{1}{12x}$ **61.** $\dfrac{7x}{x+2}$ **63.** $\dfrac{x}{6}$ **65.** $\dfrac{x+3}{x+4}$ **67.** $\dfrac{x+5}{x}$ **69.** $\dfrac{-(x+4)}{x(2x-1)}$

71. $\dfrac{x-2}{x+2}$ **73.** $\dfrac{(3x^2 - x - 6)(x+3)}{(6x^2 + x - 9)(x-2)}$ **75.** $\dfrac{(4x-5)(2x-1)}{(x+4)(x+1)}$ **77.** $\dfrac{9x^3 - 6x^2 + 4x}{(9x^2 - 12x + 4)(9x^2 + 6x + 4)}$

79. $-\dfrac{3x-2}{x^2}$ **81.** $\dfrac{x+3}{2x-1}$ **83.** $\dfrac{x-1}{x-8}$ **85. a.** See page 331 **b.** Answers will vary **c.** Answers will vary

87. a. $x = 4$ **b.** $x = 10, x = -10$

Exercises 5.2, Pages 348 – 350

1. 3   **3.** 2   **5.** 1   **7.** $\dfrac{2}{x-1}$ **9.** $\dfrac{14}{7-x}$ **11.** 4   **13.** $\dfrac{x^2-x+1}{x^2+x-12}$ **15.** $\dfrac{x-2}{x+2}$

17. $\dfrac{4x+5}{2(7x-2)}$ **19.** $\dfrac{6x+15}{(x+3)(x-3)}$ **21.** $\dfrac{x^2-2x+4}{(x+2)(x-1)}$ **23.** $\dfrac{x^2+3x+6}{(x+3)(x-3)}$

25. $\dfrac{8x^2+13x-21}{6(x+3)(x-3)}$ **27.** $\dfrac{3x^2-20x}{(x+6)(x-6)}$ **29.** $\dfrac{-4x}{x-7}$ **31.** $\dfrac{4x^2-x-12}{(x+7)(x-4)(x-1)}$

33. $\dfrac{4}{(x+2)(x+2)(x-2)}$ **35.** $\dfrac{-3x^2+17x+15}{(x-3)(x-4)(x+3)}$ **37.** $\dfrac{4x-19}{(7x+4)(x-1)(x+2)}$

39. $\dfrac{-7x-9}{(4x+3)(x-2)}$ **41.** $\dfrac{4x^2-41x+3}{(x+4)(x-4)}$ **43.** $\dfrac{-2x^2-4x+15}{(x-4)(x-2)}$ **45.** $\dfrac{x^2-4x-6}{(x+2)(x-2)(x-1)}$

47. $\dfrac{6x+2}{(x-1)(x+3)}$ **49.** $\dfrac{5x+12}{(x+3)(x+1)}$ **51.** $\dfrac{9x^3-19x^2+22x+12}{(3x+1)(x+3)(5x+2)(x-1)}$

53. $\dfrac{5x+1}{(y-3)(x+1)}$ **55.** $\dfrac{5xy-8y+2}{(y-4)(y+1)(x-2)}$ **57.** $\dfrac{6x^2-12x+5}{2(2x+1)(4x^2-2x+1)}$

59. $\dfrac{14x-43}{(x^2+6)(x-5)(x-2)}$ **61.** Answers will vary

Exercises 5.3, Pages 354 – 355

1. $\dfrac{4}{5xy}$ **3.** $\dfrac{8}{7x^2y}$ **5.** $\dfrac{2x(x+3)}{2x-1}$ **7.** $\dfrac{7}{2(x+2)}$ **9.** $\dfrac{x}{x-1}$ **11.** $\dfrac{4x}{3(x+6)}$ **13.** $\dfrac{7x}{x+2}$

15. $\dfrac{x}{6}$ **17.** $\dfrac{24y+9x}{18y-20x}$ **19.** $\dfrac{xy}{x+y}$ **21.** $\dfrac{y+x}{y-x}$ **23.** $\dfrac{2(x+1)}{x+2}$ **25.** $\dfrac{x^2-3x}{x-4}$ **27.** $\dfrac{x+1}{2x-3}$

29. $-\dfrac{2x+h}{x^2(x+h)^2}$ **31.** $-(x-2y)(x-y)$ **33.** $\dfrac{2-x}{x+2}$ **35.** $\dfrac{-x^2y^2}{x+y}$ **37.** $\dfrac{R_1R_2}{R_2+R_1}$

Exercises 5.4, Pages 365 – 367

1. $x = 7$ **3.** $x = -\dfrac{74}{9}$ **5.** $x = \dfrac{1}{4}$ **7.** $x = \dfrac{3}{2}$ **9.** $x = 4$ **11.** $x = \dfrac{10}{3}$ **13.** $x = \dfrac{1}{4}$

15. $x = -\dfrac{3}{16}$ **17.** $x = -3$ **19.** $x = -39$ **21.** $x = \dfrac{62}{7}$ **23.** $x = -3$ **25.** $x = 22$ **27.** $x = \dfrac{2}{3}$

29. $x = -2$ **31.** No solution **33.** $x = \dfrac{7}{11}$ **35.** $x \le -4$ or $x > 0$

37. $x < -6$ **39.** $x < -9$ or $x > -3$

41. $2 < x < \dfrac{5}{2}$ **43.** $x > 7$ **45.** $\dfrac{7}{5} \le x < 4$

47. $-9 < x < -\dfrac{4}{3}$ **49.** $x \le -4$ or $0 \le x < 3$ **51.** $r = \dfrac{S-a}{S}$

53. $s = \dfrac{x - \bar{x}}{z}$ **55.** $R_{\text{total}} = \dfrac{R_1 R_2}{R_1 + R_2}$ **57.** $P = \dfrac{A}{1+r}$ **59.** $x = \dfrac{b - yd}{yc - a}$ **61. a.** $\dfrac{4x^2 + 41x - 10}{x(x-1)}$

b. $x = \dfrac{1}{4}, 10$ and $x \ne 0, 1$

Exercises 5.5, Pages 375 – 377

1. 10   **3.** 14   **5.** $\dfrac{12}{7}$ **7.** 15, 9 **9.** 2, 5   **11.** \$1,500   **13.** 1875 miles   **15.** $1\dfrac{4}{5}$ hours   **17.** 6 hours

19. 120 mph, 300 mph   **21.** 250 mph, 500 mph   **23.** 50 mph   **25.** 4.5 days, 9 days

27. boat: 14 mph, current: 2 mph   **29. a.** 5 and 7 **b.** 2 and 4

Exercises 5.6, Pages 383 – 387

1. $\dfrac{7}{3}$ **3.** 2   **5.** 10   **7.** 36   **9.** 24   **11.** $-\dfrac{27}{5}$ **13.** 40   **15.** 54   **17.** 32   **19.** 27   **21.** 256 feet

23. 6 in **25.** 254.34 in.^{2} **27.** 6   **29.** $R = \dfrac{kl}{d^2}$, 15 ohms   **31.** $F = kAv^2$, 2025 lb   **33.** $E = \dfrac{kml}{A}$, 0.0073 cm

35. $L = \dfrac{kwd^2}{l}$, 1890 lb   **37.** $F = \dfrac{km_1 m_2}{d^2}$, 9×10^{-11} N   **39.** Answers will vary

Chapter 5 Test, Pages 391 – 392

1. $\dfrac{x}{x+4}$ **2.** $-\dfrac{x^2 + 4x + 16}{x+4}$ **3. a.** $5 - x$ **b.** $x^2 + x - 2$ **4.** $\dfrac{x+3}{x+4}$ **5.** $\dfrac{3x-2}{3x+2}$

6. $\dfrac{-2x^2 - 13x}{(x+5)(x+2)(x-2)}$ **7.** $\dfrac{-2x^2 - 7x + 18}{(3x+2)(x-4)(x+1)}$ **8.** $2x^2$ **9.** $\dfrac{x^2 - 7x + 1}{(x+3)(x-3)}$ **10. a.** $\dfrac{3x}{2-x}$

b. $\dfrac{x-2}{x}$ **11.** $x = -\dfrac{7}{2}$ **12.** $x = -1$ **13.** $x \le -\dfrac{5}{2}$ or $x > 3$

14. $x < -\dfrac{5}{3}$ or $x > -\dfrac{1}{2}$ 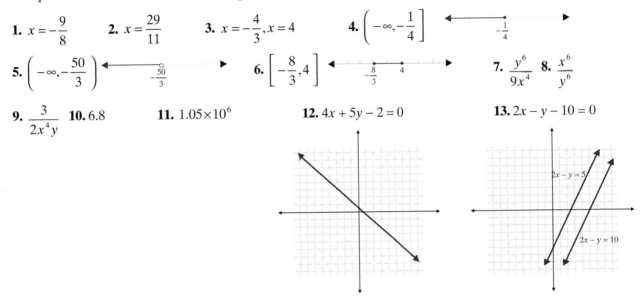 **15.** $\dfrac{2}{7}$ **16.** 4 hr **17.** 42 mph-Carlos; 57 mph-Mario

18. 11 mph **19.** $\dfrac{400}{9}$ **20.** $\dfrac{15}{2}$ cm

Chapter 5 Cumulative Review, Pages 392 – 395

1. $x = -\dfrac{9}{8}$ **2.** $x = \dfrac{29}{11}$ **3.** $x = -\dfrac{4}{3}, x = 4$ **4.** $\left(-\infty, -\dfrac{1}{4}\right]$

5. $\left(-\infty, -\dfrac{50}{3}\right)$ **6.** $\left[-\dfrac{8}{3}, 4\right]$ **7.** $\dfrac{y^6}{9x^4}$ **8.** $\dfrac{x^6}{y^6}$

9. $\dfrac{3}{2x^4 y}$ **10.** 6.8 **11.** 1.05×10^6 **12.** $4x + 5y - 2 = 0$ **13.** $2x - y - 10 = 0$

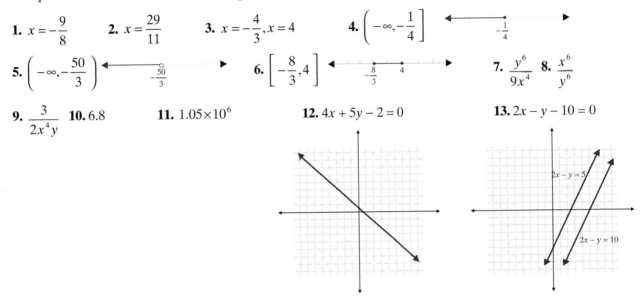

14. $x = 2, y = -1$ **15.** $x = \dfrac{15}{4}, y = \dfrac{33}{8}, z = -\dfrac{15}{8}$ **16.** $a = 5, b = 1$ **17.** $x = 1, y = -5, z = 2$ **18.** $\det(A) = -102$

19. $(3x + 2)(5x + 4)$ **20.** $(x + 4)(2x^2 + 3)$ **21.** $2(2x - 3)(4x^2 + 6x + 9)$ **22.** $x^{-3}(2x + 1)(x - 3)$

23. a. $P(2) = 15$ **b.** $x - 2$ is not a factor of $P(x)$ as $P(2) \neq 0$.

24. a. $x^2 + 9x + 20 = 0$ **b.** $x^3 - 6x^2 + 11x - 6 = 0$

25. 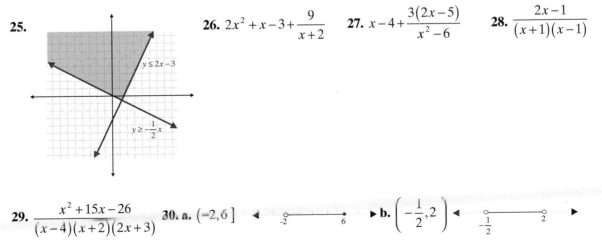 **26.** $2x^2 + x - 3 + \dfrac{9}{x + 2}$ **27.** $x - 4 + \dfrac{3(2x - 5)}{x^2 - 6}$ **28.** $\dfrac{2x - 1}{(x + 1)(x - 1)}$

29. $\dfrac{x^2 + 15x - 26}{(x - 4)(x + 2)(2x + 3)}$ **30. a.** $(-2, 6]$ **b.** $\left(-\dfrac{1}{2}, 2\right)$

31. a.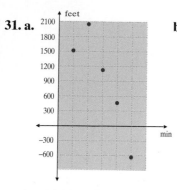

b. $528, -968, -616, -1144$ **c.** Juan is accelerating at a rate of 528 feet per minute, decelerating 968 feet per minute, decelerating 616 feet per minute, decelerating 1144 feet per minute.

32. a. Not a function **b.** Function, $D = \{-7, -3, 0, 5, 6\}, R = \{-2, 1, 4\}$ **c.** Function, $D = (-\infty, \infty), R = (0, \infty)$

33. 256 feet   **34.** 24 feet   **35.** 16, 18   **36.** $x = 3, y = 11$ **37.** $\frac{2}{3}$ hr or 40 minutes   **38.** 120 sq yds.

Chapter 6

Exercises 6.1, Pages 410 – 411

1. 0.02   **3.** 32   **5.** 67.082   **7.** 0.02   **9.** 2.3208   **11.** $2\sqrt{3}$ **13.** $7\sqrt{2}$ **15.** $-9\sqrt{2}$

17. $2\sqrt[3]{2}$ **19.** $3\sqrt[3]{4}$ **21.** Non-real   **23.** $2yx^5\sqrt{6x}$ **25.** $ac\sqrt[3]{a^2b^2}$ **27.** Non-real   **29.** $2x^3y^4$

31. $9ab^2\sqrt[3]{ab^2}$ **33.** $5xy^3\sqrt{5x}$ **35.** $2bc\sqrt{3ac}$ **37.** $-5x^2y^3z^4\sqrt{3}$ **39.** $2xy^2z^3\sqrt[3]{3x^2y}$ **41.** $5|y|$

43. $-8|a^3|$ **45.** $4x^2y^4\sqrt{2}$ **47.** $3b^3\sqrt[3]{4a}$ **49.** $3xy^2\sqrt[3]{3x^2y}$ **51.** $\frac{\sqrt{x}}{8x}$ **53.** $\frac{-\sqrt{6y}}{3y}$ **55.** $\frac{y\sqrt{10x}}{4x}$

57. $\frac{2\sqrt{2y}}{y}$ **59.** $\frac{y\sqrt[3]{2x}}{3x}$ **61.** $\frac{\sqrt[3]{30a^2b^2}}{5b}$ **63.** Answers will vary   **65.** Answers will vary

Exercises 6.2, Pages 420 – 422

1. 3   **3.** $\frac{1}{10}$ **5.** -512 **7.** Nonreal   **9.** $\frac{3}{7}$ **11.** -4 **13.** -5 **15.** $\frac{1}{4}$ **17.** $-\frac{27}{8}$ **19.** $\frac{9}{16}$ **21.** $\frac{2}{5}$

23. $\frac{1}{81}$ **25.** $-\frac{1}{16,807}$ **27.** 2187   **29.** 4.6416   **31.** 0.0131   **33.** 158.7401   **35.** 7.7460

37. 1.0605   **39.** 1.6083   **41.** $8x$ **43.** $3a^2$ **45.** $8x^{\frac{5}{2}}$ **47.** $5a^{\frac{13}{6}}$ **49.** $a^{\frac{8}{5}}$ **51.** $x^{\frac{1}{2}}$

53. $a^{\frac{7}{6}}$ **55.** $a^{\frac{1}{4}}$ **57.** $\frac{y^{\frac{1}{2}}}{x^{\frac{4}{3}}}$ **59.** $\frac{1}{a^{\frac{3}{4}}b^{\frac{1}{2}}}$ **61.** $\frac{x^{\frac{3}{2}}}{16y^{\frac{2}{5}}}$ **63.** $\frac{-x^2y^4}{z^4}$ **65.** $\frac{c^3}{3ab^2}$ **67.** $\frac{8b^{\frac{9}{4}}}{a^3c^3}$

69. $x^{\frac{1}{4}}y^{\frac{5}{4}}$ **71.** $\frac{y^{\frac{2}{3}}}{50x^{\frac{4}{3}}}$ **73.** $\frac{6a}{b^2}$ **75.** $\frac{b^{\frac{5}{12}}}{a^{\frac{11}{12}}}$ **77.** $\frac{3x^{\frac{1}{2}}}{20y^{\frac{2}{3}}}$ **79.** $x^{15}\sqrt{x^4}$ **81.** $\frac{1}{x^{12}\sqrt{x}}$ **83.** $\sqrt[12]{a^5}$

85. $\sqrt[10]{x}$ **87.** $\sqrt[4]{a}$ **89.** $a^9b^{18}c^3$ **91.** $a^{20}b^5c^{10}$

Exercises 6.3, Pages 429 – 431

1. $-6\sqrt{2}$ **3.** $5\sqrt{x}$ **5.** $-3\sqrt[3]{7x^2}$ **7.** $10\sqrt{3}$ **9.** $-7\sqrt{2}$ **11.** $20\sqrt{3}$

13. $3\sqrt{6}+7\sqrt{3}$ **15.** $20x\sqrt{5x}$ **17.** $14\sqrt{5}-3\sqrt{7}$ **19.** $11\sqrt{2x}+14\sqrt{3x}$ **21.** $4\sqrt[3]{5}-13\sqrt[3]{2}$

23. $x^2\sqrt{2x}$ **25.** $4x^2y\sqrt{x}$ **27.** $3x-9\sqrt{3x}+8$ **29.** $24+10\sqrt{2x}+2x$ **31.** 2 **33.** $13+4\sqrt{10}$

35. -3 **37.** $6+\sqrt{30}-2\sqrt{3}-\sqrt{10}$ **39.** $5-\sqrt{33}$ **41.** $49x-2$ **43.** $9x+6\sqrt{xy}+y$

45. $12x+7\sqrt{2xy}+2y$ **47.** $-\dfrac{3\sqrt{3}+15}{22}$ **49.** $\dfrac{3\sqrt{6}-\sqrt{42}}{2}$ **51.** $4\sqrt{5}+4\sqrt{3}$ **53.** $\dfrac{-5\sqrt{2}-4\sqrt{5}}{3}$ **55.** $\dfrac{59+21\sqrt{5}}{44}$

57. $8+3\sqrt{6}$ **59.** $\dfrac{x^2+4x\sqrt{y}+4y}{x^2-4y}$ **61.** $\dfrac{1}{\sqrt{7}+2}$ **63.** $\dfrac{2}{\sqrt{15}-\sqrt{3}}$ **65.** $\dfrac{1}{\sqrt{x}-\sqrt{5}}$ **67.** $\dfrac{2y-x}{x\sqrt{2y}+x\sqrt{x}}$

69. $\dfrac{1}{\sqrt{2+h}+\sqrt{2}}$ **71.** 4.33975 **73.** 31.60000 **75.** -57.00000 **77.** 251.94353 **79.** 0.40863

81. a. $l^2-l-1=0$ **b.** 97.08 feet **c.** The yellow rectangle is "golden".

Exercises 6.4, Pages 439 – 441

1. a. $\sqrt{5}$ and 2.2361 **b.** $\sqrt{9}$ and 3.0000 **c.** $\sqrt{50}$ and 7.0711 **d.** $\sqrt{4}$ and 2.0000 **3. a.** $\sqrt[3]{27}$ and 3.0000

b. $\sqrt[3]{-1}$ and -1.0000 **c.** $\sqrt[3]{-8}$ and -2.0000 **d.** $\sqrt[3]{24}$ and 2.8845 **5.** $[-8,\infty)$ **7.** $\left(-\infty,\dfrac{1}{2}\right]$

9. $(-\infty,\infty)$ **11.** $[0,\infty)$ **13.** $(-\infty,\infty)$ **15.** E **17.** B **19.** A

21.

23.

25.

27.

$y=2\sqrt{3-x}$

29.

$f(x)=-\sqrt{3-x}$

31.

$y=\sqrt[3]{3x+4}$

33. 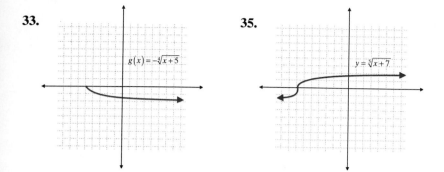 **35.**

$g(x) = -\sqrt[4]{x} + 5$

$y = \sqrt[3]{x} + 7$

Exercises 6.5, Pages 448 – 449

1. Real part is 4, imaginary part is –3   **3.** Real part is -11, imaginary part is $\sqrt{2}$

5. Real part is $\dfrac{2}{3}$, imaginary part is $\sqrt{17}$ **7.** Real part is $\dfrac{4}{5}$, imaginary part is $\dfrac{7}{5}$ **9.** Real part is $\dfrac{3}{8}$,

imaginary part is 0.   **11.** $7i$ **13.** $-8i$ **15.** $21\sqrt{3}$ **17.** $10i\sqrt{6}$ **19.** $-12i\sqrt{3}$ **21.** $11\sqrt{2}$

23. $10i\sqrt{10}$ **25.** $6 + 2i$ **27.** $1 + 7i$ **29.** $2 - 6i$ **31.** $14i$ **33.** $\left(3 + \sqrt{5}\right) - 6i$

35. $5 + \left(\sqrt{6} + 1\right)i$ **37.** $\sqrt{3} - 5$ **39.** $-2 - 5i$ **41.** $11 - 16i$ **43.** 2 **45.** $3 + 4i$ **47.** $x = 6$,

$y = -3$ **49.** $x = -2, y = \sqrt{5}$ **51.** $x = \sqrt{2} - 3, y = 1$ **53.** $x = 2, y = -8$ **55.** $x = 2, y = -6$ **57.** $x = 3, y = 10$

59. $x = -\dfrac{4}{3}, y = -3$ **61. a.** No **b.** Yes

Exercises 6.6, Pages 454 – 456

1. $16 + 24i$ **3.** $-7\sqrt{2} + 7i$ **5.** $3 + 12i$ **7.** $1 - i\sqrt{3}$ **9.** $5\sqrt{2} + 10i$ **11.** $2 + 8i$

13. $-7 - 11i$ **15.** $13 + 0i$ **17.** $-3 - 7i$ **19.** $5 + 12i$ **21.** $5 - i\sqrt{3}$ **23.** $21 + 0i$

25. $23 - 10i\sqrt{2}$ **27.** $\left(2 + \sqrt{10}\right) + \left(2\sqrt{2} - \sqrt{5}\right)i$ **29.** $\left(9 - \sqrt{30}\right) + \left(3\sqrt{5} + 3\sqrt{6}\right)i$ **31.** $0 + 3i$ **33.** $0 - \dfrac{5}{4}i$

35. $-\dfrac{1}{4} + \dfrac{1}{2}i$ **37.** $-\dfrac{4}{5} + \dfrac{8}{5}i$ **39.** $\dfrac{24}{25} + \dfrac{18}{25}i$ **41.** $-\dfrac{1}{13} + \dfrac{5}{13}i$ **43.** $-\dfrac{1}{29} - \dfrac{12}{29}i$ **45.** $-\dfrac{17}{26} - \dfrac{7}{26}i$

47. $\dfrac{4 + \sqrt{3}}{4} + \left(\dfrac{4\sqrt{3} - 1}{4}\right)i$ **49.** $-\dfrac{1}{7} + \dfrac{4\sqrt{3}}{7}i$ **51.** $0 + i$ **53.** $-1 + 0i$ **55.** $0 + i$ **57.** $1 + 0i$

59. $0 - i$ **61.** $x^2 + 9$ **63.** $x^2 + 2$ **65.** $5y^2 + 4$ **67.** $x^2 + 4x + 40$ **69.** $y^2 - 6y + 13$

71. Answers will vary   **73.** $a^2 + b^2 = 1$

Chapter 6 Test, Pages 461 – 462

1. 4   **2.** $\dfrac{1}{27}$ **3.** $4x^{\frac{7}{6}}$ **4.** $\dfrac{7x^{\frac{1}{4}}}{y^{\frac{1}{3}}}$ **5.** $\dfrac{8y^{\frac{3}{2}}}{x^3}$ **6.** $\sqrt[3]{4x^2}$ **7.** $2^{\frac{1}{2}}x^{\frac{1}{3}}y^{\frac{2}{3}}$ **8.** $\sqrt[12]{x^{11}}$

9. $4\sqrt{7}$ **10.** $2y\sqrt[3]{6x^2y^2}$ **11.** $\dfrac{y}{4x^2}\sqrt{10x}$ **12.** $17\sqrt{3}$ **13.** $(7x-6)\sqrt{x}$ **14.** $8\sqrt[3]{3}$ **15.** $5-2\sqrt{6}$

16. $-xy\sqrt{y}$ **17.** $30-7\sqrt{3x}-6x$ **18. a.** $-\left(\sqrt{3}+\sqrt{5}\right)$ **b.** $\dfrac{1+\sqrt{x^3}}{1+x+x^2}$ **19. a.** $\left[-\dfrac{4}{3},\infty\right)$ **b.** $(-\infty,\infty)$

20. a.   **b.**   **21.** $16+4i$

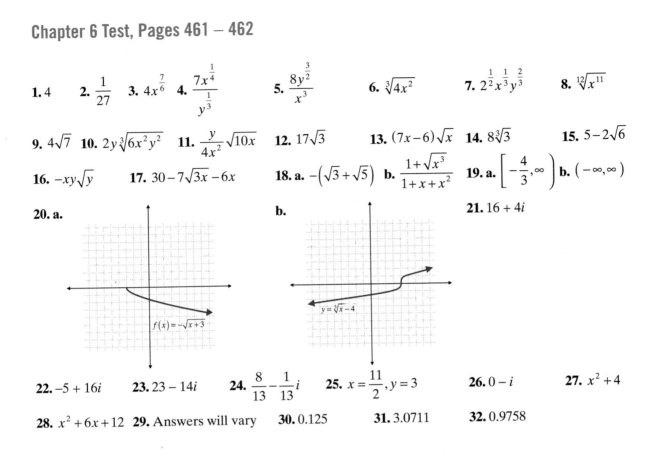

22. $-5+16i$ **23.** $23-14i$ **24.** $\dfrac{8}{13}-\dfrac{1}{13}i$ **25.** $x=\dfrac{11}{2},\ y=3$ **26.** $0-i$ **27.** x^2+4

28. $x^2+6x+12$ **29.** Answers will vary   **30.** 0.125 **31.** 3.0711 **32.** 0.9758

Chapter 6 Cumulative Review, Pages 462 – 465

1. $2x^3-4x^2+8x-4$ **2.** $6x^2+19x-7$ **3.** $-5x^2+18x+8$ **4.** $n=\dfrac{s-a}{d}+1\ \text{or}\ \dfrac{s-a+d}{d}$

5. $p=\dfrac{A}{1+rt}$ **6.** $(4x+3)(3x-4)$ **7.** $(7+2x)(4-x)$ **8.** $5(x-4)(x^2+4x+16)$

9. $(x+4)(x+1)(x-1)$ **10.** $\dfrac{4x^2-12x-1}{(x+3)(x-2)(x-5)}$ **11.** $\dfrac{4x^2+6x+17}{(2x+1)(2x-1)(x+3)}$ **12.** $\dfrac{x^2-1}{2x-4}$

13. $\dfrac{x+6}{x-1}$ **14.** $x=-\dfrac{5}{7}$ **15.** $x=\dfrac{83}{4}$ **16.** $\left(-2,\dfrac{3}{5}\right]$ ◄──────► -2 $\dfrac{3}{5}$

17. $\left[-2,\dfrac{1}{3}\right)$ ◄──────► -2 $\dfrac{1}{3}$ **18.** $\dfrac{50}{3}\text{in}^3$ or $16.6\overline{6}\text{in}^3$ **19.** 8 ohms   **20.** $(x-16)(x+3)=0$

$x=-3$ and 16 **21.** $(2x+3)(x-2)=0$ $x=\dfrac{-3}{2}$ and 2 **22.** $(5x-2)(3x-1)=0$ $x=\dfrac{1}{3}$ and $\dfrac{2}{5}$ **23.** -333

24. $(1, -2)$

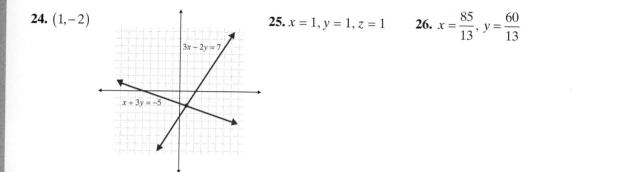

25. $x = 1, y = 1, z = 1$

26. $x = \dfrac{85}{13}, y = \dfrac{60}{13}$

27. a. $P(3) = 0$ **b.** $P(4) = 0$ **c.** $P(1) = 0$ **d.** $(x-1)(x-3)(x-4)$ **28. a.** $x^2 - 11x + 28 = 0$ **b.** $x^3 - 11x^2 - 14x + 24 = 0$

29.

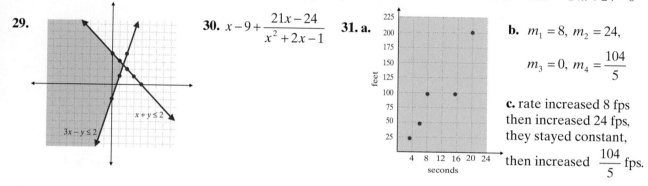

30. $x - 9 + \dfrac{21x - 24}{x^2 + 2x - 1}$ **31. a.**

b. $m_1 = 8$, $m_2 = 24$,

$m_3 = 0$, $m_4 = \dfrac{104}{5}$

c. rate increased 8 fps then increased 24 fps, they stayed constant, then increased $\dfrac{104}{5}$ fps.

32. a. Function $D = (-\infty, \infty), R = (-\infty, 0]$ **b.** Not a function **c.** Function $D = (-\infty, \infty), R = [-1, 1]$

33. $15, 17$ **34.** $x = 1$ **35.** $x = \pm\sqrt{12} \approx \pm 3.46, \pm\sqrt{6} = \pm 2.45$ **36.** $\dfrac{1}{16}$ **37.** $x^{\frac{7}{3}}$ **38.** $12\sqrt{2}$ **39.** $2x^2 y^3 \sqrt[3]{2y}$

40. $14 - 2i$ **41.** $-\dfrac{8}{17} - \dfrac{19}{17}i$ **42.** 10 mph **43.** 7.5 hours **44.** \$35,000 in 6% and \$15,000 in 10%

45. 60 pounds of first type (\$1.25 candy) and 40 pounds of second type (\$2.50 candy)
46. $x \approx -1.372, x \approx 4.372$ **47.** $x = 1, x \approx -2.303, x \approx 1.303$ **48.** $x = -4, x = 1, x = 5$ **49.** 279,936 **50.** 0.04
51. 1.30268 **52.** 6.45522

Chapter 7
Exercises 7.1, Pages 477 – 478

1. $x^2 - 12x + 36 = (x-6)^2$ **3.** $x^2 + 6x + 9 = (x+3)^2$ **5.** $x^2 - 5x + \dfrac{25}{4} = \left(x - \dfrac{5}{2}\right)^2$

7. $y^2 + y + \dfrac{1}{4} = \left(y + \dfrac{1}{2}\right)^2$ **9.** $x^2 + \dfrac{1}{3}x + \dfrac{1}{36} = \left(x + \dfrac{1}{6}\right)^2$ **11.** $x = \pm 12$ **13.** $x = \pm 5i$ **15.** $x = \pm 3i\sqrt{2}$

17. $x = 9, x = -1$ **19.** $x = \pm 2\sqrt{3}$ **21.** $x = 1 \pm \sqrt{5}$ **23.** $x = -8 \pm 3i$ **25.** $x = 5 \pm i\sqrt{10}$ **27.** $x = 1, x = -7$

29. $x = 4 \pm \sqrt{13}$ **31.** $z = -2 \pm \sqrt{6}$ **33.** $x = -1 \pm i\sqrt{5}$ **35.** $y = 5 \pm \sqrt{21}$ **37.** $x = \dfrac{5 \pm \sqrt{5}}{2}$ **39.** $x = \dfrac{-1 \pm i\sqrt{7}}{2}$

41. $x = -2 \pm \sqrt{7}$ **43.** $x = -1 \pm i\sqrt{3}$ **45.** $y = 1,\ y = -\dfrac{4}{3}$ **47.** $x = \dfrac{-7 \pm \sqrt{17}}{8}$ **49.** $x = \dfrac{1 \pm i\sqrt{11}}{4}$

51. $y = \dfrac{-3 \pm i\sqrt{11}}{2}$ **53.** $x = 2 \pm \sqrt{2}$ **55.** $x = \dfrac{-5 \pm i\sqrt{7}}{2}$ **57.** $x^2 - 5 = 0$ **59.** $z^2 - 4z + 2 = 0$

61. $x^2 - 2x - 11 = 0$ **63.** $x^2 + 49 = 0$ **65.** $y^2 + 5 = 0$ **67.** $x^2 + 6x + 13 = 0$ **69.** $x^2 - 4x + 7 = 0$
71. Answers will vary

Exercises 7.2, Pages 484 – 486

1. 68, two real solutions **3.** 0, one real solution **5.** −44, two nonreal, complex solutions **7.** 4, two real solutions **9.** 19,600, two real solutions **11.** −11, two nonreal, complex solutions **13.** $k < 16$

15. $k = \dfrac{81}{4}$ **17.** $k > 3$ **19.** $k > -\dfrac{1}{36}$ **21.** $k = \dfrac{49}{48}$ **23.** $k > \dfrac{4}{3}$ **25.** $x = \dfrac{-3 \pm \sqrt{29}}{2}$

27. $x = \dfrac{5 \pm \sqrt{17}}{2}$ **29.** $x = \dfrac{-7 \pm \sqrt{33}}{4}$ **31.** $x = 1,\ x = -\dfrac{1}{6}$ **33.** $x = \pm\sqrt{\dfrac{4}{3}}$ **35.** $x = \dfrac{9 \pm \sqrt{65}}{2},\ x = 0$

37. $x = \dfrac{-3 \pm \sqrt{5}}{2},\ x = 0$ **39.** $x = -1,\ x = 4$ **41.** $x = \dfrac{-4 \pm i\sqrt{2}}{2}$ **43.** $x = \pm\sqrt{7}$ **45.** $x = 0,\ x = -1$

47. $x = \dfrac{7 \pm i\sqrt{51}}{10}$ **49.** $x = -2,\ x = \dfrac{5}{3}$ **51.** $x = \pm\dfrac{3}{2}i$ **53.** $x = \dfrac{2 \pm \sqrt{3}}{3}$ **55.** $x = \dfrac{7 \pm i\sqrt{287}}{12}$

57. $\dfrac{2 \pm \sqrt{2}}{2}$ **59.** $x = \dfrac{-7 \pm \sqrt{17}}{4}$ **61.** $x = 60.4007,\ 2.5993$ **63.** $x = 2.0110,\ -0.7862$

65. $x = -0.5806,\ -4.1334$ **67.** $x = -4.7693i,\ +4.7693i$ **69.** $x^4 - 13x^2 + 36$, Answers will vary

Exercises 7.3, Pages 491 – 496

1. 6, 13 **3.** 4, 14 **5.** −6, −11 **7.** $-5 - 4\sqrt{3}$ **9.** $\dfrac{1 + \sqrt{33}}{4}$ **11.** $7\sqrt{2}$ cm, $7\sqrt{2}$ cm **13.** Mel: 30 mph, John: 40 mph

15. 4 feet×10feet **17.** $32\,\text{cm} \times 12\,\text{cm} \times 4\,\text{cm}$ **19.** 40 seats **21.** 17 inches, 6 inches **23.** 3 inches
25. 2 amperes or 8 amperes **27. a.** $307.20 **b.** 45 cents or 35 cents **29.** $13 and $22 **31.** 64 mph
33. Sam: 7.5 hours, Bob: 12.5 hours **35.** 150 mph **37.** 190 reserved, 150 general
39. a. 6.75 sec **b.** 3 sec, 3.75 sec **41. a.** 7 sec **b.** 2 sec, 12 sec **43.** 14.1421 cm **45. a.** 94.2 ft, 706.5 ft^2

b. 84.84 ft, 449.86 ft^2 **47. a.** No **b.** Homeplate **c.** No **49.** 8.49 cm **51.** $x = \dfrac{-b \pm \sqrt{b^2 - 4ac}}{2a}$

Exercises 7.4, Pages 501 – 502

1. $x = 3$ **3.** $x = 13$ **5.** $x = 3$ **7.** $x = 2$ **9.** $x = -4,\ x = 1$ **11.** $x = -5,\ x = \dfrac{5}{2}$

13. $x = -2$ **15.** $x = \pm 5$ **17.** $x = 2$ **19.** $x = 4$ **21.** $x = 0$ **23.** $x = 5$

25. No solution **27.** $x = 4$ **29.** $x = -1,\ x = 3$ **31.** $x = 5$ **33.** $x = 2$ **35.** $x = 6$

37. $x = -4$ **39.** $x = 12$ **41.** No solution **43.** $x = 40$ **45.** Answers will vary

Exercises 7.5, Pages 506 – 507

1. $x = \pm 2$, $x = \pm 3$ **3.** $x = \pm 2$, $x = \pm\sqrt{5}$ **5.** $y = \pm\sqrt{7}$, $y = \pm 2i$ **7.** $y = \pm\sqrt{5}$, $y = \pm i\sqrt{5}$

9. $z = \dfrac{1}{6}$, $z = -\dfrac{1}{4}$ **11.** $x = 4$, $x = \dfrac{25}{4}$ **13.** $x = 1$, $x = 4$ **15.** $x = \dfrac{1}{8}$, $x = -8$ **17.** $x = \dfrac{1}{25}$

19. $x = -\dfrac{1}{3}$, $x = \dfrac{3}{8}$ **21.** $x = 0$, $x = -27$, $x = -8$ **23.** $x = 1$, $x = 2$ **25.** $x = -3$, $x = -\dfrac{7}{2}$

27. $x = 0$, $x = 8$ **29.** $x = -1$, $x = -\dfrac{1}{2}$ **31.** $x = \pm\sqrt{1+i}$, $x = \pm\sqrt{1-i}$ **33.** $x = \pm\sqrt{1+3i}$, $x = \pm\sqrt{1-3i}$

35. $x = \pm\sqrt{2 \pm i\sqrt{3}}$ **37.** $x = \pm\dfrac{1}{5}\sqrt{5}$, $x = \pm 1$ **39.** $x = \pm\dfrac{1}{2}\sqrt{6}$, $x = \pm\dfrac{1}{3}i$ **41.** $x = -\dfrac{1}{4}$ **43.** $x = -4$, $x = 1$

45. $x = -\dfrac{1}{2}$ **47.** $x = -7$, $x = -\dfrac{3}{2}$ **49.** $x = \dfrac{26}{5}$ **51.** Because of the square root, the solution must be positive.

Chapter 7 Test, Pages 510 – 511

1. a. ± 4 **b.** $\pm 4i$ **2.** $x = -\dfrac{1}{2}$, $x = 0$ **3. a.** $x^2 - 30x + 225 = (x - 15)^2$ **b.** $x^2 + 5x + \dfrac{25}{4} = \left(x + \dfrac{5}{2}\right)^2$

4. a. $x^2 + 8 = 0$ **b.** $x^2 - 2x - 4 = 0$ **5.** $x = -2 \pm \sqrt{3}$ **6.** 73, Two real solutions **7.** $k = \pm 2\sqrt{6}$

8. $x = \dfrac{-1 \pm i\sqrt{7}}{4}$ **9.** $x = \dfrac{3 \pm \sqrt{41}}{4}$ **10.** $x = \dfrac{2 \pm i\sqrt{2}}{2}$ **11.** $x = 1$ **12.** $x = 0$, $x = 36$ **13.** $x = \pm 1$, $x = \pm 3$

14. $x = \dfrac{3}{2}$, $x = -1$ **15.** $x = 0$, $x = -1$

16. Triangle is not a right angled triangle, because $6^2 + 8^2 \neq 11^2$

8 ft, 11 ft, 6 ft

17. a. $t = 7$ seconds **b.** $t = 6.464$ seconds   **18.** 12 inches, 16 inches   **19.** towards home 50 mph, away 40 mph
20. 0.0714, -175.0714

Chapter 7 Cumulative Review, Pages 511 – 513

1. $x = 6$ **2.** $x = \dfrac{7}{8}$ **3.** $\left[-\dfrac{19}{2}, \infty\right)$ **4.** $\left(-\infty, \dfrac{7}{5}\right]$

5. $y = -\dfrac{3}{2}x + 3$ **6.** $y = -\dfrac{3}{2}x + 10$ **7.** $\dfrac{1}{x^5}$ **8.** $x^3 y^6$ **9.** $9y^{\frac{1}{2}}$ **10.** $\dfrac{27x^2}{8y}$ **11.** $-3x^2 y^2 \sqrt[3]{y^2}$

12. $2x^2 y^3 \sqrt[4]{2xy^3}$ **13.** $\dfrac{9}{2}\sqrt{2}$ **14.** $\dfrac{4}{3}\sqrt{3}$ **15.** $4x^2 + 17x - 15 = 0$ **16.** $x^2 - 2x - 19 = 0$

17. $x = -1,\ y = -2$

18. $x = 5,\ y = 4$ **19.** 73 **20.** $x = 1,\ y = -1,\ z = 3$ **21.** $x = -\dfrac{3}{2},\ x = \dfrac{2}{5}$ **22.** $x = \dfrac{-7 \pm \sqrt{33}}{8}$

23. $x = -1$

24. $x = -2,\ x = \dfrac{4}{3}$

34. x-int:$(-1.58, 0)$ and $(1.58, 0)$

25. a. 0 **b.** -32 **c.** 156

26. a. -2 **b.** is not a factor
   c. Remainder Theorem

27. a. 5.9136 **b.** 14.8306 **c.** -5.8284

28. $5\left(\sqrt{3} - \sqrt{2}\right)$

29. $\left(x + 9\right)\left(\sqrt{x} - 3\right)$

30. $\sqrt{5}\left(\sqrt{6} - 1\right)$

31. $4 + 2i$

32. $19 + 4i$

33. $\dfrac{-11}{13} + \dfrac{16i}{13}$

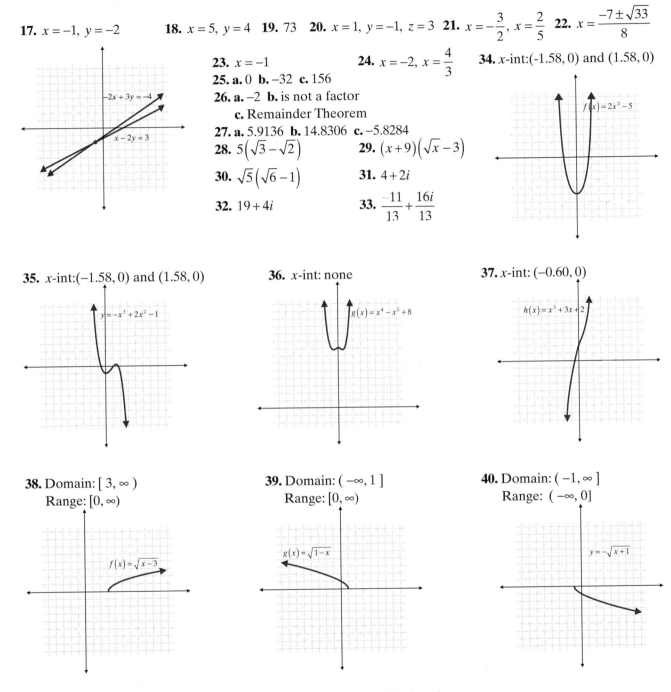

35. x-int:$(-1.58, 0)$ and $(1.58, 0)$

36. x-int: none

37. x-int: $(-0.60, 0)$

38. Domain: $[\,3, \infty\,)$
   Range: $[0, \infty)$

39. Domain: $(\,-\infty, 1\,]$
   Range: $[0, \infty)$

40. Domain: $(\,-1, \infty\,]$
   Range: $(\,-\infty, 0\,]$

41. $\$35$ **42.** $20, 26$ **43.** $12, 14, 16$ **44.** length of the base $= 19$, altitude $= 8$

45. If any vertical line intersects the graph of a relation at more than 1 point, then the relation graphed is not a function.

Chapter 8

Exercises 8.1, Pages 527 – 530

1. $x = 0, (0, -4), \{x | x \text{ is real}\}, \{y | y \geq -4\}$ **3.** $x = 0, (0, 9), \{x | x \text{ is real}\}, \{y | y \geq 9\}$

5. $x = 0, (0, 1), \{x | x \text{ is real}\}, \{y | y \leq 1\}$ **7.** $x = 0, \left(0, \dfrac{1}{5}\right), \{x | x \text{ is real}\}, \left\{y \middle| y \leq \dfrac{1}{5}\right\}$

9. $x = -1, (-1, 0), \{x | x \text{ is real}\}, \{y | y \geq 0\}$ **11.** $x = 4, (4, 0), \{x | x \text{ is real}\}, \{y | y \leq 0\}$

13. $x = -3, (-3, -2), \{x | x \text{ is real}\}, \{y | y \geq -2\}$ **15.** $x = -2, (-2, -6), \{x | x \text{ is real}\}, \{y | y \geq -6\}$

17. $x = \dfrac{3}{2}, \left(\dfrac{3}{2}, \dfrac{7}{2}\right), \{x | x \text{ is real}\}, \left\{y \middle| y \leq \dfrac{7}{2}\right\}$ **19.** $x = \dfrac{4}{5}, \left(\dfrac{4}{5}, -\dfrac{11}{5}\right), \{x | x \text{ is real}\}, \left\{y \middle| y \geq -\dfrac{11}{5}\right\}$

21. a.   **b.**

c.   **d.**

23. a.   **b.**   **c.**

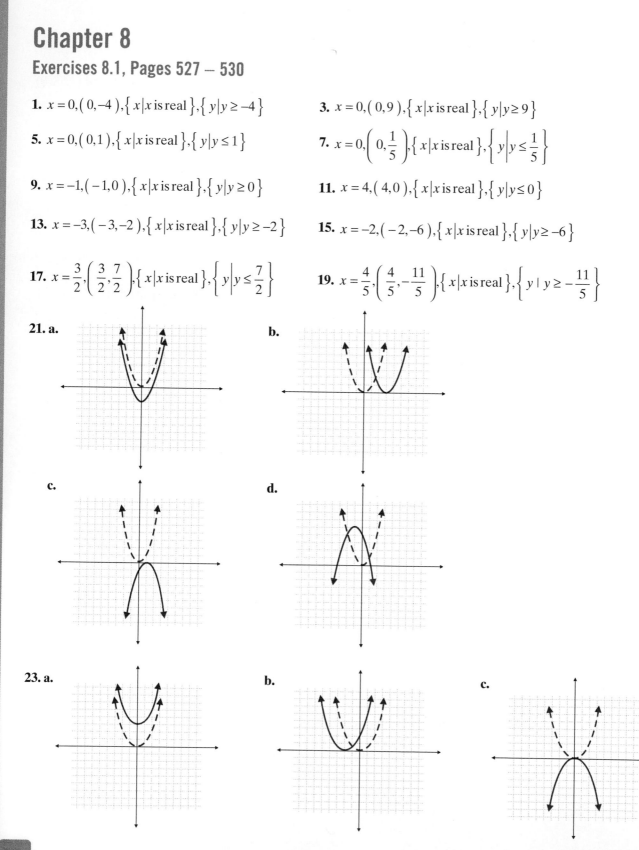

d.

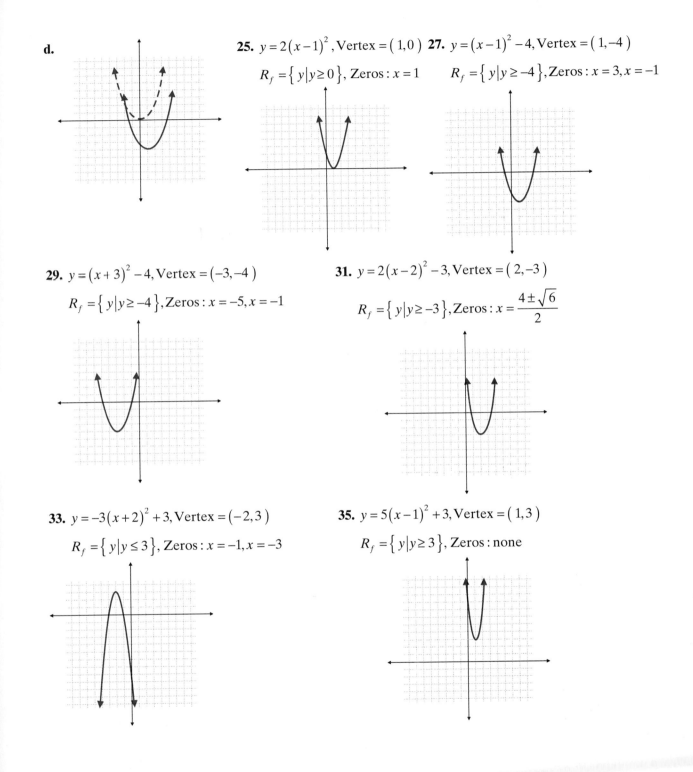

25. $y = 2(x-1)^2$, Vertex $= (1, 0)$ **27.** $y = (x-1)^2 - 4$, Vertex $= (1, -4)$

$R_f = \{ y | y \geq 0 \}$, Zeros : $x = 1$ $R_f = \{ y | y \geq -4 \}$, Zeros : $x = 3, x = -1$

29. $y = (x+3)^2 - 4$, Vertex $= (-3, -4)$

$R_f = \{ y | y \geq -4 \}$, Zeros : $x = -5, x = -1$

31. $y = 2(x-2)^2 - 3$, Vertex $= (2, -3)$

$R_f = \{ y | y \geq -3 \}$, Zeros : $x = \dfrac{4 \pm \sqrt{6}}{2}$

33. $y = -3(x+2)^2 + 3$, Vertex $= (-2, 3)$

$R_f = \{ y | y \leq 3 \}$, Zeros : $x = -1, x = -3$

35. $y = 5(x-1)^2 + 3$, Vertex $= (1, 3)$

$R_f = \{ y | y \geq 3 \}$, Zeros : none

37. $y = -\left(x + \dfrac{5}{2}\right)^2 + \dfrac{17}{4}$, Vertex $= \left(-\dfrac{5}{2}, \dfrac{17}{4}\right)$

$R_f = \left\{ y \,\middle|\, y \le \dfrac{17}{4} \right\}$, Zeros: $x = \dfrac{-5 \pm \sqrt{17}}{2}$

39. $y = 2\left(x + \dfrac{7}{4}\right)^2 - \dfrac{9}{8}$, Vertex $= \left(-\dfrac{7}{4}, -\dfrac{9}{8}\right)$

$R_f = \left\{ y \,\middle|\, y \ge -\dfrac{9}{8} \right\}$, Zeros: $x = -1, x = -\dfrac{5}{2}$

41.   **43.**

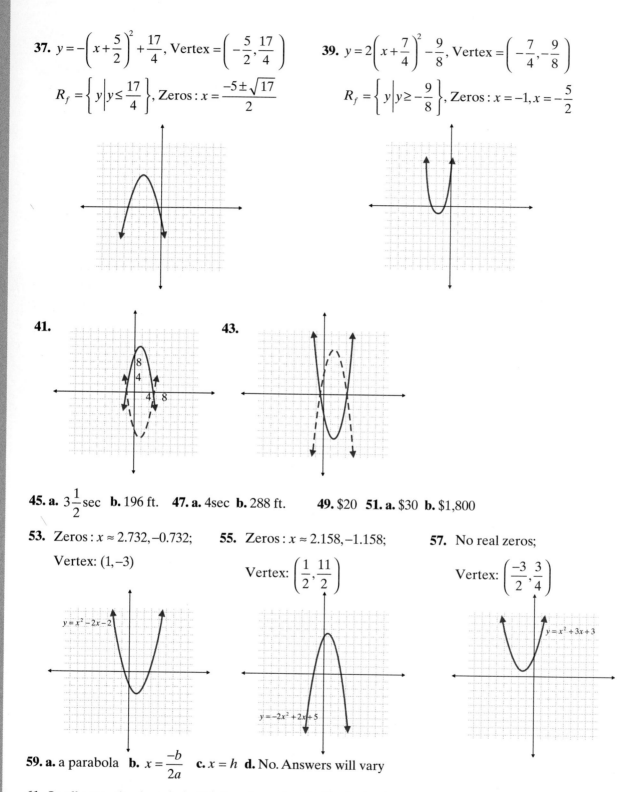

45. a. $3\dfrac{1}{2}$ sec **b.** 196 ft.   **47. a.** 4 sec **b.** 288 ft.   **49.** \$20   **51. a.** \$30 **b.** \$1,800

53. Zeros: $x \approx 2.732, -0.732$;   **55.** Zeros: $x \approx 2.158, -1.158$;   **57.** No real zeros;

Vertex: $(1, -3)$

Vertex: $\left(\dfrac{1}{2}, \dfrac{11}{2}\right)$

Vertex: $\left(\dfrac{-3}{2}, \dfrac{3}{4}\right)$

$y = x^2 - 2x - 2$

$y = -2x^2 + 2x + 5$

$y = x^2 + 3x + 3$

59. a. a parabola   **b.** $x = \dfrac{-b}{2a}$ **c.** $x = h$ **d.** No. Answers will vary

61. In all cases the domain is R (all real numbers). For $|a| > 0$, the range is the interval $[k, \infty)$. For $|a| < 0$, the range is the interval $(-\infty, k]$.

Exercises 8.2, Pages 539 – 541

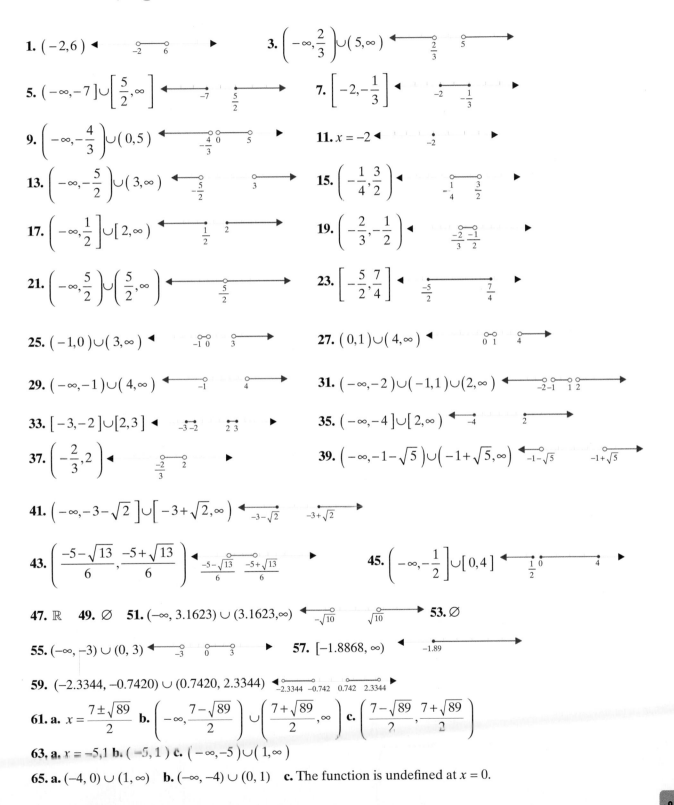

1. $\left(-2,6\right)$

3. $\left(-\infty,\dfrac{2}{3}\right)\cup\left(5,\infty\right)$

5. $\left(-\infty,-7\right]\cup\left[\dfrac{5}{2},\infty\right)$

7. $\left[-2,-\dfrac{1}{3}\right]$

9. $\left(-\infty,-\dfrac{4}{3}\right)\cup\left(0,5\right)$

11. $x=-2$

13. $\left(-\infty,-\dfrac{5}{2}\right)\cup\left(3,\infty\right)$

15. $\left(-\dfrac{1}{4},\dfrac{3}{2}\right)$

17. $\left(-\infty,\dfrac{1}{2}\right]\cup\left[2,\infty\right)$

19. $\left(-\dfrac{2}{3},-\dfrac{1}{2}\right)$

21. $\left(-\infty,\dfrac{5}{2}\right)\cup\left(\dfrac{5}{2},\infty\right)$

23. $\left[-\dfrac{5}{2},\dfrac{7}{4}\right]$

25. $\left(-1,0\right)\cup\left(3,\infty\right)$

27. $\left(0,1\right)\cup\left(4,\infty\right)$

29. $\left(-\infty,-1\right)\cup\left(4,\infty\right)$

31. $\left(-\infty,-2\right)\cup\left(-1,1\right)\cup\left(2,\infty\right)$

33. $\left[-3,-2\right]\cup\left[2,3\right]$

35. $\left(-\infty,-4\right]\cup\left[2,\infty\right)$

37. $\left(-\dfrac{2}{3},2\right)$

39. $\left(-\infty,-1-\sqrt{5}\right)\cup\left(-1+\sqrt{5},\infty\right)$

41. $\left(-\infty,-3-\sqrt{2}\,\right]\cup\left[-3+\sqrt{2},\infty\right)$

43. $\left(\dfrac{-5-\sqrt{13}}{6},\dfrac{-5+\sqrt{13}}{6}\right)$

45. $\left(-\infty,-\dfrac{1}{2}\right]\cup\left[0,4\right]$

47. $\mathbb{R}$ **49.** $\varnothing$ **51.** $(-\infty,3.1623)\cup(3.1623,\infty)$ **53.** $\varnothing$

55. $(-\infty,-3)\cup(0,3)$ **57.** $[-1.8868,\infty)$

59. $(-2.3344,-0.7420)\cup(0.7420,2.3344)$

61. a. $x=\dfrac{7\pm\sqrt{89}}{2}$ **b.** $\left(-\infty,\dfrac{7-\sqrt{89}}{2}\right)\cup\left(\dfrac{7+\sqrt{89}}{2},\infty\right)$ **c.** $\left(\dfrac{7-\sqrt{89}}{2},\dfrac{7+\sqrt{89}}{2}\right)$

63. a. $x=-5,1$ **b.** $\left(-5,1\right)$ **c.** $\left(-\infty,-5\right)\cup\left(1,\infty\right)$

65. a. $(-4,0)\cup(1,\infty)$ **b.** $(-\infty,-4)\cup(0,1)$ **c.** The function is undefined at $x=0$.

Exercises 8.3, Pages 552 – 556

1. a. 12 **b.** 4 **c.** $a + 8$ **3. a.** 4 **b.** 31 **c.** $x^2 - 4x - 1$ **5. a.** 1 **b.** $4a + 5$ **c.** $4x + 4h - 3$ **d.** 4   **7. a.** 0

b. $a^2 - 6a + 5$ **c.** $x^2 + 2xh + h^2 - 4$ **d.** $2x + h$ **9. a.** -3 **b.** $2a^2 - 8a + 5$ **c.** $2x^2 + 4xh + 2h^2 - 3$ **d.** $4x + 2h$

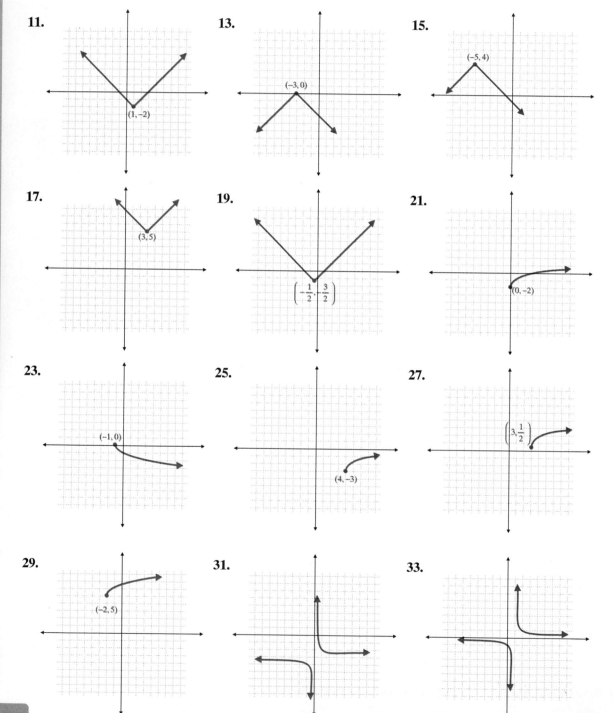

35.

37.

39.

41.

43.

45.

47.

49.

51. iii **53.** ii

55.

$y = 2x^2$

$y = -3x^2$

57.

$y = x^2 - 4$

$y = (x+1)^2 - 4$

59.

$y = -x^2 + 1$

$y = -3(x-2)^2 + 1$

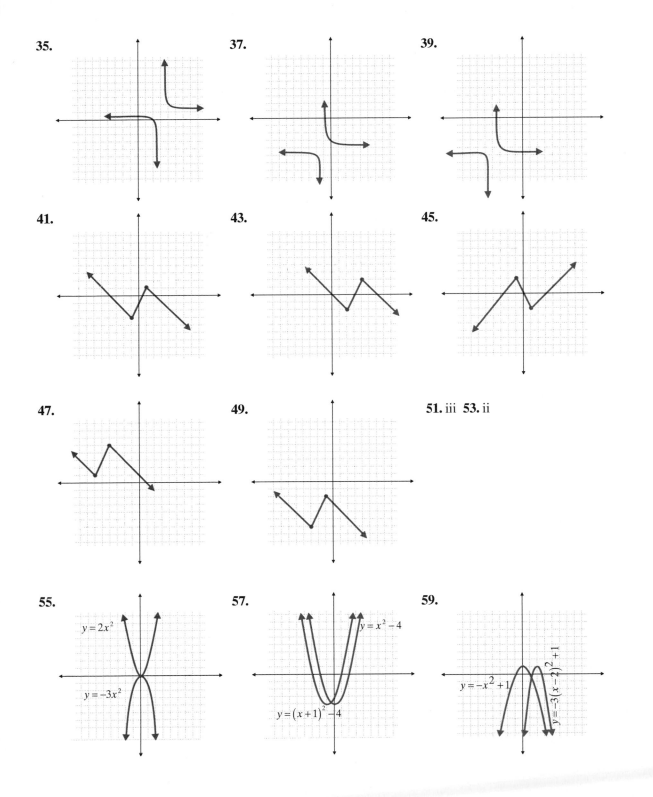

Exercises 8.4, Pages 563 – 564

1. Vertex : $(4,0)$, y – intercepts : None

Line of symmetry : $y = 0$

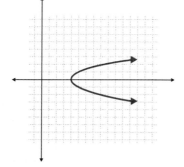

3. Vertex : $(-3,0)$, y – intercepts :

$(0,\sqrt{3}),(0,-\sqrt{3})$ Line of symmetry : $y = 0$

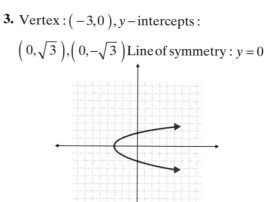

5. Vertex : $(3,0)$, y – intercepts : none

Line of symmetry : $y = 0$

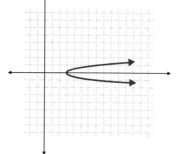

7. Vertex : $(0,3)$, y – intercepts : $(0,3)$

Line of symmetry : $y = 3$

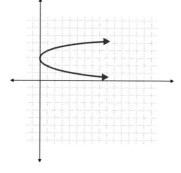

9. Vertex : $(4,-2)$, y – intercepts : none

Line of symmetry : $y = -2$

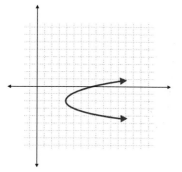

11. Vertex : $(-1,1)$, y – intercepts : $(0,0),(0,2)$

Line of symmetry : $y = 1$

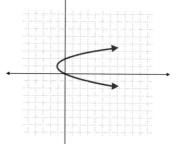

13. Vertex: $(0,-2)$, y-intercepts: $(0,-2)$

Line of symmetry: $y = -2$

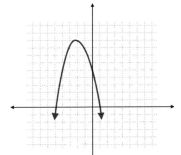

15. Vertex: $(0,4)$, y-intercepts: $(0,4)$

Line of symmetry: $y = 4$

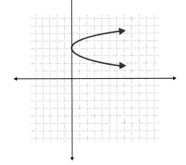

17. Vertex: $(-2,9)$, y-intercepts: $(0,5)$

Line of symmetry: $x = -2$

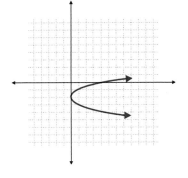

19. Vertex: $(-3,-4)$, y-intercepts: $(0,5)$

Line of symmetry: $x = -3$

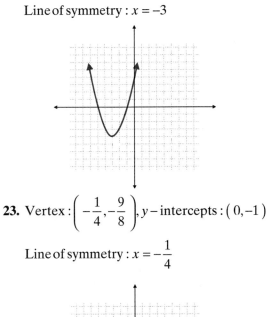

21. Vertex: $(1,2)$, y-intercepts: $(0,1), (0,3)$

Line of symmetry: $y = 2$

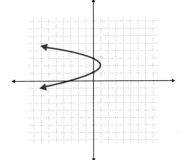

23. Vertex: $\left(-\dfrac{1}{4}, -\dfrac{9}{8}\right)$, y-intercepts: $(0,-1)$

Line of symmetry: $x = -\dfrac{1}{4}$

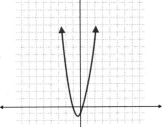

25. Vertex: $\left(-8,-1\right)$, $y-$intercepts:

$\left(0,-1+\dfrac{2}{3}\sqrt{6}\right),\left(0,-1-\dfrac{2}{3}\sqrt{6}\right)$

Line of symmetry: $y=-1$

27. Vertex: $\left(\dfrac{9}{8},\dfrac{5}{4}\right)$, $y-$intercepts: $\left(0,\dfrac{1}{2}\right),\left(0,2\right)$

Line of symmetry: $y=\dfrac{5}{4}$

29. Vertex: $\left(\dfrac{3}{2},0\right)$, $y-$intercepts: $\left(0,9\right)$ **31.**   **33.**

Line of symmetry: $x=\dfrac{3}{2}$

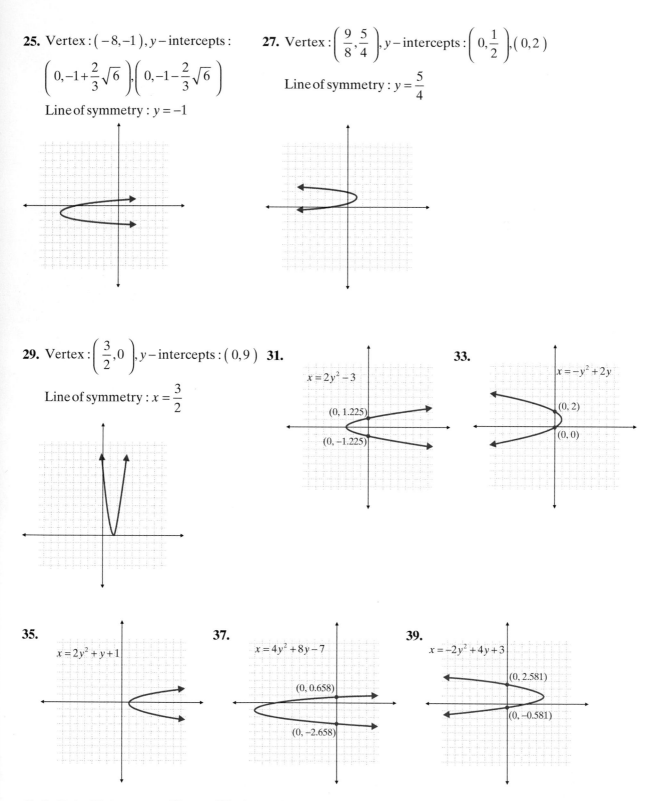

$x=2y^2-3$
$(0, 1.225)$
$(0, -1.225)$

$x=-y^2+2y$
$(0, 2)$
$(0, 0)$

35.   **37.**   **39.**

$x=2y^2+y+1$

$x=4y^2+8y-7$
$(0, 0.658)$
$(0, -2.658)$

$x=-2y^2+4y+3$
$(0, 2.581)$
$(0, -0.581)$

41. ii   **43.** i   **45.** Answers will vary. The larger $|a|$ is, the more open the graph will be.

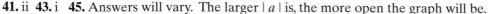

Exercises 8.5, Pages 575 – 578

1. $5; (4, 5.5)$ **3.** $13; (3, 4.5)$ **5.** $\sqrt{29}; (2, 4.5)$ **7.** $3; (5.5, -3)$ **9.** $\sqrt{13}; (6, -3.5)$ **11.** $17; (-3, -4.5)$

13. $x^2 + y^2 = 16$ **15.** $x^2 + y^2 = 3$ **17.** $x^2 + y^2 = 11$ **19.** $x^2 + y^2 = \dfrac{4}{9}$ **21.** $x^2 + (y - 2)^2 = 4$

23. $(x - 4)^2 + y^2 = 1$

25. $(x + 2)^2 + y^2 = 8$

27. $(x - 3)^2 + (y - 1)^2 = 36$

29. $(x - 3)^2 + (y - 5)^2 = 12$

31. $(x - 7)^2 + (y - 4)^2 = 10$

33. $x^2 + y^2 = 9;$ Center: $(0, 0)$, $r = 3$ **35.** $x^2 + y^2 = 49;$ Center: $(0, 0)$, $r = 7$

37. $x^2 + y^2 = 18$

Center: $(0, 0), r = 3\sqrt{2}$

39. $(x + 1)^2 + y^2 = 9$

Center: $(-1, 0), r = 3$

41. $x^2 + (y - 2)^2 = 4$

Center: $(0, 2), r = 2$

43. $(x + 1)^2 + (y + 2)^2 = 16$

Center: $(-1, -2), r = 4$

45. $(x + 2)^2 + (y + 2)^2 = 16$

Center: $(-2, -2), r = 4$

47. $(x - 2)^2 + (y - 3)^2 = 8$

Center: $(2, 3), r = 2\sqrt{2}$

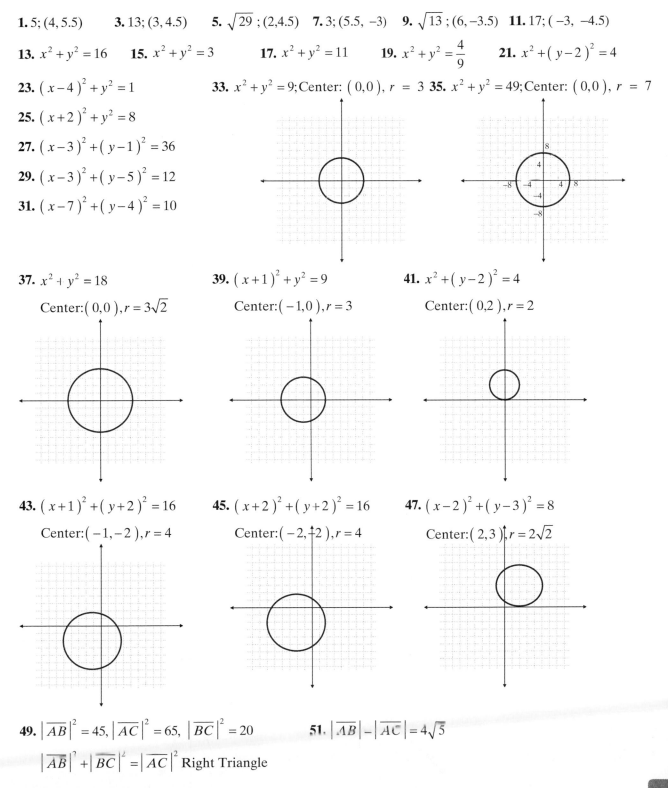

49. $\left| \overline{AB} \right|^2 = 45, \left| \overline{AC} \right|^2 = 65, \left| \overline{BC} \right|^2 = 20$ **51.** $\left| \overline{AB} \right| - \left| \overline{AC} \right| = 4\sqrt{5}$

$\left| \overline{AB} \right|^2 + \left| \overline{BC} \right|^2 = \left| \overline{AC} \right|^2$ Right Triangle

53. $\left|\overline{AB}\right| = \left|\overline{AC}\right| = \left|\overline{BC}\right| = 4$ **55.** $\left|\overline{AC}\right| = \left|\overline{BD}\right| = \sqrt{61}$ **57.** $10 + 4\sqrt{5}$ **59.** $\sqrt{41} + \sqrt{65} + \sqrt{10}$

61.   **63.**

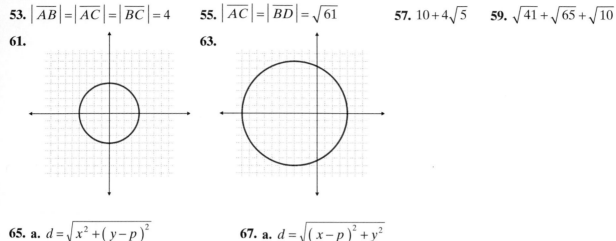

65. a. $d = \sqrt{x^2 + (y - p)^2}$ **67. a.** $d = \sqrt{(x - p)^2 + y^2}$

    b. $d = y + p$ **b.** $d = x + p$

    c. $y + p = \sqrt{x^2 + (y - p)^2}$ **c.** $x + p = \sqrt{(x - p)^2 + y^2}$

      $(y + p)^2 = x^2 + (y - p)^2$ $(x + p)^2 = (x - p)^2 + y^2$

      $y^2 + 2py + p^2 = x^2 + y^2 - 2py + p^2$ $x^2 + 2px + p^2 = x^2 - 2px + p^2 + y^2$

      $x^2 = 4py$ $y^2 = 4px$

Exercises 8.6, Pages 588 – 590

1. $\dfrac{x^2}{36} + \dfrac{y^2}{4} = 1$ **3.** $\dfrac{x^2}{25} + \dfrac{y^2}{4} = 1$

5. $\dfrac{x^2}{1} + \dfrac{y^2}{16} = 1$ **7.** $\dfrac{x^2}{1} - \dfrac{y^2}{1} = 1$ **9.** $\dfrac{x^2}{1} - \dfrac{y^2}{9} = 1$

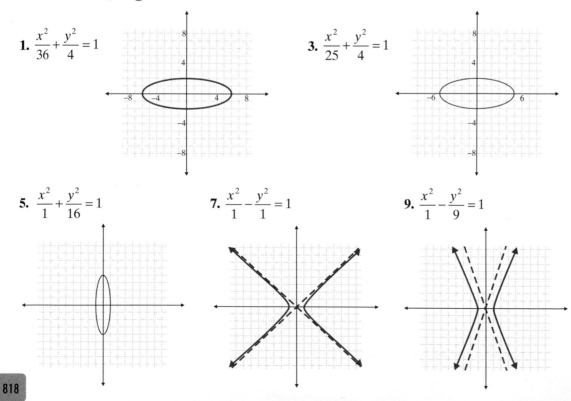

11. $\dfrac{x^2}{9} - \dfrac{y^2}{4} = 1$

13. $\dfrac{x^2}{4} + \dfrac{y^2}{8} = 1$

15. $\dfrac{x^2}{20} + \dfrac{y^2}{4} = 1$

17. $\dfrac{y^2}{9} - \dfrac{x^2}{9} = 1$

19. $\dfrac{y^2}{8} - \dfrac{x^2}{4} = 1$

21. $\dfrac{y^2}{18} - \dfrac{x^2}{9} = 1$

23. $\dfrac{x^2}{6} + \dfrac{y^2}{9} = 1$

25. $\dfrac{x^2}{5} + \dfrac{y^2}{4} = 1$

27. $\dfrac{x^2}{25} - \dfrac{y^2}{15} = 1$

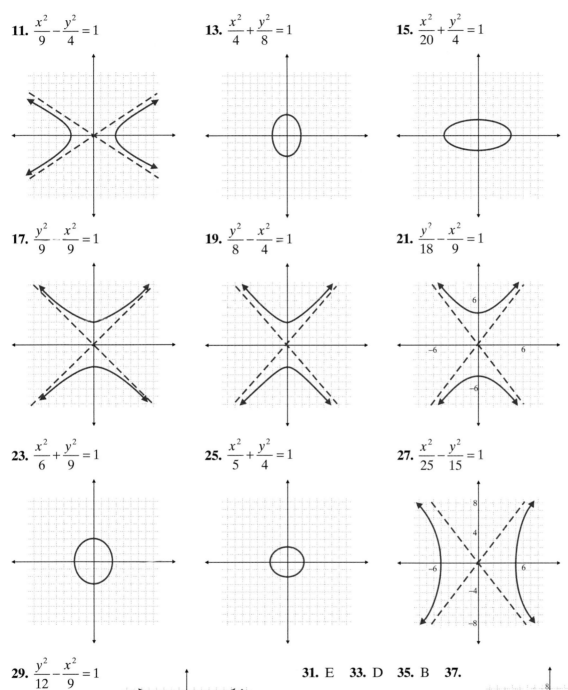

29. $\dfrac{y^2}{12} - \dfrac{x^2}{9} = 1$

31. E **33.** D **35.** B **37.**

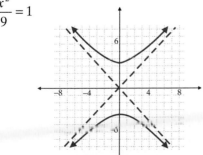

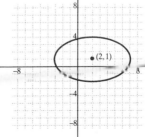

819

39.

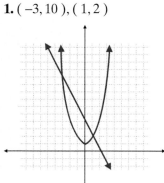

41.

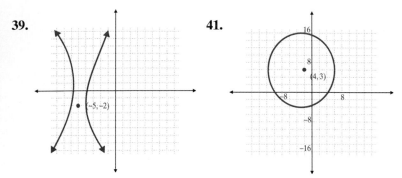

43. b. set up the equation

$$\sqrt{(x+c)^2+(y-0)^2} +$$

$$\sqrt{(x-c)^2+(y-0)^2} = 2a$$

and square both sides twice, then simplify.

c. at the y-intercept $(0, b)$ a right triangle is formed with hypotenuse a and sides b and c. The Pythagorean Theorem gives $a^2 = b^2 + c^2$.

Exercises 8.7, Pages 596 – 597

1. $(-3, 10), (1, 2)$

3. $(1, 1), (2, 0)$

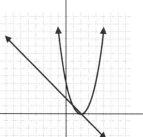

5. $(-2, -4), (4, 2)$

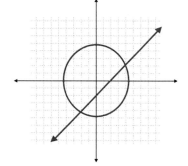

7. $(5, 3)$

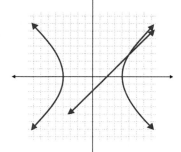

9. $(-3, 0), (3, 0)$

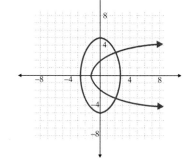

11. $(2, 3), (2, -3)$

13. $(-2, 4), (1, 1)$

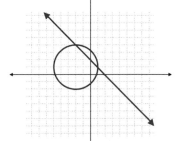

15. $(-3, -2), (-3, 2)(3, -2), (3, 2)$

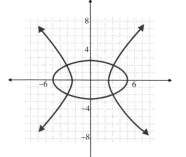

17. $\left(-3\sqrt{5},5\right),\left(-6,4\right),\left(3\sqrt{5},5\right),\left(6,4\right)$ **19.** $\left(1,3\right),\left(-1,3\right)$ **21.** $\left(-3,\sqrt{11}\right),\left(-3,-\sqrt{11}\right),\left(3,\sqrt{11}\right),\left(3,-\sqrt{11}\right)$

23. $\left(-\dfrac{3}{2},-1\right),\left(\dfrac{1}{2},\dfrac{1}{2}\right)$ **25.** $\left(4,4\right),\left(-2,-2\right)$ **27.** $\left(5,-3\right),\left(-5,1\right)$ **29.** $\left(0,3\right),\left(2,3\right)$

31.   **33.**   **35.**

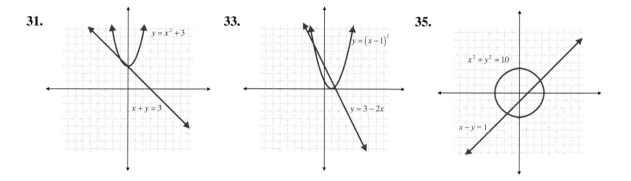

Chapter 8 Test, Pages 602 – 603

1. $y=\left(x-3\right)^2-1$

Vertex: $\left(3,-1\right)$

Axis: $x=3$,

Range: $y\geq-1$

Zeros: $x=2,4$

Domain: All Real Numbers

2. $y=-2\left(x-\dfrac{3}{2}\right)^2+\dfrac{15}{2}$

Vertex: $\left(\dfrac{3}{2},\dfrac{15}{2}\right)$ Axis: $x=\dfrac{3}{2}$

Range: $y\leq\dfrac{15}{2}$

Zeros: $x=\dfrac{3\pm\sqrt{15}}{2}$

Domain: All Real Numbers

3. $y=2\left(x-3\right)^2-9$

Vertex: $\left(3,-9\right)$

Axis: $x=3$,

Range: $y\geq-9$

Zeros: $x=\dfrac{6\pm3\sqrt{2}}{2}$

Domain: All Real Numbers

4. a. 13

b. $2x^2+6$

c. $2x^2+4x+7$

d. $4x+2h$

5. $\left(-\infty,-3\right]$ or $\left[5,\infty\right)$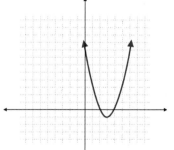

7. $\left[1,3\right]$

6. $\left(-4,-\dfrac{1}{2}\right)$

8. $\left(-0.6697,1.4231\right)\cup\left(5.2466,\infty\right)$

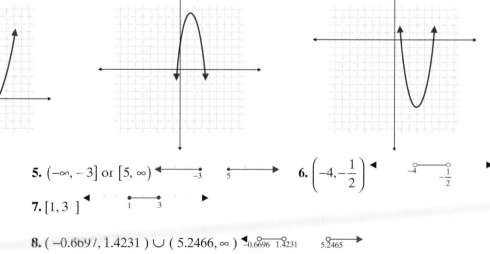

9.
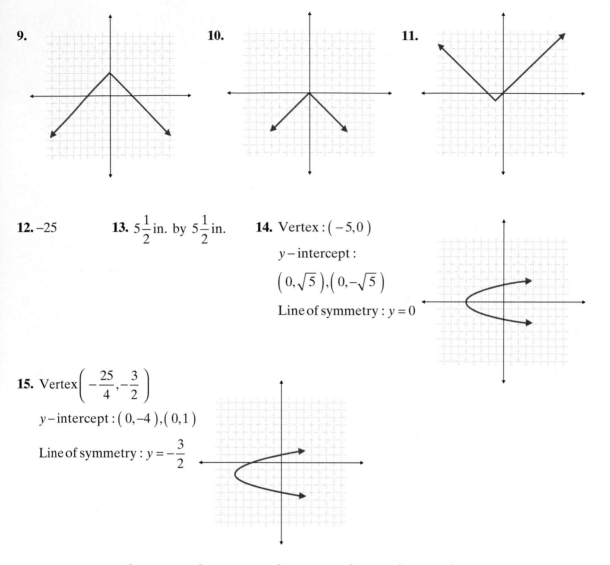

10.

11.

12. -25 **13.** $5\frac{1}{2}$ in. by $5\frac{1}{2}$ in.   **14.** Vertex : $(-5,0)$

y – intercept :

$\left(0,\sqrt{5}\right),\left(0,-\sqrt{5}\right)$

Line of symmetry : $y = 0$

15. Vertex $\left(-\dfrac{25}{4},-\dfrac{3}{2}\right)$

y – intercept : $(0,-4),(0,1)$

Line of symmetry : $y = -\dfrac{3}{2}$

16. $3\sqrt{10}$ **17.** $\left|\overline{AB}\right|^2 = 52, \left|\overline{AC}\right|^2 = 104, \left|\overline{BC}\right|^2 = 52, \left|\overline{AB}\right|^2 + \left|\overline{BC}\right|^2 = \left|\overline{AC}\right|^2$ **18.** $(x+3)^2 + (y+1)^2 = 25$

19. $x^2 + (y-1)^2 = 9$

Center: $(0,1), r = 3$

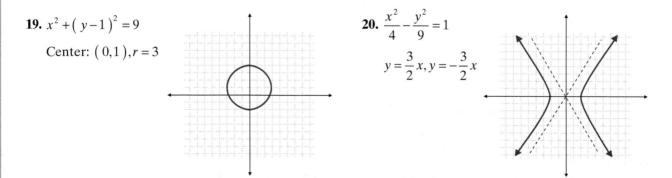

20. $\dfrac{x^2}{4} - \dfrac{y^2}{9} = 1$

$y = \dfrac{3}{2}x, y = -\dfrac{3}{2}x$

21. $\dfrac{x^2}{9}+\dfrac{y^2}{\frac{9}{4}}=1$

22. $\dfrac{y^2}{9}-\dfrac{x^2}{16}=1$

$y=\dfrac{3}{4}x,\ y=-\dfrac{3}{4}x$

23. $\dfrac{x^2}{4}+\dfrac{y^2}{25}=1$

24.

25.

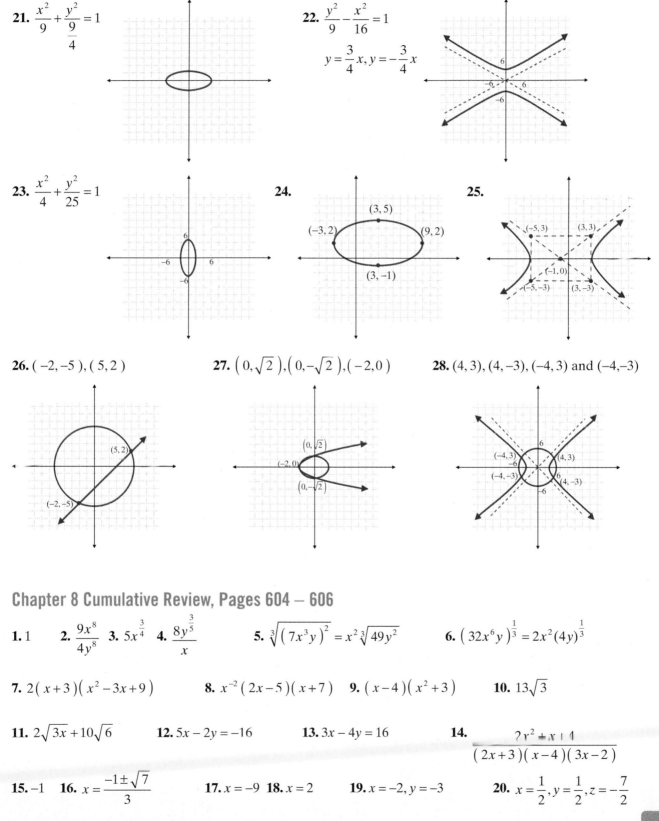

26. $(-2,-5),(5,2)$

27. $\left(0,\sqrt{2}\right),\left(0,-\sqrt{2}\right),(-2,0)$

28. $(4,3),(4,-3),(-4,3)$ and $(-4,-3)$

Chapter 8 Cumulative Review, Pages 604 – 606

1. 1 **2.** $\dfrac{9x^8}{4y^8}$ **3.** $5x^{\frac{3}{4}}$ **4.** $\dfrac{8y^{\frac{3}{5}}}{x}$ **5.** $\sqrt[3]{\left(7x^3y\right)^2}=x^2\sqrt[3]{49y^2}$ **6.** $\left(32x^6y\right)^{\frac{1}{3}}=2x^2(4y)^{\frac{1}{3}}$

7. $2\left(x+3\right)\left(x^2-3x+9\right)$ **8.** $x^{-2}\left(2x-5\right)\left(x+7\right)$ **9.** $\left(x-4\right)\left(x^2+3\right)$ **10.** $13\sqrt{3}$

11. $2\sqrt{3x}+10\sqrt{6}$ **12.** $5x-2y=-16$ **13.** $3x-4y=16$ **14.** $\dfrac{2x^2+x+4}{\left(2x+3\right)\left(x-4\right)\left(3x-2\right)}$

15. -1 **16.** $x=\dfrac{-1\pm\sqrt{7}}{3}$ **17.** $x=-9$ **18.** $x=2$ **19.** $x=-2,\ y=-3$ **20.** $x=\dfrac{1}{2},\ y=\dfrac{1}{2},\ z=-\dfrac{7}{2}$

21. $y = \dfrac{1}{2}(x+0)^2 - 3$ Vertex: $(0, -3)$

Axis of symmetry: $x = 0$,

D_f = All real numbers

$R_f = \{\, y \mid y \geq -3 \,\}$,

Zeros: $x = \pm\sqrt{6}$

22. $y = -(x-2)^2 + 0$ Vertex: $(2, 0)$

Axis of symmetry:

$x = 2$,

D_f = All real numbers

$R_f = \{\, y \mid y \leq 0 \,\}$,

Zeros: $x = 2$

23.

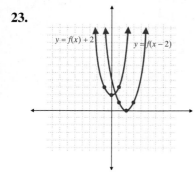

24. $x \geq 5,\ -1 \leq x \leq 0$ **25.**

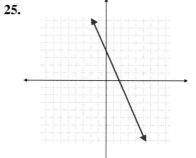

26.   **27.**   **28.**

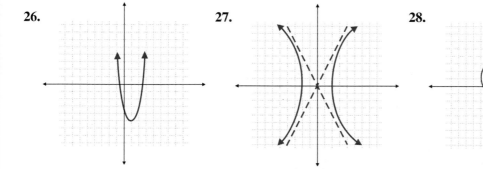

29. a. 5 **b.** $4x - 11$ **c.** $4x - 4$ **d.** 4   **30. a.** 13 **b.** $2x^2 + 3x - 3$ **c.** $2x^2 - 5x + 1$ **d.** $4x + 2h + 3$ **31.** \$3600 at 7%;

\$5400 at 8%   **32.** 36   **33. a.** $t = 2\frac{1}{2}$ sec **b.** 148 ft   **34.** \$15

35.   **36.**   **37.**

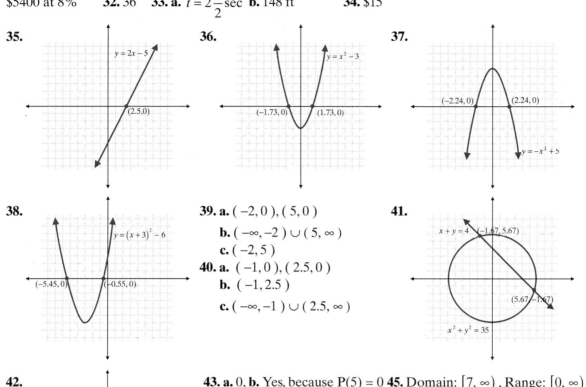

38.   **39. a.** $(-2, 0), (5, 0)$ **41.**

   b. $(-\infty, -2) \cup (5, \infty)$

   c. $(-2, 5)$

40. a. $(-1, 0), (2.5, 0)$

   b. $(-1, 2.5)$

   c. $(-\infty, -1) \cup (2.5, \infty)$

42.   **43. a.** 0, **b.** Yes, because $P(5) = 0$ **45.** Domain: $[7, \infty)$, Range: $[0, \infty)$

   44. $a^2 + b^2 = c^2$

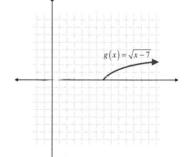

Chapter 9
Exercises 9.1, Pages 614 – 618

1. a. $2x - 3$ **b.** 7 **c.** $x^2 - 3x - 10$ **d.** $\dfrac{x+2}{x-5}$ **3. a.** $x^2 + 3x - 4$ **b.** $x^2 - 3x + 4$ **c.** $3x^3 - 4x^2$ **d.** $\dfrac{x^2}{3x-4}$

5. a. $x^2 + x - 12$ **b.** $x^2 - x - 6$ **c.** $x^3 - 3x^2 - 9x + 27$ **d.** $x + 3$ **7. a.** $3x^2 + x + 2$ **b.** $x^2 + x - 2$ **c.** $2x^4 + x^3 + 4x^2 + 2x$

d. $\dfrac{2x^2 + x}{x^2 + 2}$ **9. a.** $2x^3 + 2$ **b.** $8x$ **c.** $x^4 - 14x^2 + 1$ **d.** $\dfrac{x^2 + 4x + 1}{x^2 - 4x + 1}$ **11.** 9   **13.** $-a^2 - a - 1$ **15.** 27 **17.** $\dfrac{8}{5}$ **9.** -31

21. $\sqrt{2x-6}+x+4$, Domain: $[\,3,\infty\,)$ **23.** $3x^2-19x-14$,   Domain : $(-\infty,\infty\,)$

25. $\dfrac{x-5}{\sqrt{x+3}}$, Domain : $(-3,\infty\,)$ **27.** $-3x\sqrt{x-3}$, Domain: $[\,3,\infty\,)$ **29.** $\sqrt[3]{x+3}+\sqrt{5+x}$, Domain : $[-5,\infty\,)$

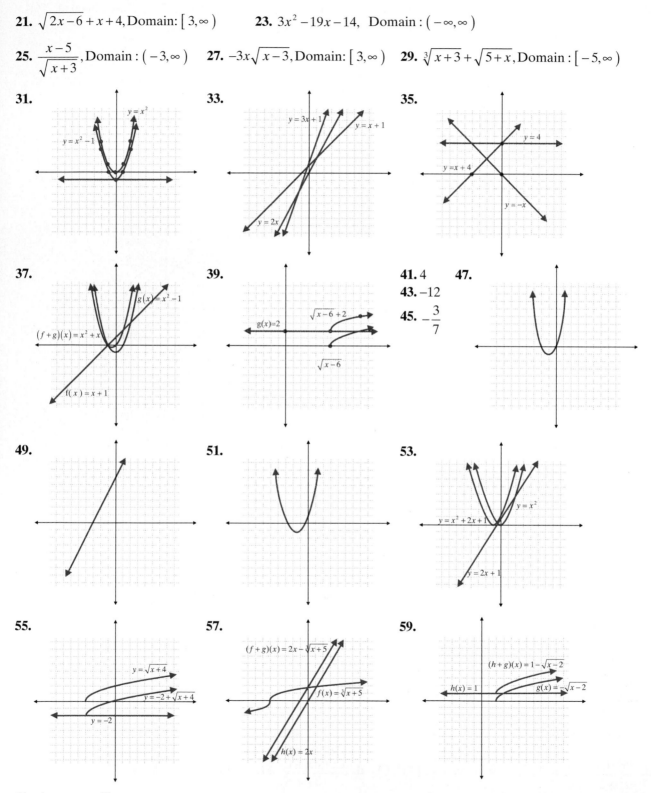

31.

33.

35.

37.

39.

41. 4   **47.**

43. −12

45. $-\dfrac{3}{7}$

49.

51.

53.

55.

57.

59.

61. Answers will vary

63. a.   **b.**   **c.**

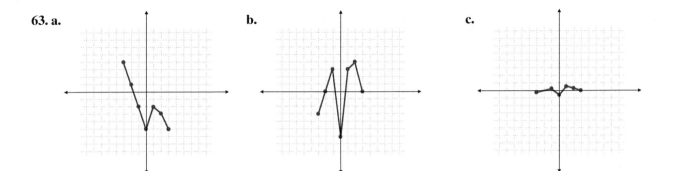

Exercises 9.2, Pages 630 – 633

1. $f(g(x)) = \dfrac{3}{2}x + 11;\ g(f(x)) = \dfrac{3}{2}x + \dfrac{9}{2}$ **3.** $f(g(x)) = 4x^2 + 12x + 9;\ g(f(x)) = 2x^2 + 3$

5. $f(g(x)) = \dfrac{1}{5x - 8};\ g(f(x)) = \dfrac{5}{x} - 8$ **7.** $f(g(x)) = \dfrac{1}{x^2} - 1;\ g(f(x)) = \dfrac{1}{(x-1)^2}$

9. $f(g(x)) = x^3 + 3x^2 + 4x + 3;\ g(f(x)) = x^3 + x + 2$ **11.** $f(g(x)) = \sqrt{x - 2};\ g(f(x)) = \sqrt{x} - 2$

13. $f(g(x)) = \sqrt{x^2} = |x|;\ g(f(x)) = \left(\sqrt{x}\right)^2 = x$ **15.** $f(g(x)) = \dfrac{1}{\sqrt{x^2 - 4}};\ g(f(x)) = \left(\dfrac{1}{\sqrt{x}}\right)^2 - 4$

$$= \dfrac{1}{x} - 4$$

17. $f(g(x)) = x;\ g(f(x)) = x$ **19.** $f(g(x)) = (x - 8)^{\frac{3}{2}};\ g(f(x)) = \sqrt{x^3 - 8}$

21.   **23.**   **25.**

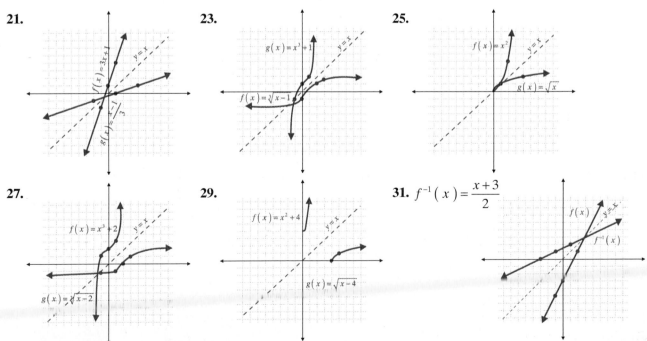

27.   **29.**   **31.** $f^{-1}(x) = \dfrac{x + 3}{2}$

33. $g^{-1}(x) = x$

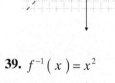

35. $f^{-1}(x) = \dfrac{x-1}{5}$

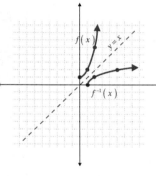

37. $g^{-1}(x) = \dfrac{1-x}{3}$

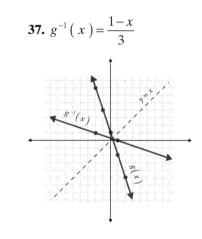

39. $f^{-1}(x) = x^2$

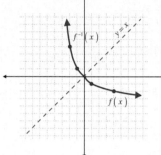

41. $f^{-1}(x) = \sqrt{x-1}$

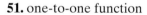

43. $f^{-1}(x) = -x-2$

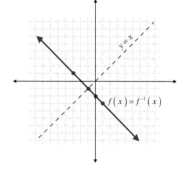

45. one - to - one function

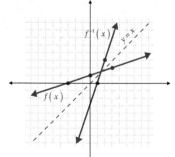

47. Not a one-to-one function

49. Not a one-to-one function

51. one-to-one function

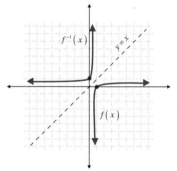

53. one - to - one function

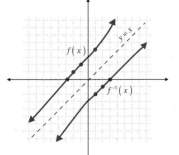

55. Is a 1-1 function

57. Is not a 1-1 function

59. Is a 1-1 function

61. Is a 1-1 function   **63.** Is not a 1-1 function

65.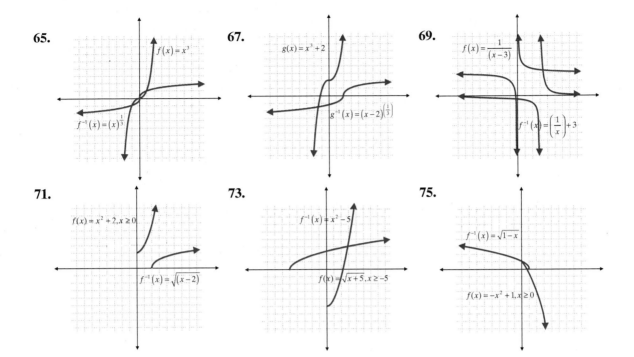

67.

69.

71.

73.

75.

Exercises 9.3, Pages 644 – 646

1.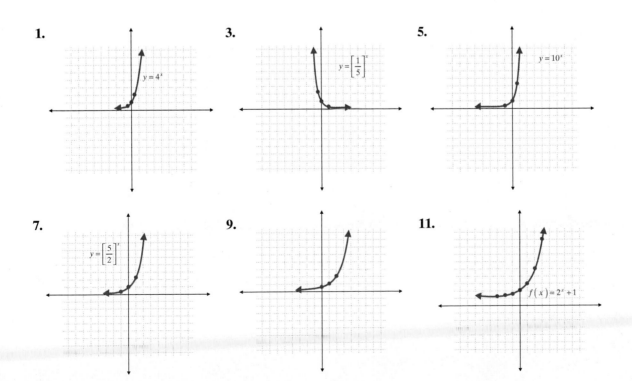

3.

5.

7.

9.

11.

13.

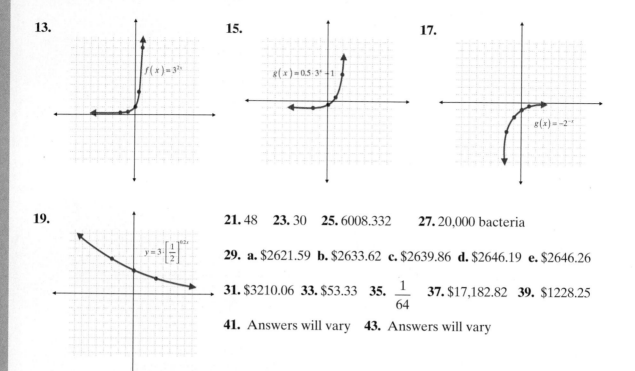

$f(x) = 3^{2x}$

15.

$g(x) = 0.5 \cdot 3^x + 1$

17.

$g(x) = -2^{-x}$

19.

$y = 3 \cdot \left[\frac{1}{2}\right]^{0.2x}$

21. 48   **23.** 30   **25.** 6008.332   **27.** 20,000 bacteria

29. a. $2621.59 **b.** $2633.62 **c.** $2639.86 **d.** $2646.19 **e.** $2646.26

31. $3210.06 **33.** $53.33 **35.** $\dfrac{1}{64}$ **37.** $17,182.82 **39.** $1228.25

41. Answers will vary   **43.** Answers will vary

Exercises 9.4, Pages 657 – 659

1. $\log_7 49 = 2$ **3.** $\log_5 \dfrac{1}{25} = -2$ **5.** $\log_2 \dfrac{1}{32} = -5$ **7.** $\log_{2/3} \dfrac{4}{9} = 2$ **9.** $\ln 17 = x$ **11.** $\log 10 = 1$ **13.** $3^2 = 9$

15. $9^{1/2} = 3$ **17.** $7^{-1} = \dfrac{1}{7}$ **19.** $e^{1.74} = N$ **21.** $b^4 = 18$ **23.** $n^x = y^2$ **25.** $x = 16$ **27.** $x = 2$

29. $x = \dfrac{1}{6}$ **31.** $x = 11$ **33.** $x = 32$ **35.** $x = -2$ **37.** $x = 1.52$ **39.** $x = 3$

41.

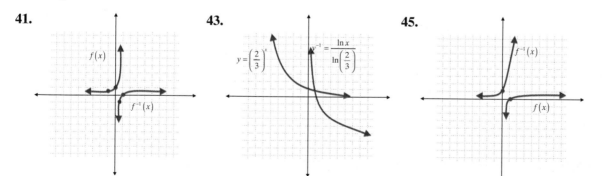

$f(x)$

$f^{-1}(x)$

43.

$y = \left(\dfrac{2}{3}\right)^x$

$y^{-1} = \dfrac{\ln x}{\ln\left(\dfrac{2}{3}\right)}$

45.

$f^{-1}(x)$

$f(x)$

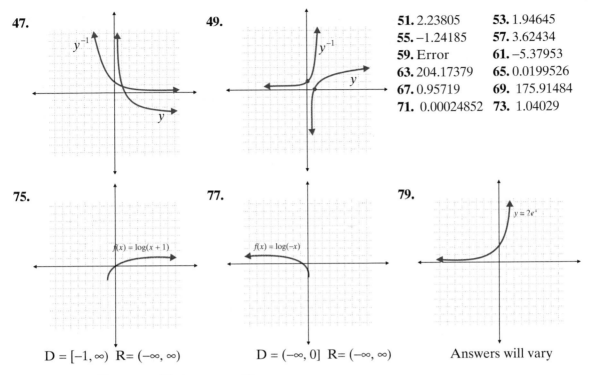

47.

49.

51. 2.23805   **53.** 1.94645
55. −1.24185   **57.** 3.62434
59. Error   **61.** −5.37953
63. 204.17379   **65.** 0.0199526
67. 0.95719   **69.** 175.91484
71. 0.00024852   **73.** 1.04029

75.

77.

79.

$D = [-1, \infty)$ $R = (-\infty, \infty)$ $D = (-\infty, 0]$ $R = (-\infty, \infty)$ Answers will vary

81. Answers will vary   **83.** Answers will vary

Exercises 9.5, Pages 666 – 668

1. 5   **3.** −2   **5.** $\dfrac{1}{2}$ **7.** 10   **9.** $\sqrt{3}$ **11.** $\log 5 + 4 \log x$ **13.** $\ln 2 - 3 \ln x + \ln y$ **15.** $\log 2 + \log x - 3 \log y$

17. $2 \ln x - \ln y - \ln z$ **19.** $-2 \log x - 2 \log y$ **21.** $\dfrac{1}{3} \log x + \dfrac{2}{3} \log y$ **23.** $\dfrac{1}{2} \ln x + \dfrac{1}{2} \ln y - \dfrac{1}{2} \ln z$

25. $\log 21 + 2 \log x + \dfrac{2}{3} \log y$ **27.** $-\dfrac{1}{2} \log x - \dfrac{5}{2} \log y$ **29.** $-9 \ln x - 6 \ln y + 3 \ln z$ **31.** $\ln \dfrac{9x}{5}$ **33.** $\log \dfrac{7x^2}{8}$

35. $\log x^2 y$ **37.** $\ln \dfrac{x^3}{y^2}$ **39.** $\ln \sqrt{\dfrac{x}{y}}$ **41.** $\log \dfrac{xz}{y}$ **43.** $\log \dfrac{x}{y^2 z^2}$ **45.** $\log (2x^2 + x)$

47. $\ln \left(x^2 + 2x - 3 \right)$ **49.** $\log \dfrac{x^2 - 2x - 3}{x - 3}$ **51.** $\log \dfrac{x + 6}{2x^2 + 9x - 18}$ **53.** Answers will vary

Exercises 9.6, Pages 676 – 678

1. $x = 11$ **3.** $x = 9$ **5.** $x = \dfrac{1}{6}$ **7.** $x = \dfrac{7}{12}$ **9.** $x = \dfrac{7}{2}$ **11.** $x = -2$ **13.** $x = -3$

15. $x = 4, x = -1$ **17.** $x = 1, x = \dfrac{3}{2}$ **19.** $x = -2, x = 3$ **21.** $x = 2$ **23.** $x = 0, x = -\dfrac{3}{2}$

25. $x = 3, x = -1$ **27.** $x \approx 0.7154$ **29.** $x \approx 7.5098$ **31.** $x \approx -3.648$ **33.** $x \approx 24.7312$ **35.** $t \approx -653.0008$

37. $t \approx -1.5193$ **39.** $x \approx 3.322$ **41.** $x \approx -1.4307$ **43.** $x = 1$ **45.** $x \approx 1.2203$ **47.** $x \approx -1.6467$

49. $x \approx 1.1292$ **51.** $x \approx 4.854$ **53.** $x \approx 1.252$ **55.** $x \approx 25.1189$ **57.** $x \approx 31.6228$ **59.** $x = 0.0001$

61. $x \approx 4.953$ **63.** $x \approx \pm 0.3329$ **65.** $x = 3$ **67.** $x = 100$ **69.** $x = 6$ **71.** $x = 20$

73. $x = \dfrac{25}{2}$ **75.** $x = 1001$ **77.** $x = -2.99$ **79.** $x \approx 1.1353$ **81.** $x \approx 22.0855$ **83.** $x = -10, x = 8$

85. 2.2619 **87.** 0.3223 **89.** -0.6279 **91.** 2.4391 **93.** -1.2222 **95.** 2.3219

97. 3.1133 **99.** 0.839 **101.** Answers will vary   **103.** Answers will vary, $7^{1+x}, 7^{2x}$

Exercises 9.7, Pages 682 – 685

1. $4027.51   **3.** 13.9 years   **5.** $f = \dfrac{3}{10}$ **7.** 1.73 hours   **9.** 8166 bees   **11.** 12.28 lb per sq in

13. 2350 years   **15.** 2.3 days   **17.** 8.75 years   **19.** 9 years   **21. a.** 13.86 years **b.** 6.93 years

23. 294.41 days   **25.** 100   **27.** 8.64 million   **29.** 2083, 2437, 2744

Chapter 9 Test, Pages 690 – 691

1. a. $\sqrt{x-3} + x^2 + 1$ **b.** $\sqrt{x-3} - x^2 - 1$ **3.** Not inverse to each other   **a.**

c. $\left(\sqrt{x-3} \right) \cdot \left(x^2 + 1 \right)$ **d.** $\dfrac{\sqrt{x-3}}{x^2+1}$

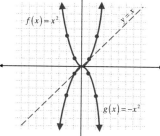

 e. a. $x \ge 3$ **b.** $x \ge 3$ **c.** $x \ge 3$ **d.** $x \ge 3$

2. a. $-4x^2 + 1$ **b.** $-8x^2 + 40x - 47$

b. Inverse to each other   **c.** Both inverse to each other

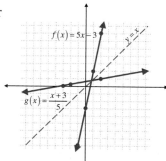

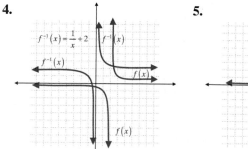

4.

5.

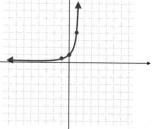

6. a. $x = -4$ **b.** $x = -3$ **7.** 25,981

8. a. $\log_{10} 100{,}000 = 5$ **b.** $\log_{\frac{1}{2}} 8 = -3$ **9. a.** $e^4 = x$ **b.** $\frac{1}{9} = 3^{-2}$ **10. a.** $x = 343$ **b.** $x = \frac{3}{2}$

11.

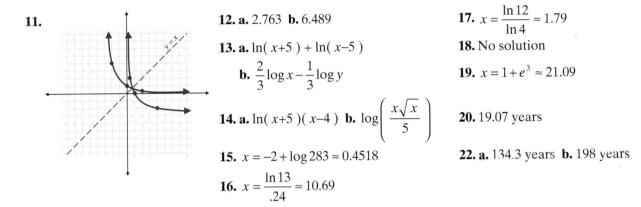

12. a. 2.763 **b.** 6.489

13. a. $\ln(x+5) + \ln(x-5)$

   b. $\frac{2}{3}\log x - \frac{1}{3}\log y$

14. a. $\ln(x+5)(x-4)$ **b.** $\log\left(\dfrac{x\sqrt{x}}{5}\right)$

15. $x = -2 + \log 283 \approx 0.4518$

16. $x = \dfrac{\ln 13}{.24} \approx 10.69$

17. $x = \dfrac{\ln 12}{\ln 4} \approx 1.79$

18. No solution

19. $x = 1 + e^3 \approx 21.09$

20. 19.07 years

22. a. 134.3 years **b.** 198 years

Chapter 9 Cumulative Review, Pages 691 – 695

1. 1 **2.** $-\dfrac{x+3}{x+1}$

3. $\dfrac{2}{x+4}$ **4.** $\dfrac{x-4}{x+1}$

5. $\dfrac{x^{\frac{1}{6}}}{y^{\frac{1}{3}}}$ **6.** $\dfrac{x^{\frac{1}{2}}}{2y^2}$

7. $x^2 y^{\frac{3}{2}}$ **8.** $x^{\frac{2}{3}} y$

9. $x = 2, y = 5$

10. $x = 1, y = -1, z = 2$

11. Vertex: $(3, -11)$ Range: $y \geq -11$
   Zeros: $3 \pm \sqrt{11}$

12. Vertex: $(-2, -5)$ Range: $(y \geq -5)$
   Zeros: $x = -2 + \dfrac{\sqrt{10}}{2}$

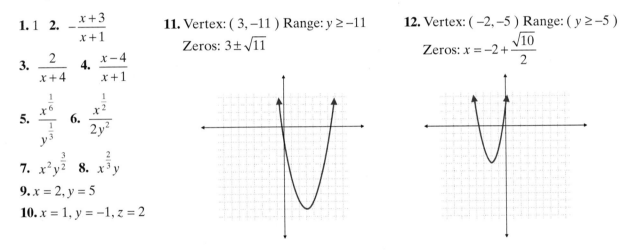

13. $x = \dfrac{-5 \pm \sqrt{33}}{2}$ **14.** $x = \pm 2, x = \pm 3$ **15.** $x = 6$ **16.** $x = 4 \pm \sqrt{6}$ **17.** $x = -0.9212$ **18.** $x = 5 + e^{2.5} \approx 17.18$

19. $x^2 + y^2 = 12$ **20.** $(x-1)^2 + (y-2)^2 = 9$

21.

22.

23.

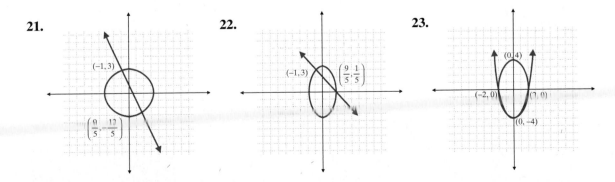

24. Is a function   **25.** Is a function   **26.** Is not a function   **27.** Is a function

28. $\{(-2, 13), (-1, 8), (0, 5), (1, 4), (2, 5)\}$ **29.** $\{(-2, -28), (-1, -6), (0, 0), (1, -4), (2, -12)\}$

30.   **31.**   **32.**

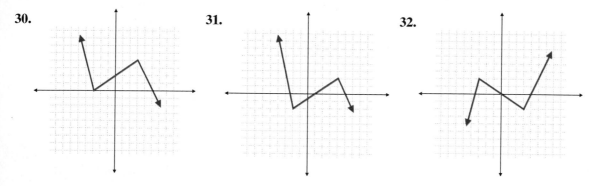

33. Is not a 1-1 function   **34.** Is not a 1-1 function   **35.** Is a 1-1 function   **36.** Is a 1-1 function

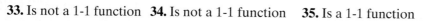

37. a. $x^2 + x + \sqrt{x+2}$ **b.** $x^2 + x - \sqrt{x+2}$ **c.** $\left(x^2 + x\right)\sqrt{x+2}$ **d.** $\dfrac{x^2 + x}{\sqrt{x+2}}$ **e. a.** $x \geq -2$ **b.** $x \geq -2$ **c.** $x \geq -2$

d. $x > -2$ **38. a.** $x^2 + 2x + 4$ **b.** $x^2 - 2x + 2$ **c.** $2x^3 + x^2 + 6x + 3$ **d.** $\dfrac{x^2 + 3}{2x + 1}$ **e. a.** All real numbers

b. All real numbers **c.** All real numbers **d.** All real numbers except $x = -\dfrac{1}{2}$

39.   **40.**   **41.**

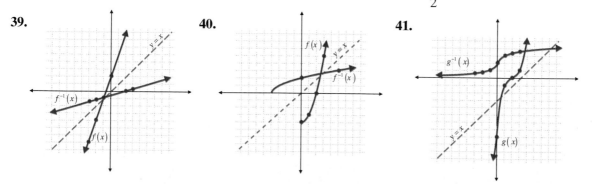

42.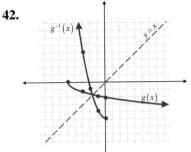

43. 13 clothbound, 30 paperback **44.** 10 mph, 4 mph   **45.** 14.616

46. $\left|\overline{AB}\right|^2 + \left|\overline{AC}\right|^2 = \left|\overline{BC}\right|^2 = 65$ **47.** $\dfrac{7}{8}$ **48.** \$609.20

49. 17.33 centuries   **50.** 4.6 sec

Chapter 10
Exercises 10.1, Pages 703 – 704

1. 1, 3, 5, 7   **3.** $2, \dfrac{3}{2}, \dfrac{4}{3}, \dfrac{5}{4}$ **5.** 2, 6, 12, 20   **7.** 2, 4, 8, 16   **9.** $-2, 5, -10, 17$ **11.** $-\dfrac{1}{5}, \dfrac{1}{7}, -\dfrac{1}{9}, \dfrac{1}{11}$

13. 1, 0, −1, 0   **15.** 0, 1, 0, 1   **17.** $\{4n+1\}$ **19.** $\{(-1)^{n+1}(2n-1)\}$ **21.** $\{n^2\}$ **23.** $\left\{\dfrac{1}{n+2}\right\}$

25. $\{n^2+1\}$ **27.** Decreasing   **29.** Decreasing   **31.** Increasing   **33.** $\left\{250\cdot\left(\dfrac{2}{5}\right)^n\right\}$; 6.4 cm when $n=4$

35. $\left\{20,000\cdot\left(\dfrac{97}{100}\right)^n\right\}$: 17,175 students when $n=5$

Exercises 10.2 Pages 708 – 709

1. 2, 7, 15, 26   **3.** $\dfrac{1}{2}, \dfrac{7}{6}, \dfrac{23}{12}, \dfrac{163}{60}$ **5.** 1, −3, 6, −10   **7.** $\dfrac{1}{2}, \dfrac{3}{4}, \dfrac{7}{8}, \dfrac{15}{16}$ **9.** $-\dfrac{2}{3}, -\dfrac{2}{9}, -\dfrac{14}{27}, -\dfrac{26}{81}$

11. $2+4+6+8+10 = 30$ **13.** $5+6+7+8+9 = 35$ **15.** $\dfrac{1}{2}+\dfrac{1}{3}+\dfrac{1}{4} = \dfrac{13}{12}$ **17.** $2+4+8 = 14$

19. $16+25+36+49+64 = 190$ **21.** $3+1+(-1)+(-3) = 0$ **23.** $6+(-12)+20+(-30) = -16$

25. $\dfrac{1}{2}+\dfrac{2}{3}+\dfrac{3}{4}+\dfrac{4}{5}+\dfrac{5}{6} = \dfrac{71}{20}$ **27.** $\displaystyle\sum_{k=1}^{5}(2k-1)$ **29.** $\displaystyle\sum_{k=1}^{5}(-1)^k$

31. $\displaystyle\sum_{k=2}^{6}(-1)^k\left(\dfrac{1}{k^3}\right)$ **33.** $\displaystyle\sum_{k=4}^{15}\dfrac{k}{k+1}$ **35.** $\displaystyle\sum_{k=5}^{12}\dfrac{k+1}{k^2}$ **37.** 7   **39.** 48   **41.** 10   **43.** 295 **45.** −152

Exercises 10.3 Pages 718 – 719

1. Arithmetic sequence $d = 3, \{3n-1\}$ **3.** Arithmetic sequence $d = -2, \{9-2n\}$ **5.** Not an arithmetic sequence   **7.** Arithmetic sequence $d = -4, \{10-4n\}$ **9.** Arithmetic sequence $d = \frac{1}{2}, \left\{\frac{n-1}{2}\right\}$

11. $1, 3, 5, 7, 9$; arithmetic sequence   **13.** $-1, 4, -7, 10, -13$; not an arithmetic sequence

15. $-1, -7, -13, -19, -25$; arithmetic sequence   **17.** $\frac{20}{3}, \frac{19}{3}, 6, \frac{17}{3}, \frac{16}{3}$; arithmetic sequence

19. $\frac{1}{2}, \frac{1}{4}, \frac{1}{6}, \frac{1}{8}, \frac{1}{10}$; not an arithmetic sequence   **21.** $\left\{\frac{2n+1}{3}\right\}$ **23.** $\{9-2n\}$ **25.** $\left\{\frac{17}{2}+\frac{3}{2}n\right\}$

27. $\{63-5n\}$ **29.** $\left\{\frac{81}{2}+\frac{3}{2}n\right\}$ **31.** 232 **33.** 44 **35.** 7 **37.** 19 **39.** 154 **41.** 235 **43.** 126 **45.** 231 **47.** $\frac{143}{3}$

49. 132 **51.** 171 **53.** -100 **55.** 9 days   **57.** 1625 cm   **59.** Answers will vary

Exercises 10.4, Pages 730 – 732

1. Not a geometric sequence **3.** Geometric sequence   **5.** Geometric sequence   **7.** Not a geometric sequence

$r = -\frac{1}{2}, \left\{3\left(-\frac{1}{2}\right)^{n-1}\right\}$ $r = \frac{3}{8}, \left\{\frac{32}{27}\left(\frac{3}{8}\right)^{n-1}\right\}$

9. Geometric sequence $r = -\frac{1}{4}, \left\{48\left(-\frac{1}{4}\right)^{n-1}\right\}$ **11.** $9, -27, 81, -243$; geometric sequence

13. $\frac{2}{3}, \frac{4}{3}, 2, \frac{8}{3}$; not a geometric sequence **15.** $-\frac{8}{5}, \frac{32}{25}, -\frac{128}{125}, \frac{512}{625}$ geometric sequence

17. $3\sqrt{2}, 6, 6\sqrt{2}, 12$; geometric sequence   **19.** $0.3, -0.09, 0.027, -0.0081$; geometric sequence   **21.** $\left\{3(2)^{n-1}\right\}$

23. $\left\{\frac{1}{3}\left(-\frac{1}{2}\right)^{n-1}\right\}$ **25.** $\left\{\left(\sqrt{2}\right)^{n-1}\right\}$ **27.** $\left\{\frac{1}{3}(3)^{n-1}\right\}$ **29.** $\left\{-5\left(-\frac{3}{4}\right)^{n-1}\right\}$ **31.** $\frac{1}{4}$ **33.** $\frac{32}{9}$ **35.** $\frac{1}{4}$ **37.** $n = 4$

39. 363 **41.** $\frac{1023}{64}$ **43.** $-\frac{333}{64}$ **45.** $\frac{422}{243}$ **47.** $\frac{75}{128}$ **49.** 4 **51.** $-\frac{1}{3}$ **53.** $\frac{2}{9}$ **55.** $\frac{4}{11}$

57. $\$13{,}248.23$ **59.** $\$4352$ **61.** $64\frac{4}{5}$ grams

63. a.   **b.**   **65.** $S_n, r^n \to \infty$ (or $r^n \to -\infty$)

if $|r| > 1$

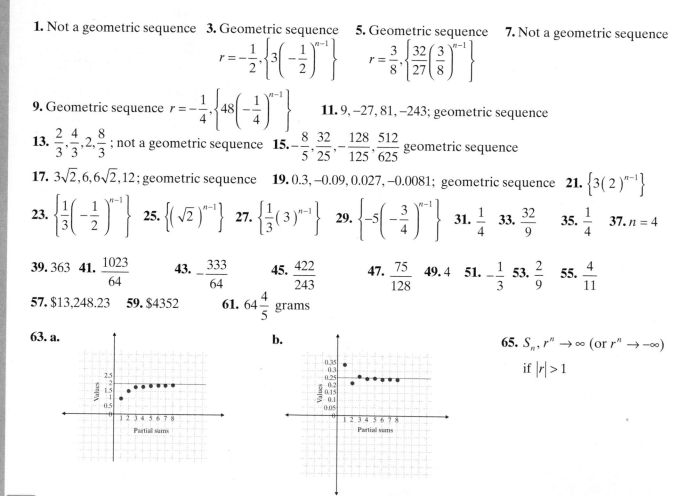

Exercises 10.5, Pages 741 – 742

1. 56 **3.** $\dfrac{1}{15}$ **5.** 4 **7.** $(n-1)!$ **9.** $(k+3)(k+2)(k+1)$ **11.** 20 **13.** 35 **15.** 1

17. $x^7 + 7x^6 y + 21x^5 y^2 + 35x^4 y^3$ **19.** $x^9 + 9x^8 + 36x^7 + 84x^6$ **21.** $x^5 + 15x^4 + 90x^3 + 270x^2$

23. $x^6 + 12x^5 y + 60x^4 y^2 + 160x^3 y^3$ **25.** $2187x^7 - 5103x^6 y + 5103x^5 y^2 - 2835x^4 y^3$

27. $x^{18} - 36x^{16} y + 576x^{14} y^2 - 5376x^{12} y^3$ **29.** $x^6 + 6x^5 y + 15x^4 y^2 + 20x^3 y^3 + 15x^2 y^4 + 6xy^5 + y^6$

31. $x^7 - 7x^6 + 21x^5 - 35x^4 + 35x^3 - 21x^2 + 7x - 1$ **33.** $243x^5 + 405x^4 y + 270x^3 y^2 + 90x^2 y^3 + 15xy^4 + y^5$

35. $x^4 + 8x^3 y + 24x^2 y^2 + 32xy^3 + 16y^4$ **37.** $81x^4 - 216x^3 y + 216x^2 y^2 - 96xy^3 + 16y^4$

39. $243x^{10} - 405x^8 y + 270x^6 y^2 - 90x^4 y^3 + 15x^2 y^4 - y^5$ **41.** $3360x^6 y^4$ **43.** $1{,}140{,}480x^8$

45. $-27{,}500x^6 y^{18}$ **47.** 1.062 **49.** 0.808 **51.** 64.363 **53.** 0.851

Exercises 10.6, Pages 747 – 748

1. 840 **3.** 24 **5.** 120 **7.** 60,480 **9.** 1,814,400 **11.** 110 **13.** 336 **15.** 72 **17.** 360 **19.** 64 **21.** 576 **23.** 288 **25.** 69,300

Exercises 10.7, Pages 751 – 753

1. 35 **3.** 1 **5.** 84 **7.** 6 **9.** 120 **11.** 816 **13.** 792 **15.** 190 **17.** 30 **19.** 66,528 **21.** 14,700
23. 840 **25.** 600 **27. a.** **b.** **c.** **29.** 45

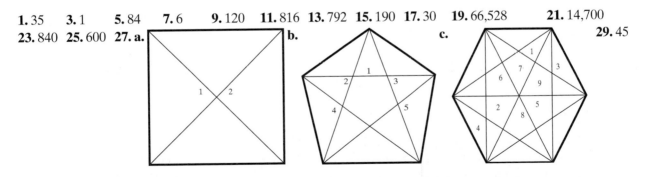

Chapter 10 Test, Page 757

1. $\dfrac{1}{4}, \dfrac{1}{7}, \dfrac{1}{10}, \dfrac{1}{13}, \ldots;$ neither **2.** $\left\{\dfrac{n}{2n+1}\right\}$ **3.** 26 **4.** $a_n = 8 - 2n$ **5.** 243 **6.** $\dfrac{1}{8}$ **7.** $a_n = \left(\sqrt{3}\right)^{n-2}$

8. $\dfrac{21}{16}$ **9.** 68 **10.** $-\dfrac{40}{729}$ **11.** $\dfrac{15}{100} + \dfrac{15}{10,000} + \ldots = \dfrac{5}{33}$ **12.** 74 **13.** \$13,050.16 **14.** 462

15. $32x^5 - 80x^4 y + 80x^3 y^2 - 40x^2 y^3 + 10xy^4 - y^5$ **16.** $5670x^4 y^4$ **17.** 151,200 **18.** 792 **19.** 720 **20.** 168

21. Answer will vary

Chapter 10 Cumulative Review, Pages 758 – 761

1. $11x + 3$ **2.** $-x^2 + 3x + 5$ **3.** $(4x+3)(16x^2 - 12x + 9)$ **4.** $(3x-5)(2x+9)$

5. $(2x+1)(5x+7)(x-2)$ **6.** $\dfrac{11x+12}{15}$ **7.** $\dfrac{-6x-4}{(x+4)(x-4)(x-1)}$ **8.** $\dfrac{1}{x^2}$ **9.** $\dfrac{8^{1/2}\,y^{1/3}}{x^2}$ **10.** $\dfrac{2x^{\frac{4}{3}}}{3y}$

11. $3\sqrt{3}x$ **12.** $\dfrac{-13+11i}{29}$ **13.** $x > 3$ ◀   **14.** $\dfrac{1}{3} \le x \le \dfrac{13}{3}$ ◀

15. $-\dfrac{5}{2} < x < \dfrac{9}{4}$ ◀   **16.** $x = \dfrac{26}{7}$ **17.** $x = \dfrac{-2 \pm i\sqrt{2}}{2}$ **18.** $x = 4$

19. $x = \dfrac{39}{17}$
20. $x = 5$
21. $x = e^{2.4} \approx 11.02$
22. $n = \dfrac{A-P}{Pi}$
23. $x = 2,\ y = -5$
24. $x = 0,\ y = 2,\ z = -1$
25. a. $y = \dfrac{x+7}{2}$ **b.** $2x^2 - 5$ **c.** $2x + 1$

26.   **27.**

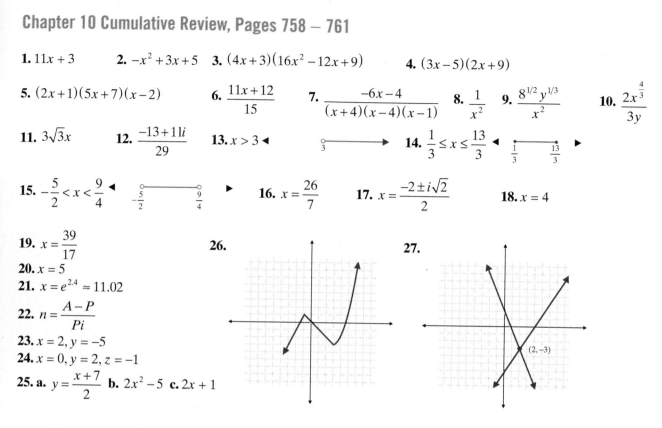

28.   **29.**   **30.**

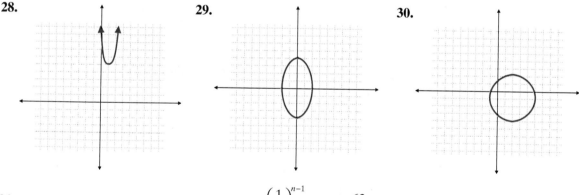

31.a. $a_n = 10 - 2n$ **b.** -10 **32.a.** $a_n = 16\left(\dfrac{1}{2}\right)^{n-1}$ **b.** $\dfrac{63}{2}$

33. $x^6 + 12x^5 y + 60x^4 y^2 + 160x^3 y^3 + 240x^2 y^4 + 192xy^5 + 64y^6$

34. 210 **35.** 1680 **36.** 2002 **37.** 20 mph, 60 mph   **38.** 16 lb at \$1.40, 4 lb at \$2.60   **39.** 16 ft by 26 ft
40. 12.56 hrs   **41.** \$16,058.71   **42.** 443.7 liters   **43.** 12   **44.** 3024
45. 150 **46.** $x \approx -0.4746266,\ 1.395337$ **47.** $x \approx -1.9646356,\ 1.0580064$ **48.** $x \approx 0.24083054,\ 2.7336808$
49. $x = 1$ **50.** $x = 1, -3, 2$

INDEX

A

Abel, 467
Absolute value bars, 17–18, 28
  rewriting equations without, 40–41
  rewriting inequalities without, 70–72
Absolute value equations
  of form $|ax + b| + c = d$, 40
  of form $|ax + b| = |cx + d|$, 40–41
  solving, 18–19, 40
Absolute value function
  definition of, 546
  graph of, 547–548
Absolute value inequalities
  definition of, 69
  of form $|ax + b| < c$, 70
  of form $|ax + b| > c$, 71
  solving, 70–72
Absolute value
  definition of, 17–18, 39
  symbols, 17–18
Abstract products, 266
ac–method of factoring, 286
Addition and subtraction of rational
  expressions, 342
Addition and subtraction with complex
  numbers, 446
Addition method
  definition of, 181
  nonlinear systems solved by, 595
  systems of linear equations solved by,
    181
  variables eliminated by, 182
Addition property of equality, 35
Addition property of inequality, 66
Addition
  associative property of, 11
  commutative property of, 11
  complex numbers, 446–447
  fractions, 331
  functions, 609
  identity property of, 11
  inverse property of, 11
  polynomials, 256
  radical expressions, 423–424
  rational expressions with common
    denominators, 331, 341–342
  rational expressions with different
    denominators, 344–348
  rules for real numbers, 11, 19
Additive identity, 11
Algebra of functions, 609
Algebra
  systems of equations, 189
Algebraic expressions
  combining like terms, 32
  definition of, 32
  evaluating, 33–34
  terms of, 32
Algebraic notation, 64, 362

Algebraic operations with functions,
  610–611
Alternating sequence, 701
Analysis of factoring by the ac–method, 287
And, 9–10
Angles
  measures of, 44
Annuity, 726
Applications
  algebra, 189
  area, 379
  arithmetic sequence, 717
  average, 57
  circumference, 8, 45, 379
  combined variation, 381
  compound interest, 301, 640, 681
  consecutive integers, 308–309
  cost, 55–56, 490–491
  difference quotient, 545
  direct variation, 379
  distance–rate–time, 54
  earthquake intensity, 681
  exponential growth and decay, 679–680
  fractions, 368–369
  geometry, 46–47, 490
  Golden Ratio, 431
  gravitational force, 380
  half–life, 682
  Hooke's Law, 379
  interest, 56, 188
  inverse variation, 380–381
  joint variation, 381
  Newton's law of cooling, 680–681
  number, 52–53
  percent–mixture, 187
  profit, 55
  projectiles, 489
  proportion, 359–360
  Pythagorean Theorem, 310, 488
  rate, 373–374
  real numbers, 21–22
  strategy for solving word problems,
    51–52, 368, 487
  symbolic equivalents of English phrases,
    52
  systems of linear equations in three
    variables to solve, 200
  systems of linear equations in two
    variables to solve, 189
  triangle, 46, 359–360
  variation, 378–383
  water pressure, 379
  work, 188, 369–372
Area
  circle, 45, 379
  maximizing, 527
  of geometric figures, 45
Arithmetic average, 57
Arithmetic rules for rational numbers
  (or fractions), 331
Arithmetic sequences

applications of, 717
  common difference of an, 712
  definition of, 711–712
  nth term of an, 713
  partial sum of, 715
  sum of a finite, 716–717
Array of signs, 223
Associative property
  addition, 11
  multiplication, 11
Asymptotes
  of a hyperbola, 583
Augmented matrix, 206
Average
  definition of, 57
Axes, 105
Axis
  of a parabola, 517
  of symmetry, 517
  x, 105
  y, 105

B

Back substitution, 36, 179–180
Base, 27
  exponent, 27, 76
Base–10 logarithms, 652
Base–e logarithms, 654
Binomial coefficient, 736
Binomial expansion, 734
Binomial Theorem, 734, 738–741
Binomial(s)
  definition of, 256
  dividing polynomials by, 273–277
  expansion of, 262–263, 265
  multiplication of, 262–263
  multiplying form $(a + b)(a - b)$, 262–264
  multiplying form $(a - b)^2$ or $(a + b)^2$,
    264–265
  multiplying using FOIL method, 263–264
Boundary line, 158, 237
Braces, 8, 28
Brackets, 28
Brahmagupta, 329
Briggs, 607
Briggsian logarithms, 607

C

Calculator(s)
  $a^{\frac{m}{n}}$, 418–419
  absolute value equations, 317–318
  absolute value inequalities, 318–319
  approximating solutions of systems of
    equations, 183–184
  Binomial coefficient, 737

caret key, 90, 149, 418
circles, 573–575
common logarithms evaluated on, 653
compound interest, 640
cube roots, 407
determinants, 225–226
equations, 151–152, 213
evaluating exponential expressions, 418
evaluating expressions, 428
factorials, 735
functions, 151–152
GRAPH key, 149
horizontal parabola, 561–562
inverse log, 653–654
line in the form $y = mx + b$, 123–124
linear inequalities, 162–164, 239
matrix, 213–216, 225–226
odd powers, 414
permutations, 747
polynomial equations, 315–317
polynomial inequality, 537–539
properties of exponents, 90–91
radical expressions, 401, 428
radical functions, 437–439
rational exponents, 418–419
roots, 401, 418
square roots, 401
systems of equations, 183–184, 213–216
systems of linear inequalities, 239
table of values, 438
TRACE key, 150–151
using, 147–148
WINDOW key, 149, 314
Y= key, 149
ZOOM key, 149
Cartesian coordinate system, 105
Celsius to Fahrenheit equation, 44, 359
Center
    of circle, 570
    of ellipse, 579, 586
    of hyperbola, 582, 587–588
Change-of-base formula, 674
Changing the form
    quadratic function, 522
Characteristics of slopes and graphs of lines, 120
Checking equations, 36, 67
Circle(s)
    area of, 45, 379
    center of, 570, 572–573
    circumference, 8, 45, 379
    definition of, 570
    diameter of, 45, 570
    equation of, 570–571, 592
    finding center and radius of, 571
    graphing, 573–575
    perimeter of, 45
    radius of, 45, 570, 572–573
    standard form, 571
    writing equation given center and radius, 571–572
Circular cylinder
    surface area of, 486
Circumference
    circle, 8, 45, 379
Classification of polynomials, 256

Closed circle, 10
Closed half–plane, 158
Closed interval, 64
Closure property
    addition, 11
    multiplication, 11
Coefficient, 33, 255
    binomial, 736
    matrix, 206, 220
Collinear, 123
Column of a matrix, 205
Combination, 749–751
Combined variation, 381
Combining like terms, 33
Common "log" key
    on calculator, 653
Common denominator
    adding and subtracting radical
        expressions with, 423
Common difference
    of an arithmetic sequence, 712
Common errors, 266, 334, 342, 451, 482
Common logarithm(s)
    definition of, 652
    evaluating, 653
Common ratio
    of a geometric sequence, 721–722
Common
    factors, 332–334
Commutative property
    addition, 11
    multiplication, 11
Completing the square
    quadratic equations solved by, 474–475
    steps to solve by, 472–473
Complex conjugates, 451
Complex fraction(s)
    definition of, 351
    simplifying by multiplying by common
        denominator, 353
    simplifying numerator/denominator and
        dividing, 351
Complex number(s)
    conjugate of, 451
    definition of, 443–444
    division of, 451–453
    equality of, 445
    evaluating form i^n, 454
    finding powers of i, 443, 453
    imaginary part of, 444
    multiplication of, 450
    real part of, 444
    solving equations involving, 446
    standard form of, 444, 451
    sum or difference of, 446–447
Complex rational expressions, 351–353
Composite functions, 620–621
Composition (composite), 619
Compound inequalities
    definition of, 9
    graphing, 10
    intersection of two sets, 10
    solving those involving "and", 10
    solving those involving "or", 10
    union of two sets, 10
Compound interest

applications of, 301, 640, 681
continuous, 641, 681
formulas for, 301, 640, 681
Compounded continuously, 641, 681
Condensing logarithmic expressions, 665–666
Conditional equation, 38
Conic sections
    circle and distance formula, 570
    circle center and radius of, 571
    circle defined, 570
    circle equation of, 571
    definition of, 557
    ellipse defined, 579
    ellipse equation of, 580–581
    ellipse foci of, 579
    ellipse major axis, 580
    ellipse minor axis, 580
    ellipse with center at (h,k), 586
    ellipse with center at origin, 580
    hyperbola asymptotes, 583–584
    hyperbola defined, 582
    hyperbola equations of, 584
    hyperbola foci of, 582
    hyperbola vertices of, 584
    hyperbola with center at (h,k), 587
    parabola and graphing calculator, 561–562
    parabola defined, 558
    parabola horizontal, 558
    parabola vertical, 558
Conjugates
    complex, 451
    definition of, 425
    division of, 451–453
Consecutive
    even integers, 308
    integers, 308
    odd integers, 308
Consistent equation, 177, 179, 181, 236
Consistent systems
    of equations, 179, 181, 199, 236
    solution of, 177
Constant of variation, 378, 380
Constant term (or constant), 32
Continuously compounded interest
    formula for, 643
Contradiction equation, 38
Contradictions
    solving, 39
Coordinate of a point
    in a plane, 105
    on a line, 67–68
Coordinate system
    Cartesian, 105
Corresponding
    angles and sides, 360
Cost
    applications of, 55–56, 490–491
Counting numbers, 3
Cramer's rule for 2 x 2 matrices, 230
Cramer's rule for 3 x 3 matrices, 231
Cramer's rule
    definition of, 229
    inconsistent and dependent systems with, 231

system of linear equations in three
    variables solved using, 232–233
system of linear equations in two
    variables solved using, 229, 232
Cross–multiplication property, 1, 329
Cube root(s)
    definition of, 406
    evaluating, 406–407
    examples of, 765–767
    simplifying, 407–408
    symbol for, 406
Cubed, 27, 765–767
Cubes of integers from 1 to 10, 406
Cubic equation, 306, 482
Cubic
    polynomial, 256
Cylinder
    surface area of, 486
    volume of, 381

D

Decimal approximations
    finding, 8
Decimal notation
    converting to and from scientific
      notation, 89
Decimals
    fractions expressed as, 4
    irrational numbers written as, 4
    rational numbers written as, 4
    repeating, 4
    terminating, 4
Decreasing sequence, 702
Definitions of algebraic operations with
    functions, 609
Degree
    monomial, 255
    polynomial, 255
    zero, 255
Denominator(s)
    least common (LCD), 343
    negative exponents in, 80, 82
    rationalizing rational expressions, 425
    rationalizing those containing one term,
      408
    solving inequalities containing rational
      expressions, 361–364
Dependent equation, 177, 179, 181, 236
Dependent systems
    of equations, 179, 181, 199, 236
    solution of, 177
Dependent variable, 106
Derivative, 544
Descartes, 105
Descending order
    polynomials written in, 255
Determinant(s)
    array of signs for, 223
    definition of, 220
    evaluating, 221
    expansion by minors, 222
    in Cramer's Rule, 230–231
    inconsistent/dependent systems, 231
    linear systems of equations in three

variables solved using, 223
linear systems of equations in two
    variables solved using, 221
of 2×2 matrix, 221
of 3×3 matrix, 222
of a square matrix, 220
Diameter
    circle, 570
Difference of two cubes, 264–265, 295–296
Difference of two squares, 264–265, 285
Difference quotient, 544
Difference
    arithmetic sequence, 711–712
    complex numbers, 447
    functions, 609
    polynomials, 257
    radical expressions, 423–424
    rational expressions, 342, 344
    real numbers, 20
Dimension, 205
Direct variation
    applications of, 379
    Hooke's law and, 379
    powers with, 379
Directly proportional, 378
Directrix
    definition of, 577–578
    of parabola, 577–578
Discriminant
    definition of, 482
    finding, 483
    for determining number and type of
      solutions, 483
    using, 483–484
Distance formula, 44, 54, 372, 568
    Pythagorean Theorem and, 566–567
Distance
    between two points, 568
Distance–rate–time problems
    solving, 53–54, 372
Distributive property
    combining like terms by using, 33
    multiplying polynomials and, 262–263
    removing parentheses and, 11
    simplifying expressions and, 11
Division by zero, 26
Division of rational expressions, 336
Division
    algorithm, 272–273
    complex numbers, 451–453
    definition of, 25
    fractions, 331
    functions, 609
    long, 272
    polynomial by binomial, 273–277
    polynomial by monomial, 271
    polynomials, 271–277
    rational expressions, 336
    rules for, 25–26
    simplifying complex rational expressions,
      353
    symbols, 25
    synthetic, 275
    zero, 26
Domain
    axis, 140

definition of, 140, 433
function, 518
function in x, 609, 620
radical function, 433–435
relation, 140
Double root, 305, 469, 483
Double subscript, 208
Downward opening parabola, 519

E

e, 6, 608, 642
    deriving, 642
Earthquake intensity
    applications of, 681
Elementary row operations, 207
Elements, 8
    of a set, 8
Elimination method
    solving system of linear equations by,
      210–212
    steps to solve by, 210
Ellipse(s)
    center at (h, k), 586
    center of, 579
    definition of, 579
    equation of, 580–581, 592
    foci of, 579
    graphing those centered at origin, 580
    intercepts of, 580
    major axis, 580
    minor axis, 580
Ellipsis (…), 3
Empty set, 8, 18, 38
    symbol for, 8
Endpoints, 569
English phrases
    translating into algebraic expressions, 52
Entry, 205
Equal symbol, 1
Equality of complex numbers, 445
Equality
    addition property of, 35
    multiplication property of, 35
Equation(s)
    absolute value, 39
    area, 379
    checking, 36, 67
    circle, 570–571, 592
    circumference, 8, 45, 379
    complex numbers, 446
    compound interest, 301, 640, 681
    conditional, 38
    consistent, 177, 179, 181
    contradiction, 38
    dependent, 177, 179, 181, 236
    determinants, 224
    direct variation, 378
    distance, 568
    ellipse, 580–581, 592
    exponential, 670–672
    extraneous solutions, 357
    Fahrenheit to Celsius, 44, 359
    finding inverse, 626

first–degree, 34
form $ax + b = c$, 34
graphing, 107
gravitational force, 380
half–life, 682
Hooke's Law, 379
horizontal line, 119
horizontal parabolas, 558
hyperbola, 584, 593
illumination, 383
inconsistent, 177, 179, 181, 236
inequalities with rational expressions, 361
inverse variation, 380
involving rational expressions, 356–359
known roots, 475–476
linear, 34
linear in two variables, 108
linear system of, 176
logarithmic, 648, 673–674
midpoint, 569
Newton's law of cooling, 680
nonlinear systems of, 593–595
parabola, 518, 592
parallel lines, 130
perpendicular lines, 131
point–slope form, 126–127
quadratic, 304, 469
quadratic in form, 503–505
rational, 356
slope–intercept form, 116–118
solution of, 37
solving form $b^x = b^y$, 670–671
solving those containing absolute values, 40
solving those containing radical expressions, 498–501
solving those containing rational expressions, 356
solving those quadratic in form, 504–505
standard form, 107, 113, 126
variation, 378, 380–381
vertical line, 119
water pressure, 379
Equivalent, 36
Euler, 6, 515
Evaluating a function, 434–435, 543–544
Evaluating algebraic expressions, 33–34
Evaluating formulas, 46
Evaluating logarithms, 649–650
Even integers
consecutive, 308
Every real number
complex number of, 445
Expanding a binomial, 262–263, 265
Expanding by minors, 222
Expanding logarithmic expressions, 664–665
Exponent rules
summary of, 415
Exponent(s)
base of, 27
definition of, 27
integer, 77
logarithm, 649
negative integers as, 78
negative rule for, 78, 415
one, 76, 415

power rule, 81, 415
power rule for fractions, 86, 415
power rule for products, 84, 415
product rule for, 77, 415
quotient rule for, 80
simplifying expressions containing, 79–82
square roots of, 405
summary of properties for, 88, 415, 669
zero, 78, 415
Exponential decay function, 637–638, 679–680
Exponential equation(s)
applications of, 679–682
properties for solving, 670
solving, 670–672
writing with logarithmic notation, 671–672
Exponential function(s)
definition of, 635
general concepts of, 638
inverse, 647
Exponential growth function, 636, 638–639, 679–680
Exponential notation, 76
Expression(s)
algebraic, 52
evaluating, 52
exponential, 76–82, 84–88
radical, 399
rational, 331
simplifying those containing exponents, 335–336, 405
Extraneous root, 357
Extraneous solution, 357, 497

F

$f(x)$ notation, 434, 542
Factor Theorem, 307
Factor(s)
common, 332–334
definition of, 22
greatest common (GCF), 283
least common multiple (LCM), 343
polynomial, 274
product, 22, 283
Factorial notation, 735
Factorial(s)
evaluating, 736
n, 735
zero, 735
Factoring
ac–method, 286
by grouping, 297
by special products, 264
completely, 284
FOIL method, 263
greatest common factor (GCF), 283
monomial from polynomial, 271
negative exponents, 298–299
polynomials, 264
polynomials by grouping, 287, 297
quadratic equations solved by, 469–470
quadratic equations zero factor property, 468

rational expressions simplified by, 335
special forms, 264
trial and error method, 289
trinomial whose leading coefficient is 1, 289
trinomials by grouping, 287, 297
trinomials perfect square, 264
trinomials whose leading coefficient is not 1, 289
zero–factor property, 303, 468
Factorization, 469–470
prime, 765–767
Fahrenheit to Celsius equation, 44, 359
Fibonacci, 697
Field properties of real numbers, 11
Finding the square root, 399
Finding an equation given the roots, 306
Finding the inverse ln of N, 656
Finding the inverse log of N, 654–655
Finding the roots, 303
Finite, 8
Finite sequence, 698, 716
First coordinate, 105
First terms
in binomial, 263
First–degree equations
definition of, 34, 104, 107
First–degree inequalities
definition of, 65
solving, 66
First–degree polynomials, 256
Focus
ellipse, 579
hyperbola, 582
FOIL method
definition of, 263
factoring by grouping with, 286
factoring completely with, 289–290
factoring trinomials with, 291
mnemonic device, 263
multiplying two binomials, 263
order, 263
polynomial multiplication, 264
square of a binomial and, 264
Forms of equations, 127–129
Formula(s)
area, 45, 379
Binomial Theorem, 739
change–of–base, 674
circle, 570–571, 592
circumference, 8, 45, 379
combination, 749
compound interest, 301, 640, 681
continuously compounded interest, 643
definition of, 44
difference quotient, 544
direct variation, 378–379
distance, 44, 568
exponential growth and decay, 636–637, 639
Fahrenheit to Celsius, 44, 47, 359
for factoring perfect trinomials, 264
general term of arithmetic sequence, 713–714
general term of geometric sequence, 722–723
gravitational force, 380

Hooke's Law, 379
illumination, 383
interest, 44, 56
inverse variation, 380–381
IQ, 44
midpoint, 569
parallelogram, 45
partial sum, 705, 715, 725
perimeter, 45–46
permutation, 745
Pythagorean Theorem, 309–310, 487–488, 566
quadratic, 479
rectangle, 45, 47
simple interest, 44
slope, 114, 116
slope–intercept, 47
solving for specified variables, 46–48, 359
solving for variable in, 46–48
special product, 264
square, 45
sum of angles, 44
trapezoid, 45
triangle, 45–46
variation, 378, 380
vertex of parabola, 523
water pressure, 379
Formulas of squares, 285
Fourth root, 412–413
Fraction bar, 28
Fraction(s)
    addition of, 331
    complex, 351
    definition of, 331
    division of, 331
    exponents, 412
    expressing as decimals, 4, 5
    Fundamental Principle of, 331–332
    multiplication of, 331
    radical, 403, 405, 408–409
    reciprocal of, 331
    subtraction of, 331
Fractional exponents, 78, 412
Function notation, 434
Function of a function, 619
Function(s)
    absolute value, 546–548
    addition of, 609
    algebra of, 609
    composite, 620
    composition of, 619–621
    definition of, 140–141, 433, 516
    division of, 609
    domain of, 140, 433
    evaluating, 543–544
    exponential, 635
    exponential decay, 637–638
    exponential growth, 636, 638
    graphing from a table of data, 436–439, 517
    horizontal translation, 545–546, 548–552
    inverse, 624
    linear, 146
    logarithmic, 647
    multiplication of, 609
    notation, 434, 542

one–to–one, 622–624
polynomial, 258–259
polynomial inequalities, 533–536
quadratic, 516
radical, 433–434
range of, 140, 433
reflection, 550–551
subtraction of, 609
vertical line test, 433, 517
vertical translation, 545–546, 548–550
zeros of, 150, 516, 523–525
Fundamental Principle of Counting, 743
Fundamental Principle of Fractions, 331–332
Fundamental rectangle of a hyperbola, 584

G

Galois, 467
Gauss, 715
Gaussian elimination, 207, 210
GCF, 283
General concepts of exponential functions, 638
General quadratic equation, 479
General term
    of arithmetic sequence, 713
    of geometric sequence, 723
Geometric figures
    formulas for area, 45
    formulas for perimeter, 45
Geometric sequence
    applications of, 726–727
    common ratio of, 721–722
    definition of, 721–722
    nth term of a, 723
    partial sum of, 725–726
Geometric series
    infinite, 728–730
Geometry
    applications of, 490
Golden ratio, 431
Graph(s)
    absolute value function, 547–548
    absolute value inequalities, 70
    circle, 573–575
    domain and range found from, 147
    ellipse, 580–582
    equation in two variables, 108–109
    exponential decay, 637
    exponential growth, 636
    horizontal line, 119–120
    horizontal line test and, 622–623
    horizontal parabola, 558–561
    hyperbola, 583–585
    inequalities, 10–11, 237–238, 363–364
    intervals of, 64, 363
    inverse function, 625, 627–629
    linear equations, 107
    linear function, 147
    linear inequalities, 159–161
    linear system, 178
    logarithmic function, 652
    one–to–one function, 622–623
    ordered pair, 107
    parabola, 517–522

parallel lines, 131–132
perpendicular lines, 130–132
point–slope form, 128–129
quadratic function, 518–522
radical function, 436–439
real numbers, 10
slope, 114–115
slope–intercept form, 117–118
sum of two functions, 611–613
systems of linear equations, 178
systems of linear inequalities, 237–238
systems of nonlinear equations, 593–595
vertical line, 119–120
vertical line test and, 142–144, 517
vertical parabola, 518–522
x– and y–intercepts, 109–110
Graphing calculator
    $a^{\frac{m}{n}}$, 418–419
    absolute value equations, 317–318
    absolute value inequalities, 318–319
    approximating solutions of systems of equations, 183–184
    Binomial coefficient, 737
    caret key, 90, 149, 418
    circles, 573–575
    common logarithms evaluated on, 653
    compound interest, 640
    cube roots, 407
    determinants, 225–226
    equations, 151–152, 213
    evaluating exponential expressions, 418
    evaluating expressions, 428
    factorials, 735
    functions, 151–152
    GRAPH key, 149
    horizontal parabola, 561–562
    inverse ln, 656
    inverse log, 653–654
    line in the form $y = mx + b$, 123–124
    linear inequalities, 162–164, 239
    LN, 608, 655
    LOG, 653
    matrix, 213–216, 225–226
    odd powers, 414
    permutations, 747
    polynomial equations, 315–317
    polynomial inequality, 537–539
    properties of exponents, 90–91
    radical expressions, 401, 428
    radical functions, 437–439
    rational exponents, 418–419
    roots, 401, 418
    square roots, 401
    sum of two functions, 613–614
    systems of equations, 183–184, 213–216
    systems of linear inequalities, 239
    table of values, 438
    TRACE key, 150–151
    using, 147–148
    WINDOW key, 149, 314
    Y= key, 149
    ZOOM key, 149
Graphing method
    for solving systems, 213–216
Gravitational force

formula for, 381
Greater than, 8, 64
    symbol for, 8
Greater than or equal to, 8, 64
    symbol for, 8
Greatest common factor (GCF)
    definition of, 283
Group theory, 467
Grouping method, 286
Grouping
    factoring by, 286–289
Growth and decay, 636–639

H

Half–life
    applications of, 682
Half–open interval, 64–65
Half–plane, 158, 237
    closed, 158, 237
    open, 158, 237
Higher terms
    rational expression, 332
Hooke's Law, 379
Horizontal and vertical lines, 120
Horizontal and vertical translations, 546, 548
Horizontal axis (or x–axis), 105
Horizontal distance, 113
Horizontal line test
    one–to–one functions and, 622
Horizontal line
    equation of, 119
    graph of, 119
    slope of, 118, 120
Horizontal parabola
    definition of, 518, 558
    equations of, 558
    graph of, 558–561
    vertex of, 560–561
    y–intercepts of, 559
Horizontal shift
    function, 545
    parabola, 520
Horizontal translation(s), 520, 545
How the use information about slopes, 133
Hyperbola
    asymptotes, 583–584
    center at (h,k), 587–588
    equations of, 584, 593
    foci of, 582
    fundamental rectangle of, 584
    graph of, 583–585
    intercepts of, 584
    vertices, 584
Hypotenuse, 309, 488

I

i^2, 443, 450
i
    notation, 443
    powers of, 453–454
Identities, 11

Identity equation, 38, 359
Identity
    additive, 11
    multiplicative, 11
Illumination
    formula for, 383
Imaginary number, 444
Imaginary part
    complex number, 444
Important comment about the graphs of
    polynomial functions, 315
Inconsistent equation, 177, 179, 181, 236
Inconsistent systems
    of equations, 179, 181, 199, 236
    solution of, 177
Increasing sequence, 702
Independent variable, 106
Index of summation, 705
Index
    radical, 406, 413
Inequalities
    absolute value, 69
    addition property of, 66
    English sentences and, 64
    first–degree, 65
    infinitely many solutions, 65
    interval notation for, 64
    linear, 64–65
    multiplication property of, 66
    on a number line, 64
    properties of, 13, 66
    quadratic, 533–536
    rational expressions, 361
    solutions of, 362
    solving, 66, 363, 532
    symbols for, 8
    systems of, 236–238
    with three parts, 68–69
    word expressions to, 64
Inequality symbols
    reversing direction of, 65
    using, 64
Infinite, 8
Infinite geometric series
    sum of, 728–730
Infinite repeating decimal, 4
Infinite sequence, 698–699
Infinite series, 728
Infinity, 65, 727
Infinity symbol, 65, 641, 727
Information about zeros of polynomial
    functions, 314
Inside terms
    in binomial, 263
Integer exponents, 77
Integer(s)
    consecutive, 308
    definition of, 3, 7
    negative, 3
    positive, 3
    set of, 8
Intelligence quotient (IQ), 44
Intercept
    x–, 109
    y–, 109
Interest rate, 44

Interest
    compound, 301, 640, 681
    simple, 44, 56
Intersection
    graphing, 10
    sets, 9
    solution sets of two inequalities, 10, 237
Interval notation
    solution of rational inequality, 361–362
Interval(s)
    closed, 64
    half–open, 64–65
    inequalities, 64
    open, 64–65
Inverse functions
    definition of, 621, 624, 626
    finding, 624, 628–629
    graph of, 625, 627–629
    notation for, 624
Inverse ln N, 656
Inverse log N, 653–654
Inverse property
    addition, 11
    multiplication, 11
Inverse variation
    equations, 380
    problem solving, 380–381
Inversely proportional, 380
Inverses, 624
Irrational numbers, 3–5, 7
    as square roots, 8
    written as decimals, 4–6
Irreducible, 284, 292

J

Joint variation
    solving problems involving, 381

K

Key words, 52
Known roots
    equations, 475–476
Kowa, 175

L

Last terms
    in binomial, 263
Leading coefficient, 255
Least common denominator (LCD)
    steps to find, 343
Least common multiple (LCM)
    steps to find, 343
Legs
    of a right triangle, 309, 488
Less than, 8, 64
    symbol for, 8, 64
Less than or equal to, 8
    symbol for, 8

Like radicals, 423
Like terms
    combining, 32–33, 423
Limiting value (limit), 641, 698
Line of symmetry, 517, 520
    deriving, 522
    horizontal parabola, 558
    vertical parabola, 517
Line(s)
    equation of point–slope form, 127
    equation of slope–intercept form, 116
    graphing using slope and y–intercept, 117–118
    horizontal, 120
    parallel, 130
    perpendicular, 131
    slope of, 113
    vertical, 120
Linear equation(s)
    graphing, 108
    graphing by using intercepts, 109
    horizontal line, 118–120
    point–slope form, 127
    properties of equality for solving, 35
    slope–intercept form, 116
    solving algebraically, 189
    solving by combining like terms, 36
    solving graphically, 178
    standard form, 107
    systems of, 177
    vertical line, 118–120
Linear equations in one variable, 34–38
    applications of, 51
    steps for solving, 36
    types of, 38
Linear equations in three variables, 194
Linear equations in two variables, 104, 107
    graph of, 108
    intercepts of, 109
    ordered pair solutions of, 106
    point–slope form of, 127
    slope–intercept form of, 116
    standard form of, 107
    summary of forms of, 133
    systems of, 176
Linear function(s)
    definition of, 104, 146
    degree of, 104
Linear inequalities in one variable, 64
    graphs of, 67
    solving, 66
    steps for solving, 66
Linear inequalities in two variables, 158
    graphs of, 159–161, 237
Linear inequalities
    addition property of, 66
    consistent, 236
    containing fractions, 67
    definition of, 64–65, 104
    dependent, 237
    division by a negative number, 65–66
    in one variable graphing, 64
    in two variables graphing, 237–238
    inconsistent, 236
    multiplication by a negative number, 65–66

multiplication property of, 66
    properties of, 66
    solving, 66–68, 237
Linear system(s)
    solution by addition, 181
    solution by Cramer's Rule, 229
    solution by determinants, 220
    solution by Gaussian elimination, 210
    solution by graphing, 178
    solution by substitution, 179
Linear systems of equations, 176, 194
Linear
    polynomial, 256
Logarithm(s)
    change–of–base, 674
    common, 652–653
    definition of, 647–648
    equations, 648
    evaluating, 649–650
    exponential form of, 648–649
    graphs of, 651–652
    natural, 654–655
    negative number or zero, 653
    power rule of, 663
    product rule of, 661
    properties of, 651
    quotient rule of, 662
    summary of properties of, 664
    translations, 648
Logarithmic equation(s)
    properties for solving, 670
    solving when the base is different, 671–672
    solving when the base is the same, 670
    solving with logarithms, 673–674
Logarithmic expressions
    condensing, 665–666
    expanding, 664–665
Logarithmic function(s)
    common, 652–653
    definition of, 647
    logarithmic notation and, 648
    natural, 654–655
Logarithmic notation, 648
Logarithmic properties
    basic properties, 651
    change–of–base formula, 674
    power rule, 663
    product rule, 661
    quotient rule, 662
Long division, 272, 274
Lower limit of summation, 705
Lower terms
    fraction, 332
    rational expression, 332

M

Main diagonal, 209
Major axis
    of ellipse, 580
Mathematicians
    Abel, 467
    Brahmagupta, 329
    Briggs, 607

Descartes, 105
Euler, 6, 515
Fibonacci, 697
Galois, 467
Gauss, 715
Kowa, 175
Napier, 607
Oresme, 1
Pascal, 738
Pòlya, 51
Recorde, 1, 253
Matrix (matrices)
    2×3, 205
    array of signs, 223
    augmented, 206
    coefficient, 206, 220
    column, 205
    Cramer's rule, 229–231
    definition of, 205
    determinant, 220
    dimension, 205
    double subscript, 208
    elementary row operations, 207
    entry, 205
    Gaussian Elimination, 207
    graphing calculator, 213–216, 225–226
    inconsistent and dependent systems identified with, 213
    linear systems solved using, 207–208
    main diagonal, 209
    minors, 222
    ref form, 210
    row, 205
    row echelon form, 210
    row–equivalent, 207
    row operations, 207
    square, 205, 220
    subscript, 208
    systems of equations solved using, 207–208
    triangular form, 209
    upper triangular form, 209
Matrix of the coefficients, 220
Maximum values
    quadratic function, 525–527
Mean, 57
Method for solving equations with radicals, 497
Midpoint formula, 569
Midpoint
    line segment, 569
Minimum values
    quadratic function, 525–527
Minor axis
    of ellipse, 580
Minor
    expansion by, 222
Missing powers, 277
Mixture
    applications of, 187
Monomial(s)
    definition of, 254, 255
    degree of, 255
    factoring from polynomial, 271
    multiplication of, 262
    polynomials divided by, 271

Multiple
    least common (LCM), 343
Multiplication of rational expressions, 335
Multiplication property of equality, 35
Multiplication property of inequality, 66
Multiplication property of zero, 26
Multiplication
    algebraic expressions, 23
    associative property of, 11
    binomials and, 263
    commutative property of, 11
    complex numbers, 450
    FOIL method of, 263
    fractions, 331
    functions, 609
    identity property of, 11
    inverse property of, 11, 13
    polynomials, 262–263
    radical expressions, 424–425
    rules for, 23–24, 26
    symbols, 23
    terms with the same base, 76
Multiplicative identity, 11
Multiplicative inverse, 11, 13

N

n compounding periods per year, 679
n factorial, 735
$n!$, 735
    permutations, 744
Napier, 607
Napierian logarithms, 607
Natural "ln" key
    on calculator, 655
Natural logarithm(s)
    definition of, 654
    evaluating by calculator, 655
Natural numbers
    definition of, 3, 7
    set of, 8
Nature of solutions, 483
Negative coefficient
    factoring out GCF, 284
Negative exponent rule, 78, 415
Negative exponent(s)
    definition of, 78
    evaluating, 79
    factoring, 298
    integers, 78
Negative integers, 3
Negative number(s)
    characteristic of logarithms, 653
    cube root of, 406
    exponents, 78
    multiplying both sides of inequality by, 65
    number line, 17
    square root of, 443
Negative or positive, 3, 17, 362
Negative
    fractions, 333
    rational numbers, 333
    reciprocal, 131
    signs, 17, 333
    slope, 117

square root, 400
Neither increasing nor decreasing
    sequence, 703
Newton, 386
Newton's law of cooling
    applications of, 680–681
Nonlinear systems of equations
    solving by addition method, 595
    solving by graphing, 593–595
Nonnegative, 18
Nonreal number, 445
Not equal to, 12
    symbol for, 12
Not factorable, 284, 290, 292
Notation
    algebraic, 9, 71, 362
    decimal, 4–5, 89
    exponential, 76
    $f(x)$, 434, 542
    factorial, 735
    function, 434, 542
    interval, 64, 362
    inverse, 624
    $P(x)$, 258
    radical, 398, 413
    scientific, 89
    set–builder, 8, 362
    sigma, 705–706
nth partial sum, 705
nth root, 412
    simplifying expressions, 417
nth
    term of a geometric sequence, 723–724
    term of an arithmetic sequence, 713
    term of a sequence, 700
Null set, 8
    symbol for, 8
Number line
    definition of, 7
    inequalities on, 64–65
    numbers graphed on, 10
    opposites on, 17
Number of solutions, 38
Number(s)
    absolute value, 17
    additive inverse of, 11
    complex, 443
    counting, 3
    cube roots of, 406
    factors of, 343
    imaginary, 444
    integers, 3
    irrational, 3–5
    mixed, 4
    multiplicative inverse of, 11, 13
    natural, 3
    negative, 3
    opposite, 3, 17, 39, 334
    positive, 3
    prime, 343
    rational, 3–4
    real, 3, 6
    reciprocal, 13
    roots of, 412
    scientific notation, 89
    square roots of, 399

whole, 3
Numerator(s)
    fraction, 4
    negative exponents in, 80–82
    rationalizing, 430
Numerical coefficient, 33, 255

O

Octants, 194
Odd integers
    consecutive, 308
Odd powers, 413
Odd roots, 413
One
    exponent rule of, 415
    multiplicative identity of, 11
    multiplicative inverse of, 11
One–to–one correspondence, 7, 105
One–to–one function
    definition of, 621–622
    finding inverse of, 624–625, 628–629
    horizontal line test for, 622
Open circle, 10
Open half–plane, 158
Open interval, 64–65
Operations
    addition and multiplication, 11
    order of, 177, 179, 181, 236
    real numbers, 11, 19–20, 23, 25
    research, 175
Opposite of x, 17
Opposite(s), 3, 17, 334
Or, 9–10
Order of operations
    mnemonic device, 28
    rules for, 28
Ordered pair(s)
    components of, 105
    definition of, 105
    plotting on a graph, 108–109
    relations, 145
    solution to system of linear equations, 177
    solutions, 106
Ordered triples, 194
    solution to system of linear equations, 199
Oresme, 1
Origin, 105, 109, 518
Original equation, 36, 356
Outside terms
    in binomial, 263

P

$P(x)$ notation, 258
Pairs
    ordered, 105
Parabola(s)
    axis of symmetry, 517
    directrix, 577–578
    downward opening, 519

equations of, 518, 592
graph of, 517, 558
horizontal, 518, 558
horizontal shift of, 559–561
leftward opening, 561
minimum/maximum values, 525–527
rewriting equation in standard form, 522
rightward opening, 559
symmetry of, 517
translation of, 519–520
upward opening, 517, 519
vertex formula for, 523
vertex of, 517
vertical, 518–522, 524–525
vertical shift of, 519
x–intercepts of, 523–525
y–intercepts of, 559
Parallel line(s)
definition of, 130
equations of, 130
graph of, 131–132
slope of, 129
writing equations for, 133
Parallelogram
area of, 45
perimeter of, 45
Parentheses, 23, 28
distributive property, 11
in interval notation, 64–65
order of operations, 28
simplifying algebraic expressions with, 28–29
Partial sum
arithmetic sequence, 715
definition of, 705
geometric sequence, 725–727
using sigma notation, 705
Pascal, 738
Pascal's Triangle, 738
Percent–mixture
applications of, 187
Perfect cube, 406
Perfect square, 399
Perfect square trinomials, 264–265, 285
Perimeter
of geometric figures, 45
triangle, 45–46
Permutation, 744
Perpendicular line(s)
definition of, 131
equations of, 131
graph of, 130–132
slope of, 130
Phrases
algebraic expressions written from, 52
Pi (π), 6, 763–764
Plane
coordinates of points in, 105
Plotting ordered pairs, 108–109
Plus or minus
symbol for, 1
Point(s), 107, 517
coordinate of, 105
Point–slope form
definition of, 127
equations of parallel and perpendicular

lines and, 129–132
writing equations using, 126–129
Pòlya, 51
Polynomial division
by monomial, 271
division algorithm, 272
Remainder Theorem, 278
synthetic division, 275
Polynomial equation(s)
consecutive integers, 308
Factor Theorem, 307
Pythagorean Theorem used for
obtaining, 310, 488
quadratic, 304, 469
Remainder Theorem and solving, 278
solving by factoring, 304
Polynomial inequalities, 318, 532
Polynomial multiplication
FOIL method used in, 263
special products, 264
vertical format, 267
Polynomial(s)
addition of, 256
classification of, 256
degree of, 255–256
descending order, 255
division algorithm, 272
division by monomials, 271
evaluating, 259
Factor Theorem, 307
factoring by grouping, 286
functions defined by, 258–259
greatest common factor (GCF) of, 283
least common multiple (LCM) of, 343
long division of, 272
multiplication of, 262–263
negative coefficient, 284
operations on, 256–257, 262, 272
prime, 284, 292
Remainder Theorem for, 278
special products of, 264
subtraction of, 257
synthetic division, 275–277
terms of, 256
types of, 256
Positive (or principal) square root, 400
Positive integers, 3, 309
Positive number(s)
on number line, 17
scientific notation of, 89
Positive or negative, 3, 17, 362
Positive
slope, 117
Possibilities if $D = 0$, 231
Power rule for exponents, 81, 415
Power rule for fractions, 86, 415
Power rule for products, 84, 415
Power rule of logarithms, 663
Power
definition of, 27
Powers of i, 453–454
Prime factorization, 765–767
Prime numbers, 343
Prime polynomials, 284, 292
Principal, 56
Principal (or positive) square root, 400

Problem(s)
algebra, 189
area, 379
arithmetic sequence, 717
average, 57
circumference, 379
combined variation, 381
compound interest, 301, 640, 681
consecutive integers, 308–309
cost, 55–56, 490–491
direct variation, 379
distance–rate–time, 54
earthquake intensity, 681
exponential growth and decay, 679–680
fractions, 368–369
geometry, 46–47, 490
Golden Ratio, 431
gravitational force, 380
half–life, 682
Hooke's Law, 379
interest, 56, 188
inverse variation, 380–381
joint variation, 381
Newton's law of cooling, 680
number, 52–53
percent–mixture, 187
profit, 55
projectiles, 489
proportion, 359–360
Pythagorean Theorem, 310, 488
rate, 373–374
real numbers, 21–22
strategy for solving, 51–52, 368, 487
symbolic equivalents of English phrases, 52
systems of linear equations in three
variables to solve, 200
systems of linear equations in two
variables to solve, 189
triangle, 46, 359–360
variation, 378–383
water pressure, 379
work, 188, 369–372
Procedure for adding and subtracting
rational expressions with different
denominators, 344
Procedure for solving inequalities with
rational expressions, 364
Product rule for exponents, 77, 415
Product rule of logarithms, 661
Product(s)
a positive real number and a negative
real number, 23
complex numbers, 450–451
definition of, 22
factors, 283
fractions, 331
functions, 609
polynomials, 262
rational expressions, 330–331
two positive real numbers, 23
Projectiles
applications of, 489
Properties of equations with exponents and
logarithms, 670
Properties of exponents, 415

Properties of inequality (order), 13
Properties of one, 11
Properties of square roots, 402
Properties
    equality, 35
    exponents, 88, 415, 669
    inequalities, 13, 66
    logarithms, 651, 664
    sigma notation, 706
Proportions
    definition of, 359
Pure imaginary number, 444
Pythagorean Theorem
    applications of, 310, 488
    distance between two points, 566–568
Pythagorean Triple, 313

Q

Quadrants, 105
Quadratic equation(s)
    applications of, 487–491
    definition of, 304, 468–469, 592
    discriminant of, 482–483
    factoring to find roots of, 305
    formation of, 479
    formula for, 304, 479
    fractional exponents and, 503–504
    graphs of, 592
    solving by square root property,
        470–472
    solving in x by completing the square,
        473–475
    standard form of, 304, 469
    steps to solve by factoring, 304
    types of solutions for, 483
    writing given the solutions, 306
Quadratic formula
    deriving, 479
    discriminant in, 482
    quadratic equations solved with, 480–481
Quadratic function(s)
    analysis of, 517
    finding vertex and intercepts, 523–525
    graphing, 520–521
    graphs of $y = a(x - h)^2$, 518–520
    graphs of $y = a(x - h)^2 + k$, 518, 521–522
    graphs of $y = ax^2$, 518
    graphs of $y = ax^2 + k$, 518–519
    graphs of $y = ax^2 + bx + c$, $a \neq 0$, 516,
        518, 521–522
    minimum and maximum values, 525–527
    writing in form $y = a(x - h)^2 + k$, 522
    zeros of, 516, 523–525
Quadratic in form
    solving equations, 504–505
    steps to solve, 503
Quadratic inequalities
    algebraically solving, 533–536
    definition of, 532
    graphing method for solving, 537–539
Quadratic
    polynomial, 256
Quotient rule for exponents, 80, 415
Quotient rule of logarithms, 662

Quotient(s)
    fractions, 4, 331
    functions, 609

R

Radical equation(s)
    definition of, 497
    isolating the radical term, 499
    method for solving, 497
    solving, 498–501
    solving by squaring each side once,
        498–499
    solving by squaring each side twice, 500
    solving those containing nth roots, 500
Radical expression(s)
    adding and subtracting, 423–424
    changing to and from expressions with
        rational exponents, 416
    definition of, 399
    evaluating cube roots, 406–407
    multiplying, 424–425
    rationalizing the denominator, 408
    square roots and, 403
    square roots with variables and, 404
    variables and, 405
Radical function
    definition of, 433–434
    domain of, 435
    evaluating, 435
    graphing, 436–439
Radical notation, 398, 413
Radical sign, 398–399, 413
Radical(s)
    adding and subtracting like, 423
    definition of, 399, 413
    equations containing, 498–501
    evaluating square roots, 400
    expression, 399
    like, 423
    notation, 398–399, 413
    radicand, 399
    rationalizing denominators, 408, 425
    sign, 398–399, 413
    simplest form, 402, 407
Radicand
    definition of, 399, 413
    perfect power factors of, 399
Radius of a circle, 45, 570
Range
    axis, 140
    definition of, 140, 433
    function, 140, 518
    radical function, 433
Rate, 56
Rate problems, 373–374
Ratio, 190, 359
Ratio (rate) of change
    slope, 134
Ratio for a geometric sequence, 721–722
Rational equation(s)
    applications of, 359–360
    definition of, 356
    extraneous solutions, 357
    solving, 356

solving for specified variable, 359
Rational exponent(s)
    conversion, 416
    definition of $a^{\frac{m}{n}}$, 415–416
    odd powers, 413
    principal nth root, 413
    properties of, 415
    simplifying expressions with, 417
    simplifying radical notation, 418
Rational expression(s)
    addition of those with common
        denominators, 331, 341
    addition of those with different
        denominators, 344
    applications of, 368–375
    definition of, 330–331
    division of, 331, 336
    equations involving, 356
    finding least common denominator
        (LCD), 343
    inequalities involving, 361
    multiplication of, 331, 335
    properties of, 331
    reciprocals of, 331, 336
    reducing, 332
    simplifying complex, 351–353
    simplifying product, 335
    simplifying quotient, 336
    simplifying negative exponents, 335
    subtraction of those with common
        denominators, 331, 341
    subtraction of those with different
        denominators, 344
    summary of operations with, 331
Rational inequalities
    definition of, 361
    solving, 361–364
    steps to solve, 364
Rational number(s)
    definition of, 3, 331
    Fundamental principle of, 3, 331–332
    writing as decimals, 4
Rationalization, 426–427
Rationalizing denominator
    containing one term, 408
    rational expression, 425
    simplifying radical expressions, 408
Rationalizing denominators with sum or
    differences of square roots, 426
Rationalizing numerator, 430
Real number lines, 7
Real number(s)
    absolute value of, 17
    applications of, 21–22
    definition of, 3, 6–7, 444
    division of, 25–26
    field properties, 11
    multiplication of, 23–24
    number line, 7
    order of operations, 28
    properties for inequalities, 13
    properties of, 11
    reciprocal of, 13
Real part
    complex number, 444
Reciprocal(s)

definition of, 13
fraction, 87, 331
negative exponents and fractions, 87
rational expression, 336
Recorde, 1, 253
Rectangle
area of, 45
fundamental, 584
perimeter of, 45
Rectangular coordinate system
plotting ordered pairs on, 105
quadrants of, 105
Reduce, 332
Reduced rational expressions to lowest
terms, 332
Ref form, 210
Reflection across the x–axis, 550–551
Relation
domain and range, 140
functions of, 140, 433
Remainder Theorem, 278
synthetic division and, 278–279
Repeating decimals, 4–5
Replacement set, 66
Reverse
sense of an inequality, 65
Right angle, 309
Right triangle, 309, 488
Rise, 113–114, 117
Root of multiplicity two, 305, 469
Root(s)
by calculator, 401
cube, 306, 406, 765–767
extraneous, 357
negative, 400
nth, 412
of equation, 303
principal, 400
square, 398, 765–767
Roster form, 8
Row echelon form, 210
Row equivalent, 207
Row of a matrix, 205
Row operations, 207
elementary, 207
on augmented matrix, 207
Row–equivalent, 207
Rule for negative exponents, 78
Rules and procedures
adding/subtracting rational expressions
with different denominators, 344
solving a first–degree equation, 36
solving a first–degree inequality, 66
solving inequalities with rational
expressions, 364
Rules for adding real numbers, 19
Rules for finding LCM for a set of
polynomials, 343
Rules for multiplication and division with
real numbers, 26
Rules for order of operations, 28
Rules of exponents, 76–81
Run, 113–114, 117

Satisfying the equation, 36, 106
Scientific notation
computations with, 90
converting to and from decimal
notation, 89
definition of, 89
number written in, 89
problem solving with, 91
using to compute, 90–91
Second coordinate, 105
Second–degree inequalities, 236
Second–degree polynomials, 255, 468
Second–degree systems of equations, 176
Second–degree trinomial, 256
Second–order determinants
evaluating, 221
Sense of the inequality
changing, 65
Sequence
alternating, 701
arithmetic, 711–712
decreasing, 702
definition of, 698
Fibonacci, 697
finite, 698
geometric, 721–722
increasing, 702
infinite, 698–699
neither increasing nor decreasing, 703
nth term, 700
term, 698–699
writing terms given general term for,
700–701
Series
definition of, 727
infinite, 728
infinite geometric, 728–730
Set of simultaneous equations, 176
Set(s)
definition of, 8
elements of, 8
empty, 8
finite, 8
infinite, 8
intersection of, 9
null, 8
real numbers, 9
solution, 37, 106
union of, 9
Set–builder notation, 8
domain of rational function expressed
in, 8, 362
Sigma notation
definition of, 705
properties of, 706
Similar (like) terms
combining of, 32–33
Similar triangles, 359–360
Simple interest, 44
Simplified form of a radical, 402
Simplifying complex fractions
multiplying common denominator, 351
simplifying numerator/denominator then

dividing, 353
Simplifying complex rational expressions
dividing, 353
multiplying common denominator, 351
Simplifying exponential expressions, 76–82,
84–88
Simplifying expressions containing rational
exponents, 417
Simplifying expressions
order of operations, 28
raised to negative powers, 79
raised to zero power, 77–78
Simplifying radical expressions, 404, 407
Simplifying rational expressions, 335–336
Simultaneous equations, 176
Slope(s)
definition of, 113
finding from equation, 117
formula for, 114
graphing line using y–intercept and,
117–118
horizontal line, 119–120
negative, 117
parallel lines, 129–130
perpendicular lines, 131
positive, 117
rate of change, 134
vertical line, 119–120
zero, 119–120
Slope–intercept form
definition of, 116
linear equation, 116, 126
Solution of an equation, 106
Solution of system of equations, 177
Solution of system of inequalities, 236
Solution set, 18, 34, 106
equation, 34, 37, 106
inequality, 66
system of linear equations, 177
system of linear inequalities, 236
Solution(s)
definition of, 34, 106
extraneous, 357, 497
first–degree equations, 35, 37
first–degree inequalities, 66
nonlinear system in two variables,
593–595
three variables, 194
two variables, 106
Solving
a polynomial equation, 315–317
a polynomial inequality with a graphing
calculator, 537
absolute value equations, 40, 317–318
absolute value inequalities, 70–72
an equation, 35, 36, 106
equations by factoring, 303
equations in quadratic form by
substitution, 503
equations with two absolute values, 41
exponential equations, 670–672
first–degree equations, 36
formulas for specified variables, 46–48,
359
inequalities with three parts, 68–69
linear inequalities, 67

logarithmic equations, 673–674
polynomial inequalities algebraically, 533–536
quadratic equations by completing the square, 474–475
quadratic equations by using the square root property, 471–472
word problems, 51–52, 368, 487
Special forms
difference of two squares, 264, 285
factoring, 285
perfect square trinomials, 264, 285
sum and difference of cubes, 264
Special products of polynomials, 264
Special products
factoring by, 265–266
multiplying radicals with, 265
Specified variable
solving for, 46–48, 359
Square root of expressions with even and odd exponents, 405
Square root of x^2, 404
Square root property, 471
Square root(s)
by calculator, 401
definition of, 398, 400
domain of function, 433, 435
evaluating, 400
evaluating functions, 435
examples of, 765–767
function, 433
graph of function, 436
negative, 400
negative numbers as multiples of i, 453
negative numbers in terms of i, 443
of two, 6
principal, 400
simplified form, 402
symbol, 398
Square
area of, 45
binomial difference, 264, 285
binomial sum, 264
examples of, 765–767
matrix, 205, 220
perfect, 399
perimeter of, 45
Squared, 27
Squares of integers from 1 to 20, 399
Squaring, 399
Standard form for equations of hyperbolas, 584
Standard form of a linear equation, 107
Standard form
complex number, 444, 451
equations of circles in, 571
equations of ellipses in, 580
equations of parabolas in, 558
equations written in, 107, 113, 126
quadratic equation in, 469
Standard notation
converting between scientific notation and, 89
Standard window
graphing calculator, 149, 314
Strategy for Gaussian Elimination, 210

Strategy for solving word problems, 51–52, 368, 487
Subscript, 208
Substitution method
systems of linear equations solved using, 179
Subtraction
complex numbers, 446–447
definition of, 20
fractions, 331
functions, 609
polynomials, 257
radical expressions, 423–424
rational expressions with common denominators and, 331, 341–342
rational expressions with different denominators and, 344
Sum of two cubes, 264, 295
factoring, 295–296
Sum of two functions
graphing, 611–613
Sum of two squares
factoring, 469
Sum or difference involving square roots, 425
Sum
angles of a triangle, 44
arithmetic sequence, 714–717
complex numbers, 447
finite arithmetic sequence, 716–717
functions, 609
geometric sequence, 724–725
infinite geometric series, 728–730
partial, 705, 715, 725
polynomials, 256
rational expressions, 341–348
real numbers, 19–20
Summary of formulas and properties of straight lines, 133
Summary of properties of exponents, 88, 415
Summary of relationships among various types of numbers, 7
Summation notation
properties of, 706
Summation
index of, 705
lower limit of, 705
upper limit of, 705
Symbol(s)
absolute value, 17
cross sign, 23
cube roots, 406
division, 25
element of, 8
elements in sets, 9
ellipsis, 3
empty set, 8
equivalents for English phrases, 8, 23
fraction bar, 3, 25
function composition, 619–620
function notation, 434
greater than, 8
greater than or equal to, 8
grouping parentheses, 11
inequality, 8
infinity , 65

intersection, 9
inverse of function, 624
is similar to, 360
less than, 8
less than or equal to, 8
multiplication, 23
not equal to, 12
nth roots, 413
null set, 8
opposites (or additive inverses), 11
parentheses, 23
principal square root (radical), 400
radical sign, 398, 413
raised dot, 23
sigma in adding terms of sequence, 705
square root, 398
such that, 8
sum, 705
union, 9
Symbols for multiplication, 23
Symmetric about the line $y = x$, 625
Symmetry of a parabola, 517
Symmetry
axis of, 517
Synthetic division
polynomials divided using, 275–277
Remainder Theorem and, 278–279
Systems of equations
addition method used for solving, 181
consistent, 177
dependent, 177
elimination method used for solving, 210–211
graphing method used for solving, 178
inconsistent, 177
matrices used for solving, 205, 207
Systems of inequalities, 236
graphing, 237–238
solving, 237
Systems of linear equations in three variables
consistent, 198
elimination method for solving, 211
graphs of, 195–196
inconsistent, 199
matrix method for solving, 207–208
solving, 196
Systems of linear equations in two variables
addition method for solving, 181
consistent, 177
Cramer's rule and solving of, 229
definition of, 176
dependent, 177
elimination method for solving, 210
graphing method for solving, 178
inconsistent, 177
matrix method for solving, 205
substitution method for solving, 179
Systems of nonlinear equations
addition method for solving, 595
graphing method for solving, 593–595

T

Table of values
  functions, 435–436
Tables
  creating, 106
Temperature
  Fahrenheit to Celsius, 44, 359
Term(s)
  arithmetic sequence, 713–714
  definition of, 32
  degree of, 45
  geometric sequence, 723–724
  like, 423
  nth, 700
  polynomial, 254
  sequence, 698–699
Terminating decimals, 4
Test value, 362
Theorem for distinct permutations, 746
Third–degree equation, 306
Third–degree polynomial, 256
Third–order determinants
  definition of, 222
  evaluating, 223
Time of work, 369–372
To find
  inverse of a 1–1 function, 628
  LCM for a set of polynomials, 343
  value of $a^{\frac{m}{n}}$ with a calculator, 418
To graph a linear equation in two variables, 108
To rationalize the denominator of a radical expression, 408
To simplify
  complex fraction (first method), 351
  complex fraction (second method), 353
To solve
  first–degree (or linear) equation in one variable, 36
  linear inequality, 66
  polynomial inequality, 532
  polynomial inequality with a graphing calculator, 537
  quadratic equation by completing the square, 473
  rational equation, 356
  system of linear equations by addition, 181
  system of linear equations by substitution, 179
  system of two linear inequalities, 237
  equation by factoring, 304, 469
  three linear equations in three variables, 196
To write a fraction with complex numbers in standard form, 452
Transitive property of inequality, 13
Translation
  function, 542, 545–552
  parabola, 519–520
Trapezoid
  area of, 45
  perimeter of, 45
Trial–and–error method of factoring

trinomials, 286, 289
Triangle
  area of, 45
  finding lengths of the sides, 46, 568
  Pascal's, 738
  perimeter of, 45
  right, 309, 488
  similar, 359–360
Triangular form, 209
Trichotomy property of inequality, 13
Trinomial(s)
  definition of, 256
  factoring form $ax^2 + bx + c$ by grouping, 286
  factoring perfect square, 264, 285
  factoring those whose leading coefficient is not 1, 289–292
  factoring those whose leading coefficient is 1, 289–292
  factoring with FOIL, 289–292
  prime, 284, 292
Triple
  ordered, 194
Two absolute values, 40
Two methods for graphing linear inequalities, 158
Two–order determinants
  definition of, 221
  evaluating, 221
Types of equations, 38

U

Undefined number, 13, 26, 78, 653
Undefined slope, 119–120
Union
  linear inequalities, 10
  sets, 9
Unit, 8, 17, 69–70
Unit of time, 369
Unlike terms, 33
Upper limit of summation, 705
Upper triangular form of a matrix, 209

V

Value of a 2×2 determinant, 221
Value of a 3×3 determinant, 222
Value
  test, 362
Variable(s)
  definition of, 106
  equations solved for specified, 46–48
Variation
  applications of, 378–383
  combined, 381
  constant of, 378, 380
  direct, 378
  equations, 378, 380
  inverse, 380
  joint, 381
Varies
  directly, 378

inversely, 380
jointly, 381
Vertex (vertices)
  deriving, 522
  formula, 523
  hyperbola, 584
  parabola, 517–518
Vertical (or y–axis), 105
Vertical distance, 113
Vertical format, 257, 267
Vertical line test
  definition of, 142, 433, 517
  graphs of functions, 621–623
  using, 142–144, 517
Vertical line
  equation of, 119–120
  graph of, 119–120
  slope of, 119–120
Vertical parabola
  axis of, 517
  definition of, 518
  equation of, 518
  vertex of, 517, 558
Vertical shift
  function, 545
  parabola, 519
Vertical translation(s), 519, 545
Vertical
  line, 119–120
Volume
  cylinder, 381

W

Wasan, 175
Water pressure
  formula for, 379
Whole numbers
  definition of, 3, 7
  set of, 8
Window
  graphing calculator, 149, 314
Word expressions to algebraic equivalent, 52
Word problems
  solving, 51–52, 368, 487
Work problems
  solving, 188, 369–372
Writing equations with known roots, 475–476

X

x–axis, 105, 109, 516
x–coordinate, 105
x–intercept
  locating, 109
  parabola and, 523–525
x–value(s)
  ordered pair solutions and, 106

Y

y–axis, 105, 109, 559
y–coordinate, 105
y–intercept
    graphing line using slope and, 117–118
    locating, 109
    parabola and, 559
    slope–intercept form and, 116
    writing equation of line given slope and,
        117–118
y–value(s)
    ordered pair solutions and, 106

Z

Zero(s)
    additive identity, 11
    definition of, 3
    degree of monomial, 255
    denominator, 13, 26
    exponent rule, 78, 415
    Factor Theorem, 307
    factorial, 735
    function, 516, 523–525
    multiplication property, 26
    polynomial function, 314
    power, 78, 88
    quadratic function, 523–525
    slope, 118
Zero–Factor Property, 303, 468

CHAPTER 6 — Roots, Radicals, and Complex Numbers

Properties of Square Roots:

1. If $b^2 = a$, then b is called the **square root** of a $(a \geq 0)$.
2. $\sqrt{ab} = \sqrt{a}\sqrt{b}$
3. $\sqrt{\dfrac{a}{b}} = \dfrac{\sqrt{a}}{\sqrt{b}}$
4. $\sqrt{x^{2m}} = \left|x^m\right|$, m is a positive integer
5. $\sqrt{x^{2m+1}} = x^m\sqrt{x}$ m is a positive integer

Properties of Radicals:

1. If $b^n = a$, then $b = \sqrt[n]{a} = a^{\frac{1}{n}}$, n is a positive integer.
2. $a^{\frac{m}{n}} = \left(a^{\frac{1}{n}}\right)^m = \left(a^m\right)^{\frac{1}{n}}$ or $a^{\frac{m}{n}} = \left(\sqrt[n]{a}\right)^m = \sqrt[n]{a^m}$

Complex Numbers:
Numbers of the form $a + bi$.

Powers of i:
$i = \sqrt{-1}$
$i^2 = -1$

CHAPTER 7 — Quadratic Equations

Square Root Property:
If $x^2 = c$, then $x = \pm\sqrt{c}$.
If $(x - a)^2 = c$, then $x - a = \pm\sqrt{c}$ $\left(\text{or } x = a \pm \sqrt{c}\right)$.

Quadratic Formula:

$x = \dfrac{-b \pm \sqrt{b^2 - 4ac}}{2a}$

Discriminant: $b^2 - 4ac$
$b^2 - 4ac > 0 \rightarrow$ Two Real Solutions
$b^2 - 4ac = 0 \rightarrow$ One Real Solution
$b^2 - 4ac < 0 \rightarrow$ Two Nonreal Solutions

CHAPTER 8 — Quadratic Functions and Conic Sections

Parabolas:

Vertical Parabolas:
Parabolas of the form $y = ax^2 + bx + c$:
If $a > 0$, the parabola opens upward.
If $a < 0$, the parabola opens downward.

Vertex: $\left(-\dfrac{b}{2a}, \dfrac{4ac - b^2}{4a}\right)$

Line of Symmetry: $x = -\dfrac{b}{2a}$

Parabolas of the form $y = a(x - h)^2 + k$:
Vertex: (h, k)
Line of Symmetry: $x = h$

Horizontal Parabolas:
Parabolas of the form $x = ay^2 + by + c$ or $x = a(y - k)^2 + h$
If $a > 0$, the parabola opens right.
If $a < 0$, the parabola opens left.
Vertex: (h, k)
Line of Symmetry: $y = k$

Vertical and Horizontal Translations:
Given a graph $y = f(x)$, the graph of $y = f(x - h) + k$ is:
1. a horizontal translation of $f(x)$ by h units and
2. a vertical translation of $f(x)$ by k units.

Distance Formula (distance between two points):

$d = \sqrt{\left(x_2 - x_1\right)^2 + \left(y_2 - y_1\right)^2}$

Midpoint Formula:
$\left(\dfrac{x_1 + x_2}{2}, \dfrac{y_1 + y_2}{2}\right)$

Circles:
Standard form: $(x - h)^2 + (y - k)^2 = r^2$
Center: (h, k)
Radius: r

Ellipses:
Standard form: $\dfrac{(x-h)^2}{a^2} + \dfrac{(y-k)^2}{b^2} = 1$ or $\dfrac{(x-h)^2}{b^2} + \dfrac{(y-k)^2}{a^2} = 1$; $a^2 \geq b^2$
Center: (h, k)
Length of Major Axis: $2a$
Length of Minor Axis: $2b$

Hyperbolas:
Centered at the origin:

1. Standard form: $\dfrac{x^2}{a^2} - \dfrac{y^2}{b^2} = 1$

   Curves open left and right.
   x-intercepts: $(a, 0)$ and $(-a, 0)$
   Asymptotes: $y = \dfrac{b}{a}x$ and $y = -\dfrac{b}{a}x$

2. Standard form: $\dfrac{y^2}{a^2} - \dfrac{x^2}{b^2} = 1$

   Curves open up and down.
   y-intercepts: $(0, a)$ and $(0, -a)$
   Asymptotes: $y = \dfrac{a}{b}x$ and $y = -\dfrac{a}{b}x$

Centered at (h, k):
Standard form: $\dfrac{(x-h)^2}{a^2} - \dfrac{(y-k)^2}{b^2} = 1$ or $\dfrac{(y-k)^2}{a^2} - \dfrac{(x-h)^2}{b^2} = 1$